Also by William L. Shirer

NONFICTION

Berlin Diary
End of a Berlin Diary
Midcentury Journey
The Challenge of Scandinavia
The Rise and Fall of the Third Reich

FICTION

The Traitor
Stranger Come Home
The Consul's Wife

JUVENILES

The Rise and Fall of Adolf Hitler
The Sinking of the *Bismarck*

THE
COLLAPSE
OF THE
THIRD REPUBLIC

An Inquiry into the Fall of France in 1940

by

WILLIAM L. SHIRER

SIMON AND SCHUSTER · NEW YORK

SBN 671-20337-1
Library of Congress Catalog Card Number: 72-91306
Designed by Edith Fowler
Manufactured in the United States of America

To the memory of my brother John,
who died suddenly
as the last lines of this book
were being written

CONTENTS

Book Five   THE COLLAPSE OF THE
THIRD REPUBLIC

FOREWORD

This is the second book in which I have attempted to set down out of my own experience and from the mass of historical material that eventually became available what happened to a great European nation in the years that were climaxed by the Second World War. In the first work I wrote of the rise and fall of Nazi Germany and how it came that a cultured, Christian people lapsed into barbarism in the midst of the twentieth century, gladly abandoning their freedoms and the ordinary decencies of human life and remaining strangely indifferent to the savagery with which they treated other nations, other races. I was aided in that task by the availability of a unique source of information: the secret archives of the Third Reich, which were captured by the Allies at the end of the war. I was helped too, I feel, by a personal acquaintance with Nazi Germany, in which I had lived and worked during more than half its twelve years of existence.

The lack of the perspective of time for all who labor in the field of contemporary history is more than compensated, I believe, by the experience of having lived through the events themselves, by the firsthand knowledge one acquires of the leading characters caught up in them, by the *feel* one gets for the nature and mood of the country, the society, the institutions, and above all the people at a time of crisis. *The History of the Peloponnesian War* does not suffer, it seems to me, for Thucydides "having lived through," as he tells us, "the whole of the war," of which he has left us such an unforgettable account. One is grateful to him for not leaving the writing of it to others who came later.

I lived and worked in France for a good many years, beginning in 1925 when the country was not only the greatest power on the continent of Europe but, to me at least, the most civilized and enlightened. In the ensuing years I watched with increasing apprehension the Third Republic go downhill, its strength gradually sapped by dissension and division, by an incomprehensible blindness in foreign, domestic, and military policy, by the ineptness of its leaders, the corruption of its press, and by a feeling of growing confusion, hopelessness, and cynicism (*Je m'en foutisme*) in its people. And though at the beginning of the 1930s I left for assignments elsewhere, I returned frequently to Paris throughout the decade and thus was able to keep in touch with the deterioration one could see—or at least feel—all around.

From the very beginning I liked the country and the people, became sympathetically involved in discussion and study of their problems, their leaders, their politics, their journalism, their literature, and like Jefferson and many other Americans who have lived and worked there, came to feel that Paris was my second home, a sentiment that has never left me. Though I did not try to hide my sympathies and prejudices, I was, after all, a foreigner, and this gave one a certain objectivity, keeping one out of the partisan battles and making one skeptical of many claims from the Right, Left, or Center. Since the extreme Right and Left in the thirties wanted, for opposite reasons, an end of the Third Republic, my affinities were with the Socialists on the Left, the Radical-Socialists in the Center, and the moderate conservatives slightly right of Center. These represented the vast majority of Frenchmen, were the bulwark of the Republic, and one hoped they would know how to preserve it through thick and thin.

Obviously the fall of France and the collapse of the Third Republic the summer of 1940 is a painful subject to Frenchmen and they would sooner forget it. Not many French historians have yet tackled it. René Rémond, the political scientist and historian, deplored in 1957 the lack of books on the last ten years of the Republic. Not only historians but journalists, he said, stayed off the subject, and even the learned journals were wary of approaching it. Since then a beginning has been made. Jacques Chastenet and Edouard Bonnefous have rounded out their multivolumed histories of the Third Republic with accounts of its last years and end. Earlier, E. Beau de Loménie wrote well of its "death," and other French historians have covered various aspects, among them Pierre Renouvin, Maurice Baumont, François Goguel, René Rémond, J-B. Duroselle and Pierre Dhers.

In no country, including my own, have I ever received such coopera-tion in the work of research as I got in France from historians, editors, librarians, and some of the leading political figures in the drama itself. The first three, besides offering new insights, guided me to material I would not otherwise have obtained and often provided it themselves from their own private sources. Paul Reynaud, the Premier during the last climactic months of the Republic, sent me letters and memoranda of great length in answer to my queries and supplemented them with long talks in his apart-ment behind the old Chamber of Deputies. Edouard Daladier, who was either Premier or Minister of Defense, or both, for four years until replaced by Reynaud toward the very end, talked with me for hours. These were the two key political figures during the last years of the Republic.

There were difficulties, to be sure. The main one was a law which forbids making available to scholars, or to anyone else, confidential state documents until they have gathered dust in the files for fifty years. But even after fifty years the French government holds back. I was informed in writing, for example, by the technical counselor of the Ministry of the Armies, M. de la Fournière, that "unfortunately" the archives of the Historical Section of the Army were not available to researchers—"not even," he added, "to the generals of the French Army"—for any period later than 1900. The French Foreign Office kindly sent me a copy of an order releasing for the perusal of scholars certain *dossiers* "up to 1815," others "up to 1849," still others "up to 1896." It seemed to shy away from the twentieth century. Recently, however, the Foreign Office has begun to publish its confidential papers for the 1930s, though it has been handicapped by the loss of many of its original documents, burned in the courtyard of the Quai d'Orsay on May 16, 1940, in a moment of panic when reports reached frightened officials that German tanks and troops were approaching the capital. Winston Churchill was among the notables who watched the bonfire from a second-story window.

André Chamson, director of the National Archives, wrote that he was "deeply grieved" that he could not make accessible the Riom Court papers I had asked to see. "But we have to stick very firmly," he added, "to the 'law of 50 years,' especially in the matter of papers covering the last war and the occupation." Chamson's grief is genuine. He is a noted author and member of the Académie Française, and understands a writer's problems. He was not, unfortunately, in this instance, the law. Even the eminent Professor Pierre Renouvin of the Sorbonne, himself in overall charge of the postwar publication of the state's secret papers, was complaining in 1958 that "the French archives . . . are still not accessible, even to privileged researchers." And Reynaud and Daladier complained to me that, because of the law, they were being denied access to their own state papers acquired when they were in office, though Reynaud must have taken the bulk of his with him, for they pile up in his published memoirs.

French historians have fretted and fumed about the famous, or, as they say, "infamous" *loi de cinquante ans*. Still, I found in the end, as they did, that most of the confidential material could be obtained—without breaking the law. For one thing, the political leaders and generals, particularly the latter, have made them available either in their memoirs or in their sworn testimony at the postwar trials of collaborators, especially those of Pétain and Laval, or during exhaustive questioning by the Parliamentary Investigating Committee, which was charged by the National Assembly to look into the "events that took place in France from 1933 to 1945." It heard testimony and accumulated documentation for five years, from 1945 to 1950. It became a rather common sight to see former cabinet ministers, diplomats, generals, and admirals appear on these occasions and, as they testified, pull out of bulging briefcases sheafs of secret documents which they had retained and which they used to bolster their case. The Parliamentary Investigating Committee published several hundred key documents, many of them left by those it interrogated, others pried out of a reluctant government. The Committee's nine volumes of testimony of nearly all the principal figures of the last years of the Republic, all of them subject to searching cross-examination, provides much firsthand material.

In fact, before I had finished my research in Paris in the late 1960s, the material was becoming mountainous, and it took some time to make one's way out of the thick woods of documentation and testimony into the clearing.

The so-called "Wilhelmstrasse Documents," published by the German Foreign Office in 1941 and covering events in France from May 29, 1939, to June 3, 1940, are of considerable value. These consisted of a selection from 1800 cartons of secret papers from the French Foreign Office (apparently all that had not been burned) and 30 cartons of confidential military documents, including many papers of General Gamelin, the Commander in Chief of the French armies in 1939–40. German troops had found them in June 1940, in a French railroad train stalled by bombing at a village on the Loire.* To lend authenticity to its publication, which it entitled "The Secret Documents of the French High Command," the Wilhelmstrasse included in its volume the photostats of the originals.

It would have been impossible to write of the Battle of France without having at hand the secret orders and reports of the French High Command and of the commanding generals in the field. (We already have those of the Germans from their captured papers.) Despite the restrictive law, most of these are now available through the writings of Colonel Pierre Lyet, the semiofficial military historian, both in his book on the battle and in articles in the *Revue Historique de l'Armée,* of which he is editor. Other officers, some from the Service Historique de l'Armée, presided over by the genial and learned General de Cossé-Brissac, have revealed further orders, dispatches, and decisions in that publication and also in the invaluable *Revue d'Histoire de la Deuxième Guerre Mondiale.* General Gamelin in his three volumes of memoirs gives many more, as does General Weygand, his successor, in his memoirs. General Roton, Chief of Staff to General Georges, who commanded actual operations during the battle, has added still more in his published journal. Though they are not nearly as complete as the French military papers published after the First World War, when France was victorious, and which included two volumes of orders and dispatches, they suffice to give an accurate picture of what happened and, especially, what went wrong.

---

* They were recaptured by the American army in Thuringia, Germany, on April 14, 1945, and returned to Paris a fortnight later, where they have been under lock and key ever since.

The memoirs, journals, and diaries of the prominent figures in government, Parliament, the Army, and diplomacy, of which there has been a virtual torrent since the end of the last war, have a value, I think, far beyond the run of such sources ordinarily. With the usual reservations for the special pleading of the authors (Gamelin's, Weygand's, Paul Baudouin's, and Georges Bonnet's are at times staggering), they not only provide firsthand information of what was said and done—and sometimes plotted—but they are full of the texts of secret documents often not obtainable elsewhere. And they can be checked not only against the writings of each author's French rivals but against the confidential dispatches and memoranda of the British, Germans, and Americans in their dealings with the French, most of which are now available.

All in all, I have come to the conclusion that by one means or another, despite the "law of fifty years," we now have almost all the essential documentary material concerning the last years of the Republic and its collapse in July 1940.

As with the book on the Third Reich, I have found it necessary to go back a bit in history. This seemed to me to be especially important for the story of the Third Republic's end. I have not tried to write its history. That would take several volumes. But it was necessary to delve into it in some depth in order to comprehend not only what was lost when it went under but how and why it became ripe for its fall. A great nation, though it experiences the worst of luck, does not suddenly collapse out of the blue. The seeds of its ruin are planted long before. The threads that lead to ultimate disaster can be traced back. This was particularly the case with the Third Republic. The seeds can be seen planted during the nineteenth century; the threads are not hard to pick up and follow.

France, it is true, fell as the result of one battle that raged for six weeks in the spring and summer of 1940. But as Montesquieu observed: "If the hazard of a battle, that is, a particular cause, ruins a State, there was a general cause which determined that this State had to perish from a single battle." Yet only a quarter of a century before the Third Republic had been strong enough, its government, Army, people, and institutions tough enough, to survive a succession of bloody and disastrous battles. In the ensuing twenty-five years something happened that sapped that strength and toughness so that at the first visitation of adversity the Republic floundered and expired. This is the subject of most of this book.

Deliberately I have avoided drawing lessons from this story for the benefit of those living in or running the democracies of the Western world today, though it would not be difficult, I suppose, for the reader to draw his own conclusions. History must speak for itself. A historian is content if he has been able to shed some light. As the French poet-diplomat Paul Claudel once observed: "It is not enough to know the past. It is necessary to understand it." The lessons follow from that.

Where is France? What became of the French?
—GEORGES CLEMENCEAU, at the time
of the Dreyfus Affair

*Whatever form the final triumph may take, it will
be many years before the stain of 1940 can be effaced.
. . . It was the most terrible collapse in all the long
story of our national life.*
—MARC BLOCH, before his execution
by the Germans in 1944

*The General Staff in 1914 was prepared for the
war of 1870, and in 1940, for the war of 1914.*
—GUY LA CHAMBRE, Minister of Air, 1938–40

*History with us has become a sort of permanent
civil war. It teaches us to hate one another.*
—FUSTEL DE COULANGES

*We reached those last days when we could endure
neither our vices nor their remedies.*
—TITUS LIVY, on the decline of Rome

*Quand, dans une République, il y a des factions, le
parti le plus faible n'est pas accablé plus que le plus fort,
c'est la République qui est accablée.*

*Si le hasard d'une bataille, c'est à dire, une cause
particulière ruine un Etat, il y avait une cause générale
qui faisait que cet Etat devait périr par une seule
bataille.*
—MONTESQUIEU (*Grandeur et Décadence
des Romains*, Ch. XVIII)

*It is not enough to know the past. It is necessary to
understand it.*
—PAUL CLAUDEL

Prologue

1

DEBACLE!
Summer 1940

The collapse of the French Third Republic in the balmy May-June-July days of 1940 was an awesome spectacle.

In the span of six weeks during that spring and early summer of weather more lovely than anyone in France could remember since the end of the previous war, this old parliamentary democracy, the world's second largest empire, one of Europe's principal powers and perhaps its most civilized, and reputedly possessing one of the finest armies in the world, went down to utter military defeat, leaving its citizens, who had been heirs to a long and glorious history, dazed and then completely demoralized.

Before they could recover their senses an eighty-four-year-old, nearly senile Marshal, a legendary hero of the First World War, aided and indeed prodded by a handful of defeated generals and defeatist politicians, completed the debacle by jettisoning in mid-July, with the approval of a stampeded parliament, the Third Republic and its democratic way of life, and replacing it with a fascist dictatorship that attempted to ape a good many aspects, though not all, of the totalitarian regime of the Nazi German conquerors.

By this means these Frenchmen hoped not only to alleviate the bitter consequences of defeat but to wipe out their country's admittedly imperfect democracy, which, though it had heaped honors and favors on them and afforded them vast opportunities to further their professional careers and enrich their lives and, more often than not, their pocketbooks, they had long despised, and which now, in its agony, they scorned, claiming that it was responsible for the terrible defeat.

The twentieth century, strewn as it was with the wrecks of many a mighty empire, had not previously seen such a sudden cataclysm. One had to go back to the previous century to find even the faintest parallel.

In 1806 the France of Napoleon I had quickly brought Prussia to heel. In 1870 the France of Napoleon III had been crushed by Prussia in forty-two days. But in the First World War, France, with the help of her allies, not only had held out for four years against the onslaught of the ancient foe but had emerged victorious in 1918. Little wonder that in June 1940 the swift annihilation of France by Hitler's Germany stunned the minds of vanquished and victor alike and of most men who had followed the course of battle from near or from far. It seemed beyond the power of the mind to grasp.

"It was the most terrible collapse," a French historian sadly recounted, "in all the long story of our national life."[*1] To the Catholic philosopher Jacques Maritain it was an "unprecedented humiliation of a great nation."[2]

In Paris, the fallen capital, I noted in my diary on June 17: "I have a feeling that what we're seeing here is the complete breakdown of French society—a collapse of the army, of government, of the morale of the people. It is almost too tremendous to believe."[†3]

How, I wondered, had it come about? How was it possible? What were the terrible weaknesses, the defects, the blindness and the stumblings that had brought this gifted people to such a low and pitiful state? Sometimes in history, I tried to remember, a nation went down not so much because of its own flaws as because of the attacking nation's unexpectedly tremendous strength. Was this but the latest example? For years from Berlin I had watched Nazi Germany's mercurial rise in military might, which the sleeping democracies in the West did little to match. I had followed too at first hand Hitler's cynical but amazingly successful diplomacy, which had so easily duped the West and which had paved the way for one quick military conquest after another. But still—and notwithstanding—the French debacle in the midst of which I now found myself was quite incomprehensible. Not even the German generals I had talked with in Berlin had expected it. Though they knew some of its weaknesses and had planned to take advantage of them, they had had a decent respect for the French army, acquired by personal experience in the 1914–1918 war and by their remembrance of history that went back to the Napoleonic wars.

About noon that day, June 17, I had come into Paris on the heels of the rapidly advancing German army, with which I was an accredited, neutral, American correspondent, the United States not yet having been

---

* This was Professor Marc Bloch of the University of Paris. A Jew, a hero of the Resistance, he was arrested, barbarously tortured, and shot by the German Gestapo in France on June 16, 1944, a few weeks before the liberation.

† Three weeks before, on May 26, Georges Mandel, French Minister of the Interior, told General Sir Edward L. Spears in Paris: "There is no will to fight. . . . There has been a collapse of the whole French nation."[4] Mandel, also a Jew, was later murdered by the French fascist militia, with the connivance of the Nazi Germans.

shoved into the war by the Japanese and by Hitler. It was one of those lovely June days, bright and sunny under a cloudless sky and not too warm, that had often made life seem so wondrous in this ancient and beautiful metropolis, where I had worked and lived for some years between the wars before moving on to other European capitals and eventually to Berlin —though there never was a year that I did not return to Paris on some kind of assignment or pretext and thus was able to follow at first hand, to some extent, the troubled affairs of a country that had become, spiritually, my second home.*

On this June day the usually teeming streets were empty of the French. On the sidewalks there was scarcely a human being to be seen except for an occasional group of strolling German soldiers in their dark-gray uniforms gaping like tourists at the familiar landmarks of the great city. The stores were closed, the iron shutters drawn tight over the shop windows, the blinds closed snugly on the windows in the residential quarters, much as they would be in an ordinary August when half the Parisians deserted the city for vacations at the seashore or in the countryside or up in the mountains.

Now, most of them had fled. According to police estimates, only 700,000—out of five million—inhabitants were left in the city by June 14, the day the Germans entered.[5] Two days before, when a great pall of smoke from burning oil depots in the suburbs hung over the nearly deserted capital, a stray herd of cows from a dairy farm at Auteuil could be seen meandering about the Place de l'Alma in the center of Paris almost under the shadow of the Eiffel Tower across the Seine.[6]

There was now, in this third week of June, a horde of more than eight million panic-stricken refugees strung out for hundreds of miles on the roads south of Paris between the rivers Seine and Loire and beyond. Before the Parisians fled en masse on the approach of the Germans, six million others, including two million from Belgium, had abandoned their homes and farms in the north and northeast and lit out by any means available toward the south to keep from being captured by the enemy. Many of them had experienced life under German occupation in the first war and were determined to spare themselves and their children that fate this time. Since almost all roads in France led to Paris, many of these refugees had passed through the capital during the last fortnight of May, a considerable number in the relative comfort of packed railroad trains. Their passing had been quite orderly and some had remained in the city in the belief that Paris, as in 1914, would be held. Their arrival, however, increased the feeling of uneasiness among the Parisians, who, without accurate news of the collapsing front from their government and army chiefs, fed on mounting rumor and began to fear the worst.

There had been a bad scare toward the end of the first week of battle, on May 15, when it was learned that the Germans had broken through at the Meuse river crossings at Sedan and north of that ill-fated city, whose

---

* "France is every man's second country," Thomas Jefferson once wrote.

fall had doomed France in 1870. The High Command had informed the government—to its amazement—that there was nothing to stop the enemy armored columns from reaching Paris within twenty-four hours.

"Last night," Premier Paul Reynaud had wired the new British Prime Minister, Winston Churchill, urgently, "we lost the battle. The route to Paris is open."[7]

Seized by panic, high officials at the French Foreign Office began dumping secret state documents out of the windows to bonfires in the yard below, and the smoke had drifted up the Seine to the nearby Chamber of Deputies, giving its members pause for thoughts about getting away in time. Word spread over Paris, and many citizens hastily departed. But the German panzer columns had bypassed Paris and raced unimpeded westward to the Channel, cutting off the flower of the French army, all of the Belgian army, and nine of ten divisions of the British Expeditionary Force in Flanders. This had given Paris a respite.

On Sunday, May 19, the day after Marshal Henri Philippe Pétain, eighty-four, the hero of Verdun, had joined the government as Vice-Premier, and the very day General Maxime Weygand, seventy-three, the aide of Foch in the first war, replaced the faltering Generalissimo Maurice Gamelin, sixty-eight, a former aide of Joffre, as Commander in Chief, the members of the government and Parliament, led by the President of the Republic and the Premier, had gone to pray at Notre Dame for the miracle of deliverance.* No doubt they were thinking of the "miracle" of the Marne that had stopped the onrushing Germans before Paris in the second month of battle in 1914 and turned the tide of the whole war. But now on barely the tenth day of battle there was neither a Joffre nor a Foch nor a Galliéni to lead and inspire the French army. Their successors, Gamelin and Weygand and Georges, were of a different stripe.

The prayers, led by the Cardinal Archbishop of Paris, had not been answered. The Germans, after rounding up the trapped French forces which had not been able, or willing, to get away by sea with the British at Dunkirk—the Belgian army had surrendered unconditionally on May 28—resumed their offensive on the Somme and Aisne on June 5. The French defenders, now outnumbered two to one and assisted by only one British division, quickly gave way. By June 9 the enemy armor was close enough to Paris to prompt the government to decide to depart the next evening. When the Parisians learned of the government's flight they joined it.

Between June 9 and 13, when the Germans arrived at the gates of the city, two million Parisians, men, women, and children, took off in utter panic toward the south, packing a few belongings on the roofs of their small cars

---

* "An exquisite day . . . nothing could lessen the loveliness of the chestnut trees in bloom, the shimmering beauty of the Bois, the Champs Elysées, the Seine," Vincent Sheean, an American correspondent and writer, remembered. But watching outside the cathedral when the dignitaries departed, he noted the "blank, polite indifference in the faces turned to them from the crowd."[8]

or on the racks of motorcycles or bicycles or in baby carts, peddler's carts, wheelbarrows, or in any wheeled contrivance they could lay a hasty hand on, for many were on foot.* They had no idea of their destination; they wanted only to keep out of the clutch of the Germans, who under Hitler's brutal rule were rumored to be even more barbarian than the Germans of Kaiser Wilhelm II, who had shot so many hostages when they overran Belgium and northern France in 1914.†

No provision for food, drink, and lodging had been made for so many suddenly uprooted millions. The authorities had not foreseen such a massive and pitiful exodus. At night these desperate people, when they were not on the move, slept in their cars or in the fields. By day they scrounged for food where they could find it and sometimes pillaged. The towns and villages through which they inched their way on the jammed roads were usually emptied of their own dwellers, who, in a sort of chain reaction, had joined the first column of refugees that appeared, so that the food stores and bakeries were closed or their shelves empty. A few peasants along the route dispensed food and even water, sometimes at a highly profitable price, but this was but a drop in the bucket.‡

In Paris we heard from returning correspondents of this frightened, leaderless swarm of citizenry fleeing down the roads so choked with traffic and so snarled that even when the gasoline held out and the overheated motors continued to revolve, a man was lucky to make twenty-five or thirty miles in twenty-four hours in a car packed tight with the members of his family and bulging with baggage roped down on the roof under a mattress to protect, it was somehow hoped, against bombs from the sky. For the German Luftwaffe, which first had terrorized the French troops, was now bombing civilian refugees, especially those crowding the approaches to bridges and crossroads, which might have been military objectives had they been defended by French soldiers. For a week the German aviators had been joined by the Italians, who seemed to the terror-stricken refugees to outdo the Germans in attacking them.[12]

On June 10 Italy had entered the war on the side of Germany and had tried to assault what was left of a stricken France.§ The Italian army had not had any success for a week, nor would it to the end, against the handful

---

* Tens of thousands, packing the Paris railroad stations like sardines, managed to get away in trains. Between June 8 and 13, some 198 passenger trains, 87 freight trains, and 37 mail trains, all jammed with men, women, and children, left the city's stations for the southwest. In the debacle the French railways seem to have been by far the best-organized body in the country. They were responsible also for moving most of the troops.[9]

† In all, 29,660 French hostages would be executed by the Germans during World War II.[10]

‡ There was a peasant near Chartres who stood by the pump on his well and addressed a large group of milling, thirsty refugees: "Come on! Get out your money! Ten sous a glass of water, two francs a bottle!"[11]

§ Prompting President Franklin Roosevelt, who was speaking that evening at Charlottesville, Virginia, to say: "On this tenth day of June 1940, the hand that held the dagger has plunged it into the back of its neighbor."

of determined French troops defending the Alpine passes and the entrance to the Riviera. But against the logjams of terrified civilians on the roads the Italians, from the safety of the undefended air, were more successful.

Along the congested thoroughfares French soldiers were now enmeshed with civilians in the wild scramble to keep out of the reach of the pursuing enemy. Most of these troops, cut off from their units in the confusion of retreat, had thrown away their arms. They blended quickly into the columns of fleeing refugees. Units that were still intact and armed milled around in the towns or villages or at the approaches to bridges waiting for orders that never came. The President of the Republic, Albert Lebrun, himself fleeing with the government from Tours to Bordeaux on June 14, noted that "the towns and villages are full of idle troops. What are they doing there, inert, when one needs them so badly elsewhere?" It was for him, he added, a "mystery."[13]

By blocking the roads the refugees not only impeded the movement of those troops that did try to move forward to stem the German tide but often held up the retreat of units until they were overrun by enemy armored formations and captured. The General Staff of the French Seventh Army, drawing back from the Seine to the Loire, complained that its "movement has been rendered almost impossible by the afflux of refugees encumbering the roads with their cars and carts. The villages and crossroads are places of indescribable bottlenecks."[14]

Most demoralizing of all to army units still trying to fight were the efforts of civilians to prevent them from offering further resistance that might damage their homes and shops. At one village on the River Indre the local inhabitants extinguished the fuses of explosives already lit by army engineers to blow the bridge there and slow down the German advance. French troops digging in at Poitiers were surprised to see the mayor driving out with a white flag to surrender the town to the Germans. He was backed by the inhabitants, who had threatened to tear down the barricades erected by the soldiers.[15] French civilians, like so many of the troops, had no more stomach for the fighting that had started only a month before.

Perhaps it made little difference now. The remaining French armies that had tried to stand on the Somme and Aisne and then along the Seine and Marne had either been chewed to pieces by German tanks or were in disorderly retreat toward the Loire and upper Seine east of Paris. On June 11 General Alphonse Georges, commanding the collapsing front, estimated he had left the equivalent of only thirty divisions—out of sixty in line the week before—from the sea to the beginning of the Maginot Line, and they were exhausted from trying to fight by day and retreat by night. On June 12 the great Maginot Line of fortifications in the east, which had not been penetrated by the enemy, was abandoned on the orders of General Weygand. But the move came too late, and four days later the 400,000 retreating fortress troops were encircled by the Germans.

On the abandonment of Paris, Supreme Headquarters had been moved temporarily to Briare, on the Loire east of Tours, where General Weygand, backed by Marshal Pétain, spent much time relaying the increasingly catastrophic news to the government and urging it to acknowledge defeat and give up the hopeless struggle.

The government itself was in disarray. After struggling all night to get their cars through the mass of refugees on the clogged roads, the cabinet members and their skeleton staffs had arrived from Paris at the Loire on the morning of June 11 and scattered to various châteaux in the region of Tours. There was only one antiquated telephone in each castle (usually in the downstairs toilet), none of them in good working order and each connected only with the nearest village, where the operator insisted on taking off the customary two hours for lunch and closing down at 6 P.M.

There was little communication between the cabinet ministers and none at all with the outside world. Paul Baudouin, Undersecretary of Foreign Affairs, who was in charge of the displaced Foreign Office, found his only source of news in a portable field radio which the British Ambassador had thought to bring along. When Baudouin, on the afternoon of the 11th, went to see the President of the Republic at the Château de Cangé, he found the nation's chief magistrate "entirely isolated, without news from the Premier, without news from Supreme Headquarters, depressed, overwhelmed. He knows nothing."[16]

Parliament, which might have helped to sustain the bewildered government in its determination to fight on in spite of the faltering generals, could not be assembled during such a headlong flight. Everyone knew that the halt on the Loire would be brief because of the approaching Germans, but no one knew where the government would flee to next. On the 12th, Reynaud, weary and disheartened but still resolved to continue the fight, tried to persuade his colleagues to agree to the government moving westward into the Brittany peninsula, where he hoped a stand could be made with the help of the British. But he was overruled. Bordeaux, to which the government had gone temporarily in 1914 at the time of the Marne, seemed a safer haven to the majority. General Weygand himself had urged the government to remain in Paris even at the risk of capture, prompting President Lebrun to exclaim that the general "must be mad."[17]

To one foreign observer they all seemed a little mad, the leaders of government and of the army, as they thrashed about the Loire quarreling as to what to do next. "A mad-house," General Sir Edward L. Spears, Churchill's liaison officer with Reynaud, called it. He had been exasperated when on the morning of June 13 he arrived at the Château de Chissay to see the Premier.

In the courtyard, I saw to my utter astonishment Madame de Portes in a dressing-gown over red pyjamas, directing the traffic from the steps of the main entrance. She was shouting to the drivers where to park.[18]

Countess Hélène de Portes, Reynaud's mistress, was reputed to have a strong and strange hold over the Premier, and the dismayed British general felt that she was now making the most of it. She had joined Pétain, Weygand, Baudouin, and other defeatists to try to wear him down to the point of taking France out of the war.

There had been another titled lady very much in the picture until a few days before. This was the Marquise de Crussol, the mistress of Edouard Daladier. The two women had been as bitter rivals as were their illustrious lovers. By their driving ambition on behalf of their respective men they had added to the intrigues, the confusions—and the titillation—of French politics. But Daladier, one of the political bulwarks of the Third Republic for a decade, and Premier and Minister of Defense when France entered the war, had fallen from power when Reynaud, who had succeeded him as Premier on March 21, finally eliminated him altogether from the government on June 5 in the midst of the debacle. The Countess de Portes now had the stage to herself, so far as a woman was concerned, and she would flutter on and off it, raging, ranting, weeping, and intriguing to make the man she supposedly loved and for whom she had been so ambitious do what he seemed resolved not to do.

The day the German army entered Paris, June 14, the French government fled from its temporary halting place on the Loire to Bordeaux in the southwest corner of France. The end was approaching. Late that evening the haggard cabinet ministers, after struggling through the traffic jams of milling refugees and troops, straggled into the port city, exhausted and demoralized. General Spears, who saw Reynaud at midnight, found him "worn out . . . forlorn and undecided."[19]

General Weygand, the Commander in Chief, journeyed to Bordeaux more leisurely in his special train, arriving the following afternoon in fighting trim to pit himself against the Premier, who, though weary and depressed, still stubbornly refused to give up. The general was convinced that further fighting against the Germans was senseless. He intended to concentrate on fighting Paul Reynaud and a government he despised.

The showdown between these clashing temperaments came at Bordeaux on the weekend of Saturday–Sunday, June 15–16. Reynaud insisted on General Weygand asking for a cease-fire while the government moved on to French North Africa to continue the war from there. Weygand refused, declaring that such a step would be contrary to the honor of the French Army. He demanded that the government which had declared war on Germany now ask for an armistice. The venerable Marshal Pétain backed him up. At a cabinet meeting on the morning of June 16 he submitted his resignation, in writing. The government, he stated, must immediately "cease hostilities." Many ministers, led by the other Vice-Premier, Camille Chautemps, the great compromiser, began to side with the military.

Feeling himself opposed by the majority of his cabinet and by the High Command, Paul Reynaud gave in and resigned shortly after 8 P.M. on June 16. The President of the Republic, who already had caved in, immediately named Pétain to succeed him. At thirty minutes past midnight of that fateful Sunday the new French government of the Marshal, with Weygand as Minister of Defense, asked the Germans for an armistice.

Six days later, on June 22, 1940, in the little clearing in the Forest of Compiègne at Rethondes north of Paris, on the exact spot where the defeated Germans had signed an armistice on November 11, 1918, I watched the French, in their turn, capitulate. Hostilities ceased at thirty-five minutes past midnight on June 24, after the French had signed that evening in Rome an armistice with Italy. The day before, Pierre Laval, who had been so long in eclipse, since 1936, and deeply resented it, was named a Minister of State in the Pétain government. In the chaotic corridors of Bordeaux he had already set to work to bury the Third Republic, which had accorded him the highest political honors but which he could not forgive for keeping him out of office the last four years. It had "vomited" him, he said, and now he was going to "vomit" it.[20]

He and Pétain and Weygand and others of like mind accomplished this at Vichy on July 10, 1940, when they stampeded a frightened National Assembly into voting to abolish itself and the Third Republic and to set up a dictatorship of the aged Marshal, behind whom Laval began to pull the strings.

By this date, July 10, I had returned to my post in Berlin, where I heard over the German radio the news of the vote of the National Assembly at Vichy. It was difficult to believe. We did not know then the pressures which had been brought upon the members of the Assembly, nor the extent of the confusion in which they met, nor the awesome dimensions of their moral collapse, nor the machinations of Laval and his followers, nor the nature of the ideas and ambitions of the half-senile octogenarian Pétain, though, as anyone who had been in France during the last tragic days could see, the hero of Verdun had emerged as a shining light of hope to the stricken, beaten people. Still, it seemed incomprehensible to me that the French, despite the shattering debacle, could in one frantic step go back on their own history and so basely betray their national character and their democratic institutions.

How, I kept asking myself, as during the mid-June days in Paris, had the French fallen to this state? What were the reasons for the swift military defeat and the sudden political and moral collapse? Had the French truly fought, as in the previous war against the Germans? I myself had seen little sign of it, but I had not seen all the battlefields, and in fact had seen very little of the fighting. It had moved too fast to catch up with. And, admitted that a crushing military defeat often brings down a regime held responsible for it, as had happened in France in 1870 and in Germany and Austria-Hungary in 1918, and in Russia in 1917—was it necessary for the Third Republic to commit hara-kiri as it apparently had done at Vichy on July 10, 1940? Certainly the French people had not been consulted.

And who was responsible for the staggering collapse of the army and the government? The generals, who had prepared and led the army so badly? The politicians, who, as Vichy had already begun to charge, had failed to provide the army with the necessary arms? Or did the main responsibility lie with the French people themselves, who, as the Vichyites—and some of the Catholic clergy—were beginning to say, had gone soft under the "godless" Republican regime? What responsibility fell on the extreme right, with its antipathy to the Republic, its sympathy for the Fascist dictators, and on the extreme left, whose Communists had slavishly followed the dictates of Moscow even when, as happened after the Nazi-Soviet Pact of August 1939, they opposed France's vital interests? Did the fall of France prove, as Laval was saying, that democracies in our time could not stand up to the dictatorships? Was democracy in the Western world, as Vichy—after Rome and Berlin—proclaimed, finished? Was France's collapse inevitable, the logical consequence of one of those straight, descending lines of history which some historians, Spengler and Toynbee for example, claimed, after the event, they could detect?

Had it been inescapable because the price of victory in 1918—nearly a million and a half Frenchmen killed in battle—was too murderously high to allow France to recover sufficiently to oppose the more numerous and more highly industrialized Germans so soon on anything like equal terms? Could the British, who had furnished so relatively few troops and planes even after the eight months of grace provided by the "phony war," have done more? And, if so, would it have been enough to stop the Germans, as had happened in France in 1914, when the British contribution had been even smaller because the fighting then had started immediately after the declaration of war? Would the French debacle have been averted if there had been time for American intervention, as there was in the first war?

Sitting in Berlin that summer of heartbreak when almost everyone in Europe, except in Britain, believed—and was this not true also in the United States?—that the Old World must come under the ruthless rule of Adolf Hitler and the self-styled German Master Race, I pondered these questions. The Germans, the men of Vichy, and even some Americans were sure that Hitler represented the "Wave of the Future." To many of us who had lived through the Nazi time in Germany it was clear that a Europe dominated by the German *Herrenvolk* would be doomed to a long night of mindless barbarism. Pétain and Weygand do not seem to have understood this, and Laval perhaps didn't care.

Even during that dark summertime of 1940 I could not bring myself to believe, as my broadcasts, dispatches, and diary show, that Europe was destined to such a sorry fate. I never lost hope that in the end Hitler would be brought down, his savage empire destroyed, and some semblance of decency restored in the world. Then I would try to find out how it was that Europe came to the brink of such an abyss. First there would be the task of trying to get to the bottom of the German story and to learn, if possible, out of my own experience and whatever documentation came to light, how it happened that a great and cultured people, the Germans, succumbed in the twentieth century to the barbarism of the Third Reich. Then I would turn to the French, with whom admittedly I was more in sympathy, to try to find out why this people, equally great and more civilized, and for most of the last century and a half the champions of personal freedom, of equality and fraternity among men, went down so quickly and easily that early summer of 1940 in a collapse more terrifying and more complete than any other in their long history.

Chance had made me an eyewitness to a good part of both of these cataclysmic events. But though I had seen them unfold and reported what I saw daily over the turbulent years, there was a great deal, obviously, that a journalist, working under the pressure of daily deadlines and largely ignorant of the secrets of state, did not know or understand.

Two decades later I accomplished the first task, concerning the rise and fall of the German Third Reich, as best I could. I then turned to the second one, an inquiry into the collapse of the French Third Republic. The roots of this story go far back—to the very birth of the Republic, and even further.

BOOK ONE

The Rise
of the Third Republic
1871–1919

2

A FREAKISH BIRTH
AND EARLY GROWING PAINS
1871–1891

By the very nature of its freakish birth and of the dissensions it inherited from the turbulent years after the great revolution of 1789, the Third Republic seemed destined for a short and stormy life. It is a wonder it was born at all, since a large majority of the National Assembly, elected to choose a new regime to succeed the fallen Empire of Napoleon III, preferred a monarchy. It is almost a miracle that it survived as long as it did—longer than any other form of government since the overthrow of Louis XVI—for most of the upper classes, backed by such powerful institutions as the Church, the Army, and the bureaucracy of permanent high officials, including the judiciary, opposed its very existence and for long fought to undermine it and bring it down.

It came into being by a fluke. The National Assembly, elected in 1871 after the debacle of France's swift and humiliating defeat by Prussia, had not wanted a republic. Nearly two thirds of its members—some 400 out of 650 deputies—were Monarchists. But they could not agree on a king. Some wanted the Comte de Chambord, the legitimate Bourbon heir; others wanted the Comte de Paris, the Orleanist pretender. A few hoped for the return of still another Bonaparte.

"There is only one throne," Adolphe Thiers, the President of the Provisional Republic, told the Assembly in 1873, "and three men can't sit on it." Thiers himself, who once had served the Orleanist King Louis-Philippe as chief minister, was being reluctantly won over to the republic. "It divided us least," he said later, thus putting his finger on one of the weaknesses which dogged it to its end—its negative and compromising character, its inability to win over all the nation and unite it.

Since 1792, when Louis XVI was finally deposed, arrested, tried, and guillotined, the French had tried almost every conceivable form of government: a short-lived republic culminating with the Terror of Robespierre and replaced in 1795 by a sort of constitutional republic under a Directory that lasted until Napoleon Bonaparte took over as First Consul in 1799; the Napoleonic Empire from 1804 to 1814; the Bourbon Restoration under Louis XVIII and Charles X from 1814 to 1830 (except for the 100 days when Napoleon returned from Elba); the Orleans "bourgeois monarchy" under Louis-Philippe from 1830 to 1848; the Second Republic from 1848 to 1852; and then the Napoleonic Second Empire under Louis Napoleon, the Republic's first and only elected president, who had already taken over dictatorial power in 1851 and proclaimed himself Emperor the next year. He and his Empire came crashing down in 1870 with France's crushing defeat by Prussia. On September 4, two days after the Emperor was made prisoner at the capitulation in Sedan, Léon Gambetta, at the head of a revolutionary mob, proclaimed a new republic in Paris. But it was not until nearly five years later that the members of the National Assembly, anxious at last to adopt some kind of permanent regime that would give the country the political stability it so badly needed after so long a period of uncertainty, and weary of the futile attempt to agree on a king to sit on the throne of a monarchy most of them wanted restored, in one fashion or another, reluctantly chose a republic.

The story of the inability of the Monarchist majority to reach an accord on who should be king is too long and complicated to be adequately treated in a book of this kind. French historians, depending on their political views, give varying accounts and explanations. But most of them agree that it was mainly the intransigence of the Legitimist Pretender, the Comte de Chambord, out of touch with the realities of life and public opinion in France after decades of exile in a provincial Austrian castle, which cost him the chance to restore the Bourbons to the throne. The two candidates for the throne were Chambord, the grandson of Charles X, and the Comte de Paris, the grandson of the Orleanist King Louis-Philippe. What seemed to be a reasonable solution of the rivalries of the two Bourbon houses was reached by 1873 when it was agreed that Chambord, who was fifty-three and childless, should become king, and that Paris, who was thirty-five and had a growing family, should be his heir. In this way the choice of king would be settled and the rival houses reunited.

But in a series of ill-timed, ill-conceived manifestos Chambord showed himself so uncompromising that even most of his supporters came to the conclusion that he would never do. He insisted, for one thing, that the flag of France must be not the tricolor of the Revolution, which the Orleanist king had found no difficulty in accepting, but the white fleur-de-lis banner of the earlier Bourbon kings. In the minds of most Frenchmen, the blue-white-red flag was a symbol of the overthrow of feudalism by the Revolution and of the social and political gains which had followed it. Chambord seemed to threaten these solid achievements and to be determined to bring about a fundamental counterrevolution. "I do not wish to become the legitimate king of the Revolution," he declared, and when his own backers in the Assembly suggested that he would have to make some sacrifices and compromises he replied: "I have neither sacrifices to make nor conditions to accept."

His stubbornness doomed him—and the monarchy. As Thiers, then President of the Provisional Republic, quipped: "Henceforth people will denounce only one person as the founder of the Republic in France— M. le Comte de Chambord. Posterity will christen him the French Washington!"

The matter, of course, went deeper than Chambord's obstinate inflexibility. The divisions among Frenchmen, which played so fateful a part in the life of the Third Republic, were a major factor. Though the Legitimists and the Orleanists did seem to reach agreement in the end, since both were Monarchists, a world separated them. As René Rémond has pointed out, they represented "two systems, two religions, two histories, two societies. Between them lay an abyss."[1]

But that was not the only split among Frenchmen in the early 1870s. A growing minority were Bonapartists who yearned for the return of another Napoleon. And a much larger and faster-growing minority, which would soon become a majority, were Republicans, who thought that France had had enough of kings and emperors, Bourbons or Bonapartes, and who believed it was high time that France seriously try a republic. The failure of the Monarchist majority to select a king played into their hands.

And so the lawmakers at Bordeaux, weary from four years of futile argument as to who should sit on the throne, sort of backed into the harness of a republic as if it were the least of evils—and by a majority of one vote in the Assembly, 353 to 352, though there would have been a tie had one deputy, who was against it, not been late in arriving for the balloting. Even then it was not clear to many members that they were actually choosing a republic. The day before, they had rejected it, or thought they had.

After four years of marking time the Assembly had finally got around to discussion of a constitution. A thirty-member committee had prepared several drafts of a constitution in 1874. All had been rejected. Now, in January 1875, a new draft was being debated. Time was pressing. The mandate of the Assembly was nearing an end. If it did not agree on some form of government there would be anarchy or another coup d'état, of which the French were now weary. There were rumors of plots to restore a Bourbon or a Bonaparte king by force. Two right-wing military men of royalist sympathies, Marshal MacMahon (of Irish descent), as President, and General Cissey, as Premier, were at the head of the provisional government. They could facilitate a military takeover.

Toward the end of January two amendments came up for a vote. The first, offered by a deputy named Laboulaye, read simply: "The Government of the Republic is composed of two Chambers and two Presidents." It was voted down by the Assembly on January 29 by 359 to 336. "Decidedly," as one French historian wrote, "the Assembly did not want a Republican form of government."[2] The next day an amendment by a former provincial professor of classics named Wallon was taken up and seemed destined for rejection by the same vote. It read: "The President of the Republic is elected by absolute majority vote of the Senate and the Chamber sitting as the National Assembly. He is elected for seven years and is re-eligible." There seemed to be nothing very new in this. Marshal MacMahon's term as "President of the Republic" had already been set by the Assembly in 1873 at seven years, because the Monarchist majority had believed that within that time the differences between the two royal houses could be settled and the President would then step aside for a king. But the Wallon amendment was hotly debated, and Wallon himself, a moderate man who did not consider himself a Republican, apologized to God and to the Assembly for even introducing it.[3] It squeezed through, 353 to 352, on January 30, 1875.

Confusing though it must have been to members of the Assembly, the acceptance by one vote of the seemingly innocent Wallon amendment would be considered afterward by politicians and historians alike as the act which established the Third Republic. By mid-July 1875 the Assembly had completed its task of drawing up the constitutional laws on which the Republic was to be based. Almost immediately the fledgling Republic was plunged into a constitutional crisis which nearly wrecked it at its very inception, the first of many political crises which plagued Republican France until the end and brought the overthrow of 107 cabinets—an average of almost two per year.

The constitution which gave France modern history's first parliamentary Republic provided for a legislature of two houses, the Chamber of Deputies and the Senate, a cabinet responsible to them, and a President with considerable powers, including the right to dissolve the Chamber with the consent of the Senate. In the minds of the Monarchists the presidency could easily be converted into a throne; indeed most of them saw in the patchwork constitution a framework for a monarchy. In the meantime the Republicans would be kept in their place by a strongly conservative President, Marshal MacMahon, and by a Senate which by the very rules of its election was bound to be a conservative force.

One fourth of the 300 members of the Senate were to be elected for life, first by the expiring National Assembly and thereafter by the Senate itself. The rest, who would serve for nine years, one third of them to be renewed every three years, were to be chosen indirectly by electoral colleges in which the rural councils were predominant. Each commune had one vote regardless of population, so that the conservative villages were vastly overrepresented compared to the large towns and cities. A senator had to be at least forty years old. Thus the Senate was designed to be a bulwark of conservatism and a strong check on the Chamber of 618 members, who were to be elected by universal manhood suffrage.* The Republic, as Thiers had insisted, was to be conservative "or there would be no Republic."

But how conservative? That question was soon to be resolved by a political crisis which shook the country, put to rout the extreme conservatives, and finally established by vote of the people what was to be called a "Republic of Republicans." The event is remembered in modern French history by its date: *Seize Mai,* May 16 (1877). It gave France the kind of republic it was to have until the catastrophic finale in 1940.

THE CRISIS OF THE SIXTEENTH OF MAY

The first elections under the new constitution, early in 1876, had given the Senate, as was inevitable, a Conservative-Monarchist majority and the Chamber of Deputies an overwhelming majority of Republicans—some 363 against 180, of whom 75 were Bonapartists. Léon Gambetta, the fiery orator who had been the chief inspiration of the Republican victory in the Chamber—though the three Republican groups, even at this beginning, had been unable to unite in a coalition—was the logical candidate to head the first government. But President MacMahon refused even to consider him. He was too Republican, too radical, for the arch-conservative Marshal. The President chose instead as the first Premier of the Third Republic a colorless moderate named Dufaure, and when he was quickly overthrown MacMahon picked a conservative Republican, Jules Simon. But Simon, a university philosopher and prolific author, was not conservative enough to suit the old soldier who was President. MacMahon wrote the Premier a sharp letter of reprimand, which left Simon no alternative but to resign. MacMahon's letter was dated May 16—hence the crisis is known by that date.

The President, on the urging of the Monarchist clique that surrounded him, named the Duc de Broglie as Premier, but the Chamber refused to accept him. MacMahon thereupon dissolved the Chamber and called for new elections. Though the President himself stumped the country and the de Broglie government used every conceivable form of pressure and intimidation to "make" the elections, the electorate nevertheless returned a sizable Republican majority to the Chamber. MacMahon, undaunted, appointed a general as Premier. The Chamber would have none of him. Plots of Monarchists and generals to seize power by a military coup and abolish the Republic were launched, but the Marshal, as honest as he was reactionary, declined to support them. He finally gave in and reluctantly appointed a Premier acceptable to the Chamber. In 1879, when partial elections in the rural councils surprisingly gave the Republicans a majority

---

* Women did not get the vote in France until after World War II.

in the Senate—the villages in France had finally staged their own quiet revolution—this was more than MacMahon could swallow, and he resigned. He was replaced by Jules Grévy, a moderate, austere country lawyer and a dedicated Republican.

The crisis of May 16, 1877, and the resignation of President MacMahon two years later were decisive. They established the Third Republic as a going democratic, parliamentary regime. They marked the final routing of the Monarchists and the end of their hope to restore a monarchy to France. It was a crushing defeat for the right-wing conservatives and for the Army and Church, which had so bitterly fought the rise of Republicanism, though it was a blow that they would never quite accept as final.

There were other consequences of the *Seize Mai* which were not so favorable for the future of the Third Republic. The constitutional laws had given the President considerable powers to balance those of the Parliament. Never again after MacMahon's experience did a French President dare to invoke his constitutional right to dissolve the Chamber. The President of the Republic became a figurehead. Moreover, the National Assembly tended to pick weak and mediocre men as chief magistrate.* Clemenceau, who himself was defeated for the office by a much lesser man, once declared: "I always vote for the most stupid." The popularly elected Chamber of Deputies became all-powerful, subject only to the slight restraint of the Senate. It became not only the chief legislative branch but in practice the executive organ of government as well, for premiers and their cabinets existed only on its sufferance.

Freed from the threat of dissolution, the deputies were guaranteed four years in office and could not be disciplined by their parties nor influenced by their constituents with the threat of having to face an early election. This helped lead to a multiplicity of loosely organized parties which made a stable majority in the Chamber impossible. Governments came and went, on an average of nearly two each year, but the Chamber changed only every four years. Majorities were created and dissolved, not by decision of the electorate during those four years, but by bargains struck in the corridors by the deputies, many of them avid to become ministers. Ministries followed one another with dizzy speed, but the same ministers often remained in office, regardless of the supposed change in the complexion of the government. For many politicians it became a game of musical chairs. Such instability and political frivolity was ill-suited to facing the challenging social and economic problems that began to confront every Western country caught up in the industrial revolution in the last quarter of the nineteenth century.

But these inherent weaknesses could not be easily discerned in the

---

* At bottom was the Republicans' fear of a man on horseback taking over and becoming a dictator. Memories of the two Napoleons were still fresh. That the fear was well grounded would soon be shown in the Boulanger crisis.

heady days at the end of the turbulent 1870s, when the majority of the French people finally made it clear by their votes that they wanted a republic. For nearly a decade after their unexpected and humiliating defeat by Prussia, there had been bickering and uncertainty over the form of government Frenchmen would live under. Now a choice finally had been made. And while the Church and the military and the Monarchists and the archconservatives predicted that only anarchy and disaster could ensue from a democratic regime based on the will of the masses,* most Frenchmen appear to have felt that a new day for them was dawning. At last they would have the individual liberty—if not the equality and fraternity—promised by the Revolution ninety years before. At last they would be masters of the government and not its servants and victims.† For them, if not for the sizable, powerful minority, the prospects for the Third Republic appeared bright.

And yet . . . If one looked closely at the structure of French society it could be seen that though the anti-Republican right had lost its political dominance it still held on to administrative and social positions which conserved for it great strength in the nation. It continued to dominate the Army, the Navy, diplomacy, the magistrature, and most of the machinery of public administration. The world of private finance and business and of the liberal professions was largely in its hands. By controlling most of the press it was in a position to keep public opinion in line. It had the strong backing of the Roman Catholic Church. Over the two remaining decades of the nineteenth century it would demonstrate its power in three crises which shook the fledgling Republic to its foundations. These were provoked by the Boulanger episode, the Dreyfus Affair, and the bitter struggle between church and state. Though the denouement of each of them served to strengthen the Republic in that the forces of anti-Republican reaction were in the end defeated, all three of them further deepened and exacerbated the divisions among Frenchmen which in the end were to prove so fatal to the survival of the Republic.

THE THREAT OF GENERAL BOULANGER

When, in January 1886, General Georges Boulanger became Minister of War, he was generally regarded as the most Republican of generals—indeed as one of the few Republican generals in the Army.‡ That was why

---

* During the "parliamentary" regime of the Orleanist monarchy, 1830–48, the electorate was restricted to 200,000 men, mostly the local "notables," as they were called. Universal manhood suffrage, introduced by the short-lived Second Republic in 1848, suddenly multiplied the electorate by fifty times.

† True freedom of the press was only established in 1881; freedom to set up trade unions in 1884; and freedom of public assembly in 1907. It is significant that even the Third Republic, regarded as it was by the ultraconservatives as "dangerously radical," was so slow in establishing such basic freedoms.

‡ Just as half a century later Marshal Pétain was believed by many to be one of the most Republican of the generals and even relatively liberal politically.

Georges Clemenceau, the uncompromising leader of the Radicals* in the Chamber, had insisted on his appointment.

The Army, which had changed over from the old professional force of the Second Empire to one based on universal conscription, was badly in need of reorganization and reforms. The staunchly Republican ministry of Freycinet wanted to see the changes directed by a general it could trust. It was scarcely a secret that most of the higher Army officers were Monarchists at heart.

Boulanger, a much-decorated veteran of campaigns in the Crimea, North Africa, Indochina and of the Franco-Prussian war, set to work with energy to overhaul and strengthen the Army. He weeded out the more zealous royalist officers such as the Duc d'Aumale,† uncle of the Orleanist pretender to the throne; quickly improved the living conditions, the discipline, and the morale of both officers and men; and modernized the instruction, training, and weapons of the troops. He had a flair for personal publicity, and the public soon became aware that the handsome young general was remaking the Army into a force that might soon challenge the Prussians and that moreover it was a Republican army of the people.

When on July 14, Bastille Day, the great national holiday, General Boulanger staged a dazzling military parade at Longchamp and, mounted on his famous black charger and surrounded by Spahis in their resplendent uniforms, contrived to make himself the center of attention, the huge crowd acclaimed him deliriously. Overnight he became the darling of the people, his praises sung in the music halls and in the streets. No one since Gambetta had so fired the imagination of the masses. Within a few weeks Boulanger had become the most popular man—by far—in France.

The politicians, even those Radicals like Clemenceau, who had insisted on making the general Minister of War, were not pleased. The old fear of a general on horseback returned to haunt them. Moreover, Boulanger seemed to be pushing France to a new showdown with Prussia. Hitherto the hero of the Republican masses, he began to be courted by certain right-wing leaders, including the expelled Orleanist and Bonaparte pretenders, who saw in him a possible leader who could not only restore a monarchy but avenge the 1870 defeat by Prussia. *"Général Revanche,"* they began to call him, approvingly. In the Reichstag in Berlin, Bismarck complained that Boulanger was threatening peaceful relations between France and Germany. At one point, in the spring of 1887, Boulanger demanded a general mobilization because the Germans had arrested a French customs officer at the border.

---

* The word "Radical" does not have the same political connotation in France that it has in American parlance. In American terms perhaps "liberal" is more accurate. The so-called "Radical Republicans" in French politics were not very radical. They were solidly middle-class and quite conservative in economic and social affairs.

† To whom he owed his promotion to general.

The cabinet and its supporters in the Chamber became alarmed. The Minister of War was becoming not only too popular but too belligerent. He would have to go. For his part, Boulanger quickly perceived his waning support in the government and in Parliament at the very moment the people were acclaiming him as their hero. Perhaps what he did next was inevitable, seeing what hero-worship does to most men. He turned on Parliament. He demanded the dissolution of the Chamber, a revision of the Constitution, and the establishment of a strong executive to be the head of a sort of authoritarian republic. He left no doubt that he felt himself to be the only possible candidate for that post. All the elements of the Right embraced him. But such was the confusion in France that he also continued to enjoy great popular support among many Republican Radicals and even among some of the Socialists.

Convinced that the flamboyant Minister of War had become a threat to the very existence of the Republic, the moderate Republicans took advantage of a change of government in May 1887 to drop Boulanger from the cabinet and assign him to an army command in the provinces, where it was hoped he would soon be forgotten. But this was based on a false estimate of the demagogic appeal of the general and the state of mind of the masses. Though still on active service and therefore ineligible to run for public office, he allowed his name to be placed on the ballot in several by-elections for the Chamber, which he easily won. The government finally retired him from the Army, thus making him eligible for office. Within a week he was elected to the Chamber from a constituency in the north where the votes of coal miners and peasants gave him an overwhelming majority.

He had been aided by a scandal which in the fall of 1887 erupted in the presidential palace itself and brought down both the government and the President of the Republic, the austere and venerable Jules Grévy, whose son-in-law, a deputy by the unlikely name of Daniel Wilson, had been found to be selling government decorations, honors, and favors from his quarters in the very seat of the presidency. It was the first of a long series of shabby affairs revealing corruption in high places—two "Republican" generals and several politicians were also involved—that were to plague the Third Republic and weaken public faith in the integrity of its leaders and institutions until toward the end, in the early 1930s, as we shall see, a succession of them so undermined the Republican regime as to make it ripe for the fate which shortly would overtake it.

Many of the criticisms of the regime that were to receive widespread support in the last decade of the Republic's life could now be heard as Boulangism became a threatening movement. A French historian of the Left later summed them up: the sterility of political quarrels, the repetition of ministerial crises, the emptiness of parliamentary debates, the delay in adopting fundamental reforms often promised the people, including the revision of the Constitution.[4] Almost despite himself—for he was a man of shallow mind who lacked any real political conviction—Boulanger became the leader of the discontented, on both Left and Right, and the champion of revision and reform.

On June 4, 1888, Boulanger, now a deputy, mounted the tribune of the Chamber to read a manifesto calling for the revision of the Constitution. In words similar to those used a half century later by Marshal Pétain and General Weygand he said: "France has suffered for several years from material and moral ills which cannot be prolonged without damage to all." Parliament, he added, had become merely a scene of fruitless debates that got the country nowhere.

Clemenceau, until recently his political backer and mentor, answered him:

These debates, which you deplore, honor us all. They show above all our ardor in defending the ideas we believe just. These debates have their inconveniences, but silence has even more. Yes, glory to the lands where men speak out! Shame to those where men keep silent! . . . It is the Republic itself which you dare bring down!

The Premier, Charles Floquet, was more biting:

I keep wondering what it is that brings our colleague to take before this assembly such a lofty attitude and to speak like General Bonaparte.

But be assured! At your age, *monsieur le général* Boulanger, Napoleon was dead!*

Although defeated in his effort to induce the Chamber to dissolve itself and submit to a new election—Parliament was not yet ready to commit suicide—which he formally moved on July 12, 1888, Boulanger was far from finished. His curious array of backers, from some Socialists and Radicals on the left to Bonapartists and Royalists on the right, now received generous financial backing from the Duchesse d'Uzès, heiress of the immensely profitable Veuve-Cliquot champagne concern, who turned over nearly a million dollars to the cause in the belief that she was somehow helping to restore the Bourbon monarchy to France—the confusion wrought by Boulangism apparently had no end. With such a sum, aug-

---

* Considering these and other words spoken by the Premier in a subsequent session as personally insulting, Boulanger challenged him to a duel with swords. This was fought on July 13. Though Floquet was sixty-five and the general only fifty, and though a military officer presumably would have had more experience with a sword than a sedentary lawyer and politician, the Premier wounded Boulanger in the neck in the second round and was judged victor. The general was accompanied to the scene by Madame Marguerite de Bonnemains, a beautiful young divorcee with whom he had recently fallen violently in love and who had become his mistress. Her decisive influence on him and his career was soon to be shown. It was not the last of such influences, as we shall see, on some of the important figures of the Third Republic.

mented by other contributions from the wealthy Right, the general and his aides were able to launch a daily newspaper, publish and distribute millions of pamphlets and handbills, and lavishly finance electoral campaigns. With general elections due in 1889 Boulanger's strategy now was first to get himself elected in a number of by-elections for the Chamber and with this impetus go on to win a national majority the following year. Perhaps there might be a shortcut to power by way of a coup d'état if enough of the by-elections proved his overwhelming popularity. Some of his advisers flaunted the idea. They believed, not without some reason, that the Army and the Paris police might not seriously oppose such a step.

On August 19, 1888, the general easily triumphed in three provincial by-elections. On January 27 of the following year it was confidently believed by his supporters that his moment had arrived. He stood for election that day in a constituency of Paris, which since the Revolution had been the stronghold of radical Republicanism. If he were elected here, it would show that the French, not only in the countryside but in the "red" capital, wanted him to take over the affairs of the nation. He had but to walk over to the Elysée Palace, oust the President, and assume supreme power. As a matter of fact, this was what he nearly did.

The various Republican groups buried their differences and agreed on a single candidate to oppose what they now called a military adventurer. They warned that Boulanger would try to overthrow the Republic if he won this election in the capital of France. They campaigned vigorously in every precinct. But to no avail. Boulanger was elected by 240,000 votes to 162,000. When the result became known large crowds surged into the streets demanding that their hero march to the presidential palace and take over. As it happened, he was not far away, having dined in a private room of the nearby fashionable restaurant Durand in the rue Royale with his aides while the election results were coming in. Outside in the crisp night air could be heard the wild shouts of the crowd: "To the Elysée!" His lieutenants urged him to lose no time. His hour, they said, had struck.

Actually, this was no idle boast. Several cabinet members hastily began to evacuate their ministries. At the Elysée Palace itself, where the President of the Republic had convoked an emergency cabinet meeting, there was near panic. All realized the precariousness of their position. As one historian later described it:

This evening Boulanger is the master of the Capital. . . . He has the crowd, he has the police, the Republican Guard, a part of the Army. . . . If he wishes to march on the Elysée who is there to bar the way?[5]

But the military hero wished to go elsewhere. Instead of going to the presidential palace to take over the dictatorship of France he went home to be with his mistress. At this most crucial moment of his life the company of Madame de Bonnemains meant more to him than staging a coup d'état.

When he returned later that night to the restaurant his disheartened aides told him it was too late. He never received another chance.

The imperiled Republic was saved not by any resourcefulness of its sworn leaders but by a denouement straight out of comic opera. The Boulanger threat quickly faded out in the same ludicrous vein. The government, relieved to find that the dashing general was not after all made of the stuff of heroes, concluded that he did not even have the courage to be a martyr. A mere tip that the government planned to hale him before the Senate, sitting as the High Court of Justice, for plotting to overthrow the regime was sufficient to send the general in headlong flight across the border to Belgium on April 1. The authorities, who really feared to bring such a popular figure to trial, secretly facilitated his getaway.

The precipitate flight burst the bubble of Boulangism. The great hero who had come within an ace of destroying the Third Republic had turned out to be a bogus hero. Two years later Marguerite de Bonnemains, who had contracted tuberculosis, died in her lover's arms in Brussels. Two months after that General Boulanger went to her grave there, took out his revolver, and shot himself in the temple. He could not, he said in a suicide note, go on without her.

"Though Boulangism," wrote a British historian, "ended as a farce, it had been a force."[6] It had almost brought down the young parliamentary Republic. Though the Right had used it as a tool to overthrow the regime, a considerable part of the masses on the Left had seen in it an expression of their resentment against not only the corruption in government but the failure of government to do something about the economic and social problems brought on by the advancing industrial revolution and the theory and practice of laissez-faire. These masses, their numbers swollen by a rapidly growing body of urban workers, had practically no representation in Parliament, where their interests were ignored.

"The Republic toward which I march," Boulanger had promised, "will protect the weak, the humble, the little men." Millions of little men had— naively—believed him. And though disillusioned by the swift deflation of their hero, they did not abandon their aspirations for some improvement in their miserable economic and social status. The more the bourgeois-dominated democratic regime denied them their due, the more they became alienated from the nation, thus further sapping its strength.

As for the Right, it was thoroughly discredited by its support of so spurious an adventurer. The cause of the Monarchists and Bonapartists, whose pretenders had in the end so ardently backed the preposterous general, was irretrievably lost. Never again would they become a serious threat to the Republic. This, at least, was one gain for the struggling parliamentary regime. The haunting fear of a man on horseback, of new coups d'état such as had overthrown the First and Second Republics, was largely banished.

The Third Republic was given a breathing space. Quietly it weeded out a few more anti-Republicans from the Army and the top civil service ranks. Not so quietly it began to settle certain accounts with the Church, which had joined with the rest of the Right behind Boulanger to try to bring the Republic down. But the forces of reaction, though for the moment in disarray, were far from spent. Five years after the collapse of Boulangism they rose again as the Dreyfus Affair burst upon the nation and tore it apart.

3

THE DREYFUS AFFAIR
1894–1906

Three days before Christmas in 1894 Captain Alfred Dreyfus, a thirty-five-year-old probationary officer on the General Staff, was found guilty by court-martial of treason for having turned over military secrets to a foreign power. He was sentenced to dishonorable discharge, military degradation, and life imprisonment on Devil's Island, a barbarous French penal settlement off the steaming South American coast of Guiana. Many in France, including the great Socialist leader Jean Jaurès, thought that Dreyfus should have been shot for such a terrible deed.

Dreyfus was a Jew. His conviction for treason set off in France a wave of violent anti-Semitism that already had been kindled by the Panama scandal* and apparently convinced a large section of the public that the Jews were responsible not only for shocking corruption in high political and

---

* In 1888 the company formed by Ferdinand de Lesseps, the renowned builder of the Suez Canal, to build a canal across Panama had gone bankrupt, with a loss to stockholders, most of them small bourgeois investors, of some $300,000,000. Subsequent revelations by government investigators and of various trials in court revealed an astonishing corruption in which several cabinet ministers, some 150 members of Parliament, and nearly every important newspaper in France were found to have been heavily bribed by the company in an effort to stave off a financial crash. Of all the lot, several of whom were prosecuted in the courts, only one man was ever found guilty and sentenced, and in his case only because he was the sole politician to confess. (As some French historians have facetiously noted, this confirmed the wisdom of the advice once given by a nobleman about to be strapped to the guillotine: "Above all, never confess!")

But in all the clamor over the Panama scandal it was not so much the bribed politicians and newspaper publishers who were blamed but three financial promoters who had handled the actual bribing for the company, all of whom were Jews. From this fact sprang a new wave of anti-Semitism in France. There was another consequence, similar to the one which would follow further financial scandals in the 1930s: the little man lost faith in the politicians who were running the Third Republic and in the Republic itself.

financial circles but for betraying military secrets to the hated Germans and thus jeopardizing the security of the nation, still in the throes of recovering from the defeat by Prussia in 1870. Most of the few remaining Jewish officers in the Army and a good many more Protestants, whose patriotism was also questioned, were driven out of the service by the fanatically Catholic and nationalist officers who controlled it.

The whole truth about the Dreyfus Affair probably never will be known.[1] French historians are inclined to believe that there was one General Staff officer, never apprehended, who did turn over military secrets to the Germans.[2] A second officer, not on the General Staff, was involved in this treason and exposed, but even the extent of his guilt is far from clear. The facts, as finally elucidated by the High Court of Appeals after twelve years of turmoil and fierce argument, add up to so fantastic a tale as to be beyond the powers of imagination of any writer of fiction. What concerns us at this point, however, is not so much the story itself of the Dreyfus Affair, absorbing and highly dramatic as it is, but the light it sheds on the rocky course of the Third Republic. Further seeds of what was to come, like the fatal elements which begin to build up in a Greek drama, were planted in French society in this unhappy time. The divisions of a divided people were deepened, the gulf between the Right and Left widened, and the chances of eventual conciliation between the two made more difficult, if not impossible.

The sole piece of evidence produced by the prosecution against Dreyfus at his court-martial, which began in Paris on December 19, 1894, was so flimsy that had the War Minister not engaged in a piece of illegal skulduggery in a desperate effort to procure the conviction of the Jewish captain an acquittal would most probably have been pronounced. This evidence consisted of one document, called the *bordereau,* an innocent enough term since it signifies in French merely an itemized list of papers or documents being handed over to someone, but which was to become famous throughout the world during the *Affaire.*

This particular *bordereau,* however, was not an innocent piece of paper. It was an itemized list of secret military documents that had been turned over by a French Army officer to the German military attaché in Paris, Colonel Max von Schwartzkoppen, believed by the French to be the head of Germany's military espionage network in France. The colonel received the documents but not the *bordereau* listing them. This was filched from the German Embassy by a French agent and delivered on September 26, 1894, to the Section of Statistics of the Second Bureau of the French General Staff. The famed *Deuxième Bureau* was the Intelligence department and the Section of Statistics was in charge of counterespionage.

For at least three years the counterespionage office had suspected that Schwartzkoppen had a contact in the French General Staff who was furnishing him secret military information. Military maps had disappeared as well

as papers revealing the nature of new explosives, French plans for mobilization and for cooperation with Russia, with whom France, hitherto isolated
by Germany, had signed a military alliance in 1892. A few small fry had
been caught and convicted. But the counterespionage bureau had been
under increasing pressure from the General Staff to ferret out the traitor in
its ranks. The *bordereau,* listing as it did highly secret information about a
new 120-mm. gun, its performance and use, a reorganization of French
artillery, and the latest Firing Manual for Field Artillery, could only have
come from an officer within the General Staff or from one who had a con-
federate in it. The word came down from the Minister of War himself,
General Auguste Mercier, to find the guilty one.

Scraps of evidence implicating the German and Italian military attachés were reexamined. There was a message from Schwartzkoppen to his
assistant instructing him to pay 300 francs to "the man of the Meuse forts,"
or to his mother, for more frontier maps. There was an intercepted note
from Schwartzkoppen to his Italian colleague, Colonel Panizzardi, the
Italian military attaché (both officers signed their letters to each other with
the name "Alexandrine"), which began: "Enclosed are twelve detail maps
of Nice that the scoundrel D_____ left with me for you."

It was thought highly unlikely in French Intelligence circles that the
attaché would give the real initial of his agent but the suspicion of the
General Staff fell on a clerk at the Cartographic Institute, where the maps
were made, by the name of Dubois, who also had a mother, which cast
further suspicion on him as perhaps the "man of the Meuse forts." But
nothing could be pinned on Dubois after a careful investigation. As a mere
clerk he would not have access to the kind of information disclosed in the
bordereau. Only someone in the General Staff could know of such things.
Because most of the documents dealt with artillery, he must be an artillery
officer, but one who knew what was going on in other branches of the
service as well. That definition would fit a probationer, who had not yet
been assigned to any one branch of the General Staff but who worked
temporarily in them all. Breathlessly, Colonel Jean Sandherr, chief of
counterespionage in the Second Bureau, went down the list of probationers
whose name began with "D." His eyes fell on the name Dreyfus. It rang a
loud bell in his mind. Just a year before he had made a formal protest
against the appointment of this young artillery officer to the General Staff.
He had called him a "security risk," but had been overruled. Now, in a
flash, he was sure he had found the traitor. It was the Jew, whose appointment only he had had the foresight to oppose.

His first move was to compare specimens of Dreyfus' handwriting
with that of the *bordereau.* Just as he had suspected, they were remarkably
similar. Handwriting experts were called in. Though they differed, the
consensus was that Captain Dreyfus might well have written the *bordereau.*
On the basis of this, and of this alone, Dreyfus was arrested on October 15

on suspicion of having committed high treason and lodged in the military prison of Cherche-Midi.

Before his trial by military court could be held he was convicted a hundred times over by the Parisian press, whose irresponsibility and venality would help to poison French society under the Third Republic until it was beyond healing. Abetting the press in finding an officer guilty even before his trial was the Army itself. Key officers, including Major Hubert Henry of the Second Bureau, and General Mercier, Minister of War, fed the Paris newspapers with material "proving" the treason of Dreyfus.

In separate interviews with two of the leading newspapers in France, *Le Matin* and *Le Figaro,* weeks before the trial, the War Minister declared there was no doubt of Dreyfus' treason. "The General Staff has known," General Mercier was quoted as saying, "that for more than three years Dreyfus was in contact with agents of a foreign power which was neither Italy nor Austria-Hungary." The inference was plain; Dreyfus was a spy for Germany. On November 1, 1884, a fortnight after the captain's arrest, the anti-Semitic *La Libre Parole,* which was being fed tips by Major Henry, "confirmed" the inference and added further details. Helped by this peculiar officer, the newspaper had been the first to reveal the identity of the captain arrested on suspicion of treason.

The miserable, shameful officer who has sold the secrets of the defense of our country and thus committed treason is Captain Dreyfus. . . . Arrested fifteen days ago he has made a full confession. There is absolute proof that he has sold our secrets to Germany.

Soon the other newspapers were repeating that the traitor had "confessed" to his terrible crime and adding fanciful details of their own. *L'Intransigeant* declared that Dreyfus was a gambler who lost two or three thousand francs a night. *Le Temps* and *Le Matin,* two of the most conservative and apparently responsible newspapers in Paris, explained to their readers that Dreyfus had become a spy because of his mad love for an Italian beauty in Nice, a *"magicienne d'amour,"* a lady of "noble birth," who was a secret Italian agent and had seduced the Jewish captain into giving her confidential material from the French General Staff. Gaston Méry in the *Libre Parole* found that Dreyfus had other love interests which led him to ruin, that he was intimate with "certain women of high Jewish society in Paris who maintained a veritable center of espionage and treason." Other journals implicated Dreyfus as the traitor who had sold the Germans the secret formula of the new melanite shell when he was stationed at the powder factory at Bourges.

Now the truth about all these charges was not difficult to come by. Dreyfus had first worked at Bourges long *after* the secrets of the new shell had been obtained by the Germans. He had not confessed while awaiting trial; indeed he had vehemently affirmed his innocence. As to his gambling and lurid love life, the chief of the Paris police, Lepine, at the request of the Army, had conducted an investigation. He had found a Dreyfus with a bad record, but his first name was Max. Lepine reported back to the Army that Captain Alfred Dreyfus, a relatively wealthy young man, was a homebody who rarely left the bosom of his happy family.* Since he was a man of ample means it was unlikely he would commit treason for any financial gain.

But above all, the French press, especially that part controlled by militant anti-Semites and Catholics, held that Dreyfus' guilt was obvious because he was a Jew and because "international Jewry" was conspiring to ruin France. Commented the Catholic daily *La Croix:* "Dreyfus is an agent of international Jewry which has decided to ruin the French people." *La Libre Parole* declared: "Jews like Dreyfus probably are only minor spies who work for the great Israelite financiers. They are the wheels of the great Jewish plot which is delivering us bound hand and foot to the enemy."

Soon the press was reporting that the Jews were bringing pressure on the government to suppress the Dreyfus case and free the guilty captain. Actually the government was hesitating to go ahead with the trial because of the lack of evidence. By the first of December every newspaper reader in France had been led to believe that Dreyfus was guilty. It was not that they wanted the captain to have his day in court. They wanted a court-martial to confirm what they had been told and now believed, and to assess the fullest penalties of the law against the Jewish traitor. Some newspapers were already demanding the death penalty, though that had been abolished some years before. Bowing to the clamor of the press. the government set December 19, 1894, as the date for the court-martial to begin.

Because the only piece of evidence against Dreyfus was the *bordereau,* and the handwriting experts could not agree that the captain had written it, and he himself testified at length with much conviction that he could not possibly have written it since he was not aware of much of the information in it, it seemed by the end of the first day of the trial that the military court would have to acquit the accused because of lack of evidence. The War Minister's official observer at the trial, Major Georges Picquart, so reported. But Picquart, whose stubborn honesty was to make him eventually the greatest hero of the *Affaire,* at the cost of military disgrace and, for the time being, of his military career, did not know that his Chief and also one of his colleagues on the General Staff, Major Hubert Henry, the number three officer in Counterespionage, were determined now, at any cost and regardless of the law, to have Dreyfus found guilty.

Henry made the first move. He was the only officer on the General Staff who had risen from the ranks. Aristocratic officers quailed at his rough, burly, sergeant-major's manner, but they did not doubt his patriotism or his honesty. On the insistence of the government and over the protest of

---

* Later evidence suggested that Dreyfus, like many officers, had had affairs with other women, though he denied it at his interrogations.

the defense the military trial was being held *in camera*. Henry brought forward a grave accusation. He testified that "an unimpeachable gentleman" had warned him that there was a traitor in the Ministry of War. "And there is the traitor!" Henry roared, pointing an accusing finger at the prisoner in the dock. When Dreyfus' attorney demanded the name of the "unimpeachable gentleman"* on the grounds that under French law the accused had the right to be faced with his accuser, Henry, touching his cap, answered: "There are secrets in the head of an officer that are kept even from his kepi." The presiding judge came to his aid. "You do not have to name the person. It will suffice," he said, "if you swear on your word of honor as an officer that this person told you the traitor was Dreyfus." Major Henry again roared out: "I swear!"

This was a damaging blow to Dreyfus but an even more devastating one was to come at the end of the four-day trial—indeed after it had ended and the military judges had adjourned to deliberate their verdict. In the War Ministry, General Mercier, with the aid of a bizarre figure, the Marquis Mercier du Paty de Clam, a major on the General Staff, had concocted a secret file on Dreyfus which he was sure would sway the judges after they had finished hearing evidence and had retired to make their decision. Though to present it without the knowledge of the defense was plainly illegal, as General Mercier fully realized, he was now desperate. The Jew had to be found guilty.

Like so many men involved in the Dreyfus Affair, Major Paty de Clam, scion of an ancient family, was an odd character. Bored with life in the bourgeois society of the Third Republic he lived in a peculiar world of childish fantasy and intrigue. In common with many other reactionary officers he was obsessed with the idea that France was crawling with spies and that most of them were Jews. Not all, though. For two years he had had one of his cousins shadowed because the man spoke several foreign languages and traveled abroad a good deal and therefore must be a spy.

For the War Minister the marquis now drew up a sort of criminal biography of Dreyfus which purported to show that the Jew's whole military career had pointed toward treason. Dreyfus, he wrote, was undoubtedly "the man of the Meuse forts," who was selling secret maps to the enemy. It was the Jew who had given the Germans the secret formula for melanite at Bourges. It was Dreyfus to whom Colonel Schwartzkoppen referred when he wrote of "that scoundrel D⸺." Into General Mercier's secret file on Dreyfus went a further piece of "evidence" which had turned up a fortnight after the Jew's arrest. This was a telegram to Rome from Colonel Panizzardi, the Italian military attaché which the French had decoded.

---

* The "unimpeachable gentleman" was probably the Marquis de Val Carlos, a former Spanish military attaché and a somewhat shady character about town. He had once warned an agent of the Second Bureau: "There's a wolf or two in your sheepfold." There is no evidence that he ever named Dreyfus, but by this time Major Henry was convinced that the Jewish captain was the culprit and he would stoop to anything to make it stick.

Panizzardi, like his German colleague, had been puzzled by the arrest of Dreyfus and by the lurid revelations in the Paris press. On November 2 he had wired Rome in code: "If Captain D. had no relations with you, a denial would be welcome to avoid press comment."

By the time Major du Paty had doctored the telegram to further the case against Dreyfus, it read: "D. arrested. Precautions taken. Emissary warned." It was as such that it went into the Second Bureau's Dreyfus file. Paty's singular biography of the "traitor," the documents it referred to, and a terse covering letter from General Mercier were put in a sealed envelope and unobtrusively slipped by Paty himself to the presiding judge of the court-martial on conclusion of the taking of testimony. The judge was requested to read its contents to his colleagues before they reached a verdict and then return it sealed to Paty. General Mercier, as was later revealed, intended to destroy his own contribution and disperse the original "documents" in the files.

His covering letter to the judges had said, among other things: "The traitor's name begins with D. . . . General inference: the above facts may be applied to Dreyfus. . . . The D. who betrayed the Nice maps, the writer of the *bordereau,* and Captain Dreyfus can only be one and the same person."

The defense lawyer, as he later said, could have torn such "evidence" to shreds and made mincemeat of General Mercier's hasty deductions. But he did not learn of them until much later. Even then he could not believe at first that the General Staff and the venerable Minister of War could possibly have concocted such false "evidence" nor presented it *in camera* without his knowledge in plain violation of Article 101 of the Penal Code.

The French Army procured its conviction. The verdict of guilty by the court-martial was unanimous. And after a public degradation of the convicted traitor on the parade grounds of the *Ecole Militaire,* whose utter barbarity sickens the stomach in the mere reading of a description of it seventy years later—the condemned officer's epaulets and his red General Staff trouser stripes were ripped off and his sword broken while the mob shouted "Death to the Jew!"*—Dreyfus was shipped off to Devil's Island, where the deadly, steaming, unbroken heat of day and night slowly wasted his life away. On the orders of the French government he was kept for a long time confined to his tiny stone hut twenty-four hours a day and at night his ankles placed in double irons attached to an iron bar across the foot of his cot. Since there would seem to have been not the slightest chance of his escaping from this remote island off the coast of South America, his treatment could only have been interpreted as a form of torture ordered by a civilized government from the ultracivilized city of Paris.

---

* Commented *La Libre Parole* the next day: "It was not an individual who was degraded here for an individual crime. The shame of an entire race was bared in its nakedness."

So fas as the government, the Army, and the general public were concerned the Dreyfus case was closed. A traitor had been caught, tried, and sentenced according to law. And yet in a few minds—in those of his wife and brother, in that of his lawyer, Edgar Demange, an elderly, highly respected, devout Catholic, there was a certainty that Dreyfus was innocent, that if there was treason it had been committed by another officer. Even in the mind of Major Georges Picquart, who did not like Jews in general nor young Captain Dreyfus, whose supervisor on the General Staff he was, in particular, there were vague doubts. As the War Minister's official observer at the trial he had been troubled by the paucity of evidence. Six months after the trial had ended Picquart was named head of counterespionage of the *Deuxième Bureau.* He was asked by his superiors to look into the motives which could have prompted Dreyfus to betray his country—a matter which still puzzled the Army leaders. Picquart never found any motives but he uncovered something else, which transformed his life almost as violently as that of Dreyfus and which plunged his country and his Army into a new tumultuous crisis and in the end enabled justice to prevail.

For the next twelve years France would be torn by strife over the rights and wrongs of this case that at times bordered on bitter, if bloodless, civil war. Families were torn asunder, old friendships destroyed, duels fought, governments overthrown, careers ruined. Some men went to prison, some committed suicide. There were riots in the streets and mobs threatened the lives of leaders courageous enough to express doubts of the guilt of the condemned Jew. The President of the Republic was spat upon and caned. The whole country seemed to be consumed by blind hatred and intolerance. It was hopelessly and hysterically divided between those, mainly on the Right, who believed Dreyfus guilty, and those, mainly on the Left, who over the years became convinced that he was innocent—the victim of a vicious miscarriage of justice engineered by the reactionary, anti-Semitic, Army Officer Corps and maintained by it even after the High Court of Appeals had exposed the perjured and forged evidence.

Long before the end of the *Affaire,* as the French called it, the question of the guilt of Dreyfus became almost lost in the melee, giving way to a fundamental conflict over the very moral concepts of French society which cast its shadow over the Third Republic from then on to the end. For to the Army leaders and their backers in the Church, and among the conservative classes, the supreme issue became not whether Dreyfus was guilty (though they believed he was) but that even if he was innocent it were better that he suffer the tortures of the damned (as he was literally doing on Devil's Island) than that the prestige and the honor of the French Army, on which the defense of the country depended, be impugned. Of what significance was the life and honor of one individual compared to the life and the honor of *la patrie?** Of what significance indeed were naked truth and naked justice for the individual and even respect for the human personality regardless of race or religion if adhering to them undermined the confidence of the people in the leaders of the Army and sapped their faith in the constituted authorities and thus weakened the fiber of the nation? Above everything else lay the national interest and throughout history individuals had been sacrificed for it, as had truth and justice.

Characteristic of this moral concept on the Right was the postscript which the writer Paul Léautaud appended to his contribution to a fund being raised for the widow of Colonel Hubert Henry, who would confess to forging documents against Dreyfus and would kill himself when placed under military arrest: *"For Order, Against Justice and Truth!"*† Colonel Henry, despite his admitted forgeries that helped condemn an innocent man, would become a hero to the *anti-Dreyfusards*. A rising young poet and journalist, Charles Maurras, who would found the royalist and ultranationalist movement of Action Française on the debris of the Dreyfus Affair, first attracted attention by an article in the Monarchist *Gazette de France* defending Colonel Henry for his crookedness, not only on patriotic but on moral grounds. Henry's forgeries, he wrote, were an act of "patriotic devotion." They were done "for the good and honor of all." The colonel's sacrifice," added Maurras, was that of a "moralist or a statesman." He promised that it would "remain immortal."

But there were other moral values in France that were far older and more universal than those of the Right, and once aroused in the minds and hearts of a growing number of citizens by the revelation of new evidence that Dreyfus had been the victim of a cruel injustice they finally triumphed, though not without many setbacks over a stormy decade. These concepts were simply that truth was truth and justice justice no matter where they led or to what consequences, and that no society, and no army, for that matter, could endure—or should endure—unless they were based on absolute respect for them. If the Army had committed an injustice in sentencing an innocent man for treason let it rectify its mistake. From this conclusion sprang the demand, at first only a whisper but then gradually growing into a clamor, for the "revision" of the Dreyfus case.

Nor would those who insisted upon it, Radical Republican politicians

---

* Adolf Hitler once gave his own answer to the question: "What is life? Life is the Nation. The individual must die anyway. Beyond the life of the individual is the Nation."[3]

† The anti-Semitic daily newspaper *La Libre Parole,* which organized the fundraising, omitted the word "Against" so that the phrase appeared as "For Order, Justice and Truth." Léautaud protested and threatened legal action unless the mistake was rectified. "You make me say," he wrote the journal, "that I am *for* justice and truth, whereas I am *against*." Among the other contributors listed was Paul Valéry, who would later become a well-known poet and essayist and member of the Academy, and who noted that his contribution was made "not without reflection."[4] A young army captain by the name of Weygand contributed ten francs for a monument to Colonel Henry. His political position was already evident.[5]

such as Georges Clemenceau, Socialist leaders such as Jaurès, writers such as Emile Zola, Anatole France, and the almost saintly young poet Charles Péguy, university professors and public-school teachers, be put off by accusations that they were harming the nation or the Army. It was in the name of national honor that Péguy asked for justice for Dreyfus, for to him the honor of a nation had to be based on truth and was tarnished by a lie. "The passion for truth, for justice," he wrote later of those days, "the impatience with things false, the intolerance of the lie and of injustice, occupied all our hours and used up all our forces." In the end they would be rewarded.

Le Petit Bleu: the Case Reopened

One day in March 1896, more than a year after Dreyfus had begun to serve his life term on Devil's Island, the French Intelligence Service intercepted a letter from the German military attaché in Paris to a French Army officer. It asked "for a more detailed explanation of the question in suspense." It was addressed to Major Count Ferdinand Walsin-Esterhazy, 27 rue de la Bienfaisance, Paris. It was written on a *pneumatique,* what the French called a *petit bleu* because of the color of the paper used in this form of note sold by the Post Office for circulation in Paris by means of pneumatic tube. The *petit bleu* was to become as famous a piece of paper in *l'Affaire* as the *bordereau.*

"What, another spy?" Picquart asked when the paper was placed on his desk by a junior officer. After glancing at it he ordered a routine check on Major Esterhazy, who turned out to be a descendant of one of the leading families in Hungary—the Esterhazys were known throughout Europe. Though born in Paris, he had fought in the Austrian army against Prussia in 1866 and in the French army against the same foe four years later. His war record was excellent; his private life something else. An obsessive gambler, he was constantly in debt. He had squandered his wife's dowry, engaged in various shady financial transactions, and had trouble with various mistresses. At the moment he was commander of a battalion of the 74th Infantry Regiment at Rouen. For some time he had been applying for a post on the General Staff Intelligence Service, stressing that he knew seven foreign languages and had a good background in German, Austrian, and Italian affairs. He had one friend in Intelligence, Major Henry, who had been backing him in his application.

That written application had come to Picquart and there was something familiar, he thought, as he pondered the *petit bleu,* in the handwriting. He went back to the Dreyfus file, which he had been studying in his spare time, and got out the *bordereau.* Excitedly he called in some handwriting experts. He even called in Major du Paty, whose belief in his own expertness in graphology had first led him to conclude that Dreyfus had written the *bordereau.* Now the marquis was just as sure that Esterhazy had written it. "Of course, it's the same writing!" he exclaimed. The experts agreed. Picquart now became convinced that Esterhazy, already shown by the *petit bleu* to be in treasonable correspondence with Colonel Schwartz-koppen, was the author of the *bordereau* and therefore the officer who had been selling military secrets to the Germans. Dreyfus, therefore, must be innocent.

He confided his thoughts to General Charles Gonse, Deputy Chief of the General Staff, and urged that the Army take the initiative in reopening the Dreyfus case in order to allay criticism that it was trying to perpetuate an injustice. He reminded his chief that the Dreyfus family, backed by a growing number of important politicians, was pressing for a new trial. The Army, he argued, should act first. Had General Gonse accepted this sound advice the Army might have been spared the loss of confidence it would soon earn, and the country most certainly would have been spared the crisis which shook it to the roots. It was an opportunity for the Army to retreat with honor by merely recognizing that an injustice might have been done.

But General Gonse was not the kind of officer to wish to compromise the Army in this way. He scolded Picquart, who had just been promoted to lieutenant-colonel, for trying to mix the two cases. "The Dreyfus case," he said firmly, "is closed. Besides," he added, "what do you care if this Jew is on Devil's Island or not?"

"He is innocent," Picquart replied.

The general studied the upstart young colonel a moment and finally said: "If you keep silent, no one need find out anything."

"General," Picquart cried out, forgetting rank, "what you say is abominable. I do not know what I shall do. But I will not carry this secret to my grave."

The next thing Picquart knew was that General Gonse ordered him off to duty on the frontier of Tunisia, where sporadic fighting was taking place with the Arabs and from where, according to later court testimony, some of the generals hoped the troublesome colonel might not return alive.

But Picquart was made of sterner stuff than his superiors realized. He was different in other ways from the general run of army officers. A deep student of history, philosophy, and literature, his cultivated mind had never ceased to grow, so that his horizons were broader than those of most of his colleagues. Even more important, he was a man of strong character who had a burning allegiance to abstract justice that outweighed any considerations of career. He had meant what he said when he warned his superiors that he would not carry the secret of Dreyfus' innocence to the grave.

On April 2, 1897, he wrote a private letter to the President of the Republic stating his conviction that Dreyfus was innocent, that the real traitor was Esterhazy, and that Dreyfus had been framed. He did not mail the letter, but two months later, while on leave in Paris, left it with his friend and lawyer, Louis Leblois, with instructions that it be sent to the President in case of his death. Under a pledge of secrecy he confided to his lawyer the evidence he had uncovered. Later he agreed that Leblois could divulge the story to certain reliable members of Parliament who had concerned themselves with the case on condition that he not be named as the source. It was this last act which would eventually make the generals and the other anti-Dreyfusards fume and result in Picquart's disgrace and imprisonment and in Leblois being for a time suspended from the French bar.

But the truth was now out, and it began to circulate. The venerable Auguste Scheurer-Kestner, Vice-President of the Senate, a conservative industrialist, and, like Dreyfus, Picquart and Leblois an Alsatian, became interested. So did Georges Clemenceau, a Radical Republican politician and editor from the Vendée who looked like a Mongolian and had a character of solid rock, a deep skepticism about the erring human race, and a raging passion for justice no matter who stood in the way of obtaining it. At first convinced, as was almost everyone else, of the guilt of Dreyfus, he had denounced the "traitor" with customary vehemence. But when the truth started sifting in he took up the cudgels for Revision, hammering away day after day over the years at the Army and the government, until by the end he had penned more than 800 articles on the *Affaire* in his daily paper, *L'Aurore.* Soon he would throw his columns open to an article by a famous novelist, which blew the case sky-high just at the moment the constituted authorities believed that it had been stifled once and for all.

Events now proceeded at an accelerating pace. On November 16, 1897, Mathieu Dreyfus, who had been devoting all of his time to try to clear his brother, publicly denounced Esterhazy as the author of the *bordereau.* Esterhazy demanded a court-martial to clear himself, received it, and on January 11, 1898, after the judges had deliberated for three minutes, was unanimously acquitted. That evening great crowds jammed the streets shouting "Long live Esterhazy! Long live the Army! Death to the Jews!" The next day Colonel Picquart, who had testified against Esterhazy, was arrested and lodged in the military fortress of Mont Valérien.

On the following day, January 13, an open letter to the President of the Republic from the novelist Emile Zola burst upon the scene. It was published in *L'Aurore* and Clemenceau, in a flash of editorial genius, gave it a title that would make it world-famous: *"J'Accuse!"*—"I Accuse!" It marked the great turning point in the Dreyfus Affair and seemed to demonstrate that in France the pen after all was mightier than the sword.

Zola at this time was at the height of his fame as a controversial novelist, acclaimed, attacked, and widely read not only in France but throughout the Western world. The twenty novels of the *Rougon-Macquart* series lay behind him. He was finishing *Paris,* the third of the trilogy called *Three Cities.* His world reputation had brought phenomenal sales of his books and a good deal of money. He had no need of further publicity, though he was now accused by the anti-Dreyfusards of seeking it.

The language of his letter was violent, the accusations scathing. He accused the generals by name and especially Paty de Clam, now a colonel, of having deliberately framed Dreyfus, and the Army itself of having *ordered* the acquittal of Esterhazy, the real traitor. He closed by daring the government or the Army to hale him before the courts for defamation.

The dare was accepted. The Government, urged on by the Army, moved immediately to prosecute Zola. But, firm in its resolve not to open the Dreyfus case, it limited its charge only to Zola's accusation that the Army had ordered the acquittal of Esterhazy. This would prevent the defense from introducing evidence of the military frame-up of Dreyfus.

The tumultuous trial lasted two weeks but the jury took less than an hour to find Zola guilty. He was given the maximum sentence, a year in prison and a 3,000-franc fine. Perhaps he was lucky to get home that day alive. The mob, which had invaded the corridors of the Palace of Justice, shouting "Death to Zola! Death to the Jews!" wanted to lynch him, and that evening his residence was stoned by angry demonstrators.* Even Premier Jules Meline joined in the anti-Semitic outbreaks. "The Jews," he told the Chamber, "who have foolishly unloosed this prepared campaign of hatred, brought down upon themselves a century of intolerance—the Jews and that intellectual elite which seems to enjoy poisoning the atmosphere and inciting bloody hatred." He promised "from today on" to apply "the full rigor of the law against them." The Chamber applauded his words and by a vote of 428 to 54 passed a resolution of its own:

> The Chamber invites the government to repress energetically the odious campaign . . . subsidized by foreign money to rehabilitate the traitor Dreyfus, who was unanimously convicted by the testimony of twenty-seven French officers and who has confessed his guilt.

Colonel Picquart, now almost as much an object of hatred in the Officer Corps as Dreyfus, had testified quietly but firmly in the Zola trial that the chief document cited by the Army against Dreyfus, the one in which the Italian military attaché had named Dreyfus as the spy, appeared to be a forgery. Three days after Zola's conviction, on February 26, 1898, Picquart was dismissed from the Army for conduct unbecoming an officer. His lawyer, Leblois, was suspended from the bar for six months because of his implication with his friend and client.

The Dreyfus Affair seemed to have been squelched at last. And it might have been—permanently—had it not been for the overconfidence of the Army and of a new War Minister, a loyal Republican deputy by the name of Godefroy Cavaignac, who had become convinced of Dreyfus' guilt. On July 7, 1898, Cavaignac rose in the Chamber determined to end the Dreyfus agitation once and for all. He announced that the Army had

---

* Zola's conviction was quashed on a technicality and a new trial ordered. He was convicted again by a court at Versailles on July 18, 1898, after declining to appear at his trial. Before he could be arrested to serve his prison sentence he fled to London on the advice of his lawyers. Apparently he despaired, or his lawyers despaired, of anyone's obtaining justice in France in the climate of those days.

irrefutable proof of the guilt of Dreyfus and for the first time made it public by reading to the deputies three incriminating documents in which the German and Italian military attachés had talked "of that scoundrel D_____" and Colonel Panizzardi had actually named Dreyfus as a spy. The whole Chamber wildly applauded Cavaignac for his courage. It voted unanimously to post the text of the speech on the official billboards of the country's 36,000 communes. The new civilian Minister of War became the hero of the day and, encouraged by his success, proposed to the cabinet that the leading backers of Dreyfus, Senator Scheurer-Kestner, Clemenceau, Zola, Picquart, and a score of others be brought before the Senate sitting as the High Court for plotting against the security of the state.

Then his house started to cave in on him. On July 10, Picquart, now dismissed from the Army, wrote a letter to the Prime Minister, which Clemenceau promptly published in *L'Aurore,* regretting that the good faith of Cavaignac had been abused.

Since the War Minister cited to the Chamber three of these secret documents on which the guilt of Dreyfus was presumably established, I consider it my duty to inform you that I am in a position to establish before a suitable court that the two documents dated 1894 do not refer to Dreyfus and that the one dated 1896 has all the marks of a forgery.

Enraged, Cavaignac ordered Picquart arrested for revealing state secrets. Esterhazy was also arrested—not on suspicion of treason, but on charges of moral conduct unbecoming an officer. The pot was coming to a boil again.

In order to answer Picquart's charges of forgery the War Minister had instructed a young General Staff officer, Captain Louis Cuignet, to reexamine the Dreyfus file and make sure of the authenticity of the documents he had cited. To the dismay of Cavaignac the young officer soon discovered that one of the three documents cited by the War Minister in his great speech as "irrefutable proof" of Dreyfus' guilt, a letter from the Italian military attaché to Schwartzkoppen in which Dreyfus was named as the guilty one, had been forged—most likely by Colonel Henry. The colonel was called on the carpet by the Minister of War himself and there, in the presence of the Chief of the General Staff and his deputy, Henry confessed to the forgery. He was immediately arrested and lodged in the fortress of Mont Valérien and the press was informed of his confession. The next day Henry was found dead on his cot. He had slit his throat with his razor.

Though admitting his forgery, he furnished no details to Cavaignac. Knowledge of them, however, did not go with him to the grave. Later they became known. In 1896, as the agitation for a new trial for Dreyfus began to mount, Colonel Henry had decided that more "evidence" against the condemned captain might be useful. A note from Colonel Panizzardi on the stationery of the Italian Embassy inviting Colonel Schwartzkoppen to dinner had been intercepted by French Intelligence and brought to Henry. Seeing an opportunity, he had called in a shady character named Lemercier-Picard, who had a certain expertness at forging handwriting. On a blank piece of paper as identical to that of the Embassy stationery as they could find, Henry had Lemercier-Picard write an interesting message:

Dear friend, I read that a deputy will question the Minister on Dreyfus. If asked by Rome for new explanations, I will, of course, say that I have never had any dealings with that Jew. If asked, will you say the same? No one should ever find out who was associated with him.

Henry then pasted this to the Embassy stationery along with Panizzardi's signature from the original. It was this document which Captain Cuignet discovered, on close examination, to be a forgery. Cuignet never forgave himself for having thus opened a hornet's nest. He was filled with remorse for having unwittingly caused so much embarrassment to the Minister of War and the Army, and, often on the verge of a nervous breakdown, spent the rest of his life trying to atone for it by actively asserting in his writings and speeches that Dreyfus was guilty.

Lemercier-Picard did not long survive Henry. One day, shortly after being visited by a former adjutant of Henry, he was found hanged in his room.

On the news of Henry's suicide, Esterhazy, though perhaps relieved by the thought that a number of secrets implicating him now would never come to light, nevertheless decided that it would be best to leave the country. After his arrest he had been tried by a military court on morals charges and retired from the Army. Now he fled over the Belgian border and from there went to London. General Boisdeffre, the venerable Chief of the General Staff, who had testified in court at the Zola trial that the document was genuine, resigned his post, admitting that he had been duped by Colonel Henry. Cavaignac too resigned, though sticking stubbornly to his belief that Dreyfus was guilty despite Henry's forgery. Probably he did not know the extent of the colonel's forgeries. Apparently he was unaware that the scheming colonel, in his zeal to pin guilt on Dreyfus, had also composed out of thin air seven letters from Dreyfus to the Emperor of Germany himself and one reply from Wilhelm II. A résumé of these, provided by Colonel Henry, had been published in Rochefort's *L'Intransigeant* on December 12, 1897.

They purported to show Dreyfus writing to the Kaiser asking for a commission in the German Army. Wilhelm II had replied, through the German Ambassador in Paris, that Dreyfus could serve Germany best by remaining in the French Army as a German spy. Further letters "showed" that Dreyfus had accepted this advice, though at least once the Emperor complained that "the scoundrel" was getting more and more demanding but was worth the bother. When the French government on the day of publication issued a formal denial and asserted that the "letters" did "not exist and have never existed," Rochefort assured his readers that under the circumstances the government had "to lie" and that the letters were genuine. The originals, he claimed, had been returned to the German Embassy, but photographs of them had been placed in the Army's files and shown to the judges at the court-martial of Dreyfus. It was on the strength of these, Rochefort added, that the Jew had been convicted of treason.

"Where is France? What became of the French?" Clemenceau would soon lament. Where indeed, when, as the jailed Colonel Picquart now publicly swore, a man had been convicted of treason on evidence that had been forged, and presented illegally to boot; where an Esterhazy could be whitewashed by a military court and a Zola found guilty by a civilian one; where a colonel who had confessed to faking evidence against the Jewish captain and who had killed himself rather than face the consequences could be hailed as a martyr to truth. A foreigner, confused by such a topsy-turvy moral world, asked a young French journalist, Paul Brulat: "Where are the honest men in this country?" And the reply was: "They are frightened."*[6]

In this poisoned atmosphere of fright and hatred the Third Republic was being further weakened. At least two factions judged the time and climate ripe to try to overthrow it. Madame Lucie Dreyfus, the wife of the condemned officer, had formally petitioned the courts for a revision of the verdict, and on October 29 the Criminal Branch of the High Court of Appeals agreed to review the case. Weeks before, in anticipation of this decision, a new storm had blown up in the press and in the Chamber. The judges of the criminal court were accused of being on the point of selling out France to Germany. They were branded as traitors. Rochefort in L'Intransigeant suggested that the eyes of each judge be put out—that was the only way to handle the traitors. Editors and deputies shouted that if the secret documents in the Dreyfus case were shown the judges of such a court the papers would turn up in the Kaiser's hands the next day.

In the midst of the turmoil the Royalists, who had been thought dead, revived. The official representative in France of the exiled Orleanist pretender was so encouraged that he began to draw up lists of the king's future ministers, prefects, and magistrates and telegraphed urgently to the Duc d'Orléans, who was on a hunting trip in Bohemia, to be back in nearby Brussels by October 24, on the eve of the opening of the fall session of Parliament. A few months later, when a new crisis arose during the funeral of the President of the Republic, the pretender was perched on the Franco-Belgium border, ready to make the short journey to Paris and there be crowned king.

---

* As a good many honest Americans were during the McCarthy era in the 1950s.

Félix Faure, a former hide merchant from Le Havre who had long served in the Chamber of Deputies and in various cabinets before becoming President of the Republic, died suddenly of a stroke in his office at the Elysée Palace early on the evening of February 16, 1899. It is quite probable that the rumors which swiftly spread over Paris about the circumstances of Faure's demise were based on fact. These spoke of a pretty young wife of a painter having been present on a divan in the President's office during the hours preceding his stroke. She was spirited out of this exalted spot by a side door before the wife was called. But more important than the circumstances of death, however much the telling of them might help relieve for the moment the tension of the Dreyfus Affair—the newspaper of Paul Déroulède, the fiery nationalist leader, charged that the Jews had killed the President—was the fact that his passing removed one of the most powerful of those who had staunchly opposed reopening the Dreyfus case.

Emile Loubet, a moderate small-town lawyer, who two days later was elected by the National Assembly to succeed Faure, was known to favor giving Dreyfus a new day in court. This was reason enough for hysterical outbursts against him in the anti-Dreyfus press. When the newly elected President returned from the election at Versailles he was greeted by hostile mobs in the street organized by Déroulède and his ultra-nationalist *Ligue des Patriotes*. Déroulède, an old Boulanger supporter, was urged to lead his mob into the Elysée Palace and chase out the new President. He decided to wait until the funeral of Faure on February 23.

With a ringing proclamation calling for the abolition of the 1875 Constitution in his pocket, Déroulède, accompanied by the writer Maurice Barrès, gathered with his followers, augmented by a number of anti-Semitic and Royalist hooligans from other organizations, at the Place de la Nation. His plan was to stop the troops returning from the funeral cortège and persuade their commanding officer to join him in marching on the presidential palace, where he would take over. He is said to have known of the presence of the Duc d'Orléans on the frontier and to have been unhappy about it, for he was a strong Republican who merely wanted a different kind of republic, one based, as Boulanger (and Louis Napoleon) had once asked, on rule by plebiscites instead of by Parliament.

When General Roget arrived at the head of his troops, Déroulède stopped him and implored him to lead the march back to the Elysée. But the general, on horseback, was too prudent to become interested. Brushing the agitator aside with his sword he led his troops on to the nearby barracks, where he had Déroulède and his followers arrested for disturbing the peace. Though it ended in a farce, the attempt might have succeeded had any of a number of other generals more sympathetic to Déroulède been in the place of General Roget.

Once again the Republic had been threatened. When, during the following August, Déroulède, in league with the Orleanists, Bonapartists, and the anti-Semitic leaders, plotted a fresh attempt against the regime, the government, now led by a more energetic premier, Waldeck-Rousseau, arrested the conspirators and haled them before the Senate sitting as the High Court. Déroulède, who earlier had been quickly acquitted by a Paris jury for his part in the February 23 affair, was now convicted and sentenced to ten years' banishment from France.

Intimidated by the clamor of the anti-Dreyfus forces that the judges of the Criminal Chamber of the High Court were traitorously conspiring to clear the name of the condemned Jew, the Chamber of Deputies—quite unconstitutionally—passed a law transferring jurisdiction of the appeal to all three branches of the High Court sitting as one. It was believed that the majority of justices of the full court were anti-Revisionists.

Whatever their previous opinions, the forty-six justices, after hearing the evidence and the report on the case drawn up by the President of the Civil Branch of the Court, delivered an opinion on June 3, 1899, annulling Dreyfus' conviction and ordering a new trial before a military tribunal at Rennes. Dreyfus, after nearly five years of imprisonment on Devil's Island, was brought back to face a new court-martial. Marquis du Paty de Clam, incidentally, was incarcerated in the military prison of Cherche-Midi on a charge of forging documents in the Dreyfus case. Colonel Picquart, after 324 days in prison, was released. Zola returned from eleven months of exile in England believing that justice at last had triumphed.

Because of the confession and suicide of Colonel Henry, the arrest of Paty, and above all the decision of the High Court of Appeals which threw out the "evidence" by which Dreyfus had been originally convicted, it was generally believed that the court-martial at Rennes would quickly acquit him. But this was to underestimate the folly of the French Army High Command and the madness of the reactionary anti-Dreyfusards, who now clamored for a death sentence for the captain and the deportation of all the Jews in France.

In the dreary town of Rennes the new court-martial began on August 7, 1899, and lasted for four weeks. Dreyfus, only two months away from his fortieth birthday, appeared to be an old man, his hair turned gray, his body enfeebled by the hell of five years on Devil's Island, but his mind alert and his determination to prove his innocence as strong as ever. His heart seemed to sink when all the old generals took the stand to again proclaim their belief in his guilt and resurrect all the evidence which had been thrown out by the High Court as forgeries. General Mercier, now retired but soon to be elected to the Senate, led the pack. It was he who had slipped alleged evidence to the first court-martial without the knowledge of the defendant, a violation of the law which the High Court had duly noted. Unabashed, he declared that it had been his moral and patriotic duty to do so, and he proceeded to rehash all the old material, forgeries and all. Because of his rank and reputation he overwhelmed the younger officers of the court.

After a month of listening to testimony—the court had had to adjourn temporarily when the chief defense lawyer, Fernand Labori, was shot and wounded by a fanatic, who was never apprehended—the seven judges delivered their verdict on September 9. By 5 votes to 2 they found Dreyfus guilty of treason, but with extenuating circumstances. His sentence was reduced to ten years in prison.

To all except the fanatical anti-Dreyfusards, the verdict was ridiculous. How could there be extenuating circumstances in the committing of treason? Once again Clemenceau in *L'Aurore* despaired of justice in France.

> Extenuating circumstances indeed! . . . Tomorrow the people, stupefied, will ask what remains of the historic traditions that once made us the champions of right and justice for the whole earth. . . . France is now a country with no security either for the liberty, the life, or the honor of her citizens.

Premier Waldeck-Rousseau also despaired of the Army ever meeting its obligations to the truth. He was determined not to let the Rennes verdict stand, but he knew a third court-martial would only do what the first and second had done. He decided to have the President of the Republic pardon the condemned man. Clemenceau, Picquart, and others who had defended Dreyfus at the cost of their careers, objected. If Dreyfus accepted a pardon, they argued, he would be acknowledging his guilt. And it would leave a shadow over Picquart, who, though released from military prison by the Government, was still in disgrace in the Army.

The Rennes verdict had overwhelmed Dreyfus. He suffered a nervous breakdown. It seemed doubtful that he could survive another long interval in which the High Court would have to review the finding of the second court-martial. In these circumstances and on the advice of his family and most of his friends he agreed to accept a pardon, but not without appending to his acceptance a letter to the President of the Republic, drafted by Jaurès:

> The government of the Republic gives me back my freedom. It means nothing to me without honor. From today on I shall continue to seek reparation for the atrocious judicial error of which I am still the victim. I want the whole of France to know by force of a final judgment that I am innocent.

On September 19, 1899, nearly five years after he had first been condemned as a traitor, Dreyfus walked out of the military prison at Rennes a free man.

Eventually the "final judgment" he had asked for cleared his name and restored his honor, as it did that of Colonel Picquart. Seven years later, on July 12, 1906, the three branches of the High Court of Appeals, sitting again as one, quashed the verdict of Rennes. Holding that there existed no evidence whatsoever against the condemned man, that he had in fact been convicted "by error and wrongfully," it forbade any further trial. It had taken twelve and a half years to achieve justice in this turbulent Republic where prejudice and passion ran so high; but it had been achieved.

Parliament approved a government bill to rehabilitate both Dreyfus and Picquart in the Army. Dreyfus was promoted to major and made a Knight of the Legion of Honor. Colonel Picquart, who had suffered stoically the indignities heaped upon him by his brother officers in the Army, was promoted to brigadier-general with top seniority, and in 1908 became Minister of War in Clemenceau's government. A man of great nobility to the end, he showed no vindictiveness toward the generals who had so unmercifully persecuted him. In upholding the innocence of Dreyfus after he had seen the evidence, he had only followed his conscience, believing that he had best served the Army and the country by a steadfast devotion to truth and justice.

It was not until 1931, thirty-seven years after Dreyfus' first conviction, that the testimony of the one man who at any time could have revealed who was guilty of selling military secrets to the Germans—Dreyfus or Esterhazy—saw the light of day. Some of the posthumous papers of Schwartzkoppen, who had died in Berlin in 1917, were finally published.[7] Though they did not clear up all the points in the *Affaire,* they did exonerate Dreyfus completely and reveal that Major Esterhazy was the French Army officer who had sold military secrets to the German military attaché in Paris and who was the author of the celebrated *bordereau.* Schwartzkoppen justified his lifelong silence, when he knew that speaking out would have prevented—or soon corrected—a horrible miscarriage of justice, on the grounds that the Chief of the German General Staff and even Kaiser Wilhelm II himself had forbidden him to reveal the truth. After all, it was to Germany's advantage to see France rent and weakened by the Dreyfus affair. And who would have believed Schwartzkoppen had he spoken out at the time, since an officer in the spying business automatically denies his deeds? And since he was, after all, getting valuable military information from Esterhazy long after Dreyfus had been put in irons on Devil's Island how could he possibly reveal his real contact? In his papers he maintained that on taking formal leave of Paris in November 1897, when he was returned to duty in Berlin, he had assured the President of the Republic on his word of honor as an Army officer that he had had no dealings whatsoever with Dreyfus and that, so far as he knew, the condemned man was innocent. He had not, of course, mentioned Esterhazy.

But his papers tell in considerable detail of his relations with that individual, who first came uninvited to his office in Paris on July 20, 1894, and, explaining that he needed money, offered to supply the Germans with secret French military documents. He described further frequent visits from Esterhazy, including one on September 1, 1894, when the French officer handed him over documents which later were listed in the *bordereau* and for which he paid 1,000 francs ($200) in cash on the spot. Thereafter for nearly two years, Schwartzkoppen says, Esterhazy visited him at the German Embassy on an average of once a fortnight, turning over to him French military secrets of "great value." In March 1896, more than a year after Dreyfus had begun to serve his life sentence on Devil's Island and the very month that Picquart discovered the *petit bleu,* which Schwartz-koppen admits to having written, the German officer says he broke off relations with Esterhazy because he had no more information to sell. It may have been too, though Schwartzkoppen does not say so, because he felt the French security service was getting hot on his trail.

In his memoirs he shed light on one more point. He declared that "the scoundrel D_____" referred to in one of his intercepted messages to Colonel Panizzardi as one who had turned over twelve military maps of Nice, and who, General Mercier had told the two courts-martial, could only have been Dreyfus, was in reality the clerk in the Cartographic Institute named Dubois whom the French had first suspected and then cleared. He says Dubois sold numerous military maps to both the Germans and Italians over a long period.

Schwartzkoppen's revelation that both Esterhazy and Dubois continued to furnish him with secret maps and papers long after Dreyfus was sentenced would seem to corroborate the belief of the *Deuxième Bureau* that confidential military information had continued to flow to the Germans even though it no longer could have come from Dreyfus.*

More than any other upheaval the Dreyfus Affair sheds light on the fatal fissures in French society during the time when the Third Republic was moving into the twentieth century. The Radical Republicans, supported by most of the Socialists, had finally triumphed over the forces of the Right, but the bitterness between them had been exacerbated almost

---

* Not all the anti-Dreyfusards in France were convinced by the revelations in the Schwartzkoppen papers. In 1964 a book was published in France written by Madame Henriette Dardenne, the daughter of the former War Minister Cavaignac, who, it will be remembered, had convinced himself of Dreyfus' guilt despite the confession of forgery he obtained from Colonel Henry.[8] His daughter was still convinced of that guilt, and with a stunning absoluteness. It may be true, as the historians have written, that no one who did not live through the *Affaire* can have the faintest conception of the fierce and ugly passions it aroused in France. But reading Madame Dardenne's book helps. More than half a century after the event she is as raucous and passionate and as blind to the evidence and the forgeries as any violent, hysterical anti-Dreyfusard of the time. To her there is not the shadow of doubt that Dreyfus was guilty of treason, that Colonel Picquart himself was a despicable traitor, and that most of the unsavory characters who, on all the evidence put before the highest French court, framed the innocent Jewish captain, were virtuous, patriotic heroes, fiercely devoted to the truth.

beyond hope of repair. They seemed to dwell more and more in two separate, hostile worlds, divided not only politically but by their fundamental attitudes toward morals and religion. There was no tolerance, no breadth of understanding, which might have led toward reconciliation in the interest of national unity. One more imposing layer was added to the wall which had been raised between the two Frances by the Revolution and which had been built up ever higher, layer by layer, by the successive crises of the June Days, the Second of December, the Commune, the Sixteenth of May, and Boulangism.*

Not only the Army, which had played such an inglorious role in the Dreyfus controversy, was weakened, but also the country, which, because of its obsession for a whole decade with the *Affaire,* had given little attention to other pressing problems: the static economy, lagging social welfare, labor-management strife, the fall of the birth rate, foreign policy— and this at a moment when a new threat was rising beyond the Rhine from a unified, dynamic, militarist, and increasingly restless and belligerent Germany.

---

* These are historic dates and events in nineteenth-century French history, not all of which can be chronicled in a work of this kind. The June Days saw the savage suppression of the workers of Paris by the Republican general Louis Cavaignac after the uprising of 1848 had overthrown the Orléans monarchy and a Republic had been proclaimed. The Second of December was the day in 1851 on which Louis Napoleon staged his coup overthrowing the Republic. The Commune of 1871 was the bloodiest of all events in Paris during the nineteenth century and had a lasting impact on French life until the end of the Republic, contributing more than any other happening to the alienation of the working class. This revolt of Parisian workers and other Republicans, shortly after the siege of Paris by the Prussians, was put down with terrible brutality by Thiers and regular French government troops. Some 20,000 persons were killed in Paris in the savage fighting—more than died in the Reign of Terror during the Revolution—and 4,000 *Communards* were afterward condemned to death, including twenty women, though not all were executed. Thousands were deported.

Further seeds of the catastrophe of 1940 were planted during this time and there are some deadly parallels between the the defeatism of the conservative politicians and generals in the 1870 war with Prussia and that of the same types in 1939–40.

4

THE CONSOLIDATION OF THE REPUBLIC
1880–1914

THE STATE VERSUS THE CHURCH

Because the Catholic Church, and especially a large number of militant priests and monks from such orders as the Assumptionists, had taken an active and verbally violent part in the bitter campaign to deny justice to Dreyfus and discredit the troubled Republic, the Church now had to face the consequences. Though the new Premier, René Waldeck-Rousseau, was a moderate, his government (1899–1902) was dominated in Parliament by a coalition of Radical Republicans and Socialists who, believing that the very existence of the Republic had been endangered by the Boulanger and Dreyfus affairs, in which the Catholic clericals had played so important a role, were now determined to curb the power of the Church to undermine the regime.

The first objective was to stamp out the Church's hold on education, which, in the view of the Republican majority, was turning the young against the Republic and all it stood for. Already a start in this direction had been made in the early 1880s under the tenacious anticlerical leadership of Jules Ferry. Until that time the Church had dominated primary and secondary education in France. Half of the boys and nearly all the girls attended Catholic parochial schools, partly because there were not enough public schools available. In numerous villages the only school was Catholic. Even in the public schools many of the teachers were priests, monks, and nuns, and religious instruction in them was obligatory. To a growing number of ardent Republicans this Catholic education was a threat to the Republic. It was fashioning the youth into enemies of the Republican way of life.

Against such a long-established and entrenched institution as the Church, Ferry had moved gradually but firmly. In a series of legislative enactments which he sponsored over the first half of the decade religious instruction in all public schools was forbidden, members of religious orders were prohibited from teaching in them (after a transition period of five years), tuition was abolished, and large sums were appropriated for the building of additional public schools and numerous normal schools for the training of lay teachers. Parochial schools were permitted to continue, but public funds could no longer be given them. There was an outcry among the clericals, who denounced the lay public schools as "atheist and immoral" and warned that the Ferry reforms were but a first step. In this they were right. Under the impact of the Dreyfus agitation the Republican government now, as the first decade of the new century began, took further and more drastic measures.

The most vocally anti-Republican of the Catholic orders, the Assumptionists, was dissolved early in 1901. Shortly afterward the so-called Associations Act of 1901 was passed to curb the other orders. *"Congrégations,"* as the various orders were called, were permitted to continue to exist only if they were formally authorized by Parliament, and no member of them could teach in any school in France unless his order was authorized. Waldeck-Rousseau wished not to suppress the great Catholic orders but to regulate them and remove them from politics. He expected that Parliament would be reasonable in "authorizing" the *congrégations* that behaved themselves.

And so it might have been had the Catholic clericals not participated so violently in the spring national elections of 1902 against the coalition which had passed the Associations Act. The coalition was maintained in power by the electorate but its leaders were exasperated and enraged at the Church whose militants once more had tried to overthrow them.

Sensing that the new Parliament would go much further in enforcing the law against the *congrégations* than he desired, Waldeck-Rousseau resigned in June 1902 and was replaced as Premier by Emile Combes.* This was a man of a different stripe. Waldeck had been a sophisticated, highly successful lawyer in Paris and was the most tolerant of men. Combes was a country doctor who at first had studied for the priesthood in a seminary, where he had written a thesis on St. Thomas Aquinas and then, recoiling from becoming a priest, had turned to medicine. But in the process he had turned bitterly against the Church and now, in 1902, a little old man of seventy, with long years of experience in the Senate, where he had battled the clerical interference in politics, he was determined with all the zeal of an Inquisitor to settle accounts once and for all with the Catholics.

Three weeks after assuming office he closed down all primary schools for girls maintained by the religious Sisters. A month after that, in July 1902, he gave all 3,000 remaining parochial schools in France eight days

---

* Waldeck's government lasted three years, the longest in the history of the Third Republic. He was the only Premier, I believe, who ever resigned on the morrow of an electoral triumph.

to shut down for good. Riots broke out up and down the land as irate parents, priests, nuns, and monks defied gendarmes and troops sent to enforce the order. But the schools were closed.

Combes then tackled what he considered the main enemy. He persuaded Parliament to reject the request for "authorization" of a'l fifty-four *congrégations* which had asked for it. In one stroke they were thus dissolved and many of the 20,000 monks affected fled abroad. Finally, in July 1904, he completed the liquidation of the orders by pushing through a law forbidding "the teaching of any kind in France by the *congrégations.*" Even those few orders previously authorized to teach were suppressed but in some cases they were given ten years to wind up their affairs. Some 16,000 "teaching monks" found themselves out of work.

Then Combes took on the Holy See itself. For years he had been enraged at the refusal of the pope to accept the nomination of certain French bishops named by the state, though by the terms of the Concordat signed by Napoleon Bonaparte and Pope Pius VIII in 1801 the French government had held the right of appointment. Combes threatened to break off diplomatic relations with the Vatican.

In the spring of 1904 a new pope, Pius X, protested bitterly against a state visit of the President of the Republic, Emile Loubet, to the king of Italy in Rome, which twenty years before had been occupied by the troops of the newly unified kingdom and proclaimed the capital, thus depriving the papacy of its last temporal sovereignty. The Vatican had never recognized the Italian occupation of Rome and Pius X resented France's apparent recognition of it by the state visit of Loubet. But his resentment was mild compared to Combes' reaction to his protest. The Premier called it an "intolerable" interference in France's conduct of its foreign affairs and recalled his Ambassador to the Holy See. The Chamber overwhelmingly (427 votes to 95) supported him, and by autumn it had taken up a new law denouncing the Concordat and proclaiming the separation of Church and state.

The law was passed the following year, in 1905, even though Combes, for reasons other than clerical, had been forced out of office. And though the pope condemned the law, forbade its acceptance by French Catholics, and excommunicated every deputy who voted for it (there were 341 of them in the Chamber), the French government went ahead with the task of separating Church and state once and for all. Title to all Church property was taken over by the state, priests and bishops were removed from the public payroll, and the handling of worship was given to associations of Catholic laymen. For a couple of years there was considerable strife and great confusion, but in the end, under the more tolerant administration of a rising young Socialist, Aristide Briand, who had drafted the separation law and then administered it as Minister of Cults, a compromise was worked out. The Church buildings were put at the disposal of the clergy and the French Catholic hierarchy was permitted to resume its authority over Church affairs—for the first time without interference from the state.

Once more the Republic had triumphed, as it had against its enemies during the Boulanger and Dreyfus crises. In twenty-five years, from 1880 to 1905, it had relentlessly curbed the position and the power of the Church, cutting off its financing by the state, chasing it from the schools, dissolving its powerful orders, taking over its remaining property, and excluding it from politics. But in one respect the Church gained. The separation of Church and state freed the Church from government control and interference. Though Catholicism declined for at least a decade, as was shown by the decrease in attendance at worship and in the sharply rising number of civil marriages and equally sharp drop in baptisms, it would thereafter begin to show a new vigor. Anticlericalism, now that it had won the big battles, would begin to decline, though it remained a force, albeit diminishing, to the very end of the Republic.

But there were scars left by this struggle, as by all the others. Many Catholics resented what they felt was persecution by the state. Most of them found themselves excluded from the political circles that dominated public life. As for the Republican majority, many, despite their triumph, remained suspicious of the Church and hostile to its more ardent adherents. Freemasonry helped to keep the fires burning. Though its membership was small it was politically potent and ever on the alert to discover and combat an upsurge in political Catholicism. In return, the Freemasons were feared and despised by the Church. They were resented by most of the generals, especially after General André, Minister of War from 1900 to 1904, in an effort to Republicanize the Army, enlisted the aid of the Masonic lodges in weeding out the most zealous Catholics from the Officer Corps.

In some ways the Army proved more difficult to deal with than the Church. The great military chiefs, with scarcely an exception, were Catholic and Royalist. To expel them all would have weakened the Army fatally. There were simply not enough Republican generals to man the High Command. Yet, despite the uproar in Parliament when his arrangement with the Freemasons was revealed (it brought his downfall), General André, and his immediate successors succeeded in getting rid of at least some of the worst reactionaries in the top military posts. He reformed the system of promotions, which had been exclusively in the hands of a Catholic-Royalist clique. Younger officers, not so zealous as their elders for monarchy and Church, were brought forward. And though the morale of the Army remained as low as its prestige for nearly a decade, a new spirit set in around 1910 which would rejuvenate the military establishment and prepare it, just in time, for the great ordeal of 1914.

By 1905, then, the Third Republic had finally and definitely established itself. Its political leaders had successfully met all challenges and con-

solidated the regime. Monarchism became a lost cause. Bonapartism too.*
The French, as a whole, were no longer interested in having a king or a
man on horseback. Representative democracy, Republican in form, despite
all its fumblings and shortcomings, was widely accepted. The alliance of
Church and Army, if not broken, had been greatly weakened by the drastic
curbing of the first and the partial purging of the second after the Dreyfus
case. It no longer possessed the strength to overthrow the Republic.
Almost without anyone noticing it amid the distractions and passions of
domestic strife a vast overseas empire, second only to that of Great
Britain, had been built up. German efforts since 1871 to keep France
isolated in Europe had been frustrated. The alliance with Russia in 1892
and the Entente with Great Britain in 1904 had given France some assurance that henceforth she would not have to stand alone against the
traditional enemy beyond the Rhine, by now become the strongest military
power in Europe and the most threatening.

France, under the Third Republic, could now turn its attention and
its energies from its domestic upheavals to the new challenges of the new
century both at home and abroad.

THE CHALLENGES OF THE TWENTIETH CENTURY

In the heat of the Dreyfus Affair and the State-Church conflict these
challenges had scarcely been perceived. Obsession with the great domestic
issues had blinded the stalwart Republicans, who controlled Parliament
and government, to the urgency of the economic and social problems which
beset all the rapidly industrializing Western nations at the turn of the
century, and from which France could not escape.†

In the industrial revolution, from which the new economic and social
problems grew, France was falling behind the other leading nations, behind
Great Britain and the United States, and, above all, behind rival Germany.
The French were having difficulty in changing over from the age of wood,
wind, and water to the more complicated age of coal, steam, iron, and
steel, and on the whole they did not much like the transformation or at
least the speed with which it was being carried out in other countries. They
stuck to sailing ships long after others had abandoned them for steamers.
At the beginning of the Republic, France had been the world's second
greatest industrial and trading nation. By 1914 it had fallen to a poor
fourth, behind Germany, Great Britain, and the United States, and per
capita income was only one half of that in America.

Lack of an adequate supply of coal in France helped to put a brake

---

* In the Chamber elected in 1898 the Royalists, who now called themselves
Conservatives, had 80 members of various monarchist nuances. The Bonapartists were
reduced from a recent strength of 100 deputies to none.

† In the opinion of some, on both the Left and the Right, the Republican leaders had kept the pot boiling on the Church issues in part at least because they wanted
to divert the attention of the masses, who backed them in their anticlerical policies,
from much-needed and long-retarded economic and social reforms.

on industrial development. But there were more important reasons that lay in the French character and temperament and in the history of their economic evolution. For one thing, the Frenchman was too individualistic to submit willingly to the inexorable demands of the machine or to accept fully the new disciplines—and abuses—of unbridled capitalism, which was spurring rapid industrial growth abroad. Instinctively the French disliked and distrusted bigness in business, in finance, in farming, preferring if possible to keep such enterprises down to family size. In 1914, on the eve of a world war which was to devour the products of industry on a scale never before dreamt of in the Western world, one half of all workers in France were engaged in shops employing fewer than a hundred men; one third of all workers labored in tiny enterprises of ten workers or less. Quality, in which the gifted, industrious artisan had such pride and which was appreciated by the French customer, was preferred to quantity, which was made possible by the new steam-driven machines, whose goods, in the French view, were shoddy.

French exports, insofar as any were possible under the extremely high domestic tariffs, which priced most French products out of world markets, were largely in luxury goods—silk textiles, vintage wines, perfumes, and women's dresses and hats designed and made in the fashion center of the world, which Paris was. These were exquisite products, enjoyed by the French as well as the foreign consumer who could afford them. But in a Europe drifting, as the twentieth century got underway, toward war, world supremacy in turning out fine silks and the best of wines, perfumes, and ladies' hats hardly compensated for the big blast furnaces in the Ruhr just across the Rhine turning out steel for Krupp's big guns.

The course a people chose to take depended on the kind of society it wanted. And on the whole the French were satisfied. Though agriculture was backward despite a fertile soil and favorable climate, France produced 90 percent of all the food its people consumed. For the most part the country was quite self-sufficient. Its well-being was not very dependent on the whims of an erratic, impersonal world market which brought periodic depressions to so many other peoples. Though lagging behind the others in making steel and iron and their products, the French (with the exception of the city and rural workers) felt reasonably happy with their lot. They had considerable economic stability and prosperity, and their government, much as they distrusted it, gave them a balanced budget and a currency seemingly as solid as gold. Was not the French way of life the envy of the world, especially of the Germans?*

FLAWS IN THE STRUCTURE

Yet there were flaws in the economic and social structure which few saw or understood—or, if they did, admitted—and which, if corrected, as

---

* French writers liked to quote a German saying, often attributed to Goethe, that the good life was "to live like God in France."

they might have been by a more resolute, honest, and judicious leadership in government, Parliament, and the world of business and finance, would have made France stronger and better able to compete with the other Great Powers. Some of the flaws were a consequence of history. Others were the result of the shortsightedness and greed of a small possessing class, which feared that too-rapid industrialization might endanger its entrenched wealth. And there was a connection between history and this age-old human failing.

Those who had gained control or ownership of the most lucrative commercial, industrial, financial, and transportation enterprises in France owed their good fortune in most cases to grants from the state. Not just from the Third Republic, but from all the other regimes which had preceded it and set the precedent. One remembers the famous remark usually attributed to Louis-Philippe, the Orleanist "bourgeois king" between 1830 and 1848, but actually pronounced by one of his ministers: *"Messieurs, enrichez-vous!"* And it could not be said that the bankers and businessmen did not act on the advice. One state concession after another enabled them to get rich, or richer. The practice went back to the old Bourbon monarchy, when, especially during the eighteenth century, there took place financial operations on behalf of the court which, in the words of a Swiss historian, "developed into a state-organized looting of the national wealth."[1]

The king was beheaded, the *ancien régime* overthrown, as that century came to an end, but the custom of the state granting profitable concessions to favored individuals and families continued under republics, two Bonaparte dictators, more monarchies and more republics. During the closing decades of the eighteenth century and throughout the nineteenth, most of the great family fortunes, and what an interesting right-wing contemporary French historian has called *Les Dynasties Bourgeoises* were founded as bounties from the national government.*

Napoleon showed how generous the state could be to its friends shortly after being crowned Emperor. In a message to the Senate in 1808 he declared: "It is for us to assure the well-being and the fortunes of the families which place themselves entirely at our service." The next year he turned over most of the state-owned canals, then one of the principal means of transport, to some of his favorites for private exploitation. Highly profitable mining concessions followed. It had been the practice of the old monarchy, for all its corruption, to let out mining concessions for brief

---

* E. Beau de Loménie *Les Responsabilités des dynasties bourgeoises,* in four volumes. This is an interesting work presenting a minority view. A pungent writer, a long-time Royalist who criticizes the abuses of the bourgeois-capitalist world in almost the same strident tones as the Marxists, whom he deplores, Beau de Loménie argues in his central thesis that France from Napoleon's time to the end of the Third Republic was dominated by the "bourgeois dynasties," consisting of a small group of families who established business and financial empires largely through state concessions and who because of their position and money controlled the press and wielded such political power that Parliament and government usually did their bidding.

periods only. Now Napoleon, by a law of 1810, turned the mines over to private ownership in perpetuity, and what is more, for free, demanding only that 5 percent of the net profits accrue to the state. Already before becoming dictator, Napoleon had established the national bank, the Bank of France, which, though it helped restore order to the nation's chaotic finances, quickly rendered its narrow circle of investors, who had provided only a small nominal capital (2 million francs),* fantastically high profits. Almost all the capital came from the deposit of state receipts, to which was added income from the bank's commissions on discounting all commercial bills.

It was around the citadel of the Bank of France, whose shareholders became immensely wealthy without having had to risk any money or even put up much, that the important business and financial interests entrenched themselves. They too were spared risking their capital or contributing very much of it. For as the nineteenth century progressed they were the lucky recipients of state charters for new banks and insurance companies, of concessions for more mines and canals, and, what was even more lucrative in the new age of steam and steel, concessions for railroads, public utilities, public works, shipping, and for the exploitation of a vast new colonial empire.

The state, in its generosity, furnished most of the capital for these enterprises, guaranteed the fortunate new owners against losses, subsidizing their operations when necessary, and, to put frosting on the cake, began to build up high tariff walls, which spared French entrepreneurs from foreign competition and guaranteed them huge and easy profits. In such a system it was inevitable that businessmen and bankers, fighting and grabbing for such profitable favors from the state, would corrupt politicians who could throw plums their way. And while this state of affairs was not limited to France (the state legislatures in the U.S.A. yielded nothing to the French Parliament in such corruption) it had a demoralizing effect on the Third Republic that would help to undermine it in the end. Nowhere more than in France did the good citizens become so skeptical of the morals of their parliamentary representatives or, for that matter, of the ethics of the business and financial worlds. They could not believe that senators, deputies, and cabinet ministers, nor bankers and businessmen with whom they were in cahoots, were putting the interests of the nation and of all its people above those of their bulging pocketbooks.†

---

* $400,000. Napoleon himself chipped in 30,000 francs.

† The cynicism of some politicians was bluntly shown by Anatole de Monzie, Minister of Public Works and a perennial cabinet member for a quarter of a century, in a lecture on Talleyrand which he delivered before a select group in Paris during the winter of 1939, shortly before the outbreak of World War II. "In politics," he said, "honesty is a proof of weakness." The remark brought amused applause from the fashionable audience and warm approbation the next day from *Le Figaro,* the favorite newspaper of the upper classes, which cited the words as being "particularly witty." De Monzie, a dilettante in letters, may have been a little carried away by the subject of his lecture.[2]

Nevertheless, in France, as elsewhere in the West in this period of zooming industrial expansion, the entrepreneurs convinced themselves to an extent that today seems highly amusing that they were operating a free market open equally to all and that they owed their success and their profits to the virtues of the "free-enterprise" system, which rewarded those with imagination, initiative, and "know-how" who were brave enough to take risks. There were, to be sure, in France bold, imaginative businessmen who launched into new fields (automobiles, aviation, rubber, and chemicals, for instance), without much encouragement except in tax relief from the state. But they were the exception. What the French businessmen, like the bureaucrat and the little shopkeeper and the clerk, wanted was security against the risks of this uncertain world.

To a great extent he got it, but at a price that was paid dearly by the nation. Secure in his position thanks to state concessions, charters, subsidies, and a high tariff wall, the family dynasties who owned or controlled most of the great enterprises looked with strong disfavor on competition not only from without but from within. Thus the "Establishment," instead of encouraging the investment of a great deal of ready capital in new enterprises at home, which might make them competitive, channeled the savings of the country, especially those of the more modest folk, into foreign loans. While these brought good dividends to the little investor and profitable commissions to the banks floating the loans (as high as 19 percent), they left the French economy stagnant for lack of capital growth. By 1914, 45 billion francs* had been invested abroad (25 percent of it in tsarist Russia). Only some 60 percent of French capital was being invested at home.†

This brake on the development of French industry and commerce was bad enough economically. But it had deleterious social consequences as well. It meant that a mass of common people who might have been gainfully employed in productive work were forced to earn their living in nonproductive fields and at wages and salaries which left millions of them on the verge of poverty or in the midst of it. Many of them were absorbed in the tattered bottom ranks of the rapidly expanding government bureaucracy as *petits fonctionnaires* at pitifully small salaries. Many got concessions to run little tobacco shops under the state tobacco monopoly where, because of the growth of the smoking habit, they could eke out a living in a corner of the wall. Condemned to mediocrity, to a petty life without horizons and without hope of betterment, to a continual struggle to make

---

* Nine billion dollars.

† "Money has never been more plentiful," Baron Alphonse de Rothschild declared publicly in 1905. "Why is this money not utilized for the development of commerce and industry?" None knew better than this banker the answer to the question.

The vast sums invested abroad, especially in tsarist Russia, were wiped out in the 1914–1918 war—a disaster for the small holders.

ends meet at a very low level of existence, and forced to strictly limit the number of their children because they had no means to provide for even an average-sized family, their only consolation was that they, like the businessmen, at least enjoyed security. They were seldom displaced from their lowly jobs.

THE FALL OF THE BIRTHRATE

The fall of the birthrate was becoming a disaster to France in the struggle to keep up with the rest of the world. Later, when the Third Republic began to run downhill, some churchmen, conservatives, and generals like Weygand blamed the "atheism" of the French and the breakdown of the family and the lack of old-fashioned patriotism and morals for the decline in the birthrate that so weakened the country. Being well-off themselves, they did not see, or they refused to see, that one of the principal reasons for the severe birth control practiced by the French was economic: too many Frenchmen were without the means to support a family with more than one or two children, if that.*

At the beginning of the nineteenth century France had been the most populous country in Europe, with the exception of Russia, which had passed it in population toward the end of the previous century. In 1815, at the end of the stirring Napoleonic era, France had some 30 million people against 11 million in Prussia, 13 million in Great Britain and 26 million in the multinational Habsburg Empire. By 1870, when war with Prussia came, France had lost its lead. Germany, which Bismarck was about to unite, had 41 million, France only 36 million. The French birthrate was falling faster than the German. The decline, to be sure, was relative, but that did not make it any less costly to the nation in a world of rival powers. During the nineteenth century France increased its population by twelve millions, or 44 percent. But the other great European nations grew faster in numbers: Great Britain by 26 millions (more than three times), Germany by 32 millions, Russia by 70 millions.

---

* This, to be sure, is a complicated subject on which there is much disagreement among the demographic authorities. Dudley Kirk, an American, has argued that poverty was not the cause of France's slow growth in population at all. Most French experts such as Leroy-Beaulieu and P. Bertillon ascribed the relative fall of the French birthrate to the state of "civilization" after the industrial revolution had taken hold and created a mass proletariat and a large number of the poor lower middle class crowded together in the growing cities. But identical situations existed in Germany, Great Britain, and the United States, whose birthrates were considerably higher than the French.[3] Professor Alfred Sauvy of the Collège de France, France's leading authority on demography at the time this book was written, cites as reasons for the deliberate curtailing of births: the lowering of the infant mortality rate, urbanization, improvement of education, and the "prudence" of French parents. He points out that birth control was practiced as much in well-to-do families as among the poor. He is convinced from his own studies that the fall of the birthrate began in France around 1760, a full century before it began in most other Western countries, though he cannot account for this head start. I have been much rewarded in the study of this subject, and others, by the works of and talks with this genial and stimulating man.[4]

In several regions in France the population was standing still or decreasing. By the last decade of the nineteenth century in more than half the departments in France—49 out of 87—more persons were dying than were being born. Numerous villages became deserted; there was no one left to inhabit them. Mines and industries could not find enough native laborers to work them. By 1914 a million workers, mostly from Italy, Belgium, Luxembourg, and the Polish provinces, had been imported. Only this mass immigration enabled the country to function.

Militarily, the demographic decline caused grave concern. Whereas in 1870 Germany's population had been only slightly higher than France's, by 1914 when war again broke out the balance had been tipped strongly against the French. Then Germany had a population just short of 65 million; France but 40 million. Gravely the government and the General Staff in Paris calculated the consequences on the number of men who could be mobilized. In 1870 France and Germany could each count on roughly 4.5 million men of military age—twenty to thirty-four. In 1911, as the two nations girded for a struggle that seemed inevitable, Germany's greater population gave her a total of 7.7 million men between twenty and thirty-four. France had but 4.5 million, no more than in 1870. Gloomy prophets in Paris did not see how France could escape another military debacle if the Germans chose again to attack—unless Russia and Great Britain could mobilize quickly and come to her aid.

Or could the French themselves find compensations for their numerical inferiority to the Germans? This was a question which provoked a good deal of thought, both serious and foolish, not only in French military circles but in the government and Parliament and press, and even among the philosophers. For one thing, an increase in the term of military service would help, and in 1913, after months of stormy debate in the Chamber— for the country as a whole balked at this additional burden—it was raised from two to three years. But this still left France behind Germany. It raised the size of the French standing army to 700,000 men, but the enemy had 150,000 more in theirs, and their reserves were increasing proportionally.

A New Spirit in the Army

Something more was needed and it was believed by many in the Army and government that it had been discovered by a remarkable group of younger officers who came to the fore toward the end of the nineteenth century and by the sheer force of their intellect and willpower swept a number of cobwebs out of the minds of the generals in the High Command and raised the study of military strategy and tactics to a high level. But in doing so they let themselves be carried away to a point that would have almost fatal consequences—as often happens when finespun theories which sound convincing in the lecture hall of a Staff College are tested in the confusion of actual combat. What they demanded was that the French

Army recognize the overwhelming importance of the all-out offensive from the very start of hostilities. They preached the *offensive à outrance,* the *attaque brusquée,* ending up with the bayonet charge. They never tired of reiterating the dictum of the brilliant theorist Colonel Ardant du Picque, who had been killed at Metz in 1870 but whose searching writings had only been published at the turn of the century: *"To win you have to advance!"*

Corollary to this and perhaps owing its inception to the philosopher Bergson's much publicized theory of *élan vital* was the teaching that the French soldier was inherently superior to the German in fighting qualities. His *élan* was something especially French. His excitable Gallic temperament made him peculiarly fitted to take the offensive. There was a spirit in the French ranks which Captain Gilbert, who helped to inspire the "Young Turk" revolution in military thinking, called *furia francesa.* It could be invincible! The taking of the offensive with "French fury" would more than offset the German army's superior numbers.

"The French Army," declared Colonel de Grandmaison, the leader of the "Young Turks," "no longer knows any law other than the offensive." But the offensive at all costs, at any time, and even when the enemy has the advantage of position and superiority in firepower? The "Young Turks" answered "Yes." There could be no exceptions.

Colonel Ferdinand Foch, who, as events would prove, possessed the most original and subtle mind in the French Army, cautioned against the offensive at any cost. Named a professor at the *Ecole supérieure de guerre,* the French War College, in 1894, he stressed in his lectures, it is true, the necessity of taking the offensive in the end if a war was to be won. He did as much as any officer to change the thinking of the French Army from its obsession with the defensive to a confidence in the big attack. But though underestimating the rapidly growing strength of firepower in defense—few French officers appreciated the role of the new machine gun or barbed wire, which the Japanese had just demonstrated successfully in the campaign against the Russians in Manchuria—Foch nevertheless stressed that the all-out offensive must be subject to certain "qualification and discernment" and that recklessness in attack could lead to prohibitive losses and ultimate failure.

In a minority almost of one in those heady days was a professor of infantry tactics at the War College, Colonel Henri Philippe Pétain, who insisted in his lectures that the ratio of firepower should largely determine whether one took the offensive. If you have overwhelming superiority in guns, then attack; otherwise remain on the defensive until you have achieved that superiority. He therefore refused to go along with the "Young Turks" who wanted to take the offensive at all costs. This stubborn stand earned him a reputation in the Officer Corps as a gloomy man, almost a defeatist and certainly a heretic. Still only a colonel as 1914 approached he was nearing the age of retirement and he himself believed that his military career was about to end.* As fate would have it, it was about to begin—with consequences for the nation over the next thirty years that would be tremendous, at first good and then disastrous.

While Colonel Foch and the "Young Turks" he inspired brought about an intellectual and moral regeneration of the French Army they failed to appreciate fully the technological revolution in weapons. The older generals were even more blind to the possibilities of new arms—an ossification of the imagination that not only jeopardized France's chances to survive in 1914 but doomed those chances in 1940. To be sure, the French Army had been the first to get the magazine rifle, the Lebel, which was adopted in 1889. Two years before, the French had started producing the 75-mm. quick-firing field gun, by far the best piece of light artillery in existence and considerably superior to the German 77-mm. gun. But the famous "75" had one weakness. It had a flat trajectory. It would not have much value in the hills of Alsace and Lorraine where the French intended to launch their offensives. And so hypnotized was the High Command by the brilliant performance of the "75" that it neglected to develop heavy artillery, as the Germans were doing. In fact it deliberately refused to. Some of the politicians in Paris wondered why, and the Army told them.

As late as 1909, for instance, a representative of the Army appeared before the Chamber's Finance Committee and confidently declared: "You talk to us of heavy artillery! Thank God we have none! What gives the French army its strength is the lightness of its cannons."

The High Command was equally blind to the effectiveness of the new machine gun. It had already proved itself as a deadly defensive weapon in the Japanese-Russian War and in the campaigns in the Balkans. Yet in 1910 the Director-General of Infantry complacently confided to a group of parliamentarians that the French General Staff was having machine guns manufactured merely as a sop to public opinion. "Make no mistake," he declared, "this weapon will change absolutely nothing." When the first war started the French troops had 2,000 machine guns and the Germans 5,000. In vain Colonel Pétain had urged on the High Command the importance of this new weapon. He insisted on stating this in a new infantry manual which he had been asked to draw up, but his superiors crossed it out.

The generals were equally blind to the military possibilities of the airplane. French inventiveness had given the country a head start in the development of this exciting new machine. But the old army heads were not impressed.† Shortly before the outbreak of war the Commander of the

---

* He commanded the 33rd Infantry Regiment, in which a young lieutenant, Charles de Gaulle, had chosen to serve on his graduation from the military academy of St.-Cyr in 1912. Thus the two men whom fate would pit against each other twenty-eight years later, when one was illustrious, the other unknown, met early in our history.

† Their successors, as we shall see, were no more impressed in the 1930s despite the role of the airplane in the 1914–1918 war. The consequences of such blindness would prove much worse.

War College was witnessing an aviation show. Some of the younger officers had been urging that the Army consider the use of airplanes for observation over and behind the enemy lines and even for dropping bombs on enemy columns. The head of the War College* considered it nonsense. Watching the then rather primitive biplanes circle over the field he exclaimed to a group of fellow officers: "All that—it's a sport! For the army, airplanes are a zero!"[5]

Despite its weaknesses in men and arms, the French High Command, egged on by the "Young Turks," made the fatal decision in 1911 to scrap all of its old defensive plans and adopt a new one calling for all-out offensives as soon as the Germans attacked. This was the famous Plan XVII (the sixteen previous ones since 1870 had been defensive), worked out under the direction of the able but phlegmatic new Chief of the General Staff, Joseph César Joffre, who assumed the top post in the army in 1911.† It called for the bulk of the French Army to wage offensives in Alsace and Lorraine as soon as the Germans struck. Though Intelligence persisted in reporting that the main German thrust probably would come through neutral Belgium, Joffre and his staff did not give this much thought in their planning. Their minds were on the *French* offensive, which would liberate the two lost provinces and push the Germans back to the Rhine.

The war, the French High Command was certain, would be decided in the first great battles along the frontiers. For this reason it did not place much importance on the reserves nor did it believe the Germans did. The issue would be settled quickly by the regular armies in being. This was an erroneous conclusion by the French which would cost them dearly, for secretly the enemy had decided to throw in its reserves in the great sweep through Belgium.‡

Such in brief was the state of the French Army as the second decade of the twentieth century began and the rumblings from a restless, belligerent Germany became more ominous. Though like all armies it clung to

---

* That would be Foch.

† He replaced General Victor Michel, who was ousted because he believed that the main German thrust would come through Belgium (as it did!) and that the French army must concentrate on stopping it. To do this he wanted to double his front-line strength by attaching a regiment of reserves to each active regiment. This was rank heresy to the new military doctrinaires, whose motto had become: "*Les reserves, c'est zero!*" At a showdown meeting of the Supreme War Council in 1911 not a single general supported his chief. One of them declared that General Michel was "off his head," and the Minister of War, Adolphe Messimy, himself a former career officer who had resigned his commission in protest over the Army's refusal to revise the Dreyfus conviction, called Michel's proposed defensive plan "an insanity." It was dropped, along with him.

‡ Before 1914 as well as before 1940 the French and British governments had considered whether to move into neutral Belgium if it seemed that the Germans were about to attack her preliminary to invading France, but had decided not to until *after* the Germans invaded the little country. The disadvantages to the Allies in both periods were obvious. But the Belgians in both cases were blind to where the real danger lay. Their 1914 plans called for mobilizing three armies, one against Germany, the second against France, the third against a possible British landing.

much that was obsolete* it had been rejuvenated in spirit by Foch and the "Young Turks." It was infinitely superior to the force which had crumbled so easily before the Prussians at Sedan and Metz in 1870. If war came again much would depend on the quality of leadership of the top generals, above all on that of the Commander in Chief, about whom there were doubts among some of the more aristocratic officers. For Joffre was a true son of the Third Republic, a commoner of humble origin, who had not even graduated from the great military academy of St.-Cyr but from the *Ecole Polytechnique,* which turned out engineers, and who had little experience in staff work, and, with his phlegmatic nature and paunchy figure, which his baggy, unpressed, usually undecorated uniform accentuated, appeared to lack the martial dash of the great French captains of the past. But in him and in his field commanders France was to be better served in 1914 than in 1870 and 1940.

---

* The soldier's red trousers, for example. Even the forceful Messimy was unable to get the Army High Command or the government to adopt a less visible color, though the Germans were changing to field gray and the British had already adopted khaki. To clothe the French soldier in a drab color was unthinkable. "Eliminate the red trousers?" cried a former War Minister to a parliamentary committee which was considering it. "*Jamais! Le pantalon rouge c'est la France!*"[6]

5

CLASSES AND CONFLICT
1875–1914

An army can rarely be stronger than the country it serves. How strong was France under the Third Republic on the eve of the ordeal it was about to undergo? We have seen some of its weaknesses: its failure to industrialize as fast as the other great Western powers were doing, the decline of its birthrate, the dissensions which for so long had so deeply divided its people. Were there other flaws in this civilized society that sapped its strength?

THE BOURGEOISIE, BACKBONE OF THE REPUBLIC

Backbone of the Third Republic was the bourgeoisie, which at the turn of the century numbered between 5 and 6 millions out of the country's population of some 39 millions. This was the stalwart middle class which had made the Revolution of 1789, thrived under two Bonaparte dictators, survived the brief restoration of the Bourbon monarchy, prospered under the Orleanist king, and completely dominated the Third Republic from 1875.

Now in the early 1900s the French bourgeoisie, surfeited with its power that controlled government, industry, finance, commerce, education, the professions, the press, and that had brought its most prominent members a great deal of wealth, which they were determined to preserve and augment, began to show the first signs of decline. The sap, as Léon Blum, himself a comfortably well-off bourgeois who had devoted his life to socialism, would later say, had started to trickle out of it. It was losing its dynamism, its creativeness, its boldness, its imagination. Behind its moneybags and its entrenched position in the affairs of state and society it more and more feared change. Change threatened its great stake in this land. It might jeopardize the privileges of the bourgeoisie, just as those of the upper orders had been endangered when change overtook the decaying *ancien régime* a century before. The great middle class had gained immensely from that transfer of privilege to it from the aristocracy, nobility, and throne, and quite naturally it wished to preserve those gains from the reach of the restless masses below. There were rumblings from below, and some who were neither above nor below but outside (a few politicians, writers, philosophers, teachers) were beginning to wonder whether the glorious Revolution had not been after all merely the substitution of one selfish and greedy class for another, that of the aristocracy of money for the aristocracy of birth. The first, having amassed its pile, was becoming as blind to the interests of the nation, as distinguished from those of class, as the second had been. Being satisfied and overfed, it wanted to stop the clock and stand still, forgetting that to stand still is to begin to die.

To be sure, the bourgeoisie in France was far from being a monolithic mass. Alongside its rich and privileged were many solid citizens of modest means and station. They included the artists and writers, the intellectuals, the professors in the universities, the teachers in the lower schools, the lawyers and doctors and engineers and permanent government officials, and a myriad of small manufacturers, traders, and shopkeepers. As in all societies the well-off were in the minority, though they set the style and the pace and kept their fingers on the controls. To the differences in the size of bank accounts were added those of politics. While the big businessmen and bankers and the press they dominated were obviously conservative politically, the mass of the middle class supported the Radical Party or parliamentary groups closely associated with it in aims and ideology. To understand French politics you had to remember, as the historian André Siegfried never tired of saying, that though the middle-class Frenchman's heart was usually on the Left, his pocketbook remained on the Right.

Nearly all of the bourgeois, high, middle, and low, shared certain aspirations and determinations, and in these they were joined by the more prosperous landowning peasantry. They wanted government and society to leave them free to make money, to save it, and to bequeath it to their children. They did not want it depleted by taxes or by increases in wages for workers in factory or field or shop, or by the requirements of the newfangled policies of social welfare that certain wild-eyed Socialists under foreign and probably German influence* claimed were becoming necessary in an industrialized age.

Sometime toward the end of the nineteenth century the bourgeois temper, which had made a revolution to overthrow a centuries-old order of life, with its monstrous inequalities, became frozen. It stood solidly for law and order to protect property, investments, and savings. It fiercely

---

* Like that of Bismarck, who, partly because he hated socialism, was pioneering in social welfare for Germany in order to defeat socialism and yet adjust society to the machine age of mass production.

opposed change and reform and social agitation and disorder. And because of its greed and selfishness it refused stubbornly, just as the old nobility and aristocracy had done, to bear its fair burden of the expense of maintaining the state.

THE AVERSION TO TAXES

The aversion of the bourgeoisie to paying an equitable portion of the taxes was notorious. Evasion of taxes, of course, was not peculiar to the French; it prevailed in all other countries. In France the habit went back a long way. Under the old monarchy the Church, with its vast landholdings, was practically exempt from taxation, as were the clergy. The nobility and aristocracy, whose wealth was based mostly on great landed estates, dodged most of the taxes the crown attempted to impose, though since the time of the extravagant Sun King, Louis XIV, who needed vast sums for his wars and the luxuries of Versailles, the state had been continually on the verge of bankruptcy. And all the time the peasants in the countryside, the shopkeepers and artisans in the towns, groaned under an unbearable burden of taxation. When during the reign of Louis XV an attempt was made by Machault d'Arnouville to reduce the public debt by a tax of a twentieth, without respect to persons and with no exemptions, there was such an outcry in the *parlements*—those merciless enemies of fiscal reform and vigilant defenders of upper-class privileges—that the king had to sacrifice his minister and his plans.

But the emerging bourgeoisie was no more enamored of paying taxes than the noblesse and the aristocracy they were about to replace. When the States-General met in Versailles on May 5, 1789, the Third Estate, which represented 95 percent of the populace but which was dominated by the wealthy and propertied middle classes, insisted on as light a burden of taxes as possible though proclaiming its belief in "equality of taxation." After carrying through the Revolution that year these good people were in a position to protect themselves—even from equality.

The Third Republic never pressed them to assume a fair share of the burden of taxation. Toward the end of the nineteenth century it had become evident to most economists in the West that a tax on income was the best method not only of assuring equity in taxation but of raising the bulk of the large sums needed by a modern, heavily armed state. Moreover the income tax could be adjusted up or down to meet the varying demands of the times. Great Britain had had an income tax since 1842 and Germany its *Einkommensteuer* since the end of the century. In France the very idea ran into fierce opposition from the possessing class.

From 1871 to 1914 over two hundred bills for a fiscal reform based on adoption of the income tax had been presented to the parliamentary committees, but for decades the two Chambers refused to take them up. Finally in 1896 a Radical government proposed such a tax on an extremely modest scale, progressing from 1 to 5 percent. It was greeted by howls of horror from those who would have been touched. Such a project, they said, would rob a Frenchman of his freedom. It would infest the country with an army of snooping tax collectors prying into the sacred secrets of a man's fortune. "A tax of this kind," declared the eminent economist, Paul Leroy-Beaulieu, "would poison the whole life of a democracy; it would spread defiance everywhere, cause capital to flee; . . . it would be the onset of a struggle to the death between the Treasury and the taxpayers. . . ."

The taxpayers—at least the well-off ones—were prepared for a "struggle to the death" against so monstrous an evil. The government which had dared to propose it was overthrown and replaced by one under the conservative high-tariff advocate, Jules Méline, which promised not to impose on Frenchmen this crude violation of their liberty and of the sanctity of their private affairs.

But the old system of direct taxes, which dated from the old monarchy and from Napoleon (it included a tax on the number of windows and doors in your dwelling) was simply inadequate to meet the needs of a country feverishly rearming. As it was, three quarters of the income of the state as late as 1913 came from taxes on consumption, and the total sum from all taxes amounted to only 40 percent of government expenditures. Drastic fiscal reform became an urgent necessity. In 1909 the Chamber, at the insistence of Premier Clemenceau and his finance minister, Joseph Caillaux, had passed a bill establishing a modest income tax. The more conservative Senate refused even to discuss it, and it died. This was a moment when the conservatives were pressing for drastic increases in military rearmament and a raising of the term of conscription from two to three years. But they did not want to pay for it, provoking the historian François Goguel to wonder whether "the French bourgeoisie did not prefer its gold to its sons," and leading even more cynical critics to exclaim that a Frenchman would die for his country but would not pay for it.

It was only under the shadow of war, in the summer of 1914, that Parliament reluctantly voted an income tax, and it did not become truly effective until 1916, after two years of war on such a scale that France was facing financial collapse. As it was, in 1918, the last brutal year of the devastating war, the French government's total revenues were only 12 percent of its expenditures. The nation's survival in those grim war years, with the Germans never far from Paris, was possible only through resort to loans, from its own citizens and from abroad, principally from the United States. Not even the swollen profits of the arms manufacturers and of the furnishers of other military supplies were severely taxed.

THE ALIENATION OF THE WORKING CLASS

The attitude of the prospering bourgeoisie toward the class which performed the labor of the nation was no more generous than it was toward the hated tax collector.

Alienated by bitter memories of the bloody repression of the Commune, by the neglect of Parliament to do something about its plight, by the hostility of employers toward even the attempt to form trade unions, and by the government's savage breaking of strikes by armed force, the French working class felt itself shut out from the main course—and most of the benefits—of French life. Certain consequences followed, and if they were natural under the circumstances they also led to much confusion in the minds of the workers. The labor movement proclaimed itself an enemy of political democracy.* It opposed both parliament and government, seeing no hope for relief or even for any understanding of its problems from such sources. It refused therefore to throw its support to any political party, even to the Socialists, who, under the brilliant leadership of Jean Jaurès and the more doctrinaire influence of Jules Guesde, were trying to give the working class political expression. The only salvation of the workers, as the Charter of Amiens drawn up in 1906 by the CGT (the Confédération Générale du Travail), founded nine years before, proclaimed, lay in "direct action": the overthrow of the middle-class Republican regime by the ultimate weapon of the general strike. Not Karl Marx but Georges Sorel, the penetrating but shifting bourgeois philosopher, became the chief intellectual inspiration of the revolutionary syndicalist movement in France. Sorel's cult of violence, developed in his book *Reflections on Violence,* which was to find its culminating expression in the general strike and the toppling of the government, provided a sort of philosophical basis for the aims and ideology of the French labor-union movement.†

After the Commune in 1871 the police had dissolved the chambers

---

* The grounds for this viewpoint, which seems so strange to us today, were put by one French trade-union leader at the time: "Organized democracy snuffs out minorities in favor of sheeplike and conservative majorities. Thus democracy with its universal suffrage and its political sovereignty ends by cementing the economic slavery of the working class." Not until after the 1914–1918 war did the French trade-union movement, officially at least, discard this curious idea.

† Sorel, a retired government engineer, had one of the most original if erratic minds of the century and the influence of his writings on the European labor movement and on some of its offspring was immense. Always despising the French and German Socialists as empty opportunists and becoming disillusioned with the trade unions, he flirted for a time with the extreme Right of Maurras' Action Française, only to end up toward the end of his life as an enthusiastic champion of Lenin and Communism. Possessed of a profound—though somewhat disordered—learning he corresponded with a number of thinkers all over Europe, in particular with the Italian philosopher Croce, with whom he kept up an avid correspondence for the last twenty years of his life. Sorel's influence on another Italian had historical consequences.

Benito Mussolini would later admit that the germs of Fascism were planted in him by the reading of Sorel before the First World War when he was a young revolutionary Socialist in Milan and editor of the party's organ, *Avanti.* In 1912 Sorel, after reading the Italian firebrand's editorials, made a remarkable prediction: "Our Mussolini is no ordinary Socialist. Believe me, you will perhaps see him one day at the head of a sacred battalion, saluting with his sword the Italian banner. He is an Italian of the fifteenth century, a *condottiere.* People do not yet know it, but he is the only energetic man capable of redressing the weaknesses of government."[1]

of workers' syndicates, forerunners of the trade unions, though even the dictatorship of Napoleon III had tolerated them. The Third Republic, as we have seen Thiers insisting, would be conservative or it would not be. There was no place in it for troublesome organized workingmen.

The employers, with such encouragement from the state, would have no truck with unionism. They saw in even the early feeble attempts of a few leaders to form unions a call to class struggle, to disorder if not downright revolution. In 1884 Parliament was finally forced to pass a law recognizing for the first time the legal right of workers to organize, but the law made no attempt to induce management and labor to settle their differences by peaceful collective bargaining. The employers, for their part, refused even to discuss with union leaders wages and working conditions. This intransigence helped to turn the unions toward what their members felt was their only recourse: the strike. But this brought the unions up against not only the employers but the republican government.

From 1906 until the eve of the war France was plagued by a series of strikes, many of them disorderly and most of them put down by the government with force. Army troops were often called out to intimidate the strikers. On a few occasions they opened fire and there were casualties—killed and wounded—in the streets. Even the winegrowers of the Midi went on strike and staged disorderly demonstrations in several cities. At Narbonne, where barricades were set up, the 17th Infantry refused to fire on the demonstrators and mutinied. In 1910 Premier Aristide Briand, though calling himself an independent socialist, put down a general railroad strike by arresting the union leaders and calling the strikers to the colors as army reservists. There was irony in this since Briand had begun his career as a labor lawyer who preached the necessity of the general strike!

In no other country of the West did the working class become so alienated from society as in France. In no other land was labor legislation so far behind in meeting the minimum requirements of the industrial age. Not until 1900 was the labor of women and children limited to a ten-hour day; the men still worked twelve hours. Only in 1906 did a law give the laborer one day off a week, on Sundays. There was no attempt in France to emulate the social-security legislation Bismarck had put through in Germany.

No wonder that the French workers, balked in their efforts at improving their lot by strikes or by collective agreements with employers or by social legislation, concluded that there was no hope of obtaining redress from the parliamentary Third Republic. They felt they were second-class citizens. This was scarcely their country, and it was in this time that they began to subscribe to Karl Marx's dictum that "the worker has no country." They loathed service in the army and agitated for pacifism—why should they die defending such a hostile society? Shortly, in 1914, in response to new German aggression they would bury their bitterness and join with other Frenchmen in the defense of their soil. Nevertheless their alienation added still a further fissure to those already splitting the nation and weakening it. By the time the Germans attacked still again, in 1940, this feeling of being deprived of full citizenship in the Republic, twisted by the grip of Communism, which had taken over a good part of the labor movement and whose foreign policies zigzagged recklessly at the whims and interests of Moscow and usually to the detriment of France, would add this mass of proletarian Frenchmen to the swelling groups on the Right who cared little about defending the republican regime—even against the old enemy. I myself would live to see the June days in 1940 when the Communists, like the French reactionaries whose motto was "better Hitler than Blum," would welcome the Germans into Paris, appeal to them to release their comrades from French prisons, and servilely ask them for the political recognition their own government, during the crisis of the war years, had denied them.

THE EXTREME RIGHT

On the other side of the strikers' barricades, so to speak—beside the bourgeois Radicals and moderate Republicans who dominated the government—were the conservatives and the remnants of the once powerful monarchist Right. As the new century opened they began still another comeback, at least in spirit if not in political force. They embraced a new, raucous authoritarian and chauvinistic nationalism that, ironically enough, helped to strengthen France in the First World War but, losing sight of the true national interests in the weird confusions of the 1930s, would help to sap her strength until there was not enough left to assure the Republic's survival at a moment of adversity. Like the labor movement, this new nationalism was antidemocratic and *anti-parlementaire* and looked toward the eventual overthrow of the bourgeois republican regime. It was also anti-intellectual, glorifying naked force, disdaining reason, contemptuous of the critical spirit of free inquiry which the eighteenth-century philosophers had made one of the glories of France. And it was violently anti-Semitic.

The seeds of Fascism, in truth, were sown at this time—earlier than is generally recognized and in this unexpected place. In France at the turn of the century, as in Italy and Germany a quarter of a century later, the soil was not exactly unfertile for their germination.

An unexpected reversal of class ideologies suddenly took place. Ever since the Revolution of 1789 it had been the Left which was nationalist, patriotic, chauvinistic even, and militarist, and this spirit had enabled the new France not only to successfully defend the frontiers against a monarchist European coalition but, under Napoleon, to conquer most of Europe with her invincible armies. In 1870–71, it had been the Left, as the Republicans were known in those days following the collapse of the Bonaparte Second Empire, which under the leadership of the fiery Gambetta had wanted to continue the war against Prussia. In vain he had appealed to the patriotism of all Frenchmen. The Right, the dominant monarchists, had insisted on peace, even though it meant national humiliation and military occupation by the Prussians. In 1814–15 the French royalists had welcomed the entry into Paris of foreign sovereigns whose armies had just defeated Napoleon and who brought with them a Bourbon king to be restored and with him a host of Legitimist exiles who had plotted against their country on alien soil.

By 1900 the roles were reversed. The Left, especially the Socialists and trade unionists, were becoming pacifist. Even the nationalism of the moderate Republicans was becoming diluted. They grudged the expense of increasing the size of the army and rearming it. They no longer harbored a spirit of revenge against the Germans nor had much passion for regaining Alsace and Lorraine by force of arms. Almost forgotten amongst them was the old cry of Gambetta about the lost provinces: "Never speak of them; never forget them!"

Out of the debris left by annihilation at the polls, the fiasco of Boulanger, the denouement of the Dreyfus Affair, and the severe curbing of the Church by the Republic, all the disparate elements of the old Right, the royalists, the Bonapartists, the Boulangists, the anti-Dreyfusards, and the unrepentant Catholics sought desperately for survival in some new form. They had no leaders, no banner, no national organization, scarcely any doctrine—only bitter and impotent hates.

For two decades at the end of the nineteenth century they had tried to organize, but without much success and always in confusion. There had been the Ligue des Patriotes, founded in 1882 by nationalist-minded Republicans to prepare the country morally and physically for revenge against Prussia. But it had been carried by the tide of Boulangism into the ultranationalist, *anti-parlementaire* camp. There was the Ligue Antisémite of Jules Guérin. It had floundered toward the end of the Dreyfus Affair with the trial and exiling of its comic-opera leader. Finally in 1899 a third league had sprung up, the Ligue de la Patrie Française, whose aim was to combat the radical, democratic, pro-Dreyfus Ligue des Droits de l'Homme and foster conservative nationalism. Within a year of its founding it had attracted a hundred thousand members, including the bulk of the intellectual notables of the Académie Française and of the other exalted academies of the Institute. But its success had been ephemeral.

Succeeding all the Leagues in an attempt to resolve the tangled yearnings of the disunited rightist enemies of the Republic there sprang up at the turn of the century a curious organization, strongly led by a strange and rather unlikely figure, which would give them a doctrine, a faith, a confidence, a goal of sorts, and a coherence that, while it would never achieve political power, would wield an influence on the country out of all proportion to its numbers, and toward the end, by poisoning the well-springs of democracy and further dividing the French, help mightily, with the aid of Nazi German bayonets, to dig the grave of the Third Republic it so despised.

The organization was called "Action Française." Its undisputed leader for half a century was Charles Maurras, a stone-deaf poet from Provence, steeped in Greco-Roman classicism, out of touch with the modern world, which he loathed, a brawling, formidable pamphleteer and journalist (his followers believed him to be a profound philosopher) whose genius lay in his capacity to hate and to stir up hatred with his poisonous pen. His hates were endless: the Revolution, the Republic, democracy, Parliament, the common people, popular education, the rights of man. He had a specially brewed venom for what he called "the four alien poisoners of the motherland": Protestants, Jews, Freemasons, and naturalized foreigners—whom he cursed as *metèques.** An agnostic who once described the Christian gospels as fairy tales written by "four shabby Jews" (his anti-Semitism was notorious) and Christianity as a religion for the rabble, Maurras would seek and—until the pope finally stepped in in 1926—receive the support of the Church and the militant Catholics. He had a flair for gathering around him provocative writers such as Léon Daudet, the boisterous son of the novelist Alphonse Daudet and for a time the husband of the granddaughter of Victor Hugo, and Jacques Banville, a brilliant if erratic historian, and he made his daily newspaper, *L'Action Française,* the most livelily written journal in Paris. Though it preached royalism and all other sorts of foolish reaction—the idea of restoring the monarchy was dead as a doornail in France by this time—it was an interesting journal to read, no doubt in part because it was so scurrilous, venomous, and vituperous. Though Maurras, if memory serves (I read him daily for years), could grow dull when he left off character assassination or a call to bump off some Republican scoundrel and indulged in pseudo-metaphysical speculation, displaying his considerable classical learning, Léon Daudet, a lighthearted Parisian to the core, was almost always amusing and sometimes hilarious. He had an impish, Rabelaisian mind—most of his novels were considered *risqué* if not somewhat porno-graphic—a boyish love of scandal and a passion for exposing it, a fantasti-cally rich and vulgar vocabulary for vituperation, and a carelessness about the truth which often got him into the clutches of the law. He also had a passion for literature, in which he was widely read, and a certain tolerance of human foibles which Maurras, a misanthrope, lacked, and an abiding love for the Parisian scene, with all of its *chinoiseries,* its excitement, and its beauty. I was often astonished at the waste of such a talent on such a forlorn and lost cause, but I confess that in my years in France I usually began my day at breakfast by turning to the front page of *L'Action*

---

* It was an honorable term in ancient Greece, which Maurras worshiped. In the heyday of Athens "metics" were foreigners in the city who were accorded many privileges, allowed to serve the state but not accorded full citizenship rights. Under Maurras' aegis it became in French a word of opprobrium.

Française and the outrageous outbursts of Daudet, Maurras, and their frenzied collaborators.

How could one take them seriously? In truth, not many did. Circulation of the newspaper never got much above 50,000 and paid membership in the organization was somewhat less. But the readers and the members formed a certain elite, fairly numerous among writers and journalists, high permanent officials, lawyers and doctors, and the restless students and the younger instructors in the universities who instinctively revolted against the corruption, logrolling, and drabness of republican rule. Army officers and priests and bishops, smarting under the blows of the Dreyfus Affair and the curbing of the Church, and remnants of the old nobility and aristocracy still dreaming of the restoration of a throne to kneel to, read *L'Action Française* avidly, contributed to the movement's coffers, and encouraged their sons to join the Camelots du Roi,* who were beginning to brawl in the streets. Thus *L'Action Française* not only had a fairly profound influence on the intellectual climate of France but it introduced a new technique of political warfare to the Right. The streets before had belonged to the Left, which had carried out revolution behind the barricades in them. Now the young toughs of the Camelots du Roi disputed possession of the streets with Socialists and trade unionists and with the police, the first example of the rowdy tactics of later brownshirts and blackshirts in two adjacent lands.

What did Action Française stand for?

We have seen what it was against: the Republic, democracy, the Protestants, the Jews, the Freemasons. But what did it want? Essentially, to turn the clock back to the eighteenth century, restore the monarchy and the old hierarchical way of life, in which a king reigned supreme above all quarreling factions and the elite, the nobles and aristocrats aided by right-thinking upper-middle-class officials, carried out the royal orders, managed the affairs of the state, and gave French society the unity, the tone, and the splendid inequalities it had enjoyed during the golden days of the ancient regime. Thus would what Maurras called the *pays réel*—the real country— be reestablished. Forty kings, he preached, had made France the glory of the West for a thousand years. Bring them back and the glory would return. The masses, infected by the poisons of democracy, socialism, trade unionism, the rights of man, equality before the law, and popular education, would be put back in their place, cured of their dangerous infections and made to resume their old role as contented or at least respectful servants of their masters. The ridiculous reign of uncouth, uneducated majorities would be brought to an end and rule by the elite restored.

That at the beginning of the twentieth century the wellborn, right-

---

* Literally "Street-hawkers of the King." They were organized by Action Française chiefly from among officeworkers, shop clerks, and students for rioting in the streets. In the 1930s they would be joined by similar groups from other rightist organizations, by now inspired by the street tactics of Mussolini and Hitler, and once, in 1934, as we shall see, would almost topple the Republic.

thinking upper classes, and especially army officers, priests and bishops, writers and intellectuals, could take such drivel seriously reveals the sterility of the Right in France at this time. Agitation for the restoration of the monarchy got nowhere. The mass of the French were too intelligent to be taken in by such nonsense even when it was preached by those in high places. Here Action Française failed completely. None of the exiled Orleanist pretenders ever had the slightest chance of returning, however much Maurras and Daudet beat the drums for them, and in the end they repudiated their boisterous champions, who were left without even a candidate for their throne.

But Action Française had its successes. They were all negative. Maurras and his followers did succeed in inoculating an elite with a burning contempt for the Third Republic and its faltering democratic way of life. It convinced grown-up men and women, most of them educated and well-off, that the Republican regime consisted of a gang of crooked swindlers and traitors who were destroying the country. In 1914 it would temporarily put aside its hatreds and rally to the defense of the *patrie* out of an old hatred for the Germans and a patriotism rekindled by its new nationalism. This helped France to survive. A quarter of a century later, when a new challenge from the same source faced the nation, Action Française and its allies on the Right had become too full of hate and contempt for the Republic they had so unmercifully assaulted to consider it worth saving—even from the same Germans. They would make a generous contribution to the ultimate debacle.

6

THE PERMANENT POLITICAL CRISIS
1875–1914

Attacked, as we have seen, from Left and Right, the Third Republic's shaky parliamentary system of government bungled along into the twentieth century, providing continually fresh ammunition to its enemies and concern to its supporters by its incredible instability. The country lived in a state of permanent political crisis. Governments rose and fell with dizzy rapidity, some lasting but a few months, the most durable of them but two or three years, and nearly all of them set up and then soon overthrown as the result of trivial intrigues in the corridors of the Chamber of Deputies that were rarely understood and scarcely appreciated by the bewildered citizenry. No government lasted long enough to formulate long-range policies, much less to carry them out had there been any.

From the very beginning of the Republic this political chaos had prevailed. Between 1871, when the Assembly met in Bordeaux, and 1879, when the Republic became fairly firmly established, there were twelve ministries. It was, one French historian has remarked, a period of "the most total confusion."[1] The Third Republic was off to a typical start. By the beginning of the First World War there had been fifty governments, an average of one per year. After that war the rate of change would double, cabinets lasting an average of six months.

For a decade around the turn of the century a certain political stabilization appeared to have set in when the stout republicans joined together in a bloc to settle the Dreyfus Affair and the conflict with the Church. The ministries of Waldeck-Rousseau, Combes, and Clemenceau had governed for nearly nine years, exerting an uncustomary authority over the unruly Chamber and Senate. But then, despite the stark demands on the country in a Europe drifting toward war, the old political anarchy returned. From the fall of Premier Clemenceau in July 1909 to August 1914 when the Great

War began, the Republic indulged itself in the irresponsible luxury of having eleven different governments, or a little better than two a year. Most of the cabinets resigned over questions of the utmost superficiality. "One is often astonished," the historian quoted above commented in a book published in 1962, "at the triviality of motives which pushed the Assembly to overthrow governments."*[2] However disillusioned the electorate may have become with such political shenanigans by their elected representatives— and in the end their despair would become fatal—the deputies and senators themselves came to accept the annual or semiannual ministerial crisis as a normal procedure to which they were much devoted. It was a game that intrigued them.

The consequences of this strange state of affairs do not seem to have been realized by the politicians, but they were predictable. They weakened the Republic from the beginning and in the end helped pave the road to disaster. How was it possible for a government to cope with the increasingly complex problems of the twentieth century if it did not last long enough to be able seriously to plan on how to meet them? It was not possible, and what happened was that governments, whose life was certain to be short, avoided tackling long-term problems, their ministers complacently certain that it would not be they but their successors who would have to shoulder the burden of resolving them. Thus French governments found it easier to stand still, to stand pat, and this accounted for their backwardness in meeting the new challenges piling up in the country in the economic and social fields. Ministers became concerned not with trying to solve the nation's problems but with staying in office, and the best way to accomplish this was to do as little as possible and thus displease as few as possible. The term of office was inevitably short, to be sure, but a good many members of Parliament became perennial ministers, passing from one cabinet to the next with perfect equanimity. The instability of the ministries was in part, perhaps, compensated for by a remarkable stability of the ministers.† Briand, for example, participated in twenty-five governments under the Republic, and though he was the champion in this, his record was threatened by a good many others, especially after the first war when the regime began to flounder.

Part of the cause of the instability of French governments under the Third Republic was the weakness of the political party system. In all its time no single party every had a majority in Parliament or came close to

---

* This is Jacques Ollé-Laprune. He has entitled his book: "The Stability of Ministers under the Third Republic." He could hardly have called it the "stability of ministries." The differentiation is of some importance, as we shall see.

† Ollé-Laprune argues that it was quite considerably compensated for and that the key to understanding the Third Republic is the phenomenon of the "permanence of ministers." The American historian Carleton Hayes held the same view and expounded it forcefully. Though they have a point it seems to this writer that they unduly minimize the consequences of a constant change of governments in the Third Republic. Surely, stable ministries in a democracy are better than stable ministers.[3]

having one. Each government had to depend for its life on the support of at least two and usually half a dozen parties, with their conflicting interests and aims. No political party, with the exception of the Socialists, was organized on a truly national scale with its members accepting a certain party discipline. Indeed, except for the Socialist Party, united in 1905, and the center Radical-Socialist Party, formed in 1901, none of the political groups at this time even called themselves a "party." They chose instead such terms as "federation," "alliance," "union." Their names meant nothing. All conservative groups called themselves republican or democratic or liberal or even left, while the center parties, conservative in regard to economics and social affairs, often called themselves not only radical and republican but socialist. They were loosely organized and, with one exception, had few roots in the countryside, their ideology, if any, being exceedingly vague, and party discipline nonexistent. The French voter, a down-to-earth individual, often wondered what these parties stood for and was skeptical of them all, even of the party he voted for.

To comprehend French politics in the first decade and a half of the twentieth century—and especially in the brief period between the two world wars when the Third Republic began to face requirements beyond its capacity to meet—it is necessary to look into the nature of the one political party which dominated the regime during all but a few years of its final four decades.

This was the great left-center group, the so-called Radical and Radical-Socialist Party, which was scarcely radical and certainly not socialist. It has often been described by French historians as "not a party but a state of mind." More than any other group it represented in politics during these years the solid, middle-of-the-road, small-town bourgeoisie and well-off peasantry, bulwark of the Republic.

The "Radical-Socialists," as they were called, considered themselves to be the heirs of the Jacobins of the great Revolution and of Gambetta. They were anticlerical, antimilitary, anti-Bourbon, anti-Bonapartist. They championed Dreyfus, lay public schools, the rights of property and of individuals and of the little man (if he was not a worker). And their followers were imbued with a strong individualism which made them distrustful of kings, men on horseback, generals, great wealth, upper-class privilege, socialism, and strong, centralized governments in Paris, even if they dominated them. The function of the deputy, said "Alain,"* the widely read philosopher of the Radical Party, "should be to represent the ordinary undistinguished citizen against the eternal conspiracy of the strong, the rich, the powerful."

Founded in 1901 by the federation on a national scale of numerous local and *département* committees of so-called Radicals, the party owed its

---

* Professor Emile Chartier.

strength to these provincial cadres, which were accorded a large degree of autonomy.* Each was made up of more-or-less self-appointed local Republican "notables": doctors, lawyers, journalists, professors and schoolteachers, shopkeepers and prosperous peasants, some of whom were members of a Masonic lodge. These were the citizens who possessed influence in their community and by this right—for they were not elected—met in committee to choose a deputy to the Chamber and fought the election in his behalf. They made no effort to recruit a mass membership, for this would have jeopardized their tight control of the local party machine. Though party membership was small, the party vote was large, thanks largely to the French system of elections which provided for a second round of voting in each *arrondissement* where a candidate had failed to obtain a clear majority in the first round. In the second case, only a plurality was necessary and it was in these that the followers of the numerous liberal-left splinter parties usually threw their vote the second time to a Radical-Socialist in order to prevent the election of a conservative. In 1906 the party won more than 250 seats in the Chamber, emerging as the largest single party in the country. But because it was dominated by the autonomous local committees the party itself had little cohesion, almost no party discipline, and by its very nature found it difficult to formulate policies for the nation. Its deputies remained parochial in spirit and considered it their first duty—though the Constitution stipulated otherwise—to represent in Parliament first of all local interests. National interests came afterward. This was what the peasantry and the *petite bourgeoisie* wanted. Deeply rooted in the countryside of a land that was still predominantly rural, the Radical-Socialist Party became the core of most of the Republic's coalition governments and provided key ministers even in those governments which shifted temporarily to the Right or the Left. The party's strengths and weaknesses reflected those of France herself.

The weakness of the party system was compounded by the manner in which the Parliament itself functioned. Ever since the MacMahon crisis it had insisted on making the President of the Republic a figurehead and on running the government itself, without checks or balances. Parliament, and especially the popularly elected Chamber of Deputies, was the government as well as the legislature. The cabinet was merely its executive arm, but had no power, its existence being at the mercy of whimsical ever-changing parliamentary majorities. But 615 deputies comprised too large a body to constitute a government. In England a cabinet which was overthrown by the Commons could appeal to the electorate in a new election. This was constitutionally possible in France but in practice impossible. The electorate was deprived of the right to make a judgment on the conduct of the affairs of state except once in every four years when a new Chamber was elected. By

---

* France was divided into ninety departments, the chief administrative officer in each being a Prefect who was appointed by the Ministry of Interior in Paris.

that time the confusion wrought by five or six successive governments was so great and the lines separating the parties so indistinct that no considered judgment by the people was possible.

Amid so much political instability how could the Republic continue to function and its ephemeral governments manage the business of a great, powerful, and civilized nation? Three factors came to the rescue and helped to give France a certain stability. These were the temperament of the people, the continuity of ministers (despite the continued fall of ministries), and the steady hand of the permanent *Administration,** which had changed little over the centuries despite all the upheavals of revolution and changes of regime.

If politics consists of ideas and interests—and it was these which fragmented the French politically—it also is shaped by man's temperament, which lies deep in a people and which in France was a stabilizing influence. This temper is hard to define, but one French historian has attempted it.[4] He believes that far below the surface in French life at this time there existed "certain sentiments, certain affirmations, that were almost instinctive and perhaps highly irrational and which had to do with a citizen's conception of the sense of life, the nature of man, the ends of society." He argues that this wellspring made for some stability in the artificially created chaos of French politics.

The second factor was the stability of ministers, which compensated to some extent for the instability of ministries. Governments came and went, almost with the seasons, but the same ministers remained in one after another of them. It became a game of musical chairs. When the music stopped with the fall of a cabinet the ministers scrambled to retain a seat and several of them invariably landed on one—often the very ones they had previously held. Henri Queuille, one of the most durable ministers, for instance, was Under-Secretary of Agriculture three times and Minister of Agriculture eleven times in the two decades between 1920 and 1940—to skip ahead in time a little—not to mention six other cabinet posts he occupied when not handling farming for the Republic. Théophile Delcassé held the Ministry of Foreign Affairs in six different governments from 1898 to 1905 and thus was able to give continuity and stability to the conduct of external relations when the alliances which would save France in 1914 were being forged.

Aristide Briand led all the rest in the holding of ministries, figuring in twenty-five ministries between 1906 and 1932. He was Premier eleven times, Foreign Minister seventeen times (doubling as Premier in seven governments), and held various other cabinet posts in his long career. His miraculous powers of survival as a minister assured a good deal of conti-

---

* In France *L'Administration* denotes a number of government agencies, manned by permanent civil servants, which administer the laws and public services.

nuity in the offices he held. As Minister of Cults in five governments (in two of which he was also Premier) from 1906 to 1911 he was able to carry out with much tact the law of separation of church and state. As Minister of Foreign Affairs in fourteen governments between 1925 and 1932 (during which he served four times also as Premier) he brought a stability into the conduct of French foreign relations that helped Europe to enjoy one of its few periods of peace and tranquillity between the world wars.

There were many other examples of the longevity of ministers, especially after the first war, when, for example, such Radical-Socialist politicians as Albert Sarraut (equaling the record of Henri Queuille) served in twenty ministries, Camille Chautemps, Edouard Daladier and Anatole de Monzie in seventeen, and Georges Bonnet in thirteen—these are all figures we will meet in the culminating chapters of the story.

In the opinion of most contemporary French historians this curious Gallic phenomenon of the permanence of men despite the instability of institutions did much to spare the Republic from undue chaos.[5] With familiar faces appearing in one cabinet after another the constant change of governments did not have quite the consequences—at least until the last two decades—that it might have had in other Western democracies. In the Chamber and Senate it was considered a normal procedure. The ministries passed but the ministers remained. There was some truth in the quip of Clemenceau when he was criticized by a deputy for having overthrown so many governments. "I have overthrown only one," he replied. "They are all the same."

And yet? Somehow the competence of at least a few of the perennial ministers and the human compromises made in the corridors of Parliament, where the fates of governments were really decided, enabled the Republic for long to scrape through. But the time would come when such a shaky parliamentary system, dominated as it was by permanent crisis, simply would not prove good enough to sustain the Third Republic in the cruel and demanding years of the 1930s when the economies of the Western world collapsed, the Communists captured most of the working class, Fascism began to spread its poison among the well-to-do, and the threat of a new Germany, Nazified, rose beyond the Rhine.

Perhaps what held the country together more than anything else and enabled the Republic to function tolerably well was the third factor making for stability: the permanent Administration, which played a key role in French government and life. This comprised various organs, run and staffed by permanent civil servants, which administered the law, the legislation passed by Parliament, and the acts and services of government. To the very end of the Republic the Administration changed little in outlook or methods of work since the days of the Capetian kings. In its strange but steady exertions we can see much of the secret of the solidity and continuity of French life over the centuries despite the toppling of thrones, dictatorships, and republics and the incessant changes of regimes and governments.

In the twentieth century a good deal of this bureaucracy seemed to be an anachronism, an apparatus musty from age. In reality it was one of the foundations of the Republic, as it had been of the ancient and modern monarchies and of the Napoleonic dictatorships.

Forty kings would come and go, some of them whiling away much of their time amid the refined pleasures of Paris, Versailles, and Fontaine-bleau; Parliaments might be suppressed or take a long vacation; ministers might spend most of their time hunting or fishing or making love. The permanent bureaucracy, the officials high and low, the jurists, the book-keepers, the lowly clerks, saw to it that the machinery of government ground away, that taxes were collected, treaties made, armies raised, accounts kept, justice dispensed, and public services and civil order for the most part maintained. Despite all the turmoil over the centuries of French history the bureaucracy, it could be said, never surrendered or died—or changed. Since the reign of King Philip Augustus (1180–1223) these permanent officials stood like a Rock of Gibraltar against the chaotic currents of whatever times. Honest to a degree unknown or unpracticed among the old nobility and aristocracy (from the earliest days they were recruited mostly from the bourgeoisie) and the later parliamentarians and cabinet ministers, industrious in a plodding sort of way and fairly efficient, possessed of a strong sense of public duty, of a remarkable *esprit de corps,* and of a pride in their professional code, but also woefully unprogressive, and unresponsive to the demands of evolving society, they were a pillar of the state.

We can see them surviving into the modern age in the paintings and drawings of Daumier, crowlike figures in their ermine robes or dress uniforms, full-bearded, stern-eyed, a little pompous, the judges among them leaning heavily over their benches, the lesser officials in black scarecrow coats poring ponderously over huge ledgers, a quill pen in hand. Even in my own time in Paris between the wars one could see such figures in the corridors and in the courtrooms of the Palais de Justice, the parliament building of the old monarchy, or more modest ones in the endless crannies of the ministries. In the dusty rabbit warrens of the Cour des Comptes (Chamber of Accounts), which administers the fiscal affairs of the state, you could still see the accountants scribbling in thick ledgers with their quill pens, adding and subtracting figures with their minds and lips, engrossed in a form of bookkeeping that had been used without interruption or improvement since medieval days. The news of the invention of the typewriter and adding machine (the computer had not yet been developed) obviously had not penetrated these thick walls, nor had double-entry bookkeeping been heard of.[6]

At the pyramid of the bureaucratic institutions stood the venerable Conseil d'Etat, or Council of State. It had jurisdiction over the entire administrative machine, ruling supreme over the instruments of state power and interpreting the content of laws passed by Parliament and decrees issued by the government and seeing that they were carried out according to its own lights. It also served as tribunal in judging disputes between the state, departments and communes, and the citizen, and in this role protected the rights of the little man against the powerful public authority. There was also the Cour de Cassation, or Supreme Court of Appeals, which we have seen meting out justice to Dreyfus after Army courts-martial had denied it. It had the final word in interpreting civil law as the Council of State had in public law. There was the Inspectorate of Finance, a sort of general staff of the Treasury, whose civil servants, the Inspectors of Finance, were regarded as the cream of the permanent bureaucracy and who usually attained the highest rank in the Civil Service before being lured away to top positions in private business and especially in finance. There was the corps of ninety Prefects who ruled the ninety departments on behalf of the Ministry of Interior in Paris. They were entitled to wear the uniform of a major-general and were as secure in their rank, and usually as autocratic, as any general in the regular army. There was the group of civil servants who manned the colonial services and another the diplomatic and consular corps. In the latter, men like Philippe Berthelot and Alexis Léger (the poet Saint-John Perse) virtually dominated the French Foreign Office for years regardless of who was Foreign Minister, carrying out the tradition of Talleyrand, who in an earlier time served the ancient monarchy, the Revolution, Napoleon, the Restoration and Louis-Philippe. And, finally, there were the vast bureaucracies that ran the postal services (which also handled savings accounts), the telegraph and telephone systems, and the state-owned railways; and there were the hundreds of thousands of teachers in the public schools and universities, which, unlike our own, were organized and financed on a national scale. It has been estimated that one out of twenty Frenchmen was a paid functionary of the state.

France actually had two sets of governments,* a Parliament which passed the laws and established the policies and services of the state, and the Administration which carried them out—and often in a way that the popularly selected representatives of the people had not intended or wished. Thus the permanent bureaucracy served as a check upon Parliament—there was no other—and saw to it that the business of government got done even at the most chaotic moments. As even the liberal, fiercely democratic American historian of French birth and education, Albert Guérard, once exclaimed: "So long as the bureaucrat is at his desk, France survives!"[8]

True, but a price was paid by the Third Republic. The permanent bureaucracy was bound to attract men of narrow and conservative vision who became more hidebound as their years in office went by. "In France,"

---

* Two constitutions too, at least in the opinion of a conservative historian, Daniel Halévy. "Republican France," he wrote in 1931, "has, in reality, two constitutions: one, that of 1875, is official, visible and fills the Press—it is parliamentary; the other is secret, silent, that of *l'An VIII*—the Napoleonic constitution which hands over the direction of the country to the administrative corps."[7]

"Alain" wrote in 1906, "all the *chefs de service* [i.e., the top bureaucrats] are reactionary. He who fully understands that has the key to our politics."[9] It was natural for such men in the more responsible positions to look with increasing alarm and aversion on the tergiversations of the parliamentary regime. A growing hostility to the Third Republic spread and deepened in their ranks, especially among those in the Council of State, the Inspectorate of Finance, the diplomatic service, the courts, and in the university branches from which most of them had come: the Law School and the School of Political Science. In the end many of them, attracted by the reactionary royalism of Action Française or the fascism of the Croix de Feu and the Cagoule and related groups, would help to betray the Republic they were sworn to serve.

7

THE ACHIEVEMENTS
OF THE THIRD REPUBLIC
1875–1914

For all its political chaos and its inability or unwillingness to solve its economic and social problems and keep in step with the feverish industrial developments of the other great Western nations, France under the Third Republic could look back on the eve of war in 1914 to some splendid achievements. In the realm of the spirit they were dazzling. But even in more prosaic fields they were considerable. Indeed, later Frenchmen would look back on the era before 1914 as *"la belle époque"*—the good old days.

The general standard of living had improved a good deal. Between 1870 and 1914 total national income was nearly doubled, industrial production tripled, and foreign investments were up by six times. Prices, which had slumped by 40 percent in the stagnant decades of the 1870s and 1880s, had recovered by that amount by 1914 and real wages had increased by 50 percent. Foreign trade was up 75 percent. Some 125,000 miles of new public highways were constructed, giving France by far the best system of roads in Europe for the automobile, which was just coming into popular use. France had pioneered in building motorcars and in 1913 turned out 45,000 of them, more than any other country in Europe. Some 56,000 miles of new railways were constructed; the old harbors were deepened and enlarged for the new ocean liners and battleships and two new great ports built at Le Havre and St.-Nazaire.

In the new age when the manufacture of iron and steel made a modern country industrially and militarily strong France became a major producer in this all-important field too. Thanks to faulty work by German geologists in 1871 which had led the German government to draw the frontiers of the newly annexed Lorraine so as to include all *known* iron deposits, the French came into possession of the largest iron field in Europe just inside their shrunken frontier around Briey. Because of its high sulphur content the iron in the mines in French Lorraine at first could not be worked, but the development of the Gilchrist-Thomas smelting process in the early 1880s suddenly gave France the basis of a great iron and steel industry. By 1914 twenty plants in French Lorraine were producing two thirds of the country's pig iron and steel, and France had become the world's largest exporter of iron ore. Her iron reserves were estimated as amounting to nearly one fifth of the world's available supply.

Even in agriculture, which remained inefficient and backward despite a fertile soil, advances were made. The annual value of farm products rose from 6 billion francs in 1860 to 11 billions in 1913. As we have seen, the French raised 90 percent of the food they consumed. They were third, behind the United States and Russia, in exporting wheat, and of course led the world in sales abroad of wines.

Added to the resources of the rich land of France were those of the enormous new colonial empire which Jules Ferry and a remarkable group of energetic army officers, civil-service chiefs, and commercial adventurers had acquired almost without notice by the people and the Parliament. Colonial expansion never excited the minds of the French as it did the British. The Socialists opposed it and the Radicals, who controlled the government, just barely condoned it. Suddenly France found itself with a colonial empire in North and Central Africa and in Asia (where Indochina was conquered) second only in size and population to that of Great Britain. For the handful of soldiers who carried out the conquests it provided an outlet not available at home for martial energies and an opportunity to regain for the Army some of the prestige lost in the military disaster of 1870 and in the mishandling of the Dreyfus Affair. The Church also participated enthusiastically in the colonial conquests since they gave the missionaries vast new fields in which to convert the "heathen" to Christianity. Gradually Frenchmen began to see that possessing a great colonial empire made France more of a world power—far ahead of a jealous Germany in this respect. Economically the new colonies not only opened up fresh sources of raw materials for France but provided a growing market for French goods and for enterprises such as the building of railways and harbors. Some 13 percent of the country's exports now went to the newly acquired possessions and 10 percent of foreign investments. The annual trade with the colonies rose from 350 million francs in 1879 to 2 billions in 1913.[1]

But it was in arts and letters and in the art of living that France at this time became the foremost land in Europe—or, for that matter, in the world. Paris, with its incomparable beauty and spaciousness, its air of civilized sophistication, became the modern Athens of the Western world. Like a magnet it attracted the poets, the playwrights, the novelists, the artists, even the philosophers, not only from the provinces but from the four corners of the earth—and with them the many who appreciated their ferment, their creativity, and the way of life in this City of Light. Where else in the world—certainly not in London or Berlin or New York or even in Rome—was the climate so propitious for the cultivation of the mind and the spirit? "As an artist," proclaimed Nietzsche, "a man has no home in Europe save in Paris."* Even many Americans, including some who were not artists, shared the feeling, if not always for the arts then for the art of living, subscribing to the words of a forgotten fellow citizen that "good Americans, when they die, go to Paris."†

Three men had made a deep impression on French thinking in the first three decades of the Republic: Auguste Comte, with his philosophy of Positivism; Ernest Renan, with his deep skepticism which stemmed from a familiar tradition of the French; and Hippolyte Taine, with his emphasis on a Cartesian sense of logic and clarity. All three men had cast off the romanticism of the earlier decades of the nineteenth century which in literature had reached its climax in the towering figure of Victor Hugo. They were imbued with the new scientific spirit which set in in the West in the last third of the century with the spectacular advances of science, and which in turn led to almost an obsession that the key to the secret of life lay in the discovery of the bare, dry, ascertainable facts. Emile Zola asserted the new scientific rationalism in his cascade of widely read naturalistic novels. Anatole France, whose novels reached almost as large a public as those of Zola, reflected the skepticism of Voltaire and Renan, writing with gentle irony in an almost classical prose of the foibles of the French bourgeoisie and their pompous political and military leaders. And before them had been Gustave Flaubert, whose best remembered novel, *Madame Bovary,* had been published under the Empire, and whose last, unfinished, *Bouvard et Pécuchet,* had come out in 1881, a year after his death. In both he had depicted, with an objectivity and a naturalistic art which was devastating, the hypocrisies and spiritual drabness of bourgeois provincial life.

In literature, to be sure, the France of the Third Republic had not brought forth such formidable novelists as Balzac and Stendhal,‡ those two geniuses whom one must read to understand French life in the first half of the nineteenth century; or such a gifted poet as Baudelaire or such a penetrating literary critic as Sainte-Beuve. But no other country perhaps saw

---

* And added, in the same book (*Ecce Homo*): "I believe only in French culture, and regard everything else in Europe which calls itself 'culture' as a misunderstanding." As for culture in his native land the German philosopher added: "I do not even take the German kind into consideration."

† Thomas Gold Appleton. Oliver Wendell Holmes made the saying popular by quoting it in *The Autocrat of the Breakfast Table.*

‡ Stendhal was not appreciated in France, except by Balzac, until long after his death in 1842. His works were little read by his contemporaries and seldom even reviewed; many were not even published at the time. But he was sure that some day he would be read. Writing to Balzac in 1840 he remarked that he did not "expect to be read until 1880." Earlier he had predicted that he "would be read by 1935" and in his unfinished biography he addresses "the reader of 1880 or 1900." Never in literary history has a writer's prediction about himself been so amply fulfilled.

develop so many good and widely read writers: Flaubert, Zola, Anatole France, Alphonse Daudet, Paul Bourget, Maurice Barrès, the brothers Goncourt, the short-story writer Maupassant, culminating in the greatest of all, Marcel Proust, the first volume of whose long novel, *A la recherche du temps perdu,* published at his own expense on the eve of the war (1913), attracted little notice, but whose place and influence in modern French literature was to be immense. The influence of Barrès, little known in America, was also great, not only in literature but in politics and in ideology, for in his writings and career could be found all the contradictions of life and thought in the Third Republic. He was a Republican who became the darling of the Royalists, a man of the right wing in politics who leaned toward socialism, an unbeliever who supported the Church.

In this time France had its poets too, Rimbaud, Mallarmé, Verlaine, the three symbolists, and a little later, Péguy, Claudel, Valéry, and Apollinaire. In painting there was a virtual renaissance as the Impressionists and then other schools burst upon the scene. Merely to recall some of the names: Monet, Manet, Degas, Cézanne, Renoir, Van Gogh, Picasso, Derain, Matisse, reminds one of the flowering in France of one of the oldest and greatest arts. Of sculpture, too, for there was Auguste Rodin.

In philosophy we have seen the influence of Bergson on the military mind; but perhaps it was even greater on the writers, artists, and educators in the decade before the war. He became the theorist of anti-intellectualism and denied the value of positivism, rationalism, and reason as very important forces in life. The impact of his *Creative Evolution,* published in 1906, was immense, stressing as it did the prime importance of intuition and the irrational as the springs of man's creativity, and of *élan vital* (vital urge) as the driving force in men and societies. The poets and the painters were quick to adopt this view to their work. It led to Sorel, to Proust, and to Freud. But Bergsonianism did not endure much past his lifetime (he died in Paris during the Second World War) and there were critics who, though praising the originality and provocativeness of Bergson's thought and the eloquence with which he expressed it, believed that its shortcomings were many and stemmed partly from his ignorance of history.

Despite the scandalous neglect by the national government, which financed and ran the universities, in providing French scientists with adequate laboratories for research (Pasteur and the Curies, for instance, were forced to carry out their early experiments in the most primitive and makeshift laboratories) science made remarkable progress during the last decades of the Republic before the war. A remarkable group of men sprang up to leave their mark on the world of science: Henri Poincaré in mathematics, Marcellin Berthelot in chemistry, Henri Becquerel (who introduced the nuclear age in 1896 by his discovery of the radioactivity of uranium salts) and Pierre and Marie Curie (who discovered radium) in physics and chemistry, Pasteur in medicine, and Jean Charcot, Freud's mentor, in psychopathology.

"Literature is civilization itself," proclaimed Victor Hugo, and the French agreed. Nowhere else did writers (and artists) achieve such eminence and their works receive so much public esteem. Authors were not only more popular than politicians (businessmen never had the status they enjoyed in America) but were considered more important. Their lives as well as their novels, plays, and poems were celebrated and chronicled in the press and became one of the chief topics of conversation among the people. In fact in this land they became gods or demigods, enthroned on Olympus, in Paris.

If the history of a nation is largely the history of its ideas* and its art, then the ferment in the artistic, literary, scientific, and intellectual world made this period—the first forty years of the Third Republic—one of the most interesting and fruitful eras in the long life of the nation. Moreover, there was peace and some prosperity and a good and meaningful life for many. From the debacle of 1870 France had once again risen to the level of a great world power. The Republic, for all its shortcomings, was proving a success. As the historian Maurice Reclus pointed out, if France had had a king or an emperor during these forty years, the four decades would have been hailed as marking one of the great reigns in French history.[2]

The precious liberties which kings and emperors had largely denied a Frenchman now had, and he cherished them. He was free to say and write and do what he pleased. The centuries of almost unbroken political and civic oppression seemed but a memory. And in this land individualism was enthroned, cultivated, practiced, respected. Other countries might turn out more iron and steel, produce more horsepower and more goods per man-hour, show more national discipline in getting things done, encourage fiercer competition between businesses, provide more social services and more comforts for the people, but these evidences of "progress" by others did not unduly concern Frenchmen. They tended to look upon the new-fangled machines, the belching blast furnaces, the dreary factories with their assembly lines and their adjoining slums, as a necessary evil inflicted upon the new times. A modern society had to have them, but they must not be allowed to become the center of civilization nor be permitted to dominate it. What did they all matter—and this went for most of the other gadgets of the twentieth century so dear to the Americans: modern plumbing, clean toilets, full-size bathtubs, elevators and telephones that worked—compared with the pleasures of being an untrammeled individualist who preserved his own mind and the right to express it and who had no interest in or intention of becoming an organization man and submitting to the growing conformity of a business-minded, mechanized world?

Yet, did not this cult of the individual, so strong and so extensively cultivated in France in these years, contribute to the weaknesses of the nation and its society, which Frenchmen thought better and more blessed

---

* "It is the ideas and sentiments which pervade a people," Alexis de Tocqueville contended, "that are the true cause of everything else."

than any other? Did it not make for an undue selfishness of persons and closely knit families which some foreign friends thought they saw in the French? The practice of charity, for instance, of which the Anglo-Saxons were so proud, scarcely existed among these people. And did this fierce individualism not almost fatally weaken the state by weakening its government at a time when a strong state with a strong government was necessary for national survival? There was no doubt that this individualism led most Frenchmen to subscribe wholeheartedly to the axiom that the best government was the one which governed least. Anatole France never tired of reiterating that the Republic was the best regime for the French because it was the most feeble; it weighed least on the individual. "All the bonds are relaxed," he said. "And while this enfeebles the state it lightens the burden on the people. . . . And because it governs little, I pardon it for governing badly."[3]

How little and how badly, we have noted. But in one field it did well. In foreign affairs the blindness and the paralysis which would set in in the 1930s (in England too) with disastrous consequences for the Third Republic had not yet begun to develop. On the contrary, under Clemenceau and Raymond Poincaré and a brilliant Foreign Minister, Delcassé, French foreign policy was bold and imaginative, with a sharp eye always on the protection and promotion of French national interests, and it was conducted with a firm and cool resolve in the face of growing German provocation abroad and ideological quarrels and, at times, a strange disinterestedness, at home.

Escaping from the isolation in which Bismarck had trapped it after 1871, France, as we have seen, had formed a military alliance with Russia in 1894, and Delcassé had strengthened it in 1899 so that each power was committed to come to the aid of the other in case either was attacked— Russia by Germany and Austria-Hungary, France by Germany. In 1904 the centuries-old enmity of Great Britain and France had been buried in the face of the threat of Germany, and a convention signed bringing an end to their ancient feuds and their more recent colonial rivalry (in 1898 they had almost gone to war over possession of Fashoda in the Sudan) and paving the way for an Entente which, in 1907, thanks largely to the endeavors of Clemenceau, was expanded into the Triple Entente with the inclusion of Russia. This was a counterweight to the Triple Alliance of Germany, Austria-Hungary, and Italy and gave France further assurance that if her two principal neighbors, Germany and Italy, attacked, they would not find her fighting alone.

Not that there was much danger from Italy, despite her commitments in the Triple Alliance. Delcassé saw to that. In 1902 he negotiated a secret treaty with Rome in which France and Italy agreed to remain neutral in case the other was attacked. This secret accord in fact took Italy out of the Triple Alliance, as would be demonstrated when the test came.

Thus Germany, in part because of the bullheadedness of her emperor and his sabre-rattling government but also because of the shrewdness and tenacity of French diplomacy, found herself becoming increasingly isolated in Europe, opposed by the three other greatest powers in Europe, supported only by an Austria-Hungary which was visibly crumbling and by a not very strong Italy, in whose word it had little faith. In its anger and frustration the government in Berlin proceeded to provoke a crisis in Morocco in order to frighten France and Great Britain with the threat of war. The Entente Cordiale of 1904 had been made possible by France's agreeing to give Britain a free hand in Egypt and the Sudan in return for British support for France's taking over Morocco. Germany, which had not looked kindly on Britain and France seizing most of the African continent, decided to prevent France from grabbing Morocco and at the same time warn Britain that Germany could not be excluded from sharing in the remaining spoils of Africa.

By threatening war Germany took the first step that would lead inexorably to history's first world conflict, the bloodiest and most costly the quarreling planet had yet suffered.

8

THE COMING OF
THE FIRST WORLD WAR
1905–1914

On March 31, 1905, the impetuous Kaiser Wilhelm II, accompanied by his chancellor, Prince von Bülow, landed at Tangier and proceeded to deliver one of his bellicose speeches. He warned that Germany would insist on Morocco remaining an independent state and that all powers must be accorded equal commercial opportunities in the country. Germany would not countenance France gaining control of it.

This was a calculated slap in the face to France by the hated enemy, and Delcassé wanted to call what he believed to be the Kaiser's bluff. But the French Premier, Maurice Rouvier, a former banker, did not want to take the risk. He realized that the Germans had timed their provocation shrewdly. For France's ally, Russia, was being badly beaten by the Japanese in Manchuria in a war that had glaringly exposed the military weakness of the Russians. The cream of their armies had been slaughtered in the Far East and their navy, including the Baltic Fleet, sunk. Moreover a revolution had broken out in 1905 throughout the land and threatened to topple the shaky, reactionary tsarist regime. If Germany now invaded France, as Paris feared, Russia could not lift a finger to help. The French themselves, the government well knew, were ill prepared for war. The country was still rent by the Dreyfus Affair and the church-state conflict, and the morale of the Army, as we have seen, was at its lowest ebb as the result of these domestic quarrels and also because of the reduction of military service from three to two years. The humiliated French government swallowed its pride, sacrificed Delcassé as Foreign Minister and agreed to an international conference at Algeciras in Spain at the beginning of the following year when the Big Powers, at Germany's insistence, agreed to respect the territorial integrity of Morocco and the rule of its sultan and maintain an open door there for all the European nations.

For the moment France was balked by Germany in its determination to add Morocco to its swelling North African empire. More important, the French, smarting from the German slap, believed that the government in Berlin, bent on taking advantage of Russia's temporary paralysis and Britain's hesitation to augment the Entente Cordiale with France by a military pact, was now resolved to make war. Instinctively Frenchmen felt that the Tangier crisis marked a definite turning point toward a war which the Germans would soon provoke and which France could not escape. The discerning mystic poet-journalist Charles Péguy sensed it that very morning when the news of the Kaiser's speech at Tangier was published in the Paris press. "Like everyone else," he wrote, he had come into the city at nine o'clock that morning, and "like everyone else I knew at half-past eleven that, in the space of those two hours, a new period had begun in the history of my life, in the history of this country, in the history of the world."[1] The Europeans were approaching the great watershed of 1914 and began to sense it.

The militarists in Berlin, like Adolf Hitler a generation later, were making it clearer each day what Germany intended to do with the most powerful army in the world. General Friedrich von Bernhardi, the great German military historian, was laboring on a book, *Germany and the Next War,* which would be published in 1911 and in which, echoing the heady teachings of Fichte, Hegel, Treitschke, and lesser Germanic minds, he would forcefully reiterate the old Teutonic cry that "war and conquest are a biological necessity" and that, specifically, "France must be so completely crushed that she can never cross our path again."[2]

At the time this book was being published in 1911 the Germans were provoking a new crisis in Morocco which made it seem as if they believed the hour to crush France had arrived. On the first day of July that year the German gunboat *Panther* put into the Moroccan port of Agadir ostensibly to "protect German interests" but in reality to again intimidate France, whose troops six weeks before had occupied Fez, the capital, in response to an appeal by the Sultan, who was besieged there by rebel forces. Again there was panic in the chancelleries of Europe and fear that Agadir was but the prelude to Germany's launching a European war. The sudden appearance in such waters of a German warship, even if it were only a gunboat, was bound to alarm the British Admiralty. When Lloyd George, the fiery Welsh Chancellor of the Exchequer, warned Germany in a public speech that Great Britain would support the French in this crisis, Berlin backed away. The French, though firm, were conciliatory, and in a convention signed with the Germans on November 4 they ceded them two large slices of the French Congo and agreed to maintain the "open door" in Morocco in return for Germany at last promising no longer to oppose a French protectorate over it. Once again a Franco-German war had been averted, but just. Still, Germany had lost ground. It had been forced to abandon its stand against French control of Morocco.

And though perhaps the rulers in Berlin did not quite realize it, they had forced Britain into a closer relationship with France. Seven weeks after the beginning of the Agadir crisis the Imperial Defense Committee held a secret meeting in London presided over by Prime Minister Asquith in which it was agreed that in case of a German attack on France which brought Britain into the war, the British would immediately rush over an army of six infantry divisions and one cavalry division to fight on the left flank of the French armies. Staff talks between the two countries had already worked out the details. Small though this contribution seemed in comparison to the two million soldiers which France and Germany each intended to throw into the battle, it would prove important beyond its numbers in an hour of bitter need.

Berlin seemed determined to alienate and provoke the two western democracies and turned a deaf ear to sentiment in both London and Paris that sought some kind of honorable and friendly understanding with Germany. For even in the French capital there were at least two powerful forces that sought a *rapprochement* with the Germans. Both miscalculated the German temper. The French Socialists, inspired by Jaurès, believed that their German counterparts, the Social-Democrats, the largest socialist party in the world, would prevent German militarism from triumphing and marching the country off to war. Joseph Caillaux, the new French Radical leader, believed that a peaceful understanding could be reached with Germany through business and financial ties.

Caillaux had just become Premier for the first time in 1911 when the Agadir crisis broke out. A brilliant financier who had risen to the top civil-service post in the Ministry of Finance before going into politics, and a liberal one at that, for he had championed the income tax, and a man of immense self-confidence and chilly arrogance, he did his best to prevent the German provocation at Agadir from developing into a Franco-German war. Secretly negotiating with the Germans behind the back of his own Foreign Minister, Caillaux reached agreement with them on November 4. He hoped the settlement would be the preliminary to a wider accord which ultimately would give Germany commercial access to most of the world's colonial territories and lead to Franco-German economic collaboration in Europe. His enemies in France, who were legion, for he had a talent for antagonizing even those who agreed with him, suspected that he really wanted to abandon France's alliance with Russia and her Entente Cordiale with England in order to achieve a lasting accord with Germany, which, in their view, would put France at the tender mercies of the Germans. Caillaux himself believed that achieving a Franco-German reconciliation was the only way to prevent a European war, which Germany would probably win.

Berlin did not respond to his overtures. Wilhelm's Germany preferred to win its place in the sun on its own, chiefly by its invincible army, and its rapidly growing navy, that was threatening Britain's supremacy of the seas. Caillaux, like his Radical-Socialist successors in the 1930s, did not learn, until it was too late, that to appease the Germans when they felt like conquerors only whetted their appetites. The Chamber, which reluctantly approved his ceding a large chunk of the French Congo to Germany, overthrew him for having done so. He was replaced in January 1912 by Raymond Poincaré who, perhaps in part because he came from Lorraine, believed that Germany could not be appeased, that it was intent on launching war at any moment, and that the first duty of a French government was to be prepared to meet a new German onslaught.

Could this "first duty" be accomplished in a republican France still plagued by political dissension and instability and still, at heart, pacifist? Later Poincaré, who over the bitter opposition of Clemenceau was elected President of the Republic by the National Assembly on January 16, 1913, would be charged with being a warmonger and with helping to provoke war with Germany. *"Poincaré, c'est la guerre!"* became the cry of some of his enemies. Whether there was any substance to the charge is doubtful, but at any rate the French people did not want war. Clemenceau himself seemed to express the mood of the country when he declared in the Senate on February 10, 1912: "We want peace. We want it because we need it to remake our country. We are pacifists, but we are not submissive. If war is imposed on us we will not flinch."

In August 1913 the Chamber and the Senate had reluctantly voted an increase in the term of conscription from two to three years, but only because Germany had augmented the size of her army the month before. The three-year service, which still left the French standing army inferior in numbers to the German, was unpopular in the country and the general election in the spring of 1914 returned an imposing majority of Radicals and Socialists who, united in a *bloc des gauches,* had campaigned for the return of the two-year term. The election was truly a plebiscite for peace. Moreover Jaurès, whose Socialist Party had won a resounding 104 seats in the Chamber, and Caillaux, whose Radical-Socialist group had won even more—some 172 seats—both wanted peace with Germany and believed it was possible. Perhaps they might have succeeded, slim though the chances were, had there not occurred in that tense spring and early summer of 1914 three assassinations which upset not only France but all Europe.

Two occurred in Paris and one in a far-off little Balkan town. On March 16, 1914, the wife of Caillaux shot and killed Gaston Calmette, the editor of *Le Figaro.** On July 31 Jaurès was assassinated by a right-

---

* *Le Figaro* was one of the leading conservative daily newspapers, and on January 5, 1914, Calmette had launched a series of signed articles against Caillaux of a violence that shocked even Parisians, accustomed as they were to vituperation in their venal press. Calmette set out to destroy Caillaux for reasons which he believed sufficient: because Caillaux was responsible for trying to force the income tax on France, an act of "robbery by violence" which *Le Figaro* and all good conservative newspapers hysterically opposed; and above all because Caillaux had carried his pro-

wing fanatic in a Paris café. The chiefs of the two largest parties in France, which dominated Parliament and which were working for peace, were abruptly removed from the political scene, for Caillaux immediately resigned his post as Minister of Finance.

Between these two assassinations in Paris there occurred another, a thousand miles away. On June 28 Archduke Francis Ferdinand, heir to the Habsburg throne, was slain, with his wife, by a youthful Serbian fanatic in the Bosnian town of Sarajevo. This struck the spark that set off the First World War.

Bismarck, who had been dismissed as German Chancellor in 1890 by the headstrong young Wilhelm II, but who had lived on in bitterness of mind and spirit until 1898, had predicted it. "Some damned foolish thing in the Balkans," he had said shortly before his death, would provoke a European war.[3] Having forged modern Germany by making war, he had striven for a long peace in which his newly united country could consolidate its gains.

Few Frenchmen, absorbed as they were in their domestic quarrels and by the drama of the Madame Caillaux affair, understood why the assassination of an Austrian archduke in a far away Balkan town should lead inexorably to a European conflict of arms. Perhaps few Englishmen, Germans, Austrians, and Russians either. Perhaps not even their statesmen, for with the exception of the Austrian, they strove almost hysterically at the last moment to avert war, and even the Austrian political leaders, wooden-headed though they were, thought that by crushing little Serbia, whose government they believed implicated in the murder of Francis Ferdinand and responsible for the Slav unrest in the crumbling Austro-Hungarian Empire, they would be fighting only a local war they were sure to win in short order.

But the growing national rivalries, the feverish rearmament, the division of the great powers into two hostile armed camps, the Balkan wars of 1912–13 which had driven the Turks out of Europe except for the bridgehead of Constantinople and aggravated relations between the new independent Balkan states and Austria-Hungary and between Vienna and St. Petersburg and between their respective allies in Berlin and Paris—

Germanism to what Calmette charged was the border of treason. No holds were barred by the embattled editor, and his series culminated in the publication of facsimiles of passionate love letters which Caillaux had written to his eventual second wife (signed "Your Joe") when both had been married to others and which his first wife had stolen. This was too much for the second Madame Caillaux and on the late afternoon of March 16, 1914, she called at the offices of *Le Figaro* and greeted its editor with six pistol shots in the stomach. Her trial for murder began in July and all but blotted out news of impending war from the Paris dailies. Though Parisians fed on scandal and particularly on *crimes passionnels* this case, with its daily revelations of the intimate love life of a Prime Minister, outshone all previous ones. Madame Caillaux's defense was that her pistol went off six times "by itself" and a jury of gallant Frenchmen acquitted her on July 28, on the very eve of the mobilization of millions of men in Europe for a war the coming of which the readers of the Paris press, feeding avidly on the juicy tidbits of the trial, were scarcely aware.

all these happenings had brought tension in Europe to a breaking point. It resembled, as has been said, a powder keg, and once the spark from Sarajevo was put to it, it was bound to blow up. The puny little human figures in the frantic European chancelleries seemed powerless to do anything about it.

Austria-Hungary mobilized against Serbia and declared war on her on July 28. Russia mobilized against Austria-Hungary on July 30. The next day Germany sent an ultimatum to Russia demanding that it revoke mobilization within twelve hours, and when no reply came herself mobilized on August 1 and declared war on Russia. Ultimatums were now hurtling out of Berlin. On July 31 one had been sent to Paris demanding to know within eighteen hours whether France would remain neutral and, if so, stipulating that she hand over to the German army the key French fortresses of Toul and Verdun, which blocked the routes the Germans could take over their border to France. On August 1 the French government replied that it "would act in accordance with its interests"—it did not demean itself by even replying to the insolent demand that France turn over to the Germans its means of defense. The same day it ordered general mobilization and on August 3 Germany formally declared war on France. Berlin, now in the throes of a great war fever, was taking on all comers.

Only the question of what Great Britain would do remained open and the German government settled it on August 4 by invading Belgium, whose neutrality Britain, along with the other Great Powers, had solemnly guaranteed. The vacillating British government now got out an ultimatum of its own. Britain could never stand idly by while a German army occupied Flanders across the Channel. It demanded that the Germans respect Belgian neutrality and so declare by midnight August 4. But the Germans then, as on a second similar occasion which will be treated in the climactic chapters of this work, had no comprehension of the British temperament. The German Chancellor, Bethman-Hollweg, indignantly stormed at the British Ambassador in Berlin that Britain was doing "this unthinkable thing . . . to a kindred nation . . . *all for a scrap of paper!*" Being the kind of German he was the Chancellor did not realize that the expression would resound around the world to the detriment of Germany and would indeed haunt her until another German Chancellor a quarter of a century later, again regarding Germany's written word to Belgium "as a scrap of paper," made the practice seem customary to *any* German government.

War!

When its ultimatum to Berlin on Belgium ran out at midnight August 4, Great Britain declared war on Germany. And so began the First World War, which, contrary to the belief of all the belligerents that it would be a brief one because no nation had resources immense enough to fight a long one, lasted 1,564 days and became the bloodiest and costliest armed conflict the world had yet seen.

On the one side were the nations of the Triple Entente: France, Great Britain, and Russia. On the other side Germany had only Austria-Hungary, for on August 3 the third power in the Triple Alliance, Italy, had declared her neutrality on the grounds that her German and Austrian allies had provoked aggressive war without consulting her, in violation of the terms of their pact. Italy's declaration of neutrality relieved France of having to fight a war on two fronts. The perspicacious Delcassé, as we have seen, had made this possible by his secret deal with Rome.

By midnight of August 4, though, the French knew that the great bulk of the world's mightiest army was being hurled against them. Unlike a similar summer day forty-four years before, however, they knew (thanks also to Delcassé's diplomacy) that this time they would not be fighting the powerful enemy alone. To the east the Russians were assembling sizeable armies on the German and Austro-Hungarian borders. And now at this very hour of midnight the British had finally made up their minds that in their own national interests they must come in on the side of France. Yet because Britain's army was amazingly small—for a great European power —the French realized that the first heavy blows of the enemy in the west must be borne by themselves.

If the confident militarists in Berlin were sure that the armies of the Republic could not stand up to them, it must be added that there were many in Paris, even among the staunch patriots, who had grave doubts that they could. They feared that the revolutionary syndicalists and Social-ists would disrupt the country with a general strike, as they had often warned they would do if war threatened. The government could not be sure that the mass of the workers, whose leaders had agitated against the Army and war, would answer the call for mobilization. The murder of Jaurès on the evening of July 31, less than twenty-four hours before the mobilization orders would be issued, stunned the government, which was apprehensive that the assassination of the great Socialist leader would provoke the workers to man the barricades and refuse to respond to the call to the colors. The 2nd Regiment of Cuirassiers, about to entrain for the frontier, was ordered to remain in the capital in order to provide a force of cavalry to put down a possible insurrection.

But the wobbly government of Premier René Viviani had failed to judge the temper of the French people in this hour of mortal danger to the country. The response of the workers to the murder of their leader was to march calmly to their mobilization centers like everyone else. Charles de Gaulle, then a young lieutenant hurrying off to his first war, would later recall with bursting pride that though the General Staff had estimated that 13 percent of the reservists might refuse to report for military service, less than one and a half percent failed to do so, that the recruiting offices were besieged by 350,000 volunteers, and that 3,000 peacetime deserters returned to join the army. Of the 2,501 suspected left-ists and pacifists (including a young left-wing Socialist, Pierre Laval) listed on "Carnet B," who were to be arrested on the day of mobilization because it was believed they would try to sabotage it, some 80 percent eventually volunteered in the army. The Minister of Interior revoked the order of arrest for every Frenchman on the list.

What happened immediately in France was not further strife—all the bitter old quarrels were buried—but union. President Poincaré had called for it on August 4 when his war declaration was read to a wildly applauding Chamber of Deputies. But the establishment of the *"Union sacrée"* was more than a response to the inspiring words of the President. It came spontaneously from the French people resolved to defend the soil of the country. As a French historian would write: "The first days of 1914 were among the most glorious our country has ever lived. . . . This spirit of union from the very first saved the country. . . . Because the Republic made this possible it deserved the gratitude of the patriots."[4]

On August 28 the Radical government was replaced by one represent-ing all the political parties from the extreme Left to the Right, with Viviani remaining as Premier. Parliament, after unanimously approving the govern-ment's decision to fight, had adjourned with the tacit understanding that in this moment of peril the country would have to be run by the military High Command without interference from the civilian politicians. No longer did even the Radical and Socialist members of Parliament fear that the generals would lag in their zeal to defend the country or conspire to jettison the Republic. There would be this time, they felt confident, no Sedan, no Metz, no Bazaine. They trusted the generals to fight and to halt the invasion of the ancient enemy.

But by the end of August the generals and their troops had suffered a series of shattering defeats that appeared to be as bad, if not worse, than those experienced at the beginning of the Franco-Prussian war. The French armies and the small British Expeditionary Force to the north and northeast of Paris were in headlong retreat. The sound of artillery fire began to be heard in the capital itself, and on September 2, the forty-fourth anniversary of Sedan, the government fled to Bordeaux. France faced a disaster no less overwhelming than that of 1870, and from the same foe in the same way.

As we have seen in the opening chapter, France faced a similar catastrophe for the third time in 1940. And since this last challenge is the principal concern of this study we must try to see what it was that France had in August–September 1914 that saved it from the debacle of 1870 and—what is more important for us—from that which would come in May–June 1940.

9

THE THIRD REPUBLIC'S FINEST HOUR
1914–1918

Above all else the France of the Third Republic in 1914 had a resolute and united people and government, and a determined, cool-headed Commander in Chief who at the darkest moments of seeming calamity never lost his nerve nor his confidence in himself and his troops. Though the government, on the advice of the High Command, moved to Bordeaux to escape possible capture, it remained—after a brief panic the last week of August—united and determined to fight to the finish. The people too. And the troops and their officers and the High Command, and, at the top of the military pyramid, General Joffre—despite the rapid retreats of the first three weeks, one quick defeat in battle after another, and staggering losses in killed and wounded.

As in 1940 so in 1914 the main German blow came on a front where the French generals least expected it. They were warned in plenty of time where the Germans most probably would strike, but they did not believe the warnings. Besides, they had plans for mighty offensives of their own in places of their own choosing.

The strategy of the German General Staff for a quick victory over France, after which the Russians would be disposed of, had long been dominated by the teachings of Count Alfred von Schlieffen, Chief of the General Staff from 1891 to 1906, who bequeathed to his successors what became known as the Schlieffen Plan. While Russia, incapable of mobilizing rapidly, would be held by only nine divisions, the bulk of the German army—seven eighths of it—would be hurled against France. Like the Franco-Prussian War it would be a quick campaign of no more than six weeks, ending, as in 1870, with the destruction of all the French armies and a small British force, if England was foolish enough to get entangled in the war. Then the mass of the victorious German army, one million men strong, would be rushed by rail to the east, where it would similarly crush the ponderous Russians, who would just be getting their armies into line.

The core of the Schlieffen Plan lay in its concentration of an overwhelming force on the right wing, which would sweep into Belgium through the Liège-Namur gateway, press westward toward the Channel ("Let the last man brush the Channel with his sleeve," Schlieffen advised), then turn sharply south across the Somme and the Seine and finally eastward south of Paris, rolling up the French armies against their fortifications on the borders of Alsace and Lorraine. First evolved in 1894, the plan was revised and perfected by Schlieffen until the final version was ready in 1905, a year before his retirement. The violation of Belgian neutrality, solemnly guaranteed by his own country and the other great powers, did not bother Schlieffen any more than it did his immediate successor nor his ultimate successors in Berlin in 1940. When he died at eighty in 1913, on the eve of war, his only thought was on the strategy of victory through Belgium. On his deathbed he is said to have muttered: "Keep the right wing strong!"

His successor, General Helmuth von Moltke, namesake and nephew of the field marshal who had crushed the French in 1870, heeded his last words—but not quite completely. He was tempted to dilute his master's plan a little by subtracting some divisions from the German right wing and adding them to the left wing in Alsace and Lorraine, opposite the French fortifications. He thought this might enable him to bring off a double envelopment, on both flanks, as Hannibal had done against the Romans at Cannae in 216 B.C. Thus he sowed some of the seeds of later disaster. Whereas Schlieffen had insisted that the right wing be seven times as strong as the left, Moltke watered it down by 1913 to a ratio of three to one. Nevertheless his modified Schlieffen Plan called for as quick progress on the right as the original. The road past Liège was to be cleared by the twelfth day of mobilization, Brussels occupied by M-19, the French border traversed by M-22, a line running east from St.-Quentin achieved by M-31, and the entire French Army destroyed south and east of Paris by M-39. A six weeks' war, just as in 1870 (and, to skip ahead, 1940!).

Despite many warnings the French High Command simply refused to believe that the main German onslaught would come through Belgium. As far back as 1904, when Schlieffen was putting the final touches to his plan, an officer of the German General Staff had sold its contents to the French Army. They revealed that the Germans intended to strike their main blow through Liège, Namur, and Charleroi in Belgium and then sweep into France down the valley of the Oise, which is just what they did ten years later. The Chief of the French General Staff at the time, General Pendezac, was inclined to take the bought secrets seriously, but his colleagues were skeptical. Perhaps the documents were a plant. General Joffre, the new Chief of Staff, and his right-hand man, the able General de Castelnau, later convinced themselves that the main German attack would come through the plateau of Lorraine. They did not believe the Germans had enough front-line troops to extend themselves so far west as Belgium. They did not know that, under Schlieffen's earlier prodding, the enemy had introduced a revolutionary new concept into modern war: the use of reserves as front-line troops. As we have seen, the French rejected the idea that reserves could be of much value in actual combat.

We have seen too that at least one leading French general feared that the Germans would make their main attack through Belgium.* This was General Michel. As Commander in Chief–designate in time of war, he submitted a report in 1911 predicting a massive German offensive through Belgium and proposing that it be met by a French army of one million men dug in along a line between Verdun and Antwerp and running through Namur on the Meuse. This was anathema to his fellow generals for two reasons: it foresaw a German attack in an area where they were sure it could not possibly take place; and it would put the French armies on the defensive, whereas the whole doctrine of the new army was offensive. General Michel, in their opinion, compounded his errors by urging that the French double their front-line troops by throwing in a reserve unit for each regular unit. This was what the Germans were doing, but the French did not believe that either. General Michel, as has been mentioned, was dismissed as a crackpot for his heresies—and, as events would show, for having been absolutely right.† He was replaced by Joffre, who with new aides, notably Foch and Castelnau, dismissed Michel's recommendations ("A piece of foolishness," Joffre called them) and proceeded to draw up new plans in which the French armies would take the offensive in Alsace and Lorraine and leave the Belgian border virtually undefended.

They were embodied in Plan XVII. Completed in the spring of 1913, it called for two major offensives, one to the north and the second to the south of the German-fortified line of Metz-Thionville, with the latter supported by an attack further south in Alsace which was expected to carry the French to the Rhine and achieve in the first weeks of the war the liberation of one of the two lost provinces. The plan stressed that the French must take the offensive all along the line. "We must get to Berlin by going through Mainz," said General Foch, who was now in command of the XXth Corps at Nancy, 120 miles from the town on the Rhine. All in all the French would deploy five armies (against seven German armies) stretched from Belfort in Alsace, near the Swiss border, to Hirson, some one hundred miles up the Franco-Belgian frontier. This left two thirds of that border, from Hirson to the Channel, uncovered, the very region where General Michel had urged the army to concentrate its main force.

---

* See above, p. 83, footnote†.
† General Michel was not the only French officer who would prove right. In 1913 Colonel Grouard published a book, *La Guerre éventuelle,* in which he warned: "It is above all the German offensive through Belgium on which we ought to fix our attention. . . . If we take the offensive at the outset we shall be beaten."

Indeed, by the third week of August 1914 the main force of the German army, which had burst through the Belgian fortresses of Liège and Namur, was sweeping over the Franco-Belgian border west of Hirson, and between its advancing columns and Paris there was very little to stop it—only the battered French Fifth Army and the five divisions of the British Expeditionary Force, both retreating rapidly. The war for the French seemed lost—before the month was out.

"MIRACLE" ON THE MARNE

There then occurred what many historians—not very soundly or accurately—would later describe as the "Miracle of the Marne" and what, to the surprise of both sides, would suddenly and dramatically turn the tide of battle and of the great war itself. On the banks of the little Marne river just east of Paris, and on a boiling front that in fact extended for more than 250 miles from Paris to Lorraine and Alsace, where the French First and Second Armies were locked in fierce battle with the forces of Crown Prince Rupprecht, the French, aided by the small British force of five divisions whose commander, Sir John French, had wished to pull out entirely, stood and fought. From September 6 to 13 the Battle of the Marne raged. At its beginning the Germans were almost within sight of Paris and, as it seemed to them, of final, glorious victory. A cavalry patrol of General von Kluck's First Army, which had led the sweep on the outer flank through Belgium and northern France, had got close enough to the capital to see the Eiffel Tower. By the end of the battle the great German sweep had been stopped and thrown back. France, though its mining and industrial northern provinces remained in German hands, had been saved —to fight another day, for four long years, as it turned out.

To most of the world, including the German, it seemed that a miracle had happened at the Marne, and Bergson compared it to the "miracle" of Joan of Arc. The truth was more prosaic and complex.

Despite the German threat on his left, General Joffre had stubbornly insisted on following Plan XVII, and French offensives were duly mounted at the opening of hostilities in Alsace and Lorraine and then in the center through the Ardennes. All three failed. As late as August 20, the day the Germans entered Brussels and it seemed evident to everyone except the generals of the French High Command that the main German thrust was coming through Belgium, General Joffre insisted on launching his offensive in the Ardennes, as called for in Plan XVII. He seems to have believed that victory in the center would force the German right wing to stop and turn back. But this attack was stopped cold by a superior German force within three days. In the meantime three German armies were fighting their way across the Franco-Belgian frontier further west. The French Fifth Army of General Lanrezac, who since the first week of hostilities had vainly tried to warn Joffre that the heaviest German blow was coming through Belgium against his one army, was defeated by the Second and Third German Armies at Charleroi on August 22–23, and forced to retreat southward over the border into France. On August 23 General von Kluck's powerful First Army had defeated the outnumbered British at Mons. The French frontier had been breached. Only the small British force and the badly mauled retreating French Fifth Army stood between the Germans and Paris.

At last Joffre awoke to realities and in the midst of the shattering of so many French illusions and the wreckage of so many hopes he now displayed a mettle—courage and cool-headedness and resolution and a will and mind to take desperate corrective action—that had been lacking in Marshal Bazaine in 1870 and, alas, would not be found in Gamelin and Weygand in 1940, when these illustrious generals found themselves in the same seemingly hopeless plight. Where they panicked or froze or gave up, he remained calm, collected, resolved, even confident. Without this man and his indomitable spirit in the face of crushing adversity France would not have survived September 1914. Had Joffre been possessed of a deeper and more flexible mind he might have avoided some of the errors of the first month of battle. But there is no doubt that his strength of character and his amazing imperturbability kept the faltering French armies in being when they were about to disintegrate.

In the final trial he was aided by another remarkable general, Joseph Simon Galliéni, who self-effacingly had declined the post which Joffre had received in 1911. In poor health, he had retired from active service in April 1914, on reaching the age limit of sixty-five. Suddenly on August 25 he was called back to become Military Governor of Paris and to do what he could to defend the capital against the approaching Germans. Galliéni was one of the more intellectual generals of the French Army. Invariably wearing a pince-nez, he might have been taken for a professor of mathematics in a university. A student of languages, among other things, he kept a diary in German, English, and Italian which he called *Erinnerungen of my life di ragazzo*.[1] He had made his military reputation mostly in France's conquest of colonies and had been hailed as the conqueror of Madagascar. With a quicker mind than Joffre's, he was the first to size up the opportunities offered by German mistakes which would lead to the Battle of the Marne. Against the opposition of Joffre he had insisted on the importance of trying to hold Paris—not only because this would buck up the nation's morale but because the capital was the soul and brain of the country, its communications and transport center, an immense depot, and its industries one of the chief sources of military supplies. He had opposed powerful forces in the government and even in the High Command which in the last days of August had wanted—as Weygand would insist on in 1940—to declare Paris an open city so as to spare it destruction. On August 3, the day after the government pulled out for Bordeaux, a placard appeared on the walls of the capital:

The members of the Government of the Republic have left Paris to give a new impulse to the national defense. I have received an order to defend Paris against the invader. This order I shall carry out to the end.

GALLIÉNI

With the energy of a man half his years and despite his illness—he was suffering from prostatitis—Galliéni, with no great help at first from Joffre, set out to scrape up troops and guns and organize the defense of Paris.* But, like Joffre, his mind was receptive to an even greater opportunity—halting the whole German juggernaut now approaching the capital and throwing it back before the great city could be directly attacked. He saw that opportunity in a flash on September 3 and he convinced Joffre, who was rather slow to see it, to seize it. The imperturbable Commander in Chief had not been inactive in doing something to meet the German threat on his extreme left. For several days he had been withdrawing, at great risk, whole army corps from his hard-pressed armies in the east, rushing them by rail across France and reassembling them in the neighborhood of Paris. With these divisions and others extracted from the last available reserves, he had created two new armies, the Sixth, under General Michel Joseph Maunoury, which he placed on the extreme flank of his line, on the left of the BEF, and the Ninth, under General Foch, to plug a growing gap between the French Fourth and Fifth Armies, the latter having been battered for three weeks by the advancing German First and Second Armies. On the day Foch left his beloved XXth Corps, fighting valiantly and successfully before Nancy, to take his new command, he received the news of the death in battle of his only son. On the way to his new post he picked up hastily at a railroad station a cavalry officer to be the chief of his makeshift staff. This was Colonel Maxime Weygand, who was to become the chief aide of the future Allied generalissimo and was to command the French armies in the final weeks of the great debacle of 1940.

Joffre was now achieving at least equality in numbers to the enemy approaching Paris. The first serious German strategic error of the war gave him his opportunity. On the last day of August, General von Kluck, commander of the First Army on the German flank, whose orders had been to sweep west and south of Paris, changed his direction and made an inward wheel that would take him *north* and *east* of Paris. He believed the small British army directly in front of him was finished and that the French had no forces to outflank him on the west. He was confident that he could now smash the remnants of the French Fifth Army east of Paris and bring the war to a quick and victorious conclusion.

---

* Among those he called up was Major Alfred Dreyfus, now fifty-five, who was assigned to the artillery, his old branch of the service. It was the martyr's final vindication.

Kluck's First Army, whose great flanking sweep through Belgium and northern France was the key to the success of the modified Schlieffen Plan and which so far had brilliantly fulfilled its mission, suddenly found itself outflanked, though the German commander did not at first realize it. The French High Command learned of Kluck's turn to the southeast the next day, on September 1, from orders taken from a dead German cavalry officer. But Joffre did not immediately sense the opportunity it gave him to attack Kluck on his exposed western flank. On September 2 he ordered a further retreat to the Seine, southeast of Paris. There, "within a few days," he said, he planned to make his final stand and, if possible, throw the enemy back.

Galliéni was outraged. Joffre was sacrificing the capital and seemed, to him, blind to the opportunity to hit the Germans on their flank. Though Joffre had not informed him of the intelligence received on September 1 of Kluck's change of direction, he had got wind of it from his own sources. On the morning of September 3 he confirmed it beyond doubt from the report of a French pilot who had flown over Kluck's columns and had seen them heading southeast toward the Marne instead of toward Paris. Later in the day a second French pilot and two British aviators brought further confirmation. The German flank was open. It remained for Galliéni to convince Joffre of this and to get him to take advantage of it while there was still time. Though it was not exactly his job, but Joffre's, he must also persuade the British, who, though as battered as the French Fifth Army and as utterly fatigued by constant battle and retreat, were in a crucial position just south of the Marne. He knew that the British commander, Sir John French, was so discouraged he was pulling the BEF out of the battle and thinking of withdrawing on his own to the sea, leaving the French in the lurch. This would have ensured German victory. But if the BEF could be persuaded to halt and fight, it and the Fifth and Sixth Armies on its flanks, weak as they were, might turn the tide if the French armies further to the east also halted and counterattacked. Aerial reconnaissance early on the morning of September 4 showed Galliéni that Kluck's flank was now wide open to attack by this combined Anglo-French force. Without waiting for Joffre's approval he gave Maunoury preliminary orders to move the Sixth Army into position for the attack on Kluck's rear. He then turned to the not inconsiderable task of convincing his Commander in Chief and his British ally to play their part in time.

After numerous appeals on the telephone ("The real Battle of the Marne," he would later quip, "was fought on the telephone") Galliéni won over Joffre that evening to order the great counterattack for September 6. Earlier that day of the 4th he had journeyed to British Headquarters, but Sir John was not there and he had got nowhere with his staff. Later in the day General Franchet d'Esperey, the energetic new commander of the Fifth Army who had just replaced Lanrezac, got further. Though Sir John again failed to show up for an agreed rendezvous, his deputy, General

Henry Wilson, agreed with d'Esperey to throw the BEF into the crucial counterattack toward the Marne. Sir John French, though, seemed to the French High Command to be still hesitating, and on the afternoon of the 5th, on the eve of the planned battle that Joffre now felt would decide the fate of France, the Commander in Chief journeyed 115 miles to BEF headquarters at Melun, southeast of Paris, to make a final effort to induce the British commander to join in the counterattack the next morning. It was to prove Joffre's most eloquent moment. Gone was the phlegmatic manner. He spoke passionately with stabbing gestures most unlike him. "I cannot believe," he said, "that the British Army will refuse to do its share in this supreme crisis." And pounding his fist on the table for perhaps the first and last time in his life, he concluded: *"Monsieur le Maréchal* (General French was a field marshal), the honor of England is at stake!" The Englishman's face turned crimson and tears formed in his eyes. He agreed to halt the retreat of the BEF and throw it into battle the next day.

That battle, resounding down history as the first Battle of the Marne (there would be a second in 1918 when the Germans made their last desperate bid for victory) was won by the Allies, who in four hot, dusty September days turned almost certain and final defeat into victory. German military might, seemingly so invincible, met its match at the very moment when the invaders believed triumph already achieved. In the climactic trial by battle the German army was stopped and hurled back. This was not, as was for so long believed, a miracle. It was the logical result of German mistakes committed because some of their field commanders became too confident—Kluck above all—and because a handful of French generals, principally Galliéni and Joffre, keeping their heads in the midst of apparent debacle, took advantage of those mistakes, and because their troops, French and British, disheartened and utterly fatigued though they were from three weeks of lost battles and constant retreat, summoned up some last reserve of strength that enabled them for the first time to go over to the offensive against what had seemed until then to be a vastly superior foe. If there was any miracle at the Marne the spirit of the weary Anglo-French troops was it.

The defeated Kluck, who had had a poor opinion of the enemy forces he had pushed back so easily the first weeks, understood this afterward. "The reason that transcends all others" for what happened on the Marne, he said in 1918, "was the extraordinary . . . aptitude of the French soldier [he might have added, the British too] to recover quickly. That men will let themselves be killed where they stand—that is well-known and counted on in every plan of battle. But that men who have retreated for ten days, sleeping on the ground and half dead with fatigue, should be able to take up their rifles and attack when the bugle sounds, is a thing upon which we never counted. It was a possibility not studied in our war academy."[2]

If the belligerent commander of the key German First Army was surprised by the *élan* of the French soldier, the German High Command was even more surprised by the sudden Allied counteroffensive. Kluck's Chief of Staff, General von Kuhl, later testified to it.

Neither the Supreme Command nor First Army headquarters had the remotest idea of an immediately imminent offensive of the whole French Army. The continuation of the French retreat was accepted as settled. There was only a question of our flank being threatened from Paris. . . . The great offensive on the whole front . . . came as a complete surprise. No sign, no prisoner's statement, no newspaper tattle had given us warning of it.[3]

For this surprise General Joffre was mainly responsible. Unlike Bazaine in 1870 (and Gamelin and Weygand in 1940) he had known how to retreat in order to keep his armies in existence. His armies on the left wing had been defeated and forced back because he had not at first realized, despite the timely warnings of Lanrezac, that the principal German blow was coming through Belgium. He had partly rectified his error by directing a skillful retreat. His Fifth Army, which had borne the brunt of the major German attack and suffered heavy losses, had not been destroyed or cut off. His Fourth and Third Armies further to the right had been drawn back to keep pace with the retreating Fifth Army and BEF so that there was no German breakthrough as in 1940, or envelopment as in 1870.

In his new headquarters in Luxembourg, far behind the boiling front, General von Moltke, as gloomy and unsure of himself despite his victories as Joffre was cheerful and confident in the face of his defeats, had begun by the end of August to appreciate the overall situation, though his field commanders, each seeking his own glory on his own segment of the front, had not. "Where are the prisoners?" he began to ask, as one general on the line after another reported that the French were finished. On September 3 General von Bülow, commander of the Second Army on Kluck's eastern flank, arrived on the Marne and wired Moltke that the French Fifth Army was "decisively beaten" and retreating "utterly disorganized to south of the Marne." The next day Kluck advised that he feared nothing from Paris.

Moltke knew better. He knew what Kluck and Bülow were not yet aware of: that Joffre, while carrying out a skillful retreat, had shifted several corps from the eastern front to the vicinity of Paris and that the German right flank was in danger. "We must not deceive ourselves," Moltke told a cabinet officer visiting his headquarters on September 4. "We have had success but not victory. . . . When a million men oppose each other in battle the victor has prisoners. Where are our prisoners? . . . It seems to me the French are conducting a planned and orderly retreat."

This, at any rate, was his estimate of the situation and that night Moltke acted on it—to the consternation of the Kaiser, who was prancing around headquarters playing his role of War Lord and getting in the way of the commanding general, and to the stupefaction of his commanders in the field. He issued a General Order halting the great wheeling movement of his armies. He instructed the First and Second Armies to stop their advance south of the Marne and face west toward Paris and thus protect the German flank against an attack from the capital. He told the field commanders bluntly what they had refused to believe. "The enemy," he said, "has evaded the enveloping attack of the First and Second Armies. It is bringing up new formations and concentrating superior forces in the neighborhood of Paris to protect the capital and threaten the right flank of the German armies."

This was also true and Moltke was sound in ordering what he did to meet the situation. But his orders came too late, and Kluck, who could scarcely believe them, at first refused to follow them. Joffre, to the surprise of the Germans, had now, by the evening of September 5, established actual superiority of numbers where he needed it. Between Verdun and Paris, where the next day he would make his final stand by attacking, he had 56 infantry divisions, including 5 British, and 9 cavalry divisions; the Germans had 44 infantry and 7 cavalry divisions.

By keeping his head, Joffre had, as Moltke finally acknowledged, managed to conduct a "planned and orderly retreat," had thereby kept his armies intact, and, when he at last grasped the German strategic plan, had successfully initiated the classic maneuver—as old as war itself—of making himself superior in strength at the place of decisive battle. When the enemy, because of Kluck's premature inward wheel, offered him its flank just northeast of Paris he—with the prompting of Galliéni—struck.

Attacked on his weakly held flank on the afternoon of September 5, the day before Joffre's target date, by the advance guard of Maunoury's makeshift Sixth Army, Kluck was forced to withdraw his army in haste from south of the Marne in order to meet this unexpected threat. In doing so he opened a gap between him and the Second Army of Bülow that soon became 30 miles wide. It was into this gap that the small but crucially placed BEF of five divisions and the larger force of d'Esperey's Fifth Army poured. On the right of the Fifth Army, Foch's improvised Ninth Army bore the brunt of a succession of severe attacks from the German Third Army and part of the Second between the Marne and the Seine. It was during this part of the battle that the future Allied generalissimo sent a famous message to Joffre: "I am being beaten back on my right and on my left. I am attacking in the center." He held, and carried out his key mission of protecting the flank of the principal Allied attack further west. To the east, on both sides of Verdun and on the Moselle in Lorraine, Moltke had ordered his four armies there to continue the attack while the First and Second Armies near Paris halted. There was fierce fighting on this eastern part of the front but the French, though depleted by the units taken by Joffre for the Marne, held stubbornly. On the Marne and Ourcq rivers just east of the capital the battle was decided.

The climax came on the fourth day, September 9. On the extreme flank Maunoury's Sixth Army was in trouble that morning as the full force of Kluck's army, which had pulled back from south of the Marne to the Ourcq, turned against it. It was here at this moment that something happened that grew into one of the great legends of the Battle of the Marne: that it was won by Galliéni's famous "taxicab army," rushed out of ·Paris to a critical front. The facts are interesting and dramatic enough. Hard-pressed already on the 8th, as Kluck began throwing more of his Army against him, Maunoury, who had only seven divisions, four of them second-rate reserve units hastily scraped together, called desperately for reinforcements. Galliéni had the IV Corps, which was just arriving in Paris by train from the east. Requisitioning 600 taxicabs and an odd assortment of buses and trucks, he stuffed them with 6,000 troops from the corps and shooed them off to Sixth Army's threatened front. The taxis, which made the 35-mile trip twice during the night, carried the men, and the other vehicles their supplies. From this brilliant improvisation, which materially aided Maunoury—he was also helped by the heavy guns of the Paris forts—the legend of the "taxis of the Marne" grew to great proportions.

In the meantime the BEF and the French Fifth Army were plunging into the gap between the German First and Second Armies. Their progress slowed by their own fatigue after an unbroken fortnight of retreat and battle, by the necessity of having to get over three rivers (the Grand and Petit Morin and the Marne, which were too deep to be forded and had to be bridged), and by the stubborn resistance of the Germans, they reached the Marne on the morning of September 9 above and below Château Thierry and advanced beyond it. Faced with a breakthrough between their two armies Kluck and Bülow shortly after noon ordered a general retreat back to the Aisne. The gap between them remained until next day but the French and British were too weary and perhaps too cautious to exploit it fully. The Germans, equally weary, were able to fall back in fairly good order and without serious pursuit, and thus escape disaster, though they lost 30,000 prisoners. By September 13 the fighting had died down. The Germans withstood all Allied attempts to dislodge them from the Aisne. Farther east their armies were pulled back to straighten out the line. The next day, September 14, Moltke was dismissed. The six weeks' timetable for crushing France had run out. It had been enough to destroy the French armies in 1870 and would prove sufficient in 1940. But in 1914 it had ended in a defeat.

Paris was saved, and France, the Germans halted and thrown back, the legend of their invincibility destroyed. They had made a tremendous and daring bid for quick victory, had almost grasped it, and then seen it slip through their fingers. Over the long run, for four murderous years of trench warfare, they would do no better, though once, four summers

later, they again would come close to victory on this same Marne only to
see it once more snatched from them, after which came quick and final
defeat.

VICTORY: LONG LIVE THE REPUBLIC!

Those four years of terrible trial marked the Third Republic's finest
hour. Out of the depths of their long history and national character the
French had summoned sources of strength sufficient to repel the invader.
The British had helped save the day in the first crucial weeks and would
help much more as the ghastly slaughter increasingly decimated the men of
the country. Toward the end the Americans would also aid, throwing in
fresh divisions to help their tiring, depleted allies. But it was mainly
the French who turned the tide that September week of 1914 from the
Marne to Verdun and Lorraine. And they bore the brunt of battle to
the end.

Not even in the most splendid times of the ancient monarchy, or in
that of Napoleon, had France proved so great in adversity as during these
four years under the Third Republic. As in all the fateful moments of a
country's history, when it succeeds in mastering fate, the Third Republic
found a few men of greatness to lead it—both political and military:
Clemenceau and Poincaré; Joffre, Galliéni, Pétain, and Foch. Each of
them, civilian and military, was unflinching in the darkest moments,
determined to halt the invader and drive him from the land. As President
of the Republic, Poincaré, cold and precise in manner, never wavered in
his steely resolve to fight to the end. Clemenceau, a veritable French Cato,
who had hurled taunts at the government and the Army for their failings
for three years, was brought back to power as Premier in November 1917,
at perhaps the blackest moment of the war. France had suffered more than
four million casualties, of whom nearly a million had been killed in action
—most of them in futile, bloody offensives which had got nowhere. Defeatism was rife in the country, in the army, the government, Parliament,
the press, and especially among the workers, and treason in fairly high
places was spreading. There were strikes in the factories, and mutinies in
the army were so serious that for a month in the summer of 1917 the
French army was almost out of action. Ruthlessly the old Tiger, as
Clemenceau was known by his friends and enemies (of whom the latter
far outnumbered the former) set to work to stamp out defeatism, jail the
traitors, real and alleged, including Caillaux, the former Premier, and
Malvy, the Minister of Interior, and restore confidence in ultimate victory.
For the last year of the war he was virtually a dictator. Without him the
Third Republic might have faltered fatally.

Without Pétain too. Called in 1916 to defend Verdun from the
heaviest offensive yet launched by the Germans, he had successfully held
it to become in time the legendary "hero of Verdun." When Joffre had
been ousted as Commander in Chief at the end of 1916, and then Nivelle in

1917, Pétain had succeeded to the top post on May 15, 1917, at the age of sixty-one. His immediate job was not only to halt an imminent general enemy offensive but to preserve the French army from completely disintegrating as the result of widespread mutiny that had begun on April 29. With a mixture of firmness and of understanding for the real grievances of the men in the trenches, he quickly improved the living conditions of the troops, saw that more leaves were granted them, forced the government to take better care of their families, and impressed both officers and men with his insistence that henceforth the French armies would only undertake the offensive when they had adequate artillery support and were ready.* He became known as the one general above all others who refused to sacrifice his men unnecessarily. There would be no more futile bloodbaths as long as he was in command. There would be no toleration of mutiny either. Officers were ordered to restore discipline; a small number of mutineers, some selected arbitrarily from the ranks of units that refused to return to the trenches, were executed after summary and swift courts-martial, and others sentenced to prison. By the end of 1917 Pétain had succeeded in restoring the morale of the French Army.

There was a flaw, though, in his character which began to show itself in the desperate days toward the end of the war when it seemed to him that as the result of the last great German offensives the British army was finished and that the French, which he then commanded, would soon be too. At a high-level meeting of Anglo-French military and civilian leaders at Doullens on March 26, 1918, at a moment when the British Fifth Army had been destroyed and the rest of the BEF faced withdrawal to the sea and separation from the French armies, which would have been doomed by such a move, Pétain, according to Clemenceau, pointed to the British Commander in Chief, Sir Douglas Haig, and whispered: "He will have to surrender in the open field in fifteen days, and we shall be very lucky if we are not forced to do the same."[4] Contrary to Joffre in the first years of the war and to Foch in the last, Pétain became increasingly pessimistic and even defeatist when the war took such an apparently hopeless turn for the Allies that last spring and summer of the conflict. This developing trait in a general who had showed so much steadfastness and resourcefulness in defending Verdun and in rebuilding the army after the mutinies, eventually came to dominate him and would have fatal consequences for the Third Republic in its dark days in 1940.

We have seen what contributions Galliéni and especially Joffre had made in saving France from quick defeat in 1914. Joffre's indomitable

---

* Long before, when he was teaching infantry tactics at the War College, Pétain, as we have seen, had been alone in opposing the offensive at any cost which Grandmaison and Foch had made the new doctrine of the French Army. He had stressed the supreme importance of firepower and tried to warn that offensives begun without superiority in guns would be futile and that an army should remain on the defensive until it achieved that superiority. These views, as has been pointed out, earned him a reputation in the Officer Corps as a gloomy man, almost a defeatist. See above, p. 81.

character, his ability to withstand panic when all seemed lost, his coolness in conducting a retreat that kept his armies in being, his decisive action to withdraw at great risk several army corps from the eastern front to give him superiority around Paris for the decisive battle, his ruthless cashiering of generals in the field who proved incompetent or worse— these were what did more than anything else to turn the tide on the Marne. We shall find them lacking in the two Commanders in Chief in 1940.

Finally there was Foch. His confidence in himself, in the Army, and in ultimate victory, had been as soaring and unfaltering as that of Joffre. At the Doullens meeting, despite his lower rank—he had been without a command since the fall of Joffre at the end of 1916—he had intervened against the pessimism of Pétain. "You are not fighting!" Clemenceau remembered him later as saying. "I would fight without stopping. I would fight before Amiens. I would fight in Amiens. I would fight behind Amiens.* I would fight all the time!"[5] At the suggestion of Haig, General Foch was then and there named coordinator of the Allied armies. Three weeks later, on April 14, 1918, with British and American agreement, he was made Commander in Chief of all the Allied armies on the Western front. By midsummer he had stopped Ludendorff's last desperate bid for victory and was leading the Allied forces in a great counteroffensive to final triumph.

At 5 A.M. on November 11, 1918, in a little clearing in the Forest of Compiègne at Rethondes, the Armistice was signed by the Germans in the railway car of Marshal Foch. At 11 A.M. the fighting came to an end and in the Allied capitals the church bells rang out and the crowds deliriously celebrated the victory and the end of the massacre of the war. It had cost the French 1,357,800 dead, killed in action, 4,266,000 wounded, and 537,000 made prisoner or missing—exactly 73 percent of the 8,410,000 men mobilized to defend the land.† The northern third of the country was in ruins from four years of battle and deliberate German destruction, the nation's treasury was empty, the war debts piled so high that they were almost beyond counting.

But these staggering costs, even the fearful bloodletting, the deepest wound of all to the country, were momentarily forgotten in the general rejoicing over the victory and the termination of the mass slaughter. France had survived the greatest ordeal in her history. By burying for the moment their age-old quarrels and forging a sacred union, by achieving a magnificent spirit of self-sacrifice and an iron resolve to endure unconquered, the French, despite human failings and some faltering the last two years, had survived a threat more deadly than they had ever faced before. The Third

---

* Amiens, the vital link between the British and French armies, was threatened by one of the German offensives. Foch demanded that it be held at all costs.
† British Empire casualties were 3,190,235, or 35.8 percent of the total mobilized, of whom 908,371 were killed in action. American casualties totaled 350,300, or 8 percent, of whom 126,000 were killed in action.[6]

Republic, so shaky and so uncertain during its rough passage through the last quarter of the nineteenth century and the first decade of the twentieth, had proved to be as strong a regime as France had ever had. The autocratic monarchy of Germany had been toppled. The democratic Third Republic of France stood more solid than before. In the elation of victory during those late fall days in 1918 it seemed destined to continue as long as men could foresee, immensely fortified and unified by the triumph to which the mass of the people had given so much.

And yet . . . Probably few French read, or would have believed if they had, the strangely prophetic words of Jules Cambon, one of two brothers famous as diplomats at this time—he had been Ambassador to Berlin before the war. As a young man Cambon had fought as a soldier in the Franco-Prussian war and tasted the bitter dregs of the humiliating defeat. "France victorious," he cautioned in those heady autumn days of 1918, "must grow accustomed to being a lesser power than France vanquished."

How could that be? Allied victory had left Germany prostrate, shattered her allies, Austria-Hungary and Turkey, and Russia was rent with revolution and civil war and Italy by civil strife. These had been the other principal powers on the Continent. Now triumphant France, triumphant in military power at least, towered above them all.

BOOK TWO

Illusions and Realities of Victory
1919-1934

10

VICTORIOUS FRANCE—
"THE GREATEST POWER IN EUROPE"
1919–1931

W hen, in 1925, fresh out of college, I had first come to live and work in Paris in the midst of a summer as lovely as the one just fifteen years later which would see its fall, France was the greatest power on the continent of Europe.

Her hegemony, though frowned upon by her two principal allies in the victory of 1918, Great Britain and the United States, was acknowledged by all the nations. Her army, far superior to any other, stood watch on the Rhine. It supported French foreign policy, whose objective was to keep Germany disarmed, wring from her the promised payment of reparations, and make viable the new smaller nations to the east of Germany which had risen from the debris of the fallen Austro-Hungarian Empire and which were now allied with France.

No other country on the Continent could challenge France's supremacy. The nightmare of the German threat, which had haunted the French for so long, had been erased. Germany, still shaken by her defeat, her army and navy reduced to a token force, forbidden by the Versailles Treaty to build warplanes or tanks or heavy guns or submarines or battleships, and saddled with the burden of reparations, was no longer a menace. The Habsburg Empire, whose headstrong leaders had so recklessly taken the lead in plunging Europe into war, had ceased to exist. Russia, under the Bolsheviks, was just staggering back on its feet after the upheaval of revolution and years of devastating civil war. For the moment it was still withdrawn from a hostile Europe. If Great Britain had not withdrawn, it had resumed more and more its island aloofness, striving to hold together a restive overseas empire whose members, India above all, were beginning to clamor for independence. It had not been able to regain its old predominant economic and financial position in the world, which had been shattered by the Great War. It was ridden with unemployment, which was growing like a festering sore. And though it still maintained the world's largest navy it had, like the U.S.A., disbanded its army. Italy, weakened by years of civil strife and national paralysis, had been taken over by the Fascists, who, though they made the trains run on time, were finding it as difficult to make the Italian peninsula, bereft of natural resources, into a first-class power, one that could rival France, as had their disunited democratic predecessors.

Besides being dominant in Europe, France also had a great empire, augmented by new territory in Africa and the Near East taken from Germany and Turkey under a so-called mandate, a sort of trusteeship, from the League of Nations. Sprawling over four and a half million square miles of territory in Africa, the Near East, and Asia, the French Empire had a population of one hundred million, more than twice the population of the homeland. It had been a valuable asset during the war, furnishing not only badly needed raw materials but military manpower. No fewer than 449,000 native troops saw combat in France and 187,000 more served in military labor battalions. Now, in the mid-twenties, the French colonies, besides giving status to France as a world power, were proving to be of considerable economic value. They furnished a profitable outlet for capital and for engineering and construction firms. They supplied raw materials. And more and more, especially after the world depression set in in 1929, they would provide French manufacturers with an expanding market. By the mid-thirties nearly one third of French exports were going to the countries of the Empire.

THE CITY OF LIGHT

Supreme in Europe, powerful in the world—such was the France in those days of the mid-twenties. But that was not all. Paris again bloomed as the cultural capital of the world. Attracted by its lights, its splendor, its beauty, its charm, its civilities, its balmy air of freedom, its appreciation of the arts and of artists and the life of the mind and the spirit, students, teachers, writers, painters, sculptors, designers, and a swarm of tourists flocked from the four corners of the earth to the great city and appeared, at times, almost to overrun it.

This was especially true of Americans, fleeing the arid land of Coolidge, Prohibition, and the Scopes "monkey trial."* Besides the hordes of Yankee tourists, who came to have a good time and, in some cases, to imbibe a little culture—to gawk at the Gothic wonders of Notre Dame and the Sainte

---

* I myself had got away from America on a cattle boat the week the trial started. Scopes, a high-school teacher in Dayton, Tennessee, prosecuted by William Jennings Bryan, twice a candidate for President and a former Secretary of State, among other things, and defended by Clarence Darrow, for having taught the Darwinian theory of evolution contrary to the teachings of the Holy Bible, was found guilty and fined $100 on July 21, 1925. The trial seemed to many of my generation an example of the inanity of American life in that silly time.

Chapelle, at the Arc de Triomphe at the summit of the Champs-Elysées and the artistic treasures of the Louvre, to drink alcoholic beverages in freedom and eat better than at home and enjoy the night spots on Montmartre—there were the American expatriates, for whom Paris was heaven on earth. Many of them were young writers, and out of this happy exile, this dramatic episode in American literary history, as Van Wyck Brooks called it, some major figures were beginning to emerge.

A young newspaperman living on the Left Bank soon encountered them: Hemingway, Fitzgerald (usually at the Ritz Bar on the Right Bank), Cummings, MacLeish, Elliot Paul, Gertrude Stein (who held court in her salon in a house off the Luxembourg Garden), Kay Boyle, Hart Crane, Harold Stearns, Glenway Wescott, Djuna Barnes, Ezra Pound, Eugene Jolas, editor of *transition*, which raucously proclaimed the "revolution of the word," and others. An Irish expatriate was the guiding genius of them all: James Joyce. Some were not expatriates, preferring to do the bulk of their writing at home, but they came in and out of Paris: Sinclair Lewis, Dos Passos, Sherwood Anderson; and from Ireland, Yeats. Across the street from this writer's hotel on the rue de Vaugirard, Santayana lived for a time, rather remote from what must have seemed to him a dizzy decade and not much taken by the French *esprit,* perhaps because he had remained, at heart, though he wrote in English and had had his entire academic career at Harvard, very much a Spaniard. In a top-floor studio behind the Dôme in Montparnasse, an American woman of genius held open house. This was Isadora Duncan, the great dancer. Though no longer young she was still beautiful, with large, luminous blue eyes, almost classical features, and a fine head of luxuriant reddish hair. To pay her court, artists, writers, journalists, diplomats, and politicians came nightly to her studio, where there was much gaiety, good talk, music, and, as the night wore on, perhaps a solo dance by the great artist herself.

Mostly the expatriate writers lived in a little American world of their own between Montparnasse and the Seine, being too preoccupied with their own problems of creation in their own language to have much to do with the French literary world, though a few consorted with the noisy Dadaists and the surrealists.

French writing was in fact in full ferment in those days and was dominated by the "Big Four": the poets Paul Claudel and Paul Valéry; Marcel Proust (who had died in 1922 but whose influence was just beginning to be felt as successive volumes of his long novel *A la recherche du temps perdu,* finished just before his death, came out—the last in 1927), and André Gide. To so many who lived in Paris in those rather golden days, whether they were old or young, French or foreign, the literary world, and especially what was coming out of it in books and plays and combative little reviews, was a source of wonder and excitement. In this luminous, civilized capital the product of man's imagination was not only taken seriously but seemed more important than anything else: than how one gained a living or what the bankers and businessmen, politicians and statesmen, were up to. Even the Paris newspapers, dominated as they were mostly by big business and big finance, reflected this. A new book or play, the annual *Prix Goncourt* for a novel, a squabble between two rival schools of writers, an author's marriage or divorce or death—these were matters that received front-page notice, as did the latest art show, or a new painting by Picasso, Braque, Léger, Rouault, Matisse, Modigliani, and other painters, or a new sculpture by Bourdelle. When Anatole France died in 1924 he received a funeral such as Paris usually gave only her hero-statesmen or soldiers.

Unlike most of my compatriots in Paris, who were writing poems, short stories, novels, and plays, or intending to, I was in the newspaper business, whose chief concern had to be not with the literary life but with the life of the nations in Europe, the foremost of which was France. They were struggling to recover from the most devastating war in history and to settle down in peace.

RECOVERY

To all appearances France, despite her terrible bloodletting and the destruction of her richest *départements* in the north and northeast, had made a remarkable comeback. She had spent eight billion dollars to repair the flooded mines, rebuild the factories, public buildings, shops and homes, the railways, the roads and canals, and clear the farms of the war's debris and the thousands of miles of trenches, and restock them. The Germans, whose reparations were supposed to pay the bill, had been almost completely successful in dodging payment, and the French had had to raise the money on their own. Production, which had fallen in 1919 to 57 percent of the 1913 level, had begun to mount. By 1923 it had risen to 88 percent, surpassing the prewar level the next year and soaring to 126 percent in 1926.

The country was prosperous, the people relaxed, the Continent at last at peace. The hatred and intolerance, the frenzy and fear, which very soon would begin to grip this land and the rest of Europe had not yet set in to poison men's minds. That October of 1925 the Pact of Locarno was signed. It brought back defeated Germany into the community of Western nations. Freely signed by a democratic German government the Locarno agreement appeared to guarantee peace for as long as statesmen could foresee. The frontier between France and Germany and between Belgium and Germany, over which armies had poured for centuries to bring on war, was solemnly guaranteed by the four big powers, France, Great Britain, Germany, and Italy. And by the terms of the accord Germany was welcomed into the League of Nations, which, inspired by President Woodrow Wilson but scornfully rejected by his blinded country, had joined together most of the nations in a world organization to settle future disputes between countries by peaceful means. All of Europe relaxed in the new spirit of Locarno. Everywhere, and above all in France, there was a growing confidence in the League and even a feeling that its new member, Germany, was at last mending its ways, won over finally to the merits of democracy and a durable peace.

Yet in Paris, despite the general euphoria, there were some darkening clouds. French governments were falling faster than ever before, and so was the French franc, once as solid as gold. The second development was largely the cause of the first. From April of 1925, when the *Cartel des Gauches* government of Edouard Herriot fell, to July of the following year, when the conservative Poincaré returned to power, seven cabinets were overthrown by the Chamber of Deputies or the Senate—all over disputes about how to solve the monetary crisis, restore the shaky finances of the state, and save the franc. Yet Raymond Poincaré, the austere Lorrainer, the first President of the Republic ever to become afterward a Prime Minister, at the age of sixty-five assuming that post for the second time in the postwar era on July 26, 1926, was able quickly to restore national confidence, put government finances on a solid basis, halt the fall of the currency, and finally in 1928 peg the franc at twenty-five to the dollar, or one fifth of its prewar gold value. Poincaré saved the government from bankruptcy and the nation from financial collapse, but his success was not without its cost. Hundreds of thousands of Frenchmen of the solid bourgeois class found their life savings, usually in the form of prewar or wartime government bonds, reduced in value by four fifths. This was bound to shake their confidence in the government—any government—and to embitter them with a feeling that they had been cheated by the Republic.

Still, the prosperity was pretty general. Production increased, exports soared, the swarming tourists brought in 10 billion francs a year and the Treasury, which had been empty in 1926, built up a surplus of 19 billion francs by 1929. There was a lessening of tensions between the nations, especially between the defeated and the victors of the Great War. Even Germany, fully recovered thanks largely to unlimited American loans from her financial and economic debacle of the early twenties, seemed to be settling down under a democratic government dominated by the conciliatory Gustav Stresemann, one of the architects of the Locarno peace. Paris was relieved to hear less talk of ultimate revenge from Berlin. A troublesome ultranationalist agitator in Bavaria, named Adolf Hitler, who had thundered that France, like Carthage, must be destroyed, had been imprisoned and then silenced by the government, and his party banned. For the French, the German "danger" seemed to have passed into history. In 1923 military service was reduced from three years to a year and a half and in 1928 to a year. By the end of 1930 the last of the French troops of occupation had left the demilitarized Rhineland.

From 1926, the year after I arrived, until the worldwide depression began to be seriously felt in 1931, there was a period of five years that later was remembered by French historians and memoirists as one of the happiest times of the Third Republic. Not since Napoleon, and before him Louis

XIV, had France enjoyed such well-being. And in the last golden years of the 1920s the well-being was more equitably distributed than before. Even a young foreigner like myself felt he was living in as much of a paradise as could be found on this imperfect earth. Civilization seemed to have reached a shining peak here.

And yet? Questions began to be asked by a few, raising a faint ripple of uneasiness. Were there flaws in the magnificent picture? Had these good people perhaps been living for a decade under a great illusion? Was there more appearance than reality in their happy state? Was there, under the glittering surface—as the prosperous, peaceful 1920s neared their end and Poincaré retired because of failing health and the American financial crash in 1929 threw up dark clouds across the Atlantic—a feeling that the fruits of victory in 1918, for which the French had sacrificed so much, were slipping away? Had the nature of that victory, its real cost and its limitations, been lost on even so logical a people as these?

To seek the answers it was necessary to go back to the beginning of 1919 when the Allies, giddy with their triumph, gathered in Paris to draw up the treaty of peace and, as they believed, to make it impossible for Germany ever again to resort to war. The conflict just ended had exacted a greater price than anyone dared face up to.

THE PRICE OF VICTORY

The 134 billion gold francs' worth of goods and property that had gone up in the smoke of battle eventually could be replaced but not the nearly million and a half dead. One out of ten Frenchmen had been killed at the front, and, as always in a long war, the youth, on whom the future of any nation depends, had been decimated most. Three out of ten of them between eighteen and twenty-eight had been snuffed out. The intellectuals, so vital to the life of a country, had suffered the next heaviest casualties. Twenty-three out of every hundred men who had belonged to the liberal professions had perished in the trenches. Of 4,266,000 men wounded, a million and a half remained permanently maimed. Such casualties were bound to weaken the nation for decades to come.[1]

That was not all. The ghastly losses would have grave demographic consequences for a country which, as we have seen, was already suffering before the war from a decline in the birthrate. It has been calculated that between 1915 and 1919 there were 1,400,000 fewer births than there would have been had there been peace. Moreover there was a loss of half a million further births between 1932 and 1939, which would have occurred had there been a normal birthrate during the war. There were 1,400,000 fewer parents by then. Nearly a million and a half war dead, more than two million fewer births—this was the price of victory for the country, which at the end of the war had fewer inhabitants than when it started, despite the addition of nearly two million citizens from regained Alsace and Lorraine. France emerged from the conflict with a population of thirty-nine millions. It faced a Germany with sixty-three millions. And soon the Germans would be increasing in number at twice the rate of the French.

As far as births were concerned the French were not increasing at all. Only a massive immigration organized by the state made possible a slight growth in population. Two million foreigners, mostly Italian and Polish male workers, were brought into France after the war. Without them French industry, mining, and agriculture could not have recovered. They accounted for 80 percent of the 2,700,000 increase in French population between the wars. Actually after 1935 a depopulation set in as the death rate exceeded the birthrate and immigration was curtailed because of unemployment stemming from the 1931 depression. Except for the two years immediately after the war, when the surviving soldiers came home and there was a quick rise in the number of children born, the birthrate continued to decline, even compared to the prewar rate. Because of the war's consequences the structures of the population had changed too. There was a surplus of old people, many of them necessarily unproductive. In fact France had the largest proportion of aged people in Europe. But there was a shortage of young people. When the second war came in 1939 France had less than half as many men between twenty and thirty-four as the Germans—roughly four million to nine million.[2]

THE PEACE OF VERSAILLES

The moment of glory had come for the France of the Third Republic on November 11, 1918, when the Germans, after fighting for four years on French soil, their armies never very far from Paris and time and again on the verge of breaking through, finally capitulated. In the delirious rejoicing that the savage war was over, that it had been won and that the living that day would live, it was only human for the French to overlook for the moment the frightful cost of the victory and the stark fact that though their armies had borne the brunt of the fighting and suffered by far the highest casualties, the triumph had come only because of the aid of her two democratic allies, Great Britain and—at the last but decisive moment—the United States. Alone, France could not have defeated Germany. The Germans had too many men and too many industries turning out arms. The French had too few of both. And this would always be.

But did it matter now, as the new year came and the heads of the triumphant Allied governments prepared to gather in Paris on January 18, 1919, to draw up the terms for peace? Germany was prostrate and in chaos. The Kaiser had fled, the monarchy had fallen, a Republic had been proclaimed in Berlin, and it was being threatened from the Left and the Right. The exhausted Germans were fighting among themselves with seemingly their last ounce of energy. However soon and however much they restored order, for which they had such great respect, and recovered, they would be forced by the Allied peacemakers to remain disarmed, to keep behind the Rhine, which was the only natural barrier between them and their western neighbors, and to pay for the devastation they had wrought in Belgium and northern France. The French had no doubts about that. Their Finance Minister, Louis-Lucien Klotz, and Britain's great wartime Prime Minister, Lloyd George, had proclaimed that the Germans would pay. The generalissimo of the victorious Allied armies, Marshal Ferdinand Foch, had insisted that the Franco-German border be pushed back to the Rhine to give France the military protection she needed. And in the gala opening of the Peace Conference on January 18, 1919, in the gilded hall of the Quai d'Orsay in Paris, President Poincaré, in his high-pitched, nasal voice and in his chilly manner, had said:

> Justice is not inert. . . . When it has been violated it demands first of all restitutions and reparations for peoples and individuals who have been despoiled and mistreated. In formulating this legitimate claim it shows neither hate nor an instinctive and thoughtless desire for reprisals. It pursues a double object: to render to each his due and to discourage the renewal of the crime by impunity.

What the French wanted above all else from the peace settlement was a guarantee of their security, and for reasons difficult now to comprehend their chief allies, Great Britain and the United States, never quite understood this—perhaps because Woodrow Wilson, the American President, and Lloyd George, the British Prime Minister, lacked a sure grasp of European history. The French could not ignore that history. They could not forget that since the days of the Huns invaders had broken into their fair country some thirty times from across the Rhine. Five times within a century, in 1814, 1815, 1870, 1914, and 1918, the people of Paris had heard the thunder of Prussian artillery and thrice watched the Germans parade through their streets as conquerors. Since the humiliation of France by Prussia in 1870—for nearly half a century—every Frenchman had lived in fear that "they would come again," and in 1914 they had come. Now in 1918 they had been defeated and expelled. Every citizen of France had one overwhelming determination: "Never again!" Let the peacemakers see to that.

What Wilson and Lloyd George failed to see was that the terms of peace which they were hammering out against the dogged resistance of Clemenceau and Foch, while seemingly severe enough, left Germany in the long run relatively stronger than before. Except for the return of Alsace-Lorraine to France in the west and the loss of some valuable industrialized frontier districts to the Poles, from whom the Germans had taken them originally, Germany remained virtually intact, greater in population and industrial capacity than France could ever be, and moreover with her cities, farms, and factories undamaged by the war, which had been fought in enemy lands. In terms of relative power in Europe, Germany's position was actually better in 1919 than in 1914, or would be as soon as the Allied victors carried out their promise to reduce their armaments to the level of the defeated. The collapse of the Austro-Hungarian Empire had not been the catastrophe for Germany that Bismarck had feared, because there was no Russian empire to take advantage of it. Russia, beset by revolution and civil war, was for the present, and perhaps would be for years to come, impotent. In the place of this powerful country on her eastern border Germany now had small, unstable states which could not seriously threaten her and which one day might easily be made to return former German territory and even made to disappear from the map.*

There was much idle talk at the Conference of Paris about the disappearance of four mighty empires, German, Russian, Austro-Hungarian, and Turkish. But the cynical Clemenceau, at the head of the French delegation, knew that the strongest of them remained—even though it had reluctantly become a Republic. His task at the peace parleys, as he saw it, was to see that Germany was permanently weakened, or, if this could not be achieved, confronted for at least a generation with an Allied coalition which, having won the war, would keep the peace by guarding France's northeastern border to make sure that any future invasion from across the Rhine would be met by overwhelming force.

Prodded by the implacable Foch, Clemenceau at first demanded that Germany's western border be fixed at the Rhine, with the French army standing guard on the left bank and the German population on that side formed into an autonomous state dominated by France. Lloyd George and Wilson would have none of it. "You're trying to create another Alsace-Lorraine," Wilson charged.

Lloyd George suggested a compromise. If France relinquished her claims on the Rhine, Britain and the United States would guarantee France's boundary against future German aggression. Wilson agreed and treaties to that effect were drawn up. Marshal Foch, pressed by the uncompromising Poincaré, made one last desperate effort to save for France the only natural barrier there was against the hereditary enemy. On March 31, he demanded to be heard in person by the Big Four, Wilson, Lloyd George, Clemenceau, and the Italian premier, Orlando, who were responsible for drawing up the peace terms.

If we do not hold the Rhine permanently [Foch told them] there is no neutralization, no disarmament, no written clause of any nature, which can prevent Germany from breaking out across it and gaining the upper hand. No aid could arrive in time from England or America to save France from complete defeat.

---

* By 1922, General Hans von Seeckt, commander of the German armed forces, was secretly advising his government: "Poland's existence is intolerable, incompatible with the essential conditions of Germany's life. Poland must go and will go." He added that Poland's obliteration "must be one of the fundamental objectives of German policy. . . . With the disappearance of Poland will fall one of the strongest pillars of the Versailles Peace, the hegemony of France."[3]

It was a prophetic pronouncement. But Clemenceau gave in. In return for abandoning the Rhine he accepted solemn guarantees of his country's frontier from his two great allies. Neither ally kept its word. Both houses of the British parliament approved the Treaty of Guarantee in July 1919, but on condition that the United States also ratify it. The U.S. Senate refused to approve either it or the Versailles Treaty, and the British assent was nullified.

The French regarded this as a betrayal. It was. They spoke of being cheated by their wartime allies. They were. Clemenceau, whose outspoken sympathies for Britain and America (he had been a newspaper correspondent in the United States shortly after the Civil War, had learned American English and married an American) had earned charges from the Right before the war that he was an Anglo-Saxon "tool," was embittered and disillusioned. As the Premier who had pulled France together in the closing period of the war, he realized what so many Frenchmen tended to forget, that without British and American help the war could not in the end have been won. He saw too that without Anglo-American promises of military aid in the future it would be beyond France's power to repel the next German invasion. He had been promised that aid in return for giving up the security of the Rhine, which his generals had demanded. Now France had neither.

The deceit of the Allies would have fateful consequences. Germany, even under Hitler, would never have risked invading France again if her rulers and her generals had known in advance that Britain and America would oppose it by military force. The U.S. Senate's rejection of the Treaty of Guarantee brought a certain responsibility on the United States for the subsequent course of events which pushed western Europe to the brink of destruction by Germany, though this was scarcely recognized in America. The Senate's action did not spare the American republic in the end. It only made the reconquest of western Europe from the Germans, when the Second World War came, infinitely more costly in American lives and treasure than it would have been had a President's word been honored in the first place by the Senate. The United States, supremely complacent in its shortsighted isolation, was lost as a factor in guarding the peace of Europe it had helped to win, and in which its fate would always be intertwined.

THE QUESTION OF REPARATIONS

On reparations too the French felt that in the end they were cheated not only by the Germans but by their own allies, who backed away from making the loser pay. France never received from Germany enough to pay for more than 20 percent of the cost of rebuilding the devastated regions in the north. For this the French were largely to blame themselves. At the Peace Conference they were too greedy; they asked for too much. And they would not face the fact that only a fully recovered, prosperous enemy could pay substantial sums in reparations. They saw only that such a Germany would also be powerful enough to take revenge for its defeat. This was the dilemma. The French attempted the impossible: to keep Germany economically weak and at the same time to squeeze from her huge reparations. In the long run they failed to achieve either objective.

At the outset French claims were reasonable enough. As the Armistice terms made clear, the Allies asked only that Germany pay for the damage done to Belgium and northern France. This was but simple justice, recognized even by the Germans. But as the Paris Conference began the French *and* the British increased their demands. They insisted that the enemy pay for all the Allied *costs* of war and for pensions for the families of the war dead and disabled soldiers as well. President Wilson strenuously opposed this. A compromise was made and it called for the Germans to pay only for the "damages" of war (including the immense losses in shipping, mostly British, sunk by German submarines) and pensions.

But the peacemakers at Paris could not agree on the amount of the bill. After months of wrangling they finally decided that the figure and the rate of payment would be left to the findings of a Reparations Commission, which would make its decision by May 1921. In the meantime, the Treaty of Versailles stipulated, Germany would pay an advance on reparations of 20 billion gold marks ($5 billion), two fifths of it earmarked for Belgium. On the eve of the deadline, on April 28, 1921, the Reparations Commission fixed a total figure for German reparations of 132 billion gold marks ($33 billion), of which France would receive 52 percent. This was to be paid off in annual installments of half a billion dollars a year plus an amount in gold currency or in goods equal to 26 percent of German exports.

Given the feeble state of her economy at this time, Germany could not meet such a burden. Nor was she willing to pay what she could, if she could possibly avoid it. There were plenty of opportunities for the Germans to scale down payments by taking advantage of Allied dissensions, especially those between Paris and London. By 1921 the British had decided that the restoration of the German market, which had been so profitable to them before the war, would be more beneficial to their own sluggish economy than receiving any great amount of reparations. The Americans had their eyes on the potential German market too, and their bankers were eager to lend money at profitable interest rates to bring about German recovery. The Anglo-Saxon democracies showed little understanding or sympathy for the French, who had suffered materially much more than they from the war, and who believed that as a matter of simple justice Germany should pay at least enough to cover the immense costs of their own reconstruction.

Alone among the victors during each of those first years of peace France had been forced to spend more annually in rebuilding her ruins than in fighting the war. And the burden was not lightened in French minds by the knowledge that Germany herself had no devastated regions to rebuild.

By the end of 1921 Germany began defaulting on her reparation payments, pleading inability to pay. Deferments and moratoriums were granted her but the patience of the French began to wear thin. Much was made in England and America then and subsequently of the intransigence of Poincaré, who had become Premier in January 1922 and who was accused in London and Washington of wanting to squeeze the last sou from Germany even if it bankrupted her. But in retrospect he appears more conciliatory than he seemed in Anglo-Saxon eyes. At inter-Allied conferences in London in December 1923, and in Paris the following month, he agreed to a moratorium on German payments for two years (the Germans had asked for two and a half years). He proposed that 82 billions of the total reparations figure of 132 billion gold marks be floated as bonds to pay inter-Allied war debts owed to Britain and the United States, mainly by France, and that only the rest, 50 billions, be paid directly to the victors as reparations. Since the French share of this was one half, the 25 billions would have paid for only 20 percent of their costs of reconstruction. Britain turned the proposal down.

Eight days later, on January 11, 1923, Poincaré sent French troops in to seize the Ruhr, the industrial heart of Germany, which produced 73 percent of its coal and 83 percent of its iron and steel. With a finical legalism befitting the lawyer he was, Poincaré had waited until the Reparations Commission officially certified that Germany had defaulted on its payments in kind to France. Under the Versailles Treaty, France was entitled to take just such a sanction in these circumstances.

The rest of the world, especially Britain and the United States, howled in anger against this French "aggression." The German government itself replied by proclaiming a massive passive resistance in the Ruhr. It ordered and financed a general strike of the workers. It made management close down the mines and factories. The blast furnaces were extinguished. Not a ton of coal was mined or a ton of steel produced. The railroads in the Rhineland ceased to run. In Berlin the government deliberately organized the destruction of the currency, the mark falling to 4 million to a dollar by August and eventually to 25 billions, becoming worthless.

Poincaré stubbornly persevered. By sending in French and Belgian engineers and workers he was able to get the mines, mills, and railroads functioning well enough to extract something from the Ruhr.* A separatist Rhineland movement was secretly subsidized and supported, and when its German leaders proclaimed a Rhineland Republic it was feared in Berlin that the Reich might permanently lose its richest region. Without the Ruhr,

---

* A balance, after expenses, of 106 million dollars' worth of goods, of which the French took 91 million, turning over the rest to Belgium and other allies to whom reparations were due.

which had been sealed off by Poincaré so that the rest of Germany received not a single ton of coal or steel, the country could not exist. On September 26 the German government capitulated, decreed the end of passive resistance in the Ruhr, and agreed to discuss the resumption of reparations.*

In Paris the more rabid nationalists, led by the President of the Republic Alexandre Millerand (a former Socialist become reactionary), and Marshal Foch, urged Poincaré to take full advantage of the German surrender. "It's the greatest event since the Armistice!" cried Millerand, and Foch exclaimed: "We're going to see whether we again bungle an opportunity, as we did with the Armistice and the Peace!" What Millerand and his friends wanted was for Poincaré to meet immediately with the discouraged German government and with the industrial tycoons of the Ruhr and force them to turn over to the French a considerable share in the ownership of the Ruhr industries. Then the coal field of the Ruhr and the iron mines of Lorraine would be joined in a massive Franco-German cartel which would produce most of Europe's steel and durable goods and make the Continent, under France's dominance, supreme economically in the world.

But Poincaré's ambitions for France did not go so far. He had maintained from the first that he had gone into the Ruhr only to make Germany honor its obligations under the Versailles Treaty to pay reparations. Further he would not go. He would take from Germany what she was obligated to pay, but he would not steal from her. And he believed that despite all the bad blood between Paris and London over the Ruhr seizure, in the long run an Anglo-French entente, which he hoped could be restored, was the only effective guarantee against future German aggression. This was to take the long view. But probably Poincaré, for whom the Anglo-Saxon world always seemed somewhat incomprehensible, did not realize as he wound up the Ruhr adventure—this could be seen only in retrospect—that his firm action would mark the last time a French government would act on its own, in defiance of Britain, in its dealings with Germany. Henceforth it would proceed only with British support.

This policy might have had beneficial results had governments in London been blessed with leaders of foresight who understood and faced the realities of political life on the old continent, above all those in Germany. But the British—and the French—were not to have such good fortune. Ramsay MacDonald, Stanley Baldwin, and Neville Chamberlain, who would dominate the British government and Parliament in this time, lacked the qualities needed. There were some in Paris, mostly on the Right, who believed that the country would be better off to act more independently of Britain. They thought that one of the lessons of history was that no great nation could, with impunity, allow its destiny to be decided largely by another, with different interests and outlooks, and those mostly and

---

* Six weeks later, on November 8, Adolf Hitler, unknown in Germany outside of Bavaria, took advantage of the chaos caused by the wild inflation and of the popular resentment against the Republic for surrendering to the French in the Ruhr to stage an armed uprising in Munich, later to be remembered as the Beer Hall Putsch.

naturally selfish.* But by the end of the twenties the more thoughtful French, even on the Right, were beginning to feel that their nation was not strong enough, in the face of a resuscitated, revengeful Germany, to go it alone. Only in collaboration with the British could France cope with the potentially stronger enemy beyond the Rhine.

German reparations did not continue for very long. Under the Dawes Plan worked out in 1924, which reduced Germany's annual payments, the French received over the five years it was in effect some one billion dollars, two thirds of which was in deliveries in kind. The Young Plan of 1929 lowered the annual German payments still further. Two years later, the worldwide depression, the 1931 Hoover moratorium on reparation and war-debt payments, and Germany's refusal to pay any more brought the end of reparations. On July 9, 1932, at Lausanne, France and Britain, with their allies, signed an agreement with Germany to abolish reparations. As a sop to public opinion in the Allied countries Germany agreed to make a final token payment of 3 billion Reichsmarks ($750 million) to be deposited with the Bank of International Settlements.

Of the 132 billion gold marks assessed Germany for reparations in 1921, Germany had paid a total in money and goods of 22,891,000,000 (five and a half billion dollars), of which France received 9,585,000,000 (a billion and a third dollars).[4] Actually, on balance, Germany never had to pay a single mark out of her own resources. Her borrowings from American bankers, which were never repaid, amounted to more than her total reparation payments. Naive American investors footed the German reparations bill.

It had been loudly proclaimed in Germany, and believed in Britain and the United States and even in large circles in France, that once the last French troops evacuated the demilitarized Rhineland and the Allies canceled German reparations, the people of the Reich would feel greatly relieved, if not grateful, and that these generous gestures by the former victors, which wiped out most of the burdens—and reminders—of defeat, would save democracy in Germany, bolster it, and give the beleaguered Republic, attacked from the extreme Right and Left, a new lease on life.

Just the opposite happened. On June 30, 1930, the French withdrew their last troops from the Rhineland. Less than three months later, on September 14, Adolf Hitler's Nazi Party, which made no secret of its enmity to democracy, the German Republic, and France, won a resounding election victory. It increased its vote from 810,000 (in 1928) to 6,409,600, raising the number of its deputies in the Reichstag from 12 to 107. From the ninth and smallest party in Germany it became the second largest. On July 31, 1932, three weeks after the Allies abolished German reparations,

* A lesson pondered, preached, and practiced by President Charles de Gaulle in the 1960s.

the German people responded in a national election by giving the Nazi party a still greater electoral triumph. It polled 13,745,000 votes and won 230 seats in Parliament, becoming easily the largest political party in the country.

Allied help did not save the faltering German republic. Six months after this election the Nazis took over political power in Berlin, quickly destroyed the democratic republic, and began to prepare for revenge against France for the defeat in 1918 and the Versailles *Diktat*.

THE WRANGLE OVER WAR DEBTS

Though the United States refused to take a cent of reparations from Germany, its government and Congress insisted that its Allies, especially Britain and France, pay their war debts in full and with interest. The British government had proposed at the Peace Conference that all inter-Allied debts be canceled on the principle that money lent during the war was a contribution to the common victory. The French, heavily in debt to both Britain and America, agreed. President Wilson rejected the very idea. As the inimitable President Calvin Coolidge would later say: "They hired the money, didn't they?"

Britain and France during the war had both "hired" money and lent it. The British government had borrowed $4 billion from the United States and lent its Allies, chiefly France, nearly twice that amount. When, in 1922, being pressed by Washington for repayment, Britain announced that she would ask only enough from her Allied debtors and from German reparations to cover her payments to the United States, this was equivalent to canceling three quarters of the total amount due her. France had borrowed $3.5 billion from the United States, nearly half of it after the Armistice. She had lent *her* allies over $5 billion, half of it to Russia, which, now under the Bolsheviks, refused to pay back a ruble. The French felt that their own sacrifices in human life, so much greater than those suffered by the Americans, to achieve Allied victory might be somewhat compensated for by the sacrifice of Yankee dollars.

But Washington was adamant. It demanded that its former allies pay up. By 1929 most of them had reluctantly agreed: the British to pay over sixty-two years some $11 billion dollars on their $4 billion debt (the accrued interest nearly trebling the original debt) and the French $6.75 billion on their original debt of half that amount.[5] Cries of "Uncle Shylock!" could be heard throughout western Europe in those days. Though the American government refused to recognize any connection between reparations and war debts the French made it clear they would never pay Washington more than they received in reparations from Berlin.

The Lausanne conference, which canceled reparations, doomed further payment of inter-Allied debts. The Allies at that meeting agreed not to ratify the ending of reparations unless the United States, in effect, assented to the cancellation of their war debts. The American government refused,

and the Lausanne Treaty consequently was never ratified, though its provision that Germany need pay no more reparations was honored. Payments
to America by Britain and France ceased, except for token offerings by the
former in 1933. When Premier Herriot insisted on France meeting her
payment of $19 million due Washington on December 15, 1932, he was
overthrown the day before by an angry Chamber of Deputies—403 votes
to 187. The United States Congress was equally angry. It passed a resolution to the effect that it was "against the policy of Congress that any of the
indebtedness of foreign countries to the United States should be in any
manner canceled or reduced." In 1934 Congress passed a law forbidding
defaulting nations to float loans in America. But it had no effect. Not only
reparations but war debts were dead. Only little Finland continued to pay
its modest debt, for which it was much esteemed from coast to coast.

For more than a decade the wrangling over war debts blew ill-feeling
to and fro across the Atlantic. By the time Hitler came to power in Germany
at the beginning of 1933 the great alliance of the three Western democracies, which had humbled the Nazi dictator's predecessors in 1918, was in
ashes. It was not to be revived, so far as the Americans were concerned,
until Hitler had conquered France, put Britain in mortal peril, and declared
war on the United States.

11

DECLINE, I
POLITICAL AND FINANCIAL CHAOS,
AND THE POINCARÉ RECOVERY
1924–1930

Deprived of the bulk of reparations, which they had counted on and to which they thought they were entitled, badgered by the United States to repay the war debt, faced with the enormous expense of rebuilding the devastated regions and with the Treasury drained dry by the huge expenditures of four years of war, various French governments of the Right and the Left, none of them lasting very long and most of them committing incredible follies, struggled for eight years to stave off national bankruptcy.

For a couple of years after the peace they declined to do anything at all, even to face their problems. The slogan of the politicians that the Germans would pay blinded government and Parliament to the necessity of providing for enough revenue by taxation to meet the major part of expenses. Instead of raising taxes the government raised loans, a habit it had acquired during the war, when taxes, which were scarcely augmented despite the dire necessity, paid for but 17 percent of the total wartime expenditures of 210 billion gold francs ($42 billion), the rest coming from massive borrowing and advances from the Bank of France. Year after year during the 1920s, whether the cabinet was conservative or radical, the borrowing and the advances continued until there came a time—several times—when the short-term loans could not be repaid when they fell due and the advances from the Bank of France were halted and the Treasury was literally empty.

It seemed obvious that taxes would have to be raised and some financial sacrifices made by those best able to afford them. But this did not seem obvious to Parliament. For five years after the war it declined to vote any substantial increase in taxes. When the Finance Minister of the conservative *Bloc National* government in 1923 asked for six billion francs in new taxes he was turned down. At the beginning of 1924 the Treasury could not meet its short-term obligations and Parliament finally approved Poincaré's demand for a rise of 20 percent in all taxes, direct and indirect. This fell hardest on the poor, since indirect taxes on consumption accounted for nearly half the state revenues, and the income tax—full of glaring loopholes and scandalously evaded by all who could get by with it, the rich above all—for less than a quarter. The selfishness of the moneyed class in avoiding any financial sacrifice to help put the country back on its feet later struck many French historians as shocking. The possessors and the manipulators of most of the country's wealth simply contrived to escape shouldering a fair share of the burden of paying for the war and the reconstruction.

They stubbornly and successfully opposed all efforts of Parliament and government to increase income taxes adequately and fairly or even to clean up the rotten tax structure which weighed so much more heavily on the poor than on the rich. And in their fanatical regard for their capital and profits, which was matched only by their disregard for the salvation of the country, they spirited their capital abroad to such a massive extent as to make inevitable a fall of the currency, the bankruptcy of the Treasury, and a lack of capital at home to finance badly needed reconstruction and in particular to enable the farmers, the little businessmen, and the shopkeepers to get a new start in the difficult postwar world. When in the spring of 1925 the Herriot government asked Parliament for a law to control the headlong flight of French capital abroad the measure was bitterly attacked in the capital's leading afternoon newspaper, *Le Temps,* organ of the steel trust, Le Comité des Forges, as "rank socialism" which would destroy the capitalist system. Parliament refused to approve the law, the massive movement of capital abroad continued without hindrance, and though the Treasury was again emptied and the franc fell further France was saved from this sort of "rank socialism."

But the government was not saved from the necessity of finding money to carry on the affairs of state. When the debate in the Chamber of Deputies on where to find it began in November 1924, a Socialist leader, Pierre Renaudel, made a suggestion that raised a howl of protest from conservatives in Parliament and the Press. *"You have to take the money from where it is,"* he argued. Indeed, one might ask, from where else?* But the very idea of asking those who had the money to shoulder the main burden of increased taxation frightened them to death and there was a new exodus of capital to safer foreign havens. "Above all else," cried the influential *Journal des Finances,* "there must be a stop to this worrying of the pos-

---

* The answer of the business and financial interests was given in the Chamber by one of their spokesmen, a deputy named Bokanowski: "We are told you have to take the money from where it is. I maintain that first you have to leave it where it is." And that is where it was left.

sessors." Perhaps so, though the possessors seemed easily prone to worry. The worries of the dispossessed were not mentioned, nor was the worrying of the government by hostile acts of the financial community, led by the Bank of France, which in the spring of 1925 launched an offensive against the "leftish" Herriot cabinet with the object of bringing it down and terminating the threat against its moneybags.*

The flight of capital itself, in which the great financial houses took the lead, was, aside from the damage it did to the country, a form of blackmail against the government not to raise taxes and especially not to consider a tax on capital. The banks resorted to other forms of blackmail. They offered to lend the Treasury money for twenty-four hours in order to cover up the advances of the Bank of France above the legal limit in return for the government overlooking evasions of income tax and refraining from clamping on a control of the export of capital. Suddenly, at the beginning of April 1925, as the final assault on the Herriot government began, the banks refused further loans, even for a day, so that the surpassing of the legal limit of advances from the Bank of France had to be published. As a result the franc fell and further panic ensued.

Actually, during the conservative Poincaré regime prior to 1924 the Bank of France had often advanced to the Treasury more than the law allowed. Moreover it had put at Poincaré's disposal certain "secret funds" of the Bank, which were considerable. Now, in April 1925, it denied to the Cartel government what it had been pleased to accord the more moderate Poincaré cabinet. On April 1 and again on April 6 the Bank of France warned the government that the legal limit of its advances to the state— 41 billion francs—was about to be reached, that it would be illegal to advance more, and that the government would find itself without means to meet its obligations, even the payroll of its employees. Secretly the Bank leaked the news to the press, most of which, including the large-circulation daily newspapers, had vociferously supported the financial powers in their offensive to bring down the Cartel government. The influence of the French press, dominated by large business and financial interests, in undermining not only a popularly elected government but—more important— the Third Republic itself in these declining years was growing.

Anatole de Monzie, Herriot's Minister of Finance, a curious figure who was both a Radical politician and a dilettante man of letters, had tried

---

* "Leftish" in French terms but not, it must again be emphasized, in American. The *Cartel des Gauches* (Cartel of the Left Parties) which triumphed in the general election of May 11, 1924, on a platform opposing Poincaré's foreign policy, above all his occupation of the Ruhr, and his domestic policy, above all his raising of *all* taxes by 20 percent, was dominated by the Radical-Socialist Party, a middle-of-the-road group no more radical than the Democratic Party in the U.S.A. and, of course, not "socialist" at all, despite its name. The Cartel was supported in Parliament by the Socialist Party, which, however, refused to join the Herriot government. The Communist Party, with 28 elected deputies in the Chamber, opposed the Cartel, as did the Conservative parties, though naturally for different reasons.

to counter the attack of the financiers by asking the Chamber on April 9 to approve two drastic measures to restore the finances of the state: first, to raise the legal limit of currency circulation (governed by advances from the Bank of France) from 41 to 45 billions, and second, a forced loan of 10 percent on one's capital. There were renewed howls of anguish in the press, but when the Chamber, by voting its confidence in the government that very day, indicated that it would approve the two measures, the business and financial powers turned desperately to the Senate as the last hope of overthrowing the Herriot government and preventing what they regarded as a dangerous inflationary step and an even more dangerous assault on their capital. There was no time to lose.

The Senate promptly obliged—the next day. This assembly of old men, each member elected indirectly by local councils for nine years, was more conservative than the Chamber of Deputies and more fearful of change. Tending to lag behind public opinion by the very nature of its composition, which could only be changed by election of one third of the senators every three years, it looked with suspicion on the Cartel of the Left Parties, which dominated the Chamber and which seemed bent on solving the country's financial crisis in a revolutionary way. Without waiting for Monzie to lay before it his two measures, it began on April 10 a debate on the general financial policies of the Herriot government and before the day was over, a question of confidence having been posed, overthrew it by 156 votes to 132.

The question of whether the Senate had the constitutional right to overthrow a government supported by the majority of the popularly elected Chamber of Deputies had never been quite settled in France. Only twice before, in 1896 and in 1913, had a Senate dared to do so, and there were some who urged Herriot to refuse to resign and to provoke a dissolution of the Chamber, after which he could appeal to the country in a general election. He declined to do so, apparently because of the fear that the state might go bankrupt before an election could be held and that in such circumstances the *Cartel des Gauches* could hardly hope to win it. Perhaps, as some believed, he recognized that no French government, no matter what its popular majority in the Chamber—or in the country—could stand up to the private financial and business interests. They opposed higher direct taxes and they were ready to fight to the death against a forced loan on capital.

A year afterward, Professor Gaston Jèze, an eminent professor of law and no radical, who had served on a Committee of Experts named by the government to draw up a plan to restore the state's finances, put his finger on the situation.

Personally [Professor Jèze commented in the *Journal des Finances*] I believe that taxes on acquired wealth would be the fairest solution. But such taxes have met an invincible resistance among the possessors, who are the most powerful. That is a fact. The selfishness of the possessing classes is not reducible. We have to adapt to it.[1]

But to "adapt" to it meant for the Republic to capitulate to it, which it did.

THE POWER, THE GREED, AND THE FEARS OF THE UPPER CLASS

We confront here, in the fall of Herriot that spring of 1925, and in the frank remarks of an eminent jurist a year later when the financial predicament of the state was even worse despite the frantic efforts of six successive governments to cope with it, some of the abuses of the Third Republic which during the next and last fifteen years would so fatally sap its strength.

The power of a small elite which possessed most of the wealth was greater than the power of the republican government elected by the people, presumably to run the country in the interest of all the citizens. This group was determined to preserve its privileged position and thus its money. In effect, since the triumph of the Republic over President MacMahon there had been a virtual alliance between the possessor class and the Republic, which it manipulated through its control of the Press, the financing of political parties, and the handling of its vast funds to influence the fiscal policies of government. The mass of the people might elect a radical Chamber of Deputies, as it had in 1924, with a mandate to enforce economic, financial, and social reforms on the country. No matter. The bankers and the businessmen had learned the technique of how in a democratic society to thwart the majority, as the fall of Herriot had demonstrated. Not only in the elections of 1924 but again in those of 1932 and 1936, as we shall see, the voters sent leftish majorities to the Chamber. But they quickly melted away, not because of a change of mind in the electorate (there were no elections in between) but because of political trading in Parliament by the elected representatives, who in each case, after approving a government of the Left, shifted their support to a government either of the Right or of the safe center.

Worried for a moment by the outcome of the elections, the upper classes were soon reassured, at least for a time, by the ability of parliament to frustrate the will of the majority of the electorate. And more and more, as the last years of the Third Republic ticked off, the wealthy found it difficult to put the interest of the nation above that of their class. Faced with specific obligations to the country if the state were not to flounder in a financial morass, they shrank from meeting them. The Republic might go under but their valuables would be preserved. In the meantime they would not help keep it afloat by paying a fair share of the taxes. The tax burden was for others to shoulder. If that were understood by the politicians, the Republic could continue. If not . . . were there not other forms of government possible which promised more security for entrenched wealth? The thoughts of some of the biggest entrepreneurs began to turn to the Fascist "experiment" in Italy and to the growing success of the Nazi Party in Germany.

One of these entrepreneurs was the electricity magnate Ernest Mercier, who with the support of some of his business colleagues launched in 1926 one of the first anti-parliament movements, *Redressement Français,* or "French Resurgence." It argued that a parliament of *politicians* was incompetent to handle the affairs of state in the complicated postwar world where the intricacies of national and international business and finance called for specialized knowledge. It wanted to see parliament and government run by "technicians," who knew how modern society functioned, and it assured the country that the great business and financial enterprises could furnish these trained men. In other words, it wanted its own men to control directly what up to now they only controlled indirectly. Mercier and his band inspired "technocracy," whose leaders if not ideas would play a certain role in burying the Third Republic and in setting up its short-lived successor. Among these technocrats around Mercier in *Redressement Français,* was a strange and murky figure named Raphaël Alibert, who in the 1920s was an ardent royalist in Action Française and who would shortly emerge as the political mentor of Marshal Pétain.

Another businessman who had begun to despair of parliamentary democracy was François Coty, who had made a huge fortune manufacturing perfume and whose business had greatly profited from the devaluation of the franc. In 1922 he had bought the conservative morning newspaper, *Le Figaro,* and then as the financial crisis deepened had begun to subsidize numerous right-wing anti-parliament movements, some of them openly fascist. Flattered by the politically discontented, who used his money to assault the Republic, Coty began to conceive himself as a savior of the nation who one day not too far off might be called upon to take over the helm of state and save it from democracy. Ridiculous as the thought was, for Coty was a political nincompoop, he seems to have taken it with growing seriousness. And though he never came near his goal—his millions were far from enough—he did succeed in contributing, like so many other short-sighted Frenchmen of wealth, to the undermining of the Third Republic, under which he had so greatly prospered.

One can begin to see at this time, in the mid-1920s, the possessing class in France alienating itself from the rest of the nation. Since the bulk of the working class, felt *itself* somewhat cut off from the nation—for opposite reasons—the Republic obviously was in more trouble than many realized.

Despite its power, the upper bourgeoisie, which had dominated the Third Republic since the beginning, was in decline. It had begun to feel itself on the defensive in a world in which the masses were threatening its privileged position by demanding more equity in the distribution of wealth and in sharing the burden of the increasing costs of government. And by the very workings of the democratic system the masses, which had the overwhelming majority of votes, might succeed in getting what they wanted. The great principle of democracy was no longer so dear to the high bourgeoisie as it had been toward the end of the eighteenth century, when its leaders used it as a means of overthrowing the monarchy and nobility and grabbing their political and economic power for themselves. When the struggle was won and the gains achieved the doctrine began to lose interest for this now dominant class. As the nineteenth century unfolded it commenced to inspire fear. In 1848, and even more in 1871 at the time of the Commune, the upper middle class turned against democracy and defended its privileges with the same pitiless brutality and egotism it had employed in wrenching them from the nobility. The rise of socialism and trade unionism toward the end of the nineteenth century further frightened the possessors, and the Bolshevik Revolution in Russia in 1917 and the founding of Communist parties in western Europe, above all in France, in 1920 aggravated their fears.

They had subscribed to democracy, within limits, for more than a century because it had enabled them to procure and then to protect their rich holdings. Now in the mid-1920s democracy as it functioned in the wobbly Third Republic appeared to them to threaten their entrenched position and, worse, their property and pocketbooks. That the threat was largely a fantasy did not make it seem less real to them. It was in this uneasy state of mind that they began to join together to save, not France or even the Republic, but their class and its wealth.

In the back of the minds of some of them at this time the idea began to sprout that perhaps the nation could be saved—and with it their class and its privileges—by return to an autocratic regime, even a dictatorship. They looked across the Alps to Italy. Mussolini had put an end to democracy and all its threats by crushing it with the greatest of ease. In Germany, it was true, Hitler, just out of prison, apparently had been squelched and was no longer in the news. But as the Nazi chief began his comeback in the late twenties his program of doing away with parliamentary democracy again was heard of in France and not without some sympathy in extreme Right circles. They began to think that perhaps an authoritarian regime in France would not only be a good thing in itself but would enable the country to live in peace and harmony with similar regimes in Germany and Italy, much as the European autocracies had lived after Metternich brought them together at the Congress of Vienna on the overthrow of Napoleon and emboldened them to stand pat against the dangerous threats of democracy and other tides of history.

That the Nazi German Fuehrer, as he had made clear in *Mein Kampf,* published in 1925, had no tender feelings for the French nation and people did not occur to the business and financial elite in France until it was too late. In the end they would prove wrong about Mussolini's attitude toward their country too.[2]

THE SHORTCOMINGS OF THE LEFT

If the possessor class in France was too selfish, greedy, and shortsighted to consent to a fair and decent solution of the state's financial crisis, the leftist Cartel majority in the Chamber of Deputies, representing the Frenchman of modest means, was at the same time too ignorant, too confused, and too timid to force one on the country, as it had the constitutional right and power to do. The Left too bears a heavy responsibility for keeping the government on the edge of bankruptcy. With its large majority in the Chamber at the beginning of 1924 it could have enacted the laws necessary to give the state the revenue it needed, curb inflation, and put a brake on the flight of capital and the widespread evasion of the income tax. But it could not make up its mind to do so. By threatening to do something, such as carrying out a forced loan on capital, converting short-term into long-term bonds, raising the income tax and decreasing its evasions, it frightened the rich and drove their money abroad. By doing nothing, despite the threats, it helped to empty the Treasury, weaken the currency, and add greatly to the chaos.

Ignorance of economics on both the Right and the Left played a role in compounding the mess. On the Right, bankers and businessmen were trying to apply classic nineteenth-century capitalist doctrines to the twentieth century, whose problems, were much more complex. On the Left most of the politicians in the Chamber were small-town lawyers, small businessmen and farmers, with a liberal sprinkling of professors, who had little comprehension of the problems of financing a state so terribly burdened by the costs of the most destructive war in history.

Edouard Herriot himself, the Premier of the Cartel government, was a good example. Highly intelligent, a gifted though florid orator, educated at the *Ecole Normale,* a brilliant professor of literature who had written his doctoral thesis on the interesting subject of the beautiful Madame Récamier and later a fascinating book on the life of Beethoven—for music, as well as literature and history, was one of the many interests of this highly cultured man—a passionate radical politician in the tradition of Gambetta and still obsessed by old issues such as the state against the church, which had been largely solved by the beginning of the century, he, like most of his political colleagues, was ill equipped by education, political experience, and character to solve the financial and economic problems of the postwar world. Herriot was a genial man, courteous to his opponents, ready to compromise, and not ambitious enough to be ruthless in achieving his ends. At the center of politics the last sixteen years of the Third Republic (he had been elected to the Senate in 1912 as its youngest member), twice a Premier, often a holder of other cabinet posts, for long stretches to the very end the President of the Chamber of Deputies, a post he liked best, he was typical of almost all the Left and Center leaders the Republic spawned in the final chapter of its existence. They lacked a toughness to fight through to the end for their beliefs and their programs.

They shied away from facing the fact that not only were temporarily drastic and unpopular measures necessary to restore fiscal sanity but the whole administration of the business of the state was badly in need of a fundamental overhaul. All through the interwar years this administration was in a state of lamentable confusion. An impenetrable fog seemed to lie over the Ministry of Finance. No proper books were kept. No proper government statistics of the nation's economy were compiled and no proper audits of government accounts were made. In 1924, in the midst of the general confusion, 4 billion francs' worth of National Defense bonds disappeared from the Treasury without trace. Forty years later, an eminent French economist-historian, tried—but failed—to unravel the mystery. He suspected that certain "resolute and highly placed individuals got away with a gigantic exploit" such as to pale into insignificance certain financial swindles which a decade later would rock the Republic. But he could not prove it—for lack of evidence.[3]

To mask the huge Treasury deficits after 1918 the government resorted to three budgets. The "ordinary" budget was always balanced and the Finance Minister could assure the country that all was well. But the second and larger budget, called the "extraordinary" one, provided for no receipts at all. It was all expenses, and in 1919, the first year it was tried, amounted to 29 billions, three times the amount of the ordinary "balanced" budget. Then a third budget was created called "recoverable expenses," based on the hope of German reparations. But since these never amounted to much the items of expense in this phantom budget remained largely "unrecoverable."

This financial juggling did not long conceal the fact that the state was spending a great deal more than it was taking in—17 billions more in 1920 and from 7 to 12 billions more annually the next four years. In these circumstances a debt that the state simply could not continue to shoulder, or at least hope to honor by repaying, piled up. In the end the state, in effect, repudiated most of it by allowing the franc to fall until it was finally stabilized in 1928, at one fifth of its prewar value.

A Cascade of Cabinets

There were other weaknesses of the Third Republic exposed—or reexposed—during these fitful years between the wars. No government lasted long enough, even if it had had the capability, to come to grips with its problems, which in this period were largely fiscal—for, paradoxically, the economy expanded and prospered all through the 1920s. During the fourteen months that followed Herriot's overthrow by the Senate on April 10, 1925, there were six successive governments—a veritable cascade of ministries. Some were overthrown by the confused and fickle Chamber of Deputies, others simply resigned in order to reshuffle their ministers and maintain a precarious majority in the Chamber for a few weeks or months. Paul Painlevé, a brilliant mathematician from the Sorbonne but a rather ineffectual Radical-Socialist politician, who had been Premier for two months in 1917 during a dark period of the war, succeeded Herriot. His two governments lasted seven months, from April to November 1925, the second one being overthrown by three votes in the Chamber, which could not quite stomach his bold proposal to get the government out of hock by imposing a 1 percent tax on capital annually over fourteen years.

Aristide Briand, the perennial Premier of the Third Republic, then took over, forming during the next seven chaotic months no fewer than three governments, his eighth, ninth, and tenth, the ninth lasting but three months and the last but three weeks. By that time, mid-July of 1926, the Treasury was empty, billions of francs in short-term loans had come due and could not be repaid, the franc itself had fallen to 50 to the dollar, a mob was howling outside the Chamber, blaming the deputies for the latest crisis, some of the rioters across the Seine on the Place de la Concorde were stoning buses full of Yankee tourists, who were held responsible, with their compatriots at home, for plotting the currency's fall (and cursed for taking advantage of it by living it up in Paris on devaluated francs), and the directors of the Bank of France were informing the government—and under-handedly the Press—that the legal limit of its advances having been reached it would not give the Treasury a centime more. Along the boulevards large crowds of women were storming the department stores and the smart shops in a frenzy to convert their falling francs into something more durable.

In the citadel of finance at the Bank of France, the governor and the Regents, sacred trustees of the famous "two-hundred families," who were popularly—and rightly—believed to possess or control most of the wealth of the country, were congratulating themselves on their firm attitude toward the government, which they were now determined to bring down. As it happened, the government was headed for the moment by the same hated man, Edouard Herriot, whom they had helped to topple fourteen months before. He had taken four days to form one, and on July 21, when he presented it to the Chamber for approval, it was toppled by a vote of 290 to 273. Outside the Palais-Bourbon, where the assembly met, a mob pressing against the closed steel gates became so threatening that the Prefect of Police had to call for reinforcements of mounted Republican Guards to prevent it from invading the premises and roughing up the legislators. The "mob," was well organized. It had been assembled by the various anti-parliament leagues that were mushrooming on the Right. They were taking to the streets, as the Brown Shirts in Germany and the Black Shirts in Italy had done—and for the same purpose.*

---

* With the fall of the Briand government on July 17, 1926, Joseph Caillaux, a storm-center in the tumultuous life of the Third Republic for a quarter of a century, disappeared for good from the ranks of cabinet ministers. But he was far from finished politically, continuing for another decade to play a role, albeit a disruptive one, in the Radical-Socialist Party and in the Senate, where he headed the powerful Finance Committee. Authoritarian by nature, as was his bitter enemy Clemenceau, rude, insolent and vain in manner (this writer never observed him without a monocle), and unpopular in Parliament and in his party, his faults of character were somewhat compensated for by a brilliant and incisive mind.

His comebacks in political life became legendary. Overthrown as Premier in 1912 because of his costly appeasement of Germany, he was back in the cabinet as Finance Minister the next year. In 1914, after his wife had murdered Calmette and

At midnight of that stormy July 21, the President of the Republic called on Raymond Poincaré, now aged sixty-five, to form a new government of "National Union," to save, if he could, the government from bankruptcy and the franc from becoming entirely worthless. On July 27, the Chamber of Deputies, which had been selected in 1924 by a popular majority to get rid of Poincaré and all his policies, foreign and domestic, now approved him by an overwhelming majority, 358 votes to 131. Herriot, who had replaced Poincaré in 1924 and always opposed his policies, became a cabinet minister in this new government.

Such were the political ways of the Third Republic. Regardless of the expression of the will of the voters, majorities in the Chamber melted away, turning from one direction to another. When the majorities were of the Left, as after the 1924 election, they turned to the Right. This became a habit that could not be broken, but which defies rational explanation, during the rest of the life of the Republic, adding to the confusion and frustration in the land.

Yet in 1926 a certain strength was generated from this fickleness of Parliament which could not be summoned up again a decade later when the supreme crisis for the Republic began. Despite the Gallic passions which political disagreement aroused so violently, there came a moment in that summer of 1926, as there had come in the summer of 1914 but would never occur again, when in the face of danger, the political quarrels were temporarily buried and the ranks closed in the interest of preserving the Republic.

"We never see you except in times of trouble!" a Communist deputy shouted at Poincaré the day he presented his government. If meant as an insult, it nevertheless contained a large measure of truth. The country was in trouble again and all the political parties except the Socialists and Communists gathered behind Poincaré. Five former Premiers joined his government. There was a political truce.

---

he had defended her gallantly in court and helped win her acquittal, Caillaux had seemingly retired from active politics for good. His experience toward the end of the war appeared to have finished him. Long suspected of being secretly in touch with the Germans and known to favor stopping the war and negotiating a compromise peace, he was deprived in 1917 of his parliamentary immunity at the insistence of Clemenceau and arrested and jailed on January 14, 1918, on the charge of correspondence with the enemy and plotting against the security of the state in wartime. Finally brought to trial in 1920 before the Senate sitting as the High Court of Justice he was found guilty by a vote of 150 to 91 of communicating with the enemy, though "without premeditation." He was condemned to three years in prison and the loss of civic rights for ten years.

From that blow Caillaux also recovered. Amnestied along with many others in 1924, he soon got himself elected to the Senate, appointed to two cabinets in 1925–26, and, for a time, chosen as head of the Radical-Socialist party. Throughout his life he believed in rapprochement with Germany, whether she was led by Wilhelm II or by Adolf Hitler. He spoke out for it in the Senate to the last, at the time of Munich and thereafter to the final days of peace. Caillaux died on November 21, 1944, at the age of eighty-one, just as France was being liberated by her allies.

THE POINCARÉ RECOVERY

Before the new President of the Council had time to formulate new fiscal policies confidence returned. The franc rose. Capital began to flow home. The Regents of the Bank of France, who had more admiration for Poincaré than he had for them—for though conservative he was a man of utter integrity, a staunch Republican and a fierce patriot—were happy. Businessmen breathed a sigh of relief.

Well they might. Poincaré had no miracles up his sleeve nor radical solutions to offer. Conservative and orthodox in his ideas of government finance, he had no intention of unduly rocking the boat, but since it was aground he was determined to refloat it. He would honor the state's debts when they became due and thus restore government credit. He would cut expenses and raise revenue until they were balanced. And he would stabilize the franc.

All these things he quickly did. To refund government loans he set up a Sinking Fund run by an agency made independent of the Treasury. This was the *Caisse d'Amortissement.* A special law reserved for it the revenue from certain taxes and from the tobacco monopoly which the Treasury was forbidden to touch.

Taxes were raised, but the distribution of their burden remained essentially unchanged. Most of the sharpest increases were in indirect taxes, which weighed heaviest on those of modest means. The general income tax was reduced by half, from 60 percent to 30 percent, though the additional special income tax on salaries and on farmers' profits was raised from 7 to 12 percent. Business and financial circles were pleased, their confidence that Poincaré was not going to soak the rich restored. Their affairs prospered.

The incoming Premier was too honest and shrewd, however, to let them off scot-free. He was going to get at least part of the additional money he needed to balance the budget "from where it was." In the atmosphere of restored confidence he rushed through Parliament practically without debate a number of laws calling for new taxes and increase of old ones which the bankers and businessmen and the political Right would never have accepted from a less "conservative" government. For the first time in France's history he imposed a tax on part of the Frenchman's capital—a 7 percent levy on real-estate capital when it changed hands. The low tax on business profits was raised by half—from 10 to 15 percent and on income from nonregistered foreign securities from 14 to 25 percent.

By the end of the year 1926, Poincaré, though in office a little less than six months, could look with pride on his accomplishment. Government revenue was up over the previous year by 6.5 billion francs, a billion and a half had been repaid to the Bank of France, the receipts of the Sinking Fund enabled it to meet without trouble the obligations of the short-term debt, and there was a budget surplus of a billion francs against a deficit of one and a half billions the year before. Not only was the fall of the franc halted; the currency began to rise. From 50 to a dollar in July, and plunging, the franc doubled its value by the end of the year. In six months Poincaré had stabilized the franc *de facto* at a rate that was to be legalized and tied to gold two years later.

There was—there had been all along—plenty of French money to restore the finances of the state. Poincaré, who at first had thought of forcing the Banks to buy government bonds in order to get immediate revenue, had listened to some advice from the director of the United States Federal Reserve Bank.

Why not turn to those who have more capital than all your banks together? To those who have more than ten billion francs in securities or gold abroad? Why not turn to your own Frenchmen?[4]

The Premier had not turned to them alone but his ability to restore confidence had resulted in the return of the bulk of French capital salted away abroad. He had imposed on the poor a heavy burden in increased taxes and a higher cost of living, for prices rose all through the last half of 1926 and for the next three years. But most Frenchmen, even many of modest means, were apparently thankful that anything had been saved at all—the state from bankruptcy, the franc from sliding to zero—and that business generally prospered. When election time came in 1928 the people gave Poincaré a vote of confidence. The Center and Conservative parties received a majority of seats in the new House. The floundering Third Republic under Poincaré's leadership and with the cooperation of the Left and Right had surmounted another crisis and achieved for the country a remarkable recovery.

But not, as was inevitable, without cost. The financial sacrifices needed were relatively light and fell heaviest on the poor and on those, many of modest means, who had bought government bonds before and during the war with gold francs and now found them reduced by four fifths in value by the devaluation of the currency. Some families had most of their life savings virtually wiped out. Others whose income came mostly from fixed rents and interest were in a similar fix. A certain proletarianization of a good many solid citizens of the middle class took place at this time. Like the workers they found it increasingly difficult to make ends meet, but contrary to the workers they turned politically not to the Left but to the extreme Right in hope of salvation. They felt that the state under the Republic, which many of them had distrusted anyway, had not honored its promise to pay them back, with interest, what they had lent it and that, in effect, it had cheated them of 80 percent of their savings.

Moreover the severe inflation of the early twenties caused by the fall of the franc, the rise of prices, and the paralysis of government finances brought about a deep neurosis about the currency in the French people. The whole foundation of the world of the solid bourgeoisie was shaken.

Sudden impoverishment, the difficulty of establishing a family budget, the futility of trying to save when your bank account or your investments might be halved in value by the plunge of the franc—all these upset the very conceptions on which the good middle class had lived for a century. Frenchmen became obsessed with the idea that the "Poincaré franc," shrunk though it was, must never again be devalued, lest they be ruined anew. The obsession became a national neurosis which would greatly add to the nation's difficulties when the world-wide depression came in the early thirties and the British devalued the pound and the Americans the dollar and the French held stubbornly—and disastrously—to their 1928 franc.

The financial crisis of the mid-twenties had another profound effect on French public opinion which would further divide the citizenry and weaken the Republic. The bankers, industrialists, and businessmen, and even the more thriving peasants and shopkeepers, came to believe with a certainty that brooked no compromise that the political "Left," which, aside from the small Communist Party, was in reality little more than reformist and middle-of-the-way, was incapable of governing the country. They believed that unless the conservatives, who had rallied behind Poincaré, dominated Parliament and government France was lost. As was natural, and as is the case with such people in all countries, or was at this time, they could not see their own shortcomings, above all their selfishness, their reluctance to make a fair share of the sacrifices needed, and their blindness to the need in a modern industrial society of some measure of social security and a more equitable distribution of both wealth and the increasing tax burden. In social welfare France in this period lagged behind all other nations in the West except the more affluent United States, and in wages and conditions of labor it was the worst of all.

A few visionaries, not all from the Left, urged Poincaré to take advantage of the vastly improved situation after 1926 to overhaul the whole old-fashioned, nineteenth-century structure of French society, modernizing the government and the economy, building new housing so urgently needed, rescuing agriculture from its unmechanized stagnation, encouraging responsible trade unionism and responsible collective bargaining of labor disputes, and instituting a bold program of social security, comparable to that which had worked so well for so long in Germany. In a country where despite the general recovery the workers and peasants were just able to exist* and a considerable section of the lower and middle bourgeoisie was being proletarianized by inflation and the devaluation of the franc, and where the birthrate, as a consequence, continued to fall much faster than across the Rhine or almost any place else, this would have strengthened the nation for the unseen but inevitable ordeals that lay ahead.

Poincaré responded—but only feebly. The country, at least as it was

---

* Wages of industrial workers in 1930 averaged $1.80 (45 francs) a day, those of farm laborers 88 cents a day (22 francs). Prices were lower in France than in the United States, but by not more than one half, and in many goods not even that.[5]

represented in Parliament, was not ready for such a far-reaching regeneration. Finally, on April 5, 1928, just in time for the elections, the Chamber and Senate approved a modest program of social insurance, limited mostly to the sick and the aged, with wage and salary earners contributing 5 percent of their pay, the employers an equal amount, and the state defraying the cost of the operation. Characteristically, the Parliament provided a delay of twenty-two months in the implementation of the law.* The Third Republic was never in a hurry.

The Left had its blind spots too in these troubled years of the 1920s. It was no less convinced than the Right that it alone was fit to govern the Republic in the true interests of the country and that Conservative rule would ultimately ruin the fair land. The masses believed that the "miracle" of the Poincaré recovery had been achieved mostly at their expense. And they were convinced that there was a vast conspiracy of the *Mur d'Argent,* the "Wall of Money," to overthrow the Left Cartel governments which they had put in power in free elections and which in their view had only wanted a little more equity in French life. They were bitter at the realization that the "conspiracy" had succeeded, that the Cartel was out and the Poincaré conservatives in. Their beliefs and feelings were not without some justification. But like those on the Right they failed to recognize their own shortcomings. They did not seem to comprehend their own responsibility for the financial mess of the government, which lay primarily in their indecision, in their inability to agree on—let alone enforce—any policy which might have put the government in the black and stopped the financial panic, the flight of capital abroad, and the disastrous fall of the franc.

In this time, too, the gulf between the Right and Left, between the possessors and the masses, between the popular press and its readers, was further enlarged, despite a brief political truce under Poincaré. More and more, as the 1920s came to an end and the clouds threatening a world-wide depression appeared over New York, Frenchmen faced one another across a widening chasm that made hearing over it, even if one listened, more difficult and mutual understanding, in the absence of reasonable communication, almost impossible. Each side hardened in its belief that the other was unfit to govern the Republic.

In November 1928 the Radical-Socialists, who had lost heavily in the elections largely because of their support of Poincaré, withdrew from his coalition government. After carrying on with a purely conservative cabinet, the sixty-nine-year-old Premier, exhausted by three years of untiring labor, and ill from a prostate which had to be operated on immediately, resigned his high post for the last time on July 26, 1929, after forty-one years in politics, and retired to his native Lorraine on the border of Germany,

---

* Characteristically, too, the various employers' associations, having lost their fight to prevent Parliament from enacting the modest social-security legislation, continued their well-financed campaign in the press and on billboards to render it ineffective and to get it repealed.[6]

which he had so long hated and which he still mistrusted and feared. There he settled down to write the last five volumes of his ten-volume memoirs, *Au service de la France,* and to turn out articles for the press. A long and successful life in politics as deputy, senator, minister and President of the Republic had not brought him wealth, as it had so many other politicians—his integrity about his personal finances had been fierce and fanatical—and he had had to write to earn a living. A man of somewhat narrow vision, for whom the world outside of France remained almost incomprehensible, cold and austere in temperament, often petty in his dealings with others, he was nonetheless possessed of considerable intelligence, a clarity of thought, a broad culture, and a character that could not be corrupted. He never wavered in his devotion to the Republic and to his country, which he loved with a passion that often carried him into chauvinism. As the French said, Poincaré, despite his faults, deserved well of his country.

He lived on until October 15, 1934—long enough to see his world, at home and abroad, cracking up. The world-wide depression and a series of inept French governments of both Right and Left—it made little difference which—had by then undone most of his domestic accomplishments, and both his own foreign policy of trying to keep Germany in check and that of Briand in attempting to bring the two ancient enemies together in a lasting peace were already in ashes. Hitler had taken over in Berlin twenty-one months before and embarked brashly on a course which Poincaré, as President of the Republic, had had to grapple with just prior to 1914. Wilhelm II then, and now Hitler. Dying in his native Lorraine, Poincaré, it is said, glanced uneasily over the nearby frontier toward Germany and feared that "they would come again."

THE PASSING OF THE OLD GUARD

All the old figures who had dominated the Third Republic for a generation, guiding her into the unsettled twentieth century and through the grim war years and the chaotic postwar era, were passing. New and younger and untried men were emerging to preside over the country as it faced the uncertain years of the 1930s. Clemenceau, the old Tiger, had died in 1929 at the age of eighty-eight. Embittered by his defeat for the presidency in 1920 by a lesser man who had turned out to be out of his mind, he had endured his political retirement in a dark and desolate mood. "Everything I have done," he had said in 1922, "has been wasted. In twenty years France will be dead."

Briand, another pillar of the Third Republic, eleven times Premier, seventeen times Foreign Minister over a period in office that stretched for a quarter of a century, died on March 7, 1932, at seventy, he too, like his enemy Clemenceau, shattered at being rejected for the presidency in favor of a mediocre man and, like both Clemenceau and Poincaré, disconsolate at the realization that almost all he had done was in shambles.

Much less doctrinaire than Clemenceau and Poincaré, despite his debut in public life as a left-wing Socialist, Briand had applied himself for the last seven years of his life—from 1925 to 1932—as Foreign Minister in eleven successive governments, four of them his own, to achieving a decent and durable peace. With perseverance and skill he had sought to conciliate Germany, rebuild the entente with Great Britain, make the League of Nations effective in maintaining the peace, bring about a general disarmament, outlaw war, and launch the idea of an eventual United States of Europe. He may have been naive in his belief that the human race was ready to abandon war. He was proved to have been naive in his trust of the Germans under Stresemann, with whom he shared the Nobel Peace Prize in 1926.* No doubt he overestimated the capability of the League of Nations to keep the peace. But for seven years he carried his own country with him, and even Britain and to some extent the German republic, in his quest for it. No one who listened to his eloquent, emotional oratory those years in the Chamber of Deputies in Paris and in the League of Nations Assembly in Geneva, as this writer did, can lose from his memory the impact of the golden voice, the glowing words, and the flowing gestures made with hands so delicate and artistically expressive that they reminded one of those of Paderewski at the piano.

Lacking any firm belief in doctrines of the Left or the Right, he was essentially a conciliator, believing that compromise could in the end settle the most bitter disputes. In France, as we have seen, he had conciliated the Catholics after the separation of church and state and for nearly a decade he labored as Foreign Minister in conservative as well as radical governments to achieve a decent accord between the nations of the West. But reason and compromise and conciliation could not suffice to meet the harsher realities that hardened as the 1930s began. They had begun to fail in Briand's dealings with the German Republic, which, after every concession, demanded a new one, and when Hitler came they would prove useless. In France, too, as divisions widened and intolerance grew, they were losing their effectiveness. Briand served his last two terms as Foreign Minister under the premiership of Pierre Laval, who scorned his policies and who, as 1932 came, dumped him, finishing off the long and distinguished career of a man broken now and disillusioned and ill. Death mercifully took him seven weeks later.

A new breed of men were coming to the fore in France, as elsewhere. The era of Briand was dead. Dead, too, or dying, were the great illusions: that France victorious could forever impose its will on the vanquished, that the democratic allies of the war would remain allies in the postwar world, that the League of Nations could keep the peace—in short, that life in the Western world would remain pretty much as it was and that France under the Third Republic could muddle through the twentieth century without

---

* The memoirs of Stresemann, published after his death, make that abundantly clear.

changing its ways much. Yet, if the illusions were lost, the stark realities emerging from behind them were not squarely faced. The convulsions of the century's third decade, ushered in by the world-wide depression and soon exacerbated by the advent of Hitler and the throw-back barbarism of National Socialism in Germany, shook the Third Republic and jarred it to its foundations. France, like the United States and Great Britain, was ill prepared for the succession of shocks. It was at this time that the Republic began the final slide down toward catastrophe.

In Paris there was again a cascade of ministries of the Right and Left, none of them remaining in office long enough to cope with the unfolding crises. Though the elections of 1928 had returned a conservative Chamber of Deputies and those of 1932 a radical one, there was no stable parliamentary majority for any policy or any cabinet and the Chamber or the Senate massacred governments on the slightest pretext. Five cabinets were overthrown in seventeen months following the resignation of Poincaré in July 1929. Between June 1932 and February 1934 six governments came and went, lasting an average of three months. On January 30, 1933, the day Hitler became Chancellor of Germany, France was without any government at all, the five-week-old Paul-Boncour cabinet having been overthrown on January 28 and a new one, Edouard Daladier's first, not being formed until January 31. It made no difference to the Chamber what was happening abroad and how it might affect France. Five years later, on the day Hitler marched into Austria, France would again find itself without a government.

THE WEAKNESS OF THE PRESIDENTS

The weakness of the presidency and the mediocrity of the politicians who held it in the last years of the Third Republic contributed to the instability of French governments. We have seen Clemenceau confessing that in the elections of the National Assembly for President of the Republic he always voted for the most stupid candidate. His parliamentary colleagues were no different, and this attitude brought about Clemenceau's own defeat for the highest office in 1920. It was a blow that finished his long political career and left him bitter and despondent over the nine remaining years of his life. As the "Father of the Victory" Clemenceau enjoyed so immense a prestige in the country and in Parliament that his election to succeed the retiring Poincaré as President of the Republic seemed assured. No doubt his stern and dictatorial rule as Premier during the last year of the war had caused resentment among certain Senators and Deputies and his old anticlericalism, which Briand cited in intriguing against him, disqualified him in the minds of some on the Right. But the country was shocked when on January 17, 1920, the National Assembly sitting in Versailles elected not Clemenceau but Paul Deschanel, an elegant, urbane deputy who was President of the Chamber and who had few political enemies because he had few convictions. There was a further irony. Deschanel was on the verge of insanity and soon passed over the line. One night not long after his election the President of the Republic jumped off a presidential train steaming through the countryside and, clad only in pajamas, presented himself, after a short walk in the dark through the brush along the rails, to the guardian of a forlorn grade-crossing draw-bar. When the President identified himself the guardian took him for a lunatic and called the gendarmerie. A little later the President was dis-covered floundering about like a wounded carp in a pond near the presi-dential château at Rambouillet and near to drowning. Finally, on Septem-ber 21, nine months after defeating Clemenceau for the Presidency, Deschanel was forced to resign his high office because of incapacity.* He was replaced by Alexandre Millerand, the former Socialist who had now become a staunch conservative, and who four years later would share the fate of MacMahon in being forced to resign because a rebellious majority in the Chamber of Deputies refused to form a government until he did so.

The members of Parliament preferred not only weak and mediocre men for President but men who were considered "safe." Though the elections of 1924 had returned the Left majority of the *Cartel des Gauches,* the National Assembly that year, disregarding the expressed will of the electorate, chose as President the moderate Gaston Doumergue, President of the Senate, over Paul Painlevé, the candidate of the supposedly victori-ous *Cartel.*

In 1931 the National Assembly chose the moderate, plodding Paul Doumer over the one statesman in France of world-wide reputation, Aristide Briand. It had now become almost a custom to choose a President of the Senate to be President of the Republic. On May 7, 1932, the day before the second balloting in the national elections (in which the first round on May 1 had shown a shift to the left), Doumer was assassinated by a demented White Russian while presiding over the opening of a book fair in Paris. The election runoff the next day made certain a strong left majority in the Chamber and it was generally assumed that the returns would in-fluence the choice of a new President. The old Parliament, with its conserva-tive majority sitting as the National Assembly, however, picked Albert Lebrun, President of the Senate, a decent but colorless man who had re-frained from the electoral battle, thereby offending neither the Left nor the Right. He was elected President of the Republic on May 10, 1932. For the next eight and last years of the Republic France would have a typical President. In the climactic crisis of the troubled regime a typical man at the top was not good enough.

---

* Notwithstanding his mental condition, Deschanel was promptly elected to the Senate from the district of Eure-et-Loire.

12

DECLINE, II
THE EROSION OF MILITARY POWER
1925–1934

Not only the old political figures but the old military chiefs who had led the French and Allied armies to victory in 1918 were passing from the scene. Marshal Foch, the Allied generalissimo, died at seventy-eight in 1929, disillusioned by the way he thought the peace had robbed his country of the fruits of victory. The Treaty of Versailles, he had said in 1919, gave not peace but "an armistice for twenty years," a prophecy, like that of Clemenceau, of terrible accuracy.

Marshal Joffre, the hero of the Marne, died at seventy-nine in 1931, defeated in his last efforts to get the country to fortify the northern as well as the northeastern frontier. He believed the Germans, if another war came, would again attack through Belgium, but he was not heeded.

Only Marshal Pétain, of the great military triumvirate, lingered on. Covered by a halo of glory for his defense of Verdun and continuing to hold his post as Commander in Chief of the French Army for thirteen years into the peace, he seemed indestructible. He was seventy-five, ten years over the age limit, when he finally retired in 1931.* Possessed of the vigor of a man twenty years his junior, he was retained on the *Conseil supérieur de la guerre,* the War Council, where his eminence, towering high above that of any other general, allowed him for another five years to dominate French military thought and policy. Even after that, as he emerged into his eighties and began to take a belated interest in politics, he was far from finished.

Pétain's successor in 1931 was General Maxime Weygand, sixty-four, brilliant wartime aide to Marshal Foch, cocky as a bantam rooster, which he resembled, and suspect in republican political circles because of his outspoken royalism and his fanatical Catholicism. (Clemenceau, who

---

* For the top post in the Army the age limit could be stretched from 65 to 68.

admired him, once remarked that "of course, he is up to his neck in priests.") To balance this appointment the government selected as Chief of the General Staff General Maurice Gamelin, sixty-one, former aide of Marshal Joffre, who was credited with having drawn up, junior officer though he was at the time, the actual plans for the Battle of the Marne in 1914. A staunch republican who in the reactionary circles of the military hierarchy was suspected of being a "liberal," Gamelin, a short, mild-mannered, wispy man, who succeeded Weygand in the top post in 1935, had had an exceptional career as a combat as well as a staff officer and was reputed to have the finest intellect of any general of his aging generation. Because of his experience in leading large units in hard-fought battles the last two years of the Great War—unlike that of General Weygand, who had never commanded combat troops in the field—there seemed in the mid-thirties no reason to believe that General Gamelin lacked the will to action that would match and complement his subtle and cultivated mind.

No reason but his age. He was sixty-five when he took over from the sixty-eight-year-old Weygand in 1935.* Not only the Commander in Chief but all the other generals holding important posts were getting old. The French Army was being run, one prominent newspaper editor said, by an odd assortment of Methuselahs. They had become generals during the war, when promotion was necessarily rapid. (Pétain had risen from colonel to full general in two years.) And they had clung to their posts after 1918, blocking promotion of younger, more vigorous officers with new outlooks.

Charles de Gaulle, despite—or perhaps because of—the attention his probing mind began to attract after the war among his superiors as a teacher of history at Saint-Cyr and as a provocative writer on military subjects, remained a captain for twelve years, being promoted to major only in 1927 when he was thirty-seven years old. Thousands of junior officers, graduates of the Military Academy of Saint-Cyr or of the engineering college, the famous Ecole Polytechnique, seeing no prospect for normal advancement and unable in the inflationary years to support their families on the meager salaries paid to those in the lower grades, resigned their commissions to go into business or a civil profession. They felt they could not otherwise fulfill themselves or earn a decent living. Other officers were simply let out, some one thousand of them in 1933–34 when the military budget was cut by two billion francs, the full effect of the Depression having just hit France. The budget of 1933, in fact, called for eliminating one sixth of the Officer Corps, 5,000 men out of 30,000, causing panic in the High Command until the project was dropped.

This was the beginning of the period of the "lean years" in the

---

* General Weygand, like Marshal Pétain before him, held the post of Vice-President of the War Council and Inspector-General of Armies, a title which also designated him as Supreme Commander in time of war. General Gamelin, when he stepped up in 1935, retained his post as Chief of the General Staff, combining it with the top job.

number of men available for military service caused by the drastic drop of the birthrate during the war of 1914–1918. Less than a quarter of a million able-bodied youths came of military age each year. "For every Frenchman between the ages of twenty and thirty," de Gaulle pointed out in *Vers l'armée de métier,* one of his disturbing books that so annoyed the military hierarchy and left the country so cold, "there are two Germans." Since the conscripts served but one year under the colors and that year had to be devoted to training them, France was left without much of an army in being. Only the 62,000 professional soldiers, many of whom were detailed to training the raw draftees, and 72,000 colonial troops provided a slim basis for a small standing army. The disastrous consequences of this state of affairs would soon be demonstrated.

By the time the Depression came at the beginning of the thirties, the French Army, theretofore generally believed to be the strongest in the world, was withering away—not only because of the dwindling manpower available and the shrinking military budgets but for other reasons just as substantial. The Army was suffering from sclerosis in the High Command, from a wave of pacifism in the country, and from an utter confusion in Parliament, the government, and public opinion as to what kind of army to have to meet the minimum needs of national defense, the extended commitments of French foreign policy, and the consequences of the postwar revolution in military science brought about by the swift technological advances in the development of the airplane and tank, in both of which arms the French had pioneered and excelled in the closing years of the Great War.

SCLEROSIS IN THE HIGH COMMAND

The generals not only had clung to their posts after 1918. They had held on tightly and blindly to the ideas that had brought them success on the battlefield. Their minds were closed. Much later, as his long life neared its end, Marshal Pétain, frankly admitted it. "After the war of 1914–1918," he told a Parliamentary Investigating Committee, "it was finished for me. My military mind was closed. When I saw the introduction of other tools, other instruments, other methods, I must say they didn't interest me."[1] As late as January 1935, just before his retirement, General Weygand, an old cavalryman, urged the War Council to be "prudent" in pushing the mechanization of the army, asked it "not to forget that horses are always useful," and declared that more horses, "especially saddle horses" were urgently needed for the army.[2] What was good enough, including horse cavalry, to bring victory in the First World War would be good enough to win in the second. "This is what I did, and it succeeded," Marshal Foch admonished a group of young officers not long before his death. "We must always do the same." It seemed almost as if most of the army leaders had not yet heard of the development of the combustion engine, which by the end of the 1920s was making possible faster planes (for fighters), heavier and longer-range planes (for bombing and transport), and heavily armored tanks that could carry a 75 mm. gun and move over rough country at 40 miles an hour.

There was one old general with a young and fresh mind who contended that it was revolutionizing warfare. This was General Estienne, called in France "the father of the tank" (he had developed it in 1915 quite independently of the British, who claimed to be its inventor). He had bludgeoned the High Command into building tanks, had first led them into battle in 1916, and at the end of the war commanded several thousand of them. He believed that he had discovered one of the vital arms that made victory in 1918 possible, for the Germans lagged far behind the Western allies in this field.* Moreover General Estienne was sure that the tank, especially when teamed up with the plane, was the chief weapon of the future in land warfare.

On February 15, 1920, when the French military hierarchy, of which Foch, Joffre, and Pétain were still blazing lights, had settled down to the comfortable conclusion that all the lessons for wars in the twentieth century had been learned between 1914 and 1918, General Estienne delivered a bold and prophetic lecture in Paris to the younger army officers, repeating it a year later in Brussels where King Albert was a fascinated listener. "I believe," he said, "that the tank will soon shake to their foundations not only the tactics but also the strategy and after that the very organization of all modern armies." And he proceeded to set forth the vision of an independent armored force of 100,000 men, 4,000 tanks, and 8,000 trucks advancing 50 miles in a day or night, piercing and disrupting the enemy and putting him to rout. This was exactly the number of men and tanks advocated by General de Gaulle in 1934, and it could have accurately described the Panzer force which the Germans hurled into France and Belgium in May 1940.

Ten years later, in refining his thoughts, General Estienne laid down the final guidelines for armored warfare. "The armored force [he called it 'assault artillery'], must be an independent arm," he argued, "for it has not the least analogy to the infantry, differing essentially from it by its methods of combat, its armament, and by its organization, which necessitate having behind it a formidable service of refueling and supply." Finally, with a glimpse into the future that appears today almost supernatural, but

---

* General Ludendorff, who, under Hindenburg, commanded the German armies, tells in his memoirs of the great Allied tank attack which began on August 8, 1918, a date he called the "Black Day of the German Army in this war." It marked the beginning of the end for the Germans. "Early on August 8," Ludendorff writes, "the British and French attacked between Albert and Moreuil with strong forces of tanks, in which they alone were superior. They broke through deeply in our front. Our divisions there were completely overrun. Their headquarters were surprised and taken by the enemy tanks. . . . Six or seven German divisions among the best we had were completely destroyed. The situation became extremely grave. . . . The employment of tanks in massive quantities proved to be our worst enemy. The eighth of August brought the end of our capacity to fight on."[3]

which he said came from the experience gained by the "hazards" of a career which had made him first a pioneer aviator and then a tankman, he stressed the importance of a close collaboration between independent armored units and *planes,* with the latter not only providing aerial reconnaissance ahead of the advancing tanks but joining them in the battle and in the pursuit.* Paraphrasing Napoleon he concluded: "Assault artillery (armored force) will henceforth determine the destinies of armies and peoples."[5]

The French High Command did not believe it. To its venerable, veteran generals all this rash talk of a great autonomous armored force breaking through the infantry and artillery was claptrap. The thing was impossible. First General Estienne and then his disciples, like the upstart Lieutenant Colonel de Gaulle were judged victims of an aberration.

THE HORSE AGAINST THE TANK

General Brécart, member of the War Council and Inspector General of the Cavalry, was for instance dead against replacing horses by mechanized monsters in his branch of the service. Writing in the military review *L'Officier de Réserve* in October 1933, he violently attacked the very idea of creating light mechanized divisions and consigning his beloved animals to pasture. "We are creating dangerous Utopias!" he exclaimed. "We have no idea where it will end!" For the sake "of the future of our country" he demanded that cavalry be restricted to horses, and after depicting the wonders of the animals bred in France, "one of our national riches," he said, he concluded with a plea: "We must safeguard the raising of horses!"

General Weygand, whose love of horses was no less passionate than that of General Brécart, was open-minded enough to suggest that armored vehicles might at least be added to a cavalry division, and in 1931 the first move in this direction was hesitantly taken. General Dufieux, Inspector General of Infantry and Tanks, objected. In particular he was against the newfangled notion of using tanks as an autonomous unit. "In my opinion," he wrote his chief, "there is no possibility that a mechanized combat detachment can ever be used to lead a complete operation by itself. . . . I cannot understand therefore why the Mechanized Cavalry Division is being formed as if it were sufficient to itself in all circumstances." The tank, he insisted, was made to accompany the infantry, never to fight in units of its own.

---

* Actually the French had made a beginning with the development of the tank-plane assault toward the end of the first war. The First Air Division was formed on May 14, 1918, and played a key role in the great tank attacks of August. The unit consisted of 432 Spad planes, precursors of the Stuka dive bomber. One young German officer who saw his front overrun by French tanks supported by the First French Air Division did not forget the experience. This was Heinz Guderian, the creator of the Panzer Army in the second war. "I drew my conclusions," he later told a French officer, "from the employment of tanks by your army in combination with your Air Division."[4]

That was the crucial point. Was the tank to be used merely as an adjunct of the infantry as in the Great War? Or, now that it was developing into a formidable offensive weapon, should it constitute an independent unit capable of operating on its own at a speed which would leave the infantry, artillery, and horse cavalry far behind? General Estienne had raised the question in 1928 and again in 1931 and insisted on an affirmative answer. The French High Command considered the question and answered it—in the negative. The Manual of "Instructions for the Employment of Tanks" drawn up in 1930 began:

Combat tanks are machines to accompany the infantry. . . . In battle, tank units constitute an integral part of the infantry. . . . Tanks are only supplementary means, put temporarily at the disposition of the infantry. They strengthen considerably the action of the latter but they do not replace it. Their action, to be effective, must be exploited by the infantry at the moment of their impact; the progress of the infantry and its seizing of objectives are alone decisive.

And to leave no doubt that the High Command considered the tank units to be pariahs, the Manual prescribed that they must always be under the command of the infantry units they served. Not until it was too late, and then only halfheartedly and piecemeal, did the French Army chiefs budge from this already outmoded stand. To the bitter end most of the French military experts, and some of them the most renowned, went on repeating, against the desperate cries of the rebellious Colonel de Gaulle and his friend Paul Reynaud, a rising young middle-of-the-road politician, the old arguments against using armor as independent, self-supporting units, as the Germans had begun to do as soon as they started building tanks, theretofore denied them by the Versailles Treaty, in 1933.

In December 1938, nine months before the second war came, the *Revue d'Infanterie* featured an article by a Major Laporte exposing the latest ideas of the High Command. "Not even the most modern tanks," he wrote, "can ever lead the fighting by themselves and for themselves. Their mission must always be to participate along with the fire of the artillery and heavy infantry arms in the protection and support of attacks. . . . On the field of eternal battle the principal enemy of the foot soldier remains the enemy infantryman, who, as our instructions recall to us, alone conquers ground, organizes it and holds it. The tank must above all be considered as one of the auxiliaries of the foot soldier."

Less than a year before the outbreak of war, the venerable Marshal Pétain put the finishing touches to the French military doctrine about armored warfare. In a celebrated introduction to a controversial book that appeared at the beginning of 1939 by General Chauvineau, a professor at the *Ecole de Guerre,* entitled "Is an Invasion Still Possible?" (which he answered in the negative) Pétain, who had long been irritated by what he thought were wild and woolly ideas sponsored by Colonel de Gaulle, spoke out from his Olympian heights.

It would be imprudent to conclude that an armored force, capable of advancing, it is claimed, 125 miles a day, forcing great strongholds and sowing panic in the enemy's rear, is an irresistible weapon. The decisive results obtained by this force would have no tomorrow. . . . Before a barrage of antitank guns and mines the armored division would be at the mercy of a counterattack on the flanks. . . . As for tanks, which are supposed by some to bring us a shortening of wars, their incapacity is striking.

Since the military chiefs were skeptical of the tank, despite the intelligence that began to arrive from Berlin shortly after the advent of Hitler in 1933 that the Germans were going to make it the basis of their future army, it is no wonder that the French were slow in developing the machine itself. With the Germans forbidden since 1919 to build tanks the French generals had had the advantage of a tremendous head start. But they were too ossified to use it. General Estienne himself as early as 1921 had worked out designs for the future thickly armored, heavily gunned and fast-moving tank which eventually would be called the B tank. By 1925 a few prototypes had been produced and successfully tested. Then for four years the whole matter was dropped by the High Command. Taken up again in 1929 it was discussed for another four years and finally in 1935 the first orders were given. By that time German production of heavy tanks was in high gear and this was the main reason the French High Command finally, if reluctantly, acted. But it was in no hurry. Production was limited to ten B tanks a month and soon fell behind even that leisurely schedule. At the beginning of 1939, after Hitler had sent his armored *divisions* into Austria and Czechoslovakia, and France had reason to think that her turn would come next, production of the B tank was eight per month.

The Army had had eighteen years since the designing of the heavy tank, fourteen years since its satisfactory tests, to push its production and thus provide the basis for the most formidable armored force in the world. For the B Tank was superior in almost every way to the best the Germans could build. A full two decades after it was designed Great Britain and the United States were content to copy it for their Churchill and General Grant tanks.

As with the tank, so with the airplane. The lethargic French High Command had no special regard for the role of aviation in warfare either. Twelve years after the end of the Great War, in which French aviation had played an increasingly important part, in reconnaissance, strafing, and bombing, the Air Force in France remained essentially unchanged, with the same old cumbersome aircraft, though of course it had been reduced in size. The High Command's Manual of Instructions, drawn up by Pétain in 1921, scarcely took notice of the plane. "By day it scouts, by night it bombards," it said, and that was all.

The succeeding Manual of 1936 went little further. Though it admitted that there had been much progress in the development of arms since 1921 it concluded that "this does not essentially modify the essential rules laid down in the previous instructions." Of the 177 pages in the Manual only three were devoted to the role of the Air Force. It was to reconnoiter with its fighters and bomb airfields and troop concentrations behind the enemy's lines with its bombers. There was no word about the plane participating in actual battle on the ground. "Direct action of air forces in the battle is illusory," Marshal Pétain laid it down. General Gamelin later agreed. "There is no such thing as the aerial battle," he proclaimed. "There is only the battle on the ground."

So after the war the French Air Force vegetated, content with its antiquated planes and its primitive tactics that had worked well enough from 1915 to 1918. Finally at the repeated insistence of some of the younger pilot officers, the High Command agreed in 1937 to install radios in fighter planes. The French bombers never got them. Both in bombers and fighters, especially in the latter, the few new planes being manufactured by that late date were inferior in every way, above all in speed and range, to those being produced in Germany, England, and even the United States. To the French High Command the Air Force was a somewhat obstreperous stepchild.

Later the French generals would complain bitterly that the Parliament and government never gave them the arms to fight with. It is true that during the first years of the Depression, Parliament cut down on military spending. In 1934 the Ministry of War approved a government decision to cut armament credits substantially. But who was Minister of War at that time? Marshal Pétain was the minister, and when General Weygand angrily demanded that he convoke a meeting of the War Council to discuss the disastrous consequences of the reduction, the Marshal refused.

The fact was that the High Command did not even spend the armament credits allotted it. Thus in General Weygand's last two years as Army Chief vast sums were left unspent—59 percent of the arms credits in 1933, and 33 percent in 1934—despite his loud cries for more money to rearm. In 1935, the year General Gamelin succeeded General Weygand, 60 percent of the armament credits were not used. Confusion in the Ministry of War and in the General Staff on how to rearm later struck a Parliamentary Investigating Committee as "unbelievable." No one seemed to be in charge. In the words of the conservative Finance Minister at the time there was "an absence of overall planning, a lack of any direction" in the Army.[6]

The ranking generals did not know what arms were needed because they did not know how the new weapons were to be employed. They had shut their minds to the possibilities of tanks and planes in future warfare. General Estienne beginning in 1921, Colonel de Gaulle after 1933 (not to mention a German colonel, Heinz Guderian, whose book *Achtung Panzer!* appeared early in the thirties) had proclaimed as urgently as they could that armor and air units, acting together, would dominate the battlefield in the next war. The French High Command with ill-concealed hostility had noted their ideas—and rejected them.

THE STAGNATION OF MILITARY THOUGHT

Why?

The answer lay largely in the atrophy of the French military mind in the comfortable years of peace after the great victory in 1918. This was reflected not only in the inability of the High Command to keep abreast of technological developments in weapons and to work out new tactics for their use but even in the teachings of the advanced military schools. The renowned Military Staff College (*Ecole Supérieure de Guerre*) struck one young officer as "having become a school of eunuchs, where it was no longer a question of raising the level of the thinking." Another youthful officer who attended it found its teaching to be "of an astonishing poverty."[7] The very highest staff school, the Center of Advanced Military Studies (*Le Centre des Hautes Etudes Militaires*) struck them as just as dead. Before 1914 the brilliant lectures of Colonel Foch and Colonel de Grandmaison at the Ecole de Guerre had electrified the young officers and rejuvenated the thinking of the French Army, instilling in it a new spirit for the offensive. But after the war the teaching stressed the defensive, emphasizing that it had proved successful from 1914 to 1918 and would so prove again. New ideas were frowned upon or summarily dismissed. No wonder that General Tony Albord, one of the pupils at the War College in those days, would later lament "the eclipse of military thinking in France after 1918." It was, he believed, "without precedent," and "the principal cause" of what would happen in 1940.

The fear of the new, of new weapons that necessitated new tactics, became an obsession. As late as 1936, when the new Manual of Instructions was drawn up by a committee of distinguished generals led by General Alphonse Georges, it was emphasized that despite the technological advances made in weapons

the Committee which has drawn up the present instructions does not believe that this technical progress sensibly modifies the essential rules hitherto established in the domain of tactics. Consequently it believes that the doctrine objectively fixed at the end of the war (1918) by the eminent chiefs who had held high commands must remain the charter for the tactical employment of large units.[8]

This is a stunning confession, however unconscious, that the minds of the French generals had ground to a halt and were already thickly coated with rust. They were clinging, as their Manual insisted, to 1918 tactics. But these were now outdated. They had been based in 1918 on infantry, supported by horse-drawn artillery, inching forward one mile an hour over shellholes and through tangles of barbed wire, slowly pressing the enemy back but never breaking through. French defensive tactics on the eve of the new war were still designed to meet that kind of plodding attack, their offensive tactics to carry it out.

Unfortunately for them, the German General Staff had by that time, in 1936, laid down an entirely new set of tactics, borrowed from a French general (Estienne) and refined by a French lieutenant colonel (de Gaulle). These provided for self-contained armored divisions, with heavy tanks accompanied by motorized infantry, engineering units, heavy artillery on caterpillar tracks, and mobile refueling services, and closely supported by combat planes, advancing ten, twenty, thirty times as fast as the foot soldier could do, sowing panic and confusion in the enemy's rear, destroying his communications and lines of supply, and blasting in a day and for good the "continuous front," which had stalemated both sides in the Great War and in which the French High Command still believed as inviolable.

"For the High Command," in the words of the Parliamentary Investigating Committee after the second war, "stagnation had become the supreme form of wisdom."

Our strategists were little more than bookworms in the library, sheltering their insufficiencies behind precedents. They had made of the Ministry of War, the War Council, the General Staff, gigantic machines where the plethoric central services reigned amid mountains of paper. . . .

The General Staff, convinced of its infallibility, made the defense of its prejudices and prerogatives the essence of its action. . . . Having retired to its own Sinai among its revealed truths and the vestiges of its vanished glory, [it] lived on the margin of events, devoting all its efforts to patch up an organization which had been superseded by the facts.[9]

An Obsession: The Defensive and the Continuous Front

The obsession of the French High Command with the defensive and with its corollary, the "continuous front," seemed logical enough. It was based on the solid experience of the 1914–1918 war, during which the French, with their allies, had successfully defended the country, worn out the invaders, and then driven them out. The continuous front had held. It had been pierced by the Germans but the breach had always been repaired. There had been serious but no finally disastrous breakthroughs. Marshals Foch, Joffre, and Pétain and later General Weygand pointed to this with pride and predicted it would be the same in the next war.

Exalted symbol of defensive war was the hero who had stopped the Germans before Verdun in 1916, Marshal Pétain. "Firepower kills!" he had drummed into his pupils before 1914 when he taught infantry tactics at the Ecole de Guerre. This was obvious, but was it equally obvious, as Pétain insisted, that firepower gave the defensive an immense superiority over the offensive? The statistics of the Great War scarcely supported it. French infantry, on the defensive for most of the time, had suffered nearly twice the rate of casualties of the German. And was it true, as the Marshal maintained as late as 1938, that "up to now, so far as operations on the ground are concerned, every new invention has been of greater benefit, generally speaking, to the defense than to the attack"? In the case of such "inventions" as the speedy, heavily armored and gunned tank and the dive bomber and the heavy bomber, protected by fast fighters, it was obviously not true, for these were offensive weapons. But Marshal Pétain believed it, and his word was accepted as if it were the Gospel in France.

His belief in the "continuous front" too. Its supreme value was laid down in the Manual of Instructions of 1921 and reiterated in that of 1936. And as late as 1938 Pétain was insisting in his introduction to General Chauvineau's book (from which the above quotation is also taken) that "the continuous front is the great revelation of the last war. It proved itself stable. . . . It will continue to suffice for everything."

General Weygand too believed in it. After he had taken over the supreme command from Pétain in 1931 he recalled that in the Great War the "front was really never broken by either side." Thus for him, he said, the conception of the "inviolable front" had been raised to "an axiom."

To the everlasting credit of Pétain, Weygand, and the other leading generals of the French Army it must be said that one of their reasons for insisting on the defensive, which was to be strengthened by vast new fortifications, was their determination to spare French blood in any future war. The holocaust of 1914–1918 had sickened them. Not only that, but they had sense enough to see that another such bloodletting would be the end of France, even if she again won. It was Pétain, as we have seen, who in the first war stopped the massacre of French infantry which General Nivelle had so recklessly perpetrated in his ill-prepared, ill-conceived, and futile offensives. Thereafter, Pétain, as the new Commander in Chief, laid it down that there would be no more offensives until the French had overwhelming superiority in artillery fire and the infantry could advance without being massacred. He became known in the ranks as the general who had compassion for his men and respect for their lives.

There were other reasons for the French adherence to the defensive. After the restoration of Alsace-Lorraine in 1918, France had no further territorial claim on Germany. She had no reason to attack her nor the country's other neighbors, Spain, Italy, Switzerland, and Belgium, who were militarily weak and, except for Fascist Italy after 1935 and Franco Spain after 1938, friendly and peaceful. The French wanted only to be secure within their own boundaries. For that a strong defensive capability was considered all that was necessary. It was known, of course, that French commitments to Czechoslovakia and Poland called for France to come to their aid by staging an offensive in the West if they were invaded by the Germans. But there had been no possibility of that as long as Germany had been kept disarmed. Even after Hitler came to power in Berlin in January 1933, withdrew from the League of Nations in October, and began feverishly to rearm, it was not believed in France that Germany would be so reckless as to attack her eastern neighbors.

Europe, the French felt, was tired of its interminable wars that had perennially massacred its youth and laid waste so much of its land. Even Hitler, a common soldier twice wounded in the last one, was frequently quoted in the Paris press as saying so. Frenchmen hoped that war with Germany was now a thing of the past. They realized that because of her greater manpower and industrial strength Germany would be, as soon as she rearmed, militarily superior to France alone. At any rate, with the "lean years" arriving in the thirties, when for at least four years the number of available new conscripts would be reduced by nearly one half, the French army would be too small to be anything more than a defensive force.

To strengthen the country's defenses, new fortifications would be necessary—to compensate not only for the numerical weakness of the army but for the loss of the shield in the Rhineland when the last French troops were withdrawn from it in 1930. The French High Command, supported by Parliament, government, and public opinion, was determined that if the Germans attacked again, the industrial and mining regions along the northern and northeastern borders must be held at all costs. It was the loss of these regions in the first weeks of 1914 which had almost knocked France out of the war, depriving her of most of her sources of iron and steel and coal and much of her heavy industry.

Strong fortifications would not only stop the Germans along the border but would provide France with the *couverture* which was absolutely essential in order to have time to mobilize the reserves and deploy them behind the frontier. Since the French Army, deficient in motor transport, depended, as in 1914, largely on the railways to move troops and supplies, mobilization and deployment would take at least a fortnight, during which time the fortress line, it was calculated, would hold any surprise attacks in force. The army-in-being, less than half the size of that in 1914, was too small to accomplish this by itself.

THE MAGINOT LINE

It was these considerations that led to the hasty construction of the Maginot Line. Studied and debated and planned for nearly a decade by the War Council under Marshal Pétain and by a special military "Committee for the Defense of the Frontiers" under General Guillaumat, the last details of the new fortress line were finally approved in 1929 by Paul

Painlevé, the Minister of War, and the first installment of a credit of half a billion dollars for its construction voted by Parliament the same year. Work began in 1930, energetically pushed by the man who would give the project its name, André Maginot, a mutilated war veteran who served as Minister of War until his sudden death in 1932 from poisoning occasioned by eating bad oysters at a New Year's banquet. The main fortifications were completed in 1935, giving France, now gripped by fears of a rapidly rearming Nazi Germany, the most formidable line of defensive works the world had ever seen—and a complex about it, "the Maginot Line complex," that paradoxically would contribute to the military debacle in 1940 which the celebrated bastion was designed to prevent.

The trouble with the Maginot Line was that it was in the wrong place. The classical invasion route to France which the Germans had taken since the earliest tribal days—for nearly two millennia—lay through Belgium. This was the shortest way and the easiest, for it lay through level land with few rivers of any consequence to cross. It was the route the Germans had taken again in 1914.

The Maginot Line did not bar it at all. Its bristling guns, protected by tons of steel and concrete which no known bomb or shell could penetrate, lay further to the east, facing Germany proper along the frontier from the Luxembourg border to the Rhine. In Alsace along the west bank of the great river a secondary system of fortifications consisting of a double row of casemates was built to halt any German attack across the wide and swiftly flowing Rhine, itself a formidable barrier. The northeast corner of France was thereby well covered.

The problem of how to defend the northern frontier facing Belgium, immediately behind which lay most of the coal mines and a great industrial complex, if the Germans should again come that way nagged at the minds of the French High Command and the government throughout the interwar period. It was, admittedly, a difficult matter to resolve. To extend the Maginot Line westward along the Belgian border from Luxembourg to the sea would cost more than the French government could afford. Besides, if somehow it could be done it would offend the Belgians, who would feel themselves abandoned to the tender mercies of the Germans, whose massive armies, as 1914 had shown, they could never hope to prevent from overrunning their country. Belgium was too small in men and resources.

To sit on the long Belgian border, which had no fortifications of any consequence, and there await a great German offensive which had gathered momentum by a sweep through Belgium was out of the question. All through the late twenties and early thirties the French War Council debated the alternatives. There were two. Either fortify certain strong points along the northern frontier from the western edge of the Maginot Line to the sea so as to block the main gateways to northern France, or arrange to rush the French army into Belgium to help the Belgians meet the enemy as far forward as possible. In 1932 Weygand and Gamelin demanded the first solution and actually obtained preliminary credits from Parliament to begin the work. Pétain, surprisingly, in view of his past teachings, insisted on the second solution: the only way to defend the northern frontier, he argued, was to advance into Belgium as had been done belatedly in 1914.

But suppose the Belgians declined to ask for help and refused to allow the French to advance into their country? Premier Poincaré raised the question at a meeting of the War Council in 1927. In 1914, he reminded Foch and Pétain, the Belgians had for several days refused the French army permission to come in, and the delay had been costly. Suppose they objected again? The French, unlike the Germans, would never go into Belgium without being asked. Pétain, despite his reputation for keeping to the defensive, answered that the French would have to go in anyway.

The showdown on what to do came on March 7, 1934, when Marshal Pétain, at that moment Minister of War, appeared before the Army Commission of the Senate to answer questions. Weygand and Gamelin, as the ranking active heads of the Army, had renewed their demand for credits to build a number of fortified strong points along the Belgian frontier. Pétain opposed them. "To build fortifications on the frontier," he said, "would not protect them [the industrial regions] because they are too close to the border. *We must go into Belgium!*"

The question of the Ardennes Forest as a possible invasion route for the Germans came up at this meeting, and Marshal Pétain gave an answer that would be recalled six years later at Sedan, which faces the southwest exit of that hilly and wooded area. *"It is impenetrable,"* he responded confidently, "if one makes some special dispositions there. Consequently we consider it a zone of destruction. Naturally the edges on the enemy side will be protected. Some blockhouses will be installed. As this front would not have any depth the enemy could not commit himself there. If he does we will pinch him off as he comes out of the forest. This sector is not dangerous."

In 1940 against the Belgians and French and in 1944 against the American First Army the Germans would show how "dangerous" it was. But in this opinion too the French High Command would follow the advice of the "victor of Verdun"—with disastrous consequences.

So the vast Maginot Line was built and in 1935 completed and the long frontier adjacent to Belgium was left unprotected except for some light fortifications constructed at a few points from Montmédy, southeast of Sedan, to Dunkirk on the sea, which General Paul-Emile Tournoux considered were little more than "phantom works."[10]

No matter, the French people felt secure behind the great Maginot Line. They developed a "Maginot Line complex." The confidence that these fortifications would stop the Germans the next time with little loss of life to the defenders responded to a feeling deep in the consciousness of the French people, still exhausted from the bloodletting of the Great War. The complex took hold of almost everyone: if another German war should come, the youth of France would not again be slaughtered in opposing the old enemy or even be called upon to endure much suffering. The great caverns of the Maginot Line, built six and seven stories deep into the ground, had many comforts: air conditioning, clean messes, shower baths, reading rooms, and cinemas. From there the guns would halt the Hun. No more bloody, muddy trenches, as in 1914–1918.

There were a few in France, in the army and out, who had some doubts whether a purely defensive war fought behind formidable underground fortifications could ever be won or the country even saved from disaster by it. Napoleon's words were recalled: "It is an axiom of the art of war that the side which stays within its fortifications is beaten." General Guillaumat, who headed the Army's Committee for the Defense of the Frontiers, issued a warning as early as 1922, when his group was still studying the plans for the Maginot Line. "It is dangerous," he said, "to let the false and demoralizing notion spread that once we have fortifications the inviolability of our country is assured, and that they are a substitute for the rude labor of preparation of wills, hearts, and minds."[11]

But the country was in no mood to heed such sensible advice. It was easier and more comforting, once the northeast fortified wall was built, to fall into the Maginot Line complex, and to conclude smugly that at last, after a thousand years, the country was secure against attack. Little wonder then that the urgent plea of Colonel de Gaulle, backed in Parliament by the politician Paul Reynaud, that the Army immediately build up an armored force that could take the offensive was resented not only in the Chamber and Senate and in most of the press but in the highest circles of the military. The generals and civilians alike were proud (and to their credit!) that France, civilized and peaceful, gave no thought to attacking another country. She had no need of offensive arms. She was concerned only with defending what she had.

On March 15, 1935, there was a great debate in the Chamber of Deputies over military policy. Reynaud, with material supplied him by de Gaulle, pleaded for the establishment of an armored force capable of taking the offensive if the Germans struck in the east against France's allies or again in the west through Belgium. General Maurin, Minister of War, answered him:

How can anyone believe that we are still thinking of the offensive when we have spent so many billions to establish a fortified frontier! Should we be mad enough to advance beyond this barrier—on I don't know what sort of adventure?

The Army, the government itself, had spoken, and Parliament and the country approved.* If the Germans came again they would be halted

---

* Though the Chamber did nothing about Reynaud's proposal for an armored force, it did vote that day, 365 to 176, to raise the term of military service from one to two years.

and broken by the guns and the traps of the Maginot Line, in, under, and behind which the French troops would be sheltered in comfort, their lives spared. The French people had been put to sleep with a pleasant dream based on a false sense of security. The unprotected Belgian frontier was forgotten.

The very next day after General Maurin uttered his complacent words Adolf Hitler in Berlin tore up the Versailles Treaty and announced that Germany would immediately establish a conscript army of half a million men. Already in the *Kriegsministerium* in the Bendlerstrasse (which was part of the journalistic beat of this writer, then a correspondent in Berlin) young officers led by Colonel Heinz Guderian had worked out the plans and the tactics for a great offensive Panzer force, and they knew that from this day on they would have the money and the material and the men to swiftly fashion it.

13

DECLINE, III
THE WORLD DEPRESSION
SHAKES THE THIRD REPUBLIC
1931–1934

The Depression, which overwhelmed the United States beginning with the "Black Friday" of October 25, 1929, when the stock market crashed, came late to France.

All through 1929 and 1930 the "Poincaré prosperity" continued, unaffected by the American slump. At the end of 1929 the Treasury showed a large surplus, the vaults of the Bank of France were bulging with gold, the country's trade balance was exceptionally favorable, and the index of industrial production had risen to a new high of 144 against 137 in January. The good citizens of the Republic celebrated Christmas and New Year with the happy feeling that France was the most prosperous country in the world. The year 1930, which saw America floundering deeper in its economic and financial morass, closely followed by Germany and Great Britain, was almost as good as the previous one in France. Though prices and production began to fall, business on the whole was off by only 3 percent and unemployment, which had been nonexistent in 1929 (812 persons out of work), remained low (11,952 in December, 1930).

It was not until the autumn of 1931, following the crash of the great Kreditanstalt bank in Vienna, the financial panic in Germany, and, above all, the abandonment by Great Britain on September 21 of the gold standard and the 40 percent devaluation of the pound sterling, that the Depression really hit France. Stocks plummeted on the Bourse, the Treasury's surplus became a deficit, the trade balance turned unfavorable, industrial production fell by 22 points, unemployment doubled, and the index of wholesale prices slumped from 626 to 440.

The Depression was never quite as bad in France as in more industrialized Germany, Britain, and the United States. Unemployment, which was so massive and corrosive in the other lands, seldom rose above half a million. But the slump was bad enough, the worst economic and financial crisis the country had experienced in more than a hundred years, and it was aggravated and prolonged by the failure of the fumbling Parliament and the rapidly changing governments of the Third Republic to take sensible measures to cope with it. It was obvious that after Britain in the fall of 1931 and the United States in the spring of 1933 devalued their currencies by 40 percent France would have to follow suit or be shut out of the world markets, dwindling though they were. But until 1936, when it was too late, successive French governments refused to consider devaluation. The French, as we have seen, had developed a deep neurosis about the franc as the result of its fall in the mid-twenties. The "Poincaré franc" had wiped out four fifths of their savings. Maintaining it at its 1928 gold level was considered to be a sacred duty of the state lest the citizens once more be swindled. No Parliament, no cabinet, dared to devalue it again. The result was that France, alone of the great capitalist powers in clinging to gold, was priced out of the foreign markets. At home the governments followed a disastrous policy of severe deflation. Production was curbed, wages and salaries cut. Misery increased. And resentment.

But whereas in England and America the resentment took the form of grumbling against the government in power (President Hoover was blasted out of office in the elections of 1932), in France, as in Germany, it was directed more against the republican regime itself. In Berlin this discontent brought Hitler to power at the beginning of 1933 and led to the quick destruction of the democratic Weimar Republic. In Paris it spawned a number of right-wing leagues whose objective was to overthrow the democratic Third Republic. By the beginning of 1934 it seemed to their leaders that their time too, like that of Mussolini and Hitler earlier, had come.

The conservatives, returned to power in the elections of 1928 thanks to Poincaré's prestige, led the country during the first years of the Depression. New political figures had emerged from their ranks, chief among them André Tardieu and Pierre Laval, each of whom was three times Premier between the fall of 1929, after Poincaré's retirement, and the spring of 1932, when the electorate voted the Left back into power.

Tardieu, who took over the government in November 1929, when the country was glowing with prosperity and well-being, the legacy of Poincaré, was regarded by friends and enemies alike as a rising star, a worthy successor to Poincaré and indeed to Clemenceau, whose protégé he had been. Intelligent, dynamic, incisive, though handicapped in politics by a bristling arrogance and a scarcely concealed contempt for the masses, he wanted to make over his country's economy and political system after the American model, which he greatly admired. It is puzzling that so intelligent a Frenchman understood his fellow countrymen, who had not the slightest desire to emulate the Americans, so little. This curious failure quickly cost him his political life. Three times Premier between 1929 and

1932 he took his case to the country in that latter year and, despite a large slush fund provided him by big business and finance, was decisively defeated. Piqued, he gave up his seat in the Chamber in 1934, eventually joined one of the Fascist leagues, and poured out his rancor in violent articles in the venal right-wing weekly *Gringoire,* denouncing what he called the "invertebrate Republic" and calling for its replacement by an "authoritarian" system.

The Advent of Pierre Laval

Pierre Laval was more subtle and more enduring. A true son of the soil, from the rugged mountain country of Auvergne, he had a peasant cunning, a toughness and tenacity and a rude manner of which he was never ashamed even after he gained political power, and with it a material fortune which made him a millionaire. His father, descended from a long line of sturdy peasants, had been an innkeeper and butcher in the village of Châteldon where Pierre was born on June 28, 1883. From his mother, tender and devout, he inherited the dark complexion and slightly Oriental features that probably came from a Moorish invasion centuries before; and from her, against his father's wishes, came the encouragement to get out of the primitive hills and seek a higher education. Working his way through the lycée and eventually getting a university degree in law in Paris in 1909, he was admitted to the bar in the same year, capping the occasion by marrying a young woman from his native town to whom he remained devoted to his dying day. His family life was simple, harmonious, and altogether exemplary, but his political life turned out quite differently.

It had begun in 1914 on the eve of the war when, at the age of thirty-one, he was first elected deputy from the working-class Paris suburb of Aubervilliers as an extreme left-wing Socialist and pacifist. He opposed the war from the outset. His name was on the "Carnet B" list of dangerous agitators who were to be arrested at the outbreak of the conflict. He was active in the minority wing of the Socialist Party which agitated for a negotiated peace and which sent delegates to Switzerland to meet with the German Social Democrats to work for it. Like all Socialists he welcomed the Russian Revolution in 1917 with enthusiasm and pleaded with the Chamber to allow French Socialists to attend a peace meeting in Stockholm which the Russian revolutionaries had convoked. But he was already beginning to make that turn which would take him from the extreme Left to the far Right. Clemenceau, a shrewd and cynical judge of men, noticed it. He offered the young firebrand Socialist an undersecretaryship in his cabinet when he took over in 1917 with the iron determination to stamp out defeatism and pacifism and win the war. To the horror of his Socialist comrades, who detested and distrusted "the Tiger," Laval wanted to accept. Party discipline prevented him. But his road out of the Socialist Party, away from Marxist, revolutionary doctrines, had begun.

His ambition for office, his greed for wealth, got the better of his left-wing Socialist principles. In 1920 when the Party split, with the majority of members declaring themselves Communists and joining Lenin's Third International and the conservative minority under Léon Blum remaining loyal to the old Socialist Second International, Laval refused to remain with either group. He became an "independent socialist" and, soon dropping that label, simply an "independent" or "nonparty" politician. And though remaining mayor of Aubervilliers to the end, despite the overwhelming Communist majority of voters in the town—this was a peculiar but not uncommon phenomenon of French municipal politics—Laval drifted steadily to the political Right, amassing a considerable fortune as he went along and winning increasing confidence in the world of big business and finance, which he had once so unmercifully castigated.

His thirst for office was first satisfied in 1925 at the age of forty-two when Painlevé made him Minister of Public Works. During 1926 he served in three cabinets of Briand, in whose footsteps he seems at this time to have wanted to follow, perhaps not unmindful of the fact that the Premier, like him, had begun political life as a rampant Socialist. He joined two governments of the conservative Tardieu between 1930 and 1932. In fact he and Tardieu traded the top post during that time, each retaining the other in his cabinet. On January 27, 1931, Laval, having moved four years before from the Chamber to the Senate, achieved the goal he had long sought. He became Premier for the first time, remaining in that office until February 1932, through three successive conservative governments. The taste for the sweets of political power never left him.

Serving as Minister of Colonies in all three of his cabinets, incidentally, was a deputy from one of the moderate center parties whose Oriental features were even more pronounced than his. This was Paul Reynaud, a peppery little man like General Weygand, who came from hardy mountaineer stock in the Alps of Savoy, and, now a dapper lawyer and an economist, represented a fashionable Parisian district in the Chamber.*

Socialists, Communists, and the Alienation of Labor

Like the nation itself as the Depression-laden 1930s unfolded, labor was divided. Like its enemies on the extreme Right, though for different reasons, it felt itself alienated from the Republic.

Trade unionism was still bitterly fought by the employers and scarcely encouraged by the government, even when the government was radical and supported by the Socialists. And the unions weakened themselves by splitting into two hostile groups.

The collapse of the general strike in May 1920 had almost destroyed the trade-union movement in France. Ruthlessly put down by the govern-

---

* Reynaud had first become a minister in 1930 when he was named Minister of Finance in the second Tardieu government. He and Tardieu later broke over the latter's bitter opposition to devaluing the franc.

ment of the former Socialist Millerand, with troops, police, and strike-breakers, the work stoppage ended with hundreds of labor leaders in jail, the CGT (General Confederation of Labor) outlawed by the courts, and thousands of workers deprived of their jobs for having walked out. In despair, workingmen left their unions in droves. Before 1920 was out the membership in the CGT had dropped from 2,400,000 to 600,000. From then on for sixteen years 90 percent of French workers remained unorganized. They sank into a deep apathy, convinced that there was no hope for them—from the unions, from a hostile government, from a rural-dominated Parliament that had no comprehension of a city laborer's lot, or from the employers, who, encouraged by the collapse of the strike, were now determined to eliminate the unions completely, deal with their employees on an individual basis and on their own terms, and even to sabotage the eight-hour day, which Parliament had voted in 1919, and the mild social-insurance legislation which the two chambers were threatening to enact, and finally at the end of the twenties did.

Without collective-bargaining power the French worker found himself deprived of a fair share of the economic gains that came as prosperity returned to France after the first war. Real wages lagged behind the increase in profits and production. By 1929 they had risen only to 109 against a rise in the index of industrial production to 140. After the Depression hit, total wages fell by one third and unemployment rose sharply. But for a decade and a half labor submitted almost meekly to this diminution. There were few strikes. Employers welcomed what they called an era of "social stability" and "labor peace." Few among the prosperous middle and upper classes were aware or, if they were, cared—such was the gulf between the classes—that beneath the economic misery of the French workers was a moral one, which was perhaps even more degrading. A sense of humiliation, of oppression, of helplessness, came over them. It is not suprising that many of them became quite indifferent to the fate of the Republic whose Parliament and government seemed to them to have combined with the employers and the moneyed classes to shut them out of the French community. They were doing its labor but they were receiving few of its benefits or privileges and had little voice in it.

This was partly their own fault. They had split in two not only in their trade unionism but in their politics, and this division had helped to diminish both their economic and their political power. For this an event in a faraway land was responsible: the Bolshevik Revolution of November 1917 in Russia, the consequent establishment of socialism for the first time in history in a large country, and the launching of a world-wide Communist movement that was as hostile to the old Socialists of the Second International as it was to the capitalists. This sudden and staggering upheaval had terrified the bourgeoisie and pulled it together in France, as in the rest of the Western world, out of concern for its very survival. It had, on the contrary, been welcomed with enthusiasm by the French working class, whose leaders, like those in Germany, thought for a moment, that it might happen in western Europe too. It had not happened; the capitalist world in the West had proved too strong.

The Bolsheviks in Moscow had set out immediately to capture the Socialist parties and the Socialist-dominated trade unions in the West for Communism. They did not capture them but they did succeed in dividing them. During the week of Christmas 1920, at a special Party Congress at Tours, the Communists took over the French Socialist Party by a three to one vote, retaining not only the bulk of the membership but the party apparatus and its newspaper, *L'Humanité*. Léon Blum, an intellectual, a writer, a bourgeois, and a Jew, led the minority out of the Congress and set about to rebuild an independent French Socialist Party from the ground up. He and his few colleagues had refused to accept Lenin's twenty-one demands, which would have put the French Party completely under the orders of Moscow.

The French Communists, like other Frenchmen, were individualists, and their refusal to knuckle down completely to the dictates of the Executive Committee of the Third International in Moscow soon got them into trouble. Trotsky demanded a drastic purge in the French party. Hatchetmen were sent to Paris to enforce an iron discipline. Most of the old leaders, including L. O. Frossard, Secretary-General of the party, were expelled or forced to resign. By 1923 membership had fallen from 130,000 to 55,000. Most of the disillusioned dissidents rejoined the Socialist Party. But what the Communists lost in numbers they made up in militancy. A new crop of leaders emerged. Whereas the old Socialist chiefs had come, like Jaurès and Blum, from the middle class, and were intellectuals, the new leaders of the Communist Party were genuinely proletarian. Maurice Thorez, who at thirty would become the Party chief at the beginning of the thirties, had been a miner and construction worker; Jacques Doriot, a steelworker; Jacques Duclos, a pastry cook. Shaped and hardened by their early employment, scornful of the ideas and ideals of the earlier leaders of the workers' movements, and completely subservient to Moscow, they would fashion the French Communist Party into a truly revolutionary organization, dedicated to the overthrow of the regime.

The Communists were less successful in their efforts to capture the trade-union movement. In 1921, a year after they had led the majority out of the Socialist Party, they attempted to take over the Socialist-oriented CGT. But the majority of the unions in the Confederation was against them and they were able to persuade only a minority to leave and form the CGTU (Confédération Générale du Travail Unitaire). Like the Communist Party, it was soon beset with dissension and torn by purges, and most of the unions would have nothing to do with it. In 1936 it abandoned its divisive struggle and was absorbed into the CGT. But for fifteen years it had split and weakened the trade-union movement* as the Communist Party to the bitter end, except for the brief interval of the Popular Front in 1936, divided and weakened the working-class political movement.

THE REPUBLIC IN TROUBLE

The Republic was by now, as the Depression deepened, in grave trouble. The French elections in the spring of 1932 had once again, as in 1924, returned the Left to political power. And once again the Socialists, who had polled more votes than any other party and elected 131 deputies to the Chamber, refused to join the Radicals in forming an all-Left government, excluding the Communists, who had lost nearly a quarter of a million votes. It was no doubt logical for the Socialists under the leadership of Léon Blum to be hesitant in joining a "bourgeois" government, since to do so, he believed, might cause many of their more Marxist followers to defect to the militant Communists. But it was unreal for them to want to shape the policies of the new Left government without also assuming the responsibilities of sharing office. And it was irresponsible of them to join their enemies on the Right to overthrow Radical governments whose policy on this or that displeased them, as they soon began to do. In massacring a succession of Radical governments they not only facilitated the return of the conservatives to power but helped to discredit Parliament in the minds of the people, who were already despairing that the assemblies, whether dominated by the Right or Left, could ever bring the country out of the morass of the Depression and end not only the economic slump but the political chaos.

Having helped to overthrow Herriot on December 14, 1932, the Socialists joined the conservatives six weeks later in felling the government of Senator Joseph Paul-Boncour, who for decades had been a prominent member of the Socialist Party and only recently had changed to an "independent socialist." To meet a budgetary deficit of 11 billion francs, Paul-Boncour had proposed an increase in direct taxes of 5.5 billion francs and a reduction of government expenses by the same amount. The Right had opposed the first and the Socialists the second, and Paul-Boncour, a rather attractive figure in French politics (being a renowned lawyer at the bar, a flamboyant orator, a man of letters, a devoted "first nighter" at the theater, and possessed of a great mane of white hair and the handsomest face in Parliament) was through for life as a President of the Council, after his first try at it.

He bowed out after a 300 to 193 vote in the Chamber against him on January 28, 1933. Two days later Hitler became Chancellor of Germany. On that day France was without a government. Only the next day did one of the rising younger men in the Radical-Socialist Party, Edouard

---

* A Catholic trade-union confederation, the CFTC (Confédération Française des Travailleurs Chrétiens), had been founded in 1919, but it was too small in numbers to be very effective.

Daladier, succeed in forming a new government—the third Radical government in the seven months since the elections. His cabinet would prove more durable, lasting nearly nine months until it in turn was discarded with the help of the Socialists. Like most of the other ministers of the Third Republic he would return to office. Thus the two men who were destined to be heads of their respective governments when the final showdown between Germany and France began, Hitler and Daladier, had assumed the office for the first time within a day of each other.*

THE ADVENT OF EDOUARD DALADIER

In 1933 Edouard Daladier inspired a good deal of confidence in the country. Many believed that he was the man the Republic was looking for. He was known to be utterly uncorruptible. He seemed tough, intelligent, tolerant, and straightforward—the very qualities needed in a Premier if the government was going to make a forthright effort to solve its problems both at home and abroad. Born in 1884, the son of a baker in the little town of Carpentras in Provence, he had, like Laval, the hardy qualities of the French peasant though he was utterly without Laval's greed. Like Laval he had worked his way through school but unlike Laval he had fought for four years as an infantryman in the trenches, survived the slaughter at Verdun, and risen from a private in the ranks to captain of a company.†

At the University of Lyon, where he was a pupil of Herriot, whose political protégé he became and then his rival in the Radical-Socialist Party, Daladier had earned the difficult and rather rare degree of *agrégé d'histoire,* which signified a rigid training in the classics and in history. For some years he taught history and never ceased studying it, frequently turning to the reading of it for guidance and inspiration on a late evening after a rough day of political battle. Named minister for the first time in 1924 at the age of forty in Herriot's initial government, he served in seven more cabinets between 1925 and 1933 as Minister of Colonies, of Public Instruction and Beaux-Arts, and of War.

By 1933, when at the age of forty-nine he first became Premier, he was thus a seasoned minister and politician. Admirers called him the "bull from Vaucluse" (his electoral district) not only because of his broad shoulders and thick neck, which resembled a bull's, but because of his stubbornness and his rather rude manner of attack. France, they said, needed such a man at this moment to straighten it out.

But was he really such a man? There were a few doubts and they would grow. His political enemies said he was a bull all right, but "with horns like a snail." Bull-like though he seemed to be in appearance and

---

* A third figure came on stage as head of government at almost the same moment. This was Franklin D. Roosevelt, who became President for the first time on March 4 that year.

† The Abbé Desgranges, a deputy from Morbihan, who had served in his infantry company, paid him a fine tribute. When asked if Daladier had been a good officer, he replied: "Better than that. He was a good soldier."[1]

manner, one could not but notice his ample, thoughtful forehead, his sad eyes, his sometimes melancholy air, that denoted more a man of thought and contemplation than a man of action. It was noted by those close to him what an agony it seemed to be for him to come to a tough decision, though this, they thought, sprang from an intelligence and a profound sense of responsibility rather than from a flaw in the will.

Though Daladier's first term as Premier lasted nearly nine months, three times longer than the average at this period, there was scarcely time enough for the new Radical leader to prove himself. He fell on October 24, 1933, over a relatively minor question of reducing the salaries of state employees. Albert Sarraut, a mediocre and colorless politician, but a power in the Radical-Socialist Party, succeeded him. His government lasted but a month, being overthrown on the same small issue as the previous one. The next government, that of Camille Chautemps, also a power in the Radical Party, whose slippery qualities were noted in the opening chapter, fared little better. After two months in office he resigned, for reasons which we shall shortly come to, without even facing a vote in Parliament.

Six governments in less than two years.* The Left majority, elected to the Chamber in 1932, simply could not agree on a program that would keep the government financially afloat and make at least a serious attempt to extricate the country from the slough of the Depression. Six radical Prime Ministers followed one another with dizzy speed but their ministers remained practically the same. The good citizens, especially those in Paris, where the boiling point of temperaments was lower than in the more stolid provinces, became less and less amused. A widespread feeling that the Parliament of the Third Republic was becoming, or had become, incapable of governing grew in intensity. Fed by the outbreak of a new financial scandal, which compromised a handful of cabinet ministers, deputies, law enforcement officers, and the courts themselves, aroused by a sensational and unscrupulous press, and exacerbated by the reckless propaganda of the mushrooming Fascist and antiparliamentary leagues, with their cries of "Down with the Robbers!", the anger of a considerable number of Parisians, especially of the middle and upper classes, exploded into violence. For the first time since the Commune of 1871 during the birth pangs of the Third Republic blood flowed in the streets of Paris and the Republican regime suddenly found itself in peril of its life.

---

* Would the women of France, surely among the most attractive in the Western World, have contributed something to the stability of the Third Republic if they had had the vote? The old men in the Senate never allowed the question to be answered. In 1919, by a vote of 329 to 95, the Chamber of Deputies had granted women equal suffrage. But the Senate refused even to discuss the matter and the bill died. The Radicals, it was said, feared that the women would vote the way the priests advised. And so alone among the democracies of the West between the wars, France refused to give women the vote. This mark of democratic progress and enlightenment would come only after the Second World War, and it was not until 1966 that French women received full legal rights that put wives on an equal basis with their husbands. The old Code Napoléon, which had made the husband the master of the household, took a long time to be liquidated.

BOOK THREE

The Last Years of the Third Republic 1934-1939

14

A FATEFUL TURNING POINT
FEBRUARY 6, 1934

$\mathbf{E}$arly in January 1934 I had come back to work in Paris. Long assignments in London and Vienna, in India and Afghanistan, and a year off writing in Spain had kept me away from France for considerable periods over the preceding four years. What struck me first on my return was the high pitch to which strife between Frenchmen had risen. Rancor and intolerance poisoned the air. There was growing resentment against the antics of Parliament and of the rapidly changing governments, which shirked responsibility for doing anything to alleviate the Depression. This was especially noticeable on the Right and among certain groups of war veterans, many of whose members in France, as in America, tended for reasons I have never understood to be led and dominated by reactionaries and demagogic know-nothings.*

Rowdy antiparliamentary leagues had sprung up like mushrooms and while a few of them seemed to be merely offshoots of the old antirepublican and anti-Semitic leagues that had come and gone during the last quarter of the nineteenth century, and were therefore traditionally French, most of them appeared to me to have a new and uglier quality that I had first seen in the Black Shirts in Fascist Italy and the Brown Shirts in Germany. In France too, they were now prowling the streets in their various colored

---

* It puzzled the political scientist René Rémond, who wrote: "While apolitical in its formal claims, the 'ex-serviceman's spirit' is in fact one of the modern components of the psychology of the man of the Right. . . . It seems to be almost a law that the war-veteran organizations move to the Right. The Stahlhelm, the American Legion, and the Croix de Feu are three examples which seem to prove it. By what mystery of political psychology does the . . . comradeship of combat, the wish to maintain the fraternity of the trenches, lead to an ideology of the Right?"[1] Though Rémond posed the question he did not attempt to answer it. Perhaps it defies rational explanation.

shirts, their jackboots echoing on the pavement, beating up decent citizens and howling for the downfall of the Republic.

Behind them, one soon learned, were certain powerful business and financial groups that were furnishing the money to keep them active and growing and which, on their own, while refraining from soiling the hands of their members in hooliganism of the streets, were spreading propaganda with the aim of inducing Frenchmen to get rid of their parliamentary democracy in favor of a totalitarian regime. The objective was no longer a form of Bonapartism or Boulangism, as it had been a half-century before. What the well-heeled reactionaries wanted was an up-to-date Fascist totalitarianism on the Italian and German model. Before the end of 1933 they felt confident enough to come out in the open and say so.

Ernest Mercier, one of the tycoons of the electrical and oil trusts, who, as we have seen, had founded the antiparliamentary movement Redressement Français, told an assembly of that group on January 24, 1934, in a capital already nervous over the growing rioting in the streets provoked by the leagues:

There is only one solution—and circumstances will soon impose it—and that is a government of authority, supported by an irresistible popular moral force. . . . This is the task to which we dedicate ourselves. And not one among us will stop until it has been accomplished.

Mercier had already lined up strong financial backing from the coal and the iron and steel industries, among others. Some of his colleagues were even more explicit. Already on November 25, 1933, the *Revue hebdomadaire,* one of the organs of the business community, had published an article by an important industrialist demanding the establishment of a corporative state on the Italian style and another piece by François Le Grix, a spokesman of big business, predicting that a *coup de force* was inevitable and imminent: "It will take place very simply and very quickly. The Chamber will be adjourned *sine die* and Paris put in a state of siege after demonstrations by taxpayers and unemployed." Leaders were already organized to carry it out, he wrote, adding: "Because the leadership may have to be ready to act within a few weeks it is better not to publish the names yet. But I can assure you that it is getting ready." Three days later the financial journal *Le Capital* informed its readers: "The best minds envisage the experiment of an authoritarian government on the model of those of Italy and Germany."

On January 29, the day after the two-month-old government of Camille Chautemps had resigned rather than face a hostile Chamber and a more hostile capital, one of the leaders of the Taxpayers League, which had been organized and financed by the peanut-oil king, Jacques Lemaigre Dubreuil, told a mass rally at Magic City: "We are going to carry out a march on the Chamber of Deputies, and if necessary we will use whips and sticks to sweep out this chamber of incapables." The popular Parisian press quoted his words on their front pages. Gustave Hervé, the old left-wing Socialist and pacifist now become a chauvinistic Rightist, took up the chant. In his newspaper *La Victoire* on January 10 he asked in bold type on page 1: "How can we get rid of this weak and rotten regime? Who is the leader who will emerge in France, as he emerged in Italy and Germany?" Though he did not publish his name that day, he had already picked the man: Marshal Pétain.[2]

The hero of Verdun was still widely regarded as the most "republican" of the generals but it was known in the upper military circles that he was losing faith in the Republic. A remark of his Chief of Staff that year that "the whole system has to be changed" was believed to represent the thinking of the Marshal.[3] He, like the other surviving marshals, Lyautey and Franchet d'Esperey, was already in touch with the antiparliamentary leagues and discreetly lending them encouragement. General Weygand himself, the Commander in Chief of the Army and a staunch royalist at heart, had been at odds with the constantly changing republican governments for years. By 1934 it was clear that the intellectual revolt of the Right against Parliament had spread to large sections of the Officer Corps. As the street riots in Paris spread all during January and the police seemed unable, or unwilling, to put them down, there were doubts in the government that the Army could be counted on to restore order.

THE LEAGUES

Middle- and upper-class youths, many from the universities or just out of them, formed the phalanx of the various leagues that in January had taken to the streets. The most active and effective of these was the royalist Action Française, whose storm troopers were organized as Camelots du Roi. Their spirits roused by the daily dose of inflammatory articles by Charles Maurras, the poet-philosopher leader of Action Française, by Léon Daudet, who possessed the most vituperative pen in Paris, and by Maurice Pujo, leader of the Camelots, in the daily newspaper *L'Action Française,* they staged their first big demonstration on January 9, the day Parliament reconvened after the holidays. They were repulsed by the police before they could get to the Chamber, though on the Place de la Concorde, just across the Seine from the Palais-Bourbon, they were able to haul the Minister of Marine, Albert Sarraut, out of his car and rough him up before he was rescued by the police.

Neither the government nor the public knew that behind the sudden activity of the royalist street brawlers as the New Year began lay more than merely a desire to take advantage of the revolt of rightist public opinion in Paris against Parliament. The leaders of Action Française had been secretly urged to become more active by the Comte de Paris, heir of the Pretender to the throne, the Duc de Guise. The young prince—he was twenty-six—believed that the time was ripe for a serious attempt to restore the Orléans monarchy to the throne of France.

At the first of the year he and his father had summoned three of the leaders of Action Française, Maurras, Pujo, and Admiral Schwerer, to Brussels, where the "royal" family lived in exile and had criticized them severely for their lack of action. The Comte was sure that the moment was at hand to bring the Republic down. The other leagues, the rightist war veterans, and the nationalist leaders who dominated the Municipal Council of Paris must, he said, be brought into a plot to stage a coup. "You failed to do anything in 1926," the Prince told the royalist leaders from Paris. "This time you have the opportunity to do something. Will you take it?"

A royalist could scarcely say no to the "king" or his heir. And though almost speechless from the unexpected dressing-down they had received, the three leaders answered yes.[4] Apparently they did not dare to remind the Prince or his father that though the other leagues and their financial bankers in industry would cooperate with the royalists in trying to bring down the government and even the Republican regime, they were not interested in bringing back a monarchy. They considered that issue dead in France. What they wanted was an authoritarian government on Fascist lines which they could dominate. Moreover they did not intend to let the Action Française take the lead in the street fighting. When the Camelots du Roi got a jump on them in staging the demonstration on January 9, they began to mobilize their own forces.

By the outset of 1934 several other leagues were getting headlines in the newspapers. Among the oldest was an organization of street brawlers called "Jeunesses Patriotes," recruited mostly from university students, which a right-wing deputy from Paris, Pierre Taittinger, had founded in 1924 during the financial crisis of that time. Its strength had waned during the Poincaré recovery but recently as the Depression grew worse and the Parliament and government more impotent it had begun to grow again. Actually it was an offshoot of the old League of Patriots of Déroulède, which had led the agitation and the street demonstrations during the Boulanger and Dreyfus affairs. It did not aim to overthrow the Republic but to make it authoritarian on Bonapartist and Boulangist lines, strengthening the executive, curbing Parliament and, borrowing from the programs (if not the practices) of Fascism and National Socialism, restrain big business and limit profits. According to the police records, it had in 1934 a membership of some 90,000 in the country, of whom 6,000 were in Paris. Its street-fighters were organized in mobile squads of fifty men, outfitted in blue raincoats and berets, and commanded by a retired general named Desofy. Though some of its young toughs had royalist sympathies the leaders considered Action Française to be a deadly rival.

Somewhat similar in ideology was an organization called "Solidarité Française," founded in 1933 and financed by the wealthy perfumer François Coty, who had continued to dabble in the backing of right-wing movements and newspapers, apparently under the delusion that like another famous Corsican (Coty's born name was Spoturno) he might end up at the top, as Napoleon had. The titular leader of the movement was Major Jean Renaud, a retired colonial army officer with a gift for rabble-rousing oratory but devoid, like his backer, of political sense. His storm troopers were oufitted in blue shirts, black berets, jackboots, and their slogan was "France for the French." Though they claimed a membership of 180,000 in the country, of whom 80,000 were supposed to be concentrated in Paris, it is doubtful if they ever numbered more than one fifth of that. At the start of 1934 they had reached their peak and were proving their militancy in the street.

The most fascist of the leagues was one calling itself "Le Francisme," which drew its inspiration from Hitler and Mussolini, and was founded on Armistice Day, November 11, 1933, by a right-wing adventurer named Marcel Bucard. It openly worked for an outright Fascist regime in France. Though its rowdies were among the most adept street-fighters it never caught on with more than a few thousand youths. Among its bright young recruits was Paul Ferdonnet who later would achieve notoriety as the "radio traitor of Stuttgart," when he sold out to the Nazis at the beginning of the second war and broadcast Nazi propaganda in French from the radio station there.

More important in numbers and in the backing it received from a surprisingly large segment of conservative circles was the Croix de Feu, founded in 1927 as a nonpolitical association of decorated war veterans and taken over in 1931 by an energetic forty-five-year-old lieutenant colonel by the name of François de La Rocque who had recently retired from active army service. He quickly transformed it into a paramilitary, antiparliamentary league, able to mobilize street demonstrators on an hour's notice and determined to stamp out Communism and pacificism and reform the Republic by curbing its erring Parliament. Though Colonel de La Rocque struck most people as a courtly gentleman, he had demonstrated his tougher qualities as early as November 27, 1931. On the evening of that day he led a mob of Croix de Feu members, assisted by storm troopers from Action Française and the Jeunesses Patriotes, into the great hall of the Trocadéro, where thousands of persons were attending the final gala meeting of the International Disarmament Congress and broke it up. Though some of the most distinguished men in France and in Europe were on the platform, including former Premier Painlevé, Lord Robert Cecil, Salvador de Madariaga and the chairman, Edouard Herriot, they were swept away by Colonel de La Rocque and his rowdies while other assault groups cleared out the audience and even the police who had been sent to protect them. All of France heard the tumult, for the proceedings were being broadcast, and La Rocque, in a sense, was made.

He was not a very intelligent man nor did he have much political sense. But he was a good organizer and he labored hard at working up a *mystique* about himself, for the movement's objectives were purposely vague so as to draw as many adherents as possible. At the time of the Trocadéro riot he was in close touch with Laval and Tardieu, who alternated as Premiers in those days, and who gave him not only moral support but—it seems certain—financial backing from secret funds of the state, which La Rocque was trying to undermine. Private funds also were not lacking, for among his backers were such business leaders as Ernest Mercier and François Coty. By the end of 1933, as the hostility against Parliament mounted in Paris, the Croix de Feu and its auxiliary bodies had some 60,000 members, of whom a third were in Paris.

Most of the veterans of the war had stuck to the two old organizations of ex-servicemen which were largely nonpolitical except as pressure groups: the UFC (Union Fédérale des Combattants) with nearly a million members, and the UNC (Union Nationale des Combattants) with slightly less. The first was dominantly liberal and radical, reflecting the mass of the electorate, especially in the provinces. The UNC was more conservative and nationalist, especially in Paris, where its leaders began to itch to get into the streets with the leagues.

But even the moderate war veterans in the UFC were becoming fed up with the shenanigans of Parliament. On November 26, 1933, after the overthrow of the three-week-old cabinet of Albert Sarraut, the council of the UFC, which was regarded on the Right as somewhat "leftish," had taken the unprecedented step of attacking the "political disorder, lack of courage," and corruptness of Parliament and of "warning it for the last time" that unless the new government then being formed by Chautemps mended its ways and did something to combat the Depression there would be a crisis not only of government and Parliament but of the *Republican regime itself*. The senators and deputies paid no heed to this warning or to any other. They seemed strangely indifferent to public opinion, at least that of Paris, and supremely unaware of their growing irresponsibility. They fiddled along in their accustomed ways while the country sank deeper into a morass and the resentment of the people, especially in the capital, simmered toward the boiling point.

It was in this charged atmosphere as the New Year of 1934 came that a new financial scandal involving not only a veteran crook but his confederates among certain politicians, cabinet ministers, police, and even magistrates of the court burst upon the front pages of the daily newspapers.

THE STAVISKY AFFAIR

The Third Republic had been plagued from time to time with certain financial scandals in which a few cabinet ministers, past or even present, and members of Parliament had been shown to be in cahoots with shady or downright crooked promoters. The Panama and Wilson scandals had momentarily shaken the country in the closing years of the nineteenth century and aroused a certain amount of feeling against the corruptness of the republican parliamentary regime. The corruptness of the press, so glaringly exposed in the Panama Affair, was overlooked, perhaps because it was taken for granted.

In 1928 there had begun a new cycle of politico-financial scandals, which the enemies of the Republic were quick to exploit and which indeed did excite public opinion. On the eve of Christmas that year, two cases of financial skulduggery involving politicians had given the antirepublican press something to bite on. Louis-Lucien Klotz, who had been Clemenceau's Minister of Justice and one of the signers of the Versailles Treaty, was arrested for passing bad checks. His passion for horse races and other forms of gambling had got him into trouble. But the affair which received the biggest headlines was the arrest at the same time of Martha Hanau (a dumpy lady of forty with short-bobbed hair and a manner that attracted certain men, including politicians), on charges of having swindled investors in her various financial enterprises of millions of francs. It became a *cas célèbre* in France for seven years, during which the redoubtable Madame Hanau was in and out of jail, once getting out by going on a hunger strike, her trial and then her appeal from conviction being continually delayed year after year. Finally in 1935 she was packed back to prison, where she promptly killed herself.

The pattern of the Hanau affair was to be repeated in subsequent financial scandals. The lady was able to defraud the public because she had "connections." She knew cabinet ministers, senators, deputies, had close relations with the French Foreign Office, and used some of her easy money to subsidize newspapers, including one of the leading Paris "leftish" dailies, *Le Quotidien.* She published her own weekly, *Gazette du Franc et des Nations,* which if it often served to "defend the franc" and the brotherhood of nations, as she said, also enticed tens of thousands of innocent investors to fork over large sums to her questionable enterprises. But how could the average citizen suspect the lady when the most eminent statesmen in France contributed articles to her publication, among them Premier Poincaré himself, and Foreign Minister Briand and Education Minister Herriot and even the Cardinal Archbishop of Paris, none of whom had the faintest notion of what Madame Hanau was up to.

Not innocent at all were the politicians involved in the next financial scandal to land on the front pages, the Oustric affair. Oustric, the son of a small-town café proprietor, had managed, after numerous business failures, to set up a small bank in Paris named after himself. His specialty was to float stocks of dubious quality, push up their value on the market by false publicity, sell them at the peak, and then rebuy them when they had fallen, and begin the operation all over again. In 1926 Raoul Péret, the Minister of Finance in Briand's seventh cabinet and so highly regarded in the Chamber that he seemed certain soon to become a Premier, authorized Oustric to float on the Paris Bourse the stock of an Italian rayon company, Snia Viscosa. The financial experts of the Treasury had opposed it because of Oustric's shady reputation as a banker, but Péret had overruled them. The commercial attaché of the French Embassy in Rome had also opposed the transaction but had been overruled by his Ambassador, Senator René Besnard. The next year, Péret, out of office but still a deputy in the Chamber, became the chief lawyer of the Oustric bank at a fat annual fee. Besnard, having quit the Rome Embassy and returned to the Senate, became the lawyer of one of Oustric's companies—at an even larger fee.

In 1930 the Oustric Bank and its subsidiaries were unable to meet their payments and closed down. The courts ordered an inquiry into the matter, but Péret, who had now become Minister of Justice in Tardieu's second cabinet, quashed it. When the facts leaked out the Senate overthrew Tardieu, and Péret and Besnard were haled before the senior assembly, acting as the High Court of Justice. Ultimately the Senate found them not guilty of breaking the law but in large circles of public opinion their *moral* guilt appeared to be proved. Once again there was an outcry in the press against the corruptness of the republican regime.

Other such scandals, too many and too detailed to be recounted here, followed, including the Aéropostale affair, which involved the financial difficulties of a leading French airline and its connections with politicians, chief of whom was the company's lawyer, Pierre-Etienne Flandin, who from 1929 to 1932 had been either Minister of Commerce or Minister of Finance in the six successive cabinets of Tardieu and Laval. The public, especially in volatile Paris, was surfeited with such doings. If Parliament and government would not clean up their own houses then the people of Paris might have to take to the street, as they had in 1789, 1830, 1848, and 1871.

It was against this background that at the beginning of 1934 the affairs of a long-time swindler with astonishing connections in the highest and supposedly most respected circles of the Republic burst into light and provoked the crisis of February 6. On the morning of December 30, 1933, as the good citizens were getting ready to celebrate New Year's Eve as best they could in the midst of a deadening Depression, the newspapers announced that a warrant for the arrest of one Serge Alexandre, alias Sacha Stavisky, had been issued in connection with the floating of fraudulent bonds by the municipal pawnshop of Bayonne. The headlines were small, the name unknown to the public, and most readers presumed that it was the case of just another crook being uncovered. Then suddenly the story burst like a fury through the press and the country. A good deal promptly became known about Stavisky and even more about his highly placed "connections" and how he used them to help perpetrate his frauds and stay out of jail.

Serge Alexandre (Sacha) Stavisky, born in 1886 in Kiev of Russian Jewish parents in modest circumstances, had come with his family at the turn of the century to Paris, where the father set himself up as a dentist in one of the poorer quarters. At twenty-two Sacha had his first brush with the authorities over a minor fraud and in 1912, when he was twenty-six, received his first sentence for another. His father, out of chagrin at the wayward life of his son, committed suicide, but this seems to have had little effect on the young man. By this time, shunning work, he had drifted into the petty underworld of Paris, living off women, drug peddling, confidence games, forgery, the disposal of stolen bonds, and an occasional armed robbery, and developing a remarkable ability to escape the clutches of the law. Gradually he rose in the world, accumulating money from this shady practice and that, frequenting the gambling salons of the French resorts, buying a theater, financing a newspaper, showing himself around with fancy mistresses, acquiring politicians and even ingratiating himself, whenever he felt the law breathing down his neck, with the Sûreté Générale, the state secret police, for whom he sometimes served as an informer in the shadowy world of crooks and adventurers.

Finally in 1926 he got into real trouble when he was arrested on the complaint of a couple of stockbrokers who charged him with mulcting them out of 7 million francs. Put behind the bars in the Santé prison in Paris, he languished there for eighteen months while the authorities were trying to unravel the tangle of his swindles. Released in 1927 on provisional liberty ostensibly to face trial, he never again had to face that inconvenience. Thanks to his friends and supporters in the Justice Department, the courts, the police, the Parliament, and in certain ministries, his trial never took place. It kept being postponed until, at the beginning of 1934, it had been put off nineteen times over a period of seven years. In the meantime Stavisky was back at his old practices, the only ones he knew, growing richer, buying two newspapers, one of the Left, the other on the Right (*Volonté* and *Rampart,* respectively), acquiring one of the capital's leading theaters, the *Empire,* and a stable of racing horses and enlarging his circle of friendships among politicians, ministers, and ex-ministers, police officials and newspaper publishers and editors. During this affluent period his murky affairs came to the attention of the police on forty-five occasions. Not once was anything done about them. The obsessive swindler seemed to be above and beyond the law.

Responsible for the nineteen postponements of his trial was the head of the Paris Parquet, Chief Prosecutor Pressard, who happened to be the brother-in-law of the Premier of the moment, Camille Chautemps, for long a power in the dominant Radical Party. The man who actually did the postponing appeared to be an assistant prosecutor in the Paris Parquet, one Albert Prince, whose body shortly would be found mangled on the rails of the Paris-Dijon railroad line.

The longer his trial was put off the more money Stavisky made in a whole string of fraudulent enterprises. One of his favorite rackets was to have himself named, through his pull with politicians, the agent for the floating of a city's municipal bonds. He would "cover" them with deposits of false or stolen jewels or by fictitious bookkeeping, discount them at a legitimate bank, and use the money to found a new company of dubious purpose. In this way he had made off with 10 million francs of municipal bonds of the city of Orléans in 1928 but had managed to repay them before he was caught. At Bayonne, practicing the same chicanery with the help of the mayor, who was also a Radical-Socialist deputy in the Chamber, he ran into trouble when he could not make good on bonds becoming due. On Christmas Eve, 1933, one of his confederates in the city government there confessed that 239 million francs' worth of bonds had been floated either by falsifying the accounts or by being "backed" by Stavisky's faked or stolen jewelry. The man was arrested, so was the mayor-deputy, as well as another Radical deputy, the publishers of two Paris newspapers Stavisky had subsidized, Albert Dubarry of the "leftish" *Volonté,* a sort of fabled blackmailer in Paris of those days, and Camille Aymard, of the "rightist" *Liberté,* and various other accomplices.

On January 3, 1934, *L'Action Française,* the first Paris newspaper to scent a scandal in the affair, published the text of two letters in which Albert Dalimier, the then Minister of Colonies, had written two years before when he was Minister of Labor and Social Welfare. Dalimier, in his official capacity, had strongly recommended to the insurance companies and other investment groups that they buy up Stavisky's Bayonne municipal bonds, which, on such assurance, they had done. Exposed, but protesting his innocence, Dalimier promptly resigned from the cabinet.*

In the meantime Stavisky had disappeared and the police, whom he had sometimes served as stoolpigeon, were unable, or unwilling, to arrest him. It was known that the *Sûreté* had recently furnished him with a false passport. Perhaps the police hoped he would flee abroad. But with the headlines in the Paris newspapers screaming that he be found and brought to justice and with public indignation mounting, the police finally tracked him down in the winter resort of Chamonix. On January 8 the newspapers announced that Stavisky had committed suicide just as the police were breaking into the villa where he had been hiding. Few Frenchmen believed it. They were sure the police had murdered the crook with so many connections to prevent him from exposing them.†

---

* The name of Georges Bonnet, the Minister of Finance in the Chautemps government, also cropped up in the scandal. The Investigating Committee of the Chamber later called it "regrettable" that Bonnet allowed a Stavisky aide to operate in the Ministry of Finance. The Committee noted also that in October 1922 Bonnet had lunched with Stavisky at Stresa during an international conference. The photograph of this meeting had been used by the swindler to show his connections in high political circles.

† A year later the special Parliamentary Investigating Committee concluded that while Stavisky "beyond a shadow of doubt" had shot himself as the police broke into the villa, his suicide had "been somewhat forced." The Committee made it clear that the police did not want to take the man alive. After describing how Stavisky had shot himself in the head, the lawmakers recounted how the police had let the wounded man lie on the floor for more than an hour without succor while he slowly died. "This extraordinary negligence," it held, "finished the task which Stavisky had begun. . . . Would it have been possible to take Stavisky alive? We believe the

Next day the tempers of a good many people of Paris rose swiftly toward the boiling point. This was the last straw, after the mounting revelations of the complicity of politicians and police with a long-time swindler. That morning, January 9, *L'Action Française* issued a ringing appeal on its front page for Parisians to gather after their day's work and march on the Chamber of Deputies to the cries of "Down with the Robbers! Down with the Assassins!" The call was really to mobilize their own forces. That evening, some 2,000 strong, they tried to reach the Palais Bourbon but were repulsed. Two nights later, on the 11th, the Jeunesses Patriotes, led by a municipal councilor, joined the royalist Camelots in a bigger demonstration. This time mounted units of the Mobile Guard had to be called out to prevent the rioters from reaching the Chamber and it was only the timely arrival of a large detachment of firemen with their hoses that held back the mob as it was breaking into the nearby Ministry of Public Works. For the first time the demonstrators tore down trees and railings and confiscated cars to form barricades in the streets. They overturned newspaper kiosks and set them on fire. They jammed the third-rail conduits furnishing electric power to the streetcars, which, along with public buses, were halted. A police report described the damage to public property as the worst in twenty years. The spirit of insurrection was spreading in the city. The next morning *L'Action Française* in blaring headlines called for "a revolt of Paris against the robbers," meaning the Parliament and government.

Premier Chautemps, underestimating the genuine resentment in Paris against the lax morals of the politicians, stubbornly refused to appoint a special committee to investigate the whole Stavisky mess. No doubt he was embarrassed by the fact that the public prosecutor responsible for postponing the swindler's trial nineteen times was his brother-in-law, and that his own brother, Pierre Chautemps, was a lawyer for one of the Stavisky companies. He saw in the growing street riots a plot by the Right to overthrow his Radical government. And being a wheelhorse politician of no deep convictions he was not unduly disturbed by revelations of a little corruption in politics. If it happened among his own people on the moderate left, he knew it also took place on the Right. Backed by a parliamentary majority in his refusal to air the Stavisky scandal, thanks to the votes of the Socialists, who feared that powerful reactionary forces were exploiting it in the hope of staging a Fascist coup supported by the right-wing Prefect of Police, Jean Chiappe, Chautemps merely threw more oil on the fire by demanding the muzzling of the press, which he held largely responsible for urging the rioters on.

The riots did go on, increasing in violence. There were large ones on January 22 and 23 and the biggest of all on January 27, which continued

answer is yes. Beyond doubt there was no attempt by the police to make a normal arrest and conserve for justice an accused of his importance."[5]

all through the afternoon and evening, during which much property damage was done and eighty police injured. That evening Chautemps, his shaky government further compromised the day before by the revelation that his Minister of Justice, Eugène Raynaldy, was involved in still a new financial scandal connected with the bankrupt Sacazan bank, and he himself finally shaken by the seriousness of the rioting that day, and perhaps by a new chant of the besieging mob that could be clearly heard in the Chamber, "Hang the Deputies!", resigned. It was the first time in the history of the Third Republic that a government backed by a solid majority in both chambers had given way to the menace of the streets. The leagues had won their first victory. They had overthrown a "leftish" government. The triumph merely whetted their appetite.

DALADIER TRIES TO STEM THE TIDE

Weeping and wailing about the chaotic state of affairs the President of the Republic, Albert Lebrun, tried to persuade a predecessor of his, Gaston Doumergue, to abandon his rural retreat in the south and return to the troubled city and form a "national government of truce." Doumergue refused on the grounds of age; he was seventy-one. Lebrun next appealed to the presidents of the two chambers, Jules Jeanneney of the Senate and Fernand Bouisson of the Chamber. They too had no relish for the job, and on their advice Lebrun turned to Edouard Daladier, a Radical-Socialist untouched by the Stavisky scandal or by any other, and who was still widely believed to be a man of strong determination who could clean up the current mess.

Daladier tried first to form an all-party government from the Socialists to the Right, but he was turned down by both groups and finally had to settle for a cabinet drawn largely from his own party, as was the previous one, with the addition of two moderates, François Pietri as Minister of Finance and Colonel Jean Fabry, a one-legged war hero, as Minister of War and National Defense. The key post of Minister of Interior was given to a young ex-Socialist, Eugène Frot, who was reputed to be a coming "strong man" on the Left but who was suspected by some of having dictatorial ambitions and of being in secret contact with the rightist leagues.

Daladier immediately promised that he would do what Chautemps had refused to do, set up a Parliamentary Committee to investigate the Stavisky affair, and that in the meantime he himself would move "fast and firmly" against those already compromised in the scandal, whether they were in Parliament, the police, or the Justice Department. Completing his cabinet on the last day of January, the new Premier proceeded to be as good as his word. According to his later testimony he sat up throughout the night of February 2 personally reading the prosecutor's dossier on the Stavisky scandal and two other confidential reports on how the two police services, the Sûreté Générale and the Paris Prefecture of Police, had handled it. Since the Sûreté, as has been noted, had had peculiar relations with the swindler, to say the least, and since the popular Prefect of Police in Paris, Jean Chiappe, had personally received the crook at least once in his office and was moreover a close friend of the shady editor Dubarry, who was already in jail for his complicity with Stavisky, and furthermore since the police file on the man was a bulging one but strangely silent on any action taken, Daladier determined to take action.

But he acted clumsily. Instead of firing the two police chiefs and Prosecutor Pressard at least for negligence he tried to kick them upstairs. Chiappe was appointed to the highest administrative post in the government service, Resident-General in Morocco. Pressard was boosted up to the High Court as a judge. And Thomé, the Director of the Sûreté, was named, of all things, Director of the great and classic state theater, the Comédie-Française, in place of an eminent man of the drama, Emile Fabré, who was in disgrace with the Radicals because he was putting on a play that winter which they considered to be "antidemocratic"—Shakespeare's *Coriolanus,* no less. "A policeman running the *House of Molière!*" exclaimed a British correspondent in Paris, Alexander Werth, and his indignation and amazement were shared by most Parisians regardless of their political color.[6] To the sober but liberal historian François Goguel, this was "vaudeville."[7]

It was also inevitably fated to kick up a storm in sophisticated, mercurial Paris. Stavisky was momentarily forgotten in the fury over the replacement of Chiappe. The temperamental, dashing Prefect of Police, a passionate Corsican, became overnight the new martyr of the Right. Anger over his being "fired" and, without much doubt, his own intrigues with the rightist leagues, which followed from his boiling resentment, helped precipitate the crisis of the next few days.

The Chiappe Affair, as it was now called, complicated and confused the issue and added to Daladier's difficulties. The Premier was accused of sacrificing the police chief in exchange for votes from the Socialists, who detested Chiappe, believing that he harbored visions similar to those of another Corsican, Napoleon, of staging a coup d'état. Moreover, they noted, as did everyone else, the contrast between the police coddling of the rightist demonstrators and the savagery of Chiappe's men to Socialist and especially Communist demonstrations. Indeed the policemen's union had protested to the Prefect the gentleness being shown the antiparliamentary rioters. Later it would tell the Parliamentary Investigating Committee that the police were given to understand that they must treat the rightist demonstrators more leniently than they had the leftist.

The Radicals and the Socialists, on whose support Daladier depended for survival, also suspected Chiappe of being secretly allied to the reactionary leagues. Chiappe's reaction to his dismissal appeared to them to bear this out.

On Saturday morning, February 3, Daladier telephoned Chiappe at his home and asked him to come to see him. When the Prefect protested that he was in bed with an attack of sciatica—the illness seems to have been more diplomatic than real—the Premier then told him over the phone of his "promotion" to the top post in Morocco. Chiappe angrily refused to be kicked upstairs. There was a heated exchange, at the end of which the police chief said menacingly, according to Daladier: "All right, you'll find me tonight in the street!" This meant to the Prime Minister that the chief of the capital's police was going to join the Fascist demonstrators in the street, and he dismissed him forthwith. Later, Chiappe would deny the statement, insisting that he had merely said he would be out in the street, ruined and jobless. Given Chiappe's hot Corsican temper and capacity for resentment, the Premier's version seems the most credible, and was buttressed by the testimony of a witness, Frot, the Minister of Interior, who was at Daladier's side and listened to the conversation, Chiappe's angry, high-pitched voice coming in loud and clear, even over the notoriously crude Paris telephones of that era.

At any rate, on February 3 Chiappe was out, the two moderate members of the cabinet, Pietri, also a Corsican, and Colonel Fabry, his close friends, resigned, and the Fascist leagues had a new cause, in addition to the Stavisky scandal, to resume fighting in the street. They seized on it avidly.

Over the weekend the streets had been quiet. On Monday evening, February 5, Colonel de La Rocque had mobilized some of his Croix de Feu shock troops for a sort of a rehearsal. They had scuffled with the police in an attempt to storm the Ministry of Interior but had been repulsed. Tuesday, February 6, the date on which the Chamber of Deputies reconvened to vote on the new Daladier government, was to be the big day for the leagues. On the morning and afternoon of that day the big-circulation dailies, as well as the political newspapers of the Right, such as *L'Action Française*, carried flaming appeals from the various leagues calling on their members and all Parisians who sympathized with them to take to the streets that evening in a massive demonstration against the government. It was a call to insurrection, or at least to violence that might lead to insurrection. The envenomed royalist journal had appealed on the 5th for bloody vengeance, singling out Frot and others by name as among those who would be "killed without mercy."

To further inflame the populace of Paris several newspapers—including such conservative journals of large circulation as *Le Jour, La Liberté* (whose director was already in jail as a Stavisky accomplice) and the usually responsible *Echo de Paris*—had carried false reports that the government had secretly brought into the capital tank squadrons, machine-gun companies, and black Senegalese troops to "mow down" the "peaceful" demonstrators. Most of the Paris press also published that day a letter to the President of the Republic from the Federation of Taxpayers protesting that "black troops, backed by tanks, cannon, and machine guns" were to be thrown by the government "against the people of Paris, who are considered the enemy."

Finally, all the great newspapers of the capital, including the sober *Temps,* published not only the hysterical appeals of the leagues to the populace of Paris to rise up against Parliament and government and chase the "robbers" from the Chamber of Deputies, reconvening that day, but carefully noted on their front pages the exact time and place for each group and its sympathizers to meet in case they had failed to receive more direct messages. The Paris press was behaving even more irresponsibly than usual. Only *Paris-Soir* among the large-circulation newspapers urged the people to remain calm.

At the last moment the Communists got into the act. On the morning of February 6 *L'Humanité,* the Communist daily, called on all party members to join the demonstrations that evening. The small Communist war-veterans group, the ARAC (*Association Républicaine des Anciens Combattants,* founded in 1919 by the writer Henri Barbusse), which had some 5,000 members in Paris, was to take the lead. Thus the Communists did not hesitate to join their worst enemies on the Extreme Right in demonstrations aimed to bring down the republican government. I had seen this duplicity in Berlin in the last months of the Weimar Republic when the German Communist unions had joined the Nazi unions in carrying out a strike that paralyzed public transport. They would do anything, they said, to topple the "bourgeois" German republican government, which at that moment was even more shaky than the French on February 6, 1934. By joining the Nazis they had helped bring it down, but in its place they had got Hitler, who proceeded to annihilate them. I was not much surprised that evening to find on the Place de la Concorde French Communists at the side of royalists and Fascists pelting the police who blocked their way to the Chamber of Deputies.

The Battle on the Place de la Concorde

Late on the afternoon of February 6 I was assigned by the Paris *Herald* to go down to the Place de la Concorde, across the Seine from the Chamber, to see if the threatened demonstrations showed any signs of developing. I had read the accounts in the morning newspapers of the meeting places of the various leagues and had noted that they formed a wide circle around the Palais-Bourbon, on which the demonstrators planned to converge. I found a few hundred young men, shock troops from Action Française, Jeunesses Patriotes and Solidarité Française, trying to shove back the police toward the bridge that leads from the great square across the Seine to the Chamber. But they were easily dispersed by the police, who numbered about one hundred, backed up by another hundred Mobile and Republican Guards. After phoning the office, I went into the Hôtel Crillon on the north side of the Place for a bite to eat. It did not look as if it would turn out to be much of a story. The demonstrations I had seen on previous evenings had been much rougher.

But when I emerged onto the Place de la Concorde an hour later— about 6:30 P.M.—the scene had changed. The square was packed with several thousand demonstrators who were standing their ground against repeated charges of mounted, steel-helmeted Mobile Guards. Over by the obelisk in the center a bus was on fire. I worked my way through the Mobile Guards, who were slashing away with sabers, to the Tuileries, which overlooks the Place on the east side from an elevation of ten or fifteen feet. A mob was crowded behind the railings, pelting the police and guards with stones, bricks, garden chairs, and iron grilles ripped up from the base of trees. It was here that I noticed for the first time Communists mingled with their supposedly Fascist enemies. Down on the broad square itself the fighting continued, with the crowd advancing and then retreating before charges of the mounted Guards. It was by no means an unequal fight. The rioters were using sticks with razor blades attached to one end to slash away at the horses and the legs of the men mounted on them and they were throwing marbles and firecrackers at the hooves. A number of horses went down and their riders were mauled. Both sides began to carry away their wounded.

To get a better view I went up to a third-floor balcony of the Hôtel Crillon overlooking the Place. About twenty journalists, French and foreign, were standing there against the railing and there was one woman whom I did not know. The first shots we didn't hear. Then the woman slumped to the floor. When we bent over her, blood was flowing down her face from a bullet hole in the very center of her forehead. She was dead, instantly.* The firing now became general—from both sides. It was difficult to see what was going on, for almost all the streetlights had been pelted or shot out. Later it would be established that a mob, mostly from Solidarité Française, had started to break through the last police barricade guarding the bridge leading to the Chamber, which the police chiefs had been instructed to hold at all costs. A few policemen and Mobile Guards panicked and opened fire with their automatic pistols, killing six rioters in front of them and the woman on the Crillon balcony across the square and wounding forty more. Finally the officers in charge got their men to stop firing. One of them, the director of the municipal police, and two senior officers were themselves injured, the latter seriously, and carried away to the Chamber of Deputies where a first-aid station had been hastily set up.

In the Chamber itself there had been pandemonium since 3 P.M. when the session called to vote on the new Daladier government had begun. The Premier himself was prevented from reading his ministerial declaration, his voice, by no means a weak one, being drowned out by the taunting shouts

---

* She was later identified as Madame Gourlan Corentine, thirty-three. She had been merely a spectator, one of three onlookers killed that night by pistol fire.

from the conservatives and Communists. The first kept yelling: "Resign!", breaking off to sing the *Marseillaise,* the national anthem. The Communists countered with shouts of "Power to the Soviets!" and broke off into singing the *Internationale.* Several times the deputies of the extreme Right and Left stepped from their benches to indulge in a free-for-all, being separated only after the intervention of the *huissiers* and the eminent and dignified quaestor of the Chamber himself. Not since June 1899, when Waldeck-Rousseau presented his government in the midst of the Dreyfus Affair, had there been such turmoil and violence in this chamber. Three times the Speaker suspended the session for fifteen minutes in order to calm the deputies, but in vain. At one interval the rightist deputy Jean Ybarnégaray strode over to the ministerial bench and tried to drag the Prime Minister off it by the coat sleeves. In the din and the confusion Daladier finally concluded that debate on the various interpellations was impossible and demanded a vote of confidence. This provoked a new uproar from the Right and a new suspension of the session.

It had hardly been resumed when the sound of firing from the Place de la Concorde was heard for the first time within the Chamber. "They're firing!" shouted Deputy Scapini, who had been blinded in the war. "You are a government of assassins!" Above the shooting could be heard the roar of the mob, and it seemed to be coming closer. A deputy shouted: "They are storming the doors of the Chamber!" Several of his colleagues quickly left the hall. Their uneasiness was not allayed by the sight of the corridors, which were now jammed with injured police and guards over whom a couple of doctors attached to the Assembly were working, administering first aid. Many wounded lay unconscious on the floor. To help restore them the valiant wife of the quaestor, Madame Barthe, sent to her rooms for several bottles of aged rum. The sight of the wounded, the sound of the clamor of the crowd and of the firing, caused a number of deputies who had left the debating chamber to steal out into the night. As one member later recalled, "the least courageous were not the last to depart." By the time the tumultuous session ended at 8:30 P.M. there were only five deputies, besides the cabinet members, on the floor of the House.[8] The Speaker, Fernand Bouisson, a dignified gentleman with a white beard, was found by one deputy to have hidden a slouch hat and an old dark overcoat under his rostrum to replace his topper and cover his formal dress suit, which the presiding officer customarily wore.[9] It would be a useful disguise in case it were necessary to make a quick getaway. For nearly an hour there was a general fear that the rioters might storm the Chamber at any moment. In the press gallery the journalists hastily scrawled a sign on the door: "NOTICE TO THE DEMONSTRATORS: NO DEPUTIES IN HERE!"

Edouard Herriot's face was too well known to the public even if he had resorted to disguise, which he did not, and as the Radical leader was making his way home on foot a band of fifty ruffians seized him, roughed him up, and, to lusty shouts of "Throw him into the Seine!", which unfortunately was nearby, began to drag him toward the river. It was the wrong river for the veteran deputy, who also doubled as mayor of his native city of Lyon, by which flows the Rhône. "Messieurs!" he cried, "At least have the decency to conduct me to the Rhône!" A platoon of gendarmes rescued him just in time.

Before adjourning, the Chamber had given the new Daladier government three successive votes of confidence, the last by 343 to 237. The decisive majority was due to the support of the Socialists, whose leader, Léon Blum, had explained during the debate: "Our vote for the government is not a vote of confidence. It is a vote of combat!" The Socialists were not forgetful of what had happened to their party and to the democratic regime in Italy and Germany when Mussolini and Hitler had taken over.

Daladier had his parliamentary majority, but on this night of wild rioting it was not enough. The rage of the Parisians had to be taken into account too. The Premier was to learn this in the next crucial hours.

Though the deputies had left the mob remained in the streets, and after the firing began its mood grew uglier and more threatening. On the Place de la Concorde and on some of the streets on the Left Bank leading to the Chamber the situation had become graver. It began to seem doubtful if the police and the guards could hold the bridge or some of the side streets leading to the Palais-Bourbon much longer. The angry demonstrators did not yet know that the deputies already had cleared out of the Chamber and that the opportunity to achieve one of their objectives, to rough up the members of Parliament and chase them from their seat of power, had been missed.

We carried the woman's body down from the balcony to the lobby of the Crillon, where a good many injured rioters and spectators were lying on the floor, attended by well-dressed ladies attempting to administer first aid as best they could. As I stepped out of the hotel onto the Concorde I saw that the Ministry of Marine next door was on fire. A band of determined leaguers, someone said, had ignited rags soaked in gasoline and tossed them through the broken windows, from which heavy smoke now billowed. A couple of fire trucks had arrived, but before the firemen could get their hoses playing on the building the demonstrators had slashed them. They were now trying to force the entrance of the smoking Ministry. Naval guards were holding them back at pistol point.

Thousands of ex-servicemen were now joining the demonstrators. Shortly before 9 o'clock, on the Place and around the beleaguered bridge, the tumult suddenly ceased, the roar of the mob subsided, the sporadic firing stopped. And then we saw marching into the square from the Champs Elysées a long column of war veterans from the UNC, their decorations pinned on their breasts, singing the *Marseillaise* and holding high their flags and banners. Many carried signs: "UNC. WE WANT FRANCE TO LIVE IN

ORDER AND HONESTY."* Unlike the leaguers they did not seem to be in a very militant mood. The forces of order treated them with marked deference, saluting their flags. The main column turned north from the square into the rue Royale. A smaller group of about a thousand, mostly members of the Association of Veterans Decorated at the Peril of their Life, headed south for the bridge. There the two leaders, General Lavigne-Delville and Colonel Josse, the latter a former deputy and senator, parleyed with the municipal police chief, Marchand, who politely but firmly refused to let them pass over to the Chamber.

In the meantime the bulk of the war veterans had turned left from the rue Royale into the rue Saint-Honoré and had headed for two vital objectives in any insurrection: the Presidential Palace, inside of which M. Lebrun was already wringing his hands in dismay at the turn of events, and the Ministry of Interior, which administered the national police and guards. The ex-servicemen, stopped at a barrier by the police, now became belligerent, fought their way through the barrier and then a second one and arrived before the Palace, where they were met by mounted Republican Guards and pushed back. They returned to the Concorde in an ugly mood, having lost fifty-three badly injured and most of the rest nursing bruises from police sticks and the long swords of the horse guards. As they retreated toward the Concorde they were joined by thousands of adherents of the leagues and a large number of Communists.

It was this force, some 10,000 strong, that at about 10:30 P.M. began a fierce assault on the bridge and almost carried it. During the next hour it made twenty successive charges and though each was repulsed before the final barricade of police trucks by the gendarmes, Mobile and Republican Guards and by firemen who kept three hoses playing on the front ranks of the attackers, the mob kept re-forming and making a new attempt. The strongest attack of the evening came shortly before 11:30. The guardians were driven back and some of them started to flee for their lives over the bridge. It was at this moment that the police and guards again opened fire, in self-defense, and the rioters were halted at the edge of the bridge.

It was now near to midnight and the crazed and bruised demonstrators, a few of whom were firing sporadically on their own, now re-formed for what looked like a final assault. It seemed doubtful whether the police, guards, and firemen could hold them this time. Exhausted by nearly six hours of fighting, weakened by the loss of more than a thousand injured, and frustrated by orders not to use their firearms (their muskets had been taken away from them before the disorders broke out and they had only their revolvers) the police and guards appeared to have neither the force nor the

---

* Probably few marchers knew that the national president of the UNC, Henri Rossignol, was on the board of a Stavisky company that had perpetrated one of the crook's last and most extravagant swindles. It had the improbable name of Caisse Autonome de Règlements des Grands Travaux Internationaux.[10]

will to withstand another serious assault. Ten of the twelve firemen had been put out of action by flying missiles and weary policemen had taken over their three hoses.

It was then that the man of the hour emerged. Colonel Simon, commander of the First Legion of the Gendarmerie, had no command that evening. Early in the afternoon he had been asked by the Paris Prefecture of Police if he could scare up some gendarmes from the suburbs and surrounding towns and he had arrived at sundown with some 500 of them and turned them over as reinforcements to the Paris police. He remained at the bridge, as he testified later, merely to see how his men were doing. A bit after 11:30, Colonel Simon realized that the forces of order were too weak and demoralized to stem the assault if they merely tried to stand their ground. Part of the demoralization, he saw, came from the lack of leadership. The Prefect of Police, Bonnefoy-Sibour, who had replaced Chiappe three days before and was inexperienced, had acted throughout the evening as a spectator, nevously chain-smoking and refusing to give one single order, and the wounding of most of the assistant police chiefs had left the forces of order without a strong and recognized leader.

Colonel Simon therefore took charge himself. Acting on his experience in the war that had taught him that sometimes the best defense was the offense, he decided that the only way in which the situation could be saved was to attack and clear the square of the riotous mob. He asked the mounted guards to lead a charge and promised to follow at the head of gendarmes and Mobile Guards on foot to mop up. In a matter of a few minutes the square was cleared—and held. The colonel had done it without firing a shot. Encouraged by the success of the operation another group of police had set off to clear the Cours-la-Reine, adjoining the river at the left of the bridge, from which snipers had been firing from the trees that line the way and covering the demonstrators below. Several policemen lost their heads and opened fire, killing six rioters and wounding seventeen.

But it was the counteroffensive of Colonel Simon which cleared the Concorde, relieved the bridge over to the Chamber, and broke the riot. Shortly after midnight it petered out and by 2 A.M., when I returned to the shambles of the square after writing my story, it was deserted. The insurrectionists, nursing their wounds, had gone home; the bloodied police had dispersed, except for small groups guarding the bridge and the Chamber.

As I made my own way wearily home on foot, for there was no public transportation, I wondered what had become of the Croix de Feu, the best organized and the most formidable of the leagues. I knew it had been called out but I had not seen it at the side of the other war veterans on the Concorde all evening. It seemed a bit of a mystery and indeed would remain so. Next day I learned that one of its two columns, 2,000 strong, which had assembled on the Left Bank, had marched down the rue de Bourgogne, had been stopped at the corner of rue Saint-Dominique, two blocks from the Chamber, by a weak force of Mobile Guards and police, and just as it was storming this barrier with ease and preparing to pour into the Palais-Bourbon where the deputies were still in session—it was 7:30 P.M.—an order arrived from Colonel de La Rocque to pull back and to circle around toward the west of the Chamber and join a second group on the Quai d'Orsay before the Foreign Office.

An hour later, when the merged columns of the Croix de Feu, numbering some 4,000, began to scuffle with the police and guards in front of the Foreign Office and were on the point once more of breaking through and reaching the Chamber a block away, another order arrived from the colonel commanding his shock troops not only to pull back but to disperse for the evening. This was at 9 P.M., when the battle in the streets was far from over, the issue still undecided, and the Croix de Feu in a better position than the other groups to capture the Chamber and drive the politicians out.

The colonel seems to have been frightened by the extent of the insurrection that evening. Though he had inveighed against the perfidy of the republican Parliament this seems to have been largely because it was at the moment in the hands of the Radicals. Most probably he had no wish to overthrow the Republic, but merely to reform it, making it more conservative and nationalist, putting it in the charge of the traditional class from which he came. Though his movement would grow to formidable proportions during the next two years his ideas remained vague. On the morning of February 7 he issued a grandiose statement: "The Croix de Feu invested the Chamber and forced the deputies to flee!" This was not true. The deputies had left on their own steam after affirming their confidence in the government. What was true was that La Rocque's storm troops *could* have taken the Palais-Bourbon, chased the deputies, and assumed the lead in setting up a provisional government.* Colonel de La Rocque had deliberately muffed that chance.

The casualties that evening were considerable on both sides. Among the estimated 40,000 rioters fourteen were killed by bullets and two died later from their wounds; some 655 were injured, of whom 236 were hospitalized and the rest treated at first-aid stations. The police and guards lost one killed and 1,664 injured, of whom 884 were able to resume service after having their wounds dressed. The guardians fired 527 revolver bullets; the

---

* This was also the view of one of La Rocque's fiercest enemies, a man at the opposite end of the political spectrum, Léon Blum, the Socialist leader. In testimony before the Parliamentary Investigating Committee on June 18, 1946, Blum declared: "If, above all . . . the [Croix de Feu] column advancing on the Left Bank under the orders of Colonel de La Rocque had not stopped in front of the slender barricade of the rue de Bourgogne, there can be no doubt that the Assembly would have been invaded by the insurrection. . . ." Blum added that there could be "no doubt" either that the deputies would have been chased from the Chamber "and a provisional government proclaimed as was done in the same place in 1848 and September 4 [1870]."[11]

number of shots fired by the rioters was never ascertained.[12] It was the bloodiest encounter in the streets of Paris since the Commune of 1871.

DALADIER GIVES UP

Daladier, who had seen four years of massive slaughter as an infantryman in the war, was appalled by the bloodshed, but as the head of government he was pledged to defend the Republic against any attempt, however bloody, to overthrow it. Shortly before midnight, just after the Place de la Concorde had been cleared and the demonstrators had begun to disperse, he issued a communiqué in the name of the government:

> There is evidence of an attempt by armed force against the security of the state. . . . The government is determined to maintain . . . the security of the population and the independence of the republican regime.

After reporting to the President of the Republic, Daladier went to the Ministry of Interior where there took place an impromptu meeting with the Young Turks of the cabinet, on whom the Premier apparently was counting to support him in resorting to stern measures to put down the insurrection. Among them was Frot, the fiery young Minister of Interior, who had remained at his post all evening and who urgently pressed for drastic action, Jean Mistler, Guy La Chambre, Pierre Cot, and the Minister of Justice, the Attorney General and his assistant. Most of the young cabinet officers urged the Premier to do three things: (1) declare a state of siege, in which case the Army would take over the responsibility of maintaining order and protecting the Republic; (2) open legal proceedings against the leaders of the riots for "plotting against the security of the state"; (3), in the meantime, put these leaders under "preventive arrest."

Daladier, who, as Minister of War in the last four governments, had been feuding with General Weygand for more than a year, did not trust the Commander in Chief of the Army, whose fierce royalist sympathies might make him, he thought, a lukewarm defender of the Republic. The Attorney General strongly objected to all three measures on the grounds that they were illegal. A state of siege, he ruled, could not be proclaimed without a special law by Parliament. Legal action for plotting against the security of the state could not be taken until there was positive proof, of which at the moment, he said, he had none. Nor could preventive arrests be carried out without a mandate of the court in each instance.

Frot decided in the last case to go ahead illegally. He telephoned the Prefect of Police and ordered him to arrest every leader of the riots he could find. When Frot next reported that both the Paris and the national police forces had been so weakened by the night's fighting that they could no longer be counted on to maintain order by themselves, Daladier overcame his doubts about the Army and ordered the concentration in the city of the 512th Regiment of tanks, twenty battalions of infantry and twenty squadrons of cavalry from outlying barracks. But there was argument about this too and in the end the Premier changed his order and directed that the military troops be brought only as far as Saint-Cloud, on the outskirts of the capital.

At 3 A.M. a weary Daladier made his way back through the now quiet streets to his residence at the Quai d'Orsay.

"What are you going to do?" the journalists asked him.

"Save the Republic," he said.

The next morning he had second thoughts. Doubts began to assail this decent but wavering man whether, in the circumstances, he was the man to save the Republic. The Young Turks had also weakened. Frot, who had been so determined during the night to put down any new outbreak, read the morning secret police reports. They frightened him. Police agents who had infiltrated the various leagues reported that their leaders were preparing an even bigger demonstration for this day, February 7, and that this time they would come armed with revolvers and hand grenades. There had been a run on every gun shop in Paris. Thousands of weapons had been hastily bought. Several groups, the police reported, had "condemned" Frot to death and intended to carry out the "sentence" before dark. The dashing young Minister of Interior caved in. Without consulting his Prime Minister he hastily telephoned the President of the Republic: "The government must resign as soon as possible." The weeping Lebrun needed little prodding. Frot then telephoned Daladier and repeated his advice.

The Premier's surprise was heightened by the attitude of the Young Turks who met with him at noon. Without exception these young men, who had been so defiant a few hours before, now counseled their chief to throw in the sponge. The Presidents of the Chamber and Senate as well as Herriot and Frossard, a Socialist leader, came in to give the same advice. By now, over the telephone, President Lebrun was insisting that Daladier step down "in order to avert civil war." Léon Blum, the chief of the Socialist Party, alone urged him to stay in power and fight. The Republic, he said, was threatened. The threat must be met. He advised asking Parliament to declare a state of siege. But deserted by all but Blum the Premier gave in to the overwhelming demand that he get out. He seems to have been obsessed at this moment by the dread thought of provoking further bloodshed in the streets. Shortly before 2 P.M. he drove over to the Elysée Palace and handed in his resignation to a relieved President Lebrun. For the second time in a fortnight—and in the history of the Third Republic— the "streets" had overthrown a government supported by the majority in a democratically elected Parliament. Daladier explained why he had stepped down in a final communication to the public:

The government, which has the responsibility for maintaining order and security, refuses to assure it today by resort to exceptional means susceptible of causing a bloody repression and a new effusion of blood. It does not wish to employ soldiers against the demonstrators. I have therefore handed to the President of the Republic the resignation of the cabinet.

In this pathetic declaration could be seen all the weaknesses of the Third Republic, of the Radical politicians who dominated it, and of Daladier, hitherto regarded as a "strong man" himself. One could not but admire the humaneness of the Premier, who had seen so much bloodshed in the war and now was appalled at the specter of Frenchmen killing one another in the streets. But if the Fascist-minded rioters would not shrink from bloodshed in order to overthrow the regime, was it not the duty of a republican government and its Premier to defend the Republic by force if necessary? From what I had seen of the mob the night before, especially its lack of determined leadership, it seemed evident that a little display of military force on the following day, the deployment of a few army tanks and some army infantry and cavalry detachments around the Palais-Bourbon and other strategic points, would have cowed the demonstrators and caused them to disperse without the firing of a shot or the shedding of one more drop of blood. But Daladier, deserted by his cabinet aides whose courage had proved so fleeting under the slightest pressure, harassed by an easily frightened President of the Republic and reviled by a venal, reactionary press, would not risk any show of force at all.

Actually the Third Republic survived the night of February 6, 1934, largely by luck, as it had survived the evening of January 27, 1883, when General Boulanger could have taken it over, and a later occasion when Déroulède seemed to be on the point of overthrowing it—"three miraculous escapes," as Blum later called them, and each due largely to the failure of the rebellious leaders to take advantage of their opportunities. On the evening of February 6 most of the leaders of the leagues stayed out of the streets themselves and were so surprised and then so shocked at the success of their storm troopers that they didn't know what to do with it. La Rocque directed his forces from a hideout and as soon as he realized how near to storming the Chamber they were, abruptly ordered them to disperse. The leaders of Action Française, whose Camelots and other groups were in the thick of the fighting and suffered the heaviest casualties —four killed and twenty-six wounded by gunfire alone—also refrained from descending into the melee. Maurras himself, the chief of Action Française, after writing his daily editorial, sat up in his home until dawn writing some verse in his Provençal dialect in honor of Daudet's wife, Pampille, and was so tired from his poetic efforts that he slept until late the next afternoon. Maurice Pujo, supposedly in command of the royalist shock troops, disappeared early in the evening and could not be found for two days, either by the police or by his friends. On the afternoon of February 7, with the leagues arming for a new try and with the young fanatics of Action Française burning for more action, Maurras was asked by some of the latter what he thought of the situation. "But I have not had time," he replied, "to see the papers yet!"

The indecision of the royalist chiefs made the proclamation of the Duc de Guise that day seem even more foolish than it was.

Frenchmen! From foreign soil where I am constrained to live by the cruel law of exile I bow with deep emotion before the dead and the wounded, who at the cost or the risk of their lives, have risen up against an evil government. To maintain itself in power . . . it has not hesitated to fire on the war veterans, on the war-mutilated, on a generous youth, the hope of the country.

Frenchmen! That is where you have been led by sixty years of a Republic, by a government of parties.

Frenchmen of all parties and of every sort, now is the hour to rally to the principle of monarchy, on which was founded over the centuries the grandeur of France and which alone can assure peace, order, and justice.

> In exile, February 7, 1934
> Jean, duc de Guise

THE CONFUSED AFTERMATH

Instead of the good duke and a restored Orléans monarchy, the rebels succeeded in getting, after Daladier left, merely another coalition republican government of all parties except the Communists and Socialists, led by the seventy-one-year-old former President of the Republic, Gaston Doumergue, who was a republican, a Radical (though a conservative one in his old age), and a Protestant and Freemason to boot, possessing all the qualifications which the royalists and right-wingers said they had rebelled against. Doumergue, a vain, mediocre, and now senile old man, who as President had become as noted for his perennial smile as President Lebrun was for his constant weeping, at first declined the latter's request that he leave his country retreat to return to Paris to form a "government of truce and appeasement." He was too old, he said, and too tired. But urged by the presidents of the two Chambers and several past Premiers, he finally gave in. Actually the intervention of Pierre Laval, nursing his frustrations at having been excluded by the Radicals from the government for two years, appears to have been decisive. Heading a delegation of conservative deputies he had called on Lebrun just after Daladier resigned. When the President, in tears, told him that Doumergue had turned him down, Laval grabbed a telephone and put through a call to the former president.[13] His powers of persuasion seem to have worked on Doumergue.

But that was not all. Laval also helped persuade the new Premier to appoint Marshal Pétain as Minister of War. Two consequences fateful for the Republic were to follow from this. First, Pétain, then seventy-eight, was bitten for the first time by the political bug. Second, there now began a strange collaboration between the aging Marshal and Laval, who was Minister of Colonies in the new government. They seemed to make the most unlikely bedfellows, for what could the great military war hero have in common with the conniving, unprincipled politician who as an extreme left-wing pacifist had opposed the 1914 war and avoided becoming a soldier in it? Before long certain observers noticed Pétain praising Laval as "the man of tomorrow" and Laval slyly hinting that a man of the Marshal's immense stature might be needed to save the country should the shaky parliamentary system break down. In the back of the mind of each there seems to have sprouted at this time the idea that the other could be useful to him in the uncertain future.[14]

Doumergue, with the illustrious Marshal and seven former Premiers in his all-party cabinet, brought a temporary appeasement to the troubled land. But it took a week for the rioting to die down. For the Left, frightened by the success of the Fascist street-brawlers in overturning a government if not the regime, determined to demonstrate that its followers too could go into the streets to prevent what had happened in Rome and Berlin.

Though the chiefs of the leagues had called off their shock troops as soon as Daladier resigned, several thousand of them, chiefly Camelots and Jeunesses Patriotes, in defiance of order, surged through the capital on the night of February 7. They were joined by thousands of hooligans from the Parisian underworld who took the lead in smashing shopwindows and looting stores. Four rioters were killed and 178 injured and the police and Mobile Guards suffered 289 wounded.

By now the Communists were in a state of confusion and embarrassment. Their leaders had deliberately thrown them into the streets on February 6 alongside the Fascist leagues. The next day the Communists rejected an appeal of the Socialists for a joint peaceful anti-Fascist demonstration on the Place de la Bastille for February 8. Instead they called for a massive Communist rally for February 9 on the Place de la République to "protest against Fascism." This time the police made arrests, carting off 1,200 demonstrators to jail, and did not even bother to sound the warning bugle before opening fire. Four rioters were shot dead and twenty-four wounded by gunfire. It made a difference whose heads were being broken, and the popular press, which had castigated the police for its "brutality" on February 6, congratulated the authorities for their firmness in putting down the Communists. Finally on February 12 the predominantly Socialist CGT staged a twenty-four-hour general strike to show their "support of the Republic against Fascism." Joined at the last moment by the still-embarrassed Communists, it succeeded in shutting down public services and industry throughout the country. Four strikers were killed by the police and several wounded. Again, as the Parliamentary Investigating Committee later found, the police did not trouble to sound the bugle before firing. Even to the conservative and hostile *Temps* the strike was impressive. For the most part orderly, it appeared to warn the country that organized labor in France would not sit supinely by, as had its comrades in Germany, while Fascists tried to overthrow the democratic Republic.

One more murky affair, an aftermath of the Stavisky scandal, threatened for a time to convulse the edgy public anew. Less than a fortnight after Doumergue took over to try to calm the country the body of a Paris magistrate involved in the shady business of keeping Stavisky out of jail was found mangled on the tracks of the Paris-Dijon railway. Apparently he had been tied to the rails after having been drugged. The popular and the rightist press in Paris immediately charged that the judge, Dr. Albert Prince, had been murdered by the police of the Sûreté at the instigation of former Premier Camille Chautemps and of his brother-in-law, Pressard, to keep him from revealing their complicity in the Stavisky business. It had been Prince, who as head of the Financial Section of the Paris Parquet, the public prosecutor's office, had granted Stavisky the nineteeen postponements of his trial, ostensibly at the command of Pressard.

Public opinion, stirred up by the venal press, was outraged at this "police murder," which seemed to resemble that of Stavisky—and for the same motive: to silence a witness to the corruption of the republican regime. The truth, as in the case of so many of these affairs in France, was never completely established, at least to the satisfaction of all. But the Parliamentary Investigating Committee concluded that it was a suicide and not a murder, that Prince had "saved Stavisky by his dilatory tactics," and that because of this involvement and certain others connected with his private life he chose, in a moment of depression, to kill himself. How the magistrate managed to drug himself to the point of unconsciousness and then tie himself to the rails before being run over was never explained.

For the press of Paris it was another field day. Since the detectives of the police force assigned to the case seemed to be dragging their heels the newspapers hired their own sleuths to solve the mystery, or rather, to prove that Prince was murdered. When three famed detectives of Scotland Yard led by its former chief, Sir Basil Thompson, hired by the mass-circulation evening paper *Paris-Soir* to investigate the "murder," quickly concluded that it was a suicide, the publisher of the journal, Jean Prouvost, refused to publish their findings. "A suicide means the loss of 200,000 readers," he exclaimed. "I have to have a murder!" To the astonished English detectives he explained that to publish their findings of suicide "would go against public opinion, which believes, or wants to believe, it was a crime. It could lead to civil war in France."[15]

But the passions that on the evening of February 6 had led the country to the brink of civil war were beginning to cool off, and not even the malodorous Prince affair could fully revive them. Both sides, the

Right and the Left, and the many caught in between, now paused to assess the February uprising and to consider what its real goals were, why it had failed by so little, and what the consequences were for the future of the Third Republic. On one point at least all the quarreling contestants agreed: that February 6 was a fateful turning point in the life of the Republic, whose course from now on would be determined by the further clash of the forces which had met and tasted blood on the Place de la Concorde that wintry evening.

In due course there was an official investigation into the events of February 6 by the Chamber of Deputies and one after the war by the Assembly. Laurent Bonnevay, the deputy who headed the Chamber's special Commission of Inquiry, which reported its findings before the end of 1934, concluded that the demonstrators had tried to bring about "the downfall of the regime," and both he and Lebrun agreed that on the night of February 6 the nation was on the threshold of what Bonnevay called "an atrocious civil war."[16]

To the National Assembly's special Investigating Committee after the war, charged with studying the events from 1933 to 1940 which led to the fall of the Third Republic,

the 6th of February was a revolt against Parliament, an attempt against the regime. The intention was by means of a popular uprising to disperse the deputies, to take possession of the Chamber, and to proclaim an authoritarian government at the Hôtel de Ville [City Hall] of Paris. The march of the columns of demonstrators toward the Palais-Bourbon, the leaflets distributed in the different quarters of the city, and the instructions given to the nationalist leagues leave no room for doubt. It was not a question of a spontaneous demonstration but of a genuine insurrection, minutely prepared.[17]

Would the Army have acquiesced in such an insurrection? Would it have declined to lift a finger in defense of the Third Republic, for which its Commander in Chief, a royalist at heart, and some of the generals had such contempt? On the night of February 6, when it became evident to Daladier that he would need the support of Army troops if he were to stay in power and restore order, General Weygand seems to have played it safe. He recounts in his memoirs that he remained at home that evening but was kept informed "about the principal incidents and the movement of troops, which was arranged by the Etat-Major in accord with the War Ministry."[18] Thus, content to follow events, he took no step himself to assure the Premier that the Army stood ready to defend the constitutional government.

There is no evidence that General Weygand was in any way connected with a plot to overthrow the government or the regime, though his second in command, General Gamelin, hints that he may have been. Reporting a stormy meeting between himself and his chief on December 17, 1933, some six weeks before the February uprising, in which Weygand bitterly attacked Daladier in person and the government in general and Gamelin tried to defend them, the latter adds: "It appeared to me that it was a question if not of a sort of plot, with political motivations, at least of a trap contrived for the Minister."[19]

Against this background of a royalist Commander in Chief's quarrels with the duly elected government, it is little wonder that Daladier doubted that he could count on the Army to restore order on the night of February 6. Weygand's name is said to have stood high on the list of suspects drawn up by the Daladier cabinet to be arrested on February 7.[20] Gamelin himself felt for a time his support of the government against Weygand had cost him his military career—he was due to become Commander in Chief in 1935, when Weygand reached the age limit and would have to retire. "I was certainly classed," Gamelin recounts, "as the military chief who would not allow himself to be drawn into a combination against the legal government. The supreme post would be barred to me, or at least I would be gotten rid of at the first opportunity."[21] This comment from the Chief of the General Staff, the second-highest-ranking officer in the Army, reveals a great deal about the attitude of the military hierarchy in 1934 toward the republican government.

The three living marshals of France, though no longer on active duty, continued to exert, because of their prestige, an immense influence on the officer corps. None of them liked the Radical governments and two of them, Lyautey and Franchet d'Esperey, were fed up with the regime itself. Lyautey, had threatened on February 7 to lead a column of the Jeunesses Patriotes, of which he was an honorary patron, on the Chamber if Daladier did not resign. Marshal Franchet d'Esperey would soon be interesting himself in two secret organizations, one in the Army led by an aide of Marshal Pétain, Commandant Loustaunau-Lacau, and another which had close connections with the armed forces. The first was known as the "Corvignolles" network, with secret cells throughout the Army. The second was called CSAR (Comité Secret d'Action Révolutionnaire) and was popularly known as "La Cagoule" and its members as "Le Cagoulards," "the hooded ones." This last was deliberately terrorist, resorting to murder and dynamiting, and its aim was to overthrow the Republic and set up an authoritarian regime on the model of the Fascist state of Mussolini, who furnished some of its arms and most of its secret funds and in whose behalf it murdered two leading anti-Fascist Italian exiles. Its leader was a former naval engineer named Eugène Deloncle and the head of its military section was General Duseigneur, a retired Air Force officer. Marshal Franchet d'Esperey would become one of the main links betweeen the two secret groups and help raise funds for them. Marshal Pétain would be kept informed of their work through Loustaunau-Lacau. The two marshals could hardly have been ignorant of the fact that though professing to be anti-Communist both secret organizations, especially the Cagoule, were also antirepublican.

So far as can be established Pétain, the most popular and influential of the three marshals, though he was in touch with some of the leagues had no part in the riots of February 6. Their significance to him was that they brought him into the subsequent government as Minister of War and launched him at seventy-eight on a political career. And yet—might he have played a key role in a new regime had the leaguers succeeded in their aims on February 6? At least one French statesman believed so.

"Who would have composed the provisional government?" Léon Blum asked himself in his testimony on the February 6th crisis before the Assembly's Investigating Committee after the second war. "I do not know, of course, what the relations of Marshal Pétain with the organizers of the riots might have been.* But I believe his name would have been on the list of members of the new government, along with those of Pierre Laval and, certainly, André Tardieu."[22]

The military hierarchy and the world of big business and finance were not the only pillars of the nation whose leaders despaired of the Republic and, in some cases, worked to undermine it. The free press, echoing for the most part the views of the industrial and financial tycoons, many of whom financed the antiparliamentary leagues, bears a heavy responsibility for what took place on February 6. For nearly a decade the big-circulation dailies of Paris had been stirring up the public against the regime by their continual attacks on Parliament and the Radical governments which it from time to time spawned. By the beginning of 1934 they

---

* M. Blum does not seem to have known that the Marshal was in contact, through one of his military aides, with La Rocque, the head of the Croix de Feu, with the Redressement Français movement, thanks to Raphaël Alibert, a fanatical royalist without political sense, to whom Pétain began to turn at this time for political education, and with Action Française, whose chief, Maurras, he helped to get elected to the Académie Française in 1938 and whom he once called "the most French of Frenchmen." All three of these groups took an active part in the February 6 demonstrations. Maurras himself at this time confided to friends: "We must bring Pétain to power. He will bring back the king." After the 6th of February an increasingly large number of leaders on the extreme right began to think of Pétain as the man who could save France from the anarchy of the radical Republic. A year later Gustave Hervé, under the influence of Alibert, published a pamphlet, "It is Pétain Whom We Need," which became a best seller. But, such was the confusion in France, it was not only the reactionaries who were thinking of Pétain as a savior. Some on the Left had the same idea. In 1935, too, Pierre Cot, a left-wing Radical-Socialist, published a magazine article suggesting that the illustrious Marshal might be the sole man capable of saving France.[23] To an American observer, John Gunther, writing of France at this time, "Pétain . . . is a 'Left' general, i.e., a good republican."[24]

had prepared the ground for drastic action against the Chamber of Deputies. Their influence in helping to incite the riots may be gauged by the fact that in the provinces, where almost all the daily newspapers were solidly republican and opposed to the new wave of Fascism, the night of February 6 passed quietly and the news of the attempt to storm the Chamber of Deputies came not only as a surprise but as a shock.

Backing the rightist opinion of the great Paris dailies were certain recently founded weeklies, whose circulation and influence mounted rapidly in the mid-thirties. *Candide,* founded in 1924, and *Gringoire,* four years later, had achieved by 1934 circulations of half a million. Of a rather high literary quality, at least at first, and attracting articles by many of France's most distinguished writers, the two weeklies gradually became more and more reactionary, pro-Fascist, anti-Semitic, and the center of the most venal propaganda against the parliamentary Republic and the politicians who dominated it. *Gringoire,* owned by Horace de Carbuccia, son-in-law of the Paris Prefect of Police, Chiappe, became especially violent and scurrilous against the regime after the police chief was dismissed in February 1934. Two years later it drove the Minister of Interior, Roger Salengro, to suicide by publishing completely false articles charging that as a soldier he had deserted to the Germans in 1915 and had been condemned to death by a French court-martial. Tirelessly it inveighed against democracy, the "corruption" of Parliament and government, and against the British—one of its editors, Henri Béraud, once attracting national attention by a front-page diatribe: "SHOULD ENGLAND BE REDUCED TO SLAVERY?" Fascist Italy was the journal's great idol and hope, and, as time went by, Nazi Germany. Widely read as they were, *Candide* and *Gringoire* helped poison public opinion against the Republic. Both weeklies became the favorite reading of a large number of Army and Navy officers.

Also popular with the Army and Navy officers, and indeed with the military rank and file, was a third weekly, *Je suis partout,* founded in 1930. Like *Candide* and *Gringoire* it glided to the extreme right and after the 6th of February became openly and violently Fascist, lauding Mussolini and Hitler, cursing the Western democracies and the Jews, and calling for the end of the Republic. By the time the second war started some three hundred soldiers clubs had subscribed to it and two hundred more had applied for subscriptions.[25]

With such weeklies sowing their poison and the great daily newspapers contributing their full share, it is little wonder that French public opinion was manipulated more and more to be so scornful of the Republic and so cynical about its policies that it cared less and less whether it survived. As the moderate historian René Rémond had pointed out, these big-circulation newspapers of general information "obeyed the same passions, supported the same prejudices,. saw the world through the same spectacles" as the avowed rightist political dailies. "It is the press of the

Right that formed public opinion," he adds. "The average Frenchman, even if he voted Left, read most often a newspaper of the Right, whose inclination was more and more toward Fascism."[26]

The riots of the 6th of February led to two developments which further divided France: one, the rapid growth of the Croix de Feu on the Right, and, two, the rise of the Front Populaire on the Left. From that chilly winter day of 1934 on, the nation seemed irrevocably split in two.[27]

15

AFTERMATH: WIDENING OF THE GULF
1934–1936

All through the two years that followed the rioting on the Place de la Concorde the extreme Right and most of the Left girded for a showdown. The essentially conservative coalition governments of "truce" were caught in the middle, and in the divided country hesitated to face forthrightly the deteriorating situation at home and abroad.

The narrow defeat of the rightist leagues on February 6th had aroused wide circles on the Left to the danger of the threat of Fascism. They were determined that it would not triumph in France as it had in Italy and Germany. Within a month three noted intellectuals, the philosopher "Alain" (Émile Chartier), a Radical-Socialist, the physicist Paul Langevin, a Socialist, and the ethnologist Paul Rivet, a Communist sympathizer, formed an Anti-Fascist Vigilance Committee of Intellectuals (Comité de vigilance des intellectuels anti-fascistes) which soon attracted over 8,000 members. On the political side three deputies, the Radical-Socialist Gaston Bergery, the Socialist Georges Monnet, and the Communist Jacques Doriot joined together to found an "Anti-Fascist Common Front." Their respective parties did not approve. Doriot was expelled from the Communist Party, Bergery forced to resign from his, and Monnet disavowed by his. The Communist chiefs in particular were furious at such "deviation" from the party line, which still loudly insisted that the Socialists were "Social-Fascists." But the three men had laid the first foundations for the Popular Front.

On the extreme Right the leagues attempted to exploit their success of February 6th by forming a National Front. But only two of them, Solidarité Française and Jeunesses Patriotes, joined it openly. Action Française would give no more than tacit support. The Croix de Feu refused to have anything to do with it.

It was Colonel de La Rocque's league which benefited most from the events of February 6th, in which it had played such a mysterious role—or non-role. Tens of thousands of Frenchmen hastened to join it or its auxiliaries, chief of which was a suborganization called "National Volunteers," recruited from those who were too young to have fought in the Great War. By 1936 Croix de Feu had some two million members and was no longer primarily a right-wing war-veteran's organization but a popular mass movement—indeed in October 1935, it adopted the name of Mouvement Social Français, from which it was only a step to its final title of Parti Social Français, which it took when the government eventually dissolved all the rightist leagues.

As a movement and then a political party it had more members than any other in France. But its very success in rapidly attracting a mass following diluted its effectiveness. Most of the hundreds of thousands of good bourgeois who flocked to its banners did so because it seemed to promise a French society based on the old-fashioned virtues of Order, Honesty, Nationalism, and Patriotism and to have outgrown its original penchant for violence in the street. Though La Rocque orated and wrote at great length—he was a bad writer and a worse orator—about forcing on the country political, economic, and social reforms in order to restore unity, stability, prosperity, and moral grandeur, he remained vague as to details. The conclusion is inescapable that the handsome colonel didn't know himself what he wanted except perhaps the power to turn back the clock. Despite its numbers the movement had practically no representation in Parliament and thus remained politically ineffective. And after October 1935, when it agreed to disarm, it lacked the means to achieve power by more direct and violent paths. Probably René Rémond was right when he concluded that the whole Croix de Feu movement became little more than the play of political Boy Scouts.[1] Most of its restless young men soon left to join more militant rightist organizations, including the terrorist Cagoule, which was pledged to overthrow the Republic by violence. They accused La Rocque of "moral swindle" because he lacked a vital program. The Left however, obsessed by the memory of what had happened in Italy and Germany, still regarded La Rocque as a potential Mussolini, if not a Hitler. Its leaders were frightened by the mass following he so rapidly built up. All through 1934 and 1935 they labored to overcome their own disunion and mutual suspicion. Amid much difficulty and pain, the Popular Front—*Le Front Populaire*—began to take shape.

THE BIRTH OF THE POPULAR FRONT

To the surprise of almost everyone in France, particularly the Socialist leaders, the Communist Party, reversing its previous stand, took the lead. For four months after February 6th, the Communist chiefs had continued to hurl insults at the Socialist Party, accusing it of selling out the workers to the bourgeoisie and appealing to its rank and file to desert to the

Communist ranks. Suddenly, in June 1934, the line changed. The Communist Party asked the despised Socialist leaders to join it in common action against Fascism.

The signal came from Moscow. At the end of May, *Pravda,* organ of the Soviet Communist Party, published in Moscow an article calling for the cooperation of Communists and Socialists, especially in France, against the Fascist danger. "It would be a crime against the working class," said *Pravda,* "to oppose such a united front." After a year and a half Moscow had finally been aroused by the threat of Nazi Germany. In Paris, Communist Party headquarters got the message immediately. On May 31 *L'Humanité,* the Party's daily newspaper, republished the *Pravda* piece. On the same day the party addressed a letter to the Socialists requesting joint talks. Léon Blum, the Socialist leader, feared a trap. He and his lieutenants were deeply suspicious of this sudden change of line. Nevertheless Blum reluctantly agreed to meet with his former tormentors on the Left. Pressure had been building up from his own followers for some kind of working-class unity. The Socialist workers in the Paris region were openly demanding it.

On July 14, in the midst of the celebration of Bastille Day, the leaders of the two parties held a crucial meeting. The Communists were so conciliatory that Blum was both surprised and puzzled. He wondered what the "intellectual explanation" for it was. On July 27 a pact between the two Marxist parties was signed in Paris. It called for joint action against the Fascist leagues, their disarmament and suppression, for the dissolution of the Chamber, the introduction of proportional representation in the election of its members, the end of the government's deflationary decree laws, opposition to "preparations for war," and an end to their own interparty quarrels. A committee of seven leaders from each party was set up to carry out the agreement. More important than what was agreed upon was the fact of agreement itself. It put an end to thirteen years of fratricidal conflict between France's two labor parties. It paved the way for the Popular Front.

Surprisingly it was the Communists, rather than the Socialists, who next insisted that the Front be enlarged to include the Radical-Socialists, who were the largest party in the Chamber, and, despite their name, were traditional representatives of the rural *petite bourgeoisie.* Without the support of this third party, without, in fact, an alliance of labor with that large segment of the middle class which voted Radical, no common front could hope to get a majority in the Chamber of Deputies and take over the government. The Radicals, like the Socialists, were suspicious of this sudden wooing by the Communists, but the latter kept pressing their suit. On October 10, 1934, Maurice Thorez, in the name of his Central Committee, appealed for "a broad *Front Populaire* to combat Fascism and for Work, Liberty, and Peace." In doing so he incidentally gave the movement the name it would finally take. Until now it had called itself *"Ras-*

semblement Populaire." "Front" was a more militant title. Gradually many of the Radical politicians in Parliament, increasingly dissatisfied with their Party's presence in the conservative coalition governments of Doumergue, Flandin, and Laval, were won over by the Communist appeals. They joined the Socialists and Communists in reviving the old prewar *délégation des gauches* to coordinate action by the Left parties in Parliament against the policies of the government.

There was another reason for the abrupt about-face of Communist policy in pushing for a labor alliance with the Left and liberal middle class. It originated in Moscow, where Stalin, if not the French Communists, had become increasingly fearful of Hitler Germany. Having given the first signal for a new line in *Pravda* in May 1934, he now, on May 15, 1935, gave a stronger one. On the occasion of the conclusion of the Franco-Soviet Pact, the evolution of which we shall shortly return to, Stalin, at the request of Foreign Minister Laval, issued a brief statement which in one blow shattered one of the basic policies of the French Communist Party and indeed, in a large measure, of the French Socialists. It read: *"Stalin understands and fully approves the policy of national defense being followed by France in order to maintain its armed strength at the level required by its security."*

For the Soviet dictator this was merely common sense. Soviet Russia could scarcely survive an attack by Nazi Germany unless the French had in the West a strong army. But the French Communists had opposed, as had the Socialists, not only strengthening the nation's military forces but the very conception of national defense. Less than a year before, Thorez had risen in the Chamber and stated the traditional Communist line: "We are against national defense. We are supporters of Lenin, of revolutionary defeatism." And he had appealed to the Socialists to oppose voting military credits for "this government which is preparing for war." Two months before Stalin spoke out, Thorez had stated flatly that even if France were invaded the Communists would not support a war "initiated by capitalist and imperialist powers."

Now, in May 1935, he accepted Stalin's new line—not meekly but with enthusiasm. He had the Party placard the streets of Paris with large posters saying: "STALINE A RAISON! STALIN IS RIGHT!"

The Bolshevik dictator's reversal of policy left the Socialist Léon Blum greatly astonished—and not a little troubled. He thought it most "unfortunate." The Socialists in the Chamber had constantly opposed French rearmament—despite Hitler's feverish rearming across the border, despite Hitler's bold act of March 16 that year of flouting the military restrictions of Versailles by proclaiming a new conscript German army of thirty-six divisions. "Without denying the duty to defend the national soil against invasion," Blum said lamely, "we refuse to identify ourselves with the military planning of the bourgeoisie."

The new line of the Communists that henceforth they would support rearmament and the strengthening of the military services made it easier for the Radical-Socialists and the other liberal bourgeois parties to join them in a common front. No longer need there be the fear that if the Germans again attacked, the Communists would sabotage the defense of the country. In the next few weeks a broad union of the Left was achieved. On June 12 the annual Socialist Party Congress at Mulhouse voted unanimously to push ahead with a common front. On June 14 the two rival labor federations, the Socialist-dominated CGT and the Communist CGTU, agreed to resume discussions for a merger. On June 17, the Comité du Rassemblement Populaire was formed under the presidency of Victor Basch, the president of the League of the Rights of Man, to stage a massive demonstration on the great holiday of July 14—an assembly "of all forces determined to defend liberty." Not only the three major Left parties, Communists, Socialists, and Radical-Socialists, and the two labor confederations pledged their support but a dozen groups of intellectuals, writers, artists, and various other liberals. Even such odd organizations as Les Travailleurs sans Dieu, Les Amis des fêtes du peuple, L'Union naturiste de France and the Association pour L'émancipation de la Corse asked to be allowed to join the great rally on July 14.

It turned out to be one of the most impressive demonstrations the Republic had ever seen. In Paris hundreds of thousands marched from the Place de la Bastille to the Cours de Vincennes and in scores of provincial towns vast throngs turned out to demonstrate. In the capital 10,000 delegates of the various front organizations gathered in the Buffalo Stadium in an Assises de la Paix et de la Liberté and took a solemn oath:

In the name of the people of France assembled today over the whole expanse of our territory,

We, delegates or members of the Rassemblement Populaire of July 14, 1935,

Inspired by the unanimous determination to give bread to the workers, work to the young, and peace to the world,

Take the solemn oath to remain united, to disarm and dissolve the seditious leagues, to defend and develop democratic liberties and to insure peace for humanity.

Daladier, who, against the wishes of Herriot, had been dragging the Radical-Socialists into the front, marched side by side with Thorez and Blum, joining them in giving the anti-Fascist clenched fist salute to the delirious crowds along the streets. "I represent the *petite bourgeoisie*," he told the organizers of the demonstration, "and I declare that the middle class and the working class are natural allies."

The great rallies throughout France and especially in Paris on Bastille Day that summer were a striking demonstration by the common people that there was still massive support for the democratic Republic despite all its shortcomings and its corruption. It was meant to show, and it did show, that the mass of the French people would not submit supinely to a Fascist take-over, as had the German masses beyond the Rhine and the Italian masses beyond the Alps. But in France they wanted more than merely to stop the Fascists. They wanted a social and an economic New Deal. This the Popular Front, which may be said to have been born at last on that great summer holiday of 1935, promised. It would take another six months for the party leaders to work out a program, but a common Front had been launched and had aroused immense enthusiasm among the masses. It was a new and dynamic force in the life of the Republic, which had seemed so moribund. For millions it offered a new hope. It promised a way out of the Depression, which weighed most heavily on the poor. It offered the prospect of an overhaul of the antiquated, inadequate, inequitable social and economic structure of French society, which was long overdue.

For the comfortable well-to-do, gripped by an increasingly hysterical fear of Communism and of the new agitation of the lower classes, the Popular Front was feared as a dire threat to their fortunes and their privileges. Both sides now began to prepare grimly for the electoral battle in the spring of 1936. Its outcome would determine which side would rule and, perhaps, what kind of Republic there would be.

Ferment for Reform and the Synarchists

Outside of the political parties, the trade unions and the intellectuals of the Left on the one hand and of the leagues and their moneyed and intellectual supporters on the other (for the extreme Right, largely because of Maurras of Action Française had attracted numerous writers, journalists, and teachers), there were a good many individuals of various political shades, or of none at all, who banded together in groups to try to think out means of rescuing the country from its corrosive divisions and from its moral, political, social, and economic morass.

But neither these groups nor even those within a group could agree on a sensible course of action. Their confusions reverberated across the land in their respective periodicals, some of a high literary quality, though they aroused little interest among the masses or even among the politicians. The very names of the reviews which sprang up overnight in the mid-thirties were revealing: *L'Homme Nouveau, L'Ordre Nouveau, Plans, Réaction, Esprit, Combat, Nouveaux Cahiers.* Their various programs and manifestos revealed a jumble of conflicting ideas. If they had anything in common it was a hostility to liberal capitalism, to Communism and Socialism, and though most of them proclaimed their scorn for Fascism their ideas of reforming the state, the government, and society reminded one of those encountered previously in Rome, Munich, and Berlin. A manifesto of *L'Ordre Nouveau* was typical. It was preparing, it said, "the revolution of order against capitalist disorder and Bolshevik oppression, against powerless capitalism and homicidal imperialism, against parliamentarianism and dictatorship." Adolf Hitler, in his rabble-rousing days in Munich, had used similar words.

During the summer of 1934 the prolific novelist Jules Romains gathered together a group of nineteen young men chosen from the leagues on the far Right to the trade unions on the Left and got them to agree on a program highly publicized that year as the July 9th Plan. It was as fuzzy as the others, like them hostile to liberalism, parliamentarianism, and the "totalitarian mystiques," and calling for general constitutional, economic, social, and moral reforms. Nothing ever came of it and it passed into limbo with the rest of the "plans."

Among the members of the novelist's group was Jean Coutrot, a brilliant graduate of France's great engineering college, L'Ecole Polytechnique, who became an economist and a technocrat and whose life as well as sudden death was wrapped in mystery, for he preferred to work in the shadows as a manipulator of men and movements. In 1931 he had founded, with the help of fellow graduates from the Polytechnique who had risen high in the elite branches of the civil service and in industry and banking, a group called the "X-Crise" for the purpose of studying the world economic crisis which had begun that year. Two years later he transformed it into Le Centre Polytechnicien d'Etudes Economiques, attracted numerous economists, sociologists, trade-union leaders, and key men in business and finance, and made of it a sort of Rand Corporation devoted to research into the economic, social, political, and even agricultural problems of the world in general and of France in particular.

Coutrot was devoured by the certainty that France, and indeed the Western world, struggling to get out of the Depression and somehow make capitalism work, could only be saved by the technicians who really ran the industries, the banks, and the trade unions and who alone, he believed, understood the complexities of twentieth-century industrialized society. The politicians and the well-meaning intellectuals simply lacked, in his view, the knowledge of what made the modern world go round. No serious reforms could be expected from them. A man with a genius and a fierce hunger for setting up organizations which he believed could solve all the new problems, he successively built up further groups with highfalutin titles such as Le Comité National de L'Organisation Française, Le Centre D'Organisation Scientifique de Travail (actually established at Coutrot's urging by the Popular Front government)—and not to neglect other fields, Le Centre D'Etude des Problèmes Humains and L'Institut de Psychologie Appliquée. It could not be said that France lacked organizations to cope with its myriad problems. Coutrot, weaving together one group after another, saw to that.

Later Coutrot would be generally credited with being the man behind a technocratic movement called *Synarchie,** which to this day,

* Apparently from the Greek, *"syn-archy,"* denoting the opposite of *"an-archy."*

despite many studies of it, remains—at least to this writer, who has pondered most of them—somewhat of a mystery. That its adherents infiltrated the highest posts in business and finance and in the government bureaucracy there can be no doubt. As a loosely knit group of like-minded individuals, graduates of the same elite schools, above all of the *Polytechnique, Ecole Normale,* and *Ecole des Sciences Politiques,* and successful in business, banking, and the top ranks of the civil service, they grew more and more influential in the last half of the 1930s, not only through the power of their strategic positions or through their work in Coutrot's various organizations, but in propagating through the press and their many contacts in high places a disdain for the fumblings of parliamentary democracy and a view, surely proved erroneous throughout the West, that men of special education and training who knew how to make private enterprise efficient and profitable were best fitted to run the government and shape the nature of modern society.

Did the Synarchists also form, as has been charged, a secret society dedicated to overthrow the parliamentary government and to replace it with a technocratic one? That some Synarchists organized as far back as 1922 a secret society with revolutionary aims has been established. It was called "Le Mouvement Synarchique d'Empire," or MSE, and its secret "Pact," containing "Thirteen Fundamental Points and 598 Propositions" for the Synarchist revolution, was discovered by the Vichy police in 1941 and published after the war.* That at one time the MSE was linked with the terrorist Cagoule also seems clear. But though no revolutionaries in all of history probably ever worked out a more detailed and flamboyant program than did the authors of this paper, this secret society of technocrats never got close to staging a revolution. Its members were too fond of writing and talking to act. Nevertheless, in hammering away at the very conception of parliamentary government, in insisting that it was incapable of solving the country's economic, social, and even political problems, the Synarchists made a considerable, if subtle, contribution—on top of all the others—to undermining the Republic.

The government of the smiling, somewhat senile Gaston Doumergue, which came into power after the events of February 6th to effect a truce between warring Frenchmen, also tried to institute reforms to strengthen

---

* A wordy document! The aim of the movement is stated as "the taking of power in order to install an appropriate synarchic regime." The "revolution would come from above." It would do away with the parliamentary system—"this potpourri emanating from the Constitution of 1875, a regime imported from abroad and inadaptable to France." In its place would be a sort of corporate regime similar to that of Fascist Italy. Both classical capitalism and socialism are rejected. So far as one can make out from reading the lengthy document the movement would set up a sort of super monopoly capitalism, with competition abolished and endless plans drawn up for production and distribution, the whole—as well as the government— to be run by knowledgeable technocrats.[2]

and stabilize the government of the Republic. But Doumergue acted too clumsily and too late. Had he pushed his proposals for constitutional revision immediately after the February riots the frightened deputies and senators undoubtedly would have accepted them. The main proposal would have permitted the President of the Republic to dissolve the Chamber without the consent of the Senate. Under such a threat, it was hoped, the Chamber would think twice before upsetting cabinets every few months. But Doumergue delayed. He decided first to take measures to cope with the financial and economic crisis brought about by the Depression. By the time he got around to his political reforms, six months had passed and the Chamber was taking its summer vacation.

Abruptly Doumergue took to the radio to announce his plans for constitutional reform. This was imprudent. The custom was for a Premier to speak to the country only from the tribune of the Chamber or the Senate. Members of Parliament resented his going over their heads. When at the beginning of November Doumergue announced that he would ask the two Chambers to approve several dozen decree laws regarding finances and then gather at Versailles as the National Assembly to vote his constitutional reforms—without prior debate in the Chamber or Senate— the Radicals revolted and left the government. On November 9 Doumergue was forced to resign. He was succeeded first by Paul-Etienne Flandin, a moderate conservative, and then by Pierre Laval, then regarded as being of a similar political stripe. Both contrived to keep the coalition government alive.

Doumergue, who had aroused such high hopes in the country when he returned to office, had not fulfilled them. He had restored calm to the streets but his deflationary policy had worsened the effects of the Depression. He had failed to achieve even a modest constitutional reform which might have restored some political stability and enabled the government to cope seriously with the economic stagnation.* In foreign affairs France was in an increasingly precarious position, and domestic dissension, scarcely patched over even temporarily by Doumergue, was paralyzing the sensible conduct of relations abroad, either with friend or foe.

Fumblings in Foreign Affairs

Since 1918, as we have seen, French foreign policy had beeen dominated by the fear of German revenge. But until Hitler came to power in Berlin in January 1933, and within a year consolidated his dictatorship

---

* The Left believed that Doumergue was secretly in sympathy and in contact with the rightist leagues and planned to go much further in reforming the Constitution than his first proposals indicated. They saw their suspicions confirmed when, on the eve of his departure from Paris, Doumergue reviewed from the balcony of his residence on the Avenue Foch a parade of the Croix de Feu in his honor. To emphasize his sympathy for this most powerful of the anti-Parliament leagues, the retiring Premier had donned its traditional *béret basque* and he had warmly saluted the parading storm troopers. Commented Léon Blum: "Doumergue has been a protégé and a protector of Fascism, not only sympathetic to it but an accomplice."

and began feverishly to rearm, the threat from across the Rhine had not seemed imminent. Now in 1934, though France was torn by internal dissension, it was necessary for any government in Paris to face soberly the consequences of the sudden rise of the Third Reich and the fanatical determination of its ruler to avenge the defeat of 1918.

It seeemed fairly clear to most French leaders, except for those on the extreme Right and Left, who were blinded by ideology, that a number of new policies had to be adopted quickly if France were to parry the German threat. These were:

1. To strengthen France's alliances and draw Soviet Russia, the only country in the East with the military and economic power to effectively restrain Germany, into them.

2. To make the Germans respect the demilitarized Rhineland zone, which was necessary if France were to come to the aid of her Eastern allies in case they were attacked.

3. To bring Italy into an anti-German front, or at least to neutralize her.

4. To reorganize and strengthen the French Army, which in 1934 could mobilize only sixty divisions, but two thirds of the number available in 1914. And at the same time to renounce the strategy of defense, expressed by the Maginot Line, and to rebuild an army capable of taking the offensive against Germany should she attack either in the east or west.

Flandin and especially Laval, who together would dominate the government for a year after Doumergue departed in November 1934, had other ideas. They were cool to the idea of an alliance with Russia. They favored a rapprochement with Fascist Italy and at least an appeasement of Nazi Germany, provided that Hitler directed his expansion toward the east. This was also roughly the view of the predominantly conservative government in London.

Under Louis Barthou, Foreign Minister in the Doumergue coalition government, the last survivor of the staunch old republican politicians of the stripe of Clemenceau and Poincaré, who had helped guide the country to victory over Germany, France during most of 1934 followed a course of firmness toward the Germans, understanding with the Italians, and a rapprochement with Soviet Russia. Indeed it was Barthou who enticed the Soviet Union into the League of Nations in September 1934, after overcoming the opposition to her entry by several powers. This was the first step in Barthou's plan to make Russia, as before 1914, France's great ally against Germany in the East.

On April 17, 1934, Barthou had taken a decisive step in halting the drift of French foreign policy. For two years the World Disarmament Conference at Geneva had been in session, without making any progress. The Allies had waited thirteen years to convene it and thus make good the promise in Article 8 of the League Covenant that eventually all the powers would disarm to the same level. The French had taken the lead in refusing to concede Germany immediate parity in arms, and Hitler in response had pulled his country out of both the Disarmament Conference and the League of Nations on October 14, 1933. He had thereupon speeded up his own secret rearmament.

The British, under Prime Minister Ramsay MacDonald, aided by Arthur Henderson, the British Labor leader, who was president of the Disarmament Conference, increased the pressure on France to concede Germany the principle of equality in armaments and to agree, to begin with, to both nations' limiting their armies to 300,000 men. The French response was surprisingly decisive. In a note to the British government on April 17, 1934, Barthou declared that France "refused to legalize German rearmament" contrary to the Versailles Treaty—and that henceforth "France will assure her security by her own means."

This dealt a deathblow to the Disarmament Conference, which expired in June, and it weakened the League of Nations, under whose auspices the Conference was held and on whose collective security French foreign policy had placed considerable hope. It meant the end of the dream of controlled disarmament. The French, by their own decision, were henceforth on their own, confronted by a Germany whose large population and industrial capacity would in the long run give her a decided military superiority.

Logically—and were not the French reputed to be the most logical people in Europe?—the consequences of the Barthou note proclaiming that France would henceforth assure her security "by her own means" should have led immediately to the strengthening of those means: her armed services and her alliances. But militarily, despite the presence in the cabinet as Minister of War of the illustrious Marshal Pétain, only feeble steps were taken: acceleration of work on the Maginot Line and a very modest—and inadequate—effort to modernize the antiquated Air Force. In diplomacy, however, Barthou moved swiftly and with determination. He set about, above all, to forge a Franco-Russian alliance.

To camouflage it in the spirit of Geneva's collective security and to overcome British doubts and Polish hostility, Barthou proposed an Eastern Locarno, in which the frontiers in Eastern Europe would be guaranteed by Germany on the one hand and by Russia, Poland, Czechoslovakia, and Romania on the other, with the support of France, and, if possible, Great Britain and Italy. But Nazi Germany had no intention of tying its hands in the East—long ago in *Mein Kampf* Hitler had outlined his ideas for conquest there—and on September 14, 1934, formally refused to have anything to do with an Eastern Locarno. Three days later Poland also rejected it. The Poles flatly refused to consider a convention that might bring Red Army troops through their country to help defend it against Germany. They feared that once there the Soviet soldiers would never leave. In fact, for some time the Polish government, dominated by a clique of politically inept generals and colonels who had served under the dictator Pilsudski, had begun to detach Poland from its traditional ally and protector, France, and approach Germany in the belief that the Reich would better protect Polish lands against the encroachment of the hated Russians.

This was pure folly. Long before Hitler, back in 1922, in fact, General von Seeckt, the chief of the German Army, had reiterated in a secret memorandum Germany's age-old policy regarding Poland. Its existence, he had said, was "intolerable, incompatible, with the essential conditions of German life." The "obliteration of Poland," he had added, "must be one of the fundamental goals of German policy."[3] But the Poles, a valiant people, had a lamentable record for losing sight of their own best interests. On January 26, 1934, Colonel Josef Beck, the anti-French Polish Foreign Minister, had signed a ten-year nonaggression pact with Nazi Germany, and thereafter the two countries, formerly so hostile to each other, had drawn closer together. For the Poles it was a trap.

Barthou was cut down by an assassin's bullet before he could proceed, after the collapse of his project for an Eastern Locarno, with forging a direct military alliance with Russia. On October 9, 1934, Croat terrorists, allegedly financed and armed by Mussolini, shot King Alexander of Yugoslavia, killing him and Barthou, who was riding at his side, in the streets of Marseilles shortly after the monarch had arrived for a state visit to France.*

Pierre Laval succeeded Barthou as Foreign Minister, a post he kept through successive governments, including one of his own, for the next fifteen months. He would thus be the chief architect of French foreign policy during this crucial period. The momentum which Barthou had generated in bringing France and Russia together in a defensive alliance against Germany forced Laval to carry on. But he did so reluctantly and with his customary cunning. He distrusted the Soviet Union, doubted that it had any great military power, and feared that an alliance with it would bring down upon France, whose weaknesses he had no illusions about, the wrath of Hitler. Moreover, he felt it would encourage the French Communists and the formation of a leftish Popular Front while discouraging—indeed enraging—his conservative and reactionary friends. What he wanted was an alliance with Fascist Italy, weak as she was, and some sort of understanding with Nazi Germany which would spare France another aggression from across the Rhine and turn Hitler's aggressive urges toward the east, that is, toward Russia.

At the beginning of January 1935, in pursuance of Barthou's aims

---

* General Georges was gravely wounded in the shooting and never fully recovered. The loss of Barthou would be increasingly felt. He was the last of the line of pre-1914 French statesmen, who had never flinched from standing up to Germany. None of his successors, Laval, Flandin, Delbos, and Bonnet, had his deep instinct for the long-range interests of the country regardless of personal ideology. I was in Berlin when the news of Barthou's assassination reached there and noted the sighs of relief in the Wilhelmstrasse.

to draw closer to Italy, Laval journeyed to Rome. There on January 7 he signed an accord with Mussolini. It broke the ice of the long hostility between the two Latin countries and no doubt encouraged Mussolini to keep at arm's length from Hitler.* What the Italian dictator wanted at the beginning of 1935 was the support of France in maintaining the independence of Austria in case Germany menaced it again. This was all the more important for him since for several months he had been planning the conquest of Abyssinia. Because this project would drain off most of the Italian army and Air Force from Europe, Mussolini knew that it would tempt Hitler again to try to seize Austria. By the terms of the Rome Pact, the French agreed to "consult" with the Italians in case of any threat to Austria's independence, and secretly to institute talks between the General Staffs of the two countries.† They also threw a few bones to the Italians in the way of stretches of desert in North Africa. This seemed a cheap price for the French to pay in return for Italian support against Germany in Europe. But secretly Laval paid a much higher price. In a private conversation with the Duce on the last evening of the parley he gave Italy a free hand in Abyssinia. This was bound to embroil France with Great Britain, which held large territories in Northeast Africa, and with the League of Nations, of which Abyssinia was a member, and which was obligated by its Covenant to halt the very aggression Mussolini planned.‡ Laval did not inform his own government of his secret con-

---

* On July 28, 1934, Austrian Nazis, with the encouragement of Berlin, had cold-bloodedly murdered the Austrian Chancellor, Dollfuss, in Vienna, and attempted to take over the government. Mussolini had quickly mobilized four divisions on the Brenner Pass as a threat to Germany. Hitler did not like it and the Duce, who regarded himself as the protector of Austria, knew it.[4]

† In June General Gamelin went to Rome and negotiated with Marshal Badoglio on joint Italo-French military action against Germany should Hitler try to grab Austria. It was agreed that the French would send an army corps to Italy to link up with Italian and Yugoslav forces for a drive on Vienna from the south. In return the Italians promised to send an army corps to the French front in the West. Gamelin says: "We gave each other a guarantee covering the whole of our frontiers: the Alps and Africa."[5]

‡ There has been a great deal of controversy among French politicians and historians as to the kind of "free hand" Laval secretly gave Mussolini in Abyssinia. There is no word of it naturally in the official text of the Rome Pact. But at least twice Laval admitted in secret French government meetings that he had indeed given the Duce a "free hand" in Abyssinia but—he emphasized—only on condition that it be achieved peacefully.

The first occasion was a meeting of the High Military Committee (Haut Comité Militaire) on November 21, 1935, in Paris, presided over by Laval, then Premier. General Gamelin, the Commander in Chief of the Army, quotes Laval as saying: "I've got in effect a secret treaty with Mussolini [about Abyssinia]."

Gamelin confessed in his diary the next day that he had become so depressed by this contact with Laval "that on returning after the meeting to my home something happened to me that had not occurred since the death of my dear mother: I broke down and wept. I wept for the destiny of my country, which up to now has always found the men it needed in the hours of crisis: not only a Joffre, a Foch, but a Poincaré and a Clemenceau. But today we have none like them."[6]

In a secret session of the French Senate on March 14, 1940, Laval elaborated on his confidential agreement with Mussolini: "We reached an agreement—this is

cession to Italy. Not even its head.*

In April 1935, despite Mussolini's no longer secret preparations to conquer Ethiopia, France and Britain drew closer to Fascist Italy. Hitler was responsible for this. On March 16, 1935, he had tested the mettle of the Versailles victors by tearing to shreds the military restrictions of the Treaty and decreeing a new German conscript army of thirty-six divisions, or roughly half a million men—nearly twice the size of the French army stationed in France. And he had got away with his gamble. Under the terms of the Treaty the French could have sent their troops into Germany and occupied it, and that probably would have been the end of Hitler. They still had the relative military superiority to do it. Instead, they feebly protested to the League of Nations against this "violation of international law." The League took no action, except to condemn Germany. Great Britain reacted even more supinely. Its government sent its foreign minister, Sir John Simon, to Berlin to talk matters over with Hitler.

Still, the Fuehrer's bold defiance of the military restrictions of the Versailles Treaty had aroused considerable fear not only in Paris and Rome but even in lethargic London. In April the heads of government of Great Britain, France, and Italy met in Stresa to consider how to restrain Hitler. This was a golden opportunity for the French and British to draw Italy definitely into an effective anti-German front. Mussolini needed no urging. Hitler's attempt to take over Austria the summer before and his establishment on March 16 of a new conscript army had awakened the Duce to the threat of Nazi Germany. At Stresa he urged a military alliance to cope with German aggression not only against Austria but against Czechoslovakia and France. But the British government could not bring itself to go so far. Stresa ended merely with an agreement "to oppose by all appropriate means the unilateral repudiation of treaties susceptible of endangering the peace of Europe," and to reaffirm their fidelity to the

---

the famous secret clause which I have in my files, but it's everyone's secret—whereby France henceforth renounced all influence whatsoever in Abyssinia and abandoned in the economic field all the advantages which she could have to the benefit of Italy. . . . But I said to Mussolini: 'Henceforth you have a free hand, but a free hand in the path of peace.' "[7]

It is difficult to believe that a man so astute—and so cynical—as Laval, could have thought for one moment that a man like Mussolini ever intended to carry out his free hand peacefully—or that the warrior tribes of Ethiopia would have permitted him. As for Mussolini's version of the "free hand," the Duce told the French Ambassador in Rome in December 1935, that Laval appeared to him disposed to leave Italy "complete liberty of action."[8]

On June 24, 1935, in Rome, Mussolini reiterated to Anthony Eden, then British Minister for League of Nations Affairs, that Laval had given him a "free hand" in Abyssinia. When the British Minister replied that Laval had assured *him* that he had given Italy a "free hand" only in economic matters, Mussolini, according to Eden, "flung himself back in his chair with a gesture of incredulous astonishment."[9]

* Flandin, the Premier at this time, recounts in his memoirs that if Laval gave Mussolini a free hand in Abyssinia, "he did not tell me so." Flandin vigorously insisted that the reports of this secret agreement were "absolutely false."[10]

Locarno Agreement and their determination to maintain the independence of Austria. Abyssinia was not even discussed, but it appears that Mussolini left Stresa with a feeling that in return for Italy's supporting France and Britain in Europe, these two powers, which had grabbed by force such huge slices of Africa in the previous century, would not seriously oppose his now taking a small slice of his own.

Still, the Stresa front, as it was called, appeared to cement Fascist Italy to the anti-German lineup the French were trying to forge. Though the British weakened it by a refusal to consider a military pact, the Stresa meeting helped spur secret military talks between the French and Italian General Staffs, which had been agreed to in January at Rome. To the French that spring it seemed that their aim of isolating Nazi Germany and building a wall of steel around her was nearing fulfillment. The Berlin government found itself friendless (except for Poland) in a world that increasingly viewed it with distrust and hostility. It remained for France to bring in Europe's last great power to complete the encirclement of Hitler's Reich.

Laval, urged on by Premier Flandin (who says his foreign minister needed a great deal of prodding)[11] and by the Radical leader, Herriot, who had been conducting further talks with the Russians, now proceeded to complete the negotiations which Barthou had begun for a Pact of Mutual Assistance with the Soviet Union. It was signed in Paris on May 2 by the Soviet Ambassador and by Laval, who a fortnight later went on to Moscow to celebrate it.*

There was really not much to celebrate. Laval, backed by French conservatives and encouraged by the British government, had seen to that. He had deliberately watered down the terms of the supposed Franco-Russian alliance to a point where there was not much left in it. It bore little resemblance to the one the two countries had concluded before 1914, which had helped save France in the first war. All the teeth in the former had been extracted in the latter. Laval was proud of his feat. As he told a meeting of the Supreme Military Committee: "I've extracted the most dangerous things from it. I don't trust the Russians."[12]

Although the two nations agreed to come to each other's aid in case of aggression by a European power (i.e., Germany) it was stipulated (at the insistence of the French) that the aggression would first have to be certified by the Council of the League of Nations. In view of the reluctance

---

* It was in Moscow, on May 15, that Laval extracted from Stalin the statement expressing his personal approval of France's policy of national defense. (See above, p. 234.) Obviously Laval thought such a word from Stalin would be helpful to France in putting a stop to the opposition of the French Communists to strengthening the armed forces. In this sense, it was helpful. But what Laval did not foresee was that it also increased the prestige of the Communist Party in France and greatly aided it in forging the Popular Front. Also, to many Frenchmen, not all conservative, it was a questionable practice to ask a foreign ruler—and a Bolshevik at that—to intervene in the internal affairs of the country.

of the League Council in the past to verify an act of aggression (in Manchuria in 1931, for instance, when the Japanese attacked) it was obvious that before the Council acted Germany would have a good deal of time to carry out its aggression. But that was not the only reservation the French insisted upon. It was also laid down in the Pact that aggression would have to be determined by the other Locarno powers: in this case, Great Britain and Italy. Thus a further delay in meeting a German attack was stipulated.

Finally, the French government, unlike its more farseeing predecessors before the first war, refused to put teeth in the alliance by concluding a military convention. All through 1935 the Soviet government pressed for a military accord. Laval refused to consider it. He had succeeded Flandin on June 7, 1935, as Premier and had retained the post of Foreign Minister for himself so that he was exclusively in charge of external affairs. His Minister of War, Colonel Jean Fabry, was even more adamant. He claimed to believe that a military pact with Russia "would lead to war." Before the end of the year he simply cut off all talk with the Soviet Union on the subject. General Gamelin, who on January 21 had replaced General Weygand as Commander in Chief of the Army, bowed, as usual, to his political chiefs. The High Command, which in the beginning had been enthusiastic for a military convention with Moscow, did not press the matter. In the meantime, all through 1935 Laval declined to ask Parliament to ratify the Franco-Soviet Pact—for fear, he said, of provoking Hitler. It would not be ratified until a month after Laval had been driven out of office, in February of the following year.* Weak as the Pact was, it therefore did not juridically take effect until nearly a year after its signing. By that time the French policy of containing Hitler was in ashes, and the Republic was more divided than ever on foreign as well as domestic affairs.

The trouble was that in France (as in the U.S.A. in the 1950s and 1960s) foreign policy was at the mercy of domestic policy and of the quarrels it engendered. The Left, which hated Fascist Italy because it had destroyed the freedoms of democracy, opposed the rapprochement with Mussolini and only swallowed the Rome Pact of January and the Stresa front of April because of its even greater hostility to Nazi Germany, just as,

---

* In his delaying tactics Laval was backed by the timid Army chiefs. As late as February 25, 1936, two days before the Chamber was due to vote on ratification, the General Staff in a secret note advised the Foreign Office that in view of German objections that the Pact violated Locarno it would be better to postpone parliamentary approval and submit the question to the Hague Tribunal and "perhaps" to the Council of the League of Nations. The Army believed that Hitler would justify occupying the demilitarized Rhineland zone on the grounds that since the Franco-Soviet Pact violated the Locarno agreements, he was no longer bound by them. The belief was correct, but, as the secret German archives make clear, Hitler would have found another excuse if the French Chamber had not on February 27 ratified the Pact with Russia. In this case the Chamber showed more courage than the General Staff.[13]

before 1914, out of fear of Wilhelm's Germany, it had swallowed the military alliance with tsarist Russia, whose tyrannical regime it heartily despised. The Left wanted France, in common with Britain and Russia, to stand up to the Fascist dictators—though not to the point of war. Its pacifism weakened its cause. The Right was equally pacifist and wished to accommodate Mussolini and Hitler, with whose ideologies it increasingly sympathized; and it was hostile to the Soviet Union. In both cases ideology—not the true interests of the country—dominated the conflicting views on foreign policy.

In the early summer of 1935 the Right, in so far as it was represented in Parliament, would have approved the watered-down alliance with Russia. It was still suffering from the shock of Hitler's proclaiming a conscript army and sufficiently in control of its senses to realize that this was a blow to France. Its leaders knew that in 1935, as before 1914, Russia was the only power in the East strong enough to give effective aid to France in case of another German attack. But as the summer lengthened the fear of Communism by the Right mushroomed to a point of hysteria. The Communist gains in the municipal elections of May, the massive Popular Front demonstrations of July 14, which we have noted, and the progress of the Left groups in forging a common front for the national elections due in the spring of 1936, spread panic among the conservative bourgeoisie. It seemed to them that the Bolsheviks were about to take over France and that the alliance with Bolshevik Russia was abetting them. These highly emotional and greatly exaggerated fears of revolution at home turned most of the conservatives against the alliance. Soon they were echoing Hitler's propaganda that the Pact with Moscow was a further move to encircle Germany and a step toward war. They began to clamor for an understanding with Germany and a free hand for Italy in Abyssinia—an alliance, so to speak, not with the traditional allies, Russia and Great Britain, but with the Fascist powers, whose domestic and foreign policies, they began to believe, were saving the world from Communism. This was folly. It blinded the Right to the true interests of the country, which had been so clear to it before 1914. Ideology had triumphed over reason. In France the foreign policy of the Right consisted of accepting the renunciation of the nation.[14]

THE WRECKING OF FRENCH FOREIGN POLICY: ABYSSINIA AND THE FAILURE OF SANCTIONS

It was in this state of confusion and division that France faced the consequences of Italy's invasion of Abyssinia on October 3, 1935, in plain violation of Article 16 of the League Covenant. The question for the French government was whether to stand up with Great Britain, Russia, and the overwhelming majority of the smaller nations in upholding the League Covenant by moving for sanctions against the aggressor, or, in the interest of keeping Italy in the Stresa front against German aggression in Europe, to seek somehow to let Mussolini get by with his aggression in Africa, as the

Duce thought Laval had agreed to in January.* Admittedly it was a difficult dilemma for the French. Laval tried both courses and, as was inevitable,
failed in each. The edifice built up by France to contain Germany collapsed and buried the hopes of French foreign policy. All the patient work
of Barthou to forge a system of alliances to stop Hitler, all the years of labor
of Briand to make the dream of collective security under the League of
Nations come true, were undone.

On October 10, 1935, one week after Mussolini's legions invaded
Abyssinia, fifty nations in the League Assembly agreed that Italy "had resorted to war" in violation of the Covenant and they voted to apply sanctions under Article 16. Yielding to the pressure of the British, who took the
lead at Geneva, and of French public opinion, Laval reluctantly went along
with the decisions of the League. But he immediately set to work to see that
no sanctions were applied which might harm Italy's effort to conquer Abyssinia. The key to sanctions was an embargo on oil to Italy, proposed by the
British. The Italians, who had to import all their oil, could not prosecute the
war without it. Laval refused to consider such sanctions. He objected to
Britain's naval concentration in the Mediterranean. He stalled on the British
request that France back Britain militarily in case Italy attacked her. Finally
on December 9, as the Italian armies, using poison gas and bombing indis-
criminately, penetrated deep into Ethiopia, Laval inveigled the British Foreign Minister, Sir Samuel Hoare, to sign an agreement—to become famous as
the Hoare-Laval Plan—which gave Mussolini more than half of Abyssinia,
including the fertile plains, and left the Emperor only the ancient Ethiopian
mountain kingdom. During the two days of talks with Hoare in Paris Laval
kept telephoning Mussolini secretly to get his approval of the sellout. It was
too much for the British public, which rose up in anger, forced Hoare to
resign and made Prime Minister Stanley Baldwin, whose government had
first approved the Hoare-Laval Pact, abandon it, along with his Foreign
Minister.

The position of Laval in France was so shaken that he too was forced
out of office six weeks later. Despite all that France had done in watering
down sanctions to the point where they were quite ineffective, Mussolini
was so resentful at the French for failing to back his aggression that on
December 28, 1935, he denounced the Rome accords of the previous January, including the secret military agreement, and also the engagements of
Stresa.

France suffered a double setback: the loss of Italy in the anti-German
front and the defeat of the conception of collective security under the League
of Nations. At the beginning of May 1936, the Emperor of Abyssinia fled,
the Italians entered the capital of Addis Ababa, and on May 9 the King of

---

* Later Flandin would boast that at a cabinet meeting on the eve of Laval's
departure for the crucial September meeting of the League of Nations Council and
Assembly he urged that if Italy attacked Abyssinia France refuse to vote for the
application of Article 16.[15]

Italy proclaimed himself Emperor of Abyssinia. The League of Nations, on which France had founded much of her foreign policy for two decades, died too that spring. It could not keep the peace; it could not prevent aggression. France was left alone to defend herself as best she could against a restless, aggressive Germany which very soon, in a year or two at the most, would be stronger on land and in the air than she. With the loss of Italy as an ally, France might have turned to Russia and worked out a military alliance. Moscow was still pressing for it. But hatred and fear of Communism, real or professed—and in France it was both—blinded the French to the necessity of this, until it was too late. Finally, the Abyssinian war put a severe strain on Anglo-French relations.

Large sections of public opinion in France, especially in conservative circles, blamed Great Britain for the fiasco at Geneva and, more importantly, for driving Italy out of the Western camp. The British, it was widely believed, had taken the lead in imposing sanctions more out of selfish imperial interests in Africa—above all to protect the headwaters of the Nile—than out of any regard for upholding the sanctity of the League Covenant. And for the sake of a savage country in Africa they had sacrificed the security of Europe against Germany. During the Abyssinian crisis the French government had asked London for definite guarantees that the British would come to the aid of France if Hitler, taking advantage of the situation, moved into the demilitarized Rhineland and tried to attack France. The British had refused to give it at the very moment they were asking for French commitments to them in the Mediterranean.

There was a final cause for the French resenting British hypocrisy. Shortly after the British government had protested Hitler's violation of the military clauses of the Versailles Treaty on March 16 and then joined Italy and France at Stresa in proclaiming their determination to uphold the sanctity of treaties, it had, behind the backs of its two Stresa allies, negotiated a naval agreement with Germany which violated the naval clauses of the Versailles Treaty and gave Hitler the right and encouragement to build all the warships his shipyards could construct for at least ten years.* The Naval Pact was signed in London on June 18, 1935, without the British government having the courtesy to consult with France and Italy or, later, to inform them of the secret agreements which stipulated that the Germans

---

* Germany agreed to restrict her Navy to one third the size of the British but was accorded the right to build submarines, explicitly denied her by the peace treaty, up to 60 percent of British strength, and to 100 percent in case she decided it was necessary to her security, which she shortly did. Germany also pledged that her U-boats would never attack unarmed merchant ships, a word that she went back on from the very beginning of the second war. As soon as the deal with Britain was concluded Germany laid down two battleships, the *Bismarck* and *Tirpitz,* with a displacement of over 45,000 tons. By the terms of the Washington and London naval accords, Britain, France, Italy, Japan, and the United States had to limit their battleships to 35,000 tons. Great Britain, as the French contended, had no legal right to absolve Germany from respecting the naval clauses of the Versailles Treaty. And, as many Frenchmen added, no moral right either.

could build in certain categories more powerful warships than any the three Western nations then possessed. The French regarded this as treachery, which it was. They saw it as a further appeasement of Hitler, whose appetite grew on concessions. And they resented the British agreeing, for what they thought a private gain, to scrap further the peace treaty and thus add to the growing overall military power of Nazi Germany.

But whatever the shortcomings of a friend and ally, and in the case of Great Britain they were calamitous, a nation in the end must shoulder the responsibility for its own failures. Because of its hesitations and the devious policies of Laval, the French government had lost all: Italy as an ally against Germany, the military backing of Russia, Great Britain as a close partner, the League of Nations as a potential force in halting aggression. These consequences opened the eyes of Hitler to his opportunities and strengthened his determination to seize them.

At home there were further consequences: one was the embitterment of Laval—at the British for opposing him on Abyssinia, losing him Italy, and hastening his fall; at French parliamentary democracy for casting him out at the beginning of 1936. An ugly sore began to fester within him, growing more poisonous with each successive year that he was excluded from office until he became consumed with a venomous and burning rage to one day get his revenge—against the treacherous British, against the ungrateful Third Republic, which, to use his own unlovely but typical expression, had "vomited" him out.

The crisis over Abyssinia tore Frenchmen further asunder. The Right fumed at the loss of Italy as an ally and blamed the Left for this setback— the Left and perfidious Albion. Anglophobia raged in the reactionary press. "I hate England," stormed Henri Béraud in *Gringoire*. "I hate her by instinct and by tradition. I say, and I repeat, that England must be reduced to slavery!" Hatred for Russia was even more vehement as the Right prepared to try to force Parliament to reject the Franco-Soviet Pact. "With Hitler Against Bolshevism!" proclaimed Coty's newspaper *L'Ami du Peuple*.

Though less virulent, the Left took up the challenge. It supported sanctions against Italy, pressed for an accord with Britain, blamed Laval's deviousness and pro-Fascism for the fiasco at Geneva, and insisted on Parliament's approving the Franco-Soviet Pact, regardless of what Hitler thought. Angry, violent words were hurled between the two camps. To the Right, France was on the verge of being taken over by the Communists; to the Left, by the Fascists. In the hullabaloo the long-range interests of the country were lost sight of.

Its foreign policy in ruins, its domestic quarrels more venomous and crippling than ever, its Army weaker than even the government knew, a divided, panicky France faced the next challenge. It came, as might have been expected, from across the Rhine.

COUP IN THE RHINELAND:
THE LAST CHANCE TO STOP HITLER
AND AVERT A MAJOR WAR
MARCH 1936

F or more than a year the French government had been receiving warnings that Adolf Hitler was preparing to move German troops into the demilitarized Rhineland.

This was the stretch of German territory on the left bank of the Rhine and a zone 50 kilometers wide on the right bank in which, by virtue of Articles 42 and 43 of the Versailles Treaty, Germany was forbidden to maintain troops or fortifications. It was part of the price paid to France in 1919 for abandoning Marshal Foch's demand that the territory on the left bank be awarded to the French. It gave France (and Belgium) some security against a repetition of the sudden German invasion in 1914. The demilitarized zone was also the key to the effectiveness of France's alliances with the new powers in the East, Poland and Czechoslovakia. Should these nations be attacked by Germany the French army could strike swiftly through the demilitarized zone to the Ruhr, the industrial heart of Germany and the center of her armament works. The Versailles Treaty had imposed the demilitarized zone on Germany, but in 1925 she had freely accepted it as part of the Locarno Pact.

As recently as May 21, 1935, following Germany's denunciation on March 16 of the military clauses of the peace treaty and the proclamation of a conscript army, Hitler in a widely heralded "peace" speech to the Reichstag had solemnly affirmed that Germany would "unconditionally respect" the *territorial* provisions of the Versailles Treaty and the obligations she had freely entered into at Locarno, including the demilitarization of the Rhineland. Actually, three weeks before making this pledge the German dictator had secretly instructed the German High Command to prepare plans for reoccupying the Rhineland. The code name given for the operation was *Schulung*. It was to be "executed by a surprise blow at lightning speed" and

251

its planning was to be so secret that "only the very smallest number of officers should be informed."[1]

There is no record in the French archives that the government or High Command in Paris ever learned of *Schulung*—until it was sprung. But those archives are full of warnings as to what Hitler had been up to in the Rhineland for more than a year.

As early as October 1934 an obscure but alert French consul general in Cologne, Jean Dobler, began to report to Paris on the first German moves. By the following spring his dispatches were becoming more ominous. A lengthy one on April 12, 1935, to the French Foreign Office detailed the measures the Germans were taking to prepare the demilitarized zone for receiving troops and warplanes. He reported that new barracks, arms and ammunition depots, military garages, airfields, rail lines, and roads were being hastily built. No one in Paris seems to have paid any attention to the consul general's warnings. As he later testified, his dispatches were never even acknowledged and he was given no encouragement to continue with his intelligence work.[2]

By the fall of 1935 more important sources in the diplomatic and military hierarchy began to sound the alarm. In October French Military Intelligence reported that the Germans were "actively preparing" for the reoccupation of the demilitarized zone. On October 21 General Gamelin, after mulling over this news, wrote the Foreign Office that "the hypothesis of a German repudiation of the Rhineland statutes must be envisaged before the autumn of 1936, at the latest."[3]

From Berlin the astute French ambassador, André François-Poncet, already had, as he later wrote, "instructed the Quai d'Orsay to this effect." On November 21 he had a lengthy talk with Hitler during which the Fuehrer launched "into a long tirade against the Franco-Soviet Pact, which he considered criminal." The German dictator's outburst convinced the Ambassador that Hitler would soon retaliate by moving into the Rhine. François-Poncet informed Paris that "Hitler's sole hesitancy now concerned the appropriate moment to act." On the last day of 1935 the Ambassador, in a mood of dark foreboding, again renewed his warning.[4] On the day after Christmas, General Gamelin had again written the Foreign Office informing it of the latest military intelligence on military construction work being rapidly pushed in the demilitarized area.[5]

As the New Year came the French government and the military High Command were well aware, then, that the Germans were preparing to move into the Rhineland in the very near future. The question could no longer be evaded: what would the French do? Both the government and the military faced the question timidly and with trepidation. Much depended, they agreed, on the British, who were obligated by both the Versailles and the Locarno treaties to join France in opposing the German move. The trickery of the British government in signing a naval pact with Hitler in the summer of 1935 behind France's back and in clear violation of the peace treaty had raised many doubts in Paris. On January 11, 1936, Laval, who was about to be overthrown, wired Corbin, his Ambassador in London, that two German army corps had been assigned to the demilitarized zone and that its "total occupation" might take place as early as January 30, the anniversary of Hitler's becoming chancellor.[6] The British government was not unduly alarmed by this news.

The last week of January, on the occasion of the funeral of King George V, Foreign Minister Flandin crossed over to London and in conversations on the 27th with Eden, who had just become Foreign Minister, and on the next day with Prime Minister Stanley Baldwin, he put the crucial question: what would the British government do if the Germans marched into the Rhineland? According to Flandin, the Prime Minister replied that the British would have to know first what France would do. Flandin replied that his personal opinion was that France would resist but that on his return to Paris he would ask his government to take an official stand and would inform Eden of it when they met in a few days at Geneva.[7]

Eden's account of Flandin's inquiries in London that January is revealing.

> I replied that the French attitude to a violation of the Rhineland was clearly a matter for the judgment of the French government. How much importance, I asked, did they attach to the demilitarized zone? Did they wish, for their part, to maintain it at all costs, or would the French government prefer to bargain with the German government while the existence of the zone still had value in German eyes. . . . I thought it desirable that the French Government, as the power directly concerned, should make up their mind about the Rhineland. If they wished to negotiate with Hitler, they should do so; if they intended to repel a German invasion of the zone, they should lay their military plans. Any forcible action would depend on France.[8]

Coming from one so knowledgeable of the balance of power in Europe, these words must have astonished the French Foreign Minister. Eden knew perfectly well how important the maintenance of the demilitarized Rhineland zone was to France. Her security dependend on it. And Britain's too. He was passing the buck, though, surprisingly, this is just what he accused Flandin of doing. "From my talk with Flandin," he later wrote, "I had the impression that, while not prepared to use force to defend the zone, he was equally reluctant to negotiate about it. He might be tempted, however, to put the blame for inaction on either account elsewhere." On Britain, that is.

To forestall this, Eden wired Sir George Clark, the British Ambassador in Paris, and "warned him against a discussion of hypothetical cases" with Flandin. "You should not give him any encouragement to hope that His Majesty's Government would be prepared to discuss the matter on the basis of a statement of the British attitude."

What that attitude was Eden made clear in a note to the cabinet on February 14 after he had consulted with the British General Staff and the

Air Staff, which warned him of the consequences to France of a German move into the Rhineland. He was convinced, he noted, that "It was improbable that France would fight for the Rhineland."

> Taking one thing with another, it seems undesirable to adopt an attitude where we would either have to fight for the zone or abandon it in the face of German reoccupation. It would be preferable for Great Britain and France to enter betimes into negotiations with the German government for the surrender on conditions of our rights in the zone while such surrender still has bargaining power.

What rights? Eden did not say. What rights could there be once you had surrendered the zone to Hitler? By mid-February 1936, then, the British, assuming that the French would not fight, and horrified at the idea of themselves having to, had decided that only a surrender would appease Hitler and prevent the guns from going off. The French did not know this.

On his return from London to Paris, Flandin turned to the military High Command to ask if the Army had the means to quickly repel a German armed incursion into the demilitarized zone. He requested Premier Sarraut to call a meeting of the Supreme Military Committee (Le Haut Comité Militaire) to answer the question.* Its response brought a swift and terrible disillusionment to the members of the government. They had not suspected how weak and flabby and unprepared the Army was, nor how timid were its ranking generals.

In the absence of Premier Sarraut, who was detained by a debate in the Senate, Flandin, according to his own account,† put the crucial question to the Supreme Military Committee: "If German troops go into the Rhineland what military measures can be immediately taken to oppose them?" To his "great surprise," he says, General Maurin, the Minister of War, replied that the French Army was organized as a purely defensive force to man the Maginot Line and that it was not prepared to take the kind of offensive necessary to stop the Germans in the Rhineland. Flandin recounts that he was flabbergasted but that he insisted that the High Command prepare to resist the Germans if the government demanded it.

At an ensuing cabinet meeting, Flandin says, the government concluded that the response of the military seemed to have been "impromptu and superficial." It decided to take a firm stand. Again according to Flandin, it (1) "confirmed" that the government would take measures to oppose the

---

* The Supreme Military Committee met under the presidency of the Premier and consisted of the ministers of the three armed services and the chiefs of the General Staffs.

† There is no record of this meeting of the Supreme Military Committee in the French archives so far made available. Flandin's account is the only one there is. Probably, as we shall see, no such meeting took place on the Foreign Minister's return from London at the end of January. He is obviously reporting on another meeting, a session of the cabinet, which took place much later—at the end of February, when time was running out. The answers of the military, however, were the same as he reports.

reoccupation of the Rhine "by all means," and, (2), authorized Flandin to inform Eden that in case of violation of the demilitarized zone the French government had decided "to put all its military forces at the disposal of the League of Nations to oppose violation of Articles 42 and 43 of the Versailles Treaty."[9]

For this action as well as for the timid response of the Supreme Military Committee we have only the testimony of Flandin. But there are secret documents which confirm the reticence of the High Command. There are more documents to show that by the middle of February neither Flandin himself nor the government was nearly as resolute as the Foreign Minister tries to make out. The action of the cabinet which Flandin reports was itself contradictory. For if the French government was to oppose German reoccupation of the Rhineland "by all means" in time, it could not content itself merely with placing its army, navy, and air force at the disposal of the League. The French would have to act swiftly on their own while the League, according to its custom, deliberated.

It is clear, however, from the French archives recently published that first the Army and then the government shrank from the prospect of opposing the Germans alone and turned more and more to the concept of concerted action under the League, which was bound to come too late if at all. This was tantamount to agreeing in advance to let Hitler get away with his gamble. Actually, as the confidential German records reveal, the Fuehrer's generals, fearful of the French army, considered it too risky a gamble to take.[10] They need not have worried had they even suspected how their opposite numbers in Paris were recoiling from the prospect of tangling with them in the demilitarized zone. Nor could Flandin, floored as he says he was by General Maurin's reply to him, continue to harbor any illusions.

The Minister of War kept him informed of the Army's hesitations all through February. On February 12 he wrote Flandin telling him of further German measures that seemed to indicate an early reoccupation of the Rhineland. What should France do, he asked, if it took place? The Minister of War suggested that the government "should immediately bring a complaint to the League of Nations that Germany had violated not only the Versailles Treaty but the Locarno accord." As to French action itself if the Germans moved, "certain measures of precaution would have to be taken" in case the enemy did not stop and went on to attack the French frontier.[11] He made no mention of the need to drive the Germans out of the Rhineland if they began to enter.

Five days later, on February 17, General Maurin again cautioned Flandin on behalf of the military.

It seems it would risk being against French interests to use our right to occupy the demilitarized zone. . . . We would risk appearing as the aggressor and thus find ourselves alone against Germany. Such an operation should not in any case be envisaged without the full accord of the British government.

In the same letter the Minister of War also replied to a fresh demand of Flandin, made on the 14th, to tell him "precisely" what "dispositions" were being taken by the military to counter the Germans in the Rhineland. He outlined progressive "measures of alert" which the Army could take on its own initiative and which would put on a war footing the troops manning the Maginot fortresses, the frontier, and the antiaircraft batteries. These were purely defensive. There could also be, the general explained, the *couverture,* which in eight days would enable the French to put an army of a million men in the field. But this, the Minister of War pointed out, could only be done by decision of the government. All in all, he concluded, these measures would be but a *preparation* "for the reoccupation of the Rhineland zone by French and other troops."[12] What the "other" troops would be the general did not say. British? Belgian? He must have known there was little prospect of these. And all these measures merely to *prepare* a riposte? Could not the French army, vastly superior at this moment to the Germans in armament and trained manpower, move into the undefended zone as quickly as the enemy? The question kept bobbing up from the civilian government. But the petrified generals had already answered it.

The French Foreign Minister had posed another question to General Maurin in his letter of February 14. In the event that there were negotiations with Germany concerning the demilitarized zone, he asked, how far could France go in agreeing to "a more liberal interpretation" of the Rhineland statutes?[13]

General Maurin included a reply to this question in his letter to Flandin of February 17. To negotiate over the Rhineland, he said, would be "extremely dangerous and should be avoided." But General Gamelin, the Army Commander in Chief, revealed after the war that the military in the end had made a more compromising answer to a more compromising question. By the time it got to him, he testified, the question from the Foreign Office was: "Under what conditions could France, if the government so decided, admit the presence of reduced [German] garrisons on the left bank of the Rhine?" And he added that the question and the pressure for an answer came originally from Great Britain. In view of Eden's querying of Flandin on January 27 mentioned above, there seems no reason to doubt the general's word on this.

The response of the Army General Staff, General Gamelin said, was as follows: France could accept a German occupation of the Rhineland on condition that the garrisons and paramilitary forces were limited, that no military supplies were stockpiled, no maneuvers held, no new airfields built, and, "above all, that no fortifications were erected." In addition, there would have to be an effective international control to see that the Germans did not cheat.[14] The question put by the Foreign Minister and the response made by the military showed a further wavering in both the government and the Army.

In the meantime, though the warnings of imminent German moves mounted, the High Command, as if gripped by paralysis, made no plans and took no steps to meet the Wehrmacht troops in the Rhineland. Later General Gamelin claimed that in January he had asked the army commanders in the frontier regions to prepare for the *couverture* and to "study certain operations for a series of local but rapid advances into German territory"— actually a few miles into the Saar.[15] But after the War the Parliamentary Investigating Committee could find no trace in the military archives of "these projects."[16] The Army chief, highly intellectual as he was, always seemed to be instituting "studies"—but no more.

Warnings of German preparations were now practically deluging him but their flood did not move him to act. On January 15, General Renondeau, French Military Attaché in Berlin, warned of an imminent German move into the Rhineland.[17] The same day Military Intelligence, in a "Very Secret" communication for the eyes of Gamelin only, gave a similar warning.[18] Apparently jogged out of his nonchalance by two such messages in one day, General Gamelin, on behalf of the General Staff, got up a note which he sent three days later, on January 18, to the Supreme Military Committee: "Recent information permits us to suppose that Germany envisages in the near future the reoccupation of the demilitarized Rhineland, or at least of the right bank of the river." What did the General Staff propose to do about it? It asked for "supplementary military credits." There is not a word in the note about military action. Moreover General Gamelin grossly exaggerates, as he was to do to the very end, the strength of the German Army.*[19]

The same day, January 18, the Supreme Military Committee met to consider the note. Though General Gamelin reported that the Germans would reoccupy the Rhineland "as soon as possible" and then fortify it, making it impossible for France to come to the aid of Poland and Czechoslovakia, no decision for any counteraction was taken. The matter would be "studied" at the next meeting.[20] Whatever studies were made—and under General Gamelin's prodding the High Command seemed to resemble more a university faculty than a group of fighting generals—it is clear that the Commander in Chief concluded from all the studies that the French Army, despite the head start it had had on the Germans during seventeen years of the latter's disarmament, and despite its consequent overall superiority, was incapable itself of repelling the Germans in the Rhineland. On February 19 General Gamelin called a meeting of the chiefs of the General Staffs of all three services to discuss "the eventuality" of a German reoccupation of the demilitarized zone. The secret minutes disclose Gamelin's timidity. "There are no grounds," he said, "for envisaging that France alone can occupy the demilitarized zone." Still, he added, "precautions" will have to be taken "in case of a surprise German reoccupation."[21] Precautions. Nothing more. The Army continued to mark time.

---

* He includes 200,000 men of the Labor Service, and 40,000 men of the SS. As this writer, who was a correspondent in Berlin at the time, can testify, neither group was then of any military value.

The government too. This was a caretaker government which was expected to mark time until the national elections at the end of April. Senator Albert Sarraut, a wheelhorse Radical-Socialist politician, had been picked to replace Laval on January 25, 1936, largely because he seemed to be the political figure who gave the least offense either to the Right or the Left, whose thoughts and energies were concentrated not, as might have been supposed, on the threat of war from Italy over the Ethiopian sanctions, or from Germany over the Rhineland, but on the coming spring elections, in which all the Left parties, including the Radicals and the Communists, of the newly formed Popular Front, were making a strong bid for victory—a prospect that sent shivers down the spines of the solid bourgeoisie, both in Parliament and in the country.

No one could say that Sarraut was of a heroic cast. He was mediocre even as a politician but he was experienced, having become for the first time an undersecretary in 1906, thirty years before, and having served as a minister eighteen times from 1914 up to then, including one term (of less than a month) as Premier in the fall of 1933. To keep the support of the center conservatives he had named Flandin as Foreign Minister. Big and strapping for a Frenchman, six feet four, and forty-eight, Flandin looked, dressed, and acted like an Englishman, and he had many friends in London among the members of Parliament and the newspaper lords, who regarded him as one of the most pro-British of French politicians. Though moderately conservative at this time, he was a staunch Republican and could boast that his forefathers had steadfastly fought kings and emperors since the Great Revolution. For all his intelligence, ability, and success he seemed to many to lack something in his character that was hard to define, a flaw, perhaps in the will and in the capacity for judgment.

Also in the cabinet was Georges Mandel, the Minister of Posts and Telegraph. A Jew, a nonparty conservative, a protégé of Clemenceau whose hatred and distrust of the Germans he shared, he had worked much of his life in the shadows. Highly intelligent, with a granite character, icy manners that fended off all but his closest friends, and a deep skepticism about the human race, he provided much needed backbone in the French government at this time, as he would later in the last days of the Republic. Allied with him in support of a firm policy toward Germany was Senator Joseph Paul-Boncour, Minister of State for League of Nations Affairs. A handsome, silver-haired ex-Socialist, an eminent lawyer, a gifted orator, a man of letters, a devotee of the theater and a bon vivant, Paul-Boncour had never quite fulfilled in politics the promise of his many talents. Twice a War Minister, twice a Foreign Minister, and once for six weeks toward the end of 1932 Premier, he was a veteran cabinet member, and as French representative at the Geneva Disarmament Conference he had had much contact with the Germans and grown to distrust them. He believed now, with the Rhineland crisis coming to a head, that France must stand up to them. Marcel Déat, a college professor and neo-Socialist, was Minister of Air. He was already traveling down the road toward defeatism which in the end would land him in the Nazi camp as an outright collaborator of the Germans. On March 2 he wrote Flandin from the Ministry of Air that a German reoccupation of the Rhineland did not "necessarily" mean that the enemy would attack France herself. "The taking of preventive measures," he added, "is likely to take us further than we want to go."[22] The French Air Force, like the Army, did not want to fight unless the frontier itself was crossed.

As February ran out the caretaker government of Premier Sarraut bestirred itself. Diplomatic and military intelligence left little doubt that the Germans were about to go into the Rhineland. At the beginning of the month the persistent consul general in Cologne, Jean Dobler, had finally been permitted, after several refusals, to come to Paris to make a personal report. He informed the Foreign Office that Hitler's preparations for reoccupation of the demilitarized zone were now "practically finished."[23] At midnight on February 13 the French consul at Düsseldorf, Henry Noël, wired Flandin that German army officers, attired in civilian clothes, had arrived to "prepare for the reoccupation of the demilitarized zone."[24]

In the light of such news, and much more like it, Sarraut decided it was time to pin the Army down as to what it was prepared to do to meet the German threat, and time too for the government itself to make up its mind. He had been considerably annoyed at the Army for having suggested to the Foreign Office on February 25 that the ratification of the Franco-Soviet Pact be postponed because of its fear that Hitler would use it as an excuse to venture into the Rhineland. It caused him, he says, "to reflect on the morale and lack of energy of the High Command." The Chamber was due to vote on ratification on February 27 and the Sarraut government intended to push it through that day. The Premier called a cabinet meeting on the morning of the 27th to consider the consequences. He at once posed the question to General Maurin, Minister of War: what were the military plans to oppose the Germans in the demilitarized zone?

To his consternation he listened to the general explain that the peacetime French army "could only take the defensive." To take the offensive strong reserves would have to be called up and "before all else," an industrial mobilization carried out.[25] In the light of this revelation, the French cabinet made its decision. Immediately after the meeting Flandin called in the Belgian Ambassador and told him in confidence what it was. In case of German violation of the demilitarized zone,

a. The French government will not take any isolated action. It will act only in accord with the cosignatories of Locarno.

b. In case of a flagrant and incontestable violation of Articles 43 and 42 [of the Versailles Treaty], the French government will immediately consult with the British, Belgian, and Italian governments with the view of concerting a common action in execution of the stipulations of the League of Nations Pact and the Locarno accords.

c. In awaiting the advice of the guarantor powers, the French government reserves the right to take all preparatory measures, including those of a military character. . . .[26]

Flandin told the Ambassador that he would inform Eden of this decision when he saw him at Geneva the following week. Why he waited nearly a week to tell the British government is not revealed. At Geneva on March 3, Flandin handed Eden a written text of the government's decision. The British Foreign Minister contented himself with saying he would take it up with his government on his return to London on March 5.[27] Later Eden recalled "there was nothing to take exception to in this as a statement of intent."[28] He seemed relieved.

By the beginning of March 1936, then, with all signs pointing to an imminent German move into the Rhineland, the British and Belgian governments knew, to their great relief, that France would not alone oppose it by force and thus risk dragging them into armed conflict with Germany, which they both wanted to avoid like the plague. While Hitler acted, the French would merely appeal to the League and to the Locarno Powers. Though there is no evidence in the German Foreign Office or military documents to show that Hitler knew this, his conduct demonstrated that he felt it instinctively, as he did so much else in the early successful years of power. The supineness of the British and French on March 16 the year before, when he tore up the military restrictions of Versailles, had convinced him that he could get away with further gambles.

On March 2 in Berlin he had a long talk with the French Ambassador, who had come to him to plead anew for a peaceful "rapprochement" between France and Germany. François-Poncet found the Nazi dictator "nervous, excited, and disturbed; he looked very impatient and very much annoyed." The Ambassador reported to Paris that Hitler had "once again launched into a long diatribe against the Franco-Soviet Pact," which he reiterated was "incompatible with Locarno" and constituted "a grave menace" for Germany. The Fuehrer demanded time for "reflection" on what could be done about Franco-German understanding. He also insisted that the visit be kept secret—a request the Ambassador thought a little strange.[29]

There were reasons for Hitler's nervousness and excitement during the interview that even so astute an envoy as François-Poncet could not know of. On that very day, March 2, 1936, General von Blomberg, on the Fuehrer's instructions, issued formal orders to the German Armed Forces for the occupation of the Rhineland on March 7. It was to be, Blomberg told his senior commanders, a "surprise move." The general said he expected it to be a "peaceful operation." If it turned out that it was not—that is, that the French would fight—the Commander in Chief reserved "the right to decide on any military countermeasures." As would be learned from the German confidential papers later, this meant the "right" to beat a hasty retreat if the French budged.[30]

THE GERMANS MOVE

At dawn on March 7, 1936, small detachments of German troops moved into the Rhineland. Despite all the warnings, the French Army at first did not believe it. At 9:45 A.M. more than three hours after the movement began, Military Intelligence telephoned to the General Staff in Paris that the Berlin correspondent of a Paris newspaper had earlier that morning reported regular German troops entering the demilitarized zone but that "there were no other indications of this nature."[31] Perhaps François-Poncet, who had taken to blowing hot and cold in the last days, had put Paris off its guard. On February 27, the day of the crucial cabinet meeting in Paris, he had wired from Berlin: "Germany will not openly violate the Locarno Pact. She will not carry out suddenly a military occupation of the Rhineland zone."[32] Even on the night of March 6, when Berlin was flooded with rumors that Germany would reoccupy the Rhineland on the morrow and when it had been officially announced that the next day Hitler would address the Reichstag after a memorandum had been given the envoys of the Locarno Powers, the Ambassador had wired Flandin: "What is Hitler going to do?" His best guess was that "Hitler would announce that Germany was ready to reenter the League of Nations on certain conditions, among which would be a modification of the Rhineland statutes." But, he added, "it was not out of the question" that the Nazi dictator would "denounce Locarno and announce an early reoccupation of the demilitarized zone." He thought, however, that the first hypothesis "was the most probable."[33] Admittedly the Fuehrer was unpredictable.*

At 10 A.M. on March 7 in Berlin the French Ambassador was brought abruptly face to face with reality when Baron Konstantin von Neurath, the German Foreign Minister, apprised him (as well as the ambassadors of Great Britain and Italy and the Belgian chargé d'affaires) of the news from the Rhineland—"a symbolic occupation," he called it—and handed him a formal memorandum in which Germany, on the flimsy pretext that the Franco-Soviet Pact had already violated it, denounced the Locarno Treaty, which Hitler had just broken, and then proposed new plans for peace! "Hitler struck his adversary in the face," François-Poncet wryly noted, "and as he did so declared: 'I bring you proposals for peace'!"[35]

Two hours later the Nazi dictator propounded those phony peace proposals in a delirious scene in the Reichstag, which this writer found both fascinating and gruesome, and which he has recounted elsewhere.[36] Hoarse

---

* My own diary note for that day in Berlin recalls the feverish atmosphere. ". . . A day of the wildest rumors. Definite, however, is that Hitler has convoked the Reichstag for noon tomorrow and summoned the ambassadors of Britain, France, Italy, and Belgium for tomorrow morning. Since these are the Locarno Powers, it is obvious . . . that Hitler intends to denounce the Locarno Treaty. . . . My guess, based on what I've heard today, is that Hitler will make an end of the demilitarized zone, though the Wilhelmstrasse savagely denies this. Whether he will send the Reichswehr in is not sure. This seems too big a risk in view of the fact that the French army could easily drive it out. . . ."[34]

from nearly two hours of shouting, Hitler concluded solemnly: ". . . We pledge that now, more than ever, we shall strive for an understanding between the European peoples. . . . We have no territorial demands to make in Europe. . . . Germany will never break the peace!"

The question was: would France break it—by opposing the Germans marching into the demilitarized zone? All that day Hitler and his generals bit their fingernails waiting anxiously for a sign of what the French would do. Early in the afternoon in Berlin I ran into General von Blomberg in the Tiergarten. His face was ashen, his cheeks twitching. He and his fellow generals (as we later would learn) already wanted to pull back. All depended now on the reaction of the French.

Shortly after 10 A.M. in Paris, when the news from Berlin and the Rhineland left no more doubt as to what was happening, Premier Sarraut summoned to his office in the Ministry of Interior three of his cabinet officers, along with General Maurin, Minister of War, and General Gamelin. It was expected that he would convoke the full cabinet, presided over as was customary by the President of the Republic, so that the government could act at once. But he did not take this step until the next day. Perhaps he wanted to consult first with those of his colleagues who he thought would be most firm in this emergency. These were Flandin, the Foreign Minister, Paul-Boncour, Minister of State for League of Nations Affairs, and Georges Mandel, Minister of Posts—"the dear and heroic Mandel," Sarraut called him.

According to Sarraut,[37] he and his civilian colleagues were for quick action to expel the Germans from the Rhineland at once. But immediately—to their dismay, they say—they ran squarely into the towering timidity of the High Command. What was the Army going to do? Sarraut put the question to the two generals. General Gamelin's answer floored him. The Army chief asked only for permission to "take the first measures of precaution," which he explained meant recalling soldiers on leave and moving up reinforcements by road and "preparing" to move more by rail if necessary.

"And that was all!" the Premier would exclaim later in recounting the meeting. "No question of an offensive operation, no question of a series of local but rapid advances into German territory which he later said he had prescribed the study of. Not a word about those things!"

Paul-Boncour intervened: "I would like to see you in Mainz as soon as possible," to which General Gamelin replied: "Ah, that is another affair. I would like nothing better. But you must give me the means." Since he was the Commander in Chief of the Army he presumably had all the means there were at the moment. But it quickly dawned on the astounded civilian ministers that what the two generals wanted was a *general mobilization,* starting with the *couverture,* which itself would take eight days to put a million men on a war footing. What was called for on that crucial Saturday of March 7, 1936, was a police action by the French to chase out a few German troops who were *parading* into the Rhineland—this was clear even to a correspondent in Berlin that weekend. But the French High Command demanded a sledgehammer to kill a fly. It feared that the slightest move into the demilitarized zone that brought French troops into hostile contact with German soldiers would provoke war.

The Premier put a question whose answer exposed this fear. He asked General Gamelin: "If we act alone against Germany, without Allies, what will be the outlook?" "I responded," the Army chief recalled later, "that at the beginning, under present conditions, we would have the preponderance, but in a long war the superiority of our adversaries in numbers and industrial capacity would play a strong part."[38] Confronted by these warnings from the military that the least French reaction to the German move would provoke a long war which the Germans, this time, might well win, Sarraut adjourned the meeting without any decisions having been taken.

Unduly frightened that the French might act on their own, the British Ambassador in Paris, Sir George Clark, on the instructions of his government, rushed to the Quai d'Orsay before the morning was out and insisted "very strenuously" to Flandin, who had left the meeting at the Ministry of Interior to confer with him and the other Locarno ambassadors, that France take no isolated action and that specifically it "take no military measures which might engage the future, before prior consultation with the British government."[39]

But the members of the British government had dispersed for the traditional English weekend.* It was impossible to consult it. Eden made it clear to the French Ambassador in London that nothing could be decided in London until the following Monday, when the Prime Minister and his colleagues would be back. That would give the Germans forty-eight hours to consolidate their hold on the Rhineland without interference. Nowhere in his own account nor in the dispatches of the French Ambassador describing their meeting does the British Foreign Secretary seem to have given thought to the consequences of such procrastination. His only thought was to discourage the French from doing anything over the weekend.

Charles Corbin, the French Ambassador in London, was a skilled, old-school diplomat—one of the last of a dying breed—who had been devoting the final years of a distinguished career to reviving the Anglo-French entente, which had saved France in 1914 and which might, he believed, save her again if the Germans came once more. Not easily dis-

---

* It was quite seriously believed in Berlin that Hitler timed his gambles in foreign policy for Saturdays, when he knew that the British cabinet members and other high officials were away from London observing their weekend in the country. The March 16, 1935, when he had declared conscription, was also a Saturday.

couraged by English ways, so incomprehensible to most Frenchmen, nor fooled either, his talk with Eden that Saturday morning in London left him, if not disillusioned—he was too experienced for that—at least considerably frustrated and depressed. He wired Paris:

> The Secretary of State abstained, despite my insistence, from giving me any indication of his own views. He maintained silence on the question of the Locarno Pact itself. . . .

In fact, Eden struck Corbin as "relieved" by the morning news.

> His attitude was that of a man who asks himself what advantages can be drawn from a new situation and not what barriers should be raised to oppose a menace.[40]

This was bad news for Paris, and after Flandin had mulled over Corbin's dispatches he got off a cable the next day to his Ambassador urging him to try to wake up the British. "Please intervene urgently with the British government," he wired Corbin, "impressing it with the danger of letting things drift."[41]

Though Flandin did not know it, the British Prime Minister already had decided to let things drift, so far as Britain was concerned. He stated his views to Eden when the youthful Foreign Secretary arrived at Chequers Saturday afternoon. The phlegmatic Stanley Baldwin, who seemed to his people to symbolize stolid John Bull, knew little of foreign affairs and cared less.

> Baldwin said little [Eden recalled later], as was his wont on foreign affairs. Though personally friendly to France, he was clear in his mind that there would be no support in Britain for any military action by the French. I could only agree.[42]

It was becoming clear in Paris that there would be very little support in France itself. Saturday evening Eden received a dispatch from Sir George Clark in Paris. Flandin had told him, he reported, "that the French Government did not wish to take up an isolated position, but to concert with the other Locarno powers in order to bring the matter before the Council of the League." Eden was pleased by this "temperate report" from Paris. It was, he says, just what he "had anticipated."[43]

At 6 P.M. Sarraut called another meeting of some of his cabinet colleagues in Flandin's room in the Foreign Office. The Ministers of Marine and Air, François Pietri and Marcel Déat, respectively, were there, accompanied by the Chiefs of Staffs of their services, Admiral Durand-Viel and General Pujo. Generals Maurin and Gamelin were also present. Despite the appearance of the top men in the three armed services no military decisions of any importance were taken nor were they requested by the military chiefs. One decision only was made: to appeal to the League of Nations.*

Some French leaders, even those out of office like Paul Reynaud, who wanted the French Army to get a move on, thought Sunday, March 8, would be the "decisive" day and that, as Sarraut had told his generals on Saturday morning, "it was now or never." But the first reactions of the Sunday press, Left, Right and even Center, disclosed that French public opinion was even less disposed than the generals and the government to see France take decisive action. Though unable to agree on anything else the morning newspapers were unanimous in their insistence that nothing be done that could lead to war.

On the extreme Right, Charles Maurras in the royalist *Action Française* thundered: "We do not have to march against Hitler with the Soviets!" For several days he would reiterate: "We do not want war!" Also on the far Right, *Le Jour,* noting that it was the military who were being "moderate, restrained and wise," warned the civilians in the government not to act stupidly "in order to please Moscow." The chant of the press of the Right was that opposing Hitler's march into the Rhineland would only serve the interests of the Russian Bolsheviki.

On the Left, the press was equally blind. The Socialist *Populaire* demanded that the government limit its action to an appeal to the League and the Locarno Powers and that it show some understanding for the German move:

It was stupid to believe that a great country of more than sixty million people would put up with, seventeen years after the war, the demilitarization of part of its territory. . . . Hitler has torn up a treaty, he has broken all his promises, but at the same time he speaks of peace and of Geneva. We must take him at his word.

As for the big-circulation Paris dailies—all conservative—the reaction of *Le Matin* was typical. Its whole front page that Sunday morning gave its readers the impression that Hitler's move into the Rhineland was a good thing for France and that the French should be grateful to the Fuehrer. He had saved them from the "Communist peril"! The newspapers' front-page headlines read:

---

* The Foreign Office documents revealed that Flandin was not nearly so much in a hurry even to appeal to the League as he pretended. By his own account, at the very first meeting with the Premier, at 10 A.M. on Saturday, he informed him that "without losing an hour" he had brought the matter to the attention of the Secretariat of the League. But the Foreign Office papers show that his message was actually sent at 6:15 P.M. the next day, or thirty-two hours later, at the end of the second day of the German reoccupation of the Rhineland. Not only in London but in Paris there seemed to be no hurry to do anything.[44]

THE DENUNCIATION OF LOCARNO BY THE REICH

IN HIS ELOQUENT AND IMPASSIONED SPEECH
ADOLF HITLER SHOWED THE COMMUNIST PERIL

"I have," he said, "warned France. . . . I tremble for Europe."

FRAN⊃O-GERMAN CONVERSATIONS ARE STILL POSSIBLE

THE COMMUNIST PERIL[45]

With such journalistic fare to feed on, the government in a full cabinet session presided over by the President of the Republic, Albert Lebrun, met Sunday morning to consider what, if anything, to do. General Maurin, the War Minister, demanded *general mobilization* in order to move against the handful of German troops that had moved into the demilitarized zone. Later General Maurin and especially General Gamelin would strenuously deny that they had asked for general mobilization—the "reinforced *couverture,*" putting a million men into the field in eight days, they contended, was all they had asked for as a first step. But their memories were faulty. There is no doubt from the evidence now available that they warned the government that a general mobilization would be necessary if French forces were sent into the zone. It was this "lack of proportion between the step proposed and the envisaged operation," as Paul-Boncour called it, that frightened the members of the government, which had already been told that to challenge the Germans by arms in the Rhineland would lead to a general war. No one in France, the politicians above all, especially with an election due in a few weeks, wanted to risk war, or upset the country by staging a total mobilization.

One young Undersecretary of State, Jean Zay, remembered later how the defeatism of the Minister of War had "settled" the issue at this Sunday-morning cabinet meeting: "General Maurin said in a stifled voice: 'The Foreign Minister talks of . . . entering the Rhineland. . . . There are risks to this.' " Someone asked if "the risks entailed war.

"No one replied. General Maurin continued: 'The present state of the French Army does not allow us to run risks.' The Minister of Air and the Minister of Marine expressed in their turn opinions equally reserved."[46] Plainly the three armed services, above all the Army, which was by far the most important of them, did not want to do anything that would risk war.

In the face of this, Flandin caved in. Turning to the Premier he said: "I see, Mr. President, there is no use insisting."[47] The cabinet thereupon approved the government's decision to appeal to the League and to consult with the Locarno Powers. An official communiqué revealing this and adding that "the movement of troops" would be followed by the "preparation of additional measures" brought a sigh of relief in Berlin.

Hitler and his nervous generals had been waiting uneasily for more than twenty-four hours for a lightning French move into the zone. Now, after the news from Paris, they were greatly relieved. In Berlin that Sunday I noted:

Hitler has got away with it! France is not marching. Instead it is appealing to the League! No wonder the faces of Hitler and Goering and Blomberg and Fritsch were all smiles this noon as they sat in the royal box at the State Opera and . . . celebrated. . . . Heroes Memorial Day.

I had just learned that the German troops had been given strict orders to beat a hasty retreat at the sight of the first advancing French. They were not prepared or equipped, it was explained, to fight a regular army.[48]

That Sunday evening in Paris, Premier Sarraut took to the air in a nationwide broadcast to try to arouse the French people to a realization of what was at stake—and perhaps to put a little backbone into the hesitant generals as well. "We are not prepared," he said, "to allow Strasbourg to come under the fire of German cannon." The speech had been drafted for him at the Foreign Office but Flandin did not like its "bellicose tone" and in particular the sentence about Strasbourg, and told him so. But Sarraut grimly determined to deliver it unchanged. Jean Zay, his Undersecretary, stood just behind him as he spoke into the microphone. "In listening to these words," he remembered later, "which aroused so many different emotions, I understood nevertheless that the matter was closed."[49]

If he had been present to listen that same evening to General Gamelin as he presided over a lugubrious meeting of the military brass, he would have been even more disillusioned. It was a conference that the Army chief merely mentions in his memoirs as having taken place, but the minutes, made available recently,[50] shed more light than any other document on the hesitations of General Gamelin. Moreover they refute—in his own words—Gamelin's contention that he never considered a general mobilization necessary to force the Germans back out of the Rhineland. Excerpts from the secret minutes tell the story.

GENERAL GAMELIN: The government has asked me: "Are you ready to hold?" I answered that if a conflict between Germany and France was limited to the land front on the frontier . . . the front would become stabilized. Only the Air Force could carry out offensive action. . . .

Admiral Durand-Viel, the Navy commander, reminded him that the government was really asking the military: "Are you prepared to push the Germans out of the zone?"

General Gamelin answered: "The fact is that as soon as we enter the zone war will break out. That will make necessary a *general mobilization*." But he did not intend to venture into the Rhineland alone. "It will be necessary to have British and Italian contingents with us, and with the

Belgians." As to measures already taken, the general announced that the Maginot Line had been manned and twenty-four-hour leave for troops canceled in the east—"but not," he said, "in the rest of the country."

That was all. The Germans had been in the Rhineland for two days—with feeble forces that had done little more than parade in behind blaring bands. Only three battalions of infantry had been sent beyond the Rhineland cities toward the French frontier, and these had traveled leisurely by train. There was no deployment for battle. No tanks had crossed the demilitarized line 50 kilometers east of the Rhine.* Yet by the end of this second day General Gamelin had taken no steps to push across the still undefended frontier some of the troops he had nearby nor to assemble a force to back them up. His timid moves had been purely defensive, as if he really expected the German army, weak as it then was, to assault the formidable defenses of the Maginot Line. He did not, as he said, even cancel leaves "in the rest of the country," where the divisions he would need for ultimate action were stationed. They were not alerted to get ready to move. The general was waiting, as he said, for British and Italian reinforcements.

In London that Sabbath day Eden was making it plain that there would be no British "reinforcements." He was even stalling on rushing into *diplomatic talks* with the French. Flandin was pleading for a meeting with the British, and with the Belgians and Italians, in Paris on Monday. But Eden found this to be impossible. He would have to attend a cabinet meeting Monday morning, the first one called to consider the crisis, and in the afternoon he would have to make a statement to the Commons.

After his meeting in the country on Saturday afternoon with Baldwin, with whom he agreed that there would be no British support for French military action, Eden had spent the rest of the weekend in London drafting a note on the Rhineland situation for the cabinet and pressuring the French to make haste more slowly.

The Foreign Secretary explained to his colleagues that "the reoccupation of the Rhineland had deprived us of a useful bargaining counter." The words seem frivolous. He advised the cabinet that "military action by France against Germany should be discouraged." Any demand for Hitler to evacuate the Rhineland "should certainly not be made, unless the powers concerned were prepared to enforce it by military action." The French, "if further irritated," might move into the Saar. "We ought to avoid such a development," Eden argued, "if we could." He also thought "we must resist any attempt to apply financial and economic sanctions [against Germany]"[52]—this from the man who for five months had been hounding the French to back just such sanctions against Italy.

---

* General Guderian states flatly that no tanks were employed in the move into the Rhineland. Germany's three Panzer divisions had been formed only six months before, on October 15, 1935, and according to Guderian, were in no state for combat.[51]

In the meantime that Sunday the French Ambassador had been trying to pin down the British Foreign Secretary for a meeting of the Locarno Powers in Paris on Monday. He reported to Paris that he was having difficulties.[53] Finally Eden relented and agreed to come over on Tuesday morning on condition "that it be understood that at Paris the representatives of the powers will not be invited to agree immediately on concrete propositions. The question raises matters of exceptional gravity," Eden told the Ambassador, "and deserves to be examined with the patience necessary. The reunion in Paris will constitute a first discussion which can be followed the next day at Geneva, in awaiting the deliberation of the [League] Council, which alone is qualified to take decisions." The first meeting of the Council, Eden suggested, should take place Friday—one week after Hitler's violation of the Rhineland statutes.[54]

This was a British delaying action of considerable magnitude. By Friday, as Eden well knew, it would be too late for the League to do anything more than to register a formal—and useless—protest against another German violation of treaties.

THE "WAR CONFERENCE" OF MARCH 9

Monday evening, March 9, while waiting for the British to arrive on the morrow, Premier Sarraut made a last attempt to stir up his dormant generals. He called an informal meeting of the Supreme Military Committee for 9 P.M. at his home in the Avenue Victor Hugo, requesting the generals to bring their war maps and their plans for quick action.* He had been amazed to find in his talks with the military over the past forty-eight hours that the Army was not only reluctant to act but had prepared no plans, despite a year of warnings, for pushing the Germans out of the Rhineland.

There was a plan in the files of the General Staff, but it was out of date. "Plan D," as it was known, had been drawn up on October 22, 1932, three months before Hitler became Chancellor. In case the Germans attempted to reoccupy the demilitarized zone it called for an immediate French advance into the Saar with three divisions of infantry, a division of cavalry, and a brigade of Senegalese. Thereafter, an army of half a million men, brought to war footing within six days by the *couverture,* would advance into the rest of the zone. Admittedly, at the beginning of March 1936 the German army was considerably stronger than in 1932. But the first conscripts called up had had only four months of training, and the Wehrmacht, because of the restrictions of Versailles, lacked the trained reserves available to the French. Nevertheless General Gamelin now estimated that it would take three times the force laid down in "Plan D" merely to penetrate a few miles into the Saar on the left bank of the

---

* Gamelin gives the date of the meeting as March 10, a day later, but Sarraut was certain in his postwar testimony that it was March 9. See footnotes 55 and 56 for sources.

Saar River—ten divisions of infantry, one of cavalry, and "five organic elements of army corps." This would have given the French just one-hundredth of the Rhineland. And to accomplish it he wanted to mobilize more than a million men.

There was a second and more up-to-date plan for a sudden French riposte in the Rhineland drawn up at the request of a previous War Minister, Daladier, by General de Vaulgrenant, who had commanded the aviation of the Army of the Rhine throughout the postwar French occupation and who had a special knowledge of the territory. But in the crisis of March 7 the General Staff did not mention it to the Premier. Apparently it had disappeared mysteriously from its files.*

Afterward, Sarraut tried to sum up his thoughts as he prepared to meet the generals that evening of March 9.[56] He knew that France was obliged to appeal to the League Council and to the Locarno Powers, and this the government had done. But he also believed that under Article II of the Locarno Pact France had a right to invoke "legitimate self-defense" and carry out by itself a police action to expel the Germans from the demilitarized zone—and this without waiting for the League or the Locarno partners to act. He says he had no illusions that they would act in time. He knew the British and the Belgians strenuously opposed France's resorting to arms.

He therefore decided, he says, to ask the Military Committee to settle with him the question of a military riposte.

. . . to examine and discuss, with the maps before us, the practical possibilities, the tactical means . . . and the risks of an armed action without necessarily launching the general mobilization which General Maurin already had asked the government for.

I thought: "The British won't march, nor will the Belgians. They even oppose our moving ourselves. But if, in defiance of them, we carry out the operation ourselves, and succeed, they will thank us." Was there therefore not the means of carrying out this project without resorting to mobilization? Did the military not have the means of striking a blow without that? It seemed out of the question that they had not at least envisaged something like an advance with an expeditionary corps made up of troops on the frontier and just behind it. Was it perhaps that they lacked the guts to try such an operation?

The answers to his questions overwhelmed him. They came mostly from General Gamelin, who has left a detailed account of them, citing

---

* Deputy Louis Marin, in cross-examining Sarraut before the Parliamentary Investigating Committee after the war, charged that the papers on the Plan had disappeared. When, during the Rhineland coup, he had asked General de Vaulgrenant to find out why, the latter was rebuffed at the Ministry of War on the ground that his plan was "not official." Marin exclaimed: "What became of these documents? How did they disappear just when they were needed?" Later Sarraut asked General Gamelin, who replied: "Ah, yes, the Vaulgrenant report. Yes, there were several like that."[55]

them in defense of himself and the High Command.[57] They are far more revealing than he seems to have imagined of what Sarraut calls "the lack of the virile faculties of initiative, audacity, and imagination" in the Army chief and his fellow generals. The admirals of the Navy and the chiefs of the Air Force, who were also present, showed the same shortcoming.

In the first place, General Gamelin explained, the very "idea of sending quickly into the Rhineland a French expeditionary force, even a more or less symbolical one, is *chimerical*." The Army, he said, had no "expeditionary force. It is nonexistent. Our military system does not provide one." Then, with that patient meticulousness for which he had so formidable a talent, he explained what the French military system did provide.

> Our active army is but the framework of the mobilized national army . . . 400,000 active troops under arms for 3 million mobilized. None of our units is capable of being put instantly on a war footing.

He then recounted that the reinforcements already sent to the Franco-German frontier were "solely to increase our defensive power. They are good only for *static* [Gamelin's emphasis] employment on our territory. They have not increased our offensive power."

To obtain offensive power, to carry out any forward movement at all into the demilitarized zone, the government would first have to decree the "reinforced *couverture*." This would put 1.2 million men on a war footing at the end of eight days. And with such a sizable force what could be done? General Gamelin's answer was to sketch two very limited moves he had in mind and which, he pointed out, would present "the least risk." These were a short advance on a narrow front into a small part of the Saar, and a move into Luxembourg, a tiny buffer principality between Germany, France and Belgium, into which the Germans had shown no signs of advancing. "Either one," he added, "would take *eight days* to prepare." This information, Sarraut recalled, "stupefied" him. He wanted the French Army to move into the Rhineland where the Germans were, not into Luxembourg, where they weren't. He also wanted to know if that was all Gamelin proposed to do.

> Any other operation [Gamelin replied] would entail to a considerable degree all the inconveniences inherent in limited actions. . . . Naturally, there is no question initially of forcing the Rhine, on which the Germans are already practically installed.

Since Kehl was across the Rhine from Strasbourg, it could not be taken, nor even Saarbrücken just across the border in the Saar. Gamelin explained why. There were "difficulties" in fighting in the streets of towns. Urban agglomerations constituted "veritable strong points. In this regard, Saarbrücken is a city that stretches out in a vast industrial region. It would be absurd to get a 'bloody nose' there."

The Army chief painted a dark picture of what might happen if the French eventually penetrated very far into the Rhineland. "There we would run into not only the forces already there," the strength of which he grotesquely exaggerated, "but into the main German army. We would then need several armies and thus the total mobilization of our forces."* He did not look forward to grappling with the bulk of the Germany army. "The resources in men and industry of Germany are far superior. . . . For a long war we would have to have allies." And he had some questions—his mind seems always to have brimmed with questions—on that subject.

> Will the Belgians let us pass through? Will we have Italy with us or against us, or neutral? What will Poland, Czechoslovakia, Russia, do to retain German forces in the east? In brief . . . if Germany fights there can be total war and the government must envisage it cold-bloodedly.

What the Premier was envisaging that evening was a police action against a small band of German troops parading into the Rhineland, and the generals were telling him to envisage, instead, total war, with all its perils. General Gamelin, with an assist from General Pujo of the Air Force, then proceeded to run through, as Sarraut recalled, "the whole gamut of the perils."

> Our going into the Rhineland can bring in response a [German] attack on us through Belgium, as in 1914, aerial bombing of Paris, of our bases and assembly points, of London, Brussels, Liège, etc. attacks by [German] submarines, artillery bombardment of our Rhine cities, Strasbourg, Mulhouse, etc.

If the generals exaggerated the threat of bombing by the German Air Force, which had only been established less than two years before and at this time was not superior to the French Air Force, their estimate of German troops in the Rhineland by March 9 was so magnified as to be ludicrous, and one can understand the feeling of the postwar Parliamentary Investigating Committee that it constituted "a sort of alibi" concocted by the High Command for not acting.

General Gamelin's minutes of the March 9 Council of War put German military strength in the demilitarized zone, *as of the moment,* at "295,000 men, with the value of twenty-one to twenty-two divisions." But of these, 235,000 men were not soldiers at all, and 30,000 more, or all but the 30,000 regular army troops, were policemen from the *Landespolizei.* The French High Command's table of German forces in the Rhineland on March 9 lists 90,000 "Army troops—30,000 from the Wehrmacht,

---

* Sarraut says he tried to point out to his generals three reasons for not resorting to total mobilization: (1), it was unnecessary for the police action he was urging, (2), it would wreck the country's economy, already severely strained by five years of depression, and (3), it would transform, as he put it, "a legitimate police action, which we had every right to take, into a veritable declaration of war, for which France alone would be held responsible by all of Europe."[58]

30,000 from the *Landespolizei,* and 30,000 from the Labor Service (*Arbeitsdienst*), forming six to seven divisions." Now, as any correspondent in Berlin knew, the Labor Service at the beginning of 1936 was not a military force. Its men trained with shovels and were engaged mostly on public works. But, as if that were not exaggeration enough, General Gamelin adds to the German forces already in the zone 205,000 "auxiliary troops, forming the base of fifteen border security divisions." These, he says, comprised "150,000 SA, 25,000 SS, and 30,000 NSKK."

This is trickery. Again, anyone who worked in Berlin at that time (as this writer did), and certainly the French military attachés, knew that these Nazi Party paramilitary groups had no military value. The SA was a rabble of flabby Party hacks, the NSKK a sort of contingent of motorcyclists who delivered messages, and the SS at this time merely an elite group of guards for Hitler and the other party chiefs.

Jean Dobler, the French consul general in Cologne, whose warnings of a German reoccupation of the Rhineland had gone so unheeded in Paris, testified after the war on this and other matters pertaining to the High Command's hesitations.

> It does not seem to me that one can consider these four formations. . . . SS, SA, NSKK and the *Arbeitsdienst* as having any military value. . . . They could not overnight have fought in the Rhineland against our forces. . . . It seems to me excessive to count the men of these formations among the troops in the Rhineland in March 1936.[59]

Yet General Gamelin not only counted them but explained to the government that "these paramilitary formations can be quickly amalgamated into the active army."[*][60] To meet this phantom force General Gamelin was asking for the reinforced *couverture,* which would give him 1.2 million men. He reminded the Premier that it would cost at least 30 million francs a day, and to coat the bitter pill General Maurin, the War Minister,

---

* While he was on the stand before the Parliamentary Investigating Committee after the War, Dobler ventured to nail down the evasions of General Gamelin and the High Command regarding action that could have been taken by the French in the Rhineland. "It was suggested to General Gamelin that he occupy Kehl and Saarbrücken. Kehl is as far from Strasbourg as the Madeleine is from the Chamber of Deputies (i.e., a few blocks). Saarbrücken is at the frontier. But General Gamelin responds that he cannot force the Rhine even after the *couverture* and that it would be dangerous to occupy Saarbrücken. After all, the Germans had been in Kehl only four days; we had been in Strasbourg eighteen years, and no measure had been taken to allow us to cross the Rhine at a time when on the German side there were no fortifications and when we had artillery which could take Kehl under fire. The gage which General Gamelin envisaged taking was the left bank of the Saar river between Saarbrücken and Mertzig, which was an insignificant stretch of territory—perhaps a hundredth of the demilitarized zone."

Dobler thereupon asked a question which gets to the core of the matter: "What security did the demilitarized zone give us if the German Army could reoccupy it in twenty-four hours and we could not produce any response before at least eight days? It is inconceivable that the General Staff had to wait until March 7, 1936, to reveal this situation to the French government."[61]

chimed in that before any action could be taken there would have to be an "industrial mobilization." Again the Premier pointed out he was asking only for a police action. "After all," he remarked to the two generals, "you have merely a symbolic force in front of you—thirty battalions or so." But the military insisted not only on mobilizing a million men but industry as well.

That was not all. There was the Navy and the Air Force. General Pujo, the Air Force chief, painted a gloomy picture of German bombs raining down on Paris and other cities. He asked—and General Gamelin said it was "only logical"—for a total mobilization at once not only of the Air Force but of the antiaircraft defenses of the country. Admiral Durand-Viel announced, in Gamelin's words, "that the Navy could do nothing important at all without its own total mobilization." Finally, the Minister of War summed up the situation: "There are only two things to do: take measures of security—we've taken them; take steps leading to a penetration of Germany in force—these can lead eventually to war." Since the Premier knew that no one—neither the government nor Parliament nor the people nor, obviously, the Army—wanted war, he felt completely stymied. The generals would not, or could not, carry out the police action he thought would suffice. After listening to General Gamelin's long and lugubrious exposition, he later remembered thinking:

Why did the Chief of our Armies not grit his teeth and pound on the table and in the presence of the government hammer out a ringing profession of his faith? Why, instead of multiplying the objections in order to discourage action, did he not cry out to his listeners: "We must march. It's our duty. We will win. There is nothing else to do."[62]

The civilian Prime Minister was not the only one disillusioned by the timidity of the Army chief. Tony Albord, then a young staff officer and later a general, listened to a similar presentation General Gamelin gave to the Superior War Council two evenings later, on March 11. He recalled it after the war.[63]

Everyone was waiting . . . for important decisions. The meeting began. General Gamelin revealed the situation as he saw it and then outlined the measures which he had proposed to the government. A profound silence came over the assembly. The general spoke in a hollow voice, his eyes lost in the distance. As his thoughts came perhaps faster than his words, he did not, as was customary with him, finish his sentences. In the middle of this jerky discourse the words "general mobilization" fell like a heavy rock.

Could we really not undertake anything without going to this extreme? Was it not rather at this moment a question of audacity and speed? That at least was the idea which abruptly came over the mind of this modest and silent assistant. But doubtlessly qualified voices were going to be raised to suggest a bold solution. Foch had certainly left some pupils in this assembly, and Mangin some disciples. . . .

Could we not throw the Strasbourg division into Kehl or Landau, the one at Nancy into Saarbrücken, the one at Metz into Treves? Obviously this was the military side of the problem. But the government, judging by its public declarations, appeared to have decided to act vigorously, immediately, and alone, if necessary. Any initiative of this kind was thus sure to receive its support. . . .

The generals of the Army, surprised, overwhelmed by the words of the Commander in Chief, remained silent for the most part or merely raised objections of detail without interest. Not one reacted or protested or became angry. The meeting dragged on, doleful, deceiving, terrible. It ended finally in confusion.

And among those leaving there were some who perceived at once that France had just suffered her first defeat. This defeat came from the sanctioning of a defective military organization, without suppleness, unadapted to new and unexpected circumstances, which obliged us to use a hammer to kill a fly or to lay down the hammer, too heavy and too dangerous to handle, without having killed the fly.

Because in 1935 and 1936 we were unable to deliver a counterstroke with the appropriate instrument of combat, we were pushed slowly but surely toward war in the near future. And we were condemned to undertake this war with a rigid military system already out of date.

MUCH TALK AND NO ACTION

Eden's speech in the Commons on Monday afternoon had not encouraged the French to expect much of him when he arrived in Paris on Tuesday morning, accompanied by Lord Halifax.* While he had affirmed to the House that Great Britain would feel "honor bound" to come to the aid of Belgium and France if they were attacked, he had added that "there is, I am thankful to say, no reason to suppose that the present German action implies a threat of hostilities." And though he told Parliament that the occupation of the Rhineland had "profoundly shaken confidence in any engagement into which the Government of Germany may in the future enter" he had added that the British government would examine Hitler's new "peace proposals seriously and objectively" to determine if they afforded a new means of preserving "the structure of peace." And he concluded "If we want peace, it is our manifest duty to rebuild."†

When the representatives of the four Locarno Powers met at the Quai d'Orsay in Paris Tuesday morning it quickly became evident that the French position, in contrast to the British, was: If we want peace, we must throw the Germans out of the Rhineland at once. The French Foreign

---

* According to one British historian, Eden was carefully watched and checked by his cabinet colleagues from the opening of the crisis. This was the reason Halifax was sent with him to Paris (though Eden in his memoirs says it was at *his own* request). The same source asserts that Eden's speech to the Commons was modified by the cabinet.[64]

† The leading editorial that day in *The Times* of London, which had already embarked on its policy of appeasement of Hitler that was to culminate two years later in the Munich crisis, was entitled: "A Chance to Rebuild."

Minister demanded economic, financial, and military sanctions to achieve it. "The gravity of Flandin's statements," Eden thought, "exceeds anything which has been said before." Flandin claims he went even further than Eden recounts.[65] He said that France was ready to chase the Germans out of the demilitarized zone with her own forces; all she wanted was the moral support of the other Locarno Powers. This was pure bluffing. Eden suspected this, but he could not be sure. He reiterated Britain's opposition to French unilateral action, and in this, to Flandin's surprise, he was supported by the Belgian Prime Minister, Paul van Zeeland, who was aghast at the slightest prospect of war.

The Italian Ambassador said nothing, declining to enter into the discussions because his country was under League sanctions. What Eden suggested, in effect, according to Flandin, was that if France refrained from armed action, Germany could be induced by negotiations, if not to withdraw from the Rhineland, at least to agree to keep its reoccupation "symbolic" and to refrain from fortifying it.* He was "glad," he told Flandin, "that there was no intention to try to reach decisions at this meeting." The only decision was that the talks would be continued, not at Geneva, as first planned, but in London, where the Locarno Powers would meet again beginning March 12 and the League Council convene on March 14. This was a diplomatic setback for France. Flandin realized this as the meeting broke up. "Negotiations," he says he told the British, "will end in nothing, or, rather, they will sanction a new retreat. And this time the retreat will be decisive for it will generate a whole series of new retreats." In this at least, the French Foreign Minister was an accurate forecaster.

In London he fared no better with the British than he had in Paris. On the evening of March 14, at dinner at 10 Downing Street, he had a crucial meeting with Prime Minister Baldwin.† The Prime Minister told him, he recounts, that "he understood the French position but that he must tell me frankly that Britain could not take the least risk that might lead to war."

> Baldwin explained that although he understood little of foreign affairs he was able to interpret accurately the feelings of the British people. They wanted peace.

> Flandin relates that he replied that the best way of maintaining it was to stop Hitler's ambitions while it was still possible.

---

* The next evening, back in London, Eden asked Hitler, through the German Ambassador, to agree to withdraw all but a symbolic number of troops from the zone and to "undertake not to fortify the zone, at least for the period necessary for the negotiation of the pacts and for the regularization of the international situation." Hitler replied the next day that he would agree not to increase the number of troops already in the Rhineland but, as Eden notes, the German Chancellor "made no mention of the fortifications."[66]

† We have only his own account and, as will be manifest, it must be taken with a grain of salt.[67] Eden does not mention the meeting in his lengthy account of the proceedings in London.

France, I added, is not trying to drag Great Britain into war. She will herself assume all the risks of what is no more than a simple police operation. . . . All that we ask is that you give us a free hand.*

Baldwin listened. He did not discuss it, but always he came back to the same refrain: Britain was in no state to risk war. When I disputed that there was any risk he ended by saying: "You may be right. But if there is even one chance in a hundred that war would follow from your police action I have not the right to commit England. England is simply not in a state to go to war."

"I understood that evening," Flandin concludes, "that I would not obtain, despite my efforts, British acceptance of our military intervention in the Rhineland."

Despite his efforts? Did he make them? Later a French military document and the testimony of Eden raised doubts. There is a minute of a meeting of the military in Paris on March 13 presided over by General Georges and called to consider an urgent telephone message from Flandin in London, who demanded a reply the same evening. The Foreign Minister wanted to know what concessions the French could make, assuming the Germans remained in the Rhineland, and also what safeguards should be asked. Would it be "inconvenient," he asked, to agree to Germany and France maintaining the same number of troops on their frontier? Would it be "inconvenient" to agree that neither country should construct new fortifications near the frontier?[69]

Flandin, despite the defiant words he says he hurled at the British, was retreating. Eden, in his account of the London meetings, contends that the French Foreign Minister said one thing in private and another in public, and that in private he accepted the reestablishment of German military sovereignty in the zone on condition that it was "symbolic" and that no fortifications were built.[70] With this knowledge the British proceeded to persuade the Locarno Powers and the League Council to accept Hitler's gamble as a *fait accompli,* to condemn it, to try to limit its consequences, and then to throw a sop to France.

On March 19, exactly twelve days after the event, the League of Nations Council duly condemned Germany for reoccupying the Rhineland in violation of the Versailles and Locarno treaties. It was a hollow gesture. Of more apparent substance were two other agreements reached the same day: one between the Locarno Powers, and a second between Great Britain and France. The Locarno Powers agreed, as Eden puts it, to "reaffirm our obligations under the Treaty"—but of what value was this when the British had just reneged on them? They requested Germany not to

---

* To which Winston Churchill in his memoirs comments: "This is certainly not true. How could Britain have restrained France from action to which, under the Locarno Treaty, she was legally entitled?"[68] In view of what we have seen Generals Gamelin and Maurin telling Flandin and the government it is patent that Flandin was either bluffing or that his memory of what he says he told Baldwin is faulty. As Gamelin had told the Premier March 9, the very idea of a police action was "chimerical."

increase her military force in the demilitarized zone and not to fortify it. They asked Germany to accept an international force made up of troops from the four Locarno guarantor powers to occupy a stretch 20 kilometers wide on the German side of the Franco-Belgian frontiers, with an international commission to watch over it. The purpose of these "requests" was to keep the German reoccupation of the zone "symbolic." If Germany agreed to them, the Locarno Powers would then be willing to open negotiations with Hitler on his "peace proposals," including a revision of the Rhineland statutes. Finally, the Locarno Powers announced that discussions between their General Staffs would be inaugurated. If this last was meant to frighten Hitler it failed. He rejected the requests.

Flandin made much of the final accomplishment in London of March 19: a letter from the British government to the effect that if the negotiations with Germany failed the British government would not only consult with France about the "new situation" but would come to her aid in the case of unprovoked aggression. The guarantee was to be reciprocal and contact between the General Staffs of the two countries was to be "established and continued." A similar letter was given Belgium. To Flandin, who obtained it, this was, he said, the equivalent of an Anglo-French military alliance—similar to the one that had saved France in 1914. He claimed more: that it was a British guarantee against any further infractions by Germany in the Rhineland and obligated Britain to come automatically to the aid of the French to prevent the Germans from increasing their forces in the Rhineland or from fortifying it.

This proved to be a rather academic point in the end. London and Berlin exchanged proposals and counterproposals for the contemplated negotiations, ending up with Eden's much publicized questionnaire to Hitler on May 7, exactly two months after the Rhineland coup.* The Fuehrer never bothered to answer it. After all, he had given his answers long before in *Mein Kampf.* The negotiations of the Locarno Powers on the Rhineland and on Hitler's "peace proposals" petered out before they had made a serious start, as did the crisis itself, leaving Germany in full military control of the demilitarized zone. Strasbourg found itself in the range of German guns.

What happened to the British guarantee of March 19? Flandin says that to succeeding French governments it "seems to have been purely and simply forgotten." When the Germans started to fortify the Rhineland and thus created the "new situation" stipulated in the Anglo-French accord, the government of the day in Paris did not think to invoke it.[72]

---

* Some of the questions were: Was Germany now ready to conclude "genuine treaties"? Did Germany intend to respect the existing territorial and political status in Europe? Did Germany subscribe to the principle of nonintervention as well as nonaggression? Was she willing to make a nonaggression pact with Russia? The questions struck most observers as rather absurd, the kind a fussy old maid of an aunt might put to an obstreperous nephew. Eden later explained that their real purpose was to "expose Hitler's intentions."[71]

CONSEQUENCES: THE RHINELAND CRISIS IN RETROSPECT

After the war the Parliamentary Investigating Committee tried to find out why France had not done something about Hitler's coup in the Rhineland and whether, if it had, the attempt would have succeeded. It heard testimony from all of the surviving principals, civilian and military.

General Maurin, who had been Minister of War, was questioned by Louis Marin, a conservative deputy, who, unlike most of his colleagues on the Right, had resisted the Germans to the end.

MARIN: General, in the days before March 7, when everyone expected the [German] move, what did the Ministry of War do?

GENERAL MAURIN: Nothing special. . . .

MARIN: But what was the plan? To prevent the Germans from crossing the Rhine something more was called for than merely putting a few troops in a state of readiness. The military certainly had a plan? The Ministry of War had a plan?

GENERAL MAURIN: No, I do not recall. To prevent the Rhine from being crossed you had to get to the Rhine. And with artillery. You had to go to war. . . . No one in the cabinet wanted war. No one in the country wanted it. The moment it was decided that no one wanted war, we had to accept it.[73]

General Gamelin, in his postwar testimony, was even more evasive. Exonerating the military, himself above all, he blamed the government for the failure to counter the Germans in the demilitarized zone. He had a remarkable talent for passing the buck. Marin tried to pin him down, as he had General Maurin.

MARIN: The General Staff was warned in advance. Why did it not prepare a riposte which could be launched automatically and which would brake or annihilate the [German] crossing of the Rhine?

Gamelin replied that the General Staff *had* prepared something, the limited advance into the Saar. Marin persisted.

MARIN: Well, if, as you say, you prepared something why was nothing done?

GAMELIN: To carry out the plan, we needed reserves. Our army of 1936 could do nothing until it was reinforced by these prior measures, prescribed by law.

He blamed the government for not giving him the means to act. He blamed it for giving in to the British.

THE PRESIDENT [of the Committee]: Did Premier Sarraut tell you why the government decided to do nothing?

GAMELIN: Yes. Because of England. He told me: "The English won't march."[74]

In his own postwar testimony[75] Sarraut also reproached the British.

> We had the right to act alone. . . . But the British said: "If you march alone, that will bring a rupture between us!" . . . In the presence of this risk the majority of my government was against taking action alone. . . . The British would not listen to doing anything, at any price. If we acted, it was the rupture—and in that case our complete isolation. There was no one else; the Belgians went along with the British; the Italians naturally followed their own game. We found ourselves completely alone.

But to blame Britain for the lack of French action was, as Churchill said, "an explanation but no excuse . . . since the issue was vital to France."[76] Reynaud agreed. He found it "a poor excuse . . . and a cover for the French government's failure."

In the perspective of a decade, the French Parliament Investigating Committee took a more tolerant view of British behavior in the Rhineland crisis. After concluding that France, with Poland and Czechoslovakia,* had a decided military superiority over Germany on March 7, 1936, it disputed the contention that Britain threatened a rupture if the French had marched into the demilitarized zone.

> In these conditions the British objections need not have impressed us. It was not a question of the rupture of Franco-British amity. . . . In the spring of 1936 Britain could not act with arms. But France, which was far from having disarmed as the British had, was able to impose the respect of international law on Hitler. . . .
>
> The documents agree. . . . Great Britain completely respected the freedom of decision of France. She insisted that we should not launch military operations. But never did the official dispatches nor the words of her statesmen threaten a rupture if France exercised alone the right of legitimate defense recognized by Locarno. . . . England loyally indicated to us her position and its possibilities. Her policy was largely influenced by our own incertitudes. The traditional pragmatism of the British statesmen would have inspired other solutions if on the morning of March 7, as soon as the Germans moved, French troops had crossed the frontier to impose respect for the demilitarized zone.[77]

Could the French army have driven the Germans out? The Parliamentary Committee, after hearing all the evidence, concluded that it could have.

---

* Poland and Czechoslovakia in 1936 had more trained troops between them than Germany had, and the Czechoslovak army, thanks to the production of the Skoda armament works, was better armed. Both governments indicated immediately that they would honor their treaty engagements and come to the aid of France if she became engaged in hostilities with Germany in the west. At no time, so far as the available documents show, did General Gamelin take into consideration the value of the Polish and Czech armies when he calculated (and exaggerated) the risk of French action.

The relation of forces in being permitted France by herself to chase the German troops from the Rhineland. But it was necessary to act at once. . . . An immediate and powerful response, carrying our troops to the Rhine and permitting us to occupy bridgeheads on the right bank, would have placed Germany in a very unfavorable strategic situation. We could then, if she intended to continue hostilities, have pushed our offensives through the valleys of the Ruhr, the Main, and the Necker, toward her most vital centers. Hitler did not have at this time the forces of 1939. . . .

But evidently we could not make the slightest response without calling to the colors a million men. . . . To chase three regiments of the Wehrmacht we had to put on a war footing the whole French Army and indeed mobilize the entire nation.[78]

If the French had budged, what would have happened? What would the Germans have done? Hitler himself later gave the answer.

If the French had marched into the Rhineland, we would have had to withdraw with our tails between our legs, for the military resources at our disposal would have been wholly inadequate for even a moderate resistance.[79]

And General Alfred Jodl, a rising star in the German High Command and one of its best brains, testified at the Nuremberg Trials: "Considering the situation we were in, the French covering army could have blown us to pieces."[80]

Would that have brought an end to Hitler and the downfall of the Third Reich (and averted the Second World War)? Hitler's own answer, made in confidence, has been preserved. "A retreat on our part," he said long afterward, in reminiscing of his Rhineland gamble, "would have spelled collapse. . . . The forty-eight hours after the march into the Rhineland were the most nerve-racking in my life."[81]

For France the failure to oppose the German reoccupation of the demilitarized zone was a disaster, and one from which all the later ones of even greater magnitude followed. The two Western democracies had missed their last chance to halt, without the risk of a serious war, Nazi Germany and probably, as we have seen Hitler admitting, to bring down the Nazi dictator and a regime bent on conquering Europe as soon as it was fully armed. They let the opportunity slip by.

The whole structure of European peace and security set up in 1919 collapsed. The French alliances with the countries to the east of Germany were rendered useless. As soon as Hitler had fortified the Rhineland, the French Army, even if it found more resolute generals, would no longer be able to achieve a quick penetration of Germany to aid the Eastern allies if they were attacked. Indeed the French Army would no longer be able to tie down in the west the main German forces. They would be free to assault Czechoslovakia and Poland. This was quickly realized in Prague and Warsaw—this and more: for if the French Army was too timid to move into the undefended Rhineland it would never do so when that region was bristling with fortifications.

The supineness of France and Great Britain on and after March 7, 1936, greatly strengthened Hitler's position in Germany. The people rejoiced at his show of strength and showed it in a plebiscite on March 29 in which 98.8 percent of them voted their approval of his action. His gamble assured him a further ascendancy over his generals, the last group in Germany with any power to curb his megalomania. They had feared the French Army; he had shown how hollow was the fear. And he had opened for them vast new possibilities for military conquests in the East.

France lost, in effect, not only her allies in the East but an ally in the West. Belgium defected from her military alliance and obtained, on April 24, 1937, a release by Britain and France even from her obligations under Locarno and the London agreement of March 19. She reverted to her old neutrality. The initiative for this foolish step was taken by the young king, Leopold III, soon after the March 7 crisis, but it was backed by all the parties, including the Socialists, and by the vast majority of the people. Not only the great Western democracies were becoming blinded to their own best interests but the little ones as well. In their joint declaration to Belgium, Britain and France agreed to come to her aid if she were attacked. But such a guarantee was of little practical value unless there were plans of the three General Staffs for military aid *in time*. King Leopold and the government ruled out all staff talks and all military understandings, taking the pose that Belgium had no more to fear from Germany than from France. This was folly.

France emerged from the crisis weakened in other ways. It had feared to act without British approval and henceforth it would do nothing without the prior consent of the government in London. It thus abandoned an independent foreign policy. This subordination to Britain might not have been so disastrous had there been resolute men, with a knowledge of history, even contemporary history, at the helm in London. But there were none. Churchill was still in the political wilderness, deprived by his fellow conservatives of a place in the cabinet. It was Neville Chamberlain who would soon succeed Baldwin as Prime Minister, and he was already obsessed with the belief that war could be avoided by the further appeasement of Hitler. Italy, which seemed a year before to be an ally against Germany, had been lost because of sanctions and already showed signs of passing to the other side.

At home the fear of war over the demilitarized zone, slight as the possibility was, served to intensify the pacifism of the Left. It staunchly supported the government for having done nothing to spoil Hitler's gamble in the Rhineland. On the Right there was further disillusionment with England and a despair that soon grew into outright defeatism. More and more, Conservative circles concluded that Nazi Germany represented the wave of the future and that France must make an accommodation with it. This was the conclusion that Flandin reached, and Laval, and many others.

Finally, the crisis of March 7 had revealed the weakness of the Army and the timidity of its High Command, especially of General Gamelin, its chief. If this revelation, which had so shocked Sarraut, Flandin, and Paul-Boncour, had provoked the government into doing something about it, into cleaning out the tired old generals and replacing them by younger and more energetic men (as Hitler had done in Germany) and in reorganizing the Army so that it could do more than huddle behind the Maginot Line, then the setback to the country might have been mitigated.

One day after the war while Sarraut was testifying before the Parliamentary Investigating Committee he was asked by Michel Clemenceau, the son of the old Tiger, who had not tolerated hesitant generals in the first war, why, since General Gamelin had shown himself to be such a defeatist and, as he said, "scarcely a great warrior," the Premier had not cashiered him. "To do that," Sarraut answered, "it would be necessary to transform the psychology of men."

Gamelin had been the aide of Joffre. It was believed that he had inherited Joffre's doctrine, his talents, his experience. He was, in addition, extremely intelligent. . . . One of the grave faults of politicians and members of government is that they have always had complete confidence, permeated by timidity, in the military. The only exception was your father. . . . The rest always have hesitated to intrude in military circles. It is stupid, but that's the way it is.[82]

For a few weeks after March 7 the Premier seems to have had his doubts about leaving Gamelin in command of the Army. On April 4 he summoned to his office the general, along with the Chiefs of Staff of the other two services and the ministers of all three and asked point-blank: "Is our land army and our air force really incapable of taking any action at all?" On Gamelin's smooth assurance that the two services were "ready for war," which the events of the previous weeks had shown they were not, Sarraut dropped the matter.[83] His caretaker government, now that the elections were at hand, was about to relinquish office. General Gamelin and General Georges, the Major General of the Armies, were left in their top posts. They would command the French armies four years later when the supreme test came—the test that might have been avoided had they been more resolute on March 7, 1936.

If on that day the military High Command was found wanting, so was the government, the Parliament, the press, the people. It was a collective failure that had paralyzed France's will to act and it had been in the making a long time. It was, as the Parliamentary Investigating Committee found more than a decade later, "the result of seventeen years of improvidence, of illusions, and of complacency. The moment the Wehrmacht crossed the

Rhine, France began to pay for the immense errors of its foreign and military policies committed since 1919. . . . Intellectual and moral weakness explain our setback."[84]

But the country was in no mood that spring of 1936 to assess the reasons for this setback or to consider its fateful consequences. It was now embroiled in the bitterest election campaign the Third Republic had seen since the epic battle between MacMahon and Gambetta, between the Right and the Left, in 1877. What mattered most to Frenchmen was not that the country had suffered perhaps a fatal blow from without but whether for the first time since the Republic's birth the voters would return a genuinely Left government, the Popular Front, pledged to reform the nation's social and economic structure, which had been defended so long and so successfully by the conservative middle and upper classes.

To the Left, a coalition of the Radicals, Socialists, and Communists, military intervention in the Rhineland would have upset its bright chances for victory at the polls. To the Right, obsessed by fear of Communism and even of radical change, however long overdue, it was more important to stop the Front Populaire in the polling booth than to stop Hitler at the Rhine.

17

FRANCE FURTHER DIVIDED—
THE *FRONT POPULAIRE*
AND THE SPANISH CIVIL WAR
1936–1937

L éon Blum, the Socialist leader and one of the principal architects of the Popular Front coalition, was unable to take an active part in the tumultuous election campaign that spring, which culminated at the polls on April 26, 1936, with the runoff a week later. He had been a victim of the current political gangsterism on the extreme Right. On February 13 a group of royalist ruffians had savagely beaten him to within an inch of his life.

Driving from the Chamber of Deputies with his Socialist colleague Georges Monnet and Madame Monnet on their way to lunch, their car was held up on the Boulevard Saint-Germain near the corner of the rue de l'Université by the funeral procession of Jacques Bainville, the royalist historian, who had died four days before. A group of young fanatics from Action Française and its Camelots du Roi, accompanying the cortège, recognized the Socialist leader and promptly set upon him. Breaking the windows of the car, tearing the doors off, the youths dragged Blum out of the car after pummeling Monnet and his wife to get at him and proceeded to beat and kick him unmercifully. He was saved by a group of construction workers repairing the walls of the nearby Ministry of War who rushed to his aid and extricated him from his assailants. Bleeding profusely, especially from a gash in his temple, he was taken to the hospital, where the bleeding was stopped and his wounds dressed. The shock and the loss of blood left him invalided for several weeks, which he spent recuperating at the home of Vincent Auriol in the south of France.

Even the right-wing deputies in the Chamber were shocked at this latest violence in the streets and joined the others in condemning it. Before the afternoon was over the Sarraut government issued a decree dissolving Action Française and two of its student organizations. Charles Maurras, the leader of Action Française, was later indicted, convicted of incitement to murder and sentenced to four months in prison.* In one front-page editorial after another he had been urging his followers to get rid of "this naturalized German Jew, or son of one, this monster of the democratic Republic," one way or another. On April 9 the year before, on page one of L'Action Française, Maurras had suggested one way: "He is a man," he wrote of Blum, "who must be shot—but in the back."

The beating up of the Socialist leader gave the Front Populaire a martyr and enhanced its election prospects. It stirred the workers and the liberal elements in the middle classes to strive harder for victory. It jolted many solid burghers into the conviction that there was a threat from Fascism at home. And the explanation in the columns of L'Action Française the next day that the assault on Blum had been a deliberate provocation, a diabolical plot, by the police, the Bolsheviks, and the British to discredit the royalists and pave the way for the Soviets' taking over the country did not increase the credibility of the extreme Right in the minds of those in the middle of the road. These moderates, who because of their numbers held the balance of power in any national election, were deeply troubled. From the Right they were warned that the triumph of the Front Populaire would bring the immediate Bolshevization of France; from the Left they were warned that only a Popular Front government could save the country from Fascism. They wanted neither Communism nor Fascism. But many of them felt it was time for a change, for a fresh attempt to lift the country out of the miseries of the Depression, as the American electorate had felt in 1932. Their votes would be added to those of the giant bloc of workers, white-collar employees, small shopkeepers, and even peasants who believed that only a Popular Front government could give the people a New Deal.

Despite a heavy rain over much of France on Sunday, April 26, a record number of voters—85 percent of those registered—turned out to cast their ballots. Though the Left Coalition showed heavy gains—the Communist vote was up by 700,000 over 1932—the results were inconclusive so far as seats won in the Chamber were concerned. In 424 out of the 598 electoral districts in metropolitan France no candidate received the necessary absolute majority and a runoff on the following Sunday was necessary. Here the Popular Front showed the value of its discipline. With few exceptions its candidate receiving the highest vote in the first balloting was solidly supported by all the Left parties against the candidates of the Right in the second one, where only a plurality was necessary.

The popular vote, though decisive, was fairly close: 5,628,921 for the candidates of the Popular Front and 4,218,345 for their opponents. But thanks to the unity shown in concentrating its votes in the runoffs the Popular Front emerged with a strong majority in the Chamber of Deputies, 378 to 220. The Socialists and the Communists were the chief gainers.

---

* Maurras was elected to the Académie Française two years later.

With 1,977,000 votes the Socialists for the first time in the history of the Third Republic became the largest party in France, increasing their representation in the Chamber from 97 to 146. Proportionately the Communists did even better. They doubled their vote to a million and a half and increased the number of their deputies sevenfold—from 10 in the old Chamber to 72 in the new. For the first time the Communists constituted a numerically important party in the Chamber.

The Socialist-Communist gains were achieved partly at the expense of their bourgeois ally, the Radical-Socialists, theretofore the largest party in the country. Their vote fell by 400,000 to 1,955,060 and their delegation in the Chamber from 159 to 116. Their participation in the conservative governments of the preceding two years and their support of the deflationary measures which those governments had carried out had driven many of their supporters farther left.

The masses were thrilled by their victory, achieved peacefully and democratically at the polls. It buoyed them up with new hopes. The misery of the workers and white-collar employees had struck one moderate French historian as utterly "stupefying," and he had added that the "selfishness and blindness of the French bourgeoisie called for a revolutionary movement."[1] At a moment when great dangers, from without and within, threatened the country, the Popular Front, he thought, as did many others, offered perhaps the last chance to integrate into the nation the proletariat, which for so long had lived in exile on its own soil. For the third time in a century the vast laboring class was knocking at the gates of the City. In 1848 and 1871, despite their successful revolutions, the workers had been turned back. Now in the spring of 1936 they felt that they would enter. The victory at the polls had at last given their elected representatives the dominant role in the government. The Socialist and Communist leaders had, it is true, warned them that a victory of the Popular Front would be no mandate for a revolution. But at least it promised long-overdue social and economic reforms: higher pay, paid vacations, shorter working hours, and collective bargaining rights for all employees; new policies for getting the stagnant economy moving, curbs on financial speculations, and "democratization" of the Bank of France so that it would serve the nation and not just the interests of the famous "Two Hundred Families" who controlled it. There would be not revolution, but reform.

Dismayed by the triumph of the Popular Front, the upper classes did not see the difference. To them the "Bolsheviks" had wrested control of the government. They saw France on the brink of red revolution. There was a panic on the Bourse. Government bonds fell sharply. Shares of the Bank of France dropped in one week from 7,830 francs to 7,365. A flight of capital and a panicky buying of gold began. By the end of the week after the elections the Bank of France had lost 2.5 billion francs from its gold reserves.

The rush by the possessors of capital to send it abroad was designed not only to protect themselves but, obviously, to sabotage the efforts of the Popular Front to regenerate the country's depressed economy by putting French capital to productive work. Capital abroad would be "safe" for the holder, but it was lost to the nation's economy, which badly needed it. This form of sabotage had been tried against the Herriot government after the victory of the Cartel des Gauches in the 1924 election, and it had worked.

Realizing that the flight of capital would be disastrous to the country, the leaders of the Popular Front, even before taking office, strove to assure the possessors of capital that their moneybags were safe at home. But the assurance fell on deaf ears. All through May, while Blum waited impatiently to take over, the rich continued frantically to convert their francs into foreign exchange and to buy and hoard gold. The inept Sarraut government declined to take measures to stop it. Blum and his designated Finance Minister, Vincent Auriol, in an effort to restore confidence in business and financial circles, promised they too would respect the capitalist's freedom to do with his money what he pleased.

Though the citizens had expressed their will by the only means afforded them in a democracy when they went to the polls that spring, it did not appear that they had narrowed the gulf which separated Frenchmen, the Haves and the Have-Nots, the Right and the Left. On the contrary. It was obvious from the hysterical reaction of the Right that the advent of the Front Populaire, despite all the declarations of Blum that he hoped to conciliate conflicting class interests for the good of society and the country, threatened to widen and deepen the old cleavage. It seemed doubtful to the objective observer—few in number in France that spring of 1936— that the course of French history in this respect could be changed.

But an attempt was made.

The very morning after the elections, on May 4, Blum announced that the Socialist Party, as the largest one in the Popular Front and in the Chamber, was ready to form a new government. For thirty years this party had refused to take part in a "bourgeois" government, even in 1924 and 1932 when a Left majority had been returned to Parliament and the then dominant Radical-Socialists had begged its leaders to join them in forming a cabinet. Blum and his party had spent their entire lives in the opposition. Now, just turned sixty-four and without any cabinet experience whatsoever, the Socialist leader was anxious to try his hand "without losing a moment."

He had few illusions about himself or his task. In his first speech after the election, on May 10, he told the National Council of his party: "I do not know whether I have the qualities of a leader for so difficult a battle," a statement that recalls to American readers similar ones made by Adlai

Stevenson. Like Stevenson, Blum was prey to self-doubts, self-criticism, and given to airing his soul-searching in public.*

He had few illusions, either, about how far the Popular Front could go in making over the nation. In a speech to the Socialist Party Congress in Paris on the last day of May, shortly before he would take office, he warned his followers that the Popular Front had not received a mandate to change the existing capitalist economic and social order. There was a difference, he explained, between "the exercise of power within the framework of capitalist society and the revolutionary conquest of power."

Neither the Socialists alone nor the proletarian parties together have a majority. The majority is based on a coalition of the working classes and the middle classes organized around the Popular Front program. Our mandate is to carry out that program.

He gave a categorical assurance to the whole nation:

We are going to act within the framework of the present regime, whose contradictions and injustices we pointed out in the course of the election. . . . The real problem that this experiment will pose is to learn if from this social system it is possible to extract the maximum of order, welfare, security, and justice for all who work and produce.

Because the old Chamber did not expire until the end of May Blum could not constitutionally assume office until the beginning of June. For a whole month the caretaker, "do-nothing" government of Sarraut would have to suffice. But the workers, so long submissive and quiet, were now flushed by the success of the Popular Front at the polls. They refused to wait. Spontaneously, without authorization from their unions (most workers were unorganized) or encouragement from their political parties, they began to launch a series of strikes that swelled like a tidal wave beyond anything the country had ever seen and which threatened to wreck the Popular Front and indeed the country before Blum and his colleagues could get at the helm and do something about them. The lame-duck Sarraut government folded its hands and did nothing.

The strikes began at various airplane factories, at Bréguet in Le Havre on May 11, at Bloch in Courbevoie on the 14th, at Nieuport at

---

* Blum's first speech after the election and Adlai Stevenson's address accepting the Democratic nomination in 1952 alluded to a well-known Biblical passage. Blum, after expressing doubts about his abilities as a leader added: "But I do not come here to say to you: 'Let this cup pass from me. I did not wish it, I did not ask for it.' Yes, I did ask for it." Stevenson after similarly depreciating his qualities for the Presidency —he wished that the Convention had chosen "a stronger, a wiser, a better man than myself"—went on: "I have asked the Merciful Father to let this cup pass from me. But from such dread responsibility one does not shrink in fear. . . . So, 'If this cup may not pass from me, except I drink it, Thy will be done.' "

Issy-les-Moulineaux on the 26th. At first they seemed sporadic and attracted little attention in the press. But from May 26 on they began to spread like wildfire. On the 27th the 35,000 workers of the country's largest automobile works, Renault, struck and it was here that the Parisians learned that the strikes were different from any previously known. Borrowing from an American example the workers staged a "sit-down," or "sit-in" strike. They simply occupied the factory, expelled the managers from the premises, or, in a few cases, locked them up in their offices. This disregard of the ancient rights of property enraged the conservatives and later Blum would frankly admit in the Chamber that the occupation of the factories was illegal. That they were peaceful and orderly, that no damage was done to property, and that the workers carried out their "sit-ins" with surprisingly good humor did not assuage the outraged feelings on the Right. The conservative *Le Temps* felt there was something sinister in the very mood of the strikers—perhaps they behaved so well because they thought they were going to take over the factories intact and run them. To the rightist *Echo de Paris* the "good humor" of the strikers portended even worse. "All revolutions commence like that. There is a very strong feeling in Paris that the revolution has begun."

In vain the leaders of the Socialist and Communist parties and of the Confederation of Labor pleaded with the strikers to resume work. By June 3, the day before Blum took office, there were 350,000 men and women on strike in the Paris region alone and nearly twice as many more in the rest of the country. In most cases they had occupied the struck plants. Unless the strikes could be speedily settled they threatened to paralyze the country. In the Elysée Palace, the edgy President of the Republic, appalled by the turn of events, thought of resigning. Lebrun disliked the Popular Front and feared, he said, its "excesses." As the strikes mounted he tried to persuade Blum to replace Sarraut at once but the Socialist leader, a great stickler for legality, refused on the ground that it would be unconstitutional.

Finally on the evening of June 4 Blum arrived at the Palace to present his new cabinet to the President. Its makeup was not as complete as he had hoped. The Communists had refused to join it. Publicly they had explained that their presence in the cabinet would give a pretext to the reactionaries to sabotage the new government. They promised nevertheless to support it "loyally and without reserve" in the Chamber. Actually they did not want to tarnish their image as a truly revolutionary proletarian party. They believed that Blum would be the prisoner of his "bourgeois" allies, the Radical-Socialists, and would be unable to achieve any important change in the economic and social structure of the country. From this they hoped eventually to benefit by attracting all the proletariat to their banner. Blum could hardly complain. For more than a decade he had persuaded the Socialist Party to adopt the same attitude toward the Radical governments. Blum had also asked the General Confederation of Labor to be represented in the new government but the CGT had also declined. The trade-union movement was opposed to direct participation in politics.

The cabinet which the new Premier presented to President Lebrun was therefore made up of Socialists, Radical-Socialists, and a few from the splinter Left parties. It was a novel cabinet in two ways. It included several relatively young men and, as undersecretaries, three women—in a country where women did not have the vote. Mme. Irène Joliot-Curie was Under-secretary for Scientific Research.

Lebrun, as always in a crisis, was in a highly emotional state that evening. He insisted that the new government, though it could not lawfully assume power before receiving a vote of confidence in the Chamber, immediately take over the ministries of the Interior and Labor "from this moment on, as of 9 o'clock," so that the strikes and the threat to public order would not get further out of hand. Blum agreed. He dispatched Roger Salengro and Jean Lebas to the Interior and Labor ministries at once.

After the members of the government had been sworn in, the President asked the new Premier to remain with him. It was a painful moment for Lebrun, who believed the Popular Front might well ruin the country, and who had little personal sympathy for Blum. He had by this time, however, abandoned his inclination to resign. If he had done so, he later said, he would have been succeeded by a Popular Front candidate, since the Left now had a majority in the National Assembly, which elected the President. "I had the illusion," Lebrun explained, "that my presence could prevent certain abuses, restrain certain excesses."[2]

"The situation is terrible," the President told the Premier. "When are you going to present your government to the Chamber?"

"Day after tomorrow, Saturday," Blum answered, explaining that it would be physically impossible to convoke the Chamber before then.

"You're going to wait until Saturday?" Lebrun asked. "You don't realize what's happening in the country?"

No one realized it better than Blum, but he kept his temper. The President insisted that the Premier do something immediately to calm the country, imploring him at least to take to the radio the very next day. "Tell the workers," he counseled, "that Parliament is going to meet, that as soon as it convenes you are going to ask it to pass immediately the measures they are demanding."[3]

Again Blum complied, though he had qualms about the "parliamentary correctness" of such a step before he had been confirmed in office by the Chamber. The Right was already predicting that the Popular Front would tear up the constitution and carry out a revolution, and Blum, extremely sensitive to this, was particularly anxious to show how groundless were such fears. The next day at noon he broadcast to the nation and particularly to the striking workers, assuring the latter that he would ask Parliament to vote without delay the laws "which you demand—the right of collective bargaining, the 40-hour week and paid vacations." On the following day,

Saturday, June 6, Blum presented his government to the Chamber and outlined the program of the Popular Front, which, besides the labor measures, called for a public-works project, nationalization of the armament industry, reform of the Bank of France, a Wheat Office to stabilize farm prices, raising of the compulsory school age, and repeal of the cuts in salaries of civil servants and pensions to war veterans. He received a decisive vote of confidence, 384 to 210.

The experiment of the Popular Front was launched.

No worse time could be imagined for its debut, with the bourgeoisie tense from fear, capital fleeing, the Treasury in difficulties, the economy moribund, and the sit-in strikes threatening to paralyze the country, while abroad, Mussolini was completing the conquest of Abyssinia in defiance of the League of Nations, Hitler was consolidating his military hold on the Rhineland and feverishly rearming, and Spain, under a newly elected *Frente Popular* of its own, was rapidly sliding into anarchy and almost certain civil war.

As if that were not enough, Blum was confronted from the outset with a wave of anti-Semitism such as France had not seen since the days of the Dreyfus Affair. It was directed against him personally because he was a Jew, the first to become Premier in the history of France. At the opening session of the new Chamber a rightist deputy, Xavier-Vallat, taunted the Premier for his Jewishness.

XAVIER-VALLAT: Your arrival in office, Mr. President, is incontestably a historic date. For the first time this ancient Gallic-Roman country will be governed——

HERRIOT (the Speaker): Be careful what you say, M. Vallat!

XAVIER-VALLAT: ——by a Jew. I have to say aloud what everyone is thinking silently—that to govern this peasant nation which is France it is better to have someone whose origins, no matter how modest, spring from the womb of our soil rather than have a subtle Talmudist.

And he warned that the country would now be run by "a small Jewish coterie." Blum for a moment was beside himself with rage but before he could respond Herriot censored Xavier-Vallat* and declared the incident closed. For the reactionary press, however, it was just a beginning.

In *L'Action Française,* Maurras and Daudet had a field day. "France under the Jew" was the title of Maurras' first editorial the day after Blum took office. "We now have a Jewish government," he warned his readers. Daudet excelled him in inventing insulting titles for the new Premier: "Blum, the gentle yid," "the radiophonic Hebrew," who presided over the "Cretin-Talmud cabinet." France, said Daudet, had returned to the times of "the traitor Alfred Dreyfus. The domination of a rabbinical Jew, Léon

---

* Xavier-Vallat ended up at Vichy as administrator of the anti-Jewish Pétain-Laval decrees.

Blum, a total stranger to our manners, customs, and ways of understanding and feeling, multiplies the peril of war by ten times." Previously the Right had assaulted Blum for his pacifism. Now it cried out that because of his hatred of Fascism he would lead the country into war against Italy and Germany. *L'Action Française* harped on the fear. "It is as a Jew that Blum must be seen, conceived, understood, fought and brought down," wrote Maurras. "This last verb may seem a little strong. I hasten to say I do not mean that Blum must be beaten down physically—until that day when his policies lead us into the war which he dreams of waging against our Italian friends. That day we must not fail to do so." Gleefully Maurras quoted some lines that André Gide, whose literary fame in the thirties had become enormous and who in 1936 was just abandoning a naive faith in Communism, had written in 1914: that Blum was "too Jewish" for his own good.

It comes [Gide had written] from the fact that Blum considers the Jewish race superior, as called upon to dominate after having been long dominated, and that it is his duty to work for its triumph with all his force. Doubtlessly he foresees the possible advent of the race. . . . He seems to think that the time will come which will be the time of the Jews.[4]

Quickly on June 5, the day after Blum took office, Gide hastened to explain that what he really meant to say in 1914 was that the Jews had a passion for justice and the truth and it was that which "animated" Blum. He was extremely happy, he added, at the triumph of the Popular Front in general and of Blum in particular. Under such leadership, he was sure, France would resume its role as a "pioneer of civilization."[5]

The Right complained that Blum had stacked his government with Jews. Henri Béraud in the anti-Semitic and Fascist-oriented weekly *Gringoire* named thirty-two Jews who, he said, had been given prominent posts in the ministries, including one by the name of Dreyfus. Even Pertinax (André Géraud), the influential press commentator on foreign affairs, would complain later that Blum had unnecessarily courted anti-Semitism "by surrounding himself in the Premier's office by ten, if not more, Jews." Actually only two Jews held prominent posts in that office: André Blumel, a former law-partner of Blum, and Jules Moch, a young naval engineer. Blum himself was the only Jew among the ministers in the cabinet. Jean Zay, Minister of Education, was the son of a Jewish father and a Protestant mother, but he had been raised as a Christian, had married one, and brought up his children in the Protestant faith.

Though a good many French Jews were proud that one of their number had become head of government for the first time, others were not so happy about it, fearing that it would provoke a new wave of anti-Semitism in the country. A prominent rabbi in Paris, overcome by this fear, tried to persuade Blum not to become Premier. No one who was not in France in those days can comprehend the hatred of Blum by Frenchmen on the Right.

They loathed him as a Jew, as a Socialist, as the head of a Left government, and even as a subtle intellectual. A "good bourgeoise lady" snapped to Pertinax: "I'd like to meet Blum—to spit in his face!"[6] On the Left the new Premier was venerated as a man who would save France from Fascism, lighten the burdens of the poor, conquer the Depression, and preserve Peace.

Hardly had Blum received the vote of confidence in the Chamber for his Popular Front government when he set to work to settle the sit-down strikes that had brought the economic life of the country to a standstill. The very next day, on Sunday, June 7, he brought together at the Hôtel Matignon, the Premier's office, representatives of the leading employers' associations and the General Confederation of Labor. With Blum presiding they began their discussions at 3 P.M. and before the night was over they had reached agreement. The workers would evacuate the factories and end their strikes in return for a wage increase ranging from 7 to 15 percent and industry's acceptance of the principle of collective bargaining, the right of unions to represent their workers in negotiations with management, and no further reprisals against employees for joining a union.

To an objective foreign observer there seemed nothing very extraordinary in the terms of the agreement. Wages in France were shockingly low—as little as 11 cents an hour. The right to organize unions and to bargain collectively had long been accepted, for the most part, in England and the United States (and in Germany before Hitler). But in France the "Matignon Agreement," as it was called, represented a radical change for both management and labor. The employers' associations had previously refused to bargain collectively, as had most of the great industrial concerns. The latter, refusing even to recognize the unions, had fired workers merely for joining them. They alone, in most cases, had dictated wages, hours, and conditions of labor. The unions were too weak in membership to stand up to the employers. Indeed the meeting in the Premier's office was the first ever held in France between the representatives of the country's chief employers and those of organized labor. Later some of the leading entrepreneurs would say that they had been forced to negotiate with a pistol at their heads, what with their plants occupied illegally by the strikers and a leftish Premier pressuring them for concessions. Actually it was management that had pressed Blum to hold the talks with the CGT. The employers were prepared to make concessions to avert, as they said, "revolution," and to get back their factories from the workers who had occupied them.

Labor hailed the Matignon agreement as a great victory, long overdue. Jouhaux, the head of the CGT, exulted: "In one historic night we caught up with and surpassed other countries that have been moving in this direction for fifty years. The victory obtained Sunday night marks the beginning of a new era." Organized labor had reason to rejoice, for besides the concessions of higher wages and recognition of the unions and their collective bargaining rights it had the assurance of the new government that Parliament would quickly legislate a 40-hour week and two weeks' vacation with pay. The shorter week, paid vacations, and the overall 12 percent wage increase, the CGT announced jubilantly, meant in reality a 35 percent boost in wages. The esteemed *Le Temps,* mouthpiece of the iron and steel trust, sourly agreed: "One might think one was dreaming. Yet the figure (35 percent) is exact."

It took some time to get the workers to accept the agreement, evacuate the plants and return to their jobs. The union leaders had difficulty in regaining control of their own followers. Four days after the Matignon accord, on June 11, the strikes reached a new peak, spreading in Paris to the department stores, whose employees were notoriously underpaid, and to hotels, restaurants and cafés. In the countryside the farm workers, emulating their city brethren, not only laid down their tools but in many cases occupied the farms. On that day the government estimated the number of strikers at 1,165,000, but the actual figure was closer to two million. All week long Blum and his fellow cabinet ministers worked night and day to persuade the workers to end the strikes. Thorez, the Communist chief, in a speech on June 11, warned them: "You have to know not only how to start a strike but how to end it." At first his plea, as well as that of Blum and his ministerial colleagues, fell on deaf ears. Leon Trotsky, fishing in troubled waters from his latest place of exile in Norway, to which he had recently moved from Paris, proclaimed during the week that "the French Revolution has begun" and urged the strikers to overthrow their "oppressors," among whom he included Blum, for whom he had the monumental contempt that so many Communists had for the Socialists. On June 12 the Parisian Trotskyite journal, *La Lutte Ouvrière,* entreated the workers to organize themselves into armed militia units. Blum ordered the police to confiscate the issue and told the Chamber that "since yesterday" certain "suspect groups, foreign to the French trade unions," were trying to take over the strikes and use them to provoke disorder.

Not so much the pleas of Blum, Thorez, and the troubled leaders of the CGT but the haste with which Parliament began to pass the promised labor legislation induced the workers to end the strikes. Never in all the years of the Third Republic did the legislators, many of them now thoroughly frightened by the specter of revolution, act with such dispatch. "Each hour counts," Blum warned the Chamber in introducing the new legislation on the day after the Matignon agreement. Four days later, on June 11, the Chamber passed the bill on collective bargaining by 528 to 7, and the bill on paid vacations by 563 to 1. There was more argument over the 40-hour week, but it too was approved the next day by 385 to 175. The more conservative Senate moved somewhat slower but on June 17 and 18 it approved the three bills by votes of 279 to 5, 295 to 2 and 182 to 64, respectively.

Within ten days Parliament, which had resisted since the end of the Great War acting on such measures, had by overwhelming votes given the country the only important social legislation of the Third Republic. Blum believed that he had not only made good his promise of giving the workers their due—and in record time—but, more important, had saved the country from civil war. At Lille the following weekend, Roger Salengro, the Minister of Interior and mayor of the city, proudly told his fellow townsmen: "We have had a peaceful revolution. Not a machine has been broken, not a drop of blood has been spilled. It has been the most formidable social upheaval the Republic has ever known."

By that weekend too the strikes had begun to subside. Led by their political and union leaders and makeshift bands the strikers paraded out of the factories to the sound of martial music and the applause of their sympathizers. At the sprawling Renault automobile works on the edge of Paris a Socialist senator and a Communist deputy headed the parading strikers. They followed a band whose musicians were wearing the Phrygian caps of the glorious Revolution of 1792.

That revolution was celebrated with a new fervor that summer on the traditional anniversary of July 14. In Paris a vast throng turned out to cheer Blum and acclaim the achievements of the Popular Front. The Premier was in an exalted mood. In a brief speech to the massive gathering he compared the year 1936—only half over—to the great years of 1792, 1848, 1870. After so long a struggle the workers had at last won entrance to the City. "Every effort," he said, "every advance toward social justice, attaches the workers of France to the Republic and to the country. The very object of the Popular Front is to furnish them with new means to defend it. . . . The cause of the workers struggling for social justice and the cause of republicans struggling for civic and political liberties must be indissolubly linked." To achieve them had been his lifelong goal and he believed he had made a good start.

Four days later, on July 18, there occurred an event abroad, on the other side of the Pyrenees, that plunged his government into a grave crisis and France into a new convulsion from which neither ever recovered.

THE IMPACT OF THE SPANISH CIVIL WAR

The Republic of Spain, which had replaced the monarchy in a bloodless revolution only five years before, and which had struggled desperately for bare survival in that retarded, anarchic, passion-torn land, also had a Popular Front government. It had been elected in February, just prior to the one in France. As in France, it had incurred the wrath of the entrenched conservatives, especially the powerful Roman Catholic Church and, above all, the generals of the Army, who had remained monarchists at heart and who because of this were being weeded out by the new government, which generously accorded them retirement at full pay in the naive belief that this would keep them happy and render them harmless. Instead, it gave them more time for plotting. General Francisco Franco, the Chief of Staff, had been dismissed from his post and sent off to command the small garrison in the Canary Islands to keep him as far away as possible from the center of things. It was known that in February he had appealed to the outgoing Prime Minister to prevent—by military force if necessary— the duly elected Popular Front government from assuming office.

The Popular Front government in Paris was quite naturally sympathetic to the *Frente Popular* regime in Madrid, not only for ideological reasons but because it gave France, faced on two of its frontiers by hostile, aggressive Fascist powers, Germany and Italy, a friendly and congenial neighbor on its southwest border. But engrossed in their own problems, Blum and his ministers had had no time to notice the deterioration in the affairs of the fledgling Popular Front government in Spain. By the beginning of the summer of 1936 it was in deep trouble. The country was falling into anarchy. The government was losing control. The workers and peasants, delirious over their electoral triumph and thirsting for revenge after years of savage repression, even under the bourgeois Republic, were burning churches and castles, and sometimes killing priests, monks, nuns, and grandees. Wild-cat strikes, many staged by the strong unions run by the anarchists, who were against *any* government, even of the Popular Front, were breaking out daily all over the country.* Political assassinations on all sides were mounting to such an extent that no leader, on the Right or Left, felt safe. And the generals, many of them unemployed, some in exile or, like Franco, in semiexile, were plotting—not only to restore order but to overthrow the Republic, bring back the king (the last Bourbon king, Alfonso XIII, had fled rather ignominiously on April 13, 1931) and restore the authority of the Church, which for centuries had been almost supreme in Spain.

On July 17, under Franco, who soon emerged as the leader, they struck in Morocco, to which the young general flew from the Canaries in a chartered British plane. The next day the military uprising spread to Spain itself. Seville and several other towns in Andalusia were seized by the rebels.

Léon Blum, as he later testified, was "completely surprised" by the news from Spain.[7] On July 18 he had received a visit from an old friend, the Spanish Socialist lawyer Jiménez de Asúa, author of the republican Constitution. When he asked his visitor how things were going in Spain, the latter replied: "Very well. We are very satisfied." Two days later, on arriving at his office, the Premier found an urgent telegram, sent *en clair* and received in Paris during the night, from the new Spanish Premier José Giral: "Are surprised by dangerous military coup. Ask you to help

---

* The anarchist trade union organization, CNT (*Confederación Nacional del Trabajo*), numbered more than a million men and women. In no other country in the world were there so many anarchists so well organized and so dedicated. Their union was as hostile to the somewhat larger Socialist labor confederation, UGT (*Unión General de Trabajadores*), as it was to the employers.

us immediately with arms and planes. Fraternally yours, Giral." The Spanish Prime Minister had bypassed his Ambassador in Paris, Juan F. de Cárdenas, who as an old-school diplomat might be expected to sympathize with the military rebels.

Blum immediately summoned Yvon Delbos, his Foreign Minister, Daladier, Minister of War, and Pierre Cot, Minister of Air (all three members of the Radical Party) who promptly agreed with him that it would be in the national interest to send the Spanish Republic what arms could be spared. Because French rightist circles had already burst forth with sympathy for the rebels, the ministers decided to keep the transaction secret for the time being. But in France this was impossible. Ambassador Cárdenas had been told of the affirmative French decision, and had loyally informed his government, but being a man of great probity, no others.* However his military attaché, a fanatical supporter of Franco, immediately communicated to the rightist press the itemized list of the proposed arms shipment. On July 23 Henri de Kerillis published the complete details in the *Echo de Paris*. This time the French Right exploded with indignation. *L'Action Française* branded Blum and Cot as "traitors." But there was a "traitor" of another sort in the French cabinet—a minister whose identity was never established—who promptly informed the German Ambassador of the details of the proposed French aid to Spain. The envoy immediately got on the wire to Berlin.

In the meantime Blum, accompanied by Delbos, had gone to London on July 23 for a scheduled meeting with the British and Belgians to consider the future, if any, of the Locarno Treaty, which Hitler had torn up when he sent his troops into the Rhineland. Blum sensed at once a certain displeasure in the British Conservative government that France should contemplate aiding the Spanish Republic. He let it be known through French journalists covering the meeting that he would not be deterred by the British. He was, he said, resolved to help a friendly, democratic government.

Anthony Eden, the British Foreign Secretary, came to his hotel in London just before his departure the next day. "Are you going to send arms to the Spanish Republicans?" Eden asked. Blum answered that he was. "It's your affair," Eden rejoined, "but I ask you one thing. I beg of you: be prudent." The timid Tory government in London, it was evident, was fearful that if France aided the Republic, Hitler and Mussolini would aid Franco, and that the European war London dreaded might come out of it. It was also evident that Britain, as in the days preceding the Rhineland coup, would pressure France not to do anything to rock the boat in Europe, despite what Hitler—or Mussolini—did.

Blum does not seem to have been much surprised or impressed by the initial British reaction to French aid to the Spanish government. But he

---

* Cárdenas resigned from his post the next day and eventually became an envoy of Franco.

was not prepared for the opposition to it which broke like a storm on his return to Paris on July 24 from many of the circles which, he thought, at first had approved it. Camille Chautemps, the shifty Radical-Socialist politician and a member of the cabinet, was waiting for him at Le Bourget airfield. He informed the Premier that in his brief absence a furious storm had blown up and that the situation was "grave." Franco sympathizers in the Spanish Embassy, he told Blum, had leaked to the rightist press details of the scheduled arms shipment and Kerillis, especially, had launched a violent campaign in *Echo de Paris* against aiding the Spanish Republic. Even the two chambers were upset.

At first Blum could scarcely believe him. He called in Jules Jeanneney, the venerable President of the Senate. He found this wise old man, he says, "in a state of extreme emotion." Jeanneney feared that aid to Madrid would land France into the war it had just avoided by doing nothing after March 7. "England," he added ominously, "will not follow us." Herriot, the Speaker of the Chamber, was just as frightened, imploring Blum: *"Ah, je t'en prie, mon petit, ne vas pas te fourer là-dedans."* ("I beg of you, my good friend, don't get mixed up in that business.") Delbos, the Radical-Socialist Foreign Minister, an upright but timid man with a limited vision of the world, was beginning to waver. Though he had agreed at the beginning of the week on the shipments to Madrid, he now began to see many difficulties and disadvantages. Later that evening he joined Daladier, Pierre Cot, and Vincent Auriol, the Minister of Finance, at Blum's private residence. Fernando de los Ríos, who had been dispatched hastily to Paris to take over the Spanish Embassy, was called in. He tried to impress the French leaders with the urgency of the situation if the Spanish Republic were to survive. Above all, he wanted planes. Despite the objections of Delbos, it was agreed that the first shipment would be sent immediately.

The next day, July 25, a crucial one, as it turned out, the Premier began to give way before the storm and the mounting opposition of his Radical-Socialist partners in the government. The newspapers of the Right that morning were more vehement than ever. Kerillis hysterically denounced the sending of planes to Madrid as "abominable" and indeed "criminal." The President of the Republic saw his worst fears of the Popular Front government confirmed. He protested to Blum during the day against this "interfering in the affairs of other countries" and demanded that no final decision be taken until there had been a meeting of the full cabinet.[8]

The cabinet met that afternoon. It was the first of three meetings over a fortnight that dealt with Spain and were to lead to the so-called Nonintervention Agreement, one of the most outrageous diplomatic farces perpetrated in Europe between the wars. Most of the Radical-Socialists in the cabinet, led by Chautemps and Delbos and finally supported by Daladier, who as Minister of War, was a key figure, now opposed the shipment to the Spanish Republic of the arms which had already been assembled for immediate dispatch. Jean Zay, the young Minister of Education and himself a Radical-Socialist, later recounted how Chautemps, just before the cabinet meeting, took several of the younger ministers aside, lectured them "energetically" about the risks of helping the Spanish Republic, and assured them "that the military insurrection would be victorious in a few weeks and that the Republican Government would crumble like a house of cards."[9] This was not the first time nor the last that this suave intriguer, a man without known convictions in politics, domestic or foreign, would cunningly spread defeatism in a French cabinet.

Blum was not effective in pushing his views. He made little effort to exert his leadership. At the end of the cabinet meeting it was officially announced that "in view of possible international complications" the French government would "suspend the shipment of arms to the Republic of Spain." But that was not quite the whole story. Blum had not yet completely capitulated. It was privately arranged that part of the shipment would go to Mexico, which would turn it over to Madrid. And no difficulties for the time being would be put in the way of private arms transactions for Spain. Pierre Cot, the Minister of Air, himself a Radical-Socialist, agreed to help out in this business, and André Malraux, who had gained world fame two years before with his novel *La Condition Humaine,* about the Chinese revolution, became the buyer on behalf of the government of Madrid. Thus a trickle of arms for the hard-pressed Spanish Republicans was assured—enough to spare them a quick overthrow but not enough, in the long run, to put the military rebellion down; not after Mussolini and Hitler intervened on a massive scale. As Jean Zay, and some of the other Young Turks in the government who were for promptly assisting the Republicans, later concluded, an insignificant amount of French aid in July would have enabled the government in Madrid to stamp out the rebellion quickly. But Blum was too taken aback by the uproar on the Right and the panic on the Left to realize this, until it was too late. He had begun his ill-fated retreat.

He almost seized an opportunity to redress the situation the following week. On July 30 three Italian Savoia bombers made forced landings in Algeria and French Morocco. Questioning of the surviving crews by the French authorities established that they were part of a contingent being rushed to Franco by Mussolini. While France hesitated, Italy was moving. Blum now had his excuse to do what he had wanted to do in the first place. But he used it only halfheartedly. He told the Senate Foreign Affairs Committee that if other nations sent arms to Franco, France would "resume its freedom of action." That was all. But the reaction in France to the Italian intervention was just the opposite of what the Premier apparently expected. In Parliament, in the cabinet, even in the moderate press, the proof that Italy was intervening on behalf of the Spanish rebels renewed fears that an ideological war would spread from the Spanish

Civil War to Europe and that France would face an attack from Germany and Italy.

At the Quai d'Orsay the nervous permanent officials, led by Alexis Léger, the secretary-general, were frightened by this prospect. To avoid it, Léger came up with a proposal: an agreement by the Big Powers and Portugal (which had begun to aid Franco from the start) not to send arms or "volunteers" to either side in Spain. Thus was born the idea of "nonintervention," one of the cruelest diplomatic hoaxes of the era.

Blum, encouraged by the British, who were still petulant at even the prospect of France aiding the legal government of Spain, embraced the idea at once. He convinced himself that it would help prevent the larger war, which he, a lifelong pacifist, was determined should never take place. Still, the cabinet session of August 1, the second on the Spanish problem, was a stormy one. Delbos presented Léger's nonintervention plan and urged its adoption, telling his colleagues that British pressure on France to observe "strict neutrality" was increasing and the international situation becoming more delicate. Cot, opposing him, argued that proof of Italian aid to Franco showed that nonintervention was bound to fail. The Fascist powers would never accept it in reality. But the cabinet backed Delbos and a communiqué after the meeting announced that France would appeal to Britain and Italy, to begin with, to join in a pact barring intervention in Spain. Until the agreement was signed, however, France reserved her "freedom of action," in view of aid being furnished Franco by other powers. Secretly, the impatient Cot was told to disregard the "Mexican deal" and get off his planes to Madrid directly. He immediately dispatched fifty-five planes, mostly bombers and fighters.

Though he had accepted the idea of a nonintervention pact, the French Premier was not happy about it. The specter of a Franco triumph, backed by Hitler and Mussolini, began to haunt him. It would be a disaster for France and, he was sure, for Britain as well. But up to now he had not been able to convince the government in London of this. A suggestion by an old friend of his, Philip Noel Baker, one of the leaders of the British Labor Party, who called on him in Paris at this moment, prompted Blum to make one more effort to impress the British government with the dangers of a Franco victory. Baker had told him that if he could convince the British Admiralty of this, the Admiralty would certainly convince the government.

Though Blum, as he later testified, was not sure of the attitude of his Army General Staff on Spain, he had noted that Admiral Darlan, Chief of the Naval Staff, agreed with him on the consequences to France and Britain of a Fascist Franco government in Madrid. Since the French admiral had developed close and friendly personal relations with Admiral Lord Chatfield, Blum sent him over at once to London to talk with the British naval chief.

Darlan's mission failed. The British Admiralty, as was to be expected, thought Franco was "a good Spanish patriot . . . who would know how to defend himself against the encroachments of Mussolini and Hitler" and Britain was certainly not going to do anything against him. Darlan was so informed in blunt naval language. The rebuff to him, Blum later said, had a "considerable influence" on the decision which was finally taken by the French government at the third cabinet meeting on Spanish affairs on August 8.

On the eve of that meeting the Socialist leader had fallen into such a severe state of depression over Spain that he was "strongly tempted," he later acknowledged, to resign.[10] He felt himself completely boxed in. His personal desire to help the Spanish Republic had been frustrated by the opposition of Britain, the poisonous divisions in his own country, and his fear of a larger war. Abroad, he told himself, France was "practically isolated in Europe on the question of Spain" and he himself felt increasingly isolated from the prevailing opinion in his own country. He had kept his promise to push the Popular Front social reforms through the two Chambers. He could now honorably step down.

He was persuaded not to do so, he said, largely by his Spanish Republican friends, de los Ríos and Jiménez de Asúa, who convinced him that a friendly Popular Front government, even if its hands were tied, was better for the hard-pressed Spanish Republic than a hostile French government. There was a tearful scene one evening in Blum's apartment when, after de los Ríos had described the heroism of poorly armed Republican militia holding off Franco's barbarous Moroccan troops in the Sierras, the French Prime Minister broke down and wept and his Spanish friend joined him.[11] After they had recovered their composure the Spaniard again implored him not to resign.

Next day, August 8, at the meeting of the cabinet, Blum, having wrestled with his conscience, took the final plunge which, though he perhaps did not realize it, spelled the doom of the Spanish Republic which he had wanted so much to save. He decided to stay on the job and go through with the policy of nonintervention in Spain. Delbos, the Foreign Minister, reported to the cabinet progress in getting the other powers to join in an embargo of arms to both sides. Italy, Germany, and Russia, he said, had accepted "in principle." It was up to France to take the lead. It did so by announcing in an official communiqué that as of the next day, August 9, all export of war material to Spain would be suspended.

This was a unilateral action on the part of France and all the more surprising because Blum was quite aware that Italy and Germany were pouring arms and planes into Franco-held Spain and, in the case of planes, pilots to fly them and mechanics to keep them flying. Indeed, on August 9, while Blum was trying to justify his policy to an angry gathering of workers at Saint-Cloud, and in London the Counselor of the German Embassy was assuring the British government that "no war materials had been sent from Germany and none will," the American consul in Seville was watching the arrival there of ten Savoia bombers from Italy and eighteen Junkers, six fighters, and six antiaircraft guns from Germany. Twenty Italian and thirty German pilots were part of the consignment.[12]

If the policy of nonintervention was to be anything but a fraud, it was essential from the start to see that all four Big Powers strictly observed it— with no cheating permitted. Now, as the German and Italian secret documents make clear, neither Berlin nor Rome, though eventually signing the Nonintervention Pact, intended to cease its aid in arms and men to Spain. On August 28, for example, the German chargé in Rome informed Berlin that though Italy would sign the Pact "it is obvious that it does not intend to abide by [it] anyway."[13] Germany signed on August 24 but the very next day, for another example, Field Marshal von Blomberg, the German Minister of War, appointed a young staff officer, Colonel Walter Warlimont, to head the German armed forces in Spain.[14]

Anglo-French diplomats and intelligence officers surely knew what Italy and Germany were up to. For one thing, the foreign correspondents in Spain, Germany, and Italy kept them informed. My own Berlin diary is full of jottings about Nazi aid to Franco at this time. It seems incredible— it seemed incredible to me at the time*—that Blum and Eden put any trust at all in Hitler and Mussolini keeping their word in regard to Spain. Yet they did. On September 6 Blum told a public meeting that he hoped, by France's example, "to challenge the honor of the other powers." The "honor" of the Fuehrer and the Duce was a frail reed on which to base a crucial decision of foreign policy as late as 1936.

In England, Anthony Eden, despite his long experience in foreign affairs and years of dealing with the Fascist dictators, acted with equal naiveté, though he later saw the error of his ways. In the absence of Prime Minister Baldwin, who was ill, he personally put through on August 19 a complete British embargo on the shipment of arms to Spain—and this at a date when Italy and Germany had not even signed the Nonintervention Pact. "I had not yet learned," he commented sadly of this step much later, "that it is dangerous to offer such gestures to the dictators, who are more likely to misinterpret than to follow them."[16] Indeed Eden pressed forward with the nonintervention farce with the same fervor he had shown in trying to get sanctions applied to Italy the year before.

The Foreign Office in London became the headquarters of the so-called Nonintervention Committee, which was hastily set up to "supervise" the embargo on arms and men to Spain and to see that it was observed

* In Berlin on November 18, the day Germany and Italy accorded official diplomatic recognition to the Franco regime, I jotted in my diary: "[Ambassador William E.] Dodd tells me our consulate in Hamburg reported this week the departure from there of three German ships loaded with arms for Spain. In the meantime the comedy of 'nonintervention' goes on in London. For two years now the policies of London and Paris have ceased making sense to me, judged by their own vital interests."[15]

by all the signatories to the Pact. Thus through the meetings of this body, which began on September 9 and continued sporadically to the conclusion of the Civil War, was hypocrisy and chicanery between the great European powers carried out to the sorry, sordid end. As the German Ambassador in London, Joachim von Ribbentrop, who like the other envoys there served on the committee, later observed with unaccustomed honesty—and humor—the group should have entitled itself "the Intervention Committee."

Brazenly, it winked at the massive violations by Italy and Germany and later at the lesser though considerable ones of the Soviet Union, which began in October (three months after the Italo-German intervention had begun, and then only after the Spanish Republic had sent most of its remaining gold reserve to Russia as a guarantee for payment), and at the small ones of France, which permitted at intervals a trickle of arms and volunteers to pass through to Republican Spain. Not until Italian submarines the next year began sinking not only Russian and Spanish but French and British ships in the Mediterranean did the Nonintervention Committee, under pressure from the British Navy, bestir itself to end Mussolini's piracy on the high seas. By that time, German and Italian aid, which included an Italian Army of 60,000 men, complete with a large Italian air force, and the Nazi German Air Force Condor Legion of some 10,000 men and hundreds of planes, supported by tanks and artillery, had assured Franco's military superiority and eventual triumph.*

The impact of the Spanish Civil War, the enormous frustrations it brought to French policy abroad, the disarray it caused at home, the feeling of moral guilt on the Left that France had let down the democracy across the Pyrenees and helped Fascism to triumph in still another Western country to the detriment of France's position in Europe, broke Blum's heart and the heart of the Front Populaire, hastening its end and leaving the Republic more divided and poisoned by hatred than it had been. The unity and the impetus of the Popular Front was shattered. To the traditional division between Right and Left were added divisions within political parties, and among Catholics and intellectuals. And in the paroxysm of ideological passions everyone again lost sight of the national interests of France.

---

* Among the achievements of the German Condor Legion was the obliteration of the historic Basque town of Guérnica on the afternoon of April 26, 1937. After three hours of saturation bombing with high explosives and incendiaries, the German pilots machine-gunned the populace trying to flee the burning rubble. Out of Guérnica's population of 7,000 souls, 1,654 were killed that afternoon and 889 wounded. Later Goering, chief of the Luftwaffe, boasted that Guérnica had been a valuable experiment. It showed the ease with which undefended towns could be completely wiped out by proper bombing. The Western world, at least, was horrified, not knowing what would happen to cities and towns when a bigger war came a little later. But the Germans had given a warning.

The Army, most of whose officers were personally sympathetic to Franco and his rebellion, declined also to give a moment's thought to the consequences to France of a Franco triumph made possible by Germany and Italy. A few planes, a few tanks, a few batteries of artillery, a scattering of "technicians," rushed over the border, as Blum had first planned, would have enabled the Spanish Republic to quash the rebellion in a few days or weeks, before the aid from Italy and Germany, which were further away, could come by sea to save the military junta. This would have been a telling blow to Hitler and Mussolini and would have left France with at least one friendly neighbor on her borders. Yet there is not one line in General Gamelin's voluminous memoirs indicating that he and the General Staff gave the matter the slightest consideration until it was far too late.* To the retired General de Castelnau, one of the heroes of the First World War, the conflict in Spain was "between Muscovite barbarism and Western civilization" and he hammered away at this theme in the columns of the *Echo de Paris,* the most widely read daily newspaper among French officers. This was the theme in the big-circulation newspapers too, which echoed the partisan journals of the Right in insisting that a victory of the Spanish Republic would bring Bolshevism not only to Spain but to France.† Several newspapers that winter of 1936–37 featured articles on their front pages predicting a "Communist coup." Patriots were urged to get ready. In the minds of the French reactionaries civil war in France, following that in Spain, seemed imminent.

It seemed possible, and for a time imminent, to some on the Left too, but coming not from a Communist uprising, of which there was not the slightest sign or possibility, but from a rightist coup, similar to the attempted one on February 6, 1934, but this time with the support of the military, as in Spain. Later Blum himself gave some credence to this view. He became convinced that by his policy of nonintervention in Spain he had not only saved Europe from war in 1936 but spared his own country a civil war. In a letter dated July 9, 1942, from the prison at Bourassol to which Pétain had confined him without trial, Blum wrote to a French friend in New York:

What our American friends perhaps do not perceive . . . is . . . that

---

* Not until March 15, 1938, nearly two years later. Then, prodded by Blum, General Gamelin drafted a note for the government reluctantly conceding that the consequences for France of a Franco victory, made possible by German and Italian intervention, were "dangerous" and "alarming."[17]

† Actually in 1936 the Communists were a small minority in the Spanish Republic, having but 14 out of 473 seats in the Cortes and only 10,000 members in the country. Government and parliament were overwhelmingly non-Communist. This would change as the Republic's position worsened and it became increasingly dependent for survival on belated Soviet aid. Then, as Soviet and Comintern agents swarmed into Spain with the Russian arms and the International Brigades, the power of the Communist minority grew rapidly and was probably dominant at the end, when the Republic was doomed. But French reactionary circles called the non-Communist Spanish Republican government "Bolshevist" from the start.

civil war would have broken out in France. . . . The Spanish affair was deeply imbedded in the social crisis. . . . As soon as the situation had been stretched to the danger point, we would have had in France a counterpart to the Franco *coup de force*. There would have followed civil war with slight chance of victory for the republic.[18]

He reiterated this contention in a speech after the war:

I have realized since that time that we in France were also on the eve of military coup d'état. . . . I had a presentiment of it at the time. Since then I know it.[19]

THE POPULAR FRONT RUNS AGROUND

To the frustrations of the Spanish Civil War were added the domestic ones. Economic and financial difficulties, beyond the capacity of the Blum government to solve, brought the Popular Front experiment to an early end.

The trouble was that the Socialist Premier felt that in domestic as in foreign affairs his hands were tied. He had not, he believed, received a mandate to overhaul the capitalist system of a free economy now wallowing in its fifth year of depression, much less to substitute his own Socialism for it. He could only try to get it moving again on its own terms, and for this he needed—and rather naively expected to get—the cooperation of the business and financial worlds. But after the sit-down strikes of labor, he was now confronted by a sit-down strike of capital. Its owners either spirited it abroad or sat on it at home. In both cases it became unproductive. In a report to Parliament in June 1936, Vincent Auriol, the Finance Minister, calculated that there were some 60 billion francs "missing" from the national economy, of which 26 billions had been sent out of the country. He asked the holders of capital to reflect on "the historic fate of social classes or regimes which did not foresee or consent in time to the sacrifices needed for the safety of the country." It was a vain appeal.

The industrialists themselves, resentful at having been pressured into raising wages and shortening working hours, made little effort to try to find new markets and increase production and employment. Even the conservative-minded generals, who were uneasy about the Popular Front, were surprised to find a lack of enterprise in the armament industries, to which they now began to give large orders. Most of the firms had poor engineering staffs and deficient and too few tools. They hesitated to expand for fear the investment would not pay off handsomely enough in the end. The makers of tanks and planes, of which thousands were needed in quick order, found excuses to delay deliveries and to keep their production down despite lucrative contracts from the government.

After a time Blum suspected that the businessmen and especially the financiers were determined to bring the Popular Front government down by making things as bad as possible, and he was not far wrong. But he remained deaf to the pleas of some of his tougher colleagues to crack down on industrialists and bankers, as Hitler had done in Germany. Instead he strove to conciliate them in the belief that if he won their confidence they would take the lead in stirring up the sluggish economy.

Parliament adjourned on August 13, after passing the bulk of the Popular Front social reforms and promising on its return to consider others. Aside from the labor laws, already noted, new legislation provided for a three-year public works program of 20 billion francs to stimulate the economy and alleviate unemployment, the nationalization of the armament industry if this was found necessary, a reform of the Bank of France designed to transfer control of it from the "two hundred families" to the state, raising of compulsory schooling to the age of fourteen, and the establishment of a Wheat Office to boost and stabilize the low and fluctuating prices of farm products. Altogether 133 laws were passed in 73 days— something of a record in French parliamentary history.

Some of the reforms were not as drastic as the laws governing them seemed to indicate. Most of the gun and munition makers managed to retain possession of their firms. Only the airplane works in the end were nationalized and they thereafter showed some improvement in production, thanks to government orders for military aircraft, but fell far short of what was needed. On paper the revision of the statutes of the all-powerful Bank of France seemed to wrest control from the principal private stockholders, mostly bankers, and turn it over to the state. The fifteen Regents, who ran the Bank and who were elected by the two hundred largest stockholders—the famous "two hundred families" who most Frenchmen believed really governed the country* and who, in the opinion of the Left, were ruining it—were abolished and replaced by twenty Councilors, most of whom were appointed by the government and who for the first time included representatives of the trade unions, the cooperative societies, and farm groups. But somehow the Bank continued to be the citadel of conservative, orthodox finance. An advisory committee set up to draft the bill had recommended nationalizing the Bank but Blum, fearing to antagonize the bankers, had disregarded the recommendation. He still hoped that by showing moderation he could win over the financial community to helping get the country out of its mess.

Not only the Bank of France needed more drastic overhauling but, even more important, the whole credit structure of the country, which

---

* Daladier, seventeen times a cabinet minister and three times Premier in the last fifteen years of the Third Republic and a typical representative of the solid lower-middle bourgeoisie, summed up the general attitude in a speech at the annual Congress of the Radical-Socialist Party in 1934: "Two hundred families are masters of the French economy and, in fact, of French politics. They constitute a force which a democratic state should not tolerate, which Richelieu would not have tolerated in the kingdom of France. The influence of the two hundred families weighs heavily on the fiscal system, on transportation, on credit. The two hundred families place their delegates in the seats of power. They operate on public opinion, for they control the press."

seemed to be more in tune with the eighteenth century than the twentieth. France had considerable capital but it had to be brought home and put to work. Neither the government nor industry could borrow from private sources the substantial amounts it needed. French financiers apparently had not yet learned what had become obvious in most of the other Western lands: that the imaginative use of credit, especially in depressed times, was the chief primer for expanding the economy. They had the money but not the knowledge nor the will to use it. If the Socialist and Radical members who made up the government were aware of the urgent need to expand credit, they did little about it, waiting vainly, for the impetus to come from private enterprise. This proved to be a forlorn hope.

What was needed most that summer and fall of 1936 as the country's financial situation worsened and the economy showed few signs of reviving was to stop the flow of capital abroad, corner it at home, and utilize it— by force, if necessary. It would have been easy enough for the government simply to prohibit the exportation of gold or foreign exchange except by permit to industries needing raw materials from other countries. But neither Blum nor his Socialist Finance Minister, Vincent Auriol, would go so far. They feared it would further alienate the bankers and business-men and destroy confidence in the free economy. Indeed, Blum seemed to think it would be a "totalitarian" act, such as Hitler had taken in Germany (on the insistence of the banking wizard, Dr. Hjalmar Horace Greeley Schacht) with great success. So he continued to plead with the holders of capital to consider the interests of their country, refrain from sending any more of it abroad, and bring back what they had sent out. The plea was in vain.

By the end of September 1936 the Bank of France had lost 16 billion francs in gold since the beginning of the year. Public announce-ment of the cabinet decision of September 7 to allot a special credit of 14 billions for swift and urgent rearmament caused a new panic in financial circles and brought a further exodus of capital. Before the month was out the gold reserves of the Bank were down to 50 billions, the minimum considered necessary to keep the country afloat. The possessors of capital knew as well as anyone, and better than most, that sizable new credits for strengthening the armed forces were absolutely necessary in face of Germany's massive rearming if France were to have any chance of surviv-ing another invasion. On August 24 Hitler had raised the term of military service in Germany from one to two years. His standing army would soon be doubled in size. France, because of its smaller population, could not keep up in such a race, as the years before 1914 had shown. It already had a two-year term for conscripts. As the General Staff pointed out in a secret memorandum of September 8, France could only respond to the German move by a large increase in its armament—in tanks and planes, above all.[20] This was obvious to everyone, even to bankers and business-men. Yet all through September they continued frantically to get their money out to safe havens, knowingly weakening the country for monetary gain. Such was the patriotism of this traditionally patriotic and nationalistic class at this troubled time. It would not change very much down to the day the country was overwhelmed.

On September 26 the Popular Front government was forced to do what it had promised it would not do: devaluate the franc. Blum had assured the Chamber on June 6, the first day he met it, that his government would not carry out a "monetary coup d'état" by again devaluating the currency. He had hoped that an economic upsurge and the return of capital would enable him to avert it. Neither had happened, and the step was now overdue.

Ever since the British and then the Americans had devalued their currency by 40 percent, Paul Reynaud, the moderate-conservative gadfly deputy, a voice in the wilderness in those days, had been urging successive governments to follow suit in order to allow France to price itself back into the world markets and start digging itself out of the Depression. Neither his conservative friends nor his Radical and Socialist opponents had paid him any attention. Frenchmen, rich and poor, still had a deep neurosis about tampering with the franc. Maintaining the "Poincaré franc" of 1928, which itself had wiped out four fifths of a family's savings, was considered a sacred duty of all governments. Blum realized this, but by September 1936 he had no other recourse but to realign the franc with the dollar and the pound.

For a few months the devaluation, of roughly 30 percent, did stimulate the economy. Industrial production rose from 81 in September to 93 (1928 = 100) in the following March. But otherwise the hoped-for improvement did not materialize. The Treasury made a "profit" of 17 billion francs by the devaluation, of which 10 billions was placed in the newly created Exchange Stabilization Fund, but by January 1937 the 10 billions in the Fund had been used up. One of the main purposes of devaluating the franc had been to attract capital back home. It failed. This was largely because the lawmakers, in a quite commendable effort to prevent the speculators from making a 30 percent profit, had provided that returning capital in gold or foreign exchange could only be exchanged for francs at the old rate. There was no profit incentive to return capital. It stayed abroad. And speculation against the franc and raids on the dwindling gold reserves of the Bank began again. Prices rose and the trade unions and government workers insisted on salary increases to meet them. Strikes broke out. Harassed from Right and Left, Blum in desperation asked for a "pause."

The government's deficit at the end of 1936 amounted to 16 billions. Committed to spend large sums on rearmament the Premier was faced with the utter necessity of cutting down other expenditures. In February 1937 he had to tell the government workers, who constituted one of the main props of his Socialist Party, that justified as were their demands for higher salaries to keep in step with rising prices, the government didn't have the money to grant them at once. It would have to cut down in a number of places, even at the expense of some of the social reforms. "A 'pause,' " he said, "has become necessary."

On March 7, the government announced a number of specific measures designed to carry it out: reestablishment of a free market in gold (its holders could now reap the 30 percent profit denied them at the time of devaluation), a halt to all new government spending, reduction of the Treasury deficit by 6 billions, and appointment of a special committee to advise on the operations of the Exchange Stabilization Fund, whose initial holdings of 10 billions had been so quickly exhausted. The makeup of the Committee exasperated the Left. Blum chose as members, besides the Governor of the Bank of France, three of the most conservative financiers in the country, Jacques Rueff, Charles Rist and Paul Baudouin. Their advice was predictable, though apparently not to Blum.

If the "pause" that spring aroused deep resentment among the Communist and Socialist allies in the the Popular Front, who regarded it as a "retreat" if not a "betrayal," it aroused only scorn in the very business and financial groups Blum was trying to appease by it. They regarded it as a confession of failure by the Popular Front. *Le Temps* commented gleefully: "This is not a pause. It's a conversion." Actually this latest attempt of Blum's at conciliation did nothing to dampen the bitter feelings so many Frenchmen had for one another. Two incidents, one a few months before, the other just after this time, revealed the depth of passions in the Republic. In the first a decent and upright man, a public figure of note, was driven to suicide by the calumnies of irresponsible and unscrupulous men of the extreme right. This was Roger Salengro, a lifelong moderate Socialist, mayor of the northern industrial city of Lille, a deputy in the Chamber and Minister of Interior in the Blum government.

On July 14, 1936, the royalist journal, *L'Action Française,* boiling with indignation that its leader, Maurras, had been sentenced to prison for incitement to murder (of Blum), launched a campaign against Salengro, accusing him of having left his post in the trenches in October 1915 and deserted to the Germans.* *Gringoire,* by now the most scurrilous of the weeklies and the most widely read, with a circulation of half a million, including many in the Army and many more in extreme right-wing circles, took up the cry. It contended that Salengro, then a battalion dispatch rider, on the pretext of going out one night into no-man's-land between the trenches to try to bring back the body of a close friend, had really gone over to the Germans to bring them vital information about the French positions. It stated flatly that for this treasonous deed he had been condemned to death in absentia by a divisional court-martial. *Gringoire's* most notorious contributor, Henri Béraud, wrote an open letter to the

---

* The charge had first been made several years before by the Communists, fighting Salengro and his Socialist Party in the local elections in the north.

President of the Republic, claiming that no fewer than fourteen poilus in Salengro's battalion were witnesses to his desertion and had testified at the court-martial which condemned him to death. Béraud demanded that Lebrun throw the cowardly Minister out of the government and save France from further disgrace.*

Though Salengro proclaimed his innocence, so great was the storm aroused by the public accusations that Blum appointed General Gamelin himself to head a Court of Honor to look into the facts. The Court quickly found from the archives that a court-martial had indeed tried Salengro for desertion, but that it had acquitted him. It was established that the young soldier had been given permission by his platoon commander to go out one night beyond the barbed wire to try to bring back the body of a friend, that he had been surprised by a German patrol and made prisoner. The only court-martial that had condemned him was a German one—for refusing as a war prisoner to work in an arms factory, for which he was given two years in prison. Gamelin says he tried "discreetly" to give the facts in the case to the journals leading the slanderous campaign, but that they showed no interest in learning the truth.

Even after Blum announced to the Chamber on November 13 the results of the investigation of Gamelin's Court of Honor, *Gringoire, L'Action Française* and other publications of the extreme right claimed that it was a "whitewash" and stuck to their accusations. Salengro, "a sweet, timid and extremely sensitive man," according to Jean Zay, who sat next to him at cabinet meetings, was in despair. Though the Chamber on November 13 by a vote of 427 to 103 (some 40 of the latter votes were later changed to yeas) cleared the Minister of Interior of the charges, he remained deeply depressed as the reactionary press continued its calumny against him. The death of his wife the year before had also contributed to his despondency. Four nights after the overwhelming vote of confidence in him in the Chamber he returned to his lonely, unheated apartment in Lille, looked at a cold supper the maid had left on the kitchen table, went to the stove and turned on the gas.[21]

To the Rightist newspapers which cooked up the charges, Salengro's suicide was, they wrote, "a confession of guilt."†

---

* Béraud was condemned to death as a collaborationist after the Liberation but the sentence was commuted to life imprisonment at hard labor and he was released some time before his death in 1958.

† Salengro's successor as Minister of Interior, Marx Dormoy, a tougher-fibered man, also met an untimely end. During his confinement under house arrest during the war by the Vichy government in a hotel at Montélimar, a bomb went off one night under the mattress of the bed on which he was asleep and killed him. It had been planted by the terrorist Cagoule, which, when he was Minister of Interior, he had exposed.

Jean Zay, who continued as Minister of Education in all the successive governments, resigned his post in September 1939 to fight as a second lieutenant at the front. Condemned by the Vichy government on trumped-up charges of desertion he was imprisoned throughout the period of the Occupation. On June 21, 1944, on the eve of the liberation, he was murdered by the Vichy militia.

Salengro had aroused the ire of the extreme right because, as Minister of Interior, he had signed the government decree dissolving the Fascist leagues on June 18, 1936, a fortnight after the Popular Front took office.* Colonel de La Rocque, the chief of the Croix de Feu, quickly replaced it with a political party which he called the "French Social Party"—Parti Social Français, or PSF. Jacques Doriot, expelled from the Communist Party, as we have seen, for having prematurely propounded a Popular Front, formed a political party of his own, the Popular French Party—Parti Populaire Français, or PPF. This was violently anti-Communist, anti-Soviet, and Fascist and demanded that France line up with Germany and Italy. It quickly attracted substantial funds from industry and finance, whose leaders suddenly—if secretly—embraced this former firebrand of Bolshevism.

It was a meeting of one of these new rightist parties, the PSF, provocatively held in the working-class Paris suburb of Clichy, that brought about the second incident revealing the depth of political passions and the spirit of violence at this time. To protest the PSF rally on the evening of March 16, 1937, the Socialist mayor of Clichy and the Communist deputy who represented it called on their Popular Front followers to stage a counterdemonstration in front of the local movie house where the rightist meeting was taking place. A riot ensued and the police fired on the Popular Front demonstrators, killing five of them and wounding 150 others. Among the wounded was André Blumel, Blum's *chef de cabinet,* who had rushed to the scene to try to help restore order. Two bullets felled him. Blum himself was at the Opéra that evening and on being apprised of the news hurried to Clichy attired in his silk top hat, white tie, and tails, a costume which appeared somewhat grotesque among the blood-spattered working-class *manifestants* and which both the Communists and the rightists made use of to deride him.

The mild-mannered Socialist Premier was horrified by the sight of the dead and wounded from his own ranks. He thought of resigning. He felt that as head of government he had to protect the right of the opposition, no matter how reactionary, to hold public meetings and that in the last resort he was responsible for maintaining order in the streets. He was deeply hurt at charges that he was acting like "bloody Noske," the German Socialist leader in 1919, a former butcher, who had so ruthlessly put down the Communist rioters in Berlin. His own working-class followers were disenchanted with him, the extreme Right highly pleased at his predicament. One of the latter's publications, *L'Insurgé,* published an oversize cartoon by Ralph Soupault depicting a blood-spattered Blum standing in a pool of blood at Clichy and proclaiming: "Who said I had no French blood?" The cartoon was headed: "Murderers! Resign!"

---

* *Le Temps* protested the dissolution of the leagues, calling it a "new and grave attack on the principle on which rests one of the most important of our public freedoms: the right of association."

The bloodshed at Clichy left a further stain on the Popular Front government and generated more tension in the charged atmosphere which hung over the country. Blum was visibly tired and discouraged. In foreign affairs, dominated by the Spanish Civil War and the hypocrisy of "nonintervention," he was doing no better. German and Italian aid to Franco was making certain that France would soon have another unfriendly Fascist power on its borders. Italy was irretrievably lost so far as Blum could see. Mussolini had confirmed it in a speech at Milan on November 1, 1936, proclaiming the "Rome-Berlin Axis." Ten days before, on October 21, though Blum may not have known it, Count Galeazzo Ciano, Mussolini's son-in-law and foreign minister, had signed a secret protocol in Berlin which outlined a common policy for Germany and Italy in foreign affairs.[22]

In the fall of 1936 Belgium had defected from its alliance with France, leaving the unfortified French border on the north open to a German sweep through Belgium. Blum and his Foreign Minister, Delbos, held a number of secret meetings with the Belgians to try to dissuade them from embarking on neutrality, but they ran up against the stubbornness of the young King Leopold.* To the harassed French Premier the Belgian action was not only a blow to France's military position but a further sign of the growing lack of confidence abroad in French leadership and in collective security. "I sensed with cruel anguish," Blum told the Parliamentary Investigating Committee after the war, that Belgium's defection "was a new sign, a new symptom of the progressive dismantling of all our European positions."[23]

It continued with France's allies in the east of Europe. This, as Blum recognized, was due in large part to the failure of France to act when Hitler reoccupied the Rhineland. French efforts to strengthen the alliances with the Little Entente (Romania, Yugoslavia, and Czechoslovakia) failed. The first two were now engaged in trying to mend their fences with Germany. Even the Czechs began sounding out Berlin about an "understanding." As for Poland, under the guidance of Colonel Josef Beck, the Foreign Minister, it was drifting closer to Nazi Germany. Blum personally tried to stem this drift with offers of financial and military aid. On September 6, 1936, the French government agreed to advance Poland two billion francs over the next four years to finance its rearmament, but this generous gesture had no effect in changing Warsaw's pro-German foreign policy.

Blum also attempted to strengthen the ties with Russia by reaching a military accord, for which the Soviets had been pressing for a year. Without Russia to take on a sizable part of the German army and air force in the East, France was doomed if war should come.

All this would have seemed to be self-evident in Paris, but it was not

---

* After futile negotiations with the Belgians all through the winter of 1936–37, France and Britain on April 24, 1937, gave Belgium a unilateral guarantee against unprovoked aggression.

—not to French conservatives, blinded by their obsessive fear of Communism, not even to the High Command, for the same reason. A few persons in Paris saw it clearly enough. One was Paul Reynaud, who all through 1935, 1936, and 1937 conducted a lonely campaign for a military alliance with the Soviet Union, thereby drawing upon himself the wrath of the Center and the Right in Parliament and in the press. Before he set off to Moscow in the fall of 1936 to become Ambassador, Robert Coulondre went to see Reynaud, who received him standing before a large map of Europe on the wall of his study. "Look at the map," the deputy said to the Ambassador. "On it is written our foreign policy. Geography made necessary the alliance of the Third Republic with tsarist Russia against the Germany of the Kaiser. Today it makes necessary the alliance of the same Third Republic with the Russia of the Bolsheviks against the Germany of the Fuehrer."[24] But in this, as in his campaign to prod the High Command into establishing armored divisions, Reynaud was a voice in the wilderness. His own political colleagues lamented that he had become "soft on Communism."

Blum, despite his Socialist's suspicion of the Communists and distrust of the Soviet Union, decided, as soon as he took over the Popular Front government, to do something about the Franco-Soviet Pact, which had become somewhat forgotten since its signing a year before. The Russians had been urging that it be strengthened by a military convention. But out of fear of antagonizing Hitler, alienating Poland and Romania, France's allies in the East, and arousing the displeasure of Britain, the government had stalled and the General Staff had shown little interest. In November 1936 Blum instructed the High Command to begin secret negotiations in Paris with the Soviet military attaché to determine whether there was a real basis for general-staff talks between the two countries. He named General Schweisguth, Deputy Chief of the General Staff, to conduct the negotiations for the French.

This was a singular choice. Earlier that fall General Schweisguth had returned from observing the annual maneuvers of the Red Army and given a highly unfavorable report, concluding that it was not capable of "fighting a war against a major European power." Blum, as he later testified, was struck by the difference between this report and that of General Loiseau, who had witnessed the Russian maneuvers the year before.[25] The latter had concluded that the "Red Army is probably one of the strongest armies in Europe. . . . Its technique is on a particularly high level." The Premier says he had "some difficulty" in getting the General Staff to produce the earlier report for him and it did so only after "a certain delay." He had begun to run up, he adds, against "if not a resistance at least a reticence on the part of the General Staff" to approaching the Russians about a military accord. The High Command, the Premier found, considered the Polish Army superior to the Russian or in any case more important to France "except perhaps in aviation." And it did not believe that Soviet military aid to France could be of much account because Russia was separated from Germany by buffer states and these, especially Poland and Romania, would not permit Red Army troops to pass through their territories to engage the Germans.

On this last point were to flounder all the efforts to achieve a Franco-Russian military alliance. "If the Bolsheviks come through Poland," General Smigly-Rydz, the chief of the Polish Army, had told General Gamelin in Warsaw in July, "they will never leave."*[26] He had refused even to discuss the question of Russian aid in case of a German attack. During the negotiations in September for the 2 billion-franc advance to Poland, Blum and Delbos made no effort to attach a condition that Poland consent to the entry of Soviet troops in case Germany attacked Poland and France. The subject was not mentioned.

There was one further consideration which made not only the French General Staff but the government cautious about a military pact with the Soviet Union. Blum's timid Foreign Minister, Delbos, pointed it out to Coulondre when he gave him instructions for taking over the Embassy in Moscow. He kept asking himself, he said, "if the Soviets were not trying to push France into a war with Germany."[27] General Schweisguth, returning from Moscow at the same time, was more specific. A long talk with the Soviet War Minister, Marshal Voroshilov, had convinced him, he reported, that Russia wanted to land France into a war with Germany, in which case the Soviets could provide little aid because of the lack of a common frontier with Germany. On the other hand, the general reported, if there were a military alliance, Russia would expect France to attack Germany with full force should the Germans invade the Soviet Union (presumably through the Baltic states).[28] The feeling, then, in both the High Command and the French Foreign Office was that it would be prudent to go slow in the military negotiations for fear, among other considerations, of being pushed into a war with Hitler in which the Russians would give little aid.

The Soviets persisted. On February 17, 1937, Blum had a showdown meeting with the Russian Ambassador, Vladimir Potemkin. The French official minutes of the meeting have been preserved.[29] They disclose that in case of a German attack on France or Czechoslovakia the Soviet government was prepared "to lend assistance with all its military forces" on condition that Poland and Romania "fulfill their duty" and allow the passage of Soviet troops through their territories "either by their

---

* The Polish government also feared that the Russians would bring with them their Communism and attempt to plant it in Poland. This was not an idle fear, as the events after the second war showed. The Polish attitude also stemmed from a historic hatred of the Russians, especially since the Partition. General Smigly-Rydz told Gamelin that "the Russians of the tsars as well as the Bolsheviks had been more odious than the Germans, whom we detest." But the Poles could not, despite their feelings, afford the enmity of both their giant neighbors. Nor in case of attack were they strong enough to defend themselves successfully against one without the aid of the other.

own decision or that of the League of Nations." Moscow was willing, Potemkin said, to specify exactly what military action it would take and put it down in definite military accords drawn up between the interested states. "If," he added, "for incomprehensible reasons Poland and Romania oppose the Soviet Union lending aid to France and Czechoslovakia and do not permit the passage of Soviet troops through their territories, then the assistance of the Soviet Union will be necessarily limited." In that case Russia would send troops to France by sea and fly air force units to France and Czechoslovakia. It would lend what naval support it could and it would furnish the two countries with food, oil, raw materials, especially manganese, arms, planes, and tanks. Having outlined what Russia would do, the Soviet Ambassador asked Blum what France would do if his country were attacked by Germany. The Premier promised to answer later. The French reply was not hasty. Drawn up by General Gamelin on behalf of the General Staff on May 10, nearly three months later, it typified the hesitation of the French Army chief to commit himself to more than vague generalities and his penchant for raising objections that put off taking any action. Gamelin had not grown bolder since the crisis of March 7, 1936. He proposed the following response to the Russians:

1. On the question of the assistance which France could lend to the Soviet Union if she were attacked by Germany:

France, if she herself is not attacked by the main forces of Germany, is ready to take the offensive according to the circumstances of the moment and in the framework of conditions laid down by its pacts of mutual assistance to various countries and subject to its obligations under the Pact of the League of Nations.

All French forces will be devoted to this offensive action in the measure where they will not be needed on other fronts or in our foreign possessions.

2. Concerning the question of the passage of Soviet troops through the territories of Poland and Romania:

The conversations which France has had with these two powers have not led to a solution of this problem.

The French General Staff points out that the only immediate [Soviet] aid which can now be envisaged is that of aviation and motorized forces since Poland and Romania will have need of all their rail lines for the transport of their own troops.[30]

In view of this negative response of the French High Command, there seemed little point to either party in continuing the talks. As a matter of fact Blum had decided to drop them months before. He revealed the reason only after the war.[31]

At the end of 1936, he told the Parliamentary Investigating Committee, he received confidential word from the President of Czechoslovakia, Edouard Beneš, an old and close friend of his, advising him to observe the greatest caution in his negotiations with the Soviet General Staff. According to the Czech Intelligence Service, Beneš said, the leaders of the Russian General Staff were involved in "suspicious relations" with Germany. The implication was that any French military plans passed on to the Russians would be made known to Berlin by the Soviet General Staff, whose leaders were alleged to be plotting with Hitler to overthrow Stalin and set up a pro-German government in Moscow. Soon thereafter Marshal Tukachevsky, Chief of the Russian General Staff, and several other high officers as well as a number of "Old Bolsheviks," such as Zinoviev, Bukharin, Rykov, and Radek, were arrested by Stalin, charged with treasonous dealings with the Germans, and after a series of long-drawn-out trials, found guilty and shot. Beneš had quickly passed along his "intelligence" to Stalin.*

In view of the fact that the Soviet High Command and Army were decimated by the purge—some 5,000 officers and officials were believed to have been liquidated—the French General Staff saw all the more reason to shun further military talks with the Russians. Blum himself, as he told the Investigating Committee, felt "sort of paralyzed" by the warning of Beneš and made no further effort to prod his generals on the matter. He seems to have made no effort to verify the Czech information or to reflect that the charges of treason against Tukachevsky and the others might be, as was later believed, largely trumped up by Stalin to rid himself of opposition in the Party and in the military. In the light of this, Blum's excuse for halting the negotiations seems less than candid. It is difficult to escape the conclusion that he was more influenced by the opposition of the French General Staff itself and by that of a large section of the press and of Parliament, including his Radical supporters, who believed, or professed to believe, that a military alliance with Russia had few advantages and many disadvantages, among the latter being that it would provoke Hitler to attack France and that even if this did not take place it would open the floodgates to Communism in France and make France the pawn of the Bolshevik power. Marshal Pétain had, on the eve of the election in April 1936, warned against the consequences of the Franco-Soviet Pact, though he had been Minister of War in the government when Barthou laid the foundations for it and presumably had approved it: "In holding

---

* Churchill, to whom Beneš recounted the story much later, in January 1944, believed there was "some evidence" that the Czechoslovak President's information came actually from the OGPU, the Soviet secret police, which "wished it to reach Stalin through a friendly foreign source."[32] Another version—of the many that were subsequently bandied about—was published in the Paris newspaper *Le Monde* on October 23, 1948. According to it, the Soviet secret police learned of the alleged plot only at the last minute, thanks to the treachery of General Dybenko, Commander of the Central Asia Military Region. Arriving in Moscow to take part in the coup with other high generals, he got cold feet and informed the secret police of what was up. *Le Monde* says that General Dybenko was the principal state witness at the trials. Shortly after this service to Stalin, it says, he himself was shot.

out our hand to Moscow we have held it out to Communism. We have admitted Communism to the circle of acceptable doctrines. We will certainly regret it."

Not only the Army but the government, Parliament, press and most of the people seemed relieved when negotiations for a military pact were quietly dropped. They would be resumed, indeed frantically pursued, by the French government three years later—when it was too late.

Disdaining the prospect of Russian aid which had been so important in 1914, and aware that Great Britain had no army to land in France, as it had had at the beginning of the Great War, the High Command now knew that except for the help in the east of Czechoslovakia and Poland,* France would have to confront Germany alone. The large new credits approved in September 1936 gave it a chance to seriously rearm on land and in the air and thus to catch up with the Germans. Blum and his War Minister, Daladier, left it to the generals as to how they would use the money—a mistake they later regretted. The question was: would the French emulate the Germans in building up self-contained armored divisions to be supported by dive bombers, as Lieutenant Colonel de Gaulle was urging, or be content merely to strengthen the defensive fortifications, add to their stocks of conventional weapons, and stick to the old tactics which had served so well in the 1914–1918 war, as most of the aging generals complacently suggested? All through 1936 and the following year the Superior War Council, made up, as de Gaulle remarked to Reynaud that year, of "good-humored sexagenarians,"[34] studied the problem under the prodding of the schoolmasterly Gamelin, who continued to make up in studious pursuits what he lacked in the urge for action.

At a meeting of the Council on April 29, 1936, just before the Popular Front took office, General Gamelin argued against following the Germans in establishing armored divisions. The Reich at this time was building up its first three panzer divisions. "The problem of constituting similar units," said Gamelin, "has been studied in France since 1932. But we have renounced the idea because of the development of antitank weapons."

It appeared to us [he continued] that a tank attack cannot succeed against a well-held front unless it is supported by a great deal of heavy artillery knocking out the enemy's antitank weapons. Only a large force, supported by artillery and capable of using behind the tanks strong infantry units, can obtain important and durable results.

---

* Even that was doubtful. In a highly secret note to the Superior War Council on June 4, 1936, General Georges warned that "there is complete uncertainty about Poland." He even envisaged Poland fighting with Germany, in which case, he remarked, the twenty-six German divisions which the General Staff had calculated would be held down in the east by the Poles, could be employed in the west against France.[33]

He did not believe, he said, that the German armored divisions were designed "to rupture a well-organized front but merely to carry out rapid action against relatively weak forces in open country such as in Czechoslovakia, Poland, and Belgium." The most he recommended was to establish a second light mechanized division to replace another horse-cavalry division.[35]

Still, the French Army had no intention of giving up on the horse! More than a year and a half later, at a meeting of the War Council on December 15, 1937, under the chairmanship of War Minister Daladier and in the presence of the illustrious Marshal Franchet d'Esperey and all the top generals save Marshal Pétain, who was absent, it was decided on the urging of General Massiet, Inspector General of the Cavalry, with the support of General Gamelin, that two horse-cavalry regiments which were to be replaced by a third light mechanized division be retained in the Army. This was advisable, General Massiet said, not only because it was important to keep up the raising of horses in France but because horse-cavalry regiments were still extremely valuable for reconnaissance. He was warmly supported by General Prioux, who deplored a shortage of 50,000 saddle horses, urged that more be bought and that the cavalry be "rejuvenated" by replacing the present rather aged mounts with younger ones.[36]

Horse cavalry for reconnaissance at this time in history, the end of 1937! Time stood still for the French generals.

Perhaps not quite. It budged. By the fall of 1936 a little light seems to have penetrated the mind of Gamelin, if not the minds of many of his fellow officers. At a meeting of the Superior War Council on October 14 Gamelin surprised his listeners by a slight shift of position on the question of the panzer division. The Germans, he said, had conceived the idea of an armored division "as the means of carrying out a sudden attack and of exploiting it in depth. We lack such an offensive instrument. We need to have one." General Prételat, one of the ranking generals, objected. The tank division, he argued, was not the answer. But Gamelin persisted— in his way. He "invited" the members of the Council to "study" the matter.[37]

The "studies" seem to have been leisurely. It was not until fourteen months later, at the meeting of the Council on December 15, 1937, in which the retention of horses occupied so much attention, that the generals considered again the question of establishing divisions of heavy tanks. According to the confidential minutes of the meeting,[38] General Gamelin suggested that an armored division was an "extremely interesting tool for carrying out a counterattack or playing a role in exploiting a breakthrough." General Dufieux, Inspector General of Infantry and Tanks, agreed that it was "interesting" but stressed the "dangers and risks" of putting all the heavy tanks into an armored division. At any rate, he said, there would not be enough of these tanks to form a division before 1939. There was much discussion as to how to constitute a panzer division, just what to put in it in the way of artillery, motorized infantry, transport, and air support. The question raises "many problems," Gamelin conceded. Finally the Council agreed "to continue studies and experiments during the year of 1938 regarding the eventual composition of an armored division and its possibilities of employment." The generals were obviously in no hurry.

Why the need for more study? Fifteen years before, General Etienne, the "father" of the tank, had patiently explained what a panzer division should be like. For two years. Colonel de Gaulle had publicly and privately outlined in great detail the composition of such a unit. The Germans, who had taken their ideas first from Etienne and then from de Gaulle, had already established three armored divisions, and the French High Command had learned exactly how they were made up. On November 20, 1935, General Renondeau, the French military attaché in Berlin, had sent a detailed report to the General Staff in Paris, on the composition of each of the three German panzer divisions.[39]

At the meeting of the War Council that December of 1937, Daladier, who as Minister of War presided, had suggested to the generals that they ought to consider having a special attack plane to accompany the armored divisions. The minutes suggest that his proposal was received in silence. The Germans already were developing just such a plane, the Stuka dive bomber. A French manufacturer, Lioré-Nieuport, Daladier knew, had built a plane of this type before the Germans—in 1935. Neither the French Army nor Air Force had shown any interest in it. When in 1937 Daladier tried to get the Air Force to buy the plane, General Vuillemin, its Commander in Chief, told him it was of no value for operations over land but that perhaps the Navy could use it on its aircraft carriers "for attacking enemy ships."[40] The French Navy ordered fifty of them.

When it was too late Blum "bitterly reproached" himself for not using the authority of the government in combating the inertia of the High Command, especially in forming armored divisions. In October, 1936, he had invited Colonel de Gaulle to his office for a talk and had pointed out to him that the large new military credits just approved would give France large quantities of tanks and planes and enable the High Command to establish armored divisions and the necessary assault planes. De Gaulle tried to explain to him that the planes envisaged would be "for interception, not for attack" and that the General Staff was still opposed to putting its tanks in armored divisions, preferring to disperse them with the infantry. Blum bridled a bit, ending the interview by saying: "The use of credits is the affair of Daladier [Minister of War] and General Gamelin."

"No doubt," de Gaulle replied. "But permit me to point out that the national defense is a responsibility of the government."*[41]

---

* Commenting on the tendency of Parliament and government "to relegate preparation of the national defense solely to the military," the Parliamentary Investigating Committee after the war concluded: "There are very important aspects of war

"I have many times bitterly reproached myself," Blum told the Parliamentary Investigating Committee after the war when he recounted how he had failed to keep after the High Command to use its ample credits for building up a great armored force. "Only later did I realize the error, or the illusion, into which I had fallen. I should have been more skeptical and severe in investigating and verifying what was done."[43]

He would not have had much time. As spring arrived that year, 1937, it became obvious that his days in office were numbered.

The Fall of the Popular Front

The pattern of events which had brought the early downfall of every leftish or liberal government since the Great War, regardless of its majority in the Chamber, now was repeated.

The Depression deepened. The funds in the Treasury ran out. The flight of the franc continued. From March to June 1937 industrial production dropped from 93 to 88. By June 15 the balance in the Treasury was down to 2.5 billions. In the first three weeks of the month the Bank of France lost another 8 billions in gold. The reserves in gold and foreign exchange of the Exchange Stabilization Fund, which had been set up to keep the currency reasonably stable, were again exhausted and some 8 billions in metal had to be borrowed from the Bank. Even then, the franc dropped from 20 to 23 to a dollar. With tax receipts lower than anticipated because of the decline in business and personal income the government tried to raise money by short-term borrowing, but there were no lenders. The banks, and those for whom they acted, preferred to buy gold or foreign exchange. By the middle of June it seemed doubtful that the Treasury could meet its obligations for the rest of the month. Two of the three financial experts whom Blum had appointed in March to watch over the Stabilization Fund, Rist and Baudouin, resigned on June 14 because the government would not follow their bankers' advice to drastically reduce expenditures, raise taxes, and restore an absolutely free market in foreign exchange. The next day Blum, with the encouragement of his Finance Minister, Auriol, reacted almost violently.

They finally had concluded that their policy of appeasing the financiers by allowing them to send their capital abroad had failed. They had tried to attract it back by maintaining a relatively free exchange, but this policy had only brought the government to the brink of bankruptcy, for the capital had not returned. "French capital," Blum told the Chamber, had simply gone on "strike." Auriol used stronger words to the hostile Senate. He compared the flight of capital to "desertion in wartime. If every Frenchman," he said, "had done his duty, we would have nothing to fear." Behind the actions and attitudes of big finance Blum and Auriol saw an

---

which escape, and will always escape, the soldier. . . . A government worthy of the name must never shelter behind the military but, on the contrary, imprint on it the essential impulsions."[42]

attempt to overthrow the Popular Front government. When Baudouin resigned on June 14 he told Auriol that what was needed most was "a different majority"—that is, a more conservative government.[44]

On June 15 Blum held an emergency meeting of the cabinet. He and Auriol decided to get tough with those who were speculating against the franc and causing the drain on capital. "If they [the speculators] wish to strangle us," Auriol told the press after the meeting, "let them be certain it will not come without a fight." The cabinet agreed to ask Parliament for plenary power to take all necessary measures by decree to cope with the financial crisis. This was the power which Parliament had denied Herriot in 1925 when there was a similar financial crisis but which had been readily granted to Poincaré and later to Laval. Blum and the Socialist Party had always opposed such a drastic step, but now, struggling to keep the Popular Front government from sinking, they were desperate.

The Chamber, despite the misgivings of the Radical-Socialists, approved decree powers to the government by a vote of 346 to 247. The Senate dominated by the Radical-Socialists, who were a part of the Popular Front government but now soured on it, balked. It voted down Blum's proposed bill by a large majority and approved a much weaker version of its own. Once again the Chamber, at Blum's request, voted to give him the plenary powers he had asked for, and once again the Senate, on June 20, rejected them.

It seemed that evening that France might be thrown into a constitutional crisis. The right of the Senate to overthrow a government had never been settled, and there were many supporters of Blum in the cabinet meeting that followed who urged that he defy the upper House. It was suggested that he request the Senate and President of the Republic to dissolve the Chamber and set new elections. But the Radical members of the government, already weary of being allied with the Communists and, privately, out of sympathy with Blum's projected policies to get tough with capital, refused to agree to such a step. Blum himself, worn out from a frustrating year in office, was in no mood to provoke a constitutional crisis, which he felt would so weaken the country that it might collapse. A quarreling, bankrupt country might tempt Hitler and Mussolini to attack.

At 2 A.M. on June 22, 1937, he handed in the resignation of his government to the President of the Republic. "I have had enough!" he told the American Ambassador, William Bullitt. "Everything that I have attempted to do has been blocked."[45] He had tried for just a year. In that brief time the experiment—and the experience—of the Front Populaire had run its course.

It had had its successes—and its failures. There were social gains—the greatest achieved in the Third Republic's history—but also economic setbacks, so that the advantages that came to the workers, the peasants, and the poor from the former were largely offset by the hardships that came from the latter. Substantial wage and salary increases won in June 1936, for example, had been largely wiped out by the following June, when the government fell, by the increase in the cost of living. Still, labor had won the right to organize and bargain collectively, and, like the middle classes, have a fortnight's vacation with pay. It had won the 40-hour week, but this had decreased production, especially of badly needed armaments —at a time when the regimented German workers were toiling 60 hours a week, mostly on arms.

The inability to improve the economy and the nation's finances was the greatest failure of the Popular Front. There was not much it could do as long as Blum felt bound to work within the old moribund economic system whose bankers and businessmen refused to cooperate with him or do anything on their own. The French economy was simply out of date, many of its industries, as Charles Spinasse, the Minister of National Production, found, "organized and equipped as they were in the Middle Ages or in the seventeenth century." No one attempted seriously to renovate it, neither the government nor the businessman.

Blum himself blamed the bourgeoisie, forgetting how reluctant he was, as Premier, to prod it into the twentieth century.

> Was it not evident [he asked in a book written during the second war] that the bourgeoisie had not found in itself any reserves of energy, any resources of the imagination, any capacity for renovating and rebuilding, to overcome the economic depression? Was it not evident that in every sphere of productive activity—industry, agriculture, commerce, banking—it dawdled along in its routine traditions?[46]

But Blum failed to use the power of government to stop the "dawdling." Instead, he tried to win the confidence and support of the bankers and industrialists by leaving them to their own devices. Above all, Blum's failure to stop the flight of capital by strict control of the export of gold and foreign exchange prevented the economy from reviving and landed the country in a financial mess. As the first Socialist—and Jewish—Prime Minister in the history of France he was determined to keep his word, as he said, "to exercise power only within the framework of capitalism." His scruples do him credit. But in a harsh world of conflict, in which it was evident that the economic and financial elite were out to destroy his government—at whatever cost to the country—his lack of boldness, of toughness, proved his undoing.

There was another failure. Despite all the genuine efforts of Blum to bring about a civilized reconciliation between the warring classes and interests, the Popular Front experiment left France more divided than ever. The overthrow of the Popular Front made the masses bitter and disillusioned. Many believed that since a peaceful revolution had failed to curb the power of the financial and industrial oligarchy, a bloodier one was necessary, and these flocked to the Communist Party. The Right, relieved at the demise of the Front Populaire, was nevertheless still fearful of Communism and of the anarchy it believed the masses had fallen into. Many on the Right turned more and more to the belief that a savior for France must be found beyond the frontiers.

Gustav Hervé, the once fiery Socialist and pacifist, now become the opposite, pointed the way: "Anything but this filthy anarchy! . . . How many must be mumbling between their teeth these days: *"Ah! Vive Mussolini et vive Hitler!"*[47]

It was at this time, I remember, that one began to hear in upper-class circles in Paris a remark that became almost a chant: "Better Hitler than Blum."

There had been during the fleeting months of the Popular Front one further achievement—in the sphere of humanity. Life had become a little better for the masses. There was something in the atmosphere fostered by the Popular Front which writers, philosophers and historians, as well as leftish politicians, later looked back to as *l'Esprit de 1936,* the Spirit of 1936. For the poor there was a feeling of liberation. At last they felt a sense of participation in the life of the nation. They had helped to elect a Parliament and government that shared their aspirations and had tried to achieve some of them.

One of Blum's innovations had been to establish a subcabinet office for "leisure and sports" and to put at its head as undersecretary an imaginative and energetic young Socialist, Léo Lagrange.* Within a couple of months, in time for the traditional August vacations, he had wangled for the poor cut-rate fares from the railroads, reduced prices from the resort hotels, and had increased the number of camps and youth hostels (*auberges de la jeunesse*). That August millions of workers and their families, taking advantage for the first time of paid vacations, flocked to the seashore, the mountains, and the countryside, invading premises theretofore occupied mostly by the more well-to-do, who were not always pleased by the presence of what they called the "new paid vacationers" indulging in this newfangled "proletarian tourism."

"Let us open the gates of culture to the people," the youthful Jacques Soustelle proclaimed in the new liberal weekly *Vendredi,* founded by the young writers André Chamson and Jean Guéhenno, who sang of the spiritual side of the revolution of 1936. "You have a right," Jean Giono, the novelist, wrote, addressing the common people, "to the harvests, a right to happiness, a right to the real world, a right to the true riches here below, right away, now, in this life." The Popular Front encouraged the novel idea.

---

* Lagrange was killed in action in June 1940. "He was a man we all loved," Malraux said of him after the war.

By the year's end Léon Blum, with considerable justification, could say in his New Year's Eve broadcast:

We see again in the country a hope, a feeling for work, a feeling for life. France has another look, another air. Blood flows faster in our rejuvenated body. Everyone feels that in France the human condition has improved.

He never lost his conviction that, whatever its failures, the Popular Front had brought, as he told his judges during his trial at Riom on March 11, 1942, "a sort of beauty and light into lives that had been difficult and obscure," giving them "hope for the future."[48]

The Popular Front, with Blum's overthrow by the Senate, was dead though it would not be buried for another year. The myth of it hung on, or was clung to by the three quarreling parties of the Left which had forged it and which, together, still had a decisive majority in the popularly elected Chamber—if one counted seats and overlooked the fickleness of those who held them. Blum himself helped to keep the myth alive by agreeing to serve as Vice-Premier in the government of Camille Chautemps, who succeeded him. The Communists helped too by promising to support the new cabinet in the Chamber.

But the fire of the Popular Front had gone out. It had not been strong enough to overcome its own divisions and to stand up to the determined opposition of industry and finance, the onslaughts of the reactionary press, and the fierce enmity of the upper and middle classes. This government, which by its promulgation of mild and long overdue social reforms had inspired so many fears, did not have the force to justify them.[49]

Dominated now by the Radical-Socialists, who were solidly bourgeois at heart, distrusting the Socialists and hating the Communists, and led by the suave Chautemps, for whom the demands of the hour were beyond his limited capacities, and by a similar type of Radical politician, Georges Bonnet, as Minister of Finance, the new Popular Front government proceeded by stages to liquidate itself and to whittle away the gains the first one had achieved.

Once again, as after 1924 and 1932, the people who had elected to the Chamber a majority of the Left, felt cheated. As if by some inscrutable law of French politics this majority for the third time in a decade melted away into conservatism, which also was a spent force. The enfeeblement of the Third Republic, in an apprehensive Europe whose peace was being increasingly threatened by the growing belligerence of the Fascist dictators, continued apace.

18

DISSENSION AND DISARRAY: FRANCE AND THE *ANSCHLUSS*
MARCH 1938

When on the night of March 11–12, 1938, Adolf Hitler engineered the *Anschluss* and sent his troops into his native Austria to add that ancient country to the domains of the Third Reich and establish Nazi Germany in the heart of Central Europe, there was little reaction from Paris. There was, in fact, no French government in being that day.

The day before, on the 10th, the wobbly Radical government of Camille Chautemps had resigned without even asking the Chamber for a vote of confidence, which undoubtedly would have been granted, though grudgingly. His government, like all recent ones, was in financial difficulty and again he had asked for decree powers to try to deal with it. But the main reason for Chautemps stepping down was his reluctance to face Hitler's latest aggression, which had been in the making, quite publicly, for some days. As the Wehrmacht troops marched toward Vienna Léon Blum, at the instigation of the President of the Republic, was trying frantically to form a cabinet that at least would give France a government to cope with the new crisis abroad. By the 12th, when Hitler officially proclaimed the *Anschluss* and set off from Germany for Austria to take it over, the Socialist leader had not yet succeeded. In the face of Hitler's aggression and yet another financial crisis at home, he was striving to form a coalition government which finally would unite all Frenchmen from the extreme Left to the extreme Right. But he was not succeeding. The conservatives were giving him the cold shoulder.

For nearly a year after replacing Blum, the weak and ineffectual Chautemps had presided over the destinies of the Republic and the country had slid a little further downhill. The franc had become worth a little less, the state of finances a little worse, the economy a bit further depressed, the Popular Front majority in the Chamber still further divided and diluted.

At the first of the year, 1938, the Front Populaire had been practically buried when Chautemps, in a moment of pique, told the Communists he could do without them, and the Socialists, led by Vice Premier Blum, had resigned in protest. Chautemps had carried on for two months with a minority government composed exclusively of Radicals and then thrown in the sponge.

The next evening Hitler seized Austria. It took him less time to accomplish this than it did the French to change governments that March weekend. While France under Chautemps had drifted, Germany under Hitler had prepared to act.

Four months before, on November 5, 1937, the Nazi dictator had called in his military chiefs and his Foreign Minister for a highly secret briefing in Berlin and in a harangue that lasted more than four hours had told them that he intended to increase Germany's "living space"—*Lebensraum*—by taking, to commence with, Austria and Czechoslovakia, peacefully if possible, by war if necessary. When his Army chief, General Werner von Fritsch, and his Foreign Minister, Baron Konstantin von Neurath, proved hesitant in embracing his program for aggression he sacked them. On February 4 he himself took over personal command of the armed forces, cashiered sixteen senior generals along with Fritsch, reorganized the High Command, and replaced Neurath at the Foreign Office with an insufferable ignoramus named Joachim von Ribbentrop, a former champagne salesman. Hitler was now ready to act on his plans without any interference from the Army or the Foreign Office.[1]

On February 12 he had summoned the Austrian Chancellor, Kurt von Schuschnigg, to Berchtesgaden, and after lambasting and insulting him for the better part of a day, had presented him with an ultimatum demanding, in effect, that he turn over Austria to the local Nazis or face an attack by the German Army.[2] Schuschnigg had submitted, but when he saw that the nazification of Austria was but a prelude to German annexation, he called for a plebiscite in a forlorn attempt to let the Austrian people decide their fate. This was on March 9. The next day Hitler, in a state of rage at the Austrian Chancellor's display of independence, ordered the German army to march into Austria not later than March 12.

As had been the case with Hitler's coup in the Rhineland two years before, the French government received plenty of warning of Hitler's plans. On February 18, General Gamelin was given by a "personal friend" a detailed account of the Hitler-Schuschnigg meeting and the ultimatum that followed. It was confirmed by the French Minister in Vienna. Gamelin says that he immediately went to see Daladier, the Minister of War, to point out "the grave consequences to us of a German occupation of Austria." These were not difficult even for a layman to understand. As Gamelin explained to Daladier, they would put the Germans in a position of flanking Czechoslovakia on three sides and render the Czech "Maginot Line" of fortifications useless, since they could now be attacked from the rear. The

French Army chief also took care to point out—he states it in his memoirs
—that as soon as the Germans had finished their fortifications on the
Rhine, "they would be the masters of Central Europe because we could
no longer effectively intervene." He adds that the War Minister agreed with
him that this time, unlike on March 7, 1936, France ought to "do something."[3]

But nothing was done. The Chautemps government was too weak to
do anything. The Army, as in the spring two years before, made no plans
to counter a German move. And again, as on the morning when the
Wehrmacht troops marched into the Rhineland, France turned to Britain
before budging, leaving the decision whether to oppose Hitler up to London. No one in Paris could have had any illusions as to what the British
decision would be. As far back as November 1937, Lord Halifax, who had
called on Hitler at Berchtesgaden, had left him with the distinct impression
that the new Chamberlain government would not seriously oppose the
Anschluss. In February, Halifax had become British Foreign Minister,
replacing Anthony Eden, who had resigned because of his opposition to
Chamberlain's policy of appeasing the Fascist dictators. Just to make sure
of Britain's attitude, Ribbentrop, the newly appointed German Foreign
Minister, journeyed to London on March 9 ostensibly to wind up his affairs
at the Embassy, where he had been Ambassador. He saw the King, the
Prime Minister, the Archbishop of Canterbury, and, on the 10th, the day
Hitler decided to march into Austria, Lord Halifax. That evening he reported to the German dictator from London: "England will do nothing in
regard to Austria."[4]

France got the message two days later. On the afternoon of March 11,
when the news from Vienna left no more doubt as to what Hitler was up to,
Gamelin says he was informed by the government, which was expediting
current affairs until a new cabinet could be formed, that "no military measures were to be taken." Nothing would be done, he was told, until London
had been heard from. Later, in his postwar testimony before the Parliamentary Investigating Committee, Daladier would claim that France wanted
to act.

> I wanted to do something to maintain the independence of Austria. I saw
> Premier Chautemps, who had just resigned, several times. The General Staff
> agreed that it was time to act.

On the morning of March 12 Daladier met with the Premier, Delbos,
the Foreign Minister, and Bonnet, the Minister of Finance. "I told them,"
Daladier testified, "that we had decided to apply the military measures
already envisaged, on condition that we obtain the collaboration of Britain,
which the Foreign Office already had asked for."[5]

What the "military measures already envisaged" were Daladier did not
say, and his fellow ministers must have wondered. Gamelin later recalled
them. They consisted of canceling leave for the troops on the German

border! The Army Commander in Chief says he told Daladier that "if France once again gives way, we shall have to intensify our effort." Whereupon he asked for an extra credit of 174 million francs to strengthen the Maginot Line.[6] The timidity of Gamelin staggers one. At this very hour several German divisions were marching through Austria. In a few days they would surround Czechoslovakia on three sides. France's whole position in the East would be in jeopardy. And all the Commander in Chief of the French Army could think of doing to counter this blow was to cancel leaves of the troops on the German frontier and ask for a little more money to bolster the Maginot Line!

At 5 P.M. that afternoon the reply of the British government reached Paris. Gamelin says that Léger, the Secretary-General of the French Foreign Office, who passed it along to the government and to him, was "heartbroken" by it. But surely not surprised. Britain, as expected, declined to do anything more than register a protest in Berlin against Hitler's aggression. France fell in line. Austria was abandoned to its fate. Later the French politicians again blamed Britain for their own inaction. But in truth they were glad of the "out" which London gave them. They had never intended to act, nor had they made any plans to do so.

The Germans knew it all along. Their confidential documents, captured after the second war, reveal how accurately they assessed the French weakness. On the morning of March 12 Count Johannes von Welczeck, the German Ambassador in Paris, assured Berlin that France would do no more than protest. Two days later he reported that the French were resigned to the *Anschluss*.[7] German Military Intelligence also quickly satisfied itself that the French army would not budge.

> High Command . . . reports at 1:20 A.M., March 13, by phone from France from a reliable agent:
> 1. The Maginot Line is manned throughout, but exclusively for defensive purposes.
> 2. Military measures are not to be expected from France except in case of an attack on the Czechs.

. . . . .

> War Ministry reports by telephone, March 13: Reports of our agents in France tell in general of prevailing calm and normal routine in the Army.[8]

Without firing a shot and without interference from Great Britain, France, and Russia, whose combined military forces could have overwhelmed him, Hitler by swallowing up Austria had added seven million more subjects to the Reich and gained a strategic position of immense value to his future plans. Not only did his armies flank Czechoslovakia on three sides but he now possessed Vienna. As the capital of the old Austro-

Hungarian Empire, Vienna had long stood at the center of the communications and the trading systems of Central and Southeast Europe. Now that nerve center was in German hands.

Perhaps most important to Hitler was the demonstration again that neither Britain nor France would lift a finger to stop him. Nor would they concert with Russia to forge a ring around the Reich, as they had done prior to 1914. On March 17, less than a week after the *Anschluss,* the Soviet government had proposed to London and Paris a conference of powers, within or without the League of Nations, to consider means of halting further German aggression. Prime Minister Chamberlain, intent now on trying further to appease Hitler and Mussolini, despite what had just happened in Austria, received the Russian suggestion coolly and quickly rejected it.

The inevitable consequence of any such action [he told the Commons on March 24] would be to aggravate the tendency towards the establishment of exclusive groups of nations which must . . . be inimical to the prospects of European peace.

Apparently Chamberlain did not mind such "exclusive groups of nations" as those joined in the Rome-Berlin Axis or in the tripartite Anti-Comintern Pact of Germany, Italy, and Japan, nor that group which he was now trying to revive—the so-called Four Powers, of Britain, France, Germany, and Italy—which excluded Soviet Russia. Once again France took its cue from Britain and cold-shouldered the Russian proposal.* Robert Coulondre, the astute French Ambassador in Moscow, mentions in his memoirs the Soviet proposal, which was issued while he was en route to Paris on leave. He affirms that he took it up with the Foreign Minister when he arrived in Paris and urged that it be accepted in order to assure Russian help for Czechoslovakia, which obviously was next on Hitler's list. He went further: he said it was "urgent to begin military talks with the U.S.S.R."[10]

No nation, not even the victim, Austria, bothered to appeal to the

---

* In his memoirs (*Au Cœur de la Mêlée,* pp. 258–259, and in the abridged English language translation, *In the Thick of the Fight,* pp. 179–181) Paul Reynaud expresses his surprise that the Russian proposal "passed unperceived" by the French Foreign Office or government. But this cannot be true. Reynaud quotes Blum as testifying that neither he nor his Foreign Minister, Paul-Boncour, had it brought to their attention. And Paul-Boncour does not mention it in his three volumes of memoirs. French records thus far available are also strangely silent on the matter. But the captured German documents make clear that the French Foreign Minister did have the Russian proposals "brought to his attention." On March 19, the German Embassy in Paris wired Berlin that the Soviet Ambassador had called on the French Foreign Minister and discussed with him "Litvinov's proposal to call a conference in order to prevent a repetition of attacks similar to that on Austria." The Embassy reported that the Foreign Minister "expressed interest" but stressed that the Russian suggestions would "require thorough study and painstaking research before they can be given practical expression." This was diplomatic language for stalling—indefinitely. The French Foreign Minister of the day was Paul-Boncour.[9]

League of Nations, whose statutes guaranteed Austria's independence and obliged all the other member states to come to her aid if attacked. The dream of Woodrow Wilson, the hope of the world, embodied in the League, were dead.

By March 14, the day Hitler entered Vienna, having proclaimed Austria out of existence,* Léon Blum had finally formed a French government. But, as he told the Chamber, it was not the one he had hoped—and tried—to form. Called upon for the second time in a moment of crisis to constitute a government, Blum realized that a new Popular Front regime would not be strong enough to meet the deteriorating situation in Europe caused by the German dictator's latest act of aggression. He therefore appealed to the Right to join the Left in a government of National Union, "from Thorez to Marin." Thorez was the leader of the Communist Party, Louis Marin the chief of the principal conservative group, the Republican Federation.

Never before in the history of the Republic had the Left taken the initiative in forming a government of all the republican parties in order to unite the nation in a time of peril. Hitherto this had always been done—in 1914, in 1926, in 1934—by the Right. And the Right had made these coalition governments essentially conservative, especially in domestic affairs. Now in 1938, with the country again facing a crisis, the Right hesitated to join a united government headed by a Socialist. Blum offered to step down in favor of another if the Conservatives would agree to participate in a national government.

Saturday, March 12, was the crucial day. In Vienna the night before Chancellor Schuschnigg had been forced to resign by Hitler and had been temporarily supplanted by a stooge local Nazi government under the "quisling" Seyss-Inquart, who was holding the capital until Hitler and his Wehrmacht troops could arrive and take over. In Paris that morning Blum quickly won over his own party, the Socialists, and also the Communists and the Radicals, who formed the Popular Front majority. He then appealed to the Center and the Right to join a National Union government. Reynaud of the Center, Louis Marin of the Right, were sympathetic, but most of their followers, led by Flandin, were hostile. Blum, undaunted, proposed that they call a meeting of their deputies to hear his appeal.

At 6 P.M. that early evening in the Salle Colbert in the Palais-Bourbon Blum addressed the opposition deputies in one of the most eloquent—and, as he later mused, pathetic—speeches of his life.† The Left parties of the

---

* Hitler's proclamation of March 13 began: "Austria is a province of the German Reich."

† As Vincent Auriol said much later, when he was the President of the Republic (the Fourth):

"In the face of Hitler's expansion, in the face of the peril of war . . . Blum addressed the most pathetic, the most heartrending appeal that a man has ever made

Front Populaire had that day given him a mandate, he said, to unite with the parties of the Center and the Right for the good of the country. It was "inconceivable" to him, he declared, that the parties of the conservative opposition, with their long tradition of patriotism, would refuse to join together with the majority to give unity to the hard-pressed nation. It was so inconceivable to Blum that, as he later told his judges at Riom, he left the Chamber hall convinced that he had won the opposition deputies over. After he had gone the Center and Right leaders spoke. Reynaud strongly urged his colleagues to join a National Government. When some members protested against joining a government that included Communists, Reynaud retorted: "It is not Stalin who enters Vienna today, who will menace Prague tomorrow. It is Hitler. . . . I say today France must unite." He was supported by Marin, Mandel, and even the mercurial Kerillis, all further to the Right.

Those present later said it was Flandin who turned the tide. He had visited Berlin the previous December, talked to several Nazi leaders, and had been so impressed that he had returned with the conviction that Germany had become too strong to contend with and that henceforth France must accommodate herself to her more powerful neighbor instead of opposing her,* and take the same attitude toward Fascist Italy. A government dominated by the Popular Front, he argued, would only aggravate the Fascist dictators and, moreover, displease the Tory government of Britain.

The idea that France should restrict her governments to those which pleased not only her friends but her foes does not seem to have shocked the conservative deputies. They knew, of course, that Flandin's principal objective in refusing to cooperate with the Popular Front was to destroy it and prepare the way for the return of a conservative government in which he might again become a minister. He had been out of a cabinet job for two years and, like Laval, resented it. Flandin's intervention was decisive, despite the moving appeal of Reynaud, backed by Marin, Mandel, and Kerillis, to join in a government of National Union.

The assembled opposition deputies rejected Blum's proposal overwhelmingly, by 152 to 5.

Unable, as he said, to conceal his "surprise" and his "sadness," Blum formed his second Popular Front government the next day. "Everybody knew that it would be brief," he told the Riom court long afterward, "and I assure you, I knew it as well as anyone else."[12]

It lasted less than a month.

---

to opponents, that they unite and join with him so that a unified government might protect a threatened country and its liberty."

Auriol's tribute was made in an oration at Blum's funeral on April 2, 1950.

* Churchill, visiting Paris a few days later, had a long talk with Flandin and noted: "He was quite a different man from the one I had known in 1936; . . . Now out of office [he was] completely convinced that there was no hope for France except in an arrangement with Germany. We argued for two hours."[11]

The opportunity to unite the country was missed—because of the recalcitrance of the Right. Paul Reynaud, taking to the radio on March 19, bitterly regretted it.

France is making a terrible spectacle of herself. All the quarrels, all the rancor, all the bitterness of political strife, have come to the surface. Is it not time that we rise above ourselves, forget our party and class differences and become children of the same country, children of a country in danger? . . . Can it be that France has lost its instinct of self-preservation?

It was acting, he added, as if it had.[13]

Xavier-Vallat on the extreme Right again greeted Blum with an anti-Semitic outburst when the Premier presented his new government to the Chamber. Defending the refusal of the conservatives to unite with the Popular Front in an all-party government he exclaimed:

Personally, it strikes me as unseemly to try to reunite the French around a man who represents so intensely the people whom a divine malediction has condemned to be without a country.

For this remark, according to the *Journal Officiel,* there was "applause from the Right, vigorous protests and prolonged rumbling from the extreme Left to the Left."

In foreign affairs Blum moved quickly to pick up the pieces left by Hitler's seizure of Austria, Chamberlain's growing appeasement of the Fascist dictators, Franco's mounting successes in the Spanish Civil War made possible by Italian and German aid, and the failure of Chautemps for a year to react to these events.

On March 14, the day after he assumed office, he called in the Czech Ambassador and in the presence of Paul-Boncour, the Foreign Minister, solemnly assured him that France would unreservedly honor her commitment to Czechoslovakia to come to her aid if attacked by Germany. Count Welczeck, the German Ambassador in Paris, informed Berlin the next day that it was a "binding pledge" and that this time France would not wait for the League of Nations to act or for Britain to react. "The Supreme Military Council," he added, "summoned for this afternoon will deal with the matter and work out details of military measures relating to the new commitment." The "period of inaction" in France, the Ambassador stressed, "is to end." And he warned Berlin that the new Blum government was going to be tough not only in defense of the Czechoslovaks but in Spain. "Accordingly," he wired, "German and Italian intervention in Spain is to be countered and French intervention apparently is to be intensified, above all by means of war material and provision of technical assistance."[14]

The German envoy, with contacts among pro-German politicians in

Parliament and probably even in the government, was well informed—about intentions. Blum called a meeting of the Permanent Committee on National Defense for the afternoon of March 15, his second day in office, to discuss French commitments to Czechoslovakia and to consider intervention against Franco in Spain. Had the German Ambassador seen the minutes of the meeting[15] he would have been less worried than he appears to have been. The hesitations of the French generals and of the Minister of War, Daladier, reached a new peak.

Paul-Boncour posed the first fundamental question: what help could France give to Czechoslovakia in case she were attacked by Germany? Not much really, was the answer of Daladier and General Gamelin. The only aid France could give, Daladier explained, was to mobilize her forces on the frontier and thus pin down the bulk of the German army in the West. Gamelin, emboldened for a moment, thought the French could go one step further "and attack." But then he drew back, pointing out that he would have to assault "a zone already fortified" and that "this could lead us to operations lasting a long time."

"But Russia would intervene," Blum interjected.

"I do not see what effective aid Russia could give initially," Gamelin responded coolly, resorting to his habitual technique of multiplying the difficulties involved. Poland and Romania, he said, probably would not give Soviet troops the right of passage, and even if they did, their railroads were insufficient for the task and their highways, if motorized troops were used, in bad shape. General Vuillemin, chief of the Air Force, was equally pessimistic about support from Russia in the air. In the first place, he said, Poland and Romania would first have to give permission for Russian planes to fly over their territories, and this was doubtful. Even if it were forthcoming there were only forty airfields in Czechoslovakia to receive the Soviet aircraft, and these, he said, could quickly be destroyed by German bombing. The defeatist Air Force general delivered the real coup a few minutes later when discussion centered on the risks of a general war. Given the superiority of the German Luftwaffe, General Vuillemin said, *"the French air force would be wiped out in fifteen days."*

This alarming information gave the meeting pause for thought and Marshal Pétain contributed to the disillusionment by adding: "In aviation it is less the initial force than the potential of construction that counts. And this potential we do not have." Guy La Chambre, the Minister of Air, supported him. Whereas, he pointed out, France was turning out 3,000 planes a month at the end of the last war, its present production was 40 planes a month, which he hoped to raise shortly to 60. Marshal Pétain, the minutes say, "compared this to the 250 planes a month being produced by Germany."

Deep gloom fell over the session. It was not dispersed when the Prime Minister posed what he called the "second question: *How can we intervene in Spain?"* Could France, he asked, make good on an ultimatum to Franco giving him twenty-four hours to renounce the support of Germany and Italy or face French intervention in the Spanish Civil War? Hitler, Blum reminded his colleagues, had successfully used such an ultimatum with Austria a few days before.

The Premier's questions, judging by the minutes, caused consternation. Gamelin replied immediately that "the conditions were not the same." Germany, he stressed, had a standing army of 900,000 men, France had only 400,000. Daladier was more blunt: "You would have to be blind," he declared, "not to see that intervention in Spain would unleash a general war." Léger, of the Foreign Office, supported him. "Germany and Italy," he affirmed, "would regard French intervention in Spain as a *casus belli.* No doubt about that." Here the weakness in the fundamental attitude of the French was exposed: French intervention but not Italo-German intervention (which already was massive) in Spain would bring about a European war. This was a grave confession of inferiority and helplessness. Daladier summed up the consensus as the doleful meeting came to an end:

> Such an intervention, not motivated by new facts, would risk leaving us alone to face Germany and Italy, with only the feeble aid of a Russia, distant and weak, and without being assured at all of the help of Great Britain.

This fear of being left alone to face the Fascist dictators was to haunt the French leaders, military and civilian, from then on and to paralyze any initiative in foreign policy that might have strengthened France in Europe, wrought an anti-Axis coalition, and discouraged Hitler and Mussolini from further aggression. It was based on two serious errors of judgment: an underestimation of Soviet military strength and a failure to recognize the basic need of Great Britain, for its own preservation, to stand by France against Germany and Italy.

The meeting of the Defense Committee, which had begun at 6:15 P.M., mercifully came to an end at 8 o'clock. At least Blum and Paul-Boncour knew the limitations on their freedom of action. They could not intervene in Spain. And in the light of what the generals and the Minister of War had said, France could do little to save Czechoslovakia from being overrun. She could of course honor her word to that country, as Blum had just said she would, and by proclaiming it perhaps deter Hitler. The question was: would France honor her word? For the next six months it would be raised and debated, affirmed and doubted, with increasing intensity and passion, in Paris, Berlin, London, Moscow, Rome, and Prague until the Indian summer days that hung over a jittery Europe on the brink of war at the end of September that year brought a final answer.

Marshal Pétain, through a former adjutant, Major Loustanau-Lacau, who, as we have seen, had succeeded in forming anti-Republican cells in the Army and was in close touch with the terrorist Cagoule, leaked the Defense Committee's discussion on intervention in Spain and in an exaggerated form to the reactionary press the next day. Headlines telling of a government decision to intervene in Spain and to send three divisions to Catalonia to repulse Franco appeared on the front pages of the rightist Parisian press. They brought the nervous British Ambassador, Sir Eric Phipps, scurrying to Paul-Boncour to demand an explanation. The equally edgy Spanish Ambassador in Berlin demanded what the Germans would do in the face of this French move. The Germans were not worried. General Wilhelm Keitel, Chief of the High Command of the Wehrmacht, assured the German Foreign Office that there was little likelihood of the French moving into Spain. "The lack of internal unity and the weak position of the present French government," Keitel said, "make it appear improbable."*[16]

The German High Command, like Hitler, was watching very closely the signs of "lack of internal unity" in France—not for the assurance it gave about Spain but about Czechoslovakia. Soon, on April 21, as we know from the German documents, Hitler would call in Keitel to discuss the operational plans, already drawn up the year before, for a "lightning" attack on Czechoslovakia.

The lack of internal unity in France, on which the Germans were keeping such a close watch, brought an end to the second Blum government on April 8, 1938, and buried the Front Populaire once and for all. A series of strikes, especially damaging to rearmament, broke out again, just as they had when Blum first took office two years before. This time the employers, certain that the leftist government would not last, made no effort to settle them, though as soon as Blum had departed they quickly did so— "an extraordinary coincidence," it seemed to Auriol.

In Parliament tempers on the Right again reached the boiling point. On April 6, when debate began in the Chamber on the government's financial and economic proposals, which most conservatives conceded were "coherent and constructive,"[17] the Speaker had to suspend the session to quell a riot. "Death to the Jews!", shouted a rightist deputy, Duboys-Fresney, in the midst of the melee, and Montigny, a Radical, charged that the decree powers Blum had asked for until July 1 to inaugurate his program would allow the Socialist Premier to "legally carry out the revolution." Flandin, continuing his fight to bring down the Popular Front, was outraged that the new government should dare to propose control of foreign exchange, though the need to halt the continual flight of capital, which for so long had so weakened the country, was conceded by everyone.

What the Blum government proposed was to give France for the first time since Poincaré a bold and comprehensive program for the economic and financial regeneration of the country, putting capital to productive use, vastly increasing credit, controlling foreign exchange, and substituting financial order for the prevailing chaos. Ironically for a man who for years had

---

* Keitel, incidentally, informed the Foreign Office in the same note that he "assumed" that "we continue to maintain the *fiction* that no German troops are committed in Spain."

opposed increasing military credits, Blum based his program on a vastly
augmented output of armaments in the belief that to cope with Hitler the
Army, Air Force, and Navy must be immediately and drastically strengthened and that the expansion of the war industries would greatly stimulate
industrial production as a whole.

> Such, gentlemen [he told the Chamber], are the measures proposed. . . .
> They are dominated by the immense obligation . . . on all Frenchmen to assure
> the defense of the country. Certainly it is a kind of tragic irony that a nation
> devoted to peace and human progress is compelled to strain and concentrate all
> its resources for a gigantic military effort. . . . But we shall prove that free
> peoples can rise to . . . their duties, that democracies are capable, through a
> voluntarily accepted discipline, of deploying strength that is not obtained else-
> where except through blind obedience.

But the French democracy, or at least the Parliament which was supposed to speak for it, was in no such heroic mood. Politics as usual prevailed. The Chamber, still dominated by the Popular Front majority,
approved the program 311 to 250, though nearly half the Radical-Socialists
deserted the coalition to vote against. On April 8, the Senate, again led by
the embittered Caillaux, once more overthrew a Blum government, this
time by a vote of 214 to 47. It had lasted twenty-six days. Its collapse
interred the Front Populaire despite its majority in the Chamber—such
was the fickleness of the elected deputies. For the third and last time since
the Great War, a union of the Left, victorious in the elections, dominant
in the Chamber, had fallen apart and lost the reins of government.

Edouard Daladier, the Radical-Socialist who had led his party into the
Popular Front and been one of its staunchest supporters, succeeded Blum
as Premier. After receiving unprecedented votes of confidence in both the
Chamber (514 to 8) and the Senate (290 to 0) and the power to govern
temporarily by decree, which the Senate had refused to Blum, the new
Premier, who from now on would preside over the destinies of the Third
Republic almost to the bitter end, moved quickly to the Right. The absence
of the Socialists, who refused to enter his government though promising to
support it in the Chamber, and of the Communists, who were not asked to
join it though also pledging Parliamentary support, made it easy for
Daladier to receive conservative backing. He took into his cabinet two
moderate conservatives, Reynaud and Mandel, and several from his own
party who had soured on the Popular Front.

Among the latter was Georges Bonnet, who replaced Paul-Boncour
at the Foreign Ministry. This vain, tricky, conniving Radical politician,
"a foul ferment without morality but with a taste for intrigue," as the
usually chivalrous General Gamelin said of him after getting to know him
at the Quai d'Orsay, was scarcely the man to conduct foreign affairs in the
midst of the worst crisis in Europe in a generation. The presence in the
cabinet, however, of Mandel and Reynaud, moderately conservative though

they were in domestic matters, promised to counter the "pernicious influence" of Bonnet, to quote Gamelin again, in conducting France's relations with other powers, friend and foe. They wanted France at last to stand up to Hitler and Mussolini and they strove to make her strong enough, through rearming and strengthening her alliances—not only with Britain but with Russia—to do so. Only in this way, they believed, could peace be saved.

Bonnet too wanted peace, passionately, but at almost any price, especially if other countries that lay athwart Hitler's ambitions could be maneuvered into paying it. His appointment as Foreign Minister, as Daladier frankly told Paul-Boncour when he named Bonnet to replace him, signified a change of French foreign policy. On April 10, when Daladier had called in Paul-Boncour to discuss the Foreign Ministership in the government he was forming, the latter had told him that if he remained in the post he would insist on a strong French stand in support of Czechoslovakia, warning that if that country were left in the lurch Poland would follow and Hitler would be the master of the Continent. Daladier had replied: "Your policy is fine, but I don't believe France is strong enough to follow it. I'm going to pick Bonnet."

"If you wish thus to change our foreign policy," Paul-Boncour says he responded, "you couldn't have made a better choice." Events would soon confirm his judgment.[18]

19

THE ROAD TO MUNICH, I
April 27–September 13, 1938

On April 27, 1938, the day of his departure with his Foreign Minister for talks in London with the British government, Daladier handed General Gamelin a curt note in his own handwriting: "Let me know precisely what military action France can take against Germany to assist Czechoslovakia, it being understood that mobilization is only the first step."[*][1]

The Army chief replied in writing the next day, in time for the Premier to have the benefit of his views in his talks in London. They were typically cautious. France had no military convention with Czechoslovakia to supplement its pact of mutual assistance, Gamelin pointed out. If the French mobilized they could take the offensive—but subject to certain conditions. Once again he raised a number of them, as he had during the Rhineland coup and the *Anschluss*. Action would depend on how many French troops the Italians held down in North Africa and in the Alps. Its "effectiveness" would depend also on what Russia did, and Britain, and Romania and Yugoslavia.[3]

In the talks in London on April 28 and 29 Daladier and even Bonnet were bolder than their generalissimo. Hitler's real aim, the Premier told the British, was not to gain concessions for the Sudeten Germans but to use their grievances as a pretext to destroy Czechoslovakia and eventually to secure "a domination of the Continent in comparison with which the ambitions of Napoleon were feeble."

---

[*] The view of the French Foreign Office, according to Bonnet, had long been that mobilization itself, without fighting, was enough to fulfill France's obligations to come to the aid of Czechoslovakia if attacked by Germany. This, it was held, would pin down a good part of the German army in the west.[2]

Today it is the turn of Czechoslovakia. Tomorrow it will be the turn of Poland and Romania. When Germany has obtained the oil and wheat it needs, she will turn on the West. Certainly we must multiply our efforts to avoid war. But that will not be obtained unless Great Britain and France stick together, intervening in Prague for new concessions but declaring at the same time that they will safeguard the independence of Czechoslovakia. If, on the contrary, the Western Powers capitulate again they will only precipitate the war they wish to avoid.[4]

Brave words and full of foresight. Catching the spirit of his Premier, Bonnet backed them up, reiterating that Hitler's goal was "purely and simply to wipe Czechoslovakia from the face of the map." It was therefore necessary, he added, for France and Britain to adopt "a common attitude of firmness, resolved to stick to it whatever the risk. In any case," he declared, "France will honor her word."

As the French ministers must have expected, Prime Minister Chamberlain would not heed their appeal. In a speech to the House a month before, the Prime Minister had been very careful to point out that Britain was not obligated to come to the aid of France if she became involved in war with Germany over Czechoslovakia. Privately he had already written off the little country.

You have only to look at the map [he had written his sister on March 20, one week after the *Anschluss*] to see that nothing that France or we could do could possibly save Czechoslovakia from being overrun by the Germans, if they wanted to do it. . . . I have therefore abandoned any idea of giving guarantee to Czechoslovakia or to the French in connection with her obligations to that country.[5]

He now made this clear to the French, after chiding Daladier for his pessimism. He did not believe, he said, that "the picture was really so black as M. Daladier had painted it. He doubted very much [in the words of the British minutes in indirect quotation] whether Herr Hitler really desired to destroy the Czech State, or rather a Czech state." But if he did, Chamberlain "in all frankness did not see how it could be prevented."

From this craven attitude stemmed all that followed. The French argued in vain. On the afternoon of the second day, April 29, Chamberlain withdrew to discuss the impasse with his cabinet, returning to the conference with a compromise that meant nothing. Britain would agree to join France in asking the Czechs to go as far as possible in meeting the demands of the Sudeten Germans. At the same time the British government would ask Berlin for "moderation."

"The only thing we obtained," Daladier reported later, "was that Britain would join us in a common action—but purely diplomatic." He returned to Paris dejected—and perplexed—by his first meeting with the British Prime Minister.

Hardly had the distinguished French visitors left Downing Street to board their plane when the new British Foreign Minister, Lord Halifax, summoned the German Chargé d'Affaires, Theodor Kordt, to assure him that the French and British had not been cooking up anything against Germany. Britain, he said, had made "no further military commitments" to the French. In fact, Kordt wired Berlin, Lord Halifax, "with obvious emotion," had stressed that "the best thing would be if the three kindred nations, Germany, Britain, and the United States, could unite in a joint work for peace."[6]

In Berlin the British Ambassador, Sir Neville Henderson, who had been sent to Germany by Chamberlain to try to open a new era in Anglo-German collaboration, handed the Wilhelmstrasse a written memorandum about the Franco-British talks, explaining that "His Majesty's Government are particularly desirous that the German Government should not be kept in ignorance of certain of the subjects under discussion with the French Ministers. . . ."[7] By May 10 the First Secretary of the British Embassy was assuring the Germans that the Sudeten-Czech question could be settled by Britain and Germany alone, without the participation of other powers, and that

If the German Government would advise the British Government confidentially what solution of the Sudeten German question they were striving after, he believed that he could assure us that the British Government would bring such pressure to bear in Prague that the Czechoslovak Government would be compelled to accede to the German wishes.[8]

At this stage of the game the German government had no intention of advising the British, even confidentially, what their "solution" was. In London, at the end of April, Daladier had tried to tell Chamberlain what it was, but the Prime Minister had thought him too pessimistic. As early as April 21 Hitler had called in his Wehrmacht chief, General Keitel, to discuss revisions of *Case Green,* the code name for surprise attack on Czechoslovakia, which had been drawn up the year before. One problem was how to "justify" the attack and Hitler told Keitel that the best way would be a "lightning action based on an incident (for example, the murder of the German Minister in the course of an anti-German demonstration)."[9] He had planned just such an "incident" to justify a German invasion of Austria when Ambassador Franz von Papen in Vienna was to have been done away with, though it later proved unnecessary. In Hitler's gangster world German envoys abroad were certainly expendable. As to the tactics of the Sudeteners in Czechoslovakia, Konrad Henlein, their leader, had received instructions from Hitler personally in a three-hour conference in Berlin on March 28, a fortnight after the German annexation of Austria. Henlein was told to keep presenting "demands which are unacceptable to the Czech government."[10] Thus the plight of the German-speaking minority in Czechoslovakia* was for Hitler a mere pretext for cooking up a stew in Central Europe which would enable him to take another country he coveted.

Despite the ardent British appeasement of Germany that spring, which had led to the offer by London to give Hitler what he wanted in Czechoslovakia, the Fuehrer grew restless for military action as summer approached. On May 16, less than a week after the British had assured Berlin it would make the Czechs accept any "solution" the Germans desired, Hitler got off from his mountain retreat at Berchtesgaden "an urgent and most secret" telegram to OKW, the High Command, asking how many divisions on the Czech frontier were "ready to march within twelve hours in the case of mobilization." OKW responded immediately: "Twelve divisions." Hitler wanted to know more. "Please send the numbers of the divisions," he wired back. The numbers of ten infantry divisions were promptly provided by OKW, which added there was also one armored division and one mountain division ready.[11]

THE MAY CRISIS

Events now moved rapidly toward the first crisis over Czechoslovakia, which took place the weekend that began on Friday, May 20, 1938. On May 9 Henlein had broken off talks with the Czech government and gone to Germany. Nazi-fostered riots were beginning to break out in the Sudetenland and Goebbels, the Nazi Propaganda Minister, was whipping them up in the press and on the radio into bloody tales of "Czech terror" against poor defenseless Germans. On May 18 Czech Intelligence reported German troop concentrations on the frontier and the next day a newspaper in Leipzig seemed to confirm them. It reported German troop movements near the border. General Ludvik Krejči, the Chief of the Czech General Staff, now considered that he had "irrefutable proof," as he told the German military attaché, "that in Saxony a concentration of from eight to ten [German] divisions had taken place." This, as we have seen, was somewhat less than the twelve divisions OKW had assured Hitler were on the Czech frontier, but the Germans denied there had been any "concentration." Nevertheless on the afternoon of May 20, following an emergency cabinet meeting at Hradčany Castle in Prague presided over by President Beneš, the Czech government ordered a small mobilization. One class was called up along with some technical reservists, and the fortifications were fully manned. The Czechs, in contrast to the Austrians two months before, did not at this juncture intend to give up without a fight.

Hitler was outraged at this display of spunk by one of his intended victims, and his feelings were not assuaged by the messages that arrived

---

* The Sudeten Germans had never belonged to the German Reich (except as part of the loosely formed Holy Roman Empire), but only to Austria. Chamberlain seems to have been ignorant of this fact of history. He continually referred to the Sudeteners being "returned" to Germany.

for him at Obersalzberg from the German Foreign Office in Berlin telling of continual calls by the British and French ambassadors throughout the weekend warning Germany that aggression against Czechoslovakia meant a European war. The British and the French, not to mention the Czechs, seemed to be standing up to him. I remember the feeling of crisis in Europe that May weekend, which I spent in Vienna and then in Prague, on the telephone continually with Berlin, Paris, and London. The Europeans felt they were nearer to war than at any time since the summer of 1914. To a continent still under the shock of the German military occupation of Austria two months before, it was understandable that the reports of German military concentrations on the Czech border would be believed and provoke alarm.

Actually there was no evidence, so far as I know, of any *new* concentration or movements of German troops that weekend. There were only the twelve German divisions mentioned by Keitel, "ready to march within twelve hours." As Colonel Jodl informed the Wilhelmstrasse on May 21 some of them naturally were engaged in "peacetime maneuvers."

On the morning of Friday, May 20, the OKW chief had dispatched to Hitler the text of the revised plan for *Case Green* to be signed by the Fuehrer. Actually, he himself had written most of it, stressing that the Czechs must be "smashed" within four days. Because he was confident that the French would not fight, the Directive provided for only a "minimum cover in the west" and it was emphasized that "the whole weight of all forces must be employed in the invasion of Czechoslovakia." While French reaction was ruled out, Hitler "expected attempts by Russia to give Czechoslovakia military support." What Great Britain might do is not even mentioned.[12]

In his mountain chalet above Berchtesgaden that weekend Hitler mulled over the revised plan for his next aggression. But his pleasure at contemplating it was spoiled by the humiliation he felt at the action of the Czechs and by the support given them in London, Paris, and Moscow. He convinced himself, Jodl reported, that he had suffered a loss of prestige, and nothing could put him in a blacker, uglier mood. Swallowing his pride, he ordered the Foreign Office in Berlin to inform the Czech Minister in Berlin on Monday, May 23, that Germany had no aggressive intentions toward Czechoslovakia and that the reports of German troop concentrations on her borders were without foundation.

In Prague, London, Paris, and Moscow the government leaders breathed a sigh of relief. The Czechs demobilized. The crisis swiftly passed. Hitler, it was believed in the West, had been given a lesson by the firmness of the other great European powers and by the determination of a small one that seemed threatened. The relief all over Europe was great, but the belief that Hitler had been taught a lesson was groundless. Also groundless was the impression, created by Britain's surprisingly energetic diplomatic action in Berlin that weekend, that the Chamberlain government was prepared to give military aid to the French automatically if they went to war with Germany over Czechoslovakia.

In the midst of the May crisis the British government had secretly given France a stern warning. It came late on the evening of Sunday, May 22, just as a jittery Europe was beginning to panic over the prospect of war and a fearful Paris felt most the need of staunch support from London.

That afternoon General Gamelin had been hastily recalled from an inspection tour in Brittany and at 6 P.M. had been received by Daladier and Bonnet, who told him the situation was grave. "I shall attack," said the general blandly, and then, as usual, cited all the difficulties in his way—"the German fortifications in front of me, the bulk of the Germany army," and so on. It would be easier to attack through Belgium, he explained, but he was told that the Belgians had just been holding maneuvers along the French frontier in order, the Belgian Foreign Minister had explained to the French Ambassador in Brussels, "to show you that if you come our way in order to support Czechoslovakia you will run up against the Belgian army." Gamelin noted that Daladier and Bonnet were disturbed at the failure of the Czechs to go further in their concessions to the Sudeteners and their other minorities. He warned them, he says, that if the concessions were carried too far, Czechoslovakia would "disappear from the map and Germany would then have a free hand in Poland and then against us." He reminded Daladier that only the day before he had urgently requested authorization to form three more infantry divisions and set up three armored divisions to strengthen the Army. Apparently the Premier did not think the situation was *that* grave, for he refused the authorization. He also told the general that the firm attitude of Great Britain that weekend appeared to be saving the Continent from war.[13]

But not precisely in the way the Premier envisaged. A few hours later, at 10:30 P.M., Sir Eric Phipps, the British Ambassador in Paris, a nervous little man whose previous tour of duty in Berlin seemed to have left him with a mighty fear of Hitler's wrath, appeared at the Quai d'Orsay to see Bonnet and to read to him a highly confidential communication he had just received by wire from Lord Halifax. The urgency of the matter was not lost on the French Foreign Minister, who had never been called on before by the Ambassador on the Sabbath and who knew moreover that the British Foreign Secretary did not customarily pen important telegrams on that day, the sanctity of the British weekend being what it was. Also the hour was late for a diplomat to be about.

The message from Lord Halifax, which the Ambassador says he "read slowly" to Bonnet, who "took copious notes and thoroughly understood," was as follows:

1. It is of utmost importance that French Government should not be under any illusion as to attitude of His Majesty's Government . . . in the event of failure to bring about peaceful settlement in Czechoslovak question.

2. His Majesty's Government have given the most serious warnings to Berlin. . . . But it might be highly dangerous if the French Government were to read more into those warnings than is justified by their terms.

3. His Majesty's Government would of course always honour their pledge to come to the assistance of France if she were the victim of unprovoked aggression by Germany. . . .

4. If, however, the French Government were to assume that His Majesty's Government would at once take joint military action with them to preserve Czechoslovakia against German aggression, it is only fair to warn them that our statements do not warrant any such assumption.

5. In the view of His Majesty's Government the military situation is such that France and England, even with such assistance as might be expected from Russia, would not be in a position to prevent Germany over-running Czechoslovakia. The only result would be a European war, the outcome of which, so far as can be foreseen, . . . would be at least doubtful.

6. His Majesty's Government fully realize the nature and extent of French obligations but they feel that in the present highly critical situation the French Government should take full account of the preceding considerations. . . .[14]

This was the real British position, and would remain so, except for moments of wavering when it seemed that Hitler would force Britain into supporting France over Czechoslovakia, almost to the end. The French government cannot be blamed for keeping it constantly in mind during the anxious months that followed. The trouble was that Bonnet seized upon it as an *excuse* for doing nothing to save Czechoslovakia and to halt Hitler while the West, with Russia, still had the strength to do so. Instead of combating this British stand and endeavoring to get London to see the light and change it, he welcomed it and used it to give his country a temporary and, as it turned out, disastrous out. Hit by the slow reading of Halifax's communication the real Bonnet quickly surfaced and revealed itself. Phipps disclosed this in his next dispatches to London.

Reporting to Halifax at 1 A.M. that night on his meeting with Bonnet, the Ambassador wired:

M. Bonnet repeated to me that he would readily put any pressure on Czechoslovak Government that you might think at any moment desirable. . . . I pointed out that it behooved the Czechs to be more reasonable, for alternative for them would be total annihilation. His Excellency [Bonnet] heartily agreed. Moreover, he said, *if Czechoslovakia were really unreasonable the French Government might well declare that France considered herself released from her bond.*[*][15]

By the next evening, May 23, when Phipps again saw Bonnet, the

---

* The italics are mine.—W. L. S.

French Foreign Minister was plunging with mounting enthusiasm into playing Britain's game. He was getting tough with the Czechs and praising the Germans for their "reasonableness." Phipps duly reported this to London the next day.

M. Bonnet tells me that after I saw him last night he again spoke with the utmost severity to M. Osusky [the Czech Minister in Paris] and urged him to return at once to Prague in order to convince M. Beneš of the vital necessity of acting quickly and generously. M. Osusky seemed very much impressed and returned to Prague by air this morning.

The French Foreign Minister agreed with the Ambassador that Beneš, the President and the cofounder of Czechoslovakia in 1918, was the real culprit.

I [Phipps reported further] expressed the hope that very firm and persistent pressure would be brought to bear upon M. Beneš by the French Government for it would be intolerable if he were to be allowed to wreck the now brighter chances of a peaceful settlement. M. Bonnet entirely agreed and promised that this should be done.

It does not seem to have occurred to these two men, despite their responsible positions, despite the evidence, despite recent history, that it was Hitler, not Beneš, who was threatening to "wreck" that peace. In fact Bonnet, judging by what he told Phipps, had now convinced himself that Hitler was being reasonable.

M. Bonnet [Phipps concluded his telegram] paid tribute to reasonable attitude of the German Government and agreed that the Czechs must now on their side make a large and generous contribution to the cause of peace.[16]

While Bonnet and Phipps were praising Berlin's moderation Hitler was sulking at Obersalzberg, gripped by a burning rage to get even with Czechoslovakia and particularly with President Beneš, who, he believed, had deliberately humiliated him. On May 28 he suddenly appeared in Berlin and summoned the ranking officers of the Wehrmacht to hear a momentous decision. He himself told the Reichstag of it on January 30, 1939.

I resolved to solve once and for all, and this radically, the Sudeten question. On May 28 I ordered:

1. That preparations should be made for military action against this state by October 2.

2. That the construction of our western defenses should be greatly extended and speeded up. . . .

3. The immediate mobilization of 96 divisions was planned, to begin
with . . .

To his assembled confederates, Goering, Generals Keitel, Brauchitsch,
and Beck, Admiral Raeder, Ribbentrop, and Neurath, he thundered: *"It
is my unshakable will that Czechoslovakia shall be wiped off the map!"*

Case Green was again brought out and revised. One significant change
was made. Whereas the Directive, as of April 21, had begun: "It is not my
intention to smash Czechoslovakia in the near future," this was now altered
to read: *"It is my unalterable decision to smash Czechoslovakia by military
action in the near future."*

What the "near future" meant was explained by General Keitel in a
covering letter. *"Green's* execution," he ordered, "must be assured by October 1, 1938, at the latest."

It was a date which Hitler would adhere to through thick and thin,
through crisis after crisis, and at the brink of war, without flinching.[17]

THE QUESTION OF RUSSIA

Much depended on Russia.

The Soviet Union, like France, had a pact of mutual assistance with
Czechoslovakia which obligated it too to come to the aid of that country
in case of unprovoked aggression. But it contained a significant reservation: it came into effect only if France *first* honored her commitment to
the Czechs. Moscow, it would seem, had its doubts about the French as
early as May 16, 1935, when the treaty with Prague was signed. Ironically,
the French government had urged the Czechs to accept the condition out
of fear that otherwise Russia might use the pact to unleash a European
war.

The question that spring of 1938 was not only whether France would
honor her word to Czechoslovakia but whether the Soviet Union would, and
if so, how. She had no common frontier with Czechoslovakia, being separated by slices of Poland and Romania.

This was a problem which Bonnet took up with the Soviet Foreign
Commissar, Maxim Litvinov, on May 12, 1938, during a meeting of the
Council of the League of Nations at Geneva. The Czech crisis was already
brewing. If Germany attacked, Bonnet asked, what would Russia do?
Honor her commitments, Litvinov replied, if France does.

"But how," Bonnet says he insisted[18], "since you have no common
frontier? Are you ready to force a passage of your troops and planes
through Poland and Romania, if necessary?"

The Soviet Foreign Minister replied that Russia had no wish to go to
war with Poland and Romania. If she could not obtain the permission of
those two countries for the passage of her troops and planes she would not
cross them. But, he added, France was an ally of both Poland and Romania
and had great influence with them. She was therefore in "a good position"

to obtain from them the right of passage if the Czechs were attacked. Bonnet promised to try.

But his heart was not in it. During the next crucial months he would bring the matter up with the governments of Poland and Romania but he would never really press it. Like Chamberlain in England, like all previous French governments, like the French Army, Bonnet distrusted the Bolshevik Russians and, shuddered at the thought of the Western powers becoming involved in a war allied to the Soviet Union. And this despite the fact that Russia was the only military power in the East comparable to Germany, that its aid in a struggle with the Reich would be crucial to Britain and France, themselves so deficient in armament, and that as General Gamelin would say, when it was too late, "from a military viewpoint all depended on Russia."[19]

It is understandable that Poland and Romania, with shaky right-wing regimes, would oppose the passage of Soviet troops. It was feared they would never leave—at least not until they had spread Communism and undermined the government. The Poles and Romanians did not see that their choices for survival had narrowed and that to reject Russian aid was to make them both ripe for being swallowed up by Germany. They were too weak to defend themselves, even with French help. Bonnet contends he tried to tell them this. But he did not force the issue. Instead, he used the reluctance of the Russians to fight their way through Poland and Romania to come to the aid of the Czechs as a ground for proclaiming that the Russians would not honor their commitment to Czechoslovakia.

One Frenchman who saw the value of Russian military strength and the necessity of tying it to that of the West if Czechoslovakia were to be saved and Hitler halted was the French Ambassador in Moscow, Robert Coulondre. Immediately after the *Anschluss* he had told his Foreign Minister that "if the French government intended to make a stand at Prague it was more urgent than ever to open military talks with the U.S.S.R."[20] In the pursuit of that aim he returned to Paris on the eve of the May crisis, and on May 20 he saw Bonnet in an effort to win him over to his views.

He believed at first that he had won him over. Bonnet advised him to see General Gamelin, then draw up a proposal and submit it to Daladier and himself. Gamelin, the Ambassador found, was "favorable to military talks." With the help of Léger and René Massigli, the top ranking permanent officials at the Quai d'Orsay, Coulondre wrote out his memorandum. On the advice of Massigli, "so as to avoid inopportune foreign reaction," the paper stipulated that the military talks would be secret and *"a deux,"* that is, bilateral—between the French and Russians, the French and Czechs, and the Russians and Czechs. Three days later, on May 23, the day the crisis began to ease, Coulondre brought his written proposal to Bonnet. He found him changed.

What had happened to him since May 20? He was now hesitant. . . . He feared, he said, that the prospect of Soviet military support would incite certain French elements to be bellicose.

The hesitant Foreign Minister, however, "authorized" him to see the President of the Republic and to submit his paper to Daladier. The Premier was also hesitant but approved,

though in recommending the greatest prudence in order to avoid the reactions of Hitler and insisting that the [military] talks be secret and never *à trois.*

The same evening, May 23, the persistent Ambassador returned to Bonnet.

He was still hesitant. He repeated his misgivings about the military situation of France and Great Britain, which had just begun to rearm, the attitude of Poland,* the ambiguity of Soviet policy. . . . I reminded him that in endeavoring to save the Peace at any price one risked being pushed into war. I repeated to him my conviction that if France and Britain wanted to halt Hitler, the best place to do it was in Czechoslovakia. I myself did not perceive that the U.S.S.R. was ambiguous about Prague. The only way to ascertain the value of her support was to have the military talks I proposed.

The Ambassador added that he thought the French were attaching too much importance to Poland and too little to Russia.†

I told M. Bonnet that the Kremlin did not regard Poland as capable of maintaining a front. . . . For Hitler the only two fronts were those of Russia and France. It was those, in conjunction with our British alliance, which perhaps could still restrain Hitler. . . . The time had come to make Poland decide for or against us.

Coulondre says that Bonnet thereupon "finally approved the opening of military conversations." The Ambassador returned to Moscow think-

---

* Poland that May weekend had emphasized to the French that not only would it oppose the passage of Soviet troops by military force but that it would not back France, despite the Treaty of Mutual Assistance between the two countries, if it went to war with Germany over Czechoslovakia.

On May 25 Bonnet had a stormy meeting with the Polish Ambassador in Paris, Lukasiewicz, whom he describes as "a passionate and vehement man, who blindly served the designs of his Foreign Minister, Colonel Beck, whose megalomania had become unbelievable." To Bonnet's request that Poland line up with France and Britain to defend Czechoslovakia, the Ambassador replied that "it was a country condemned to death. To wish to defend it was a mistake on the part of France and Great Britain." When Bonnet broached the question of the passage of Russian troops through Poland Lukasiewicz cried: "We shall oppose it by force! And that means war between Russia and us!"[21]

† It will be recalled that when Blum assumed office in 1936 he found that the General Staff considered the Polish Army more important than the Russian—a view that apparently still held.

ing that "at last" he had made some progress. But not for long. "The winds of fear," he noted a little later that summer, "soon swept away, along with much else, the tender hope I had brought back from Paris."[22]

In Moscow he persisted as long as he could. But his own government was strangely uncooperative and uncommunicative. On July 1 the Czech Minister in Moscow showed him a copy of a dispatch which Osusky in Paris had just sent to his government in Prague. "The French government," it said, "will not follow up for the time being the military talks with the Soviets. It does not want to arouse the susceptibilities of the British conservatives." In this roundabout way the French Ambassador learned of the decision of his government. He realized, he says, that his efforts to bring Russia into a military coalition to stop Hitler had failed. And the suspicion began to sprout in him that the Russians, shunted aside by Great Britain and France in their hectic efforts to please Hitler, had about decided that two could play that game. One day early in the summer Litvinov had hinted to him that if Poland attacked Czechoslovakia (over Teschen) the Soviet Union might attack Poland. The Ambassador concluded that Russia would not move against Poland without "a prior understanding with Germany." The thought, he says, "troubled" him.[23] It was more prophetic than he realized.

The crisis over Czechoslovakia subsided during the hottest days of summer but it was obvious to nearly everyone that it was the calm before the storm. In mid-July the King and Queen of England paid a state visit to France, and Paris and Versailles glittered with formal receptions and banquets which Republican France could be so ingenious and so tasteful in organizing. The French, watching the colorful ceremonies, relaxed. The weather was beautiful. People forgot the Sudetenland, Beneš and Hitler. The fear of war receded. Little diplomacy was transacted during the royal visit. Only one hour, on July 20, was allotted to political talks. On that day Lord Halifax told Daladier and Bonnet that the British government was sending Lord Runciman to Czechoslovakia to try to mediate the dispute between the Sudeten Germans and the Czech government. The French Premier and Foreign Minister approved.

On July 26 Chamberlain announced the visit to the House of Commons, stressing that Runciman was going on his mission "in response to a request from the Czechoslovak Government." This was not strictly true. Runciman, with French approval, had been forced down the throats of the Czechs by the Prime Minister. There was a second deceit in Chamberlain's move in sending an "arbitrator" to Prague. He knew that the Sudeteners were not free agents. They took their orders from Germany. Any honest mediation would have to take place between the governments of Berlin and Prague.

The British Prime Minister's position by this time was no longer a secret. As early as May 14 certain American newspapers had published dispatches from their London correspondents about "off-the-record" remarks made by Chamberlain to them at a luncheon given by Lady Astor. He had told them, they reported, that neither Britain nor France, nor probably Russia, would come to the aid of Czechoslovakia in the case of a German attack, and that Britain favored, "in the interest of peace," turning over the Sudetenland to Germany. Despite angry questions in the House of Commons the Prime Minister had not denied the veracity of the American dispatches.

On June 1 Chamberlain had uttered similar words in confidence to British journalists, and two days later *The Times* had made their tenor public in the first of its editorials which were to help undermine the Czech nation, by suggesting that Prague grant "self-determination" to the country's minorities "even if it should mean their secession from Czechoslovakia." On June 8 the German Ambassador in London informed Berlin that the Chamberlain government would be willing to see the Sudeten areas separated from Czechoslovakia—provided that it was done peacefully.[24]

Lord Runciman, reflecting Chamberlain's views, puttered about in Czechoslovakia that August, spending most of his time dining, wining, and golfing with the Sudeten aristocracy—with Prince Ulrich Kinsky, with Prince Max von Hohenlohe, and others—and moving toward the recommendation which his government, to avoid a clash with Hitler, wished.

Bonnet, in Paris, approved. On August 9 he called in the German Ambassador for "a frank talk," and according to the latter said

he still considered the sending of Runciman to be right and proper in spite of the fact that the Czechs sought to represent him as a pronounced friend of Germany. We would have to go to the extreme bounds of compromise in the Sudeten question, even if this did not suit the Czechs.*[25]

Like Bonnet, the French generals were also getting cold feet about the prospect of fighting Germany in support of the Czechs. The more the Army chiefs, Gamelin and Georges, thought about it the less enthusiastic they became. In mid-August, the chief of the Air Force, General Vuillemin, after a visit to Germany, panicked. Riding back to the Embassy in Berlin with Ambassador François-Poncet from a gala luncheon at Goering's country palace after a week of visiting the humming German aircraft factories and watching air maneuvers, General Vuillemin expressed his stupe-

---

* In his own version of the conversation Bonnet says he told the Ambassador that if Germany attacked Czechoslovakia, France "would intervene . . . and there would be war."[26]

The Parliamentary Investigating Committee questioned Bonnet about the part of the German Ambassador's telegram which I have quoted. He denied "absolutely" that he had said any such thing.

"Then the German Ambassador was lying?" a Committee member asked.

"Surely," Bonnet replied.[27]

faction at what he had seen.* "If war comes this autumn, as you fear," he told the Ambassador, "there will not be one French plane left after fifteen days."[29]

General Gamelin was not so pessimistic about the Army. But he was cautious. When the Foreign Minister asked him on August 26 about the state of preparedness of the Army, Gamelin says he replied: "We're ready. We have only to press the button."[30] Actually, as he made clear a few days later when Daladier cornered him, he saw almost insurmountable obstacles ahead. Both he and General Georges grossly exaggerated the strength of the German army in the west and held the German fortifications there to be much more formidable than they were. The generals were extremely doubtful about the French being able to take the offensive in time to be of any help to the Czechs. General Georges, especially, was against risking sending the Army "beyond the frontier" for a good long time.

The timidity of the French generals is all the more interesting in the light of the pessimism of the German generals. At this very moment there was a revolt in the German General Staff without precedent in the Reich's military history. It was led by no less a figure than the Chief of the General Staff, who was convinced that it would be disastrous to fight a war with the Western powers. Moreover, a plot was hatching among some of the generals, led by the Chief of the General Staff, to do away with Hitler if he tried to plunge Germany into war. This also was unprecedented in the annals of the Prussian-German Army. It was not that the German generals were opposed on moral grounds to military aggression against Czechoslovakia. They had enthusiastically supported Hitler's taking of Austria in the spring. They simply believed that Germany was not ready to take on the Western powers and Russia. "The opinion of the Army is," Colonel Jodl, Chief of Operations of OKW, noted in his diary on May 30, "that we are not as yet equal to them."[31]

All that summer General Ludwig Beck, Chief of the Army General Staff, penned eloquent memoranda to General Walther von Brauchitsch, the new Commander in Chief of the Army, insisting that the Army prevent Hitler from going to war.[32] A sensitive, intelligent, intellectual, highly cultivated, but indecisive man, Beck was a sort of German equivalent of Gamelin. On May 5, in a long note to Brauchitsch, he laid down his fundamental position. A German attack on Czechoslovakia, he said, would provoke a European war in which Britain, France, and Russia would oppose Germany and in which the United States would be the arsenal of the Western democracies. Germany simply couldn't win such a war. On July 16 he demanded that the Army tell Hitler to halt his preparations for war.

---

* The French Air Attaché in Berlin, General de Geffrier, and his assistant, Captain Paul Stehlin, were surprised at General Vuillemin's stupefaction. For two years they had been filing detailed reports on German aircraft production and on the performance of the Messerschmitt 109 and 110 fighters, the Heinkel III twin-motor bomber and the Stuka dive bomber—the planes with which the Germans would fight World War II in the air.[28]

In full consciousness of the magnitude of such a step but also of my responsibilities I feel it my duty to urgently ask that the Supreme Commander of the Armed Forces [Hitler] call off his preparations for war and abandon the intention of solving the Czech question by force until the military situation is fundamentally changed. For the present I consider it hopeless, and this view is shared by all the higher officers of the General Staff.

It certainly was shared by the field commanders who would have to defend the western frontier against the French. On August 10 General Gustav von Wietersheim, Chief of Staff of Army of the West under General Wilhelm Adam, told Hitler that with the Army committing almost its whole force against the Czechs, the country was defenseless in the west and would be overrun by the French. In fact, he said bluntly, the unfinished Siegfried Line could not be held for more than three weeks.

The Fuehrer [Jodl recounted in his diary] becomes furious and flames up, bursting into the remark that in such a case the whole Army would not be good for anything. "I say to you, Herr General, [Hitler shouted at Wietersheim] the position will be held not only for three weeks but for three years!"[33]

General Adam, who had been selected to command the German forces in the west, also dared to speak up. He had reported to a secret meeting of the senior generals on August 4 that in the west he would have only five active divisions and that they would be overwhelmed by the French.* Late in August General Adam, a blunt and able Bavarian officer, joined Hitler, who was making a tour of the western fortifications in a special train full of party propagandists and spouting to the world that the "West Wall" was impregnable. The general told the Fuehrer that the fortifications could not be held with the troops assigned him. The Supreme Commander, according to both Jodl and Adam, became hysterical.

"The man who doesn't hold these fortifications," Hitler shouted to the general, "is a scoundrel!"[34]

General Beck resigned as Chief of the Army General Staff on August 18. He had urged a "generals' strike," but not a single general followed him. Still, a few of them joined him and a handful of civilians in a plot to overthrow Hitler if he went to war.†

At the center of the conspiracy was General Franz Halder, who succeeded General Beck. The first Bavarian and the first Roman Catholic ever to be elevated to that high military post, Halder resembled his predecessor in his intelligence and wide intellectual interests. Since the Army had the only physical means capable of overthrowing the Nazi dictator by force

---

* At this very moment General Gamelin was estimating the German strength in the West at fifty divisions "to begin with," and General Georges was saying there would be sixty divisions. Far from thinking that they could "overwhelm" the Germans, they were hesitating even to plan to attack them.

† I have described the conspiracy that summer and fall in considerable detail in *The Rise and Fall of the Third Reich.*

he and Beck enlisted the aid of various generals who commanded the units stationed in and around Berlin. A few civilians led by Dr. Hjalmar Schacht, President of the Reichsbank, were drawn in. The civilian group kept the British informed of what was up and asked for their cooperation. On September 5 Theodor Kordt, Counselor of the German Embassy in London and a member of the conspiracy secretly informed Lord Halifax of the date of Hitler's attack on Czechoslovakia (October 1), of the plans to overthrow the Nazi dictator on its eve, and begged Britain and France to stand firm against Hitler's threats until the revolt was launched. Halifax the same day discussed the development with Chamberlain, who was most skeptical. Neither man breathed a word to the French ally.

Because of this and even more because of the shortcomings of French Intelligence, neither Premier Daladier nor General Gamelin ever learned of the crisis in the German army's leadership, of the resignation of General Beck in mid-August* or of the military plot to oust Hitler if he ordered an attack on Czechoslovakia. This information would have been of the greatest importance to the French General Staff, with its constant overestimation of the strength of the German Army, and even more to the French government, which daily, as the Czech crisis rose toward a climax in September, lost a little more of its nerve because of its increasing fears of German military might. Yet Daladier assured me in 1964 that he had learned of these developments in Germany only after reading my book on the Third Reich twenty-three years later.†

Nevertheless, the Premier and General Gamelin learned enough of Germany's mounting, if unannounced, mobilization and the buildup of her troops on the Czech frontier to lead them to take certain countermeasures.

---

* Hitler forbade any mention of Beck's resignation in the press or even in the official government and military gazettes and ordered the retired Chief of the General Staff and his fellow officers to keep it strictly to themselves. It was a well-kept secret and I can find no evidence that the French High Command heard of it until after Munich.

† Daladier referred me to an article—one of three—he had written in the French weekly *Candide* in the autumn of 1961. In the issue of September 14–21, he wrote: "We did not know then [1938] the documents published by William Shirer in his . . . history of the Third Reich: the resignation of the Chief of the General Staff, General Ludwig Beck on August 18, which was kept strictly secret on the menacing order of Hitler; the declarations to Hitler of General von Wietersheim on August 10 and those of General Adam, Commander in Chief in the West, that the fortifications [of the Siegfried Line] would not be completed by the end of August and that they had not been given enough troops to hold them.

"We remained ignorant also of what Shirer has written in his book on 'the birth of a conspiracy.' . . . It is regrettable that the confidences of the German conspirators were never made known to us and that after they had informed London they did not consider it useful to inform us also."

In the course of a long conversation the former French Premier also expressed his regret that the British government had never tipped him off.

Finally, there is not a word in General Gamelin's voluminous memoirs or in his lengthy testimony, and in that of General Georges, before the Parliamentary Investigating Committee after the war, to indicate that they ever suspected the crisis in the German Army.

At the beginning of September the first steps toward the *couverture* were initiated. Certain reservists were called up and the class of conscripts due to be released at the end of the month was held over. But as partial mobilization continued General Gamelin remained in doubt as to what to do if war came.

On September 12, the day all Europe waited nervously to hear what Adolf Hitler would say about Czechoslovakia in his concluding speech at the annual Nazi Party rally at Nuremberg, Daladier, after a cabinet meeting, put the key question to his three top generals, Gamelin, Georges, and Billotte. "What can you do," he asked them, "to help Czechoslovakia?" According to his own notes Gamelin responded:

> We cannot defeat the German Army before it has taken the most important part of Czechoslovakia, but all will be restored by the Peace Treaty. . . .
> Nothing can be done on the Rhine. . . . Only through Belgium. But she will not let us pass and we will not go that way without her assent.[35]

There remained the region between the Rhine and the Moselle, including the Saar. But it was too small, the general explained, to maneuver in. In that narrow space each side, he added, would have from fifty to sixty infantry divisions* and though the French would take the offensive "as soon as possible" the result would be "a modern version of the Battle of the Somme."† Daladier, a slogging infantryman for four years in the First War, did not relish seeing such slaughter again. There were also risks if the French committed the bulk of their forces in the narrow Palatinate and General Gamelin was quick to point them out. The Germans then, he explained, might move through Switzerland or "more likely, through Belgium and march on Maubeuge," as they had in 1914. The danger of being thus outflanked must be considered. How the Germans could march through Belgium, let alone through Switzerland, when in reality they would have only twelve divisions in the west, seven of them weak reserve units, was a question not raised, since Gamelin was insisting that the enemy would have five times that strength. As for Russia, Gamelin assured Daladier that her "role would initially be secondary."

General Georges, who would have command of the French forces in the northeast, was even more cautious. Since the Germans even at the beginning would be equal in size to the French, he said, and moreover would be protected by "fortifications of value," there could be no "quick decision." It would therefore be "wise," he counseled, "not to engage the first French forces beyond the frontier." It would be better not to take the offensive "until the coalition will have permitted the realization of a certain

---

* He overestimated the initial German strength by four or five times.

† In that battle during the summer of 1916 the attacking Anglo-French armies lost 246,000 killed and wounded, failed to achieve a breakthrough, and gained very little ground.

equilibrium of forces." What the "coalition" would be he did not say. Apparently, he meant to wait for the British, who had no army of any consequence in being. Or for the Americans, who were in the same fix.

The Americans, as the September crisis began to worsen, were giving no encouragement at all. On September 4, on the occasion of the dedication of a monument to the American war dead of the First World War at Pointe de Grave near Bordeaux, Ambassador William Bullitt, under pressure from Bonnet and with the authorization of President Roosevelt, had warned that "if war broke out in Europe no one could predict whether or not the United States would be drawn in." It was a feeble statement for a great power but isolationist sentiment was still so strong in America that five days later Roosevelt practically repudiated it. "Those who count on the assured aid of the United States in case of a war in Europe," he was quoted in the French newspapers as telling a press conference, "are totally mistaken. . . . To include the United States in a Franco-British front against Hitler is an interpretation that is 100 percent false." Toward the end of September when an armed conflict in Europe seemed imminent, the American government informed France in writing that if war came the Neutrality Law would prevent it from delivering the planes which the French had ordered in May. This was a blow to Daladier, who had counted on the American aircraft to help make up the deficiencies in the French air force.[36] He was already concerned with General Vuillemin's estimate that all his planes would be destroyed after a fortnight of war. "Even after taking into account the pessimistic temperament of General Vuillemin," he later confided, "his opinion weighed heavily on my decisions."[37]

Still, as September came and Hitler seemed more and more intent on going to war, Daladier gave signs of stiffening. The British Ambassador noted it in a talk with the Premier on September 8.

M. Daladier declares most positively [Phipps telegraphed to London] that if German troops cross the Czechoslovak frontier the French will march to a man. They realize perfectly well that this will not be for the *beaux yeux* of the Czechs but for their own skins, as, after a given time, Germany would, with enormously increased strength, turn against France.

Sir Eric Phipps, as defeatist by this time as Bonnet, was distressed by Daladier's firmness and he tried to crack it. He "enquired," he reported, about the difficulties of attacking the Siegfried Line and about the "internal situation" in France, remarking to Daladier that "there seemed still to be a certain number of strikes going on." But the Premier was optimistic on both accounts and so obviously determined that the Ambassador felt constrained to remind

M. Daladier of the promise of the French Government to keep us fully informed and to consult us before taking measures of force.

He assured me the promise would be kept, but my impression is that French actions would follow pretty soon on any German attack upon Czechoslovakia.[38]

For a moment, as the middle of September approached, the mood of London too appeared to be stiffening. On the 11th, as all of Europe waited uneasily to hear what Hitler would say at Nuremberg, the British Foreign Office issued an "authorized statement" meant no doubt to impress the German dictator before he spoke and to assure the French. It asked the German government not to indulge in "illusions" and not to believe that it could carry out an attack on Czechoslovakia without facing "the possibility of intervention by France and thereafter by Great Britain."

The Paris press hailed the statement as proof that the British government had at last made up its mind to stand by France. But the French government soon learned better. Secretly Lord Halifax conveyed to it quite another tune. On September 10, the day before the British communiqué was issued, Bonnet, apparently on the prompting of Daladier, had put the fundamental question to Phipps: "Tomorrow Germany may attack Czechoslovakia. If so, we will march. Will you march with us?" The Ambassador had passed the question on to the British Foreign Secretary and two days later, on September 12, Lord Halifax replied, in a letter to Phipps which was to be shown to the French Foreign Minister:

> So far as I am in a position to give any answer at this stage to M. Bonnet's question, it would have to be that while His Majesty's Government would never allow the security of France to be threatened, they are unable to make precise statements of the character of their future action, or the time at which it would be taken, in circumstances that they cannot at present foresee.[39]

Thus the British position remained the same as it had been on May 22 when in the midst of the spring crisis it had secretly warned the French not to count automatically on Britain coming to the aid of France if war broke out over Czechoslovakia. Bonnet did not receive this reiteration in the form of Halifax's letter until September 14. By that time, as the high-strung Phipps wired to London, the French Foreign Minister has suffered "a collapse."

Those mid-September days that year were feverish ones in a Europe facing the prospect of another great war so soon after the previous one, though much of what went on remained unknown to the jittery public since the statesmen and generals and diplomats operated in that secrecy which President Wilson had so deplored at the time of the first war. The British communiqué of the 11th was of course public knowledge and meant to be so, but not Halifax's confidential note to the French dodging the issue. Also on the 11th General Gamelin had taken the unusual step of calling in the German Military Attaché in Paris, Lieutenant General Erich Kühlenthal, and asking him to inform the German High Command of the military measures he was taking toward mobilization in view of the German mobilization. The general had denied that Germany was mobilizing.

There was nothing secret about Hitler's speech on September 12 at the Party rally at Nuremberg for which Europe had been waiting breathlessly for a week fearing that it might be the signal for war. All week long the Nazi leaders had been working up the party faithful to a state of hysteria over the alleged Czech persecution of the Sudeten Germans. On the 10th Goering, with his characteristic elegance, had shouted to the mob: "A petty segment of Europe is harassing the human race. . . . This miserable pygmy race [the Czechs], without culture—no one knows where it came from—is oppressing a cultured people, and behind it is Moscow and the eternal mask of the Jew devil."

Actually, the substance of Hitler's speech on the evening of September 12 was moderate enough to deceive Europe and give it a false sense of relief. I was in Prague that day and listened to the harangue over the radio. I had never heard a speech of Hitler so full of venom, of hate, of spitefulness, nor heard the party hacks at Nuremberg so stirred to bedlam by him, though I had attended two or three Nuremberg Party rallies in the previous years. But in what he said he shrank back from the precipice of war. He demanded that the "terrible persecution of the martyred Sudeten Germans by the Czechs cease" and that they be given the right of self-determination—that is, that the Sudetenland be turned over to Germany. But he refrained from saying that Germany would attack Czechoslovakia, and the capitals of Europe, which, with the exception of London, did not know that he had secretly set the date of October 1, less than three weeks hence, for that assault, were grateful.

Grateful, but still worried. In Paris members of the French government began to panic. The news from Czechoslovakia the next day was frightening. Fired up by the Fuehrer's speech the Sudeteners rose up in arms, plentifully supplied by Germany, and in half a dozen towns attacked police barracks, railroad stations, post and telegraph offices, and other public buildings. The Czech government declared martial law, rushed in troops and after two days of fighting put down the revolt, but not until twelve Czechs and nine Germans had been killed and hundreds wounded on both sides. The evening of the 14th in Prague, I remember, the Czechs expected a German attack before midnight. But by then certain things had begun to happen in the capitals of the major powers that transferred the conflict from Czech soil to the summits of Big Power diplomacy.

In Paris on September 13 Bonnet, in the words of the British Ambassador, "collapsed." Daladier faltered. The urgent telegrams of Sir Eric Phipps that evening tell much of the story. At 6:15 P.M. he wired London briefly that Bonnet "seems completely to have lost his nerve and to be ready for any solution to avoid war."[40] At 7:10 P.M. the Ambassador got off a longer telegram to Halifax explaining what had happened.

> I saw Minister for Foreign Affairs this afternoon after Ministerial Council.
>
> M. Bonnet was very upset and said that peace must be preserved at any price as neither France nor Great Britain were ready for war. Colonel Lindbergh . . . declares Germany has 8,000 military planes and can turn out 1,500 a month.* M. Bonnet said that French and British towns would be wiped out. . . .
>
> He said there had been rumors that today's Council had decided upon mobilization; this was quite untrue. On the contrary, no further military measures were contemplated, and peace must be maintained at any price.
>
> M. Bonnet was glad to receive from me yesterday a copy of your telegram of May 22 with our warning about not being automatically obliged to take arms if France resisted German aggression. He indicated most confidentially that he had found this useful with certain bellicose French ministers. He hoped warning still applied. I said it most certainly did. . . .[41]

From this day, September 13, Bonnet was determined that France should not fight to save Czechoslovakia—or itself.† He had caved in.

"M. Bonnet's collapse," Phipps concluded his long telegram, "seems to me so sudden and so extraordinary that I am asking for an interview with M. Daladier."

He saw the Premier a few minutes later and found him not collapsing but certainly faltering—a quite different man than he had seemed a week before, on the 8th, when last they had talked. At 8:30 P.M. Phipps got off a telegram to Halifax describing the meeting.[43]

> I have seen M. Daladier.
>
> I was careful not to give away M. Bonnet, for . . . this might have led to a Cabinet crisis with deplorable results. . . .
>
> The President of the Council said that he was gravely perturbed by bloodshed in Czechoslovakia and felt every minute was now precious. . . .
>
> I finally asked M. Daladier point-blank whether he adhered to policy expounded to me by him on September 8. He replied, but with evident lack of enthusiasm, that if Germans used force French would be obliged also. He added, however, that of course he would have to be sure in regard to rights and wrongs of recent bloodshed in Czechoslovakia.
>
> M. Daladier said he had sent two officials to Prague by air . . . to im-

---

* So far as first-line planes and their production was concerned, Lindbergh, if Bonnet quoted him correctly, overestimated both by at least four times.

† The French press knew it. That very evening, according to a private letter Phipps sent Halifax on September 16, Bonnet told the French diplomatic correspondents "that France rejected any solution by recourse to arms."[42]

press M. Beneš how essential it was . . . to make every possible concession to Sudeteners. . . . He spoke bitterly of M. Beneš, as did M. Bonnet previously. . . .

To resume, M. Daladier of today was quite a different one to the M. Daladier of September 8, and tone and language were very different indeed.

I fear French have been bluffing, although I have continually pointed out to them that one cannot bluff Hitler. . . .

M. Daladier said he would perhaps telephone to the Prime Minister.

This the Premier did later that evening. Both Bonnet and Daladier had asked Phipps to suggest to London the calling immediately of a three- or four-Power conference to try to settle the Sudeten problem and avert war. To urge that and, if the British declined, as Phipps had indicated they would, to suggest that Chamberlain get in contact with Hitler directly and affirm Franco-British solidarity, Daladier got through on the telephone to the Prime Minister in London shortly after 9 P.M. He says the connection was bad.[44] Apparently he was unable to get through his message.* But he says he "understood" Chamberlain to reply "that he had come to a decision some time before, a decision he believed would be useful, and that he would tell me about it later."

Thus the Prime Minister put off the Premier of the allied nation. He declined even to hint to Daladier what he had in mind. We know now what it was. A little later that evening, at 11 P.M., Chamberlain got off an urgent message to Hitler.

In view of the increasingly critical situation, I propose to come over at once to see you with a view to trying to find a peaceful solution. I propose to come across by air and am ready to start tomorrow.

Please indicate earliest time at which you can see me and suggest place of meeting. I should be grateful for a very early reply.[46]

---

* Realizing that because of the faulty telephone connection Chamberlain had not caught his remarks, Daladier that evening asked the British Ambassador to relay "a very important message immediately to the Prime Minister." This was dispatched by telephone at 10:10 P.M. Fearing that "matters risk getting out of control almost at once" and emphasizing that "entry of German troops into Czechoslovakia must at all costs be prevented" because if it were not, "France will be faced with her obligation, viz: automatic necessity to fulfill her engagement," Daladier proposed two measures:

"1. Lord Runciman to make known his plan publicly and immediately.

Should above procedure not be sufficient, I propose:

"2. An immediate proposal to Hitler for a meeting of the Three Powers, viz: Germany for Sudetens, France for the Czechs, and Great Britain for Lord Runciman, with a view to obtaining that pacific settlement advocated by Hitler in his speech last night."

So the French Premier was pleading with the British to get France off the hook of her commitments to Czechoslovakia.[45]

Two hours before, the German Chargé d'Affaires in London, Theodor Kordt, had wired Berlin that Chamberlain's press ·secretary had informed the German correspondents in London that the Prime Minister "was prepared to examine far-reaching German proposals, including plebiscite, to take part in carrying them out, and to advocate them in public."[47]

The surrender that was to culminate in Munich had begun.

20

THE ROAD TO MUNICH, II
SEPTEMBER 15–28, 1938

The next step was taken two days later, September 15, at Berchtesgaden, where Chamberlain conferred with Hitler without the presence of the French. The two men soon got down to business.* Hitler demanded self-determination for the Sudeten Germans. To obtain it, he said, he "would face any war, even a world war." The British Prime Minister was impressed. Personally, he said, "he recognized the principle of the detachment of the Sudeten areas." But he would first have to obtain the agreement of his cabinet and of the French government. He said nothing about getting the Czechs to agree. He proposed another meeting within a few days and asked Hitler in the meantime to refrain from military action. The Fuehrer agreed to both, and Chamberlain was pleased.[1] As he remarked privately a few days later: "In spite of the hardness and ruthlessness I thought I saw in his face, I got the impression that here was a man who could be relied upon when he had given his word."[2]

Arriving back in London on the evening of September 16 Chamberlain at once called a cabinet meeting, which Lord Runciman, hurriedly summoned by air from Prague, joined. The British "mediator" proved immensely helpful to the Prime Minister. Admitting that he had "a great deal of sympathy for the Sudeten Germans," he proposed handing over immediately to Germany the areas where they had a clear majority. That, in effect, was what Chamberlain had agreed to with Hitler. But Runciman went further. He strongly recommended that the Czechoslovak government "prohibit" either "parties or persons" from continuing their hostile

---

* I have described the meeting in detail in my history of the Third Reich.

"agitation" against the country's "neighbors." And that, moreover, she should "so remodel her foreign relations as to give assurances to her neighbors that she will in no circumstances attack them or enter into any aggressive action against them arising from obligations to other states." That even a man as ignorant and prejudiced as Lord Runciman should be concerned with the danger of agitation and aggression from a rump Czech state against Nazi Germany staggers the mind. But his fantastic recommendations seem to have impressed the British cabinet and most certainly bolstered Chamberlain's resolve to meet Hitler's demands.[3]

Having rallied his cabinet to his position the Prime Minister summoned the French to London to get their backing. In view of what Phipps reported that very day, the 16th, from Paris in a personal letter to Halifax, Chamberlain must have realized that this would not be very difficult.

> Bonnet repeated to me this morning [Phipps wrote] that he and the French Government would accept any plan advocated by the Prime Minister or Runciman and impose it upon the Czechs; if the latter were recalcitrant they would be told that France disinterested herself from their fate; *but* if meanwhile the Germans attacked the Czechs the French would have to fulfil their treaty engagements.

After reporting that the French Foreign Minister on September 13, the day of his "collapse," had told the diplomatic correspondents that "France rejected any solution by recourse to arms," the British Ambassador summed up his personal impressions:

> I feel pretty certain that the French will by no means resort automatically to arms, even if the German forces cross the Czechoslovak frontier. They will, I believe, examine very closely the circumstances in which the "aggression" takes place, and I do not suppose we shall blame them for caution in this respect.[4]

Blame them! The British were insisting upon such caution. However, they had little to worry about, as the course of the Anglo-French meeting on September 18 in London, attended by Daladier and Bonnet, quickly disclosed. Recounting to his guests his conference with Hitler, Chamberlain stressed that "the situation was much more urgent and critical than I supposed," and revealed that he personally favored accepting Hitler's demand for self-determination for the Sudeteners. Daladier, firm at first, tried to explain to his British hosts that "Germany's real aim was the disintegration of Czechoslovakia and . . . a march to the East. Romania would be next. . . . The result: Germany would soon be the master of Europe and then would turn on France and Britain."

Chamberlain had gingerly raised this question at Berchtesgaden, inquiring whether the "return" of the Sudetenland would be Hitler's "last territorial demand," or whether he was aiming, as some in Britain believed, at "the dismemberment of the Czechoslovak state." The Fuehrer had given his "assurance" that this was his last such demand*—he wanted no Czechs in the German Reich—and the British leader had accepted his word. "The Prime Minister," as the English minutes of the meeting record him telling the French, "had derived the impression while watching Hitler and talking to him that he would be better than worse than his word and that he could be relied upon unless something quite unexpected occurred."[5] Though Daladier did not agree, he was not the man to conquer the stubbornness of the Prime Minister or to open his eyes. After affirming that France would honor her commitments to Czechoslovakia if she were attacked by the Germans, he began to give ground. The British minutes indicate the turning point.

The problem is [the Premier said] to discover the means of preventing France from being forced into war as the result of her obligations, and at the same time to preserve Czechoslovakia and save as much of that country as is humanly possible.

The means were quickly found and agreed upon. The Czechs would be asked, and pressured, if need be, to cede to Germany all territory in which the Sudeteners comprised more than one half of the population. In return for this sacrifice Great Britain agreed to participate in "an international guarantee of the new boundaries . . . against unprovoked aggression." But this assurance was made conditional on the Czechs abrogating their treaties of mutual assistance with France and Russia.

And there was the cant. In the joint note which the British and French governments handed to President Beneš the next day calling upon him to abandon the Sudetenland it was stated:

Both the French and British Governments recognize how great is the sacrifice thus required of the Czechoslovak Government in the cause of peace. But because that cause is common both to Europe in general and in particular to Czechoslovakia herself, they have felt it their duty jointly to set forth frankly the conditions essential to secure it.

The Anglo-French statesmen were in a hurry. They could not keep Hitler waiting. The joint note concluded:

The Prime Minister must resume conversation with Herr Hitler not later than Wednesday, and earlier, if possible. We therefore feel we must ask for your reply at the earliest possible moment.[6]

The proposals reached Prague at noon on Monday, September 19. Not much time was given the Czechs. But they did not need much. The

---

* In 1935 Hitler had given a similar assurance after the Saar was restored to Germany.

next day they rejected them, explaining—prophetically—that to accept them would put "Czechoslovakia sooner or later under the complete domination of Germany." After reminding France of her treaty obligations and also of the consequences to the French position in Europe should the Czechs yield, Prague's reply offered to submit the whole Sudeten question to arbitration under the terms of the German-Czech treaty of October 1925.

The British and French, frightened that Hitler might go to war at any moment unless the Czechs yielded, refused to accept their rejection. To make Prague change its mind they now resorted to the sharpest—and the shabbiest—kind of diplomatic pressure. And they compounded their deceitfulness by insisting that the Czechs, despite the threat of attack by an already mobilized Germany, refrain from even beginning their own mobilization. London and Paris feared that such a step might further "provoke" the German dictator. Thus at the very moment France and Britain were justifying their policy of sacrificing Czechoslovakia partly because she was not strong enough to defend herself they were trying to prevent her from taking the only measures by which she could do so.

This duplicity was too much for the chief of the French military mission in Czechoslovakia, General Foucher. He knew that the formal request of the Czech General Staff for military talks with the French to concert common action in case of German aggression which had been made to General Gamelin in July had gone unanswered.[7] This had given him the painful thought that his country might not honor her commitments. But when he learned on September 15 that Daladier himself had informed the Czechs of his uneasiness over their first modest measures of precaution he wrote, and then telegraphed, Gamelin that unless the country now mobilized it could not put up a fight against the Germans.[8]

The easygoing Gamelin was finally aroused—if only because he realized, as he wrote to Daladier on September 18, that an unmobilized Czechoslovakia would be unable to "hold down an important part of the German forces"—that is, spare the French from facing them. Two days later, shortly after returning from London, the Premier asked the general: did he, in effect, approve of the Czechs mobilizing? Gamelin was typically evasive. While Czechoslovakia, he answered, could not defend herself "without a total mobilization . . . this was a matter for the Czech High Command to decide. The question is whether France and Britain want to give Czechoslovakia complete freedom of action, without conditions. That is a question beyond the competence of the French High Command."[9] It was up to the government to decide.

That very night—of September 20–21—the French government in fact made a decision, but on another issue, and under circumstances that are still a matter of controversy but, on the basis of the available evidence, smack of deceit. The leading role in that tense evening's developments was taken by Bonnet, who many years later was still defending what he did as justified and honorable.

Shortly before 9 P.M. on the evening of September 20, the French Minister in Prague, Victor de Lacroix, was dictating a telegram to be telephoned to Paris recounting the Czech rejection of the Anglo-French proposal when he received a call from the Prime Minister, Dr. Milan Hodja, requesting him urgently to come to see him at once. Hodja, the leader of the Agrarian Party and somewhat at odds with President Beneš, was already faltering—partly out of fear of the Germans and partly out of fear that the French were faltering. He wanted to make sure that France, as he suspected, would renege on its commitment to Czechoslovakia. He put the question bluntly to Lacroix, who described the tense meeting in testimony before the Parliamentary Investigating Committee after the war.[10]

Hodja asked me if I was certain that France would evade its obligations in case of a conflict. I told him that I was not aware of this but that I would telegraph immediately to Paris and obtain a firm answer to his question. He objected that this would take too much time and added: "I admit *a priori* that France will not march with us, and if this very night you can get from your government a telegram confirming it the President of the Republic will give in. It is the only means of saving the peace."

M. Hodja said moreover, in response to my questioning, that he was acting in accord with Beneš and the General Staff, which estimated that without the support of France a war against Germany would be equivalent to suicide.

The French envoy testified that he immediately informed his government of this conversation. But . . . "in examining the archives of the Foreign Ministry later I found that my telegram had been amputated. The first question of M. Hodja and my dubitative answer had been cut out."*

By the time Bonnet got through with the telegram, which he later published in his memoirs as the "integral" text,[11] it read:

The Prime Minister has just told me that if this very night I can assure M. Beneš that, in case of war . . . over the Sudeten Germans, France, because of her engagements with England, will not march, the President of the Republic . . . will give in.

The Czech leaders need this cover in order to accept the Anglo-French proposal. . . . M. Hodja declares that the procedure which he suggests is the only means of saving the peace. He wishes that all be done before midnight if possible, or in any case during the night.[12]

---

* "I believe that the mutilation of my telegram," Lacroix told the Parliamentary Investigating Committee, "is a heavy burden for the French government to bear, for it seems to indicate that, without wishing to admit it, it had decided not to hold to its engagements."

Lacroix also told the Committee that this was not the first telegram of his during the crisis which was tampered with in Bonnet's Foreign Office. A few days before, on September 17, he had sent a long dispatch recounting a confidential conversation with Beneš. "In going through the archives of the Foreign Office later I found that my telegram had been falsified."

So, according to Bonnet, the Czechs wanted a "cover." But whereas he insists that the Czechs wanted it merely as an excuse to accept the London proposals, Lacroix seemed to believe that they wanted it *only* in case France was determined not to honor her word and was willing to say so. Bonnet makes clear he did not see the difference. "We were prepared," he wrote later in self-justification, "to give the Czech government the 'cover' it asked for and we gave it our word on it."[13] He was "prepared," that is, for the French government to give its word that it would not honor its word.* This was now quickly done.

Daladier joined Bonnet at the Quai d'Orsay, where the Foreign Minister, aided by Léger and Jules Henry, the director of the Foreign Office cabinet, were drafting the "cover" reply. There was no time to call a meeting of the cabinet but it was deemed necessary to at least inform the President of the Republic, who was at the country palace at Rambouillet. It was near to midnight and Lebrun, an early riser, was already asleep. He was awakened and Bonnet explained the situation to him on the telephone. Lebrun suggested they take a little more time "to reflect" and call a meeting of the full cabinet before taking such a painful decision. But Bonnet insisted that a reply had to be made immediately and the President assented. At thirty minutes past midnight the French "cover" note was telephoned to Lacroix in Prague.

France, in accord with England, has set forth the only procedure which it judges in the actual circumstances can prevent the Germans from marching into Czechoslovakia.

In rejecting the Franco-British proposal the Czech government assumes the responsibility for Germany resorting to force. It thus ruptures the Franco-British solidarity which has just been established and by doing so it removes any practical effectiveness of assistance from France. . . .

Czechoslovakia thus assumes the risk which we believed to have been removed. She must herself understand the conclusions which France has the right to draw if the Czechoslovak government does not accept immediately the Franco-British proposal.[15]

In the opinion of Bonnet and the French government, then, it was the Czechs and not the Germans who "assumed" the responsibility for a German attack on their country. At any rate, unless Prague agreed "immediately" to the Anglo-French proposals to hand over the Sudetenland to Hitler, the two Western allies would wash their hands of the whole affair. In his postwar testimony before the Parliamentary Investigating Committee, Bonnet declared that he telephoned London that night and that the British

---

* On the evening of September 20, when Bonnet and Daladier were mulling over the "cover," the British received further evidence that the French would not fight. The British military attaché in Paris wired London on the 21st: "Yesterday evening I had an interview with Col. Gauché [chief of the Deuxième Bureau]. He [declared]: 'Of course there will be no European war, since we are not going to fight. . . .'"[14]

told him: "We cannot refuse the Czechoslovak government the cover it needs."[16] Actually there is no mention of a "cover" in the British Foreign Office papers. But there is plenty of mention of the British joining the French to increase the pressure that night on Prague.

At 10:45 P.M. Sir Basil Newton, the British Minister, had wired Halifax from Prague: "A solution must be imposed. . . . If I can deliver a kind of ultimatum to Beneš . . . he and his government will feel able to bow to *force majeure*."[17] The British Foreign Secretary obliged with a message telephoned to Newton in Prague at 1:20 A.M. It instructed him to join with his French colleague and point out to the Czech government that its refusal

if adhered to would . . . in our opinion lead to an immediate German invasion. You should urge the Czech Government to withdraw this reply and urgently consider an alternative that takes account of realities. Anglo-French proposals remain in our view only chance of avoiding immediate German attack. . . . We therefore beg Czech Government to consider urgently and seriously before producing a situation for which we could take no responsibility.[18]

The British government, like the French, was now putting the responsibility for a German attack not on the attackers but on the recipients. And unless Prague gave in, they were leaving her to her doom.

Armed with these ultimata from their respective foreign ministers, Newton and Lacroix drove to Hradčany Palace in Prague shortly after 2 A.M. and fetched Beneš out of bed—the second President of a Republic to be aroused from his sleep that night. It was obvious to the two envoys that he had not expected the call and that he knew nothing of his Prime Minister's having asked the French to confirm that they would not honor their commitments. After the French Minister had read his telegram Beneš almost collapsed. He began to sob. He felt, he said later, as if he had been clubbed. After Newton had read *his* telegram a short discussion ensued. Beneš promised an answer and the ministers said they would wait for it, but when the President explained that it would take time to consult the cabinet and the Army and that the reply could not be ready before noon they left. It was now 3:45 A.M. On parting the President had asked the French minister to put the French note in writing—Lacroix had been instructed by Bonnet to deliver it only verbally. Obviously Beneš saw no hope now, but he had an eye on history. He and his government and the Army had shown great courage in the face of enemy threats. Now, as the Czech leaders deliberated throughout the day of September 21, they began to crumble at the desertion of their friends and allies.

During the day some encouragement came from the Russians. Early in the afternoon at the League of Nations Litvinov affirmed in a speech that the Soviet Union would stand by its treaty with Czechoslovakia. A few minutes later the Soviet Minister in Prague called on Beneš to reaffirm the declaration. But the President realized that the pact with Russia called for Soviet aid only on condition that France honored her commitments. And the French had just reneged—and were putting it in writing.

Shortly before 5 P.M. on September 21 the Czech government capitulated and accepted the Anglo-French plan. "We had no other choice," an official Czech communiqué explained bitterly to the people, "because we were left alone." Privately Beneš put it more succinctly: "We have been basely betrayed."

The next day the Hodja cabinet resigned and General Jan Sirovy, Inspector General of the Army, became the head of a new government of all the parties. The day, September 22, brought other happenings. In Prague, General Foucher tore up his French passport and joined the Czech Army. In Paris, Reynaud, Mandel, and Champetier de Ribes resigned from the cabinet in protest against their government having brought such pressure on the Czech government.* In London the morning papers carried a ringing statement issued at midnight by Winston Churchill, who had just returned from a two-day visit to Paris where he had urged Reynaud and Mandel not to resign because, he had argued, the French government could not spare "its two most capable and resolute men." "The partition of Czechoslovakia," Churchill declared, "under pressure from England and France amounts to the complete surrender of the Western Democracies to the Nazi threat of force. Such a collapse will bring peace or security neither to England nor to France. On the contrary, it will place these two nations in an ever weaker and more dangerous situation."[19]

Finally, on that eventful day, the British Prime Minister set out for Germany by plane from London for the second time in a week to see Hitler again, happy and relieved that the Czechs had facilitated his task of giving the Nazi dictator what he had threatened to take by force. Once in the company of the ferocious Fuehrer at Godesberg on the banks of the Rhine, Chamberlain's euphoria quickly evaporated.

With evident self-satisfaction, as one eyewitness noted, Chamberlain explained to Hitler at their first meeting at 5 P.M. the Anglo-French plan which the Czechs had just been forced to accept.

"Do I understand," Hitler asked, "that the British, French, and Czech governments have agreed to the transfer of the Sudetenland from Czechoslovakia to Germany?" He was astounded, as he later told Chamberlain, that the concessions to him had gone so far and so fast.

"Yes," replied the Prime Minister, smiling.

"I am terribly sorry," Hitler said, "but after the events of the last few days, this plan is no longer of any use."

Chamberlain, Dr. Paul Schmidt, the official German interpreter, later remembered, sat up with a start. His owllike face flushed with surprise and anger. When he had recovered he said, according to both the English and German minutes of the meeting,[20] that he was

---

* At the insistence of Daladier, they withdrew their resignations.

both disappointed and puzzled. He could rightly say that the Fuehrer had got from him what he had demanded. In order to achieve this he [Chamberlain] had risked his whole political career. . . . He was being accused by certain circles in Great Britain of having sold and betrayed Czechoslovakia, of having yielded to the dictators, and on leaving England that morning he actually had been booed.

The Fuehrer was unmoved by the personal plight of the British Prime Minister. The Sudeten area, he said, must be militarily occupied by Germany at once. The problem "must be completely and finally solved by October 1 at the latest." He had a map handy to indicate what territories must be ceded immediately. They went far beyond the areas in the Franco-British plan.

"Full of foreboding," as he later told the Commons, Chamberlain withdrew across the Rhine to his room in the Peterhof high above the river. There seemed so little hope for a peaceful solution that after telephone consultations with his own cabinet and with the French government it was agreed that London and Paris should inform the Czech government the next day, the 23rd, that they could "not continue to take responsibility of advising them not to mobilize."* The Germans also drew certain conclusions from the day's talks. At 7:20 that evening General Keitel telephoned Army headquarters from Godesberg: ". . . Continue preparations according to plan. If Case Green occurs, it will not be before September 30. If it occurs sooner, it will probably be improvised."[21]

All day long on September 23 the two heads of government sulked in their respective hotels along the Rhine, communicating only by letter. After breakfast Chamberlain dispatched a note to Hitler saying that while he was willing to submit to the Czechs the Fuehrer's new demands for immediate military occupation of the Sudetenland he did not think they would be accepted. Late in the afternoon Hitler replied by letter. He refused to modify his position. Chamberlain answered briefly that if Hitler "would be good enough" to put his proposals in writing, "together with a map," he would consider it his "duty, as intermediary," to forward them to Prague. "I do not see that I can perform any further service here," he concluded. "I propose, therefore, to return to England."

Before doing so he came over once again to the Dreesen for a final meeting, which began at 10:30 P.M. Hitler produced his demands in the form of a "memorandum," with an accompanying map. Chamberlain noted a new time limit. The Czechs were to begin the evacuation of the ceded territory by 8 A.M. on September 26—two days hence—and complete it by September 28.

"But this is nothing less than an ultimatum!" Chamberlain exclaimed.

"Nothing of the sort," Hitler retorted. When Chamberlain answered

---

* Czech mobilization began at 10:30 P.M. on September 23.

that the German word *Diktat* applied to it, Hitler responded: "It is not a *Diktat* at all. Look, the document is headed by the word 'memorandum.' "

At this moment an adjutant brought in an urgent message for the Fuehrer. He glanced at it and tossed it to Dr. Schmidt, who was interpreting. "Read this to Mr. Chamberlain."

Schmidt did: "Beneš has just announced over the radio a general mobilization in Czechoslovakia." The room, Dr. Schmidt recalled later, was deadly still. Then Hitler spoke: "Now, of course, the whole affair is settled. The Czechs will not dream of ceding any territory to Germany."

There followed a heated argument as to who had mobilized first.

> The Czechs had mobilized first [said Hitler]. The Prime Minister retorted that Germany had mobilized first. The Fuehrer denied that Germany had mobilized.

The talks went on to well past midnight. Finally, after Chamberlain had inquired whether the German memorandum "was really his last word" and Hitler had replied that it was, the Prime Minister answered that

> there was no point in continuing the conversations. He had done his utmost; his efforts had failed. He was going away with a heavy heart, for the hopes with which he had come to Germany were destroyed.

These words brought from the Fuehrer a "concession."

"You are one of the few men for whom I have ever done such a thing," Hitler said. "I am prepared to set one single date for the Czech evacuation —October 1—if that will facilitate your task." He grabbed a pencil and changed the dates himself. This, of course, was no concession at all. September 30 or the next day, October 1, had been X-Day all along.

But Chamberlain was impressed. "He fully appreciated," Schmidt recorded him as saying, "the Fuehrer's consideration on the point." While not in a position himself, he said, to accept or reject the proposals he promised to transmit them to Prague.

Back in London the next day, September 24, the Prime Minister attempted to do the very thing he had informed Hitler he would not do: persuade his own cabinet and the French and the Czechs to accept the Godesberg demands. The cabinet refused. The French refused. The Czechs refused.

The reaction of the French government to Godesberg was to speed up its mobilization. During the night of September 23–24 white posters appeared on the billboards of every city, town and village in France calling up reservists whose mobilization cards numbered "2" or "3"—roughly a million men. The sight of them on the morning of Saturday, the 24th, was the first Frenchmen had had since the summer of 1914, twenty-four years before. As the German chargé d'affaires in Paris wired to Berlin the next day, the "new mobilization is being carried out in a calm and orderly manner throughout the country."[22]

Already General Gamelin was deploying strong forces close to the German frontier. On the afternoon of the 24th Ambassador Phipps telegraphed London that General Gamelin had informed his military attaché that besides bringing the Maginot Line to full war strength "seven more divisions would reach the border this morning. This makes a total of fourteen divisions dispatched to the frontier in the last 48 hours."

The British Ambassador was not entirely pleased with this demonstration that the French might fight after all. He added some other information in the same telegram.

> M. Flandin called on me today spontaneously [sic] to say that all peasant class were against war. . . . My own impression is that the Government can decree mobilization but not war without a vote in the Chamber and Senate. . . . If . . . a vote were taken today . . . the issue would be doubtful.[23]

This telegram was dispatched at 3 P.M. on the 24th. Later that afternoon, at 5:45 P.M., Phipps got off another one submitting his "purely personal impressions." "War now," he wired, "would be most unpopular in France.

> I think therefore that His Majesty's Government should realize extreme danger of appearing to encourage small, but noisy and corrupt, war group here.*
> All that is best in France is against war, *almost* at any price.[26]

Before departing on Sunday, September 25, for London for another meeting with the British leaders, Daladier held a cabinet meeting in Paris. At 11 A.M. he had received a copy of the Godesberg Plan with map and the Army's Deuxième Bureau (Intelligence) had explained to him that if it were accepted Czechoslovakia would be deprived of almost all her fortifications and "Bohemia would be strangled." The Council of Ministers thereupon rejected it. How willingly Bonnet went along is not known since no

---

* This passage raised eyebrows in the British Foreign Office. The next day Sir Alexander Cadogan, the Under-Secretary, wired Phipps: "We do not entirely understand your reference to 'small but noisy and corrupt war group here.' By 'war group' you surely do not include all those who feel that France must carry out her treaty obligations to Czechoslovakia. If so, . . . what are your reasons for describing it as 'corrupt'?"[24] Phipps replied on September 26: "By 'small but noisy and corrupt war group' I meant the Communists, who are paid by Moscow and have been working for war for months. A well-known French Minister has also been advocating a preventative war for many months."[25] Presumably Phipps referred to either Mandel or Reynaud, who were simply advocating that France honor her commitments to Czechoslovakia.

minutes of French cabinet meetings are kept. But General Gamelin noted: "Sunday, the 25th, the President [Daladier] tells me that he is having difficulties in his ministry. M. Georges Bonnet is threatening to resign." [27]

Late in the afternoon the Premier and his vacillating Foreign Minister flew to London. At 9 P.M. they gathered at 10 Downing Street with Chamberlain, Halifax, and their principal ministers and advisers. After the Prime Minister had briefed his visitors on his talks with Hitler at Godesberg the statesmen considered what to do. From the British minutes of the conference[28] it is evident that the French urged standing up to the Nazi dictator and that the British, doubtful of the military strength of France and under no illusions about their own, were for further appeasement of the Fuehrer in order to avoid war. The talk was frank and the clashes between Daladier (Bonnet said scarcely a word) and his hosts frequent and sharp.

The French government, Daladier said, had "unanimously" rejected the Godesberg proposals because it realized that Hitler wished

not so much to take over three and a half million Germans as to destroy Czechoslovakia by force, enslaving her, and afterward realizing the domination of Europe, which was his object.

Chamberlain then set out to remove what he called "French misunderstandings" about Hitler's Godesberg proposals and in doing so actually defended them, "explaining" that the Fuehrer wanted to send in German troops immediately "only to preserve law and order." But Daladier saw through this and replied that the Godesberg demands "amounted to the dismemberment of Czechoslovakia and German domination of Europe" and the French would not accept this.

Balked by the Premier's stubbornness, Chamberlain finally asked: "What then do you propose to do next?"*

DALADIER: "Our next step should be to say to Hitler that he should return to the Anglo-French proposals."

CHAMBERLAIN: "And if Hitler refuses?"

DALADIER: "In that case each of us will have to do our duty."

CHAMBERLAIN: "I think we shall have to go a little further than that."

DALADIER: "I have no further proposal to make."

Chamberlain replied that he "thought we could not fence about this question. We had to get down to the stern realities of the situation. . . . Hitler had said very definitely that his memorandum represented his last word. If we refused, he would at once take military measures. . . . What would the French attitude be in such an event? . . . Would France declare war on Germany?"

"The matter is clear," Daladier answered. "The French government will fulfill her obligations."

---

* I have put into direct discourse the indirect discourse customarily employed in British government minutes, changing the verb tenses but not the substantive wording.

"But how?" the Prime Minister persisted. He said he wanted to know "whether the French General Staff had got some plan, and, if so, what the plan was."

There now ensued what Daladier later described as "a running fire of questions" from Chamberlain and his cabinet colleagues about how France could fight.[29]

Did the French "contemplate," Sir John Simon asked, "the invasion of Germany?" Was the use of the French air force "over Germany contemplated?" When Daladier replied that it "certainly" was, Simon replied that "this would constitute an attack." Apparently in the mind of this great legal splitter of hairs the idea of the French as aggressors was already taking root. Daladier tried to cut short the inane questions. Addressing himself to Simon he replied:

I would consider it ridiculous to mobilize the French land forces only to leave them . . . doing nothing in their fortifications. It would be equally ridiculous to do nothing in the air. . . . I believe therefore that after the French troops have been concentrated an offensive should be attempted by land against Germany. As regards the air, it should be possible to attack certain important German military and industrial centers.

The French premier was warming up despite the chilly mood of his British hosts. He said he wished to talk also of "moral obligations." They had asked the Czechs, "who were human beings," to make heavy sacrifices, but those did not "suffice" Hitler. "At what point," he asked the British, "are you prepared to stop and how far will you go?" He, too, wanted peace. But he would not accept the Godesberg demands "come what may." He had urged an international commission to supervise Germany's taking over of the Sudeten areas. "Why should not this proposal be put to Hitler? Surely we need not accept every demand he chooses to make."

But that was pretty much what Chamberlain had been doing since his first meeting with Hitler at Berchtesgaden. He now told Daladier he was convinced the Nazi dictator would not accept an international commission. "What would we then do," he asked, "if faced with a German invasion of Czechoslovakia?" The Prime Minister thereupon took a new tack, questioning the ability of the French to save the Czechs or to wage effective war against Germany.

M. Daladier had indicated that the French plan was to undertake offensive operations . . . and also to bomb German factories and military centers. He wished to speak quite frankly and say that the British Government had received disturbing accounts of the condition of the French Air Force. . . . He felt he must ask what would happen if . . . a rain of bombs descended upon Paris, upon French industrial districts, military centers, and airdromes? He would also like to ask what assurances France had received from Russia. The

British Government . . . had received very disturbing news about the probable Russian attitude. And again, the tone of the French press today did not sound very bellicose. . . .

And then this final shot:

It would be a poor consolation if, in fulfilment of all her obligations, France attempted to come to the assistance of her friend but found herself unable to keep up her resistance and collapsed.

Daladier replied cheerfully by putting some questions himself.

He was always hearing of difficulties. Did this mean that we did not wish to do anything? . . . Was the British Government ready to give in and to accept Hitler's proposals?

As to Chamberlain's point about the French press he suggested that it was not in the press that one had to look for the real feelings of the French people but in the people themselves, who understood what was at stake. "A million of these Frenchmen are now at the frontiers. It is in them that you will find our true national sentiment."

We must face up to the facts and decide what we want to do. If Hitler put forward certain demands must we agree to them? . . . Must we always give way to Hitler's ultimata? If we were agreed to do so, it was useless to have meetings. . . . A moment came to call a halt and that moment . . . had come. . . . Mr. Chamberlain had indicated that Hitler had spoken his last word. Did the British Government intend to accept it?

This was the key question, but the British ministers dodged it. Still Daladier persisted. He posed three questions.

1. Did His Majesty's Government accept Hitler's plan?
2. Did His Majesty's Government think of bringing pressure on the Czechoslovak Government to accept Hitler's plan when we knew that they would certainly not do so and would prefer to die rather than accept it?
3. Did His Majesty's Government think that France should do nothing?

Chamberlain replied to each question in turn:

1, that it was not for the British or French Governments to accept or reject Hitler's proposals. That was a matter for the Czechoslovak Government. 2. We could not exert pressure upon the Czechoslovak Government since we had no means to compel them to reverse their decision. We were concerned with what would happen when that decision had been transmitted to Hitler. 3, he did not think it was for the British Government to express an opinion, but . . . for the French Government to decide.

After the Prime Minister had asked if General Gamelin could attend the session the next day and Daladier had said that he could, the meeting adjourned. The Premier had stuck to his guns and the Prime Minister had been unable to move him. Still, Daladier was discouraged by the British fear of Hitler, as General Gamelin learned on his arrival in London the next morning. The Premier was also doubtful, if the generalissimo can be believed, of his own Foreign Minister. Before the day, September 26, was out, Gamelin himself was more than doubtful; he felt himself to be the victim "of a very painful affair which," he later wrote, "originated in the intrigues of M. Georges Bonnet."

Stopping first at the French Embassy in London before proceeding to 10 Downing Street, Gamelin found the French delegation still somewhat depressed from the meeting with the British the night before.

The British [he was told] do not feel themselves ready for action. . . . They want to gain time. . . . I must accompany the President [Daladier] to see Chamberlain this morning. But M. Georges Bonnet must be kept out of it. He discourages everyone.

After the Prime Minister and the Premier had conferred alone for a few minutes, General Gamelin was asked to join them. Pulling papers and maps out of his briefcase he proceeded to give Chamberlain his estimate of the military situation. According to his own notes jotted down the next day he gave the following resumé:

1. French land forces: 5,000,000 men; 100 divisions to start with; a fortified system which guarantees us freedom of maneuver; an inferior air force but capable of operating at short-range in support of the army.

2. German weaknesses: A High Command which realizes dangers it faces. A fortified system not yet finished. Great deficits in cadres . . . lack of trained reserves. Difficulty of a long war because of a lack of raw materials, especially oil. Certainly a superior air force. . . .

3. Italian weaknesses: Morale of the country. Impossibility of fighting a long war.

At this Chamberlain broke in to say: "If we march, Italy won't march." Gamelin granted that was "possible."

4. Possibilities of Czech resistance: 30 divisions being mobilized against 40 German divisions. If they hold in the north and south of Moravia they can save their army, though having to abandon a part of their territory. . . .[30]

The rest of the morning the French generalissimo conferred with

Britain's three defense ministers and the chiefs of the General Staffs of the three services.* Except for the Navy, he found his hosts "feeling they were not ready for war." Toward the end of this meeting an urgent telephone call came in for Gamelin from Paris. It was from General Jeannel, his Chief of Staff, with a message from Marshal Voroshilov, the Russian Commissar for Defense, in Moscow.

The Soviets have now 30 infantry divisions, a mass of cavalry, numerous tank formations and the bulk of their air force ready to intervene in the West.[32]

Gamelin passed this information along to his British colleagues but it was "evident," he saw, "that the hypothesis of Russia invading Poland scarcely pleased our ally."

The most important development of this morning of September 26 in London, of which no record has been found in the British Foreign Office papers, had taken place in the private conversation between Chamberlain and Daladier before General Gamelin joined them. The Prime Minister had undergone a change of mind overnight after reflecting on the Premier's firm stand the previous evening. He was now convinced that the French would honor their commitments to Czechoslovakia. If Hitler forced them to do so Britain had no other recourse but to stand by France. He explained to Daladier that he was that very morning sending his confidential adviser, Sir Horace Wilson, by plane to Berlin to deliver a personal letter to Hitler containing a last plea to avoid war by negotiating directly with the Czechs the taking over of the Sudetenland peacefully. If Hitler's response was "negative," Sir Horace Wilson was instructed to read to him the following statement of British intent:

The French Government has told us that in case of a German attack against Czechoslovakia it will faithfully fulfil its obligations. If in carrying out these obligations deriving from its treaties, France became actively engaged in hostilities against Germany, the United Kingdom would feel obliged to come to her aid.[33]

This concession was late, but it represented a decisive change in British policy and was of enormous importance to France. Chamberlain reiterated it when he met with the French delegates later in the morning.

We now knew [the Prime Minister conceded] that the Czechoslovak Government were determined to resist. The French Government had said plainly that if so they would fulfil their treaty obligations. We had said publicly several times that we could not afford to see France overrun or defeated by Germany, and that we would come to her assistance if France were in danger.

---

* According to the British interpreter's notes of Gamelin's meeting with them, the generalissimo, when pressed to give an estimate of how long the Czechs could hold out, replied: "Certainly for a few weeks but perhaps not for a few months."[31]

His Majesty's Government had no intention of going back on what they had said.

The view had long been held in London that if in 1914 the British government had made known that it would support France, the Kaiser would have hesitated to declare war on her. Now the present German ruler would be told of what Britain intended to do if he went to war. Hitler was scheduled to make a speech at the Sportpalast in Berlin that evening of the 26th and it was the British hope—and the French—that the warning might induce him not to burn his bridges. At 4:10 P.M. the Prime Minister got off by telephone a message to Wilson, who was to meet the Fuehrer in Berlin at 5 P.M.

Since you left, French have definitely stated their intention of supporting Czechoslovakia by offensive measures if latter is attacked. This would bring us in; and it should be made plain to Chancellor [Hitler] that this is inevitable alternative to a peaceful solution.

A sudden and, in view of recent events, surprising firmness was developing in both London and Paris. Even Ambassador Phipps in Paris became aware of it. At 2:15 P.M. on this eventful day of September 26, he telephoned London:

Opinion has undergone a complete change. . . . I have just seen President of the Chamber [Herriot], who confirmed the complete swing-over of public opinion since Hitler's demands had become known. He assures me that an overwhelming majority in the Chamber will now be for resistance.[34]

He saw the President of the Senate, Jeanneney, that evening and received the same message.

[He] feels that war is now practically unavoidable [Phipps reported]. If we give way to Hitler's last demand we should only be postponing the evil day and he would then turn with renewed prestige and strength against France. M. Jeanneney assured me feeling in the whole country . . . was absolutely firm. . . .[35]

In Britain, too, apparently. Early in the evening of the 26th, as if to further warn Hitler before he made his speech, Lord Halifax authorized a communiqué to the press.

. . . The German claim to the transfer of the Sudeten areas has already been conceded by the French, British, and Czechoslovak Governments. But if in spite of all efforts made by the British Prime Minister a German attack is made upon Czechoslovakia the immediate result must be that France will be bound to come to her assistance, and Great Britain and Russia will certainly stand by France.[36]

All these utterances seemed plain enough, but there were certain key figures, French and British, who were displeased with them and who began now to try not only to stem the tide of firmness but to reverse it. Foremost among these was Bonnet. Far from being pleased with the British communiqué reiterating that Britain would stand by France, he was "greatly astonished," he says, "by this unexpected communication," and demanded an "explanation" from Phipps.[37] But he went further than that: he tried to suppress its publication in the French press and deliberately spread the word that it was a "fabrication." His behavior is all the more inexplicable since he had heard with his own ears that morning in London Chamberlain make a similar declaration and had heard him also assure the French delegation that the statement would be delivered to Hitler personally by Sir Horace Wilson during the day. Moreover, he knew that the Prime Minister had given Daladier the statement *in writing* at the conclusion of the London meeting. The importance of the communiqué issued by the British Foreign Office the evening of September 26 was that it made public the new British commitment to France, giving a much-needed assurance to the confused French people and to the Czechs and a warning to the German public, which, as I can testify from personal experience in Berlin at that moment, was as fearful of war as the British and the French.

Defending his strange reaction in his memoirs, Bonnet relates that the British Ambassador explained to him that the "declaration had been fabricated by Churchill and Vansittart"* and that he was to pay no attention to it.[38] This is surely untrue.† He admits that he told a group of deputies who called on him that he doubted the authenticity of the communiqué. "This was because," he says, "I was already informed that it was a fabrication." The Foreign Minister advised the French press to treat the declaration with "reserve." No wonder that the next morning the widely circulated *Le Matin* branded the "so-called communiqué" as "a clever lie" and several other Paris newspapers made similar comments.

Bonnet went still further. Though the French Embassy in London had also wired the text of the communiqué and the semiofficial French news agency, Havas, had telegraphed a second confirmation of it after consultation with the Foreign Office, Bonnet forbade its circulation among the departments of the Quai d'Orsay. This was confirmed by Pierre Comert, the

---

* Sir Robert Vansittart had been Permanent Under-Secretary in the Foreign Office from 1930 to 1938, and was now Chief Diplomatic Adviser to the Foreign Secretary. That he was passionately pro-French and anti-German was no secret to anyone, not even to Bonnet.

† There is not a word in Phipps' innumerable dispatches published by the British Foreign Office after the war to substantiate this. Bonnet also recounts that "Chamberlain's broadcast" an hour after the communiqué had been given the press was a "decisive denial" of the Foreign Office declaration. But Chamberlain did not make a broadcast that evening. He did issue a statement to the press shortly after midnight commenting on Hitler's speech and reiterating his plea for conciliation. But no word in his statement "denied" the British commitment to France.

extremely able and courageous Press Chief of the French Foreign Office, whom Bonnet would soon kick downstairs.

> M. Georges Bonnet [Comert told the Parliamentary Investigating Committee] forbade the distribution of the Embassy's telegram in the services of the Foreign Ministry and also prohibited Havas from giving the text of the communiqué to the press.[39]

In Berlin that same day, September 26, Sir Horace Wilson, wilting before the furious outbursts of Adolf Hitler, also failed in his duty to inform the Fuehrer of the new British commitment to France, which he had been urgently instructed to do.

"Very violent hour," he wired Chamberlain as soon as he returned from his interview with Hitler, which had begun at 5 P.M. At one point, when informed that the Czechs had rejected his Godesberg demands, the Fuehrer leapt up, shouted that there was "no sense at all in negotiating further" and bounded for the door. It was a "terribly painful scene," Dr. Schmidt, the German interpreter, recounted. "For the first and only time in my presence, Hitler completely lost his head."[40] And according to the three startled British diplomats present, Wilson, Ambassador Henderson, and Ivone Kirkpatrick, the Embassy counselor who kept the minutes, the aroused dictator shouted and screamed, at one point hollering: "The Germans are being treated like niggers! . . . On October first I shall have Czechoslovakia where I want her! If France and England decide to strike, let them! I do not care a pfennig!"[41]

This was surely the moment for Wilson to deliver the formal assurance that Britain *would* back France if it came to war, but inexperienced in diplomacy as he was and lacking the granite to stand up to the raving Nazi dictator, he let it slip by. He explained this omission in a dispatch to Chamberlain that evening.

> In view of intense emotion and frequent references to tonight's speech it seemed better not to deliver special message and I am to see him again tomorrow morning. . . .

But in view of Hitler's forthcoming speech a few hours later, there was all the more reason, as Daladier later declared, to confront the Fuehrer with the British warning. Had Wilson done so, Daladier said, "it might perhaps have led Hitler to modify the tone of his discourse that evening at the Sportpalast, and when made known among his entourage, it might have encouraged the opposition described by Shirer in his book."[42]

Chamberlain apparently agreed—or almost. At 1 A.M. on the 27th, he wired his special emissary in Berlin:

We do not consider it possible for you to leave without delivering special message, in view of what we said to French, if you can make no progress. But message should be given more in sorrow than in anger.

By that time, 1 A.M., Hitler had burned his bridges in his Sportpalast speech, or so it seemed to those of us who listened in amazement (despite all our previous experience) to his mad outburst before a delirious crowd of Germans in the great hall in Berlin. Shouting and shrieking in the worst paroxysm I had ever seen him in, he venomously hurled personal insults at "Herr Beneš," declared that the issue of war or peace was now up to the Czech President, and that, in any case, he would have the Sudetenland by October 1—four days thence. He had told Wilson a few hours before that he must have a reply from the Czechs accepting his Godesberg demands within 44 hours—by 2 P.M. on September 28. Amidst the frenzy of his speech he did pause once to reiterate that this was his last territorial claim in Europe. "We want no Czechs!" he muttered contemptuously.

I noted that Hitler had slumped into his chair at the end of his speech utterly exhausted. But he was fully recovered when he met Sir Horace Wilson at noon the next day, September 27. All he was interested in, he said, was whether Czechoslovakia accepted or rejected his demands. If they rejected them, he declared, "I shall destroy Czechoslovakia!" He kept repeating the threat with obvious relish.

The repetition finally moved Wilson to stand up, clear his throat, and, as he reported to London, "say one more thing in a tone which the Prime Minister would have used had he been himself present." Apparently he meant "more in sorrow than in anger." He read the declaration ("very slowly," he told London) that Britain would come to the aid of France if hostilities broke out.

"I can only take note of that position," Hitler replied with some heat. "It means that if France elects to attack Germany, England will feel obliged to attack her also." Though Wilson started to argue that he had not said that, and that he did not know that "in fulfilling their obligations France would attack Germany," the Fuehrer showed that he had comprehended the message. Raising his voice to a shout he said: "If France and England strike, let them do so! It is a matter of complete indifference to me! Today is Tuesday. By next Monday we shall be at war!"

Those were ominous words, and Wilson was obviously impressed, if not frightened. "A catastrophe must be avoided at all costs," he said in taking leave. "I will try to make those Czechs sensible." But Hitler had not spoken his last word. That evening, in fact, after Wilson had flown back to London, the Chancellor sat down and dictated a shrewdly worded letter to the Prime Minister.

There were good reasons for writing it. At first, still smarting from his scene with the British envoy, Hitler had moved closer to war. At 1 P.M., as soon as Wilson had left, he issued a "most secret order" directing assault units comprising seven divisions to move forward to their jumping-off positions on the Czech frontier. A few hours later he ordered a further step in Germany's concealed mobilization. Among other measures, five new divisions were mobilized for the west.[43] But even as Hitler went ahead with his military moves, there were developments—in Berlin and elsewhere—during this day of September 27 to make him ponder his course.

From the German military attaché in Paris came a telegram marked "Very Urgent" and addressed not only to the Foreign Ministry but to OKW (the German High Command) and the German General Staff. It warned that France's partial mobilization was so much like a total one "that I reckon with the completion of the deployment of the first 65 divisions on the German frontier by the sixth day of mobilization." That would be by the end of the week. Against such a force the Germans had, as Hitler knew, barely a dozen divisions, half of them reserve units of doubtful value. The five new divisions he had just ordered mobilized for the west were of even less value and at any rate could not be deployed for several days. The German military attaché in Paris had further news, none of it good. "It appears probable," he wired, "that in the event of belligerent measures by Germany . . . an immediate attack will take place, in all probability from lower Alsace and Lorraine in the direction of Mainz." Finally, this officer informed Berlin, the Italians were doing absolutely nothing to pin down French troops on the Franco-Italian frontier.[44] Mussolini, the valiant ally, seemed to be letting Hitler down at a crucial hour.

To worsen matters the President of the United States and the King of Sweden were butting in with pleas for peace that put the onus on Germany if war came. The Swedish monarch, a staunch friend of Germany, as he had proved in the 1914–1918 war, had gone further. During the afternoon of the 27th a dispatch arrived in Berlin from the German Minister in Stockholm, saying that the King had hastily summoned him and told him that unless Hitler extended his time limit of October 1 by ten days a world war would inevitably break out, Germany would be solely to blame for it, and moreover just as inevitably would lose it "in view of the present combination of powers."[45] In the cool, neutral air of Stockholm, the shrewd King was able to assess at least the military situation more objectively than the heads of government in Berlin, London, and Paris.

President Roosevelt, as perhaps was necessary in view of the strong American isolationist sentiment, had weakened his peace appeals by stressing that the United States would not intervene in a war. But Hans Dieckhoff, the German Ambassador in Washington, thought it necessary to get off a "Very Urgent" cable to Berlin during the day warning that if Germany resorted to force and was opposed by Britain he had reason to assume "that the whole weight of the United States [would] be thrown into the scale on the side of Britain." The Ambassador, usually a timid man when it came to warning the Fuehrer, added: "I consider it my duty to emphasize this very strongly."[46] He did not want the German government to stumble into the same mistaken assumptions it had made about America in 1914.

And Prague? Were the Czechs going to submit to Hitler's demands? In the evening came a telegram to Berlin from Colonel Toussaint, the German military attaché in Prague. It was addressed to OKW, the Supreme Command: "Calm in Prague. Last mobilization measures carried out. . . . Total estimated call-up is 1,000,000; field army, 800,000. . . ."[47] That was as many trained men as Germany had for two fronts. Together the Czech and French armies outnumbered the Germans by more than two to one.

The news from London was no better. At 8 that evening the order went out for the mobilization of the British Fleet, the greatest, at that time, in the world and capable of blockading Germany as it had during the first war. Whether Hitler knew of this when he sat down that evening to dictate his letter to the Prime Minister is not known. The official British announcement was not broadcast until 11:38 P.M. What Hitler did know was that Prague was defiant, Paris rapidly mobilizing, London stiffening, his own people apathetic, his leading generals dead against him, and that his ultimatum to the Czechs to accept his Godesberg terms expired at 2 P.M. the next day. Dr. Schmidt, who was called in to translate the letter to Chamberlain into English, had the feeling that the Fuehrer was shrinking back "from the extreme step."

His letter was shrewdly calculated to appeal to the British Prime Minister. Moderate in tone, it denied that his proposals would "rob Czechoslovakia of every guarantee of its existence" or that his troops would fail to stop at the demarcation lines. He was ready to negotiate details with the Czechs; he was prepared to "give a formal guarantee for the remainder of Czechoslovakia. I must leave it to your judgment," he concluded, "whether, in view of these facts, you consider that you should continue your effort. . . ."[48] This was the kind of invitation which he knew by now was most likely to appeal strongly to the Prime Minister.

Hitler's letter, telegraphed urgently to London, reached Chamberlain at 10:30 on the night of September 27. It came at the end of a busy day for the Prime Minister.

The disquieting news of Hitler's intransigence which Sir Horace Wilson brought back from Berlin early in the afternoon had spurred the British government to action. It was decided to mobilize the Fleet, call up the Auxiliary Air Force, and declare a state of emergency. Already trenches were being dug in the parks and squares for protection against bombing and the evacuation of London's schoolchildren had begun.

Also, the Prime Minister, after listening to Wilson, got off a message to President Beneš in Prague warning that his information from Berlin "makes it clear that the German army will receive orders to cross the

Czechoslovak frontier immediately if by tomorrow [September 28] at 2 P.M. the Czechoslovak Government have not accepted the German conditions." But having honorably warned the Czechs, Chamberlain could not refrain from admonishing them, in the last part of the message, "that Bohemia would be overrun by the German army and nothing which another power could do would be able to save your country and your people from such a fate. This remains true whatever the result of a world war might be."[49] Thus Chamberlain, as he had tended to do since Hitler provoked the crisis, was putting the responsibility for peace or war not on the Nazi dictator but on the Czech President. And he was giving not only a military opinion on the outcome of the war but a diplomatic opinion about the ultimate peace terms in regard to which, to say the least, he lacked competence. Moreover during the day, he tried the same argument with the French.

In Paris the government, assailed by the antiwar groups of both Right and Left (except the Communists), undermined by what General Gamelin termed the "intrigues" of Bonnet and discouraged by the bluntly expressed defeatism of the chief of the Air Force, was again wavering behind the façade of firmness which the smooth mobilization and the formal rejection of the Godesberg ultimatum had helped to establish. On September 26 the semiofficial *Le Temps* had published a letter from Flandin, who as a former Premier and Foreign Minister and still leader of the principal Center Party, the Alliance Democratique, carried considerable weight in Parliament and in the country. "I oppose," wrote Flandin, "the military intervention of France in the struggle between the Sudeten Germans and the Czechoslovak state." The next evening he had posted on the walls of Paris flamboyant posters:

YOU ARE BEING DECEIVED!

People of France, you are being deceived! A cunning trap has been set . . . by occult elements to make war inevitable. . . .

Though the police, on the orders of Sarraut, the Minister of Interior, promptly tore the posters down, Flandin's message was published in Doriot's Fascist afternoon *La Liberté,* subsidized by Nazi Germany. Police confiscated as much of the edition as they could.

On the Left, too, there was concerted action against war. The pacifist wing of the CGT, the Confederation of Labor, issued a violent manifesto against "an imperialist war" in support of "a country arbitrarily created," as it termed Czechoslovakia. On September 27 two powerful unions, that of the public-school teachers and the employees of the PTT (Post, Telephone, and Telegraph) published in the press a proclamation saying that war would be "a collective suicide" and that the "people were being lied to" about fighting to defend the Czechs.

The same afternoon a delegation of deputies from the Right, led by Flandin, called on the Foreign Office "for an explanation." Bonnet seemed glad to see them and did his best, according to the available evidence, to encourage them to continue their efforts for peace at any price, casting doubt on Britain's word by saying he had "no confirmation" of the Foreign Office communiqué of the 26th and backing Hitler's contention that there was really no difference between the Godesberg demands and the Anglo-French plan, which the Czechs had been forced to accept. According to one of the deputies, Jean Montigny, Bonnet told him, "with tears in his eyes": "Reynaud is crazy. We're heading for disaster. I beg you to do everything you can."[50] The delegation had rushed off to see the President of the Republic and the Premier, but Lebrun refused to see it "on constitutional grounds" and Daladier because he was too busy.

The meeting of the cabinet that morning had been confused. Daladier shrunk back from asking approval for a general mobilization but it was decided to go ahead with the calling up of several classes, which would put more than a million men in the field. Debate on giving in to Hitler's ultimatum, which expired at 2 P.M. the next day, brought out sharp divisions in the cabinet. According to a "Very Urgent, Top Secret" telegram "for the Reich Foreign Minister personally" dispatched by the German Chargé in Paris, whose Embassy had a very highly placed informant,* Bonnet, along with two other cabinet members, was "for yielding." According to Pierre Renouvin, one of the few French historians to have access to some of the still unpublished confidential state papers, Bonnet said flatly: "We must not give Czechoslovakia armed support."[52]

In that frame of mind the French Foreign Minister that morning had proposed to the British that they agree on a German occupation on October 1 of the Sudetenland as outlined in the Anglo-French plan—that is, of the territory with more than 50 percent Sudeten inhabitants, though there had

---

* This informant, mentioned in the telegram as such, was Count Fernand de Brinon, a notoriously pro-German French journalist whose confidential contacts included Bonnet and even Daladier. Cofounder in 1933 of the Comité France-Allemagne and its president thereafter, he used this organization, which had been organized ostensibly to foster better Franco-German relations, to further German Nazi propaganda in France. An early friend of Otto Abetz, the chief Nazi agent in Paris, and of Ribbentrop, the Nazi "specialist" on foreign affairs and by this time, 1938, German Foreign Minister, he fed confidential information to the Nazi government, not only through the Embassy in Paris but directly during his frequent visits to the Reich. He boasted of having had five private talks with Hitler between 1933 and 1937. His marriage to a wealthy Jewish widow did nothing to dilute his pro-Nazi sentiments. Brinon was one of a number of Frenchmen who at this time began to sell out to Germany. Named Vichy's Ambassador to the German occupation authorities in Paris (1941–45) he became one of the leading French collaborators with the Nazi occupiers. After the war he was tried for high treason, convicted, and condemned to death on March 6, 1947 and shot on April 18. The German Chargé's dispatch of September 27, 1938, warns Berlin that Brinon already was under French surveillance and that because of this "he will probably call on me this evening at my house."[51]

not yet been time for anyone to ascertain exactly what its limits were. Phipps wired Bonnet's proposal to Lord Halifax at 6:35 P.M., adding that "M. Bonnet feels we must . . . do everything possible to avert a conflict for which both our countries are undoubtedly ill-prepared."[53]

Actually Bonnet's proposed concession to Hitler went further than even the British thought of going at that moment. Before it was received in London Halifax had wired Ambassador Henderson in Berlin to propose merely a German token occupation on October 1 of the strip around Eger and Asch, which jutted into Germany and from which the Czech forces already had been withdrawn. Halifax further suggested that German, Czech, and British representatives meet on October 3 to delimit the new frontier, work out plans for its peaceful turnover to Germany, and arrange for the entry of Hitler's troops on October 10.[54]

The British Foreign Secretary was playing for time but his Ambassador in Berlin did not like it. He fired back a telegram to London the next day reporting that he had given the Germans the British proposal but that it was "quite useless since there is not the slightest chance that Hitler will accept it or even consider it. Facts must be faced," he admonished his chief in Downing Street.

Unless Czechs by tomorrow notify German Government that they are prepared [to accept] memorandum the invasion of Czechoslovakia begins Thursday [September 29] or very soon after. If a general conflict with all its dangers to us and its certain disaster to European civilization is to be averted this can only be achieved by Czechoslovak acceptance of German memorandum.

Henderson had just seen a copy of the telegram from Phipps on Bonnet's latest proposal, and he could not refrain from commenting:

It is useless and fatuous of M. Bonnet to talk of our two countries being unprepared for such a conflict and at the same time to refuse to put necessary pressure on Czechoslovakia to yield by informing her at once before midday September 28 categorically that if she does not do so we shall not support her.[55]

In the meantime the British had renewed their pressure to convince the French government that nothing could save Czechoslovakia except surrender to Hitler's ultimatum. Late in the afternoon of Tuesday, September 27, Chamberlain, as we have seen, had sent such an admonition to Beneš in Prague. Some three hours later, at 8:30 P.M., Halifax wired Phipps instructing him to see Bonnet, or, if possible, Daladier, and impress on the French government the uselessness of trying to save Czechoslovakia.

General Gamelin made it plain to us on Monday that, in his view, if German forces now invaded Czechoslovakia, Czech resistance is likely to be of extremely brief duration. . . .* If therefore our efforts for peace fail, and instead German troops enter Czechoslovakia on Thursday [September 29], as now seems probable, we may expect to be faced in a very short time with a *fait accompli,* so far as Czechoslovakia is concerned. No declarations or actions of France or ourselves in the meantime can prevent this sudden and overwhelming result. . . . The latest information requires us to face the actual facts. . . .

Halifax then proceeded in his telegram to ask the French government to "concert its action" with Britain

especially as regards measures which would be likely immediately and automatically to start a world war without unhappily having any effect on saving Czechoslovakia.

We would be glad to know that French Government agree that any action of an offensive character taken by either of us . . . shall only be taken after previous consultation and agreement.[57]

The British government at this late hour was bluntly demanding a veto over any French military action in support of its commitments to Czechoslovakia.

The French Foreign Minister quickly conceded it. Just before midnight Ambassador Phipps was able to telegraph a reply.

Minister for Foreign Affairs [Bonnet] tells me that the French Government are in entire agreement not to take any offensive measures without previous consultation with and agreement by us.

---

* This opening sentence in the Foreign Secretary's message, which Bonnet omitted in the version of the document he published in his memoirs, led to bitter charges by General Gamelin against the French Foreign Minister. "It was for me," the generalissimo wrote in *his* memoirs, "a very painful affair. It originated solely in the intrigues of M. Georges Bonnet." Declaring that at the London meeting on September 26 he had not himself spoken to Lord Halifax, Gamelin says he "learned later what I always suspected: that Lord Halifax got from Bonnet the declaration which he attributed to me. And Bonnet used it to declare that I was opposed to an energetic solution."

While General Gamelin's views about the ability of the Czechoslovak army to hold out were certainly not optimistic—as late as September 12 he had told Daladier, it will be remembered, that "we cannot defeat the German army before it takes most of Czechoslovakia"—he had told Chamberlain on the 26th that if the Czech forces retired into Moravia "they would continue to exist as a fighting force." And anyway, as he had always argued, much depended on what France, Britain, and Russia did. Bonnet, Gamelin charges, continued to falsify his position in order to show that France could do nothing to save Czechoslovakia. On September 29, the generalissimo noted in his diary: "M. Bonnet, it appears, is saying in the corridors of the Chamber: 'the best proof that we can do nothing is that General Gamelin has advised the Czech High Command to beat a retreat.' "[56]

The Ambassador added:

His Excellency feels more and more that it behooves us both to be extremely prudent and to count our probable and even possible enemies before embarking on any offensive act whatever.*[58]

Bonnet was desperately looking for a way out. The British seemed to offer the best way. For if London withheld "agreement" on French "offensive action" this would be a good excuse for not taking it. Daladier and the majority of his cabinet had not yet gone so far. On returning from the London meeting the day before, September 26, the Premier, as he later testified, had felt certain that war was inevitable. He says he drew up the order for general mobilization and also prepared the text of a broadcast to the nation "to explain to the French people that despite all our efforts for peace we had to intervene in the face of German aggression."[60]

Later in the afternoon of the 27th came a blow from his Air Force chief that made him again waver and which, he frankly admitted to this author in a long conversation in Paris a quarter of a century later (1964), was perhaps the chief consideration that forced him to make the crucial decisions of the next four days. The previous morning General Vuillemin had conferred with Guy La Chambre, the Minister of Air, and repeated the warning he had made to the Defense Committee on March 15 and to Ambassador François-Poncet in Berlin in August: that the French Air Force was too weak to fight effectively if war came and would be quickly wiped out by the Germans. At the Minister's request he put his jeremiad in writing and this came to the attention of Daladier the next day. It was a chilling document.[61]

France had only 700 planes, General Vuillemin reported: 250 day fighters, 320 bombers, and 130 reconnaissance craft. They would be greatly outnumbered by the German Luftwaffe, and the French planes were not much good anyway. The "day" bombers, he explained, could only operate by daylight a short distance into Germany and then only if the weather was favorable, that is, "by using cloud cover." They were meant "normally for night operations" but even at night "they would run into great difficulties in discovering their objectives." Thus the value of their attacks on enemy troop concentrations and on war factories would be "limited."

On the all-important matter of losses, the Air Force chief was somewhat more optimistic than he had been in March and August when he

---

* Bonnet was beginning to see even certain Czech diplomats as enemies. The next morning Phipps sent a special telegram to Chamberlain: "Bonnet assures me that M. Beneš, through his Ministers in London and Paris, has been carrying on a regular campaign against yourself and French Government and working with all the forces in favor of a 'preventive war.' "[59] Bonnet and Phipps appear to have convinced themselves that to resist German aggression was to fight a "preventive war."

had warned that his entire "aviation" would be wiped out in a fortnight. Now he estimated that the

losses during the first weeks would be very heavy and could not be replaced. They would amount to 40 percent of the initial strength by the end of the first month of hostilities, and 64 percent of the remainder by the end of the second month.

Thus the French Air Force cannot carry out its missions without extreme difficulties and at the price of heavy losses. I must add that the reserves of materiel in the depots are practically nonexistent.

There was no use counting on effective British aid in the air, he admonished. "The British contribution agreed upon by the General Staffs will not add much to our strength." He conceded that the British bombers were of good quality but would arrive very late: 120 planes on D-Day plus 7; 120 more by D-Day plus 25.

So much for the woeful inadequacy of the democratic allies in the air. But General Vuillemin did not stop there. He next dwelt at length on the disastrous consequences of this to the *land* forces and to the armament industries and centers of population.

Without sufficient aerial reconnaissance, he said,

the Army High Command will be very poorly informed of the intentions of the enemy, while he, on the contrary, will know in time of all our preparations. Thus the operations of large army units will be considerably troubled and the performance of various arms (artillery, infantry, tanks . . .) will be seriously diminished.

The Air Force chief went on and on—behind Gamelin's back, as the generalissimo complained two days later*—to bolster his contention that without suitable aviation the French land army would be hard put to accomplish anything.

Thus the concentration of French land forces can be gravely troubled and subjected to very important delays. It will be the same for its transport.

Also, land operations will be rendered very difficult as the result of the power and frequency of enemy air intervention at the rear of the armies and on the field of battle itself.

Finally, General Vuillemin wrote, enemy air attacks on war industries, especially on factories producing planes, would "greatly reduce production,"

---

* "On the 28th, I learned indirectly," writes General Gamelin, "that without telling me, despite my role as Chief of the *Etat-Major* of National Defense, the Minister of Air and the Chief of the Air Force advised Daladier that our aviation was incapable of fighting a war. General Vuillemin acknowledged this to me only several days later." [62]

whereas French bombers could do very little damage to German industries. And in his concluding paragraph the Air general warned of the consequences of "massive and repeated enemy air attacks on the great centers of population."

The report of the Air Force chief was enough to frighten any civilian minister, and the Premier was profoundly depressed by it. He braced himself—the long day of September 27 was not quite over—to listen to what the British Prime Minister would say in his broadcast at 8:30 P.M. to the British people. Its content did not much improve his spirits, for it expressed not only Chamberlain's horror of war but his doubts that one was worth fighting for Czechoslovakia, and it closed on an ambiguous note: The Prime Minister had not abandoned hope for peace but on the other hand he did not see what further he could do to preserve it.

> How horrible, fantastic, incredible it is that we should be digging trenches and trying on gas masks here because of a quarrel in a faraway country between people of whom we know nothing!

Hitler, Chamberlain said, had got the "substance of what he wanted" and Britain had guaranteed that the Czechs would give it.

> However much we may sympathize with a small nation confronted by a big and powerful neighbor, we cannot in all circumstances undertake to involve the whole British Empire in a war simply on her account. If we have to fight, it must be on larger issues than that.
>   . . . I shall not give up . . . hope . . . or abandon my efforts for peace as long as any chance for peace remains. But at this moment I can see nothing further I can usefully do in the way of mediation.

Nothing further? An hour and a half after the broadcast, at 10:30 P.M., came Hitler's letter, and as the Fuehrer must have foreseen, the Prime Minister grasped at the straw. He sat down immediately and replied.

> After reading your letter I feel certain that you can get all essentials without war and without delay.
>   I am ready to come to Berlin myself at once to discuss arrangements for transfer with you and representatives of Czech Government, together with representatives of France and Italy if you desire.
>   I feel convinced we could reach agreement in a week. . . . I cannot believe that you will take the responsibility of starting a world war which may end civilization for the sake of a few days delay in settling this longstanding problem.*[63]

---

* Daladier says he did not learn of this letter until several weeks later when it was published in a British White Paper. But the British Foreign Office documents make clear that the text was wired to Paris the next morning, the 28th. Indeed Halifax instructed Phipps: "Please inform French Government and enlist their support."[64]

This "last appeal," as Chamberlain called it, to the Nazi dictator in Berlin was followed by another to the Fascist dictator in Rome. Apprising Mussolini of what he had written to Hitler, the Prime Minister asked the Duce to support his proposal, to urge Hitler to accept it, and to inform the German Chancellor that Italy would be willing to join in a conference at Berlin to work out the transfer of the Sudetenland to Germany.[65]

The idea of a conference had been in the back of the Prime Minister's mind for some time. As far back as July, Sir Neville Henderson had suggested it on his own in a dispatch to London, proposing that four powers, Germany, Italy, Britain, and France, settle the Sudeten problem. But both the Ambassador and the Prime Minister had been reminded by the Foreign Office that it would be difficult to exclude other powers from such a conference, that is, Russia, which had a pact of mutual assistance with Prague, and Czechoslovakia.[66] Chamberlain had returned from Godesberg convinced that Hitler would never consent to any meeting which included the Soviet Union. Nor did the Prime Minister himself desire the presence of the Russians. Though it was obvious—or should have been—that in case of war with Germany, Soviet participation on the side of the West would be of immense value, as Churchill had repeatedly tried to remind the government, this was a view that apparently had escaped the Prime Minister.

But until Wednesday, September 28, when his letter was delivered to Hitler, he had not yet gone so far in his thinking as to exclude the Czechs from a conference. Indeed, on the 25th, after Prague had rejected Hitler's Godesberg demands, the Prime Minister had called in Jan Masaryk, the Czech Minister in London, and proposed that Czechoslovakia should agree to negotiations at "an international conference in which Germany, Czechoslovakia, and other powers could participate." On the following day the Czech government had accepted the proposal. And in his message to Hitler on the night of the 27th Chamberlain had specified that "representatives of Czechoslovakia" should be included in his proposed conference of Germany, Italy, Great Britain, and France.

Deep gloom hung over Berlin, Prague, London, and Paris as September 28 dawned. "Black Wednesday," some would call it, remembering that morning when war seemed inevitable.

"A great war can hardly be avoided any longer," Colonel Jodl quoted Goering as saying as the day began. "It may last seven years, and we will win it."[67]

In London the digging of trenches, the evacuation of the schoolchildren, the emptying of the hospitals, continued. In Paris there was a scramble for the choked trains leaving the city, and motor traffic out of the capital was jammed. There were similar scenes in western Germany, where an imminent French attack was feared. Jodl jotted in his diary that morning reports of German refugees fleeing from the border regions. At 2

P.M. Hitler's time limit for Czechoslovakia's acceptance of his demands ran out. There was no sign from Prague that they would be accepted.

To some of the German generals and to General Halder, Chief of the General Staff, above all, the time had come to carry out their plot to remove Hitler and save the Fatherland from plunging into a European war which they felt it was doomed to lose. All through the tense days of September the conspirators had been busy working out their plans. On the 27th they decided to act on the 29th. On the morning of "Black Wednesday," the 28th, General Erwin von Witzleben, who as commander of the troops in the Berlin area was to carry out the coup, exclaimed to his fellow conspirators: "The time has come!"

But they, as well as almost everyone else in Berlin and in the other capitals, were unaware of what was up at the very top. They knew nothing of Bonnet's proposal, which Ambassador François-Poncet received in Berlin at 4 A.M. on the 28th, to let the Germans occupy the preponderantly Sudeten districts with their troops on October 1. Nor were they aware of an even more important development: Chamberlain's proposal to Hitler for a conference of the Big Four powers and his appeal to Mussolini to back it.

All morning long that "Black Wednesday" in Berlin the French and British ambassadors tried frantically to present their proposals to Hitler before he dispatched his armies into Czechoslovakia. The attack, they believed, had been set for 2 P.M. But as the minutes and then the hours ticked away the Fuehrer showed no sign of wishing to receive them. François-Poncet had phoned at 8 A.M. for an appointment. When by 10 o'clock no response had been received he rushed off his military attaché, General Renondeau, to the Army General Staff to emphasize to the German generals, he says, "the responsibility of the High Command in case of war and to inform it of the message I was . . . as yet unable to deliver."[68] He also enlisted the aid of Ambassador Henderson, who was pleased to hear the French would at last go so far to meet the dictator's demands. Henderson telephoned Goering, who promised to try to make the appointment for the French Ambassador.

In the meantime Mussolini had acted. At 11 A.M. he got through on the telephone to his Ambassador in Berlin, Bernardo Attolico. The Germans listened in and recorded the call.

MUSSOLINI: This is the Duce speaking. Can you hear me?

ATTOLICO: Yes, I hear you.

MUSSOLINI: Ask immediately for an interview with the Chancellor. Tell him the British government asked me . . . to mediate in the Sudeten question. The point of difference is very small. Tell the Chancellor that I and Fascist Italy stand behind him. He must decide. But tell him I favor accepting the suggestion. You hear me?

ATTOLICO: Yes, I hear you.

MUSSOLINI: Hurry![69]

Out of breath, his face flushed with excitement (as Dr. Schmidt, the interpreter noted), Ambassador Attolico arrived at the Chancellery to find that the French Ambassador was already closeted with Hitler. François-Poncet had finally made it. Hitler had received him at 11:15 A.M. and the Ambassador had brandished a crude and hastily drawn map which showed large chunks of Czech territory which Bonnet was now ready to hand over to Germany on October 1. The Fuehrer seemed impressed—especially, as Dr. Schmidt noted—by the map, with its generous markings.

At 11:40, the interview was suddenly interrupted by an official who announced that Attolico had just arrived with an urgent message from Mussolini. Hitler left the room, with Schmidt, to greet the Italian Ambassador, who was attempting to catch his breath.

"I have an urgent message to you from the Duce!" Attolico, who had a naturally hoarse voice, shouted. After delivering it, he added that Mussolini begged the Fuehrer to refrain from mobilization.

It was at this moment, says Schmidt, the only surviving eyewitness to the scene, that the decision for peace was made. It was now almost noon, two hours before the time limit on Hitler's ultimatum to the Czechs ran out.

"Tell the Duce," Hitler said, with obvious relief, to Attolico, "that I accept the proposal."[70]

The rest of the day was anticlimactic. Ambassador Henderson followed Attolico and François-Poncet to the Fuehrer's presence.

"At the request of my great friend and ally, Mussolini," Hitler told Henderson, "I have postponed mobilizing my troops for twenty-four hours." He had already mobilized all the troops he had with any training, but the Ambassador was relieved. The Chancellor added that he would inform him further on the proposed conference after he had again consulted with Mussolini. A few minutes before 2 P.M. on September 28, just as his ultimatum was about to expire, Hitler made up his mind and invitations were hastily issued to the heads of government of Great Britain, France, and Italy to meet the Fuehrer at Munich at noon on the following day to settle the Czech question. No invitations were sent to Prague or Moscow. Russia, the coguarantor of Czechoslovakia's integrity in case of German attack, was not to be allowed to interfere. The Czechs were not even asked to be present at their own death sentence.

At five minutes to three on "Black Wednesday," the British Prime Minister had begun to address the House of Commons in London. The situation, which he depicted in great detail, was still uncertain, he declared, but it had improved. Mussolini, he said, had succeeded in getting Hitler to postpone mobilization for twenty-four hours. Chamberlain had spoken for an hour and twenty minutes and was about to finish when at 4:15 he was interrupted. A note was handed him.

Whatever view honorable members may have had about Signor Mussolini [Chamberlain was saying] I believe that everyone will welcome his gesture . . . for peace.

The Prime Minister paused, glanced at the note, and smiled.

That is not all. I have something further to say to the House. I have now been informed by Herr Hitler that he invites me to meet him at Munich tomorrow morning. He has also invited Signor Mussolini and Monsieur Daladier. Mussolini has accepted and I have no doubt Monsieur Daladier will accept. I need not say what my answer will be. . . .

There was no need. The ancient chamber, the Mother of Parliaments, reacted with a mass hysteria without precedent in its long history. There was wild shouting and a wild throwing of order papers into the air and many were in tears and one voice was heard above the tumult which seemed to express the deep sentiments of all: "Thank God for the Prime Minister!"

And what of the German conspirators who were on the point, or so they later said, of overthrowing Hitler and who shortly before noon on that fateful Wednesday believed, as General Witzleben declared, that their time had come. They called off the coup. They said Chamberlain, by agreeing to go to Munich, had made it unnecessary. They were prepared to oust the dictator to prevent him from launching Germany into a hopeless war. But now there would be no war.

General Halder, the Chief of the General Staff and the head of the conspiracy, explained it after the war.

It had been planned [Halder said] to occupy by military force the Reich Chancellery and [other] government offices. . . . On the day [September 28] Witzleben came to see me . . . during the noon hour. We discussed the matter. He requested that I give him the order of execution. We discussed other details —how much time he needed, etc. During this discussion the news came that the British Prime Minister and the French Premier had agreed to come to Hitler for further talks. . . . I therefore took back the order of execution because . . . the entire basis for the action had been taken away. . . .

We were firmly convinced that we would be successful. But now came Mr. Chamberlain and with one stroke the danger of war was averted. . . .*[71]

---

* For a detailed account of the conspiracy against Hitler just before Munich, see the author's *The Rise and Fall of the Third Reich,* Chapter 12.

The news that the heads of government of the Four Powers would meet in Munich to "settle the Czechoslovak problem" came as a deathblow to Prague, which had no illusions as to what would be done. In desperation Beneš wired Chamberlain through the British Minister in Prague.

I beg Mr. Chamberlain to do nothing at Munich which could put Czechoslovakia in a worse situation than under Anglo-French proposals. . . . I beg therefore that nothing may be done in Munich without Czechoslovakia being heard. . . .[72]

Already the Prime Minister had sent—the wires crossed—the Czech President an assurance "that I shall have the interests of Czechoslovakia fully in mind." As a sop to Prague, Halifax got off a message a little later that evening "advising" the Czech government to have a "suitable representative, authorized to speak on their behalf, available to go to Munich at short notice tomorrow."

The invitation on the afternoon of Wednesday, September 28, to come to Munich was accepted by Daladier with alacrity. It brought immense relief to Paris. During the morning, when all seemed black, the Premier had announced that he would broadcast to the people that evening. He intended to announce general mobilization and to affirm that France would honor its commitment to Czechoslovakia. The invitation to Munich caused a drastic change in his intentions. He went on the air briefly that evening, announcing that he would join the heads of governments of the other three powers at Munich, and explaining that in view of the coming negotiations it was his "duty to adjourn the explanations" which he had planned to make. He promised to continue his efforts "to safeguard the peace and the vital interests of France." The broadcast had a hollow sound. But all depended on how he stood up to Hitler—and indeed to Chamberlain—at Munich on the morrow.

The newspapers and politicians of all parties save the Communists hysterically welcomed his decision to go to Munich. Léon Blum in Le Populaire exclaimed that the news of the conference had raised "an immense response of joy and hope." It would have been "criminal," he wrote, to break off negotiations. "The sacred flame of peace," he concluded, "which had been flickering, has been rekindled." The moderate L'Aube urged further concessions to Hitler if necessary to save the peace.

Bonnet himself dodged accompanying his Premier to Munich. "I preferred," he says, "to remain in Paris and I asked M. Léger (the Secretary-General of the Quai d'Orsay) to replace me at the side of the head of government." He claims he set down in a memorandum the limits of concessions France could make to Germany. But his real thoughts were surely those he confided to his friend, the British Ambassador, who wired Halifax the next morning:

> Minister for Foreign Affairs last night and again this morning, when we saw Daladier off, begged me to urge you how absolutely vital he felt it was that an arrangement should be reached over Sudeten question at Munich at almost any price.[73]

General Gamelin made one feeble effort to keep that price from being ruinous to Czechoslovakia and disastrous to France. Daladier had asked him what, from a military viewpoint, were the limits of concessions which the West could make.

> I told him [Gamelin recounts] that if Czechoslovakia lost her natural frontiers, she would cease to have any effective military value. At the very least it was necessary to maintain in her hands her whole system of fortifications and to leave intact her main railway communications between the eastern and western parts so that she could remain "an economically viable state."

"I hope," Gamelin quotes Daladier as replying, "that we will not be reduced to that."[74]

21

THE CONFERENCE AT MUNICH
SEPTEMBER 29–30, 1938

$\mathbb{A}$rriving at Munich early in the morning from Berlin on his special train, Adolf Hitler continued on to Kufstein on the former Austro-German frontier to meet Mussolini in his special train from Rome. He was anxious to set up a common basis for action at the conference in case Chamberlain and Daladier proved stubborn or tried to stall for time. In his private car coming up to Munich the Fuehrer was in a bellicose mood, explaining to the Duce over maps how he intended to "liquidate" Czechoslovakia. Either the talks beginning at noon must be immediately successful, he said, or he would resort to arms.

"Besides, the time will come," he added, "when we shall have to fight side by side against France and England." Mussolini agreed.[1]

Chamberlain made no similar effort to see Daladier beforehand to work out a joint strategy for the two Western democracies with which to confront the two Fascist dictators. Indeed, it became evident to many of us in contact with the British and French delegations in Munich as the day progressed that Chamberlain had come to Munich absolutely determined that no one, certainly not the Czechs, and not even the French, should stand in the way of his reaching a quick agreement with Hitler. In the case of Daladier no precaution perhaps was necessary, but the Prime Minister took no risks.

The talks, which began at 12:45 P.M. on September 29, at the Fuehrerhaus on the Koenigsplatz at Munich, were informal, rather disorganized, and quite friendly. Dr. Schmidt, the indomitable interpreter, was struck by the "atmosphere of general goodwill." Ambassador Henderson remembered that "at no stage of the conversations did they become heated." No one presided. Each of the four heads of government spoke out as he wished. Argument was mostly on a low key. And it quickly became evident that in face of Hitler's adamant stand Chamberlain and Daladier were prepared to give in to him on every essential point.

Mussolini got the conferees down to business. "In order to bring about a practical solution of the problem," he said, "I wish to make the following proposal," whereupon he read it out.

Its origins are interesting and remained unknown to Chamberlain, I believe, to his death, and to Daladier, he himself told me in 1964, until the revelations of the Nuremberg trials. What the Duce now fobbed off as his own compromise plan had been hastily drafted the afternoon before in the German Foreign Office in Berlin by Goering, Neurath, and Weizsaecker behind the back of Foreign Minister Ribbentrop, whose judgment the three men did not trust. Hitler approved it, and it was hurriedly translated into French by Dr. Schmidt and passed along to the Italian Ambassador, Attolico, who telephoned the text to the Italian dictator in Rome just before he entrained for Munich. Thus it was that the "Italian proposals," which provided the informal conference not only with its sole agenda but with the basic terms which eventually became the Munich Agreement, were in fact German proposals concocted in Berlin.*

This must have seemed fairly obvious from the text, which closely followed Hitler's rejected Godesberg demands. But it was not obvious to Daladier and Chamberlain or to Sir Horace Wilson, or to the British and French ambassadors in Berlin who joined the discussions later in the afternoon. The French Premier, according to the German minutes (the only substantial ones kept), "particularly welcomed the Duce's proposal, which had been made in an objective and realistic spirit," and the Prime Minister "also welcomed the Duce's proposal and declared that he himself had conceived of a solution on the lines of this proposal." Wilson found them "a reasonable restatement of much that had been discussed in the Anglo-French and Anglo-German conversations." As for Ambassador Henderson, as he later wrote, he thought Mussolini had tactfully put forward as his own a combination of Hitler's and the Anglo-French proposals; while Ambassador François-Poncet got the impression that the conferees were working on a British memorandum "drawn up by Horace Wilson."[2] It was not difficult to dupe the Anglo-French statesmen and diplomats even at such a crucial moment in history as this!

---

* Erich Kordt, chief of the German Foreign Office Secretariat, recounted the German origins of Mussolini's proposals in his testimony before the U.S. Military Tribunal IV at Nuremberg on June 4, 1948, in the case of *U.S.A. v. Ernst Weizsaecker*. A summary from the official trial script is published in DGFP, Vol. II, footnote, p. 1005. Kordt also tells the story in his book *Wahn und Wirklichkeit*, pp. 129–31. Dr. Schmidt in his memoirs (*Statist auf diplomatischer Buehne 1923–1945*, p. 415) substantiates Kordt's account, remarking that translating the Duce's proposals at Munich "was easy" because he had already translated them the day before in Berlin. Ciano, the Italian Foreign Minister, in a diary entry of September 29–30 from Munich, tells of Mussolini's producing his document "which in fact had been telephoned to us by our Embassy the previous evening, as expressing the desires of the German Government." (*Ciano's Hidden Diary, 1937–38*, p. 167.)

Two minor arguments developed during the early part of the talks and in both cases the Western democracies gave in to Hitler. Chamberlain wanted to know who would compensate the Czech government for public property which would pass to Germany in the Sudetenland. He also objected to the stipulation that the Czechs moving out of the Sudetenland could not even take with them their cattle. "Does this mean," he asked, "that the farmers will be expelled but that their cattle will be retained?"

Hitler exploded. "Our time is too valuable to be wasted on such trivialities!" he snapped at Chamberlain. The Prime Minister dropped the subject.

He did insist at first that a Czech representative ought to be present, or at least, "be available." His country, he said, "could naturally undertake no guarantee that the [Sudeten] territory would be evacuated by October 10 [as Mussolini had proposed] if no assurance of this was forthcoming from the Czech government." Daladier gave his lukewarm support. The French government, he said, "would in no wise tolerate procrastination in this matter by the Czech government," but he thought "the presence of a Czech representative, who could be consulted, if necessary, would be an advantage."

But Hitler was adamant. He was "not interested," he said, "in an assurance from the Czech government." He would not suffer the presence of any Czechs. The two Western Prime Ministers began again to give way. "If the presence of a Prague representative will cause difficulties," Daladier said, "I am ready to forgo this." Finally, Chamberlain suggested "the presence of a Prague representative in the next room, in order that assurances could be obtained from him," and this was agreed to.

And so during the afternoon session two Czech representatives, Dr. Vojtech Mastny, the Czech Minister in Berlin, and Dr. Hubert Masarik, from the Prague Foreign Office, did arrive and were ushered into an adjoining room, out of sight. There they cooled their heels from 2 P.M. to 7, when the bad news began to be broken to them. At 7 o'clock Frank Ashton-Gwatkin, who had been a member of the Runciman mission and who, like his chief, had been charmed by the Sudeteners but not by the Czechs, came to give them an inkling of what the four statesmen were doing. They had reached a general agreement, the details of which he could not yet give them, he said, but which were much "harsher" than the Franco-British proposals which the Czechs had been pressured by London and Paris to accept. When Masarik asked if the Czechs could not be heard, the Englishman answered, as the Czech envoy later reported to his government, "that I seemed to ignore how difficult was the situation of the Great Powers, and that I could not understand how hard it had been to negotiate with Hitler."

Three hours later, at 10 P.M., the two unhappy Czechs were taken to Sir Horace Wilson, the Prime Minister's faithful adviser. On behalf of Chamberlain, Wilson informed them of the main points of the Four-Power

Agreement and handed them a map of the Sudeten areas which were to be evacuated at once. When the two envoys attempted to protest, the British official cut them short. He had nothing more to say, he stated, and promptly left the room. The Czechs continued to protest to Ashton-Gwatkin, who remained with them.

"If you do not accept," he admonished them, as he in turn prepared to go, "you will have to settle your affairs with the Germans absolutely alone. Perhaps the French may tell you this more gently, but you can believe me that they share our views. They are disinterested."

This was the truth, as the two Czech emissaries would quickly learn. Shortly after 1 A.M. on September 30, 1938,* Hitler, Chamberlain, Mussolini, and Daladier, in that order, affixed their signatures to the Munich Agreement providing for the German Army to begin its march into Czechoslovakia on October 1, as the Fuehrer had always said it would, and to complete the occupation of the Sudetenland by October 10. Hitler had got what had been refused him at Godesberg.

There remained the painful matter—painful at least to the victims—of informing the Czechs of what they had to give up and how soon. Hitler and Mussolini were not interested in this part of the ceremony and withdrew, leaving the task to the representatives of Czechoslovakia's ally, France, and of her friend, Great Britain. The scene was vividly described by Masarik in his official report to the Czech government.

At 1:30 A.M. we were taken into the hall where the conference had been held. There were present Mr. Chamberlain, M. Daladier, Sir Horace Wilson, M. Léger [Secretary-General of the French Foreign Office], Mr. Ashton-Gwatkin, Dr. Mastny, and myself. The atmosphere was oppressive: sentence was about to be passed. The French, obviously nervous, seemed anxious to preserve

---

* The agreement was dated September 29, though not actually signed until the early morning hours of September 30. It stipulated that the German occupation "of the predominantly German territory" should be carried out by German troops in four stages, from October 1 through October 7. The remaining territory, after being delimited by the "International Commission" would be occupied "by October 10." The commission was to consist of representatives of the four Big Powers and of Czechoslovakia. Germany, France, and Italy agreed "that the evacuation of the territory shall be completed by October 10, without any existing installations having been destroyed, and the Czechoslovak Government would be held responsible for carrying out the evacuation without damage to the said installations."

Further, the International Commission would arrange for plebiscites "not later than the end of November" in the regions where the ethnographical character was in doubt and would make the final determination of the new frontiers. In an Annex to the accord, Britain and France declared that "they stand by their offer . . . relating to an international guarantee of the new boundaries of the Czechoslovak State against unprovoked aggression. When the question of the Polish and Hungarian minorities . . . has been settled, Germany and Italy, for their part will give a guarantee to Czechoslovakia."[3]

The pledge of plebiscites was never carried out. Neither Germany nor Italy ever gave the guarantee to Czechoslovakia against aggression, even after the matter of the Polish and Hungarian minorities was settled; and, as we shall see, Britain and France declined to honor their guarantee.

French prestige before the court. Mr. Chamberlain, in a long introductory speech, referred to the Agreement and gave the text to Dr. Mastny. . . .

The Czechs began to ask several questions, but

Mr. Chamberlain was yawning continuously, without making any effort to conceal his yawns. I asked MM. Daladier and Léger whether they expected a declaration or answer of our government to the Agreement. M. Daladier was noticeably nervous. M. Léger replied that the four statesmen had not much time. He added hurriedly and with superficial casualness that no answer was required from us, that they regarded the plan as accepted, that our government had that very day, at the latest at 3 P.M., to send its representative to Berlin to the sitting of the Commission, and finally that the Czechoslovak officer who was to be sent would have to be in Berlin on Saturday in order to fix the details for the evacuation of the first zone. The atmosphere, he said, was beginning to become dangerous for the whole world.

He spoke to us harshly enough. This was a Frenchman. . . . Mr. Chamberlain did not conceal his weariness. They gave us a second slightly corrected map. Then they finished with us, and we could go.[4]

I remember from that fateful night the light of victory in Hitler's eyes as he strutted down the broad steps of the Fuehrerhaus after the meeting, the cockiness of Mussolini, laced in his special militia uniform, the yawns of Chamberlain and his air of pleasant sleepiness as he returned to the Regina Palace Hotel.

Daladier [I wrote in my diary that night], on the other hand, looked a completely beaten and broken man. He came over to the Regina to say good-bye to Chamberlain. . . . Someone asked, or started to ask: "*Monsieur le President,* are you satisfied with the agreement?" but he was too tired and defeated and the words did not come out and he stumbled out of the door in silence.[5]

Chamberlain was not through conferring with Hitler about the peace of the world. Early the next morning, September 30, refreshed by a few hours of sleep and obviously pleased with his labors of the previous day, he sought out the Fuehrer at his private apartment in Munich to discuss further the state of Europe and to obtain a small concession which he apparently thought would improve his political position at home. After a long and rambling monologue which on rereading thirty years later (from the notes of Dr. Schmidt[6]) seems incredible coming even from him,* the

---

* Among other things, Chamberlain expressed his "confidence" that Germany would "adopt a generous attitude in the implementation of the Munich Agreement" and renewed his hope that the Czechs would not be "so unreasonable as to make difficulties," and that, if they did make them, Hitler would not bomb Prague "with the dreadful losses among the civilian population which it would entail." He went on and

Prime Minister pulled out of his pocket a sheet of paper on which he had written something which he said he hoped they would both sign and release for immediate publication.

We, the German Fuehrer and Chancellor, and the British Prime Minister, have had a further meeting today* and are agreed in recognizing that the question of Anglo-German relations is of the first importance for the two countries and for Europe.

We regard the agreement signed last night and the Anglo-German Naval Agreement as symbolic of the desire of our two peoples never to go to war with one another again.

We are resolved that the method of consultation shall be the method adopted to deal with any other questions that may concern our two countries, and we are determined to continue our efforts to remove possible sources of difference, and thus to contribute to assure the peace of Europe.

Hitler read a German translation and quickly signed it—"with a certain reluctance . . . only to please Chamberlain," Schmidt, the interpreter felt. The British leader, he adds, was highly pleased and "thanked the Fuehrer warmly." The deluded Prime Minister did not know, of course, that, as we have seen, Hitler and Mussolini had already agreed at this very meeting in Munich that in time they would have to fight "side by side" against Great Britain and France.

Before going to bed on the night the Munich Agreement was signed Chamberlain had dispatched a telegram to the British Minister in Prague to make sure that the Czechs did not balk.

You should at once see President . . . and urge acceptance of plan. . . . You will appreciate that there is no time for argument; it must be plain acceptance. Your French colleague has received similar instructions. . . .[9]

---

on: to propose further cooperation in bringing an end to the Spanish Civil War (which German and Italian "volunteers" were winning for Franco), in furthering disarmament, world economic prosperity, political peace in Europe and even a solution of "the Russian problem."

* Behind France's back, as was the signing of the Anglo-German Naval Agreement of 1935. Bonnet declares that he and Daladier learned of the meeting of Chamberlain and Hitler and of the declaration they signed only from the newspapers. They immediately queried the British Foreign Office, which said it knew nothing about it. Finally they sent Ambassador Corbin in London to ask Chamberlain for an explanation. According to Bonnet, the Prime Minister "replied with his habitual sincerity," explaining that the Anglo-German declaration had not been "premeditated" but that during the course of their conversation Hitler had been so "reassuring on a number of proposals concerning Anglo-German relations" the Prime Minister had considered it advisable to put them down in writing.[7] We have it on the word of Dr. Schmidt, who as interpreter was the only other person present at the Chamberlain-Hitler meeting, that the Prime Minister "pulled out of his pocket" a copy of the declaration which he had already written out before he arrived.[8] Such were the petty deceits practiced even by one democratic ally toward another in those days.

Indeed, at 3:30 in the morning of the 30th, Daladier had got off an urgent telegram to the French Minister in Prague instructing him to see Beneš immediately "and assure his acceptance." The Minister was also instructed "to express the great emotion I have felt at the outcome of this meeting, at which it was not my fault if a representative of Czechoslovakia was not associated."[10] The petty deceits among supposed Allies continued. To the world the French Premier was already beginning to justify what he had done. To the French journalists at Munich he said: "I believe we have done the reasonable thing. Should fifteen million Europeans have been killed in order to oblige three million Sudeteners, who wished to be German, to remain in Czechoslovakia?" To the German official news agency, DNB, he declared: "Thanks to the great understanding of the representatives of the Great Western Powers war has been avoided and an honorable peace assured to all peoples."

Inwardly, as he later admitted, he felt "a great bitterness" at the abandonment of "a faithful ally."[11] He feared he would be booed on his return to Paris. Seeing a huge crowd at Le Bourget as his plane approached the landing field at 3:30 P.M., on the 30th, he asked the pilot to circle the field until he could regain his composure and prepare a few remarks to quiet what he was sure was a hostile crowd. It turned out to be just the opposite. He was wildly acclaimed—as was Chamberlain on his return to London—and half a million Parisians turned out on the route between the airfield and the Ministry of Defense in Paris to cheer him. To the nation he said over the radio at Le Bourget:

I return with the profound conviction that this accord is indispensable to the peace of Europe. We achieved it thanks to a spirit of mutual concessions and a close collaboration.

To General Gamelin, waiting among the crowd of notables at the airport, he whispered: "It wasn't brilliant, but I did everything I could." Gamelin was thinking of the 35 Czech divisions lost, and Reynaud needled him by asking: "Where are you going to find 35 new divisions now?" Daladier, who was Minister of Defense as well as Premier, could not fail to think of them too. Still surprised at the tumultuous welcome along his route back to the capital he is reported to have turned to an aide and said: "The imbeciles—if they only knew what they were acclaiming!"[12]

In Prague the stunned Czechs sought to face the fact that the Munich Agreement spelled the end of their centuries-old dream for true independence which they had enjoyed for so brief a time—nineteen years. When the French and British ministers called at the Foreign Office to tell the government that it would have to accept the Four-Power Pact and to express their sympathies, Dr. Krofta, the Foreign Minister, cut them short. "Everything is at an end," he said bitterly. "Today it is our turn, tomorrow it will be the turn of others." The cabinet sat all morning with the military leaders at the Hradčany Palace under the presidency of Beneš. At ten minutes to one on September 30 it accepted the inevitable and surrendered, "under protest to the world," as the official statement put it. "We were abandoned," General Sirovy, the new Premier, explained to the people in a broadcast at 5 P.M., "We stand alone."

Back in Paris, General Gamelin, the most reflective of military chiefs, reflected on what had happened at Munich. *"C'était fini,"* he later recalled thinking. "Germany had won a new victory and a great one."[13]

But the French people, in the government, in Parliament, in the press, in the streets, rejoiced that peace had been preserved. That was their only concern. The irrepressible Flandin dashed off a telegram of congratulations to Hitler, who replied: "I am grateful for your efforts . . . on behalf of an understanding and complete collaboration between France and Germany. . . ."*

The press, with few exceptions, was delirious in its praise of Daladier and Bonnet for having joined with Chamberlain, Hitler, and Mussolini to "save" the peace. Even Léon Blum in *Le Populaire* was carried away.

There is not a woman or a man in France who will refuse MM. Neville Chamberlain and Edouard Daladier their just tribute of gratitude. War is spared us. The calamity recedes. Life can become natural again. One can resume one's work and sleep again. One can enjoy the beauty of an autumn sun.

The press of the Right expressed not only jubilation that war had been avoided but vituperation against the handful of Frenchmen who had sought to have the government stand up to Hitler and honor its word to Czechoslovakia. "Peace is won," exulted Stéphane Lauzanne† in *Le Matin.* "It is won over the crooks, sellouts, and madmen." *Le Temps* expressed its relief that "a few farsighted and courageous leaders had triumphed over the 'war party.' "

There was also the fatuity. Colonel de La Rocque exclaimed in *Le Petit Journal:* "What a marvelous and extraordinary people we are!" He contended that France had showed "prodigious firmness, good sense and wisdom." Bonnet, greatly enjoying his momentary popularity as the chief French architect of Munich, was happy to note that "many newspapers, even on the extreme Left, presented the Munich Agreement as a success for the skillfulness and the firmness of French diplomacy." He believed, he wrote, "that France was *sans reproches.*" And to his local constituents

---

* It was later established that he sent similar congratulations to the other three heads of government.

† Lauzanne was convicted as a collaborator after the war and sentenced to a long term in prison.

he was quoted in the capital's largest newspaper, *Le Petit Parisien,* as saying:

> There is one criticism which I refuse to accept, and that is that France was not loyal to her signature. France's signature is sacred. Czechoslovakia wasn't invaded, was she?[14]

On October 4, after a brief debate during which Daladier passionately defended the Munich Agreement, it was approved by the Chamber by 535 to 75. Besides the 73 Communists only two deputies, Kerillis on the Right, and Jean Bouhey, a Socialist, voted against. It was a vote which faithfully reflected the feelings of the French people. As the eminent historian Pierre Renouvin noted: "This policy of abandoning the treaty of alliance received the assent of the majority of the cabinet and of Parliament. And finally it was approved by the bulk of public opinion."[15]

On October 5, the day after the overwhelming vote in the French Chamber, Beneš, under pressure from Berlin, resigned as President of Czechoslovakia, and having been warned that his life was in danger, flew a few days later to London and exile.

That day, too, Winston Churchill spoke out in the House of Commons. "We have sustained a total, unmitigated defeat," he began by saying, but he was forced to pause until the storm of protest against such a statement subsided. He went on.

> We are in the midst of a disaster of the first magnitude. The road down the Danube . . . the road to the Black Sea, has been opened. . . . All the countries of Mittel Europa and the Danube valley, one after another, will be drawn in the vast system of Nazi politics . . . radiating from Berlin. . . . And do not suppose that this is the end. It is only the beginning. . . .

But Churchill at that time was a voice in the wilderness, excluded from the Conservative government, which regarded him as a maverick, and with but a handful of followers in the House. The overwhelming majority, in the Commons as in the country, like that in the French Chamber and among the French people, had only one feeling: relief that they had been spared war.

In Berlin the German generals breathed a sigh of relief too—in private. Like the recently resigned Chief of the General Staff, General Beck, and like the new one, General Halder, they knew what Chamberlain and Daladier were ignorant of: that the German Army in the fall of 1938 was not strong enough to fight a European war with any hope of winning it. They were doubtful if it even had the power to penetrate the Czech fortifications, and they had no illusions that in the West, where the Siegfried Line was a mere skeleton, as Jodl said, their 12 divisions, most of them half-trained reserves, could hold out against the 100 well-trained divisions of the French Army. At the Nuremberg trial after the war the generals frankly admitted this. Asked on the stand what the reaction of the German military leaders was to Munich, General Wilhelm Keitel, chief of OKW, replied:

We were extraordinarily happy that it had not come to a military operation because . . . we had always been of the opinion that our means of attack against the frontier fortifications of Czechoslovakia were insufficient. From a purely military point of view we lacked the means for an attack which involved the piercing of the frontier fortifications.[16]

General van Manstein, who would become one of the most brilliant of the field commanders when war finally came, testified similarly on the German position at the time of Munich.

If a war had broken out, neither our western border nor the Polish frontier could really have been effectively defended by us, and there is no doubt whatsoever that had Czechoslovakia defended herself, we would have been held up by her fortifications, for we did not have the means to break through.[17]

Even Hitler became at least partly convinced of this after he had inspected the Czech fortress line. He later told Dr. Carl Burckhardt, League of Nations High Commissioner of Danzig:

When after Munich we were in a position to examine Czechoslovak military strength from within, what we saw of it greatly disturbed us; we had run a serious danger. The plan prepared by the Czech generals was formidable. I now understand why my generals urged restraint.[18]

As in 1936, when the French Army had not budged after the Germans sent a handful of troops into the Rhineland, Hitler's generals were surprised that the Western democracies had not taken into account again in 1938 the overwhelming superiority of the French Army in the West. Colonel (later, General) Jodl, who had said that in 1936 on the Rhine the French "covering force could have blown us to pieces," also testified at Nuremberg on the military position in the West at the time of Munich.

It was out of the question, with five fighting divisions and seven reserve divisions in the western fortifications, which were nothing but a large construction site, to hold out against 100 French divisions. That was militarily impossible.[19]

If, as these German generals concede, Hitler's army lacked the means of penetrating the Czech fortifications, and Germany, in the face of France's overwhelming strength in the West, was in a "militarily impossible" situation there, and further, since, as we have seen, there was such grave dissension among the generals that the Chief of the Army General Staff himself was prepared to overthrow the Nazi dictator in order to avoid a hopeless war—why then did Chamberlain and Daladier abjectly surrender to Hitler at Munich? Was it because Franco-British Military Intelligence had completely broken down and was incapable of rendering a factual estimate of German military strength? Here we confront one of the mysteries of the Munich time that has not yet been cleared up. Neither the British nor French documents so far released shed much light on it.

It is clear from what evidence we have that the French High Command grossly overestimated the strength of the German Army in the West. On September 12 Generals Gamelin and Georges had told Daladier that the Germans would have on the Western front "50 to 60 divisions from the start," an exaggeration of four or five times.[20] Did they exaggerate German strength, as they had in 1936 at the time of the Rhineland coup, in order to have an excuse for their holding back? If not, then what was their reason? Gamelin in his lengthy memoirs does not answer the question. Presumably he knew nothing of the crisis in the German High Command, of the resignation of General Beck an August 18, of General Adam's warning to Hitler that he could not possibly hold in the West because he lacked the troops and because the Siegfried Line was far from completed. The French generalissimo does not mention them except obliquely when he recounts what he told Chamberlain in London on September 26 of "German weaknesses: A High Command which realizes the dangers it faces; a fortified system not yet finished; great deficits in cadres, lack of trained reserves; lack of raw materials, especially oil." And we have the word of Daladier, who was in close touch with his Army chief, that he knew nothing of these weaknesses in the German Army, or of General Halder's conspiracy to overthrow the Fuehrer.*

It was later argued by the supporters of Munich that the sacrifice of Czechoslovakia gave Britain and France nearly a year's respite in which to catch up with Germany in rearming. The fact is that the breathing space, as subsequent events would prove, left the Western allies much weaker in relation to Germany than they had been at Munich. The tempo of German production of planes and tanks and guns was far ahead of that of the democracies and to it was shortly added not only the output of the Czech Skoda works, the third largest armament producer in Europe, but the vast stores of military equipment eventually taken over from the Czechs. The equivalent of 35 divisions that the Czechs had trained was subtracted from the overall strength of the French, and Hitler would make good use of the "respite" by training vast reserves and finishing the Siegfried Line in the West. Finally, and most important of all, the Western democracies lost Russia as an ally in the interval.

---

* See above, p. 354, footnote.

For France, though few in Paris realized it or wished to realize it, Munich was a disaster. Her military position in Europe vis-à-vis Germany was destroyed. Because her army, when the Reich was fully mobilized, could never be much more than half the size of that of Germany, which had nearly twice her population, and because her ability to produce arms was also substantially less, France had laboriously built up her alliances with the small powers in the East on the other flank of Germany—and of Italy: Czechoslovakia, Poland, Yugoslavia, and Romania, which together, if they hung together, had the military potential of a Big Power. The loss of 35 Czech divisions, deployed behind their strong mountain fortifications and holding down an even larger German force, was in itself a crippling blow to the French Army. Moreover, Munich, following the *Anschluss,* gave Germany a stranglehold on the entire Danube and Balkan region, bolstering her economic strength, which had been relatively weak until 1938.

There was another loss. After Munich how could France's remaining allies in Eastern Europe have any confidence in her word? What value now were alliances with France? The answer in Warsaw, Belgrade, and Bucharest was: "Not much"; and there was a scramble in those capitals to make the best deal possible, while there was still time, with the Nazi conqueror, and to abandon France.

And how did the one Big Power in the East, linked, like Czechoslovakia, to France by a Pact of Mutual Assistance, feel about France's word? The answer was given on October 4, the day the Chamber so overwhelmingly approved the Munich accord, by the *Journal de Moscou.*

> Who will believe again the word of France? Who will remain her ally? Why would the French government, which has just annulled "of her own accord" her pact with Czechoslovakia, respect the Franco-Soviet Pact?

The Soviet government might be clumsy in its behavior but it was not naïve. It realized perfectly well that at Munich Hitler had not only humbled France and Britain but had forced them to join him in excluding Russia from the concert of powers disposing of a country which it had pledged to help to defend if France did. And it resented being kept out in the cold. The Germans made no secret of their elation over this aspect of Munich. As the *Hamburger Fremdenblatt* exulted: "Germany has succeeded in eliminating Soviet Russia from the concert of the Great Powers. Such is the historical aspect of Munich." And Field Marshal Keitel later told the Nuremberg tribunal: "The object of Munich was to get Russia out of Europe."

On the morning the Munich conference began Halifax had tried lamely to explain to the Soviet Ambassador in London why Russia had not been invited to the meeting. The fact was, he told him, "as he very well knew, that the heads of the German and Italian governments would not be willing in present circumstances to sit in conference with Soviet representatives." The Foreign Secretary begged him "not to misinterpret the fact" and "assured him that there was no desire on our part to see the Soviet Government in any way excluded."

Such an astute and tough envoy as Ivan Maisky was not impressed by such hypocrisy and he "pressed" him, Halifax reported, with a great many questions, which the Foreign Secretary, by his own account, tried to dodge as best he could. The Ambassador's "attitude," Halifax recounted, "seemed to me, as indeed it was likely to be, one of some suspicion."[21]

In Moscow suspicion gave way to a determination to draw the inferences of Munich and to act accordingly. When on October 4 Ambassador Coulondre, on the instructions of Bonnet, went to the Foreign Office in Moscow to "explain" the Munich Agreement (his throat was "rather dry," he says, "at the prospect of such a disagreeable mission"), Vladimir Potemkin, the acting head in the absence of Litvinov in Geneva, responded coolly at first and then emotionally.

I take note that the Western Powers deliberately kept Russia out of the negotiations. . . . My poor friend [he said after a long silence], what have you done? You have opened the way to a fourth partition of Poland.

The implication did not escape the French Ambassador. A new partition of Poland could only take place with the collusion of Russia and Germany. That evening Coulondre got off a long dispatch to Bonnet warning him that the Soviet Union most probably would now "return to the entente with Germany which it abandoned in 1931" and eventually join with her in carving up Poland between them. "From France," he added, "the U.S.S.R. expects for the moment nothing more." On October 18 the Ambassador saw Litvinov, who had just returned from Geneva, and reported to Paris: "We must count on the Kremlin soon approaching Berlin . . . to sound out its intentions."[22]

The German Embassy reported the same reaction in Moscow to the Munich Pact. On October 3 the counselor of the Embassy, Werner von Tippelskirch, got off a dispatch to Berlin on the "consequences" of Munich for Soviet policy. He thought Stalin "would draw conclusions"; he was certain the Soviet Union would "reconsider her foreign policy," become less friendly to her ally, France, and "more positive" toward Germany. As a matter of fact, the German diplomat advised Berlin that "the present circumstances offer favorable opportunities for a new and wider German economic agreement with the Soviet Union."[23]

A week after Munich, then, both the French and German governments were made aware of a change in the wind in Moscow which, within ten months, would have momentous but differing consequences for both.

The surrender at Munich further exposed the growing weaknesses of the Third Republic. The government, the Parliament, the Army, the press, the people, drew back on the brink from honoring the nation's word and from standing up to Hitler. The French, paralyzed by the fear of war, mindful that the last one against Germany had bled them white and nearly destroyed them, lost track of the long-range interests of the country, sacrificing them for immediate gains, or what they thought were such, though this was an illusion. Gripped by paralysis they were unable to assess their own strength and, even more important, the strength of the coalition which might have allied the Western democracies with Russia and the smaller states in the East in a combination powerful enough to destroy the aggressive ambitions of Nazi Germany once and for all. To be sure, Great Britain, which suffered a similar blindness to its long-term national interests and was equally fearful of war—and of Hitler—had brought, as it had at the time of the Rhineland coup in 1936, much pressure on France to join her in giving in. But a great nation must stand on its own feet if it is to survive. Since 1936 France had abdicated its independence in foreign policy, subordinating it to that of Great Britain. On the road to Munich it was Britain which called the tune in making one concession after the other to Hitler, cajoling France into following her disastrous lead.

The military High Command had scarcely been a source of strength in the crisis. Having closed its mind, as we have seen, to the revolutionary changes in modern war caused by the development of the tank and plane and having also become mired in a stale and static philosophy of defense behind the Maginot Line, it shrunk back, as much as did the politicians, from the risk of war. The general commanding the Air Force panicked. And he panicked the government at a crucial moment by his cry that the air arm was good for nothing in a conflict. The leading Army generals, with Gamelin at their head, seemed to share the general paralysis. To the government they deliberately exaggerated, as they had in 1936, German strength in the West as an excuse for their timidity. Even worse, they took no resolute action either on their own or in influencing the government to work out military plans with the Russians and the Czechs which would have greatly enhanced the chances of an anti-German coalition to crush Hitler if he launched war. The generals, as well as the statesmen, rebuffed all the efforts of the Russians to institute staff talks. And despite France's commitments, they refused even to hold staff talks with the Czechs. There is something shocking—but also pitiful—in the letter of General Gamelin to the Commander of the Czech Army, General Sirovy, on September 27— at the very climax of the crisis—saying that "in the present situation I cannot enter into relations with the Czech General Staff."[24] How could France honor its commitments to Czechoslovakia if the head of the French Army was forbidden, or thought he was, to "enter into relations" with the head of the Czech Army?*

---

* Actually, according to the terms of a secret agreement signed by the foreign ministers of France and Czechoslovakia January 26–31, 1924, which General Gamelin publishes in his memoirs (Vol. II, page 469), staff talks between the two

For that matter, how could she honor them when her Foreign Minister was prepared to go to any length by whatever deception to get out of them? Daladier, as he showed at the two London meetings in September, understood what Hitler really was up to—domination of Europe—but he lacked the iron will or even the persuasiveness to prevail either with the British government or within his own.

In the last resort and particularly in a representative democracy, the people are responsible. Henri Noguères has observed that during the Czech crisis public opinion in France, as in England, "pushed its fear of war to a point of collective cowardice." It is understandable that the French people, hardly recovered from the Great War, had no stomach for another blood-bath. What is more difficult to understand is that they had no instinctive understanding of one of the lessons of history: that fighting a war is sometimes necessary in order to survive if a nation is faced by an aggressive, power-hungry enemy bent on her ultimate destruction or enslavement. True, the government and the press failed to impress this upon them. The leading newspapers backed the Bonnet line, and many of them that of Flandin. Of what importance were the Czechs, or France's word to them, or the consequences of surrendering to Hitler? The only thing that counted was peace.

Nor did the public realize how it was being poisoned and misled, not only by Fascist-minded leaders and newspapers, small in number but growing in influence, who on ideological grounds wished to accommodate Hitler and Mussolini, but also by Frenchmen who were being manipulated by German agents and German money. It was at this time that Otto Abetz, the genial "Francophile" Nazi German agent in Paris, became most effective. Easily penetrating political, business, social and cultural circles he worked tirelessly at winning their sympathies for Nazi Germany. He engineered trips with all expenses paid, for numerous politicians, intellectuals, industrialists, and leaders of the war veterans' groups to Germany, where they were wined, dined, and otherwise feted, and fed with Nazi propaganda. He obtained lucrative contracts for French writers to have their books translated and published in Germany. He arranged interviews for French journalists with Hitler so that the Fuehrer could reiterate that he wished only peace and friendly relations with France. He was believed by the French secret police, which constantly shadowed him, to be the chief source of Nazi funds for buying French journals, journalists, and others of influence. Doriot's openly Fascist daily, *La Liberté,* was almost entirely subsidized by Berlin. This was probably an exception. As Pierre Comert, the chief of

---

countries were explicitly provided for. The agreement, Gamelin himself writes, "provided that the General Staffs of the two countries will continue to collaborate 'both in matters concerning the establishment of concerted plans to meet an aggression directed against one of the two countries by a common enemy and in matters concerning the study of respective means of assistance in the case of their common interests being menaced.' "

the Press Service at the Quai d'Orsay, testified to the Parliamentary Investigating Committee later: "The German agents at this time didn't buy
newspapers. They bought journalists. It was cheaper. And it was more
effective."[25]

Aside from the cheapening of moral values which followed inevitably
from the abandoning of Czechoslovakia, the Munich settlement further
deepened and complicated the already calamitous divisions among the
French. At first sight this seems paradoxical since a majority of the Right
and Left appeared united in welcoming the safeguarding of peace at the
mere price of sacrificing a small nation in Central Europe. Actually, to
the traditional differences between the Right and the Left was added a
split within each group. A small but powerful minority in each camp opposed
Munich, and the bitterness between it and the majority was for a time
greater than that between the Left and the Right. But the new fracture, as
the historian Goguel remarked,

left intact the old ones. Remembrance of the political struggles pursued since
1936 continued to poison the atmosphere. . . . On one side and the other the
recent events were judged in the light of the old criteria, neither of them realizing that these had become in a large measure inadequate to the concrete
problems facing France at the end of the thirties.[26]

France just after Munich was difficult to comprehend for an old
friend and admirer such as this writer. I spent a few days there after covering
the Munich conference.

Paris [I wrote in my diary from the capital on October 8, 1938] . . .
completely surrendered to defeatism, with no inkling of what has happened to
France. . . . The guts of France—France of the Marne and Verdun—where
are they? Outside of Pierre Comert no one at the Quai d'Orsay with any idea
at all of the real Germany. The French Socialists shot through with pacifism;
the French Right, with the exception of a few like Henri de Kerillis, either
Fascists or defeatists. France makes no sense to me any more. . . .

What had happened to the great country? Brooding in Moscow after
Munich, Ambassador Coulondre began to realize. Later he put it down in
writing.

Munich tolled the bell for a certain France, *la grande France* of former
times and even of 1914. . . . The tolling bells do not kill a sick man; they
announce his death. The accord of Munich did not provoke the fall of France.
It registered it.[27]

No one of course could know for sure as the eventful year of 1938 drew toward a close. Disastrous it had been for France, and that this was scarcely realized in the country made the disaster worse. But the future is never certain, however predictable it may seem. In this old and splendid civilization lay deep sources of strength which could renew it.

I fled the city that autumn. Not all the lights and beauty and the sight of familiar, loved places and of old friends could relieve the foreboding one felt for the year ahead.

22

THE TURN OF POLAND
1939

After the Czechs, the turn of the Poles, who also were allies of France.

This was as evident as that night follows day—except to the Polish political leaders, blinded by their foolish illusions and driven by a fateful flaw that some historians have seen in the national character of this brave and dashing people, which urged them toward self-destruction, making them their own worst enemies. "Glorious in revolt and ruin; squalid and shameful in triumph," Winston Churchill had called them.[1] Re-created by the victorious Allies at Versailles after a century and a half of partition among Germany, Russia, and Austria, Poland had not used its new freedom and independence very wisely or with much restraint. It had scarcely been established by its Western friends before it was waging war against Russia, Germany, Lithuania, and even Czechoslovakia—in each instance to grab disputed territory.

Its western borders had never been really accepted by Germany, nor its eastern borders by Russia. The Germans, long before Hitler, bitterly resented the establishment at Versailles of the Corridor, which gave Poland access to the sea but cut off East Prussia from the Reich. Nor did they accept as final the detachment of the old Hanseatic port of Danzig from Germany and its creation as a so-called Free City under the supervision of the League of Nations, but dominated economically by Poland. Even the weak and peaceful Weimar Republic was determined one day to undo what it regarded as the Polish mutilation of the German Reich. In 1922, General Hans von Seeckt, the chief of the Reichswehr, had defined—secretly—the attitude of Germany.

Poland's existence is intolerable and incompatible with the essential conditions of Germany's life. Poland must go and will go—as a result of her own internal weakness and of action by Russia—with our aid. . . . The obliteration of Poland must be one of the fundamental drives of German policy . . . [and] is attainable by means of, and with the help of, Russia.[2]

Russia, now Bolshevik, had not forgotten that Poland in two years of warfare against her in 1920–1921—while she was weakened by the losses of the Great War, by civil war and by the attacks of the Western Allied nations—had, at the expense of the Soviet Union, pushed the Polish frontier 150 miles east of the ethnographic Curzon Line, a frontier which had transferred four and a half million Ukrainians and one and a half million White Russians to Polish rule. Thus Poland's western and eastern borders were considered subject to change by Germany and Russia respectively—a fact which seems to have been lost sight of by the Poles and by the Western democracies when they first learned to their consternation that Berlin and Moscow, implacable enemies though they had been since the advent of Hitler, showed signs in the summer of 1939 of drawing together.

A virtual military alliance with France had saved Poland in 1920 when its armies, after occupying Kiev, the capital of the Ukraine, on May 8, had been hurled back in July by a Russian counteroffensive to the gates of Warsaw. A French military mission under General Maxime Weygand had been rushed to the Polish capital to help reorganize its defenses and plan a counterblow. Among the French officers serving in the Polish combat forces was a young captain who had been captured by the Germans at Verdun in 1916 and shortly after his return from a prisoner-of-war camp had joined the 5th Division of Polish Chasseurs. This was Charles de Gaulle. His leadership won him a citation from General Weygand, whom fate would pit him against twenty years later, and the gratefulness of the Poles, who awarded him the Cross of St. Wenceslaus and persuaded him to remain in Warsaw as a professor in the new War College.

Thanks largely to General Weygand, his French officers and French arms, the Poles drove the Russians back in a great counteroffensive launched on August 14, 1920. The following year, on February 19, 1921, the illustrious Marshal Foch himself signed a secret military agreement with Poland by which the two allies agreed to support each other in case of German or Russian aggression. The French promised to arm the Polish army and train it. A "permanent" collaboration of the two general staffs was established. Poland, the largest of the newly created countries in Eastern Europe, became the bastion of the French system of alliances against Germany in the East. And France became Poland's virtual protector.

Then suddenly at the beginning of 1934 the Polish leaders faltered and played into the hands of Hitler. At the Fuehrer's urging they signed a ten-year Pact of Nonaggression with Germany on January 26. The two governments agreed not only to renounce force against each other but to settle their problems "by direct negotiations." For Hitler, it was a shrewd move; for Poland, it was bound to lead to disaster.

As long as Danzig and the Corridor existed as they were, there could be no lasting peace between Poland and Nazi Germany. But in the meantime, by inducing the Poles to negotiate with him directly, Hitler could bypass the League of Nations, which Germany had just left, weaken its drive toward "collective security" from which Poland stood to gain so much, undermine the system of Versailles, to which Poland owed its rebirth, and begin to detach Warsaw from its close ties with France, which had sustained the Poles for fifteen years. Most of the sources of strength which enabled Poland to exist were to be abandoned. Though Marshal Pilsudski, the strong man of Poland and its virtual dictator, signed the Nonaggression Pact with Germany, he was already a sick man and died the following year. The man largely responsible for pushing Poland into the German trap was Colonel Joseph Beck, Foreign Minister since 1932. He had harbored a grudge against the French ever since 1923, when, as Polish military attaché in Paris, he had been expelled for allegedly selling documents stolen from the French Army. For the Nazi dictatorship he had felt a warm sympathy from the beginning and after the signing of the Pact at the beginning of 1934 he brought Poland closer and closer to Germany—and farther and farther from France.

The day after the Munich Agreement he had, in cahoots with Hitler and against the pleas of France, sent an insulting ultimatum to Czechoslovakia demanding that she turn over Teschen to Poland, and on October 1 had sent Polish troops like hyenas, to grab this bit of territory from a stricken Czechoslovakia, thus helping to weaken her further and to make her ripe for Hitler's final designs on her.

These designs were carried out on March 15, 1939, after Hitler had achieved a masterpiece in trickery and deceit. On March 14 he had engineered a proclamation of "independence" by Slovakia, thus breaking up the Czechoslovak nation. That evening he received the aging, frightened Czech President, Emil Hácha, in Berlin and after threatening that Prague would be bombed to ruins "within two hours" and the rest of what remained of the country, Bohemia and Moravia, devastated by the German army and air force, forced him to "request" the Fuehrer to take the Czech people under his protection. This was done the next day, when German troops poured into the stricken country, occupied Prague without resistance, and enabled Hitler to proclaim from Hradčany Castle the German Protectorate of Bohemia and Moravia.*

Czechoslovakia had ceased to exist. Britain and France, which had guaranteed the little country against unprovoked aggression after they had

---

* A detailed account of Hitler's machinations in taking over Czechoslovakia is given in my *Rise and Fall of the Third Reich*.

sacrificed so much of it at Munich, declined to honor their word, contenting themselves with feeble protests in Berlin, which were scornfully rejected. Slovakia too "appealed" for the Fuehrer's "protection" in a telegram that actually had been drafted in Berlin, and Hitler quickly obliged by sending German troops into that land.* They now surrounded Poland, which had so obligingly helped with the dismemberment of Czechoslovakia, on three sides.

Hitler's occupation of Czechoslovakia on March 15, 1939, jolted the French and British governments, awakening them at last to the true nature of the German dictator and his ambitions. After Munich they had complacently proceeded on the assumption that the Fuehrer was now satisfied and would allow Europe to rest in peace. Had he not solemnly declared that the Sudetenland constituted his last territorial demand in Europe and that he "wanted no Czechs"? Chamberlain, as so often before, had taken him at his word, as had Bonnet.

The French Foreign Minister, basking in what he thought was his triumph in saving the peace at Munich, had persuaded the cabinet to approve his signing a Declaration of Friendship with Germany similar to the one wrung by Chamberlain from Hitler the morning after the Munich Conference. It pledged Germany and France to maintain peaceful and friendly relations and to consult about mutual problems. I happened to be in Paris on December 6, 1938, the day it was signed by Bonnet and Ribbentrop, and noted the frosty atmosphere in the streets and in the corridors of the Chamber and Senate. The Presidents of the two Chambers, Herriot and Jeanneney, several cabinet members, and many leading figures in political, literary, and social circles declined to attend the public functions accorded the Nazi Foreign Minister. One got the impression that the French, after their defeatist panic of the Munich days, were beginning to recover their senses and regain their distrust of Berlin. Nevertheless, Bonnet regarded the Declaration as a further triumph for himself and for his diplomacy of getting along with the Germans. Ribbentrop left Paris with his own interpretation of his talks with the French Foreign Minister and quickly passed it on to Hitler. This was that France had given Germany a free hand in Eastern Europe. Bonnet would later deny it. But the Fuehrer had already been convinced of it by the French surrender at Munich. It was not quite true. France, after all, had an alliance with Poland and a Pact of Mutual Assistance with the Soviet Union. The question, after March 15, 1939, was: what were they worth?

Bonnet was consternated by the news that the Germans had occupied Czechoslovakia. But his first concern was that, despite the Franco-British

---

* Hungary, which had been given a large slice of Slovakia shortly after Munich, was pressured by Hitler to occupy Ruthenia in the eastern regions of the old Czechoslovakia and did so on March 15.

guarantee, nothing be done about it except to protest. "Bonnet maintains
. . . we cannot intervene in any way," Ambassador Phipps wired Halifax.[3]
"A *fait accompli*," Bonnet explains in his memoirs. "It is too late to take
military measures just as it is also too early, since we are still not ready."[4]
He seems always a man who wants it both ways, or neither way.

Daladier was more serious. Though shocked like everyone else in the
West by what he termed Hitler's "act of brutality," he was not much surprised. Had he not told the British during the two meetings in London during the previous September that the German dictator's real aim was not to
grab the Sudetenland but to destroy Czechoslovakia, then turn on Poland
and finally on the West? Now he tried to face up to the consequences of
Hitler's latest aggression. The Munich Accord and the Franco-German
Declaration, he told a secret meeting of the Foreign Affairs Commission of
the Senate on March 19,

are in ruins. The events of the last few days have created an entirely new
military and strategic situation. If France does not face up to the consequences
there will be a stampede among the friendly countries which until now have
been firm. It will be a rush toward servitude. . . . And we must have no
illusion as to what will happen thereafter. New invasions will come to our
country and threaten to submerge it.[5]

Without waiting for Hitler's next conquest the French shortly after
Munich had bestirred themselves to strengthen their military capability of
eventually opposing him. On November 12, 1938, Daladier had notified
General Gamelin that the government would provide special credits of 25
billion francs for rearmament in 1939 and suggested that most of it go to
the Air Force for new planes. No mention was made of tanks. On December 5 the Permanent Committee of National Defense met to decide on how
to spend the money. The extent of the effort to be made by the country was
stressed by the new Minister of Finance, the energetic Paul Reynaud. The
military credits of 25 billions plus the regular military budget of 15 billions,
or a total of 40 billions for defense, he explained, amounted to 85 percent
of the expected receipts of the government in 1939.

But it developed that even more money would have to be spent.
Daladier announced that the American government had secretly agreed to
sell 1,000 military planes of the latest model to France for two and a half
billion francs and to deliver them by the summer of 1939. Combined with
her own production this would give France 3,000 new planes by the end of
the year and thus considerably close the dangerous gap between the French
Air Force and the Luftwaffe. It was decided to buy the American aircraft.

The problem of the British dragging their feet in rearming came up.
General Gamelin remarked that the British could put in France only two
divisions at the outset of hostilities and but 120 planes. It would be a long
time before her army could provide any substantial support—"several

years," he said. Paul Reynaud, pro-British though he was, bristled. "We shall have to ask the British," he said acidly, "to make a greater effort—if they do not want to accept a German hegemony on the Continent." But Daladier cautioned about being too "brusque" with the English. "They have finally recognized," he said, "the bankruptcy of their disarmament policy. They are beginning to rearm. We cannot really reproach them."

Finally, the question of France's weakness in the air having been dealt with, General Gamelin brought up the other glaring military weakness of France. Tank production, he said, must be stepped up. "The Germans," he warned, "have five armored divisions and two mechanized divisions. We have two of the latter, will soon have a third, plus one armored division."* But instead of demanding that the French try to catch up with the Germans in armored divisions the generalissimo again showed that resignation that was so characteristic of him. "Unfortunately," he added, "we cannot do more. . . ."[6]

Three days before, on December 2, at a meeting of the War Council attended by Marshal Franchet d'Esperey (Marshal Pétain was listed as absent) and fifteen ranking generals, Gamelin had taken up the question of tanks—with his customary reserve and timidity. He who just two years before had scoffed at the wisdom of the Germans' building armored divisions† had now come around to see their value. But he still did not understand very well how to use them. The War Council had been called primarily to decide on the "composition" of an armored division, though the French military attaché in Berlin, as we have seen, had already reported in detail on the makeup of the German version as far back as 1935 and the Army, at Gamelin's urging, had been "studying" the matter ever since. A lively discussion began between General Gamelin and General Pierre Héring as to what the armored division should be made up of and how it should be used. The generalissimo, though now—finally—conceding that the unit was "a rare and precious instrument," argued that it must be "reserved . . . for exploitation of force at a decisive point in the battle. It must not be used, except rarely, at the beginning of an action. With the development of antitank obstacles and guns it should not be employed until our regular large units have cleared the way." This was a fatal error. The Germans already had decided that the armored division, acting on its own, or in an armored corps, quite independent of the regular forces, must spearhead an offensive in order to achieve a decisive breakthrough, with the regular infantry and artillery, motorized if possible, following as quickly as they could to exploit and occupy the gap. Gamelin, in essence, was putting the cart before the horse. He could only conceive of the armored division,

---

* A mechanized division was composed mostly of light tanks and armored cars and was designed essentially for reconnaissance, the role formerly taken by the horse cavalry. An armored division was made up mostly of heavy and medium tanks, with its own motorized artillery and infantry.

† See above, p. 318.

as the minutes say he stressed, "acting within the framework of the regular army corps."

General Héring disagreed. He argued that the armored division must have the autonomy to act on its own.

General Gamelin [the minutes reveal] objects . . . The armored division is not made for operating in the dark but within the framework of large regular units already in the line which will provide the necessary security. General Georges is of the same opinion.

General Georges was already designated to command the northeast front against the Germans and ultimately did so. His ideas of armored warfare were thus of considerable importance. He took issue with General Héring, declaring that to make the armored division completely self-supporting and powerful enough to assume the mission of piercing the enemy defenses would necessitate making it too cumbersome. "One cannot conceive," he said, "of giving the means of organic exploitation to the armored divisions, which will not have the occasion to utilize them except rarely." But this was exactly the role to which the Germans had assigned them. However, Gamelin and Georges maintained that the tank units would always be dependent upon the regular infantry and artillery.

General Héring [the minutes continue] says he is disturbed at the idea that the far-reaching action of the armored division should be limited in such a regrettable way by being obliged to advance in successive jumps according to the classic process of slow attacks based on the movement of infantry and artillery. . . . If we really want to do something new we must not attach the armored division to the regular artillery. The tanks have their own artillery and can also be supported by attack planes.

But his two superiors rejected any such idea.

How little they understood the use of armored divisions as a means of lightning warfare was shown in a bizarre discussion that now ensued. The confidential minutes of the meeting disclose that General Garchery pointed out that "at night the tanks must be retired, refueled, and repaired." At this point, he said, they must be guarded by the infantry. General Gamelin agreed. "In all probability," he said, "the action of the armored division will be terminated before nightfall and by that time the regular reconnaissance forces or the light mechanized divisions will have caught up with them."

The question of the size of motorized infantry and artillery units to be integrated into an armored division was then discussed. Gamelin submitted that both must be small. Again, though General Héring continued to protest, Gamelin insisted that regular units of infantry and artillery would largely suffice to support the tank divisions. Anyway, Gamelin concluded, it was "premature" to decide "definitely" on such matters. Premature at the end of 1938! It was finally agreed that a second armored division would be formed but General Colson, Chief of the Army General Staff, "added" that the two armored units would not be fully constituted before the beginning of 1941. Two years hence! Despite the ominous happenings beyond the Rhine the French generals were still in no great hurry.[7]

Why not? General Gamelin certainly understood the significance of those happenings. And it made him pessimistic. His true feelings were conveyed to Daladier the next day, December 3, in a letter to the Premier, who was also Minister of Defense, accompanying a confidential report of the Army General Staff on the situation as of November 30. The rapid buildup of the German army and air force, Gamelin wrote, is such

that one can say that by next spring Germany will be in a position to wage war simultaneously against Poland and France. . . . If we continue to be faced with the ambitions of Rome and Berlin, France will be in no condition to attack Germany initially with any chance of success. If France is content to maintain herself within her own boundaries she will soon be unable to retake, without important British help, a Belgium which Germany can rapidly submerge. Soon perhaps France will be powerless even to attack Italy over the Alps. . . . The situation can very quickly become quite grave, even for the defense of our territory.[8]

The general's intelligence enabled him to see the situation quite clearly. But the lack of an urge to act made him resigned. He could tell his Prime Minister that the situation was grave, that militarily France was becoming progressively weaker relative to the Rome-Berlin Axis. But he could not bring it upon himself to insist resolutely that France do much more to strengthen itself than it was doing. As he would say on December 5: "Unfortunately we cannot do more."

The generalissimo's apprehensions were further deepened the following spring (1939) by what seemed to him, and to many others, the recklessness of the British, jolted by Hitler's occupation of Czechoslovakia, in suddenly giving—what they had refused to give the Czechs—unilateral guarantees to the remaining small countries in Eastern Europe that Germany coveted—and by France following, as usual, uncritically, in Britain's wake.

In London, Chamberlain, who had staked so much on the appeasement of Hitler and gone so far in it, was a little slow to react to the Fuehrer's takeover of Czechoslovakia. In the Commons on March 15 he excused his decision not to honor his country's guarantee to Prague on the grounds that the "declaration" of Slovakia's "independence," which he knew to have been engineered by Berlin, "had put an end by internal disruption to the state." The Prime Minister refused to accuse Hitler of breaking his word. "I do not wish to associate myself," he said, "with that charge." He even maintained the next day in the House that "so far" no protest had been sent to Berlin. This, at least, was true, for the British note to the German government on March 15, after stating that "His Majesty's Government have no desire to interfere unnecessarily" . . . merely added that it "would deplore any action in Central Europe which would cause a setback to the growth of . . . confidence."

Even Bonnet had gone further than that. He had instructed Ambassador Coulondre, who had moved from Moscow to Berlin, to tell the Germans that they had violated both the Munich Agreement and the Franco-German declaration of December 6 and that France refused to "recognize" the *fait accompli* in Czechoslovakia.

Suddenly and unexpectedly on March 17, two days after Hitler rode triumphantly into Prague, the British Prime Minister experienced a great awakening. That evening he was scheduled to make a speech in his home city of Birmingham and he had drafted an address on domestic matters with emphasis on the social services. On the afternoon train going up to Birmingham the awakening occurred. He scrapped his prepared speech and jotted down notes for a new and quite different one. Apologizing for his "very restrained and cautious . . . somewhat cool statement" to the Commons two days before, he now publicly proclaimed that Hitler had deceived him, that the Munich accord had been "wantonly shattered" and that Great Britain would "resist to the utmost of its power" any attempt by Germany to swallow up a new country.

On the last day of March he announced to the Commons a unilateral British guarantee of Poland. If she were attacked Britain would lend her "all support in their power." Stung, as he was, by Hitler's deceit, the peace-loving Prime Minister now proceeded recklessly to add guarantees to other countries in Eastern Europe that felt threatened by Nazi German ambitions, persuading France to follow him. Already on March 23 the British and French had issued a formal declaration that they would intervene militarily in case of aggression against Holland, Belgium, or Switzerland. On April 13, a week after Mussolini, jealous of Hitler's successes, had invaded and occupied little Albania, which gave Italy a springboard for an attack on Greece, a joint Anglo-French declaration promised armed support of Greece and Romania if they were attacked. The same day the French government publicly and formally confirmed the Franco-Polish alliance, each state "guaranteeing the other immediately and directly against any menace, direct or indirect, which threatened their vital interests." A month later, on May 12, Great Britain concluded a treaty of mutual assistance with Turkey, and France followed suit on June 23 after ceding the disputed territory of the sanjak of Alexandretta to the Turks.

This was, on the part of the British, a sudden reversal of policy which, as Churchill said, had no parallel in history. But having foolishly given so much away their position was much weaker and that of Germany much stronger. They now showered their guarantees right and left without much thought as to how they could give them weight. How could Britain, it was asked in Paris, help Poland or Romania—or for that matter, France—when it had no army? The French naturally welcomed the spate of British guarantees since they themselves were already committed to Poland and, to a slightly lesser extent, to Romania and Yugoslavia. Yet there were misgivings in Paris at the British being so precipitate. It would take time, the French knew, to organize a military coalition with the Eastern countries and it would take time for the British to reestablish an army—they had only decided to resort to the draft on April 27. In the meantime, Germany could, as General Gamelin had warned Daladier, strike—both in the East and in the West.

In Paris the generalissimo followed the intense diplomatic activity of the Quai d'Orsay and the British Foreign Office with some apprehension. He regretted, he says, that the French General Staff had not been consulted about taking on so many commitments. He wondered why Yugoslavia, whose army was the strongest in the Balkans, was left out when the guarantees were being scattered about and he concluded that it was done so as not to offend Italy, whom Bonnet was now trying to woo away from Germany. Above all, he says, had he been consulted, he would have proposed "precise military conversations parallel with these political declarations. It is all right to engage in a noble gesture. But it is better to know where it leads." He wondered why "we had not demanded anything in exchange from Romania and Greece"? He was thinking, as subsequent events would show, of Romanian oil going to Germany and of the use of Salonika in Greece as a possible front against the Germans, which it became in the first war.

And finally, he asked, "could we not profit from the occasion by settling the thorny question of the eventual collaboration of Poland and Russia, which risked being the stumbling block to an entente with the latter country?"[9]

So General Gamelin saw, or says he did, what should have been obvious to everyone in the West, but was not—that Russia was the key to the situation that uneasy spring not only for the Western democracies but also for Germany.

THE FRANCO-BRITISH TALKS WITH RUSSIA: I

On March 18, 1939, three days after the disappearance of Czechoslovakia, Litvinov had proposed—as he had just a year before, immediately after the disappearance of Austria—a conference, this time of six powers, France, Britain, Poland, Russia, Romania, and Turkey, to meet at once in Bucharest to establish a "peace front" to stop Hitler. The proposal was received coolly in Paris and London. Bonnet does not mention it in his voluminous memoirs, and there is no record of what he did about it, if anything. To the British Prime Minister the idea was "premature." His government, he told the Commons on March 23, was not "anxious to set up in Europe

opposing blocs." He was still highly distrustful of Moscow.* The furthest
he would go, he told Bonnet on March 21 when the French Foreign Minister arrived in London with President Lebrun, who was paying a state visit,
was to suggest that France and Britain join Poland and the Soviet Union in
a formal declaration stating that they would "consult immediately" about
steps to halt further aggression in Europe. Bonnet agreed and the same day
the suggestion was put to Colonel Beck in Warsaw, who rejected it so far as
including Russia was concerned. He was even more distrustful of the Soviet
Union than Chamberlain and moreover shared the British Prime Minister's
views about the worthlessness of Russian military aid.

Thus in declining to respond to the Soviet proposal for an immediate
conference to set up an anti-Hitler coalition Britain and France deliberately
muffed the first opportunity to line up Russia on their side.† Even Bonnet
understood that without the military help of Russia Poland could not be
defended. Suddenly alarmed at the prospect of letting the Soviet Union go
by default he asked Daladier to call a meeting of the Committee of Defense
to consider the matter. The Easter holidays had brought further news that
increased the tension in Paris. On Good Friday, April 7, the Italians had
invaded Albania. The next day, Gamelin records, there had been an "alert"
after Intelligence had reported significant moves of German troops on the
borders. Rumors were rife of a Nazi coup in Danzig. The Polish Foreign
Minister had felt it necessary to warn the Germans that such an action
would bring war between the two countries. Though most of the cabinet
members had left Paris for the holidays, the key ones were asked to return
and General Gamelin was summoned from an inspection tour of the Alps,
where the French were hastily reinforcing their troops on the frontier with
Italy. The urgent meeting of the Defense Council took place late on Easter
Sunday, April 11.

A good part of the discussion was taken up with Italy and it was
decided that in case of hostilities the French armed forces would concentrate at first on a knockout blow against the Italians. But Bonnet was concerned chiefly about Russia. Poland, he said, refused to talk to Russia. He
therefore proposed the opening of direct diplomatic talks with Moscow in
an effort to get the Russians to agree to come to the aid of Poland and
Romania if they were attacked. The French would then undertake to clear

---

* "I must confess," Chamberlain wrote in a private letter on March 26, "to
the most profound distrust of Russia. I have no belief whatever in her ability to
maintain an effective offensive, even if she wanted to. And I distrust her motives.
. . ." (Feiling: *The Life of Neville Chamberlain*, p. 603.)

† In explaining to the Soviet Ambassador in London, Ivan Maisky, on March
19 why the Russian proposal for a conference at Bucharest was "not acceptable," Lord
Halifax said that no minister of the Crown could be spared for the moment to go to
Bucharest. This initial rebuff seems to have soured the Russians in the subsequent
negotiations with the British and French. Maisky later told Robert Boothby, a Conservative member of Parliament, that the rejection of the Soviet proposal for a
conference had been "another smashing blow at the policy of effective collective
security" and that it had sealed the fate of Litvinov.[10]

the matter with Warsaw and Bucharest. But this was being unrealistic. On March 20 the Soviet government had gone out of its way to explain in a public statement that there could be no question of Russia giving Poland and Romania a guarantee of assistance unless they asked for it, which they had not done. The Defense Committee nevertheless approved Bonnet's proposal, and also a second one: to have the French military attaché in Moscow take up with Marshal Voroshilov the military aspect of the problem.[11] This second suggestion was also unrealistic. For the Russians had made it plain, as we have seen, that in their opinion serious military talks between France and the Soviet Union, which they had urged for years, could only be held at the General Staff level. The French had put them off. Though the confidential minutes of the meeting, which Gamelin published in his *Mémoires,* say that he acquiesced in the proposal to have the French military attaché in Moscow get in touch with Voroshilov, they make clear that he did not push the matter nor suggest that military conversations be held between the General Staffs. He remarks complacently in a footnote to the minutes that in the subsequent military talks he did not himself receive any "precise information" and "obviously" was only interested in their "general sense."[12]

It is clear that at this point in time, with the Germans quite obviously preparing an attack on Poland and with Italy pushing into the Balkans, the French—and the British—were not very serious about lining up the Russians in a military alliance against Hitler. Apparently they did not understand that at this juncture they needed the Soviet Union more than it needed them. They were committed to the defense of Poland and Romania. Russia was not. It still had a choice. Moreover, the Franco-British guarantees of Poland and Romania had added to Russia's security on her western frontiers, without her having had to give anything in return. If honored, they would make it more difficult for the German armies to drive through these two buffer states to the Soviet border, since Britain and France were obligated to attack Germany in the West.

At any rate, it was obvious, or should have been, that the hardheaded dictator in the Kremlin did not intend to risk committing his country to the Western Allies unless he could get guarantees that they would really honor their word this time and specify exactly by what military measures and with what military forces they would carry out their commitments. After Munich the Kremlin remained highly suspicious of the West. It feared that Chamberlain and Daladier were more concerned with pushing Germany into a war with the Soviet Union than with forging a Triple Alliance to stop the Germans, as it had in the first war.

Stalin had issued a warning to the West five days before the Nazi occupation of Czechoslovakia. On March 10, 1939, speaking to the Eighteenth Party Congress in Moscow, he had castigated France and Britain for abandoning Austria and Czechoslovakia and for trying to "embroil" Germany in a war against the Soviet Union. They were, he said, pushing the Germans further eastward, promising them an easy prey and saying: "Just start a war with the Bolsheviks, everything else will take care of itself!" This looks very much like encouragement. . . . It looks as if the purpose . . . was to engender the fury of the Soviet Union against Germany . . . and to provoke a conflict with Germany. . . .

In conclusion, Stalin laid down certain "new tasks," the chief of which was, he said, "not to let our country be drawn into conflict by warmongers, whose custom it is to let others pull the chestnuts out of the fire for them." This attitude in Moscow must be kept in mind when we follow subsequent events.

On April 15 Britain and France made their first proposals to Moscow. The British asked merely that the Soviet Union make a Declaration to Poland and Romania similar to that given by the Western Allies. The French went a little further. They proposed that the three Big Powers agree to come to the aid of one another if one of them became engaged in war with Germany. But that was not going far enough to suit the Russians.

Two days later, on April 17, Litvinov countered with a proposal for a virtual Triple Alliance between the three countries. Not a vague one, such as Paris envisaged, but detailed and far-reaching. Not only would the parties agree to provide mutual assistance but they would back it up with a specific military convention defining just what their respective armies, navies, and air forces would do in case of war. The signatories, to be joined by Poland if it desired, would guarantee all the states of Central and Eastern Europe, including the Baltic states, whether they liked it or not, against aggression. Military conversations were to start at once along with political talks.

This was Litvinov's last bid for an alliance with the West against Germany, and the Soviet Foreign Minister, who had staked his career on a policy of stopping Hitler by collective action with France and Britain, apparently thought that at last he had succeeded. Ambassador Coulondre thought the Soviet offer was almost too good to believe and urged its acceptance. Churchill agreed, telling Chamberlain that "there is no means of maintaining an eastern front against Nazi aggression without the active aid of Russia." Later he wrote that such an alliance would have been a blow to Germany and might have prevented Hitler from launching war. But in London the Soviet proposal caused consternation and in Paris at least the usual reticence. Influential French circles—and not only on the Right—were against any military alliance with the Soviet Union. A fortnight before, on March 28, Deputy Jean Montigny, a Radical-Socialist, had proposed an interpellation in the Chamber on what he called "the error and the illusion of any foreign policy based even partly on confidence in the power of the Russian army outside its frontiers and on the loyalty of the Soviet government."

Over the last fortnight of April the talks with Russia stalled. On the 22nd, the French cabinet reluctantly agreed to accept the Soviet proposals as a basis for negotiations. But it could not win over the British. Chamberlain and Halifax insisted that first Russia should give a unilateral guarantee to Poland and Romania similar to Britain's and that only afterward would they examine an accord with the Soviet Union, which they pointed out in an *aide-mémoire* to the Quai d'Orsay, "is less immediately menaced." On the 29th Bonnet made a new stab at the problem by proposing to Moscow a pact of mutual assistance between the three powers to come into effect if they became involved in a war with Germany as the result of "an attempt by force to modify the *status quo* in Central or Eastern Europe." This got around the vexing problem, Bonnet thought, of getting the Poles to accept Russian aid. But Moscow was unimpressed and London distinctly cool.

Stalin was getting impatient with the West and on May 3 he took a decisive step to show it. On that day, tucked away on the back page of the Moscow newspaper *Pravda,* organ of the Communist Party, in a column called "News in Brief," appeared a small item: "M. Litvinov has been released from the Office of Foreign Commissar at his own request." He was replaced by Vyacheslav Molotov, Chairman of the Council of People's Commissars.

Though the significance of Litvinov's abrupt dismissal would have seemed to be obvious to all—the Germans certainly quickly grasped it—it does not seem to have been understood in Paris and London. Bonnet makes clear that he was quite satisfied with the assurance given him by the Soviet Ambassador the next day that Litvinov's departure "did not denote any change in Soviet foreign policy." Even Ambassador Coulondre, despite all his experience in Moscow, seems to have lost his analytical powers. On May 4 he informed Bonnet from his new post in Berlin of a conversation he had just had with the Soviet chargé d'affaires, who, after assuring him that Litvinov's disappearance would not change in any way Soviet foreign policy, added:

With Molotov, member of the Politburo, depositary of the thoughts of Stalin, Soviet foreign policy can only gain in clarity and precision, and France and England will have no reason to regret it.

Coulondre added that "these indications are reassuring. Of course we shall have to wait and see if they are confirmed by the facts."*[13]

He had not long to wait to see how little they would be confirmed.

Actually, as the Germans saw at once, Litvinov's "disgrace" signified a sharp turn in Soviet foreign policy. To make sure that the German government understood the significance of it, Georgi Astakhov, the Soviet chargé

---

* In his book Coulondre does not mention this dispatch. Instead he writes: "I was very much struck by Litvinov's disgrace. . . . He could not have been dismissed except for reasons of foreign policy."[14]

d'affaires in Berlin, made one of his rare calls on the Foreign Office on May 5. There he talked with Dr. Julius Schnurre, who had been conducting trade negotiations with the Soviet Embassy until they were broken off in February.

> Astakhov touched upon the dismissal of Litvinov [Schnurre reported] and tried . . . to learn whether the event would cause a change in our attitude toward the Soviet Union. He stressed the great importance of the personality of Molotov [and his] importance for future Soviet foreign policy.[15]

The Soviet envoy also invited the Germans to resume the trade negotiations.

THE SECRET RAPPROCHEMENT OF BERLIN AND MOSCOW: I

This was not the first feeler put out by the Russians in Berlin. A fortnight before, on April 17, the very day that Litvinov had proposed to the French and British the forming of a Triple Alliance against Germany, the Soviet Ambassador in Berlin, Alexei Merekalov, had made his first call on Ernst von Weizsaecker, the State Secretary of the German Foreign Office, since assuming his post nearly a year before. He had asked the Secretary "point-blank," the latter reported, what he thought of German-Russian relations. After Weizsaecker had replied that Germany wished to live "in a mutually satisfactory condition of economic exchange with Russia," the Ambassador went considerably further.

"Ideological differences," he suggested, "need not disturb relations between Russia and Germany."

> Russia [the Secretary reported him as saying further] had not exploited the present friction between Germany and the Western democracies against us, nor did she wish to. . . . There was no reason why Russia should not live on a normal footing with us, and out of normal relations could grow increasingly improved relations.

Weizsaecker felt that the Ambassador had been "steering the conversation" toward this last remark and made a note of it for his foreign minister.[16]

As early as April, then, the Russians had begun playing both sides of the street.* Very soon the Germans would respond to their overtures with more realism—and cynicism—than the Western Allies were capable of. If

---

* If some credence can be cautiously given the alleged journal of Litvinov (published as *Notes for a Journal*) Stalin had been contemplating approaching the Germans soon after Munich, the exclusion from which had increased his suspicion of the West. Toward the end of 1938, according to an entry in this journal, Stalin told Litvinov that "we are prepared to come to an agreement with the Germans . . . and also to render Poland harmless." In January, 1939, Litvinov notes that all his communications with the Soviet Embassy in Berlin must go through Stalin and that Ambassador Merekalov, on Stalin's instructions, is about to begin negotiations with Weizsaecker in order to let Hitler know "in effect: 'We couldn't come to an agreement until now, but now we can.' "

Stalin could play a double game so could Hitler, who was a master of it. No matter that he had based his domestic policy on anti-Communism (all the German Communist leaders were in jail, or had fled) and his foreign policy on the exclusion of Russia, as he had insisted on at Munich, from European affairs. Despite his burning contempt for the Soviet Union, which he had first expressed so vehemently in *Mein Kampf* and reiterated ever since, Hitler realized that she might well prevent him from carrying out his next act of aggression if she allied herself with the West. But if he could make a deal with Moscow to detach her from Britain and France, he would then be free to carry out his plans on schedule.*

Those plans already had been formulated at the beginning of April, a few days after Chamberlain had announced Britain's unilateral guarantee of Poland. On April 3 Hitler approved a top-secret directive to the armed forces concerning "Case White." This was the code name for the operation to destroy Poland. The Polish armed forces were to be "destroyed by a surprise attack." The target date was set for September 1. And like the date Hitler had set the year before for taking the Sudetenland—October 1, 1938—this more important date of September 1, 1939, would also be kept. In such matters as timing the Nazi dictator was as good as his word.

To set the stage, Hitler moved quickly. In a speech to the Reichstag on April 28 he denounced the Anglo-German naval treaty and, more important, the nonaggression pact with Poland. Perhaps even more important, as I, who sat through the two-hour address, noted, the Fuehrer omitted his customary attack on the Soviet Union. There was not a word about Russia. This seems to have encouraged the Soviet government. For on May 17 the Russian chargé d'affaires in Berlin again saw Dr. Schnurre at the Foreign Office and after discussing the resumption of trade negotiations passed to larger matters. "There are no conflicts in foreign policy between Germany and the Soviet Union," Astakhov told him, "and therefore there is no reason for any enmity between the two countries."[18]

Three days later, on May 20, the German Ambassador in Moscow, Count Friedrich Werner von der Schulenburg, who as an old nationalist had always worked for closer Russo-German ties, had a long talk with Molotov, who, he reported, was in a "most friendly mood." The newly appointed Commissar for Foreign Affairs informed the Ambassador that economic negotiations could be resumed "if the necessary *political* bases for them were created."[19] Schulenburg was intrigued. The Russians, he grasped at once,

---

* On April 30 General Karl Bodenschatz of the German Air Ministry had tried to explain this to a very surprised young assistant air attaché of the French Embassy in Berlin, Captain Paul Stehlin, whom he had befriended. When Bodenschatz, a close friend of Goering and a confidant of Hitler, had remarked that "something was going on in the East," Stehlin had expressed his astonishment that Hitler, the arch anti-Bolshevist, could turn toward Russia. "Don't take his words too seriously," Bodenschatz had answered. "Hitler is a soldier. When it comes to carrying out a plan, juridical or ideological considerations play no part. Hitler is no longer thinking of regulating the German-Polish conflict without Russia. There have already been three partitions of Poland. Well, believe me, there will be a fourth."[17]

were willing to go much further in their approach to Germany and work out agreements not only for increased trade but for a *political* understanding.

The carefully concealed and still wary feelers between Berlin and Moscow did not escape the watchful eyes of the French Ambassador in the German capital. Coulondre, as we have seen, had warned of a possible Russo-German rapprochement after Munich before leaving the Embassy in Moscow. Now, as the spring of 1939 got under way, he began to note further signs in Berlin. He was much impressed by Captain Stehlin's report of his talk with General Bodenschatz on April 30* and on May 7 forwarded it to Bonnet in Paris with his own comments. Because of Bodenschatz's position, he said, he believed his remarks reflected "pretty accurately the designs of Hitler." Still, he warned, the feelers to Russia might be merely a diplomatic maneuver designed to force the Western Allies to make more concessions to Moscow. "It is difficult," he concluded, "for Hitler to arrive at a collusion with the Soviets since not only his domestic but his foreign policies have been built on an anti-Bolshevist edifice."†[20]

Two days later, however, on May 9, he wired Bonnet: "For the last 24 hours Berlin is full of rumors that Germany has made, or is going to make, proposals to Russia leading to a partition of Poland."[22] And on May 22 he got off a long telegram to Paris on what was going on in the mind of the Nazi Foreign Minister. Ribbentrop, he reported, was convinced that Poland "sooner or later must disappear, partitioned again between Germany and Russia. In his mind this partition is closely linked with a rapprochement between Berlin and Moscow. . . . One of the objectives is to get Russia to play, in the dismemberment of Poland, the role that this latter country played with regard to Czechoslovakia."[23] A week later, on June 1, the Ambassador informed Bonnet that Hitler

will risk war if he does not have to fight Russia. On the other hand, if he knows he has to fight her too he will draw back rather than expose his country, his party, and himself to ruin.

Coulondre added that Hitler's two top generals, Keitel, Chief of the High Command, and Brauchitsch, Commander in Chief of the Army, had told the Fuehrer that if Germany had to fight Russia she would have "small

---

* In his book, page 270, Coulondre gives a wrong date (May 6) for it, and misspells the captain's name.

† Still, Coulondre regarded the Bodenschatz information so highly that he asked Captain Stehlin to fly to Paris and present it personally to the Quai d'Orsay. He gave the air attaché a personal letter to Bonnet suggesting that the latter question him further about his two-hour talk with Bodenschatz. Stehlin reports that Bonnet declined to receive him, that all his efforts to penetrate the French Foreign Office were greeted by "evasive and discourteous responses," and that after cooling his heels in Paris for six days he flew his plane back to Berlin. Later he was warned by a friend in the Quai d'Orsay, that it thought it better for an air attaché to mind his own affairs and not intrude in diplomacy![21]

chance of winning the war." The Ambassador, who for years had been urging a Franco-Russian military alliance, concluded by stressing to Bonnet the "urgency" of reaching at once an agreement in Moscow between Britain, France, and Russia.[24] The implication was, as it had been in all of his recent dispatches, that if the Western Allies didn't hurry the Germans might beat them to it.

Hitler, as he later told his generals, was quite confident of this though at the beginning of June he was in no hurry.* He had just tied Italy to Germany, which gave him a certain leverage against France and Britain. On May 22 the so-called "Pact of Steel" between Italy and Germany had been signed in Berlin. It was an outright military alliance with each party pledged in the event of "warlike complications" to come to the aid of the other "with all its military forces on land, at sea, and in the air." The next day, May 23, the Nazi dictator summoned his military chiefs to the Chancellery in Berlin, informed them that "we must burn our boats," that Poland would be attacked "at the first suitable opportunity," that "Danzig is not the subject of the dispute at all," that "it is a question of expanding our living space in the East" and that "there will be war."

War with France and Britain as well as with Poland, he conceded, but probably not with Russia. "It is not ruled out," he said, "that Russia might disinterest herself in the destruction of Poland."[26]

What the Western Allies were trying to do at this moment was to interest Russia in the *defense* of Poland. And in fact the Russians were interested because their own defense was involved. But the Poles were not. There arose the same stumbling block that had occurred during the Czech crisis the year before: the refusal of the Poles to agree to the passage of Soviet troops through their territory to meet the Germans.

The French had a chance to bring the Poles to their senses about Russian help when the Polish Minister of War, General Kasprzycki, accompanied by Colonel Jeklicz, Deputy Chief of the Polish General Staff, arrived in Paris in the middle of May to work out a military convention with France. Here was an opportunity for General Gamelin, who conducted the talks for the French, not only to insist that Poland, in its own interests, agree to accept Russian military aid but, indeed, to make France's military commitments to Warsaw conditional upon it. Gamelin, however, did not even mention the matter during a whole week of negotiations. Without even inquiring how the Polish General Staff planned to stem the Germans without Soviet aid he

---

* "I was convinced," he said to his generals on August 22, "that Stalin would never accept the English offer. . . . Russia had no interest in maintaining Poland. . . . Litvinov's dismissal was decisive. It came to me like a cannon shot as a sign of change in Moscow toward the Western Powers. I brought about the change toward Russia gradually. . . ."[25]

signed on May 19 an accord promising that the French Army would launch a major offensive in the West if the Germans attacked Poland.* There is no record of Daladier having pressed his generalissimo to bring up the question of Soviet military assistance to Poland, nor of Bonnet's having done so, though the latter did his best to sabotage the Polish military agreement by refusing to sign an agreed political accord on which it depended. This is a curious incident, giving further insight into the character and ways of the French Foreign Minister, and the chaotic manner in which the business of government was conducted in Paris that spring as the crisis over Poland mounted. It had a direct influence on certain subsequent events.[27]

General Gamelin and General Kasprzycki finished drafting the military convention on May 18, and before signing it the French generalissimo took it to Daladier that afternoon to get his approval. This was given the next day and Gamelin then signed the compact, adding a letter to the Polish War Minister stating that the Convention would come into effect only after a new political treaty had been signed between France and Poland. This political accord, he had been told, had already been drawn up and agreed to and would be signed probably that very day, May 19. But it was not.

Bonnet claims that when he learned on the 18th "by chance" that Gamelin had signed the military convention he was "stupefied."[28] He asserts that because the Poles demanded that the political treaty include a clause stating that a German seizure of Danzig would be considered by Poland as a *casus belli* he had "refused to sign it." This was not unreasonable. The French government was reluctant enough to go to war if Poland itself were attacked. It did not wish to be drawn into conflict over Danzig. But was this the reason for Bonnet's turning down the political treaty? The evidence is against him.

Gamelin publishes in his memoirs[29] the text of a letter which Bonnet wrote Daladier May 18 enclosing a copy of the projected Franco-Polish political agreement and declaring that "this text, corresponding to your public declarations, was unanimously approved by the cabinet on May 12" and "should be signed shortly." It included a declaration that the French Foreign Minister "took note" of the Polish position that "Danzig was a vital interest to Poland." Bonnet made no objection to this in his letter.† According to the Polish Ambassador in Paris, M. J. Lukasiewicz, Bonnet had assured him on May 17 that he had no objection to the declaration on Danzig and had agreed that the political convention would be signed two days later.[30]

It was not (not until September 4, four days after Poland had been attacked by Germany), and General Gamelin drew some important conclusions that had an effect on what followed. When he learned the following week that the French government had "renounced" signing the political

---

*How General Gamelin hedged in his own interpretation of the promise both at the time it was made and when the time came to fulfill it will be duly recounted.

† Bonnet does not publish this letter in his memoirs.

accord, he concluded, he says, "that in consequence our military protocol had no value and did not tie us." He admits that "at heart, I was satisfied."[31] This is revealing. He seems to have been relieved at getting out of any formal obligation to do very much to help the Poles if the Germans attacked them, apparently forgetting that by the secret military treaty of February 19, 1921, with Poland, signed by Marshal Foch, France obligated herself in case of German aggression to provide her ally "effective and rapid support."*

But regardless of how "effectively and rapidly" France supported Poland by attacking in the West to draw off German strength in the East— and General Gamelin makes clear in his interpretation of the promises to the Poles in the May talks that he did not intend to attack with too much too soon[33]—he knew that Poland could not be saved from being overrun by Hitler's armies unless she received timely and direct support from the Soviet armed forces.† He repeatedly tells us he knew it. Noting in his memoirs his

---

* Bonnet's torpedoing of the political pact further poisoned the already bad blood between him and General Gamelin which had been so evident at the time of Munich. In his memoirs Gamelin castigates Bonnet for his mishandling of the negotiations with Poland in May. And then with that little turn of the knife at which he was so adept he adds: "Let there be no misunderstanding. I am certainly not pretending that Bonnet was a traitor, as I have been accused of saying. But I submit . . . that his action was harmful to the interests of France." Bonnet lambasts the generalissimo for signing the military accord in the first place and then, after the belated signing of the political treaty on September 4, for continuing to claim that it was "nonexistent." After the German occupation Bonnet gave an interview to a Paris newspaper in which, after pleading for Franco-German collaboration, he boasted of having refused in May 1939 to increase the military obligations of France to Poland.[32]

† At that, the confidence of the French General Staff in the worth of the Polish army increased as the summer proceeded. So did that of the French, British and American military attachés in Warsaw. This struck such an unmilitary civilian observer as this writer as strange, as did the blindness of the Poles to their disastrous strategic position and to the necessity of Russian military aid. I had spent the first week of April in Poland and noted in my diary on April 2 from Warsaw:

Attended a pitiful air show this Sunday afternoon, my Polish friends apologizing for the cumbersome slow bombers and the double-decker fighters— all obsolete. They showed a half-dozen modern fighters that looked fast enough, but that was all. How can Poland fight Germany with such an air force?

On April 6, the day the British and Polish governments announced that they would sign a pact of mutual assistance, I noted from Warsaw that with the backing of Britain and France the Poles would fight. Still, I felt "uneasy" about three things:

Poland's terrible strategic position (flanked on three sides since the German occupation of Czechoslovakia): the (German) West Wall, which, when completed next winter, will discourage France and Britain from attacking Germany in the West and thereby aiding Poland; and, finally, Russia. I have dined and drunk with a dozen Poles this week—from the Foreign Office, the Army, and the old Pilsudski legionnaires who run *Polskie Radio*—and they will not bring themselves to realize that they cannot afford the luxury of being enemies of both Russia and Germany and that they must choose and that if they bring in Russia along with France and Britain they are saved. They point out the dangers of Russian help. To be sure, there is a danger . . . that the Red Army, once on Polish soil, will not leave, that it will Bolshevize the

"extreme annoyance" at the sudden arrival of General Kasprzycki in Paris on May 14, he comments:

> I had not wished to have any precise conversations with the Poles before . . . we were able to have talks with the Russian General Staff. It was evident that a prolonged resistance by Poland was inconceivable without the help of the U.S.S.R.

He realized that, and he realized the main difficulty. "Now, I knew very well," he goes on to say, "that the Poles would never even discuss this with the Soviets."[35] Yet by his own account he shrunk back from facing the consequences. Nor did he take the lead in trying to force the Poles to come down to earth. As in so many other matters where military policy was directly concerned, he was content to leave the initiative to the civilian government. But initiative was just what was lacking in the Daladier government, as it was in the Chamberlain-Halifax government in London. As the summer of 1939 got under way the statesmen in Paris and London appeared to be in no hurry to solve the problem of Soviet aid even though it was beginning to dawn on them that without it Poland was doomed and perhaps the West as well.

The French Parliament itself had not brought any pressure on the government to come to grips with the issue. All through the spring it had seemed half-asleep about foreign policy, though it had aroused itself to a fairly high pitch in the debate over introducing proportional representation, a measure designed by the Conservatives to make impossible the election of a new Popular Front majority, which the Chamber finally passed in June just before adjournment. The vote (339 to 234) caused the deputies, as one editor noted, "to depart [on June 27] in great tumult and disorder"—a further reminder that France would face the summer's crisis as divided as ever.

The mandate of the Chamber, elected in 1936, expired in May 1940, and Daladier feared that when the deputies returned for the new session at the end of August, at the very moment the German-Polish crisis most probably would be at its height, they would simply start preparing for their re-election and further disrupt the unity the country would sorely need. Having been given the power to govern by decree law in the interim, he promulgated a decree on July 30 prolonging the life of the Chamber until May 1942. There was less hullabaloo in the country than he expected. Most politicians didn't mind having their job automatically extended for two years, and the mass of the people, who had no exaggerated confidence in the possibility of getting better elected representatives, did not seem to care. This Chamber of Deputies, it will be remembered, had had in the beginning a

---

country with its propaganda (this country has been so misruled by the colonels that no doubt it does offer fertile ground to the Bolsheviks), and so on. . . . Then make your peace with the Nazis. . . . Never! they say.[34]

Popular Front majority, but in the peculiar politics of this House which we have tried earlier to fathom, the majority, without any new general election having intervened, had become conservative. The men were the same; their alignments, their policies, had changed. At any rate, the country would have to do with this fickle Chamber for another three years—if the Republic lasted that long.

23

A SUMMER'S INTERLUDE IN PARIS
May–July 1939

In the beautiful French capital, always at its loveliest in June and July, the summer season was as glittering as ever despite the war clouds on the horizon. The Republic was celebrating the one hundred and fiftieth anniversary of the glorious revolution. Jean Zay, the Minister of Education, who was charged with organizing the anniversary celebrations, hoped that they would "symbolize all that was being menaced on our frontiers." On May 5 the festivities were inaugurated at Versailles, where a brilliant assembly of officials, notables, and foreign diplomats gathered first at the Hôtel des Menus Plaisirs (where just 150 years before the three Estates had met to sound the death knell of the ancient monarchy), and then moved on to the Galerie des Glaces in the great palace of Louis XIV to hear a ringing oration by Edouard Herriot, who was not only President of the Chamber of Deputies but an eminent historian and the Republic's most florid and sonorous orator.

Besides the patriotic festivals there were many elegant social fetes. Some remembered later that the women of fashionable Paris had never seemed so beautifully dressed. The salons of the great couturiers, Schiaparelli, Maggy Rouff, Lanvin, Robert Piguet, Marcel Rochas, were jammed. The styles that summer were described in the press as "extremely feminine." Men liked them. The craze for dancing seemed to rival that of 1925. The night clubs were packed. The hit movie that summer was entitled *Toute la ville danse.* The theaters were also enjoying their best season in years. Even the ancient house of Molière, the Comédie-Française, departed from its classical repertoire to present a new play, *A souffert sous Ponce-Pilate,* by Paul Raynal. Louis Jovet, with a new partner, Madeleine Ozeray, was triumphing at the Athénée in Jean Giraudoux's *Ondine.*

For almost everyone in France, even for the lowly, times were getting better, and it seemed incredible to them that the improvement, after nearly a decade of depression, should be spoiled by war. A good harvest was in the making. Industrial production was up 17 percent in June over a year before. Over the same period unemployment had decreased by 20,000—to 343,000. The cost of living had risen in the preceding twelve months by only 3 percent and against that was a rise of 5 percent in hourly wages and even more in salaries. The flighty franc was at last stable. The export of gold had ceased. The balance of payments had reached an equilibrium and on the Bourse stocks were up by 16 percent over the previous year. The wave of strikes had completely subsided. On May Day, the European Labor Day, French workers had foregone the usual day off and reported for work. Most of them were looking forward to a fortnight's paid vacation in August. Life was looking up in the summer sunshine. The average Frenchman could not grasp—what the newspaper headlines and radio bulletins stressed—that Hitler seemed bent on war over faraway Poland. War was the last thing a Frenchman wanted.

In the smaller circle of the educated and literate—a larger circle than in almost any other country in the world—new books were selling unusually well: *Terre des hommes* by the sensitive aviator-writer Saint-Exupéry, *Gilles* by Drieu La Rochelle, whose fine talents were beginning to be wasted by his aberration for Fascism, *Scandale de la vérité* by Georges Bernanos, *La Douceur de vivre* by Jules Romains and *Mémorial de la guerre blanche* by the physician-author Georges Duhamel. Two talented young writers attracted attention that summer: Jean-Paul Sartre, the thirty-four-year-old existentialist philosopher, novelist, and essayist, with *Le Mur,* a book of short stories; and Albert Camus, a youth of twenty-six, with *Noces,* a series of sketches of life in Algeria, where he was born of a French family and still lived. The uneasiness of the times was reflected in most of these works though none forecast what lay ahead at the summer's end. The last novel to be written by Luc Durtain appeared that season. Ironically, it was entitled *La Guerre n'existe pas.*

The possibility, though, even the probability, of imminent war existed in the minds of many Frenchmen, especially among the political and social elite. Later when they looked back on the most brilliant and colorful social affair of the summer they recalled their forebodings. By all accounts the gala soirée in the elegant gardens of the Polish Embassy, then housed in the Hôtel des Princes de Sagan, on the night of July 4–5 was the climax of the Parisian social season. All remembered how toward 3 o'clock in the morning the Polish Ambassador and five members of his staff took their place opposite six elegantly gowned Polish women, including Madame Artur Rubinstein, wife of the celebrated pianist, and swung into a mazurka that went on and on ever faster and more frenetic while hundreds of august guests looked on clapping their hands and stamping their feet to the increasing tempo of the music until, as one observer noted, "everyone was carried away." This observer was Pierre Lazareff, the youthful and dynamic editor of the mass circulation *Paris-Soir*. Himself carried away by the dancing and "by this beautiful summer night under a sky pierced with stars, in a fairy-tale garden where Chinese lanterns, festoons of electric lights, and the flames of Bengal torches made iridescent the balustrades and the great sphinx of white marble with all the colors of the rainbow," he felt suddenly "that the realities and menaces were far away."

In this happy mood he ran into Paul Reynaud, who recalled him to reality. "It is scarcely enough to say," Reynaud remarked sharply, "that they are dancing on a volcano. For what is an eruption of Vesuvius compared to the cataclysm which is forming under our very feet?"[1]

To the writer Alfred Fabre-Luce, who like his friend, Drieu La Rochelle and quite a few other Frenchmen had gone from the Left to the extreme Right, the Polish gala party was "a farewell—everyone knew it." Georges Bonnet had gone on to the Polish Embassy with General Gamelin and other notables after a dinner of the France–Grande-Bretagne Association, where Hore-Belisha, the British War Secretary, had declared that "France has the greatest army in the world, commanded by our General Gamelin." The Foreign Minister did not linger long. "This sumptuous fete," he later wrote, "marked for me the end of an epoch. I returned to the Quai d'Orsay, thinking of the wind of folly which was blowing all these carefree dancers toward a catastrophe without precedent."[2]

Two other events of this first fortnight in July aroused different feelings. On July 2, General Weygand, speaking at Lille, declared: "The French Army is in a better state than at any time in its history. It possesses a materiel of the highest quality, fortifications of the first order, an excellent morale and a remarkable High Command. No one in our country wants war, but if we are obliged to gain a new victory, we shall gain it." This optimistic judgment, from one whose military prestige in France was second only to that of Marshal Pétain, was prominently displayed on the front pages of the newspapers and brought much encouragement to the public.* Monzie, still in the cabinet, feared it would stimulate "bellicose feelings." By this time he was for peace at any price.

The event which gave Frenchmen the most confidence in their Army and Air Force was the traditional military parade down the Champs Elysées on July 14, Bastille Day, which capped the Republic's celebration of the 150th anniversary of the Revolution. The Army chiefs had planned to make it especially impressive, not only to give a fitting climax to the summer's anniversary, but to instill confidence in a populace which had doubts about

---

* Long afterward and in the light of events General Weygand made excuses for his optimistic words. "When I pronounced them," he wrote, "I had been out of the High Command for four years, during which I had never been consulted about anything. My role as an old chief was to maintain morale on the eve of a war that everyone knew was imminent, and not to lessen confidence in an army which at this hour it was no longer possible to modify."[3]

the capacity of France to stand up to Hitler's Germany. Contingents in colorful uniforms from the far-flung Empire alternated with those from the metropolitan army and to these was added a detachment of British grenadier guards in their resplendent scarlet uniforms and tall horsehaired busbies —35,000 troops in all. The applauding crowds that packed the broad avenue did not miss the significance: here was evidence of the might of not only the French Empire but the British, joined together. And despite all the talk about Anglo-French inferiority in the air, the sight of 350 French planes, joined by a squadron from the British Air Force, flying in formation above the Champs Elysées, appeared to give the crowds, at least, a feeling that the two allies had strength in this arm too. And in tanks and artillery. The latest heavy tanks, reputed to be the best in the world, clattered down the pavement followed by detachments of awesome-looking long-range guns.

The Army, Bonnet noted, gave an impression "of order, discipline, and irresistible force. How could one fear Germany?" The Foreign Minister, who had plenty of fears himself and who thought the parade might raise false hopes, ran into the venerable President of the Senate, Jules Jeanneney, who as the last drumbeats faded away, was exclaiming in a voice loud and proud: "A good thing that the German Ambassador and his military attaché have been able to see at first hand the force of our army. Germany must henceforth understand that it can no longer count on any concessions from us. With such an army French public opinion will not support it."[4] And the writer Joseph Kessel was so transported by the military spectacle that he exclaimed to friends next to him: "There will be no war! I guarantee that a morning such as this will make M. Hitler reflect!"[5]

Confidence that France could and would stand up to Germany and its threats of war spread all over Paris. Jean Fabry, former Minister of War and for long somewhat soured on the Republic, wrote in *Le Matin,* a champion of appeasement of Germany:

We are 106 million people behind the same frontier, which stretches from Scotland to the Sahara . . . : 46 million British, 42 million French, 18 million North Africans; 106 million people who have behind them all the free seas and all the resources of their Empires.[6]

And André Tardieu, the former Premier, who since 1934 had despaired of the Republic and finally of his ability to reform it, suddenly beamed with confidence.

The enemy—his acts the last four years prove it—neither desires war nor can make it. He lacks raw materials, gold reserves, a treasury, and cash. He lacks . . . a stable interior. . . . He is bluffing. The [Rome-Berlin] Axis is inflicting on us a war of nerves. If we stand firm the Axis will retreat. The secret of Hitler . . . is that of a virtual fugitive who, to avoid a clash, hurls menaces.[7]

But there were others—some in high places—who did not believe it or, for that matter, have any faith in the strength of France to resist the ancient enemy. There were a good many who did not wish to resist, some out of fear, others because of their pro-German and Fascist convictions and their hatred of the democratic Republic. On July 10 Marcel Déat, who had gone from Socialism to Neo-Socialism and now made no bones of his sympathies for totalitarian Fascism which within a year would carry him to outright collaboration with the Germans, published an editorial in *L'Œuvre* which soon became famous—and to many, infamous. *"Why Die For Danzig?"* it was entitled, and his conclusion that to die for Danzig was "idiotic" was no doubt shared by many Frenchmen in the confusion of the hour. Déat, despite his reputation as one of the most intellectual of the politicians, did not understand what Hitler had told his generals: that Danzig was not the issue at all. At issue, as Hitler had also made clear to them, was the German destruction of Poland as a further step toward German hegemony in Europe. Flandin, former Premier and Foreign Minister and still the head of the center party in Parliament, perhaps saw this. To avoid getting in the way of Germany he was for ditching Poland as he had been the year before for abandoning Czechoslovakia. He was urging all summer, as he later admitted, that France should denounce her commitments to Poland.[8] He too was now, like Monzie, for peace at any price whatsoever.

Among those who had been most successful in persuading Frenchmen of the "idiocy" of dying for Danzig was Otto Abetz, the suave German Nazi agent in Paris.* On July 2 Daladier had finally bestirred himself to expel Abetz—an action he had put off for months so as not to anger Hitler and Ribbentrop. The pusillanimous Nazi Foreign Minister was beside himself with rage. Abetz was not only his protégé but the Paris representative of the so-called *Dienstelle Ribbentrop* in France, which had given him one of his covers.

"I have no intention whatsoever," Ribbentrop wired his Ambassador in France, "of accepting this action . . . and intend to send Abetz back to France." Count Welczeck was instructed to tell Daladier this personally, and if the Premier proved adamant, to tell him further that "as far as he knew, Abetz was already back in France," which the Ambassador, no friend of the Nazi agent, dutifully did. As might be expected, Bonnet stepped in with a compromise designed to smooth the ruffled feelings in Berlin. He invited Welczeck to his country home on August 10 and the next day the Ambassador wired Berlin:

Bonnet intends to propose to Daladier that Abetz should be given a clear statement of his good faith to the effect that he was neither suspected of espionage nor had in any other way broken French laws. . . . When the wave of political excitement had subsided in a few weeks, an entry visa for Abetz might again be considered.[9]

---

* See above, pp. 411–412.

The "Declaration of Honor" which Bonnet had proposed was duly published in *Le Temps* as an official communiqué of the French government. That was not the last France would see of Abetz. He would return as Hitler's Ambassador in Paris after the German occupation, and this time, in a far stronger position, resume his efforts to poison the French against themselves.

Already a few French writers, some out of conviction, were doing this. A good example was Count Alphonse de Chateaubriant, the celebrated author of *La Brière,* who made a pilgrimage to Nazi Germany in 1937 and quickly became converted into a fanatical worshiper of Hitler, whom he saw as a Christ-like figure, and into an unblushing admirer of National-Socialist Germany, which he found full of humanism and Christian ideals, wishing only peace with her neighbors, above all with France, and having nothing of the "beast of prey" in its noble spirit. In exalted language the Count put all this rubbish into a book, *La Gerbe des forces,* which had an immediate and considerable impact on his native land. Reading it, Henri de Kerillis, who had led the press campaign against Abetz but who admired Chateaubriant for his talents and for his "honesty as a man," was horrified. "One goes," he wrote, "from surprise to surprise, from stupefaction to stupefaction." And no wonder.

> Hitler [Chateaubriant wrote] is immensely good. . . . If he salutes the masses with one hand he holds out the other faithfully toward God. . . . The thoughts of Hitler have their roots deep in the profound waters of the Christian sea. Hitler is trying to raise a Christian temple for Germany. . . . The National Socialists are the beginning of the work of God.

And so on *ad nauseam*—from a celebrated French writer who, as Kerillis admits, "was neither venal, corrupted, nor bought by German propaganda." Strange as it may seem, the book was widely read in French military circles. Kerillis recounts meeting one day at the Cercle Interallié a general, who pulled Chateaubriant's book out of his pocket and asked him what he thought about it. When the editor replied that it was one of those books that poisoned the country the general looked surprised, shrugged his shoulders, and exclaimed: "You always go to extremes!" The general, he says, was Weygand.[10]

Chateaubriant had not been bought. He had merely lost his senses. But others were purchased and as war approached Daladier reluctantly began to put them out of business. Two journalists, Loys Aubin, chief news editor of the esteemed *Le Temps,* and Poirier, a former administrator of that journal and presently an advertising manager of *Le Figaro,* were arrested, charged with "having relations with foreign states." Aubin was reported to have admitted receiving several millions from Germany.

Who cared for the welfare of the Republic now? Certainly the mass of the people, untouched by corruption above, and the vast majority of the members of Parliament and the government, confused by events though they were. Even most of the newspapers and magazines. But subtle and influential forces were working against it.

On June 8 Charles Maurras, the leader of the royalist movement, Action Française, and a bitter enemy of the Republic, was formally received into the venerable Académie Française, thus becoming one of the "Forty Immortals," as they were sometimes called. To be elected to the Academy (Maurras had been chosen the previous June shortly after getting out of prison) was to reach the height of prestige in France, whether one was a writer, politician, general, or philosopher, and the significance of Maurras' elevation to this august body was not lost on anyone. Georges Bidault, the young editor of the liberal Catholic daily *Aube*, called it a "defy" to the Republican regime and, along with other editors, demanded that the President of the Republic refuse to validate it. The easygoing Lebrun declined to use his veto, though he refused to receive the newly elected member, as was customary.*

The Church in Rome also moved to help the French royalists. A month after the reception of Maurras into the Academy, on July 7, 1939, the new pope, Pius XII, lifted the ban on Action Française, making it easier for French Catholics in good conscience to work through it to undermine the Republic.† In this matter too, Georges Bonnet had a hand. Behind the back of his Ambassador to the Holy See, Charles-Roux, and against the wishes of the majority of the cabinet, Bonnet conducted a number of private conversations with French royalists and representatives of the Vatican. When the Nuncio in Paris, Valerio Valeri, asked the French Foreign Minister whether the government did not oppose lifting the sanctions against Action Française, Bonnet replied that it was a religious, not a political, matter and that a pardon for the royalists would not inconvenience the government. This was the signal for a go-ahead and the new pope took quick advantage of it.‡[11]

The lovely summer began to fade, and the euphoria left by the gala

---

* On April 5, 1939, Albert Lebrun, thanks largely to the politicking of Daladier, had been reelected by the National Assembly to a second seven-year term as President of the Republic. He received 506 of the 994 votes. It was not a thumping majority for the colorless, sixty-eight-year-old former senator. It was generally felt in the Assembly that the country, facing a growing crisis in Europe, needed a more energetic and forceful figure—in 1914 it had had Poincaré—but the members of Parliament could not agree on a stronger man, and perhaps there was none. The choice would soon add to France's misfortunes.

† Eugenio Cardinal Pacelli was elected pope on March 2, 1939. He had spent, as some French newspapers were quick to point out, twelve years in Germany as Nuncio first in Munich and then in Berlin. As Papal Secretary of State he had negotiated and signed a Concordat with Nazi Germany on July 20, 1933, which had given the new Nazi regime some badly needed prestige at the time. His silence on Nazi Germany's massacre of the Jews would provoke a great deal of controversy after the war and inspire the much-debated play, *The Deputy*, by Rolf Hochhuth, a German Protestant.

‡ Bonnet does not mention this affair in his memoirs.

celebrations of the Revolution, by all the glittering parties of the capital's most brilliant social season in years, by the general good times and by the workers' plans for their paid vacations, gave way to uneasiness. The head-lines from Berlin became more and more ominous. Fear of war grew. The hope that the Republic could save the peace, or, if not, forge the coalition with Britain and Russia which had defeated Germany the last time, was not great. Instinctively one felt that the country was weaker, more divided, less confident, than it had been on the eve of the great test of 1914.

24

THE TALKS WITH RUSSIA
SUMMER 1939

THE FRANCO-BRITISH TALKS WITH RUSSIA: II

Most of Bonnet's time that summer was spent on more important diplomatic negotiations than the dubious ones with the new pope to strengthen the anti-Republican royalists in France. He wanted to line up the Soviet Union with France and Britain against Germany before she attacked Poland and plunged Europe into war. Though devious, Bonnet was not unintelligent. It is evident from the record that he realized quite well—much more than the British—that all depended on Russia. If she joined the West, Hitler would hesitate to go to war; if he did go to war Russia's military power, allied with that of the West, would defeat him.

As June came the talks with Russia were still stalled. One June 1, Monzie, who sat in the Cabinet as Minister of Public Works, noted in his diary that "the Anglo-French–Soviet negotiations have arrived at a blind alley. Actually, the project is dead, but it will not be buried, in order to give the impression that it is not dead."[1] Perhaps the wish was father to the thought. At any rate the notation expressed the sentiment of several ministers in the government. Daladier and Bonnet felt that the British were dragging their feet and that this was due largely to Chamberlain's attitude. The Prime Minister was not only distrustful of the Russians but did not believe they had enough military power to be of much use to the Western Allies.* However, on May 27, bowing to a storm of criticism in the Commons led by Winston Churchill, Lloyd George, and Anthony Eden, he finally instructed the British Ambassador in Moscow to agree to begin discussions of a pact of mutual assistance, a military convention, and

---

* This was the view of the British military experts. On March 6 that year, for instance, the British military and air attachés in Moscow had filed long dispatches to London to the effect that while the defensive capabilities of the Soviet Army and Air Force were considerable they were incapable of mounting a serious offensive.[2]

guarantees to the countries threatened by Hitler. This step, as the German Ambassador in London reported to Berlin, was taken "with the greatest reluctance" and only after the British government had got wind of "German feelers in Moscow."[3]

The Russians urged the British to send their Foreign Secretary to Moscow to speed up the negotiations. But Lord Halifax declined to go. "It was really impossible," he told the Soviet Ambassador, "to get away."[4] Anthony Eden, though out of office, offered to go in his place. Chamberlain would not hear of it.[5] Instead, he decided to send William Strang, a capable career official whose previous tour of duty in Moscow had not given him much liking for the Bolsheviks and who was little known either in his own country or outside it. To Churchill this appointment was "another mistake. The sending of so subordinate an official," he thought, "gave actual offense."[6] The Russians themselves made this quite clear. It was further evidence to them that Chamberlain was not very anxious to get down to business about a real alliance to halt Hitler.

Already on May 31, in his first public speech since becoming Commissar for Foreign Affairs, Molotov had castigated the Western democracies for their hesitation. If they were serious, he said, in joining Russia to stop aggression they must get down to brass tacks and agree on three main points:

1. Conclude a tripartite mutual-assistance pact.
2. Guarantee the states of Central and Eastern Europe, including *all* European states bordering on the Soviet Union.
3. Conclude a definite military agreement on the form and scope of the immediate and effective aid to be afforded one another and the smaller states threatened by aggression.

The same day he called in the French and British ambassadors and insisted that because of the delays in League of Nations procedures the contemplated guarantees be automatic, without reference to the League, as the British had proposed, and that the guarantees to the Baltic states, including Finland, be given regardless of their consent and against their wishes, if necessary.

Though the French government quickly agreed, the Soviet proposal was too much for the British government to swallow. It refused to join in a guarantee of a country against its will. This was an admirable position from an ethical point of view. But since Poland, Romania, and the Baltic states had made it plain they did not wish to be guaranteed by Russia, it meant in effect, as Bonnet continually pointed out to London all through June, that no effective alliance with Russia was possible. Chamberlain and Halifax finally gave in, on condition that the smaller countries would be guaranteed *secretly*. By now the Western democracies were making all the concessions, the British most reluctantly and the French out of desperation.

By July 4 only two serious differences between the two sides remained: an agreement on the definition of "indirect aggression" and on whether the political accord should be signed before a military pact was concluded. On the first question the British had argued that only the government of a state itself was qualified to decide whether or not it was the victim of aggression. But the Russians had cited the case of Czechoslovakia, where a government under extreme pressure had *consented* to a foreign military occupation. Molotov insisted that such a contingency be faced and proposed that "indirect aggression" cover "the case of an internal coup d'état or a political change favorable to the aggressor." He feared that the Baltic states, under threats from Berlin, might simply "invite" the Germans to march in, as Czechoslovakia had done, thus bringing Hitler's troops to the frontier of the Soviet Union.

The British, though willing to provide against a case such as Czechoslovakia, refused to go all the way with the Russians, pointing out to the French, who were willing to give in here too, that under the Soviet proposal a mere change of government in a guaranteed state would give Moscow the pretext for intervening and thus launching a European war. This question provided a stumbling block that would persist to the end.

On July 8, however, after a conference with the Allied ambassadors, Molotov seemed—at least to the French—willing to compromise further on the matter. But he insisted that no political treaty could be signed until a military accord had been concluded. This last demand angered London and "upset" Bonnet, who protested that it was "dangerous and contrary to all precedents." He admits that the Soviet government might have had in mind the "precedent" of France refusing to conclude a military convention after signing a mutual-assistance pact with Russia in 1935. He might have added, though he does not, that the French themselves as recently as May had declined, as we have seen, to synchronize a political and military pact with Poland. Bonnet finally proposed to the British a compromise: agreement with the U.S.S.R. to sign a political accord, including in it Molotov's definition of "indirect aggression," with the provision that it would not become effective until a military convention had been concluded.

But London was at the end of its patience. It told the French so in an *aide-mémoire* on July 13 declaring that the British government rejected the Soviet proposals both for defining "indirect aggression" and making the political accord subject to the conclusion of a military one.

> We have arrived at a point [the note said] where we can no longer continue the process of accepting each new demand of the Soviet government.

And after listing six concessions made to Moscow, it concluded:

> Our patience is almost exhausted, and the Soviet government must not count henceforth on our being ready to give in each time it formulates a new demand. His Majesty's Government may have to reexamine her entire position.[7]

It must be said for Bonnet that his own patience, in contrast to that of the British, was inexhaustible. He refused to accept the British position as final and began firing off telegrams to the Foreign Office in London through his Ambassador there and through the British Ambassador in Paris. On July 18 he asked Ambassador Corbin to see Lord Halifax immediately and "insist" that instructions be sent to the British Ambassador in Moscow "this evening" giving him "sufficient freedom of action to achieve the political accord on the best conditions still possible."[8] The next day, the 19th, he called in Sir Eric Phipps and handed him a personal letter to be wired to Halifax appealing to the British government to drop its reservations and sign the political treaty.

Our negotiations have been going on for four months. . . . The Premier and I believe it is of primary importance to bring them now to a successful conclusion. . . .

The same day he got off "pressing instructions" to Corbin to insist with the British government that "all the Soviet demands be accepted and that military talks start at once."

The hesitation of the British government on the threshold of the decisive phase of negotiations risks compromising not only the reaching of an accord but the consolidation of our diplomatic and strategic position in Central Europe. . . . All the bulwarks of our security in Europe will be destroyed. . . .[9]

The next day the British agreed to the commencement of military talks but still declined to accept the Russian definition of "indirect aggression" for fear, as Corbin wired to Bonnet on July 20, that it would give Russia "the right to interfere in the domestic affairs of certain third states and to exercise on them a pressure incompatible with the maintenance of their independence."[10]

On July 24 the French and British ambassadors in Moscow saw Molotov and to their surprise found him in a conciliatory mood. According to a dispatch to Paris of the French envoy, Paul-Emile Naggiar, the usually unbending Soviet Commissar conceded that since they had reached agreement on the main points of the political mutual-assistance pact—the differences over the definition of "indirect aggression" were "secondary"—they could now proceed to draw up a military convention which would spell out the obligations of the first. The Soviet Union, he added, was ready to begin at once.

France too. Daladier had already appointed General of the Army André Doumenc, formerly Deputy Chief of Staff under General Weygand, and considered to be one of the most brilliant officers in the French Army, to head the French military mission and instructed him to be ready to proceed to Moscow at once. But the British again dragged their feet. Chamberlain had been less than lukewarm to the whole business of staff talks and had not publicly announced his agreement to them until July 31, when he informed the Commons.*

The officers he selected for the military mission raised eyebrows both at home and abroad. The chief delegate, as might be supposed, was a naval officer, Admiral Sir Reginald A. R. Plunkett-Ernle-Erle-Drax, who had been Commander in Chief, Plymouth, until the year before. To a young army captain on the French mission he looked as though he had "descended from a portrait of Rodney"—a blunt, honest, seadog who, as would shortly become apparent, was completely out of his depth in high-level negotiations with the Russians, who seemed to him to be men from another planet. The Royal Air Force was represented by Air Marshal Sir Charles Burnett, a brilliant pilot who had risen from the ranks but who understood neither grand strategy nor diplomacy. The Army's representative was Major General T. G. G. Heywood, a capable officer with diplomatic experience.

The German Ambassador in London, Herbert von Dirksen, described the British delegation in a dispatch to Berlin August 1 in which he first pointed out the skepticism in London about the outcome of the Moscow talks with the West.

This is borne out [he wrote] by the composition of the British military mission. The Admiral . . . is practically on the retired list and was never on the Naval Staff. The General is also purely a combat officer. The Air Marshal is outstanding as a pilot and instructor, but not as a strategist. This seems to indicate that the task of the Military Mission is rather to ascertain the fighting value of the Soviet forces than to conclude agreements on operations. . . . The Wehrmacht attachés are agreed in observing a surprising skepticism in British military circles about the forthcoming talks with the Soviet armed forces.[12]

Indeed, so skeptical was the British government that it neglected to give Admiral Drax written authority to negotiate—an oversight, if it was that, which Marshal Voroshilov complained about when the staff officers first met.

But if Admiral Drax had no written credentials he certainly had secret written instructions on how to proceed at the meeting in Moscow. He was admonished "to go very slowly with the [military] conversations, watching the progress of the political negotiations," until a political agreement had been concluded.[13] It was explained to him that confidential military information could not be imparted to the Russians until the political pact was signed. It is obvious from the confidential British and French papers that the Chamberlain government was determined to take its time in spelling

---

* Cool, too, was William Strang, who had been sitting in on the talks in Moscow since June 14. "It is indeed extraordinary," he wrote the Foreign Office on July 20, "that we should be expected to talk military secrets with the Soviet Government before we are sure that they will be our allies."[11]

out the military obligations of each country, especially its own, in the proposed mutual-assistance pact.*

Though the French were in more of a hurry, the instructions given General Doumenc by General Gamelin on July 27 were, as the astute young staff officer Captain Beaufre saw immediately, "vague on essentials and terribly negative on the very points which would become crucial."† Obviously by the first of August, with the German army already concentrated in overwhelming strength on the Polish border, the most important point was the question of the support the Red Army could give to the Poles. But General Gamelin tried to dodge it.

The Poles [his instructions read] cannot admit officially in time of peace the intervention of the Russian forces on their territory in case of a conflict. But no doubt, at the moment of danger, they will accept the support of the Soviet Air Force and perhaps even of mechanized units. The possibility of their opening their frontiers to Russian forces of all categories remains improbable.[16]

Thus as August came, the month when the harvests of Europe were in and war could start, as it had in 1914, and now threatened to again, General Gamelin complacently accepted Poland's intransigence about Russian aid, though, as we have seen, he knew it to be disastrous. He showed, even at this late hour, as Beaufre says, that France had not yet taken seriously the question of Russian help because it did not yet see that this was the foundation of successful resistance—not only of Poland but of the West—to Germany. Ironically, the Germans saw it.

By now, perhaps Daladier too. On July 31 the French Premier received General Doumenc for a farewell talk. "Bring us back an accord—at any price," he told him.[17]

But there seemed to be no hurry about it, either in Paris or London. A plane would have got the Franco-British military mission to Moscow in a day. But it was decided by the two governments that it should proceed to Russia by slow boat, the 9,000 ton passenger-cargo vessel, *City of Exeter*,

---

* A copy of the British instructions to Admiral Drax was given the French on July 31. According to the then Captain André Beaufre, a member of the French military mission, who studied them, they "recommended proceeding with the greatest prudence, no important information was to be given, the possibility of a German-Soviet collusion was always to be kept in mind, and the negotiations were to be conducted as slowly as possible in order to gain time."[14] That the members of the British military mission understood their instructions was made clear by Air Marshal Burnett in a letter to the Chief of the Air Staff from Moscow: "I understand it is the Government's policy to prolong the negotiations as long as possible. . . ."[15]

† Gamelin, so detailed in his memoirs about so many things, does not mention them. Historians owe a debt to General Beaufre (as he later became) for revealing them and for giving the only comprehensive and documented account yet available (in 1967) of the French version of the military talks in Moscow. The British government has given its version fully in DBrFP, VII, especially in Appendix II, which gives the minutes of all the meetings as well as confidential notes and dispatches relating to them.

formerly used on the South African run. Its speed, as the Deputy Soviet Commissar for Foreign Affairs, Vladimir Potemkin, noted, "did not exceed 13 knots." He figured it would take the Allied mission six days to get to Moscow, and that was what it took. The *Queen Mary* could have conveyed it across the Atlantic to New York in less time.

On August 5 the *City of Exeter,* with an Indian crew, sailed from Tilbury with twenty-six officers of the Franco-British mission and steamed toward the Baltic and Russia.

Aboard the good ship the members worked out a draft for a military convention and Captain Beaufre thought it well defined the spirit with which the Allied military men entered into negotiations with their opposite numbers in Moscow. The key article (Number Seven) began:

The defense of the Polish and Romanian territories is essentially the task of the military forces of these two Powers.

However, if the two countries asked for help, the three Allies would respond, particularly with "air assistance, war material, and specialists."[18]

The Western military experts did not yet have an inkling of how far short this fell from the Soviet demands—or indeed from reality. They were soon to find out. But even to begin with, there was the great gulf between the Russian and Western worlds. Beaufre felt it as they arrived in Leningrad at midnight, August 9–10, under the pale northern sky. While the Indian crew busied itself with the docking, the British and French officers, standing on the bridge attired in dinner jackets, looked down on a shabbily dressed crowd. "It would have been difficult to better synthesize," he later noted, "the contrast between the two worlds which were about to meet." Soon after the two worlds met—and collided—Air Marshal Sir Charles Burnett, who, Beaufre thought, looked like a Colonel Bramble, a figure out of an old English engraving of a fox hunt, would be writing home of his impressions of the two ranking Soviet generals he faced across the table: "I have rarely seen such disagreeable faces."[19]

The Franco-British military mission finally reached Moscow on August 11 and met with the Soviet delegation, headed by Marshal Kliment E. Voroshilov, Commissar for Defense, and General Boris M. Shaposhnikov, Chief of the General Staff of the Red Army, for the first working session the next day.

By then it was very late.

THE SECRET RAPPROCHEMENT OF BERLIN AND MOSCOW: II

Perhaps too late.

The Germans also had turned to Moscow. All through May and June Hitler had blown hot and cold over the thorny question of making advances to the despised Soviet Union in order to thwart the Allied negotiations with it. On May 25 the German Foreign Office was informed that the Fuehrer wished "to establish more tolerable relations between Germany and the Soviet Union" and instructions detailing the new line were drafted for Ambassador Schulenburg, who was asked to see Molotov "as soon as possible." Hitler first approved the draft and then the next day changed his mind and forbade dispatching it. Four days later, on May 30, he changed his mind again and ordered a "modified approach" to Molotov. Talks were resumed in Moscow on a new trade treaty, but on June 29 Hitler abruptly called them off.

The initiative for their resumption came from the Russians. On July 18 they informed the Germans that they were prepared to "extend and intensify" German-Soviet economic relations. Hitler, badly in need of raw materials from abroad for his war, was interested. Instructions were given to conclude a trade agreement "at the earliest possible moment" and Schulenburg was told to "take up the threads" again of his previous political discussions with Molotov. He was advised of secret conversations between the Wilhelmstrasse and the Soviet Embassy in Berlin in which the Germans for the first time suggested that they had more to offer Russia than the Western democracies, especially with "respect to Soviet vital interests in Poland and the Baltic." This is the first mention of the subjects on which the Germans felt a deal with the Soviet Union might be based— the kind of deal at the expense of Poland and the Baltic states which the Western Allies could not, or would not, make. Schulenburg was instructed to emphasize this to Molotov. A note of urgency crept into the messages he received from Berlin. On July 31 he was told in an "urgent and secret" telegram to try to see Molotov at once and get down to business. The date is worth noting; it was on this last day of July that Chamberlain announced to the Commons that an Allied military mission was being sent to Moscow.

The announcement spurred on the Germans. August 3, two days before the Anglo-French military delegation sailed for Russia, was a crucial day in Berlin. The German government had made up its mind, and Ribbentrop personally so informed Ambassador Schulenburg in two "Secret–Most Urgent" telegrams supplemented by a third wire from Weizsaecker.[20] The German Foreign Minister informed his envoy in Moscow that in a conversation with the Soviet chargé, Astakhov, the day before

I expressed the *German* wish for remolding German-Russian relations and stated that from the Baltic to the Black Sea there was no problem which could not be settled to our mutual satisfaction. In response to Astakhov's desire for more concrete conversations on topical questions . . . I declared myself ready for such conversations. . . .

In a second telegram he revealed that he had "dropped a gentle hint (to Astakhov) at our coming to an understanding with Russia on the fate

of Poland." Weizsaecker's message, telegraphed in between the two messages from Ribbentrop, informed Schulenburg, who was seeing Molotov
that evening, that "we are anxious to continue in more concrete terms . . .
in view of the political situation and in the interests of speed."

The Germans were now in a hurry. Less than a month remained before
Hitler's target date of September 1 for the onslaught on Poland. When
Schnurre saw Astakhov that same day of August 3 he stressed the importance of making "use of *the next few days* . . . in order to establish a
basis as quickly as possible."* Not only were the Germans more in a
hurry than the French and the British; they were prepared to go to greater
lengths to reach an understanding with the Bolsheviks.

The astute French chargé d'affaires in Berlin, Jacques Tarbé de St.-
Hardouin, noted the change in the atmosphere in the German capital. On
August 3, the very day of so much German-Soviet diplomatic activity, he
reported to Paris:

> In the course of the last week a very definite change in the political
> atmosphere has been observed in Berlin. . . . The period of embarrassment,
> hesitation, inclination to temporization or even to appeasement, has been suc-
> ceeded among the Nazi leaders by a new phase.[21]

Hitler had finally and definitely made the decision to outbid the West-
ern democracies in Moscow. He was now confident that he would succeed.
As the French diplomat had clearly observed: the period of uncertainty in
Berlin had ended. With Russia lined up, the German war could begin.

It would, in fact, begin at the end of August, the Fuehrer told Count
Ciano at Obersalzberg on the 12th, explaining that the fall rains in October
would make the primitive Polish roads impassable. Toward the end of the
meeting a "telegram from Moscow," as the German minutes put it, was
handed to Hitler. After perusing it, he turned to the Italian Foreign Minister. "The Russians," he said, "have agreed to a German political nego-
tiator's being sent to Moscow."[22]

Though no "telegram from Moscow" was ever found in the captured
German documents there can be no doubt that Hitler was referring to a
teleprint he received on August 12 from the Foreign Office in Berlin. The
Soviet Embassy had informed it that very day that Molotov was now ready
to discuss the questions raised by the Germans, including "the Polish
question," and that the Soviet government proposed Moscow as the place
in which to discuss them. The talks, however, Molotov had stressed, would
have to be undertaken "by degrees."[23]

But Hitler could not wait for negotiations with the Russians "by
degrees." The attack on Poland had to begin by September 1, and it was
now nearly the middle of August. If he were successfully to sabotage the
Anglo-French talks in Moscow—the first military conversations had begun

---

* Emphasis in the original document.

this same day, August 12—and swing his own deal with Stalin, it had to be done quickly, not by stages but in one big leap.

Monday, August 14, was another crucial day for the Germans. At 10:53 P.M. Ribbentrop dispatched a long "Most Urgent" telegram to Schulenburg, "For the Ambassador Personally," directing him to call on Molotov and read him the contents verbatim. A "speedy clarification of German-Russian relations," he wired, was necessary. Likewise an agreement on "territorial questions in Eastern Europe. Since . . . this clarification can be achieved only slowly through the usual diplomatic channels, I am prepared to make a short visit to Moscow in order, in the name of the Fuehrer, to set forth the Fuehrer's views to M. Stalin. It should not be impossible to lay the foundations for a final settlement. . . ."

The nature of those foundations was shrewdly put, and especially designed to appeal to Stalin. The Western democracies, Ribbentrop said, "are trying to drive Russia into war with Germany." That was exactly what Stalin had told the Party Congress in March. But the bait the Germans offered was calculated to appeal to the Soviet dictator the most.

There exist no real conflicts between Germany and Russia. . . . The Reich government are of the opinion that there is no question from the Baltic to the Black Sea which cannot be settled to the complete satisfaction of both countries. Among these are such questions as: the Baltic Sea, the Baltic states, Poland, Southeastern questions, etc.[24]

This was a bid to the Soviet Union to divide up Eastern Europe, including Poland, a bid which France and Britain could not—and obviously, if they could, would not—match, though the Russians had gingerly felt out the Allied military missions on the subject, at least in regard to the Baltic, where the former Russian provinces lay. The German proposal offered Stalin a double advantage: staying out of a war with Germany, which he greatly feared and wished to avoid; and getting back—on a platter, so to speak, without the risk of costly conflict—all the territories taken from the Soviet Union under Western pressure at the end of the Great War in the Baltic, Poland, and Romania. To go with France and Britain, on the other hand, meant certain involvement in a war with Germany in which the Western democracies might sit tight while Hitler's mechanized armies swept through Poland and Russia. And even if victory were finally won, there might be little left of the Soviet Union, including its Bolshevik regime, and no prospect of regaining the lost lands. These factors, as Stalin saw them, must be kept in mind as we return to the negotiations with the Western Allies in the Soviet capital.

THE FRANCO-BRITISH TALKS WITH RUSSIA: III

August 14 was also a crucial day in the military talks in Moscow. They had not gone well from the beginning of the first meeting two days before when Marshal Voroshilov protested Admiral Drax's lack of written credentials to negotiate after he and General Doumenc (who had an *Ordre de Service* signed by Daladier) had produced theirs.*[25] This seemed to the bureaucratic-minded Russians to show a lack of seriousness by the British in the negotiations. And their confidence in the Western Allies was not increased in the second and third sessions on the 13th when the Soviets pressed for facts and figures on Franco-British forces and plans and General Doumenc and Admiral Drax did their best to follow instructions by imparting as little information as possible, some of which was obviously less than the truth.

"The least that can be said," commented Captain Beaufre on General Doumenc's exposition of the forces which France would hurl against Germany if she attacked Poland, "is that it stretched the truth a little." Among other things, the French general told the Russians that the Maginot Line now extended "from the Swiss frontier to the sea," whereas any newspaper correspondent knew that it did not cover half that length and indeed left the French army exposed to a long undefended border south of Belgium. Even the French, who knew the facts, were surprised at the size of the British Army which General Heywood said his country would put in the field: 16 divisions "in the early stages of a war" and 16 divisions more later. Beaufre figured this was "three to four times" greater than the British had promised the French in staff talks recently. But Voroshilov, who, the British and French officers had already conceded, conducted himself like the proverbial Russian bear, was not to be put off. "How many divisions will you have if war breaks out soon?" he asked, finally forcing the British general to admit, after he manfully tried evading an answer, that all England had at the moment was "five regular divisions and one mechanized division." Beaufre says he felt at this moment that "the Soviet delegation understood better than it had the immense weakness of the British Empire."

All through the two meetings on August 13 the "terrible Voroshilov," as the French army captain calls him, not without a touch of affection, kept putting searching questions to the visiting military delegations, most of which they had been instructed to evade, if possible. What forces, the Marshal asked, will Poland have against Germany and what is their plan of defense? All the unhappy Doumenc could say was that he did not know. What about Belgium? asked Voroshilov, having in mind no doubt how the Germans had swept through that little country in 1914. The defense of Belgium, Doumenc answered, was "primarily the task of her own forces. French troops cannot enter unless and until they are asked to, but France is ready to answer any call."

Then at the close of the afternoon session on August 13 Voroshilov posed the crucial question: *How did the French and British General Staffs*

---

* In Note 25 will be found the principal sources on which I have based this section on the military talks in Moscow and the repercussion in Paris, London, and Warsaw. Specific numbered source footnotes have been dispensed with in order to avoid cluttering the text. But each statement, quotation, dispatch, and note is fully documented from the sources given.

envisage the action which the Red Army could take in the event of aggression against Poland and Romania, since Russia, having no common frontier with Germany, "must take action on the territory of other states?" He asked for an answer by the next day. This was the key question and its putting by the Russians and its evasion by the Western Allies led to the crisis of August 14 and to the events which followed.

At first Admiral Drax and General Doumenc tried to put Voroshilov off when he began the meeting on the 14th by insisting on an answer to his question. It was the duty of Poland and Romania, the French General argued, "to defend their own frontiers, but the Three Powers must be ready to help them when they ask for assistance." Voroshilov replied that they "might ask for help too late" and be overrun by the Germans in the meantime. Admiral Drax then declared that he was sure they "would ask for help as soon as they had been driven back from their frontiers. If they did not ask for help when necessary" [he added], "and allowed themselves to be overrun, it may be expected that they would become German provinces."

The last thing the Russians wanted on their borders were German provinces, full of German troops, and Voroshilov jumped up, bristling, and said that the Soviet delegation "noted with interest" the Admiral's statement and that he hoped all present would also carefully note it. Beaufre thought it had impressed the Russian officers in the worst possible way. The Admiral, he says, had suggested making the point in discussions aboard ship the week before but the French had "begged" him not to.

Admiral Drax may have realized that he had blundered for, according to the British minutes, he asked for an adjournment. Voroshilov opposed it. His face flushed a deep crimson (according to Beaufre), he rose, and for the fourth and final time put his questions. This time he was specific.

1. Will the Soviet forces be allowed to move against East Prussia through Polish territory and, in particular, through the Wilno Gap?

2. Will the Soviet forces be permitted to advance through Polish Galicia in order to make contact with enemy troops?

3. Will Soviet forces be allowed to use Romanian territory in the event of German aggression against that country?

"We ask for straightforward answers to these questions," he added. "In my opinion, without an exact, unequivocal answer it is useless to continue these military conversations."

A brief adjournment was taken for the British and French to take counsel. As the officers walked out to the garden Beaufre heard Admiral Drax exclaim: "I'm afraid our mission is ended!" After a few minutes' consultation the visiting delegations drew up a written reply, which General Heywood read to the Russians. It did not help matters.

It must not be forgotten [it said] that Poland and Romania are sovereign states, and that the authority required by the Soviet mission must be obtained from these two governments. This becomes a political question, and we therefore suggest that the Soviet government should ask the Polish and Romanian governments for the answer. . . .

In the meantime, in view of the possibility "that German armies will be marching into Poland tomorrow," the Franco-British statement urged that they stop "wasting precious time" and continue the discussions on the assumption that the answer to the Russian question would be yes.

Voroshilov then asked for a recess to confer. After an hour, during which, Beaufre was sure, the Marshal was told on the telephone how to answer by Stalin himself, he read, in turn, the written Soviet reply. It was both sarcastic and tough.

The Russian military mission, it said, "had not forgotten that Poland and Romania are sovereign states." On the contrary, it said, that was why the Soviets had asked the French and British to get the permission of the two states for the passage of Russian troops. It was up to them to obtain it, since they, not Russia, had guaranteed Poland and Romania.

The Soviet military mission expresses its regret at the absence of an exact answer on the part of the British and French missions to this question of the right of passage of Soviet armed forces over Polish and Romanian territory.

[It] considers that, without a solution to this question, all the discussions which have been started regarding the conclusion of a military agreement . . . are doomed to failure. For this reason, the Soviet military mission cannot recommend to its government to take part in an enterprise so obviously doomed to failure.

To Captain Beaufre the Soviet response was "extremely frank and of a logic, unfortunately for us, irrefutable." Apprised of the crisis, the British and French ambassadors in Moscow hastily conferred and then got off telegrams to their respective capitals.

The French Ambassador and I . . . are agreed [Sir William Seeds wired] that Russians have now raised fundamental problem on which military talks will succeed or fail . . . namely, how to reach any useful agreement with Soviet Union so long as this country's neighbors maintain a sort of boycott which is only to be broken . . . when it is too late. . . . We are agreed that Soviet negotiators are justified in putting on Great Britain and France the onus of approaching those countries.

He, like the French Ambassador and General Doumenc, who sent similar telegrams to Paris, asked that the Polish government be pressured to accept at once, and stressed "the extreme urgency" of getting an immediate response. "Unfortunately," says Beaufre, "the response never came." It was not that the French and British governments did not try to bring the Poles around to reason, but that they did not try hard enough.

Georges Bonnet says he was awakened at 5 A.M. on the morning of August 15 by an official bearing a dispatch from Ambassador Naggiar with the tidings of the Soviet demand. After quickly reading it, he says he realized "its extreme gravity." He immediately telephoned the Polish Ambassador, who, unmindful of the crisis, was vacationing on a beach in Brittany. Bonnet asked him to return to Paris immediately for consultation. It was not of much use. When the Foreign Minister insisted that Poland must accept the help of the Red Army if she were to save herself, Lukasiewicz replied: "Never!" Bonnet reminded him that Hitler had recently boasted he would overrun Poland in three weeks.

"On the contrary," replied the Ambassador. "It is the Polish Army which will invade Germany—at the very outset."

The Ambassador had no idea, as Bonnet advised his own envoy in Warsaw by wire, "of the danger to his country caused by such incomprehension." Unfortunately for Poland it was also true of the men in Warsaw who ruled it. Still, the French Foreign Minister, at last aroused, tried desperately to bring the Polish government down to realities. On the night of August 16 he wired Ambassador Léon Noël in Warsaw to "insist" to Beck that he agree to accept Russian help. Bonnet's logic this time was impeccable.

You should forcefully stress [to Beck] that eventual Russo-Polish collaboration on the eastern front is an indispensable condition to the effectiveness of our common resistance to Axis aggression; that it would be dangerous to await the opening of hostilities before agreeing to it, and that . . . in refusing to discuss the strategic conditions of Russian intervention, Poland would accept the responsibility of a breakdown in the military negotiations at Moscow, and of all the consequences which would result.

General Musse, the French military attaché in Warsaw, was summoned from *his* vacation in France and rushed back to Poland to add to the pressure on the Polish General Staff. In Moscow General Doumenc, on his own hook, decided to send Captain Beaufre to support him and to explain to the Polish military leaders that "the strategic importance of Russian aid was undeniable and the importance of concluding the military pact no less so."

The situation in Moscow on the night of August 17, when Beaufre left by train for Warsaw, was, he says, "agonizing. We were on the verge of rupture . . . and we had not yet had any response to our telegrams on the main point raised by Voroshilov."

The meetings of the military missions on August 15 and 16 had not got anywhere. On the 15th, General Shaposhnikov, the Chief of the Red Army General Staff, after complaining that the French and British had given "nothing concrete" about their military plans, had exposed his own. He declared that "against aggression in Europe" the Soviet Union would

"deploy" 120 infantry divisions, 16 cavalry divisions, 5,000 heavy guns
and howitzers, 9 to 10 thousand tanks, 5,000 to 5,500 fighter and bomber
aircraft—figures which fairly took the breath out of the Western officers,
though they judged them exaggerated. But again the Russians came back
relentlessly to the same point. They could only employ such a force effectively, Shaposhnikov explained, if they could come to grips with the
Germans by first advancing through Poland and Romania.

The next day Admiral Drax and General Doumenc tried to get the
Soviets to agree to some general principles of joint action, which they had
drafted. But the Russians were not interested. "They are too abstract,"
Voroshilov declared, "and do not oblige anyone to do anything. . . . We
are not here to make abstract declarations but to work out a complete
military convention which should fix the number of divisions, artillery, tanks,
aircraft, and naval squadrons which each of the three states will contribute."
Until the Russians got an answer to the "cardinal point on the passage of
Soviet troops through Poland and Romania," he added, "it will be useless
to continue our conversations."

The next day, August 17, the inevitable climax came. Voroshilov
demanded an adjournment of the talks until a definite reply had been
received. Drax and Doumenc objected, arguing that useful staff work
could be done in the meantime and that the news that the conference had
adjourned indefinitely would have a calamitous effect on the already tense
situation in Europe. It was finally agreed to adjourn for four days—until
August 21. The unsolved question of the right of passage of Soviet troops,
all-important as it was if an effective military alliance was to be forged,
was not the only factor which made the Russians so adamant for adjournment. In the greatest of secrecy Berlin and Moscow were at that moment
drawing closer together. But this neither the French and British governments nor their military experts in Moscow knew. General Doumenc
sincerely believed that the Russians still wanted a military accord.*

As soon as the meeting on August 17 had adjourned he wired Paris
urgently:

The session for the 21st was only fixed to avoid an impression abroad that
the talks have been interrupted. . . . The U.S.S.R. wants a military pact. . . .
She does not want us to give her a piece of paper without substantial under-
takings. Marshal Voroshilov has stated that all the problems . . . would be
tackled without difficulty as soon as what he termed the crucial question was
settled. It is now indispensable that I should be authorized to respond yes to the
question.

---

* Even Air Marshal Burnett, he who had found the Slavic faces of the Russian
generals so "disagreeable," thought so. Writing to his Chief of Staff from Moscow on
August 16 he stated: "We consider that Russia wishes to come to some agreement
with the Allies, but they fear that they cannot afford to wait until Germany has overrun Poland and fight Germany on the defensive in their own territory. . . ."

The "yes" depended, however, on the Polish government and the Polish General Staff, and on the success of the French and British governments in inducing them to give it. Though both Paris and London had been reckless in giving their pledges to Poland without thought of Russia, they now realized—in mid-August—that their help in the West could not save Poland unless the Soviet Union also came to her aid in the East. For the next three days, from the 17th to the 20th, they tried strenuously to convince the Poles of this.

Armed with the new instructions from the Quai d'Orsay, which arrived in Warsaw on the 17th, Ambassador Noël and General Musse saw Foreign Minister Beck and General Stachiewicz, respectively, the next day. Both ran into a stone wall. Beck told the Ambassador that to agree to a passage of Soviet troops through Poland would provoke Hitler to attack immediately. Even if Poland agreed to accept Russian help he was certain that the U.S.S.R. would not honor its military engagements and indeed was "materially incapable" of honoring them. When Noël urged him to think it over, Beck said that he would and that after consulting Marshal Smigly-Rydz* he would give the government's definite reply the next day. "But I have little hope," he concluded. "What we Poles fear is that once the Soviet troops have entered our territory they will never leave."

General Musse fared no better with the Chief of the Polish General Staff. General Stachiewicz told him he had no faith in the Russians and that they "wanted merely to occupy Polish territory and had no intention of employing Soviet troops in offensive operations."

Though Bonnet in Paris, as his telegrams and memoirs make clear, assumed that the French military attaché was doing his best to convince the Polish General Staff that it should accept—indeed, welcome—Soviet aid, it became known later that General Musse did not have his heart in it and could not have been very effective.† He shared the Poles' distrust of Russia and their overestimation of their own strength and of Soviet military weakness. When Captain Beaufre arrived in Warsaw from Moscow on the evening of August 18 and explained the predicament of the military talks in Moscow he found little sympathy from General Musse. The military attaché told him flatly that there was no chance of Poland's accepting Soviet aid. "The hatred of the Poles and Russians make it impossible," he said and added that he too doubted the "good faith" of the Soviets. "The intervention you ask us to make here," he went on, "will play into the hands of the Russians, who have never renounced the idea of recovering the land they lost in 1921. We should not make ourselves the

* Marshal Edward Smigly-Rydz, Inspector General of the Army, ranked second to the President, but, as the successor to Marshal Pilsudki, was the actual chief of the government and the armed forces. He had the last word.

† General Gamelin, so far as his own papers and all others available show, did nothing to stir up General Musse or the Polish General Staff, though the issue was of vital importance to the French Army.

brokers for these propositions." When Beaufre argued that even the British now admitted that the Polish army could not hold out alone against the Germans for more than fifteen days and that therefore Russian aid was indispensable, General Musse responded "violently, arguing that it was absurd to underestimate such an excellent army, well-equipped and whose tactical conceptions had made great progress."

As Beaufre muses sadly, one can see how easily foreign observers on the spot "can make erroneous judgments," especially "if they have lived long in a country where a thousand ties, a thousand sympathies, attach you to it and falsify your judgments"—a finding concurred in by this writer, who in twenty years as a foreign correspondent in a dozen capitals found it terribly true of most ambassadors (Henderson in Berlin, for example) and nearly all military attachés (including the American). "In the case of General Musse," Beaufre concludes, "it was evident that he was for the Poles against the Russians and entirely disposed to defend their ideas."

Conceivably, it wouldn't have made much difference if General Musse had been more objective and farsighted. For the Poles in August 1939, like their ancestors for centuries, had become blinded to their own best interests and, as so often in their tragic past, seemed doomed to court their own destruction.

August 19 was the decisive day. Beck had promised his definitive answer by evening. In the morning the British military attaché in Warsaw joined his French colleague in a new appeal to the Polish General Staff. General Stachiewicz remained deaf to their pleas. "In no case," he said, "can Poland admit Soviet troops to its territory. No useful purpose can be served by discussing it." He conceded only, as Beck had done the day before, that the final decision would be given them that evening after consultation with Marshal Smigly-Rydz. He left no doubt what it would be.

Early in the afternoon in Paris, Bonnet, by now almost frantic, conferred with the British chargé, Sir Ronald Campbell—Ambassador Phipps too was on vacation.

> It would be disastrous [Bonnet said] if, in consequence of a Polish refusal, the Russian negotiations were to break down. . . . It was an untenable position for the Poles to take up in refusing the only immediate efficacious help that could reach them in the event of a German attack. It would put the British and French governments in an almost impossible position if we had to ask our respective countries to go to war in defense of Poland, which had refused this help.

Bonnet "hoped" the British government would continue to support him in his "efforts to persuade M. Beck." That evening in Warsaw Beck finally made it plain that neither he nor the Polish government nor the General Staff could be persuaded. The "oracle," as Beaufre describes Marshal Smigly-Rydz, had been consulted and had confirmed the decision.

Beck told the French Ambassador: "I do not admit that there can be any kind of discussion whatsoever concerning the use of part of our territory by foreign troops. We have not got a military agreement with the U.S.S.R. We do not want one."

At this fateful juncture the French and British had only one last ace to play with the Poles: to tell them that unless they reversed their decision and agreed to accept Russian aid the Anglo-French commitments of help would be withdrawn. The formal Anglo-Polish mutual-security treaty had not yet been signed, despite Beck's urging. And Bonnet was still sitting on the political accord with Poland which he had refused to sign in May. As far back as April 3, four days after Chamberlain had announced Britain's unilateral guarantee of Poland, Lloyd George had risen in the House of Commons and demanded that the government make its fulfillment conditional on the Poles accepting Soviet help.

If we are going in without the help of Russia [he said] we are walking into a trap. It is the only country whose armies can get there [to Poland]. . . . I cannot understand why, before committing ourselves to this tremendous enterprise, we did not secure beforehand the adhesion of Russia. . . . If Russia has not been brought into this matter because of certain feelings the Poles have that they do not want the Russians there, it is for us to declare the conditions, and unless the Poles are prepared to accept the only conditions with which we can successfully help them, the responsibility must be theirs.

But that far neither Chamberlain and Halifax in London nor Daladier and Bonnet in Paris were willing to go. They came close, and then hesitated to take the final step. In his talk with Campbell on August 19 Bonnet had concluded by saying he was "glad that a political treaty had not yet been concluded with Poland, since this fact perhaps gave us means of exerting pressure." But he had stopped there. Halifax nudged a little closer to the decisive step. On August 20 he wired his Ambassador in Warsaw pointing out that the Polish government had been urging

the early conclusion of a formal Anglo-Polish treaty on the ground that this would . . . reinforce confidence in Europe.

But His Majesty's Government consider that the positive effect of [this] . . . would hardly counterbalance the negative effect, which would indeed be disastrous, of a final breakdown of the Anglo-Franco–Soviet negotiations in Moscow. . . . If Polish independence is to be preserved, Poland must do everything she can to facilitate and render fully effective the assistance that is offered to her. I shall be glad if you will put these considerations to M. Beck with all the earnestness at your command.

Halifax, in his turn, stopped there. Like Bonnet, he pled with the Poles, but shrank from making the final condition which might have reversed

Beck's decision of the evening of August 19. They did not know, of course, that on that same evening in Moscow Stalin had made a fateful decision of his own.

THE SECRET RAPPROCHEMENT OF BERLIN AND MOSCOW: III

The Russians, to the immense relief of Hitler, had responded favorably to the German proposal of August 14 for talks. When Ambassador Schulenburg saw Molotov on the evening of the 15th and read to him the contents of Ribbentrop's telegram stating that the Nazi Foreign Minister was prepared to come to Moscow at once to settle all the problems "from the Baltic to the Black Sea," the Soviet Commissar replied that he "warmly welcomed German intentions of improving relations with the Soviet Union." He went further. He asked whether Germany would be interested in a nonaggression pact between the two countries and a joint guarantee of the Baltic states. These matters, he said, would have to be discussed in "concrete terms."

The first suggestion, then, for a Nazi-Soviet nonaggression pact came from the Russians—at the very moment they were negotiating with France and Britain to go to war, if necessary, to oppose further German aggression.* There could be no doubt what Hitler's response would be. A nonaggression pact would keep Russia out of the war and enable him to attack Poland on schedule without fear of Soviet intervention. In addition, it would probably give France and Britain cold feet.

The Fuehrer's answer came back to Moscow the next day, August 16. Schulenburg was directed by Ribbentrop to see Molotov at once and inform him "that Germany is prepared to conclude a nonaggression pact with the Soviet Union . . . and to guarantee the Baltic States jointly."

The Nazi dictator was in a hurry. Ribbentrop proposed to come to Moscow on August 18 "by airplane"—no slow boats for the Germans—

---

* On August 17 in Washington, Sumner Welles, Undersecretary of State, had tried to alert the British about what Molotov was up to with the Germans. He called in Sir Ronald Lindsay, the British Ambassador, that day, described the conversation between Schulenburg and Molotov on August 15th, outlined what the Germans had offered, and revealed Molotov's reply accurately and in detail, including the suggestion for a nonaggression pact and a deal for the Baltic. The information had come from U.S. Ambassador Lawrence Steinhardt, who had had a long talk with Molotov on August 16. Why did Molotov disclose this information to the American Ambassador? The Kremlin must have known that it would be passed on to the British. Was Stalin still undecided on August 16 into which camp to jump? Was he trying to warn the Anglo-French negotiators in Moscow that they must get down to business or else he would sign up with the Germans, who were offering him a great deal? The answer will never be known until the Soviet archives are opened. But if the Kremlin was trying to pressure the Western Allies, the move proved futile because, despite Mr. Welles' effort on the 17th, London received the information too late. British bungling here is almost unbelievable. Instead of urgently cabling London, Ambassador Lindsay sent on the information by *air mail,* which was much slower in 1939 than it is today. His dispatch was not received in the Foreign Office in London until August 22, when it was no longer of any use. Had it been received on August 17, or even on the 18th, history just possibly might have taken a different turn. For on the 18th, so far as can be learned, Stalin had not yet, not quite, made up his mind.[26]

armed with "full powers from the Fuehrer . . . to sign the appropriate treaties."[27]

The Kremlin, after its experience with the dilatory tactics of the Western democracies, was impressed by the dispatch of the Germans. On the evening of the 17th, when Molotov again received Schulenburg, he told him that the Soviet government "was highly gratified at the prospect of Ribbentrop's coming to Moscow,

since the dispatch of such an eminent politician and statesman emphasized how serious were the intentions of the German government. This stood in marked contrast to England, which, in the person of Strang, had sent only an official of second-class rank to Moscow."[28]

The wily Soviet Foreign Commissar, however, made no mention of Ribbentrop's request to be received on August 18. "The journey," he told Schulenburg, "required thorough preparation."

The captured confidential German state papers make clear that by this time—mid-August—Hitler and Ribbentrop were growing desperate. The orders for German submarines and the pocket battleships to sail for British waters were being held up until the deal with the Bolsheviks could be concluded. The warships would have to get off at once if they were to reach their appointed stations by Hitler's target date for launching his war. September 1, D-Day, was only a fortnight away. Also the two great army groups designated for the onslaught on Poland would have to be deployed, ready for the jump-off, immediately.

On the night of the 18th there went out from Hitler's summer headquarters on the Obersalzberg another "Most Urgent" cable from Ribbentrop to Schulenburg in Moscow. He must see Molotov at once and insist that the Russians agree to receiving the German Foreign Minister "immediately." He must not take no for an answer. The Nazi Foreign Minister reiterated that he was empowered by Hitler "to settle fully and conclusively the total complex of problems." The Nazis were quite blunt. Ribbentrop was ready, he said, "to sign a special protocol regulating the interests of both parties . . . for instance, the settlement of spheres of interest in the Baltic area."[29]

The telegram reached the German Embassy in the Soviet capital at 5:45 A.M. on August 19 and Schulenburg made an appointment for 2 P.M. to convey its contents to Molotov.

August 19 was the decisive day in Moscow, as it was in Warsaw. It started badly for the Germans. When Schulenburg saw Molotov at 2 P.M. the latter refused to fix a date for Ribbentrop's journey. "Thorough preparations would be required," Molotov said, "and the economic agreement would first have to be signed."

The dejected German Ambassador had scarcely returned to his Embassy before he received a telephone call from Molotov asking him to come back to see him at 4:30 P.M. Something had happened at the Kremlin in the meantime. Returning to the Embassy after his second talk of the afternoon with Molotov, Schulenburg jubilantly rushed off a wire to Berlin at 6:22 P.M.

SECRET

MOST URGENT

The Soviet Government agree to the Reich Foreign Minister coming to Moscow one week after the announcement of the economic agreement. Molotov stated that if the conclusion of [it] . . . is made public tomorrow, the Reich Foreign Minister could arrive in Moscow on August 26 or 27.

Molotov handed me a draft of a nonaggression pact.[30]

In a following telegram Schulenburg reported: "Molotov did not give reasons for his sudden change of mind. I assume that Stalin intervened."[31]

The assumption could not have been wrong. It is known that that evening, August 19, the Soviet dictator announced his decision to the Politburo.* A little earlier that day—between 3 P.M., when the first Schul-

---

* In his postwar testimony before the Parliamentary Investigating Committee,[32] Daladier produced a long Havas dispatch from Moscow, via Geneva, which purported to give the minutes of the meeting of the Politburo on the night of August 19 when Stalin announced his decision and explained it. Although Daladier said he could not "verify the authenticity" of the dispatch, he believed it "authentic." In its report of Stalin's reasoning, it has a ring of truth, especially when compared to what the dictator told Churchill in 1942. Stalin's argument, as given in the Havas dispatch at great length, may be summed up: if the U.S.S.R. made an alliance with the West, Hitler might postpone his attack on Poland and seek another *modus vivendi* with the West, "which would be dangerous for us." If Russia signed a treaty with Germany, she would be able to stay out of the war, which would surely follow, at least "until our turn came." The war would undoubtedly exhaust both Germany and the West so that neither could make war against Russia "for a whole decade." In the meantime and indeed at once, thanks to an agreement with Germany, Russia would obtain "a part of Poland, liberty of action in the three Baltic states, and regain Bessarabia." So much for this French version of Stalin's reasoning. Though the U.S.S.R. would quickly, in 1940, regain the lost territories, as Stalin predicted, his calculation about Germany's exhausting herself before she could turn on Russia proved disastrous and nearly fatal. In a talk with Churchill "in the early morning hours" on an August day in 1942, exactly three years later, Stalin explained one reason for not concluding a military pact with the Western Allies.

> "How many divisions," Stalin had asked, "will France send against Germany on mobilization?" The answer was: "About a hundred." He then asked: "How many will England send?" The answer was: "Two and two more later." "Ah, two and two more later," Stalin had repeated. "Do you know," he asked, "how many divisions we shall have to put on the Russian front if we go to war with Germany? . . . More than three hundred."[33]

Be it noted that Stalin was exaggerating. On August 16 Shaposhkinov told the Allied Military Missions that Russia would deploy in Europe 120 infantry divisions, 16 cavalry divisions, and the necessary artillery and tank units.

enburg-Molotov meeting ended, and 4:30 P.M., when the second one began
—Stalin had communicated his fateful decision to Molotov and instructed
him to inform the Germans at once.

Hitler was delighted with the Soviet response—except for one thing.
He could not wait until August 26 or 27 for Ribbentrop to sign the treaty
in Moscow. He had now about decided to advance the date for the jump-off
against Poland by six days—to August 26 instead of September 1. Swallowing his pride he got off a long personal telegram to Stalin begging the
Soviet dictator, whom he had so often and for so long maligned, to receive
his Foreign Minister in Moscow on August 22, or "at the latest," on
August 23. He said that he accepted Molotov's draft of the nonaggression
treaty as well as "the substance of the supplementary protocol desired by
the Soviet Union" (by which, as we shall see, the two countries divided up
Eastern Europe) but that the latter would have to be "clarified" and that
Ribbentrop would be able to do so with the Russians "in the shortest
possible time."[34]

For the next twenty-four hours the Nazi dictator, according to several
eyewitnesses, was in a state of suspense bordering on collapse and was
unable to sleep. Finally at 9:35 P.M. on August 21 Stalin's reply came over
the wires in Berlin.

TO THE CHANCELLOR OF THE GERMAN REICH,
HERR A. HITLER:

I thank you for the letter. I hope that the German-Soviet nonaggression
pact will bring about a decided turn for the better in the political relations
between our countries.

The peoples of our countries need peaceful relations with each other. The
assent of the German government to the conclusion of a nonaggression pact
provides the foundation for eliminating the political tension and for the establishment of peace and collaboration between our countries.

The Soviet Government have instructed me to inform you that they agree
to Herr von Ribbentrop's arriving in Moscow on August 23.

J. STALIN[35]

Shortly before midnight on this eventful day of August 21 a musical
program on the Berlin radio was suddenly interrupted and a voice came
on to announce:

The Reich government and the Soviet government have agreed to conclude a pact of nonaggression with each other. The Reich Minister for Foreign
Affairs will arrive in Moscow on Wednesday, August 23, for the conclusion of
the negotiations.

THE FRANCO-BRITISH TALKS WITH RUSSIA: IV

While Stalin on August 21 was considering his reply to Hitler, which would be sent at the end of the day, Marshal Voroshilov was sitting down with the Allied missions in a resumption of the adjourned military talks. Though Admiral Drax had proposed "to wait for another two or three days" because neither he nor General Doumenc had received replies to the Russian question on passage of Red Army troops through Poland from their governments, the Soviet Marshal had insisted on reconvening the conference at 11 A.M. on the 21st, as agreed upon when the meeting of the 17th adjourned. Presumably, as one of Stalin's right-hand men, he knew of the dictator's decision of the 19th to make a deal with Hitler.

After the session had opened on an almost ludicrous note—Admiral Drax proudly produced his written credentials, not realizing that they had arrived too late—Voroshilov demanded that the meetings be adjourned indefinitely, or at least until replies had been received to the question of Soviet troops entering Poland. If the responses did come and were negative, he did not "see any chance of meeting again." When the British and French protested further delay in the talks, the Russians recessed—no doubt to consult Stalin—and returned with a *written* answer, which Voroshilov solemnly read.

The intentions of the Soviet delegation were, and still are, to agree on the organization of military cooperation of the armed forces of the three contracting parties. . . . The U.S.S.R., not having a common frontier with Germany, can give help to France, Britain, Poland, and Romania only on condition that her troops are given rights of passage across Polish and Romanian territory. There exists no other way of making contact with the troops of the aggressor.

Here he reminded his guests that British and American troops in the last war could not have confronted the Germans unless they had been allowed to operate on French soil.

The Soviet military delegation cannot picture to itself how the governments and General Staffs of Britain and France, in sending their missions to the U.S.S.R. . . . could not have given them some directives in such an elementary matter. . . . This can only show that there are reasons to doubt their desire to come to serious and effective cooperation with the U.S.S.R. . . . The responsibility . . . naturally falls on the British and French delegations.

This was passing the buck. Voroshilov's argument, to be sure, was logical. The Allies were asking Russia to fight Germany but denying her the ground on which to fight. But to repeat the argument on August 21, two days after the Kremlin had decided to go with the Nazis, was deceitful.

Ignorant of what was passing between Berlin and Moscow but aroused at last by the urgent telegrams from General Doumenc and Ambassador Naggiar* and fed up with Polish intransigence, Daladier on August 21 decided on drastic action. According to his own account[36] he called in the Polish Ambassador during the morning, assured him that if the Poles let in Red Army troops the Western Allies would see to it that they did not linger in Poland after the fighting stopped, and demanded that Warsaw accept.

I added, moreover, that the situation appeared to me to be so grave that if we were resolved to avert war it was necessary to conclude this military pact, which was the only act capable of making Hitler hesitate and reflect. I said furthermore that he must urgently warn his government that it must choose, and that if by the afternoon I had not received from him a negative response I would wire General Doumenc myself authorizing him to sign the military convention with Russia.

At 4:15 P.M., when no word had been received from the Polish government, Daladier got off his telegram to Doumenc:

You are authorized to sign, for the furtherance of our common interests . . . the military convention, with the reservation that it must be approved by the French government.

But this was an idle gesture, as long as Poland had not agreed, and a futile one in view of Stalin's decision two days before. Besides, there was no "military convention" to sign. None had yet been drawn up because of the stalemate over the answer to the Soviet question. The French Premier seems to have been acting in a daze on this critical day. He subsequently testified that during the afternoon he asked London to send a similar telegram to Admiral Drax (whom he calls "Diaz") and that the British "agreed." He may have thought so, but it was not true. The confidential British Foreign Office papers reveal that London took no action on Daladier's request. Not even the next day. When Admiral Drax on August 22 wired London asking whether it agreed to the British mission backing General Doumenc in giving an affirmative reply to the Russian question he got no response. "It was not possible," Strang noted later on the dispatch, for the record, "to send a reply to this telegram as no decision was taken."[37]

In Moscow General Doumenc received Daladier's wire at 10:30 P.M. He immediately informed Voroshilov that he had been authorized to sign a military convention which would acknowledge Russia's right to deploy her troops through Poland, and arranged to see him the next evening. Again it was too late. An hour after the French general received the wire from

---

* Naggiar had wired on August 20 asking for "an affirmative answer" and demanding that "General Doumenc receive without delay authorization to negotiate and sign, in the common interest, the military pact."

Paris the Berlin radio was announcing that Germany and the U.S.S.R. had agreed to conclude a nonaggression pact and that Ribbentrop was going to Moscow two days hence to sign it.

Indeed, by the time Doumenc saw Voroshilov at 7 P.M. on August 22, the Nazi Foreign Minister had already taken off by plane from Berlin on the first leg of his flight that would get him to the Soviet capital at noon the next day. The burly Soviet Marshal did his best to let down General Doumenc, for whom he seems to have acquired respect and even a liking, as gently as possible. He pointed out that the French response was meaningless in the absence of any word from the British and the Poles.

I fear one thing [Voroshilov said]. The French and English sides have allowed the political and military discussions to drag on too long. That is why we must not exclude the possibility, during this time, of certain political events.

Those "certain political events," as the unhappy French general must by now have foreseen, took place the next day, August 23. Whereas the talks between Russia and the Western democracies had dragged on for five months—since the last days of March—those between Ribbentrop and Stalin were successfully concluded in twelve hours between noon and midnight on August 23. The Germans, unlike the Western Allies, quickly made every concession the Russians asked for. In exchange they got the one thing they wanted: a solemn assurance that the Soviet Union would stay out of Hitler's war. This was given in the published treaty of non-aggression. The price Hitler paid was set down in the "Secret Additional Protocol" to the treaty, which only became known after the Second World War with the capture of the German documents. By its terms they simply divided up Eastern Europe. Russia was given a third of Poland, all the territory east of a line bounded by the rivers Narew, Vistula, and San. She got two of the three Baltic states, Latvia and Esthonia, while Germany was to have Lithuania; and Finland, which had belonged to Russia as an autonomous state before the first war, was put in the Soviet Union's "sphere of interest." Russia's "interest" in Bessarabia, which she had lost to Romania in 1919, was recognized by Germany.

Once again Germany and Russia, as in the days when they were ruled by kings and tsars, had agreed to a partition of Poland. And Hitler had given Stalin a free hand to regain Russia's lost lands in the Baltic and the Balkans.

The Allied military missions met with Voroshilov for the last time on August 25. Dazed by what had happened, they asked whether the Russians wished "to continue the conversations." The Marshal's answer was short. "In view of the changed political situation," he said, "there is no sense in continuing the conversations." Why the French and British officers remained for two days in Moscow to await such an inevitable response can only be explained by the shock and confusion in Paris and London at the signing of the Nazi-Soviet pact.*

As late as the evening of August 23, when Ribbentrop and Stalin were putting their signatures to the pact and beginning to drink their grotesque toasts to each other,† a long telegram arrived for Doumenc in Moscow from Gamelin which revealed how little the French generalissimo, who had been content to let the military talks drift with no lead from himself, understood what had happened.

> Molotov, as well as Marshal Voroshilov, were still affirming yesterday their willingness to collaborate in a policy of resistance to aggression.‡ The progress of German military preparations makes the eventuality of German aggression against Poland appear imminent. . . .
>
> The negotiations in Moscow therefore run the risk of being passed by events. . . . It is thus necessary to ask the Russians if they are ready to join us against aggression and to urgently conclude the military accord on the minimum bases immediately realizable. . . . Even if it is imperfect this affirmation will cement the resistance front to German aggression. . . .[40]

Like everyone else on the Allied side, General Gamelin bestirred himself too late. With his prestige as generalissimo he might have brought the Polish General Staff to its senses and if he had failed he was influential enough in the French government, especially with Daladier, who regarded him as a military genius, to induce it to make Polish acceptance of Russian aid a condition for maintaining France's commitments to Poland. But, easygoing as he was, he had refrained from doing the one thing or the other. He had not even answered, as Beaufre, who was on the spot, makes clear,

---

* On August 22 the French and British ambassadors advised their governments that it might be "useful" for the military missions to remain in Moscow in case, as one dispatch puts it, "the Soviet and Ribbentrop fall out." The two governments agreed.

† For example, Stalin's toast to Hitler: "I know how much the German nation loves its Fuehrer. I should therefore like to drink to his health."[38]

‡ This, of course, was far from the truth. Molotov saw both the French and British ambassadors on August 22 to explain to them the announcement of the midnight before that Germany and the U.S.S.R. had agreed to sign a nonaggression pact and that Ribbentrop was coming to Moscow to conclude it on the 23rd. He claimed that the Soviet government had only agreed to negotiate with the Germans after it had become convinced that the Western Allies did not want a military alliance —which also was rather far from the truth. General Gamelin probably based his statement on a sentence in Ambassador Naggiar's dispatch reporting his talk with Molotov.

> Molotov told me that the fundamental policy of the U.S.S.R. had not changed and that his government remained firmly attached to the maintenance of peace and to resistance to aggression.[39]

But even General Gamelin should have seen through such hokum. Incidentally, he makes no mention in his memoirs of his telegram. Its text is given by Beaufre, *op. cit.*, pp. 173–174.

General Doumenc's frantic requests to send him an affirmative answer to the question of the passage of Soviet troops.

The blindness of the Poles to their predicament after the announcement that a Nazi-Soviet Pact would be signed, remained complete. On August 22, the next day, the French Ambassador in Warsaw reported to Paris:

> Beck is quite unperturbed, and does not seem in the slightest worried by this *coup de théâtre*. He believes that, in substance, very little has changed.[41]

25

ON THE EVE OF WAR
AUGUST 23–31, 1939

Georges Bonnet was not so stupid. He saw at once—what was obvious—that the whole balance of power in Europe had been abruptly changed, to Germany's advantage. He was sitting at his desk at the Quai d'Orsay on the night of August 21 mulling over a telegram just received from Naggiar in which the Ambassador in Moscow warned that unless the Allied talks with the Russians were promptly concluded Hitler might offer Stalin a partition of Poland and Romania, and some of the Baltic states, and that Stalin might accept. A few minutes before midnight the director of Havas telephoned him the news from Berlin that Germany and Russia had agreed to sign a nonaggression pact and that Ribbentrop was leaving for Moscow to conclude it. Bonnet was taken aback. He immediately called Daladier, who had gone to bed. The Premier, Bonnet says, thought the report must be a "journalist's prank," but asked him to check it. Bonnet called the French Embassy in London. Roger Cambon, the chargé, told him that Reuter was just flashing the Berlin announcement on its wires. That was all he knew. Desperate, the Foreign Minister wired Naggiar to find out what he could.

The next day, when Molotov himself confirmed the bad news, Bonnet realized that for France "it was a disaster." And though he told the British chargé that morning that the best thing was to "keep completely calm," his own thoughts were turning back to the defeatist line he had taken at the time of Munich. "I considered," he says, "that a war against Germany to sustain Poland, without the assurance of Russian help, was an enterprise full of unknowns and perils."

In this frame of mind he saw Daladier on the morning of August 23 and urged him to convoke the Defense Council immediately in order to find out whether France's military chiefs were ready for war under such unfavorable circumstances. "Should we not," he asked the Premier, "reconsider our engagements to Poland?" If they could be wiggled out of—the implication was clear—France might be spared going to war. Bonnet put the question to the military leaders when the Defense Council convened at the War Ministry at 6 P.M. The Foreign Minister's own mind was made up, as he later boasted. "I thought," he wrote subsequently, "that France must try to avoid a war in which the full weight would fall on her, given the Russian withdrawal, British unpreparedness, and American isolationism."[1]

But it was up to the Defense Council, Bonnet said, to advise whether the French could fight or not. Its meeting for so crucial a decision was held in such secrecy that even such important cabinet ministers as Mandel and Reynaud did not learn of it until after the fall of France. Present beside Daladier, who as Premier and Minister of Defense presided, and Bonnet, were César Campinchi, Minister of Marine, Guy La Chambre, Minister of Air, Admiral Darlan, Commander of the Navy, General Vuillemin, Commander of the Air Force, General Colson, Chief of the Army General Staff and General Gamelin, whose title now was Chief of the General Staff (*Etat-Major*) of National Defense. Attention was centered on the generalissimo, who would make the final pronouncement as to the readiness of the armed forces.

Bonnet recounts that on arriving at the meeting he ran into General Decamp (whose name he misspells), chief of Daladier's military cabinet, whose abbreviated minutes of the proceedings would lead to bitter controversy, and expressed the hope that General Gamelin would "tell us whether the French army was capable of defeating the German army."

"You will have a lot of trouble getting a straight answer from General Gamelin," Bonnet quotes Decamp as saying. "He's as slippery as an eel."[2]

Daladier opened the meeting, the minutes say, by asking for an answer to three questions.

1. Can France remain inactive while Poland and Romania, or one of them, are being wiped off the map of Europe?
2. What means has she of opposing it?
3. What measures should be taken now?

Bonnet, after summing up the grave consequences of the defection of Russia, then put the question which was to remain uppermost in his mind to the end.

In view of this situation had we better remain faithful to our engagements and enter the war forthwith, or reconsider our attitude and profit from the respite thus gained to strengthen our military power, it being well understood that France runs the risk of being attacked in her turn within perhaps a few months?

The answer to this question is essentially of a military character.

He turned toward General Gamelin and Admiral Darlan. According to the minutes, they both responded

that the Army and Navy were ready. In the early stages of the conflict they can do little against Germany. . . . But the French mobilization itself will bring some relief to Poland by tying down a certain number of large German units on our frontier.

How typical of Gamelin! The Army is ready, he says, but it can do little against the Germans at first—at the only moment, that is, when it can possibly save Poland by launching, as promised, a major offensive in the West. The Army will mobilize but it will not, to begin with, fight. Daladier asked him how long the Poles could hold out under such circumstances.

I believe [he responded] that Poland will put up an honorable resistance which will prevent the bulk of the German forces from turning against us before next spring. By that time England will be at our side.

At heart General Gamelin was even more pessimistic about what the French Army could do than the brief official minutes make him out. He makes this clear, though not intentionally, in the long second chapter in the opening tome of his memoirs which he entitles "The So-Called *'Procès-Verbal'* of the Meeting of August 23, 1939." It is based largely on memoranda he submitted in his defense at his trial before the Court at Riom.

Arguing that General Decamp's minutes were so abbreviated as to be misleading ("How is it possible," he asks, "to summarize in three pages a discussion which lasted for an hour and a half?"),* Gamelin recounts what he recalls he actually said at the meeting. In so doing he quite unconsciously strengthens one charge against him: that for a generalissimo he was remarkably timid and wavering, utterly lacking that boldness of mind that had characterized Foch the last time the French and Germans resorted to arms.

Take his version of what he believes he said in answer to Daladier's and Bonnet's questions regarding "the disappearance of Poland."

If, after annihilating Poland . . . Germany turns against France with almost all her forces . . . France will have great difficulty in mobilizing and effecting its concentrations. In this case it would no longer be possible to engage in the struggle.

This is difficult to follow. Surely France would be fully mobilized and its "concentrations" completed by the time Poland caved in. And Gamelin had given his listeners the impression that the Poles could hold out until

---

* In his subsequent testimony before the postwar Parliamentary Investigating Committee Daladier agreed that the minutes were not a regular *procès-verbal*. They were, he explained, "notes taken by General Decamp, whose intellectual and moral probity is not contested by anyone." (*Evénements,* Vol. I, p. 54.)

spring. He and General Georges, moreover, had in May promised the Polish General Staff, as we have seen, that on the fifteenth to seventeenth day after mobilization began they would mount a major offensive in the West with the "bulk" of their forces.

But did the generalissimo say, as the minutes have it, that the "honorable resistance of Poland would prevent the mass of the German forces from turning against France before the following spring"?

> I certainly was not so formal or so simple [says Gamelin]. . . . I simply meant that even if Germany vanquished Poland before winter, she would not have, after turning against us, the power she wished before spring. I concluded that by spring, with the help of Britain and the material support of America, I hoped we would be capable of fighting, if necessary, a defensive battle. I added that we could not hope for victory in any but a long war. My opinion has always been that we could not take the offensive before roughly two years —1941–42.

His promise to the Poles, then, to take the offensive not at the end of two years but within seventeen days had been an empty one.

Finally Gamelin denied saying, in answer to Bonnet, that the Army was ready.

> I could not have said that—in the sense that the materiel of the Army was complete. . . . I merely said that the Army was ready for carrying out mobilization and concentrating its forces.[3]

Such evasiveness, such timidity, on August 23, 1939, must be kept in mind in following Gamelin's brief career as generalissimo in the war that was now but a week away.

After an hour and a half of discussion, a decision was finally reached and recorded in General Decamp's sketchy minutes.

> In the course of the many exchanges of views it is pointed out that if we are stronger a few months hence, Germany will be even stronger because she will have the Polish and Romanian resources at her disposal.
>
> *Therefore France has no choice.*
>
> The sole solution is to adhere to our engagements to Poland, engagements which moreover were assumed prior to the opening of negotiations with the U.S.S.R.*[4]

---

* Only one copy of General Decamp's minutes was made. Daladier in May 1940 had a second one drawn up for Bonnet, who in December of that year, after the fall of France, published it in the notoriously Fascist and collaborationist weekly, *Gringoire*. By then Bonnet appeared anxious to show that he had opposed the war and had questioned the wisdom of entering the conflict for the sake of Poland.

Gamelin says that Bonnet gave the minutes to the Riom court, which the Vichy government of Pétain set up to try the generalissimo and several political leaders for forcing the country into a lost war. "It was this so-called *procès-verbal*," Gamelin later testified, "which served in the beginning as the ground for charges against Daladier, Guy La Chambre, and me, namely: 'Lightheartedly and irresponsibly, you plunged France into war.'"[5]

A decision, then, was reached and it was one that did the country honor. This time, unlike a year before when France had reneged on her promises to Czechoslovakia, she would keep her engagements to Poland —and this despite its putting her in a far worse predicament than she had been in in 1938 when the Soviet Union had promised her support against German aggression. Still, General Gamelin, backed by Admiral Darlan, had assured the government that the Army and Navy were ready.*

Though there was a feeling of relief among most of the participants that at least a decision, fateful as it was, had been made, the course of the meeting aggravated the old rancor between Gamelin and Bonnet.

Repeating with his usual evasiveness that he had not meant to say that the "Army was ready" but merely that "our mobilization and concentration were ready," Gamelin later explained to Daladier that he had hesitated to point out the Army's weaknesses in front of Georges Bonnet.

Naturally [I told him], I did not feel I should underline the deficiencies still existing in our armament and in our industrial mobilization. You knew them. They did not concern Georges Bonnet.

"You were right," Gamelin quotes Daladier as replying. "If you had exposed them the Germans would have known of them the next day." And once again, as in his recounting of the May episode with the Poles, the generalissimo turns the knife.

Let no one misunderstand me. The Premier did not mean to say that Georges Bonnet was a traitor and in touch with the Germans. But there was evidently in his mind the feeling that Bonnet was so imbued with the idea of avoiding war that he was capable of repeating that we did not have all the armaments necessary, which would have been spread rapidly in certain circles and passed on to the agents of Germany in France.[7]

"The meeting of August 23," Daladier later explained, "did not decide on war."[8] That decision, he knew, was up to Hitler. What he did not know was that the Nazi dictator had made it on the day before—"irrevocably," as he told his generals.

He had summoned them to his mountain villa above Berchtesgaden as soon as he got direct and personal word from Stalin late on the night of August 21 that the Soviet Union would conclude a nonaggression pact

---

* General Vuillemin, Chief of the Air Force, as was his custom, did not open his mouth at this meeting. But in a letter to the Premier three days later he backed up the rather optimistic estimate of the strength of the French and British air forces which Guy La Chambre, the Air Minister, had given on August 23. The Minister had assured his colleagues that in fighter planes the Western Allies were roughly equal to Germany and Italy, and he had stressed that "the situation of our aviation must no longer weigh on the decisions of the government as it had in 1938." It will be remembered that the year before, shortly before Munich, General Vuillemin had warned the government that in case of war the Germans would wipe out the French air force in a couple of weeks. Now he assured Daladier that the "situation is no longer comparable at all to that of September, 1938."[6]

with Germany when Ribbentrop arrived in Moscow on the 23rd. "I have called you together," Hitler told his military chiefs as the meeting began in the spacious hall of the Berghof at noon on August 22, "to give you a picture of the political situation in order that you may have some insight into the individual factors on which I have based my irrevocable decision to act. . . ." After lecturing his top military commanders on his own greatness,* Hitler turned to the political situation.

"England," he said, "is in great danger. France's position has also deteriorated. Decline of the birthrate. . . ." He thought it "highly probable" that the West would not fight now that Russia was lost, but the risk that it might fight had to be accepted. As for Daladier and Chamberlain, they were "little worms. I saw them at Munich." He then explained how he had got the Soviet Union in the bag.

I was convinced that Stalin would never accept the British offer. . . . Russia has no interest in maintaining Poland. . . . Litvinov's dismissal was decisive. It came to me like a cannon shot as a sign of a change in Moscow toward the Western powers.

I brought about the change toward Russia gradually. . . . Finally a proposition came from the Russians for a nonaggression treaty. Four days ago I took a special step which brought it about that Russia announced yesterday that she is ready to sign. The personal contact with Stalin is established. Day after tomorrow Ribbentrop will conclude the treaty. Now Poland is in the position in which I wanted her. . . . A beginning has been made for the destruction of Britain's hegemony. The way is open for the soldier, now that I have made the political preparations.

The one thing he feared was that Chamberlain and the French—or perhaps Mussolini—might try for another Munich. "I am only afraid," he said, "that some *Schweinehund* ["dirty dog"] will make a proposal for mediation."

After a luncheon recess, Hitler devoted the rest of the meeting to bucking up his generals. The notes made by some of the participants indicate its tenor.

The most iron determination on our part. No shrinking back from anything. . . . A life and death struggle. . . . The destruction of Poland has priority. . . . I shall give a propagandist reason for starting the war—never mind whether it is plausible or not. The victor will not be asked afterward whether he told the truth or not. In starting and waging war it is not right that matters, but victory.

---

* "Essentially," he said, "all depends on me . . . because of my political talents. . . . No one will ever again have the confidence of the whole German people as I have. There will probably never again be a man with more authority than I have. . . ." See the author's *The Rise and Fall of the Third Reich*, pp. 528–532 for a more detailed account of this crucial meeting, based on the notes kept by some of the participants, especially General Franz Halder, Chief of the Army General Staff, who jotted down voluminous notes in his old-fashioned Gabelsberger shorthand.

Close your hearts to pity! Act brutally! Be harsh and remorseless! Be steeled against all signs of compassion! . . . Whoever has pondered over this world order knows that its meaning lies in the success of the best by means of force. . . .

After these Nietzschean exhortations, Hitler calmed down and went over his directives for a swift campaign that would annihilate Poland before the autumn rains came. Because those rains might come early and make the Polish roads impassable, he would "probably," he said, "advance the jump-off date from September 1 to Saturday morning, August 26—four days hence. The next day he did. General Halder noted in his diary on August 23: "Y-Day definitely set for Saturday, the 26th. There will be no more orders concerning it or X-Hour. *Everything will roll automatically.*"*[9] X-Hour, the jumping-off time against Poland, was set at 4:30 A.M.

Though Daladier did not know that the date for the German attack on Poland had been set for August 26, he told the British chargé in Paris on the 23rd that he thought Hitler would march into Poland "in two or three days."[10] Ambassador Coulondre in Berlin had warned the day before that the attack was "imminent."[11]

The French Premier began to move. During the day of August 22 he gave the signal for the *Alerte,* which set in motion the *Couverture,* putting the frontier defenses and the Maginot Line on a war footing. Since the beginning of the month the reserves had begun to be called up. By August 25, according to confidential information given the British, France had increased its armed forces to 1,900,000 men.[12] Two days later, according to General Gamelin, the total effectives of the armed services had reached a figure of 2,674,000, of whom 2,438,000 were in the Army.[13] And this without declaring a general mobilization.

Obviously the Premier meant business this time. But there was dissension in his cabinet over these warlike moves. On August 22 Gamelin had seen Daladier shortly after a cabinet meeting.

He told me there were two currents running in the cabinet. Paul Reynaud and Mandel on one side who say: "The military are timid and not resolute enough." The other, Bonnet and Chautemps, "a clan for peace at any price." . . . Daladier tells me that his own decision has been made. If the cabinet does not follow him he will go. I assure him that, in that case, I shall go with him.[14]

The generalissimo made no mention of one cabinet member, Monzie. But his name appeared in a confidential dispatch of Campbell, the British chargé, to London the next day. It quoted the Minister of Public Works

---

* General Halder's emphasis.

as saying that after the Nazi-Soviet pact "there was now nothing to do but to allow Germany to have her way."[15]

The cabinet met again on August 24. Daladier did not mention the meeting of the previous day at which it was decided that France had no choice but to fight if Germany attacked Poland. Ignorant of it, Reynaud and Mandel were restless, fearing that Bonnet, Chautemps, and Monzie were maneuvering for another Munich—this time at Poland's expense.

The next day, August 25, was a critical one for a Europe already jittery with fear that war would break out at any moment. The drama was now centered in Berlin. I remember the almost unbearable tension in the German capital throughout that day. Shortly after noon all radio, telegraph, and telephone communication with the outside world was cut off on orders of the German government. That seemed to confirm reports we had that Hitler had ordered his troops to march into Poland at dawn the next day. (We did not, of course, then know of his definite orders of the 23rd.) The night before, the 24th, the last of the French and British correspondents and nonofficial civilians had hastily left for the nearest frontier. The German Foreign Office, we learned, had wired the embassies and consulates in Poland, France, and Great Britain, requesting that German citizens leave by the quickest route. The weather was warm and sultry, and everyone in Berlin, especially in the Wilhelmstrasse, where most of the ministries and Hitler's Chancellery were, was on edge.

The opposing sides had now made clear they would not budge from the stands they had taken. On August 23 the British Ambassador in Berlin had flown down to Berchtesgaden and delivered to Hitler a letter from Chamberlain affirming that despite the Nazi-Soviet pact Great Britain would honor its commitments to Poland with "all the forces at its command." The Fuehrer, the Ambassador reported, had flown into a rage and replied that if Britain attacked, Germany would be found "prepared and determined. I am fifty years old," he added. "I prefer war now to when I shall be fifty-five or sixty."[16]

Two days later, on this crucial day of August 25, certain events occurred which made him change his mind—for the moment.

The French government had approved the text of Chamberlain's letter to Hitler but had made no similar communication itself. It got a chance to do so when the Fuehrer, now back in Berlin, summoned the French Ambassador to see him at 5:30 P.M. It was plain now that he was making a last attempt to persuade France and Britain to stay out of the war over Poland.* To Coulondre he said he had a declaration to make which he wished him to pass on to Daladier.

---

* At 1:30 P.M. Hitler had called in the British Ambassador and made what he called a "last offer" to Britain. It was quite ridiculous. He was ready, he said, to "guarantee the existence of the British Empire" but only *after* "the solution of the German-Polish problem." And he added: "This is my last offer. If you reject it, there will be war."[17]

I have no hostility toward France. I personally have renounced Alsace-Lorraine and I have recognized the Franco-German frontier. . . . The thought that I should have to go to war with France because of Poland is very painful to me. . . . I shall not attack France but if she starts a conflict I shall go to the very end. . . . I believe that I shall win, and you think you will win. But what is certain is that German and French blood will flow, the blood of two peoples equally courageous. I say again it is extremely painful for me to think we will end up that way. Tell that to M. Daladier, please.

Hitler rose from his chair to end the one-sided conversation. But Coulondre was not the man to be put off. "I am not after all," he says of himself in describing the meeting, "a mere post-office box." Standing there he assured Hitler as solemnly as he could that if he attacked Poland he would find France "with all her forces, fighting on her side."[18] Bonnet recounts that when the ambassador's dispatch recounting the interview reached the Quai d'Orsay shortly before midnight he immediately telephoned Daladier the contents. The Premier's immediate reaction, he says, was to stress "the necessity of accelerating our military preparations."[19] In a nationwide broadcast that evening Daladier had reiterated that France would stand by her commitments to Poland if she were assaulted.

By 6 P.M. on Friday, August 25, then, Adolf Hitler knew at last that if he attacked Poland—and at 3 P.M. he had reaffirmed the order for the attack to begin at dawn the next day—he would have to fight France and Britain too. If he had any lingering doubts about the British these were finally extinguished at that very hour when news from London was received that Britain and Poland had just signed a pact of mutual assistance. Dr. Paul Schmidt, the official interpreter, who was in Hitler's office when the report arrived, remembered later that the Fuehrer, after reading it, sat brooding at his desk.[20]

His brooding was interrupted by equally bad news from Rome. That morning he had got off an urgent personal letter to Mussolini warning him that a German attack on Poland might take place at any moment. "In case of intolerable events in Poland," he wrote, "I shall act immediately." Hitler did not ask specifically for Italy's help. By the terms of the Italo-German alliance that was supposed to be automatic. The letter was telephoned by Ribbentrop personally to the German Ambassador in Rome and reached Mussolini at 3:20 P.M.[21] A prompt answer was requested—and received.

It was handed over to Hitler by Ambassador Attolico "at about 6 P.M.," according to a notation on the original.[22] It struck the Fuehrer, according to Schmidt, who was present, like a bombshell. For the Duce informed Hitler bluntly that if he went to war over Poland he must count Italy out. "The Italian war preparations," he explained, were simply not ready. The country could not "resist the attack which the French and English would predominantly direct against us." And Mussolini reminded his fellow dictator and supposed ally that "at our meetings the war was envisaged for 1942, and by that time I would have been ready."

By the time Hitler had finished reading the letter and somewhat recovered his composure ("The Italians are behaving just as they did in 1914!" Schmidt heard him mutter) it was 6:30 P.M. of August 25. The eventful day had now forced him to face certain realities: that Italy would remain neutral and that Britain and France would oppose German aggression "with all their forces." That aggression was scheduled to begin in ten hours. As darkness came the troops were already moving up to their final jump-off positions. The Nazi tyrant was faced with the most crucial decision of his life.

Suddenly—about 7 P.M.—Schmidt saw General Keitel, Chief of the OKW, dash out of Hitler's study. He shouted to his adjutant: "The order to advance must be delayed again!" At Nuremberg Keitel explained to the court: "I was suddenly called to Hitler at the Chancellery. 'Stop everything! At once!' he said."[23] An entry in the German Naval Registry that evening tells the story concisely.

August 25. Case White, already started, will be stopped at 20:30 [8:30 P.M.] because of changed political conditions (Mutual Assistance Pact England-Poland . . . and information from Duce).[24]

It took some doing to halt the German army that evening, for many units were already on the move. In East Prussia the order calling off the attack did not reach General Petzel's I Corps until 9:37 P.M. and only the frantic efforts of several officers who were rushed out to the forward detachments succeeded in stopping the troops. The motorized columns of General von Kleist's corps to the south had begun to move at dusk up to the Polish frontier. They were halted just short of it by a staff officer who made a quick landing in a small scouting plane and waved them back. In a few sectors the orders did not arrive until after the shooting began, but since the Germans had been provoking incidents all along the border for several days the Polish General Staff apparently did not suspect what had really happened. It did report on August 26 that numerous "German bands" had crossed the border and attacked blockhouses and customs posts with machine guns and hand grenades and that "in one case it was a Regular Army detachment."

The attack had been postponed, but no more than that. It had not been abandoned.* Again General Halder's invaluable diary reveals Hitler's state of mind at this juncture. "Fuehrer considerably shaken," he noted

---

* There is no evidence in the French and British papers so far available that Paris or London ever learned of the postponement. But they did get wind that Hitler might go into Poland on or about August 26. On August 24 the French General Staff informed the British it had learned that "the attack will commence between August 26–28."[25] Sir Nevile Henderson in his memoirs (pp. 266, 271) states that "definite information" reached him that the attack had been fixed for the 25th or 26th.

on the evening of August 25 after the news from Rome and London had induced Hitler to draw back from the precipice of war. But the next afternoon the General Staff Chief noticed an abrupt change in the Leader. "Fuehrer very calm and clear," he jotted down in his diary at 3:22 P.M. There was a reason for this and Halder gives it. "Get everything ready for the morning of the 7th Mobilization Day. Attack starts September 1." The order was telephoned by Hitler to the Army High Command.

Hitler then would have his war with Poland. It would be launched September 1. That was settled. But in the ensuing five days he would make one final effort to keep France and Britain out of it. A further entry in Halder's diary on the 26th sheds light on this: "Rumor has it that England is disposed to consider comprehensive proposal.* . . . Plan: We demand Danzig, corridor through Corridor, and plebiscite on the same basis as Saar. England perhaps will accept. Poland probably not. *Wedge between them.*"

The emphasis is Halder's and no doubt it accurately reflected—up to a point—what was in Hitler's mind. He would contrive to drive a *wedge* between Poland and Britain and give Chamberlain an excuse to get out of his pledge to Poland.

And France? Hitler seems to have been sure that France would follow Britain's lead as it had since the crisis of the Rhineland coup in 1936. Moreover, he was aware of the dissension in France and the growing opposition there to go to war "for Danzig" or even for Poland. In Halder's diary entry cited above, the general adds a brief note on the subject: "In France more and more representations to the government against war."

Some of these "representations" came from influential men in French politics. One of these was Flandin, still a force in Parliament. Since Munich he had advocated, by his own admission, that France "denounce" her commitments to Poland.[26] Now on the Sunday morning of August 27 he went to see Daladier at the War Ministry "to beg him," he says, "not to let himself be dragged into war." He had been "authorized," he adds, by his political friends to tell the President of the Council "that we would give our complete support to a compromise which would avoid war.

I had a long conversation with him and pointed out the diplomatic situation so unfavorable for France, her inferior military position, the additional trouble which the Russian defection, especially in regard to the attitude of the French Communist Party, was going to cause to the morale of the nation. I found him quite calm and objective. He disputed neither the unpreparedness of the Army nor the deficiencies in the Air Force. . . . He insisted that the question of Danzig and the Corridor had little importance. It was now bigger than that. Poland was our last ally in the East. The German General Staff wished to eliminate the second front of France's security before attacking

---

* I.e., Hitler's offer of August 25 to "guarantee" the British Empire.

France herself. . . . He believed the Polish Army would put up an honorable resistance. I disputed it, but he opposed me with the opinion of General Gamelin."

On leaving, Flandin ran into the generalissimo, who, he says, was most optimistic about the Polish forces.

. . . When I rejoined that Hitler believed he could destroy Polish resistance in three weeks General Gamelin reproached me for believing in the predictions of Hitler: "I know the Polish Army very well. The troops are excellent, the High Command up to its job. The Poles will hold out and give us plenty of time to come to their help.". . . When I asked how we were going to bring that help he replied with the utmost conviction: "The Poles will hold out at least six months and we will come to their aid by way of Romania."

"I left the War Ministry," Flandin concludes, "dumfounded."*[27]

Dumfounded, but still believing fervently, as Monzie and many others in high places did, that France must avoid war at all costs—regardless of what Hitler did, or the British. Rightist circles in Paris made no secret of their belief that Great Britain was dragging France into war.

On August 26, the day before Flandin's meeting with Daladier, the German chargé d'affaires in Paris was wiring Berlin the text of a front-page editorial that morning by Charles Maurras in the royalist *L'Action Française,* a writer and a newspaper widely read by Army and Navy officers. It warned that the British and the Jews were pulling strings to land France in a war—the very theme of the Nazi press in Berlin. Mandel, Campinchi, Jean Zay, and Paul Reynaud (the four cabinet members who were imploring Daladier to stand up to Hitler) were depicted by Maurras as belonging "to the European clique that would like to disturb the peace of the world.

Jews or friends of Jews, these gentlemen are in closest contact with the powerful Jewish clique in London. . . . If today our French people allow themselves to be slaughtered unsuspectingly and vainly at the will of forces that are English-speaking Jews, or at the will of their French slaves, then a French voice must be raised to proclaim the truth."[29]

In 1914 the men of the Right in France, including Maurras and his royalist followers, had been one with all other elements in insisting that France stand up to Germany come what might. Now, twenty-five years later, they were clamoring for the opposite, deepening the divisions in a country divided for so long.

The pacifists, swelling in numbers and increasingly vocal and influential, were clamoring for essentially the same thing: avoid war at any

---

* General Gamelin later contended that Flandin had "misunderstood" the "sense" of his words.[28]

cost. Paul Faure had won over the majority of the powerful Socialist Party from Blum in support of his policy of peace at any price. Some of the largest and—paradoxically—most left-wing of the trade unions, led by the Confederation of Schoolteachers and those of the postal employees and civil servants, were agitating for peace, filling the air with their pronunciamentos. Monzie recounts the "pacifist parade" to his office during that last week of August. Many were Socialist deputies and union leaders.

There were also the Communists, now one of the largest of the political parties and comprising a strong segment of the working class. Since the signing of the Nazi-Soviet pact on August 23, which, no doubt on instructions from Moscow, the French Communist press had slavishly welcomed as "saving the peace," they seemed lost to the nation. Or so Daladier, embittered by the duplicity of Moscow and angered by the *volte-face* of the French Communist Party, which only the day before had been hysterically demanding that France ally herself with Russia to stop Hitler, thought. On August 26 he suppressed the two Communist daily newspapers in Paris, *Humanité,* and *Ce Soir.*

Even the more farsighted men on the Right, who were not angered but relieved that the Soviet Union had defected, since it spared France the onus of having to fight on the side of the detested Bolsheviks, and who personally would not have cared if every French Communist had been dumped into the Seine with an iron grating around his neck, thought Daladier's move was hasty and ill-advised. For in reality Stalin's cynical deal with Hitler had thrown the French Communist Party into complete disarray. For three days after the announcement on the night of August 21 that the pact would be signed, the top Communist leaders, Maurice Thorez, Jacques Duclos, and Gabriel Péri, maintained an unaccustomed and embarrassed silence. Péri, the foreign-affairs expert of the Party, sat slumping at his desk in the offices of *Humanité* the three days overwhelmed, unable to write and practically unable to speak. The unholy task of grinding out editorials praising the pact and hailing Stalin as the "savior of the peace" was left to underlings.

Realizing that the mass of their followers would not swallow such a line, the Communist group in the Chamber issued on August 25 a communiqué in the form of a declaration by Thorez pledging Communist support to the nation.

If Hitler launches war, let him know that he will find the people of France, with the Communists in the front rank, united against him. . . . The Communist Party approves the measures taken by the government to guard our frontiers and to give, if need be, aid to the country menaced by aggression to which we are tied by a treaty of alliance.

But it was too late. The Communist Party had been torn asunder by Stalin's about-face. "It is a deathblow to the Communist Party here," Léon Blum told Sir Eric Phipps on August 25, adding that "it would be a mistake for the government to dissolve it."[30] If left alone, he—like others—was sure it would quickly expire. But Daladier would not listen to their advice. He suppressed the Communist press—and shortly afterward the Party—thus, as one French historian, a conservative, judged, "rescuing it from its profound embarrassment and opening to it the vast advantages of going underground."[31]

To the forces of the Right, who opposed the war because they hated the Republic and looked kindly on Hitler and Mussolini, were soon joined those on the Communist Left, millions of them, who though they felt betrayed by Stalin, resented the harassment of the police, the courts, and the government, which treated them as outlaws. They, too, turned against the war, sabotaged the armament factories, and sowed defeatism in the armed services—until Hitler attacked Russia and it was too late to help save their country.

But that is not all, as one contemplates the shaky state of the Republic on the eve of war. The cabinet, as we have seen, was divided. Bonnet, Chautemps, Marchandeau, and Monzie were determined to keep France out of war. Reynaud, Mandel, Champetier de Ribes, and Jean Zay were equally determined that France should go to war if Hitler attacked Poland. Added to this was the growing personal rivalry between Daladier and Reynaud. Though they were not far apart in their belief that this time France must make a stand and fight, if necessary, they had developed a mutual distrust that had waxed since Munich, which Reynaud had opposed. Moreover, Reynaud, an extremely self-confident man, believed that Daladier was not strong enough or able enough to lead France through the ordeal of war and that he himself was better qualified. Since Reynaud scarcely disguised his ambition Daladier became increasingly concerned that his Minister of Finance was scheming to replace him.

This mutual distrust was exacerbated by the women currently in their lives, Countess Hélène de Portes, the mistress of Reynaud, and the Marquise de Crussol, the mistress of Daladier. Ambitious to further the careers of their respective friends, avid for power for them and for themselves—this was especially true of the Countess, a driving force of formidable proportions—they stirred up the muddy waters of rivalry and intrigue between the two most important leaders in the government.

"History has a right to discuss her," Pertinax, the forthright editor-columnist once argued in justifying his comments on the role of the Marquise de Crussol.[32] He exercised that historical right to make even fuller comments on the Countess de Portes. A good many other French writers and historians have done likewise, especially in explaining the acts and influence of the energetic and persistent lady who was Reynaud's mistress. Reynaud himself does not mention her in his voluminous memoirs, nor did he once pronounce her name in the innumerable conversations and in the correspondence I had with him after the war. Obviously he regarded the matter as his private and personal affair, which others had no right to pry into. Daladier, when I saw him, took the same attitude, and I respected it in both cases. But as a small but important bit of history, especially in regard to Reynaud when he held the reins of government in a critical moment, this was more than just a personal matter. In the closing months of the life of the Third Republic the role of Madame de Portes in public affairs was, as we shall see, considerable, just as was that of the Marquise de Maintenon in the reign of Louis XIV and, even more so, that of the Marquise de Pompadour in that of Louis XV. The latter virtually ruled France for twenty years (1745–64). Madame de Portes never got that far—her time was too short—but she tried. Her influence on Reynaud and on the events which soon would come tumbling down upon him must find due notice in this narrative.

Who were these two titled women who had attached themselves to Daladier and Reynaud? Both came from wealthy bourgeois families, both married into the aristocracy, and with titles and money for a base proceeded to seek political power by liaisons with the politicians who seemed most likely to reach the top.

The Marquise de Crussol was born Jeanne Beziers, daughter of a businessman at Nantes who had made a large fortune canning sardines. Seeking a suitable title she had married the Marquis de Crussol, grandson of the redoubtable Duchesse d'Uzès, who at one time had courted Hélène de Portes. Soon Parisian wits were referring to the Marquise de Crussol as *"la sardine qui s'est crue sole"* ("the sardine which took itself for a sole")—a play on words in French, *"crue sole"* having the same pronunciation as her name. Daladier's wife had died after ten years of marriage. At the time he met the Marquise he was living in a modest and rather gloomy apartment in the rue Anatole-de-la-Forge where his sister kept house and helped him look after his two young sons. Madame de Crussol soon introduced him to a more glittering life and began to further his career in the more fashionable places of Paris.

To Pertinax, she was "a spirited woman, rather attractive with her arched nose but grasping and covetous" and dominating.[33] To André Maurois she was "a graceful and beautiful woman, blond and youthful in appearance" but with "a taste for power and an unfortunate passion for economic and political doctrines"[34]—about which apparently she knew very little. Both writers agree that unlike Madame de Portes she was content to keep herself in the background and to exercise her power and influence discreetly.

Hélène de Portes was the daughter of a wealthy contractor and shipping magnate in Marseilles named Rebuffel. Bright, intelligent, full of energy and ambition, she married Count Jean de Portes, son of the Marquis de Portes and the Duchesse de Gadagne, who promptly went to work in one of her father's establishments in Marseilles. As Lazareff remarks, the two titled husbands, Portes and Crussol, "left their wives a good deal of freedom."[35] The Countess, like the Marquise, set off to conquer Paris.

There Madame de Portes was introduced to Reynaud, who was twice her age, by André Tardieu. At first there was only a mild flirtation and, indeed, the ambitious young lady became a close friend of Madame Reynaud. But not for long. When Hélène de Portes realized that Reynaud's star was rising she became his mistress. Pertinax has described the consequences.

The two women clashed fiercely around their victim, and those who realized that the affair had long blossomed by mutual consent could only wonder at that belated explosion. From morning to night the two furies spied on and pursued each other. This quarrel became a public performance. If he went out with one, Reynaud had to fear that the other would show up.

In 1938 Reynaud moved out of his home and took a bachelor apartment on the Place du Palais-Bourbon, where he lived to the end of his long life. There the Countess had him to herself. The mystery of her hold over this brilliant and strong-willed man has never been pierced. Many who knew her have left their impressions of the lady. To General Sir Edward L. Spears, who had occasion to see her more frequently than he could stand, she was

of medium height, dark [and] her curly hair brushed upwards looked untidy. Her mouth was big and the voice that issued from it was unharmonious. . . . She seemed to the ordinary male observer to be devoid of charm. . . . She had good ankles but her complexion was sallow.[36]

Lazareff, who also saw her more often than he wished, thought her "a little dumpy . . . with pretty eyes and pretty legs, always dressed badly and with an untidy hairdo." He saw in her slightly protruding teeth a mark "of one who loved power."[37] Clare Boothe Luce, an American expert on the female world, thought the lady was a "homely, talkative little woman. . . . She looked as much like a *Hausfrau* as a French *maîtresse* can. . . ."[38]

André Maurois, the eminent man of letters and member of the prestigious Académie, could scarcely contain himself when he thought of Hélène de Portes.

She was slightly mad, excitable, meddlesome and, as the course of events was to show, dangerous. . . . Her dominant characteristic seemed to be ambition. It was not enough for her that Reynaud was Minister of Finance; she was determined at all costs to make him Premier. She filled the salons of Paris with accounts of Daladier's lack of energy, and gave everyone to understand that it was urgent that Reynaud should succeed him. Naturally these remarks were repeated the same evening to Daladier and the latter's detestation of Reynaud grew considerably stronger. . . .[39]

Maurois recounts seeing Reynaud a couple of months after he *did* become Premier.

He was depressed and nervous. On his desk were three telephones, one connected with the Ministry, the second with the outside, the third with the room of Madame de Portes. This last instrument rang unceasingly. Reynaud would lift the receiver, listen for a second and then cry out in an exasperated tone: "Yes . . . Yes, of course. . . . But that's understood. . . . But I implore you to let me do my work. . . ." Finally he stopped answering.

All agree that Reynaud's Egeria was extremely excitable. Lazareff recounts that twice she went abroad to take a cure for her nerves and that in Vienna, where she took one of her treatments, she met a number of Austrian and German Nazis. He believes that back in Paris she kept in touch with French sympathizers of Hitler and that she became attracted to Nazism. The further Reynaud advanced toward the Left, he noted, the more Madame de Portes turned to the Right.[40]

And so in a Republic already torn by dissension Reynaud battled with Daladier, their mistresses battled with each other and with the man of the other, each determined that her friend should have the top place. At the moment Daladier possessed it, but Reynaud and Madame de Portes waited impatiently their hour.

And, finally, at this crucial time for the country Marshal Pétain and Pierre Laval resumed contact with each other, entering upon a new phase of a seemingly unlikely relationship between two most disparate individuals. Toward the end of August, Pétain, who had been named Ambassador to Franco Spain that spring, made discreet inquiries of Laval as to how he sized up the political situation in Paris. The country was on the verge of war and the eighty-three-old Marshal was its most illustrious warrior. But since first serving in the Doumergue cabinet as Minister of War in 1934 he had been bitten by the political bug. Now, in August 1939, he was interested not only—as was natural—in the condition of the Army but in the political state of his country facing war.

Laval, chafing at having been out of power so long, had for years been cultivating the Marshal with the idea that one day he could make him a figurehead Premier or President behind whose immense prestige he could run France. As early as 1932, when Laval was still in office, he campaigned in the corridors of Parliament for the election of Pétain as President of the Republic by the National Assembly that year. The Marshal asked him to desist. On the day of the funeral of the assassinated Barthou in 1934 Pétain repaid Laval by advising Doumergue to appoint him Foreign Minister, which the Premier did. At another funeral a year later, that of Pilsudski in Warsaw, the two men found themselves together and compared notes. Pétain advised Laval, then Premier, to go beyond his Parliamentary opposition and do what was necessary "in the national interest." And Laval, after explaining that this was difficult for a politician to do, suggested that Pétain, with his great prestige and his position above parties and politics, was the only man in France who could do it. The Marshal dismissed the idea on the ground of his "inexperience."[41] But the seeds of authoritarianism were sprouting in both men. They found agreement in their sympathy for Franco in the Spanish Civil War. By 1937 a confidant of Franco was reporting to his chief the gist of a secret conversation with Laval in Paris in April in which the former Premier pledged support to the Spanish Nationalist rebels and added a tip about Pétain.

Laval was of the opinion that the salvation of France lay in a Pétain government and that the Marshal was determined to assume this responsibility. . . . He is in touch . . . with Pétain.*[42]

Laval and Pétain were much too discreet to see each other openly too often. But in Count René de Chambrun, who had married Laval's only daughter, Josée, in 1935, they found a useful intermediary. According to Chambrun he saw the Marshal two or three times a week, when both were in Paris, right up to the beginning of the war.[43]

Another intermediary was Major Georges Loustaunau-Lacou, the adventurous former aide to the Marshal who for years had sown right-wing ideas in the Army. It was to him that, toward the end of August 1939, Pétain spoke in the French Embassy at Saint-Sebastien where the major had been his guest. "You are going to Paris," Pétain said. "Go and see what Laval thinks of the situation. I lack information at this tragic moment."

Laval was not backward in answering. Loustaunau-Lacou recounted it at the postwar trial of Pétain.

The situation, Laval responded, is very simple. We must get rid of Daladier. Tell the Marshal that this Daladier is a dunghill and a swine (*un fumier et un salaud*), and I can prove it.[44]

Laval declared, the major reported in a long letter to the Marshal (in which he omitted the vulgarities), that a "Pétain government was now indispensable." Lest the Marshal fear taking on such an onerous task at his advanced age, Laval assured him that he and others could relieve him of "everyday matters."[45] Soon, according to later testimony of one of the Embassy secretaries, the illustrious Ambassador took to drawing up cabinet lists suggested to him by Laval and by other rightists who now began to flock to his side, flattering him, feeding his considerable ego, and gradually convincing him that he could be the savior of France and rid it of the rotten Republic.

---

* This report was given to the German Ambassador in Salamanca, who forwarded it to Berlin, and it turned up in the German Foreign Office papers captured after the war. This is the first, but far from the last, inkling that the Nazi government received of what Pétain and Laval were up to in France.

Daladier, as he later testified, was unaware of the Laval-Pétain intrigues. He knew only that his cabinet (Parliament was still in recess) and his country were divided. He was now, as August ran out, certain that Hitler would attack Poland within a few days and he was determined that, weak as France was, and divided, his government would honor its pledge to Poland. On August 26 he made one last attempt to convince Hitler of this and to bring, if possible, the Nazi dictator to reason. In an eloquent letter in answer to Hitler's personal message of the day before,* which was wired to Berlin at 2:50 P.M., he told the Chancellor that "the fate of peace still rests in your hands alone" and appealed to him to preserve it. But if he did not—

Unless you attribute to the French people a conception of national honor less high than that which I myself recognize in the German people, you cannot doubt that France will be true to her solemn promises to other nations such as Poland.

Reminding Hitler that he, like him, was a soldier in the last war and that both therefore knew war's "horrors and disasters" and that there was no need to repeat them, Daladier concluded:

If the blood of France and Germany flows again, as it did twenty-five years ago, each of the two peoples will fight with confidence in its own victory, but the most certain victory will be that of destruction and barbarism.[46]

Ambassador Coulondre delivered the letter at 7 P.M. and studied Hitler's "hard" face as he read it. "I realized," the Ambassador says, "that the battle between us would be desperate." Hitler read the letter and started to speak, his voice "hard and dry." Once again he reiterated the argument that was becoming so stale to the French and British ambassadors in Berlin: there was no hope of a peaceful solution because the Western Allies, by their guarantees to Poland, had made her impervious to reason. "Nothing in the world," says Coulondre, "could have stopped the words which now rose from my heart to my lips." They were, he admits, full of emotion.

I adjured him [Coulondre reported to Paris by telegram that evening] in the face of history, in the name of humanity, not to miss this last chance (for peace). For the repose of his conscience I begged him not to let blood flow, not only the blood of soldiers but of women and children. I reminded him of the terrible responsibility he was assuming toward Western civilization. . . .

It was all in vain. "Ah! The women and children—I have often thought of them," Hitler murmured, and then turned to Ribbentrop, who,

* See above, p. 479.

Coulondre says, had been standing near the door with "a face of stone." The two Germans conferred in whispers. "I had a minute of foolish hope," the Ambassador recounts. " 'Foolish' is certainly the word." Hitler returned to him, his face "hard and savage" and remarked: "There's no use. Poland will not return Danzig. But I will answer M. Daladier's letter."

Back at the French Embassy Coulondre telephoned Daladier in Paris. "The Chancellor turns down your proposition," he told him.

"But you ought to have read him my letter and commented on it!" Daladier exclaimed.

"Mr. President," the Ambassador said, "for forty minutes I exhausted all the arguments, all the exhortations, all the adjurations."

In his dispatch to Bonnet later that evening Coulondre wired that he had "the sadness" to report his failure: "I moved Hitler perhaps. But I did not change his mind. He stands pat."[47]

Except for Hitler's fatuous formal reply by letter to Daladier the next day, this was the last diplomatic exchange between France and Germany in Berlin until the end.

The Premier seems to have realized that any further diplomacy in Berlin was useless. But his Foreign Minister could not quite bring himself to face the brutal truth that war was now inevitable because Hitler was determined to wage it. He began to clutch wildly at straws—in Berlin, in Warsaw, and then in Rome.

For a couple of days at the end of August, Bonnet pinned his hopes on the belief that Hitler had agreed to genuine negotiations with the Poles. He not only urged but badgered Warsaw to accept. But the truth of the matter, as so often during these last frenzied days of peace, was more complicated and quite different than Bonnet was willing to see.

On the evening of August 29 the British Ambassador in Berlin had had what he termed a stormy interview with Hitler. The day before, the British had proposed to the Chancellor direct talks between the German and Polish governments and had informed him that Poland was willing. Now on August 29 Hitler had replied in a formal note which he handed to Sir Nevile Henderson that while "skeptical" of the prospects and "solely" to please the British government he agreed to direct conversations with the Poles. But there was a catch. The Polish government must send to Berlin an emissary with full powers to conclude the negotiations. And he must arrive on Wednesday, August 30, which was the next day.

"That sounds like an ultimatum," Henderson complained, but Hitler insisted it was not. Time was pressing, he said. It was now the evening of August 29. The Polish plenipotentiary must arrive the next day. The Ambassador recounts that he left the Reich Chancellery that night "filled with the gloomiest forebodings."[48]

But that was not the reaction of Bonnet when at midnight he received from Ambassador Coulondre in Berlin an account of the Hitler-Henderson meeting. He immediately wired his Ambassador in Warsaw that Hitler "for the first time" had agreed to direct talks with the Poles and that it would be "difficult to answer with a brutal refusal." The next day he instructed Noël in Warsaw to urge the Polish government to agree at once. Bonnet did not see through Hitler's game. Even Coulondre was momentarily taken in. At 2 A.M. on August 30 he telephoned Bonnet advising that the Polish government "ought to accept the designation of a plenipotentiary." Twelve hours later, after he had seen the text of Hitler's "offer," he had second thoughts. He telephoned Bonnet that the German proposal was "brutal and resembled more a *Diktat* imposed on a vanquished country than the acceptance to negotiate with a sovereign state."[49]

What the French Foreign Minister did not see—or want to see—was that there are various kinds of "direct talks" between two governments. What Hitler was demanding was that Poland within twenty-four hours send an envoy empowered to sign an agreement which he would force down his throat under the threat of armed invasion—exactly as he had done with Chancellor Schuschnigg of Austria and President Hacha of Czechoslovakia.

General Halder saw Hitler's game at once. On August 29, when he learned of his chief's offer for direct talks with the Poles, he jotted in his diary:

Fuehrer hopes to drive wedge between British, French, and Poles. Strategy: Raise a barrage of demographic and democratic demands. . . . The Poles will come to Berlin on August 30. On August 31 the negotiations will blow up. On September 1 start to use force.

The Poles were trying to get ready to meet that force but their efforts were being impeded by the French and British Ambassadors in Warsaw. On the afternoon of August 29 Count Szembek, the Polish Vice-Minister for Foreign Affairs, called in the French and British ambassadors and informed them that in view of the gravity of the situation the Polish government had decided to decree general mobilization. The ambassadors protested at once against "the untimeliness of taking this extreme measure," arguing that it would provoke Hitler to attack. Germany was by this time fully mobilized for the assault on Poland but the Ambassadors did not think Poland should act similarly for fear of provoking the German dictator. When Daladier saw the dispatch from Ambassador Noël reporting this he immediately telephoned Bonnet and instructed him to inform Warsaw at once that neither he nor the General Staff wished to do anything to prevent the Polish government from mobilizing if it judged such a step indispensable. Bonnet comments complacently that he explained to the Premier that Ambassador Noël had merely advised the Poles to give their mobilization "the least publicity possible."*

---

* This was not true. Though Bonnet omits from the French *Yellow Book* Noël's telegram which aroused Daladier, the British Foreign Office documents reveal

The Polish government actually held up announcement of general mobilization until noon the next day, August 30. Beck tried to explain to the two Allied ambassadors that it was impossible to keep mobilization secret since it could not be carried out "without posting the decree." He also asked them if they would take the responsibility for advising Poland not to mobilize "and thus jeopardize their existence?"[50] It was this question which had aroused Daladier. The delay in mobilizing would cost the Poles dearly.

Throughout the day of August 30 Bonnet continued to put pressure on the Poles to agree to "direct talks." He admits he was "preoccupied" by the time limit of twenty-four hours fixed by Hitler. He claims he was acting in accord with the British, though it is evident that London did not share his view that the Poles should comply with Hitler's ultimatum by sending an emissary with plenipotentiary powers to Berlin before the day was out. Halifax made that clear in two telegrams to Berlin. The first, dispatched at 2 A.M., informed Ambassador Henderson that "it is of course unreasonable to expect that we can produce a Polish representative in Berlin today and German government must not expect this." At 6:50 P.M. he wired Henderson again: "We cannot advise the Polish Government to comply with this procedure, which is wholly unreasonable."[51] At 7 P.M. the British Foreign Secretary instructed his Ambassador in Warsaw to inform Beck of this, to reassert that Britain would stand by its commitments but to advise the Polish government to "make known to the German Government that they confirm acceptance of principle of direct discussions." This was far from acquiescing in Hitler's demand for a Polish plenipotentiary to show up before the end of this day, as Coulondre (and Henderson) had at first recommended and as Bonnet was urging. Beck promised the French and British ambassadors in Warsaw a definite reply by noon the next day.

To Bonnet this was stalling and he fumed against Beck for his "prolonged silence and for not realizing how tragic the situation was." Actually the situation was more "tragic" than even Bonnet realized and for this Hitler, not Beck, was to blame. One of the last pieces of trickery of the power-drunk Nazi dictator took place at midnight of August 30–31 while the jittery French Foreign Minister was pacing his office in the Quai d'Orsay waiting for word from Warsaw.

At precisely that hour in Berlin, Henderson called on Ribbentrop and handed him the British reply to Hitler's note of the 29th. It was both conciliatory and firm. There then ensued a dramatic confrontation, which Dr. Paul Schmidt, the only observer present, later described as "the

---

that the French and British ambassadors in Warsaw strongly protested the Polish decision to mobilize. See dispatches of Sir H. Kennard in DBrFP, Vol. VII, No. 473, p. 364, and No. 482, pp. 370–371. Bonnet's misleading account is in his memoirs, *op. cit.*, Vol. II, p. 325.

stormiest I have ever experienced during my twenty-three years as interpreter." Henderson found Ribbentrop

aping Hitler at his worst. . . . His intense hostility increased in violence as I made each communication in turn. He kept leaping from his chair in a state of great excitement and asking if I had anything more to say. I kept replying that I had.

At one point, says Schmidt, both men leaped from their seats and glared at each other so angrily that the German interpreter thought they were coming to blows. But what is important for history is not the grotesqueness of this meeting but what followed toward its end. Ribbentrop scarcely glanced at the British reply or listened to Henderson's attempt to explain it. When the Ambassador asked for the German proposals for a Polish settlement which had been promised the British in Hitler's last note, Ribbentrop retorted contemptuously that it was now too late since the Polish emissary had not arrived by midnight. However, he added, the Germans had drawn up the promised proposals and he would read them out.

He read them in German "at top speed, or rather gabbled to me as fast as he could, in a tone of utmost annoyance," Henderson reported to London. Of the sixteen articles the Ambassador was able to gather the "gist" of six or seven, but even then he was not sure. He therefore asked for the text. Ribbentrop refused, throwing the document with a contemptuous gesture on the table and saying it was now out of date.*

It may have been out of date, since the Germans chose to make it so. But what is important is that these German "proposals" were never meant to be taken seriously or indeed to be taken at all. The Poles never received them. In fact, they were a hoax. They were a sham to fool the German people and, if possible, world opinion into believing that Hitler had attempted at the last minute to reach a reasonable settlement of his claims against Poland. The Fuehrer admitted it. Dr. Schmidt later heard him say:

I needed an alibi, especially with the German people, to show them that I had done everything to maintain peace. This explains my generous offer about the settlement of the Danzig and Corridor questions.†

---

* On the stand at Nuremberg, which condemned him to death, Ribbentrop, who said that Hitler had personally dictated the sixteen points and expressly forbidden him to give them to Henderson, denied that he had read them too fast for the Ambassador to grasp them. Schmidt testified that Ribbentrop did not "particularly hurry over them." The interpreter felt that Henderson's imperfect knowledge of German may have contributed to his inability to understand.[52]

† Compared to his demands of recent days, they were indeed "generous." Hitler demanded only that Danzig be returned to the Reich. The future of the

Henderson returned to his Embassy in the early morning hours of August 31 convinced, he later said, "that the last hope for peace had vanished." In Paris, Bonnet refused to admit it. "We did not have the right," he says, "to lose hope."

At 10:20 A.M. on the last day of August, Coulondre rang him up from Berlin with ominous news. Henderson had just told him he had learned on the best possible authority that if no Polish response was received by noon the order to attack Poland would be given immediately. In his excitement the usually cool French Ambassador recommended that the Polish government instruct Ambassador Josef Lipski to get in touch with the Germans as a plenipotentiary—that is, with the power to negotiate. Bonnet says he at once telephoned London to urge the British government to advise Warsaw to accept this, including, he admits, "the conditions indicated by our Ambassador in Berlin." At 11:45 A.M. Bonnet got through to Noël in Warsaw and pointing out the "extreme gravity of the situation" instructed him to again put pressure on Beck to agree to direct talks. Noël told him that Beck's reply was coming shortly—at noon. On the strength of this Bonnet telephoned Coulondre at 12:30 P.M. that "Warsaw has accepted direct conversations with the Germans" and instructed him to notify the Wilhelmstrasse at once. He also telephoned his premature news to London, urging that the British government immediately inform Berlin of Poland's favorable reply. "There is not a minute to lose," he warned.

Beck did reply to the French and British Ambassadors at noon on the 31st, informing them that the Polish government "confirm their readiness for a direct exchange of views with the German government on the basis proposed by the British government." This meant they agreed to talk, but on British, not German terms. Beck said he had instructed Lipski to seek an interview with the German Foreign Minister to inform him that Poland accepted the British proposals for direct talks.

At 1 P.M., a few minutes after receiving these instructions, Lipski telephoned the German Foreign Office and requested a meeting with Ribbentrop. After cooling his heels for a couple of hours he received a telephone call from Weizsaecker, who asked him whether he was coming as an emissary with full power "or in some other capacity."

"I replied," says Lipski, "that I was asking for an interview as Ambassador, to present a declaration from my government."

Another long wait followed. At 6:15 P.M., more than five hours after

---

Corridor would be decided by a plebiscite after a period of twelve months when tempers had calmed down. Poland would keep the port of Gdynia. Whoever received the Corridor in the plebiscite would grant the other party extraterritorial highway and railroad routes through it. There was to be an exchange of populations and full rights accorded to nationals of one country in the other. Had these proposals been offered seriously—the Polish government never received them—they would have formed the basis of serious negotiations and might well have spared the world its second great war in a generation.

he had requested the interview, Lipski was received by Ribbentrop. The meeting did not last long. The Ambassador read his written communication:

> The Polish government are favorably considering the British government's suggestion (for direct negotiations), and will make a formal reply on the subject during the next few hours.

This was something less than Beck had promised the Allied ambassadors in Warsaw, but by now it made no difference. When Ribbentrop asked Lipski whether he had come as an emissary empowered to negotiate, the Ambassador replied in the negative. Ribbentrop thereupon dismissed him, saying he would inform the Fuehrer.

"On my return to the Embassy," Lipski later related, "I found myself unable to communicate with Warsaw. The Germans had cut my telephone."

MUSSOLINI PROPOSES ANOTHER MUNICH

Early that afternoon of August 31 in Paris, Bonnet had seen another straw and he had clutched at it desperately in the hope that the peace might still be saved. At 12:50 P.M. Ambassador François-Poncet had telephoned him urgently from Rome to say that Mussolini was offering, if France and Great Britain accepted, to invite Germany to a conference on September 5 for the purpose of "examining the clauses of the Versailles Treaty which are the cause of the present difficulties." Count Ciano had made the same proposal to the British. He asked for a quick reply.

This obviously was a bid for another Munich, and Premier Daladier and Prime Minister Chamberlain, the unhappy veterans of that surrender, quickly saw it as such. At 1:15 P.M. Ambassador Corbin telephoned Bonnet from London to say that Chamberlain feared it was a trap. Daladier's reaction was even stronger. Sir Eric Phipps reported it promptly to London.

> M. Daladier has just told me (3:30 this afternoon) that he has instructed the French Ambassador to inform the Prime Minister that he (Daladier) will not accept Mussolini's invitation to a second "Munich" in Italy on September 5. M. Daladier remarked to me that he would rather resign than accept this invitation.[53]

But that was not the way Bonnet felt about it. "I welcomed with emotion this intervention," he says. "It brought us new hope. . . . It was sincere." And he explains that at such a conference "Poland could more easily justify before her public opinion the concessions which she would be led to make."[54] Bonnet recounts that he argued it out with Daladier, who after raising certain objections based on his experience at Munich, finally said: "You're right! We cannot turn down this proposition." This seems unlikely in view of what Daladier had told Phipps. At any rate, the Premier promised to call a cabinet meeting for 6 P.M.

It turned out to be a stormy and confusing session. Bonnet, backed by Monzie, pled for acceptance of the Italian proposal for a conference. The Foreign Minister added that the British government was urging him to inform it of the French response as soon as possible so that London and Paris could agree on a joint reply. At this point there occurred what Bonnet describes as an "incredible incident" between him and Daladier.* The Premier, Monzie noted, had turned his back on Bonnet, his "pouting" face showing "scorn or disgust." Daladier now told the cabinet that, contrary to what Bonnet said, the British were in no hurry to reply to Mussolini. He had just telephoned Corbin in London and the French Ambassador, who had just seen Chamberlain, had so informed him. Whom were the ministers to believe? Their perplexity and confusion were further increased by a new incident which further embarrassed Bonnet. An Army officer from the Premier's military cabinet broke into the meeting bearing a personal letter from Coulondre to Daladier. Whereas Bonnet had been arguing that only acceptance of a conference could save the peace, Coulondre now strongly advised from Berlin that peace could only be saved by France standing firm against Hitler. The Nazi dictator, he reported, was wavering.

The trial of force is turning to our advantage. I learn from a reliable source that for the last five days Hitler has been hesitating, that there is a wavering in the party, and that all their reports tell of a growing discontent among the people. . . . Hitler is now trying to find a way out of his impasse. The only thing for us to do is to hold firm![56]

Daladier read the message to the cabinet, on most of whose members it seemed to have a pronounced influence.† Monzie says that it stopped the debate. But Bonnet's persistence was rewarded. It was agreed to send an acceptance to Rome after agreeing with the British on its content. All evening long Bonnet was on the telephone to London trying to get British assent to his sending the response during the night. Halifax and Chamberlain declined to oblige him. It would be time enough to answer the next day. Finally toward midnight Corbin told Bonnet on the telephone that it was useless to persist. Halifax had left the Foreign Office for the night.

Monzie also persisted. He, too, was on the telephone to Bonnet.

Georges, . . . if the project for a conference fails . . . we will be caught up and pulverized in the wheels of war. If we do not resign tomorrow, the next day will be too late. . . . Let us leave together.

"Impossible, my dear friend," Monzie says Bonnet responded. "If we leave it will surely be war."[57]

In truth all these frantic, eleventh-hour efforts of the weary and

---

* Reynaud called it "the most painful scene he had ever witnessed."[55]
† Bonnet does not mention this scene in his account.

exhausted diplomats and ministers on this last day of August 1939, to save the peace, and all the noble, heartrending pleas of the pope, President Roosevelt, the King of the Belgians and the Queen of Holland, were but a flailing of the air, completely futile. As for the Germans, all their acts were deliberately deceptive.

For at 12:30 P.M. on August 31, before Lord Halifax had urged the Poles to be more accommodating and before Lipski had called on Ribbentrop to agree to direct talks and before Mussolini had tried to intervene with his proposal for a conference and before Bonnet had agreed to that conference, Adolf Hitler had taken his final decision and issued the decisive order that was to throw the planet into its bloodiest war.

SUPREME COMMANDER OF THE ARMED FORCES

MOST SECRET

Berlin, August 31, 1939

Directive No. 1 for the Conduct of the War.

1. Now that all the *political possibilities* of disposing by peaceful means of a situation on the Eastern Frontier which is intolerable for Germany *are* exhausted, I have determined on a *solution by force.**

2. The *attack on Poland* is to be carried out in accordance with the preparations made for Case White. . . .

Date of attack: September 1, 1939.

Time of attack: 4:45 A.M. . . .

Adolf Hitler[58]

---

* The emphasis is in the German original.

26

THE LAUNCHING OF WORLD WAR II
September 1–3, 1939

The news of the German attack on Poland reached Daladier and Bonnet at 8 A.M. on September 1. The Foreign Minister remembered later that it was difficult for "the terrible news" to penetrate his mind. At any rate his first thoughts were not on how France could honor its commitments to Poland but on pushing the Italian proposal for a conference—despite the German aggression. When the Polish Ambassador called on him at 9 A.M. to confirm that aggression, Bonnet, by his own account, explained that the Constitution prevented France from engaging in any act of war against Germany or even from presenting her with an ultimatum until Parliament had acted. The Chamber and Senate, he added, would meet the next day. The members needed twenty-four hours, he said, to get back from their vacations.

He then bombarded London with telephone calls in an effort to get the British to agree to French acceptance of Mussolini's conference. (According to Reynaud, Bonnet told the cabinet that he had been trying to get in touch with Halifax, but was told he was at his dentist.)[1] Finally, at 11:50 A.M., after London had said it would not object to the French response, he personally dictated the reply to Ambassador François-Poncet in Rome. It effusively thanked the Italian government for its efforts to save the peace and pledged French cooperation in any effort to settle the German-Polish conflict peacefully. It accepted with pleasure the project of a conference, making only one condition: that Poland be invited to it.

The British reply, made at the same time, was more in tune with the demands of the hour. Halifax thanked the Italians for their efforts to avert hostilities but added that in view of the morning's news "the German government had rendered it impossible."

Not for Bonnet. The Italians, he says, asked him to get a favorable response for the conference from Poland, and this he set out with great energy to obtain. He told Ambassador Noël in Warsaw to press the Poles for a quick and affirmative reply. "I consider it important," he said. "In the present situation no effort must be spared to try to save the peace." Communication with Warsaw by telephone was difficult because of what was going on that day in Poland. Bonnet got through to Noël with his instructions at 4 P.M. but the line was bad and he was not sure he had been fully understood. He reaffirmed his message to the French Embassy in Bucharest and told it to telephone it on to Warsaw.

Noël wired back Beck's reply at 9:31 P.M.

We are in the midst of war as the result of unprovoked aggression. It is no longer a question of a conference but of common action which the Allies should take to resist aggression.*[2]

The Ambassador added his own observation that "the time has passed for accommodation." He also reported to Bonnet that several Polish cities were under incessant German bombing and that, according to Beck, there had been numerous civilian casualties.†

At 10:30 A.M. on September 1 the French cabinet met briefly to consider the country's response to Hitler's aggression. It was decided to decree general mobilization, to convoke Parliament for the next day and to ask it to vote the necessary credits to wage war. This in the view of the majority, though not of Monzie, would get around asking Parliament for a declaration of war. The Constitution of 1875 stipulated that the President of the Republic could not declare war without the prior assent of the two chambers. But constitutional authorities had held that if they voted war credits that could be considered an "assent." That was what Daladier proposed to do. He shrank back from asking for an outright declaration of war.

There was some concern in the cabinet as to whether Italy would attack in support of Hitler. But during the meeting Bonnet received from London a copy of a dispatch from the British Ambassador in Rome sent late the night before. Ciano had informed him that the Italian government had made its decision: "Italy will not fight against either England or France." The news was received by the cabinet with relief.

---

* Noël's telegram did not reach Paris until 3 P.M. of the following day. Bonnet makes no mention of it in his detailed account of the day's events. Nor did he tell the British in his numerous telephone calls to London that he was attempting to bring Poland to a conference. A British Foreign Office minute of September 2 notes: "H.M. Government were neither consulted nor informed of this *démarche*."[3]

† Despite this message and others from Noël about German bombing of Polish cities, including one dispatch filed at noon September 2 that the Germans were not limiting their bombings to military objectives, Bonnet told the British Ambassador on September 2 that "so far Germans have not bombed open towns in Poland but only military objectives."[4]

The problem now was how to make good on the guarantees to Poland and to act in unison with the British. It was obvious that a joint note would have to be delivered to Hitler before the day was out informing him that the two Allied governments would honor their commitments. The British wanted to take a firm line in Berlin and demand that the Germans immediately withdraw their troops from Poland. Bonnet says he explained to London that that would be an ultimatum, and that the French government could not send an ultimatum without prior authorization of Parliament, which could not meet before the morrow. At 5 o'clock Halifax telephoned Bonnet to urge that the British and French ambassadors in Berlin ask for their passports that very evening. Bonnet recounts that he asked the Foreign Secretary to wait the vote of the French chambers. He also told the British that he disagreed with their negative attitude toward the Italian proposal for a conference. However, he finally gave ground on the nature of the Allied declaration to Germany and agreed on the text of a note which the Allied ambassadors in Berlin presented to the German government during the evening.

Unless the German government are prepared to give the French government satisfactory assurances that the German government have suspended all aggressive action against Poland and are prepared promptly to withdraw their forces from Polish territory, the French government will without hesitation fulfill their obligations to Poland.[5]

No time limit for the German reply was given, an omission that would cause much friction between Paris and London during the next forty-eight hours. In Berlin the two ambassadors had asked to be received together to emphasize the unity of their two governments, but Ribbentrop had declined. He saw Henderson at 9 P.M. and Coulondre an hour later, mouthing to both what the French envoy described as "a few more lies," such as that Poland, not Germany, was the aggressor. He said he would transmit their notes to Hitler.

September 2, while the German armies smashed further into Poland and the Luftwaffe rained down bombs on her towns and cities, was a nerve-racking day of waiting for all concerned. Mussolini tried desperately to get Germany and Britain to agree to his bid for a conference (France had already accepted), Chamberlain and Halifax grew increasingly impatient with what they regarded as stalling on the part of France, and Bonnet played for time in the hope that another Munich might spare France from fighting.

At 9 A.M. the excited Polish Ambassador arrived at the Quai d'Orsay to protest to Bonnet France's dilatoriness in honoring her obligations. He demanded to know if the French had set any time limit in their note to Berlin.

"No time limit. We can do nothing without the authorization of

Parliament," Bonnet replied. "It meets this afternoon and after it votes we can send our ultimatum to Germany."

"When will this ultimatum expire?" the Ambassador asked.

"At the end of forty-eight hours, I suppose."

"This delay is much too long! Poland has been at war for thirty-six hours!"*6

According to Reynaud, Bonnet added: "Do you want the women and children of Paris to be massacred?"8 Perhaps the Ambassador was thinking of the women and children of Poland who already were being slain.

As the morning progressed the British government grew increasingly impatient with the French. Lord Halifax expressed it in a message to Phipps in Paris at 11:55 A.M.

Delays in Paris and attitude of French government are causing some misgiving here. We shall be grateful for anything you can do to infuse courage and determination into M. Bonnet.9

This was a tall order. But Bonnet was not the only important figure in Paris who was insisting on going slowly. Daladier told his Foreign Minister that Gamelin and the General Staff were demanding as much time as possible in order to complete the general mobilization without risk of air attack and to evacuate the civilians from the border districts. They wanted, he said, no hostilities until at least 9 P.M. on September 4. If the Anglo-French ultimatum to Berlin was delivered this evening of the 2nd, the generals insisted on a time limit of forty-eight hours before it expired. Gamelin later admitted that it was he and the General Staff who were putting the pressure on Daladier not to hurry.

The British [he wrote] were insisting that hostilities should begin as soon as possible in order to give some useful assistance to Poland without delay. They feared, I believe, that we would hesitate at the last moment. They continued to distrust our Foreign Minister. I turned, I must confess, a deaf ear to this demand, for we had to gain time for our preparations, *which would in no wise delay the hour when we would be able to attack.*†10

What General Gamelin's idea of an "attack," for which he needed to gain so much time, was, we shall shortly see.

___

* Though Bonnet himself recounts this conversation with the Polish Ambassador he denied to the British later in the day that the envoy had asked for help. Sir Alexander Cadogan, the permanent Under-Secretary at the Foreign Office, rang up Bonnet at 5 P.M. and, among other things, asked him "whether the Poles had [asked] for help from France on the grounds that there was a big battle." The Foreign Office record of the talk records that Bonnet answered: "Not yet." Bonnet added "that he would telephone London when the Polish Ambassador in Paris made representations."7

† The emphasis is provided by Gamelin.

The differences between Paris and London lay, of course, in the differing military roles of the two countries. The British were thinking at first, as was natural, primarily of the war at sea. In London it was the Admiralty which was pressing the government to declare war at once so that the British Navy could seize German shipping on the high seas— the great German liner *Bremen* was a day or two out of New York eastbound—and attack German U-boats emerging into the North Sea before they could take up their stations along the Atlantic shipping routes, which constituted Britain's lifeline.

The French General Staff, just as naturally, was concerned with completing its mobilization and the deployment of its armies without being harassed by German air attack, which Gamelin much feared, especially after the news of massive German bombing in Poland. After all, it was the French who for the moment would have to do all the fighting in the West against the Germans. There would not be a single British trooper to aid them for several days and no British army worth mentioning for several months, if then.

In the midst of these irritating exchanges between London and Paris on when to go to war with Germany the matter of Mussolini's conference again popped up, accentuating the differences between the British and the French. On the morning of September 2 the Duce had sent a message to Hitler.

. . . Italy . . . still has the possibility of getting France, Britain, and Poland to agree to a conference on the following bases:

1. An armistice, which leaves the armies *where** they now are.

2. Convening of a conference within two or three days.

3. Settlement of the Polish-German dispute, which, as matters stand today, would certainly be favorable for Germany.

The idea, which originally emanated from the Duce, is now supported particularly by France.

Mussolini reminded Hitler that with Danzig already in his hands as well as slices of Polish territory overrun by the swiftly advancing German army, Germany had achieved her "moral satisfaction" and got pledges which guaranteed her the greater part of her claims. If she accepted the proposal for a conference she "would achieve all her aims and at the same time avoid a war which even now looks like becoming general and of extremely long duration."[11]

Ribbentrop had replied that Hitler would answer "in a day or two" if Rome confirmed that the Anglo-French notes of the evening before were not "ultimata."

At 2 P.M., just as, Bonnet says, all hope of saving the peace seemed lost, a telephone call to him from Ciano in Rome revived his hopes. Stretching a point, the Italian Foreign Minister told him that Hitler was

---

* Emphasis of Mussolini.

"not opposed" to the project of a conference but wanted to know if the Anglo-British notes had been "ultimata," in which case he would not consider a conference, and also whether he had until noon of the 3rd to reply to them.

Bonnet, according to the recording of the telephone conversation,[12] "warmly thanked Count Ciano for his communication" and told him (1) that the French note had not been an ultimatum, and (2) that he thought the German reply to it could be held up until noon, Sunday (September 3), but that he would have to discuss this with Daladier and the British government.

Bonnet says that "the unexpected news that Hitler had accepted a conference" reawakened in him "a feeble hope" and that he was determined to use all his forces to "arrest hostilities, if there was still time." But Ciano had not told him that Hitler had accepted—by now the Foreign Minister was grasping at straws that were not even there. He says he "rushed" to Daladier with the good news and that the Premier agreed with him not to send an ultimatum to Berlin until noon Sunday and that in any case hostilities could not begin until the night of September 4–5. On Daladier's urging to get in touch with the British, Bonnet rang up Lord Halifax at 3 P.M.

He found that the British Foreign Secretary had also received a telephone call from Ciano but had reacted to it less warmly than he. While Halifax had confirmed to Ciano that the British note was not an ultimatum —one marvels at the splitting of hairs over a single word, for the Anglo-French notes spoke for themselves, unequivocally—he had told him that in his personal opinion, which he was sure was that of the cabinet, there could be no question of a conference unless Germany first agreed to withdraw her troops from Poland.

According to a British minute, Bonnet, in his talk with Halifax, said he thought it "probably true that Hitler would be unable to accept the condition of withdrawal, though that was obviously desirable. He added that he thought a conference might be contemplated provided that Poland was represented. That was really the essential point." Bonnet does not mention this part of the conversation in his memoirs or in his notes of the conversation published in the French *Yellow Book*.

But "the essential point" to the British was something else than Bonnet's. At 5:20 P.M. Halifax telephoned his French colleague to say that the British cabinet was "unanimous" in opposing a conference unless the Germans first agreed to pull back their troops.[13] At 6:38 P.M. Halifax telephoned Ciano in Rome to give him the same message. The Italian Foreign Minister replied that he did not think Hitler would accept such a condition. "Try your best," Halifax told him. But Ciano felt it was useless to try further.

It isn't my business [he wrote in his diary] to give Hitler advice that he would reject decisively, and maybe with contempt. I tell this to Halifax, to the two ambassadors and to the Duce, and, finally, I telephone to Berlin that unless the Germans advise us to the contrary we shall let the conversations lapse. The last note of hope has died.[14]

The idea of a conference was dead—to all except Bonnet, who, to Ciano's surprise and scorn, tried desperately for another twelve hours—throughout that night—to revive it. There remained between Paris and London the problem of trying to agree on the timing of a final ultimatum to Hitler to inform him that unless he agreed to withdraw his armies from Poland forthwith the Western Allies would go to war. In London the Commons was becoming restive at the delay in honoring Britain's word and at what seemed to many members the stalling of France. At 1:30 P.M. on September 2 Halifax wired Phipps in Paris asking for French "concurrence" in a statement the Prime Minister would make to the House at 3 P.M. It would declare that the British government did not intend to wait much longer for a German reply to the Anglo-French notes of the evening before but that in order to act in concert with Paris it must wait for the action of the French Parliament, which was convening at 3 P.M.

At that hour the Chamber of Deputies and Senate, which despite the mounting crisis of the past days had been kept on vacation by Daladier, finally met. Weary, like all the other statesmen in Europe, from the round-the-clock ordeal of the past few days, the Premier, his face drawn but his manner resolute, mounted the tribune of the Chamber to read a rather hackneyed message from the President of the Republic and to deliver the declaration of his government. It was the finest speech of his career, firm and yet conciliatory. Indeed it was his words expressing even at this late hour a wish for conciliation which drew from the deputies, fearful of war as they were, the loudest and most prolonged applause. When he declared: "What we have done before the commencement of this war (to save the peace), we are ready to continue to do. If measures of reconciliation are renewed, we are still ready to join them," every member of the Chamber arose and applauded.

If combat is halted, if the aggressor regains his frontiers, if a free negotiation can still take place, the French government will spare no effort to assure its success in the interest of world peace.

Again there was prolonged applause.

But time presses. France and Britain will not stand by and witness the destruction of a friendly people prior to new enterprises of violence directed in their turn against Britain and France.

Is it merely a question of a German-Polish conflict? No. It is a question of a new phase in the march of the Hitler dictatorship toward domination of Europe and the world. . . .

We are told that once the German demands on Poland are satisfied

Germany will promise the world to respect the peace for ten, twenty, twenty-five years, or forever. Unfortunately we know those promises.

France, he said, would keep her engagements.

> It concerns not only the honor of our country but the protection of her vital interests.
> For a France which let this aggression be accomplished would soon be a France scorned, isolated, discredited, without allies and without support, and soon, have no doubt, subjected herself to a frightful assault. . . . The aggressors, rendered more powerful by their conquests, gorged by the booty of Europe, master of inexhaustible natural resources, would soon turn against France with all their forces.

In conclusion he once more expressed both determination and willingness for conciliation.

> Our duty is to finish with aggression and violence. By peaceful means, if we still can, and we will keep on trying to the end. By using our force, if all moral sense and reason have disappeared from the aggressors.

The Premier was given a standing ovation as he left the tribune. The emotion in the Chamber was intense. But this did not mean that all the deputies by any means were in favor of going to war. When the Finance Committee met during a brief recess to approve the demand for 70 billion francs in war credits some members asked Daladier whether such approval would be considered by the government as an authorization to declare war. Daladier answered that if war had to be declared, he would "come back" to Parliament. From this response ensued the later charge made by Flandin and other opponents of the war, that Daladier had not only gone back on his word by declining to ask Parliament for an actual declaration of war but that taking France into war was itself unconstitutional since Parliament had not specifically given its assent.

Reynaud, who, as Minister of Finance, was present at the Committee's deliberation, concedes that Daladier did promise to "come back" to Parliament for the war declaration. "But after the meeting," Reynaud recounts, "he changed his mind. He thought it was not necessary for a second vote." Reynaud, along with most French constitutional authorities, was certain that voting the war credits was tantamount to voting war and that the constitutional requirements were fulfilled.[15] President Lebrun later contended that each member of Parliament, in freely casting his vote, "knew precisely what he was doing." To him there was no violation of the Constitution.[16] But the quarrel over this point further divided the political leaders and the charge of evading the Constitution would be used against the government when its fortunes worsened. Pierre Laval later insisted that the government had gone to war in 1939 without the assent of Parliament.

Just before the two Houses met the leaders of all the political parties, including the Communists, had agreed to a government request that there be no debate before the vote on war credits. Alone in the Senate, Laval insisted on speaking. He had not appeared at the tribune since the elections of 1936, but he had been nursing his grudges against those who he felt had kept him out of power so long. He now chose this day to begin his public comeback and to prepare the ground for the kind of future he envisaged for France with the help of Marshal Pétain. Despite a storm of protest from all sides he attempted to speak, demanding that the government work with Italy, as he said he had done in 1935, to keep the peace. But his words were drowned out by shouts of protest and he resumed his seat.

In the Chamber, too, there was but one voice of dissent, though later many deputies claimed they would have spoken up if they had been given the opportunity. The lone dissenter was the maverick Gaston Bergery, who, like so many other politicians in France, had been making a rapid journey from the far Left toward the Right—he had been an ardent supporter of Munich. He insisted that the Chamber sit in secret session and debate going to war, but he, too, was drowned out by hostile protests.

The vote for the war credits in both Houses was taken by a show of hands and according to the *Journal Officiel* was unanimous. But even on this point there was subsequent controversy. According to a later account by Deputy Jean Montigny, made after he had become a fervent Vichyite, and by Benoist-Méchin, who would be condemned to death for his collaboration with the Germans, Speaker Herriot, after asking those in favor to raise their hands, declined to ask for a show of hands against. "The meeting is adjourned," he suddenly proclaimed.*[17]

Bonnet did not attend the meeting of the Chamber. In agreement with Daladier, he says, he decided it was more important for him to remain at the Quai d'Orsay in touch with London by telephone. At 5:20 P.M. Cadogan rang him up to say, as we have seen, that the British government rejected the Italian proposal for a conference unless Hitler pulled back his troops from Poland. But more important for the British was to get the agreement of the French for the timing of a final ultimatum to Hitler which, if not accepted within a few hours, would bring the Allies into war in consequence of their engagements to Poland. The British government, Cadogan now told Bonnet, intended to fulfill their guarantee to Poland if by midnight Hitler had not agreed to withdraw his troops.

Bonnet objected to such haste. According to the British Foreign Office record of the conversation, the French Foreign Minister asked the London government to "reflect on this. If they insisted on the midnight ultimatum

---

* Beau de Loménie, no friend of the government, believed that 100 deputies had voted against by not raising their hands. The Communists, he says, voted for.[18]

they would incur a grave responsibility *vis-à-vis* France, because French evacuation is incomplete and will take two days more to complete."[19]

In his own account, Bonnet, who thought he was talking to Lord Halifax, recounts that he reminded "Lord Halifax that we have not yet terminated the evacuation of our large cities. All our railroad stations are bulging with passengers and we risk exposing them to a frightful carnage in case of air attack." He says Lord Halifax was "very much moved" by his words and promised to discuss the situation with the cabinet.[20] The British version records only that Cadogan, who was the man on the line, asked when the French cabinet would make up its mind about the "time limit" in the ultimatum and that Bonnet responded: "by 9 P.M."

London's impatience with Paris was now approaching the boiling point. At 6 P.M., shortly after Bonnet and Cadogan had hung up, Halifax telephoned to Sir Eric Phipps in Paris.

> The position of the French government [he said] was very embarrassing to His Majesty's Government. A statement had to be made to Parliament this evening but up to the present there was no agreement on . . . what should be the time-limit to be inserted in the eventual ultimatum.
> Sir Eric Phipps said that the French Government . . . were unable to agree to less than 48 hours . . . explaining that that period would begin to run from the moment of delivery of the ultimatum.
> The Secretary of State explained that a period of 48 hours was quite impossible for his Majesty's Government. The naval authorities complained that with so long a delay the Germans might be able to make all kinds of dispositions without interference from us. Was it possible to persuade M. Daladier to agree that the ultimatum should expire at midnight tonight?
> Sir Eric Phipps said that the attitude of the French Government was that that was quite impossible in view of the fact that the evacuation of women and children was still in full swing. . . . He added that the French Cabinet were in session and were expected to rise between 8 and 9 this evening.[21]

An hour later Phipps rang up London to say that Daladier agreed to the Prime Minister's statement to be made in the House "although M. Bonnet had made difficulties." With growing disquietude London awaited the results of the French cabinet meeting.

It had convened shortly after the Parliamentary vote of the war credits and some of its members rebelled against being pushed so rapidly into war, as they put it, by the British. When one member said it was "deplorable" for the two governments to disagree on their timing of the ultimatum, Monzie replied that "for once we can afford the luxury of being a step behind the British." By this time Monzie was blaming the British for the war. The day before, when Hitler had launched it, he had noted in his diary: "The obstacle to peace is . . . without doubt in London." Taking Bonnet aside after the cabinet meeting, which ended at 8:30 P.M., Monzie says he "pressed" him to ignore the British pressure. "To demand the withdrawal of German troops in Poland," Monzie says he told him, "is an insupportable pretension, which the Minister of Foreign Affairs should have labeled as such."

Monzie says he suggested a compromise: to ask the Germans to make a "symbolic withdrawal." He was dining shortly with the Italian Ambassador. Could he suggest this "honorable proposal" to the Italians?²² Bonnet, who claims that there was "no discussion" in the cabinet about France fulfilling her obligations to Poland now that Parliament had acted, told Monzie he could.

If the British pressure on the French to hasten the ultimatum to Berlin was considerable, the pressure on the British government from the House of Commons for speed was perhaps even greater. At 9:50 P.M. Chamberlain himself rang up Daladier to tell him about it and Cadogan, listening in, made a minute of the conversation.

> The situation here [the Prime Minister said] was very grave. There had been an angry scene in the House of Commons after he had made his statement. . . . If the French government were to insist on a time-limit of 48 hours to run from midday tomorrow, it would be impossible for the Government to hold the situation here.
>
> The Prime Minister said that he quite realized that it was France which must bear the burden of the German attack, but . . . the situation here was such that some step must be taken this evening. He proposed as a compromise that we should announce that the Ambassadors had been instructed to present the ultimatum at 8 A.M. tomorrow and that if the German government had not given the required assurance by midday we should consider ourselves to be in a state of war as from that hour.

Daladier was evasive. Like Bonnet, he still clung to the hope that "a Five-Power conference" might save the peace. Dodging at first the issue Chamberlain had raised, the Premier talked at length about Ciano's initiative.

> . . . Count Ciano [the British minute reports Daladier as saying] had observed that there was still a hope of German agreement if we could put off our *démarche* until midday tomorrow, and the French cabinet had endorsed this view. If between now and midday tomorrow the German government gave a refusal, it would then be possible to address an ultimatum to the German government.

Daladier then gave a little turn to the knife. General Gamelin had become possessed of an unholy fear of German air attack despite the fact that he knew the Luftwaffe was fully engaged in Poland, and he had communicated his fear to the Premier. Moreover Britain had not yet agreed to throw in her air force if France should suddenly be bombed, unlikely as that prospect actually was. If the British sent over planes immediately, that might make a difference, and Daladier now reminded Chamberlain of this.

Unless British bombers were ready to act at once [Daladier said] it would be better for France to delay, if possible, for some hours attacks on the German armies.

At this point Daladier abruptly broke off the conversation, declaring "he could not say anything more definite on the telephone."[23]

Scarcely half an hour later, at 10:30 P.M., the impatient British Foreign Secretary rang up the French Foreign Minister, and Cadogan again listened in and made a minute. Bonnet does not include this conversation in his notes on his various telephone talks published in the *Yellow Book,* but he does give an account in his memoirs. As might be expected, it differs somewhat from the British version. The latter records Halifax proposing

that the Ambassadors should call on the [German] Minister for Foreign Affairs at 8 A.M. (on Sunday, September 3) and inform him that if he could not give a satisfactory reply by midday then after that hour we should be free to take action to fulfill our obligations to Poland.

If the French government could not agree to this timetable the British government would propose that it itself go ahead on its own and

send separate instructions to His Majesty's Ambassador [in Berlin] to act without his French colleague, *provided the French Government would give assurance that they would follow suit* within 24 hours.*

Again Bonnet objected to the British being in such a hurry. What difference, he asked, did a few hours make? Hostilities, in any case, could not begin until forty-eight hours after the ultimatum was presented since the French needed that additional time to complete their mobilization and evacuate the women and children.

I described to the Secretary of State [Bonnet recounts] the spectacle at the Gare d'Orsay where I had just seen the long lines of women, with their infants in their arms. If there was a serious air attack there would be a frightful massacre. I also insisted on the deplorable impression which separate action by our ambassadors in Berlin would make. . . .

Bonnet says that Lord Halifax was "very much shaken" by his "reflections" and promised to reexamine the question with the cabinet. But that is not what the British minute records.

The Secretary of State repeated that it seemed very doubtful whether the Government could hold the position here. . . . He did not see any grave objection to our acting at 8 A.M. and the French Government at midday. In any case it was impossible for His Majesty's Government to wait until the latter hour.

---

* Author's emphasis.

It was finally agreed, according to the British minute, though Bonnet does not mention this, that the British would deliver their ultimatum at 8 A.M. and the French theirs at noon. Bonnet's parting shot to the British was similar to Daladier's a few minutes before. "If the British bombers," he said, "could be ready at once to reply to bombing attacks the position might be different."[24]

Chamberlain and Halifax in their telephone conversations with the French had not exaggerated the precarious position of the Tory government in the seething House of Commons. At 2 A.M. that night Ambassador Corbin rang up Bonnet to warn him that the Chamberlain government risked being overthrown unless it could assure the Commons when it met at 10 A.M. that the British ultimatum, with a time limit of a few hours, had already been delivered in Berlin. Corbin added that the British government had finally decided to deliver the ultimatum in Berlin at 9 A.M. with hostilities, so far as Britain was concerned, commencing at 11 A.M.

Corbin also asked if Paris could not "shorten the delay." Bonnet recounts that he telephoned the Ministry of War to ask it and was answered:

Ask London if it can put the British Bomber Force at our disposition tomorrow morning. In that case the French General Staff can accept a reduction of the delay.

The message, says Bonnet, was relayed by Corbin to the British Foreign Office but the British General Staff could not make a decision immediately. "Once again," the Foreign Minister recounts, "we are halted by the insufficiency of our means of action."[25] One wonders why Daladier and Bonnet insisted on British bombers. Fighters, not bombers, would have been the "means" of halting a German air attack. And the French had enough fighters to turn back any bombers the Germans could spare from Poland.

The telephone calls to Paris of the British Prime Minister and Foreign Secretary had not left the French government unmoved. At midnight Bonnet, in accord with Daladier, sent a telegram to Coulondre in Berlin saying that "tomorrow morning I shall send you the terms of a new *démarche* which I ask you to make at noon September 3 to the Wilhelmstrasse." Even then the Foreign Minister shrank back from using the word "ultimatum." Did he still hope Mussolini might get France off the hook? If so, this final hope was dashed just as the long night was ending. At 5 A.M., Bonnet says, Monzie, who had sat up most of the night with the Italian Ambassador discussing his spurious "peace offer"— and also, it appears from his diary, cursing the British for their intransigence—telephoned him.

Guariglia has rung up Rome to find out if Hitler will accept a withdrawal of his troops to permit the conference to be held. Ciano has responded: "Impossible!"

Ciano's version of this last-minute French effort to avoid a war with Germany was confided to his diary.

> During the night I was awakened by the Ministry because Bonnet has asked Guariglia if we could not at least obtain a symbolic withdrawal of German forces from Poland. Nothing can be done. I throw the proposal in the wastebasket without informing the Duce. But this shows that France is moving toward the great test without enthusiasm and full of uncertainty. . . .[26]

The view of the German Embassy in Paris as to how France was moving toward the great test had been wired by the chargé at 12:20 P.M. on September 2.

> The general mobilization proclaimed yesterday has been accepted quietly by the French population and . . . is being carried out in an orderly manner and according to plan. . . .
> That France will fulfill her treaty obligations to Poland cannot be doubted. It is however an open question whether France will in consequence immediately enter into hostilities. . . .[27]

At 8 A.M. on Sunday, September 3, 1939, Bonnet went to the War Ministry to confer with Daladier about the time limit in the French ultimatum which would be presented in Berlin at noon. The Premier, who was also Defense Minister, set the opening of hostilities for Monday at 5 A.M. The General Staff, he explained, refused to accept a shorter delay. Returning to the Quai d'Orsay, Bonnet proceeded to draft the French ultimatum, "weighing each word," he says, "of this historic dispatch." It instructed Ambassador Coulondre to present himself at noon to the Wilhelmstrasse and to ask for the German response to the French note of September 1.

> If the reply . . . is negative . . . you will notify the German Minister of Foreign Affairs, or his representative, that from 5 A.M. tomorrow September 4 France will be obligated to fulfill her obligations to Poland, which are known to the German government.[28]

Even at this final hour Bonnet shrank back from a formal declaration of war. He telephoned the text of the French ultimatum to Ambassador Coulondre in Berlin at 10:20 A.M.

By this time Ambassador Henderson had delivered the British ultimatum to the German government. Promptly at 9 A.M., as instructed from London, he had appeared at the Foreign Office in the Wilhelmstrasse. He had been told that Ribbentrop would not be "available" but that he could leave his communication with Dr. Paul Schmidt, the official interpreter.

On this historic morning Schmidt had overslept and barely got to the Foreign Office by taxi in time to see the British Ambassador mounting the steps. Henderson read to him the British ultimatum. Unless the German government, it said, gave satisfactory assurances by 11 A.M. that it would withdraw its troops from Poland, *"a state of war will exist between the two countries as from that hour."* The British were no longer pussyfooting about words.

Schmidt hastened down the Wilhelmstrasse to the Chancellery with the British ultimatum.

> When I entered the room [Schmidt later recounted] Hitler was sitting at his desk and Ribbentrop stood by the window. . . . I stopped at some distance from Hitler's desk, and then slowly translated the British ultimatum. When I finished there was complete silence.
>
> Hitler sat immobile, gazing before him. . . . After an interval which seemed an age, he turned to Ribbentrop, who had remained standing by the window. "What now?" asked Hitler with a savage look, as though implying that his Foreign Minister had misled him about England's probable reaction.
>
> Ribbentrop answered quietly: "I assume that the French will hand in a similar ultimatum within the hour."[29]

At that hour in Paris the French were still having trouble agreeing on the time limit of their ultimatum. Shortly after dispatching his instructions to Coulondre, Bonnet received a call from London—from whom, he does not say—but presumably the French Embassy. "The news has spread there," he was told, "that France would not enter the war until Monday at 5 A.M. and it was producing in England an unfortunate impression very prejudicial to the Allied cause." He called Daladier, who had received the same news. The Premier said he would make one final effort to get the General Staff to shorten the time limit on the expiration of the French ultimatum.

Time was pressing. It was now 11:30 A.M. and in Berlin Ambassador Coulondre would be leaving the Embassy in twenty-five minutes to deliver his communication to the Wilhelmstrasse. At 11:30 Daladier called back Bonnet and said that he had wrung a concession from General Colson, Chief of the Army General Staff. The timetable for opening hostilities was advanced by twelve hours, to 5 P.M. on this Sunday of September 3. Bonnet put through an urgent call to the Embassy in Berlin. It came through at 11:45 just as Coulondre was getting ready to depart. Bonnet dictated to him the new time limit of 5 P.M. and the Ambassador corrected in his own handwriting the text of his ultimatum. Suddenly Coulondre was seized by doubts. Was it actually the French Foreign Minister who was speaking? He demanded confirmation from someone else at the Quai d'Orsay whose voice he was more familiar with. Bonnet put Léger and Bressy on the line to confirm the new instructions. The Ambassador was satisfied and immediately left the Embassy for the Foreign Office.

Ribbentrop was not at once available to the French Ambassador at the noon hour. He was taking part in a little ceremony at the Chancellery, where the new Soviet Ambassador, Alexander Shkvarzev, was being warmly welcomed by Hitler—an occasion that lent a bizarre note to this historic Sabbath in Berlin. Coulondre, insistent on following the letter of his instructions to call at the Wilhelmstrasse at precisely twelve noon, was therefore received by Weizsaecker. To the Ambassador's inquiry as to whether the State Secretary was empowered to give a "satisfactory" answer to the French, Weizsaecker replied that he was not in a position to give him "any kind of reply."

There now followed at this solemn moment in history a minor diplomatic comedy. When Coulondre attempted to treat Weizsaecker's response as the negative German reply, which he fully anticipated, and to hand to the State Secretary France's formal ultimatum, the latter declined to accept it. He suggested that the Ambassador "be good enough to be patient a little longer and see the Foreign Minister personally." Thus rebuffed—and not for the first time—Coulondre cooled his heels for nearly half an hour. At 12:30 P.M. he was conducted to the Chancellery to see Ribbentrop.

Though the Nazi Foreign Minister knew what the Ambassador's mission was, he could not let the opportunity, the very last such one, slip by without treating the French envoy to one of his customary prevarications of history. He who two days before had assured Coulondre that Poland, not Germany, was the aggressor, now threw in a few lies about Germany having accepted the Italian proposal for a conference. Mussolini had informed him, he said, that France approved it. "Yesterday," he went on, "Germany had informed the Duce that she also was prepared to agree to the proposal. Later in the day the Duce reported that his proposal had been wrecked by the intransigence of the British government."

But Coulondre over the past months had heard enough of Ribbentrop's falsifications. He listened impatiently a little longer to the Nazi Foreign Minister, who went on to say that if France felt bound to keep her engagements to Poland and go to war he would regret it because

we have no feeling of hostility toward France. Only if France attacks us first will we fight her, and that will be on her part a war of aggression.

Coulondre then broke in with the question he had come to ask:

"Did the Foreign Minister's remarks mean that the response of the German government to the French communication of September 1 was negative?"

"*Ja*," replied Ribbentrop.

"In that case," Coulondre said, "I must, on behalf of my government, recall to you for the last time the heavy responsibility assumed by the German government in attacking Poland without a declaration of war and in refusing to accede to the suggestion of the French and British governments to halt the aggression against Poland and withdraw its troops.

"I now have the painful duty to inform you that from 5 P.M. today, September 3, the French government will be obliged to fulfill her engagements to Poland, which are known to the German government."

"Then France will be the aggressor," Ribbentrop said.

"History will be the judge of that," Coulondre replied.[30]

On that Sunday afternoon in Berlin all the participants in the final act of the drama seemed intent on calling upon the judgment of history.

So France, in fulfillment of her word to Poland, would be at war with Germany by 5 P.M. But this was too soon for General Gamelin. At 4:30 P.M., a half hour before the hour stipulated in the French ultimatum ran out, he issued secret instructions to the Army, Navy, and Air Force to delay opening hostilities for twelve hours after the deadline.

> Our ultimatum [his order read] expires at 5 P.M. today unless the Germans accept it. But to act in accord with the British Air Force we have decided not to commence operations until tomorrow morning at 5 o'clock.[31]

The hesitations of France's generalissimo began in the very first hour of the war.

In the streets of Paris and the other cities and towns of France there was no shouting when war came. There was none of the enthusiasm, passion, and ringing belief in the righteousness of the country's cause which Frenchmen of all classes had felt and manifested when the soldiers marched off to war in 1914 just twenty-five years before. The millions of men called up responded to mobilization stoically but most of them did not have their heart in a war whose coming had surprised them and whose causes they did not understand—though Hitler's aggression in Poland and Hitler's ambitions would seem to have been clear enough to almost anyone. Many were stupefied by the suddenness of the calamity.

On the surface, France appeared to have refound a certain unity. The general mobilization went off smoothly, as did, for the most part, the evacuation of the civilians from the war zone and the dispatch of many women and children from the cities. Parliament had overwhelmingly voted the war credits. The press, heavily censored to be sure, was almost unanimous in approving the government's honoring of its word to Poland. And though there was no enthusiasm for war, there was a good deal of resignation to the feeling that Hitler had made it inevitable, that the recurring crises provoked by the Nazi dictator since 1936 could not go on forever, and that perhaps it was best "to get it over now" and free France and Europe from the ever-recurring German threat.

Underneath the surface, though, there were stinging doubts in many Frenchmen as to the wisdom of the government in having got the country into war, and in some there was bitter opposition to the course it had taken.

Few dared to voice this at the moment. This they would do later in their memoirs or in articles when it was safe to do so. Thus Senator Lémery, a close friend of Marshal Pétain and later an ardent supporter of Vichy, would write: "The declaration of war plunged France into a stupor. How could her leaders have deceived themselves and deceived her. And why this war?"[32] Monzie, who in the cabinet had fought to the last minute against going to war, would write in his diary, which he published after the defeat: "This September 4, France at war does not believe in the war."[33]

In his memoirs, written in a French prison in Algiers in 1944, Flandin, the leader of the Center Party, reveals how bitterly he was opposed to France's entering the war. In the process he reveals a confusion that was shared by many. He held, as we have seen, that the government violated the Constitution by declaring war without the explicit consent of Parliament. He suggests that the government feared that the Chamber of Deputies and "perhaps" the Senate would refuse to vote a war declaration. He denies that France was obliged automatically to come to the aid of Poland when she was attacked, arguing that her commitments to the Poles were linked with her commitments to the League of Nations, which first must decide whether any aggression had taken place. In fact, he insists that France should have gone first to the League for its opinion before entering the war![34] These three politicians were then regarded as among the pillars of the Republic.

On the extreme Right the opposition to war was even more irrational. Lucien Rebattet, a writer not without talent, a royalist now lost to Fascism, and already one of the bright young men of the Fascist *Je Suis Partout,* would write:

So, the war has been launched by the most hideous buffoons of the most hideous Jewish and demagogic regime. . . . We are supposed once more to save the Republic, and a Republic worse than the one in 1914. . . . No. I do not feel the least anger against Hitler, but much against all the French politicians who have led to his triumph.[35]

It was this sort of aberration, inspired in part by Dr. Joseph Goebbels, the Nazi propaganda master in Berlin, which would lead Rebattet, a number of other gifted young writers who had drifted to the far Right, and not a few former Leftist politicians who had taken the same route, to the sorry end of outright collaboration with the Nazi Germans. But they formed a lunatic fringe which at this time carried little weight with the country.

Of more importance on the Right were those who had already carried great responsibility in the Republic, such as Marshal Pétain, France's most illustrious soldier, who privately was against the war and contemptuous of the Republic. As we have seen, he was now in contact with Laval, a former Premier and Foreign Minister, who also opposed the war and the government and was beginning to maneuver for the Marshal to take over. Fundamentally, the Right, for ideological reasons, did not want to fight Nazi Germany. It admired Hitler's mindless dictatorship and shared his contempt for democracy. The Left, on the other hand, much larger in numbers, though despising Nazi totalitarianism, did not want to war on Germany, or on any other country, because of a devotion to pacifism which sprang from a deep conviction, nourished in the public schools since 1919, that all wars are evil and senselessly destructive to man, his property, and his morals, and must be avoided at all costs.

In the midst of so much division and confusion it is little wonder that France entered the war as a House divided. But there was an even more fundamental reason for the uneasiness that stirred just below the surface. The war had come too soon for France. She had not yet fully recovered from the exhaustion of the last one, which had ended scarcely two decades ago. Instinctively the French knew they could not survive another such bloodletting in a second war against Germany, no matter who won. And even if they won, with the help of the British and later perhaps of the Americans, like the last time, would they not again lose the peace, as they believed they had after 1919? "What's the use of fighting, then?" many are said to have asked. Senator Lémery recounts meeting one of his lawyer friends at the Palais de Justice on mobilization day. The man had had a brilliant record as a soldier in the first war. "This time," he said, "I'm going to lie low. I'm not going to get myself killed for Poland."[36]

The fear of another bloodbath haunted not only the mass of Frenchmen but also Daladier, who had spent four years in the trenches the last time, and, to their credit, the generals, who were determined to spare French blood in this war. This was a humane and civilized attitude but it left unanswered the question of how France was to avert defeat and surrender. Could it do it without severe fighting and the consequent heavy casualties?

For the next eight months it seemed—miraculously—that it could. To the surprise of the French and to their immense relief there now ensued in the West one of the strangest intervals in the history of warfare. It would be called in French *La Drôle de guerre,* in German, the *Sitzkrieg,* and in English, with less elegance, the *Phony War.* There would be no serious fighting and no bloodletting, and many illusions would sprout. It would be but the prelude, however, to the shattering of all the illusions and of the Third Republic itself.

BOOK FOUR

The War and the Defeat 1939-1940

27

LA DRÔLE DE GUERRE
SEPTEMBER 3, 1939–APRIL 9, 1940

Poland was quickly crushed by the overwhelming might of the German Army, and France, with 85 divisions facing an enemy with little more than a covering force, did little in the West to keep its commitment to help her gallant ally. Great Britain did no more. Its small contingent of two divisions did not reach the "front" until September 26. By then it was too late for the Allied armies in the West to be of any help whatsoever to the Poles.

They were vanquished in eight days. By the afternoon of September 8, the 35 divisions of the Polish army—all that there had been time to mobilize—had been either shattered or caught in a vast pincer movement that closed in around Warsaw. That afternoon the German 4th Panzer division reached the outskirts of the Polish capital. Directly south of the city, racing up from Silesia and Slovakia, General Walter von Reichenau's Tenth Army captured Kielce and General Wilhelm List's Fourteenth Army arrived at Sandomierz at the junction of the Vistula and San rivers. There remained little for the Germans to do except to mop up, and this phase was completed by the 17th, except in the Warsaw triangle and further west near Posen where pockets of Polish troops held out valiantly for a few days more.

On the night of September 6, after the fall of Cracow, the country's second largest city, the Polish government, its members dazed by the debacle, had fled from Warsaw to Lublin. On the 15th, after being unceasingly bombed and strafed by the Luftwaffe, it reached the Romanian frontier and crossed over. It was now time for the Russians, in agreement with the Germans, to move in on the stricken country to grab a share of the spoils.

The Soviet Red Army invaded eastern Poland on September 17 and the next day made contact with the German troops at Brest-Litovsk, where exactly twenty-one years before a newly formed Bolshevik government, severing its country's ties with the Western Allies, had accepted from the German Army separate peace terms of great severity. For the proud but blinded Polish nation it was all over. On September 29 Germany and Russia, for the fourth time in history, partitioned Poland. They swallowed it up completely.*

With Poland obliterated, Hitler now turned his attention to the West.

ALL QUIET ON THE WESTERN FRONT

What had happened there, or rather, what had not happened, had puzzled the Germans but not actually surprised them. As early as August 14 General Halder, Chief of the Army General Staff, had drawn up in considerable detail an estimate of what would happen in the West if Germany attacked Poland with the great bulk of her army. He thought a French offensive "not very likely." He was sure the French army would not move through Belgium "against Belgium's wishes." He concluded that the French would remain on the defensive.† On September 7, with the Polish armies already beaten, the Staff Chief noted in his diary plans for transferring the troops in Poland to the West. That evening he added a few lines on Hitler's view of the situation in the West which the Fuehrer had just conveyed to General Walther von Brauchitsch, Commander of the German Army.

Operations in the West not yet clear. Some indications that there is no real intention of waging war. . . .

That very night of September 7–8 General Gamelin launched his "offensive" in the West supposedly designed to relieve the German pressure

---

* At first Hitler and Stalin seemed to have considered setting up a rump Poland somewhat similar to Napoleon's Grand Duchy of Warsaw in order to mollify world public opinion. According to the secret German diplomatic papers the initiative to divide up all of the country came from Molotov and Stalin. On September 19 the German Ambassador in Moscow wired Berlin:

> Molotov hinted that the original inclination entertained by the Soviet government and Stalin personally to permit the existence of a residual Poland had given away to the inclination to partition Poland along the Pissa-Narew-Vistula-San line.[1]

On the evening of September 25 Stalin summoned Ambassador Schulenburg to the Kremlin and stated

> he considered it wrong to leave an independent residual Poland. He proposed that from the territory to the east of the demarcation line, all the province of Warsaw which extends to the Bug should be added to our share. In return we would waive our claim to Lithuania.[2]

The deal, on Stalin's terms, was signed in Moscow at 5 A.M. on September 29 by Ribbentrop and Molotov.

†This is the first entry in Halder's diary.

on Poland. Light French forces crossed the frontier on a 15-mile front along the "Cadenbronn Salient" southeast of Saarbrücken, where the border bulged southward. On the morning of September 9 they were followed by stronger units from the Fourth and Fifth Armies advancing, according to a later German report, in battalion strength. The French met little opposition as the German covering forces withdrew toward the Siegfried Line eight miles north of the frontier. The French, moving cautiously, were slowed mainly by mines and booby traps. To the West units of the Third Army were thrust forward to occupy a smaller salient, the Wendt Forest, southwest of Saarbrücken. There was no serious fighting; only light skirmishing.

The French had an overwhelming superiority in men, guns, and tanks. Against their fully armed 85 divisions on the whole front the Germans had 34 divisions, all but 11 of which were reserve units with little training and lacking adequate arms, munition, and transport. All the panzer divisions, all the motorized divisions, had been reserved for Poland. On September 10 some nine more reserve divisions were added but they would have been of little value against a serious attack.

Fortunately for the Germans a serious attack was never mounted nor did the highly cautious French generalissimo ever contemplate one. By September 12 the French forces had moved forward some five miles on a 15-mile front and occupied twenty deserted villages. General Gamelin thereupon commanded them to halt and on that very day, September 12, to prepare to beat a retreat to the safety of the Maginot Line should the Germans attack through Belgium.

The battered Poles protested such monumental inaction and General Gamelin replied with the sort of equivocation for which he had so often chastised Georges Bonnet. On September 9 he received radio messages from Marshal Smigly-Rydz and from the Polish General Staff telling him of the plight of their forces in face of the devastating German attacks, asking him what he was doing to draw off enemy strength and imploring him to "accelerate" whatever he was doing. The next day the Polish military attaché put the two key questions bluntly to the generalissimo.

Has the French air force already begun action against the German air force and German territory?

Will you be able to accelerate your combined action? I must report these matters to Marshal Smigly-Rydz.[3]

General Gamelin responded the same day in writing:

More than half of our active divisions on the northeast front are engaged in combat. Beyond our frontier the Germans are opposing us with a vigorous resistance. . . . Prisoners indicate the Germans are reinforcing their battle-front with large new formations.

Air action from the beginning has been under way in liaison with ground operations. We know we are holding down before us a considerable part of the German air force.

I have thus gone beyond my promise to take the offensive with the bulk of my forces by the fifteenth day after mobilization. It has been impossible for me to do more.[4]

This incredible reply reveals more than we have yet learned of the generalissimo of the French armies. For the truth was quite different from what he reported. By his own account only 15 French divisions were engaged in the entire operation of the "Saar offensive," and most French military writers put the figure at 9—out of 85 divisions on the northeast front.* There was no action in the air except for a few reconnaissance missions. French and British pilots were forbidden to bomb German territory for fear, as General Gamelin put it in a report to Daladier on September 9, "of the heaviest consequences."[5] There was no "vigorous resistance" on the part of the Germans. After almost bloodless skirmishes they drew back toward the Siegfried Line. And the reinforcements of "large new formations" were, as we have seen, 9 reserve divisions incapable at that moment of giving serious battle. Not a single German division or tank or plane was diverted from Poland to reinforce the West.

To the then Colonel de Gaulle, commanding the tanks of the Fifth Army, the Saar "offensive" consisted merely of "a few demonstrations." To the then Captain Beaufre, just back from Moscow, "it was nothing. General Gamelin, true to character, decided to make no more than a gesture. . . . That was our aid to Poland!"[6]

"It's a little test, you see. A little test," Gamelin had said to General Sir Edmund Ironside, the Chief of the British Imperial General staff, when at their meeting on September 5 he had jabbed away at a map and explained what he called the *sortie* in the Saar.[7] That was at least truthful. And Gamelin had been frank too when on September 1, the day Poland was attacked, he had written Daladier that the only way to bring "effective and rapid help to Poland" was for the French army to move against Germany through Belgium. If it was the "only way," then was it not clear that he had no intention of attacking seriously in the Saar?

The quick defeat of the Poles, to be sure, relieved the pressure on Gamelin to continue the Saar "offensive." And it raised new problems. For soon the Germans would be able to bring back their main forces, including all their armored divisions and their superior air force, and in due time hurl them against the French—possibly by way of Belgium, as they had in 1914. By September 12, when his "offensive" was coming to a halt,

---

* Colonel A. Goutard: *1940. La Guerre des occasions perdues,* p. 120. He writes that the "offensive" was carried out "not by 35 divisions but by 9 divisions, of the Fourth and Fifth Armies." The Third Army, which occupied the Wendt Forest, seems to have employed 2 divisions.

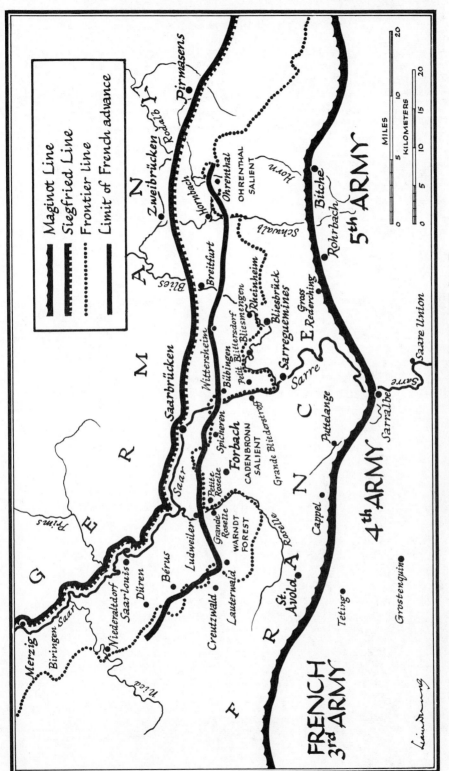

THE FRENCH "OFFENSIVE" IN THE SAAR
SEPTEMBER 1939

these considerations were much on Gamelin's mind. On that day he issued secret Personal Instruction No. 4 to his forces to discontinue their advance. Because of "military events in Poland," he said, "there is no more need of establishing a base for an eventual attack against the Siegfried Line." Indeed, he added, the front of the Fourth and Fifth Armies must be established far enough away from the German fortress line so that the enemy would not be able to use it as a base for counterattacks. So not only would there be no assault on the Siegfried Line, but the French would keep out of its artillery range! In view of a possible German move through Belgium, Gamelin further advised, the army commanders must consider the "eventuality" of withdrawing from German territory—small as the slice they held was.[8]

That afternoon, at a hastily summoned meeting of the Allied Supreme War Council at Abbeville, the generalissimo informed the British that he was calling off his "offensive" in view of the developments in Poland. "I received the impression," Gamelin says, "that my report brought a sense of relief to everyone."[9] Relieved at the prospect of doing nothing! The British and French were of one mind.

On September 21, Gamelin says, he renounced "any intention of continuing the offensive." On that date he issued orders that if the Germans counterattacked in strength the French forces should retreat to the shelter of the Maginot Line. "If the bulk of the German Army is brought back to face us," he added, "we have no interest in fighting a defensive battle except on our fortified position on French soil."[10] A week later, on September 30, the generalissimo decided, he tells us, that "the hour had come to retreat." Realizing that this would be a blow to the government, which had been making a great deal of propaganda about the French "invasion" of Germany, General Gamelin and General Georges went to see Daladier to explain to him the reasons for retreating in the Saar. The Premier was not pleased. "He feared," he said, "the reaction of public opinion not only in France but throughout the world.* But out of "profound patriotism," as Gamelin puts it, he acquiesced. To avoid any leaks to the Germans it was decided not to inform the cabinet, some of whose members, now that Poland had fallen, saw no reason for continuing the war. Only the President

---

* Not only the French and British, but the American press had grossly exaggerated the French "offensive" in Germany. In Berlin I remember my astonishment at scanning the headlines when the first newspapers from home arrived. They told of great Allied "victories" as the French "offensive" moved deeper into Germany. My own New York office of Columbia Broadcasting System wondered why I was so silent about the "Western front" in my broadcasts from Berlin that first fortnight of September. Though I did not believe a word of Nazi propaganda I did know officers of the German High Command whose word I trusted. They assured me that the action in the Saar consisted of mere skirmishes and pointed out that, for reasons astonishing to them, the French and British air force had not once intervened in the "battle" to strafe or bomb. This lack of air support seems to have been one signal to the German High Command that General Gamelin had no intention of waging a serious attack.

of the Republic was told. The French withdrawal was to be as secret as possible.[11] Indeed in his order of September 30 Gamelin, after advising General Georges that he "considered it urgent" to begin the retreat at once, instructed him to be sure to get away in the dead of night so that the enemy would not know of it.[12] "Operate only at night," he admonished. A light screen of troops was to be left in the forward positions. The withdrawal of the main French forces began that night and was completed on October 4.

Ten days later, though the Germans had not had time to transfer any forces worth mentioning from Poland to the West, General Gamelin convinced himself that the enemy was about to launch a great attack. He therefore issued on October 14 a ringing Order of the Day. It makes strange reading in view of what happened.

> Soldiers of France! At any moment a battle may begin on which the fate of the country will once more in our history depend. The nation and the whole world have their eyes fixed on you. Steel your hearts! Make the best use of your weapons! Remember the Marne and Verdun!

On October 16 the awaited attack began. The fate of France never depended less on a battle. The Germans attacked with light forces, usually in company or battalion strength, disdaining to use even the few tanks they had. The French screening forces withdrew quickly, as planned, and by the night of the 17th German territory had been cleared of the invaders. In two days, with a handful of infantry troops, the Germans took back what the French had taken two weeks to gain. Gamelin says the Germans suffered "important losses" from the fire of French artillery, which he had directed "not to spare its ammunition." Actually, the Germans listed 198 killed in the entire action, which was probably a fairly accurate figure. The French High Command put the best face possible on its withdrawal, stressing in its communiqués that the Germans were merely occupying territory evacuated by the French. General Prételat, Commander of Army Group II, whose forces had conducted the Saar "offensive," praised his troops for the "happy manner" in which they had effected their retreat. They deserved, he said, "the highest praise." But in truth, as more than one general reported, the retreat without a fight began to sap the morale of the French soldiers. It did not improve the morale of the civilians at home. After six weeks of being at war the great French Army had been unable— or unwilling—to bring the slightest relief to Poland. Its "invasion" of Germany had ended in a fiasco.

"After the prologue of the 'phony offensive,' " wrote Colonel Goutard, "we were ripe for the 'phony war.' "[13]

The phony "offensive" in the Saar revealed, at the very beginning of the war, something about the French nation, government, army, the High

Command, and General Gamelin. "The nation," Alfred Sauvy, the eminent French economist and demographist, would write of this time, "refused the war"—on the battlefield and at home. Daladier, in his postwar testimony before the Parliamentary Investigating Committee, explained why his government had not pressed Gamelin to fight on the Western Front that September.

"The collapse of Poland," he said, "was unexpected and completely surprised the High Command. General Gamelin had said he hoped the resistance of the Polish army would last over the winter, which would permit us to act in the spring." Daladier then posed the key question: *"Should the French Army have attacked?"*

The War Committee studied this problem . . . and decided that France at this moment should not carry all the burden of an offensive against Germany. It observed that Britain had sent but two divisions and that even these were far from complete, and that it was to our interest to first neutralize Italy, if possible, to increase war production and to stimulate war production in America so that the United States could furnish solid and effective help. . . . The High Command also decided to wait for spring or summer to do anything on the French front though there were possibilities of doing something at Salonika. . . .

At the very first meeting of the Supreme Allied War Council at Abbeville on September 11 Daladier had proposed that the British and French establish an "Eastern front" at Salonika, as they had done in the first war. The Franco-British forces would be joined by the armies of the Balkan Entente, which presented, the Premier emphasized, "a force of 110 divisions, equal to what the Western Allies had been able to put in the field." It was the first time, but not the last, that the French would propose fighting on other fronts than their own. Daladier revealed he had received the secret agreement of the Greek government for an Allied front at Salonika. Despite this and his pleas to Chamberlain, the British government, he says, turned him down. It feared, he added, hostile Italian reaction.[14]

Daladier came away from the meeting with a marked distrust of Chamberlain. He confided this to William Bullitt, the American Ambassador in Paris, saying that he had come to the conclusion at Abbeville that the British meant to have France fight the war alone. Thus from the beginning of the conflict, as had been the case in the last nerve-racking weeks of peace, there was tension and friction and mistrust between the democratic allies. It would grow worse as the war intensified and the French came more and more to feel that the British were not pulling their full weight in the common struggle. In the end it would become critical. Actually at the moment most of the Allied action in the war was at sea, and this was being conducted by the British Navy.

The decision not to do any serious fighting on the German front in September, either to relieve the Poles or to take advantage of Germany's temporary weakness in the West, cast further light on General Gamelin as a man and a soldier. Here again, though at a more crucial moment, was displayed his obsession with the defensive,* his cautiousness and timidity, his constant overestimation of opposing strength, and his ingeniousness in finding excuses for inaction, which we have seen growing in him since the Rhineland coup of 1936 when he also failed to act against the then feeble German army and lost an opportunity even greater than in 1939. If in September 1939 he could not deal a heavy blow to the German army when nearly all its strength, especially in tanks and planes, was concentrated in Poland, when on his side he enjoyed a marked superiority in men, guns, and armor, what could he hope to do when the enemy eventually faced him with all its might?

That he blandly let pass an opportunity that seldom comes to a great commander in chief in war was the opinion of the German generals as well as that of at least one of his own. To General Halder, who toward the end of September had told his officers: "I no longer believe in a French attack. They have missed their opportunity," the inaction of the French, though he had predicted it, still occupied his mind. Later, at Nuremberg, he would testify:

> The success against Poland was only possible by our almost completely baring our Western border. If the French . . . had used the opportunity presented by the engagement of nearly all our forces in Poland they would have been able to cross the Rhine without our being able to prevent it and would have threatened the Ruhr, which was decisive for the German conduct of the war.

General Siegfried Westphal believed the French could have advanced from the Saar to the Rhine in two weeks had they tried.

> During September [he wrote later] there was not a single tank on the German Western front. The stock of ammunition would have lasted for three days of battle. We had no serviceable reserve in the rear. All the flying units of the Luftwaffe were in service in Poland, leaving only a few reconnaissance planes and obsolescent fighters available for the West.

Every expert serving at that time in the Western Army felt his hair stand on end when he considered the possibility of an immediate French attack. It was incomprehensible that no such attack should take place, that the appalling weakness of the German defense should be unknown to the French leaders. . . . The German forces were much too weak to block the path of a French assault. . . . Yet nothing happened, absolutely nothing, apart from a few

---

* Visiting the Maginot Line during the middle of August as the guest of Generals Gamelin and Georges, Winston Churchill had been struck by this obsession with the defensive. "What was remarkable," he wrote, "was the complete acceptance of the defensive which dominated my . . . French hosts. . . . In talking to these highly competent French officers one had the sense that the Germans were the stronger and that France had no longer the life-thrust to mount a great offensive."[15]

insignificant sorties which the French undertook in the region of Saarbrücken and Perle.

The French inaction was equally incomprehensible to General Wilhelm Keitel, Chief of OKW.

We soldiers had always expected an attack by France during the Polish campaign, and were very much surprised that nothing happened. . . . A French attack would have encountered only a German military screen, not a real defense.

General Jodl, his Operations Chief at OKW, added:

If we did not collapse in 1939, that was due to the fact that during the Polish campaign the approximately 110 French and British divisions in the West were held completely inactive against the 23 German divisions.

At least one French general agreed. General Henri Giraud, who commanded the Seventh Army, believed that the Germans "had almost nothing on the left bank of the Saar. From Saarbrücken to Trier the field was clear. We could have gone through with the VI Corps."[16]

Not only did the Germans have little in the way of troops or guns or tanks to oppose a serious French attack but the Siegfried Line, before which General Gamelin seemed to quaver, forbidding his troops to get too close, was still unfinished and could not have held up the attackers for long. It was, says General Westphal, "a gigantic bluff."

Could it have been that some of the French generals were beginning to believe, as certain civilians were, that with Poland gone there was no sense in continuing the war? That was the line the Germans, with the support of the Russians, had commenced to take. I remember listening with some surprise to Hitler's speech in the Guild Hall in Danzig on the afternoon of September 19. "I have no war aims against Great Britain and France," he said. As if mindful of the lack of enthusiasm in the French Army for any attack on Germany, he added: "My sympathies are with the French *poilu*. What he is fighting for he does not know." And he called upon the Almighty "to give other peoples comprehension of how useless this war will be . . . and to cause reflection on the blessings of peace." This from a man who had just destroyed in war a valiant nation!

On September 26 the German press and radio launched a peace offensive. In Berlin I recorded the propaganda line in my diary: "Why do France and Britain want to fight now? Nothing to fight about. Germany wants nothing in the West."

Two days later the Germans enlisted the support of the Russians in their propaganda campaign for calling off the war in the West. Ribbentrop arrived in Moscow early on the evening of September 28 to sign a treaty euphemistically called the "German-Soviet Boundary and Friendship Treaty," which partitioned Poland between the two countries and gave Russia a free hand in the Baltic states. To add insult to injury Molotov and Ribbentrop concocted and signed at the same time a ringing declaration for peace. It began with the usual cant, at which the two ministers were so adept. Their governments, it said, after having

definitely settled the problems arising from the disintegration of the Polish state and created a firm foundation for a lasting peace in Eastern Europe, mutually express their conviction that it would serve the true interests of all peoples to put an end to the state of war between Germany and England and France. Both governments will therefore direct their common efforts . . . toward attaining this goal as soon as possible.

Should, however, the efforts of the two governments remain fruitless, this would demonstrate the fact that England and France are responsible for the continuation of the war. . . .

Hitler, having started the war, and Stalin having made it possible for him to start it, now blamed the Western democracies for continuing it! The Nazi dictator made his formal proposal for peace in a lengthy speech to the rubber-stamp Reichstag on October 6. To me, listening in the balcony, it sounded like an old gramophone record being played for the fifth or sixth time. How often before I had heard him from this same rostrum, after his latest conquest, and in the same apparent tone of earnestness, propose what sounded—if you overlooked his latest victim—like a decent and reasonable peace. His words, not without their usual eloquence, were shrewdly calculated to appeal not only to the German people, who after the easy conquest of Poland desired an end to the war, but even more to the peoples of France and Great Britain, for whom there had not yet been any experience of war and who, Hitler believed, had no determination to see it through. To France he declared:

My chief endeavor has been to rid our relations with France of all trace of ill will and to render them tolerable for both nations. . . . Germany has no further claims against France. . . . I have always expressed to France my desire to bury forever our ancient enmity and bring together these two nations, both of which have such glorious pasts. . . .

To Britain:

I have devoted no less effort to the achievement of Anglo-German understanding, nay, more than that, of an Anglo-German friendship. At no time and in no place have I ever acted contrary to British interests. . . . I believe even today that there can only be peace in Europe . . . if Germany and England come to an understanding.

At the end came the fervent plea for peace.

> Why should war in the West be fought? For restoration of Poland? Poland of the Versailles Treaty will never rise again. . . . The question of the reestablishment of the Polish state . . . will not be solved by war in the West but exclusively by Russia and Germany. . . . It would be senseless to annihilate millions of men . . . in order to reconstruct [this] state. What other reason exists? War in the West cannot settle any problems.

In Paris there were quite a few Frenchmen, including some in the cabinet, who agreed. And Hitler, thanks to reports from the Italian and Spanish ambassadors in Paris which were passed along to Berlin, knew it. As early as September 8 Berlin received a report from the Spanish Embassy in Paris stating that "Bonnet, in view of the great unpopularity of the war in France, is still endeavoring to bring about an understanding as soon as the operations in Poland are concluded. There are certain indications that he is in contact with Mussolini to that end."[17] On October 2 in Berlin, Ambassador Attolico handed State Secretary Weizsaecker a copy of the latest "information" from the Italian Ambassador in Paris. It stated that the majority of the French cabinet were in favor of a peace conference and that it was now mainly a question of "enabling France and England to save face." In this regard "one of the most distinguished members of the French government had confirmed" to the Italian Ambassador that "the question of form is the most important consideration." It was explained that while France and Britain at any proposed conference would have to raise the question "of the resurrection of a Polish state" they would settle for one "of a more or less symbolic character." This was the view of the cabinet majority, the Italians reported, but the position of Daladier, they added, was not quite clear.[18]

The Premier made his position clear the very day after Hitler made his peace proposal in the Reichstag. He did so, Monzie, who says he was for "mediation," complains, "without consulting us." In a nationwide broadcast Daladier declared: "We took up arms against aggression. We shall not put them down until we have guarantees for a real peace and security, a security which is not threatened every six months." Chamberlain made a similar reply in the House of Commons on October 12. The next day an official German statement issued in Berlin declared that the Western allies, by rejecting Hitler's offer of peace, had deliberately chosen war. Now the Fuehrer had his excuse.

Was that what he had been looking for all along? Perhaps he did not quite know himself, although he was pretty sure. Probably the key to his real thoughts lay in what he was telling his generals. On September 25 General Halder had noted in his diary receipt of "word on Fuehrer's plan to attack in the West." On September 27 Hitler called in the Army Command for a conference at the Chancellery in Berlin and informed it of his decision to "attack in the West as soon as possible, since the Franco-British army is not yet prepared." According to General Brauchitsch, the Commander in Chief of the Army, Hitler even set a date for the attack: November 12.[19]

Then, on October 10, three days before Chamberlain's reply, Hitler again convoked his military chiefs, read to them a long memorandum stating that Germany's "war aim" was the "final destruction of the West" and threw at them Directive Number 6 for the Conduct of the War ordering them to prepare an attack on France through Belgium, Holland, and Luxembourg, whose neutrality he had solemnly guaranteed, and stipulating that "this attack must be carried out . . . at as early a date as possible."[20]

In Paris, where the German warlord's secret directives and iron determination to destroy the West "as soon as possible" were, of course, not known, the sentiment for getting out of the war continued to flourish. Bonnet thought Hitler's peace offer "merited some attention" from the government. He felt it had been "brutally repulsed." He says the "proposition could have been studied, while hostilities were suspended." By this time he seems to have lost any contact with reality. He argues that since Germany and Russia now had a common frontier, the Franco-Soviet Pact, "whose validity Molotov had reaffirmed on August 25" would "act to our advantage if we were victim of a new German aggression, exactly as had the Franco-Russian alliance in 1914."[21] Bonnet must have been the last cabinet minister in Europe to remain ignorant of the fact that the Franco-Soviet Pact was as dead as cold stone. But by this time Daladier had removed him from the Foreign Office and the direction of foreign affairs. On September 13 he had been demoted to Minister of Justice. Still, in the cabinet he could work for peace.

Monzie, Minister of Public Works, too. His diary those days was full of fulminations against the war. On October 6, for example, the day of Hitler's peace proposal, Monzie filled his diary with the text of a long letter from a deputy serving at the "front" which concluded: "We must quickly put an end to this foolish and stupid adventure." The Minister replied that he entirely agreed.*[22]

A good number of middle-of-the-road intellectuals also agreed. A manifesto issued by a group of liberals led by Alain, the philosopher of the Third Republic, Georges Dumoulin, a trade-union leader, and Marcel Déat, the Neo-Socialist author of the famous editorial "Why Die for Danzig?", called for "immediate peace. The entire world," it said, "is going to be drowned in blood. . . . The war is condemned by almost all patriots—at the front or at home. Therefore we must obtain peace. Let us not wait until it is offered us by the makers of war. The price of peace will never be so ruinous as the price of war."

On the Far Right there was also opposition to war, though a severe

---

* Gamelin says that he himself was warned by a "political figure" of "the existence of a peace offensive backed by Laval, Chautemps, and Flandin, relying on Marshal Pétain."[23]

government wartime censorship prevented its leaders from openly publishing their views. The Communists, who since the Hitler-Stalin Pact had also opposed war against Germany, were more skillful in publishing their views clandestinely. Though the party was dissolved by government decree on September 26 it succeeded in spreading its propaganda among the workers and even among the troops. Raked over the coals by Moscow for not having properly understood the Nazi-Soviet Pact in August and severely condemned for having voted for the war credits on September 2, the French Communist Party got back on the proper line immediately thereafter. It hailed the Soviet invasion of Poland on September 17 as bringing the "liberation" of the Ukraine and White Russia. And on October 1, in support of the Molotov-Ribbentrop declaration calling on the Western Allies to make peace and putting on them the responsibility for the war if they didn't, the Communist delegation in the Chamber addressed a letter to Speaker Herriot demanding that the House be convened to deliberate in a public session the "proposals for peace which are going to be made." Blaming the war now on the Western "imperialists" and on "Hitlerite Germany," it declared that the Soviet Union stood ready to assure a "just and durable peace . . . and safeguard the independence of France." The letter "nauseated" Léon Blum, and even the pacifist wing of the Socialist Party, which was opposed to the war, denounced the contents of the letter as "an impudent lie." On September 25, the day before the government dissolved the Communist Party, the CGT, the Confederation of Labor, broke its ties with the Party, accusing it of "treason against the workers."

Defeatism too spread in Paris. Even Alexis Léger, the Secretary-General of the Foreign Office, despaired after Poland fell. Contemptuous of Bonnet, his chief, he had done all he could during the tense August days to move the government to stand up to Hitler. He had opposed Bonnet's acceptance of Mussolini's proposal for a conference at the beginning of September. But now on the last day of that month, as the last remnants of the encircled Polish forces surrendered to the Germans—or to the Russians—Léger confessed to Ambassador Bullitt that he had lost all hope. "The game is lost," he told him. "France stands alone against the three dictatorships. Great Britain is not ready. The United States has not even changed the Neutrality Act. The democracies are again too late."[24]

With the Republic so divided, Daladier had failed in his effort to form at the very beginning of the conflict a government of National Union such as had galvanized the nation in 1914. Party politics, whose triviality and passion had not diminished when the country found itself faced with mortal danger, contributed to his failure. Louis Marin, the conservative leader, refused to join the government if it included Léon Blum. The Socialists had answered that it must be either Blum, their party leader, or no one. As a result of this petty feuding neither Marin nor Blum was asked to join the government. A few of their followers took minor posts.

Resolved to get rid of Bonnet, the Premier offered the post of Foreign

Minister to Herriot, Speaker of the Assembly and a power in the Radical Party. He accepted on condition that Daladier bring Marshal Pétain into the government—not only to add prestige to it but to placate the two Fascist powers on France's borders, Spain and Italy, the dictators of which well knew the Speaker's antipathy toward them and their totalitarian regimes. Daladier summoned the Marshal back from the Embassy in San Sebastian on September 8 and implored him to join the government. Pétain asked for time to think it over, and consulted some of his friends, most of whom, such as Laval, were now begging him to consider taking over the government himself. On the 11th the Marshal saw General Gamelin and confided to him that he had no intention of joining a government that included Herriot. "It would provoke Franco and Mussolini," he said. He asked the generalissimo if he could not use his influence with Daladier to drop the idea of having Herriot in his cabinet. Gamelin, who greatly admired the Radical leader, was as cautious in politics as in war. He replied that he made "it a rule never to mix in politics."[25]

Pétain returned to Spain without calling on Daladier again, sending him a letter declining his offer.

The cabinet which you propose [he wrote] does not respond to the exigencies of the actual situation. It is established almost entirely on a political basis. It appears thus to be scarcely qualified to assure the general conduct of war.[26]

The illustrious hero, despite his age—he was eighty-three—now began to wade into the treacherous waters of politics. He invited Senator Henry Lémery, generally considered a "reactionary," to confer with him at San Sebastian. The senator was at first wary of the meeting, fearing the government might suspect a plot was in the offing to overthrow it, but he finally arrived in great secrecy on October 10. He told Pétain that "things were going badly in the army. You must prepare yourself to form a government to carry on the war, as Clemenceau did."

"The war, yes," the Marshal replied. "But politics for me is a joke. It is not my profession to direct a government."

The senator assured him that he himself could get up a government for him, and rattled off some names, including that of Laval. "Give him the Ministry of Interior," he advised.

At the mention of Laval, with whom, as we have seen, Pétain already was in discreet contact, the old man's ears pricked up.

"How did he make his fortune, that one?" Pétain asked. Lémery brushed the question aside.

At the end of the conversation, Pétain, though obviously flattered— and he liked flattery—declared that "in no case" would he take over power.[27] But his flatterers did not take this for a final answer. They decided to continue to work on him and wait for a more propitious moment—perhaps, it is clear from their own words, when defeat threatened.

Laval was not idle. Reporters found him in the corridors of Parliament and in the restaurants frequented by the politicians pushing the idea of a Pétain government. On October 27 Laval had a long talk with Elie J. Bois, the editor of the *Petit Parisien,* the morning newspaper with the largest circulation in France. No one but Pétain, he said, could form an effective government to carry on the war. The Marshal could "rally round him the best and most energetic men." When Bois objected that Pétain was too old, that he was, after all, "drawing to the end of his days," Laval replied:

"That doesn't matter. What will be asked of him? To be a statue on a pedestal. His name! His prestige! Nothing more!"

Bois says that Laval continued to "develop his plan." After the editor left him the "fugitive thought" flashed across his mind that Laval foresaw "a Pétain cabinet, of which he would be the instigator, the kingpin, the producer, and of which he would retain the real direction."[28]

The German government soon learned something of what was up. On November 16 in Berlin Weizsaecker noted in a memorandum the latest information from the Italian Embassy in Paris.

Marshal Pétain is regarded as the advocate of a peace policy in France. . . . Pétain believes that even in the event of victory France would not enjoy its fruits. If the question of peace should become more acute in France, Pétain will play a role.[29]

As the year 1939 approached its end, Daladier limped along with a divided cabinet of mostly aging, tired, mediocre politicians which gave little inspiration to a country at war. He seems to have been unaware of the intrigues around Pétain. The High Command too was headed by aging men, with little vitality or imagination or stomach for action. They did little, in the absence of real hostilities, to whip the army into a confident, fighting force. There were vital lessons to be learned from the Polish campaign, in which the German blitzkrieg tactics of using armored divisions and swarms of bombers, working together, to achieve and exploit the break-through had quickly overwhelmed the Polish troops. This was new. It marked a revolution in warfare. But the lessons were not learned. The revolution was not even understood.

On November 11 the irrepressible Colonel de Gaulle, who commanded the tanks of the Fifth Army, had addressed to General Headquarters a note on the "lessons" of Poland. "The gasoline engine," he concluded, "knocks out our military doctrines just as it will knock out our fortifications. We have excellent material. We must learn how to use it as the Germans have." He urged that the French tanks, then widely dispersed as support for infantry, be put together in armored divisions. But the two generals in charge of tank warfare rejected the advice of the impetuous colonel. General Dufieux, former Commander of Tanks, wrote to Gamelin: "In my opinion Colonel de Gaulle's conclusions must be rejected." He and General Keller, who was Inspector General of Tanks, pointed out that the German panzer divisions would find France quite different from Poland. Said General Dufieux: "How can these armored units hurl themselves unsupported against our lines, as in Poland, and penetrate deep into them without risking almost complete destruction?" And General Keller reiterated the obsolete French doctrine: "In future operations the primary role of the tanks will be, as in the past, to facilitate the progress of the infantry in reaching its objectives."[30]

The High Command put so little value on its tanks, despite what had happened in Poland, that it authorized the sale of them to friendly foreign countries. Of the last 500 model R-35 tanks produced up to May 1940, some 235, or nearly one half, were dispatched abroad—to Poland, Romania, Yugoslavia, and Turkey. Only 90 of these new tanks were at the French front when the Germans finally attacked. Not only tanks, but considerable quantities of arms continued to be exported despite the shortages of them in the French units. A total of 830 25mm. antitank guns were sold abroad in this period and more than 500 pieces of artillery with ammunition.[31]

The distrust between the two leading figures in the government, Daladier and Reynaud, was matched by that between the two top commanders in the army, General Gamelin, the Commander in Chief, and his Deputy Commander, General Georges, who was also designated as Commander of the Northeast front, that is, the Franco-German front. When General Spears visited General Georges at his headquarters at La Ferté-sous-Jouarre on November 1 he found the French general bitter at both Gamelin and Daladier. The Premier, he said, "detested" him.* "The struggle between Georges and Gamelin," the British officer found, "was extremely bitter. Georges was persuaded that Gamelin was an intriguer, utilizing Daladier to maintain his authority regardless of efficiency and elaborating . . . devices to keep control and tie Georges' hands."[33] Georges, as he later explained to the Parliamentary Investigating Committee after the war, had the responsibility for the Army's operations against Germany but not the authority for planning and organizing them. That remained in Gamelin's hands.

As France drifted toward the supreme crisis, the High Command, like the government—and the people—remained divided. Through that first

---

* Gamelin confirmed in his postwar testimony before the Parliamentary Investigating Committee that Daladier "was always extremely cool toward General Georges." Gamelin recounted that when, in January 1939, he had asked the Premier to name Georges Chief of the Army General Staff, Daladier had refused on the ground that he personally lacked "complete confidence" in him. "He is too much attached to a clan," Daladier told him. "As long as I am Minister of War I won't have him as Chief of the Army General Staff."[32]

autumn and early winter of the war, to be sure, few Frenchmen seemed to believe that such a crisis would ever come. Daladier and Gamelin, and the men around them, began to count on the Allied blockade to gradually weaken Germany. After a couple of years, they calculated, with a sizable British army in the field aside the French, bolstered by American arms and perhaps by American troops, as the last time, the West could administer the *coup de grâce* to the enemy. In the meantime there was no need to fight, to shed French blood, as long as the Germans did not attack. The *Drôle de Guerre,* so unique an experience in history, was not so bad a thing—for the soldiers at the "front" as well as for the civilians at home.

In Paris and in the smaller cities and towns the feeling grew that in this peculiar war there was no need to suffer, to deprive oneself of the good, easy life. Sacrifice was not this time needed. Or not much sacrifice, at any rate. True, at night the cities and towns were blacked out as protection against air attack. Gas masks were distributed to the populace. But the air raids never came. Soon life at home returned to almost normal. The theaters, operas, music halls, and cinemas, which had been closed on the first day of war, were reopened. By November the old favorites were playing to packed houses. Maurice Chevalier and Josephine Baker were back at the Casino de Paris, the wonderful Lucienne Boyer resumed singing at her *boîte* in the rue Volney. Henri Bernstein wrote and produced a new play called *Elvire* with Elvire Popesco in the leading role. It was a great success, as was *Ondine* by Jean Giraudoux, who now served—with less success— as High Commissioner of Information. There was a new Baty production of *Phèdre* at the Théâtre Montparnasse and popular revivals of *Cyrano de Bergerac* and *Madame sans Gêne* at the Comédie Française. In the darkened capital, night life went on almost as usual. The only annoyance was that public places, including restaurants, had to close at 10 P.M. and that it was a little more difficult to get around in the blackout. There was no food rationing. Not until January 1940 were two meatless days a week introduced, but as the journals noted, there was no restriction of the purchase of food on the other days. Gasoline, all of which had to be imported, was not rationed either. One could still use his car for weekends in the country or for getting about the city.

The intellectual life continued to flourish. Books were published and reviewed. The universities went on as before, deprived only of the youths who had been called up. A lecture by the poet Paul Valéry before a gala meeting of the five academies on *Pensée de l'art français* was praised at length in the newspapers and reviews. Though Parliament rarely met, being content to let the government prosecute the war as it saw fit, a subcommittee of the Chamber urged in November that the winter sports centers and the vacation places on the Côte d'Azur be opened as usual.

While the good folk at home continued to enjoy life, the two million troops in the field stagnated. In the absence of fighting there was nothing much to do but while away the time digging fieldworks of little value. "Our units," General Laffargue wrote later, "vegetated in an existence without purpose, settling down to guard duty and killing time until the next leave or relief." Some officers such as de Gaulle urged that the idle troops be given intensified training not only to prepare them for the blitzkrieg tactics which the Germans had used so successfully in Poland but, by keeping them busy at learning how to soldier, to raise their morale. But the ossified High Command shrunk back from such an intensive program. "We could allot but one half day a week to training because labor jobs came first," General Ruby of the First Army complained, and General Menu found that as late as March 1940 "many infantry units had still not fired a rifle or tried out their antitank and antiaircraft guns." No effort was made by Gamelin and Georges to hold exercises in divisional strength so as to give the officers and men the experience of operating in large units. "Not one of my divisional commanders," said General Grandsard, commander of the ill-fated X Corps at Sedan, "ever had his division assembled around him."[34]

Sheer boredom overcame the troops and became such a problem that the government and High Command finally bestirred themselves to do something to combat it. Recreation centers were set up in the overcrowded cantonments, theater companies were sent out from Paris to entertain the soldiers, and more frequent and extended leaves were given the men. Many in uniform tried to escape boredom through drink. "Alcoholism" became so excessive among the rank and file that it began to alarm the commanders. "The spectacle of our men in the trains and railroad stations was not always very comforting," General Ruby noted. "Drunkenness had made an immediate appearance and in the larger railway stations special rooms had to be set up to cope with it—euphemistically known as *salles de dés-éthylisation!*"

The troops in the field, like the civilians at home, began to believe that in this droll war no serious fighting would be necessary. And the soldiers increasingly resented work details, which, not without reason, they believed to be futile. Many junior officers, civilians in uniform, agreed. General Ruby noted "a general apathy and ignorance among the ranks. No one," he says, "dared give an order for fear of making a mistake or being criticized. Military exercises were considered a joke and work unnecessary drudgery."

There was also German propaganda to counter. Even General Gamelin, who admits that because he spent his time exclusively with the high brass he was "not in sufficiently close touch with the spirit of the troops," concedes that he was concerned with Nazi propaganda directed at the soldiers. By loudspeakers and large signs the Germans constantly chided the front-line French troops about "dying for Danzig, for the Poles, for the British." "Don't shoot! We won't, if you don't!" Daily this message came over no man's land from the German lines by loudspeaker or by signs held high over the bunkers. And often the French *poilus* would hoist a crude sign signifying an O.K. German planes dropped leaflets to the French soldiers further back on the Maginot Line or in their cantonments giving the text of the Fuehrer's "peace offers"—and perhaps even more effective, especially among the Communists, the statements of Molotov blaming France and Britain for continuing the war.

The "front" itself, along the Rhine north from Basel and then westward from the river to Luxembourg, was usually as quiet as a graveyard. Only occasional patrols broke the silence of the night, or an occasional burst of an artillery shell that of the day. Along the 90 miles of the Rhine which separated France and Germany and their armies not a shot was fired. Troops of each side, in full view of the other, worked desultorily at fieldworks and gun emplacements, often pausing to gaze across the river at the "enemy." Once from the German side I watched some Wehrmacht troops cheering a soccer game that some French troops were playing across the river. On the morning of October 10 I had gone up by train from Karlsruhe to Basel on the German side of the Rhine and noted in my diary:

> No sign of war and the train crew told me not a shot had been fired on this front. . . . We could see the French bunkers and at many places great mats behind which the French were building fortifications. Identical picture on the German side. The troops seemed to be observing an armistice. They went about their business in full sight and range of each other. For that matter, one blast from a French "75" could have liquidated our train. The Germans were hauling up guns and supplies on the railroad line, but the French did not disturb them. Queer kind of war.[35]

According to Colonel Goutard, the French forces along the Rhine river front were expressly forbidden to fire on the Germans. He quotes General Gamelin: "Open fire on the German working parties? The Germans would only respond by firing on ours!"[36]

It is understandable, of course, that Daladier and Gamelin did not want to risk spilling French blood until the British were at hand in some force to share the sacrifice. And Britain, devoid of any army when hostilities began, needed time to build up one that could be of any help to the French. By October 11 she had sent four infantry divisions—158,000 men —to France. "A symbolic contribution," Churchill called it, and General Fuller, the British military historian, noted that the first British casualty— a corporal shot dead on patrol—did not occur until December 9. "So bloodless a war," Fuller was moved to comment on the Western front that fall and winter, "had not been seen since the Battles of Molinella and Zagonara."

A similar comment could have been made on the "war" in the air. There was no strategic bombing by either side. At night a few bombers dropped propaganda leaflets. That was all. "A confetti war"!

Adolf Hitler could scarcely be blamed for concluding that the British and French had no stomach for a real war—except at sea. But he had plenty of stomach for one, as he showed as soon as he returned to Berlin from the romp through Poland. On September 27, as we have seen, he had informed the Army High Command of his decision to attack in the West as soon as possible and had actually set a date: November 12. On October 10 he had issued Directive Number 6 ordering his generals to prepare an offensive through neutral Holland, Belgium, and Luxembourg and to be ready to carry it out "at as early a date as possible." The generals, who had a healthy respect for the French army, and who needed time to refit the divisions, especially the armored units, returning from Poland, had balked and stalled for time. One of them, but only one of them, so far as the German records show, argued against attacking the West that fall, not only because the army was not up to it but on moral grounds. This was General Wilhelm Ritter von Leeb, commander of Army Group C opposing the French on the Rhine and along the Maginot Line. In a written memorandum to his army chief, General von Brauchitsch, he submitted that the whole world would turn against Germany if "for the second time in twenty-five years it assaults neutral Belgium." But Brauchitsch did not have the courage to show it to Hitler, who, impatient with the timidity of his generals, called them in on October 27 and told them the attack in the West would start on November 12.

On November 5, the day the movement of troops to their jump-off positions was scheduled to begin, the Fuehrer had a showdown with General Brauchitsch. Armed with memoranda from General Halder and the principal field commanders, the Army chief tried to argue that an offensive in the West now would end in disaster. The bad weather would prevent support from the Luftwaffe, he pointed out, and besides the Army was not ready. Hitler flew into a rage, throwing Brauchitsch into such a state of jitters that his fellow officers later recalled him staggering into headquarters at Zossen, 18 miles from Berlin, still so shocked that he was unable at first to give a coherent account of what had happened.*

The day after provoking his Army chief to the edge of a nervous breakdown Hitler busied himself with composing the texts of proclama-

---

* It was on this day, November 5, that a second military plot to overthrow Hitler, a sort of successor to that led by General Halder just before Munich and as timidly planned, was supposed to reach its climax. It was known as the "Zossen Conspiracy," Zossen being the headquarters of the German Army High Command and General Staff, where the plot was hatched. Halder was again the center of it and General Beck, his predecessor as Chief of the General Staff, was one of the principal ringleaders. The plan was to remove Hitler unless he agreed to abandoning the attack in the West that fall. General von Brauchitsch had more or less agreed to arrest Hitler if during his meeting with him on November 5 the Fuehrer proved adamant. Hitler so proved, but the Army chief, as we have seen, lost his nerve and when, shattered by his dressing-down from the dictator, he returned to headquarters his fellow officers saw that he was in no shape to take any action whatsoever. Nor were they willing to, in his place. As Halder explained to Beck, Brauchitsch was the Commander in Chief of the Army. "The final responsibility," said Halder, "was his." That was the end of the "Zossen Conspiracy." (For a detailed account of it, see the author's *The Rise and Fall of the Third Reich,* pages 647–651.)

tions to the Dutch and Belgian people justifying his attack on them. Halder noted the pretext in his diary: "French march into Belgium."

But the next day, on November 7, in view of the weather "and the railway transport situation," the Nazi warlord postponed the attack by three days. This was the first of fourteen postponements ordered by Hitler throughout the fall and winter. On November 9 the offensive was postponed to November 19; on November 13, to November 22; and so on, with the bad weather usually stated as the reason. Actually he probably deferred to his hesitant generals, but there were other reasons. The strategic and tactical plans had not been fully worked out, and when they had been, as we shall see, they fell into the hands of the Allies. But at no time, as the captured German military records show, did Hitler abandon his determination to deliver a smashing blow in the West "as soon as possible." Unlike the Allied leaders he used the hiatus of the phony war to plan and prepare for real war.

Then, on the last day of November, real war came to Finland. Soviet Russia suddenly attacked the little country, causing reactions in the West that were morally commendable, but otherwise foolish and futile, exposing the basic weaknesses of the Allies and the strengths of Germany in a consequent and brief struggle for Scandinavia, which itself formed an ominous prelude for what was to follow in the May days of 1940.

The Repercussions of the War in Finland

The naked, unprovoked aggression of Russia against a small, peaceful neighbor provoked great indignation in the West. And the gallant resistance of the Finns, who, though greatly outnumbered, stopped the Red Army cold for two months, aroused a tremendous wave of admiration and sympathy. In France the war against Germany was for the moment forgotten and Stalin replaced Hitler as the great enemy of the democratic Republic. Pressure mounted quickly in the press and Parliament for France, which had done so little to help Poland, to come to the aid of Finland. Shipment of arms to the beleaguered country began on December 13. And on the 19th, at a meeting of the Allied Supreme Council, Britain and France agreed to step up the dispatch of war material to Finland.

By New Year's, 1940, the French were determined to do more. On January 4 General Gamelin discussed with his commanders the question of a naval expedition to Petsamo on the Arctic Sea, though this Finnish port already had been captured by the Russians. On January 16 he addressed a long memorandum to Daladier outlining his plans for a landing at Petsamo and for occupying the western ports and airfields of Norway as a staging area for Allied troops bound for Finland. He also envisaged the "possibility" of extending the operations into the Swedish ore fields at Gullivare, from which Germany received more than half of its iron. He emphasized that this would not only deprive Germany of the iron ore it needed to make arms but that by opening up a new front it might draw away sufficient German forces to prevent the enemy from launching a major offensive against France in the spring.[37]

From the beginning of the Russo-Finnish War certain differences as to objectives had risen between the British and French governments. London realized from the outset that the two countries lacked the means of bringing effective military aid to Finland in time to save it before the Russians, with their vastly superior manpower and armament, crushed it. Besides, as the British made plain to the French at a Supreme Council meeting on December 19, they wished to do nothing to add the Soviet Union to the enemies of the Western Allies. As Daladier later told a secret meeting of the Chamber, there had been profound disagreement on this point. The French Premier, urged on by the Right, which had been so lukewarm about fighting Germany, had recklessly proposed a rupture with Russia, even if it meant hostilities.[38]

What the British government wanted was to use the *pretext* of aid to Finland to occupy the Western ports of neutral Norway: Trondheim, Bergen, Stavanger, and especially Narvik. For one thing, if the Allies got there before the Germans, it would deprive the latter of harbors and airfields from which they could more easily and effectively wage war against Britain with submarines and bombers. Even more important, seizure of these Norwegian bases, above all Narvik, would cut off the winter supply of Swedish ore to Germany, on which the Reich depended for its very existence. In the summer this ore came down by boat from Sweden through the Gulf of Bothnia. But during the long winter season this sea was frozen and the ore had to be shipped by rail from northern Sweden to the Norwegian port of Narvik, from where German ships, taking shelter against British submarines, surface warships, and bombers in the territorial waters of Norway, sailed unmolested to Germany. Since the end of September, Winston Churchill, then the First Lord of the Admiralty, had been proposing that the British Navy mine the Norwegian Leads to stop the German ore traffic. Prime Minister Chamberlain, not wishing to violate Norway's neutrality, had turned him down.

Franco-British differences were resolved at a meeting of the Supreme Council in Paris on February 5. The French agreed to drop the project for an expedition to Petsamo on the Arctic Sea. The British agreed to the sending of an Anglo-French expeditionary force of some 30,000 troops to Finland. They would be called "volunteers" so as to avoid, if possible, getting into a war with Russia. The expedition would be prepared to sail early in March. To where? At first to Narvik, and then over the ore railroad to Sweden and thence to Finland. General Gamelin got the impression from this meeting that for the British "the problem of direct aid to Finland was secondary to getting possession of the Swedish ore mines" and that they were thinking "of sending only part of the Allied forces on to Finland."[39] The rest would stay put at Narvik or along the railway to the Gullivare iron mines in Sweden. Since the Germans, it was known, were counting on eleven million tons of this ore annually—out of a total consumption of fifteen million tons—the proposed Allied, or British plan, would be a severe blow to the Reich.

Hitler realized this all too well. In the very first weeks of the war the Navy had suggested to him the value of bases in Western Norway, and on October 10 Admiral Erich Raeder, Commander in Chief of the Navy, had pressed him about the matter. But the Fuehrer was at that moment preoccupied with preparing an offensive against France. In fact it was on that very day, the 10th, that he had handed his generals Directive No. 6 calling for an offensive through Belgium and France at the earliest possible moment.

The Russian attack on Finland on November 30, 1939, radically changed the situation in Scandinavia, immensely increasing its strategic importance not only for the Western Allies but for Germany. Reports that France and Britain were preparing an expeditionary force for Finland, which could only reach its destination by crossing Norway and Sweden, stirred Hitler to action. On December 14 in Berlin he had a long talk with Vidkun Quisling, leader of a small Norwegian Nazi party, for whom the Navy, in cahoots with Nazi Party officials, had planned the sort of role played by Seyss-Inquart in Austria at the time of the *Anschluss.* Quisling, with the help of his storm troopers trained in Germany, was to seize power in Oslo and call on Germany for help. Later that day Hitler, apparently impressed by the scheme (if not by Quisling), ordered OKW to work out a plan for the military occupation of Norway—and, for good measure, neighboring Denmark. By January 27, 1940, the operation had a code name, *Weserübung* (Weser Exercise).

Angered by an incident on the night of February 16–17 in which sailors from a British destroyer boarded a German naval supply ship, the *Altmark,* in a Norwegian fjord, killed four German crewmen, and liberated 299 captured British seamen, Hitler on the 19th ordered the High Command to hurry its preparatioins. On the 21st he appointed General Nikolaus von Falkenhorst to command the expedition to Norway, and on March 1 issued the formal Directive for the Weser Exercise. The objective, it stated, was to prevent "British encroachment on Scandinavia," and while "guaranteeing our ore base in Sweden" to afford "our Navy and Air Force a wider starting line against Britain."[40]

As both sides suspected, they were now in a race to seize Norway. The sudden end of the Russo-Finnish War on March 12 seemed to rob them both of an excuse to grab the Norwegian bases.* The French and

---

* On February 1 the Red Army had begun an offensive against the Mannerheim Line between Lake Ladoga and the Gulf of Finland. Massing guns, tanks, and men on the short front, they had achieved a major breakthrough on February 11 and on February 22 Marshal Gustav Mannerheim, the Finnish Commander in Chief,

British could no longer pretend that they needed them as a staging area for their expedition to Finland. Nor could the Germans justify occupying them in order to prevent the Allies from using them as bases for their forces destined for the Finnish front. Colonel Jodl noted in his diary the embarrassment in Berlin. "Conclusion of peace between Finland and Russia," he jotted down on March 12, "deprives England, but us too, of any justification for occupying Norway." Still, both sides went ahead with their plans.

The sudden capitulation of Finland also embarrassed Daladier, who already was under heavy attack in Parliament for not doing more to save that country. To recoup his political fortunes he now showed unusual energy in pushing the project to occupy Norway. On March 14 he sent a strongly worded note to London reminding the British government that the defeat of Finland had been a sharp setback for the Allies and that it was urgent that they regain the initiative. They should, he insisted, stop the material aid Norway and Sweden were giving to Germany despite their professed neutrality. To begin with, he said, they should now put an end to the shipment of Swedish ore to Germany by seizing the Norwegian ports. He would, he added, welcome a reaction to this by Germany since it would give the Allies a theater of war in Norway and Sweden. The French Premier, like the High Command, apparently wanted to fight the Germans on any other front but the main one in France.[41]

The British government politely touched on this last point in a reply on March 27. It argued that the best way of regaining the initiative was to take some direct action against Germany itself. London again urged, as it had for some weeks, that the French agree to a secret operation which the British had prepared of launching mines in the Rhine and other German rivers and in the canals and thus disrupt traffic on Germany's inland water routes, on which the Reich depended for a great deal of its transportation —a project which the French had strenuously opposed for fear of reprisals.

---

had advised his government to try to make peace while his forces, though being beaten, were still intact. He realized that no appreciable help from the West could be expected. It was not until February 5, when his forces were under heavy attack on the Karelian Isthmus, that he received the first formal offer from France and Britain of a small expeditionary force, and not until March 7, when a Finnish delegation was already on the way to Moscow to negotiate the best peace terms it could, that General Sir Edmund Ironside, Chief of the Imperial British General Staff, informed him that France and Britain were ready to dispatch a force of 57,000 men and that the first contingent of 15,000 men could reach Finland by the end of March if Norway and Sweden would allow them transit. But Mannerheim knew that five days before, on March 2, both Nordic countries had again categorically refused transit on the ground that it would violate their neutrality. And anyway, by March 7 it was much too late.

The French and British governments and High Commands never seemed to face the fact that there was little likelihood of Norway and Sweden permitting the transit of their troops to Finland. Both of these small, neutral powers feared the reaction of Russia and Germany and, quite rightly, had no confidence that the Western Allies could ever defend them against it. The British understood this best perhaps, since from the beginning, as we have seen General Gamelin noting at the Supreme Council meeting on February 7, they were preoccupied not with getting troops to Finland but to Norway to cut off the iron-ore shipments to Germany.

The British also pointed out that now that spring was at hand the shipments of German ore would be resumed down the Gulf of Bothnia and that seizing the Norwegian ports at this time would have no effect on it. Besides, it would offend the neutrals, "especially the United States."[42]

Again the differences between the Allies were resolved at a meeting of the Supreme Council in London on March 28. Instead of occupying the Norwegian ports it was decided to mine the shipping lanes south of Narvik used by the Germans. The mining of these Norwegian territorial waters would be done on April 5 after a joint note to Norway and Sweden was delivered on April 1 stating that the Allies reserved the right to take what action they deemed necessary to halt the flow of material to Germany from the two neutral Nordic countries. So far as the record shows, no new plans were made to land forces in Norway in case of a strong German reaction to the mining. While the French were all for mining Norwegian waters they were still reticent about the British project for mining German waters. It was finally agreed that, subject to approval by the French War Committee, British teams would launch mines in the Rhine from shore on April 4 and proceed to drop mines in other German rivers and in canals by air on April 15.

Among other agreements at this meeting of the Supreme Council was one pledging not to make a separate peace. Such an agreement had been made in the first weeks of World War I, but since September Daladier had steadfastly opposed it. Now on March 28, seven months after the beginning of World War II, the French Premier gladly signed it. This was Paul Reynaud. Seven days before, Daladier had fallen.

THE FALL OF DALADIER

On March 14, two days after Finland was forced to sign harsh peace terms with Russia, the parliamentary offensive against Daladier began. The Senate met that day in secret session and it became evident at once that Daladier was to be blamed, not for inaction against Germany, but for inaction against Russia in Finland—and elsewhere. And long before the debate was over it was equally evident that the overwhelming majority of the Senate, from Right to Left,* wanted France to add the Soviet Union to her enemies in the war, as if Germany were not enough. Moreover, Daladier made it clear that his government too wanted to take on Russia and that only the opposition of Britain—and of Turkey—had so far made this impossible. Early in the session Senator Charles Reibel set the tone for the debate by demanding that France fight Russia not only in Finland but in the Caucasus. The Caucasus? Indeed the senator was touching upon a highly secret plan of the French government and High Command to destroy the main Russian oil fields, which lay in the Caucasus, not only to prevent Soviet oil from going to Germany, as it was, but to knock out Russia.

---

* The Communists, being outlawed, were no longer represented in either chamber.

Daladier had launched the idea on January 19, 1940, when he instructed General Gamelin and Admiral Darlan to prepare a study "on an eventual intervention to destroy Russian oil." The study, he told them, should be based on three hypotheses.

1. Interception of oil transported in the Black Sea for Germany—especially on German ships. In this case there will be no Russian belligerence.
2. Direct intervention in the Caucasus.
3. Without taking direct action against Russia, to facilitate revolts among the Muslims of the Caucasus.[43]

Although, as we have seen, Daladier at the Allied Supreme Council meeting on December 19, 1939, had urged the British—unsuccessfully—to break with the Soviet Union, he was now, a month later, typically cautious. Only the second hypothesis would be certain to bring France into war with Russia.

On January 31, at a meeting with the British High Command at his post at Vincennes, General Gamelin discussed the matter, but his guests were distinctly cool. The generalissimo admits he was under considerable pressure from his own side. Parliament already, he says, was demanding "resolute action" against the Bolsheviks. And he cites a letter he received from General Weygand, commander of French forces in the Near East, who was put in charge of carrying out the plans for the Caucasus operation, saying: "I believe it is of the utmost importance to break the back of the U.S.S.R. in Finland . . . and elsewhere."[44] The emphasis in French circles was shifting, as Weygand's words indicate, from helping Finland and trying to cut off shipments to Germany of Russian oil, to dealing the Soviet Union itself a heavy blow by destroying her sources of petroleum.*

Gamelin says that he himself realized the "consequences" of such action—war with Russia as well as with Germany—but that he did not think he had the "right" to oppose the government. Again the generalissimo's towering timidity! The matter certainly concerned the French High Command, which already was fearing a German onslaught in the West as soon as the spring arrived, and had no troops or arms or planes to spare for war against Russia too. But, dutifully, Gamelin went ahead working on plans to blow up the Russian oil fields. He seems, though, to have been

---

* Colonel de Gaulle noticed this during a visit to Paris in March. "Certain circles," he later wrote, "saw the enemy in Stalin rather than in Hitler. They busied themselves with finding means of striking Russia, either by aiding Finland or bombarding Baku or landing at Istanbul, much more than in coming to grips with Germany."[45]

Captain Paul Stehlin, who had been assistant air attaché in Berlin and who was now assigned to the French military mission in Finland, recounts how he was briefed by General Bergeret, Deputy Chief of Staff of the Air Force. The General explained to him the secret project to bomb the Russian oil fields, after which General Weygand's forces were to advance through the Caucasus and north toward Moscow where they would meet the Finnish and Allied forces sweeping down from the north. The thirty-two-year-old captain says he was "stupefied" to hear it. He could not believe that the French High Command had so lost its senses.[46]

troubled by the effect on the French government of a farewell dispatch from the departing Ambassador in Moscow, Paul-Emile Naggiar. The French envoy had confided to the American Ambassador in a talk on February 2 what his advice to Paris had been:

He told me in the strictest confidence [Laurence A. Steinhardt reported to Washington] that he had advocated to his government a complete rupture of diplomatic relations with the Soviet Union and that it was his personal opinion that Great Britain and France should declare war on the Soviet Union. . . . He would endeavor to press these views on his government. . . .[47]

In the Foreign Office in Paris Alexis Léger needed no pressing. William Bullitt, the American Ambassador, had had a long talk with him on January 15 and reported to Washington that evening.

Léger expressed the opinion that the British were entirely idiotic in believing that they could detach the Russians from the Germans and that they could finally obtain the support of the Soviet Union against Germany.

He went on to say that the French Government had proposed to the British Government that the British and French fleets should enter the Black Sea and bombard Batum and send airplanes to bomb Baku and thus cut off both Germany and the Soviet Union from supplies of oil. The British Government had replied that no British ship would be fitted for any action in the Black Sea hostile to the Soviet Union.

Bullitt added his own conclusions from the talk:

The French position is that France will not break diplomatic relations with the Soviet Union or declare war . . . but will if possible destroy the Soviet Union—using cannon if necessary.[48]

The idea that France could destroy the distant Russian colossus when after six months of war it had been unable to deliver the slightest blow against Germany on its frontiers staggers the mind—even at this distance in time. But General Gamelin thought there was a way to do it.

He had not been hasty in answering the Premier's instructions of January 19 to study means of striking at Russia's oil fields in the Caucasus. He did not reply until February 22, when he presented Daladier with a detailed plan. It was later found by the Germans when they captured the papers of the French High Command. The intellectual general called it a "study." It recommended concentrating the Allied effort on the bombing of Baku on the Caspian Sea where the main oil wells and refineries were located and which accounted for 75 percent of the Soviet Union's supply of petroleum. If bombing could wipe out this source, Gamelin explained, not only would Germany be deprived of Soviet oil but Russia itself would be put in such a "critical situation" for lack of petroleum that "in a few months it might face a total collapse."[49] Gamelin, like Weygand, Daladier, and the members of Parliament, had become more interested in knocking out Russia, with which France was not yet at war, than knocking out Germany, with which she had now been at war for half a year. By mid-March plans for the Caucasus operation were progressing rapidly, as Gamelin informed Daladier in a "Very Secret" communication of March 12. The British Command in the Near East, led by General Sir Archibald Wavell, was now working with General Weygand and the problem of using intermediary air bases in Turkey, Iraq, and Iran, for the Allied bombers was being worked out.

Personally [Gamelin added in a postscript in his own handwriting] I believe it is important to pursue rapidly these studies for an attack (principally by air) on Baku and Batum. These operations will be a happy complement to those to be carried out in Scandinavia. But if these last are impeded that will be all the more reason to act in the Caucasus.[50]

By this time the Kremlin had got wind of the Allied intentions to destroy the Caucasus oil fields. There is no evidence in the papers so far available that Paris and London knew this. But the United States government certainly did. On March 9 the alert American Ambassador in Moscow cabled Washington:

Informed . . . that an extensive movement of Russian troops from Moscow to the Caspian Sea area will begin tonight. . . . Voroshilov [the Commissar for Defense] left for the Caspian area on March 6 [because of] fear by the Soviet government of some act of aggression by the British and French, especially with respect to the Baku oil fields and pipelines.

Steinhardt added that one reason the Kremlin had suddenly agreed to negotiate peace with Finland was "Soviet concern about the Black Sea and the Caucasus."[51]

When the French and British met at the Supreme Council meeting in London on March 28 their time was taken up mostly with the project to mine the inland waterways of Norway. But there was some discussion of the project to bomb the Russian oil fields, with the British again wary of getting involved in war with the Soviet Union. It was decided to ask a group of Franco-British "experts" to "study" whether the operation would yield "effective results," what would be the "probable repercussions in the U.S.S.R.," and what would be the attitude of Turkey.[52]

Reynaud, who attended the Allied meeting for the first time as Premier, makes a great deal in his memoirs on how he opposed what he calls the "foolish adventure of the Caucasus, which," as he puts it, "would have pitted us against one more enemy—and what an enemy!"[53] Actually, the evidence shows that he was all for it—even if it pitted the Allies against such a powerful enemy as Russia. And he chided the British for shrinking back from such a prospect. An interesting document showing his position was found by the French Parliamentary Investigating Committee after the war. It was the text of a note Reynaud sent to the British government on March 25, four days after becoming Premier and just prior to the meeting in London. He urged the British to support "the decisive operation in the Black Sea and in the Caucasus not only in order to restrain Russian oil going to Germany but, above all, to paralyze the whole economy of the U.S.S.R. before the Reich can organize it for her profit." As to the British government's reluctance to add Russia to the West's enemies, Reynaud argued: "The French government believes we must not hesitate to assume, if necessary, the responsibility for a rupture with the U.S.S.R."

. . . The French government [he added] is ready, if the British government judges it necessary for the carrying out of military action in the Caucasus, to examine immediately with the British cabinet the best justification to invoke for putting an end to our diplomatic relations with a government whose latest spoliations [in Finland] we condemn and whose collusion with the Reich government we denounce.[54]

Later some Frenchmen would look back and shudder at the thought of what might have happened had the Anglo-French expeditionary corps ever reached the Finnish front to engage in battle with the Russians, and if the Western Allies had carried out their plan to bomb the Soviet oil fields in the Caucasus. France and Britain would have found themselves at war with Russia as well as with Germany—at war, that is, with the two greatest military and industrial powers in Europe. One thought too of the confusion that would have ensued. In a little more than a year Germany would be at war with Russia, in which case the enemies in the West would have been allies in the East, fighting the same opponent!

Events over which France and Britain had no control saved them in the end from the consequences of such folly. One was the termination of the war in Finland, which put an end to the project for sending Franco-British troops to fight Russia on the Finnish front. The second was the sudden advent of war closer home which caused the Allies to abandon their plans to bomb the Soviet oil fields.

But the consequences of the Allies' going to war with Russia and indeed of the reckless action of the French government in proposing it seem to have escaped the minds of the quarreling French legislators as they sat in secret session that early spring and began their assault on Daladier for not having drawn the sword against the Bolshevik power.

The attack was led by two conservative politicians—Laval in the Senate, Flandin in the Chamber—who had opposed France's declaring war on Germany. Laval, as we have seen, after years of sullen silence, had attempted to speak out in the Senate on September 2 against the voting of war credits—that is, against France's going to war—but had been howled down by his exasperated colleagues. Now in the secret session of March 14, two days after the signing of the Russo-Finnish peace treaty, he rose to speak again—this time to much applause. A shrewd politician, he spoke shrewdly, at times camouflaging his real position, at other times exposing it just enough to make his case against the Daladier government, which, it will be recalled, he had told Pétain at the outbreak of the war, was a "dunghill," and which he was secretly moving to replace by a government of the aged Marshal in which he would pull the strings.

It was France, Laval reminded the Premier, which had declared war against Germany and it had done so without "sufficient military and diplomatic preparation." Of course, he continued, France must win the war "and win it quickly," after which he proceeded to show that it could not be won quickly: the Siegfried Line was too strong, the blockade too ineffective, the number of troops lined up against Germany too few. He criticized the government for its feeble conduct of the war, for letting Poland down and then Finland, for not bringing Italy in as an ally. Had Daladier let him go to Rome at the beginning of the war, he said, he could have accomplished this feat—he the friend of Mussolini, he added, and of Franco, whose Spanish dictatorship France had needlessly kept at arm's length. Finally he crept up to his main point, the one he would soon be utilizing to destroy the Republic: *that France had been irresponsible in going to war.*

"You engaged yourself lightheartedly in a formidable adventure!" he exclaimed, arguing again that the government should have first lined up more allies, especially Italy, and should have had a war plan to meet the situation. On going to war with Russia, Laval was rather circumspect, asking Daladier whether "we are, in fact, at war with the country which is Germany's chief source of supplies and her ally? I am not saying we should go to war with the Soviets because I do not have your dossiers and I am prudent." But he asked the government to tell the Senate what its stand was.

Later in an exchange on the floor Laval made his own view plain enough. Senator Henry Lémery, the close friend of Pétain, who, as we have seen, had been secretly urging the venerable Marshal to take over the government, was demanding war with the Soviet Union.

LÉMERY: We are at war. We need not discriminate between our enemies except to ask ourselves which is the most vulnerable in order to defeat it first.
LAVAL: *Très bien!*
LÉMERY: There is no doubt. It is the U.S.S.R. . . . . You had in Finland an almost miraculous opportunity to vanquish the Soviet Union. You let it slip by. France weeps over it! Her heart bleeds![55]

In a secret session of the Chamber of Deputies on March 19 Flandin took the same line. He who had vehemently opposed France's going to war with Germany over Czechoslovakia in 1938 and over Poland in 1939 violently attacked Daladier for not going to war with Russia over Finland in 1940. He reproached the government for not sending an army to Finland "the moment war broke out there." Besides sending arms and an army to help the Finns on the main front in the south, he said, France should have sent an expedition to the Arctic Ocean, not only to recapture Petsamo but to attack the main Russian port at Murmansk. Then for several minutes Flandin castigated the Premier for not daring to break with Russia. "You did not want to break with her because you believed that we could bring Russia to the Allied side to help us against Germany," he charged, arguing that such a policy was based on pure fancy. "You lost the support of all the forces in the world which consider Bolshevism the principal enemy. I defy you to explain why you make war against Germany and not also against Russia." That Bolshevik Russia, not Nazi Germany, was the principal enemy, Flandin had no doubt. Like Laval in the Senate, Flandin was loudly applauded when he sat down.[56]

In both houses Daladier had defended himself and his policies at length, citing the refusal of Norway and Sweden to grant transit rights as the reason for the failure of an Allied force to reach Finland, and blaming the opposition of the British government for his inability to get a declaration of war against the Soviet Union.[57] But at times, during the lengthy debates, he appeared worn and discouraged. In January, while weekending with Mme. de Crussol at a friend's estate near Rambouillet, Daladier had been thrown from a horse and had suffered a fractured foot. The accident had immobilized him for several weeks and had hampered him in the conduct of affairs and also in parrying the intrigues he felt were being spun all around him.* Now he seemed exhausted by the effort to meet the assault on him.

To both houses he had said that if they did not approve of the way he was conducting the war they must say so and vote him out. The Senate had given him, despite the intervention of Laval, a vote of confidence of 236 to 0, with 60 abstentions. But feelings against him in the Chamber ran higher. The vote there on March 20 was 230 to 1. But 300 deputies abstained from voting. Daladier had lost his majority and though constitutionally the favorable vote cast enabled him to remain in office, he decided that since he no longer had the support of the majority, he would go. He resigned immediately after the vote.

PAUL REYNAUD AT THE HELM

Embittered by his unexpected overthrow in the fickle Chamber—at the previous secret session scarcely six weeks before, on February 9, it had given him a unanimous vote of confidence, 534 to 0—Daladier refused

---

* At the close of the debate in the Senate, Daladier had for the first time openly spoken of these intrigues. "The worst thing in time of war," he had said, "is the intrigues in the corridors of Parliament substituting for responsibility." He was hitting especially at Laval, regarded for years as the past master of intrigues in the corridors, but no doubt he also had his rival for the premiership, Paul Reynaud, in mind.[58]

President Lebrun's request to form a new government. The President thereupon called on Paul Reynaud.

This was an obvious choice for a Parliament which had been demanding a more vigorous prosecution of the war. Reynaud had a reputation for great energy, for decisiveness, for innovation. For years, practically alone in Parliament, he had been urging a renovation and modernization of the Army. Since 1935 he had pled, though in vain, for the creation of armored divisions to match those of Germany. He had opposed the surrender to Hitler at Munich and had insisted on France going to war if Germany attacked Poland. As Minister of Finance in Daladier's government he had pushed the purchase of war planes and other arms from the United States. During the first six months of the war he had made no secret of his conviction that he could prosecute the war more vigorously than Daladier. He had kept in close touch with his friend Colonel de Gaulle, with whom he agreed about stirring up the moribund army, getting rid of the deadwood in the High Command, and organizing armored divisions with the excellent tanks which the Army now had in considerable numbers.

Reynaud had also established close contact with Winston Churchill, whose ideas he shared and whose energies and imagination he admired, and had conferred with him frequently in Paris since the outbreak of the war—to the displeasure of Daladier and many others, who thought the Finance Minister was too anglophile.* Some considered Reynaud "the French Churchill." And they did seem alike in many ways: in their drive, their combativeness, their fanatical determination to defeat Nazi Germany and bring down Hitler, and in their effort to stir up their respective governments and military establishments.† Both believed that the heads of their own governments—Chamberlain in London, Daladier in Paris—were not giving strong enough leadership in a time of crisis and were lacking in vigor and imagination in fighting the war against Germany. Each believed he could do better. Now Reynaud had his chance, and Churchill would soon have his.

Paul Reynaud was sixty-two when he became Premier for the first time. Born of sturdy mountain folk from the Basses-Alpes, where he maintained a home until the end of his long life, he was small of stature, but trim and athletic, keeping in shape until old age by strenuous exercise, which

---

* Some circles, especially on the Right, accused Reynaud of conspiring with Churchill to help him get the Premiership. They later charged that the two men held secret meetings in Paris during February and early March on how best to achieve this, and that Gaston Palewski, Reynaud's *chef de cabinet,* and General Sir Edward L. Spears, Churchill's man of confidence in France, also had a part in the proceedings.[59] Churchill did not disguise his delight with Reynaud's appointment as President of the Council. The day after it took place, on March 22, he wrote his friend from London: "I cannot tell you how glad I am that all has been accomplished so successfully and speedily. . . . I rejoice that you are at the helm. . . ."[60]

† "We have thought so much alike during the last three or four years," Churchill wrote to Reynaud in the letter already referred to. "I share, as you know," he added, "all the anxieties you expressed to me the other night about the general course of the war, and the need for strenuous and drastic measures. . . ."[61]

included cycling, boxing, and gymnastics, so that physically he resembled a jockey, or as some said, a gamecock, for he had a bristling, combative nature. His slanted squint eyes and highly arched eyebrows gave him the appearance of an Oriental. Thanks to his father having made a fortune in a cotton textile enterprise in Mexico by the time he was thirty-five, the young Reynaud had been able to attend the university and law school in Paris, where after graduation he soon became a brilliant young lawyer and married the daughter of Henri Robert, one of the great defense lawyers of the Paris bar. Elected deputy from his mountain district in 1919 at the age of forty-one, defeated for reelection there in 1924 and reelected in 1928 from the silk-stocking district of the Bourse in Paris, a seat he held until the end of the Republic, Reynaud became a cabinet minister for the first time in 1930, when Tardieu appointed him Minister of Finance. By 1940 he had served seven times as Minister of Finance, Colonies, or Justice in the governments of Tardieu, Laval, and Daladier. Yet, as he later remarked in his memoirs, he remained throughout "a lone wolf" in French politics. Until 1938 he sat nominally as a member of the Alliance Démocratique, a group of moderate conservatives, resigning from that body when Flandin, its leader, issued his flamboyant posters at the time of Munich charging that the Republic was being "tricked" into war. This lack of a broad party base from which to operate was to cost him dearly as he now set out to form a government to replace Daladier.

What helped him was his reputation for energy, for getting things done, for displaying a sharp and brilliant intelligence and an ability to get to the heart of complicated problems and, having mastered them, to act. It was generally felt that these were the qualities needed by the head of the government in the seventh month of the curious war, in which the country had dragged its feet and shrunk from fighting. This was not felt by all. Many politicians, especially on the Right, did not like him. He was not for them a good enough party man or a staunch enough conservative. And as is so often the case with such a figure in so many parliaments of the democratic West—in London and Washington as well as in Paris—many members were suspicious or resentful of his brilliant, quick mind. They distrusted it. And it was perhaps true, as some said, that Reynaud appeared to be a man so possessed by his bursting energy, by his passion to get quickly to the root of a complex problem and solve it, by his restlessness to start things moving, that he was incapable of stopping for a moment to reflect where he was going and what the consequences of his lightning decisions might be. He seemed unable to find time for reflection. He was, some found, all fits and starts. Was he too vain for his own good, and too ambitious? His rivals thought that he was.

Reynaud's lack of a broad political base from which to operate in the treacherous waters of French parliamentary politics, which had not subsided—even in wartime—almost cost him the chance to serve as Premier. Daladier and his Radical-Socialist Party, the second largest after the Socialists, in the Chamber, tried to sabotage him from the first, being bitter about their own fall from power and convinced that Reynaud was largely to blame for it. When the Premier-designate asked Daladier to join his government as Foreign Minister, a post he had held as well as that of Premier and Defense Minister, and explained that he himself intended to take over the Defense post, Daladier would not hear of it. "I considered," Reynaud says, "that in time of war the head of government should be in direct contact with the army chiefs. Daladier, who had been in charge of national defense for nearly four years, refused to leave that post."[62] Realizing that without Daladier and the 116 votes in the Chamber of his Radical-Socialist Party he could not form a government, Reynaud first decided to give up trying to form a ministry. Then he capitulated. He left Daladier at the Defense Ministry. This was a severe setback. It meant that Daladier would continue to preside over the Army, which he had shaped for so long, and which Reynaud believed needed a drastic shakeup.

Reynaud says he also tried to give the country a government of National Union such as it had had in 1914. But he did not quite dare to bring in Léon Blum, the Socialist leader, a personal friend for whom he had the highest regard, out of fear of provoking the Right. "In order to maintain a balance," he says, "I did not therefore include Louis Marin," who was chief of the conservative Fédération Républicaine. The moderates refused to join his cabinet because of Flandin's opposition. Thus as Reynaud faced the Chamber on the morning of Good Friday, March 22, to seek its approval of his government he faced the solid opposition of the Center, his own group, and of the Right. His cabinet was something of a hodgepodge, with six Socialists, eleven Radical-Socialists, and the rest made up from the left-of-center moderates.

Missing from the cabinet list was a perennial minister, Georges Bonnet, who had served in fifteen governments in the past fifteen years. Reynaud had not been able to stomach him since Munich and would not have in his cabinet a man he believed still wanted to make peace with the Germans. According to one French editor, Bois, Bonnet could not believe his eyes when he first saw the proposed ministerial list.[63] According to this journalist, who is supported by Pertinax,[64] Bonnet, at Reynaud's request, had used his power as Minister of Justice to issue a decree to shorten the legal delay between divorce and remarriage so that Reynaud could quickly marry the Countess de Portes. Did the Premier-designate have no sense of gratitude? Bonnet was beside himself with rage. Having done nothing to save Daladier, he now, according to Bois, waged a campaign in the corridors the like of which, the editor says, he had seldom seen in forty years to induce the Chamber to turn down Reynaud. But in vain, and Georges Bonnet, who has figured so largely in these pages and who figured so largely in French politics for fifteen years, and in the shaping of foreign policy for the last two, passed quickly into the limbo of history. It was not felt by his enemies that the country was any the poorer.

Colonel de Gaulle, a good writer as well as a good soldier, had been called in by Reynaud to draft the government declaration and it was unusually brief. Reminding the deputies that France was engaged in a total war, and that "the stake in a total war is total—to conquer is to save everything, to succumb is to lose everything—" it declared that the new government's only purpose was "to arouse, reassemble, and direct all the sources of French energy to fight and to conquer."

The vote came quickly and it gave Reynaud a majority of one— 268 to 156, with 111 abstentions. The negative votes and the abstentions thus totaled 267 against 268 for. Of the 116 Radical-Socialists, whose party had been given eleven posts in the cabinet, three of them to former premiers, only 33 voted for the new government, 10 voted against, and 70 abstained. The center and Right voted solidly against Reynaud. "I could not even rally," the new Premier lamented, "the support of the majority of my own group."[65] As it was, it took considerable finagling on the part of Reynaud's supporters to line up the one-vote majority. At the last moment several abstentionists were pressured to vote affirmatively, and after the session the Speaker, Herriot, was heard to mutter that he was not sure that Reynaud had received even the one-vote majority.

"You will have to resign!" Chichery, the parliamentary leader of the Radical-Socialists, shouted at the Premier after the vote. "I would have, too," Reynaud comments, "if there had been anyone beside him to take over."[66] That evening Laval telephoned General Jacques de Chambrun triumphantly: "His resignation is inevitable!"*[67]

Thus, on the eve of what almost everyone felt might well be a fateful ordeal for the country—for there were signs that the phony war was approaching its end and that the Germans were about to launch a real one, an assault, with overwhelming force, on France itself—the Republic was once more rent asunder. The thin veneer of wartime national unity had cracked wide open. The divisions among Frenchmen had become wider than ever. Half the Chamber opposed the government. The Premier and the Defense Minister were at loggerheads. Petty party politics prevailed over the vital interests of the threatened nation.

Colonel de Gaulle, after drafting the government declaration, had watched the sorry scene in the Chamber from a balcony.

It was horrible [he wrote]. After the declaration of the government had been read to a skeptical and gloomy Chamber, one scarcely heard during the debate anything but individuals or spokesmen for groups who complained that

---

* A few days later, on April 3, Hans Thomsen, the German chargé in Washington, reported to Berlin some information on Laval which he said an agent of his had got from the director of the code room in the State Department. The source was a dispatch from the American Ambassador in London, Joseph P. Kennedy, who had learned from Paris: ". . . Laval is emerging as Reynaud's probable successor."[68]

they had been slighted in the distribution of offices. The danger for the country, the need for a national effort, the collaboration of the free world, were invoked only to decorate the pretensions and the rancors. Only Léon Blum, for whom no place had been found, spoke on a lofty plane. It was thanks to him that Paul Reynaud won out, though by the narrowest of margins. The Ministry obtained a vote of confidence by one vote. Even then, as Herriot, the President of the Chamber, was to tell me later: "I am not quite sure that he got even that."[69]

Before rejoining his post the troubled colonel stayed on a few days in Paris, giving Reynaud what assistance he could.

It was enough to make me see to what degree of demoralization the regime had fallen. In all the parties, in the press, in the administration, in the trade unions, very influential groups were openly supporting the idea of ending the war. Well-informed circles affirmed that this was the view of Marshal Pétain, Ambassador in Madrid, who was supposed to know through the Spaniards that the Germans were quite willing to come to terms. "If Reynaud falls," it was said on all sides, "Laval will take power with Pétain at his side. The Marshal, in effect, is in a position to make the High Command accept an armistice."* Thousands of copies of a pamphlet were circulated, carrying on its three pages a picture of the Marshal, first as the victorious leader of the Great War, with the caption: "Yesterday a great soldier! . . ." then as ambassador: "Today a great diplomat! . . ." and finally as a great, shadowy figure: "Tomorrow? . . ."

. . . Many spoke loudly of their admiration for Mussolini. . . . The Communists, who had resoundingly rallied to the national cause so long as Berlin was against Moscow, cursed the "capitalist war" as soon as Molotov and Ribbentrop got together. As for the masses, disoriented, feeling that at the head of the state there was nothing nor anyone capable of dominating events, they drifted in doubt and incertitude. It was clear that a grave reverse would risk provoking in the country a wave of stupor and fright that would carry all away.[72]

If the state of the country and of parliament depressed de Gaulle, that of the army made him feel even worse. On January 26 he had made what he calls "his last effort" to arouse the High Command and the government from their lethargy and to warn that France faced imminent disaster unless it shook itself free from the doldrums of the *drôle* war and its politi-

---

* On March 19, 1940, the German Ambassador in Spain had reported to Berlin the latest Spanish information from Paris: "Pétain is said to have told his close associates that in view of his advanced age he would be reluctant to join a French government. France's greatest mistake, he said, had been to enter the war."[70] Pétain had spent three days in Paris at the end of January visiting with old friends. He had asked Senator Lémery to call off his campaign to put his name "to the fore." All he wanted, he said, was to return to Paris to render what services he could to the High Command. "But Daladier is against it because he sees in me a rival," he added. To an old friend, General Vauthier (retired) he wrote on his return to Spain: "I have long asked myself how I could best serve my country. And I've come to the following conclusion: my physical condition is no longer such that I could take over the government and I have therefore abandoned the idea." Thus, he admitted that he had previously been entertaining such an idea.[71]

cal and military leaders drastically reorganized the Army to fight the kind of modern war which the Germans had unveiled in Poland. The obstreperous colonel took the unusual step of addressing his warning to no fewer than eighty "principal personalities," as he says, "in government, in the High Command, and in politics." Probably any other officer would have been quickly retired for bypassing the chain of command, but the High Command and the Ministry of War, though they had often blocked his promotion, had learned to live with the bold and outspoken colonel ever since, five years before, he had castigated them for not bolstering the army with armored divisions. Besides, de Gaulle had friends among some of the most powerful politicians, above all Reynaud, on whom he showered his ideas, and who was receptive to them, and Blum, who had proved sympathetic to them and to him.

In his memorandum of January 26, de Gaulle, as he later wrote, tried to convince the powers that be

that the enemy would take the offensive with a very powerful mechanized force both on land and in the air; that because of this our front could at any moment be broken; that if we ourselves had no equivalent force with which to reply there would be a grave risk of our being destroyed; that it was necessary to decide at once on the creation of the desired instrument; that while pushing forward the production of what was needed, it was urgent to group together in a mechanized reserve corps those units already in existence or being organized which at a pinch could do.

"I concluded," he says:

The French people must not at any price fall into the illusion that the present military immobility conforms to the character of this war. On the contrary. The motor gives to the means of modern destruction a power, a speed, a range of action, such that the present conflict, sooner or later, will be marked by movements, by surprises, by eruptions, by pursuits, the extensiveness and speed of which will infinitely surpass the most amazing events of the past. Let us not fool ourselves! The conflict which has begun can well be the most widespread, the most complex, the most violent, of all those which have ravaged the earth. The political, economic, social, and moral crisis from which it comes is so profound . . . that it will end fatally in a complete overthrowing of the situation of peoples and the structures of states. . . .[73]

Few prophesies have ever proved so accurate. But his memorandum, de Gaulle says, provoked "no tremors." The generals had turned down his ideas long ago. They were going to meet the German attack, if it occurred, by the tried and trusted methods of the 1914–1918 war, in which they had won their spurs. As for the politicians, they meant to avoid the awful spilling of French blood that had so weakened the country in that war. They hoped there wouldn't be any great German offensive this time. They certainly would not countenance any massive French attacks on the Germans such as those in the first three years of the Great War, which had proved so futile and had cost hundreds of thousands of lives.

Daladier had made that clear from the outset, and Reynaud, despite his promise to prosecute the war more vigorously, clung to the same line. "It would be absurd," Reynaud told a secret meeting of the Senate on April 18, "to throw ourselves head-on against the Siegfried Line. There is no question of our doing that.

How, then, [he asked] can we prosecute the war? By depriving Germany of the supplies which are vital for her in making war—iron ore from the north, oil from the south. . . . It is only in engaging in these distant operations against the enemy that we can employ our sole superiority over Germany— naval power.

Let me sum up our war policy: Defensive on land, offensive in blockading Germany."

It was not very different, after all, from the policy of his predecessor. And illusions were sprouting in the new Premier's mind. To cut off the German supply of petroleum from Russia, he told the Senate, "operations have been planned not only to achieve that but to paralyze, if necessary, the Russia of the Soviets."[74] To a secret session of the Chamber the next day he gave vent to another illusion. "It is extremely doubtful," he said, "that Hitler has the means of taking the offensive."[75]

Such was the position of the new Reynaud government. It would prosecute the war in "distant operations" while remaining on the defensive at home. As for the Right opposition in Parliament, a large fraction, it seemed to de Gaulle that bitter spring, "wanted peace with Hitler and an *entente* with Mussolini."

Dejectedly, de Gaulle, after his brief sojourn in Paris in March, returned to his post, where Gamelin informed him of his appointment to command the Fourth Armored Division, which was scheduled to be formed on May 15. Reynaud had tried to keep the colonel in Paris as his military adviser and had offered him a post as Secretary of the War Cabinet, which he had just set up, after the British example. But Daladier, stung by years of criticism from the colonel, vigorously opposed it. To Reynaud's proposal he replied (according to de Gaulle): "If de Gaulle comes here, I shall quit this office, go downstairs, and telephone Paul Reynaud to ask him to put him in my place."[76]

Reynaud therefore appointed Paul Baudouin, Director General of the Bank of Indochina, to the post and, in addition, made him an Under-secretary of State. This, as many predicted at the time, was a disastrous choice—for Reynaud above all—and even some of the Premier's most ardent admirers never understood why he picked this particular man. Baudouin, a graduate of the Ecole Polytechnique and a product of the Inspectorship of Finance, those two institutions from which so many top

men in the Treasury and in banking came, appeared to stand for everything which Reynaud opposed.* He admired Mussolini and Fascist Italy.
Before the war he had advocated that France make her peace with Nazi
Germany, which "deserved," he said, "her place in the sun." He held it
to be "a crime against our country to assert that war with Germany is
inevitable," and even after the war came he asserted that "to reject *a priori*
all idea of negotiations before the total collapse of the might of Germany is
impossible."[78]

Like a good many Inspectors of Finance who had risen high both in
the Finance Ministry and in banking, Baudouin became something of a
technocrat, believing that the time had come to curb parliamentary democracy as practiced in France, reduce the powers of the Chamber and
Senate, and establish a strong executive "of the real elite of the country"
—of an elite of technicians, that is—"strong enough to protect itself from
demagogy by subduing it" and taking "firmly in hand the task of putting
the nation once more in order."[79] These ideas, which he publicly proclaimed in various reviews, derived mainly from Rome and Berlin, and
they must be kept in mind when we follow the doings of Baudouin in the
crucial weeks ahead.

His relations with the Countess de Portes must also be remembered.
Though he asserts in his memoirs that on the day Reynaud appointed him
to office, Easter Monday, March 25, 1940, he was seeing her only for the
third time—she was presiding over dinner in the bachelor flat on the
Place du Palais-Bourbon behind the Chamber of Deputies to which
Reynaud had moved in 1938—he concedes that thereafter he would
have with her "one or two conversations each day" and that "acting
like a director of the cabinet" this redoubtable lady, this "whirlwind,"
as he calls her, would press heavily not only on the new Premier but on
his collaborators.

It has always seemed a mystery to historians that Mme. de Portes, who
professed to love Reynaud, who had striven with all her might to propel
him into the top post, would ceaselessly work to undermine his resolve,
once he was Premier, to fight the war to the bitter end and to save, at
all costs, the Republic. But the mystery dissolves somewhat if one considers
the influence on her of Baudouin. It waxed from day to day.†

"The great reproach that I make against Reynaud," Paul-Boncour told
the Parliamentary Investigating Committee after the war, "is that he, who

---

* Monzie, for whom Baudouin figures in his diary as "my charming friend,"
was convinced, as he wrote in his journal March 23, that the new cabinet secretary
"professed ideas quite contrary to the warmongering of his new chief."[77]

† Elie J. Bois argues that "Baudouin took possession of Hélène de Portes' brain;
he became the dictator of her conscience. She would no longer think except through
him!"[80] But why, one asks, was not the influence of Reynaud, a man of much
greater caliber, stronger than that of Baudouin? And why was the will of Reynaud,
for long regarded as the strong man in the cabinet, not sufficient to cope with the will
of his flighty mistress? Pertinax speaks of "her rule over Reynaud" which "had kept
on increasing over the last two years."[81]

professed to lead the war to the bitter end, took in, or maintained, defeatists in his government. . . . Thus Reynaud kept in his cabinet Chautemps . . . who was not a partisan of war to the bitter end. . . . He had Baudouin. . . ."[82] The attitude of Chautemps to the war had been noted early in March by Sumner Welles, the American Undersecretary of State, during his visit to Paris on a mission for President Roosevelt to try to ascertain in the capitals of the belligerents, and in Rome, if there were any prospects for peace. Chautemps thought there were. Welles talked with him for two hours on March 8 and reported to Washington: "Chautemps indicated an entirely receptive attitude towards the possibility of the negotiation of a peace with the present government of Germany. . . ."[83] This veteran Radical-Socialist Party chief and perennial minister, who, like Laval, was a master at working behind the scenes, remained in the new government as Vice-President of the Council, or Deputy Premier.

There was also a figure named Yves Bouthillier who would soon become prominent in the peace group opposing Reynaud. Like Baudouin an Inspector of Finance, he had been a member of Laval's brain trust in 1935. Left unemployed by the Popular Front Government, he had been forced to take a minor job at the City Hall until Reynaud, as the latter says, "dragged him out of obscurity" and made him Secretary-General of the Ministry of Finance when he took it over in 1938. Apparently Bouthillier never forgave his chief for rescuing him from oblivion and indeed, toward the end for making him Finance Minister, for even more than the others he would in the last days turn vengefully against his benefactor.

As spring came and the supreme ordeal for the Republic approached, a cabal against the Premier was forming among those closest to him, including his mistress. It would soon be joined by more important and powerful figures, the two greatest surviving military heroes of the first war and disgruntled, reactionary, antiwar politicians, the foremost of whom was Pierre Laval. Strangely enough for so astute and experienced a politician, Reynaud did not yet suspect what was up. Nor did he seem to realize— no one in France, statesman or general, seemed to realize—how imminent and how terrible was the blow which the Germans were preparing to deliver. De Gaulle had warned of it, but his dire predictions had gone unheeded.

First, there was a preliminary blow to the Western Allies. Though the Danes and the Norwegians had been warned by their intelligence services before the end of March that a German concentration of ships and troops in the Baltic ports indicated an attack on them they had done nothing about it nor had they tipped off the Allies. The Norwegian government seemed more concerned with the threat of the British to mine their territorial waters against German shipping. On April 3 the British War Cabinet discussed the latest intelligence, especially from Stockholm, about the German buildup in the northern ports, which seemed to presage a move into Norway. But nothing was done about it, and, so far as the record shows, the French ally was not informed.

General Gamelin's notes on his activities during the first week of April disclose that his mind was on anything but Norway.[84] He spent the week conferring with General Weygand about reinforcements for the Near East and the preparations to bomb the Russian oil fields, and with his other generals and with Daladier and Reynaud about various problems concerning Belgium, Italy, and North Africa. On the night of April 6–7 the main German fleet, with troops aboard destined for Narvik and Trondheim, had sailed for the north and were discovered the next morning by British aircraft and submarines. Again there is no record that this information was passed on to Paris. On the morning of the 8th the German fleet had engaged and sunk a British destroyer off Trondheim, but not before the destroyer had reported to the Admiralty the presence of the German naval squadron heading north.

Gamelin says that he did not learn of the German move until the evening of April 8 when Military Intelligence reported fifty German naval vessels passing through the Danish straits. This information was two days late. Gamelin says he telephoned the news to Daladier and that "the British were advised." He says nothing about taking any action. Earlier in the day, he declares, the High Command had approved the embarking of two battalions of Alpine troops on April 12. They were to sail from Brest to Scotland, and there held in readiness, along with a small British force, to land in Norway should the Germans react to the mining of Norwegian territorial waters, which had been carried out early that morning by the British Navy.[85] The news of the German armada putting to sea did not provoke Gamelin to do any more.

Reynaud, in his memoirs, gives a different account. He says the government learned that evening (April 8) of the Germans heading toward Norway, not from Military Intelligence but from a dispatch of Reuter, the British news agency. He immediately rang up Gamelin, he recounts, "who knew nothing about it."

"I hope," he told Gamelin, "that you have prepared a thundering riposte."

He also had an aide telephone Admiral Darlan, who, he says, "did not hide his astonishment."

"How do you know it?" asked the Commander in Chief of the French Navy.

"I've just read it in Reuter," said the Premier's aide.

"Then I shall make inquiries," responded Darlan.[86]

The surprise, the reaction, the inaction, of the ranking chiefs of the French Army and Navy on learning the news of Germany's move on Norway was a foretaste of what was now to come. Reynaud, in office as Premier for only a fortnight, was taken aback at the complacency of his military commanders and at the obvious failure of their Intelligence to keep them informed of what the enemy was up to. They, and he, had had to wait for a Reuter news dispatch to find out! He realized that the *Drôle de Guerre* was over. After seven months of not fighting the Germans on land or in the air, France—and Britain—were now suddenly confronted in Norway with the real thing, with the kind of all-out war de Gaulle had predicted. And though for Hitler this was but a prologue to a larger and more ferocious attack against the heart of the enemy in the West, the stakes for both sides were high.

28

ON THE EVE: THE WAR IN NORWAY,
THE THREAT TO BELGIUM
AND THE CRISIS IN PARIS
SPRING 1940

At 8:20 on the morning of April 9 General Gamelin arrived at the office of Reynaud at the Quai d'Orsay to find the Premier and some of his aides poring over a map of Norway and indulging, he says, in "bitter recriminations" against the Army and Navy for having let "the Boche" once more get the jump on the Western Allies. The news was ominous. The Germans had already occupied some of the principal Norwegian ports: Trondheim, Bergen, Stavanger. But the generalissimo was imperturbable.

"What do you think of the news?" Reynaud asked him. "What can we do about it?"

Gamelin, according to Baudouin, who took notes of the meeting, was unmoved, "merely moving his hands as if giving a benediction," and "replying gently."

"You are wrong to get excited," he told the Premier. "We must wait for more complete information. This is a simple incident of war. Wars are full of unexpected news."

"You consider the invasion of Denmark and Norway as entirely unexpected news?" Reynaud asked impatiently. He inquired about the Audet mountain division which had been earmarked for Norway and which he thought was at Brest ready to embark. Gamelin said it was still in the Jura mountains on the other side of France—two days away by train. Then, as was his custom, he put the blame elsewhere.

"The British have been put in charge of this operation," he began to explain. "It is up to the British Admiralty to make the decisions. I have no business intervening."

Reynaud exploded. "Have you given the British leave to fight for you?" He urged the general to consider new plans to cope with the German

561

landings in Norway. The old plans, he said, had been based on the hypothesis that the Allied occupation of the Norwegian ports would be unopposed. But he urged in vain.

"I ask you again," Gamelin replied, "not to be impatient. We must not take measures which have not been sufficiently studied. We must await events."

The meeting broke up so that the War Committee could meet at the Elysée Palace under the presidency of Lebrun. Riding to the Palace with Daladier, Gamelin says he told the Defense Minister: "There is no use in getting excited about this."

But the volatile Reynaud was excited—more by his generalissimo's complacency than by the news from Norway, alarming as it was. He exclaimed to Baudouin, as they prepared to go to the Palace: "Gamelin acts more like a bishop than a great military chief. This cannot go on!"[1]

The meeting of the War Committee went off more smoothly, thanks, Gamelin says, to the President of the Republic, "who reestablished calm and order in the discussion." Lebrun, who believed that the British were not pulling their weight in the Alliance, was apparently relieved at the prospect that Britain would now have to shoulder the main burden of fighting in Norway. The Committee decided that it was important for the Allies to retake Trondheim and Narvik and if necessary to push on from this latter port to occupy the Swedish iron-ore mines beyond the Norwegian border. It was agreed that Reynaud, Daladier, and Darlan should fly to London that afternoon to work out plans with the British to drive the Germans out of Norway.

Admiral Darlan, to the surprise of Gamelin, whom he had not consulted beforehand, proposed to counter the German thrust in the north by going into Belgium and pressuring the government in Brussels to agree to it immediately. Reynaud, trying to goad Gamelin and Darlan into acting in Norway, frowned on the admiral's proposal. It was the beginning of a dispute about strategy that would grow increasingly bitter to the very end.

Gamelin records that after the meeting of the War Committee he himself had some "bitter regrets," namely that he had not insisted on stationing the mountain division designated for Norway in Brest, where it could have been immediately embarked for action. But then, as so often, he passes the buck. Darlan had objected. "Was it not," Gamelin says, "the admiral who was responsible and who was the best judge?"[2] During this day Gamelin had managed to pin the responsibility for action—or inaction—in Norway first on the British and then on Admiral Darlan. He did not convince at least one French Army officer. Colonel de Villelume, liaison officer between the Foreign Office and the High Command, and from this time on military adviser to Reynaud, thought that the generalissimo himself should have taken some initiative in pushing new plans to reoccupy Norway. As he testified later, Gamelin lacked the "will" to do it.[3]

The lightning speed with which the Germans carried out their move into Norway amazed the French High Command, as it did, for that matter, the British. By the time the meeting of the War Committee in Paris broke up shortly before noon on April 9 the Wehrmacht troops had occupied the five principal Norwegian coastal ports, Narvik, Trondheim, Bergen, Stavanger, and Kristiansand and had captured Oslo, the capital—in each case after scarcely firing a shot. The Norwegians, refusing to heed the many warnings they had received, were taken by surprise and put up little resistance. The German naval losses, however, from British and Norwegian counteraction were considerable and would soon increase to a point that left the Fuehrer's navy badly crippled.

Besides swiftly occupying all the principal ports and the capital the Germans also succeeded in capturing by noon all of the main airfields in Norway, including the largest and most important one at Sola outside Stavanger. This feat would prove decisive in the ensuing days. It gave the invaders absolute control of the air, enabling them not only to cover their troops, which, after securing the harbors, spread out to conquer the rest of the country, but to prevent any sizable Allied landings. Moreover German bombers kept the superior British Navy at bay so that its powerful ships could not get in close enough to support the landings or to bombard the German-occupied ports. This marked the first time in history that land-based air power triumphed over naval power. It proved to be a turning point in warfare.

And so by noon of April 9 the far-flung operation over a thousand miles of coast had been successfully accomplished by a handful of German troops, 9,000 men in all, landed and supported by a fleet in the very teeth of the British Navy, which could have blown it to bits had it been alert enough to catch the enemy. It was one of the quickest, most daring and bloodless military occupations ever carried out.

Impatiently Reynaud pressed his War Minister and High Command to get a move on and join the British in rushing strong forces to Norway. On April 11 he sent a sharply worded letter to Daladier and asked him to show it to Gamelin and Darlan.

> Our High Command, [he noted] has been surprised by the speed of the German action. On the day it started our expeditionary corps, instead of being massed at the port of embarkation, was dispersed and far away.
> The battle which has begun [he wrote] is a battle for iron. The outcome of the war can depend on the outcome of this battle. Thus the Norwegian operation is of vital importance to us. . . . Our objective must be not merely the clearing of the Norwegian west coast but to send an adequate force of troops ready to occupy the Swedish iron mines.

Above all, he said, speed was necessary. He demanded that the Audet division be embarked "by tomorrow morning" and that "two or three more divisions be massed in ports within a week."

To such speed on such a scale General Gamelin and Admiral Darlan were unaccustomed and unprepared. They replied the next day that all they could do was to dispatch to Norway *"one division per month."* The Germans were transporting three divisions in the initial assault, with four more to follow in the next couple of weeks.

Balked by the stalling of his top commanders, the Premier called a meeting of the War Cabinet for the early evening of April 12. He told Baudouin he intended to "call General Gamelin to account."

"I've had enough of his stalling," he said. "I would be a criminal to leave this gutless man, this philosopher, at the head of the French Army."*4

Even so, the peppery Reynaud did not quite grasp how deep the lethargy of his generalissimo really was. He did not know, for instance, that on that very morning Gamelin, while conferring with General Georges and General Doumenc, his top commanders, about how they were going to raise the two or three additional divisions the Premier had demanded for Norway, told them, as he wrote later, "that the question is far from being as urgent as M. Paul Reynaud thinks."5 For the phlegmatic, philosophical generalissimo nothing ever seemed to be very urgent even when the house showed signs of falling down on his head, as it now did.

For this very reason Reynaud intended to have a showdown with him that evening. It turned out to be, for Gamelin, as he later wrote, "one of the most painful days of my life."6 For Reynaud too, as the minutes of the conference would show.

The civilian members of the War Cabinet, Reynaud, Daladier, and Chautemps, along with César Campinchi, Minister of Marine, Laurent-Eynac, Minister of Air, Raoul Dautry, Minister of Armaments, and Georges Monnet, Minister of Blockade, met at 6 P.M. April 12. The three service chiefs, Gamelin, Darlan, and Vuillemin, were scheduled to join them an hour later. Reynaud lost no time in attacking Gamelin for his "utter failure" to respond to the German invasion of Norway. When he had finished he asked his colleagues if they agreed. There was a long silence. Finally Daladier, who had listened to the onslaught against the general for whom he, as Minister of Defense for four years, felt responsible, "shrugging his shoulders, his jaws set," spoke up. The Premier's criticism of the generalissimo, he said, was "unjustified." The British, he contended, were responsible for operations in Norway because it was primarily a naval problem. The British and French High Commands had agreed on a plan of action. He himself considered that there was no need to "criticize it nor to modify it." Moreover, he concluded, this was the last time that he was going to attend a meeting of this kind.

The hostility between the two rivals had reached a climax. Reynaud stuck to his guns. He "disagreed," he said, with Daladier. The plans the Defense Minister lauded, he declared, had been drawn up before the

---

* Though Baudouin is not always a reliable witness, the words he here attributes to the Premier appear to be authentic. This is borne out by Reynaud's comments on Gamelin at the subsequent meeting of the War Cabinet and later.

German aggression. They had been passed by events. The British and French, he said, "now had to act without delay and without hesitation." As for the French High Command, "it was not sufficiently aroused to the necessity of prompt action."

At 7:10 P.M. Gamelin, Darlan, and Vuillemin who had been cooling their heels in a corridor for half an hour, were let into the meeting. "On entering," the generalissimo says, "we encountered a glacial atmosphere. It was as if one had said: 'Bring in the accused.' " And Reynaud, in effect, adds Gamelin, "launched into his case against the Ministry of War and the High Command."

If not a great fighter, Gamelin, at least in this instance, is a good storyteller.

"Suddenly," he recounts, "Daladier got up from his chair and went to the foot of the table. I followed him and sat down next to him. Admiral Darlan joined us." It would seem to a detached observer that the men who were responsible for the French government and armed services were behaving, at this moment of crisis, like spoiled schoolboys.

Finally the discussion resumed. Reynaud called on Gamelin to outline the situation in Norway. The general passed the buck to the admiral, who, he said, "was in a better position to give the latest information." Darlan gave a brief summary of the extent of the German occupation. Then Reynaud got back to the general. He wanted to know, he said, what Gamelin proposed to do in Norway. What the generalissimo proposed to do, Gamelin now made it clear, was to leave everything up to the British.

"This operation," Gamelin said, "is being directed by the British High Command. It is under the command of General Ironside. I do not believe it is up to me to intervene."

But Reynaud would not accept such shirking of responsibility. It was up to the French, he said, to pressure the British to strike fast and powerfully. It was up to the French to greatly increase their own participation in Norway. But the Premier could not move his complacent military chief.

General Gamelin [in the words of the official minutes], supported by the brief remarks emitted from time to time by Daladier, declared that his conception of the High Command and its responsibilities did not meet the desires of the Premier, who wished to modify a military plan at the moment that its execution had just begun.

This was the whole point of the argument between Reynaud and the military leaders. The Premier insisted that the military plan, which had been made by the Franco-British commands for an unopposed landing in Norway, had to be changed to meet an entirely new situation as the result of the German invasion. Gamelin wanted to abide comfortably by a plan that no longer made any sense. "Let's have confidence in the British High

Command," he admonished Reynaud. And Darlan chimed in to say that "it was impossible to hasten matters" and that the augmentation of French forces for Norway "was very difficult."

The quarreling members, civilian and military, finally agreed to have Admiral Darlan request additional shipping from the British to transport more French troops to Norway and to urge them to occupy Narvik without delay.

Baudouin says he left the meeting "overwhelmed by the painful spectacle of the *impuissance* of the Premier." Reynaud had been unable to stir up his military chiefs to take decisive action. In his office a few moments later Baudouin met with some of the ministers: Georges Monnet, Raoul Dautry, and Laurent-Eynac. They all agreed, he says, that "the government was paralyzed, that it could not go on this way, that General Gamelin had made a bewildering impression."

Dautry went further, according to Baudouin.

Back the Premier in getting rid of Gamelin. This general is incapable of acting, incapable of giving an order. His fear of responsibility is obvious. He only turned over the command of the Norwegian operation to the British so he could wash his hands of it, if it turns out badly.

Gamelin had urged Reynaud to have confidence in the British but as he left the meeting he realized that the Premier no longer had confidence in him. Returning to his gloomy headquarters in the dungeon of Vincennes he "once again," he says, wrote out his resignation.

Finding myself in disagreement with the President of the Council on the very principles which I believe must regulate the general conduct of the war, I ask to be relieved of my functions.

The next morning, he recounts, he took his letter to Daladier, who, as Minister of Defense, was his immediate chief.

I share your feelings [he says Daladier told him]. I too would like to go. And if you resign, so shall I. But in the actual state of the war we have no right *vis-à-vis la France* to provoke a government crisis out of wounded *amour-propre*. The situation is even worse than it seems. There is intrigue everywhere. But I ask you to be patient.

"Mr. President," Gamelin says he replied. "I shall be patient. But my letter of resignation remains written. I leave it in your hands." Perhaps sooner than he expected he would have occasion to use it again.[7]

Denmark had fallen to the Germans before noon on April 9 without resistance. But the Norwegians, after abandoning their principal ports and their capital, recovered from their surprise and shock and tried to fight back. King Haakon VII and his government, whom Hitler had hoped to capture at Oslo, escaped to the north.* Colonel Ruge, commander of the Army, began to organize resistance to the Germans, who, after establishing themselves in the capital, moved north toward Bergen and Trondheim. It was to help these Norwegian forces and to retake Narvik, far to the north, that the Allies finally spurred themselves to action.† But with too little—and too late.

Abandoning a bold plan to take Trondheim, a key port and city halfway up the Norwegian coast, by direct naval assault, the Allies decided to capture it the slow way by landing troops north and south of it. Between April 18 and 20 they disembarked a British brigade at Andalsnes, 100 miles southwest of Trondheim, and a British brigade and three battalions of French Chasseurs Alpins at Namsos, 80 miles to the north of it. But in their hurry—or what to them was a hurry—they neglected to provide their troops with antiaircraft guns and artillery. The French had sent a large steamer, *Ville d'Alger,* to Namsos loaded with flak, artillery, and tanks but it was discovered that it was too long to dock at this small harbor—a detail, Reynaud comments, "that was overlooked" by the French Command. After an initial drive southward toward Trondheim, the Allied forces were soon halted by the Germans and withdrew to their base, which was continually bombed. The smaller force at Andalsnes joined up with Norwegian contingents down the Gudbrandsdal and succeeded in slowing up three German divisions driving up from Oslo. But they had no air cover—the Allies had also neglected to find an airfield, though there were two nearby—and no artillery or tanks, and could do no more than fight delaying actions.

On April 27, seven days after the small expeditions to capture Trondheim had landed, the British government ordered their withdrawal. Reynaud protested this bitterly at a meeting of the Allied Supreme Council in London

---

* Though the disorganized Norwegian army put up no resistance at Oslo, which was occupied by five companies of German airborne troops, Norwegian shore batteries and naval craft turned back a powerful German squadron in Oslo Fjord, disabling the pocket battleship *Lützow* and sinking the 10,000-ton cruiser *Blücher* with the loss of 1,600 men.

† At a meeting of the Allied Supreme Council at Paris on April 22, it was decided to concentrate on the recapture of Trondheim and Narvik. The strong Norwegian garrison at the latter port, a key objective for both sides since it was the port through which Germany received its iron ore during the winter, was commanded by Colonel Konrad Sundlo, a fanatical follower of the traitor Quisling. He surrendered at 8 A.M. on April 9 to General Eduard Dietl's two German battalions without firing a shot. Fooled by an act of treachery of the German naval commander, Admiral Fritz Bonte, two Norwegian ironclads in Narvik Fjord, which had halted his squadron of 10 destroyers, were blown up by the Germans with the loss of most of their crews—300 men.

On April 23 the Supreme Council decided another matter. In view of the necessity of concentrating all available military aircraft for Norway and for eventualities on the French front, it decided, as General Gamelin puts it, "if not to abandon the bombing of the Russian oil fields in the Caucasus, at least to adjourn the operation *sine die.*" Happily for the Allies this was the end of that foolhardy project.

on the same day, pointing out that it would "be a veritable disaster from the moral and political point of view." But he gave way to the military, who explained that it would be a disaster to leave the troops in central Norway, where they would soon be wiped out or captured by the Germans. It was agreed, however, that Narvik would be retaken and the ore railroad occupied up to the Swedish border. From there, if necessary, the Allied forces could occupy the Gullivare iron mines in Sweden. German airpower had defeated the Allies in central Norway and kept them out of the south. At Narvik, which lay beyond the range of German bombers, and where the British had overwhelming naval superiority, the Allies believed they would be more successful. Capturing and holding it would achieve the original principal objective of the Allies of cutting off the winter iron-ore shipments to Germany and of placing their forces in a position to seize the mines themselves should the Germans threaten to occupy them through Sweden. It would also block the Arctic shipping route to northern Russia, which the Germans had made good use of that winter, and protect that route for the Allies should the Soviet Union and Germany fall out. Moreover, possession of Narvik would provide the King and the government of Norway, which had just been evacuated from near Andalsnes, with a seat from which they could still function on Norwegian soil and govern the northern quarter of their country.

On April 13 a British naval squadron wiped out all ten German destroyers as well as all but one of their cargo ships at Narvik and Admiral Whitworth advised London that the port be quickly taken. He could smash the small German land force with the fire from his battleship. But the British Army commander, General P. J. Mackesy, who arrived the next day with an advance contingent of three infantry battalions, was a model of caution. He landed his forces at Harstad, 35 miles to the north, and whiled away a whole month before daring to attack. He began to move, cautiously, only after he had assembled a Franco-British force of 25,000 men, which outnumbered the Germans 5 to 1 and had strong naval support, which the defenders completely lacked. It was not until May 28 that the Allied army, under a new commander, General Auchinleck, and with the main attacking force led by a French officer, General Béthouart, occupied the port.

By this time, however, British and French troops were urgently needed to meet the Germans closer to home. On orders from London and Paris they abandoned Narvik on June 8, and General Dietl's forces, which had taken to the mountains on the Swedish border, reoccupied the port.

The battle for Norway was but a curtain raiser for a much bigger and more decisive battle that approached as the April days gave way to May. It was a warning, but one that came late, of Allied weaknesses and German strengths. Whereas the Germans had been bold and daring, willing to take great risks, the British and French had been timid and cautious and unwilling to take any risks at all. In each case in Norway the Allies were too late with too little.

The Norwegian affair also afforded a warning of the might of air power in modern war. Complete control of the air greatly facilitated the progress of the German ground troops in central Norway and doomed the Franco-British and Norwegian infantry trying to stop them. Even more important, it showed for the first time that land-based bombers were more than a match for an enemy navy, no matter how powerful. After the first taste of aerial bombing the British Navy decided that it could not risk its capital ships to such attacks and withdrew them from the waters off central Norway. At the meeting of the Supreme Council in London on April 27 Reynaud had found the Admiralty "terrorized by the effects of the bombing."[8] And General Gamelin recounts that the day before, Sir Dudley Pound, the First Sea Lord, had told him frankly: "It is impossible to do anything against the enemy's superior air power."[9]

POLITICAL AND MILITARY CRISIS IN FRANCE ON THE EVE

The sorry Allied failure in Norway, the responsibility which the lethargic French High Command shared in it, and Reynaud's determination to find a new generalissimo to fire up the Army before the German attack in the West, which all the signs showed was imminent, provoked a new political and military crisis in Paris on the very eve of the great ordeal.

Driving out to Le Bourget on Saturday, April 27, from where he was to fly to London for the meeting of the Supreme Council, Reynaud told Baudouin, according to the latter, that he was determined to take over the Defense Ministry so he could direct the war, and that he intended to replace Gamelin by Weygand. "He has decided to act tomorrow, Sunday, or, at the latest, on Monday," Baudouin noted. In the meantime he instructed Baudouin to see the President of the Republic and get his support for the shakeup.[10]

But the high-strung and ineffective President was no help at all. Baudouin says he found the nation's chief magistrate "ignorant, or feigning ignorance, of the situation within the government." When Baudouin read him the minutes of the meeting of the War Cabinet on April 12, at which the Premier had castigated Gamelin for his failure to act in Norway, Lebrun replied: "Unbelievable! How is it possible! I knew nothing about it! Very grave! Very grave!" But the President refused to go along with the cashiering of the generalissimo or the removal of Daladier from the Defense Ministry to the Foreign Office, as Reynaud proposed.

"The President of the Council," he said, "should not be so nervous. Tell him to be patient. Time arranges many things."[11]

Returning from London on the evening of April 27 Reynaud came down with the grippe. At Le Bourget, Baudouin found him "fatigued, shivering, drawn." At his home on the Place du Palais-Bourbon a doctor found him suffering from a pulmonary congestion and ordered him to bed for a week. "For the second time," Baudouin noted, "Gamelin is saved."

The Premier's illness gave the Countess de Portes further opportunity to enlarge her control over the affairs of state. Pierre Lazareff, the young editor of *Paris Soir,* has recounted how the government functioned while Reynaud was down with the grippe. That weekend Lazareff tried to telephone the Premier. He had an important matter to discuss with him. Madame de Portes picked up the phone.

"*We* are horribly busy, my dear," she said. "But come over anyway."

When I arrived [Lazareff recounted] I found Hélène de Portes sitting behind Paul Reynaud's desk. Surrounded by generals, high officials, members of parliament, and functionaries, she was presiding over a council. She did most of the talking, speaking rapidly in a peremptory tone, advising and giving orders. From time to time she opened a door and I could hear her saying:

"How are you feeling, Paul? Keep resting. You need the rest. We are carrying on."

When Lazareff asked if he could see the Premier alone for a moment she replied: "No, he is ill. I'm doing my best to replace him."

A moment later the lady left the room to confer with the Premier. As soon as the door was shut, says Lazareff, everyone started to curse her for trying to run the government. They blamed her and the Marquise de Crussol for the worsening relations between Reynaud and Daladier. One official recounted that at a recent weekend in the country at Madame Paule de Beaumont's, the titled mistresses of the two most important men in the French government "had almost come to blows."

But when the door reopened [Lazareff concludes] everyone stopped talking. The beautiful Hélène de Portes took her place behind the desk and each man began again to discuss with her the affairs of state in the most serious manner imaginable.[12]

In such way was the government of the Republic carried on in the midst of war and growing crisis. As one official commented while the Countess was out of the room: "Formerly such women were content to intrigue in the shadows." But not Madame de Portes. Not now. She had begun to flaunt her power in the open.

"There is intrigue everywhere," Daladier had told Gamelin on April 13 when he talked him out of resigning. No doubt he was thinking of the woman and the men around Reynaud, but probably he was unaware of intrigue in wider circles. Neither he nor Reynaud seems yet to have suspected Pétain.

The venerable war hero was back in Paris on the first of May. On the third he saw Monzie, who found him "more grave than usual." They exchanged, says the diarist, "gloomy predictions."*[13] Two days later the Marshal called on Admiral Darlan at his headquarters at Maintenon. Impressed by the efficiency and orderliness of the place in contrast to the three headquarters of the Army, Pétain told the admiral: "Well, at least here things seem to be working smoothly. I congratulate you." And then he added: "We must keep in close touch. Can I count on you?"[17] Reynaud recounts that the next day, May 6, Pétain called on him, but there is conflicting testimony as to what was said. The Premier contends that the Marshal requested permission (which Daladier had refused) to return from Spain to attend the meetings of the War Committee, of which he was a life member. "That can be easily arranged," Reynaud says he responded. "Resign as ambassador to Spain and we will be happy to see you back in the War Committee."[18] According to other testimony Reynaud went further than this. He asked the Marshal to join his cabinet as a Minister of State. Major Bonhomme, Pétain's aide, for instance, noted in his daily record

---

* A notation in Monzie's published diary for March 30 purporting to quote a remark made to him that day by Pétain would later arouse much controversy and form part of the indictment against the Marshal at his postwar trial for treason. Monzie recounted that on that date Pétain called on him at his Ministry and told him that he wanted to return to Paris. On leaving, Pétain remarked: *"They'll have need of me the second fortnight of May."*[14] How did the Marshal know on March 30, it was asked, that the government would have need of him in six weeks? Had he learned in Madrid that the Germans would attack France in the middle of May, and kept the secret to himself? Had he already assumed that the French army would be defeated and that "they" would recall him to take over the stricken country? Reynaud in his memoirs and his testimony at the Pétain trial made much of this remark in Monzie's diary to show that the Marshal already—in March—was plotting to take over the government, as soon as the Germans delivered a decisive blow—a blow he fully anticipated. Most French historians have also used the Monzie quotation to advance the same argument. And it seemed buttressed by the deposition at the Laval trial of Armand Gazel, counselor of the French Embassy in Spain under Pétain. He swore that the Marshal, long before March, had given a good deal of thought to taking over the government in Paris.

> On several occasions [Gazel deposed] he (Pétain) showed me small lists of six or seven ministers with whom he would form his government in case he was called to power. I recall two names which were on every list: Laval and Lémery.[15]

Monzie's diary entry of his talk with Pétain in Paris on March 30 thus seemed to fit in with other evidence of the Marshal's growing political ambitions.

But thanks to the careful study of the evidence and testimony at the Pétain trial by Louis Noguères, former President of the Haute Cour de Justice, the question raised by Monzie has been cleared up and his evidence thrown out.[16] Noguères has established from the records of the French Embassy in Spain that Pétain was in Madrid on March 30 and could not have seen Monzie in Paris on that day. The former judge suggests that Pétain might well have told Monzie, when he saw him in Paris on May 3, that he would be needed the second fortnight of May since Reynaud had just asked him to join his government and that, in accepting, he had asked for a few days in which to return to Madrid and liquidate his diplomatic business there. But he had not made the remark on March 30. However, such was the confusion at the Marshal's subsequent trial that both the defense and the prosecution accepted the Monzie diary entry of March 30 as a fact. Then they compounded the confusion by dating it back to January. Thus the chief prosecutor argued that at the very beginning of the year, Pétain had told Monzie that "he would replace the chief of government."

book that the Marshal called on Reynaud on the day of his return to Paris, May 1 (not May 6) and that the Premier asked him to join his government.

The marshal accepted [Bonhomme recorded] but asked for a few days to return to Madrid in order to wind up certain urgent matters.

The aide added a couple of lines, apparently after his chief had told him of the meeting.

Situation is grave.
Hostility continues between P. Reynaud and Daladier.[19]

General Gamelin supports Bonhomme's version in part. He recounts that on May 6 he called on Pétain at his old office on the Boulevard des Invalides and that the Marshal told him that Reynaud had wanted him to join his cabinet but that he had declined. The generalissimo seems to have sensed what was in the back of the old hero's mind. "He gave me the impression," Gamelin relates, "of wishing 'to save himself for a more solid cabinet.' "[20]

The month of May that year brought the finest spring I had seen in my fifteen years in Western Europe and many said they could not remember so bright a one since the end of the last war. The skies were clearing, the air becoming balmy, and the roads were drying up from the early spring thaw. It was the time when for a thousand years or more in the western lands of the Continent rival armies had stirred for action. For eight months through one of the coldest, snowiest winters in memory millions of men had stood at arms on both sides of the German western frontier. Now there were signs of imminent action. Ever since the previous autumn there had been warnings that the Germans were about to strike in the West.

There had been an alert in Belgium and France early in November 1939. On November 5 Colonel Hans Oster of the German counterintelligence and an ardent anti-Nazi conspirator, had warned the Dutch and Belgian military attachés in Berlin that Hitler had set November 12 as the date for launching his offensive in the West through Belgium and Luxembourg.[21] The information apparently did not alarm Brussels. However, on the night of the 10th, Belgian Intelligence noted intensive movements of German motorized troops toward the frontier and the General Staff, which foolishly had concentrated most of its forces on the *French* border, hastily moved them eastward to meet the threatened attack. The French were also alerted and on the nights of the 11th to 13th moved the units of Army Group 1 to the border in preparation for a dash into Belgium. As we have seen, Hitler *had* ordered an offensive in the West through Belgium to begin on November 12, but had postponed it because of bad weather and because his generals complained they were not yet ready.

Soon after the first of the year, beginning on January 10, 1940, there was a more serious alert. On that day two things happened that set it off. In Berlin at 5:30 P.M. Hitler issued the final order for the attack in the West to begin at 8:16 A.M. on January 17. Since November Holland had been added to his victims, though the main thrust, as in 1914, would be through Belgium. Earlier that day, at 11:30 A.M., a small German courier plane made a forced landing near the Belgian village of Mechelen-sur-Meuse, 10 miles north of Maastricht. When three Belgian soldiers arrived on bicycles to investigate, they found one of the plane's occupants, a Luftwaffe major, frantically trying to burn some papers which he was emptying out of his briefcase. A soldier stamped out the flames and seized the papers. The major and his pilot, also an Air Force major, were taken to the village military post where they identified themselves.

The pilot was a reserve officer, Major Erich Hoenmanns, and his passenger was Major Hellmuth Reinberger, a Luftwaffe staff officer. They told their interrogators they had got lost in the low clouds and fog on a routine flight from Münster to Cologne and had been forced to land when their motor stalled. The local Belgian commander, Captain A. Rodrique, in the meantime had spread Reinberger's papers on the table and when his back was turned momentarily the major quickly thrust them into a burning stove, which heated the room. Rodrique just as quickly snatched them out, badly burning his hand, but not before a good many sheets had been scorched beyond recognition. Major Reinberger appeared somewhat relieved, and well he might. For the papers in his briefcase had contained fragments of the highly secret German plans for the offensive set to begin on January 17, exactly a week off, though the date had not been filled in. While the papers were concerned with Air Force operations they indicated the general nature of the planned German attack which, as one document put it, was to roll westward "from the North Sea to the Moselle." Two or three sheets were specific. The German Sixth Army was to move through the Maastricht salient and destroy the Belgian forces to the West. Parachutists were to land behind the Meuse further south and take the bridges over that key defense line.

Back in Brussels the General Staff first considered whether the whole affair was a "plant," designed to make the Belgians and the French react strongly enough to reveal their plans for meeting a German offensive. But the nature of the documents themselves, the zeal with which Major Reinberger had tried to destroy them, the renewed military activity behind the German frontier, and the fact that other intelligence* had also warned of a

---

* Much of it came from Rome over the Christmas–New Year holiday. On December 26, Ciano, on the basis of a dispatch from the Italian military attaché in Berlin, warned the Dutch and Belgian ambassadors—"at the invitation of the Duce," he says—of an imminent German attack on their countries. On December 30 Ciano gave a similar warning to Princess Marie-José, wife of the Italian crown prince, and advised her to inform her brother, King Leopold. On January 2, 1940, Ciano noted in his diary: "I inform the Belgian Ambassador (Count de Kerchove de

German attack toward the middle of January convinced the Belgians that they were indeed in possession of part of the German plans for an imminent offensive. Early on the afternoon of January 11 General Van Overstraeten, the military adviser to the King and the actual leader of the army under Leopold, discussed the findings with the sovereign and with General Denis, the Minister of War. They agreed to warn General Gamelin at once.

At 5:15 P.M. Colonel Hautcœur, General Gamelin's liaison officer with the King, was called to the Palace, where General Van Overstraeten informed him of the contents of the seized German documents. But the Belgians were wily. General Van Overstraeten did not divulge how the papers had been found. And he contented himself with turning over to the French officer not copies or photographs of them but merely a two-page résumé which he himself had written out. Moreover he stressed that he was merely giving information to General Gamelin—"and to him alone"— as the military leader of the two countries which had guaranteed the "inviolability" of Belgium and that the Belgians would have to wait to see "whether the German plan respected that 'inviolability.' "[24] King Leopold, now as before, was anxious not to provoke the Germans. But he was worried that they might, without provocation, attack at any moment.

Apprised during the night by Colonel Hautcœur of the captured German papers, General Gamelin held an informal council of war on the morning of January 12 at his headquarters at Vincennes. Joining him there were Generals Georges and Doumenc, officers from the Air Force and Navy, and Colonel Rivet, Chief of Military Intelligence. Rivet was skeptical of the Belgian information. His office, he said, had not noted any "immediate preparations" for a German offensive. Gamelin declared that it would have been more helpful "if the Belgians had shown Hautcœur the originals of their documents or photographs of them and, in any case, if they had enlightened us more completely as to their nature." Nevertheless he gave the order for Alert Number 1 to Army Group 1 and to the Third Army on the left of Army Group 2 and to the units of the general reserve.[25] This comprised the main striking force of the French army. It was ordered to take up a position on the northern frontier preparatory to moving into Belgium on a moment's notice. Air force units in the south were alerted to be ready to fly to stations in the north.

Denterghem) of the possibility of a German attack on the neutral countries." Further tips from the Vatican and from Sweden confirmed the information to the Belgians.[22] Even before January 10 the German generals learned that the secret of the date of the planned offensive had leaked out. General von Bock, Commander of Army Group B, which was to carry out the main attack, told General Halder at Cologne on the 5th that the "enemy knew the date. Somewhere there is a leak." And on the 7th, after his return to Berlin from the front, Halder noted in his diary that "the adversary knows the date" and that Hitler had been informed. The next day the General Staff chief made one of his cryptic notes in his journal: "Telegram Kerchove (Belgium)–Italy." Hans-Adolf Jacobsen, the German authority on military papers, suggests that the notation "refers to a deciphered telegram from the Belgian Ambassador in Rome who had learned there of the offensive." No doubt this telegram resulted from Ciano's warning of January 2.[23]

There was little further news of importance from Brussels the next day. the 13th, and Gamelin spent most of it reviewing troops in Verdun. Nevertheless that afternoon General Laurent, the French military attaché in Brussels, who had been momentarily absent in Paris on the 11th, reported that the Belgian alarm was based on more information than was contained in the German documents taken from the plane. We now know what he was referring to. Late on January 13, the Belgian military attaché in Berlin, Colonel Goethals, got off a coded telegram to Brussels saying he had learned from "a sincere informer" that the Germans intended to attack the following day. According to General Oscar Michiels, who soon was to become the Chief of the Belgian General Staff, Belgian Intelligence knew who the "sincere informer" was. And though the general, in publishing his memoirs after the war, still did not think it "advisable" to name him, it can now be done from other sources.

He was Colonel J. Sas, the Dutch military attaché in Berlin, a close friend of Colonel Oster of the German Abwehr, from whom as we have seen, he was apprised of the planned German attack of November 16. Oster tipped him off again in January. In each case Colonel Sas had informed his Belgian colleague. General Michiels says it was Colonel Goethals' telegram on the late afternoon of the 13th, which confirmed the information taken from the downed German plane, that provoked the Belgian Command to issue an order a few hours later alerting its forces and informing them: "The German attack is almost certain for tomorrow morning at dawn." Orders were given that night to remove the barriers on the French frontier —a move which was to cost the Belgian army commander, General Van den Bergen, his job. The same evening the Belgian military attaché in Paris was instructed to inform General Gamelin that a German attack was "almost certain" for the morrow.[26]

Indeed the Belgian attaché, General Delvoie, arrived at General Gamelin's headquarters at 1:30 A.M. on the 14th to tell the generalissimo that "the attack is almost certain today, Sunday, January 14." Gamelin says he responded: "Are you going to call on us, then?" Delvoie answered that he had not yet received any orders "on that."

At the same early hour a dispatch reached the Quai d'Orsay from the French Ambassador in Brussels saying that Henri Spaak, the Belgian Foreign Minister, had summoned him in the middle of the night.

> He asked me to inform you immediately that according to all information in his hands the Belgian government considers a German attack probable today, Sunday, at dawn.

If the Germans did attack, Spaak said he would ask of France and Great Britain the assistance "stipulated in the Declaration of 1937."[27] Almost as much as the King and General Van Overstraeten, Spaak, the Socialist Foreign Minister, had been responsible for leading Belgium down the blind alley of neutrality. Now, frantically, he was, like the King and his military adviser, demanding that the Allies come to the aid of Belgium—if the Germans attacked.

For years General Gamelin had been trying to tell the Belgians that if they waited until the Germans invaded it might be too late for the Allies to bring help. In vain he had asked the Belgians for serious staff talks so that at least they could draw up plans to meet the German threat. He had also begged the Belgians to strengthen their defenses so that they could offer enough resistance to the Germans to hold them up while Allied armies rushed to their support. On September 1, 1939, the day the Germans moved into Poland, he had written Daladier about the Belgian "problem." Declaring that he fully understood the government's position that France must respect Belgium's neutrality he nevertheless pointed out:

If the Belgians only call on us at the moment when they are attacked by the Germans, there is no doubt that they lack the means of defending themselves until they are reinforced. And we would have to run the risk of a battle of confrontation with the difficulty of supporting their retreating armies. This would be an arduous task.[28]

Gamelin reveals that at the end of November 1939 the Belgians finally consented to what he calls "an exchange of ideas." In the interests of secrecy it was conducted not by the respective military attachés but by Colonel Hautcœur with the King of the Belgians. The French, he says, made their "suggestions" in writing and the Belgians responded verbally—"for fear," Gamelin adds, "that a document might fall into the hands of the Germans."* But the exchange did not go very far. For one thing, Gamelin observes, General Van Overstraeten, who dominated Belgian military and political policy, was said "not exactly to love us"—surely an understatement.

What General Gamelin really wanted, as he had made clear in his letter to Daladier on September 1, 1939, was for the Belgians to call in the Allied armies *before* the Germans attacked them so that he could organize an effective defense line in eastern Belgium. This would not only keep the Germans a considerable distance from the industrial regions of northern France but, once the Germans were stopped east of Brussels, give the Allies a strong position from which they could eventually mount a powerful offensive toward the German Ruhr, on which the enemy depended for the production of most of its guns and tanks.

Now in mid-January the French generalissimo thought that at last his opportunity had come. The Belgian King and government had advised Paris in the early morning hours of January 14 that the Germans might attack within a matter of hours. By the end of the day the alerted French army would be concentrated on the border, ready to answer the call of Belgium.

At ten minutes to four that afternoon Gamelin received a telephone call

---

* In his memoirs (Vol. III, p. 179 ff.) Gamelin gives the text of some of his "suggestions."

from Daladier. From London, Chamberlain had just informed the Premier that Admiral Sir Roger Keyes, a close personal friend of the Belgian king, was at the Palace in Brussels and that Leopold had told him he was ready to call in the Allied armies. Daladier wanted to know if Gamelin was ready to respond to the call.

My reaction is immediate. [Gamelin would later write]. I do not believe the Germans are really ready to attack. It is snowing and the aviation can do little. Conditions are not favorable for offensive operations by our enemies. We must now seize the occasion.*

Gamelin asked for a quarter hour to consult with Georges, Admiral Darlan, and General Vuillemin to see if they were ready. He then called Daladier back.

I told the Premier that in order not to lose a minute the order will be given to our troops to finish their concentration on the border tonight. Tomorrow they will cross over into Belgium—as soon as the authorization is given.

This looked like action at last, and Gamelin says the Premier was "happy" about the decision. A few minutes later Gamelin had what he calls a "disillusionment which wrung my heart." At 4:45 P.M. General Georges, who would command the Allied armies, telephoned him. He sounded troubled.

I've been thinking it over [Gamelin quotes Georges as saying]. Don't you think it would be better to advise the Belgians not to call on us? We're not entirely ready. Wouldn't it be best to wait until our aviation is stronger and our forces completely reorganized?

Gamelin recounts that though usually master of himself, he this time lost his temper. Finally, he says, he talked his reluctant general into agreeing that the move into Belgium should be carried out.†[29]

All now seemed ready. "For me," says Gamelin, "the die was cast— and in favorable conditions." It continued to snow during the night and the generalissimo felt that in such weather he would not have to fear German bombing of his troops streaming into Belgium. But when dawn came he was informed that the Belgians had not yet removed all the barriers on the frontier. They had not yet given permission to enter.

Gamelin was impatient. At 8:30 A.M. on the 15th he dashed off a letter

---

* The underlining is Gamelin's.

† General Georges, despite his hesitations, was named two days later, on January 16, Commander in Chief of Allied forces on the "Northeast front." Until then he had been Deputy Commander under Gamelin, and "designated" to command the Western front. This change did not clear up the confusion of the French High Command, which had three headquarters, one for Gamelin, a second for Georges, a third for General Doumenc.

to the Premier. The French troops, he said, had completed during the night their concentration on the border. "Now each hour lost can have grave consequences," he warned. He urged Daladier to make the Belgian government "face up to its responsibilities. I have already done that," he added, "with their High Command." At 11 A.M. he met with the Premier. It was agreed that they would give the Belgian government up to 8 P.M. to reply, though Gamelin complained that this was "very late" for his troops.

Immediately afterward Daladier called in the Belgian Ambassador, told him the French army was assembled on the border and waiting for the call to come into Belgium.

> You must tell us formally, yes or no, [Daladier said] if we can enter Belgium. If no, we shall go back to the *statu quo ante*. And let it be understood that in the case of future danger we shall reserve our attitude and the nature of our action. We will wait until 8 P.M.[30]

In Brussels the cabinet met all day without coming to a decision. It became obvious in Paris that the Belgian government and army were reluctant to take a step that would surely provoke a German attack and turn Belgium into a major battlefield. All day long the Belgians waited to see if the Germans would move. Since it was still snowing they began to believe that the attack had at least been delayed.

At 7:30 P.M. General Billotte, Commander of Army Group 1, telephoned French Headquarters that the Belgians were beginning to put back the barriers on the border. Half an hour later Daladier telephoned Gamelin. The Belgians had refused to call in the French army. The government explained "it could not take the responsibility of authorizing us to penetrate preventively into Belgium." The generalissimo was taken aback. "Once more," he told Daladier, "the Belgians have missed their destiny."[31] According to Colonel Minart, a staff officer at Gamelin's headquarters, the French High Command was "informally" advised by the Belgians "that if one of our soldiers stepped into Belgium he would be regarded as an enemy."[32]

So strong—and foolish—was the Belgian reaction that the Chief of the General Staff, General Van den Bergen, was cashiered by the King for having removed the barricades on the French frontier during the night of January 13–14. He was replaced by General Michiels. Indeed Van Overstraeten, the King's henchman—some would call him his evil genius—issued an order at noon on January 15, eight hours before the Belgian government replied to the French, ordering all barriers on the French border to be put back at once and reminding the field commanders that the order "still stood to repulse by force any foreign unit of whatever nationality which violated Belgian territory."[33]

The Belgians, like the other small neutrals in Europe, the Norwegians and Danes, for instance, remained stubbornly blind as to who their real enemy was—until it was too late. For this King Leopold and General Van Overstraeten bear a heavy responsibility, though it cannot be said that the government, and especially Foreign Minister Spaak, were much more far-sighted.* But the Belgian authorities had learned one thing from the January alert. The French concentration on the border and the readiness of the Western Allies to enter Belgium had shown them that, even if they continued to refuse to cooperate with Gamelin for mutual defense, they could count on help if ever the Germans did attack. What the Belgians refused to face was the stark fact that by then there would no longer be time.

News that a German plane had made an emergency landing in Belgium, that it carried secret military plans, and that it was not yet known whether the fliers had been able to destroy them reached Berlin late on the night of January 10. It caused consternation at OKW and sent Hitler into one of his customary tantrums. His first act the next morning was to cashier the Commander of Air Fleet 2, General Helmuth Felmy, and his Chief of Staff, Colonel Josef Kammhuber. They were sacked without an opportunity to be heard, though they were innocent. Every Luftwaffe officer knew that it was strictly *verboten* to carry military documents by air.†

Hitler conferred with Jodl and Goering over whether the attack set for January 17 should be postponed. It was finally decided that if the German plans had fallen into Belgian hands it was better to go ahead with them before the Belgians and French had time to react. At 6:45 P.M. on the 11th Hitler issued orders that the offensive would begin as planned, "at 15 minutes before dawn" on the 17th. In the meantime urgent telegrams

---

* On the night of January 16 Spaak called in the German Ambassador, Vico von Buelow-Schwante, to explain why Belgium had taken precautionary military measures. The documents captured from the German plane, he said, "contained clear proof of an intention to attack." However, Spaak appeared most conciliatory. "He could assure me solemnly and most earnestly," the Ambassador reported to Berlin, "that the Belgian government would never commit the folly of calling the Allies into the country."

It never seems to have occurred to Spaak, or to his government and his King, that the greatest folly of all was to bank on the Germans' not attacking France through Belgium, as they had done in 1914 and as the papers captured from the plane and other intelligence now showed they would do again.

I should like to add [the Ambassador concluded his dispatch] that a representative of the Court, who is very close to the King, who is himself of German extraction and whose pro-German sentiment is known, told me yesterday that the King would never permit the Belgian government to depart from the clear line of a neutral policy. . . .[34]

This dispatch must have been reassuring to Hitler and his generals, who since the previous October had been planning to smash the Belgian army on the way to France, and who in mid-January were on the point of carrying out their plan.

† Major Reinberger had intended to take the train from Münster to Cologne. But meeting Major Hoenmanns over a few beers at the officers' club at the Münster flying field on the evening of January 9 he had let himself be talked into having Hoenmanns fly him to Cologne on the following morning. The latter had explained he needed some flying time and had planned a flight to Cologne to get it and also to take some soiled laundry to his wife there.

were dispatched to Brussels and the Hague instructing General Ralph Wenninger, the Luftwaffe attaché for Holland and Belgium, who was in the Dutch capital, and Colonel Rabe von Pappenheim, the military attaché in Brussels, to interview the German fliers at once to ascertain whether they had destroyed all their papers.

By the 12th tension at OKW had risen considerably. Jodl saw Hitler that morning and conceded that "if the enemy is in possession of all the files the situation is catastrophic." Nervously they waited for the report from the military attachés in Brussels on their meeting with the downed flyers, which had been arranged for 10 A.M. The Belgian High Command was scarcely less nervous over the outcome of the confrontation. It was still not completely sure whether the documents it had come by were genuine, in which case the German threat was grave, or whether they were a plant. Belgian army electricians quickly installed secret microphones in the room where the Germans would meet. Thus it was that the Belgians heard the first, urgent question of General Wenninger to the two majors: "Were the documents destroyed?" And they heard the answer, which was not quite accurate, that they had been.* This was confirmation to the Belgians that the papers were not a plant.

Rushing back to the German Embassy General Wenninger got off an urgent wire to Berlin: "Reinberger reports that the courier baggage was burned down to insignificant fragments"—the "size of the palm of his hand," he added later.[36] Early the next morning, the 13th, General Wenninger was back in Berlin reporting to Goering: "Dispatch case burned for certain." Jodl, relieved, noted it in his diary. But he made a more important entry at 1:10 P.M.: "Order to Halder by telephone: All movements to stop." The start of the offensive was postponed "for two or three days."[37]

That evening came reports from Belgium and Holland that were described in German High Command quarters as alarming. The Belgians and the Dutch were ordering partial mobilization. They could no longer be caught defenseless by a surprise attack. Ruefully, OKW put the blame on "the considerable regrouping of the Sixth Army," which was to spearhead the attack through Maastricht and whose movements had been noted by the Dutch and Belgians. OKW concluded that the alert of the two neutral nations had also been caused by the "forced landing of our fliers" and by further intelligence "which pointed to a German attack."[38]

On January 15, when the new date had to be fixed for the attack, the weather reports were bad. More snow was predicted. Jodl argued that unless they could have at least eight days of good weather the offensive must be put off to spring. The next day Hitler, after some wavering, agreed, and at 7 P.M. on the 16th ordered the attack indefinitely postponed. From the German military papers it is clear that while the bad weather played a part

---

* The German Ambassador reported to Berlin: "It was taken for granted that the conversation was being overheard with listening devices. Consequently the content of the courier could not be discussed in detail."[35]

in the decision, as did the reluctance of the generals to launch an offensive in midwinter, the overriding reason for the postponement was Hitler's awareness that he could no longer have the benefit of surprise because of the swift reaction of Belgium and Holland, which undoubtedly would be quickly aided by the French. He told Jodl that "the whole operation would have to be built on a new basis in order to secure secrecy and surprise."[39]

The "new basis," which would be worked out in the greatest of secrecy during the next couple of months, was so completely different from the one now abandoned that Hitler's generals became confident it would catch the Allies completely by surprise. The German plan of attack for January 17 was exactly what the French High Command had counted on when it deployed its armies on the Belgian border three days before. It was merely a revision of the old Schlieffen Plan, which had nearly succeeded in 1914. It called for the main German thrust through Belgium north of the Ardennes Forest where seven of the nine available panzer divisions would spearhead the attack of Army Group B with its four motorized and 30 infantry divisions. Gamelin planned that January to meet it head-on east of Brussels along the line Antwerp-Dyle-Meuse with a force equal, if not superior, to the German except for armor. This consisted of Army Group 1, comprising the First, Second, Seventh, and Ninth French armies, and the British Expeditionary Force of 5 divisions, which would link up with the 15 divisions of the Belgian army.

Unfortunately for the Allies their plans of January, which had been agreed upon the previous November, remained frozen. It never occurred to Gamelin and his generals that the Germans, who, they believed, were not given to much flexibility or imagination, would drastically change the strategy which had been partially revealed in mid-January.

THE ALLIED PLANS TO MEET THE GERMANS IN BELGIUM

Ever since the time of the Romans the invasion route of the Germans to northern France lay through Belgium. "Geographical logic," Gamelin points out, "compelled Roman Gaul to construct its *'limes'* along the Rhine facing Germany."[40] Geography dictated the course of history here for the next couple of thousand years. The high and rugged mountain ranges of the Pyrenees, the Juras, and the Alps protected France to the southwest and the southeast. But west of the Rhine there were no natural barriers. Once over that broad and swiftly flowing river, the invader could move southwest through the plains of northern Belgium between the Ardennes Forest to the south and the confines of the lower Meuse to the north—from the line of Liège-Namur to the country of the Dutch.

Paul Reynaud, I remember, often recalled the historic invasion routes to his country and indeed he wrote an eloquent essay on the subject in his memoirs. It was through Belgium, he noted, that the Franks invaded Gaul, and that the army of Emperor Otto IV and his allies came, "the army which Philip Augustus cut to pieces on July 27, 1214, at Bouvines."

The dates and the battles clutter French history; the Spanish army in 1636 rolling into northern France from the Spanish possessions in Holland-Belgium, "creating such alarm in Paris that the population hooted Richelieu in the streets, while the bourgeois of the city fled in panic toward Chartres and Orléans." Century after century the invasions came until there was hardly a town or village in Belgium and northern France that did not have a monument marking the place of a crucial battle. The formidable Condé turned back the Spaniards once more at Rocroi, and Louis XIV the armies of Marlborough and of Prince Eugène before Paris at the beginning of the eighteenth century. From Belgium the Anglo-Prussian armies after Waterloo swept down to capture Paris. And still alive in the memories of most Frenchmen was the great sweep of General von Kluck's army through Belgium in 1914 which nearly reached the French capital in September and was only turned back at the Marne a few miles to the northeast.

Not only, as Reynaud points out, were the Belgian plains the easiest to traverse for an invading army but they offered the shortest route. Sedan, on the Belgian frontier, is twice as close to Paris as is Strasbourg at the German frontier on the Rhine.[41] Now, in the spring days of 1940, Reynaud, the Premier, and Gamelin, the Commander in Chief of the Anglo-French armies, were sure that the Germans would come again by the historic route through Belgium. The question had long been raised whether the invaders should be met in Belgium or behind the defenses of the French frontier. Pétain himself, while Minister of War in 1934, had given the answer of the French Army. When questioned on that by the Military Committee of the Senate on March 7 he had replied bluntly: "It will be necessary for us to advance into Belgium."*

When? And how far? In 1934 this presented no problem since Belgium and France had a military alliance and the General Staffs of the two countries, working closely together, had agreed that as soon as there was "political tension" and Belgium seemed threatened by Germany, French armies would move into Belgium and take over the defense of the line Arlon-Liège and provide support for the Belgian forces on the Albert Canal. But in 1936 Belgium, at the instigation of the young King, had reverted to neutrality. The military alliance was abrogated, the staff talks ceased and the Belgians informed the French that any penetration of their soil would be met by force. In 1937 both the Western Allies and Germany gave solemn assurances that they would respect the inviolability of Belgium and come to her assistance if attacked. King Leopold evidently regarded the word of Germany, despite the lesson of 1914, as as good as

---

*It was at this session that Pétain made a statement about the Ardennes which would later haunt him. "The forests of the Ardennes," he said, "are impenetrable, if one makes special dispositions there. . . . The enemy cannot commit himself there. If he does we can pinch him off when he emerges from the forests. Thus, this sector is not dangerous." Until it was too late, Gamelin held the same opinion.

that of France and Great Britain. A close study of the records makes it clear that while the Anglo-French governments and General Staffs never contemplated entering Belgium unless they were called, or unless the Germans attacked her, both the German government of Hitler and the German High Command by the middle of October 1939 were planning to march through Belgium to get at France, and that only one single German general objected on moral grounds.

Thus the problem for the Allies when the war came in 1939 of how far to penetrate into Belgium to meet a German attack depended for its solution on a number of conditions: whether the Belgians called them in time, whether they mobilized their army beforehand and strengthened their fortifications sufficiently to be able to slow up the German advance, and whether the Belgians agreed to prior staff talks to concert a common defense. Without such talks it would be impossible to allot fronts for the various armies, organize their lines of supply and communication, prepare defense lines in the proper places, and set up ammunition depots where they would be needed. But this necessity was not much appreciated in Brussels, where it was feared that staff talks and preliminary preparations would be used as an excuse by the Germans to launch an attack.

There was also disagreement within the French High Command and between the French and British General Staffs as to how far to advance into Belgium in any case. On the eve of the war the two Allied commands, however, appeared to reach a general understanding on how far to go. At a meeting in London at the beginning of May 1939, they concluded that in case of war the Anglo-French armies should advance at least to the line of the Scheldt river in western Belgium, and, if possible, if the Belgians called them in time, as far as the Albert Canal near the German border. Actually a middle solution was finally agreed on as best: to meet the Germans on the Antwerp-Brussels-Namur line, provided there was time to reach there and organize a proper defense. At this meeting, the British, according to a French officer's report of the meeting, took the lead in advocating an advance into Belgium.[42]

But by the time the war started they had second thoughts. Early in September 1939, while the powerful French army was going through the motions of a phony "offensive" in the Saar ostensibly to relieve German pressure on Poland, the British Chiefs of Staff advised their government that unless the Belgians agreed to let the Allies in before the Germans attacked it would be "unsound" to advance into Belgium. They were "strongly of the opinion that the German advance should be met in prepared positions on the French frontier."[43]

But General Gamelin could not accept that. At the end of September 1939 he won over the British to agreeing to go into Belgium as far as the Scheldt—if the Belgians consented. On September 30 he issued "a personal and secret instruction" providing for the French and British armies to advance to the Scheldt and, "if the circumstances permitted," to push

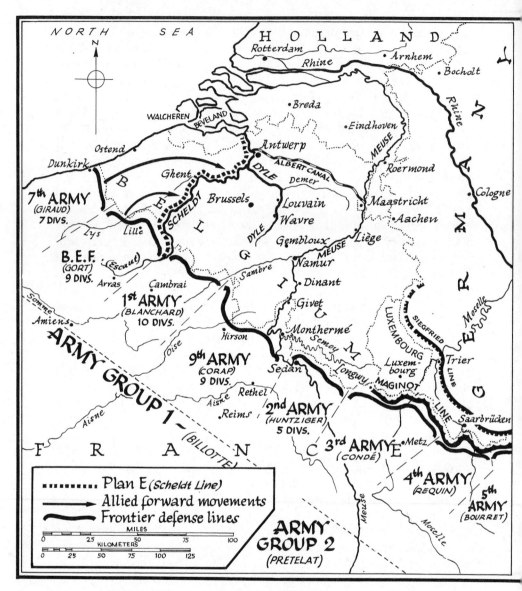

MILES

0   25   50   75   100

KILOMETERS

0   25   50   75   100   125

.... Plan E *(Scheldt Line)*
⟶ Allied forward movements
〰 Frontier defense lines

ALLIED PLAN "E" FOR ENCOUNTER IN THE WEST
AUTUMN 1939

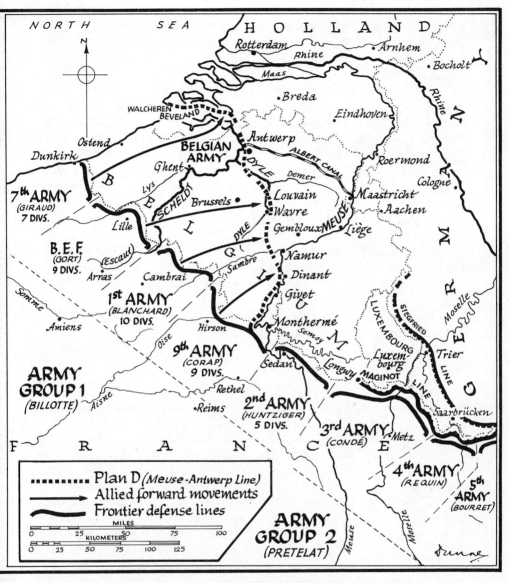

ALLIED PLAN "D" FOR ENCOUNTER IN THE WEST
AUTUMN 1939

60 miles further east to the Antwerp-Dyle-Meuse line. The advance to the Scheldt was known as Plan E (for the Escaut river, as the French called the Scheldt). The further advance became known as Plan D (for the Dyle river, which would form part of the line). The generalissimo stressed that the second position would be occupied "only if the Belgians called in time."

The turning point in fixing—and unfortunately, freezing—Allied strategy came in mid-November 1939, when a German offensive in the West seemed imminent and indeed, as we have seen, was planned by Hitler to begin. On November 5 Gamelin instructed General Georges that since Holland also was threatened the Allies advancing to the Scheldt would have to cover the mouth of the river northwest of Antwerp and occupy the Dutch islands of Walcheren and the Bevelands. If "the situation permits," the instruction added, the British and French armies would push further eastward from the Scheldt to join the Belgians on the line of Antwerp-Louvain-Wavre-Namur. The British again objected to going so far into Belgium and in a series of meetings that began November 9 Gamelin tried to convince them of the soundness of his plan. Finally, on the 13th, he informed them that the French Command insisted on sticking to it.[44]

The next day, the 14th, he met with his principal French commanders at La Ferté-sous-Jarre to assure their agreement. General Georges, who would command the operation, had doubts about the wisdom of pushing to the advanced line.

We can not push on from the Scheldt to the Antwerp-Namur position [he argued] unless the Command feels . . . it can reach the position *before* the enemy and organize it before the enemy is able to attack it in force.*[45]

The following day, nevertheless, on November 15, General Gamelin issued his "Personal and Secret Instruction No. 8," laying it down that because "of the evolution of the military situation in Belgium marked by its new measures of defense against Germany" Allied troops would not stop at the Scheldt but push forward as rapidly as possible to the Antwerp-Namur position and there organize in force. Though the generalissimo, perhaps with an eye to history, inserted several qualifications—"that it was hoped there would be time to carry out the forward move . . . if the Belgians called . . . and if the situation permitted it," his order of November 15 nevertheless surprised some of his generals, who thought the usually prudent Commander in Chief was becoming somewhat reckless and that perhaps this was due to a desire to counter charges that he lacked the offensive spirit.[46] Some of these officers felt that the push so far into Belgium to meet the Germans was beyond the capacity of the Allies, who were inferior to the enemy in armor, transport, reserves and

---

* General Georges' emphasis.

air power, and that, moreover, it incurred the danger of being caught elsewhere with inadequate forces if the main German blow should come at another part of the front.

These considerations weighed heavily on General Georges. He watched Gamelin's increasing boldness, at least in strategic planning, with growing misgivings. On November 23, at a meeting of Army Group 1 commanders at Arras, at which Georges was not present—he says he was not invited[47] —Gamelin pressed for a "study" of the problem of pushing still further into Belgium to the Albert Canal and also of sending the Seventh Army, which previously had constituted the strongest and most mobile reserve he had, north of Antwerp into Holland at least as far as Breda to forge a link between the Dutch and Belgian defenses. General Henri Giraud, commander of the Seventh Army, and General Billotte, who commanded the Army Group, raised serious objections. They pointed out that the Belgians had refused staff talks with the Dutch, as they had with the Allies, so that a common defense north of Antwerp could not be planned, and that moreover, because of the weakness of Dutch defenses, the Germans would get to Breda before the French. Billotte also rejected the proposal to advance from the Dyle to the Albert Canal unless the Belgians held out there long enough to enable the Allies to reach it in strength, which seemed unlikely.

On December 5 General Georges forwarded the "studies" of the two generals to Gamelin with a few words of his own which touched the heart of the problem and pointed out a danger that was to become only too real when the great battle finally came.

The problem is dominated by the question of available means. There can be no doubt that our defensive maneuver in Belgium and Holland will have to be conducted with the thought that we must not be drawn into engaging in this theater, in face of a German move which might be merely a diversion, the major part of our available forces. If for example, the main enemy attack came in our *center* [Author's emphasis] on our front between the Meuse and the Moselle, we could be deprived of the necessary means to repel it.[48]

This warning must be kept in mind when we come to the course of battle, for Gamelin's disregard of it would have fateful consequences.*

On November 17 the Allied Supreme Council, meeting in Paris, approved Gamelin's Plan D to push the Franco-British armies to the Dyle-

---

* Actually, at the beginning of the war Gamelin seems to have felt instinctively where the principal German blow would come. Major L. F. Ellis, in the official British history of the war in France in 1939–40, reveals that early in October 1939 General Gamelin told General Ironside, then Chief of the Imperial General Staff, that he expected the main German offensive to come through the Ardennes "sweeping south of the Meuse . . . against the whole length of the Belgian frontier, south of the Meuse to Namur, then across the Meuse and south of the Sambre to Charleroi." Gamelin does not mention this conversation in the three volumes of his memoirs, but it is clear from his papers that whatever he thought in October about where the weight of the German thrust would come, by November and thereafter he no longer thought it would come in the center.[49]

Meuse line. Chamberlain and Daladier agreed that "given the importance of holding the German forces as far east as possible, it is essential to make every endeavor to hold the line Meuse-Antwerp in the event of a German invasion of Belgium." The Dyle plan, as Colonel Lyet stresses, had become the "charter" of Allied intervention in Belgium. It did present many advantages. For the British it promised to keep German air bases at a considerable distance from the homeland and, even more important, prevent the Germans from threatening the channel ports opposite their shores. For the French it kept the Germans away from the northern industrial and mining regions, which had been lost to the enemy in the first weeks of the first war. For Gamelin, inferior numerically in first-line troops and armor to the Germans, it shortened the front by 35 miles and offered a means of slowing up and perhaps stopping the enemy onslaught before it could gather momentum. Moreover, it added to his combined strength the 20 divisions of the Belgian army. The generalissimo realized some of the disadvantages: the risk of confronting the Germans in the open field before his troops had time to organize their position, and the difficulty of meshing the Belgian army into his Allied forces because of the refusal of the King to allow prior staff talks or even to fully inform him of his operational plans and the state of his defensive positions.

What the French Commander in Chief did not seem to realize was that his own plans had to be kept flexible to meet the changing circumstances of war. In the spring of 1940, for example, the French High Command learned that the Dutch, because of the lack of cooperation from Belgium and because of their own weaknesses, had decided to withdraw their scanty forces from south of the Meuse and concentrate on defending Fortress Holland around Amsterdam, Rotterdam, and The Hague. This robbed the mission of the French Seventh Army of any purpose, since it would have to enter southern Holland where there were no Dutch forces with which to fight and which the Germans would quickly overrun. General Giraud again complained about so fruitless an operation and General Georges, who wished to have the Seventh Army held in reserve, agreed. "It's an adventure," he warned Gamelin. "If the enemy feints in Belgium he can maneuver elsewhere. Thus, we should not engage important forces in this affair. Let us avoid dreaming."[50]

But Gamelin insisted. On March 12 he ordered Georges to stick to the Dutch operation and despite renewed objections by Georges, Billotte, and Giraud over the next few weeks he made it final on April 15. The mission of the Seventh Army in Holland would be carried out. "We have to give a helping hand to the Dutch," he explained. But, as Georges had tried to point out to his chief, this left the forces that were to advance into Belgium and Holland without a single army in reserve. In fact, with eight French armies and the British army deployed on a front extending from Switzerland to the sea, there was no single army left to be held in reserve any place—only scattered divisions. This omission by Gamelin was later to baffle the experts on both sides and to confound Churchill. As late as April 14 Georges had pleaded with Gamelin to keep the Seventh Army in reserve and send a corps of two divisions from some other unit into Holland if the generalissimo still insisted on that operation. The Seventh Army, with six crack infantry divisions, largely motorized, and one light armored division, and commanded by Giraud, who was regarded as one of the most capable and energetic of the French commanders, would, if held in reserve, be invaluable in plugging any gap once the fighting started. Generals Georges, Billotte, and Giraud were now afraid it would be wasted.

Gamelin's inflexibility also led him to dismiss Georges' warning that the Germans might feint in northern Belgium and deliver their big punch in the center below Namur. Like Pétain before him, Gamelin considered that the rugged, wooded hills and narrow, winding roads of the Ardennes east of the Meuse above Sedan were obstacle enough to prevent any large army, and especially any sizable armored units, from coming through it. He made no special plans to defend there. Worse, he kept his weakest army, the Ninth, at the vital hinge just north of Sedan on which the Franco-British armies wheeling into Belgium would pivot. The vulnerable Ninth Army would have to face a good part of any enemy forces that might emerge from the Ardennes across the Meuse.

Gamelin's insensitivity as to where the Germans might concentrate their attack is all the more incomprehensible in view of the information that came to him. All through the late winter and early spring there were signs, backed by Intelligence, that the center of gravity of the German forces was shifting from the north toward the south. From the end of November to the end of January, Allied Intelligence counted an increase of German divisions on the Belgian and Luxembourg frontiers from 25 to 57 divisions. Moreover, by March, seven of the ten German panzer divisions had been located as being in a position to move westward *south* of Liège. Thus by March the deployment of German troops and armor definitely indicated that the chief enemy thrust would come in the center of the front roughly between Sedan and Namur, the sector to be held by the fragile Ninth Army.

This was now corroborated by other intelligence. On March 8 King Leopold informed his cabinet ministers that all his information pointed to the chief German thrust coming "through the Ardennes toward Dinant–Saint-Quentin with the object of cutting off the Allied armies in Belgium from Paris and rolling them up in the Pas-de-Calais." Moreover the King instructed his military attaché in Paris to inform General Gamelin of this and to stress his "certainty, based on documentary evidence, that the principal axis of the enemy maneuver would be oriented perpendicularly on the Longwy-Givet front." On April 14 General Van Overstraeten repeated the warning, adding that it now seemed evident that the Germans hoped to draw the Allied forces into Belgium and there destroy them from the south by armies coming through Luxembourg.

Three weeks before this, on March 22, Colonel Paillole, chief of the German section of French Counterintelligence, reported to the Deuxième Bureau that German Military Intelligence had suddenly begun to study the routes from Sedan to Abbeville, at the mouth of the Somme, endeavoring to ascertain what weights the bridges could carry, what water obstacles there were, how good the roads were for heavy traffic, and so on. He concluded that "an attack through Belgium toward the Channel is imminent."[51] There is no record that Gamelin paid any attention to this intelligence. The Ninth Army, woefully lacking in first-line troops, transport, antitank and antiaircraft guns, and possessing no substantial armor, was not strengthened.

Nothing was done at the headquarters of Gamelin or Georges to alter their plans in order to counter a heavy German attack between Sedan and Namur. Not even when on the last day of April the French military attaché in Berne, Switzerland, one of the best sources for news of what the Germans were up to, warned the French High Command not only of the new date set for the German offensive but exactly where its strong point would be. The attack, he said, was set for May 8–10 and Sedan would be "its center of gravity." This gave Gamelin and Georges ten days to revise their plans and redeploy their troops, but again they did nothing. So certain was the French military attaché of his information that he sent his assistant to General Headquarters at Ferté to make sure that the two top generals got the message.[52]

But they do not appear to have been impressed by it any more than they were by certain "hard" information furnished them. In March German engineers had begun in great haste to throw eight pontoon bridges across the middle Rhine between Bonn and Bingen, and on April 1 Antoine de Saint-Exupéry, the French writer and pilot, had photographed them from his Bloch 141. So many pontoon bridges in this sector clearly indicated where the Germans intended to strike hardest with their armor and motorized troops. And the Germans made it all the more clear a few days later when army engineers threw several pontoon bridges halfway across the Moselle and Ohr rivers on the border of Luxembourg, provoking panic in the Grand Duchy, which was defenseless.[53]

THE GERMANS CHANGE THEIR PLAN

The shifting of the center of gravity of the German divisions from north to south and the mounting Belgian and Allied intelligence that Hitler would launch his main offensive across the Ardennes against Sedan in the middle of the front accurately reflected a fundamental change in the German plan of attack in the West.

The change came gradually and was the subject of bitter controversy among the German generals themselves and between them and Hitler, who now regarded himself as the warlord. The original plan for *Fall Gelb* (Operation Yellow), the code name for the attack, as hastily drawn up in October, was, as we have seen, a variant of the famous Schlieffen Plan, which the Germans had tried to follow in 1914. It called for the main German drive to be carried out by the right flank sweeping through Holland, Belgium and northern France and driving the Allied forces back to the Channel and then south to the Somme. Its objectives were more modest than those of the Schlieffen Plan. The latter had envisaged the German right-wing armies, after the march across Belgium and northern France, heading south to the Seine and then turning east *below* Paris to roll up and surround the French armies and destroy them. The objective of the plan of October 1939 was merely to beat back the Allied armies in Belgium and northern France and occupy the Channel ports and the Dutch coast, securing air and naval bases from which to harass and blockade the British Isles. From a study of Hitler's various harangues to his generals that autumn it seems clear that he believed that after such a blow Britain and France would be inclined to make peace and leave him free to turn his attention to the East, that is, to Russia.

To General Gerd von Rundstedt, Commander of Army Group A on the middle of the front, and to his gifted Chief of Staff, General Erich von Manstein, this limited objective was not nearly good enough. To be sure, they resented the secondary role assigned to their Army Group, which, with only 22 divisions, none of them armored, was merely to protect the flank of Army Group B, operating to its north, against a French counter-attack from the southwest. Army Group B, under the command of General Fedor von Bock, with 43 divisions, including 9 armored and 4 motorized, was to deliver the main blow in northern Belgium.

Whatever professional jealousies were involved, Rundstedt and Manstein passionately believed that even if successfully carried out the October plan fell far short of the objectives necessary to defeat and destroy the main enemy, the French army. As Manstein put it:

> It contained no clear-cut intention of fighting the campaign to a victorious conclusion. Its object, quite clearly, was *partial* victory (defeat of the Allied forces in northern Belgium) and *territorial* gains (possession of the Channel coast as a basis for future operations). [Manstein's emphasis][54]

What Rundstedt and Manstein demanded was a plan not only to defeat the Allied armies in Belgium and drive them back but to destroy them. On October 31 they forwarded an entirely new proposal, signed by Rundstedt, to General Walther von Brauchitsch, Commander in Chief of the Army. "The success of the whole operation," Rundstedt argued, "depends on whether it will be possible completely to defeat and *annihilate* the

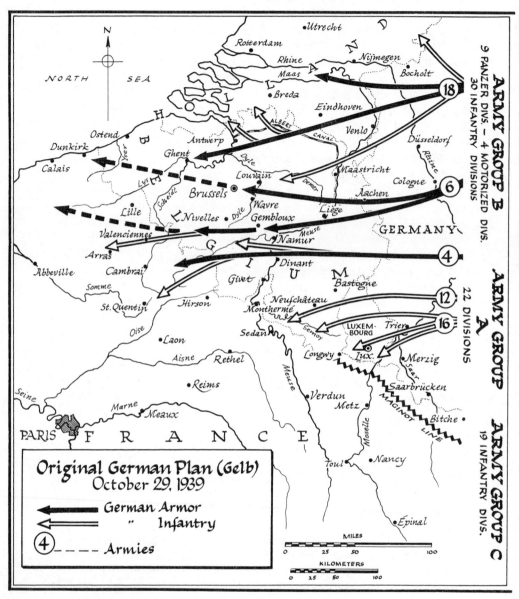

ORIGINAL GERMAN PLAN (GELB) FOR ATTACK IN WEST
OCTOBER 29, 1939

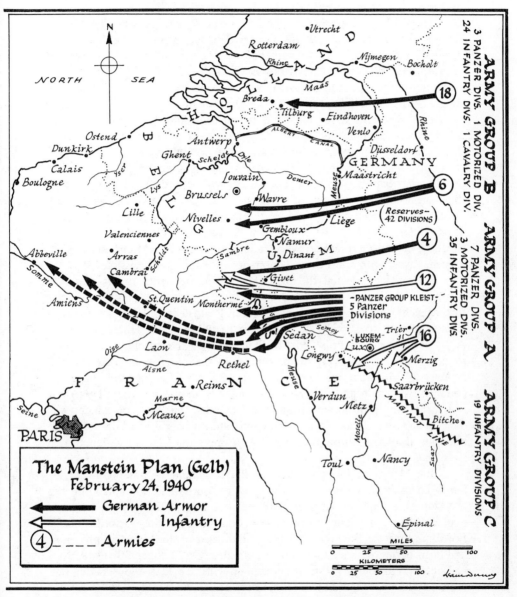

THE MANSTEIN PLAN (GELB) FOR ATTACK IN WEST
FEBRUARY 24, 1940

enemy forces fighting in Belgium and north of the Somme, not merely to push back their front line." [Rundstedt's emphasis][55]

They therefore proposed that the main weight of the offensive be shifted south from Bock's Army Group B in the north to their own, that Army Group A be greatly strengthened with additional infantry, motorized and armored divisions taken from Bock, and that it strike through the Ardennes across the Meuse to the sea at Abbeville, thus cutting off the Belgian, British, and French armies in Belgium. In the meantime a weakened but aggressive Army Group B would draw the Anglo-French forces into northern Belgium and slowly beat them back until they were attacked in the rear by Rundstedt's forces after the breakthrough and destroyed. Naturally, Rundstedt conceded, his bold plan was not without risks, but on the other hand it was the only one which promised total victory. "Both the danger and the chance of great success," he wrote, "lie with Army Group A," his own. In the back of the minds of Rundstedt and Manstein, as of Hitler, was also the thought of Russia. "To expend the offensive capacity of the German army on a *limited* victory," Manstein says he argued, "was, with the Soviet Union at our backs, indefensible."[56]

Brauchitsch rejected the plan. Halder, as he wrote in his diary on November 1, found it "lacking in positive aspects." Moreover, despite further pleas over the next few weeks from Rundstedt and Manstein, Brauchitsch refused to submit the new plan to OKW or to Hitler. Both the Army commander and his Chief of Staff resented the interference of Manstein, who was a relatively junior officer, in their high-level planning. On January 27 Manstein was removed as Rundstedt's Chief of Staff and given command of an infantry corps in the interior of the country. Though it was technically a promotion Manstein concluded that his replacement was due "to a desire of the Army High Command to be rid of an importunate nuisance who had ventured to put up an operation plan at variance with its own."

But Manstein, though exiled to the command of a second-rate infantry corps far from the front, did not give up. On February 17, on the occasion of a luncheon given by Hitler to five newly appointed corps commanders, he got a chance to propose his bold plan to the warlord himself. For some time the Fuehrer, though not informed of the Manstein proposal, had been toying with a somewhat similar idea. On October 30, 1939, Jodl had noted in his diary: "Fuehrer comes up with new idea about having one armored and one motorized division attack Sedan via Arlon." On November 9 Hitler had again brought the subject up and approved the formation of a strong armored corps to carry it out, with General Heinz Guderian, the leading tank commander, to lead it. On February 13 he had a long talk with General Jodl about the whole plan for the offensive. He feared, he said, that the mass of German armor would be wasted "in an indecisive place" and probably halted on the Maas (as the Germans called the Meuse) "by the barricaded and fortified positions of the enemy." Hitler thought it would be better to employ the bulk of the armored and motorized divisions "at Sedan, where the enemy would not be expecting our main blow." He added that the enemy, through the documents captured from the German plane on January 10, undoubtedly had been strengthened in its belief that the chief German thrust would come further north in Belgium and in Holland. Though Jodl argued back that an attack on Sedan would be a "gamble where one could be surprised by the God of War"[57] it is obvious that Hitler was receptive to the ideas of Manstein when, after the luncheon on February 17, he invited the corps commander to his study for a private talk.

For one of the few times in his life the Nazi dictator listened without interrupting, as the young general exposed in detail his plan to deliver an overwhelming blow by Army Group A through the Ardennes on both sides of Sedan and across the Meuse and then across northern France to Abbeville, cutting off the Allied forces in Flanders. After their destruction the rest of the French army would be enveloped and destroyed "with a powerful right hook." Hitler listened, asked a few questions and then agreed. "The man," he said later, "is not my cup of tea, but he certainly knows what should be done."[58]

Brauchitsch and Halder too had come around in favor of the new plan. The next day, February 18, they had a long talk with Hitler, and Halder produced a plan that went even further than Manstein's. The Chief of the General Staff had not only overcome his objections to the new proposal but now became enthusiastic about its promise of destroying the main Allied armies in Belgium. To accomplish a knockout blow on the Meuse between Sedan and Namur he would halve Bock's Army Group B in the north, and double Rundstedt's Army Group A in the middle, giving it, in all, four armies, 45 divisions and most of the armored and motorized units. This formidable force would strike on a narrow front on the Meuse between Sedan and Namur and drive to the sea—all within a few days. On the same day Brauchitsch informed the "surprised" generals, as one report recounts, who were to lead the operation, of the fundamental change of plan. On February 24 the Army High Command issued final orders for the new *Fall Gelb*, with instructions that the drastic redeployment of troops, massive and complex as it was, must be completed by March 7. Extensive measures were outlined to camouflage the move and to mislead the enemy into believing that the initial German plan, the gist of which had fallen into their hands on January 10, was being adhered to.

Thus as spring came in 1940 both sides staked their fate on the playing of one card. Unfortunately for the Allies, the German card seemed the better. The Germans were going to hit the French where they least expected it. Gamelin, by insisting on throwing the best of his forces into central Belgium, was walking into a trap. He did not of course know this, but he had received plenty of warning from General Georges that it was at least possible and in March and April he had been shown intelligence that made it seem at least probable. Part of the enigma of Gamelin, the most intellectual of the generals on either side, lies in the rigidity of his views that fateful spring. He was believed by all who knew him—and by the Germans—to possess a subtle mind. But as far back as November his mind had become frozen in a plan that he refused to reconsider in the light of ensuing developments. And he had resisted considering any alternative plans, though as a veteran high-level staff officer and also commander of troops in the first war he knew—he says so repeatedly in his memoirs—that all wars are full of surprises. This inflexibility, shared by almost all the officers of the French High Command, remains inexplicable to this day, though we have seen some of the younger officers such as de Gaulle continually complaining about the hardening of the arteries in the older generals.

The German military records make clear that the German generals had a healthy respect for the French Army and for Gamelin himself. Manstein speaks of the "reputation General Gamelin enjoyed with us," and General Guderian says that his fellow officers were aware that "France possessed the strongest land army in Western Europe and the numerically strongest tank force" and that "French tanks were superior to the German both in armor and gun caliber." Hitler in his talk with Brauchitsch and Halder on February 18 stressed that he had "no clear idea whether the enemy would automatically march into Belgium when the Germans attacked" and warned that they might not. But Guderian claims that the French Order of Battle showed that they would. He also declares that the German High Command felt it could rely on the "rigid doctrine" of the French Command. "These French strategic and tactical principles," he adds, "were well known to us in 1940."

From their Order of Battle [he wrote] it was plain that the enemy expected the Germans to attempt the Schlieffen Plan once again, and that they intended to bring the bulk of the Allied armies against this anticipated outflanking movement through Holland and Belgium. A sufficient safeguard of the hinge of their proposed advance into Belgium by reserve units—in the area, says, of Charleville and Verdun—was not apparent. It seemed that the French High Command did not regard any alternative to the old Schlieffen Plan as even conceivable.[59]

The accuracy of the German view of French strategy was shown again in mid-April. At a meeting of the War Committee in Paris on April 9, convoked principally to consider countermoves to the German invasion of Norway that morning, Admiral Darlan, as we have seen, had suggested that the Allies take advantage of the enemy's preoccupation in the North and move into Belgium, if its government agreed. General Gamelin and General Georges readily approved. Reynaud later claimed that he asked the two generals whether such a move was wise "in view of Germany's twofold superiority in aviation and effectives." If he did put that question, Gamelin subsequently testified, it escaped the notice of the generalissimo. This was the germ of an ensuing controversy between the two men, Reynaud contending that he always opposed the move into Belgium and Gamelin insisting that the Premier had never objected to it in his presence.[60]

Be that as it may, both are in accord that the War Committee finally agreed unanimously to ask the Belgians for permission to enter. Later the same day at a meeting of the Allied Supreme Council in London the British government associated itself with the decision, and the Anglo-French ambassadors in Brussels were instructed to make the necessary *démarches* in Brussels. Gamelin supported the diplomatic steps with a plea of his own to the Belgian King and General Staff and followed it up with another telegram on the 11th urging their acceptance. He asked for a definite reply by 4 P.M. so that the Allied armies could start moving "this very night."

Late in the evening came the reply. Once again the Belgians refused to allow the entry of Allied troops. They backed up their decision by rushing two divisions toward the French frontier and mining the roads and bridges behind it. "Once again," moaned Gamelin, "the Belgians have missed an opportunity." The folly of the Belgians, who knew that the Germans already had concentrated on their border a massive army and who believed they knew too, as the King had warned, where it would strike through their country, was evident. It was all the more so in the light of what was happening this very week in two other small countries, Denmark and Norway, whose neutrality had not saved them from German aggression and which, like Belgium, were not strong enough to resist successfully alone.

Once more Gamelin had showed the Belgians that he was ready to come to their aid, not only to help defend them but, as he believed, to put the Allied armies in a better position to meet the Germans. He also showed that his plans to do so, frozen since the previous November, were no longer subject to change. As May came, and with it fresh warnings not only that the Germans were about to strike, but where, he clung stubbornly to a rigid course of action that his own commander of the front, General Georges, had little faith in, that the Premier apparently frowned upon, and that in the light of some of the latest intelligence from Belgium and Switzerland that the enemy planned to hit hardest around Sedan, at the weak hinge of his forces pivoting north to the Dyle line, risked disaster.

DISARRAY IN PARIS

At this critical point, in the first lovely days of May, the Premier of France was down with the flu, his scatterbrained mistress was trying ineptly to carry on for him, Pétain was weighing his political future, Generals

Gamelin and Georges were feuding over strategy and over who should actually command in the coming battle,* and the two men who dominated the armed forces, Daladier, the Minister of Defense, and Gamelin, the generalissimo, were at odds with the head of government who, they knew, was trying to replace them. The government was shaky enough. Was the Army any better off? Was it prepared to meet a German onslaught? Not in the opinion of de Gaulle.

On May 3 the irrepressible colonel, busy as he was trying to scrape up tanks, guns, and men for the new Fourth Amored division which he was to command, got off another—and last—warning to Reynaud about the deplorable state of the Army.

Today there is no longer any possible military operation except that founded on mechanical force, as the events of Poland and Norway have proved. . . . Now, the French military system is conceived, organized, armed and commanded contrary in principle to this law of modern warfare. There exists no more absolute and urgent need than that of radically reforming this system.

The Army, he said, "will not reform itself of its own accord." The state would have to do it. What France needed, he said, was a Carnot,† and Reynaud "alone" was capable of doing what the great revolutionary had done.[62]

In the next few days Reynaud, in a way, would try, but it was too late. As General Armengaud, he who had returned from observing the Polish campaign and tried in vain to induce the High Command to absorb its lessons, pointed out:

Ideas with which one has lived a long time cannot be modified in a few days. To handle the new arms in new forms of war it would have been necessary to have new chiefs, who knew the use of these arms from experience and knew how to employ them—men of the following generation, younger by at least ten years.[63]

As it was, if the great battle came soon, the French Army would have to get along with the aging generals who believed that what they had learned between 1914 and 1918 was good enough for 1940.

Some weeks before, the right-wing deputy Pierre Taittinger and a fellow deputy, both members of the Chamber's Army Committee, had reported glaring weaknesses in the position around Sedan, the vital hinge of the pivot into Belgium. On March 8 and during the following days they had inspected the positions there and found that work on fortifications

---

* André Maurois quotes a British general, whom he does not name, on the relations of Gamelin and Georges at this time: "They are so busy making war on each other they have no time to make war on the Germans."[61]

† Lazare Carnot, one of the leaders of the French revolution, a military engineer, helped organize the republican armies and was hailed by many as "the architect of victory."

was lagging not only because of the severe winter weather but because of "the hesitations of the Command." The army brass gave, in their opinion, "an exaggerated importance to the natural obstacles of the Ardennes forest and the Meuse river."

> The defensive measures in this sector are rudimentary, not to say embryonic. . . . In certain works the concrete has not yet been poured. . . . Along the approaches the minefields which have been laid, the destructions which are envisaged, and the resistance of the blockhouses cannot hold up the enemy for more than an hour.

The deputies said they "trembled" at the thought of what a German attack would do in this sector. A mere visit to it had "left sad memories," and they recommended that "urgent measures be taken to strengthen it while there is still time."[64]

The report of the deputies was rebuffed in a mocking tone by General Charles Huntziger, Commander of the Second Army, which was deployed around Sedan. In an answer to General Georges, who had called his attention to it, he wrote sarcastically that "Taittinger seemed badly informed" and that the deputy's observations "could have been of great importance if we had awaited them before organizing our position." General Huntziger insisted that the advanced defenses north of Sedan "would considerably slow down the progress of the enemy and seriously retard him in making contact with the main defensive positions."

"I believe," the general concluded, "that *there are no urgent measures to take for the reinforcement of the Sedan sector.*"*[65]

It was in this sector, it will be remembered, that the Manstein plan called for an overwhelming strike by German armor. It would not be long before General Huntziger would rue his complacent words and seek to expunge them from the record.†

---

* The italics are mine. Strangely enough, General Huntziger apparently even opposed certain measures to strengthen the defenses of Sedan. A deposition made at the Riom Trial by an artillery officer, Major Cahier, and about which Daladier testified at the trial of Pétain (this time calling him Major Caillet) casts some light on this, though it seems almost unbelievable. The artillery officer deposed that on the Second Army front no supplementary fortifications could be built without the prior assent of General Huntziger, who never even responded to such requests without a delay of several weeks. But he seems to have gone further. Major Cahier told the court of how, with the approval of his immediate superiors, he constructed strong tank obstacles on the two main roads leading from the Ardennes forest into Sedan. The roads, hemmed in between the escarpment of the steeply rising hills and the river, were easily defendable if tanks could be held up by suitable barriers. The major finished the obstacles in March. General Huntziger, he testified, got wind of them and on May 3 ordered them demolished. A week later the German panzers came that way.[66]

† According to Reynaud, General Huntziger, when he later became War Minister of the Vichy regime, tried to remove this letter from the military archives. Thanks to the "vigilance," Reynaud says, of an officer in the Historical Branch of the Army, it was preserved.[67]

On May 4, the day after receiving de Gaulle's letter, Reynaud decided to get rid of General Gamelin. Feeling well enough after a week in bed with the grippe to leave his private apartment on the Place du Palais-Bourbon he went to the Quai d'Orsay, convoked Colonel de Villelume, his military counselor, and his two cabinet secretaries, Dominique Leca and Gilbert Devaux, and instructed them to draw up a detailed indictment of the generalissimo. He planned to read it to his cabinet, hoping that it would convince his ministerial colleagues that the hesitant Commander in Chief would have to go.

The drafters were a curious trio, but somewhat typical of the men whom the Premier now attracted around him. Colonel Marie-Joseph-Victor Paul de Villelume had for the past ten years served at the Foreign Office as a liaison officer between it and the High Command, at first dealing mostly with problems of disarmament, which had been the subject of so many conferences at Geneva. But when that subject fell into desuetude after Hitler began his feverish rearmament, the colonel, having taken a liking to the world of diplomacy, lingered on at the Foreign Ministry, and was passed by for promotion in the Army. Somehow his diplomatic status seems to have given him an exaggerated opinion of his qualities as a soldier. He disliked Gamelin, considered him incompetent, and even before Reynaud became Premier had taken it upon himself to convince Reynaud that the generalissimo ought to be replaced. Now, since March, he had redoubled his efforts. He was only too pleased to be asked to draw up an act of accusation against the Commander in Chief.

Leca and Devaux were more shadowy figures. Former Treasury officials, as were Baudouin and Bouthillier, they had been brought over from the Finance Ministry when Reynaud left that post to become Premier. Leca was a Corsican and somewhat of a *condottiere*. Devaux was intelligent, but some found him sly and even underhanded. According to Pertinax, he "was attached to Leca as was Pylades to Orestes."[68] Among other things they were adept at speech-writing, and they now joined the colonel in drafting the indictment. Reynaud added his own touches to it and by the morning of May 8 it was ready. The Premier called a cabinet meeting for the following day.

Early on the morning of May 9 he went to the Elysée Palace to apprise the President of the Republic of what he intended to do. The excitable Lebrun was horrified. He begged Reynaud not to provoke a cabinet crisis, for Daladier was sure to oppose dropping Gamelin and would resign before accepting it. With the news of German military action so menacing this was no time to have a change of government and further divide Parliament and the country.

Had the emotional President of the Republic known the facts behind the "news," he no doubt would have been even more upset than he was. And perhaps the Premier too. Time was running out for them faster than they knew.

First, there were the last-minute warnings received by the Belgian and Dutch military headquarters. On May 3 Colonel Oster of the German *Abwehr* told his friend, Colonel Sas, the Dutch military attaché in Berlin, that the attacks against the Netherlands and Belgium had been set for the next few days and, weather permitting, probably would begin on the 8th. The Dutch government promptly informed Brussels. Eleventh-hour warnings already were being received in the Belgian capital from other sources. On May 4 the papal Nuncio informed the King that the Vatican had learned the German offensive was imminent. Two days later the Pope confirmed this in Rome to Princess Marie of Piedmont, who informed her brother, King Leopold.* On May 8 two coded dispatches to Brussels from the Belgian Embassy in Berlin brought further confirmation. Viscount Davignon, the Ambassador, reported that the Wilhelmstrasse was drafting an ultimatum to Belgium, and the military attaché advised that the order for launching the offensive in the West had just been given by OKW. On the evening of May 9 Colonel Oster and Colonel Sas dined together— for the last time. The anti-Nazi intelligence officer confirmed that the attack had been set for dawn the next day. Sas tipped off his Belgian colleague and informed The Hague by prearranged code.†[69]

Actually, as the captured German documents revealed after the war, Hitler on May 1 had set the date for the attack for May 5 and then, largely because of bad weather, postponed it several times. On May 3 he put it off

---

* The Germans suspected the Vatican. On May 7 General Jodl noted in his diary: "Fuehrer greatly agitated about new postponement as there is danger of treachery. Talk of the Belgian envoy to the Vatican with Brussels permits the deduction that treason has been committed by a German personality who left Berlin for Rome on April 29." The Germans tapped the telephone lines that went over Germany between Rome and Brussels. The identity of the "German personality" who went to Rome remains unknown. In January, as we have seen, the German generals had noted a similar leak from Rome.

† I have been unable to establish how much, if any, of this information received from May 3 to 9 was passed along by the Dutch and Belgians to the Allied governments and Commands. French Intelligence was deluged with reports of when and where the Germans would strike, but it discounted them and on the 9th reported nothing "abnormal" behind the German lines. Ambassador Bullitt in a dispatch to Washington on May 3 indicated the situation as Paris saw it. "So much information reached French government recently regarding forthcoming attack on Netherlands," he cabled, "that French government convinced this information being put out by German government and it's considered probable that Hitler will turn his attention to Yugoslavia and Hungary before attacking the Netherlands." No mention of Belgium. As late as May 8 Bullitt was reporting that Reynaud and Léger continued to believe that Hitler's next move would be in the Balkans."[70]

And yet on the night of May 7–8 a French Air Force pilot, Colonel François, returning with his squadron from dropping leaflets on Düsseldorf, reported seeing a German armored column stretched out for more than 60 miles, the headlights of its vehicles shining brightly through the dark, headed for the Ardennes. At this time, though the war had been on for nine months, the French and British air forces were not permitted to drop on Germany anything more lethal than a pamphlet. So though there was no question of bombing the column the colonel promptly reported his discovery to his commanding general as a piece of important intelligence. His superiors refused to believe it.[71]

to the 6th, not only because of the weather but because the Foreign Office didn't think his proposed justification for violating the neutrality of Holland and Belgium was good enough. The next day he set May 7 as X-Day and on the following day postponed it again to the 8th. By then, as General Jodl recorded in his diary, the "Fuehrer has finished justification for *Case Yellow.*" Belgium and the Netherlands were to be accused of having acted most unneutrally. On May 7, just as his train was about to leave Berlin for the front, he again called off the attack. On the 8th, we learn from Jodl's diary: "Alarming news from Holland. Canceling of furloughs, evacuations, roadblocks, other mobilization measures. . . . Fuehrer does not want to wait any longer. Goering wants postponement until the 10th, at least. Fuehrer is very agitated; then he consents to postponement until May 10, which he says is against his intuition. But not one day longer. . . ."

On May 9 at noon Hitler set the attack definitely for 5:35 on the morrow and at 9 P.M. the irrevocable code word that set the German military juggernaut in action—*Danzig*—was flashed to the military commanders in the West. At dusk Hitler set off in his special train for his new headquarters, which he called *Felsennest* (Eyrie) near Münstereifel, 25 miles southwest of Bonn.

MAY 9, 1940, PARIS.   FRANCE WITHOUT A GOVERNMENT OR A GENERALISSIMO

Paul Reynaud returned to the Quai d'Orsay from the Elysée Palace at 10:20 A.M. on May 9, determined, despite President Lebrun's objections, to depose Gamelin and to resign if his cabinet overruled him. The other members of the government were waiting and at 10:30 the cabinet meeting began. In a "total silence," as Baudouin, who kept the minutes, noted, the Premier, his face pale and drawn and his voice hoarse from the week-long attack of flu, read for two hours the indictment of Gamelin which he and his aides had drawn up. It dealt exclusively with the Allied fiasco in Norway. While Reynaud did not gloss over British responsibility for it, he dwelt mostly on the failure of the French High Command in general, and of Gamelin in particular, to take resolute action to help counter the German invasion of Norway.[72]

Because of his sore throat Reynaud at the beginning had requested his colleagues to refrain from smoking. Halfway through the reading of his paper he noticed one of the ministers lighting a cigarette. "I beg you not to smoke," Reynaud admonished him. "I have a very bad throat." And indeed, according to Monzie, who recounts this incident, the Premier, his voice becoming increasingly hoarse, finished his reading only by a supreme act of willpower. On and on he read, piling up his case against Gamelin. "It's an execution," Monzie says Lucien Lamoureux the Minister of Finance, whispered to him.[73]

Reynaud finished reading his indictment of Gamelin at 12:30 P.M. If France continued with such a generalissimo after such shortcomings had been revealed by the handling of the Norwegian affair, he said, "we are certain to lose the war." He asked that the cabinet agree to his naming a new Commander in Chief. The request was met by utter silence. No one spoke up. "It is time," Reynaud finally said, "that each member face up to his responsibilities." At length Lamoureux spoke. The Premier, he said, had convinced him "of the impossibility of leaving General Gamelin at the head of the French armies." Then everyone turned to Daladier, Minister of Defense, and Gamelin's protector. He finally found words. He blamed the British for the fiasco in Norway. It was they who had command of the operation there. Gamelin was not responsible. As for the Franco-German front, he explained it was the "desire" of the French government not "to fire it up at present," even though the British did not "shrink" from that. France needed more time to rearm. He said he considered Gamelin "to be a great military chief."

He has tremendous prestige and a very fine military past. His great intelligence is recognized by all. And he is much more active than a great number of men of his age.

Daladier said he regretted that Gamelin had not been given a chance to defend himself. He also regretted the "grave criticisms" of the general voiced by the Premier before so many persons, even if they were cabinet members. He opposed the Premier in wishing to replace the generalissimo.[74]

Reynaud appealed to the other members of the cabinet to state their opinions but none spoke up. Daladier's stand however was decisive. "In view of such grave opposition," the Premier said, "I shall have to consider the government as having resigned." He asked his colleagues to keep it secret until a new cabinet could be formed.[75]

Gamelin learned during the afternoon of the "bitter criticism" of his command by the Premier. "Once again," he says, "I wrote out my resignation." He did not wish, he adds, to be the cause of a new political crisis.

At 1 A.M., at his command post in the Vincennes dungeon, he was awakened. A message had come in from a French agent behind the German lines: "Columns marching westward."[76]

As the greatest army ever assembled by the Germans to attack France —136 divisions, ten of them armored, backed by a formidable air armada— prepared to strike at dawn, the French Republic was without a government and without a commander in chief of its armed forces.

29

THE BATTLE OF FRANCE, I:
THE ARMIES CLOSE IN
MAY 10–15, 1940

The spring in Paris had never been lovelier. The chestnut trees along the broad avenues and the Seine were in bloom. The gardens of the Tuileries and the Luxembourg blossomed in all the bright fresh colors of May. The skies were cloudless. There had been no rain for weeks. The Parisians sunned themselves on the terraces of the sidewalk cafés along the broad Champs-Elysées and a hundred other boulevards, avenues, and streets. The stands at Auteuil were full for the annual spring racing, and betting was heavy. Crowds flocked to the spring art exhibition at the Grand Palais. The cinemas and theaters played to full houses. The windows of the great jewelry shops in the rue de la Paix sparkled with diamonds and other gems, and inside business was good. In the gilded corridors of the fashionable Ritz on the Place Vendôme, where before the first war Marcel Proust had often stationed himself to observe the comings and goings of high society, chicly dressed women paused to converse before going in for tea or lunch. Some were in uniform, among them the Duchess of Windsor, who ran a canteen for the troops. The writer Clare Boothe Luce, who had noted the presence and appearance of the Duchess in the Ritz, found the May days in Paris "insanely beautiful . . . the air sweet . . . the unstartled birds singing in the gardens . . . the flower market at the Madeleine madly colorful. . . ."[1]

On Friday, May 10, 1940, when the Germans struck, Paris awoke, one newspaper editor wrote, "in a bath of sun," and afterward he remembered "how carefree and lighthearted" everyone in the beautiful capital seemed to be—even when their radios began to blare out the first bulletins telling of a massive enemy force striking from the North Sea to the Rhine against Holland, Belgium, Luxembourg, and northeast France and of how the great German offensive had been opened at dawn by a thousand bombers attacking the airfields in the West.[2]

At 5:30 A.M., General Georges, Commander in Chief of the Northeast Front, alerted General Billotte to get ready to move his Army Group 1 into Belgium. At 6:30, informed that Belgium—at last!—had called for help, General Gamelin, Commander in Chief, telephoned Georges.

"Well, General, is it the Dyle operation?" the latter asked.

"Since the Belgians are calling on us," Gamelin replied, "do you see what else we can do?"

"Obviously, not," Georges said.[3]

Five minutes later Georges issued to Billotte an order that set his five armies of Army Group 1 into motion. General Giraud's Seventh Army was to speed north to Holland as far as Breda. General Lord Gort's 9 divisions of the British Expeditionary Force and General Blanchard's First Army were to sweep forward to the Dyle line between Louvain and Namur. General Corap's Ninth Army was to pivot northwest of Sedan and take up a position on the west bank of the Meuse as far as Namur. The left flank of General Huntziger's Second Army, already in position at the vital hinge of the great turning movement at Sedan, was to strengthen its Xth Corps there. Five light cavalry divisions—each half horse, half tanks— of the Ninth and Second Armies were to push rapidly across the Meuse to slow up the enemy moving westward through Luxembourg and the Belgian Ardennes Forest toward the river line. Army Group 1 was, on the whole, a formidable force. Yet military historians later would recall the hesitant words on the telephone early that morning of France's two top commanders as an omen for the outcome of the great battle now quickly shaping up.

General Georges, as we have seen, had been somewhat skeptical of moving so far into Belgium, fearing a trap. General Gamelin, who had conceived the operation in the belief that the Germans would strike through central Belgium around Liège, as they had in 1914, seemed, however, confident, even optimistic. At the last moment the German offensive had saved him from being cashiered—and Reynaud from resigning. At 7 A.M. the Premier sent a message to the generalissimo: "The battle has begun. Only one thing counts: to win it. We shall all work together toward that goal." Gamelin replied immediately: "*Monsieur le Président,* I see only one answer to your message. France alone counts." The feud of the day before was forgotten.

Yet Reynaud's confidence in his Commander in Chief had not been fully restored. At 7:30 A.M. Baudouin arrived at the Premier's apartment and found him dressing. "Gamelin has been saved," Reynaud said. "At last he has got the battle he has been waiting for—indeed hoping for. . . . Well, we'll see what Gamelin is worth." Baudouin describes the Premier as being "uneasy and nervous."[4]

Certainly not Gamelin that morning. Captain Beaufre, on a mission from General Headquarters at Montry, presided over by General Doumenc, saw the generalissimo shortly after 6:30 A.M. and found him striding up and down a corridor of gloomy Vincennes displaying "a martial and satisfied air such as I had never seen in him. . . . He appeared absolutely confident of success in the operations which he himself had conceived and now had launched."[5]

Gamelin himself confirms it. "I confess," he wrote later of his feelings on May 10, "that I believed in victory. I felt sure we could stop the Germans. . . . I had confidence in the Army."[6] Pierre Jacomet, General Secretary of the Ministry of Defense, saw Yves Bouthillier that afternoon. "If you had seen, as I did this morning," he told him, "the broad smile of Gamelin when he informed me of the direction of the enemy attack, you would have no cause for worry.*[7]

Actually, the generalissimo did not know that first day of battle the direction of the main German attack and never found it out, despite repeated warnings, until it was too late. He stuck doggedly to his preconceived strategy, unmindful of a famous remark of Moltke, the victor over France in 1870, whom he must surely have read since he was an avid student of military history, that "a mistake in the initial deployment of an army can never again be made good in the whole course of the war." Joffre, to be sure, had disproved that in the Battle of the Marne in 1914, and Gamelin, as phlegmatic as his chief, had helped him.

Before the German strategic surprise came the first tactical surprise. Despite all the warnings, the French army was caught napping on the early morning of May 10. Ten to fifteen percent of the troops of the front line units were away on home leave. When on the evening of May 9 Major Baril of the Deuxième Bureau called the *Etat-Major* of General Colson, Commander of the Forces of the Interior, to urge that all soldiers on leave be recalled urgently, he was told: "Why do that? They will not have to fight tomorrow. Germany is in the process of disintegrating."[9] In any case, it was too late—a refrain we shall hear often in the narrative of the next few days.

It is true that French Intelligence had been flooded for months with reports that the Germans were about to attack, and they had not attacked. The reports received were often conflicting. On May 9 for example the Deuxième Bureau was warned: "Get ready! Attack tomorrow at dawn!"[10] Yet the same day the Bureau reported that beyond the frontiers of Holland

---

* Colonel Pierre Lyet, the brilliant quasi-official French military historian, after a study of the confidential military documents not yet available to the outside, concluded that, contrary to what was said and written later, the High Command on May 10 was "highly optimistic" about the ability of the French Army to handle the Germans. The communications of Gamelin that spring, says Lyet, showed "the absolute confidence of the Commander in Chief and the total absence of a doubt, a reservation, and of any fear whatsoever of a setback." Summing up all the evidence, Lyet concludes: "For the generals Gamelin, Georges, and Billotte, the eventuality of a German attack on the Western Front was envisaged with confidence. There can be no doubt about the opinions of these three top chiefs: *the French Army was capable, at the very least, of stopping the enemy.*"[8]

and Belgium there was no sign of "abnormal German movements." Two reconnaissance flights of the Royal Air Force had been carried out there and the pilots reported seeing nothing unusual.[11]

"I can assure you," General Gamelin later told the Parliamentary Investigating Committee, "that we did not know during the day of May 9 that the Germans would attack the next day. We had no previous sign of it."[12]

No wonder the French army was caught by surprise. A number of front-line units were off to training exercises and target practice. The entire staff of the *Etat-Major* of the Second Army, which guarded Sedan, journeyed to Vouziers on the evening of May 9 to see, as one participant put it, "a very agreeable play put on by the Army theater. We got back to headquarters at 2 A.M. and were sleeping the sleep of the just when we were awakened at 5 o'clock with the news that the Boches were racing through Luxembourg and advancing toward us."* General Prioux, who commanded the First Army's Cavalry Corps and who was assigned to be the first to get away into Belgium, had spent the day of May 9 at Sissonne, far behind the frontier, directing target practice. He was awakened at dawn at Saint-Quentin, 45 miles south of the border, by German bombs falling nearby. "No one foresaw the storm," he said. Like everyone else he was taken completely by surprise. He sped toward the border to get his cavalry moving.

The dawn attacks of the Luftwaffe on the airfields of northern France had done little damage. According to General d'Astier de la Vigerie, Commander of the French Air Force on the front of Army Group 1, 4 of his planes were destroyed and 30 damaged. Forty out of 400 attacking German planes were shot down.[14] One Royal Air Force field at Condé Vraux was put out of commission when 6 of its 18 Blenheim bombers were destroyed and the rest damaged and its oil depot and offices set on fire.[15]

What concerned d'Astier most that first morning of battle was the orders he received from on high. At 8 A.M. came the first word from General Georges' headquarters: "Limit air activity to pursuit and reconnaissance." Bombing, for the moment, was not permitted! No matter that the Germans had been bombing since the break of day and that Allied scouting planes reported dense columns of German troops crossing the frontiers of Holland, Belgium, and Luxembourg, which made easy targets. There was to be no Allied bombing until further notice. After a morning of storming and protesting, d'Astier finally—at 11 A.M.—got permission

---

* This was General de Barrel, a nonparliamentary member of the postwar Parliamentary Investigating Committee. He was questioning General Gamelin on why he was taken by surprise. Gamelin argued that it was "impossible" to know what the Germans were up to until they actually attacked.[13] But was it? All through the night of May 9 German columns stretching back from the border for 75 miles to the Rhine and beyond were on the march, the headlights of their thousands of vehicles burning brightly. They were heading toward the Ardennes. Two nights before, as we have seen, a French pilot had spotted some of the columns. Apparently on the crucial night of May 9–10 no French or British air reconnaissance was carried out. At least, no record or mention of one has come to light.

to bomb the enemy columns. But General Vuillemin, the ineffectual Air Force chief, laid it down that no *"agglomerations"* were to be bombed "at any price." Since the Germans were constantly moving through towns and villages, the air general thought this was a terrible handicap. Besides, the Germans were bombing Dutch and Belgian towns at will. D'Astier recounts that a massive Franco-British bombing of German columns had long been prepared for the first night of a German offensive, and during the day the signal was given to carry it out that evening of May 10. Not only were all available French and British bombers in France to participate but an even larger contingent from Bomber Command, whose planes were based in Britain. D'Astier says that the orders of General Georges made the operation impossible and it was called off.[16] Understandably, the pages of the Air Force general's book are full of scorn of the French High Command's lack of understanding of air warfare, and peppered with instances of it.*

The Army generals became even more scornful of the Air Force. They claimed they never saw its planes, that the sky indeed was empty of them in the crucial hours when their ground troops were pinned down by murderous German bombing.† The French Air Force, inferior in numbers to the Luftwaffe, in fact never fully employed the planes it had—and this at a moment when Reynaud, Gamelin, and Georges were hysterically appealing to London for more British aircraft to help stop the enemy's incessant air attacks. Actually the French had more modern, first-line planes on hand at the end of the battle than at its beginning, a fact that "mystified" Gamelin and certainly mystifies the historian.

Simultaneous with the bombing, the German army struck, as day broke, across the frontiers of neutral Holland, Belgium, and Luxembourg, whose inviolability the German government had solemnly guaranteed. Chancellor Hitler, like Chancellor Bethmann-Hollweg in 1914 in regard to Belgium, regarded Germany's word as a "scrap of paper."

Speed and surprise and heavy bombing were the keys the Germans

---

* General d'Astier begins an early chapter of his book with an account of General Gamelin interrupting a lecture in 1939 of General Crochu at the Centre des Hautes Etudes Militaires to proclaim: "There is no such thing as a battle of the air. There is only a battle of the land." There are other quotations on the subject from General Gamelin that perhaps d'Astier did not hear of. In 1938, when questioned about the lack of planes, he is said to have replied: "We have practically no planes? No matter; we will make a war without them." Frédéric Dupont, a member of the Chamber of Deputies Army Committee, deposed that one day toward the end of July 1939, a month before the war broke out, he expressed his concern about the Air Force and that Gamelin replied: "The Air Force will not play in the next war the role which certain military commentators foresee. It will very quickly lose its effectiveness as a result of using up of its materiel and personnel. It will burn itself out in a flash."[17] Gamelin later denied saying this.

† General d'Astier de la Vigerie entitled his book in defense of the French Air Force "The Sky Was Not Empty"—*Le Ciel n'était pas vide*.

counted on to open the way for quick victory. The day had scarcely dawned before General Hans Graf von Sponeck's 22nd Airborne Division, supported by 4,000 of the 4,500 parachutists of General Kurt Student's 7th Parachute Division, descended on the Dutch airfields and approaches to vital bridges, especially those leading across the Maas (as the Meuse was known to the Dutch and Germans) estuaries to Rotterdam. Before noon they had secured strong positions within "Fortress Holland" around The Hague and Rotterdam and seized the bridges at Dordrecht and Moerdijk before they could be blown. This sealed the fate of Holland. Within five days General Georg von Kuechler's Eighteenth Army of six infantry divisions, one horse cavalry division (the only one in the German Army), and the 9th panzer division drove a hundred miles across Holland and linked up with the airborne troops. It was all over for the Dutch, who laid down their arms at dusk on May 14 and formally capitulated the next morning. The Queen and the government, whom the Germans had made elaborate plans to capture, had fled The Hague on the 13th aboard two British destroyers, which carried them to London and exile.

Further south, where more important battles were to be fought, General Walter von Reichenau's Sixth Army, which formed the southern flank of General Fedor von Bock's Army Group B (the northern flank was engaged in Holland), pushed across the Maas (Meuse) in the region of Maastricht and drove toward the Belgian first line of defense on the fortified Albert Canal.* Comprising seventeen infantry divisions and General Erich Hoepner's XVIth Armored Corps of two panzer divisions and one motorized infantry division, it was deemed a powerful enough force to lure the Allies into central Belgium east of Brussels in the belief that, like Kluck's army in 1914, it was about to strike the main blow.

To the south of the German Sixth Army, between Liège and the Moselle, the forces of General Gerd von Rundstedt's Army Group A struck across the borders of Belgium and Luxembourg. This was the main striking force of the German army, designed to obtain the great breakthrough in the center of the Allied line, roll up the Allied armies in Belgium, and bring, as Manstein had predicted, quick and complete victory. It comprised five armies, forty-four divisions, of which seven of the ten available panzer divisions were to provide the armored wedge. It was supported in the air by General Hugo Sperrle's Third Airfleet of 2,000 fighters and bombers. Crashing through the feeble Belgian defenses southeast of Liège, General Guenther von Kluge's Fourth Army of eleven divisions, spearheaded by General Hermann Hoth's XVth Armored Corps of two panzer divisions, the 5th and 7th (the latter commanded by a then unknown general, Erwin Rommel), headed for the Meuse river crossings between Namur and Dinant. To the south of them the principal armored wedge quickly cut through Luxembourg, which was undefended, and the heavily wooded and rugged Belgian Ardennes, which Pétain and Gamelin had believed to

---

* The author followed the Sixth Army during part of its drive through Belgium.

be "impenetrable" by tanks. This was General Ewald von Kleist's Armored Group consisting of five panzer divisions and three motorized infantry divisions. General Georg-Hans Reinhardt's XLIst Armored Corps of two panzer divisions drove toward the Meuse between Revin and Monthermé. General Heinz Guderian's XIXth armored corps of three panzer divisions made for Sedan.

Taken by surprise, the Allied armies were slow in getting organized and taking off on May 10. Many units were stationed some miles below the Franco-Belgian frontier and it took some doing to get them as far as the border the first day. Many divisions were broken up, some troops dispatched by road in trucks, others by rail (on which the French Command counted to a surprising extent, as in the first war), while others slogged it out on foot. Part of one division of General Giraud's Seventh Army heading toward Antwerp and Holland was transported by sea. It was 10 P.M. before the first railroad trains were assembled on the frontier. A whole day had been lost. Because of the Belgian refusal to work out prior plans with the Allies, it was difficult to find Belgian locomotives to haul them. Colonel Zeller, arriving by car at Brussels at 1 P.M., could find no one in the Ministry of Defense competent to advise him about rail transport. He was sent off to the King's headquarters at Fort Breendonck near Antwerp, where at 3 P.M. he finally was able to tell the Belgian Command that French trains would be ready at the frontier by 10 P.M. and needed locomotives to speed them on.

At some points on the border the Belgians, though their King was crying for help, had neglected to remove the obstacles that blocked the roads. It took the French Second Light Cavalry Division an hour to clear the demolitions and obstacles before it could get into Belgium to advance against the Germans pouring through the Ardennes. One unit of the British Third Division was unable to persuade a Belgian officer to remove the frontier barrier. He demanded "a permit to enter Belgium." Finally the British charged through it with heavy trucks and the division finally got under way.[18]

The French High Command had ordered the troops to move only by night to avoid losses from bombing. But since there were only eight hours of darkness at this time of year most units, when they could, ignored the order and proceeded by day. To the surprise of the High Command there was little bombing of their armies on the march. Gamelin and Georges would have been even more surprised had they known why.

They had estimated that they needed five to six days to reach the Dyle line east of Brussels and, to the south, the Belgian part of the Meuse between Givet and Namur, and prepare positions to halt the German offensive. Despite all the delays, a good part of the Allied cavalry and light armored divisions reached the line before midnight of May 10 and the next morning pushed a covering screen forward beyond the Dyle and Meuse. But the artillery and infantry were still far behind. The French and British Commands, nonetheless, were quite confident. The move into Belgium was going pretty much on schedule, which was not based on undue speed. In the French Seventh and First Armies, and in the British Expeditionary Force in between, General Billotte, chief of Army Group 1, felt he had a powerful force concentrated on a relatively narrow front—some 55 miles. Counting the immediate reserves, which followed on closely behind the main forces, it was 30 divisions strong, and contained the cream of the French Army—all three of the light armored divisions, two out of three of the heavy armored divisions, and two thirds of the independent tank battalions, motorized artillery and antiaircraft groups. It was considerably superior in numbers, guns, and even armor to Reichenau's Sixth Army driving westward to meet it. And it had, in addition, the bulk of Belgium's 22 divisions.

The two French armies, the Ninth and Second in the center, which formed the southern flank of Army Group 1, were much weaker. They were made up mostly of Series B divisions—older men with little new training—and were woefully short of armor, antitank and antiaircraft guns, and motorized transport. Indeed General Corap's Ninth Army, in the vital sector on the Meuse between Sedan and Namur, toward which the Germans were rapidly rushing with their seven panzer divisions, was having difficulty in getting its northern flank into position below Namur. Most of its units had to march on foot, and Corap, thinking there was plenty of time, was following orders by advancing only under cover of darkness. On the left flank of the Second Army, defending Sedan, General Huntziger had deployed his weakest formation, the Xth Corps, whose three divisions on May 10 were in the process of redeployment and were in no position at the moment to give serious battle. But their commanders did not expect it would be necessary for several days, if then. They had been given reason by the High Command to believe that theirs was a secondary front and that the main battle was shaping up in the Belgian plains farther north. They assumed that was why they had been given the poorest and least well-armed troops.

THE RIVAL STRENGTHS

The two opposing armies which on May 10, 1940, began hurtling toward a headlong clash on the storied battlefields of Flanders and France were, contrary to a widely held opinion then and since, and partly fostered by certain French generals anxious for an alibi for what happened, fairly evenly matched except in the air.* In numbers they were roughly equal.

---

* Thus General Georges, who was in direct command of the Allied forces in the battle, would write on December 10, 1946, in an introduction to a book full of alibis by his Chief of Staff, General G. Roton, that "in spite of the passionate discussions on the comparative effectives and armaments of the opposing sides, no one

While the generals and military historians on both sides give varying and contradictory figures about their own and the enemy's strengths, it is possible to make a fair comparison. General Gamelin, who ought to know about his own forces, gives the total Allied strength on the Northeast Front as 144 divisions and the German as 140 divisions. Hans-Adolf Jacobsen, who has made the most exhaustive study of German sources, gives the strength of Hitler's armies in the West as 136 divisions and that of the Allies as 137 divisions. The difference is not great.

How strong was the French army itself, which constituted the principal Allied force? Gamelin gives the total number of French divisions on the front as 101, including 3 light armored divisions, 4 armored divisions (the fourth was not available until May 16), and 5 light cavalry divisions (half horse, half tanks). To his 101 French divisions he adds 11 British divisions (of which one, the First Armored, did not arrive in France until the end of the month), 22 Belgian divisions, and 10 Dutch divisions, for a total of 144 Allied divisions. Lieutenant Colonel Lugand, in a study based on the archives of the French Army, puts the actual strength of the French Army a little higher. He lists 92 infantry divisions, 6 light and heavy armored divisions, and 6 cavalry divisions for a total of 104 divisions, to which he adds the equivalent of 10 more divisions of fortress troops manning the Maginot Line and other fortifications, or a total French force of 114 divisions.

If Colonel Lugand's figures for the French Army are correct, the Allied armies, when the British, Belgian, and Dutch forces were added to it, totaled 157 divisions. The Germans had 136 divisions. Whichever way the Allied strength is calculated, its forces in the West that morning of May 10 were not outnumbered.

The figures must be broken down further to ascertain the relative strengths of the armies that clashed on the active front. Foolishly, Gamelin and Georges tied down on the Maginot Line and the upper Rhine, which the Germans did not attack until they were turned, nearly a third of their forces—36 divisions, including one British division. Against them the Germans had only 19 mediocre infantry divisions of Army Group C. On the active front, where the Battle of France was decided, I have tried to work out from French and German sources the actual strengths of each side. General Billotte's Army Group 1, which bore the entire brunt of the German offensive through Belgium, contained 60 divisions, including 22 Belgian and 9 British divisions. To this must be added the 7 divisions of the French Second Army at Sedan, which was detached from him shortly after the battle began. This makes 67 divisions. Add to it the 10 Dutch

---

can contest the fact that the German Army in 1940 possessed a force superior to ours, especially in armored divisions and in aviation." Georges goes on to speak of "the flagrant inequality of the materiel and especially of the mechanized power in the means of fighting the battle."[19]

divisions, weak as they were, and the four French armored divisions, which, after first being held in reserve, joined in the battle, and the total Allied armies assembled to meet the German offensive comes to 81 divisions.

That was more than the attacking German armies had. Their offensive, as we have seen, was carried out by two Army Groups, of which Group B had 29 divisions and Group A 45 divisions or a total of 74 divisions, of which 10 were armored. If one subtracts the 10 Dutch divisions, which were overwhelmed in four days, the Allies still had 71 divisions against 74 German divisions.[20]

"Thus on balance," General Gamelin concedes, "there was an equality of forces on the front attacked, and an equality of forces on the stable front."[21] Actually on the latter front, as we have seen, the French Army had a superiority in number of divisions of more than two to one. Moreover, it was bolstered there by the strongest fortress line in the world, which the German High Command never dreamed of attacking frontally. This added greatly to the defensive power of the French and constituted the equivalent of several divisions. Finally, the French Army had a marked superiority in the number of trained regular Army officers—on active duty —39,000 of them when the war broke out. Because the German Army up to 1935 had been limited by the Versailles Treaty to 100,000 men, Hitler's forces were short of seasoned regular-army officers. For the same reason the Germans were short of trained reserves. Frenchmen had been doing their military service since the end of the last war; the Germans only since 1935.

THE QUESTION OF TANKS

Of all the myths current to this day about the French Army in 1940, one of the most unfounded—and most generally believed—is that the French forces were vastly inferior to the Germans in tanks. In the face of the facts, assembled since the end of the war, the myth explodes into thin air. The truth is that the French Army had as many tanks as the Germans and most of them were better. The trouble was that the French did not know how to use them—despite the teachings of General de Gaulle— and that the Germans did. Yet for years the Vichy government tried to pin the responsibility for the French defeat on the government of the Third Republic for having failed to provide the army with, among other things, enough tanks. A number of defeated generals, some of them directly responsible for tank warfare, aided and abetted Vichy by their surprising— to say the least—testimony.

In the question of tanks, as with other matters, French sources disagree. General de Cossé-Brissac, the genial chief of the Historical Section of the Army, kindly submitted to the author a study he had made. It contained six different sets of figures drawn up by Gamelin, the High Command, two generals, and others. After sifting through their calculations and the data in the military archives General de Cossé-Brissac concluded that on the Northeast Front the French Army on May 10 possessed 2,285 modern tanks, not including armored cars.*

Against how many German tanks? On May 10, 1940, the Deuxième Bureau issued a formal estimate of from 7,000 to 7,500 modern German tanks available for the offensive. This fantastic figure was mere eyewash. On May 13 at Georges' headquarters Daladier questioned Gamelin about it and received the astonishing reply: "This is what we call information 'to cover up'—in case the Germans do put that many tanks into action."† Later, in testimony before the Parliamentary Investigating Committee, Gamelin admitted he had been in error in reporting to Daladier such a high figure and in telling him that the German tanks were not only much more numerous but more powerful than the French. "That was not correct," he conceded.[23] He adds in his memoirs that he had "approved" the Second Bureau's obviously false figures "in order to impress French public opinion and alert it."[24]

Actually the Germans had 2,580 tanks on the Western Front, and most of them were inferior to the French. That is the figure given by Jacobsen after an exhaustive study of the German sources.[25] General Heinz Guderian, the genius of the development of armored warfare in the German army and the Commander of the XIXth Armored Corps, which made for Sedan, puts the figure in his memoirs at 2,800, of which 2,200 were serviceable in the battle.‡ "France," Guderian writes, "possessed the numerically strongest tank force in Western Europe. . . . Moreover French tanks were superior to the German both in armor and in gun caliber, though inferior in control facilities and in speed."[26]

The French superiority in what counted most in tanks in actual combat, armor and gun, was indeed striking. Roughly half of the tanks in the ten armored German divisions consisted of Mark I and II models. The first was a small 6-ton vehicle with a thin armor of 13 mm. and armed only with two machine guns. The second weighed 8 tons, and had the same armor, and mounted a small 20-mm. gun and a machine gun. Mark III was a 16-ton tank, with an armor of 33 mm. and an armament of one 37-mm. gun and two machine guns. Mark IV was the most powerful the Germans had. With an armor of 40 mm. and weighing 19 tons it carried a 75-mm. gun and two machine guns. In addition the Germans had 132

---

* "It is very difficult," the general wrote to me in June, 1963, "to ascertain the exact number of tanks on hand on May 10, 1940, for the actual battle." He cites Gamelin's figure of 2,361 tanks and Jacomet's figure of 3,468 tanks, pointing out that the latter contains tanks not yet received by the Army and those employed on other fronts.

† General Keller, Inspector General of Tanks, was still trying to cover up in 1942. Testifying against Daladier at the Riom Trial he said he believed the Second Bureau's figures were correct. "It is not for me to doubt their word today," he said.[22]

‡ Guderian gave a slightly different figure in 1946 to the Historical Section of the French Army—2,680 tanks.

Praga tanks, taken from the Czechs. This was a 15-ton tank armed with a 37- or 47-mm. gun and two machine guns and an armored turret 35 mm. thick.

Practically all of the 2,300 French tanks on the Northeast Front were superior to the German Mark I and II. This was true of the light tanks, the R (Renault) 35 and 40, the H (Hotchkiss) 35 and 39 and the FCM, which ranged from 10 to 12 tons, had armor plate 40 mm. thick and were armed with a 37-mm. gun and a machine gun. Some 2,335 machines of these models had been produced in France since 1935, though not all of them were available for the Battle of France. The H-39, particularly, was an excellent light tank and with its 40-mm. armor and a rapid-firing 37-mm. gun (model of 1938) it was, according to General Perré, Deputy Commander of the Second Armored Division, who had 99 of them, more than a match for the Mark I, II, and III German tank. Unfortunately less than half of them were armed with the new gun; the others had a 37-mm. cannon of World War I vintage. Even these were far superior to half the German tanks, the Mark I and II. The French "medium" Somua tank was heavier than the German heavy tank, Mark IV, scaling 20 tons, armed with a new 47-mm. gun and having an armor of 40 mm. Because of its speed—30 miles an hour—it was given to the light armored divisions. The D-2 was a similar tank. Finally the French heavy tank, the B-1 and B-1-bis, of which 314 had been built up to May 10, was far superior to any armored vehicle in the German Army, or anyplace else. Weighing 30 to 34 tons, with 60 mm. of armor, it carried a 75-mm. cannon and a 47-mm. antitank gun. As has been pointed out, it was so good a weapon that the Americans later copied it for their General Grant tank, and the British for their Churchill tank.

In numbers, then, the two sides were equal in tanks.* In quality the French were decidedly superior. In the battle of armor which was now shaping up toward the middle of May all depended on how each side employed its formidable force of tanks. The French High Command, traditionally skeptical, as we have seen, of the value of armored divisions and stuck with its outmoded belief that it was best to disperse most of its tanks in support of the infantry, had divided them between its seven armored divisions and those of the infantry. According to Gamelin's figures, the three light armored divisions had 600 tanks and the four heavy armored divisions 546 tanks—or 1,146 in all. Some 53 separate tank battalions with a total force of 1,215 tanks were assigned to the infantry divisions, which greatly pleased their commanders.[28] The Germans, with an entirely new and different conception of armored warfare, put all their tanks into 10 panzer divisions.

---

* Gamelin and other French military sources list the BEF as having 600 tanks. Actually on May 10 it had only 289. These were all light and medium tanks, the first carrying two machine guns, the second a 2-pounder gun.[27]

THE RIVAL AIR FORCES

In the air the Germans were supposed—then and subsequently—to have a marked superiority. General Vuillemin, the Chief of the French Air Force, later contended: "Our aviation hurled itself against an enemy five times superior in number."[29] Was this true? The facts are extremely difficult to determine—even after more than two decades. No sources on either side agree on the number of planes employed. And on the French side the figures given—even *official* figures—vary so greatly that they become a mystery which even today cannot be fully pierced. Gamelin testified several times that he could not understand the discrepancies in them. If they mystified the Commander in Chief it is little wonder that they have a similar effect on the historian. One can only attempt to arrive at an approximate evaluation, as this writer tried to do over the years of research in Paris.

The Germans, for that matter, are far from agreeing on how many planes they flung into battle on May 10, 1940. The usually careful Jacobsen gives a German total of 3,534 planes: 1,462 fighters, 1,016 bombers, 501 reconnaissance, and 555 others, but this is almost certainly too high by some 500 planes. A check with Luftwaffe officers made by General de Cossé-Brissac in 1947 gave the figure of 3,000 planes, of which only "700 to 800" were fighters, 1,200 bombers and the rest "destroyers"—the Me 110—and reconnaissance. General Kesselring cites official figures of 2,670 planes for the two Air Fleets assigned to the Western Front—1,308 fighters and 1,361 bombers, including Stuka dive bombers—but he thinks the number of fighters given is too high.[30] A total figure of 2,700 to 3,000 planes, with a thousand fighters and a thousand bombers, would seem to be roughly near the mark.

The air forces of France and Britain, together, proved considerably weaker *in the number of planes thrown into battle*. This qualification is important, not only because the British held back the bulk of their fighter planes for the defense of their island,* but because the French, for reasons never explained, also held back a substantial number of their first-line aircraft. There is a baffling discrepancy between the number of modern

---

* This was the cause of much bitterness on the part of the French against the British, compounded by unfounded charges of certain French officers and politicians and, later, historians. Major Ellis in his official history of the battle states that on May 10 the RAF had 416 aircraft (out of a total of 1,873) based in France. To these were added by the end of the first week of fighting 10 fighter squadrons. When their bases were overrun by the advancing Germans the RAF withdrew to Britain but continued fighting over France until the end. Ellis contends that during the battle 43 out of 53 British fighter squadrons were engaged over France and that all the bombers, at home and in France, were fully engaged. British losses would seem to bear him out. He gives them as 334 bombers out of 544, and 474 fighters, or more than half the total number operational on May 10. French losses in the air were slightly less.[31] It is true that the British government refused to sacrifice the bulk of its fighter force over France and withheld two thirds of it, except for missions to protect the evacuation of the BEF from France, for home defense. The wisdom of this, as Reynaud later freely conceded, would soon be shown.

planes the French had on hand in 1940 and the number they used in combat. Guy La Chambre, who was Air Minister from 1938 to 1940, told the postwar Parliamentary Investigating Committee that on the day the German offensive began the French Air Force had a total of 3,289 modern planes, of which 2,122 were fighters, 461 bombers, 429 reconnaissance, and 277 observation. But only some one third of them were on the front: 790 fighters, 140 bombers, 170 reconnaissance and 210 observation planes, or a total "front-line strength" of 1,310 aircraft. The remaining two thirds, it appears, were in the interior. A few were overseas. It seems surprising that the French did not put more of their planes at the front or in immediate reserve where they could be thrown into the battle if needed. According to the Air Minister, the French Air Force was even stronger during the fighting than the above figures would indicate. He testified that between May 10 and June 12 some 1,131 new planes were delivered to the Air Force as replacements, among them 668 fighters and 355 bombers. Thus, he declared, a total of 2,441 modern planes were available at the front during the battle. If these figures are accurate the French and British had numerical equality with the Germans—some 3,000 planes each—with the Allies being actually superior in fighters and the Germans in bombers.

A study of military archives made by General de Cossé-Brissac, which he gave me in 1963, substantially supports La Chambre's figures. He arrives at a total of 2,923 modern French planes, of which 1,648 were in line or in immediate reserve. Of the latter, there were 946 fighters (of 2,005), 219 bombers (of 433) and 483 reconnaissance and observation planes (out of 485). The Air Force Command itself advised General Georges at the beginning of May that by the 15th it could put into action 1,300 aircraft, of which 764 were fighters and 143 bombers.

So far so good. There is approximate agreement among these French sources that the Air Force had at the front between 800 and 1,000 fighters, which was about what the Germans had. The French were thus about equal in fighter strength and a little stronger if the odd 150 British fighters were added. In bombers the Allies were outnumbered two to one. But since they were fighting a defensive battle the strength in fighters seemed the more important.

To utterly confuse the picture, however, there are other sets of figures from French sources, particularly from the flying officers themselves. According to these the French Air Force was practically nonexistent. Colonel Pierre Paquier, for example, in his postwar study contends that the French had on the Northeast Front only 420 fighters and 140 bombers, backed up by 72 British fighters and 192 bombers. This seems a small number compared to the aircraft available but the Air Force colonel makes it even smaller. "Actually," he says, "the French had on the front on May 10 only 360 fighters and 122 bombers."[32] The mystery thickens. General d'Astier de la Vigerie, who commanded ZOAN (Zone of Air Operations, North), covering Army Group 1, says that he had a total of

432 fighters of which 72 were British, and 314 bombers, of which 192 were British—or a total of 746 aircraft pitted against the 3,000 planes of Germany's two air fleets. His zone comprised the entire area of the German offensive, and the general points out that he was given but one third of the available bombers and three fifths of the fighters.[33] But according to General Vuillemin, Chief of the Air Force, the French had only 580 fighters on the entire front plus 160 British fighters. General d'Harcourt, Chief of Fighter Command, testified at Riom that he had a total of only 418 serviceable fighters.[34] One can only ask: where were the rest?

The deposition of an Air Force general at the Riom trial provided what is probably the best answer we shall ever get to that question. This was General Massenet de Marancour, Commander of the Third Air Region, extending from Brittany to the Pyrenees.

. . . I was in close and frequent touch [he deposed] with General Redempt (Commander of the Air Force's special depots) about the excessive number of war planes which he deposited at my air schools because no cover for them was available elsewhere. I frequently listened to his complaints about planes he didn't know what to do with and which the Air Force High Command would not take from him. I know that nearly every evening General Redempt sent to Air Force General Headquarters the list of all planes ready for delivery, and this list was long.

The general explained that at Tours alone he had 200 war planes, of which 150 were Bloch 151 pursuit craft.

On May 10, 1940, these 150 Bloch 151's were still at Tours. . . . We had neither the necessary machine guns nor cannon but by sending trucks to Châtellerault I found immediately all the arms I needed, which proves we really lacked nothing.

At another field, the general related, he assembled 30 fighters to be thrown into the battle. "A month passed," he said. "No orders came."[35]

General Gamelin himself, reviewing the causes of defeat after the war, posed the question: "Why out of 2,000 modern fighters on hand at the beginning of May 1940, were fewer than 500 used on the Northeast Front?" Neither the generalissimo nor anyone else ever got an answer. "What is behind this mystery about our planes?" Gamelin asked while testifying before the Parliamentary Investigating Committee. "I humbly confess to you that I don't know." As to the wide discrepancies in the figures given by French military sources between the number of new planes on hand and those which participated in the battle, Gamelin comments: "We have a right to be astonished."[36] So has the historian trying to make sense of these confusing figures, and the astonishment is all the greater when one comes across the testimony of General Vuillemin himself that at the end of the Battle of France, despite considerable losses, he had more first-line planes than at its beginning.[37]

To be sure, the number of planes does not tell the whole story. In two other aspects the French Air Force was decidedly inferior to the German: in the performance of its aircraft and in their use. French fighters and bombers were slower. The Morane 406 and Potez 63 fighters had a speed of 300 miles an hour against 356 miles per hour for the German Me 109. The Curtiss P-36 did 306 m.p.h.* and the Devoitine 520 somewhat better. The British Hurricane was a match for the German fighter and the Spitfire superior. What proved most devastating to the French ground troops was not the conventional German bomber but the Stuka dive bomber, a type of plane which, as we have seen, the French Air Force refused to build despite Daladier's pleading.† It would soften up the ground for the advance of the panzers. That it would prove so effective is surprising since, with its slow speed and lack of armor and armament, it was a sitting duck for a fighter plane. French conventional bombers, few in number, were slow, carried only a light load of bombs, and were without radio to direct them.

As in the case of tanks, the effectiveness of the French Air Force would suffer from the failure to use its aircraft properly. Again as with the tanks, too many machines were assigned to the land armies, each of which had its own fighters, reconnaissance and observation planes, over which the Air Command had no control. There was confusion in the Air Command itself. Its chief, General Vuillemin, would never really control operations. No one would. Authority was divided between the Air High Command, the Air Cooperation Forces Command, whose chief, General Tetu, was stationed at General Georges' headquarters, the Zone Commands, and the chiefs of the various ground armies. Communications between them were poor, making timely air operations almost impossible. Though the French pilots had been trained principally for support of the ground troops no serious tactics had been worked out to accomplish it. Communication

---

* In 1938 and early in 1939 the French, over the vehement protests of the French aviation industry and the Air Committee of the Chamber, had purchased from the United States 200 Curtiss P-36 fighters, 215 Martin, and 100 Douglas light bombers along with 40 Chance-Vought dive bombers and 230 North American training planes, deliverable by July 1, 1939. When the war broke out the French increased their American purchases, ordering 2,065 planes at a cost of $337,000,000. In December 1939, this was increased to 4,700 aircraft costing $614,000,000, with the British to share the cost and the planes. Few of the larger orders were filled in time to be of any help. According to French official figures some 440 American planes, of which 306 were Curtiss fighters, were ready for action on May 1, 1940. By June the number was 544.[38]

† General Mittelhauser, Commander of the French troops in Norway, had warned Gamelin in April of the effectiveness of the Stuka. Though this dive bomber had been used with deadly accuracy in Poland, the French Command had paid no attention to it. "I remember [General Mittelhauser testified at Riom later] having said to General Gamelin on my return: 'We have here a new weapon. To cope with the Stukas we must have a much greater development of the fighter plane.' But it was too late. At any rate, when the Stuka was revealed to us, when we saw the British fleet giving up before Trondheim (because of it), we had the feeling that we were face to face with something quite new, and of a technical surprise whose employment would be decisive."[39]

between the ground and air was almost completely lacking. This of course was largely the fault of the Army Command, which, as we have seen, never appreciated the role of aviation in modern warfare.

FLAWS IN THE HIGH COMMAND

If confusion in the Air Command was great because of faulty organization, that in the Army High Command was even greater—for the same reason. General Gamelin, like General Vuillemin in the Air Force, would never really command operations. Indeed he would contend that such was not his business, that he had delegated that job to General Georges. But this left the latter to carry out strategic plans made by the former with formations and generals chosen and shaped by him. General Georges stressed this when he testified before the Parliamentary Investigating Committee after the war. "History," he argued, "will judge severely, I think, an organization of command placing in juxtaposition two Commanders in Chief, one of whom held the real powers while the second had the responsibility for the conduct of operations conceived and defined by the first."[40]

"A sad state of affairs," General Weygand called it. And Senator Charles Reibel, president of the Senate Army Committee, complained at the secret session of the Senate on April 16, 1940, that the setup "is so confused that we do not know who is the actual commander at the front." To General Roton, Georges' Chief of Staff, the responsibilities of the two top generals "remained confused and tangled. The arrangement made no sense."[41] It did not help that Gamelin and Georges did not get along.

To make matters worse, the High Command cut itself up into three headquarters. General Gamelin remained at Vincennes on the eastern edge of Paris at what he called his PC (Command Post).* General Georges, who was to command operations on the entire front, had his General Headquarters, Northeast, at La Ferté-sous-Jouarre, 35 miles to the east. But he spent much of his time at his residence and personal PC at Bondons, 12 miles away. Halfway between La Ferté and Vincennes was the Grand General Headquarters (GQG) at Montry presided over by General Doumenc† but under the jurisdiction of Gamelin. Here were located the Bureaus of the *Etat-Major* and the great majority of the General Staff officers. But even then some of the Bureaus and General Doumenc himself were obliged to split themselves up. The general spent the morning at Montry and the afternoon at Ferté. The Third Bureau (operations) was divided between the two headquarters, as were the Second Bureau (Intelligence) and First Bureau (personnel and organization). The Fourth Bureau (transport and services) functioned only at Montry, so that General

---

* He explains that he chose to stay there because "while being close to the government I escaped the atmosphere of Paris."[42] But Vincennes is actually on the outskirts of Paris, at the end of a subway line. And some felt that Gamelin liked the comforts and company of the capital too much to want to give them up.

† With the title of *major général*, which in the French Army means Chief of Staff.

Georges, who had to direct the actual battle, was deprived of having it ready at hand.

Three Commands instead of one! This was bad enough but it was made worse by the lamentable state of communications between them. Progress achieved in telecommunications during the 1930s apparently had escaped the notice of the French Command. There was no teletype service between the headquarters nor between them and the armies in the field. Telephone service seems to have been as bad for the military as it was for the civilians in Paris, and telegrams took a surprisingly long time to reach their destination. Dispatches went to and fro mainly by motorcycles, whose dashing drivers often ended up in the ditch trying to beat or dodge motor cars. General Beaufre, then a junior staff officer under Doumenc, tells of how his own situation reports were handled: "Every hour or so a motorcyclist took them to Vincennes for Gamelin, for we had no teletypes. Several cyclists got killed on the way in accidents."[43] What happened to their dispatches he does not say.

At Gamelin's PC at Vincennes there was no radio, not even, as one of his aides complained, any carrier pigeons! That bird, at any rate, had been got rid of. Thus Colonel Minart, the aide, explains, it was impossible for the Commander in Chief to receive direct and instantaneous reports from other headquarters or to intercept radio messages from the armies in action or from aircraft so as to get a better idea of the situation immediately.[44] Nor, or course, could he communicate by radio.* The Commander in Chief found himself from the first day of battle isolated, his headquarters, as Minart puts it, a submarine without a periscope. De Gaulle found it as quiet as a monastery. Though Gamelin occasionally did use the telephone to reach Georges, whom, he says, he wished to disturb as little as possible, his main method of keeping in touch with him was to drive by car from Vincennes to his headquarters or his residence 35 to 45 miles away. This took an hour each way on the cluttered roads. What a waste of time for the Commander in Chief in the midst of one of the most crucial and decisive battles in the history of France!

And what a loss of time between the giving and receiving—and thereby the execution—of orders, as the result of an antiquated system of communications! It would take six hours, and sometimes more, for the army to get word through to an Air Force Command to attack a specific target. It would take much longer for General Gamelin to have his orders executed. Pierre Dhers, a young historian on the Parliamentary Investigating Committee, questioned the generalissimo on that.

DHERS: Since, as you said in several of your orders, "it is a question of hours," how long did it take before they were executed?
GAMELIN: From the echelon of a commander in chief, even of a theater

---

* "At the echelon where I was," Gamelin said later, "of what use would a radio transmitter have been?"[45]

of operations, to the executory echelon on the actual front, *it generally took 48 hours. A general order issued on May 19 could not be carried out until the 21st.*[46]

Forty-eight hours! In the age of radio and teletype! The significance of the date Gamelin gave will become apparent when we reach the events of that day.

There was, and would be, friction in the German High Command, divided between OKW (High Command of the Armed Forces), OKH (the Army Command–General Brauchitsch) and the Army General Staff (General Halder). But on the whole there was little division of authority, and communications between the various headquarters and between them and the armies in the field and between ground and air were far superior to those of the French. A tank corps or division could enlist almost immediate air support or quickly receive orders from above to make a rapid move to exploit a new situation. If the German High Command had needed 48 hours to get an order executed the story that will now be related might well have been different.

The whole German Army, especially the panzer units and Air Force, were geared to a tempo made possible by the speed of gasoline-engined machines: tanks to make a breakthrough, motor vehicles to transport infantry and artillery to hold and enlarge it after the panzer raced on, and planes to disrupt the enemy's reinforcing movements in the rear and to paralyze his positions at the front at the moment of assault. The development of the gasoline engine, de Gaulle had warned time and again, had revolutionized warfare, above all in the speed of operations. The Germans had agreed; his own Command, which still stuck to the tempo of the 1914–1918 war, had not. Too much of the French Army and too many minds in its Command were geared to the three-mile-an-hour pace of the foot soldier, or at best, and only for reconnaissance and screening, to that of the galloping horse cavalry, which the tank had made obsolete. Still, the French High Command had a formidable force to throw against the invading enemy, numerically equal to it in men and guns* and tanks, though inferior in the air.

The Germans had gambled on a daring plan that might easily go

---

* The French Army probably was superior in the number and quality of its artillery pieces. They totaled 11,200 guns, from 75's to 280's. In heavy artillery it was far stronger than the Germans, with 1,600 pieces of 105's, 2,000 pieces of "short" 155's and 1,200 pieces of "long" 155's and 680 220-mm. and 280-mm. siege guns. Later it was alleged, particularly by certain defeated generals, that the army was woefully short of antitank guns. But by May 10 it had 6,000 25-mm. antitank guns and 1,280 47's, the latter capable of penetrating the armor of the heaviest German tank. In addition there were 5,300 old 75's capable of antitank defense. But though superior in artillery, the French, as was the case with tanks and planes, were victims of an outmoded conception. Most of the guns were still *horse-drawn.* The French still envisaged artillery for positional warfare. They neglected to devise means—complete motorization—for rapidly deploying their guns in mobile warfare. In antiaircraft the French army was weak compared to the Germans. Against the Germans' 6,700 37-mm. and 2,600 88-mm. flak, the French had only 2,265 antiaircraft guns of all calibers.

amiss. The French had staked all on their own plan, one which the High Command instinctively felt might have saved the day earlier, in 1914— unfortunately its mind was still on 1914—and would surely save it now. If the German High Command was confident but nervous, the French High Command was equally so. The dice had been thrown when the two Commands committed their forces irretrievably to their respective strategies. Now it would be up to the fortunes of war, often fickle and never predictable.

THE OPENING MOVES

All seemed to go fairly well the first couple of days for the Franco-British armies pushing forward to the Dyle line in Belgium, where Gamelin and Georges expected the main German blow to fall.

Daladier, returning from a meeting on May 12 at the Château de Casteau near Mons with the King of the Belgians, the BEF Command, and Generals Georges, Billotte, and Blanchard, told Gamelin that "everyone was in good form." General Blanchard, Commander of the French First Army, which was deploying in the Gembloux Gap between Wavre and Namur, where it was believed the Germans would attempt their principal breakthrough, was, said Daladier, especially happy.[47] To Winston Churchill, who had succeeded Neville Chamberlain as British Prime Minister on May 10, the day the battle began, and was plunging into his new duties as top man with customary zest, "there was no reason to suppose, up to the night of the 12th, that the operations were not going well."[48]

By then the major units of the BEF and the French First Army were getting into position on the main line of defense and General Prioux's Cavalry Corps of two light mechanized divisions—the French equivalent of light armored divisions—which had reached the Dyle on the night of the 10th, had pushed several miles ahead to form a screening front on a line Tirlemont-Hannut-Huy behind the Albert Canal and the Meuse. The BEF dug in on the Dyle river between Louvain and Wavre on a front of 17 miles, which, for its 9 divisions, was quite narrow. To the south of it the front of the French First Army defending the Gembloux Gap was somewhat wider, 25 miles. There was no river line to protect it but its force of 8 infantry and 2 light armored divisions was considered more than adequate. North of Antwerp General Giraud's Seventh Army, with 6 infantry divisions and one light mechanized division, had reached Breda and Tilburg in southwest Holland. Between it and the BEF the Belgians were taking over the front along the Scheldt and Dyle from Antwerp to Louvain.

Gamelin, by his own account, seemed not only confident but complacent. He spent the first three days, he says, mostly in smoothing out the problems of Allied cooperation and command, leaving General Georges to direct the fighting. He had an itch, he concedes, to check with Georges on the latter subject the very first day but refrained from going to see him. "I told myself," he relates, "that if I were in Georges' place I would be humiliated and offended to see the Commander in Chief of all the theaters arrive." The next day, May 11th, he did go to see him, but mostly to fuss over Georges' decision to delegate to General Billotte, Commander of Army Group 1, the direction of the British and Belgian armies. Though this seemed logical, since Billotte was in charge of the only front the Germans was attacking, from Sedan to Holland, the generalissimo says he did not hide his "astonishment" at Georges' decision. His disapproval too, for it seemed to him, he declares, "an abdication."[49]

Despite the euphoria and complacency at French headquarters and in the seats of government in Paris and London, the situation by the evening of May 11, the second day of battle, was far from reassuring. The Dutch were being overwhelmed. General Giraud, whose Seventh Army had raced to their help, found that they had hastily withdrawn north of the Meuse into Fortress Holland, leaving him to fend for himself against the Ninth Panzer Division and murderous air attacks. The whole point of his operation, to link up with the Dutch, had evaporated. The next day he withdrew to Antwerp.

The Belgians too were being overwhelmed. At dawn on May 10 German glider troops had seized the key bridges over the Albert Canal at Vroenhoven and Veldwezelt just west of Maastricht before they could be blown. A handful of troops in nine gliders, eighty men in all commanded by a sergeant, had landed at the same time on the top of Fort Eben Emael at the junction of the canal and the Meuse. This fortress had been regarded as the strongest in Europe. Constructed in a series of steel and concrete galleries deep underground, its gun turrets protected by heavy armor and manned by 1,200 men, it was thought to be impregnable. It was put out of action in a few hours and surrendered the next day at noon. Specially trained German soldiers, who had worked all winter on a model of the fort at Hildesheim, achieved this by placing "hollow" explosives in the gun turrets and air vents which spread flames and gas in the chambers below.*

With this key fort knocked out and two vital bridges secured,† three

---

* For months an air of mystery hung over the surprisingly quick capture of Eben Emael, whose fall stunned the Belgian and Allied Commands. The Germans did their best to try to deepen the mystery. A special OKW communiqué issued in Berlin the evening of May 11 announced that the fort had been taken by a "new method of attack." Dr. Geobbels, the Nazi Propaganda Minister, deliberately spread rumors that the Germans had a deadly new "secret weapon," perhaps a nerve gas that temporarily paralyzed the defenders.

† The small Belgian air force, which had been practically wiped out on the ground in the German bombings which set off the offensive, dispatched nine planes to bomb the bridges on May 11 but they missed their targets and seven were lost. At 6 P.M. the same day twelve French Le 45 night bombers, escorted by fighters, attacked three bridges west of Maastricht and German armor rolling toward Tongres, but they were ill adapted to such a mission and did no serious damage. One bomber and four fighters were lost. The next day, the 12th, the British made a suicide attempt to knock out the bridges at Vroenhoven and Veldwezelt, across which German troops and tanks were pouring, and succeeded in temporarily dislocating the latter. Of the five obsolete

corps of the German Sixth Army attacked the canal line. By noon of the 11th, General Hoepner's XVIth Armored Corps had got across the intact bridges and pushed on to Tongres, seven miles west of Eben Emael. During the night the Belgian divisions defending the Albert Canal began a general withdrawal westward. The other forts comprising the great entrenched camp of Liège held out but were simply bypassed by the Germans. This stronghold had halted the German army for seventeen days in August 1914, confounding General Ludendorff, who had had to bring up special siege guns to reduce it. Now on the eve of the second day of the German offensive it no longer counted. At dawn the next day, May 12, Hoepner's armored corps of two divisions resumed the attack toward Tirlemont, Hannut, and Huy, where General Prioux's two light mechanized divisions fought them to a standstill all day.

Prioux himself, pushing his screening force beyond the Dyle on the morning of May 11 in order to give the French First Army time to get in position athwart the Gembloux Gap, had experienced what he called a "lively deception" in finding that the Belgians had done little to fortify the vulnerable area. "No real trenches, no barbed wire, practically nothing," he reported. Five miles to the east of Gembloux he came across the so-called Cointet mobile tank obstacle, invented by a French general of that name, on which the Belgians were placing high hopes of stopping the German panzers. Prioux found it scattered here and there with large gaps in it and consequently of little value.

> I am appalled [he reported] when I think that our army, which counted on finding an organized position here, will first have to carry out its own reconnaissance and then dig in. But the enemy won't give us the time.

Learning that the Germans already had broken through on the Albert Canal and were heading toward him with powerful forces, spearheaded by two armored divisions, Prioux called the commander of the First Army, General Blanchard, at 2 P.M. on the 11th and advised pulling back to the Scheldt. "Because of the feeble resistance being put up by the Belgians," he said, "and the superiority of the enemy aviation, the Dyle maneuver will be difficult to carry out. It seems preferable to go back to the Scheldt operation"—the original Plan E. Blanchard backed him up and so informed

---

Fairey Battle bombers used, four were downed by antiaircraft guns near the bridges and the fifth forced to make a crash landing on its return. The Germans, while admiring the valor of the British pilots, wondered why their commanders had dispatched them so late. A German officer told the captured pilots: "You British are mad. We capture the bridges early Friday morning [May 10]. You give us all Friday and Saturday to get our flak guns set up all around the bridge, and then on Sunday, when all is ready, you come along with three aircraft and try and blow the thing up."[50] This matter of acting too late will become a familiar refrain as the Battle of France develops. In this case, as in many others, it was mainly due to lack of liaison and communication between the Allied commands and between ground and air within them.

Billotte a few minutes later. But it was too late. Several divisions were on the march to the Dyle and could not be turned back. General Billotte expressed his "astonishment" at the advice of his two generals on the front and told them sternly that the Dyle operation would have to be carried out. He agreed to speed up the movements of the First Army by permitting their divisions to proceed by day as well as night so that they would be in position by the 14th instead of the 15th. General Prioux was asked to try to hold up the panzers until then.*[51]

He did his best, and it was pretty good. Though the French light mechanized divisions, which General Gamelin called light armored units, were designed to carry out reconnaissance and to provide a covering screen and not to slug it out with the German panzers, that is what they were now doing. The first big tank battle of World War II had begun. All through the day of May 12, between Tirlemont and Huy, General Prioux committed his cavalry corps, the Second and Third Light Mechanized Divisions, against General Hoepner's XVIth Armored Corps, made up of the Third and Fourth Panzer Divisions. Despite the German superiority in numbers—some 824 armored vehicles to 520 of the French—the day ended in a draw. The Somua tanks, of which there were 80 to a division, proved more than a match for the German Mark III and IV, and the Hotchkiss H-35 for the two light German models. But the German armor was supported by waves of Stuka dive bombers operating unopposed in the air. Prioux received no air support at all. Further, his units were handicapped by lack of adequate radio communications—the light tanks had no radio—which made it impossible to maneuver them in large formations as the Germans did.

"We have discovered the enemy's weak point," a German tank officer reported—"their lack of maneuverability and the fact that they fight singly and in loose formations, not altogether under one command. They cannot take advantage of strength and number."[53]

The tank battle was resumed on the 13th with increased fury and it was not until evening that German superiority began to tell. The panzers gradually pushed the French back in the center west of Hannut. General Prioux ordered a withdrawal during the night. His Third Division had been badly mauled, losing 75 of its 140 Hotchkiss tanks and 30 of its 80 Somuas. But it had inflicted severe losses on the Fourth Panzer Division attacking it—164 tanks put out of commission, the French reported. And Prioux's gallant stand had given the First Army time to install itself at the Gembloux Gap.

---

* Daladier testified at Riom that when he saw Billotte and Blanchard at the Château de Casteau meeting on May 12 they did not mention Prioux's proposal. He learned of it only years later. "If I had known of the advice of General Prioux," he testified, "for I had the greatest regard for him, I would have summoned a meeting of the War Council to consider it. Since only one third of the French forces had reached the Dyle it would have been easy to stop the rest at the Scheldt. One can only ask if the course of the war might not have been changed if this had been done."[52]

If the initial resistance of the Belgians, on which Gamelin had counted so much, was "feeble," as Prioux had found in the north, and as Generals Corap and Huntziger, with equal consternation, were finding in the south —in the Ardennes Forest—their strange conception of cooperating with the French and British forces which had sped to their aid did not improve the situation.

When on May 11 Colonel Hautcœur, Gamelin's liaison officer with King Leopold, asked the Belgians to come under French command, at least for the moment, General Van Overstraeten replied testily that the Belgian Army could receive orders only from the King.[54] He was overruled the next day at the Allied conference at Casteau when the King and the British agreed to come under the command of General Billotte. But valuable time had been lost in coordinating the moves of the French and British forces with those of the retreating Belgians. For a couple of days difficulties between the British and Belgian staffs threatened to play havoc with the British occupying their assigned sector between Louvain and Wavre on the Dyle.

When early on the morning of May 11 Major General Montgomery's 3rd Division arrived on the scene it was fired upon by Belgian troops which, in the fog, mistook it for German parachutists. Fortunately only one trooper was wounded.[55] That was the beginning of a trying day for the mercurial Montgomery. His instructions were to take up a position in defense of Louvain, the ancient university city. But King Leopold had ordered the 10th Belgian Infantry Division to defend it, and it was there when Montgomery arrived.

I went to see the Belgian general [Montgomery later recounted], asked him to withdraw his division and allow me to hold the front; he refused and said he had received no orders to that effect; further only Belgian troops could hold the ancient city of Louvain.[56]

The matter was finally straightened out before the Germans attacked. The Belgians deployed further northwest. But two days were largely lost in confusion and fuming. General Emile Wanty, Chief of Staff of the Belgian VIth Corps, which on May 10 had been stationed southwest of Brussels to defend against the British and French and then moved to the Dyle to help stem the Germans, recounts that in studying the position on the 11th and 12th he found the British and Belgian troops hopelessly intermixed, each preparing their defenses in their own "divergent" ways. The lack of a common language did not help any nor, according to the Belgians, a certain British arrogance toward the foreigner. Wanty, who got along well with the British himself, laments that there were several more "incidents and accidents—arrests of Belgian soldiers, firing on each other's military vehicles, and rows over obstructions erected and mines sown without telling the other."[57]

But what concerned French headquarters the most was not the inevitable difficulties of different nationalities trying to adjust quickly to coalition warfare but reports from the very beginning that the Belgian forces were falling back rapidly in the south without fighting. Even the lethargic Gamelin was stirred.

On the evening of May 10, the first day of battle, he got off a stern warning to the Belgians, wiring General Champon, whom he had dispatched during the day to Brussels to take over liaison with King Leopold, the following message.

Army Group 1 informs me that:

1. Group K* will retire to the Meuse at Huy.

2. There will be no more Belgian troops tomorrow on the right bank of the Meuse south of the Liège-Namur line.

General Georges demands at once that the attention of the Belgians be immediately and firmly drawn to the absolute necessity of not withdrawing except under enemy pressure. They must especially maintain as long as possible their forces south of the Meuse at Huy to avoid creating a gap between the Meuse and the left of our cavalry.[58]

Gamelin and Georges were reacting to a message received from a French liaison officer at Namur that the Belgians were retiring from the Ardennes after carrying out a few demolitions and without waiting to fight behind them. It seemed obvious to the French that they were doing so on orders from the Belgian High Command. In fact, they were. What the French Army chiefs did not know was that on the previous January General Van Overstraeten had personally laid it down that the Belgian forces would not even fight a delaying action in the Ardennes, which, as General Wanty says, was the purpose for which the Chasseurs Ardennais had been created. They would carry out demolitions—mostly blowing up of bridges—and then withdraw without fighting behind the Meuse. Van Overstraeten's decision was confirmed in a secret order of the Belgian High Command on February 12, 1940. The French were not informed.[59]

THE PIERCING OF THE ARDENNES

The "impenetrable" Ardennes, as first Pétain and then the present French High Command had called it, with its narrow, winding roads threading through rugged, wooded hills, had actually been a place of battle for

---

* Named after its commander, Lieutenant General Keyaerts. It was made up of the two divisions of Chasseurs Ardennais, comprising 19 battalions of infantry and three regiments of motorized cavalry. It constituted the defense force of the Ardennes, gateway to the Meuse south of Namur, and to Sedan.

two thousand years. Caesar's legions had fought the German tribes there.*
Between 1554 and 1794 no fewer than ten campaigns had raged through
its tortuous valleys. But during the nineteenth century and the first third
of the twentieth the legend had grown in the French High Command that
the Ardennes was too "inaccessible" to be considered a possible field of
important operations. In his "Plan of War" submitted to Daladier in
February 1940, General Gamelin had not even mentioned the Ardennes.
And he had assigned, as we have seen, the weakest of all the armies, the
Ninth, to defend the vital Meuse front between Namur and Sedan at the
western exits of the Ardennes Forest.

This was where, Pétain had assured the Senate's Army Committee
in 1934, it would be easy to "pinch off the enemy" if he did emerge from
the "impenetrable" woods. In 1928 the British military historian, Captain
B. H. Liddell Hart, had journeyed through the region and concluded that
the French assumption that "the terrain would defend itself" was based
on a delusion. He had found it "well-roaded and most of it rolling rather
than mountainous country" and had warned that the "impassability of the
Ardennes has been much exaggerated."[60] But not in the French view. In
his Secret Instruction No. 82 of March 14 General Georges, in outlining
the possible moves of the enemy, had asserted that in the Ardennes "one
can count on a relatively slow development of operations because of the
poverty of rail lines and roads there."[61] In fact the High Command calculated that it would take the Germans fifteen days to bring up strong enough
forces—40 divisions with heavy artillery and 100,000 tons of munitions—
to make a serious attempt on the Meuse line from Namur to Sedan.†[62]

But by the evening of May 11, the second day of the German offensive,
it was evident—at least to the troops involved, if not to the High Command
—that the Germans were taking much less time and that, in fact, they
would be arriving at the Meuse within 24 hours in unimagined strength.
It was also evident to the French cavalry divisions in the Ardennes, suddenly mauled by the overwhelming power of seven panzer divisions, that
the enemy was striking his main blow here, where it was least expected,
where it had been judged out of the question and indeed impossible.

General André-Georges Corap's Ninth Army, defending the Meuse
from Namur south to Sedan, was far from ready. And the Xth Corps forming the left flank of General Huntziger's Second Army was in the act of
redeploying its three divisions around Sedan itself. The generals thought
they had plenty of time. Corap was carrying out a rigid, if leisurely,
schedule which gave him five to six days to get his divisions in line. Since
French territory jutted north along the Meuse to Givet, his XLIst Corps

---

* "A place full of terrors," Caesar had called it after a 10-day march through
the dark forest.

† General Halder, Chief of the German General Staff, had estimated in February
that it would take at least nine days.[63]

comprising his right flank was more or less already in position. One of its divisions, the 102nd, was a fortress division and had no transport and little artillery, being made up mostly of machine-gun battalions. It could not maneuver. The other division, the 61st Infantry to its north, was, like the divisions assigned to defend Sedan, Class B: that is, its men were relatively old and it was poorly trained and equipped. Still, these two divisions were at least in line along the steep left bank of the river.

Most of the rest of the Ninth Army, which had to wheel into position in Belgium between Givet and Namur by marches of 60 to 75 miles, was not. The 5th Motorized Division, thanks to its wheeled vehicles, got into line just below Namur by the afternoon of the 11th. But the two divisions of the XIth Corps in the center around Dinant, having little motorized transport, were slower in reaching their positions. Only half of the 18th Division's infantry battalions had reached the river by the night of May 12. The 22nd Infantry Division got 5 battalions on the line only by the next morning. But they had no antitank guns. All the division's antitank units had been sent off the week before for more training at the Sissonnes camp and never would get back in time. None of the French units arriving on the Meuse found any trace of the fortifications which the Belgian High Command had said were being built during the phony war. The foot soldiers were exhausted from three days of marching, too weary in most cases to dig in at once or to make sure that every yard of the river was covered. General Rommel, whose 7th Panzer Division arrived at the far bank on the afternoon of the 12th, was to notice this and take due advantage.

During the first day of operations on May 10, Corap and Huntziger had, according to plan, sent their cavalry into the Ardennes to ascertain the strength of the enemy, the direction of his thrust, and to slow him up so that they could complete the deployment of their forces on the Meuse, the main line of defense. General Corap, after dispatching a few scouting detachments across the river into the Ardennes during the day had hesitated to send the bulk of his cavalry beyond the Meuse until more of his infantry got into place. But at 5 P.M. he received a curt order from General Georges to get his cavalry moving as far east as possible during the night. At 2 A.M. Corap's main cavalry force, consisting of the 1st and 4th Light Cavalry Divisions and the 3rd Brigade of Spahis crossed the river and by dawn had reached a position between the Ourthe and Lomme rivers stretching from Marche through Rochefort and south to Saint-Hubert, about 15 to 20 miles deep in the Ardennes. No contact with the enemy was made.

General Huntziger's Second Army Cavalry Corps, comprising the 2nd and 5th Light Cavalry Divisions and the 1st Brigade of Cavalry, headed east on May 10 from Sedan into the southern Ardennes. By evening the 5th Cavalry and the Brigade of Cavalry had reached a line from Libramont to Neufchâteau without encountering any opposition. But further south near Arlon the 2nd Cavalry Division ran smack into the 10th Panzer Division and was stopped cold and then driven back. The next day that fate would hit the 5th Cavalry when the 1st and 2nd Panzer Divisions suddenly appeared.

If the liaison between the Belgians and French had been practically nonexistent before May 10 so far as the Ardennes was concerned, it remained virtually so thereafter. Advance units of the 2nd Army's cavalry found the Belgian Commander, General Kayaerts, at his Command Post at Saint-Hubert during the morning of the 10th and he proved difficult to deal with. The French did not then realize that he was strictly following orders: to blow the bridges according to a rigid timetable, retreat without fighting behind them, and withdraw, not west and southwest toward the Meuse, where his forces could fight at least a delaying action together with the French cavalry, but northwest toward Huy and Namur, where they could join the retreating Belgian army in the north. French cavalry officers complained bitterly to General Kayaerts that he was destroying bridges and felling trees across roads that they needed in their advance and wanted left clear in case of retreat. But the Belgian Commander of the "K" force insisted on sticking to the letter of his orders. Thus his two divisions, which, together with the French five cavalry divisions, might have provided considerable resistance to the Germans in at least slowing them up, had they been allowed to fight, were of no use whatsoever. Obstructions and destructions are of little value in retarding an enemy's advance unless they are defended. A mere two companies of Chasseurs Ardennais, which failed to receive the orders to retreat on sight of the enemy, showed what could be done if demolitions were defended with arms. At Martelange and Bodange along the Belgium-Luxembourg border they fought stubbornly behind blown bridges and piles of logs, holding up the 1st Panzer Division most of the day of May 10.[64] Later in the north the Belgian soldiers would prove their fighting qualities when they were given the chance. In the Ardennes, because of orders of the High Command, they were not allowed to.

The French were not happy about it. "Neither on May 10th nor 11th," wrote General Doumenc in his history of the 9th Army, "did the Belgian forces, with which our cavalry was making contact, halt to offer resistance, even a brief one, either on the line of demolitions or on the Ourthe or further south. This was the first regrettable effect of the lack of entente between the French and Belgian General Staffs."[65] Gamelin too was disappointed. Testifying later about the Belgians in the Ardennes he said:

They had four divisions south of the Meuse and it was hoped they would play a certain role in retarding the enemy until the French cavalry arrived. . . . But they evaporated without fighting.*[66]

---

* The Belgians would never agree. According to Lieutenant General Oscar Michiels, Chief of the Belgian General Staff, the Chasseurs Ardennais offered "a ferocious resistance."[67]

There was also a lack of entente between the cavalry corps of the Ninth and Second French Armies, and this too contributed to the ineffectiveness of the resistance they offered. Their action was not coordinated by one single command. A unit of one army would withdraw without telling the unit of the other army on its flank. Suddenly exposed, the latter would hastily pull back to keep from being outflanked. The commanders of the cavalry divisions were reporting to their respective army commands but not to each other. Thus on the afternoon of May 11, when the Second Army's 5th French Cavalry Division was attacked between Libramont and Neufchâteau and forced quickly to pull back, its withdrawal exposed the 3rd Brigade of Spahis to its north, which belonged to the Ninth Army. The latter quickly retreated to avoid being cut off.

Obviously, the five French cavalry divisions (counting the two independent brigades as one division) and the two Belgian divisions were no match for the seven German panzer divisions, backed by overwhelming airpower. Here and there the French units fought stubbornly and hard and suffered heavy losses, especially in light tanks. But what strength they had was dissipated by lack of cooperation from the Belgians and between themselves.

There was another fatal weakness, for which the sclerosis over the years of the French High Command was chiefly responsible. During their drive through the winding roads of the steeply sloped Ardennes hills the German tank divisions were extremely vulnerable. The columns of the three panzer divisions of Guderian's XIXth Armored Corps stretched back for 75 miles to the Rhine. At many points at various times they were pinned to the roads in the narrow, heavily wooded valleys and could scarcely deploy for serious combat. They were easy targets not only for bombing but for strong harassing attacks from the hills above. A few antitank guns concealed on the wooded slopes could have wrought havoc on the endless columns of vehicles moving bumper to bumper. Apparently no such tactics had occurred to the French generals and no such attacks on the flanks were made. And only on May 11 and 12 was there some Anglo-French bombing of these columns in the Ardennes, but it was too feeble to have any serious effect. The French High Command was still directing most of the Allied bombing, restricted as it was, to the north, where it felt the principal German blow was about to fall. On May 12 General Halder noted in his diary: "Enemy Air Force astoundingly cautious."

And so the seven German panzer divisions romped through the Ardennes toward the Meuse and Sedan. "The advance through the Ardennes," General Guenther Blumentritt, Chief of Operations for Army Group A, said later, "was not really an operation, in the tactical sense, but an approach march. . . . We met . . . only slight resistance in Belgian Luxembourg—from the Chasseurs Ardennais and some French cavalry. It was weak opposition and easily brushed aside."[68]

At 5:30 A.M. on May 10 Guderian's XIXth Armored Corps, made

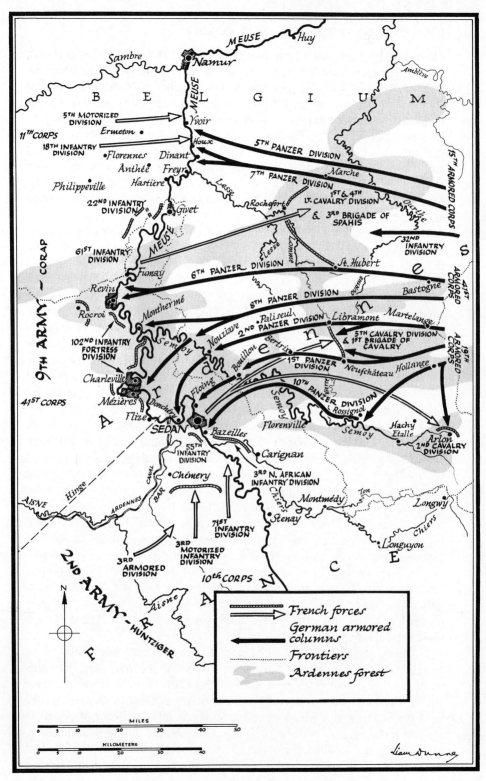

BATTLE OF THE ARDENNES FOREST
May 10-12, 1940

up of the 1st, 2nd, and 10th panzer divisions, crossed the Luxembourg frontier between Vianden and Echternach and by noon had reached the Belgian frontier. Its objective was Sedan. Farther to the north General Reinhardt's XLIst Armored Corps, comprising the 6th and 8th panzer divisions, was somewhat delayed in starting because Guderian's tanks, to its south, had priority on the few main roads. But it was soon rolling across the Ardennes toward the Meuse at Mézières, west of Sedan. Further north still General Hoth's XVth Armored Corps, with Rommel's 7th Tank Division in the vanguard and the 5th Armored following, made for the Meuse crossings at Dinant. Behind the formidable force of panzers followed several motorized infantry divisions.

By the evening of the 11th, only the second day of battle, the German armor had broken through the light French cavalry resistance all along the line. To the north Rommel's 7th Panzer had attacked the tank brigade of the French 4th Cavalry around Marche and hurled it back toward the Meuse. By the afternoon of the next day he would reach the river. To the south the three armored divisions of Guderian's XIXth Corps pushed rapidly forward all day of the 11th. By evening the 1st Panzer Division in the center had reached the Semoy river at Bouillon, ten miles north of Sedan; the 10th Panzer on the southern flank had arrived at the Semoy below Rossignol; the 2nd Panzer, on the northern flank, after being delayed by the French cavalry at Libramont and by cluttered roads, was closing up on the Semoy further west. The afternoon of the next day, May 12, the third day of the blitz offensive, German armor had reached the Meuse on an 80-mile front from Dinant to Sedan. It was 24 hours ahead of schedule. It had advanced 75 miles in three days, whereas the French had counted on holding it up for from five to six days at least. Between the XVth and XLIst German armored corps there was an enormous gap of some 20 miles filled only by one German infantry division, the 32nd, plodding along south of the XVth Corps but unable to keep up with it. The situation cried out for a French attack through the gap on the exposed flanks of the two German tank corps. But the French were in no mood for any offensive action. They thought of maneuvering only for defense, which meant pulling back whenever enemy pressure was applied. On May 12 Gamelin "suggested" to Georges that the cavalry corps being pulled out of the Ardennes be used to liquidate German parachutists behind the First Army, though these existed only in his imagination.

During the night of May 11 General Corap ordered his cavalry corps to retire behind the Meuse during the course of the next day, and this withdrawal was completed by 4 P.M. of the 12th. General Huntziger gave similar orders to the cavalry of the Second Army. Unable, at any rate, to hold the Semoy river, which extended some 12 miles in front of Sedan in Belgian territory, his cavalry retired behind the Meuse during the afternoon, abandoning the fortified points north of the river which the French had been building all winter and of which General Huntziger had been so boastful to the Chamber's Army Committee when it had called attention to their unfinished state.* Apparently it never occurred to General Huntziger to fight in Sedan itself, a town of 15,000, most of which lay on the north side of the Meuse. A stout defense in its narrow streets might have held up the German tanks considerably, and Gamelin wondered why it had not been attempted. "This town appears to have been abandoned," he noted the next day, "though it should have been defended at all costs."[70]

Late in the afternoon of May 12, after the French cavalry had passed over to the left bank of the Meuse, all the bridges across the river from Namur to Sedan were blown, with the exception of those at Mézières, where the 102nd Fortress Division held a bridgehead on the east bank. The destruction of the bridges was rigorously controlled by staff officers of the Ninth and Second Armies, who alone had the authority for carrying it out. Nevertheless a great deal of bitter controversy immediately arose over whether all the bridges had really been blown. There were rumors that they had not been destroyed, that army engineers had failed to do their duty or that fifth columnists and traitors within the Army had seen to it that many bridges remained intact for the Germans to use. Premier Reynaud himself gave authority to some of the rumors in a broadcast on the 20th which he repeated the next day to the Senate. "Because of unbelievable derelictions of duty, which will be punished," Reynaud declared, "bridges over the Meuse were not destroyed." Later in his memoirs, Reynaud expressed "regret" for his public accusation, which he admits was not true. But he said Gamelin on the 19th, and Weygand later, had told him the bridges had not been destroyed.[71] A special investigation carried out by General Dufieux after the battle confirmed that all the Meuse bridges had been blown.†

Though by the late afternoon of May 12 the German armor had reached the east bank of the Meuse and many infantry and artillery units of the French Ninth Army had not yet reached the river below Namur and three infantry divisions of the Xth Corps of the Second Army were still redeploying behind the river at Sedan, Generals Gamelin and Georges, back

---

* German aerial photographs taken early in the spring had shown what seemed to be a strongly fortified area north of the Meuse in front of Sedan. These had made some of the German generals skeptical of the plan to attempt the principal armored breakthrough here. They feared the French fortifications would hold up the German tanks for days. But an Austrian officer, an expert at interpretation of aerial photography, was called in a few days before the offensive and asked to re-examine the prints. Under his magnifying glass he discovered that the French fortifications were unfinished and probably not fully armed, as indeed was the case. He so informed General von Kleist, who was in charge of the main Armored Group of five panzer divisions, and whose XIXth Corps was designated to smash through at Sedan. Kleist was much relieved.[69]

† The legend that they had not all been destroyed died hard. As late as 1952 General d'Astier de la Vigerie was keeping it alive. In his book *Le Ciel n'était pas vide*, published that year, he recounted that aerial photographs taken by his reconnaissance planes on the morning of May 15 showed "that between Namur and Lumes our troops in retiring had left 22 out of 44 bridges intact." (Page 128, footnote.)

at their respective headquarters, were not unduly alarmed. It was believed in these high places that it would take the Germans at least a week to bring up their artillery and infantry for a serious attack on the river line. In that time the Ninth and First Armies would be ready for them. The French were still thinking in terms of the tempo of the first war. As General Doumenc put it:

> Attributing to the enemy our own conceptions of time, we imagined that he would not attempt to cross the Meuse until he had brought up the bulk of his artillery. The five or six days we supposed necessary for this would give us time to reinforce our own position.[72]

It was not only that the French High Command thought it would have plenty of time to handle the Germans at the Meuse. It still clung to its belief, despite all the evidence to the contrary, that the decisive battle would be fought not here but further north along the Dyle. In vain General d'Astier of the Air Force had been trying to point out that all his reconnaissance showed that the bulk of the German armor was concentrated in the Ardennes for a drive to the Meuse below Namur.

On the morning of May 11 he reported that his overnight reconnaissance from the air showed a strong concentration of German "motorized elements" in the Ardennes. At 11 A.M. he issued a bulletin to the Army: "The enemy appears to be preparing an energetic action in the general direction of Givet," which was on the Meuse south of Namur and Dinant. At the same hour his pilots returning from an early morning flight reported large numbers of German tanks from Neufchâteau to Arlon. This was exactly where Guderian's XIXth Corps was operating. Yet all through the day Gamelin, Georges, and Billotte instructed him to employ his planes on the northern part of the front. At 4:30 P.M. Gamelin telephoned him to ask that he employ all his aircraft to slow up the German columns coming from Maastricht toward the Dyle. And General Georges insisted that he concentrate French and British bombing on the Albert Canal.

The next day General d'Astier got off another warning.

> During the night and early morning reconnaissance shows that the enemy is making an important drive westward in the Ardennes. The columns are carrying pontoon bridging material. Large motorized and armored forces are driving toward the Meuse at Dinant, Givet, and Bouillon, coming from Marche and Neufchâteau. One can therefore conclude that the enemy is carrying out a very serious movement toward the Meuse.

Yet General Billotte's instructions to the Air Force for May 12 were to give support only to the French Seventh and First Armies and "perhaps" to the BEF in the north. At 4 P.M. General Georges intervened to order first priority to the Second Army, whose cavalry was falling back on Sedan. No mention of the luckless Ninth Army, whose cavalry was falling back with equal speed to the Meuse. D'Astier says Billotte was "astonished" at this order by his superior and that he maintained his directives to furnish two thirds of the available planes in support of the First Army in the north, and only one third to the Second Army at Sedan. Billotte too seemed unaware of the increasingly serious situation of the Ninth Army. That night French and British planes reported, says d'Astier, "an onrush, an illumination," toward the Meuse and Sedan. The Germans, they said, were driving their tanks and trucks with headlights full on. "For 48 hours then," says the general, "the Air Force had been sounding the alarm. The last doubts had disappeared."[73]

But had they? In the High Command? General Georges later testified that at the end of May 11, the second day of the German assault, when seven panzer divisions were deep in the Ardennes and approaching the Meuse between Dinant and Sedan, he still did not know where the main blow would fall. "The enemy was pushing ahead without stopping on the whole front," he declared, "so that it was not yet possible to discern the direction of his principal effort."[74] D'Astier says that at 9:30 A.M. on the 13th Billotte informed him that he did not "have the impression that the affair [on the Meuse] was imminent or that a move on Sedan would be the most important." Gamelin reveals that on the night of the 12th Georges informed him that "the defense seems well assured on the whole front along the river [Meuse]." Georges added that all the bridges had been destroyed. "So the Germans," Gamelin says he suddenly realized, "have arrived on the Meuse." But the realization did not stir him to do anything about it. He suggested, as we have seen, to Georges that the Ninth Army's cavalry corps withdrawn across the Meuse be used to chase parachutists behind the First Army front. His attention, like that of Georges and Billotte, was still there in the north. The energetic action of the Germans from the first day in that sector "appeared," said Gamelin, "to have affected all our minds. We tended to see the principal German effort as sure to come in the plains north of the Meuse. And we were rather badly informed about the progress of our adversaries through Belgian Luxembourg toward Dinant and Sedan."[75] Actually, the German attack on the Belgian, British and French forces on the Dyle line between Antwerp and Namur was about to begin. Gamelin and Georges thought it would be decisive. All their strategy, all the moves they had made in conforming to it, pointed toward this moment and this place.*

On the German side General Halder was highly pleased at this fatal miscalculation by the French. On May 13 he wrote in his diary:

---

* Daladier, at least, or so he said later at his trial at Riom, smelled a trap. Returning from the Allied meeting at Casteau on May 12 he was struck, he testified, by the fact that the vehicles of the First Army were rolling into Belgium bumper to bumper without being molested by German bombing. "I asked myself," he says, "if we were not falling into a trap, if the enemy was not drawing the French army into Belgium in order to strike a great blow elsewhere." But he was reassured, he adds, by the optimism of Generals Georges, Billotte, and Blanchard.[76]

North of Namur we are now confronted with a complete buildup of some 24 British and French divisions and about 15 Belgian divisions all together. Against this we have in our Sixth Army 15 divisions and six more in reserve, or 21 divisions in all, which, if necessary, can be renforced from the Eighteenth Army (in Holland). Should the enemy attack we are strong enough to handle it. No longer any need to bring up further forces.

South of Namur we are faced with a weaker enemy, about half our strength. Outcome of the attack on the Meuse will decide if, when, and where we will be able to exploit this superiority. The enemy has no substantial mobile forces in the rear of this front. . . .

It seemed to many of the German officers almost too good to be true. General Gamelin, for whose intelligence they had so much respect, had moved his strongest striking force into the trap, just as General von Manstein had predicted. At OKW headquarters, where Hitler was anxiously waiting to see what the Allies would do, Colonel von Lossberg exclaimed: "It looks as though the enemy is doing exactly what we hoped he would do! He is making himself strong on the northern wing and attaching less importance to Rundstedt's attack through the Ardennes."*[77] And Colonel Heusinger at OKH could not hide his rejoicing. "They have poured into Belgium," he exclaimed, "and are falling into the trap."[79] His chief, General von Brauchitsch, was quoted in the War Diary of Army Group B as saying: "There are 40 enemy divisions in northeast Belgium. . . . He says he hopes to cut them off there." The important thing, he added, was for his Sixth Army, which had drawn them into Belgium, to hold them there and "not go too far forward."[80]

On May 15 General von Reichenau, anxious to shine despite the secondary, if vital, role assigned to him, drove his Sixth Army forward. But it was stopped. Here on the Dyle and in the Gembloux Gap, where it least mattered, the Allies were a match for the Germans. The battle raged all day. The British were heavily engaged on their two flanks, at Louvain on the north and at Wavre on the south. At the latter place the Germans made a small penetration across the Dyle but were driven back by early afternoon. Around Louvain two German divisions of the XIth Corps infiltrated into the tangle of railroad tracks and buildings in the freight yards, but counterattacks by General Montgomery's 3rd Division quickly drove them out. In the Gembloux Gap south of the BEF front held by the French First Army the German attack was even stronger. Here Hoepner's XVIth Armored Corps of two panzer divisions, supported by waves of Stukas, dented the IVth Corps but heavy artillery fire and counterattacks restored the position except for one narrow sector at Ottignies.

---

* Hitler himself, according to Martin Bormann, one of his Party cronies, later boasted during one of his "bull" sessions: "When the news came that the enemy was moving forward [into Belgium] I could have cried for joy. They were walking into the trap! We calculated well to begin our attack on Liège. It made them believe we were carrying out the old Schlieffen Plan."[78]

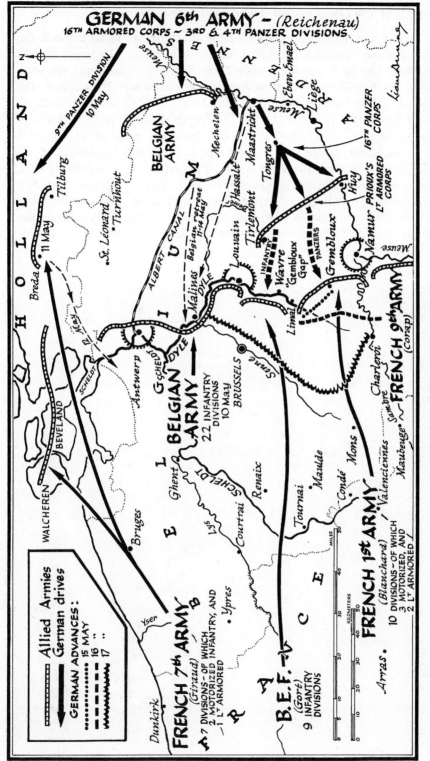

BATTLE ON THE DYLE LINE
May 12-16, 1940

At 5 P.M. Reichenau suspended the attack. It had failed to break the Dyle line, on which the Allies had pinned their hopes. The hopes seemed justified. The BEF and the French First Army had hurled the Germans back. The War Diary of German Army Group A on May 15 confirmed the setback: "The Sixth Army attacked the Dyle line from Louvain to Gembloux held by the British, Belgians, and French. Because various attacks of the panzer divisions had no success, the attack was called off at 5 P.M."[81]

The honors of the day had gone to Lord Gort, Commander of the BEF, and to General Blanchard and his First Army. They and their troops had reason to be confident of the morrow. But when the morrow came they were suddenly ordered to retreat. Their right flank was suddenly and gravely threatened by the course of battle to the south of them along the Meuse river held by the French Ninth and Second Armies. The trap was being sprung.

30

THE BATTLE OF FRANCE, II:
DISASTER AT SEDAN.
THE BREAKTHROUGH AT THE MEUSE
MAY 13–16, 1940

The little town of Sedan on the Meuse just east of where the river turns north toward Givet, Dinant, and Namur, evoked mournful memories among the French.

It was there that Emperor Napoleon III and Marshal MacMahon surrendered to the Prussians on September 2, 1870, after a short siege. This was one of the worst military disasters in the history of the French arms. Some 84,000 men, 2,700 officers, and 39 generals, after a few days of fighting, had laid down their arms and, with the emperor, become prisoners of war. France was stunned. A second military debacle, the people knew, was in the making. Marshal Bazaine, with an even larger army, 180,000 men, was surrounded and besieged at Metz. He would capitulate on October 27. But the aroused populace of Paris did not wait for that. The shattering news from Sedan was enough. On September 4, two days after the fall of the town, they overthrew the Bonaparte Second Empire and prepared to establish a Republic.

The sorry performance of Napoleon III's armies against the Prussians in the brief August days of 1870 shocked the French people. They had had no inkling that the Army was so weak. Indeed it had been reputed to be the strongest in Europe and few persons in France had realized how stagnant was its High Command, how devoid of vigor and imagination, how complacent and outdated in its conception of strategy and tactics and of the speed of military operations made possible by the recent development of railroads that could carry large forces and their supplies swiftly to the point of attack. Nor in France had there been any realistic appraisal of the Prussian army, which in 1866 had quickly routed the Austrians, though this campaign, like that in Poland in 1939, might have been profitably studied in Paris. Not much attention was paid in the French High Command to what Moltke had done in the Prussian Army in developing bold leadership in the officer corps, new strategy and tactics based on surprise and speed, and a brilliant General Staff which had prepared with Teutonic thoroughness and in the most minute detail for the invasion of France and the rapid rolling up of her armies in the centuries-old battlefields between the Meuse and the Rhine.

Now once again, exactly seventy years later, the Germans were at the gates of the ill-fated town. They had equally bold leadership and plans and their preparations were just as thorough. By the evening of May 12 Gamelin, back in Vincennes, knew that they were there, assembling in front of the blown Meuse bridges, but he still did not realize in what strength or that they were about to strike the main blow. He still looked for that farther north along the Dyle line. He thought the Meuse river, with its deep valleys, its steep, hilly banks, constituted a natural defense from Namur to Sedan strong enough to halt any secondary German effort there. Above all, he felt, it was a formidable obstacle to tanks. He knew the region well, having often inspected it, he says, in the years before the war, and he considered it, he assures us, "particularly important." Was it not there, he adds, that the German Fourth Army had "forced the passage" in August 1914? And he fills his memoirs with a lengthy description of the Meuse country and its advantages for the defender.

The key to the defense of the Sedan sector, once the town itself on the north bank was abandoned,* lay in the heights of the Bois de la Marfée just south of the river, from which King Wilhelm of Prussia had watched the battle in 1870. "From the heights of the Bois de la Marfée," Gamelin writes, "one commands the terrain right up to the edge of the Ardennes Forest 6 miles away, that is, within range of the 75-mm. gun. Tanks can go down into the valley only by roads and tracks. In any case, they must stick to them in climbing the southern bank of the river. . . . Along the whole front the river itself was defended by a series of casemates and infantry pillboxes. To the rear of them on the slopes behind the left bank there were light and medium machine-gun emplacements which could prevent Stukas from diving into the valley. . . . And the artillery on the heights of the Marfée Wood dominated the whole terrain."[2] The heights also afforded excellent observation posts, especially for the artillery, but also for any commander wishing to check German deployment at the river's edge. The defense here was favored by nature.

It had an advantage too, as Gamelin also concedes, further down the Meuse, held by the Ninth Army. From Sedan to Mézières the river is encased in rocky cliffs—"absolutely inaccessible to tanks," he says, "and very difficult even for infantry." The river here, it is true, has many ser-

---

* Gamelin says there was supposed to have been a fortress regiment in the town to defend it. "Did it disappear?" he asks. According to Colonel Goutard, it did. Its men fled with the civilian population of Sedan on the approach of the Germans on May 12.[1]

pentine bends, but these, thought Gamelin, had the advantage of flanking its bed, and at any rate were sealed off at their base by antitank obstacles and fields of barbed wire. Also there were few roads on the east bank leading down to the river on which the Germans could bring up their tanks and guns. Further north, from Givet to Namur, the river emerges from the Ardennes Forest. The slopes are not so high here or so steep, but those on the east bank dominate those on the left, where the Ninth Army units were digging in. There are also more roads on the right bank leading down to the Meuse. It was here between Givet and Namur that the German Third Army launched its offensive in August 1914, and the French chief admits that at Givet and Dinant the terrain was favorable for an attack, especially at the latter.[3] As luck would have it, this was just where the Ninth Army was weakest. On the afternoon of May 12, when the advance guard of Rommel's 7th Panzer Division reached the Meuse at Dinant, which was on his side of the river, the French 18th Infantry Division on the far shore had only five battalions in place. The rest would not arrive until the next day.

Unlike the left flank of the Ninth Army, which had had to wheel into Belgium and dig in along the Meuse south of Namur, which the Belgians had neglected to fortify, the left flank of the Second Army at Sedan had been in position since the beginning of the war and had had ample time to strengthen its defenses. Yet it too was not in readiness to repel the Germans on May 13. Though Sedan was the hinge of the whole Allied turn into Belgium, General Huntziger, Commander of the Second Army, had assigned the weakest of his two corps to defend it. The XVIIIth Corps, the better one, was stationed on the right, in the heavily fortified bridgehead of Montmèdy. The Xth Corps held the weakly fortified sector of Sedan.

When the German offensive began the Xth Corps' two infantry divisions, the 3rd North African and the 55th, held a front of 25 miles, each division reinforced by a fortress regiment. The 71st Infantry Division, which had been taken out of line on April 6 for further training, was in reserve, scattered about in several villages 35 to 40 miles behind the front. Both the 55th and the 71st were series "B" divisions, its men relatively old, ill-trained, led mostly by reserve officers and poorly armed. They lacked a full quota of antitank guns and were practically without flak. General C. Grandsard, the Corps commander, had few illusions about his troops or the strength of his position. On the eve of battle he summed up his situation: "A sector incompletely organized. Troops insufficient in number, very badly armed against tanks and planes, of rudimentary training and with an uncertain solidity." He adds that the "High Command could not have ignored this situation and that it acted as though it judged improbable an attack in force in this zone."[4]

Though he apparently shared this judgment, General Huntziger, after hesitating two days, informed Grandsard that the 71st Division was being put at his disposal and should be put into line that night, May 12, and the following night. The Corps commander decided to sandwich it in between the 55th and the 3rd North African so as to give greater density to his defense. Scattered as it was far behind the front, the 71st did not reach the line until late in the night of May 12. Its men were weary after two nights of marching and in the darkness had difficulty in finding their assigned position. Its commander, General Baudet, complained, Grandsard says, about having his division rushed so quickly into the fray.[5] There was confusion too in the two divisions on each side of the 71st. To make room for it, they had to redeploy their units in the darkness. And some of the formations, especially in the 55th Division on the left, simply withdrew to the woods behind the front planning to return to new positions on it the next night.

Despite all the confusion, considerable bombing, which upset his troops and knocked out telephone lines, and the appearance of the German armored divisions opposite him, General Grandsard was fairly optimistic as he surveyed the situation the night of May 12.

What can the enemy do on the 13th? [Grandsard says he asked himself]. Obviously he can close up on our main defense line. Can he attack? That depends on him. Will his attack succeed? The Corps Commander, though conscious of the weakness of his position, does not think so.

To be sure, the French commander conceded, the enemy

can bring up his infantry and tanks to the river. . . . But he cannot bring up his artillery, ammunition, and suitable equipment without a great deal of trouble and then only in driblets because of our artillery fire on him. . . . Moreover the tanks face an obstacle (the Meuse) unless the infantry opens the way for them, and for this they must have a long preparatory fire to achieve breaches in our line of fire.

Who will make this breach? The artillery? That does not seem possible. The tanks? Their guns lack the necessary caliber.

Their bombers? Grandsard says he had confidence in the Allied Air Force. "Thus," he concludes, "it did not seem on the evening of May 12 that the enemy would be able to attack the next day with any chance of success."[6]

It was not just that General Grandsard, like most of the other French commanders, was complacent. He had no idea, nor did the Second Army chief, Huntziger, nor Billotte, nor Georges, nor Gamelin, what would hit the Xth Corps at the vital hinge of Sedan the next day. "It was not possible," says Grandsard, even on May 12, "to evaluate the strength of the enemy forces marching toward us, since only their advance guard had engaged our cavalry." Air reconnaissance that night did report a massive body of German armor moving through the Ardennes toward Sedan with headlights full on. But nobody, he says, thought to pass along this intelligence to him.[7]

General Huntziger did get the wind up, temporarily, on the afternoon of May 12. At 3:30 P.M. he sent a telegram to General Georges which struck the latter's headquarters as "alarming." He reported severe losses in the Ardennes to his cavalry corps and to advance units of the Xth Corps, and asked for reinforcements. Georges was away at Casteau, but his Chief of Staff, General G. Roton, was sufficiently impressed to order the 3rd Armored and the 3rd Motorized divisions to head toward Sedan. General de Lattre de Tassigny's crack 14th Infantry Division, which was far to the east behind the Maginot Line, was instructed to start moving westward by rail. But at 5 P.M. Huntziger felt better about the situation and advised Roton that his front was again "calm," and that there was no urgency in sending reinforcements.

In their ignorance of what was going on just across the river, Huntziger nd Grandsard thought they had ample time to redeploy the three divisions of the Xth Corps opposite Sedan and, with that accomplished, sufficient means to throw back any German attempt to break across the stream.

Across the river, while the German tanks, guns, and assault infantry and engineers were being brought up, General Guderian conferred with his chief, General von Kleist. Guderian's three panzer divisions were far from ready and he wished to set the attack on the river crossings for May 14. The 2nd Panzer had been held up at the Semoy and only its advanced elements were at the Meuse. The 1st Panzer in the center and the 10th Panzer to the east were closing up on the river in strength but their columns stretched back for several miles into the Ardennes.

Kleist insisted that the attack begin at 4 P.M. the next day, the 13th, so that his armored force could benefit from surprise and the obvious lack of preparation of the French, who would not be expecting it so soon. Guderian readily agreed, and Kleist handed him his written orders.

The decisive effort of the Battle of the West [they read] will be made by the Kleist Armored Group, whose mission is to force the Meuse between Monthermé and Sedan, inclusive. Most of the German air force will be engaged uninterruptedly over a period of eight hours. It will destroy the French defenses on the Meuse. Thereafter, at 4 P.M. the Kleist Group will cross the river and establish bridgeheads.

Flying back to his headquarters the evening of May 12 Guderian sat down to issue specific orders to his three tank divisions. Since there was so little time, he got out of his files the orders which had been drawn up during the war games at Coblenz during the winter, wrote in a new date and time, and got them off to his units. "They were perfectly fitted," he says, "to the reality of the situation."[8]

On the west the 2nd Panzer was to cross the Meuse at Donchéry and occupy the heights of the Croix-Piot. In the center the 1st Panzer, which would make the main attack, would cross the river between Glaire and Torcy, west of Sedan, attack the key heights of the Bois de la Marfée, occupy them and advance to the line Chéhéry-Chaumont south of them. The 10th Panzer Division to the east would attack southeast of Sedan around Wadelincourt and after forcing the river occupy the heights to the south, thus protecting the flank of the other two divisions, which after establishing themselves would turn west to outflank the French Ninth Army to the north and then drive to the sea.

It was a bold plan and a daring enterprise. If the French employed their artillery with the deadliness of which it was capable the whole German attack might fail in the first hours.* For Guderian could not get a single tank over the Meuse until the assault infantry, crossing the river in rubber boats, had first established solid bridgeheads and overrun the French artillery positions. Only then could pontoon bridges be thrown over the river and the tanks brought across. In the meantime the French would have several battalions of tanks on the left bank to crush the infiltrating German infantry. There was some reason then on the night of May 12 for the guarded optimism of General Grandsard, whose single corps would have to meet the German attack.

Sedan: The Attack Begins. May 13

From 11 A.M. on, the Germans softened up the French positions by incessant dive-bombing and gunfire. Since most of Guderian's XIXth Armored Corps regular artillery had not yet come up, he employed 88-mm. flak guns and the cannon of the tanks to fire point-blank across the river at the French pillboxes and artillery posts. More damaging were the continuous attacks of the Stukas. Guderian had arranged with the Luftwaffe to carry out a sustained attack of several hours designed as much to keep the French gunners pinned down as to destroy their batteries. The uninterrupted bombing, in effect, caused relatively little damage. But besides pinning the artillerymen down so that they often gave up trying to fire, it was devastating to their morale.

The gunners stopped firing [General Edmond Ruby reported] and took cover. The infantry, cowering and immobile in their trenches, dazed by the crash of bombs and the shriek of the dive bombers, were too stunned to use their antiaircraft guns and fire. Their only concern was to keep their heads down and not move. Five hours of this punishment shattered their nerves. They became incapable of reacting to the approaching enemy infantry.[9]

---

* The 55th Infantry Division, on a front of 5 miles between Pont-à-Bar and Wadelincourt, just south and southwest of Sedan, had double the normal divisional artillery and most of the Corps' artillery, or some 140 guns, which gave it 28 pieces per mile.

Back at General Headquarters at Montry there was no particular concern. "The bombing is continuous," it reported to Gamelin, "but is not harming the troops." At noon General d'Astier was informed by the Second Army that artillery was handling the enemy and that there was no need at the moment for air support. General Gamelin recounts that early that morning he asked General Vuillemin what he was doing about air cover on the Meuse but that the Air Force chief only got around to ordering some that evening for the following day.

Time was more pressing at Sedan than the Air Force commander realized. "Unless you were blind or deaf," says General Ruby "you knew that the enemy attack was imminent." General Lafontaine, commander of the 55th Division, which was taking most of the pounding, saw that clearly enough. At 3 P.M. he telephoned Grandsard. The incessant bombing, he said, convinced him that the Germans would attack that evening. He asked for some air support to drive the bombers off. Grandsard relayed the demand, with his own backing, to Second Army Headquarters. Not a single French fighter plane, he pointed out, had appeared to disturb the Stukas all day. The complacent General Huntziger was not impressed. "You really don't need my fighters," he replied. "If I am obliged to engage them every time some threat arises they will be rapidly used up."*[10]

According to Grandsard, the Second Army chief added that it was a good thing the troops of the Xth Corps were receiving "their baptism of fire."[11] Within an hour they would receive much more than that.

At 4 P.M. on May 13 the German assault across the river around Sedan began. In the center between Glaire and Torcy, just west of the town, the 1st Battalion of the 1st Rifle Regiment of the 1st Panzer Division, along with elements of the Gross-Deutschland Regiment, started to cross the Meuse in pneumatic rubber boats. Ordinarily French artillery and machine-gun fire would have decimated them. But the pillboxes and artillery positions had either been silenced or their crews remained pinned to the ground, unable or unwilling to fire. Also the smoke from the German bombs and artillery fire made it difficult for the French to observe the river. Some boats were hit but most got across. The losses, according to Guderian, who was anxiously watching the launching of the attack, were extremely light. Soon his infantry was ashore on the left bank, reducing the casemates with machine guns, flamethrowers, and powder charges. The French infantry gave way. By nightfall the Germans had overrun the Bois de la Marfée and occupied its heights, from which French observers had been able to scan the whole battlefield. Continuing their advance in the dark they reached Chéhéry at 11 P.M. and took it. This was five miles south of the Meuse and constituted for the French a dangerous penetration.

The two other panzer divisions to each side of the 1st had not done

---

* Huntziger was also worried that his artillery ammunition would be used up too quickly. Grandsard says the Second Army commander severely rationed the number of shells he could fire.

so well. To the west the 2nd Panzer, arriving late at the river at Donchéry, had been able to get only a handful of men across by 8 P.M. But the French troops here, fearful of being outflanked by the retreat of the units to their right before the 1st Panzer, withdrew and by 10 P.M. the Germans had taken the heights of Croix-Piot on the south bank. The 10th Panzer Division on the eastern flank also had had trouble crossing at Wadelincourt. Harassed by French artillery fire from the southeast it finally got two battalions of infantry over the Meuse before dark but was unable to reach its objective, the heights of Noyers to the south.

Summing up the situation at 5:30 P.M. General Grandsard says he considered it "grave, but no more than that." The German infantry in small numbers had succeeded in getting across the Meuse. They had a bridgehead, but it was small and precarious. They had not been able to get a single tank across the river or any artillery. The French had both tanks and guns to throw the enemy back. Then, beginning about 6 P.M. the roof fell in on the anxious general. "From 6 to about 7 P.M.," he later recalled, "the situation evolved with a disconcerting rapidity toward catastrophe."[12] French troops of the 55th Division suddenly panicked!

It started not at the front, where the infantry was, but in the rear, where the artillery was supposed to be firing away. Gun spotters above Bulson could see the battle approaching as the infantry of the 55th Division fell back from the Marfée Woods. Their reports became more and more alarming. Soon there was a general cry: "Their tanks are at Bulson!" Two colonels commanding the division's heavy artillery, says Grandsard, lost their heads, abandoned their posts, followed by their frightened men but not, he adds, "by their cannon." Within 30 minutes, between 6 and 6:30 P.M. the roads were suddenly jammed with fleeing troops. The foot soldiers, having got wind that their artillery was pulling back, raced away to join the gunners in headlong flight. Most of them had thrown away their rifles but lugged their bags.

The panic spread so quickly that the men of two infantry and two artillery regiments, the backbone of the 55th division, soon were running pell-mell down the Bulson road in the wildest disorder. Their officers made no attempt to stop them. Indeed some officers were in the forefront of the terrified pack. General Lafontaine and his staff officers, seeing the fugitives approach their division's Command Post south of Bulson, went out to the road to try to stop them. They placed trucks across the road to block it. But the troops poured around them and continued their mad flight through the night, not stopping, most of them, until they reached Reims, 60 miles away. They had fled out of fear of German tanks, which they convinced themselves were at their heels. Even certain colonels swore to General Grandsard that they had *seen* German tanks approaching. Actually not one tank was across the Meuse. The Germans had done it all with infantry, without tank or artillery support, and, after 4 P.M., when they started out, without bombing. Within three or four hours the 55th Infantry Division,

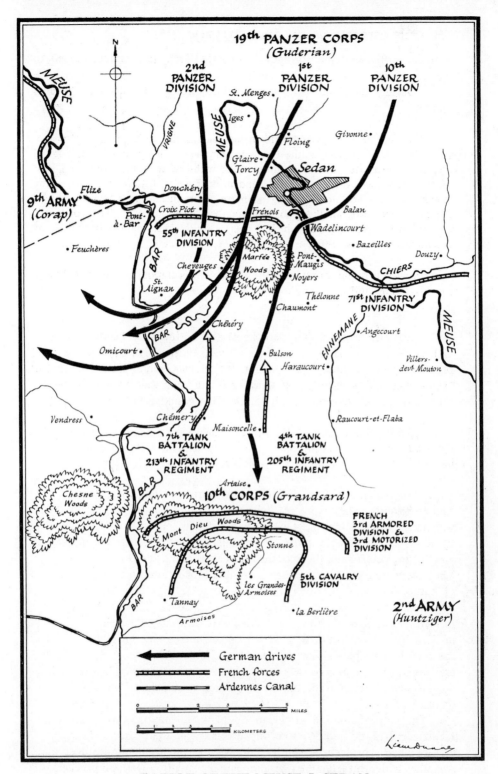

BATTLE OF THE MEUSE, I: SEDAN
MAY 13-16, 1940

with its artillery of the strength of two divisions, had almost ceased to exist.[13]

"During the night," says General Grandsard, "the situation became clearer.

First the disorder is complete in the rear of the 55th Infantry Division. . . . The heavy artillery of the Corps is completely disorganized. The colonel commanding it, after having authorized the withdrawal of the Command Post of B Group, has evacuated his PC and after 7:45 P.M. does not answer the telephone. . . . The units, having no more communications with their chiefs, get away one after another, abandoning their weapons. . . . The roads are covered with men, horses, vehicles, fleeing southward, making any kind of communication most difficult."

In such a panic, paralyzing the front, it was impossible, he concludes, for his Command "to function."[14]

The news from Sedan percolated slowly into the headquarters of Generals Georges and Gamelin. At 9:25 P.M. on the 13th General Georges passed on to Gamelin a report filed at 5 P.M. by General Huntziger that a "small slice had been bitten off south of Sedan" and that he was calling up the 3rd Armored Division. At 11:45 P.M. Georges advised Gamelin further:

From the Second Army: West of the Bar we are holding. . . . Our units fighting in the Bois de la Marfée. . . . Reinforcements (the 3rd Armored and the 3rd Motorized Division) arriving as planned. We are calm here.[15]

This was misleading. French units were no longer fighting in the Marfée Woods. They were in flight considerably south of it. And there was no mention of the disaster that had befallen the 55th Division, which by now was dissolving in panic. If Huntziger's Second Army Headquarters was "calm," as he said, those of the Xth Corps and 55th Division were not. They were struggling to prevent a complete rout after only a few hours of battle. At Army Group 1 Headquarters General Billotte was better informed than his two chiefs. At 10 P.M. he called General d'Astier, informed him that the situation at Sedan was becoming "more grave," and insisted that the Air Force make an all-out attack on the Sedan bridges "as soon as possible"—that night, if they could. When the Air Force general pointed out that it was "practically impossible" to bomb a bridge in the darkness, Billotte asked that he try: "Victory or defeat," he said, "hangs on those bridges."[16]

The actual situation at Sedan by 11 P.M. May 13, which General Huntziger had concealed from his chiefs, was this: the three panzer divisions had a bridgehead south of the Meuse roughly five miles deep and five miles wide. But from the German view the situation was still precarious.

Guderian had no tanks, artillery, or even antitank guns south of the stream. The small bridgehead was vulnerable to serious counterattack. True, the 55th Division, which had borne the brunt of the main attack, was fast disintegrating. But General Grandsard at 7 P.M. had ordered two infantry regiments and two tank battalions from his reserves to move up in its place and counterattack. To the east the 71st Division had contained the small German bridgehead of the 10th Panzer south of Wadelincourt. And the powerful 3rd Armored and the 3rd Motorized divisions were moving up to the front. The Germans were not unaware of their vulnerable position. If the French, Major Kielmansegg wrote later, had made a "spirited counterattack to remove the bulge when it was still small," they "might have destroyed all the German units on their side of the Meuse before they could be reinforced." The pontoon bridge which German army engineers were feverishly building at Gaulier for the tanks and artillery to pass over had not yet been finished.

But even if the confusion among the French units made the organizing of a counterattack most difficult the slowness of the reinforcements in coming up made it impossible to launch late that day or evening. Grandsard had actually ordered them to start moving forward at 3 P.M., an hour before the German assault started, but they had taken their time. Because of fear of bombing, which in fact had almost ceased at 4 P.M., they waited until darkness to advance. Two reserve infantry regiments and a battalion of tanks did not arrive on the positions fixed until between 3 and 5 A.M. of the 14th. The 213th Infantry Regiment was making good progress when at Chémery it ran into a horde of troops fleeing in panic. Its men were strongly tempted to turn around and join the refugees in their flight. But its officers held it together and only one company disappeared into the night. Unfortunately, alarmed by the reports from the panicky fugitives that the German tanks were coming, the commander of the regiment decided to halt there for the night. He was apprehensive, says Grandsard, about continuing forward into the woods in the darkness.

At 1:30 A.M. the Corps commander ordered a counterattack to begin at dawn the 14th. "But," says he, "not one of these four units, which constituted our reserves, executed the order it received. Not one was in place at the beginning of the night." Nor ready, even at the crack of dawn.[17] The margin of time was of the utmost importance. The German engineers had finished their pontoon bridge during the night. At 6 A.M., two hours after the break of dawn, one brigade of tanks of the 1st Panzer began to cross over. The French counterattack, which was supposed to get off at 4 A.M., had not yet begun.

It finally got rolling at 7 A.M., three hours late. On the left the 213th Infantry Regiment, led by the 7th Tank Battalion, advanced north from Chémery toward Chéhéry and at first all went well. On its right the 205th Infantry Regiment, with the 4th Tank Battalion in the vanguard, began moving north from Maisoncelle toward Bulson at 7:45 A.M. Back at La

Ferté, General Georges, cheered by faulty reporting from General Huntziger at Second Army headquarters, informed Gamelin at 7:30 A.M.: "The breach at Sedan is sealed off. Strong counterattack launched at 4:30 A.M."

At 8:30 A.M., an hour after the generalissimo received this reassuring news, the "strong" counterattack suddenly ran into the 1st Panzer Division's brigade of tanks, which had sped across the Gaulier bridge beginning at 6 A.M. and raced south. The French armored battalion stood its ground bravely but was quickly decimated, losing three quarters of its tanks. Its supporting infantry regiment fell back in disorder. This endangered the flank of the group on the right, which was ordered to beat a hasty retreat. By 9 A.M. the counterattack was liquidated. And so was the remains of the 55th Division.

On its right the 71st Division still held, blocking the advance of the 10th Panzer. But now its left flank was threatened along the Ennemane river and it began to pull back, led by the divisional commander, who hastily moved his Command Post 7 miles to the rear. His troops quickly followed, though not pressed at all by the enemy, and soon there was another scene of wild disorder as foot soldiers and and artillerymen abandoned their guns and, panic-stricken, fled down the roads southward.

Left to themselves [wrote General Ruby] the troops dissolved without even being attacked. Everyone, frightened by a menace which did not exist, fell back in disorder toward the south. By evening the 71st Division had disappeared, as had the 55th. At least the 55th had submitted to an enemy attack. The 71st faded away at the mere threat of the Germans.[18]

The morale of the French troops, sons of men who had fought at Verdun in 1916, was described by Colonel Costa, who tried to halt the fleeing men and talk them into offering further resistance. "Look here, men," he addressed them. "We've got plenty of guns and ammunition. Let's go back to the fighting."

"Colonel," he says they replied, "we want to go home, back to our little jobs. There's no use trying to fight. There's nothing we can do. We're lost! We've been betrayed!" And they resumed their flight.[19]

That evening General Huntziger himself, who just before noon had sent another optimistic bulletin to Georges saying his forces were holding out in places they actually had abandoned the previous evening—at Cheveuges and the Marfée Woods—and that "the troops were well in hand and standing up firmly," hastily moved himself and his Second Army Headquarters south from Senuc all the way to Verdun. General Grandsard thought it "premature and a little surprising in amplitude."[20]

The Xth Corps commander had been a little surprised himself, he says, that morning, when the battle still hung in the balance, to learn from Huntziger that there was no further employment for him or his corps on this particular front, crucial though it was. He received a copy of an order from the Second Army chief drawn up at midnight of May 13–14 stating that the XXIst Corps was taking over the area. Huntziger's orders directed the XXIst Corps to seal off the German bridgehead and counterattack. Such an instruction was in itself contradictory, though in line with the doctrine of the French Army. To seal off a penetration you have to disperse and spread out your troops. To counterattack you have to concentrate them at a fixed point. As Colonel Le Goyet later pointed out in assessing this order, "to put off a counterattack until you have sealed off the enemy is to lose time. And with the lost hours you lose opportunities which will not occur again."[21] But first containing a breakthrough and then striking back was what the French Army had been taught between the wars. It had often worked in the first war, though at the Marne in 1914 the French and British troops in the midst of a great retreat had suddenly turned and counterattacked, bringing the massive German offensive to a quick end. In his orders in the first hours of May 14 General Huntziger was adhering to traditional doctrine, and General Flavigny, Commander of the XXIst Corps, who received them, was going to be as much a stickler for the doctrine as his chief. This the events of May 14 and 15 would show—and disastrously.

The 3rd Armored Division, which was to lead the new counterattack and on which General Georges was pinning high hopes, had only been formed six weeks before and its units were spread out for several miles around Reims for training when the German offensive began on May 10. For the first couple of days it was not even alerted, and when orders came on the afternoon of the 12th to rush to the Sedan sector it was still dispersed. Instructed to proceed only by night it managed to reach its destination by dawn of the 14th but its tanks were out of gas, there was no fuel for them at hand, and the division had to wait for its own fuel trucks to catch up. Though its training was incomplete and it lacked a number of basic elements—antitank guns, engineering and repair companies, radios for its tanks, reconnaissance aircraft and a full complement of artillery—and though several tanks had been taken from it to reinforce two other armored divisions, it was still a powerful unit, certainly equal, if not superior, to a German panzer division with its 50 percent makeup of Mark I and II light tanks.

General Flavigny had wished to begin his counterattack at 11 A.M. on May 14 and was vexed that his armored division had not finished refueling by that time. But it started moving up to the line at noon. The plan was for the 3rd Armored, supported by the 3rd Motorized division, to advance in two groups, one from the Mont Dieu Woods and one from Stonne northward toward Chémery and Maisoncelle, respectively. This was the first step, and two more bounds, it was hoped, would carry the two divisions back to the Meuse and drive the Germans across it or destroy them before they could get over. The attack would begin about 4 P.M. when both units would be fully deployed and ready.

The moment, though General Flavigny and General Brocard, who commanded the armored division, did not realize it, was propitious. An hour or so before—around 3 P.M.—Guderian had suddenly turned the 2nd and 1st Panzer divisions westward, leaving his southern flank dangerously exposed. He knew that he was taking a risk. He had only the Gross-Deutschland infantry regiment to protect his flank and it was nearly exhausted from two days of fighting and marching. The 10th Panzer to the east had been slowed down and could not reach a position to protect his flank before nightfall. Guderian talked it over early in the afternoon with General Kirchner, commander of the 1st Panzer. They concluded that the French were incapable of mounting any more serious counterattack than that which had been so easily repulsed that morning. They did not know of the presence of the French 3rd Armored and 3rd Motorized divisions directly on their flank. It was a gamble. If their two tank divisions struck west that afternoon they might rupture the front between the Second and Ninth French Armies. Then the way would be open to Paris—or to the sea, as the Manstein Plan had calculated. They took the gamble and the two panzer divisions turned and struck west across the Bar and the Ardennes Canal.

This was a golden opportunity for General Flavigny to strike at the exposed flank of the enemy—one of those rare moments in warfare when, as at the Marne in 1914, one swift, bold move can change the course not only of the battle but of the war. The occasion is fleeting. It must be taken advantage of within a matter of hours, or even of a single hour, or the chance is lost forever.

But the commander of the XXIst Corps was not the man to seize his opportunity, or even to see it, nor was General Huntziger, who was occupied with moving his Second Army Headquarters to safer parts far south of the battlefield to Verdun. At about 3:30 P.M., one half hour after the 1st and 2nd Panzers had turned west and one half hour before his counterattack which would have caught the panzers in the flank was set to begin, General Flavigny called it off until the morrow. Not only that, but he compounded his mistake by ordering the 3rd Armored Division dispersed over a 12-mile front, instructing General Brocard to scatter his tanks so as to block every road and path down which the German armor might come. In doing so, he destroyed the possibility of an effective counterattack the next day, for the armored division, dispersed over a wide front, its units hopelessly broken up, could not quickly reassemble. He destroyed the usefulness of the only French armored division available to redress the situation at Sedan. He gave a classic example of adhering to a doctrine whose fallacy Colonel Le Goyet has pointed out.*

---

* Even after the war General Flavigny stoutly defended his decision. In a lengthy note to the Parliamentary Investigating Committee he explained that he called off the counterattack because he "felt it was bound to fail. I did it on my own hook," he added. "I wished to avoid disaster and prevent the irreparable." So many timid French

General Flavigny, to be fair about it, apparently did not know that the two panzer divisions had abruptly turned west. The confusion on his front that afternoon was tremendous and field communications had broken down as the troops of the mauled 55th Division broke and ran. Also there seems to have been no attempt at aerial reconnaissance that afternoon though General Huntziger had several pursuit and observation planes at his disposal and could count on the Air Force for more. Was a call made for them? There is no record that it was. As we have seen, General Billotte had made a desperate call for Allied planes to bomb the Sedan bridges —there was only one in operation, the pontoon bridge at Gaulier finished by the Germans during the night of the 13–14th—and the British and French fliers had responded by carrying out a suicidal attack on the 14th.

Protected by French fighters, the RAF sent out all the bombers it had left in France, some 109 Battles and Blenheims, and General d'Astier managed to scrape up some 30 French bombers. The British lost 45 of their 109 planes, the French 5 out of 30.[23] But the bridge was not destroyed and none of the returning planes noted the German panzer columns turning west, or if they did, reported it. Still, Flavigny's apparent ignorance of Guderian's move scarcely appears to excuse him. The French counterattack had been set for 4 P.M. Two powerful divisions were ready to take off. Had the general allowed them to do so, had General Huntziger energetically intervened to see that they did, the course of battle might have been changed. All that day and evening Guderian worried about his exposed southern flank. His chief, General von Kleist, was even more concerned. At 10:30 that night of the 14th the two had a bitter exchange on the telephone. Kleist ordered the 1st and 2nd Panzers to halt their advance westward until their flank could be protected by the XIVth Motorized Corps moving up in support of the hard-pressed 10th Panzer. He forbade any further advance to the west for the next day. Guderian simply refused to obey.

> I neither would nor could agree to these orders [Guderian later recounted], which involved the sacrifice of the element of surprise we had gained and of the whole initial success that we had achieved.[24]

After a lengthy and heated argument Kleist reluctantly agreed to let Guderian continue his advance the next day. He could try to reach his objective for May 15: the line Wassigny-Rethel. Rethel! The town was on the Aisne, 32 miles southwest of Sedan. Its capture would mean the complete rupture of the link between the Second and Ninth Armies. It would open the way to Paris, little more than 100 miles away, or to the sea.

General Huntziger was less than frank when he reported to General Georges on the evening of May 14. The German "pocket" now was 10

---

generals that crucial week of May! Flavigny says that General Huntziger approved his decision.[22]

miles deep on a front of 15 miles. Huntziger did not mention this. At 7 P.M. he had his Chief of Staff inform Georges that his counterattack did not get off "for technical reasons" but that the "roads had been blocked by strong forces." Half an hour later Huntziger rang up Georges and told him: "The enemy advance has been stopped and sealed off between the Ardennes Canal and the Meuse by the Flavigny Group."

Georges was not satisfied. He thought Huntziger was "hesitating too much." It was not enough to seal off the enemy. The 3rd Armored Division had been given to Huntziger for a counterattack. Georges therefore got off a new order to the hesitant Second Army chief:

The 3rd Armored Division was put at your disposal to counterattack toward Sedan. Therefore tomorrow you must energetically pursue the operation so well started today by pushing on without letup as far as possible toward the Meuse. It is the only way to regain the initiative from the enemy and to paralyze any advance toward the west or south from the enemy pocket.[25]

Though General Georges, as this order shows, was deeply concerned, he did not yet fully realize what was happening at Sedan or (as we shall see) further north. At 10:10 P.M. he had his staff telephone General Gamelin to bring him up to date on the situation:

No great change since the last report. . . . The counterattack at Sedan did not take place . . . but the German advance appears to have been blocked.[26]

To make sure that General Huntziger would not stall, General Georges at 6 A.M. on May 15 confirmed his order for a strong counterattack toward Sedan. This was more necessary than he imagined, for Huntziger had given no new instructions during the night. The confirmation was telephoned to Second Army Headquarters so that there would be no excuse for delay. Only then did Huntziger act. At 7 A.M. he ordered Flavigny to take offensive action toward Sedan "based on tanks." That was the difficulty, since the 3rd Armored Division's tanks were still dispersed over a wide front. Two companies of heavy B tanks were engaged in local actions, one along the Ardennes Canal and the other at Stonne, and could not be withdrawn. General Flavigny did not appear to be in any particular hurry to launch the attack on which General Georges put so much store. He did not get around to issuing his orders until 11:30 A.M. The whole morning had been lost. He did suggest that the attack begin at 1 P.M. but General Brocard reported that his tanks could not be reassembled before 3 P.M. That hour was then set.

By now the whole conception of the operation had changed in Flavigny's mind. He had reverted to the doctrine so dear to most French generals. The tanks would be used not en masse as a spearhead but merely to "accompany the infantry." This, he explained later, "was the kind of tactics we all understood."[27] To add emphasis to his decision he placed the armored division under the orders of the commander of the 3rd Motorized Infantry Division, to whom he had already given all of General Brocard's artillery and infantry.* Thus, as General Roton, waiting anxiously at Georges' headquarters for news of the counterattack, put it later, the power of the armored division to drive a wedge was lost and Flavigny was left with carrying out "a methodical maneuver, limited to small advances."[29]

Even this did not take place. Since the heavy tanks had not yet been completely assembled, General Flavigny postponed his attack from 3 to 5:30 P.M. At 5 o'clock he called it off entirely—for the second time in 24 hours!

One tank battalion, the 49th, failed to receive the message and started off from the Mont Dieu Woods, advancing a mile or so, but the infantry failed to follow. After running into a nest of German antitank guns and seeing that the foot soldiers had not come up behind it, the battalion withdrew. The "counterattack" was over. And so were the hopes of saving the situation at Sedan.

General Huntziger, now back in Verdun far from the smoke of battle, waited until 5 o'clock the next morning before notifying the High Command of what had happened. Even then he was evasive. "The counterattack of the 3rd Armored Division and the 3rd Motorized Division," he reported to General Georges, "did not get off at the hour fixed because of unfavorable technical conditions and also, it seems, because of mechanical breakdowns."

This dissimulation did not fool Georges. "In reality," he later told the Parliamentary Investigating Committee in discussing this message, "the 3rd Armored Division had been so widely dispersed over a broad front in order to cover every road and path in the woods, that its regroupment for the counterattack was impossible. This division . . . was not properly used."[30]

Generals Huntziger and Flavigny had to have a scapegoat for their failure. Already at the end of the afternoon of May 15, after Flavigny had called off a counterattack for the second day in a row, Huntziger wrote him:

> I learn with indignation that my orders have not been executed and that the counterattack from which we expected so much did not take place because the commander of the 3rd Armored Division did not sufficiently support the commander of the 3rd Motorized Division.[31]

Huntziger was being no more honest with himself—or with Flavigny —than he was with General Georges. He ordered the corps commander to

---

* It seems curious that as the corps commander he did not direct the two divisions himself. He later explained that he placed the 3rd Armored Division under the command of the infantry division because it "did not appear to me to be capable of acting as an armored division."[28]

"personally conduct an immediate investigation." Flavigny, who did not like General Brocard or his armored division, whose function he did not understand, was as anxious as Huntziger to find a scapegoat. Late that evening he sent a chilly message to Brocard ordering him forthwith to explain why "most of his heavy B tanks were not ready to take part in the counterattack ordered for 3 P.M., May 15."[32] This from the one who had ordered their dispersal! Brocard dutifully replied the next day with a detailed report on how it had been impossible to reconstitute in a few hours a whole armored division that had been hopelessly broken up on superior orders. But it made no difference. Before he could finish his report, and just two hours after Huntziger's deceitful message to Georges at 5 A.M. on the 16th, the Second Army chief relieved General Brocard of his command.[33]

Apparently content to have found a scapegoat, General Huntziger abandoned any idea of further counterattacks. Though he now knew that two of the three German panzers that had driven him back from Sedan had turned west and were advancing rapidly toward the Aisne, and thus were no longer a threat to him, he was satisfied merely to dig in, fight defensive local actions, and hold his withdrawn front. After all, he insisted, his army had not been broken through. General Lacaille, his Chief of Staff, later told the Parliamentary Investigating Committee it had "achieved a defensive success."[*][34] It never seems to have occurred to General Huntziger, obsessed with defensive warfare as were nearly all the French generals, to try still to mount a great counterattack, calling on his superiors to give him reinforcements from the nearby Maginot Line, where 30 divisions remained inactive. The Germans would be vulnerable for several days as their panzer and motorized divisions wheeled westward. Hitler feared just such a counteroffensive from Huntziger's sector. He was afraid another "Marne" was in the making.

But Huntziger was no Joffre or Foch. There were no likes of them in the French Army in May 1940. Huntziger's timidity, his complacency, allowed Guderian's panzers on the 14th, 15th, and 16th to sweep by the Second Army westward, roll up the southern flank of the Ninth Army defending the Meuse from just west of Sedan northward to Namur, and help trap the Allied armies in Belgium.

By this time disaster had struck the Ninth Army too. The Second Army's failure made its doom certain.

THE DEBACLE OF THE NINTH ARMY

On the late afternoon and early evening of May 12 advance elements of four panzer divisions arrived at the Meuse between Monthermé and Dinant. General Corap, the Commander of the French Ninth Army, had not expected them so soon. The High Command had calculated that the

---

* This was the officer who, when asked by the Committee if there had not been panic in the Second Army, replied: "There was no panic. On the contrary, complete order reigned!"[35]

Germans would not be ready to even try to cross the river before D-6 day, or May 15. Corap had planned to get the left wing of his army, which had wheeled from the French frontier toward the Belgian part of the Meuse south of Namur, into position by the 14th. When his cavalry corps was quickly pushed back in the Ardennes on the 11th, he had ordered his troops to speed up by forced marches. But on the evening of the 12th, as we have seen, the two divisions of his XIth Corps, which were to hold the vital sector between Dinant and Givet, were far from being in position. Their columns were strung out for several miles to the west.

The Ninth Army had not been favored by the High Command, which did not expect it to be involved in heavy fighting. Of its seven infantry divisions, only two were "active" units, and only one motorized. It was woefully deficient in antitank guns—two divisions had none at all—and it had practically no antiaircraft weapons. Except for the light tanks of its cavalry corps, most of which would be lost in the Ardennes, it had few tanks. It lacked, except for the 5th Motorized Division, the transport to enable it to maneuver or even to bring up its troops in time to the Meuse. Horses drew its vehicles and guns. The men marched. If the High Command had neglected the Ninth Army so would the Air Force, whose planes were reserved mostly for the First Army and then for the Second. It had under its own command 26 Morane fighters and 30 Potez observation aircraft. This was scarcely a match for a whole German airfleet, which would be concentrated against it on the crucial day.

Weak as it was, the Ninth Army was given the widest front to defend. On its left the crack First Army held a front of only 25 miles between Namur and Wavre. On its right the Second Army around Sedan defended a sector of 38 miles. The Ninth Army's front, extending from Namur to Sedan along the Meuse, was 75 miles long. The 5th Motorized on the north held the line for 10 miles; the 18th and 22nd Divisions, comprising the XIth Corps, in the center for 24 miles; the 61st and 102nd Fortress, comprising the XLIst Corps, in the south for 41 miles. The front of the 102nd Fortress, which had no transport and could only stand and fight, was 25 miles long, far beyond the maximum allowed by army regulations. Part of it included the sector at Monthermé where General Reinhardt's two panzer divisions were concentrating.*

It was along this river front of 75 miles against this Army, the weakest and the most extended the French had, and not even fully deployed in its vital middle, that there now fell the brunt of the second part of the one-two punch of the German breakthrough attack at the vulnerable center of the Allied defense line.

A handful of infantry troops and motorcyclists of the 7th Panzer, commanded by the energetic General Rommel, was the first to get across

---

* In addition, aside from a cavalry corps of two and a half divisions sent forward into the Ardennes, the Ninth Army had two infantry divisions in reserve: the 53rd, a "B" type unit on the right flank, and the 4th North African on the left.

the Meuse just north of Dinant. Just as at Sedan the German foot soldiers began the assault by scrambling across the river. The tanks could not be brought over until the infantry had secured a bridgehead and a pontoon bridge could be built behind it.

The French had blown the bridge at Dinant in time, but late in the afternoon of May 12 a German motorcyclist patrol discovered that the Number 5 lock, which linked the island of Houx with both banks of the Meuse 3½ miles north of Dinant, was intact. They attempted to cross over on it but were driven back by a company of the 66th Regiment, which had been temporarily stationed there to guard the passage. The company was relieved a few hours later by a battalion of the 39th Regiment which had been lent to the 18th Division. Instead of occupying the water's edge, on which enemy machine-gun and tank fire was beginning to be felt, it remained on the slopes where it was difficult to cover the lock or the island. As soon as night fell the German motorcyclists slipped across the lock without a shot being fired on them and began to infiltrate up the slopes. At 3 A.M. in the darkness they surprised and overran the battalion, which had not bothered to leave the high ground to see what was passing below, and pushed north toward Anhée.

This was the first breach in the French defenses, but it was small and carried out by only a battalion of motorcyclists armed with rifles and machine guns. The French had plenty of artillery and at least one company of tanks to support the infantry in driving the detachment back into the river. A counterattack was ordered for early in the morning but it took time to organize it, and before it could be launched it was called off shortly after 8 A.M. and the troops were instructed first to halt the German infiltrations and then to counterattack—another instance of adhering to French military doctrine. In the meantime the Germans were getting across two battalions of riflemen to bolster the motorcycle battalion.

Two miles further south, at Bouvignes, Rommel tried to ferry his 7th Rifle Regiment across in rubber boats as soon as daylight came. He immediately ran into stiff resistance from the French 66th Regiment. Rommel later described his difficulties.

> The situation when I arrived was none too pleasant. Our boats were being destroyed one after the other by the French flanking fire, and the crossings eventually came to a standstill. The enemy infantry were so well concealed that they were impossible to locate even after long search through glasses.

As he drove down to the riverbank in a Mark IV heavy tank Rommel was slightly wounded by shell splinters. However, he pressed on.

> By the time we arrived, the 7th Rifle Regiment had already succeeded in getting a company across to the west bank, but the enemy fire had then become so heavy that the crossing equipment had been shot to pieces and the crossing halted. Large numbers of wounded were receiving treatment in a

house close beside the demolished bridge. . . . As there was clearly no hope of getting any more men across at this point without powerful artillery and tank support to deal with the enemy nests I drove back to Divisional Head-quarters where I met with General von Kluge (Commander of the Fourth Army) and General Hoth (Commander of the XVth Armored Corps, of which Rommel's 7th Panzer was one of its two armored divisions).

The German generals were a bit taken aback by this unexpected opposition, which threatened to jeopardize the whole undertaking. Rommel was urged to keep on trying. But he was worried.

In Leffé (a village on the outskirts of Dinant) we found a number of rubber boats, all more or less damaged by enemy fire, lying in the streets where our men had left them. Eventually, after being bombed on the way by our own aircraft, we arrived back at the river. . . . The crossings had now come to a complete standstill, with the officers badly shaken by the casualties their men had suffered. . . . Numerous damaged boats and rubber dinghies lay on the opposite bank. The officers reported that nobody dared show himself outside cover, as the enemy opened fire immediately on anyone they spotted. . . .[36]

Rommel's account is a reminder that in a battle where, as we have seen at Sedan and will shortly see here, so many French units broke and ran under the strain of incessant bombing and at the sight, or rumor, of approaching panzers, there were French units, like the 66th Infantry Regiment at Bouvignes, that stood and fought gallantly, inflicting heavy casualties on the Germans.

But by 10 A.M. Rommel had got enough of his riflemen across to take Bouvignes and infiltrate further along the ridge toward the woods of Granges and Surinvaux. He himself had taken charge of the attack, crossing the river in a rubber boat and directing the advance of the 2nd Battalion of the regiment. Liddell Hart, who edited Rommel's papers, comments that the general's

intervention was even more crucial and decisive than he conveys. The German troops were badly shaken by the intensity of the defenders' fire when he arrived on the scene and organized the fresh effort, in which he himself took the lead.

Fortunately for his chances, the French 18th Infantry Division . . . was only in the process of taking over the position after a lengthy march on foot, and was short of anti-tank guns, while the 1st Cavalry Division had not re-covered from the tank-mauling it had received in the Ardennes.[37]

Perhaps if more French divisional commanders had shown this kind of intrepidity the course of battle might have taken a different turn. Some, of course, did. (Several generals of divisions would be killed in action.) But not enough did. They were, after all, only following French military doctrine in keeping to the rear where they believed they could best direct their units. Gamelin scolds General Corap for spending too much time with his troops instead of remaining at his headquarters to oversee the battle.

By noon of the 13th or shortly after, the German pocket was some three miles wide and two miles deep. This was not very large, and the Germans, without tanks or close supporting artillery (though their big guns were beginning to fire from across the river), were outnumbered and outgunned by the defenders, who also had some tanks. The situation called for a vigorous counterattack. Already several had been ordered.

On the northern sector of the bulge the Commander of the 5th Motorized decided at 10 A.M. to launch an attack where his first one had been called off. One infantry reserve battalion, supported by a reconnaissance group, was detailed to attack the Wastia heights just west of Houx, which the Germans had taken. But the operation was fixed to begin only at 1 P.M.—such was the view of time at French divisional headquarters. The battalion did not start moving toward the starting line until 2 P.M.—the battalion commander's conception of time was similar to his general's—and on the way it was attacked by Stukas. Its men took cover until the bombing was over and did not arrive on the west slope of the Wastia heights until 6 P.M. when it was decided it was too late to begin the attack.

Two other counterattacks were ordered to the north of the Anhée basin at 3:30 P.M. for the 5th Motorized. The same story. In the first case, a battalion of the 14th Regiment of Motorized Dragoons, supported by a squadron of tanks, arrived so late that their push had to be abandoned because of darkness. A second attack, to be carried out by another battalion of the Dragoons, never got under way because the commander, arriving on the scene, found that his starting point on the edge of the Haut-le-Wastia had been abandoned. Both counterattacks were put off to the morrow— a refrain that we have heard at Sedan.

On the southern end of the small pocket where Rommel had now taken charge of his riflemen, General Martin, commanding the XIth Corps, also prescribed a counterattack for the 18th Division. Though he issued his orders at noon, he set the attack for 7:30 P.M. Everyone on the French side seemed to have a leisurely idea of time, with no idea of the quicker tempo of the Germans, who in the meantime were ferrying over more and more troops. Martin's force was directed to attack from the Foy woods against the Germans installed in the Surinvaux forest and drive them back into the river. It was considerably stronger than anything the Germans had in its way: two battalions of the 39th Infantry Regiment, led by a company of tanks, and supported by three groups of artillery. The march to the approach line, which got off behind schedule, was slowed by enemy bombing and the advance units did not arrive until 7:30 P.M., the hour set to attack. It was reset for 8 P.M. It was then discovered that though the tanks and the artillery were ready, the infantry battalions had not yet come up. Night was falling. There was not much time. The commander decided to go ahead anyway with his tanks, supported by artillery, hoping the riflemen could soon follow. The armored company, after pre-

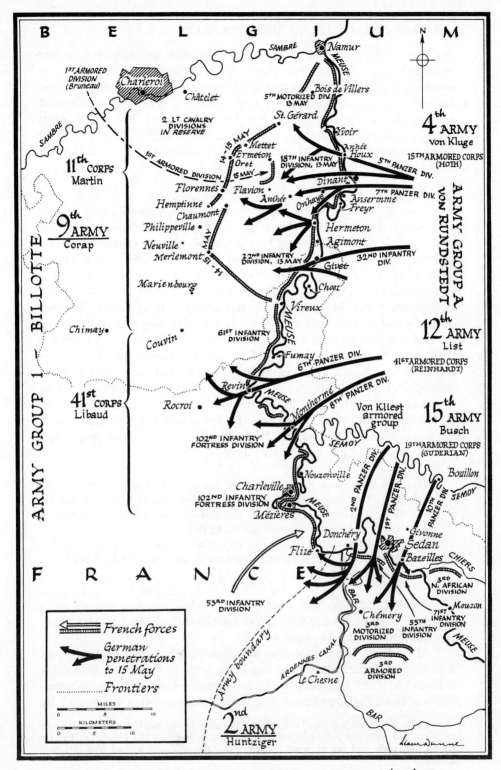

BATTLE OF THE MEUSE, II: FROM NAMUR TO MÉZIÈRES
MAY 13-16, 1940

liminary artillery fire, easily penetrated the Bois de Surinvaux, routed Rommel's motorcyclists, took many of them prisoner, mopped up the woods, and waited for the infantry to occupy it. But no foot soldiers showed up, and as darkness closed in the tanks withdrew. The one counterattack actually begun had succeeded—and then was wasted. The Ninth Army would pay dearly for its lack of diligence the next day, May 14, as the Second Army at Sedan had paid for it that same day. Here too the roof began to fall in.

Back at Ninth Army Headquarters at Vervins, General Corap and his staff took stock of this first day of battle to defend the Meuse. They had been "stupefied" on learning at 11 A.M. of the German crossing at Houx. But worse news was to follow. "Around 8 P.M.," General Véron, Deputy Chief of Staff, later recounted, "there came further bad news."[38] The Germans had also got across at Monthermé further south, at the confluence of the Semoy and Meuse. Actually this turned out to be less alarming than it sounded. The base of the loop in the river here was contained by colonial machine-gunners of the 102nd Fortress Division, who stopped Reinhardt's XLIst Armored Corps of two panzer divisions cold for two days until they were forced to retreat by developments elsewhere. One of those developments had already begun. Late that evening, says General Véron, still worse news arrived at Ninth Army headquarters. The left front of the Second Army had been broken between Sedan and the Bar. This was at the junction of the Second and Ninth Armies. The German penetration exposed the south flank of the Ninth Army.

This was very grave news. It was the germ of the whole drama, of the future debacle. This hole on the Second Army's left would be mortal for the Ninth Army. . . . General Corap took the only decision possible. He decided to sacrifice the 53rd Division by sending it to the Bar. . . .

Thus ended the day of May 13, a catastrophic day for the Ninth Army, faced with a triple menace at Houx, Monthermé, and on its right flank at the junction with the Second Army.

A catastrophic day, but, adds the general, "the situation was not really desperate." The promise of several divisions of reinforcement, he says, "gave hope of reestablishing the situation."*[39]

At La Ferté General Georges was disturbed. He had already received the bad news from Sedan. Then had come word of the Germans crossing at Houx. At 7:30 A.M. on May 14 he informed Gamelin: "The counterattack at Houx did not succeed. The infantry did not follow the tanks." He

---

* The 4th North African Division was already closing up. Other reinforcements set in motion were the 1st Armored Division, which had reached Charleroi, not far behind the front, and others more distant: the 14th, 36th, 44th, and 87th Infantry divisions.

then got off an order to General Billotte, under whose command the Ninth Army operated, to reestablish the situation on the Meuse. "The operations mounted during the 14th must be conducted with extreme energy. . . . No defections will be tolerated." Billotte, during the night, had already ordered Corap to take action on the 14th to throw the Germans back across the Meuse.

But Corap, immersed in the defensive doctrines of the French Army, was not thinking of taking the offensive, even though the German forces over the river were still weak and without tanks and therefore extremely vulnerable to strong counterattack. Instead, during the night, he drew up orders merely to contain the German bridgehead. When the German attacks had been held, and after reinforcements arrived, he intended to go over to the counterattack. This, as we have seen at Sedan, was the French Army doctrine.* General Roton, Georges' Chief of Staff, was not entirely pleased. He did not like Corap's orders for a "purely defensive deployment." They had a bad effect, he later said, on the events of May 14.[41]

The morning of the 14th appeared to start well. At dawn elements of the 5th Motorized Division on the north of the pocket, the 14th Motorized Dragoon Regiment, and the division's Reconnaissance Group began the attack on the Wastia heights which had been called off the night before. The French quickly overran the ridge, scattered Rommel's motorcycle battalion, and took forty prisoners. After this success, which seemed to give a shot in the arm to the division, the attackers were ordered to withdraw! General Corap insisted on all units stationing themselves on a line of defense further to the rear. The last chance to counterattack and drive the Germans to the river before they got their tanks over was missed.

By dawn Rommel's engineers had finished building a pontoon bridge at Bouvignes and early in the morning his tanks and artillery began to cross over. The general's plan was to clear the heights west of the river, move southwest on Onhaye, which blocked the valley leading to Philippeville, take it and advance on the latter, 25 miles away.† Though isolated French units fought stubbornly, slowing up the panzers at several village strong points, the 18th Division already was becoming demoralized and broken up by the incessant bombing, which the French Air Force did not oppose,‡ and by the first sight of enemy tanks. Not even reinforcements from elements of the 4th North African and the 1st Light Cavalry restored its morale or its cohesion. Exercise of command became almost impossible

---

* "That was the doctrine," General Vallet, Chief of Operations of the Ninth Army, later lamented. "It did not offer a response that corresponded to the situation. The situation demanded an immediate and brutal reaction."[40]

† On August 23, 1914, General Franchet d'Esperey, recognizing the importance of Onhaye, had counterattacked and retaken it from the Germans.

‡ French Air Force records do not disclose any action at all on the Ninth Army front on the 14th. All planes were concentrated for attacks at Sedan. The Luftwaffe, which had employed almost all its available planes at Sedan on the 13th, switched them on the 14th to the Dinant sector against the French Ninth Army.

during the day. Field telephone communications were destroyed by bombing. What little radio facilities there were did not work. Messages sent out by motorcyclists were delayed because the roads were jammed with fleeing refugees, by troops trying to move forward, and others trying to retreat. By afternoon there were definite signs of panic. When the day ended Rommel's 7th Panzer had taken Onhaye and Morville, halfway to Philippeville, where the division halted for the night to regroup and refuel. In the process it had surrounded a number of French battalions and rounded up their men as prisoners.

Further south on the front of the XIth Corps' 22nd Division the story was the same. Here there were no panzer divisions to confront. But units of the German 32nd Infantry Division, supported by a few light tanks, got across the Meuse north and south of Givet. After desultory fighting the Commander of the 22nd Division ordered a withdrawal to a new position six miles to the rear, abandoning its whole front along the river. "Here was another division," Colonel Goutard comments bitterly, "that disintegrated at the first blow."[42] That afternoon Ninth Army staff officers sent out to contact the forward units reported a great deal of disorder along the roads. Troops were starting to panic and to flee. To the rear, at Georges' headquarters, General Roton, attempting to get some kind of picture out of the confusion, concluded that the Germans now had a bridgehead west of Dinant some 30 miles wide and ten miles deep. "In 24 hours," he exclaims, "the forcing of the Meuse has become a *fait accompli.* . . . No one had foreseen such speed!" He could not forgive the Commander of the 22nd Division. "In the course of 12 hours of combat," says Roton, "he changed his Command Post three times, pulling back 12 miles, distancing himself each time from the zone of combat and from his Corps commander and, in fact, renouncing the command of his troops."[43]

The Corps commander, General Martin, decided at 7 P.M. to pull his two battered divisions, the 18th and 22nd, back to a new "barrier line" running from Oret in the north, south through Florennes, Chaumont, Merlemont, and then southeast to the Meuse at Vireux. There he hoped to rally his retreating infantry and, with the 1st Armored Division, which finally was coming down from Charleroi that evening, to launch a strong counterattack. His order for a new retreat struck Ninth Army Headquarters as nothing less than disastrous. It was already reeling under the "grave news," as General Véron puts it, "from the XIth Corps that the 22nd Division was completely broken through and that the 18th can no longer hold. . . . What was worse was the order of General Martin, which he made on his own initiative. This seemed to us to be a catastrophe."[44]

What followed is a matter of dispute among the French military. At 2 A.M. on the 15th General Corap called his Army Group 1 chief, General Billotte, about his critical situation. General Véron says it was a stormy and dramatic conversation. He contends that General Billotte ordered the Ninth Army to make an even bigger retreat than General Corap and General

Martin had envisaged—all the way back to a line running from Charleroi down through Marienbourg–Rocroi–Signy-l'Abbaye. General Roton gives a quite different version. According to him, Corap called Billotte, told him his troops were falling back all along the line, that the situation was grave, and that he proposed to retreat even further than anyone hitherto had suggested: back to the French frontier! Billotte agreed, but asked that the Ninth Army halt temporarily on the line mentioned above, from Charleroi south.[45]

Whoever was responsible, this new order hastened the dissolution of the Ninth Army. The disorder and the lack of communications was too great to allow for a planned retreat. Some units got General Martin's order and halted on his line. Others got Billotte's or Corap's and hastened back to their line. Still others simply made for the French frontier as quickly as they could.

What had happened to the 1st Armored Division, France's crack tank unit, which the harassed generals of the Ninth Army had hoped might stop the onrush of the panzers and even lead a counterattack back to the Meuse?

Despite all the studies and discussions among the top generals in the prewar years about forming tank divisions—or perhaps because of them—the 1st Armored Division (and the 2nd) had only been constituted on January 16, 1940, five months after the beginning of the war. Though deficient in training, in refueling facilities, in certain arms—it had no flak —and lacking suitable radios in its tanks which made communication difficult, the 1st Armored Division was a powerful unit, the equal to any German panzer and superior to some. Formed in two demibrigades, each of two tank battalions, one of heavy B's, the other of light H's, it had its own regiment of artillery, a battalion of Chasseurs and a battery of excellent 47-mm. antitank guns.

In training at Suippes north of Châlons, it was alerted on May 10 and began moving north the next morning. But immediately it became the victim of faulty army practice. While its wheeled vehicles got off by road its tanks were dispatched on flat cars by rail, the idea being to save wear and tear on their tracks. Thus until it reached its destination, which itself was uncertain, it was hopelessly dispersed and needed a good deal of time to be reassembled. The distance to its eventual assembly point north of Charleroi was only 90 miles, no more than Rommel's division, which it was fated to meet, had to make to the Meuse. If it had traveled as a unit on the roads, as the German panzers did, it could have reached its destination easily in one day.*

But in the French Army things were not so simple. To begin with, the

---

* Asked by Professor Dhers at a meeting of the Parliamentary Investigating Committee what he thought of this method of transporting an armored division partly by rail and partly by road, General Bruneau, the Commander of the 1st Armored, replied: "It was terrible. It belonged to a doctrine of the past."[46] Still another example!

division was directed to assemble in the vicinity of Saint-Quentin, 75 miles behind the First Army's position at Gembloux, which it was directed to support. This seems a little far. Then on the night of May 11, when the division was scattered over the roads and railways on its way to Saint-Quentin, it was directed to deploy north of Charleroi, directly behind the First Army. This change caused further delays and it was not until the morning of May 14, four days after being alerted, that the division was able to get in place behind the First Army. This army was expecting to meet the brunt of the German Sixth Army's attack that day or the next in the Gembloux Gap north of Namur and the 1st Armored commander, General Bruneau, was instructed on the evening of the 13th to have his tanks ready.

Hardly had he received this order when another came. While remaining prepared to carry out the mission for the First Army he was also told to get ready for another for the Ninth Army: to move south across the Sambre river for action against Dinant. All morning long on the crucial day of May 14 General Bruneau waited for definite word from on high as to which operation to carry out. As things turned out, this was a disastrous loss of time. Not until 12:45 P.M. did he receive any word at all. At that hour he was instructed to rush his division south of the Sambre in order "to counterattack and repel over the Meuse the enemy forces which have crossed at Dinant." He was told to report in person at Florennes to receive detailed orders from the Ninth Army.

Racing by car over the cluttered roads to Florennes he found there the hard-pressed commander of the scattered, retreating XIth Corps. It was now 2:15. General Martin had no idea by this time where his units were. It was finally agreed that General Bruneau would get his tanks in the vicinity as soon as possible—they were already en route—push them as far forward as he could, and "tomorrow," as the general puts it, "we would see." But General Corap, already tasting disaster, could not wait for the morrow. When General Bruneau telephoned him to advise that his division was on the way and would be in position by early morning the next day, the Ninth Army commander replied: "No, Bruneau, that is not good enough. You must counterattack this evening with all that you have. That's a formal order."[47]

Attack with what? His first tanks could not arrive before 8 P.M., an hour before dark, and the rest not before 3 A.M. They would be low on gas and need refueling. Bruneau informed General Martin that a counterattack that evening was out of the question. Again they agreed they would just have to "do the best they could" the next morning. General Martin was not optimistic after the disaster to his corps. "We'll try to make the infantry follow the tanks," he said. "But that at the least is questionable."[48]

When dawn of the 15th came and Bruneau's men were still frantically trying to refuel their tanks from the few gasoline trucks that had managed to arrive (most of them had been left in the rear of the column), the general found that there was no trace of any infantry from the XIth Corps around. They had fled to the rear of him during the night. His armored division stood there alone far in front of any foot soldiers, deployed on the road between Ermeton and Flavion, one brigade of tanks facing east, the other south, where elements of the XIth Corps were supposed to be, but weren't. There had not been time to refuel many of his tanks. Some had gasoline for only two hours of action.

Once again the French would pay dearly for their avoidable delays. Had the 1st Armored Division been dispatched on May 10 by road it could have been ready to counterattack against Dinant on the 13th, when the Germans had not a single tank over the river to oppose it. Had General Bruneau even been instructed definitely on the evening of the 13th to start moving his division that night toward Dinant,* it might have been able to mount a serious counterattack the next morning, when the 5th Motorized and the 18th Infantry were still holding fairly well, the bridge-head was small, and Rommel was just beginning to get his first tanks over at Bouvignes and the second panzer division, the 5th, had not yet begun to cross. By the morning of the 15th the situation had drastically changed. The bridgehead had been greatly expanded, two infantry divisions of the XIth Corps had been routed, and both enemy panzer divisions were across the river in full strength and driving at full speed westward.

At 9:30 A.M., supported by swarms of bombers and by their own artillery,† they fell upon the French 1st Armored, many of whose units were still refueling. The 7th Panzer (Rommel) attacked first from the south and a little later the 5th Panzer (General Walsporn) from the north. A furious battle raged for several hours. Against one panzer division the 1st Armored might have prevailed. Against two it had no chance. Besides, Rommel sent some of his tanks around the battlefield toward Florennes and Philippeville, outflanking General Bruneau's force from the south. A good many tanks on both sides were knocked out, but Bruneau, with fewer of them, suffered more than the Germans. At 2 P.M., realizing that he was being outflanked on the south, he ordered his division to pull back on a line Mettet-Oret-Florennes. But most of his units were still heavily engaged and it was difficult for them to disengage. By the time the division got back to the new line three of its four battalions had been decimated. The 28th had only 3 out of 36 heavy tanks left. Most of them had run out of gas and had had to be destroyed by their crews. Of the three companies of B tanks of the 37th Battalion, two were wiped out. Only one showed up at Mettet

---

* "General Billotte certainly thought on the 13th," says Roton, "that he would have to send the 1st Armored Division to the Ninth Army. But faithful to his first intention of engaging this crack unit for the benefit of the First Army, he kept hesitating to reroute it."[49] General Georges had specifically instructed him on the evening of the 13th to send it to the Ninth Army. The responsibility of the chief of Army Group 1 for the delay is thus considerable.

† Apparently anticipating an order to withdraw, General Bruneau had sent five of his six batteries of artillery to the rear, out of range.

fairly intact. The 26th Battalion had only six light tanks left. A good many of them too had had to be abandoned when their fuel tanks became empty. The division reported it had knocked out 100 German tanks—out of some 500—though this probably was an overestimate.

When General Bruneau that evening began to retreat on general orders further west toward Beaumont he had only 50 of the 175 tanks with which he had begun the day. When he withdrew to the French frontier at Solre-le-Château on the 16th there remained only 17 tanks, the others having been lost in the night or abandoned because of lack of fuel.* Another French armored division had been needlessly, heedlessly, sacrificed.

While the 1st Armored was making its valiant but futile stand, the Ninth Army was in disorderly retreat toward the French border. Even as daylight on May 15 broke, at 4 A.M., General Billotte had telephoned General Georges: "The situation of the Ninth Army is critical. The whole army is falling back." He suggested that General Giraud replace General Corap in order "to put some life into this wavering army." But, as usual, it was too late. What could the energetic Giraud do with an army that was fast disintegrating? By the time he arrived at its headquarters at Vervins on the afternoon of the 15th he could not even find it. The Ninth Army had ceased to exist. Four days later Giraud himself was captured.

All day long on the fatal 15th of May the Ninth Army had continued to fall apart in utter pandemonium. On the northern wing the 5th Motorized Division, the only one in the IInd Corps, fell back rapidly to keep pace with the retreat of the XIth Corps to the south. When it arrived at the French frontier near Maubeuge on the morning of the 17th it had only 1,000 men and had lost almost all its equipment. End of the IInd Corps and the 5th Motorized Division! The XIth Corps to the south, whose two infantry divisions, the 18th and 22nd, had borne the brunt of the attack by Hoth's two panzer divisions, now pulled back as rapidly as it could to the French border. Scattered units here and there blocked the enemy tanks for a few minutes or for an hour but the rest fled in panic. A few scattered men of the 18th arrived at the frontier on the evening of the 16th but the division's general could not find them. End of the 18th Division! The 22nd, to its south, met the same fate. As two French officers described it,

> The reestablishment of the 22nd Division proved to be impossible. Its units fled back in disorder in the midst of an indescribable flood of vehicles of every kind, of convoys of refugees, which the German planes machine-gunned with-

---

* No one in the High Command seems to have given any attention to the problem of refueling tanks. When General Georges was asked after the war by the Parliamentary Investigating Committee who was responsible for seeing that the tanks were quickly refueled, he replied: "That is something to be looked into. Personally I don't know."[50] No one in the High Command seemed to know.

out a letup. . . . The divisional commander realized that it was impossible to regroup any of his units before reaching the frontier. . . . The Corps Commander, seeing what panic there was, agreed.[51]

End of the 22nd Division and of the XIth Corps!*

The bewildered General Giraud, giving orders to units that no longer existed, instructed the Ninth Army to take up new positions on the "fortified sector of Maubeuge" along the French border. And a scattering of men were rounded up here and there from the debris of the Ninth to do so. They had expected to find a strongly defended line, but when they arrived no fresh troops were around to hold the fortifications. "The place was completely empty," the XIth Corps commander reported. "No troops of any kind were there. The first thing we had to do was get the blockhouses unlocked."

That proved to be difficult. When the troops had set off for the Meuse on May 10 the casemates had been padlocked. When the remnants of them returned five days later the engineers who had been left with the keys had disappeared, leaving the keys with the local mayors. But the mayors in turn had fled, joining the horde of civilian refugees trying to keep out of the hands of the Germans. No keys. The doors had to be blasted open.

The French XLIst Corps, defending the Meuse at Monthermé and Mézières against Reinhardt's XLIst Armored Corps, had done better than its neighbors to the north and south. It had stopped the attacks of the panzers for two days. On the 14th its commander, General Libaud, had realized that the German breakthrough at Dinant and Givet to his north and at Sedan to his south threatened to outflank his position on the river. But he had hopes that the counterattacks of the 1st Armored near Dinant and of the 3rd Armored below Sedan would restore the situation, and he ordered his divisions, the 61st Infantry and the 102nd Fortress, to stay put. He was surprised to receive in the early morning hours of the 15th the general order of the Ninth Army to fall back.

This was difficult to do. His troops were heavily engaged. The Germans renewed their attack at Monthermé at 7:30 A.M. on the 15th with tanks and infantry and at the same time crossed the Meuse further south at Nouzonville and descended on Mézières from the rear. Libaud's corps lacked transport with which to move. The 102nd Fortress Division had

---

* Tardily, on May 13, the 4th North African Division had been sent from its base in the forest of Saint-Michel on the frontier to reinforce the corps. Speeded up by forced marches its forward elements reached Anhée on the night of the 14th and fought well there the next morning. One of the better infantry divisions in the French Army, it was however no match for the German armored units and was pressed back to the frontier on May 16, arriving there with only a couple of thousand men minus most of its guns and equipment. The divisional commander and his staff were captured the next day.

none at all, and the 61st very little. Also his reserve 53rd Infantry Division, which had been thrown in further south to try to block the German penetration west of Sedan on his flank, could not be extricated.

The 53rd had had a typical experience. In reserve behind the XLIst Corps it had been subjected to orders and counterorders, marches and countermarches. On the evening of May 13 it had been directed toward the Meuse between Mézières and the Bar just west of Sedan, where the 2nd Panzer was trying to cross the river. It was to face north along the stream there. At 9 P.M., worried by the German thrust at Sedan on his flank, General Corap had ordered it to the Bar, facing east to meet the Germans. At 11 P.M. came new instructions countermanding the previous one and orienting it again toward the north. During the night came still a new order to proceed to the Bar after all. The result was that on the morning of the 14th the division was scattered all over the place, since some units during the night had followed one order and others a different one. "It was a record," two military historians later commented, "in the art of dispersion."[52]

There had been a further complication. On the afternoon of May 14, General Georges, increasingly concerned about the growing gap between the Ninth and Second Armies, had named General Touchon to take charge of closing it. Touchon was in command of the Sixth Reserve Army, which turned out to be an Army Command without any troops. Besides, General Touchon was at Dijon far to the south, and he did not arrive at the caving front until the night of the 14th and could do nothing until the next day. He was promised strong reserves, the 2nd Armored Division and General Lattre de Tassigny's excellent 14th Infantry Division, but they were still far behind the front and could not engage immediately in the crucial battle. Supposedly Touchon had command of the troops forming the flanks of the Second and Ninth Armies, but they had not been withdrawn from the commanders of those armies. In this situation Huntziger continued to pull his left flank southward while Corap withdrew his right flank westward. The gap instead of being closed kept widening. Touchon was helpless.

The XLIst Corps, ordered by Corap to retreat hastily from the Monthermé-Mézières sector along the Meuse, simply could not do so, heavily engaged as it was and without transport. During the day Reinhardt's two panzer divisions, the 6th and 8th, overran the 61st and 102nd divisions. The French soldiers abandoned their artillery, threw their rifles into the ditches by the roads, ran as fast as they could, and surrendered when the tanks overtook them. At the same time the 2nd Panzer Division of Guderian's armored corps driving west from the Bar overtook and decimated the ill-fated 53rd Division. Here and there units of the three French divisions stood and fought valiantly until their ammunition was exhausted. But in the chaos the XLIst Corps could not fight as a large body. By evening the German panzers were at Rethel on the Aisne and at Montcarnet even further to the west, 38 miles from the Meuse and behind the Ninth Army.

By that time the Ninth Army had ceased to exist. End of the XLIst Corps! Its 53rd, 61st, and 102nd Divisions! They were the last to hold out. Next morning, May 16, the commander of the 61st Division, General Vauthier, wandered dazedly into General Giraud's Ninth Army Headquarters to report: "Of my division I fear I am the only man left." General Portzer, commander of the 102nd, who made for the woods when the panzers overran his Command Post, roamed about for another 24 hours and then was captured.

By the evening of May 15, three days after the German panzers had begun their attack on the river line, the battle of the Meuse was irretrievably lost.* The French Second Army had failed to hold the Germans at Sedan and its failure had exposed the flank of the Ninth Army, already in deep trouble.† The Ninth Army, despite individual acts of heroism here and there, had been completely destroyed in three days. "And without really having fought," Colonel Goutard thought in later assessing the battle. "Where was there a battle fought by the Army, conducted by its Commander? One saw only a few isolated battalions fighting, and bravely, and a few tank companies without support. Then all was liquefied in the retreat."[56]

Two armored divisions had been foolishly wasted in the battle of the Meuse. The 1st, west of Dinant, had been moved to its destination too late to intervene decisively. Then it had run out of gas and had had no support at all from the Ninth Army's infantry or artillery and none from the Air Force. The 3rd, below Sedan, had been squandered by an irresponsible dispersion which robbed it of the chance to counterattack as a powerful armored unit, when it had a golden opportunity. In the case of both divisions superior officers in the upper echelons were responsible for their misuse. "I must say in all frankness," General Bruneau, Commander of the 1st Armored, told the Parliamentary Investigating Committee

---

* General Menu goes further. "At 4 P.M. on May 15," he writes, "the *war* was definitely lost for us."[53]

† Though General Corap, Commander of the Ninth Army, was cashiered, General Huntziger of the Second Army was promoted. Gamelin reveals that when General Georges relieved Corap he also suggested to the generalissimo the same treatment for Huntziger. "I dissuaded him," Gamelin admits, "saying that Huntziger had appeared to pull himself together." Later Gamelin told the Parliamentary Investigating Committee that he subsequently concluded that Huntziger "had not done all he should have done" and that he "reproached" him for not bringing up the 71st and 3rd North African Divisions in time at Sedan.[54] Soon after his failure at Sedan General Huntziger was promoted to Commander of Army Group 3. Eventually he led the French delegation at the Armistice negotiations and became Minister of War in the Vichy government. He was killed in a plane accident returning to Vichy from North Africa on November 12, 1941. As for General Corap he was later exonerated by General Georges, following an investigation of the Ninth Army by General Dufieux. After the war Georges told the Parliamentary Investigating Committee that because the Ninth Army was threatened with encirclement by the rupture of Huntziger's forces at Sedan "it is therefore not fair to put all the blame on Corap, as some have done."[55]

after the war, "that I met a total incomprehension as to the employment of this arm. The High Command did not understand how tanks should be employed."[57]

With the Ninth Army liquidated and the 2nd Army of General Huntziger showing no disposition to do more than hold south of Sedan after the panzers had passed, the way was now open for the Germans to dash to Paris—or to the sea. Nothing, as General Gamelin now calmly informed the flabbergasted Premier, Paul Reynaud, stood in their way.

PANIC IN THE HIGH COMMAND

Back at the headquarters of the top brass, of General Gamelin at Vincennes and of General Georges at La Ferté, realization of the disaster on the Meuse dawned slowly. And then suddenly it hit General Georges, who had not taken a wink of sleep since the German offensive began, and whose nerves were already frayed from purely physical fatigue.

On the morning of the 14th his situation report at 7:30 was still optimistic, indeed complacent. While he reported that the counterattack of the Ninth Army had not succeeded at Houx because the infantry failed to follow the tanks, he was apparently not yet greatly worried about Sedan. The breach there, he said, was "sealed off" and a "serious counterattack under way." To Colonel de Bardies this account showed that the High Command did not yet realize what was happening.

This report actually signifies nothing. It tries to minimize the setbacks, reassure General Gamelin, and beyond him the government and public opinion. But worse, it does not cover any of the questions essential for the Command. It gives the impression that GHQ does not yet sense a disaster and consequently does not envisage any large strokes to cope with it.[58]

This was true during the fatal day of May 15 when the disaster on the Meuse swiftly unfolded. The gap between the Second and Ninth Armies was being torn wide open by the panzers. Yet the information exchanged between Georges and Gamelin showed no recognition of the danger. At GHQ, according to a study made by Colonel Gendry, "the reports flowing into it were rather favorable. Certainly air reconnaissance signaled important concentrations in the regions of Dinant, Monthermé, Mézières, and Sedan and numerous crossings of the Meuse, but the reports from the field seemed to indicate that nearly everywhere the situation was improving."[59]

Though Colonel Minart at Gamelin's headquarters at Vincennes would later remember the day as "sad, interminable, smelling of death," he recounts that the information furnished by General Georges was "neither good nor bad, though its laconicism became more and more suspect." The colonel spent a good part of the day circulating between the three headquarters, fighting the confusion on the roads jammed with refugees from the battle zones. He could see, he says, "the progressive floundering of our organization of command, which hour by hour became more paralyzed." Still, he adds, there was "scarcely an echo of this in the vitiated air of the submarine without a periscope, which was Vincennes."[60]

Incredible as it seems, the concern of General Georges toward the end of the afternoon was not over the breakthrough on the Meuse but with the Maginot Line, which the Germans had no intention of wasting their men in attacking. At 5 P.M. Georges personally telephoned the Commander of the XVIIIth Corps, which made up the right flank of the Second Army stationed at the western end of the great line of fortifications. "You must hold at all costs the Inor-Malandry shoulder," he told him. "The whole issue of the war may depend on it." But the Germans were not attacking the Maginot Line. They had already turned west toward Paris—or the sea. Georges, judging by his orders, still did not appear to comprehend this, nor did Gamelin.

That evening the generalissimo got out a situation report of his own, destined for the commanders in other theaters of war. "To sum up," he wrote, "the day of May 15 seems to show a lessening in the intensity of enemy action, which was particularly violent on the 14th. Our front, which was 'shaken' between Namur and the region west of Montmédy, is re-establishing itself little by little."[61] In reality, as we have seen, just the opposite was happening. But the High Command persisted in its belief that, just as had happened so often between 1914 and 1918, the situation seemed bound to become stabilized as the Germans ran out of steam and the French defenses strengthened. On the evening of the 14th, in fact, Georges had telephoned Gamelin to say, among other things, that "the German advance seemed blocked. . . . All the prisoners report the German troops are tired."[62] It is difficult to comprehend this optimism and ignorance at the level of the High Command, though in part the first must have stemmed from the second.*

Actually by the 14th of May, despite all the reassuring messages, panic had begun to sprout at the three headquarters. General Georges, in fact, was breaking down. In the middle of the night on May 13–14 Captain Beaufre at GHQ was awakened by a telephone call from Georges. "Ask General Doumenc," he said, "to come over immediately." The general and his aide arrived at the Château des Bondons, Georges' personal CP, at

---

* General Gamelin appears—for the first time—to have become a little skeptical on the 14th. While conferring with Georges at La Ferté that morning Huntziger had telephoned the Commander of the Northeast Front. Afterward Georges, "justifiably upset," had turned to Gamelin: "Huntziger tells me he can see from the heights back of the Meuse French soldiers down in the valley leaving their casemates and raising their hands to surrender. He has ordered his artillery to fire on them."[63] That must have been the last time Huntziger saw his troops in action at Sedan. During the day, as we have seen, he pulled out for his new headquarters at Verdun. Since this fortress was southeast of Sedan and the German panzers were turning west, the commander of the Second Army was putting a surprisingly large distance between himself and the battlefield.

3 A.M. All the lights were out except in the map room, where Georges sat at an improvised table with his staff officers. Beaufre describes the scene.

> General Roton, Chief of Staff, is slumped in a chair. The atmosphere is that of a family gathered around a dying member. Georges rises and greets Doumenc. He is terribly pale. "Our front has been broken through at Sedan. There have been defections. . . ." He falls into a chair and sobs. He is the first man I have seen crying during this battle. . . . It gives one a frightful impression.

General Doumenc, a man of irrepressible high spirits, was "surprised," says Beaufre, "at this welcome." But he reacted immediately.

"General," he said to Georges, "*c'est la guerre*. And war always brings these things." The Commander of the Northeast Front described the breakthrough at Sedan. "There was another sob," Beaufre recounts. "All the others remained silent, overwhelmed by the event."

"Look here, General," said Doumenc. "In all wars you have stampedes. Let's look at the map and see what we can do." And poking at the map Doumenc sketched a maneuver: a powerful counterattack against the German pocket with three armored divisions, the First from the north southward, the Third from the south northward, the Second from the west toward the east. With 600 tanks between them they could push the Germans back across the Meuse. Beaufre says Georges agreed, dictated the necessary orders while he, the junior officer, woke up the cook and got him to brew some coffee to soothe everyone's nerves. Beaufre, who after the war achieved the rank of a General of the Army, believes that General Georges had never fully recovered from the serious wounds he received at the time of the shooting of Barthou in Marseilles in 1934. Now events were overwhelming him. "This brilliant and resolute man," he concludes, "had no more nerves with which to meet the uncertainties of command." And though at the hour of this dramatic meeting during the night of May 13–14 the Second and Ninth Armies were still intact, "the High Command," he felt, "had seen its own morale broken. It would never recover it."[64]

From the headquarters of General Georges at La Ferté the panic began to spread to the CP of General Gamelin at Vincennes. "Though no really disastrous news was received on the 15th," Colonel Minart later noted, "the tension grew and a collective nervousness set in. . . . Gamelin, outwardly serene, was giving way to a growing fear." While the generalissimo began to realize, as he later wrote, "the gravity of the situation," he spent a good part of this day, he confesses, pondering a gentle reorganization of the High Command. No drastic shakeup of the faltering commanders in the field such as his old chief Joffre, phlegmatic though he was, had carried out in the very first month of the war in 1914 during the great retreat, when he had dismissed forty-seven generals and replaced them with younger and more energetic men. All Gamelin could think of on this critical day of May 15, 1940, was a slight readjustment at the top staff level of command. It now suddenly looked as if the government might have to abandon Paris and the High Command move south to the Loire. In that case Gamelin thought it best to reduce the three Army headquarters to one—at last!—and confide it to General Georges—and this despite the fact that he was fast losing confidence in this bewildered and exhausted general. As for himself, he would merely remain as Chief of the *Etat-Major* of National Defense, coordinating the whole war effort. "This reorganization," he writes, "is easy to execute. I have thought about it for a long time, and everything is determined in my mind."[65] Such was the preoccupation of the Commander in Chief on the day disaster befell his armies in the field.

In the morning, to be sure, he had sent out an aide, Colonel Guillaut, to find out just what had happened to the Ninth Army. "It was the first time," he notes, "that I had sent out a personal liaison officer to an Army." Right up to the brink he had insisted on observing the static rules of the chain of command. The colonel returned to Vincennes that night and confirmed the worst. The situation of the Ninth Army, he told Gamelin, was "truly critical."

The headquarters of this army did not know exactly where its divisions were. Guillaut had met everywhere on the roads troops in complete rout. At the first sign of German motorcyclists, followed by a few tanks, everyone fell back, often in disorder.[66]

Next day the colonel was authorized to instruct General Georges' headquarters to see to it that the *gardes mobiles*—the police!—stop the fleeing troops along the roads, make those who were getting away in civilian buses and trucks get out, and "order them all to regroup and advance toward the front."[67] Gamelin himself issued a stern order to the troops, as the result, he says, of Colonel Guillaut's account of the debacle of the Ninth Army. It was Order No. 17.

You are reminded of the terms of paragraph No. 18 of Instructions for Service in the Field:
"The Commander employs all his energy in maintaining discipline, in stimulating faltering spirits, so as to keep order among the soldiers under his command. *If necessary he forces them to obey*." Any commander who does not conform to these prescriptions will be failing in his duty.

"I thought it necessary," Gamelin explains, "to put this out in view of the acts of indiscipline which had been reported to me."[68]

During the 16th the extent of the catastrophe finally began to be grasped at Vincennes. The unbelievable news came not from Georges, who remained silent for the most part, but from more direct sources. At 11 A.M., the Chief of Staff of the 2nd Military Region,* telephoned from Amiens to inform Gamelin that it had just learned that the Germans were at Montcornet, that French troops were retreating in the greatest disorder, and that 30,000 of them, from scattered units, had arrived at Compiègne, just north of Paris. Vincennes, says Colonel Minart, was "stupefied." An hour later came another call from Amiens saying that the horde of soldiers at Compiègne claimed they had retreated at the orders of a Captain de Foulonge. This caused a bizarre scene at the CP of the Commander in Chief. Minart describes it. "Who is Captain de Foulonge? The whole activity at Vincennes is concentrated on this captain. Lively criticism of him. But who is he?"

The staff officers search the records. One notation says the captain is a staff officer at the XLIst Corps; another that he belongs to the staff of the Ninth Army. "The fury grows," says Minart. "Everyone blames the captain. Poor Captain de Foulonge!"[70]

Poor Vincennes! Gamelin begins issuing orders and instructions right and left. At 1:30 P.M. he tells Georges "not to forget to destroy the oil depots in case of retreat." He wires London to implore Churchill to send over more fighter planes (though the French are not employing all they themselves have). He instructs the fleeing troops to set up knots of resistance, "even when they are encircled." He tells them that "after the wave of German tanks has passed, especially the heavy ones," they must "attack the rear of the enemy and cut his communications and supply lines."[71]

At 2:30 P.M. a strange apparition appears at the headquarters of the Commander in Chief. A Lieutenant Roger Le Bloa arrives directly from the front, with a few tattered men from the 17th Battalion of Chasseurs. They are, says Minart, "worn out and dying of hunger." They recount scenes of the debacle. At the first appearance of the panzers, they say, the French troops fled. And Minart, after listening to them, adds: "In 1814 the cry was: 'The Cossacks are coming!'; in 1870: 'The Uhlans are coming!'; and now in 1940: 'The panzers are coming!' "[72]

At the end of the day of the 16th, says Minart, "a wind of panic blew over Vincennes." Colonel Petibon, Gamelin's Chief of Staff, ordered a 75-mm. gun mounted in the courtyard pointed toward the south gate to ward off the enemy. "Everyone," Minart notes, "has lost his head." Officers began packing their bags. Cabinets were hastily emptied of papers. Documents were flung into packing cases. Maps were torn off the walls and rolled up.

---

* Colonel Minart emphasizes that the 2nd Military Region was under the jurisdiction not of the Commander in Chief nor of Georges nor of GHQ, but of the Ministry of National Defense, and that it was therefore most unusual for it to call Gamelin's CP directly.[69] Apparently by this time some bold officers were beginning to throw away the musty rule books.

General Gamelin himself [Minart adds], sad and at loose ends, inspiring a profound pity, wanders here and there between his Chief of Staff and his ordnance officers, trying to clutch at God knows what fetish. No one dares to approach him. Everyone knows that a battle has been lost.[73]

Consternation in Paris

In Paris the government of Paul Reynaud had had difficulty in learning from the High Command how the battle was going. The indefatigable Colonel de Villelume, the Premier's Military Counselor, set off each morning for the various army headquarters but usually returned empty-handed. The generals resented, he said, "the curiosity" of the President of the Council. "We know nothing," Baudouin lamented on Sunday, May 12, when the colonel after three visits to GHQ returned without any news.[74] The public was kept in complete ignorance. Strict military censorship prevented publication of any bad news. The headlines featured stories of an impending German attack in the Balkans, very little about the actual attack in the West. Life in the capital went on just about as usual. The weather continued sublime. The Parisians sunned themselves in the parks, sipped aperitifs on the sidewalk cafés, and crowded into the cinemas and theaters. They believed from what they read in their newspapers and heard on the radio that all was going well. A big battle apparently had begun in Belgium. The Germans, the communiqués assured them, were being halted.

On the afternoon of the 14th Colonel de Villelume returned to the Quai d'Orsay from Vincennes and told Reynaud that the situation was "very bad." General Huntziger's Second Army had fallen back south of Sedan. The Premier called a meeting of the War Committee. For the first time he heard from Gamelin that the French Army was in difficulty. At 7:45 P.M. he alerted Churchill by a personal message which was telephoned to London.

The situation is really very serious. The German Army has pierced our fortified lines south of Sedan. . . . Between Sedan and Paris there are no more fortifications comparable to those. . . .

He asked the new British Prime Minister, who had already sent over four additional squadrons of fighter planes, for ten more. Churchill, who could scarcely believe that the situation had become so grave so quickly, promised that the War Cabinet would give the matter "its most serious attention."[75] The British, like the French a day or so earlier, still thought there was plenty of time to act. By now the aroused Premier was beginning to know better.

The next morning at 7:30 he rang up Churchill, waking him up from a deep sleep. He spoke in English. "We have been defeated! We have lost the battle!" The Prime Minister could not quite grasp the words and said nothing. Reynaud repeated them. "Impossible!" Churchill finally replied. "Surely it can't have happened so soon."

> REYNAUD: The front is broken near Sedan. The tanks are pouring through.
> CHURCHILL: All experience shows that the offensive will come to an end after a while. . . . After five or six days they have to halt for supplies, and the opportunity for counterattack is presented. I learned all this . . . from the lips of Marshal Foch himself.
> REYNAUD: All that has changed. We're faced with a torrent of tanks.[76]

The Prime Minister concluded by saying he would be glad to come over to Paris the following day "and have a talk." "I did not comprehend," Churchill wrote later, "the violence of the revolution effected since the last war by the incursion of fast-moving heavy armor." The Prime Minister rang up General Georges, an old personal friend, who, he says, "seemed quite cool, and reported that the breach at Sedan was being plugged." A telegram came from Gamelin advising him that although the position between Namur and Sedan was "serious, he viewed the situation with calm."[77] The French generals, in contrast to the Premier, were reassuring.

At the end of the long day, the 15th, Reynaud got off another message to Churchill after he had been alerted, he says, by an "S O S on the telephone from Daladier." It was telephoned to London at 7 P.M.

> We lost the battle last night. The route to Paris is open. Please send all the planes and troops you can.[78]

The S O S from Daladier came as the result of a dramatic telephone call to the Minister of Defense from the Commander in Chief a few minutes earlier. The American Ambassador, William C. Bullitt, happened to be in Daladier's office when it occurred, and described it to President Roosevelt in an urgent cable that evening. The telephone rang. Gamelin was on the line. The Ambassador could not catch his words. But Daladier, he says, sat "totally incredulous and stupefied," listening. Finally he exclaimed: "No! What you tell me is not possible! You must be wrong! It's impossible!"

Gamelin explained that a column of German tanks had broken through and was nearing Rethel and Laon. "Then you must counterattack at once!" Daladier roared.

"What with?" Gamelin asked. "I don't have the reserves."

Daladier's face fell. He seemed, says Bullitt, to shrivel up. "Then the French Army is finished?" Daladier asked. "It's finished," Gamelin said.

"It seems obvious," Bullitt reported to Roosevelt, "that unless God grants a miracle, as at the time of the Battle of the Marne, the French army will be crushed utterly."[79]

Actually, Bullitt had seen Reynaud at 10:15 that morning and the

Premier had painted the situation as being of "the utmost gravity." The Germans had crossed the Meuse at many points north of Sedan.

> This morning at 6 o'clock Daladier had telephoned him and stated that the French troops could not hold out today against the masses of tanks and airplanes . . . and that the battle would certainly be lost quickly unless the troops could be protected from German attacks from the air.
>
> He, Reynaud, had telephoned immediately to Churchill in London and stated . . . that the war might be lost in . . . a few days . . . unless the British sent their planes from England at once.
>
> Churchill, Reynaud said, had screamed at him that there was no chance of the war being lost. . . .*

---

* Reynaud denied to me after the war that Churchill had "screamed" at him or that he had said any such thing to the Ambassador. This is but one example of Bullitt's anti-British bias, which was almost as fanatic as his anti-Russian, anti-Communist feelings. The Ambassador had a passionate love for France and the French that excluded any criticism of them, and both this and his lack of understanding for other countries and peoples tended to mar the value of his dispatches, though they are of great historical interest, especially in depicting the moods and certain utterances of the French leaders and the excitement of the unfolding drama. The historian Gordon Wright, after a study of Bullitt's dispatches (many of which, even some of the most important, are not published in the volumes of *Foreign Relations of the United States, 1940*), commented that "Bullitt's mind rattled like a machine-gun as he fired off daily schemes for saving France."[80] And not only France. As early as May 13 the Ambassador was also concerned with saving the pope, dashing off a cable to Roosevelt suggesting that the President invite the pontiff to take refuge in the United States in case of necessity.[81]

Bullitt's hysteria about Communism, which stemmed no doubt from his years as Ambassador in Russia, led to some fanciful reporting. On May 16, for example, he cabled the President that Reynaud had told him, among other things, that "the final and most horrible and incredible blow was that all the railroad workers of Belgium had gone on strike and were refusing to transport French troops."[82] Next day he was informing the President that "the Belgian railway strike was organized by the Communists on orders from Moscow. It has now been broken by the shooting of the Communist ringleaders."[83]

I can find no evidence in Belgian and French sources that there was a strike. General Gamelin did remark to Churchill on May 16, according to the French minutes of the meeting, "the Belgian railway strike was hindering the movement of troops," but he makes no mention of it in his memoirs or in his postwar testimony. Nor is there any hint of it in the records of the BEF, whose nine divisions depended in part on the Belgian railways for moving their supplies. Monzie, whose ministry in Paris had jurisdiction over working with the Belgian railways, explains that Baudouin "heard of a railroad strike in Belgium on the night of the 16th" but that when he himself looked into it that evening he found that Belgian locomotive engineers had been working 40 hours without relief hauling French troops and supplies. The rumors of a strike, he found, stemmed from the fact that the Belgian railways had been severely bombed by the Germans, causing many tieups.[84] Both Daladier and Reynaud told me they had never heard of the strike Bullitt reported.

But to the excitable American Ambassador in Paris, the Communists were responsible for a great deal that was going wrong. In a dispatch on the 17th Bullitt reported to Roosevelt that

> two infinitely more serious "fifth column" operations have taken place in the French Army.
>
> Nearly all the French heavy tanks were manned by Communist workmen from the Renault works in the outskirts of Paris. When they were given the order to advance against the German tanks they did not move. In one case

The Ambassador concluded his dispatch by saying that Reynaud had "implored" him to ask the President to rush over as many American planes as possible. "The situation," Bullitt added, "could not be more grave."[86]

To complete the bad news of the day of May 15, word was received of the formal capitulation of the Dutch Army. Giraud's Seventh Army, the most mobile one of all, had been uselessly sacrificed north of Antwerp in order to help Holland. Had it been held in reserve, as Georges had first proposed to Gamelin, it might have been thrown in behind the faltering Ninth Army on May 13 and just possibly might have saved the day. Its two motorized and one light armored divisions were now attached to the First Army and deployed behind the British and Belgians on the Dyle. Its headquarters were dispatched south to the Somme and General Aubert Frère became its new commander—another general, like Touchon of the phantom Sixth Army, for the moment without any troops.

All day long of the 15th Reynaud had become increasingly incensed with the lackadaisicalness of the High Command. According to Baudouin, the Premier, who, he says, did not want to call Gamelin directly for fear

---

when 63 French heavy tanks were ordered to make an attack only 5 went forward and 58 remained where they were. Furthermore, the men in the tanks in a number of cases smashed vital parts of the machinery.

I am informed that these men will be shot tonight.

An even more serious "fifth column" action in cooperation with the Germans on orders of the Soviet government are the Chasseurs. One regiment of Chasseurs which was composed of Communists from the Paris industrial suburbs revolted 3 days ago, seized the vital town of Compiègne on the German path to Paris and are still in possession of the town. They number 18,000 and I am informed that they will be attacked by the air force and tanks this evening.

That was a mighty big regiment! No regiment in the French Army, or in any other, contained 18,000 men.

Bullitt concluded his cable to Roosevelt:

Please for the sake of the future, nail every Communist or Communist sympathizer in our Army, Navy and Air Force.[85]

These two horrendous tales appear to have been made up out of whole cloth by Bullitt's informants (probably Baudouin, who does not mention them in his own memoirs) and swallowed by the Ambassador, who was prone to believe any tall tale about Communists. While there was some Communist sabotage in the armament factories and some defections among the troops, there is no evidence to support these fantastic accounts. Daladier and Reynaud could not believe that Bullitt had sent such reports when I questioned them about it. The detailed testimony of the commanders of all the four armored divisions, and even of the two Inspectors General of Tanks, Generals Duffieux and Keller, both of whom were extreme Rightists and as anti-Communist as Bullitt, is unanimous that the French tank crews fought magnificently before they were wiped out. As to the "regiment" of 18,000 Communist Chasseurs taking over Compiègne and about to be assaulted by the French "air force and tanks," this was pure fantasy. Actually some 20,000 troops, the debris of the destroyed Ninth Army, were milling about Compiègne at this moment, waiting for orders to reassemble. Perhaps from this chaotic scene rumors spread and Bullitt became an easy victim of them.

of offending Daladier, finally telephoned the Defense Minister to ask the reactions of the generalissimo to the collapse of the defenses of the Meuse. "General Gamelin has no reactions," Daladier replied. Reynaud, says Baudouin, was "stupefied." For the first time he brought up the name of Pétain. "Ah, if the Marshal were only here! He could do something with Gamelin! His wisdom and calmness would be a great help!" General Maurice Pujo, the former chief of the Air Force and a personal friend of Pétain, was summoned and packed off by Reynaud on the Sud-Express to Madrid to fetch the hero of Verdun. The Premier's nerves were wearing thin. When Villelume returned sometime after 7 P.M. "with a few scraps of information," Baudouin says, "he had been able to wrench from Gamelin's Staff Chief," he informed Reynaud that Colonel Petibon "had protested against the curiosity of the President of the Council." "If that continues," he quoted the colonel as saying, "I shall give no more information of any kind."

Reynaud, says Baudouin, "exploded." "It is time," he said, "to put an end to the comedy. I must take over the Ministry of Defense. Daladier will go to Foreign Affairs or depart."[87]

In the middle of the night of May 15–16, Gamelin phoned Daladier. He got General Decamp on the line. The Minister had gone to bed. Gamelin said he did not wish to disturb him. He merely wanted to leave word that the government must prepare to leave Paris. Reynaud got the word about 2:30 A.M. and this time he telephoned Gamelin directly.

"Is the situation really so grave?" the Premier asked. "You are requesting the government to leave Paris without delay? That's what General Decamp has just told me."

"I did not say exactly that," Gamelin says he responded. "I asked merely that the ministries be prepared to depart so as not to have to leave in disorder if the Germans do march on Paris."[88]

That was the subject of a hastily convened meeting at the Ministry of Interior at 3 A.M. There Reynaud and Daladier were joined by General Pierre Héring, Military Governor of Paris. According to Baudouin, Daladier was in a state of collapse. General Héring, a valiant old warrior, did not hide his emotion. He advised the government to quit the capital at once. General Gamelin, he said, had "declined all responsibility for Paris after nightfall of this day, May 16." There was no time to lose.[89]

"A morning of bewilderment," says Baudouin, "followed this troubled night." At 11 A.M. Monzie was "stupefied" by a call from Reynaud asking him to provide trucks to evacuate government files. The Germans, he was told, might be in Paris by midnight. The Premier was ordering all ministries to prepare to ship their archives south. The government, he said, must be prepared to leave Paris at any moment. At noon several ministers and the presidents of the two chambers met at Reynaud's office in the Quai d'Orsay with General Héring. When they arrived the Premier was scribbling out a proclamation to the Parisians telling them to pull out. He questioned Monzie, who, as Minister of Transport, would have to provide means of evacuating files and personnel.

"How many trains can you put at the disposition of the Parisians today?" he asked.

"Not a single one," Monzie says he replied.

"How many trucks for the two Chambers?"

"Very few."

In the light of this information cooler heads began to prevail. The flight of the government, several argued, would provoke a panic among the people and the troops. It would mean the end of the war. "Everyone," says Monzie, "talks at once." Finally Reynaud decided to postpone the evacuation. It was agreed that the government would remain in Paris until further notice.

Suddenly, says Monzie, in the midst of the deliberations there was a strange noise outside. He went to the window. Bundles of Foreign Office documents were falling past him from an upper floor and hitting the courtyard below.[90] Soon they were being fed into a huge bonfire. Smoke began to envelop the ornate palace of the Quai d'Orsay.*

CHURCHILL IN PARIS, MAY 16

Into this smoke-filled nerve center of confusion and fear came at 5:20 P.M. the new Prime Minister of Great Britain. From the moment he got out of his plane at Le Bourget an hour before, it was obvious, he says, "that the situation was incomparably worse than we had imagined." Confirmation of the worst now came from General Gamelin himself as Churchill, gathering at the Quai d'Orsay with Reynaud and Daladier, began to question the Commander in Chief. It was an eerie meeting, from the beginning.

> Everybody was standing [Churchill later recounted]. At no time did we sit around a table. . . . Outside in the garden . . . clouds of smoke arose from large bonfires, and I saw from the window venerable officials pushing wheelbarrows of archives onto them. Already, therefore, the evacuation of Paris was being prepared.

Gamelin stood before a small map mounted on a student's easel, poked at it to show where the Germans had broken through and "clear

---

* According to Pertinax, the Countess de Portes, "who prowled through the Foreign Office building when she did not bodily burst into the minister's office," exclaimed when she saw the bonfire: "What imbecile ordered that!" bursting into profanity. She was told that the Premier himself had ordered it. Later she and Reynaud put the blame on Léger. But there seems no doubt that the Premier himself gave the instructions. Pertinax adds that later in the day Madame de Portes busied herself packing at Reynaud's apartment in readiness for a quick getaway. "Suitcases," he recounts, "cluttered the entrance hall and even overflowed into the stairway."[91]

and calm," says Baudouin, "lectured as though he were giving a lesson in military strategy." The bonfires in the courtyard below were not the only source of smoke. The Prime Minister, according to Baudouin, puffed away at long cigars, producing a "volcano" of tobacco smoke.

Gamelin droned on for five minutes explaining the situation.

North and south of Sedan [he said, as Churchill remembered] on a front of fifty or sixty miles the Germans had broken through. The French army in front of them was destroyed or scattered. A heavy onrush of armoured vehicles was advancing with unheard-of speed toward Amiens and Arras with the intention, apparently, of reaching the coast at Abbeville. Alternatively they might make for Paris. . . .

When he had finished there was a long silence and finally Churchill asked: "And where is the strategic reserve?" Slipping into French he repeated: *"Où est la masse de manœuvre?"*

"General Gamelin turned to me," says Churchill, "and with a shake of the head and a shrug said: *'Aucune.'* There is none."*

"I was dumbfounded," says Churchill. It had never occurred to him, he confesses, "that any commanders having to defend five-hundred miles of engaged front would have left themselves unprovided with a mass of manœuvre. . . . I admit this was one of the greatest surprises I have had in my life."

I went back again [he says] to the window and the curling wreaths of smoke from the bonfires of the State documents of the French Republic. Still the old gentlemen were bringing up their wheelbarrows, and industriously casting their contents into the flames.†

The talks resumed. Churchill admits that he and his aides, General Sir John Dill, Deputy Chief of the Imperial General Staff, and General Ismay, Deputy Secretary of the War Cabinet, were still stunned. "We were staggered," he puts it, "at the evident conviction of the French Commander-in-Chief and leading Ministers that all was lost."

In a state of shock, unable to comprehend the extent of the disaster to the French Army, in which he had had such great confidence, Churchill now proffered some bad military advice—the last thing the French needed

---

* Gamelin later contended that he had not said "there is none," but "there is no longer any—*il n'y en a plus*."[92] It may be difficult for some to appreciate his subtlety. The fact was that on the sixth day of battle he was confessing that he had no more strategic reserves.

† The smoke drifted up the Seine to the nearby Chamber of Deputies, giving its members pause for thought. At 3 P.M. before Churchill arrived, Reynaud had thought it necessary to address the Chamber and reassure it. "We are full of hope. . . . Our soldiers are fighting bravely," he said. There was "no question," he added, of the government leaving Paris. Later that evening in a broadcast to the country Reynaud denounced as "false and absurd" the rumors that the government was contemplating leaving Paris. "The government," he said, "remains, and will remain, in Paris." In view of his instructions earlier in the day, this was less than frank.

at this juncture. This is clear from the French minutes of the meeting drawn up by Roland de Margerie, an aide to Reynaud. The Prime Minister stoutly opposed pulling back the Allied armies in the north, which were now being dangerously outflanked on the south. Instead, he proposed that those armies vigorously counterattack the Germans on *their* flank. Daladier, who had remained silent, now spoke up. His face flushed and drawn, he had been, says Baudouin, sitting in a corner "like a punished schoolboy." Now he turned to Churchill.

"The French Army has nothing left to cover Paris. We must withdraw the troops in the north."

"On the contrary," said Churchill, "they should dig in where they are."

"To do that," Daladier answered, "we would have to have some reserves. We have none."

According to the French minutes Churchill simply refused to believe that the thrust of the German armor represented "a serious menace."

"Unless the tanks are supported by infantry," he contended, "they represent a limited force. They will not be able to maintain themselves. They will have to be refueled, resupplied. . . . I refuse to see in this spectacular raid of the German tanks a real invasion. . . ."

The discussion was losing contact with reality. General Gamelin did not bring it down to earth when he broke in to say that he hoped to stem the German advance by ordering "for tomorrow a counterattack by Giraud's army." Churchill did not know that the Ninth Army, which Giraud was taking over that day, had ceased to exist.

The generalissimo, strongly seconded by Reynaud and Daladier, then demanded that the British throw in more planes—at least 10 squadrons of fighters. It was the only hope, they said, of halting the panzers. Churchill tried in vain to show that fighter planes could not stop tanks. "It is the business of the artillery to stop the tanks," he argued.

It seemed strange to him that the French High Command, which had at its disposal the greatest array of artillery in Europe, did not see this. Besides their modern guns, the French had an almost unlimited supply of 75's left over from the first war. They made excellent antitank guns. I remember thinking when, a few days later, I followed the German troops briefly through part of their push through Belgium and northern France how effective the French 75's would have been had they been strung out behind the roads down which the panzers were passing almost unmolested.

Churchill, who had already ordered four new squadrons of fighters to France, agreed at the end of the day to ask for the dispatch of six more. That left only 25 squadrons in Britain to defend the isles, a necessity that became more and more evident to the Prime Minister as the day passed. Just before midnight he received the approval of the cabinet in London for the air reinforcements and hurried over to Reynaud's apartment behind the Chamber to inform the Premier. He found it "more or less in darkness," but "after an interval M. Reynaud emerged from his bedroom in his dressing-gown, and I told him the favorable news." Churchill persuaded him to send for Daladier, who he thought also needed bucking up. The crumbling Defense Minister duly arrived. "He never spoke a word," says Churchill. "He rose slowly from his chair and wrung my hand."

According to Reynaud, the British Prime Minister rounded out the impromptu midnight meeting with a "fiery improvisation on the way to fight the enemy and announced, among other things, that the RAF would set on fire the harvest fields and the forests of Germany." Churchill says he got back to the British Embassy "about 2 A.M. and slept well." [93]

He had been wrong, he admitted later, in arguing that the Allied forces in the north should hold their ground east of Brussels. In truth, the French High Command had been in no hurry to withdraw them despite the collapse of the Ninth Army and the arrival of the German panzers at the French frontier south of Maubeuge. This put the enemy on the southern flank of the First French Army, the British Expeditionary Force, and the 22 divisions of the Belgian Army still holding out well on the line Antwerp to Namur. But General Georges appeared slow to realize the danger. He was, says Colonel Lyet, "but imperfectly informed of the situation even on the evening of May 16."[94] During the day he had issued a lengthy Order (No. 14) designed "to halt" the enemy. The armies of the north were to stay put, except that the First Army was to pull back along the Sambre on its southern flank. "The operation," Colonel Lyet wrote, "is impossible. Nothing can now oppose the march of the enemy toward the sea."

According to General Roton, his Chief of Staff, General Georges did not realize until the evening of the 16th the full extent of the disaster to the Ninth Army. Only then, says Roton, did Georges comprehend that the northern armies must begin their retreat southwest through Belgium. There seems to have been no thought of wheeling them around to counterattack the thin German armored lines extending westward. They would simply be pulled back. But not until 7 A.M. on the 17th, says Roton, was Georges' order for the retreat sent out.[95]

This was a disastrous delay. By the night of the 16th, German armored units had smashed through the feebly defended French frontier positions south of Maubeuge. Rommel's 7th Panzer had reached Avesnes; Reinhardt's armored corps had pushed to the Oise at Guise. Guderian's tanks had penetrated to Marle. As Colonel Lyet observed, nothing now stood in the way of their continuing to the sea—or to Paris.

The armies in the north, the Belgians, the British and, the French of the First Army, were not only dangerously outflanked. Worse, they were in danger of being cut off.

31

THE BATTLE OF FRANCE, III:
DISASTER IN FLANDERS AND
THE SURRENDER OF BELGIUM
May 16–June 4, 1940

The dash of the German panzers to the sea now began. Paris was bypassed. The Germans, sticking to the "Manstein Plan," which had worked so fabulously up to now, decided first to cut off and annihilate the Allied armies in northern France and Belgium. Paris and the rest of France would then be ripe for capture.

For a couple of days the French High Command tried to stem the tide along the Aisne and Oise rivers, wasting still another armored division in the effort. But both the Command and the armies were too disorganized to be able even to slow up the onrushing tanks. The Aisne held because the Germans did not try to cross it. To do so would have taken them south. Their push was westward across the Oise and beyond. On May 16, General Halder, surveying the situation as it looked to the German General Staff, began his diary: "The breakthrough develops in quite a classic form."

That same day, May 16, as we have seen, General Georges issued grandiose orders to "halt" the enemy breakthrough and go over to the counterattack. But ignorant, as his Chief of Staff says, of the extent of the disaster, he did not know exactly where his armies were, or what had happened to them. His orders had no connection with reality. For the counterattack he addressed them directly (Order No. 93, May 16) to General Giraud of the Ninth Army and to General Touchon of the Sixth Army. But the Ninth Army no longer existed and the Sixth Army had no troops. Georges stipulated that Giraud should spearhead his attack with the 1st and 2nd Armored divisions, and General Touchon his with de Gaulle's 4th Armored Division. Unfortunately the 1st Armored had been destroyed and de Gaulle's unit was just being hastily assembled. As for the 2nd, a crack division, its fate was similar to that of the 3rd at

Sedan. It too had been widely dispersed and could not be employed as an armored force. Once again the French High Command had misused a powerful division of tanks, robbing it of its effectiveness.

Orders for the division to move from its base east of Châlons did not come until noon of May 13, after the Germans had got over the Meuse at Dinant and Sedan. As in the case of the other armored divisions, it was instructed to proceed partly by road, partly by rail. But the heavy flatcars for the tanks and tracked artillery had been used to transport the 1st Armored Division northward, and until they were returned—via Paris, as it turned out—the 2nd could not budge with its chief component, the tanks. The wheeled vehicles, carrying supplies and services, got off the evening of the 13th, but the trains with the tanks and artillery were not able to start until the afternoon of the 14th and the last ones not until the night of the 15th. Thus two days were lost. In the meantime the division was scattered over 50 miles of roads and rail lines.

On the 14th, in the opinion of the division's commander, General Bruché, a golden opportunity was missed owing to the confusion in the High Command. By that time the Germans had broken through at Dinant and Sedan. The general's tanks were still waiting at the railroad yards at Châlons for transport. They could have been put on the road for Sedan (but 50 miles away) or towards Dinant (some 80 miles distant), and reached the battlefield during the night. The High Command, however, says General Bruché, believed that the division was already assembled at Charleroi west of Dinant. It therefore ordered the 2nd Division to rush by road from Charleroi to Signy-l'Abbaye behind the ruptured link between the Ninth and Second Armies. Like so many orders from the High Command it made no sense at all, having no relation to reality.

General Bruché never did get his scattered armored division assembled. The wheeled vehicles with the supplies ran into the panzers racing west from Sedan and, having no combat elements, withdrew south of the Aisne at Rethel. The tanks and tracked artillery were finally unloaded from their flatcars at various rail yards between Saint-Quentin and Hirson. By this time the German armored thrust had cut them off from their supply trains south of the Aisne. The division was hopelessly dispersed over a large triangle between Hirson, La Fère (on the Oise), and Rethel on the Aisne. The tanks were now assigned, as those of the 3rd at Sedan had been, to block the panzers at a score of widely scattered points. Another good armored division had been wasted.[1] The three heavy ones the French had, all of which on May 10 had been stationed in the Reims-Châlons area within 50 miles of the Meuse at Sedan and Mézières, which they could have reached by road overnight, had thus been squandered by the bungling of the top generals. Not one had been properly deployed to fight as an armored unit. By now, May 16, they no longer counted. There remained only the newly formed 4th, commanded by de Gaulle, and it was below strength and without divisional training.

Nevertheless it gave a good account of itself. On May 11 de Gaulle, still only a colonel, had been given command of the 4th Armored Division, which, he says, "did not yet exist." We have seen a General of the Army (Touchon) without troops. Here was a Commander of a tank division without tanks. However he began scraping them up from here and there, and by dawn of May 17, he says, he had assembled three battalions of tanks, one of heavy B's, and two of light R-35's, just east of threatened Laon. On the 16th he had personally reconnoitered the situation and what he saw nearly shattered him.

Along the roads from the north flowed lamentable convoys of refugees. I noticed among them many soldiers without arms. At this spectacle of a lost people and a military rout and from the reports of the scornful insolence of the Germans, I was filled with a terrible fury. It was too awful! The war was starting unbelievably badly. But we would have to continue it. If I lived I would fight on wherever I could as long as necessary until the enemy was defeated and this stain wiped out. That which I was able to do later, I resolved to do that day.[2]

A good deal of history turned on that defiant resolve. De Gaulle also resolved to attack the next morning with whatever forces he could rake up. His objective was to drive 12 miles northeast to Montcornet on the Serre river and there block the junction of roads which led west and south to Saint-Quentin, Laon, and Reims. Pushing aside advance units of enemy tanks, the division soon reached its objective. But again no infantry or artillery followed and de Gaulle found himself under heavy attack from German guns north of the river and from incessant bombing by the Stukas. By nightfall German tanks were infiltrating behind him. Receiving no support—"we were like lost children 20 miles in front of the Aisne," he says—he pulled back with 120 prisoners. Like all the other French armored counterattacks we have seen, this too was too isolated, piecemeal, and brief to have any effect on the battle, though it slowed up the German armor for a day.

Two days later de Gaulle, undaunted, set out again. By this time the enemy had moved farther west to the Oise. De Gaulle now drove his division northwest towards Crécy on the Serre with the object of cutting the enemy route to La Fère. The division reached the Serre, scattered various enemy tanks, but was stopped at the river by German artillery and more dive-bombing attacks. During the afternoon an order came from General Georges himself to withdraw south to the Aisne, where the French were trying to establish a defensive line to prevent the Germans, whose main force was driving west, from moving south toward Reims. For the fourth time, the High Command had wasted an armored division, though de Gaulle was able to extricate his unit almost intact. He, who for years had vainly tried to convince the High Command of the value of armored divisions, had at least shown what one could do if it was allowed

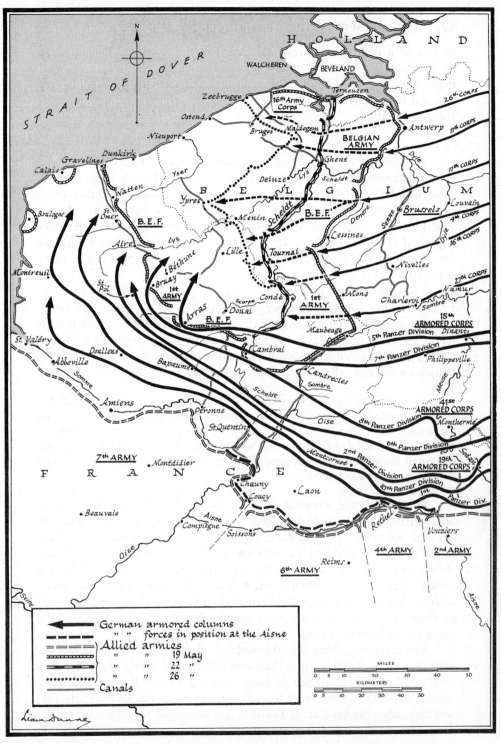

GERMAN BREAKTHROUGH TO THE SEA AND THE ROLLING UP
OF THE ALLIED ARMIES IN FLANDERS
MAY 17–JUNE 4, 1940

to fight as a unit and was resolutely led. Retreating on orders that night, de Gaulle says he could not "prevent himself" from imagining what might have happened if all the French armored strength had at this very moment been concentrated to attack the thin German panzer line on its vulnerable flank.[3]

As a matter of fact at this very moment Adolf Hitler, the Supreme German Commander, who did not know that three French armored divisions had been rendered useless, was worrying himself sick that these powerful units might attack his flank and turn his victory into defeat. The Fuehrer's mind was very much on the "Marne," where this had happened in 1914. On May 18 he wrote to Mussolini: "The miracle of the Marne of 1914 will not be repeated!"[4] His own exclamation point betrayed his uneasiness.

Two days before, on May 16, when the panzers pushed through the French frontier south of Maubeuge and headed for the Oise, the headquarters of Army Group A, which was conducting the breakthrough battle, began to think that its armored divisions were advancing westward too fast and too far, dangerously exposing the southern flank. Its War Diary entries for the day reflect a growing nervousness about the flank.

No doubt the Oise between Guise and La Fère can be crossed, probably without trouble. . . . But there is an unbearable risk there. The long line on the south flank is too thin. An attack by the enemy begs itself, especially in the region of Laon [where de Gaulle would attack the next day]. Even a local success of the enemy there threatens the progress of the operation by days, and may jeopardize it completely.

In view of this, General von Rundstedt ordered all forward operations toward the West to be halted. Crossing of the Oise must wait for his later approval.[5] On that same day General Halder noted in his diary that the French had not yet thrown in their "principal reserves" nor shown any signs of doing so. He estimated them at 30 divisions. He issued orders to keep a watch on them. But on the whole, he was not much worried. He did not believe the French High Command would get around to mounting a great counterattack against his flank before it could be made strong enough to hold.

The next day, May 17, the worries of other German generals increased—unaccountably, since there was still no sign, except for de Gaulle's local counterattack northeast of Laon, that the French were organizing a serious move to cut the breakthrough corridor from the south. Early that morning, after his 1st Panzer Division had advanced to Ribémont on the Oise, General Guderian received an order to halt his advance at once. At 7 A.M. General von Kleist arrived by air at his CP near Montcornet and promptly, Guderian says, began to "berate" him in "very violent terms for disobeying orders." The commander of the XIXth Armored Corps was so furious that he asked to be relieved of his command. Kleist accepted his request and asked him to hand over his corps to General Rudolf Veiel, which he did.

But Rundstedt did not intend to deprive himself of the service of the Army's most brilliant tank commander, and during the afternoon he sent General List, Commander of the German Twelfth Army, to straighten out the matter. List explained to Guderian that the stop order came from the Army High Command itself and would have to be obeyed. In the meantime, said List, Guderian could carry out a "reconnaissance in force." That was all Guderian needed to resume his advance. By evening his tanks were across the Oise.[6]

Back in the rarefied atmosphere of various German headquarters, the day of the 17th passed even less harmoniously. "A very unpleasant day," Halder noted in his diary. "The Fuehrer is frightfully nervous." At noon Hitler had convoked General von Brauchitsch, Commander in Chief of the Army, and Halder, the Chief of the General Staff. "Little mutual understanding," Halder noted wryly. "The Fuehrer stresses that the main danger is in the Sedan area. I see absolutely no danger there." But Hitler was not convinced. The southern flank, he thought, was dangerously exposed. During the afternoon the dictator drove to Rundstedt's headquarters at Bastogne. There he found Army Group A's commander more sympathetic. Rundstedt and his staff expected, they said, "a great surprise counteroffensive by strong French forces from the Verdun and Châlons-sur-Marne area northward . . . against the ever-lengthening left flank of the armies pressing forward." Halder, who was not present at this meeting but heard of it, kept peppering his diary all day with notations refuting the idea that the French could seriously counterattack on the exposed flank. "The enemy has only six divisions there, which is not enough to attack with. Therefore no danger." He closed his diary for the 17th, after again noting Hitler's undue nervousness: "He is worried over his own success, will risk nothing and so puts the reins on us. And all because of his concern with the left flank!" His calls and talks to the Army Groups, Halder concluded, "have caused only bewilderment and doubts."

Next day, the 18th, things were no better with the Nazi warlord and his generals. Hitler's nerves were worse than the day before. "The Fuehrer," Halder scribbled in his diary, "has an unaccountable worry over the south flank. He rages and screams that we are on the way to ruining the whole operation and risking the danger of defeat. He will absolutely not go along with continuing the operation westward. This is the subject of a most unpleasant discussion at his headquarters between the Fuehrer on the one side and Brauchitsch and myself on the other." That other military diarist, General Alfred Jodl, at OKW, was distressed at the discord at the top.

> Day of great tension. The Commander in Chief of the Army [Brauchitsch] has not carried out the intention of building up as quickly as possible a new flanking position to the south. . . . Brauchitsch and Halder are called immediately and ordered peremptorily to adopt the necessary measures at once.

These two army chiefs did not intend to let victory fall from their grasp because of the groundless fears of the World War I corporal, even though he was the warlord and now considered himself a military genius. At 6 P.M. Halder was once again with Hitler and this time he demanded, he says, that orders to resume the advance westward be given. The warlord, reluctantly, gave in. An hour later the Army High Command sent the orders out.

Halder, as his diary shows, had never worried over a great French counterattack against the widening German line across northern France. From the very beginning of the war he seems to have had an uncanny sense of the weakness of the French Army, its lack of initiative, its inability to maneuver, and its timidity in going over to the offensive as it had in 1914. His chief concern now was that his armies might not move forward to the sea fast enough to entrap the Allied armies in Belgium. Noting in his diary on the morning of May 19, as the panzers, having broken across the Oise, made for the sea, that the Allied forces in Belgium were retreating rapidly toward the Belgian-French frontier, he envisages a great battle to spring the trap. "It will last for several days. We have the advantage of the initiative. The enemy has the advantage of a stronger concentration of means."

Retreat in the North

The order for the retreat of the Allied armies in the north had been, as we have seen, disastrously delayed by the French High Command. To make matters worse, the King of the Belgians, who quite naturally hesitated to abandon Brussels without a fight, had contributed to the delay. Gamelin contends that General Billotte wanted to begin the retreat the night of May 15, when he instructed the French First Army to withdraw its right wing to Charleroi following the collapse of the Ninth Army to its south. Gamelin says King Leopold refused and thus cost the Allies 24 hours. The sovereign finally consented the next day, and the retreat of the Belgians, the BEF, and the French First Army began that night (of the 16th), Billotte having insisted on it without waiting for orders from Georges, which were not sent until the morning of the 17th.

The young King, he who had led his country out of the alliance with Britain and France five years before, already had become defeatist, and his antipathy to the Western Allies had waxed. Already he foresaw a quick

Allied defeat and, against the wishes of the government, he was determined neither to follow the retreating Anglo-French forces into France, as his father had done in 1914,* nor to flee abroad with his government, as the Queen of the Netherlands had just done. He made this clear to Premier Hubert Pierlot in a dramatic meeting at his headquarters at Breendonck on May 15.

The King explained to his Premier that as a result of the breakthrough on the Meuse the Germans would be at the channel in eight days. In that case, the surprised minister interrupted, the Belgian army must retreat first to the west and then south "in order to conserve its liberty of movement and remain in contact with the Allied armies."

"No," said the King. "Not toward the west. Toward the north." This meant that he would detach the Belgian army from the British and French and withdraw it toward the entrenched camp of Antwerp, which was already threatened by the Germans. Pierlot recounts that he thought he had not understood the King correctly but when Leopold repeated it he protested. To withdraw to the north, he said, would mean "certain capitulation" and would leave the Allies in the lurch.

The Allies? The King was scornful of them. According to his own minutes of the meeting,

He drew the attention of the government to the danger of letting itself be drawn into an Anglo-French alliance. . . . The King insisted that in no case must an alliance be concluded, especially since neither London nor Paris seemed up to now disposed to give the desired guarantees for the future of Belgium.

It does not seem to have occurred to the King that if Belgium were overrun, as now seemed probable, its only hope of eventually being freed from the Nazi German yoke lay in an ultimate victory of the Allies. Why then his stubborn stand against an alliance with them? Was he already calculating, as some have suspected, that by disassociating Belgium from the Western powers he could get better terms from the Germans?

Pierlot was disturbed and the next day, accompanied by Spaak, the Foreign Minister, and General Denis, the Minister of War, he returned to royal headquarters to have it out with the King. The three ministers, says Pierlot, were "categorical" in demanding that the Belgian army remain at the side of the Allied armies during the retreat toward France. But, he adds, the King "objected" arguing that,

once I am in foreign territory I will have to submit to the laws of that country, as will the army. Consequently the Belgian Command will no longer be free . . . and have no control over the interests of Belgium.

---

*Actually in 1914 the Allies had been able to hold a tiny strip of Belgian territory between the Yser river and the coast. There, on Belgian soil, King Albert, his government and his army, were able to function.

The ministers again protested that under no circumstances must the King "accept the eventuality of being made prisoner." They told him his duty was to accompany the government to "free territory" in order "to continue the struggle." The King would not agree, and when the ministers pointed out to him that the Queen of the Netherlands had gone to London when Holland was overrun, Leopold answered: "Was she right in leaving?" Pierlot says he and his colleagues left the meeting "without their apprehensions having been diminished. Around the King the atmosphere was defeatist. One general, pointing on a map to the channel region, said in a loud voice: 'There, in eight days, the war will be finished for us.' "

On the next day, May 17, Brussels was abandoned. The Belgian cabinet, meeting in Ostend, was concerned not only with the loss of the capital but with the attitude of the King. After a ministerial meeting Pierlot dashed off a letter to the sovereign. The government insisted, he wrote, that the Belgian army retreat in unison with the Allied forces "and not let itself be separated from them." And "in no case," he emphasized, "must the King run the risk of being captured." Leopold could not agree. He answered that

if the Allied forces were beaten . . . Belgium had no further obligations to them. . . . Belgium had assumed no other engagement to its guarantors than that of defending its territory.

Leopold repeated this to Pierlot on the following day, the 18th, when the Premier, again accompanied by Spaak and General Denis, met with him near Ghent. He seemed obsessed with the idea that after trying to defend its soil Belgium had no further obligations to the Allies, who were in reality not the country's allies but merely guarantors. The fact that Britain had sent the only army it had, and the French the best army it had, to help defend Belgium, did not seem to mean to him that Belgium owed anything to them. As the Belgian writer Marcel Thiry later pointed out,

the thought of the King was that even after the violation of our territory we had no *allies* but merely *guarantors*. This was much more than a nuance: with allies, you make war to the end, cost what it may; guarantors, on the other hand, have the unilateral obligation to aid you by all their means without you assuming any obligations toward them.[7]

This argument was backed by the Belgian Ambassador to Switzerland, Count d'Ursel, in a letter he wrote after the occupation began.

We have never admitted the thesis of the Pierlot government that there was an alliance with France and England. These two countries were our guarantors, answering our call according to their promise. Our counterpart was the engagement to defend our territory. But there never was a common cause nor a promise to link our fate to theirs.[8]

No common cause? If Belgium was overrun, how could it expect to be restored as a free country except by eventual Allied victory? The question does not seem to have arisen in the mind of the young monarch and of those around him, as later it would not penetrate the minds of Pétain, Weygand, and Laval in regard to France. In the end Leopold's attitude would cost him his throne.

For the moment he continued to pull back his troops in loyal cooperation with the British and French commands. On three successive nights, the 16th, 17th, and 18th, the three Allied armies completed their withdrawal to the Scheldt. The German Sixth Army did not follow them too closely—for an obvious reason. The German High Command did not wish the Allied northern force to retreat southwest too rapidly and too far until the panzers had sprung the trap from the south. Thus the withdrawal for the Allies became, in effect, a race against time.

The French High Command did not seem to realize this. On the morning of May 18, as the troops in the north were making ready to carry out the third step of the retreat from the Dender to the Scheldt, General Billotte sent General Georges an optimistic report from his Army Group 1 Headquarters in the north. "We are holding everywhere," he reported. "The withdrawal of the Belgians and British is going according to plan. General Giraud is content." But "holding everywhere," was the last thing his troops in Belgium should have been attempting to do. Their only hope lay in speeding up their retreat southwest into France before the panzers encircled them. It is doubtful if General Giraud was "content." His Ninth Army had ceased to exist. The Germans, after breaking across the Oise, were heading in part due west toward the sea at the mouth of the Somme and in part northwest toward the exposed southern flank of the retreating armies in the north between Bouchain and Arras. By evening General Billotte's optimism was gone. He telephoned Georges to "expose," as General Roton puts it, "the tragedy of the situation." He told his chief that they "must therefore reflect on what to do if our forces find themselves separated."[9]

On May 20, as the panzers approached the coast, there was another stormy meeting between the King of the Belgians and his ministers. Pierlot and Spaak again insisted that the King must not allow himself to be made prisoner. When Spaak asked the sovereign what he thought he could do if he remained in an occupied Belgium, Leopold responded: "I don't know, but I know it will be necessary to preserve the economic life of the country. . . . I could help to maintain the moral unity of Belgium." Spaak protested that such a course would be "disastrous" and that the King's "formula did not correspond to reality."

The government is acting on the supposition, Leopold responded, of an Allied victory, or at least that the Allies will continue the struggle. I don't believe it. Soon after the Belgians, if not at the same time, the French Army will give up fighting. In that case why should I leave the Army and Belgium and range myself on the side of the Allies, as the government wishes?[10]

That evening, May 20, the 2nd Panzer Division reached Abbeville at the mouth of the Somme. The Allied armies in the north were trapped!

SHAKEUP IN THE FRENCH GOVERNMENT AND HIGH COMMAND

In the face of the "immensity" of the developing disaster, as he put it, Paul Reynaud shook up his government and changed commanders in chief. He himself took over the Ministry of Defense, sending Daladier, who had tenaciously clung to that post for four uninterrupted years, to the Foreign Ministry. Daladier had refused to accept this arrangement in March when Reynaud, on becoming Premier, had proposed it. Now in the midst of calamity but only after, Reynaud comments wryly, "a pressing intervention by President Lebrun," he gave in. Daladier, who, as Defense Minister since 1936, was more responsible for the state of the Army than any other politician, now struck those who saw him as a broken man. Like the top generals who had fashioned it, he was stupefied to see it falling apart in nine days.

To try to pull it together, or at least, Reynaud says, to "save its honor" and also to restore the sagging morale of the country, the Premier brought back the two most illustrious surviving generals of the first war, and installed in a key position a civilian minister who was generally recognized as the man who had helped Clemenceau ruthlessly stamp out defeatism in 1917–18. General Weygand was recalled from Syria on May 17. The next day, after a cabinet meeting, Reynaud announced the changes in the government. Georges Mandel was named Minister of Interior and asked to weed out the defeatists. Marshal Pétain was appointed Minister of State and Vice-Premier.* The press was ecstatic. Mandel, the editorials proclaimed, would eliminate the traitors. Marshal Pétain, the glorious "Victor of Verdun," would once again make the Army invincible. A couple of days later, after General Weygand returned, similar praise was heaped on him. He had been, the newspapers reminded their readers, the "brilliant collaborator of Marshal Foch," architect of the Allied victory in 1918. On the evening of the 18th Reynaud addressed the nation over the radio:

---

* Reynaud also removed Léger from his post as permanent Secretary of the Foreign Office, his last act before turning the Quai d'Orsay over to Daladier, who resented being deprived of this experienced official. There seems no doubt that the Premier acted at the behest of his mistress, Madame de Portes, and of one of her henchmen, Baudouin, who could not stand Léger's independence. Léger was offered the French Embassy in Washington, but turned it down. He soon went to Washington as a private citizen and has remained there ever since. As a poet he writes under the name of Saint-John Perse. In 1960 he was awarded the Nobel Prize for literature.

. . . The Victor of Verdun, Marshal Pétain, returned this morning from Madrid. He will now be at my side . . . putting all his wisdom and all his force in the service of the country. He will remain there until victory is won.

Later Reynaud would declare that at this crucial moment he had not the least suspicion of what was really in the mind of the "Victor of Verdun" nor of the road he was already embarking on. He had the same innocence about Weygand. The Premier did not know, for instance, that on leaving Madrid to join the government the Marshal had told Franco: "My country has been beaten and they are calling me back to make peace and to sign an armistice. . . . This is the work of thirty years of Marxism. They're calling me back to take charge of the nation."[11]

If one of the friends of Pertinax can be believed, Weygand also felt, even before he returned, that there was no more hope. On May 17, the morning the general boarded a plane at Beirut for Paris, this friend talked with his assistant Chief of Staff, who told him. "He [Weygand] believes that the war is lost, and that reasonable conditions for an armistice should be accepted."[12]

Had Paul Reynaud himself by May 18, only the ninth day of battle, abandoned hope that the Germans could be stopped and the war carried on? He vigorously denied it in his postwar writings. Léger, who naturally resented the Premier's high-handed dismissal of him, later said he was "convinced" that as early as May 18 Reynaud *had* given up hope and that he wanted Pétain in his cabinet because he believed that a surrender would be easier to arrange if men like the Marshal served as a front.[13] In a frank letter to the author on August 29, 1965, Reynaud confirms that by May 18 he had little hope of accomplishing more than "saving the honor of the Army." Was that not already accepting defeat?

I called in Pétain and Weygand [he writes] in order to save the honor of the Army, hoping they could improve matters after the collapse of Corap's [Ninth] Army. This result, the only one I could hope for, was obtained. . . . My objective [was] defeat with honor.

Late that evening of the 18th Reynaud told Bullitt:

If the Germans should reach the Channel, although France would continue to fight to the bitter end, the German machine would swing down and finally take Paris. . . . The war might end in an absolute defeat of France and England in less than two months.

The French Premier, like the French generals, was already convincing himself that if France fell, Britain's fall would quickly follow. According to Bullitt, Reynaud was profoundly convinced that if the French Army should be defeated Great Britain would be strangled in short order by German submarines based on French ports and by German airplanes based on France, the Netherlands and Belgium.[14]

Now for the first time, at the approach of disaster, the suspicion sprouted in Paris and London that the ally might seek a separate peace. Bullitt, raging more shrilly than even the French against the British for not throwing in their entire Air Force in defense of France, already suspected that London was holding back in order to make a deal with Hitler. On May 18th he warned Roosevelt that "in order to escape from the ultimate consequences of absolute defeat, the British may install a government of Oswald Mosley . . . which would cooperate fully with Hitler."[15] Mosley, a former Labor minister, was the leader of a small and inconsequential British Nazi-Fascist party. Even Hitler, as I knew from my Berlin days, did not take Mosley seriously. The suspicion among the French that the British might try to make a separate peace with Hitler if France fell, or even if its fall seemed likely, mushroomed in the dark days ahead, poisoning the already worsening relations between the Allies.

In London, Churchill had his doubts about France sticking it out. On May 18, the day Reynaud appointed Pétain to his cabinet, the British Prime Minister reminded Lord Ismay, Deputy Secretary of the War Cabinet, that in considering more troops for France "one must always be prepared for the fact that the French may be offered very advantageous terms of peace, and the whole weight be thrown on us."[16]

Two days later, on May 20, Reynaud did indeed receive a peace feeler from the Germans. It was brought to him by Raoul Nordling, the Swedish Consul General in Paris. Returning from Sweden to his post he had stopped off in Berlin on May 15. Goering, he says, summoned him urgently to his headquarters and asked him to convey a message to the French Premier.

Tell M. Paul Reynaud that nothing can now change the course of events. Yesterday our panzers broke the French front on the Meuse. By the end of the month we shall be in Calais and Dunkirk. Tell Reynaud he should immediately make us propositions for an armistice. We are ready to accord France reasonable conditions. But he must hurry if he wishes to avoid a total occupation and the destruction of his country. In a few weeks it will be too late. The offers that I am authorized to make today will not be renewed. The more France delays in recognizing the facts the severer will be our conditions.

Back in Paris the Swede saw Reynaud on May 20 and gave him Goering's message. The Premier, he says, was outraged. "If I did not know you," Reynaud told him, "I would have you arrested on the spot for sowing defeatism."[17]

General Gamelin got wind on the 17th from Daladier of the recall of Pétain and Weygand. Its implications did not escape him. He would have to bestir himself. Already on that day Reynaud had telephoned him and "insisted" that he issue a new and ringing Order of the Day to the troops. And though "cool" to the idea, he says, he obeyed. The words must have had a hollow sound to the weary, retreating soldiers.

The fate of the country, that of our Allies, the destiny of the world, hangs on the battle now in course. . . . All troops which cannot advance must let themselves be killed rather than to abandon a parcel of our soil. . . . As always in the grave hours of our history the command today is: Conquer or die. We must conquer.

Next day, the 18th, the generalissimo set out by car for La Ferté to see what General Georges had in mind to do about the panzers driving to the sea. He found the general at his personal Command Post at the Château des Bondons. Georges, says Gamelin, gave "incontestable signs of weariness."

In his offices there was complete disorder. . . . I could not understand how the Chief of Staff [General Roton] was able to work. There was a continual coming and going. Liaison officers came and went. Letters and telegrams were brought in directly. Everyone talked at once. A waiting room, not a working room. As to the general himself [Georges], he was not tranquil. Officers constantly entered his room. He himself went out frequently to confer with one or another. It appeared that he worked late into the night and slept little. How could one dominate events in such an atmosphere and without withdrawing to think things over?

Gamelin says he spoke frankly about this to General Doumenc, the chief of GHQ, whom he had brought along.

He recognizes that I am right. He has not dared to speak to me until now, hoping that things would improve. But, on the contrary, they haven't.

"General," Gamelin says Doumenc then declared, "General Georges has always shown me sympathy and confidence, and I'm grateful to him. But it is going to be necessary for you to take over effective command yourself. It must be done, however, without hurting him."

"Certainly," Gamelin says he replied. "Tell me the moment and the occasion."[18]

The lethargy, the hesitancy, of the Commander-in-Chief leaves one breathless. Surely "the moment and the occasion" was now, this instant, now that he had seen Georges' "weariness" and "the complete disorder" of his Command Post at the very moment when only great boldness and clear, cool thinking could possibly save the situation, as the unperturbable Joffre, with the then young Gamelin at his side, had saved it at the Marne in 1914. But the generalissimo, now sixty-eight, had no will to act. He let the opportunity pass.

By his own account Gamelin seems to have spent this critical day as if the harsh realities of the hour and the imperative need for brutal, decisive, and immediate action scarcely concerned him. During the afternoon, while waiting at Vincennes with Daladier for a visit from Reynaud and Pétain, who had been delayed at Georges' headquarters, Gamelin observes: "It is the first time in ten days that I am left without something precise to do." He and the deposed Defense Minister whiled away the time, he says, in "affectionate and confiding conversation." How fatuous he sounds! "Daladier," he goes on to remark, "has the soul of a good Frenchman." Later that evening, at 8 P.M., he says, he sits down with his staff to a "frugal meal." He is the soul of tranquillity. "In wartime," he comments of it, "it must be an absolute rule to follow as far as possible the habits of a regular life if one is to maintain his body in a good state and the calm about one." He is pleased with the latest reports on the situation—no sign that they denote disaster. He notes them complacently in his memoirs.

The atmosphere is improving. The menace to Paris is for the moment averted. . . . The German deployment, in stretching out, becomes more vulnerable. . . . Our men, starting with the Ninth Army, galvanized by General Giraud, are digging in. . . .[19]

Does the generalissimo not know, or should he not know, that the Ninth Army, "galvanized by General Giraud" no longer exists and therefore cannot be "digging in," and that at that very moment Giraud himself, his Command Post at Le Catelet having been overrun by Reinhardt's panzers, is wandering aimlessly in the night about the countryside and by dawn will give himself up as a prisoner? One spares the reader the rest of this inane report. After dinner, Gamelin says, he signs a lengthy report on the battle up to now which Daladier had requested the day before. Reynaud, when he saw it a couple of days later, was "astonished" that "in the midst of the battle" Gamelin could spare the time to produce "such a long document, which, with its annexes, came to fifteen pages."[20]

Reynaud and Pétain finally arrived at Vincennes at 6:20 P.M., after first seeing General Georges, who had explained the situation to them and stressed, as the Premier remembered, that it "was difficult." Gamelin seemed to Reynaud to be "concerned, but elegant and fluent as usual" as he stood before a map and briefed them. The generalissimo himself concedes that he explained "what appeared to me to be the causes of our defeat." Defeat? Already, on May 18, he was acknowledging defeat? Those are his words.[21] After Reynaud and Daladier had departed the Marshal lingered on for a few moments. Shaking hands "affectionately," the old soldier said:

"My heart goes out to you," and Gamelin says he replied: "I think only of the country." He conducted Pétain to his car. The Marshal waved warmly to him. "It was the last time," says Gamelin, "that I was to see him."

The next day, May 19, the Commander in Chief was sacked. He did not suspect, he says, that it was going to be the last day of his long military career, which had begun in 1891 when he entered Saint-Cyr as a cadet. "I do not see," he says, in giving an account of his thoughts and deeds that last day, "how I can be found responsible personally for the actual situation."[22] He put the responsibility on General Georges, as Commander of the Northeast Front.

Again the fatuity of the generalissimo:

Since May 10 I have insisted to my staff that we must not intervene in the battle. That is the affair of the Northeast Command. . . . I will not go beyond my role, unanimously approved by Parliament, unless I have the impression that my duty is to bypass the rules. Today the hour has sounded. I hope it is not too late.

The hour had sounded very early that morning. At 5 A.M. General Doumenc had called him. "The moment," Doumenc said, "has come for you to intervene." They agreed to meet at General Georges' headquarters at 8 A.M. In the meantime Gamelin asked Doumenc to send over General Koeltz from GHQ to bring him "up to date." Koeltz arrived at Vincennes at 6:30 A.M. and "confirmed" Doumenc's impressions of the chaotic state of Georges' headquarters. "It realized," says Gamelin, "what ought to be done but did not take the precise decisions to carry it out. A series of partial counterattacks had been prescribed. The hour appeared to have come to carry out a broader operation."

On the way to Bondons Gamelin was filled with thoughts about Georges' failures. "I considered it particularly regrettable," he says, "that the Commander of the Northeast Front had not taken effective direction of the battle at two crucial moments, on May 10 and on May 15." On the first, the day the German offensive began, he says, Georges should have started massing strong reserves behind the Meuse front. This is interesting, since neither Georges nor Gamelin knew on May 10 where the main German thrust was coming. In fact both, as we have seen, thought it was coming further north against the French First Army and the BEF. Secondly, Gamelin says he thought, Georges on May 15, after the Meuse breakthrough, should have constituted "two masses of maneuver," one in the Arras region and the second around Compiègne, "in order to have the means to counterattack." If he thought so, why did he not, as Commander in Chief, so urge, or order? This was a retort that Georges would later make, and it seems justified.

"The hour," Gamelin goes on, "appeared to me to have come for the Commander in Chief to formulate his thoughts." He concedes that Georges had given orders at 11 P.M. the night before designed to try to save the armies in the north and cut off the panzers advancing toward the sea. "But," he adds, "this was insufficient." To give the decisive overall order to redress the situation, such as the one which Joffre had instructed him to draw up on August 25, 1914, at the Marne, now became in his mind the objective of this early morning visit to the Command Post of General Georges.

Arriving at the Château des Bondons shortly before 9 A.M. he found it in even greater disarray than the day before. Colonel Minart, one of his aides, later attempted to give a picture of it.

It is a terrible spectacle to see the elite of our Army struck down. Weary generals come and go. . . . The vestibule and adjoining rooms are cluttered with officers and staff workers. Telephones, maps, reports, dossiers, orders, and notebooks of all kinds are scattered about on ancient tables and chairs. The piano is piled with kepis. It resembles a rummage sale. To add to the disorder in this luxurious bungalow is the clatter of typewriters and telephones ringing, the sputter of motorcycles outside, and permeating the place the odors from the kitchen and from stopped-up toilet stools.[23]

General Doumenc came out to greet Gamelin as he got out of his car and again urged him to take over command of operations. Stepping warily into the pandemonium of the château, Gamelin conferred briefly with General Vuillemin on the part the Air Force should play in his proposed counterattack, and then saw General Georges. He found him, says Minart, "in a state of profound physical and moral depression." The Commander in Chief asked for pencil and paper and retired to a small room on the second floor. "I wish to work in complete tranquillity," he says, and adds

I sense the desire of all to see me take the affair entirely in hand without delay. But I do not want to inflict this humiliation on General Georges before everyone. I intend to preserve his *amour-propre* and his authority.

Gamelin thereupon wrote out with pencil on paper a general order which, he leaves no doubt, he hoped would become as effective—and as historically important—as Joffre's famous one before the Battle of the Marne which he personally, as a young staff officer, he reminds us, had drafted. It is *"Secret and Personal Instruction Number 12."* To spare Georges' feelings, he says, he began it: "Without wishing to intervene in the conduct of the battle now in course, which comes under the authority of the Commander of the Northeast Front [Georges], and approving all the measures he has taken, I consider now that . . ." —and he proceeds to sketch in very general terms what should be done to redress the desperate situation.

Though he stresses that in order to prevent the armies in the north from being encircled "the most extreme audacity is called for," there is nothing very audacious or new in his "instruction." Even a junior officer, in the midst of all the confusion at Bondons, could see what had to be done: namely to have the Allied forces in the north, the Belgians, the British, and the French First Army, fight their way south across the thin panzer corridor while a newly formed army on the Somme pressed north-ward to help break the corridor and, if possible, cut off the extended enemy armored columns that were racing, unimpeded, to the Channel coast. Be-sides advising that move, Gamelin also asked for an offensive of the Second and Sixth Armies toward the Meuse bridges at Mézières. This was the counteraction that any general, and in particular Gamelin and Georges, should have seen as urgently and immediately necessary on May 15 after the Meuse breakthrough, but nothing had been done. General Huntziger, whose Second Army had so bungled the attempt to halt the vital crossing of Guderian's Panzer Corps at Sedan, had not been urged to take the coun-teroffensive at the vulnerable spot in the German position, and he himself had been quite content to remain on the defensive after the panzers had passed him by. And Gamelin and Georges had delayed withdrawing the armies in the north when there was still time.

Was it now, on May 19, with the Germans on the Somme and the panzers approaching the sea, too late to carry out the Gamelin "sugges-tion"? Was the generalissimo, in fact, as some of his fellow generals charged, merely issuing the order for the record? Was he chiefly concerned that history should exonerate him and blame Georges? The latter could not conceal his bitterness—and his contempt—in his subsequent deposi-tion at the Riom Trial and even later—on February 12, 1948—when he testified before the Parliamentary Investigating Committee.

Commenting on Gamelin's opening line that he did not wish "to in-tervene in the battle," Georges said at Riom acidly: "Yes, I know. I'm responsible." And he adds that when Gamelin named him Commander of the Northeast Front without giving him the full powers of a commander, "I well understood that he wished to enlarge my responsibilities without increasing my attributions so as to reserve the right to disavow me, if nec-essary. . . . It allowed him, in case of success, to attribute the merit to the supreme chief, and, in case of a reverse, to blame it on the subordinate chief." As to Gamelin's "personal and secret instruction," Georges said,

> It is not an order. I would say, rather, at the risk of being trivial, that it is an *umbrella*. . . . It reveals in the supreme chief a tendency to escape respon-sibility and place it on the subordinate chief, when the situation is gravely com-promised.
> It was the Parthian shot.[24]

General Georges was no less bitter when he testified before the Parliamentary Committee eight years after the events of May 19. Re-calling again the opening lines of Gamelin's "instruction" in which he stressed that he did not wish to intervene in the battle, which was under the authority of the Northeast Front commander, Georges said:

Now on the 19th of May the situation was particularly grave. The enemy was at the gates of Saint-Quentin; the Allied forces were on the point of being cut in two.

And the Commander in Chief means to say that he is not responsible for the conduct of a great battle, the only battle that is taking place, and on which depends the issue of the campaign and the destiny of the country. He gives no orders. He confines himself to suggestions. He does not command. Strange manner, in the hour of extreme peril, to comprehend his mission of supreme chief. In such a situation, Foch, always avid for responsibilities, would not have hesitated, I believe, to throw himself into the struggle to lend all his weight to his resolution and authority.

Georges explained to the Committee that in the first phase of the war from September 3, 1939, to May 10, 1940, Gamelin addressed to him "no fewer than 140 communications of a general order."

The battle began on May 10. No more orders from the Commander in Chief until May 19, the day of his departure, when he gives me a personal and secret instruction which was really not an order but an expression of his opinion. The conduct of the battle is left to me.

After describing how he did his best to carry out the strategic plan established by Gamelin with the means given him, Georges concluded:

Thus, I accept fully the responsibility for the employment in the battle of the means given me. But the general responsibility for this battle, carried out according to a conception and form ordained to me—history, I believe, will appreciate that it is not imputable to me. And history will judge severely, I think, an organization of command placing in juxtaposition two Commanders in Chief, one of whom held the real powers while the second had the responsibility for the conduct of operations conceived and defined by the first.[25]

History, to which Georges and Gamelin appealed so fervently in the hour of their adversity, might in time judge, and surely it would place heavy responsibility for failure on both. For the moment, history could but record that on May 19, when, as they agreed, the destiny of the country hung in the balance, France's two ranking military chiefs, by their own subsequent account, appear to have been more concerned with blaming each other for impending disaster than with throwing themselves together with abandon to make one last desperate all-out effort to stave it off.*

---

* We have seen Georges' testimony on Gamelin. The latter summed up his opinion of Georges before the Parliamentary Investigating Committee on December 9, 1947—seven years after the event.

I must say [he declared] that beginning with May 15, during the course

Gamelin finished penciling his order and then added a last line: "All is a matter of hours." The armies in the north would have to strike southward at once, holding off the pursuing German Sixth Army on their heels as best they could. The troops and tanks hastily being assembled on the Somme would simultaneously have to push north to effect a junction of the separated forces. It was truly a matter of hours.

What followed at Bondons is a matter of dispute between the two generals. Georges recounts that Gamelin returned with his "paper," placed it on his desk and said: "You will read it after my departure," whereupon he took his leave. In those circumstances, Georges says he did not think "the paper was urgent. I did not open it until some moments later when I perceived it was a personal and secret instruction written in pencil. It had been a long time since I had received one! . . . I was stupefied!" Georges also denies that Generals Doumenc and Vuillemin were present during the talks. "Such a meeting," he contends, "never took place."[27] Georges' memory here—to put the best possible face on it—is faulty. Other witnesses support Gamelin in saying that he lingered on for further talks with Georges, his staff, Doumenc and Vuillemin, and conferred with the British general, Sir John Dill, Deputy Chief of the Imperial General Staff, before he left.* He even accepted Georges' invitation to stay on for lunch, a repast which Captain Beaufre still recalled with horror twenty-five years later.

The cook, disheartened like us all by the defeat, had put all his frustrated patriotism into the confection of a veritable wedding feast. With Georges pale and beaten and his principal collaborators dead with fatigue and anxiety, the luncheon had the air of a funeral repast. But, in the center, Gamelin, who now knew himself condemned by the government (Weygand's arrival had just been announced), thought it necessary to show off, to talk of one thing or another, to make jokes even. It all sounded terribly false. Finally the dessert came, an enormous concoction covered with *cheveux d'ange*. It was grotesque and pathetic. I wanted the roof to fall down. Gamelin ate it with relish, drank his coffee and left, imperturbable to the end.[29]

---

of the battle, I saw in General Georges progressively a man really fatigued because he imposed on himself an excessive load of work. Frankly, he appeared to me to be in part overcome by events. He did not sufficiently take personal direction of the battle. . . .

I must add that in my opinion it is certain that the consequences of the wounds General Georges received at the side of King Alexander accounted for a great deal of his state of fatigue. He was gravely wounded. He suffered for six months. And it appeared to me that beginning with May 10 he tried to do too much by himself and occupied himself with too many details. . . . He had never commanded a large unit on the field of battle, and his mind perhaps turned more to the questions of the General Staff than to those of Command. . . . Today [December 9, 1947], now that I have had time to reflect on events, I believe that General Georges did not take the firm and overall decisions which were necessary at certain moments of action.[26]

* Gamelin says he read his "instruction" to Georges and Vuillemin, who expressed their "accord."[28]

Imperturbable, but at one point also sly. Gamelin himself notes that during a discussion with Georges and Vuillemin he told them that if his maneuver did not succeed it would be difficult to defend metropolitan France for long. Georges agreed. Vuillemin suggested that the government ought to be warned.

> I responded [says Gamelin]: "There will be time to do that if the operations turn out badly. If we raise the possibility now they will say that we are pessimists and lost the game in advance. Should the occasion arise I shall speak to them at the proper moment. . . . Until then, the thing must remain between us three."[30]

Later Reynaud would criticize Gamelin for not informing him of this on the 19th so that plans for an eventual withdrawal to North Africa could be started at once.

Having received word that General Weygand, who had just flown in from the Levant, wished to meet him at Vincennes, Gamelin hurried back to his headquarters. While his car was making its way along the roads clogged with refugees and footloose soldiers, the members of the French government, led by the President of the Republic, the Premier, and the venerable Marshal Pétain, were praying at Notre Dame in Paris for the miracle of deliverance. It was a Sunday, the weather as lovely as it had been since the German offensive started. In the minds of Parisians gathered in the spacious square in front of the great Gothic cathedral, watching the comings and goings of the dignitaries, as well as in those of the dignitaries inside joining the priests in the litanies which called upon the glorious French saints, Sainte Geneviève, Saint Louis and Jeanne d'Arc to intercede with God for the threatened country, thoughts were on the "Miracle of the Marne" in 1914 and the chances of another one somewhere in France wherever the battle was, in 1940. After prayers, led by the archbishop, the notables dispersed to resume their more prosaic tasks.

Riding back from the services with Reynaud, Baudouin urged him to lose no time in replacing Gamelin by General Weygand. The general, dapper and jaunty despite his seventy-three years, with the figure and air of a jockey, had arrived at noon, but now that he was in Paris Reynaud hesitated to change commanders in chief in the midst of the battle. He told Baudouin that he had not quite made up his mind to relieve Gamelin. It might be better to keep Weygand at his side as Chief of the General Staff. "You can't offer Weygand half a loaf," Baudouin says he replied. "A situation as grave as this demands a sole chief."[31] At any rate, when Weygand arrived at the War Office at 2:30 P.M. Reynaud merely told him to see Georges and Gamelin and return at 7 o'clock and give him his impressions.

Weygand was already at Vincennes when Gamelin got back there. The generalissimo briefed him on the situation and on his "instruction" to

Georges. Weygand explained that the Premier had asked him "to have a look at things."

> But he did not tell me [Gamelin recounts] why and for what purpose he had been recalled. I thought it beneath my dignity to ask him.

It was beginning, though, to dawn on the imperturbable Commander in Chief what was up. On leaving, Weygand said to him: "You know that Paul Reynaud does not like you?"

"I know it," Gamelin says he replied.

At 8:15 P.M., "without any previous notice of any kind," says Gamelin, an officer arrived with a note from Reynaud.

> I have the honor to bring to your attention two decrees which the President of the Republic has just signed.* I address to you the thanks of the government for the services you have rendered the country in the course of a long and brilliant career.
>
> > Paul Reynaud

"I shall not insist," Gamelin observes, "on the cruel irony which this last phrase constituted for me." At any rate, he adds, "It was finished for me."[32]

So, in the middle of the battle he had spent so many years getting ready for—his whole life, really—General Gamelin, now sixty-eight, departed, after nearly fifty years in the French Army. He was an officer courtly of manner, gentle by nature, possessed of much intelligence, learning, and subtlety. But in the great test of ten days in May 1940 he was found lacking in determination to act and to command. In him, thought was divorced from action, and this was his fatal flaw. His mind, encrusted by the experience of the first war, which had been won, never understood the new military technology and the immensely quicker pace of the second war which the development of fast and heavy planes and tanks and of electronic communication had made inevitable, and of which the Germans, belying their reputation for ponderousness, had taken advantage.

Failure to command the army which he himself, as top man since 1935, had fashioned, was his greatest and most inexplicable fault. Not once, after the Germans had struck, did he attempt to dominate the course of battle, to counter enemy moves with those of his own, to maneuver his divisions, thirty of which were left to wither on the vine behind the unattacked Maginot Line, to vital positions in time. Though generally believed—even in Berlin—to be a brilliant strategist, he unaccountably

---

* The two decrees named Weygand Chief of the General Staff of National Defense and Commander in Chief of all operations on land, sea, and in the air, and suppressed one of the functions Gamelin had had: Commander in Chief of the land forces. Weygand, unlike his predecessor, now had authority over the Navy and Air Force.

failed to perceive the strategy of the enemy in striking at his vital and vulnerable center until it was too late, though it would seem to have been obvious by the second day of the attack. It was largely from this astonishing failure, which General Georges shared, that disaster ensued. No serious effort was made to quickly bolster the threatened forces on the Meuse, to counterattack in time the vulnerable German positions, to properly employ the armored divisions, either to halt the panzers or to attack their exposed flanks and rear. As we have seen, they were frittered away.

Not once did Gamelin intervene, as Joffre and Foch surely would have, to stir up General Huntziger, who had let the panzers cross the Meuse at Sedan and then pass him by to head west, to counterattack the bared enemy flank with reinforcements from the Maginot forts. Nor when his Ninth Army had been volatilized after only two days of weak resistance at the Meuse did he think to withdraw General Billotte's endangered Army Group 1, containing the flower of the French Army and 9 strong British divisions, pulling them back rapidly from Belgium so that they could rejoin the main French forces and live to fight another day. That at least might have been accomplished if the order for withdrawal had been given on May 14, or, at the latest, on May 15. And in the process the powerful northern armies might, in addition, have isolated the panzers, cut off their ammunition and fuel, and driven them into the sea.

The generalissimo never thought to take the initiative, seize the opportunity, go over to the attack with lightning speed, as his chief, Joffre, had done at the Marne after an equally disastrous retreat in 1914. Watching him, now that all the accounts and testimony are in, we see him at his Command Post at Vincennes paralyzed, incapable of an act of will, employing his time and mind in odds and ends that have little or nothing to do with the battle in course, mouthing inanities about this and that, and fooling himself that though he is Commander in Chief, it is "General Georges' battle" that is being fought, that he should not interfere, that he is not responsible. "A strange way to command!" as Georges later exclaimed, and as all of us who follow this crucial battle cannot but agree.

Finally Gamelin dallied too in pressing the Air Force to go all out. Even for vital reconnaissance. On May 18, for example, he made one of his rare direct approaches to General Vuillemin, the brave but incompetent Chief of the Air Force, asking him to find out what was behind the enemy panzers driving west to the channel. The Air Force general orders only two quite insufficient reconnaissance flights and reports back: "No great concentration of tanks or troops sighted. Impression calm."[33] This scanty and quite misleading air reconnaissance can be of no help to the generalissimo. Just the opposite. But he does not bestir himself to get the Air Force to make a serious effort. Instead, beginning on May 15, he fires off one telegram after another to Churchill in London beseeching him to rush over 10 more squadrons of British planes. He does not bother to see if Vuillemin is using all the French planes. Only after the war does he find out that all of them were not being employed, that because of this the Air Force would have more machines at the end of the campaign than it had at the beginning, which strikes him as a "mystery." But he does not look into the mystery when it might have done some good. Nor does he do anything about the shocking lack of cooperation between the land armies and the aviation.*

But of his shortcomings and mistakes General Gamelin, like most men, is either unaware or incapable of admitting. He concedes that he did not sleep as well as usual the night of May 19 as he contemplated the "collapse" of his life's work. But he hastens to add, as he prepares early the next morning to hand over his command to Weygand, that "in all conscience, and as a Frenchman and a Christian, I see nothing for which I can be reproached. I cannot conceive in what circumstances I would have done other than I have done."[35] Serene in his conviction that he was beyond reproach despite the debacle of the army which he had commanded for five years, he made ready for the arrival of his successor.

General Weygand showed up at Vincennes promptly at 9 A.M. The meeting between the two generals was cool and brief. "Not one single word from the heart," Gamelin complains of Weygand and asks himself: "Has this man a heart, like Joffre and Foch?" Weygand found Gamelin "relieved to be rid of his heavy load." The latter thought his successor seemed "awfully sure of himself." When Gamelin said he thought that only the execution of his last order to Georges "could save the situation," Weygand slapped his hand on his notebook and replied: "But I have the secrets of Marshal Foch!"† Gamelin says he could have responded that he himself had the secrets of Marshal Joffre "but that they had not sufficed." However, he kept his silence on that.

Weygand made little effort to question the retiring generalissimo on exactly what had happened to the various French armies, what the situation was at the moment, what had to be done urgently and immediately, and what the means, if any, were. He makes it clear he intended to get that information from General Georges, in whom, despite his near breakdown, he still had great confidence. Weygand does complain that Gamelin never mentioned the report he had sent to Daladier, at the latter's request, on May 18 on what had happened and the reasons therefor. "This document," says Weygand, who only saw it five years later, "would certainly

---

* Air Force General d'Astier de la Vigerie revealed later: "Nearly every evening [during the Battle of France] I had to pick up the telephone and myself take the initiative in informing the commanders of an army or a group of armies that I had for the next day a certain number of formations without missions, and ask them if they had any. Their response invariably was the same: 'Thanks very much. But we have no needs.'" General Girier, who commanded an assault group of 30 bombers and 40 fighters, had the same experience: "Though I could easily carry out 40 sorties a day I never received an order for a mission with designated targets from the *Etats-Majors* of an army, even from one we were attached to."[34]

† Weygand later denied saying this. But, as we shall later see, the value of his frequent denials, to say the least, is questionable.

have enlightened me." But on all the evidence it is clear that Weygand was not really interested in the views of his predecessor.*

He made it clear, though, to General Gamelin that, old royalist and anti-Republican that he was, he was interested in politics. "We must change this whole business of politics," Gamelin reports Weygand as telling him. "We must finish with all these politicians. They're all the same, one as bad as another." Gamelin says he was "shocked" to hear such words from such a mouth, but again he did not attempt to reply. The meeting was at an end. They shook hands "coolly," says Gamelin, who then departed and drove to what he calls his "comfortable but modest apartment in the Avenue Foch."[37] They would not meet again until the end of 1943 when both found themselves, along with other French notables, military and civilian, in a castle in the Tyrol as prisoners of the Germans.†

Reynaud's appointment of Weygand as Supreme Commander was as lavishly praised in the press as was his naming of Pétain as Vice-Premier. The new chief was hailed as the right-hand man of Foch who would know again how to conquer. To Emile Buré in *L'Ordre* he had been "the brains of the General Staff in the last war. . . . His is not a name of defeat or of capitulation." How little editor Buré knew! And how little the press and the politicians considered that against a German army being led by relatively young officers, none of whom had been more than very junior in rank in the first war, the government had now put at the head of the French army two *vieillards* (Pétain eighty-four, Weygand seventy-three) who had no conception whatsoever of the tempo of blitz warfare and who in the interwar years had used their immense power and prestige to prevent the French Army from adapting itself to it.

Weygand himself, though energetic, forceful, and possessed of a keen intelligence, had never commanded a sizable unit in battle. All his experience in war had been as a staff officer, and he had been a brilliant one. To the newly appointed brigadier general, Charles de Gaulle, who was busy leading the only intact armored division left, and whom Pétain and Weygand had fought—and dismissed—all through the thirties because of his stubborn advocacy of tank warfare, the new generalissimo lacked the youth, the boldness, the imagination, to take hold and save the day.

Weygand [de Gaulle would write later] was not the man to do it. He was by nature a brilliant second man. He had, in this role, admirably served Foch. He had brought courage and intelligence to his task as Chief of the General Staff. But he was neither made nor prepared to take action, to confront destiny as a great commander. In the course of his whole career he had never exercised command in battle. . . . To choose him to take command at the gravest hour in our

---

* Colonel R. Villate, among others, later testified rather devastatingly to that.[36]
† Where, as Gamelin reports, he, Daladier, Reynaud, and Michel Clemenceau, among others, refused even to speak to Weygand.[38]

military history not because he was judged capable but under the pretext that "he was a banner"—that was the great mistake.[39]

WEYGAND'S FATAL DELAY

"It is all a question of hours," we have seen Gamelin warning as he penciled his last order on the morning of May 19. But to Weygand, completely ignorant of the pace of the German armored columns, it became not a matter of hours but of days. He delayed following up on Gamelin's proposal to have the armies in the north and in the south immediately start fighting their way to a junction with each other or of launching a counteroffensive further east to cut the extended German lines just west of the Meuse. He wanted first, he says, to size up the situation himself by visiting the embattled armies, as Foch had always done in the first war. He proposed to fly to the northern forces in Belgium and talk things over with the commanders of the French, British, and Belgian armies, which were that very day, May 20, being completely encircled. For at noon on the 20th the 1st Panzer Division had captured Amiens on the lower Somme. This city, which had been so savagely fought over in the first war, had fallen without a struggle. There had been no French troops there to defend it.* That evening, as we have seen, the 2nd Panzer division reached Abbeville at the mouth of the Somme, completing the encirclement. But the Panzer divisions were strung out for nearly a hundred miles and the German infantry had not yet had time to come up. The whole rear of the German armored columns from the Somme northward was undefended. The situation cried out for Allied counter-attacks from the north and south before the Germans had time to bring up their motorized infantry. But there was not much time. Action had to be taken at once, in a matter of hours, or of a day at the most. Instead of remaining at his Command Post and galvanizing the army commanders to action and giving them a simple plan to carry out, Weygand on the morning of May 21 instead set out on a hazardous visit to the Allied commanders in Belgium.

According to Reynaud, the new generalissimo wasted a good part of his first day of command in making ceremonial visits to the political dig-

---

* To the surprise of the Germans there were only British troops in their way as they drove on Amiens and Abbeville. A British battalion had confronted the 1st Panzer Division at Albert, northeast of Amiens, and had been overwhelmed. Later in the day the British 37th Brigade had tried to prevent the 1st Panzers from establishing a bridgehead on the south bank of the Somme across from Amiens. It had been wiped out. Further west, the British 35th Brigade had tried to defend Abbeville but was annihilated by the tanks of the 2nd Panzer Division. The British units had no tanks and practically no artillery. According to the official British war history only two BEF divisions, the 12th and 23rd, stood in the way of the German armored divisions which on May 20 poured through the 30-mile-wide corridor between the Scarpe at Arras and the Somme on their drive to the sea. Both were territorial divisions with little training, no tanks, and only a few pieces of artillery. During the day of the 20th both divisions were practically wiped out.[40]

nitaries in Paris, among them the President of the Republic and the new Minister of Interior, Mandel. He did, however, spend considerable time with General Georges, whose broken condition when he had first seen him the evening before had greatly moved him. He also spent two hours with General Doumenc at GHQ. Doumenc's bubbling spirits and irrepressible optimism, he says, "comforted" him. Even General Georges seemed to him to be in better shape than the day before. "He seems to be taking hold of himself," Weygand told Reynaud later that evening.

By his own account Weygand discussed thoroughly with Georges and Doumenc what had to be done to save the Allied armies in the north but he did not stay with them to see that the counterattacks from the north and south got under way without delay. Did he hesitate, as some French officers have suggested, because his first look at the situation had convinced him that, as General Georges and his Chief of Staff, General Roton, apparently believed, the war was already irretrievably lost?* In his own recital of his meeting with Georges on the 20th Weygand says they agreed that "if the worst came to the worst, we had at least to save the honor of the French armies." And of saving the honor of the country? And even more important, of saving the country itself? From now on these last two considerations seemed subordinated in Weygand's mind to the first.

Early on the morning of May 21 the new Commander in Chief set off by plane for Belgium. Because of a number of circumstances—planes that were not ready for takeoff, landing fields where there was no motor transportation or even functioning telephones, he did not arrive in Ypres until 3 P.M. Most of the day was thus wasted away from his Command Post. He could neither issue urgent orders nor follow the worsening course of battle as the German pincers began to close in on the armies entrapped in the north.

King Leopold quickly perceived that General Weygand not only had no definite plan to close the gap but was surprisingly ignorant of the actual plight of the Allied armies. He did not know, for instance, that Abbeville had been captured the evening before. But even if Weygand had come to work out a specific timetable for action with the British, Belgian, and French commanders on the spot, this would have proved impossible, for Lord Gort failed to show up. He had not got word of the meeting until too late. When he finally arrived at 8 P.M., Weygand had departed. But not before he had been given ample opportunity to sense the defeatism of the King, his reluctance to conform to the generalissimo's advice, and his

---

* When asked by Michel Clemenceau during his testimony before the Parliamentary Investigating Committee whether by May 19 the "game was lost," General Georges replied: "I believe it was."[41] In his notes for May 19 General Roton also writes: "by May 19, the game was lost." This admission led Colonel Villate to ask: "Was it for this reason that General Weygand delayed?"[42]

scarcely concealed hostility toward his cabinet ministers, whom he refused to allow to sit in on the meeting. Nor did Weygand find his own
general, Billotte, who commanded the Anglo-French armies in the north,
displaying the determination he had hoped for.

To the King and his military adviser, General Van Overstraeten, Weygand outlined the obvious move that had to be made and which Gamelin 54
hours before had stressed should be started "within a matter of hours."
While French divisions assembling south of the Somme would attack
toward the north, as many divisions from the French First Army and the
BEF as could be withdrawn from the defensive line on the Scheldt would
push southward across the panzer corridor. To protect their rear the Belgians would have to take over most of the defensive front. To do so
effectively they would have to withdraw not only to the Lys, west of the
Scheldt, but as quickly as possible to the Yser. This would give them a
much shorter front to defend and would keep them in close contact with
the French and British forces.

Overstraeten, to whom the King left the talking, refused. The Belgian
troops were too tired, he said, to make such an extensive retreat. Besides,
the King did not wish to abandon the little bit of Belgian territory his
troops still held. It was obvious, as Prime Minister Pierlot noted (though
Weygand fails to do so in his own report), that in stating that the Belgian
Army could not, or would not, withdraw to the Yser, the King and his
Military Counselor were acknowledging defeat and, in fact, preparing the
ground for capitulation. They were also challenging the right of the Allied
Supreme Command to give orders to the Belgian Army.

When he did get the opportunity of seeing the King between the military
conversations, Pierlot bitterly protested the ruler's attitude. "Has the
French generalissimo no right to order this counterattack?" he asked. "The
King," he says, "responded in the negative, emphasizing that in reality the
unity of command did not exist." And the Prime Minister adds: "The King
considered that the situation of the armies in Flanders left little cause for
hope."

General Van Overstraeten, the King's evil genius, as many Belgians
saw him, was even more pessimistic. A little earlier he had come out to
have a word with the ministers, Pierlot, the Premier, Spaak, the Foreign
Minister, and General Denis, the War Minister, who had been kept waiting
outside the conference room like little schoolboys by Leopold.* They urged
him to accept Weygand's proposal and speed up the retreat. "The troops

---

* In an article on the Conference at Ypres published in *Le Soir* of Brussels July
12, 1947, Pierlot still expressed a sense of outrage at the exclusion of the three
cabinet ministers by the King. He called it a "humiliating experience." Not even the
Defense Minister, General Denis, a professional soldier, was allowed to sit in on the
conversations. Nor was General Michiels, the Chief of the General Staff, invited to
attend. It would be impossible to imagine the President of the French Republic or
the King of England refusing to allow Reynaud and Churchill to attend high strategy
meetings.

are too tired," he replied. "Besides, why abandon all our territory?" When they protested that conserving the Belgian army intact was more important than clinging to "a few square kilometers of territory" and Pierlot cried: "It is better to retreat than be taken!" the general responded: "But we're already taken."

I replied [says Pierlot], not without anger: "No, we are not taken. But we will be if you do not do everything to avoid it. We are not taken as long as we have arms and can move." General Van Overstraeten left without a further word.

In the midst of terrible adversity the King and his government were now at complete odds. Both sides put their bitter feelings on paper in an exchange of letters after the Ypres meeting. The next day, May 22, the monarch wrote Pierlot that their talks had made a most "unpleasant impression" on him.

I do not think I merit the reproaches of the government that I am following a policy whose objective is to lead the country to conclude a separate peace with Germany. In the accomplishment of my constitutional duty as Commander in Chief of the Army, I have, above all, the obligation to defend the national territory and avoid compromising the destiny of the army. . . . I cannot admit that the ministers have a right to judge the army or to determine when it shall retreat.

He concluded by castigating the government for the "ridiculous haste" with which the government offices had been "evacuated to France" and ended his letter on an ominous note: "This unjustifiable defection . . . leads me to the conclusion that since the opening of hostilities the government has no longer had the means of governing."

Pierlot replied the next day that the government "alone" was constitutionally responsible for the conduct of the war "and of the acts of the Chief of State." The King, he charged, had already given him the impression on May 15 and 16 that the "perspective of capitulation was already envisaged not only as an eventuality to which events outside of our choice might lead us but as a measure preferable to the inconvenience of quitting our soil." And the Premier again insisted that the "King not link his fate to that of the army to the point of losing his liberty." As to the government evacuating Brussels, he reminded the King that the ministers had left the capital only at the last hour before the Germans entered.

General Billotte, Commander of the Allied forces in the north, now arrived, having been luckier than Gort in finally finding the place of meeting. This splendid officer, like General Georges, was already showing the strain of a losing battle. Two of his own liaison officers with the BEF describe him as "discouraged and beaten, physically exhausted and prey to a profound moral depression." Weygand, who admired him, noted that his "face was marked by fatigue and anguish." According to the Belgian minutes of the meeting, Billotte informed Weygand that the French First Army was in a very confused situation, "tired and severely tested," and incapable of launching an attack. It was barely capable of defending itself. The British army, he added, "was still intact and constituted a powerful offensive force." Billotte, it is evident, did not much cheer Weygand up, though the generalissimo says he agreed to carry out his plan. No attempt, though, was made by either French general to get down to details of the attack. Nothing was said about a timetable for specific objectives and deployment. Everything was left vague. This was largely because, Weygand contends, Lord Gort had failed to show up, which, he says, he "could not understand and which greatly astonished me."

The time passed, and I still had no news of the British Commander in Chief. No one could tell me where he was. . . . I could not leave without seeing him.

But he did, driving off at 7 P.M. to Dunkirk where he boarded a French destroyer. When Gort, who had waited all day at his headquarters at Prémesque for word as to where the meeting was taking place, finally arrived at Ypres at 8 P.M., he was chagrined to find that the generalissimo had departed. From this failure to meet stemmed a good deal of subsequent military history. Weygand left Ypres with a feeling of distrust of the British, whose commander he had tried and failed to see. Gort's distrust of the French was already growing. He had received no orders from the French High Command, which had kept him largely in ignorance of the disaster to the Ninth Army and of the rapid progress of the enemy toward the Channel. Now on May 21 his British army, along with the Belgians and the French First Army, was encircled. And he had no idea what General Weygand, to whom he had to look for orders, proposed to do about it.

On May 19, when his retreating forces were reaching the Scheldt and the German panzers were nearing the sea behind him, Gort had had his Chief of Staff, General H. R. Pownall, ring up the War Office in London to warn that since the French appeared to him unable to close the gap he might have to withdraw the BEF to the coast. It was a thought that began to grip him. "I felt," he reported later, "that in the circumstances there might be no other course open to me." Weygand later would hold forth sarcastically about the "great attraction of the sea for the British." And some French officers and military commentators would charge that Gort's own words showed he had abandoned the struggle by May 19—a charge that Colonel Lyet, on the French side, convincingly refutes.[43]

Actually on May 20 General Ironside, Chief of the Imperial General Staff, had flown over to Gort with orders from the War Cabinet for the BEF to move not north toward the Channel, but south toward Amiens in conjunction with the French. And though Gort argued that such a move was "entirely impossible until the situation had been retrieved on the front of the French First Army" he agreed to follow instructions. He ordered his only two disengaged divisions to counterattack south from Arras the next day. Ironside went on that morning to Billotte's headquarters at Lens and got him to agree to throw in two infantry divisions of the French First Army for the operation. The three light armored divisions of General Prioux's cavalry corps were also to take part. Unfortunately General Blanchard, the First Army Commander, in issuing orders to his Vth Corps, which was to attack on the British left toward Cambrai, stipulated that the offensive would begin "from the 21st on"—"à partir du 21," which left it to the corps commander to decide whether it would start on the 21st or thereafter. "All the drama of the failure of the Franco-British operation," writes Colonel Lyet, "lies in those words."

As it happened, the Vth Corps informed the British it could not jump off until the 22nd.* The British attack went off on the 21st anyway, the day of the Ypres meeting, supported by the French 3rd Light Armored Division. By evening it had penetrated four or five miles south of Arras against increasingly heavy German opposition from Rommel's 7th Panzer Division, destroyed a number of enemy tanks and supply vehicles and taken 400 prisoners. The 1st and 2nd French light tank divisions did not budge, nor did the Vth French Corps. When the French started off the next day it was the British turn to stand still. General Franklyn, the British commander, merely held his ground. Once more a failure of the Allies to coordinate their action had destroyed the chance of success.

Busy most of the day of the 21st overseeing the British counterattack at Arras, Lord Gort finally got wind from the Belgians where Weygand was and set off for Ypres to meet him, arriving there at 8 P.M. The generalissimo having left, he conferred with King Leopold and General Billotte. The pessimism of the French commander had not abated during the long day. He explained again that the French First Army's divisions were too exhausted to take the offensive. Gort thereupon proposed that the French extend their defense line on the Scheldt so as to release two British divisions and that the Belgians extend theirs to free one more British division. These three divisions of the BEF would then be thrown into the counterattack. The French and Belgians assented. It was also agreed that the Belgians would withdraw at least to the river Lys. Despite the accord reached, a feeling of gloom appears to have hung over the meeting.

---

* Major Vautrin, a French First Army liaison officer with the BEF, describes the state of mind of General René Altmayer, Commander of the French Vth Corps, when he received the order for the attack: "He declares that it cannot be executed, at least not until the the 22nd, at the earliest. . . . General Altmayer, who appeared exhausted and despondent, sat on my camp bed and wept silently. He said we had to see things as they were, that his troops were finished, that he was ready to face the consequences of refusing to carry out the order and that he would get himself killed at the head of a battalion. But he would not continue to sacrifice his army corps, which had already lost half its strength."[44]

After its conclusion King Leopold briefed his rebellious ministers on it. "Lord Gort agreed to counterattack south," he told them. "But the British general considers its prospects practically null. The situation is desperate."[45]

So General Weygand, who had taken a precious day off from his Command Post in order to learn at first hand what the situation of the Allied armies in the north was, to buck up their commanders and work out a plan for their salvation, had accomplished very little. Nothing much was decided at Ypres. No definite plan for a counteroffensive was drawn up. Weygand did not learn what Gort could or would do, and the British commander did not learn at first hand what, if anything, Weygand had up his sleeve. Certainly the generalissimo left Ypres more pessimistic than when he arrived. He saw the Belgians faltering, the King at odds with his government, in no mind to accept the High Command's directives, and losing all hope. He found General Billotte, noted for his energy and drive, physically and mentally weary and with no confidence in the offensive capability of the First Army, which ten days before had been the best the French had. And the British remained a question mark. Finally, the Ypres meeting had revealed an appalling lack of confidence in each of the Allied commanders for the others. King Leopold believed the game was lost. Gort felt that the French army was incapable of taking the offensive and that the BEF would probably have to save itself. The French and Belgians began to suspect that the British were about to "desert" them and make for the sea.

To make matters worse, if possible, General Billotte was fatally injured in a car accident driving back to his headquarters that evening from Ypres. He never regained consciousness and died two days later. Now no French general in the north knew at first hand either what was in Weygand's mind for the counterattack from the north and south or of Billotte's oral agreement with Leopold and Gort at the close of the Ypres meeting for the Belgian withdrawal to the Lys and the release of three British divisions to spearhead the attack southward. The three Allied armies were left without a commander to try to coordinate their moves. General Blanchard, Commander of the disintegrating First Army, took over on his own temporarily, but he, like General Georges, was on the point of collapse. Even if he had been in better shape, he lacked the caliber of Billotte for such a command. And Weygand, who had been losing such crucially valuable time in getting a counterattack started, let more time slip by in confirming Blanchard to the new command. Not until May 25 did he get around to it.*

---

* By which time General Blanchard had given up all hope. Marc Bloch, the historian, who was on his staff, heard Blanchard say on May 26: "I am quite certain we shall see a double capitulation."[46] "How did one expect," asks Colonel de Bardies, "that General Blanchard could impose himself when General Billotte could just barely do it?"[47] At any rate, the armies in the north remained without orders from the Allied High Command for several days. As General Nyssens of the Belgian Army put it: "General Billotte was injured May 21. General Blanchard was not officially

The consequences of Weygand's delay were bound to be fatal. Between May 19, on the morning of which Gamelin gave his last order, pointing out that behind the German armored columns there was a "vacuum," and on the evening of which Weygand was named Commander in Chief—between that day and May 22, when the new generalissimo finally issued his first formal order (Number One), there had been at least a chance of the Allies closing the gap and cutting off the panzer divisions in the region of the Channel. But by the 22nd the situation had changed. After four days of strenuous effort the Germans had been able to rush forward motorized artillery and infantry to bolster both sides of their narrow corridor north of the Somme. Weygand was letting the last opportunity slip by. Gamelin, for once, was right in asking: "What would have become of the Battle of the Marne if we had let pass the days of September 5 and 6 without doing anything, or if, on May 29, 1918, when the French front on the Chemin des Dames was broken, Marshal Foch had not taken immediate measures?"[50]

Churchill flew over to Paris on May 22 to concert with the French on "immediate measures" to save the armies in the north. At noon he and Reynaud met with General Weygand at Vincennes. After listening to the generalissimo outline his plan for a joint Allied attack from the north and south through the corridor, the British Prime Minister drew up a résumé of agreement—"to make sure," he says, "that there was no mistake about what was settled." The general and Reynaud approved it, and Churchill immediately wired the text to the War Cabinet in London and to Lord Gort in Flanders.

It was agreed:
1. That the Belgian Army should withdraw to the line of the Yser and stand there, the sluices being opened.
2. That the British Army and the French First Army should attack southward towards Baupaume and Cambrai at the earliest moment, certainly tomorrow—with about eight divisions. . . .
3. That . . . the British Air Force should give the utmost possible help, both by day and by night. . . .
4. That the new French Army Group which is advancing upon Amiens and

designated to replace him until the evening of May 25. During this period of four days the Belgian Command never received a single order"—a statement confirmed by General Michiels, Chief of the Belgian General Staff.[48] Lord Gort fared no better. "Except for the . . . orders to retire from the Dyle (obtained only after I sent General Eastwood to General Billotte's headquarters to represent my views), I received no written orders from the French First Group of Armies. . . . I telegraphed to the Secretary of State pointing out that co-ordination was essential with armies of three different nations. . . . I never received any information from any source as to the exact location of our own or enemy forces on the far side of the gap; nor . . . any details of any proposed attack from that direction."[49]

forming a line along the Somme should strike northward and join hands with the British divisions who are attacking southward in the general direction of Baupaume.[51]

Now, either Churchill misunderstood what Weygand had told him or the generalissimo had misled him. There was no chance at all of implementing Paragraph Two. The British and French in the north simply did not have eight divisions to attack "certainly by tomorrow." Most of their forces were still pinned down by the Germans driving from the east. Weygand in his memoirs expresses his "regret" that Churchill misunderstood him on that. Nor was there any basis for Paragraph Four. Churchill left the meeting believing that the new French Army Group "advancing on Amiens" would strike north and "join hands" with the British attacking southward. But according to the French minutes of the meeting Weygand had been vague about this. He merely said that General Frère's forces, concentrating below the Somme, would strike northward to "increase the pressure on the enemy armor in the region of Amiens, Abbeville, and Arras." There was no word from him that this force, as Churchill believed, would push north of the river for a junction with the BEF. Weygand made this clear later in the day when he finally got around to issuing his first General Order for the counterattack. After outlining the moves to be made by the armies in the north in their attack southward, he merely added that the French force in the south would recapture the "Somme crossings," that is, the German bridgeheads south of the river. Again no word about them striking north of the Somme to help close the gap.

Though Weygand, according to the French minutes, told Reynaud immediately after the meeting with Churchill that General Frère's army on the Somme "would have tomorrow in support of the operation from the north more numerous and important units than he had believed possible a few hours before," it is clear from his own account that he never had any hope that it could mount a serious offensive beyond the Somme.

To ease the task allotted to the Northern Group of Armies [he said later] I had decided that the forces in position on the Somme should attack simultaneously in order to join up with them. . . . I was too well aware of the weakness of the numbers at my disposal . . . to allow myself to indulge in any illusions regarding the strength of this thrust from the south—that is, from the neighborhood of Amiens. But I calculated that however feeble it might be, it would at least create an additional threat to the German flank and thus increase the chances of success for the northern offensive.[52]

If this force was so "feeble," why should Weygand have exaggerated its strength to the French and British heads of government? Churchill says his understanding from what Weygand said at the meeting was that the new army on the Somme which was "to push forward from Amiens to Arras" had a strength of "from 18 to 20 divisions"—a formidable force to be thrown against the thinly held German southern flank, if it had existed.*[53]

General Weygand's General Order No. 1 of May 22 is still lacking in details of specific deployment and of timing. Moreover on some crucial points it is quite unrealistic, taking no account of the progress of the panzers up the Channel coast nor of the situation of the northern armies. There is no mention of the BEF and First French Army striking south "certainly tomorrow with about 8 divisions." No timetable for their operation is even suggested. There is no instruction, nor was there any from Georges or Blanchard, as to the role and objectives of each unit. Weygand does say that the deployment of the British and French armies is too dense, and that the entire BEF could "with advantage" be moved to the right of the attacking line. But how was this possible when all the divisions were heavily engaged along the Scheldt and in the Arras region?

Weygand reveals that he still has not got a clear picture of where the German forces are. He says the northern armies "have the imperative task of preventing the German attack from making its way to the sea." But the panzers had reached the sea two days before. Finally, contrary to what Churchill believed Weygand had told him, the generalissimo stipulates that the French forces on the Somme must merely recapture the German bridgeheads south of the river. No mention of them crossing it and pushing north.

While the talks in Paris were proceeding on May 22 and Weygand was getting out his first order, the French First Army in the north was launching its "counterattack" east of Arras toward Cambrai which General Blanchard had been unable to coordinate with the British drive from Arras the day before. It did not amount to much. Originally planned as a major effort to be carried out by the French Vth Corps supported by two light armored divisions, the scope of the attack was whittled away before it started. Instead of the Vth Corps, the 25th Infantry Division was designated to carry out the attack, and finally just the 121st Infantry Regiment, supported by two small armored assault groups. The two light armored divisions were left out entirely. The regiment jumped off at 9 A.M. between Arleux and Bouchain toward Cambrai and reached its outskirts by evening. Then to the "stupefaction" of its commander, General Molinié, it was ordered to withdraw, because the First Army Command feared it might be encircled. Thus petered out the first attempt of the Franco-British armies to fight their way southward. Unable to coordinate their attacks for the same day, each army acting on its own, the two Allied forces ended their operation on a ridiculous note with the "offensive" of the Vth Corps reduced to the employment of a single regiment, which as soon as it advanced was ordered to retreat.

---

* In reality there were only six divisions, three of them still incomplete, and stretched out on a front of 65 miles.[54]

Weygand's first order did not go out to the northern armies, as General Roton noted, until 8:50 P.M. on the evening of the 22nd—7 hours after it was issued, and by the morning of the next day Gort had not yet received it or any other directive for the "Weygand Plan." Throughout the 23rd a superior German force, led by the 5th and 7th Panzer divisions, was pushing his two infantry divisions back on both sides of Arras, though a small British garrison still held on to the town itself, repulsing several attempts of the 11th German Motorized Brigade to take it from three sides. By nightfall General H. E. Franklyn's special force around Arras was in danger of being surrounded—only two roads remained open for its escape—and about 7 P.M. Gort ordered its withdrawal to the Canal Line north and northeast, where, Gort says, "it would be well placed to take part in any further counterattack southwards." Obviously with German armor flanking it on both sides Arras could no longer have been of any use as a jumping-off place for the contemplated attack south. But the British withdrawal during the night of May 23–24 did leave the French First Army to its left in a more restricted salient, hemmed in in a quadrilateral that ran from Maulde, Condé, Valenciennes, to Douai.

General Weygand was furious when he learned on the morning of May 24 of the British withdrawal at Arras. He immediately protested in writing (and no doubt for the record) to Reynaud that

as the result of the British retreat he had advised Army Group 1 in the north that if it thought the operation planned (to attack south) could no longer be carried out, it should try to establish as large a bridgehead as possible around the three northern ports—Boulogne, Calais, and Dunkirk.

So Weygand, who would bitterly blame the British for wanting to head for the Channel, was already envisaging it himself the morning of the 24th.

The British withdrawal at Arras on the night of May 23–24 provoked a poisonous controversy between the two Allies, that continued, on the French side, long after the war. Weygand from then on blamed much that subsequently happened on this retreat and his stand was supported by most of the French generals, some seeking alibis for their own failures, and by many French military historians. Acting on Weygand's letter and on further and exaggerated reports of the British withdrawal, the French Premier got off two sharply worded telegrams to Churchill in London.

General Weygand informs me [the second one stated] that, contrary to formal orders . . . the British Army has carried out a withdrawal of 25 miles in the direction of the ports at a moment when our forces from the south were gaining ground toward the north to join up with the Allied armies in the north. This withdrawal has naturally obliged General Weygand to modify his whole plan. He is now compelled to give up his attempt to close the breach and establish a continuous front. . . .[55]

Weygand's information was inaccurate, to say the least. The British had not withdrawn 25 miles from Arras toward the ports, but 15 miles in an almost opposite direction, that is, northeast. They had not acted "contrary to formal orders" since none had been received to hold the Arras salient, though Gort can be blamed for not at least informing General Blanchard of his move until the next morning.* Finally, Weygand's information that the French forces on the Somme "were gaining ground toward the north" had no basis in fact. They were not advancing. They had made no progress even in wiping out the German bridgeheads south of the river. Notwithstanding, Weygand had wired Blanchard on the night of the 23rd that "the Seventh Army has reached the Somme at Amiens and Ham. Offensive will continue tomorrow, supported by armored forces, in the direction of Albert-Baupaume," which were north of the river.[57] It is puzzling that the top French general could so mislead the Premier, Blanchard and the British.

Weygand not only had found a scapegoat in the British. He had found an excuse in their withdrawal at Arras for calling off the counterattacks which he himself had delayed so long. He was not alone. General Besson, who on May 21 had taken over command of the Sixth and Seventh Armies on the Somme and issued a grandiose order saying: "There is no longer a question of withdrawing or merely defending. We must attack, attack, attack!" was by the evening of the 24th whistling a different tune. He rang up General Frère of the Seventh Army to say: "Army Group 1 (Blanchard) has had to withdraw to the north and the enemy is reinforcing himself in front of us. The offensive operation can therefore no longer be envisaged for the moment. We must come up to the Somme and establish ourselves in depth." For defense, not for offense, that is. Like Weygand, General Besson was using the British withdrawal at Arras to justify abandoning the counterattack.

Major Lyet, the objective French military historian, recapitulates the thinking of the French generals on this day of May 24:

> General Blanchard has sent a liaison officer to Paris to explain the *difficulties* of the projected attack to General Weygand; Weygand has seen it as *impossible* to attempt; and General Besson has given orders to *abandon* it.†[58]

Actually in the north General Blanchard and General Gort, despite the disastrous situation of their armies now encircled, had not abandoned the plan to carry out their part of the combined counterattack from both

---

* The British did inform the CP of the French 1st Light Armored Division of the pullout. That unit, on the western flank of the British, had also been steadily forced back during the day in heavy fighting. Since the French forces around Arras withdrew with the British by mutual agreement it is strange that the French First Army Headquarters was ignorant of it. Perhaps the chaos of communications was responsible.[56]

† The italics are Lyet's.

sides of the German corridor. It was still a narrow one. Only 30 miles separated the salient of the French First Army in the north from the position of the Seventh Army on the Somme near Péronne.

Already on the morning of May 23 Gort had proposed to Blanchard an attack toward the south to be carried out by two British divisions, one French division, and the French Cavalry Corps, whose three light armored divisions were now no more than at half strength. Because of the time necessary to free the British divisions from the line, he suggested the operation commence May 26. But having no illusions about the state of the French First Army troops and his own, he "emphasized," he says, "that the principal effort must come from the south, and that the operation of the northern forces could be nothing more than a sortie."[59] Blanchard agreed. Gort also asked the French commander to arrange with Weygand for the attacks from the north and south to be synchronized. The BEF commander still had no information about the French forces on the Somme which were to press northward but he seems to have taken Weygand at his word that there were some—enough to make "the principal effort"—an impression which was strengthened the next day when London informed him that "Weygand reports French Seventh Army is advancing successfully and has captured Péronne, Albert, and Amiens."[60] If true, this meant to Gort that the French divisions on the Somme had not only wiped out the strong German bridgeheads south of the Somme at Amiens and Péronne but had advanced north of the river and taken Albert. At Albert the French would be a quarter of the way on their drive to the northern armies and would have succeeded in breaking through the increasingly strong German position on the Somme. Alas for Gort, there was no truth to it whatsoever.

Despite the British withdrawal at Arras on the night of May 23, the French and British commanders went ahead loyally to carry out their end of the Weygand Plan. On the morning of the 24th Blanchard worked out the details with the British. The operation was now to be carried out with three French and two British divisions, covered by the three light armored divisions of the French Cavalry Corps and whatever tanks the British could scrape up. They were to advance south on both sides of the Canal du Nord, with the armored forces protecting their western flank against the German panzers in case the latter turned east against them from the coastal region. The offensive, a bigger one with more units than the French had yet carried out during the whole battle, was to get off May 26 with the establishment of bridgeheads south of the Scarpe. The next day the whole force would strike south toward Péronne on the Somme.

The news that the northern force was at last planning to move south caused spirits to rise in the French High Command. On May 25th Weygand visited Georges at his headquarters. Cheered by the prospect of five Anglo-French divisions fighting down from the north, supported by armor, they telephoned General Besson, who had abandoned his Somme "offensive" the day before, to resume it at once and drive with all he had northward. Weygand wired Blanchard that he was "highly pleased" with his "decision."

Later in the day the generalissimo's spirits were considerably dampened by a Major Fauvelle, who arrived in Paris from the First Army with bad news about its state and its prospects. He appeared out of the blue at a meeting in Reynaud's office attended by Pétain, Weygand, Admiral Darlan, Baudouin (who kept the notes), and General Sir Edward L. Spears. The British general had come over from London that morning to serve as Churchill's personal liaison officer with Reynaud for military matters. Half French by birth and bilingual, he had served as liaison officer between the French and British armies and then as head of the British Military Mission in France during the First World War. He knew the country and the people and liked them. The tidings that Major Fauvelle brought from the French First Army appeared to surprise Reynaud and Weygand. They shocked Spears.

There was no hope, Fauvelle said, of the First Army carrying out Weygand's plan. Blanchard, its commander, was exhausted and so were his troops. "The Army has only three divisions left," he went on, "capable of fighting. There is only one day's reserve of ammunition." According to Reynaud, he added that the British Army "appeared to be preparing to reembark and the Belgian Army to give up." His conclusion: "I believe in a very early capitulation."

The newly arrived British general listened to the major with growing horror.

I felt cold fingers turning my heart to stone [Spears writes]. I have . . . seen broken men, but never one deliquescent, that is, in a state where he was fit only to be scraped up with a spoon. . . . He was the very embodiment of catastrophe.

Pétain, says Spears, said nothing, and continued staring at the carpet. Admiral Darlan was equally silent, apparently thinking that since this was not a nautical matter it did not concern him. Weygand seemed impressed. Reynaud remonstrated.* Spears fumed. Fauvelle did make two

---

* Spears gives a vivid description of the men who now presided over the destiny of France, all of whom, except Darlan, he knew well personally. "Pétain seemed dead. . . . He looked very sad. . . . He said nothing and, head sunk, went on looking at the carpet. . . . Weygand was in khaki uniform and riding breeches, complete even to brass spurs, wizened and yellow-skinned. Like Reynaud, he looked Oriental. His sparse moustache and parchment skin, his high cheek-bones protruding from a flat face shaped like the ace of spades reversed, enhanced an impression already emphasized by his very pointed chin. But it was not his appearance, with which I was familiar, that amazed me, but his activity; he was darting about like a minnow, as fresh as a daisy, showing no sign of fatigue. . . . Reynaud's Chinese eyes . . . did not smile, but his eyebrows, which were drawn high and shaped like open umbrellas, giving him an expression of unabating wakefulness and amused curiosity, shot several times half-way up his forehead as if they had been half-closed and lifted to

constructive suggestions: that the armies in the north be permitted to move toward the sea and that General Blanchard be officially named head of Army Group 1. Weygand apparently agreed with the first and definitely with the second. Later that afternoon, four days after Billotte's fatal accident left the Army Group without a commander, he got off a telegram to Blanchard appointing him to the post and naming General Prioux of the Cavalry Corps as chief of the First Army. The generalissimo added a personal message:

You remain sole judge of decisions to take to save what can be saved, and above all the honor of the colors of which you are the guardian.[62]

To save the honor of the Army! The idea was becoming an obsession in the mind of the generalissimo. Corollary to it, another idea had begun to sprout in both Weygand and Pétain: after the honor of the Army had been saved France must ask for an armistice. The two most illustrious military men in France had given up.

Pétain even before this. Even as he left Madrid on May 17, after telling Franco, as we have seen, that France had been beaten. At least the aged Marshal made no bones about it. The very next day, while attending his first cabinet meeting in Paris, he startled the members of the government in the midst of a discussion about moving to Tours by interjecting that he himself would refuse to quit the capital, even if the Germans entered. According to Louis Marin, who was present, Pétain added "that to find himself face to face with Hitler and to talk to him did not frighten him; that, on the contrary, 'between soldiers' better conditions could be obtained than civilians could get."[63]

By May 18, then, the first day he assumed office in the Reynaud government, the "Victor of Verdun" had concluded that France would have to capitulate and that he himself could get more favorable terms for surrender than could a civilian leader. The general outline of what would have to be done was forming in his crusty mind. In that of Weygand, and even of Reynaud too.

At 6 P.M.—still on the 24th—the generalissimo telephoned Baudouin and asked him to come to see him immediately at Vincennes. The Commander in Chief was still fuming at the "retreat" of the British, which he insisted was one of 25 miles, and which he said had caused him to abandon his plan. To Baudouin, "Weygand appeared overwhelmed by this de-

avoid colliding with each other. . . . He looked not in the least rattled. I said to myself . . . : 'This is a likable, gallant little man' . . . . Admiral Darlan looked more than ever like the old salt of light comedy. . . . He conveyed an uneasy sense of unreality, of something rather bogus. . . . He also, like Pétain, evaporated from the proceedings as soon as he had sat down." Spears adds that his impression of Baudouin, "tall, clean-shaven, blue-eyed and good looking, was not an unpleasant one—a first impression," he confesses, "that was to prove to have been mistaken."[61]

fection of the British army." Overwhelmed also, he made it clear, by the pitiful state of the French army, for which as its chief in the early thirties he bore, after all, some responsibility.

The general repeated what he had said this morning at the office of the President: that France had launched itself in a war without having the materiel to fight it, neither tanks, nor antitank guns, nor flak. . . . No military preparation. No diplomatic preparation. "It is criminal," the general told me," to have declared war September 3 in these conditions. It is inconceivable that those responsible for the French army at that moment did not say to the government that the state of the army did not permit engaging in the struggle."*[64]

Baudouin, who sensed his growing power and influence—he now had the confidence of the generalissimo and the Premier and the backing of the latter's ambitious, driving mistress—says he responded to Weygand: "We must get France out of this mess. . . . The terrible tribulations which weigh on her will perhaps in the end be salutary." Baudouin swears that at these words of his the tears came to Weygand's eyes. More important, the general, he says, agreed with him, and thereupon explained "that a beaten general has no right to go on living, and that his only regret was that he had not been killed when his plane made a difficult landing on Wednesday morning."[65]

An emotional scene, but nevertheless significant. The Commander in Chief felt so defeated he wanted to die. And Baudouin, now in the center of things, wanted to get France out of the war. Pierre Dhers, a member of the Parliamentary Investigating Committee, and a sharp cross-examiner, nailed Baudouin down on this after the war.

DHERS: You have already told us that for you defeat was certain after May 16.

BAUDOUIN: Absolutely.

DHERS: Thus on May 24, the day of your talk with General Weygand, you were already for an armistice. You told us: "General Weygand convinced me of it. . . ."

BAUDOUIN: I was certain by May 24 that the battle was lost . . . and that fighting must stop. Yes, that was certain.[66]

Baudouin says he saw Reynaud at 8:30 P.M. on his return from Vincennes and that the Premier, deeply disturbed by the "British retreat," the probability that Italy would enter the war on the side of Hitler, and the low morale of the army and the population, remarked that he was wondering whether in case of moderate offers of peace from Germany,

---

*This was the general who less than a year before, on July 4, 1939, had said in a public speech at Lille: "I believe that the French Army is a more effective force than at any time in its history. Its materiel is of the first quality . . . its morale is excellent, and its High Command remarkable."

French public opinion would support him in turning them down. If not, he quotes Reynaud as saying, "since I've always been for fighting the war to the end, I would resign."[67]

Just as General Weygand by May 24 (and Marshal Pétain even earlier) appears to have accepted defeat and to have wanted to call off the fighting as soon as possible, so Reynaud was already facing up to what he might have to do: resign and let another French government consider Germany's peace terms.

All this came out at a meeting of the Comité de Guerre that got under way the next day, May 25, at 7 P.M., a few hours after the conference in Reynaud's office to which Major Fauvelle had brought such distressing news from the northern front. This was a crucial confrontation of France's military and political leaders. Much that would follow in the next crisis-ridden thirty days would stem from the words spoken here. And what certain individuals said, or were reported to have said, or denied saying, caused bitter controversy and savage recriminations in Paris that raged for years after the war. This was due largely to the fact that there were three versions of the minutes, all of them based on a résumé drawn up by Baudouin, who himself was suspect. One was uncorrected; a second was corrected by Reynaud so that one key utterance of his, which he denied saying, and which Weygand swore he *heard* him say, was scratched out; and a third version of somewhat mysterious origin published in the Paris newspaper *L'Aurore* on November 16, 1949—more than nine years after the event—which emanated from GHQ (General Doumenc) and differed from the other versions mainly in elaborating on what Weygand allegedly said.

The controversy centers over whether the Premier, the President of the Republic, the Minister of Marine, and Weygand himself first considered on this date, May 25, stopping the fighting, reneging on the promise to Great Britain not to make a separate peace, and accepting an armistice. It was over the ultimate question of an armistice that the struggle between Reynaud and some of his backers in the cabinet on the one hand, and Weygand, Pétain, and some of the ministers on the other, would be fought with increasing fierceness and not a little duplicity from this day to the end. At stake was the survival of the Third Republic.

In his report on the military situation, with which the meeting began, General Weygand said he "envisaged the worst," that is, the loss of the northern armies. In that case he would fight on the Somme "to the last extremity." But with only 60 divisions against "from 130 to 150 German divisions" he had little hope that he could do more than "save the honor of the Army and country."

France [he said] has committed the immense error of going to war without having the materiel or the military doctrine which was necessary. She must now pay heavily for this culpable imprudence. . . .

According to the *Aurore* version he added: "Conclusion: *"We must stop this war immediately."*

It was at this point that, according to Baudouin's original minutes, Reynaud intervened, declaring: *"It cannot be said that our adversary will grant us an immediate armistice."* A few days later, in correcting the minutes, he scratched out the words with his own pen.* "Consequently," he later argued, "they ought not to have appeared in the record." The question surely is not that, but whether he said them, whether he was the first to pronounce the fatal word "armistice." At first, in his subsequent testimony at the Pétain trial and later in the first version of Volume 1 of his memoirs, he admitted using the word, but only to "end the debate" and to make it clear "that nothing permitted us to believe that it would be possible to obtain an armistice conforming to the honor and vital interest of France." Later, in 1949, when Baudouin produced his minutes with the Premier's corrections in his own hand, Reynaud denied ever having used the phrase.

Weygand, before the Parliamentary Investigating Committee, swore Reynaud did utter it. "I heard the words myself," he testified. ". . . It was the first time that the word 'armistice' was pronounced."[68]

Lebrun, the President of the Republic, who presided, did not employ the word when he intervened in the debate. But that was his sense. There had been a discussion on whether the government should leave the capital and now Lebrun broke in. Would the government, he asked, not have more freedom to "examine offers of peace if this were done before the destruction of the French armies, which the general envisages?"

Certainly [he continued] we have signed engagements which prevent us from making a separate peace. But if Germany offers us relatively advantageous conditions we must, at any rate, examine them closely and deliberate with cool heads.

According to Baudouin's minutes, César Campinchi, the Minister of Marine, suggested an ingenious way out of France's obligations not to make a separate peace.

If the present government has given its word to England, another government will be less embarrassed in signing a peace treaty without a prior accord with England. The present government will only have to resign.†

All present agreed on one thing: that Reynaud must fly to London at once and examine with the British government the consequences of the

---

* It was customary in France for each minister or general to correct that part of the minutes which quoted him. It was not always a question of whether he had been quoted correctly or not but what he wanted to leave in the record as having said.

† Campinchi's friends in the government denied hearing him say this. Baudouin swore to the Parliamentary Investigating Committee that he heard him pronounce the words.[69] At any rate, they were quite out of character of this forthright man, who opposed the Armistice to the end.

destruction of the French army and the necessity, as Weygand put it, "to cease hostilities." This, added the general, is "an inter-Allied question." The Premier promised that he would go to London the next day to sound out the British government. "If offers of peace are presented," he said, "France must say to England: 'Here are the offers we've received. What do you think of them? We realize we are bound by a formal engagement to you.' "

Pétain, who as Commander in Chief of the French armies in the last years of the First World War had seen enough of the British to last a lifetime, and whose phobia toward them was now being rekindled, came to life at the discussion of the ally across the Channel.

Marshal Pétain wonders [say the minutes] whether there is a complete reciprocity of duties between France and England. Each nation has obligations toward the other in proportion to the aid which the other has given it. Now, actually, England has thrown into the struggle only 10 divisions against 80 French divisions. The comparison must be made not only between the military effort of the two countries but between the suffering they are going through.

The venerable Marshal wanted the Premier to keep that in mind when he saw Churchill.

When the meeting broke up at 9:30 P.M. one thing seemed clear, despite all the subsequent bitter wrangling as to who had said what: Pétain and Weygand, the President of the Republic and the Premier, had posed the question of ceasing hostilities and "examining" German peace proposals. And Reynaud had agreed to put it to the British on the morrow.[70]

But did he? When Baudouin fetched the Premier from Le Bourget the evening of May 26 on his return from London and asked him anxiously whether the British had agreed to release France from its word not to make a separate peace, Reynaud responded curtly: "I did not raise the question."*[71]

While he was away for the day in London a cabal had begun to form in Paris to force the harassed Premier to raise it. General Weygand assumed the leadership. On the morning of the 26th he again summoned Baudouin to Vincennes for a talk that began at 10:30 A.M. and continued for an hour. The situation of the armies in the north had become even more grave in the last 24 hours. Yet the generalissimo seemed more concerned with something else. This was the necessity of saving the French Army so that it could put down anarchy and revolution at home. He had

---

*According to Reynaud and Churchill the conversations touched mostly on concessions to be made to Italy in order to keep her out of the war. Reynaud did tell Churchill his government would be in "difficulties if the Battle of France were lost, for Pétain would come out for an armistice." Churchill says Reynaud "dwelt not obscurely upon the possible French withdrawal from the war."[72]

raised the issue toward the close of the War Committee meeting the evening before. "We must conserve the means," he had said, "of keeping order in the country. What troubles we will have if the last organized force, that is, the Army, is going to be destroyed!" Now to Baudouin, after again blaming the British "retreat" for the present mess, Weygand unburdened himself on the prime importance of "avoiding a revolutionary movement in Paris." It was all right to speak of "fighting to the last cartridge but this would only exhaust the vital forces of the country and resolve nothing. We must save honor but we must stop this thing before it leads to a senseless massacre."

Baudouin next saw Pétain, who took the same line.

The Marshal tells me he is against continuing the struggle to the end. It is easy, but also stupid, to talk of fighting to the last man. It is also criminal, in view of our losses in the first war and of our feeble birthrate. . . . We must save at least part of the Army . . . for without it to maintain order a real peace will not be possible and the reconstruction of France will not have a basis from which to begin.

The aged Marshal, says Baudouin, was in tears.

At 4 P.M. Baudouin had a talk with Camille Chautemps, the Radical Party leader and Vice-Premier.

He is terribly frightened by the situation and wonders whether it is useful to continue for long this struggle. He thinks France must rally around the Marshal for "no civilian will have the desired authority to negotiate, and we must do that very soon. . ."[73]

These four men, Weygand, Pétain, Chautemps, and Baudouin now began to form the center of a movement—Reynaud would call it a "conspiracy"—to stop the fighting and get out of the war. Pierre Laval, whom they distrusted but who, as we have seen, was in secret touch with the Marshal, would soon join.

At his daily forenoon meeting with Reynaud and Pétain on May 27 Weygand reported that he had sent "violent" telegrams to the Belgian and British Commands. "The British," he told the Premier, "not only are not attacking but they are pulling back. The Belgians are giving way. How can we avoid disaster?"[74]

This was far from being the whole story, as General Weygand well knew. The French First Army, as well as the British and Belgians, was falling back in the north—and for good reason. For two days, since May 25, the situation of all three armies had been growing increasingly desperate. On the morning of the 25th Blanchard and Gort had met with General

Sir John Dill, the new Chief of the British Imperial General Staff, and had agreed to go ahead with the offensive toward the south despite the violent German pressure on their defensive positions facing east. They realized, though, that the main Allied effort must come from the south. They did not know, because General Weygand had misled them, that this was a forlorn hope. All day long on May 25 the French First Army, fighting to hold the narrow salient at the eastern end of the Allied pocket, was heavily attacked from north, east, and south, and forced to give ground. Its plight by evening was becoming critical.

But the course of the battle further north made it even worse and suddenly threatened both the French and British armies with being cut off from the sea. Early that morning Blanchard and Gort learned that on the previous evening (of the 24th) the German Sixth Army had broken through the Belgians on both sides of Courtrai on the Lys, penetrating to a depth of 1½ miles on a 13-mile front. This at once posed a grave danger to the BEF since it threatened to separate the British from the Belgians and open a gap between them through which the Germans could advance swiftly on Dunkirk, the last Channel port in Allied hands.

Lord Gort waited anxiously throughout the day for news of promised Belgian counterattacks to plug the gap. When toward evening it became clear that the Belgians, despite a valiant effort, were unable to dislodge the enemy, that the hole between his army and the Belgians was widening and deepening, and that unless it was plugged within a matter of hours his "last hope," as he puts it, "of reaching the coast would be gone," he made his most fateful decision of the ill-starred campaign. At 6 P.M., without asking for authority from the French Command, he ordered the two divisions assigned for the push south, the 5th and the 50th, to turn north and seal the gap around Ypres, blocking the road to Dunkirk.

"With this decision," he admits, "vanished the last opportunity for a sortie (south)." But at least it kept alive the chance of saving the British Expeditionary Force and the French First Army from being captured. Gort immediately communicated his decision to Blanchard's headquarters but was unable to reach the general to explain his sudden move.

Blanchard waited a little longer to make *his* decision, though by now it had become inevitable. At 11:30 P.M. on the 25th he issued a general order saying that in view of the German breakthrough at Courtrai on the Belgian front and the withdrawal of the British divisions which were to have joined the French in the attack south, the counteroffensive set for May 26 was called off. He directed the three Allied armies in the north to "regroup progressively behind the waterline demarcated by the Aa Canal, the Lys, and the Canal de Dérivation so as to form a bridgehead covering Dunkirk in depth."[75]

Though General Weygand, according to Baudouin, was still fuming on the morning of May 27 about the British and Belgians "not attacking but instead pulling back," it is clear from the official French Army dispatches that on the morning of the 26th he received a copy of General Blanchard's order for withdrawal, approved it, and himself authorized the pullback. In fact, General Roton says the Commander in Chief was "not surprised" at the news.[76]

The "Weygand Plan," tardy offshoot of the earlier Gamelin Plan to close the gap between the northern and southern armies, was dead, officially buried on May 26 by the generalissimo himself. This did not prevent him from wiring Blanchard on the same day that Army Group 3 was "continuing its operations to cross the Somme and advance as soon as possible on the Authie river," which was 15 miles north of the Somme in the Abbeville region. At least this might have been encouraging to Blanchard and Gort, had it been true. But General Roton, who cites the message, adds, without apparent awareness of the contradiction, that after the failure of French counterattacks to wipe out the German bridgeheads south of the Somme at Abbeville, Picquigny, and Amiens, General Frère, Commander of the Seventh Army, "abandoned on May 26 all hope of realizing a junction with Army Group 1 in the north."[77]

Though this was not specifically known in London, the British government by now realized that the French "offensive" north from the Somme would never get started. When Gort returned to his Command Post on the morning of the 26th, after working out with Blanchard the details of the Allied withdrawal toward Dunkirk, he found a message from Anthony Eden, the British Secretary of State for War. In view of his "information that French offensive from Somme cannot be made in sufficient strength to [effect] junction in north," Eden advised,

safety of B.E.F. will be predominant consideration. In such conditions only course open to you may be to fight your way back to west where all beaches and ports east of Gravelines will be used for embarkation.

In a second telegram Eden told Gort that the Prime Minister had informed Reynaud, who was in London that day, of the British intention and that the French Premier had agreed to ask General Weygand to give the necessary instructions. "You are now authorized," Eden concluded, "to operate toward the coast forthwith in conjunction with the French and Belgian armies."[78]

In conjunction with the French and Belgians? The question would stir up a fresh controversy between the Allies. Eden admits that the British neglected to tell the Belgians of "the change of plan,"[79] an omission that King Leopold and his Army Staff bitterly resented. And though General Weygand had approved both Blanchard's order for withdrawal to a bridgehead "covering Dunkirk in depth" and the agreement reached on the morning of the 26th between the French commander and Gort on the details of carrying it out, nothing was said in them of an embarkation or even of a withdrawal further than the Lys.* Still, Weygand was already pondering it. Colonel P. A. Bourget, the chief of his staff at Vincennes, says that on May 26, after approving Blanchard's decision to pull back toward the sea, Weygand telephoned Admiral Darlan that it had become "necessary to examine with the British Admiralty the possibility of evacuating the forces in Flanders by Dunkirk." Bourget adds that the French Navy already had expressed reservations about whether such an operation could be carried out.[81] Reynaud states that Darlan told him it was impossible.[82]

But once again Weygand failed to keep his commanders in the field posted. Neither General Blanchard nor Admiral Abrial, in charge of the Dunkirk area, were informed by him that evacuation of the Anglo-French forces was contemplated. Blanchard thought only of a defensive stand to the bitter end around Dunkirk, with his main body of troops on the Lys. When he finally was authorized on May 29—three days later—to join the British in embarking as many of his troops as possible it was too late to assemble most of them. Indeed as late as May 28 when Gort "begged" (the word is Gort's) him to join the British in the evacuation he refused.

THE CAPITULATION OF KING LEOPOLD

At 5 o'clock in the morning of May 25 the three leading members of the Belgian government arrived at the Château de Wynendaele near Bruges to call upon the King. Pierlot, the Premier, Spaak, the Foreign Minister, and General Denis, the Minister of War, had decided to make a "last attempt," as they put it, to persuade Leopold not to allow himself to be captured by the Germans. For some days, as we have seen, Pierlot had been urging the young sovereign to follow the advice of the government, as he was bound to do by the constitution, and in case the Army was forced to give up fighting follow the ministers into exile, as the monarchs of Norway and Holland had done, and maintain a legitimate government. Leopold had stubbornly refused.

Now at the dawn meeting, with the King receiving them coolly and keeping them all on their feet, they resumed their pleas for the last time. The sovereign was deluding himself, they said, if he thought he could play any role under the German occupation. He "would be reduced to the role of a Hacha or sent off as a prisoner to Germany." Moreover, by remaining under German rule he would be deserting the cause of the Allies, "contrary to the moral obligations he contracted in calling on the Allies for help. . . . His conduct would be interpreted in Belgium, abroad, and especially in the Allied countries, as treason. . . . The monarchy itself . . . would be compromised, no doubt irremediably. . . ." But they could not move the young ruler.

---

* Gort confirms this. After describing the meeting with General Blanchard on May 26, he says: "I had not so far discussed with General Blanchard a further withdrawal to the sea. However, the possibility could not have been absent from his mind; nor was it absent from mine."[80]

"I have decided," he said, "to remain. To leave would be to desert the army—and the people. I must share their fate."

There were other reasons, he frankly admitted. "The cause of the Allies is lost," he told his ministers. "Shortly, in a few days perhaps, France must herself renounce the struggle. . . . No doubt England will continue the war, not on the Continent, but on the seas and in the colonies. But Belgium can play no part in it. Her role is terminated. . . . There is no more reason for us to continue the war on the side of the Allies."

When Pierlot asked if capitulation was certain, Leopold replied: "It is not only certain but inevitable." The Premier asked: how soon? "More or less in 24 hours," the King replied.

By this time the ministers, none of them as young as the King, were becoming weary from standing on their feet. "Sire," said Spaak, "can we not sit down and continue this conversation under conditions which permit us to talk more frankly?" After some hesitation, Pierlot remembers, "the King sat down and made a sign authorizing the ministers to do likewise."

But they got no further sitting down than standing up. After making clear that the government had decided unanimously to move to France, Spaak asked if the King intended to set up a new government in Brussels under the Germans. "Obviously," he responded, "I do not wish to be a dictator." He added that "certainly the occupant would not consent to the present one."

"If the present government pursued the war in France, would he consider it to be the 'King's government?' "

"No," Leopold answered. "This government would be necessarily against me."

So the King's course of action was clear, and it consternated the ministers. Pierlot warned him that the government would have to "disassociate itself publicly" from the sovereign.

"I understand your situation," Leopold replied. "You have a conviction. I know it is sincere. Do what your conscience dictates." His own conscience, he said, obliged him to stay. He felt he could "best serve the interests of the country from within rather than from without."

Leopold shook hands with his ministers and bid them goodbye—coolly, says Pierlot—and they drove away to Dunkirk where they took ship for England.[83]

The plight of the Belgian forces was certainly becoming desperate. All along the line from the sea north of Bruges to Ypres, which they had extended in order to release British divisions for the planned push south, they were being pushed back by an overwhelming German force. General Kuechler's Eighteenth Army, no longer needed in Holland, had reinforced General Reichenau's Sixth Army, and the bulk of these two armies was now pressing relentlessly forward against the Belgians. Moreover Leopold's troops were without air cover, were running short of ammunition and food, and their movements were entangled by a horde of two million civilians, half of them stricken refugees, milling about in the narrowing space between the crumbling front and the sea. Also, as General Michiels, the Chief of Staff, points out, the Belgian Army by the 26th felt itself being abandoned by its Allies. The British had not yet informed him of their plan to embark their forces at Dunkirk, though the day before, he adds, certain movements behind Gort's lines made him suspect it. "Thus by the morning of May 26," he later wrote, "our army was left to fend for itself."[84] The Belgians began to feel that they were being left behind merely to shield the British and French armies until they got away in boats. They thereupon began to warn their Allies that they could not hold out much longer.

During the afternoon of the 26th the Belgian Command so warned General Weygand.

Situation of Belgian Army is grave. Commander in Chief intends to carry on the fight until all means are exhausted. The enemy is attacking from Eecloo to Menin. The limits of resistance have very nearly been reached.[85]

According to General Michiels, this message went unanswered.

In the morning Gort had become worried that the Belgians instead of retreating westward toward the Yser, as he understood Leopold had promised Weygand on the 22nd, were withdrawing northward away from the BEF, thus widening the gap between the two armies. He sent a message to the Belgian Command expressing his "earnest hope" that its forces would pull back toward the Yser. The answer came back:

We regret that we no longer have any forces available to fill the gap at Ypres. As regards the withdrawal to the Yser the idea must be ruled out since it would destroy our fighting units more quickly than the battle now in progress, and this without loss to the enemy.[86]

On receipt of this message, says Gort, he urged his government in London "to bring strong pressure" on the Belgians "to withdraw their Army westwards and to maintain touch with the BEF." The Belgians, in their turn, asked the British to mount a counterattack between the Lys and the Scheldt rivers to catch the Germans on their flank. Gort replied he had no force to do so. The Allied Commands were becoming more and more at crosspurposes, and what confidence there remained between them was evaporating.

General Blanchard did not help matters when he called on Leopold at 6 P.M. to apprise him officially that he had succeeded Billotte as Commander of the three Allied armies in the north. He announced that the British were withdrawing from the French frontier positions but that (according to the Belgian account) he "did not know precisely what the intentions of General Gort were."[87] This despite the fact that only that morning Blanchard had worked out plans with the British commander for a general withdrawal to the Dunkirk bridgehead! Neither the French nor the British were being frank with the Belgians.

By noon of May 27, which would be the fatal day, the Belgian warnings became more ominous. At 12:30 P.M. a message from Leopold was telephoned to Gort's headquarters.*

Army is greatly discouraged. It has been incessantly engaged for four days and subjected to intense air bombardment which the RAF has been unable to prevent. The knowledge that the Allied armies in this sector have been encircled . . . has led his [the King's] troops to believe that the position is almost hopeless.

He fears a moment is rapidly approaching when he can no longer rely upon his troops to fight or be of any further use to the BEF. He wishes you to realize that he will be obliged to surrender to avert a debacle.[88]

Two hours later a briefer message was dispatched from Belgian headquarters to General Weygand.

Belgian resistance is at its last extremity. Our front is breaking like a worn bowstring.[89]

The Belgian Chief of Staff, who quotes the two messages in his memoirs, adds: "Thus our Allies were duly informed of our precarious state."

General Koeltz, Deputy Chief of Staff of French GHQ, arrived at 3 P.M. at Belgian headquarters on behalf of General Weygand. He noticed the King and General Van Overstraeten pacing up and down on the lawn outside wholly absorbed in an animated conversation. Leopold made no gesture to show that he wished to see the generalissimo's representative and Koeltz proceeded inside and asked to see General Michiels. The words of the Belgian Staff Chief, says Koeltz, "were rude and surly. He said the Belgian Army was in a difficult situation, that the Allies had abandoned it, that the British were no longer in touch with it. . . . General Van Overstraeten came in and in an equally vehement tone hurled reproaches at the Allies. He finished by saying:'There comes a moment when the string is so tautly stretched that it breaks.' " Koeltz says he interpreted the words as meaning that the Belgians, being so hard-pressed, would be obliged to retreat westward, as Weygand had urged them to do on the 22nd. Only later that day, he adds, did he realize what was truly meant by the Belgian generals and also why the King had declined to speak with the representative of the Allied generalissimo, under whose command he was supposed to be.[90]

---

* It was sent by Admiral Sir Roger Keyes, the British liaison officer with the King.

At 5 P.M., about an hour and a half after General Koeltz left Belgian headquarters, Leopold dispatched General Derousseaux, Deputy Chief of the Belgian General Staff, to the Germans to ask their conditions for surrender. His car was fired on by German patrols and one member wounded but eventually he reached the headquarters of the German XIth Corps. In the meantime the French and Belgian missions at Belgian headquarters were told of the move. General Champon got off an urgent wire to Weygand about it, adding that he had protested to the Belgians that they had no right to act alone. The generalissimo received it at 6:30 P.M. "This news," he says, "hit me like a thunderbolt. There had been nothing to make me anticipate it—no notice, no indication. General Koeltz, who had passed part of the afternoon with the French mission there, had given no sign of it." Weygand hastened to the War Ministry to inform Reynaud.

Lord Gort, whose army was most directly exposed in case the Belgians gave up, did not get the news until late that evening of the 27th. Just before 6 P.M. the British mission with the Belgians sent him a wire: "King asking for an armistice now." But it was not received, and anyway Gort was on the move. He had been trying in vain to find General Blanchard, and General Koeltz, after leaving Belgian headquarters, had been trying with no more luck to find him. Koeltz arrived at Admiral Abrial's headquarters at Dunkirk shortly after 6 P.M. in the midst of a heavy German bombing.

"Did you know that the Belgians have just capitulated?" the admiral greeted him.

"No," said the surprised general, "I was at Belgian headquarters at 3:15 and not a word was said about surrender."

Shortly after 11 P.M. Lord Gort arrived at the admiral's headquarters. Koeltz was still there, having been unable to find a boat to take him off.

"Do you know that the Belgians have just surrendered?" Koeltz greeted Gort.

"No," said Gort, as surprised as Koeltz had been a few hours before. "I know absolutely nothing about it."[91]

"It was the first intimation I had received," Gort said later, "of this intention, although I had already formed the opinion that the Belgian Army was now incapable of offering serious or prolonged resistance. . . ."[92]

The Belgian envoy, General Derousseaux, returned to Leopold's Command Post at 10 P.M. The German general he had met had referred his request for conditions to Hitler and the answer was: "The Fuehrer demands unconditional surrender." At 11 P.M. the King, after a brief discussion with his generals, accepted, and proposed a cease-fire for 4 A.M. on May 28. A little later that morning the German High Command sent a message to the King demanding free passage for its columns toward the sea.

"I now found myself," says Gort, "suddenly faced with an open gap of 20 miles between Ypres and the sea through which enemy armored forces might reach the beaches."[93]

For the rest of the war and long after it was over, controversy raged over the surrender of the King of the Belgians. On the morning of May 28, Reynaud, in an emotional broadcast, denounced Leopold's capitulation as an "act without precedent in history."* The Belgian Premier went on the air from Paris a few hours later and in more measured terms addressed the Belgian people. "The King has opened negotiations to treat with the enemy," he said, "against the unanimous advice of the government. . . . His act has no legal value. . . . The government will continue the struggle to deliver the country."

In London the reaction to Leopold's surrender was more restrained than in Paris. In announcing the act to the Commons on May 28 Churchill reserved judgment until all the facts were known. But on June 4, under pressure from Paris and from the Belgian government in exile, he felt it "his duty to state the truth in plain terms."

At the last moment when Belgium was already invaded, King Leopold called upon us to come to his aid, and even at the last moment we came. He and his brave, efficient Army . . . guarded our left flank and thus kept open our only line of retreat to the sea. Suddenly, without prior consultation, with the least possible notice, without the advice of his Ministers and upon his own personal act, he sent a plenipotentiary to the German Command, surrendered his Army, and exposed our whole flank and means of retreat.

Leopold was not without his defenders, both at home and abroad. They contended that he had been abandoned by his Allies, that he had held out to the last possible moment and had only capitulated to save his troops from complete destruction. They thought he had done the honorable thing by sharing the fate of his soldiers and of his people. One of the most eloquent defenses of his surrender came from General Michiels, Chief of the General Staff, who on May 27 had agreed with him on giving up. The Belgian Army, he stresses, was "abandoned." "What was the situation," he asks, "on the day of surrender?"

The armies of the north are encircled. The generalissimo, Weygand, has abandoned the effort to disengage them. The Canal line is broken. The [British] War Office has decided to reembark the BEF.

The Belgian Army has been engaged for four days in a defensive battle. All its troops are in the line. . . . There are no more reserves. The soldiers are

---

* General Spears, who was summoned urgently to the War Ministry by Reynaud on the previous evening to be told the news, says the Premier cried out to him: "There has never been such a betrayal in history! . . . It is monstrous, absolutely monstrous!"[94]

near to complete exhaustion. Part of the artillery is out of ammunition. . . .
Food is short. . . .

It would have been more heroic, to be sure, Michiels says, to fight
to the last man. "But this halo of glory," he thinks, "would have been paid
for dearly."

In a space of 1700 square kilometers between our front, the Yser, and the
sea were crowded, beside the 450,000 troops, a flood of 800,000 inhabitants and
an equal number of refugees. It was in the midst of these bewildered people that
the Germans would have pursued their attack. They, as well as the troops, would
have been mowed down, without procuring the least advantage to our Allies,
whom we could no longer help, or to ourselves, whose destruction was imminent.

It was to avoid this useless effusion of blood that the King decided, about
4:30 P.M., to send an envoy to the German Command. . . .[95]

This is understandable. But what is less so is the King's dissimulation to his Allies. Though he warned them of what he might have to do
he refused to discuss it with them. He did not raise the question with
Blanchard when the Commander of the armies in the north came to confer with him less than 24 hours before. He declined to see General Koeltz
when this general called at his headquarters at the very moment he was
discussing capitulation with General Van Overstraeten, though he knew
that Koeltz had come directly from Weygand, under whose command his
army operated. Though he warned Gort at noon by a telephoned message
that he might have to surrender any moment, he declined to discuss it with
him or even to say frankly that he had decided to give up this very day.
If Gort had known of it at noon instead of at 11 P.M., he would have had
an additional 11 hours to try to fill the gap left by the Belgian surrender.

Perhaps the King's action is not surprising when one remembers his
political attitude over the years. He had led his country out of the Franco-
British military alliance in 1936. He had insisted on Belgium resuming
its position as a neutral, though the invasion of 1914, when his father was
king, had shown how little the Germans would respect it, and he had persisted in maintaining it even after Hitler's occupation of Austria in 1937,
of Czechoslovakia in 1939, and his attack on Poland in the same year had
shown Nazi Germany's contemptuous disregard for the independence of
other neighboring countries. After the war began he had refused staff talks
with the Allies to prepare a common defense against the Germans even
when their plans for an invasion of his country fell into his hands. Only
at the last moment, after Hitler's troops were storming across his borders,
did he call on the Allies for help. Even then, when France and Britain
came to his aid, he did not regard Belgium as having any obligations to
them except to fight in its own defense. By the middle of May, as we have
seen, he was stressing this to his troubled ministers and "insisting" that
"in no case must an alliance be concluded with Paris and London." And

finally on May 25, at his last meeting with his ministers, he had told them that the Allied cause was lost, that there was no reason to continue the war on their side and that he might have to form a new government under the heels of the German occupiers.

On such evidence it is difficult to avoid the conclusion that Leopold had decided that by disassociating himself from the Allies and remaining in occupied Belgium he hoped to get more lenient terms from Hitler for his country than if he joined his government in exile and continued to defy the Nazi dictator.* Like Pétain and Weygand a month later, the King was incapable of realizing that the loss of the Battle of France did not necessarily mean that "the cause of the Allies was lost." The future, as a glimpse at history shows, is never that certain.

Though the bitter French criticism of the King's "treason" was undoubtedly sincere at the moment, it becomes somewhat hollow in view of the events which shortly will be related. And if the British felt that Leopold was letting them down, was he not justified in having a similar feeling about them? He knew that the British were beginning to evacuate their forces from Dunkirk, leaving the Belgian army to keep the Germans at bay until the embarkation was complete. Churchill confirms the British intent. In a message to Gort on the 27th he says frankly: "We are asking them [the Belgians] to sacrifice themselves for us." But until then he has not yet told the King of the Dunkirk plans, for in the same message to Gort he declares: "It is now necessary to tell the Belgians."

Even on the 27th Churchill has no plan to evacuate Belgian troops too. In a message that day to Keyes at Belgian headquarters he wired:

---

* The report of the Belgian Committee of Inquiry, which on the whole was favorable to the King, cites two pieces of further evidence. On September 6, 1940, on the instructions of Count Capelle, secretary of the King's cabinet, a message was sent out to all Belgian diplomatic missions abroad denouncing the Government in Exile for supporting the Allied war effort and laying down the new policy of the Palace in Brussels. As for the Allies, it said, "there was never a common cause nor a promise to link our fate with theirs."

This is to inform you that we cannot support in any way the ministers who, either in London or Lisbon, pursue a war which is opposed to our interest and to loyalty.

The communication ended with an exhortation to reestablish relations with the diplomatic representatives of Germany. "We are no longer at war with this country," it said.

On November 19, 1940, Leopold went to Berchtesgaden to talk to Hitler. According to his own notes, which the Committee publishes, the King asked the Nazi dictator for assurances that Belgium's independence would be reestablished. The Fuehrer was evasive and Leopold pressed him, asking if on his return to Belgium he could not give such an assurance to his people. "I would appreciate it," Hitler replied, "if you said nothing about it for the moment." Pierlot questions the propriety of the King, at the moment when the Belgian government in London was participating in the war on the Allied side, "asking the head of the enemy state for assurance on the future of Belgium and manifesting the desire to announce on his return to Brussels a favorable response from Hitler." And the Premier adds: "The King estimated that it was not on an improbable Allied Victory that Belgium must pin hopes for independence, but on the moderation of the enemy."[96]

"Presume he [the King] knows"—about the French and British evacuation at Dunkirk, that is. But he does not offer to include the Belgians. His concern is not to take out Belgian troops but only the Belgian King. "Trust you will make sure he leaves with you by plane before too late. . . . Vitally important Belgium should continue in war, and safety King's person essential." The Prime Minister does add that if Dunkirk held out for a time "we would try, if desired, to carry some Belgian divisions to France by sea." But he really does not believe Dunkirk can hold out very long. In the same telegram he says the embarkation of French and British troops will be "hazardous." And as he later wrote, he does not believe more than 45,000 men can be rescued.[97]

Whatever history's ultimate verdict about the surrender, the Belgian people, as was proper, made the final decision so far as they and the King were concerned. He was not recalled to the throne from Switzerland, where he had taken refuge after the war, until five years after it was over. A plebiscite on March 12, 1950, showed that 57 percent of those voting wished him to come back and the Christian Socialist government thereupon pushed through his reinstatement in Parliament. But the ruling party failed to realize that, in a democracy at least, kings are supposed to have the allegiance of all the citizens, not just a majority of them. Leopold returned to Brussels on July 20, 1950. But he did not remain long. On August 1 tens of thousands of aroused countrymen marched on Brussels intent on deposing him. A general strike was called, paralyzing the country. With civil war already under way the King, now forty-nine, yielded to the entreaties of his own frightened supporters who had brought him back. He stepped down, abdicating in favor of his son.

REPRIEVE AT DUNKIRK

A little before 7 o'clock on the afternoon of Sunday, May 26, the British Admiralty sent out a signal: "Operation Dynamo is to commence."

"Dynamo" was the code word for the evacuation of British and French troops from Dunkirk. Its origin went back to the previous Sunday, May 19, when, as we have seen, Lord Gort had first warned the War Office in London that retreat to a Channel port might become necessary. On the following day Admiral Sir Bertram H. Ramsay met with his naval staff at Dover to prepare a plan. No one then could know whether an evacuation would be necessary, or whether, if it eventually was, what the situation of the Anglo-Belgian-French forces in the north would be. In London it was believed that under the most favorable circumstances not more than 45,000 men could be brought out. This would doom the bulk of the BEF and the French First Army to capture. No thought was given in London to the Belgians, who had the largest army of all. And the French, at first, were not told. This neglect was very shortly to cause bitter dispute between the Allied Commands and between their armies, governments, and peoples.

The first British ship, the *Mona's Isle,* steamed off to Dunkirk two hours after the Admiralty's signal on the 26th and after taking on 1,420 British troops in the middle of a bombing that evening was shelled by long-range German artillery as she put to sea. Some 23 men on board were killed and 60 wounded. The next morning five transports underwent such heavy attack from German shore batteries that they were unable to approach Dunkirk and returned empty. It looked as if the operation was doomed before it got under way.

To complicate matters the French began to complain that they were being left out. The generals in Flanders appeared to know nothing of the British decision and the British plans to evacuate. As late as the night of May 27, just after the Belgian surrender, Gort had asked General Koeltz when they met at Dunkirk: "What do you know, since you come from General Weygand, of the plan to embark 30,000 men a day?" And Koeltz had replied: "I have never heard it spoken of." Later Koeltz would testify: "I got the impression that the British were already carrying out the plan of embarkation without having spoken of it to Blanchard or Weygand."[98]

This was not true, though General Weygand did his best to make it seem so. His attitude is strange and contradictory. As late as May 27 he professed to be "surprised" at the British "preparations for evacuation."[99] Yet, as has been recounted, already on the 26th he had approved the decision of Gort and Blanchard to withdraw to the Dunkirk bridgehead and had asked Admiral Darlan to work out with the British admiralty "the possibility of evacuating . . ." On that same day, when Reynaud was in London, Churchill says he informed the Premier of the British decision to "evacuate the BEF and requested him to issue corresponding orders."[100] Weygand records that Reynaud told him the next morning, after his return from London, of the British "decision for the withdrawal of Gort" and that later in the day, the 27th, after the news of the Belgian surrender, he realized

that it is necessary to renounce my hope of holding for a certain time a large bridgehead [at Dunkirk]. It's a question now of trying to save from capture the largest possible number of troops and to cover their embarkment from a smaller bridgehead.[101]

Indeed that same morning, at Weygand's urging, ranking French naval officers had met at Dover with the British naval chiefs and agreed on plans for the evacuation of French and British troops from Dunkirk. The French admirals, says Weygand, were "surprised" to find the British plans so far advanced. They had made none of their own, and this was to lead to grievous scenes later on the Dunkirk beaches when Gort, ignorant of the Dover accord to use all ships in common, protested the use of British transports by the French troops, who had practically none of their own.

While Weygand kept the Navy informed of his decision to evacuate, he failed to pass the word onto his hard-pressed generals in the north, or even to his close aide, General Koeltz, whom he had just sent to Belgium to size up the situation. At Cassel early in the morning of May 27, Koeltz joined Blanchard, Admiral Abrial, General Fagalde, whose XVIth Corps was already in position west of Dunkirk, and General Sir Ronald Adam, representing Gort. Final plans were worked out to defend the bridgehead. Yet neither Koeltz nor Blanchard seemed to realize yet, as the British did, that the purpose of defending the bridgehead was, as Weygand said, "to save from capture the largest possible number of troops." The generalissimo's silence had kept them in ignorance of this—though by now it might have seemed obvious. Apparently it wasn't. Indeed Koeltz, on behalf of Weygand, urged General Fagalde to try to recapture Calais, which was out of the question since the French that very moment were being driven out of Gravelines by German armor moving on from Calais. Worse, General Prioux, the new Commander of the French First Army, issued an order a few hours after the Cassel meeting saying: "The battle will be fought without thought of retreat on the Lys." If the French forces were going to join the British in getting away by sea from Dunkirk, it was folly to hold them on the Lys "without thought of retreat." The order doomed most of what was left of the once splendid First Army.

How much the British and French Commands in their hour of desperation were working at cross-purposes was brought out the next morning, May 28, at a dramatic and painful (Colonel Lyet calls it "pathetic") meeting of Blanchard and Gort at the latter's headquarters at Houtkerque. The French Commander appeared "horrified"* when Gort read him his orders from London to withdraw to the coast and evacuate.

It was then clear to me [Gort says in his subsequent report of the encounter] that whereas we had both received similar instructions from our own Government for the establishment of a bridgehead, he had, as yet, received no instructions to correspond with those I had received to evacuate my troops. General Blanchard therefore could not see his way to contemplate evacuation.

That was strange, General Pownall thought:

For what other reason did he [Blanchard] think that he and Gort had both received similar instructions to form bridgeheads? To what else could such a preliminary move lead?

Lord Gort continued his argument.

---

* At least that is how he struck General H. R. Pownall, the BEF Chief of Staff, who has left a vivid account of the British version of the meeting.[102]

I then expressed the opinion that now the Belgian Army had ceased to exist, the only alternatives could be evacuation or surrender. . . . While this discussion was taking place a liaison officer arrived from General Prioux, now in command of the French 1st Army, to say that the latter did not consider his troops were fit to make any further move and that he therefore intended to remain in the area between Béthune and Lille. . . .

I then begged General Blanchard for the sake of France, the French Army and the Allied Cause to order General Prioux back. Surely, I said, his troops were not all so tired as to be incapable of moving. . . . I could not move him.*[103]

The French then posed what for them seemed to be the vital question. "Would the British troops, regardless of the situation of the First Army on the Lys, even if it were engaged there," General Blanchard asked, "withdraw tonight north to the line Cassel-Poperinghe-Ypres?"

"Oui," responded General Pownall, translating for Gort.[104]

To General Blanchard this meant that the British were leaving the First Army in the lurch and he complained to General Weygand that Gort, despite his objections, was pulling out, "leaving the flank of the First Army completely exposed." Weygand received the message early on May 29 and asked Reynaud to protest to London. By this time the French generals not only were beginning to rail against the British for what they considered duplicity but were becoming highly confused as to what to do themselves about trying to save their encircled troops.

After his meeting with Gort on the morning of the 28th, General Blanchard had some second thoughts. During the day he and General Prioux decided after all to try to extricate as many of their troops as they could and get them to Dunkirk for evacuation. Two infantry divisions and what was left of the Cavalry Corps would move north immediately for the Channel. The five divisions of the French First Army now nearly surrounded at Lille would remain and fight to the last. Prioux decided to remain with the latter.† At 10 P.M. on the 28th, Blanchard, who only that morning had refused to consider evacuation, sent a radio message to Weygand asking permission "to embark what could be saved." Weygand replied the next morning authorizing him to move all the forces he could to Dunkirk "to permit their progressive evacuation by sea."[105] It is difficult to understand why he waited so long—three days—and he offered no

---

* According to General Pownall, Blanchard replied that "evacuation from the beach was impossible. . . . It was therefore idle to try—the chance wasn't worth the effort involved; he agreed with Prioux."

† He was captured at his Command Post at Steenwerck the next day. But his troops, the remnants of the once formidable First Army, now under the command of General Molinié, held out around Lille until late on May 31, engaging seven German divisions, three of them panzer, and thus preventing them from joining the enemy assault on Dunkirk. This gallant stand helped the beleaguered Anglo-French forces around the port to hold out for an additional two or three days and thus to save at least 100,000 more troops. "A splendid contribution," Churchill called it.

explanation for it in his memoirs and postwar testimony. In ten days since assuming command Weygand, who despite his age was noted for his energy, had fatally delayed making two vital decisions: first, to at once try to close the gap between the Allied armies separated by the German panzer drive to the sea, and, now, to get the French First Army to Dunkirk in time for evacuation. In the second case, after finally arriving at a decision, he had put off for two crucial days communicating it to his commander on the spot. By that time it was too late to save the bulk of the First Army.

But if Weygand had finally given orders to save as many French troops as possible at Dunkirk it did not follow that the French and British would or could at once act smoothly and in unison to carry out the evacuation of both forces. On May 29 Churchill laid it down to his own Command that "the French should share in the evacuations. Nor," he added, "must they be dependent only upon their own shipping." And he wired Reynaud assurances of that.

But on the 29th, when a considerable number of French troops began to arrive at the beaches the British at first refused to let them embark on their ships. Since there were practically no French vessels at hand this was tantamount to leaving them behind. Gort himself, who apparently had not been apprised by his government that the French were to be taken off in numbers equal to the British, objected to their being received on British ships—at least until all the BEF had been saved—and, he admits, wired the War Office about it. He asked, he says, "that the French should take their full share in providing naval facilities."

However, to permit embarkation of French troops to begin at once, I decided to allot two British ships to the French that night.

This was not many, considering that, as Churchill says, "850 vessels of all kinds were at work" and that 50,000 British soldiers already had been taken off, with 30,000 more scheduled to be evacuated that night. "We are in the presence of a man," Colonel de Bardies comments, in describing the conduct of Gort that day, "who is a bad combat comrade."[106]

Aside from the predictable consequences of the growing friction between the French and British, ugly incidents were bound to occur in the inferno which Dunkirk had now become. Constant German bombing and incessant artillery fire had already made a shambles of the town and harbor. Thousands of vehicles of every sort lay smashed and burning along the roads and beaches. The roads themselves were cluttered with exhausted troops and their abandoned transport. Though the British and French local Commands made valiant efforts to restore some kind of order and assign piers and beaches to units of the two armies their efforts were often unavailing in the utter confusion. They were dealing with battle-scarred men desperate to get away. On a few occasions British crewmen forced French soldiers off their boats. A French general and his aide, Reynaud complained to General Spears, were "manhandled" by British troops when they tried to push their way onto a British ship. Exhausted French soldiers arriving from the rear would make for the nearest beach only to find that it was reserved for the British. In at least one instance Welsh Guards held them off with fixed bayonets. Captain D. Barlone, a French officer who liked and admired the British—even after Dunkirk—recounted a scene on May 29, when the French began to arrive for evacuation.

> A fresh traffic block, a mile long . . . where the British have barricaded all exits so that their columns can pass through with greater ease. The French are wild. Some gunners talk of training their guns on them and shooting. . . . I take command and order two officers to take a hundred men and drag away the heavy British tractors which bar the road. Then I go out and find an English major, and in five minutes everything is arranged.[107]

Churchill flew over to Paris on May 31 to try to straighten out the situation. By then, he informed his French colleagues, 165,000 men had been taken off at Dunkirk, some 53,000 on the previous day alone.

"But how many French?" Weygand asked, acidly. "The French are being left behind?"

"Some 15,000 French," Churchill answered, explaining that many of the British taken off had been "administrative units" which had reached Dunkirk before the fighting forces. "Moreover," he added, looking straight at Weygand, "the French have not up to the present received orders to embark. One of my chief reasons for coming to Paris was to make sure the same orders are given to the French and British commanders."

"Still," Reynaud broke in, "out of 220,000 British, 150,000 have been evacuated; out of 200,000 French, only 15,000 have been taken off." The Premier strongly emphasized, he says, "that if such a disproportion was not immediately corrected it would have grave political consequences for us."

Churchill said he was fully aware of that and that he had set aside today, the 31st, as "French Day." "The French troops would be given absolute priority over the British." In the meantime Admiral Darlan had drafted a telegram to Admiral Abrial at Dunkirk to inform him of the Allied agreement and stipulating that when the Franco-British troops defending the perimeter began to embark the British would go first.

"Certainly not," Churchill interjected when that part of the message was read. *"Non . . . partage . . . bras dessus, bras dessous,"* he said, breaking into his inimitable French. The troops of the two countries would go "arm in arm" on equal terms, he insisted. "The three British divisions will form the rear-guard, since so few French have got out so far. I will not accept further sacrifices from the French."

His assurances seemed to stifle the doubts of Reynaud and Weygand

and they seemed moved when he closed the meeting with one of his eloquent perorations, declaring defiantly that the French and British must not consider themselves beaten but go on to conquer in the end.

> Even if one of us is struck down, the other must not abandon the struggle. [It] must not put down its arms until its friend is on his feet again. . . . The British people will fight on. . . .

Even Baudouin, General Spears thought, seemed carried away by the Prime Minister's fire. Actually Baudouin says he was "deeply troubled" by Churchill's words. "Does he consider that France must continue the struggle, cost what it may, even if it is useless?" he asked himself as he recorded the meeting in his diary. "We must clear that up," he concluded.

Another Frenchman at the meeting also had his misgivings. Pétain had struck Spears as "glacial and morose," and he and Churchill stopped to have a private word with him before they left the room. Already, says the Prime Minister, "Marshal Pétain's attitude, detached and somber, gave me the feeling that he would face a separate peace. The influence of his personality, his reputation, his serene acceptance of the march of adverse events, apart from any words he used, was almost overpowering to those under his spell."

Someone in the group, a Frenchman, suggested that if the present reverses continued France might have to "modify" its position.

> Here Spears rose to the occasion [Churchill recounts] and addressing himself to Marshal Pétain said in perfect French: "I suppose you understand, *M. le Maréchal,* that that would mean blockade?" Someone else said: "That would perhaps be inevitable." But then Spears to Pétain's face: "That would not only mean blockade but *bombardment* of all French ports in German hands."

"I was glad to have this said," Churchill concludes. He says he repeated: "We would fight on whatever happened or whoever fell out."[108]

Reynaud had warned the Prime Minister in London on May 26 that Pétain would come out for an armistice if the Battle of France was lost. Now five days later, after conversing with the Marshal, Churchill realized that it was not idle talk. As for Pétain, General Spears' scarcely tactful warning to him, however much Churchill admired it, could only increase his feelings of hostility toward the British. On this last day of May 1940, after only three weeks of battle, the two Western democracies in their adversity were beginning to fall out on the vital issue of continuing the fight against the Germans.

Pétain was not alone in believing that France might soon have to give up, regardless of what the British said or did. Weygand, in fact, had already taken the lead.

On May 29, the day after the Belgians had officially capitulated and ceased fighting and the day too when the French First Army was finally authorized to move to Dunkirk for evacuation, General Weygand sent a sharp note, approved by Pétain, to the head of government. He informed Reynaud that while the French Army would fight to the utmost to defend the Somme and the Aisne, the enormous disproportion between it and the enemy's forces might bring sudden defeat.

> In this case [he said] France would be unable to continue a struggle assuring the coordinated defense of its territory. . . . It is therefore necessary that the British government know that there can come a moment when France could find itself, despite its determination, in a position where it would be impossible to continue a militarily effective struggle to protect its soil.

The moment would come, he advised, when the French positions on the two rivers were ruptured. Since he had explained that such a rupture was almost inevitable and quickly so, he was warning the Premier bluntly that France might soon have to take itself out of the war—and that the British should be told.

Reynaud replied in writing the same day, saying that he was informing the British "today" of the general's note, point by point, but that he wanted to make it clear to the generalissimo that "even if the whole of the national territory could no longer be defended, this does not necessarily mean that we can suspend hostilities in conditions incompatible with the honor and the vital interests of France." He instructed Weygand to study the possibility of establishing a fortified redoubt in Brittany, through whose ports the army could be supplied, and also of making a stand in North Africa, if it came to that. He said he was calling up two new classes—a half a million men—to be sent immediately to North Africa for training and "to contribute to its defense."*[109] Despite the growing defeatism of his illustrious generals, Reynaud seemed determined to keep France in the war.

The evacuation at Dunkirk continued. May 31 and June 1 were the biggest days. Despite continuous German shelling and frequent bombing, the latter reduced considerably by British fighter sweeps from bases across the Channel, a total of 132,000 men were lifted on those two days from the port and the beaches, most of them British. But the losses in shipping were becoming prohibitive. On June 1 thirty-one vessels were sunk and eleven damaged. Two British transports laden with 2,700 French troops went down, though 2,100 men were saved by smaller craft that came to their rescue. The Germans, however, were closing in, and in view of this

---

* Despite the German superiority in numbers of divisions, the French Army had demobilized three classes—750,000 men—on the eve of the German offensive.[110]

and the heavy losses of shipping Churchill wired Reynaud proposing "closing down tonight"—June 1. The French were outraged. They immediately came to the conclusion that the British, having got out most of their own troops, were abandoning them. Lord Gort and his staff, on orders from London, had already sailed for England shortly after midnight of May 31–June 1, leaving General Alexander in charge of the British defense sector, now manned by fewer than 20,000 men. Weygand got off an angry telegram to the British High Command "insisting" that General Alexander's forces remain "side by side" with the French troops to defend the perimeter until more French could be evacuated. Some 25,000 French were still fighting holding off the enemy and 22,000 others, Weygand said, were waiting for ships to take them off. Admiral Darlan, in his turn, protested to the British Admiralty.

On the night of June 2 the British responded by sending over several ships to take out the French but most of them returned empty. Few French soldiers had been assembled to embark. At 1:20 P.M. the next day Churchill sent an urgent message to Reynaud.

We are coming back for your men tonight. Please ensure that all facilities are used promptly. For three hours last night many ships waited idly at great risk and danger.*

He was as good as his word. From the fall of darkness to midnight on June 3, some 26,746 French troops were embarked, and a further 26,175 from midnight to dawn, when the operation came to an end.

At 9 A.M. on June 4 the slaughter at Dunkirk ceased. All that was left of the once magnificent French First Army—40,000 men whose fight to the end had enabled 120,000 of their comrades and over 200,000 men of the BEF to get away safely—surrendered. Their commanding generals were not among them. On the orders of Weygand, General Blanchard, his Army Group 1 formally dissolved, had left Dunkirk on a French destroyer at 6 P.M. on June 1. Admiral Abrial and the three top commanders of the French troops, Generals Fagalde, de la Laurencie and Barthélemy, crossed

---

* That day, June 3, General Weygand seems to have been beside himself with resentment against the British. Baudouin recounts in his diary the generalissimo's outburst at the daily conference that morning with Reynaud and Pétain.

General Weygand indicates that at Dunkirk 282,000 men have been embarked, 65,000 of whom are French. Contrary to what had been settled at the Supreme Council (May 31), the rear guard is French. General Weygand is not in the least surprised at this. He adds that it is now certain that if the British, some ten days ago, ceased to march in the direction of Arras, it is because they received orders from London in that sense. Since May 16 Churchill has been playing a double game. He has abandoned France to herself. The maneuver aiming at the junction of the armies of the north with the French forces on the Somme would have succeeded, General Weygand affirms, if the British had not continually looked back toward the sea. "They do not know how to resist the call of the ports," the general declares. "Already in March, 1918, they wanted to embark."[111]

to England with the last of their evacuated men on the night of June 3–4. General Alexander, after making sure that all British soldiers had got away, himself sailed from Dunkirk in the early hours of June 3.

According to official British records quoted by Churchill a total of 338,226 troops were rescued at Dunkirk. He does not say how many French. Weygand put them at 115,000 and the military historian, Colonel Lyet, at 120,000. More undoubtedly could have been evacuated had General Weygand given his permission earlier. After he finally gave it May 29, the day also that Churchill stipulated that shipping be shared equally, a total of 139,097 "Allied," mostly French, troops, according to London's figures, were embarked against 139,732 British.[112] But the feeling that their ally had taken care of its troops first lay deep and bitter among Frenchmen and helped contribute to events which shortly will be described.

On June 4, the day Dunkirk fell, the American Ambassador in Paris invited Pétain to lunch with him alone at the Embassy residence. The Marshal said he would like to convey to President Roosevelt through Mr. Bullitt "how he personally viewed the situation." It looked dark to him.

So long as the British Army had been in Flanders the British had engaged their Air Force fully. But they had insisted that their Army should be taken off first (at Dunkirk) and that the French divisions should hold the lines fighting against the Germans while the British were embarked. Since all the British had been embarked the British had ceased to send their planes in anything like the number they had employed so long as the British Expeditionary Force was at Dunkirk.

Furthermore, at this moment when the French had almost no reserves and were facing the greatest attack in human history the British were pretending that they could send no reserves from England. . . . Moreover, they had refused to send over the British aviation. . . .

Under the circumstances he was obliged to feel that the British intended to permit the French to fight without help until the last available drop of French blood . . . and that with quantities of troops on British soil and plenty of planes and a dominant fleet the British after a very brief resistance, or even without resistance, would make a peace of compromise with Hitler, which might even evolve a British Government under a British fascist leader.

The Marshal added . . . that he felt unless the British Government should send to France, to engage in the battle which was imminent, both air force and reserve divisions, the French Government would do its utmost to come to terms immediately with Germany whatever might happen to England.[113]

Bullitt was hearing for the first time the line Pétain would now persist in to the end.

The emotional American Ambassador was greatly impressed. And his sympathy for France, his antipathy for Britain, was freshly stirred. The next afternoon, June 5, he went to see Reynaud, who told him "that he had sent this morning the stiffest note he could compose to Churchill on the subject of the withdrawal of British pursuit planes from France. . . . He considered it utterly shocking. . . . He said that if Churchill's reply was negative he would attack Churchill tomorrow as violently as he could. Either the British were allies or they were not."

The consequences of Dunkirk, it is evident, already were poisoning the air in Paris. Bullitt himself fully shared not only French resentment against Britain but Pétain's idea that the British were holding back in order to make a favorable deal with Hitler for peace. At the end of his telegram to Roosevelt recounting the meeting with Reynaud he added an opinion of his own.

If the British now refuse this essential support [planes], it will mean, I believe, that the British intend to conserve their fleet and air force and their army, and either before a German attack on England or shortly afterwards, to install eight Fascists trained under Oswald Mosley* and accept vassalage to Hitler.[114]

Did Pétain's suspicion of what the British were about to do, so stoutly supported by the American Ambassador, betray what the aged Marshal now contemplated for France?

"Dunkirk," said Weygand, "was certainly not a victory but merely the least unfortunate liquidation of what could have been a catastrophe."[115] In the Commons on June 4, when the last ships were disembarking the last men from Dunkirk, Churchill warned: "We must be very careful not to assign to this deliverance the attributes of a victory. Wars are not won by evacuations."

Yet General Weygand hailed the evacuation of a third of a million men in the teeth of German bombing and artillery fire as a "veritable *tour de force*" and Churchill felt that "there was a victory inside this deliverance." The cornered and outnumbered French and British troops had fought magnificently to hold off a far superior force until they could be taken off at Dunkirk. The British Navy, aided by what ships the French Navy could scrape up, had demonstrated the might of sea power and, in fact, had carried out the greatest naval rescue operation on a foreign shore in all of history. The British Air Force, making use of the new Spitfire plane to back up the Hurricane, showed for the first time that it was a match for the Luftwaffe. Though German bombing was at times devastating it was not enough to seriously hamper the evacuation. Several times a day RAF fighter sweeps drove off enemy bombers and brought a good many of them down. Had the Luftwaffe been able to operate continually over Dunkirk, as it had at Rotterdam and Warsaw, it is un-

---

* Leader of the British Union of Fascists. Who the "eight Fascists trained under Mosley" were, Bullitt does not say. Mosley was interned a few days later.

likely that many men would have been saved. "Deliverance," Churchill told the Commons, "was gained by the Air Force."

Luck with the weather played a certain part, as did the first serious German strategic blunder of the campaign. Throughout most of the evacuation the sea was calm and this enabled the boats to lift 98,780 men from the beaches. It also facilitated the approach of larger vessels through the difficult and shallow channels that led to the harbor itself, where 239,446 soldiers were taken off. Had the winds risen and the sea become rough the "miracle of Dunkirk" might never have happened.

More important to the Allies was the inexplicable order given by Hitler himself, on the advice of Rundstedt, to halt the panzer divisions just as they were closing in on Dunkirk. This surprising decision provoked much controversy that raged long after the war among the German generals, who were anxious to blame Hitler alone for preventing them from trapping the Franco-British army in the north and either annihilating them or forcing them to surrender. The story is so complicated, the testimony of the German generals themselves so conflicting—and full of face-saving— that I shall not go into it in detail here, having related it at length in my history of Nazi Germany, as have others in their histories and memoirs.*

The bare facts, on the basis of a study of the German records, are these. On the afternoon of May 23 General von Rundstedt, Commander of Army Group A, which had made the breakthrough from the Meuse to the sea, approved a suggestion of his generals on the spot to halt temporarily the drive of the armored divisions on the Allied pocket around Dunkirk. The next day, over the violent objections of the German army chief, General von Brauchitsch, and his General Staff chief, General Halder, Hitler issued the formal "stop" order, after conferring with Rundstedt. The reasons seemed good enough to Hitler and Rundstedt. The German panzer divisions had reported that they had only half their tanks left. The terrain south of Dunkirk was unsuited for them, being criss-crossed by canals, and much of it marshy. In fact Guderian, who later would protest loudly against the "stop" order, had already advised his superiors that "a tank attack is pointless in the marshy country . . . the infantry forces are more suitable than tanks for fighting in this sort of country."

There were other reasons for Hitler's order. He wanted to refit the tanks and redeploy the armored divisions for the next phase of the battle: the drive southward over the Somme and Aisne to capture Paris and the rest of France. Neither he nor any of his generals, being ignorant of the sea, had the faintest idea that any sizable number of Anglo-French troops could get away in boats. They believed there was plenty of time for the

---

* See the author's *The Rise and Fall of the Third Reich;* Ellis: *The War in France and Flanders. 1939–1940;* Telford Taylor: *The March of Conquest;* Colonel Goutard: *1940. La Guerre des occasions perdues;* the memoirs of Guderian and Kesselring, the entries of the German war diaries, the diaries of Generals Halder and Jodl, and the statements of the German generals in Liddell Hart: *The German Generals Talk.*

slogging infantry, supported by artillery, to close in on the enemy and destroy him. Finally, Goering had assured the Nazi dictator that the Luftwaffe alone could wipe out the remaining Allied forces crowded around Dunkirk, freeing the bulk of the Army and especially the panzers for the offensive south.

At any rate, on the orders of the Supreme Commander, the German panzer divisions halted for two days on the canal line south and west of Dunkirk. This proved to be a Godsend to the Allied forces. They were just beginning their retreat to the perimeter and the canal line was only thinly defended by French and British units hurriedly scraped up from here and there. There seems little doubt that had the German armored divisions and motorized infantry struck with the force they had on May 24, they would have overrun Dunkirk in a couple of days and cut off the Allied troops from the sea.

General Halder confided his anger and frustration to his diary.

Our left wing [he wrote on May 24], consisting of armor and motorized forces, which has no enemy before it, will thus be stopped dead in its tracks upon direct orders of the Fuehrer! Finishing off the encircled enemy is to be left to Air Force!

. . . These orders from the top [he added on the 26th] just make no sense. . . . The tanks are stopped as if they were paralyzed.

. . . The pocket would have been closed at the coast if only our armor had not been held back [he wrote further on the 30th]. . . . Now we must stand by and watch countless thousands of the enemy get away to England under our noses.

That, in fact, was what they watched.

On May 26 Hitler rescinded his "stop" order and the German advance was resumed the next day. By this time the French and British had been able to reinforce the canal line and German progress was slow. It was now too late to reach Dunkirk in time to prevent the Allied armies from getting away.

Though a third of a million soldiers had been saved to fight, at least in the case of the British, another day, they had been forced to leave behind all of their artillery and tanks and heavy equipment. The Allies had lost in all 61 divisions, nearly half the total with which they had started the battle three weeks before. The French had lost the best units they had, nearly all the army's motorized transport and armor, and half of its modern artillery. Gone were 3 light armored divisions, one heavy armored division, 2 cavalry divisions and 24 infantry divisions.

The day after the fall of Dunkirk the German offensive against the rest of France began. To meet it the French had only 60 divisions, many of them under strength, poorly armed, and without adequate transport, even horse-drawn. The Germans, flushed with victory, had twice as many divisions, nine times as much armor, and in the air, now that the RAF had been forced to withdraw from its French bases and the French Air Force was incapable of employing all the planes it had, an even greater superiority than a month before. Except for one British infantry division and part of one British armored division, which had not been involved in the fighting in the north, there were no more Allied forces in France to help.

Dunkirk, it can be seen in retrospect, was the end of the beginning for the British, but for the French it was the beginning of the end.

32

THE FALL OF PARIS
JUNE 5–14, 1940

T hough the armies of the north had been destroyed and the Channel ports from Dunkirk to the mouth of the Somme taken, most of France—at least 90 percent of its territory, comprising all that lay south of the Somme, Aisne, and the Maginot Line—still held out as the bright, warm days of June came.

There was plenty of space, which included the capital and the largest cities, in which to fight. There was room for maneuver. The question for the French High Command was whether its forces, now outnumbered two to one by the Germans, had the strength and the capability to maneuver and to carry out, if necessary, a strategic retreat, trading space for time. General Weygand did not think so. On May 25, the day before he abandoned hope of saving the northern armies, he advised the Comité de Guerre what his future strategy would be. He and General Georges had studied, he said, three "solutions" and rejected the first two as "unrealizable." These had called for shortening the front by a withdrawal to the lower Seine and thence to the Loire, in one case abandoning the Maginot Line. The third "solution" was to make a last ditch stand on the river lines now held and this, he announced, was the one he had chosen. He warned that no retreat from the Somme-Aisne front would be possible. "We will not have enough reserves to carry it out," he explained. "No methodical retreat is possible with such a numerical inferiority."[1] He had only 60 divisions, he said, against "120 to 150 German divisions" on a 400-mile front from the sea to the Rhine and Switzerland. "We must stand on the present position on the Somme-Aisne," he concluded, "and defend it to the end." The next day, May 26, he issued a general order to that effect. "The battle, on which the fate of the country depends," it said, "will be fought without thought of retreat from the position we now occupy."

General Weygand's decision has been much criticized. He was sticking to the traditional doctrine of the French Army that a continuous front must always be maintained, though the folly of this had just been shown on the Meuse and in Belgium. The idea of trading space for time, of giving up territory and retreating to fight another day, was simply beyond him, though its worth had been proved in many a war, by the Russians in 1812 when Napoleon had invaded, for example, and it would be proved again in this war by both sides in Russia and in Libya, and by the Germans in Italy. "It was senseless," de Gaulle thought, "to content ourselves with organizing on the Somme a new defensive battle line, after the manner of 1918. We should have renounced the continuous front in order to maneuver and maneuver." Even, he thought, if it meant eventually retreating all the way to North Africa. General René Bertrand, Chief of Staff to General Auguste Noguès in North Africa, agreed. "The General Staff," he testified later, "should never have committed itself to the Battle of the Somme without having another position in the rear on which to resist. This position was North Africa."[2]

De Gaulle and Bertrand were not the only generals who thought the generalissimo's view was faulty. On May 27, the day after Weygand issued his definitive order to stand on the Somme-Aisne without thought of retreat, General Bührer, in charge of colonial troops, expressed his misgivings about such a strategy to Mandel, the new Minister of Interior. The Germans, he said, would easily penetrate the thinly held line, the troops ordered to hold out would be encircled, and the enemy advance would simply pass them by. He thought it best to retreat in depth, if necessary, abandon the Maginot Line, and make a stand in the Juras and in Brittany, where the fronts would be greatly shortened. General Prételat, who commanded the group of armies on the Maginot Line, fearing that it soon would be outflanked, proposed to Weygand on May 26 that preparations be made to evacuate it so he could withdraw his forces in time to a position further south, but he was not listened to.[3]

On June 1 de Gaulle, still in command of the 4th Armored Division then counterattacking south of Abbeville, went to Weygand's headquarters and urged that the remaining 1,200 modern tanks be deployed in two groups, one north of Paris, the other south of Reims, each group supported by two or three divisions of motorized infantry with double the usual artillery, to attack the flanks of the German columns when they inevitably broke through. "At least," he remarked later, "we would have had a battle instead of a debacle." But the High Command preferred to stick to its doctrine, which already had proved so disastrous, and employ the tank divisions defensively to stop as many enemy thrusts as they could.[4]

Weygand's judgment that his forces were too weak to conduct a strategic retreat seems strange. As Major Ellis, the British military historian points out, "It is an unusual military theory that insufficiency of forces makes it impossible to withdraw from a line which is obviously too long for them to hold successfully. . . . The very fact that the Supreme Commander held this view meant that defeat was certain."[5]

Weygand had no illusions about the outcome. He warned the War Committee on May 25 that his front "could be broken through" and that in "this case fragments of the army will fight on to the end to save the honor of the country." On the 29th, a week before the German offensive was resumed, he cautioned Reynaud, as we have seen, that the moment the front was ruptured it would be impossible to continue an effective struggle.

If the Somme and Aisne could not hold, Paris was doomed to fall quickly. Notwithstanding, Weygand urged the government to remain in the capital even at the risk of capture. In fact, Reynaud and others in the cabinet began to suspect that the Supreme Commander wanted the government to be captured so as to be rid of the politicians, whom he had been cursing ever since his return to Paris. On May 26 Weygand had told Senator Louis Rollin, Minister of Colonies: "The government must remain in Paris and allow itself to be captured. That is the only thing to do." After all, said the generalissimo, there was a historical precedent.

Do you remember Titus Livy, the Roman Senator? . . . When the barbarians—and we were the barbarians then—invaded Rome . . . the senators remained in their curule chairs and continued to deliberate. . . . After a Gaul pulled the beard of a senator and the latter struck him with his rod, all the Senate was massacred. But this attitude was not without its grandeur.

The French minister and senator was so taken aback, he says, that he felt it his "duty" to hasten to the President of the Republic to impart to him Weygand's notion of grandeur. Lebrun, as was his custom when shocked, threw up his arms toward heaven, Rollin recalls, and exclaimed: "He must be mad! Does he want me to suffer the same fate as Schuschnigg?* How can a government which is prisoner freely act in the conduct of the war? It is incomprehensible! Where does he think he is leading us?!"†[6]

---

* Kurt von Schuschnigg, the Chancellor of Austria, was arrested by Hitler on March 12, 1938, when German troops entered Vienna. He was imprisoned without trial and incarcerated, mostly in the infamous concentration camps at Dachau and Sachsenhausen, until liberated by American troops in the Tyrol on May 4, 1945, shortly before he and his wife were to be murdered on the orders of Heinrich Himmler, Chief of the German SS.

† In his first published volume of memoirs, *Rappelé au service* (Page 218, footnote) which appeared in 1950, General Weygand admitted that he had been wrong in saying the government should remain in Paris and even at the risk of capture. "It should not thus have delivered itself to the enemy," he conceded.

The same day Weygand repeated his historical allusion to Baudouin, adding:

> If the government . . . wishes to avoid the development in Paris of a revolutionary movement it must affirm that it will remain in the capital regardless of the situation . . . ready to run the risk of being taken by the enemy. It is a question of domestic order and dignity.

"The general," Baudouin adds, "wants to avoid domestic troubles. Especially he wishes to avoid anarchy."[7] The secretary was not surprised. He had noted Weygand's final word to the War Committee the day before. After declaring that the French Army would be "totally destroyed if it had to fight to the end to save its honor," the generalissimo had added: "We must conserve the means of keeping order in the country."

By this time, and from now on to the end, Weygand, who had been hastily appointed Supreme Commander to try to save France from military defeat, seemed as much concerned with fighting the phantom of a red revolution in Paris, a revolution of which there was not the faintest sign, as with fighting the Germans. To preserve the Army not so much to resist the enemy, which he now deemed hopeless, as to maintain law and order in the stricken country became an obsession with him.

To get rid of the deadwood and the defeatists in the government at least—he did not dare eliminate the two leading military defeatists, Pétain and Weygand—or the deadwood in the High Command—Reynaud shook up his cabinet on June 5, the day the German offensive on the Somme began. As it turned out, though he let go Daladier, Monzie, and Lamoureux, he actually added to those in the cabinet who were now joining the generals in urging that France get out of the war.

No doubt Reynaud was glad to see the last of his bitter rival Daladier, as was the Countess de Portes, who appears to have had a hand not only in his ouster but in the naming of some of the new appointees. Pétain himself helped by insisting that Daladier go. He had never forgiven him for putting down the rioters on the Place de la Concorde on the night of February 6, 1934, and for taking a leading part in the Popular Front. The pretext for firing Daladier was the visit on the morning of June 5 of Senator Henry Bérenger, President of the Foreign Affairs Committee of the Senate and a somewhat shady character in French politics. Bérenger declared that his Committee was unanimously of the opinion that Daladier's presence at the Quai d'Orsay "was an insult to French diplomacy." The Premier offered the post of Foreign Minister to Pétain, who gingerly declined. Reynaud thereupon took over the office himself, naming Baudouin Undersecretary, a choice that he was soon to regret. Another selection he would regret even more was that of Yves Bouthillier, who was moved up from Undersecretary to Minister of Finance in place of Lamoureux. On the urging of Mme. de Portes, Reynaud named as Minister of Information Jean Prouvost, the millionaire textile magnate who had become a press tycoon with his acquisition of *Paris Soir, Match, Marie-Claire,* and other mass-circulation publications. The Premier would soon rue this one too. After some hesitation he retained Chautemps as Vice-Premier when the Radical Party leader, who was already secretly pushing for Pétain to take power, assured him that he was strongly opposed to an armistice. There would be remorse about this decision as well.

So on June 5, 1940, Daladier passed into limbo, forever. For two years, from 1938 to 1940, he had as Premier led the government and as Minister of Defense presided over the military establishment. Now with military collapse imminent, he seemed to those around him a broken man. Still, Baudouin tells us, he protested violently to Reynaud when they had a "painful" farewell meeting on the evening of June 5.

> He declared [Baudouin says] that he did not want to be dishonored. He insisted that there was nothing for which he could reproach himself and that he believed he had done his duty as Minister of War. . . . He terminated by saying that he still had the esteem of his sons and that that would suffice him.[8]

Of Edouard Daladier it might be said, I think, that he was a brave man, a staunch patriot, and a durable politician, but that in the crises of 1938–40 he proved himself unequal to the challenges that called for a statesman of much greater stature. In French politics those days though, who had had the needed qualities?

The most interesting of Reynaud's appointments on June 5, and the most important so far as future history was concerned, was that of Charles de Gaulle, Commander of the 4th Armored Division, and only a few days before promoted to be (temporarily) a Brigadier General, as Undersecretary of the Ministry of National Defense. This enraged Weygand and Pétain.

"He's an infant," Weygand protested to Reynaud. De Gaulle had just turned fifty. "He's more a journalist than an officer," the generalissimo stormed to Baudouin. "His opinion of himself is blinding."

Weygand's opinion of de Gaulle was mild compared to that of Pétain. "He's an arrogant man, an ingrate and surly," the old Marshal exclaimed to Baudouin after telling him he wished to "pour out his heart on the subject." Pétain had a long talk with General Spears on June 6, the day after de Gaulle's appointment, and poured out his heart.

> He [de Gaulle] thinks he knows all about the mechanics of warfare. His vanity leads him to think the art of war has no secrets for him. He might have invented it. I know all about him. He was once on my staff and wrote a book, or at least I told him how to do so. I gave him the outline and corrected it. . . .

When he published it he did not even acknowledge my contribution.* Not only is he vain, he is ungrateful. He has few friends in the Army. No wonder, for he gives the impression of looking down on everybody.[10]

While the venerable Marshal of France and Vice-Premier was fretting over the authorship of a book that few had read and the Premier was reshuffling his government, the German attack began on the Somme, scene of long, bloody and futile battles in the first war. At dawn on June 5 the panzers once more struck at thinly defended French lines. At 10 A.M. General Weygand addressed a flowery Order of the Day.

The Battle of France has begun. The order is to defend our positions without thought of retreat. . . . May the thought of our wounded country inspire in you an unshakable resolution to hold where you are. . . . The fate of our country, the safeguarding of her liberties, the future of our children, depends on your tenacity.

The odds, as the generalissimo well knew, were overwhelmingly against him. To confront the 95 divisions, including 10 panzer, of Bock and Rundstedt massed on a 200-mile front from the sea to Longuyon, at the beginning of the Maginot Line, Weygand had been able to scrape up only 43 divisions, of which three were armored and three cavalry. But the armored divisions had only one third of their normal tank strength—86 tanks in the 2nd Armored, 50 in the 3rd and even fewer in the cavalry units. The Germans had also concentrated their two airfleets on the front. Given the feebleness of the French air force and the lack of British air support—the RAF had had to move most of its squadrons based in France back home—the Germans would continue to have complete superiority in

---

* The remembrance of his quarrel with de Gaulle over this book continued to stir up ill feelings in the usually placid Marshal. The next day, June 7, he again showed his spleen in talking to Baudouin, who wrote in his journal: "The Marshal reproaches de Gaulle for having signed alone a book written according to his directives and corrected in large part in his own hand."[9]

It is remarkable that in the midst of the defeat and disintegration of the French Army its most illustrious living officer should have given so much thought and shown such rancor over the authorship of a book. The quarrel concerned a book by de Gaulle called *La France et son armée* which was published on September 27, 1938. Pétain claimed that it was really "a work of the General Staff" which de Gaulle had written under his direction between 1925 and 1927 "when he was under my orders." The Marshal at first forbade de Gaulle "to use a work of the General Staff which did not belong to him." But since the book was in print and the publisher intended to bring it out. Pétain relented and "authorized" its appearance on condition that a dedication to himself in laudatory terms be used. He sent the text of the dedication to de Gaulle on September 5, but it came too late, as the sheets were already off the press. Actually de Gaulle's own dedication which appeared was highly flattering to the Marshal, but Pétain was displeased because it was not his own. The quarrel between these two men, which now was to figure so prominently in French history over the next years, may be said to have begun over the authorship of a book! Writers are notoriously vain about their literary works—but generals?

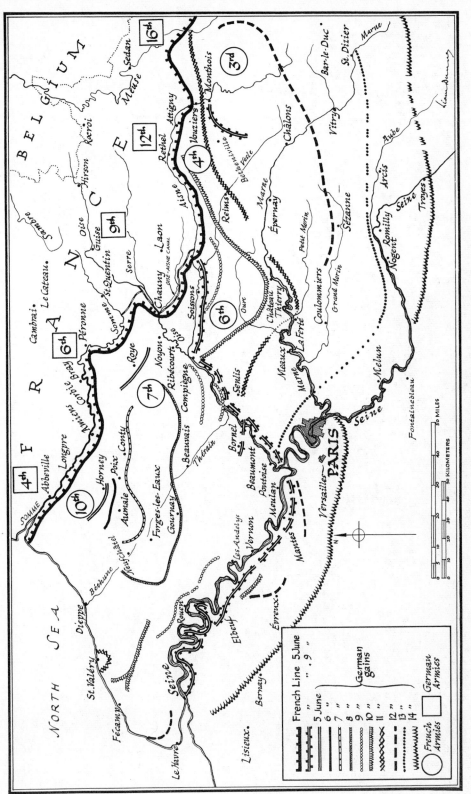

BATTLE OF THE SOMME AND THE FALL OF PARIS
JUNE 5–14, 1940

the skies. "A battle without hope," Colonel Goutard, the French military historian, would call it. Worse, since Weygand had forbidden retreat, it was bound to end in a *Götterdämmerung*.

Here and there the French troops fought with great tenacity. The French Seventh Army held so well against the attacks of four panzer divisions of the Kleist Group on the Somme between Amiens and Péronne that the German High Command was forced to renounce their further use in a drive on Paris and transfer them east to the Aisne, where a second blow was planned. After two days of fighting, the French center still held, but on the flanks, especially west of Amiens, the Germans had made considerable progress. On June 7 the situation rapidly worsened. The XVth Panzer Corps, with Rommel's 7th Armored Division in the lead, had advanced some 10 miles south of the Somme between Abbeville and Amiens on June 5 and 6 against stiff resistance. But next day, the 7th, Rommel broke through the French line, advanced 30 miles and reached Forges-les-Eaux, only 24 miles from Rouen on the Seine. This lightning thrust split the French Tenth Army in two, leaving the 51st British division, the 31st and 40th French infantry divisions, and the 2nd and 5th cavalry divisions cut off from the rest of the army, their backs to the sea and the broad mouth of the Seine.*

On June 8, four days after it began, the Battle of the Somme was lost. The Germans reached the lower Seine and on the next day occupied the river from Rouen to Vernon, bringing them on the west to within 40 miles of Paris. In the center the Seventh Army was forced to retreat to keep from being encircled. Beauvais was abandoned; Compiègne was threatened. In five days the Germans had cleared the way for an assault on Paris from the west and the north. On June 9 they launched a major attack on the Aisne. If it succeeded, the pincers could close on Paris from the east. And the Maginot Line, on which the French had pinned such high hopes, could be turned from the southwest.

After General Bock (Army Group B) on the Somme, General Rundstedt (Army Group A) on the Aisne at the eastern end of the battlefront. It was the classic use of the one-two punch, in this case, first with the right and then with the left. By a lightning shift of armor which astounded the French, who could only move their tank divisions with the greatest of delays, the German High Command shifted 4 panzer divisions from the Somme to the Aisne in two days, giving Rundstedt 8 of the 10 existing armored divisions to lead the drive over the river. Again for two days the outnumbered French forces fought tenaciously but by the evening of June 10 this battle too was lost. On the 11th Reims fell and the Germans

---

* They were cornered at Saint-Valéry-en-Caux, a small fishing port between Dieppe and Le Havre by the German 5th and 7th Panzer divisions. On the night of June 11 ships of the British Navy tried to evacuate them but could not approach the port because of heavy fog. The next morning, June 12, the force surrendered, some 40,000 men, of whom 8,000 were British (mostly from General Fortune's 51st Division) and twelve generals.

reached the Marne at Château-Thierry, where the Americans had received their baptism of fire in 1918. By this time the French armies had been reduced to the value of 30 divisions, half the strength of a week before.* Paris was now threatened from three sides.

THE GOVERNMENT DEPARTS

It had been a tense week in the French capital. With every piece of bad news—and the bad news kept pouring in—relations between the French and British became more exacerbated and the desire of Pétain and Weygand to stop the unequal struggle and opt out of the war grew more determined.

This came out clearly—and painfully—enough in the regular meeting of Reynaud with his generals on June 5, a few hours after the Germans began their assault south of the Somme. General Spears was invited to attend and immediately he clashed with General Weygand, who opened the meeting by presenting a written note of complaint against the British, which Reynaud read out.

The Commander in Chief is obliged to observe that the appeals to the British government have been of no avail. The German attack against us is being launched without our having received any further help from England. Neither fighters, nor new divisions.

Spears spiritedly protested that Weygand "was not helping the cause of the Alliance or even of France by his habit of making unjustified complaints against us."

He then proceeded to read out a telegram from Churchill about the aid Britain could now give. It was not much: one division which would start embarking in seven days, two more as soon as possible though no date could yet be given, a few more planes. Reynaud broke in to say, according to Baudouin's minutes, that he "was extremely disappointed by this message."

Reynaud declared that the British government was committing a tragic error in considering its own defense first. Now, it is to take Paris that the Germans have launched the great battle. Britain ought to throw all its forces into the balance. If it holds them back for the defense of Britain we are both going to lose the war.†

---

* According to a report of General Georges the French Army now had left: "9 light divisions and 9 normal divisions more or less complete; 11 divisions reduced to 50 percent of their combat strength; 13 divisions reduced to 25 percent; 10 divisions of which there remained only debris."[11]

† In his postwar memoirs Reynaud admits that "Churchill would have committed the greatest of mistakes if he had sacrificed in the Battle of France all of the Royal Air Force, which would soon be needed to defend Britain. . . . But in those first days of June I was entirely preoccupied by the battle being fought to cover Paris."[12]

A telegram was then drafted imploring the British government to hurry up its dispatch of troops and repeating a demand made by General Vuillemin on June 3 that the British send immediately 10 fighter squadrons and 10 more "as soon as possible." The French Air Force chief, who was incapable of employing all the planes he had, was asking for half of the remaining fighters in the RAF—a demand that Churchill wired Reynaud that night was "altogether unreasonable."

After Spears had left to send the government's message to London, the French resumed discussion among themselves. "If the battle is lost, and Paris threatened, where does the government go from here? To Brittany?" Reynaud asked Weygand. The generalissimo rejected Brittany as having "no military value."

"If the battle is lost," he declared "and France overrun, the really courageous thing to do would be to treat with the enemy." Pétain broke his habitual silence to indicate his approval of that. But Reynaud would not hear of it.

"Since I am convinced that no peace and no armistice will be acceptable, the armies must fight on as long as possible, and the government must be ready, if necessary, to leave the soil of France."

This was the core of the great argument which now pitted the Premier against his generals.

The next two days, June 6 and 7, as the French defenses south of the Somme began to weaken, there was more recrimination by Weygand against the British and more talk by him and Pétain of the necessity of ceasing the fighting. At the morning meeting on the 6th Spears noticed at once that Weygand was itching to resume the fight with him—"his face of taut parchment was working as if it would crack." He raged against the British for not fighting. General V. M. Fortune, who commanded the 51st Division at the extreme west of the Somme line, had fallen back, he charged, without orders. "General Fortune," he quipped, "should be called 'General Misfortune.'" And he asked if the retreat was ordered from London, which led him to repeat again his old charge, now so hackneyed, that the British government had ordered the British "retreat" at Arras and the evacuation at Dunkirk without consulting him. "He was now yelling in a high-pitched broken voice," Spears swears. "He was gray with rage."

"The Premier intervened," say Baudouin's minutes, "to calm the debate and turning toward Spears asked: 'but, finally, what are you going to give us?'" The unhappy British general could not give a very satisfactory answer. After he left the Premier, the generalissimo and the Marshal renewed their debate about continuing the war. When Reynaud affirmed that it *would* be continued, Weygand responded: "Continue the war? With what, if the Paris region, which produces 70 percent of our armaments, is taken?" Reynaud repeated that the army could make a stand in the Brittany peninsula. "That's a fantasy," Weygand retorted. "Then in North Africa," Reynaud persisted. "In North Africa," said Weygand, "we have but 7 divisions, most of them native. No modern arms. No anti-aircraft."

Finally Pétain spoke up. "If the present battle is lost," he said, "there is nothing left to do but to treat with the enemy—if we can obtain possible conditions." That night Baudouin ended his journal: "I am certain the battle is lost." He was now determined to desert his Premier and work with the generals for an armistice.[13]

Next day, June 8, General de Gaulle, the new Undersecretary of Defense, called on General Weygand at Montry. "A few minutes of conversation," says de Gaulle, "convinced me that he was resigned to defeat and had decided on an armistice." De Gaulle, no man even then to shrink in the presence of a Supreme Commander, despite his own relatively junior military rank,* tried to stir the mind of Weygand with thoughts of global strategy. When the generalissimo informed him that the Germans were already over the Somme, de Gaulle replied:

"All right. They're over the Somme. And after?"

"After? It's the Seine and Marne."

"Yes. And after?"

"After? *C'est fini!*"

"What do you mean, finished? What about the world? The Empire?"

"General Weygand," says de Gaulle, "broke into a laughter of exasperation."

"The Empire? Don't be childish. As for the world, as soon as I've been beaten here, England won't wait eight days to negotiate with the Reich." And he added: "Ah! If I were sure the Germans would leave me the forces necessary to maintain order!"

De Gaulle lingered on to speak to some General Staff officers at headquarters. All wanted to stop the fighting. When he returned to Paris he

---

* Two days later in Paris de Gaulle showed his loftiness, which later would become so renowned. Weygand had burst into Reynaud's office *"tout de go,"* says the young general, to the astonishment of the Premier.

The Commander [de Gaulle later wrote in describing the scene] said he had been convoked.

"Not by me," said Reynaud.

"Nor by me," I added.

"Then it's a misunderstanding," General Weygand said. "But the mistake is useful for I have to make an important communication."

His conclusion was transparent. We must, without delay, ask for an armistice. . . . The battle in France itself was lost. We must capitulate.

"But there are other perspectives," I said. Then Weygand, in a jeering tone: "Have you something to propose?"

"The government," I responded, "does not have propositions to make but orders to give."[14]

urged Reynaud to get rid of Weygand.[15] Back in the capital to carry out his new duties as Undersecretary of Defense, de Gaulle found the atmosphere no healthier than at General Headquarters.

> One tried to think that there was still a front, an active command, a people ready for sacrifices, but these were only dreams and memories. In fact, in the midst of a nation prostrate and stupefied, behind an army without faith and without hope, the machine of power turned over in irremediable confusion. . . . In the middle of the cyclone the meetings of the ministers, the instructions flung to those below and the reports received by those on high, the public declarations, the procession of officers, functionaries, diplomats, parliamentarians, journalists, who had something to report or to demand, gave the impression of a sort of phantasmagoria without object and without sense. On the bases and in the framework in which one was engaged there was no issue except capitulation. . . . A recovery like that of the Marne was possible, but only in the Mediterranean.[16]

Not only Weygand but Pétain too failed to see the opportunities of a larger strategy that now began to sprout in de Gaulle's mind of continuing the war, if metropolitan France were lost, from French territory in North Africa and in the rest of the Empire. The impetuous young general noted the Marshal's narrow view with understanding but total disagreement.

> This old soldier, who had donned the harness just after 1870, could not but consider the struggle as a new Franco-German war. Vanquished in the first one, we had won the second, that of 1914–18, with the Allies, no doubt, but they had played a secondary role. Now we were losing the third one. It was cruel but in the order of things. After Sedan and the fall of Paris there was nothing to do but end it, treat with the enemy, and, if necessary, crush the Commune, as, in the same circumstances, Thiers had once done. In the judgment of the old Marshal, the global character of the conflict, the possibilities open in our territories beyond the seas, the ideological consequences of a victory of Hitler, did not enter his thoughts. They were not things he would have had a mind to consider.[17]

On June 9, with the Germans only 40 miles down the Seine from Paris and a new enemy offensive, which began that morning in overwhelming strength, breaking over the Aisne and threatening both the capital and the Maginot Line, Pétain made a formal demand, in writing, to Reynaud to ask for an armistice.

The day before, at the regular morning meeting with the Premier, both he and Weygand had castigated Republican France for its shortcomings. These, they said, had made military defeat inevitable. Announcing that he was moving his headquarters to Briare on the Loire, south of Paris, the Supreme Commander told Reynaud: "We are at the end of our reserves. There are no more fresh units." The faithful Baudouin kept noting down his words. "He had found an army which since the beginning of hostilities, for eight months, had lived on the simple idea: 'No use of doing anything. We'll beat them.' It is necessary to destroy this tendency toward passivity, which is deeply rooted in France as the result of twenty years of abandon, feebleness, and demagogy which preceded the war."

Pétain, usually so silent at these meetings, joined in. "He supports these observations," Baudouin noted, "and declares that the discoveries he makes each day on the unpreparedness of the Army . . . stupefy him. 'Nothing has been done for months, or rather for years. Everything has to be begun over in this country.' "[18] No one, not even Reynaud, reminded the two illustrious generals that as Commanders in Chief of the French Army from the end of the first war to 1935, they bore a certain responsibility for its "unpreparedness."

By now they were gaining followers among the civilians in the cabinet. That evening, June 8, Baudouin dined with Chautemps. "He holds no more hope for the outcome of the struggle," the secretary noted. "We must put an end to it," he says Chautemps told him. "It is useless to go on. We must prevent this destruction from spreading to the rest of the country. Pétain understands this best."[19]

The Marshal's understanding of what to do was conveyed by him in writing to Reynaud at the morning conference on June 9. The Premier had discussed a little earlier with some of his cabinet members and the Prefect of Police the question of the government quitting the capital. Pétain thought that for the government to flee would be "inconvenient at a moment when the chief consideration ought to be to conserve the moral and intellectual patrimony of the country." Then, reading from his note, he came to the main point: "the necessity of asking for an armistice to stop hostilities if, of course, the conditions for an armistice, though hard, are acceptable. The salvation and the future of the country demand that we proceed in this way with courage."

Reynaud replied that "no honorable armistice with Hitler" was possible. "Besides," he added, "it would be immensely imprudent to separate ourselves from our Allies."

To this the Marshal responded icily. "The interests of France must come before those of England. England got us into this situation. Let us not be content to submit to it. Let us try to get out of it."

At this point Weygand arrived at the meeting. That morning he had issued another of his resounding Orders of the Day to the troops saying that "the enemy is at the end of his effort. We are at the last quarter hour. Hold firmly!" But he did not believe it. He described the military situation as worsening. The troops, he said, had reached the limit of their endurance. He advised Reynaud that it would be "prudent" to evacuate the ministries, though he thought the Premier and some of the key ministers should remain in Paris "to the last moment."

The question was threshed out at a full cabinet meeting that evening presided over by the President of the Republic. Lebrun remembered it in his memoirs:

General Weygand makes a complete report on the situation. Very sad impression. Marshal Pétain says nothing. He seems to be asleep, prostrated. I question him.

"Don't you wish to express an opinion, Marshal? These gentlemen are anxious to hear from you."

"I have nothing to say," he replies.

It appears that from this moment he considers defeat as an accepted fact and that there is nothing more to do about it. He had been called into the government by M. Paul Reynaud to bring it an additional force to resist. In fact, he seems to have brought it the contrary.[20]

Over the silence of the Marshal, who had said he would remain in Paris and talk with Hitler, if necessary, the cabinet decided that the government would depart the capital the next day, June 10, and set up office at Tours on the Loire to the south. It was the last cabinet meeting of a government of the Third Republic—after sixty-nine years—that Paris would ever see.

June 10, 1940, in Paris, de Gaulle remembered as "a day of agony." For the first time he attended the morning meeting of Reynaud with the generals. Pétain was absent. He had expressed his displeasure at the prospect of the arrogant young general attending these daily conferences. But Baudouin explains that the Marshal had already left for the new GHQ on the Loire.

Weygand brought his daily collection of bad news, though to Baudouin, scratching out the minutes, it seemed even worse than usual. German panzers had crossed the lower Seine in two places. The French armies to the west and north of Paris were in full retreat. Reynaud interrupted to ask when they could expect the Germans in Paris.

"In 24 hours," Weygand replied, "if the Germans know how weak we are. But probably it will be a little longer. They will encircle Paris first rather than attack directly." The generalissimo then read out a note he had composed the night before.

I am far from having lost all hope of stopping the enemy. . . . But the events of the last two days of battle make it my duty to warn the Premier that the rupture of our defense lines can come at any moment.

The generalissimo explained that he was not surprised at what was happening. "We are paying," he snapped, "for twenty years of lies and demagogy." Reynaud again urged him to prepare a stand in the

Brittany peninsula but Weygand thought it a waste of time. "It's a bad joke," he told Baudouin after the meeting. The two were consoling one another in the secretary's office. Baudouin, who had now turned on his Premier and benefactor, said he did not see how they could avoid stopping the fighting and that he "regretted" that Reynaud did not see it that way.

Weygand said he agreed with me [Baudouin noted in his journal] because the combat has reached a dead end. "It has to be stopped," the general told me. "It makes no more sense. . . ." If we are beaten why go on making the blood flow, why accumulate the material destruction, why deliver all of France to the enemy and in what a state of social decomposition, why deliver the entire army to the Germans? . . . Moreover to prolong the struggle is impossible. In North Africa? We don't have the means![21]

Weygand had clashed with de Gaulle during the meeting over the question of trying to defend Brittany and in his notes Baudouin blamed the young general "for pushing the Premier into this fantasy of the Breton Redoubt." De Gaulle tells why he supported it.

It was not because I had any illusions about the possibility of holding out in Brittany but because if the government went there it would, sooner or later, have to take to the sea . . . for North Africa.[22]

It was there, in Algeria and Morocco, that de Gaulle now envisaged France holding out. But Weygand would not hear of it.

At 4 P.M. on this day of June 10, which the leading figures in the drama would look back to as an eternity, more bad news reached Paris. François-Poncet, the French Ambassador in Rome, rang up Reynaud to tell him that at midnight Italy would enter the war on the side of Germany. Mussolini, the strutting sawdust Caesar, had waited until France was down before daring to attack her.

"What really distinguished, noble, and admirable people the Italians are to stab us in the back at this moment!" Reynaud exclaimed to Ambassador Bullitt. And that night at Charlottesville, Virginia, President Roosevelt would say: "On this tenth day of June, 1940, the hand that held the dagger has plunged it into the back of its neighbor."

The French had denuded the frontier with Italy of troops in order to throw them into the Battle of the Somme and Aisne. Only five divisions were left to defend the largely mountainous border against some 32 Italian divisions. But five were enough. They had no difficulty in stopping the Italians cold.*

---

* The French Air Force and Naval Commands, in contrast, had no desire to provoke the Italians. At the Allied Supreme War Council in Paris on May 31 the

In the opinion of Bullitt, Reynaud behaved with magnificent courage on this last day in Paris. "There is no question whatsoever," the Ambassador cabled Roosevelt, "about Reynaud's determination and the determination of the French Army to make the end of France as noble as her past. . . . I cannot express my admiration for the courage with which the French are meeting one of the most tragic situations in history."* And he added: "The British are still keeping at home three-fourths of their pursuit planes."[25] He could not forgive them for that.

Early in the evening Bullitt cabled a message from the Premier to the President of the United States.

Today the enemy is almost at the gates of Paris. We shall fight in front of Paris; we shall fight behind Paris; we shall close ourselves in one of our provinces to fight and if we should be driven out of it we shall establish ourselves in North Africa to continue the fight and if necessary in our American possessions.

A portion of the government has already left Paris. I am making ready to leave for the front. . . . It is my duty to ask you for new and even larger assistance. . . .[26]

British and French had agreed that if Italy came into the war they would bomb and bombard industrial targets and oil depots in the north immediately. Anglo-French naval and air staffs met on June 3 and worked out plans. The French put two airfields near Marseilles at the disposal of the British and the RAF began to build up a small bombing force in them. This was at a moment when Weygand and Reynaud were daily clamoring for more British planes. But on the night of July 11, when British planes were about to take off from Marseilles to bomb Genoa, Turin, and Milan, General Vuillemin, who on June 3 had insisted that the British send 20 squadrons of fighters to France, forbade the operation. When the RAF flyers tried to take off anyway, the Air Force Commander, according to the British, ordered the local populace to drive trucks, cars, and carts onto the airfields to prevent takeoff. This grounded the planes.

Admiral Darlan also took a dim view of offensive operations against the Italians. On June 14 the Third French Mediterranean Squadron carried out a heavy naval bombardment of the Ansaldo factories at Genoa and of oil tanks and refineries west of the port. Next day Darlan forbade further naval operations against Italy. Both he and Vuillemin, it was said, feared Italian reprisals on Marseilles and the Riviera.[23]

* De Gaulle was more skeptical. Recalling "this day of agony," he wrote: "The evidence of the collapse was there for all to see. The government was leaving Paris that evening. The withdrawal of the front accelerated. Italy declared war. But at the summit of the state the tragedy played itself out as in a dream. At certain moments, even, you could have believed that a sort of terrible humor spiced the fall of France, rolling from the heights of history down to the lowest depths of the abyss."

To the veteran British correspondent Alexander Werth, who regarded France as his second home, the French soldiers he saw that day did not seem very determined to make France's end as noble as her past. He noted "a mass of troops, tired, demoralized-looking, many of them drunk, all without rifles, drifting into Paris—a routed army."[24]

"This," says Reynaud, "was my last act before leaving Paris." He was, of course, not going to the front, as he told Roosevelt, but south to the Loire where the government would gather the next day. About midnight he and the lanky de Gaulle climbed into an automobile and headed for Orléans over roads jammed with fleeing, panicky refugees. General Weygand, who had so strongly urged the government to remain in Paris "even at the risk of capture," departed too—for the new GHQ at Briare, east of Orléans on the Loire. Marshal Pétain had already preceded him there by a day. The going was so slow even for the automobiles of such high official personalities in the midst of indescribable chaos along the routes continually blocked by the thousands of cars and carts of civilians in headlong flight that the Premier and the Supreme Commander did not reach the Loire, 160 miles distant, until dawn the next morning.

The plight of the refugees, utterly disorganized, eight million of them milling about on the highways and byways below Paris, without shelter, begging to buy food and water or pillaging for it, desperate to survive, to keep out of the clutch of the onrushing Germans but with no definite place to go except in the general direction of the south, stopping only when the logjams prevented further progress or when enemy planes machine-gunned them as they dived for the ditches to try to save their miserable lives, was a terrifying reminder to the leaders of the government and the High Command that the stricken French nation was falling apart.*

Would Paris, now that the government had left, and the High Command, and more than half the population, be defended as it was by the inhabitants and some troops against the Prussians in 1870, and as it surely would have been by the Army in 1914 had the Germans not been stopped a few miles away at the Marne? For in September 1914, General Galliéni, the then Military Governor of Paris, had received orders from the government, which had moved to Bordeaux, to defend the capital to the last man, and he had had the iron in his veins—and the French troops and civilians had had it in those days—to do so.

Reynaud had told Roosevelt in his message on June 10 that he would fight "in front" of Paris and "behind" it, but he had omitted to say that he would fight *in* it.† All through the last days of May and the first days of

---

* See Chapter 1 for the plight of the refugees.

† Unlike Clemenceau in 1918 when the Germans had again threatened the capital. The old Tiger had then proclaimed: "I will fight before Paris. I will fight in Paris. I will fight behind Paris." After declaring that he would fight, if necessary, on the Loire, on the Garonne, on the Pyrenees, and if driven from those mountains, on the sea, he had concluded: "But as to making peace—never!"

June there had been indecision in the government and the High Command as to whether there should be resistance in the city itself. As early as May 27 General Weygand had issued an order indicating that Paris would be defended.[27] By June 8 some 10,000 troops with 200 antitank guns and hundreds of machine guns had been rounded up to man 400 recently constructed blockhouses on the approaches to the capital. They were supported by 30 tanks and protected by several miles of antitank obstacles and ditches.[28] Even with the addition of troops from the Seventh Army falling back on Paris this was scarcely a force capable of halting the German panzer columns, though once they reached the city proper, with its tens of miles of narrow streets and solidly massed buildings, they might encounter great difficulty against determined resistance, as Leningrad and Stalingrad later would prove.

The question was: would there be French resistance? The deliberations of the French government all through the hectic day of June 9, when the sound of artillery could be clearly heard in the capital, did not touch on the matter. The President of the Republic and the Premier were more concerned with pulling the government out of Paris before it was captured. Thus the question on June 9 remained open.

It looked, though, as if the capital would be defended. That same day Weygand instructed his armies to establish a line of defense "on the position of the entrenched camp of Paris" with the newly created "Army of Paris" under General Pierre Héring, Military Governor of Paris, inserting itself between the Tenth Army on the west along the Seine and the Seventh Army north and east of the city on the Oise and Marne.[29]

On June 11, the day after the government and the High Command moved south, General Héring called in the Prefects and Police Chiefs of the Seine district and told them categorically: "The capital will be defended to the last."*[30] Apparently he thought that was what the "Army of Paris" had been created for. But in the chaos and the confusion that paralyzed the French Army he had been out of touch with his Commander in Chief. The day before, on June 10, Weygand had made his decision. Reynaud had asked him, on behalf of the City Council of Paris: "Will Paris be defended?" and the Commander had immediately responded in writing:

Paris is an Open City. . . . In order that Paris shall preserve its character as an Open City it is my intention to avoid any defensive organization around the city on the belt of the old fortifications or on that of the ancient forts.[32]

---

* That very day Churchill was urging this on the French. "I urged the French Government to defend Paris," he wrote later. "I emphasized the enormous absorbing power of the house-to-house defence of a great city upon an invading army."[31]

This vital decision was not communicated to General Héring until two days later and it took an additional day before the general, on June 13, could inform the Parisians by posters on the walls—the newspapers had ceased publication on the 10th when the government left—that their city would not be defended. By this time the Germans were beginning to envelop the capital on both east and west. They had pushed across the Seine above Vernon toward Evreux and then Dreux on the west; on the east their Aisne offensive had carried across the Marne at Château-Thierry and a force of 17 infantry and four panzer divisions was driving south of the river on Montmirail and Sézanne. General Touchon, who commanded the Sixth Army in this region, reported: "It's a carrousel of tanks. I have nothing with which to stop them."[33]

Though Generals Weygand and Georges, to their credit, were anxious to avoid the senseless destruction of the beautiful capital, they admitted later that the decision not to defend Paris was based primarily on a military judgment. The capital was declared an Open City, General Georges told the Parliamentary Investigating Committee after the war, "to prevent the encirclement of the Army of Paris and the Seventh Army." And he explained that if the two Armies had fought in Paris they would have been quickly surrounded by the Germans closing in on the south from east and west and that it was therefore better to re-form the French forces south of the city before they were cut off.[34] Weygand testified similarly at the trial of Pétain. "I made the decision," he said, "not only because defending Paris would have served no useful purpose but because the city was already being turned by the Germans on the south."[35]

The position of Paris north of the capital was abandoned on the night of June 12–13 and the next day General Héring withdrew his forces to the south of the city on a line running from the Forest of Rambouillet through the valley of the Chevreuse to Juvisy on the Seine. By evening advanced German detachments reached the outskirts of Paris on the north. They found the vast oil depots in the suburbs burning.*

The Germans now demanded the quick surrender of the city. At 5:10 P.M. on June 13 the radio post of the municipal police picked up a message from the German High Command announcing that it was sending an envoy under the protection of a white flag to discuss the rendering of the capital. He would drive down the road from Moisselles to Saint-Denis at 6 P.M. to meet with a representative of the French Command. General Héring, the Military Governor of Paris, had left the city with his troops, leaving in command General Henri-Fernand Dentz, the Commander of the Paris Region. The latter informed General Georges at GHQ at Briare of the message and

---

* No attempt was made to destroy the great factories in the industrial belt, which provided most of the armaments. Thus the Renault works, which turned out tanks and trucks, and the Schneider-Creuzot works, which turned out guns, were abandoned intact, and soon would be working for the Germans.

declared that as Commander of an Open City he did not feel himself qualified to parley with the Germans and would not do so unless so ordered.
Georges agreed.

But the Germans were not to be put off. At 2:20 A.M. on June 14 the
Paris radio post picked up a new message from the German Command. It
said its envoy sent to parley a few hours before had been killed by French
snipers, demanded that the "murderer" be apprehended, and ordered that
a French officer be sent to Sarcelles at 5 A.M. to parley. It threatened that
if this were not done Paris would be immediately attacked. General Dentz
said later that this "incident modified" his attitude. "Continued silence on
my part," he explained, "could have resulted in a catastrophe for Paris. I
therefore responded to the German message and told them I was sending
an envoy."[36]

A Major Devouges was selected for this unhappy task. Setting out
under a white flag he was met by the Germans, taken to a headquarters at
Ecouen and given the German terms, which he accepted and signed at
6 A.M.

In order to avoid that Paris becomes a theater of combat [they read], it is
demanded:

that in Paris itself and south to a line Saint-Germain, Versailles, Juvisy
. . . Meaux there must be no resistance either by troops or the population.

that in Paris there be no destruction of bridges or of public services, in
particular those supplying water and electricity and communications.

If the General-Governor cannot obtain the adoption of this pacific solution,
the resistance of the city will be broken by the sharpest means—on land and
in the air.

It was further stipulated that the municipal police would remain to
maintain law and order and that for the first 48 hours of the occupation
the population would remain indoors.[37]

A few minutes later, shortly after dawn on June 14, the jubilant troops
of Hitler, led by the 9th Division, entered Paris without a shot being fired.
The glittering city, to which the German soldiers had got so close in 1914
and in 1918 but which they could never capture in that first war, was at last
in their hands. "A great day in the history of the German Army! Since
9 A.M. German troops have been marching into Paris!" General Halder
began his diary that morning. General Bock, Commander of Army Group
B, hurried into the capital to savor the triumph. On the Place de la Concorde he held an impromptu review of troops of the 9th Division. Later he
sped up the Champs Elysées to review elements of the 8th and 28th Divisions and beam on them as they goose-stepped through the Arc de
Triomphe. "Finally," he reported in the Army Group's War Diary, "I drove
to the Invalides to view Napoleon's tomb. Then a very fine breakfast at the

Ritz." While he was breakfasting at the Ritz the swastika flag of the Third Reich was hoisted to the top of the Eiffel tower.

The great and lovely city, with all its incomparable architectural and art treasures and historic monuments, was spared destruction. Some French, some persons abroad, and of course the Germans saw in the decision not to defend Paris a further sign of the weakening of the fiber of the nation. But in retrospect one can see that it would have been a senseless thing to fight in the streets and buildings of Paris until the city, with all that was priceless and irreplaceable within it, had been reduced to rubble. The war in metropolitan France was irretrievably lost by June 14.* A savage and even prolonged stand in Paris would not have prevented the rest of France from being overrun and conquered by the German armies before the month was out. Actually, the capital could not have held out for long. There were too many mouths to feed from dwindling stocks. There were not even enough trucks left to distribute the food on hand. The fleeing officials and population had taken away almost all the motor transport and as late as the evening of June 13 General Dentz had begged GHQ to send back some trucks. "Without them," he had warned, "Paris will die of starvation for lack of means of distributing the stocks."[39] The city would have been starved out in a few weeks even if a handful of poorly armed troops and civilians had been able to hold out against the heavy shells and bombs of the besiegers.

Some made the inevitable comparison with 1870–71 but this was misleading. Then besieged Paris had held out for four months until its inhabitants and defenders had eaten the last dog, cat, and rat and were starved into surrendering. But until the end there had been hope that the Prussian siege might be lifted by a newly created French army south of Paris that grew to a force of 583,000 men. No such hope for relief existed in the summer of 1940. Also the explosive power of shells in 1870 was not sufficient to do much damage to the city. In 1940 the explosives both in shells and aerial bombs were many times more powerful and fairly quickly could have reduced the capital to rubble, as Stalingrad showed.

But comparisons with Stalingrad are also misleading. There the Russians concentrated a powerful, determined army which not only outnumbered the Germans as the battle reached its climax but had considerable superiority in artillery and air cover. Moreover, Stalingrad was not entirely surrounded. The Russians could supply and reinforce their troops in the city from across the Volga river. Perhaps what happened to Berlin in 1945 indicates what the fate of Paris would have been had the French

---

* Colonel Lyet puts the date a couple of days earlier—on June 12. "It was during this day," he writes, "that the last hope of pursuing a coordinated defense evaporated."[38]

fought in it. Though defended by fanatical SS and Hitler Youth troops, urged on by the cornered Nazi dictator himself, who remained in the capital, Berlin held out against the Russians only ten days after being besieged. It was largely destroyed, though most of the damage had been done previously by Anglo-American bombing.

The day Paris fell the French government fled from its temporary stopping place on the Loire to Bordeaux in southwestern France. The end, some sort of end, appeared to be approaching.

33

THE FLIGHT TO BORDEAUX
June 11–14, 1940

The government of the Third Republic, halting for the moment on the Loire, was in disarray.

The night of June 10–11 had been a sleepless one for the cabinet ministers and the generals as their cars inched south from Paris on the jammed roads past the hapless refugees as determined to flee the Germans as were they. Reaching the bend of the river at Orléans at dawn on the 11th they scattered to various châteaux south of the stream from Briare on the east side to Tours on the west. The old castles, though pleasant to live in for surviving aristocrats and other country gentlemen, were ill-suited for housing ministries. None had more than one telephone and it was in most cases antiquated and in poor working order. No one had thought to lay a few extra lines or to try to change the working habits of the village operator, who took off the customary two hours for lunch and closed down the exchange at 6 P.M. Sanitary facilities, none too good by twentieth-century standards even for a family, were inadequate for the skeleton ministerial staffs. Dispersed as they were in these edifices 30 to 40 miles apart the cabinet ministers found it almost impossible to get in touch with one another. The roads between the châteaux were blocked by refugees so that it often took all morning, or all afternoon, to drive from one to another. And the lack of telephones made communication by this medium difficult either between the displaced ministries or between them and the outside world. The Foreign Office had to depend on the British Ambassador's portable radio for news from abroad. The President of the Republic, installed in the impressive Château de Cangé, was found by Baudouin, the new Undersecretary of the Foreign Office, on the 11th to be "entirely isolated, without news from the Premier, without news from Supreme Headquarters, depressed, overwhelmed. He knows nothing."[1]

There was plenty of activity, though, at the Château de Chissay above the River Cher near Tours, where the Premier, accompanied by his aides and his mistress, had installed himself. The ubiquitous General Spears found it "a mad-house . . . a bedlam. The confusion was indescribable." His mind "boggled," he says, "at the thought that this was the heart of France, the brain center, . . . the place of decision." The British general was not encouraged by the sight of Countess de Portes scampering about, in the mornings at least, "in a red dressing gown over her red pyjamas." He recalled that he "had not seen red trousers on French legs since 1914," when the French infantryman wore them proudly off to battle.[2]

It was into this milieu that the Prime Minister of Great Britain flew on the afternoon of June 11 to find out, he says, "what the French were going to do." It had been a black day for General Weygand and the High Command, installed at the Château du Muguet and in a railroad train at Briare five miles away.

During the morning the generalissimo had discussed with Generals Georges, Doumenc, and Koeltz what could be done. The news that had come in overnight from the front, says General Roton, Georges' Chief of Staff, "was far from reassuring." Half of the Tenth Army had been surrounded at Saint-Valéry-en-Caux by Rommel's 7th Panzer Division and its only hope of escape was to get away that night by sea.* The rest of the Tenth Army had been driven over the Seine in three places below Paris. North of the capital the Seventh Army was retreating toward the position above the city. Further east, where the main German offensive was now raging after two days of battle, the enemy had broken over the Aisne, would take Reims during the day and reach the Marne at Château-Thierry.

To the French generals peering over their maps at the Château du Muguet that morning only two solutions seemed possible. One was to hold on to the Maginot Line and pull back the armies to the west of it on a pivot at Montmédy. This would have provided the protection of a strongly fortified line against the enemy coming from the north and east but it would have meant the abandonment of most of the country and risked having the three armies on the fortress line encircled by German forces moving southeast from the Aisne. The second solution was to abandon the Maginot Line and carry out a general retreat, which, as Weygand put it, "would cover as long as possible the heart of the country and preserve the largest number of units." He was already thinking of saving as many troops as possible from capture before an armistice stopped the fighting.

The second solution was adopted. Weygand signed the order for a general retreat. The Maginot Line was finally to be abandoned. The withdrawal would bring what was left of the French army back to a line starting from Caen at the bottom of the Cherbourg peninsula south to the Loire and then east to the Swiss border in the Jura mountains. Having signed

---

* As we have seen (p. 763, footnote) fog prevented its evacuation that night and it surrendered the next day.

the order Weygand hesitated. He instructed General Georges that it should not be carried out except on receipt of a specific order from himself, which for the moment he would withhold.[3]

Winston Churchill and his party arrived at Briare late on the afternoon of June 11 and from the doleful countenance of the French colonel who met him at the airfield he realized, he says, "how far things had fallen" since his visit to Paris a week before. But this was a mild sampling of what would confront him an hour later when he sat face to face with Reynaud, Pétain, and Weygand across the table in the Château du Muguet.

The generalissimo had a chilling tale of woe to tell.

The totality of French forces are engaged in the battle. . . . There is not one battalion uncommitted. . . . The last line of defense has been pierced. . . . The men are literally exhausted, fighting by day, marching by night, and falling asleep when they arrive at the new positions. . . . The generalissimo cannot guarantee that the lines will still be holding tomorrow. . . . General Weygand cannot intervene in the battle as Commander because he has no more reserves. . . . We entered the war lightheartedly in 1939 without recognizing the power of the German army. . . .

Apparently taken aback by this lugubrious account, Churchill requested that General Georges, whom he knew well and respected, be called in. Georges only confirmed the worst. In the last fortnight, he said, from 20 to 25 of his remaining divisions had broken up. His forces, he went on, were so thinly spread that he had nothing to oppose a powerful enemy attack.

Weygand then resumed.

If our position is dislocated, there is no hope of reconstituting it because we have nothing left in the rear. Once this defensive battle is lost the Commander in Chief sees no way of preventing the invasion of all of France. . . . If that happens we are going to have to ask how France can continue the war.

Here Reynaud intervened. "The generalissimo," he said icily, "is competent to give us the military picture. But the problem of continuing the war is a political matter and will be decided by the government." It was a tense moment in the struggle between the Premier and his general. "The two men glared at each other," Spears remembered. Then Churchill broke in: "If it is thought best for France in her agony that her Army should capitulate, let there be no hesitation on our account, because whatever you may do we shall fight on forever and ever and ever." It was a theme he kept repeating throughout the evening. Still, he was "haunted and undermined," he says, "by the grief I felt that Britain, with her forty-eight million population, had not been able to make a greater contribution to the land war against Germany, and that so far nine-tenths of the slaughter and ninety-nine hundredths of the suffering had fallen upon France and upon France alone."

He refused, though, to make a greater contribution in the air. To the desperate pleas of Weygand, Georges, and Reynaud that Britain throw *all* her fighter squadrons into the Battle of France he replied that "25 fighter squadrons must be maintained at all costs for the defence of Britain, and nothing would make us give up these." To give them up, he said, "would destroy our chance of life."

"History will say," Reynaud responded, "that the Battle of France was lost for the lack of planes," and General Georges added that he thought "it hardly likely that Britain would be attacked, and that in the meantime a massive intervention of planes on the Marne might change the situation." But the doughty Prime Minister could not be budged.*

Pétain, like Weygand, was growing incensed at the unwillingness of the British to give more help. When Churchill suggested that if the French army lost its "coordination" it might well go over to guerrilla warfare, the old Marshal responded coolly: "That would mean the destruction of the country." Again when the Prime Minister recalled to Pétain another dark day in the fortunes of Britain and France back in 1918 and how the two of them had met in Beauvais at the very moment when General Gough's British Fifth Army had been broken through and how the Marshal had saved the situation, the old soldier responded "that the analogy between 1918 and present events must not be pushed too far."

When the Army of General Gough was broken through [he said], he was able to put immediately 20 [French] divisions at his disposal, and a few days later, at the very moment he was conferring with Churchill, another 20 divisions, or a total of 40 divisions.

Pétain also "mentioned," Churchill says, that at that time, in 1918, "the British had 60 divisions in the line."

Both Reynaud and Churchill brought up the question of making a stand in Brittany, which could be supplied from England through the many ports there, but Weygand poured cold water on it. "It could not be held long," he explained. Churchill asked about "a move to North Africa," the very mention of which a week before, he says, he regarded as "defeatist," but General Georges thought there was "no hope in that."

Though Pétain had responded to him, Churchill thought, "with dig-

---

* Reynaud concedes that at the moment of this conference, the British, despite the withdrawal of most of their air force when their forward bases were overrun by the German breakthrough to the Channel in the third week of May, had on June 11, 11 squadrons—6 bomber, 5 fighter—based in France. The Premier did not know that the French Air Force was not throwing into the battle all the planes it had.

nity," the Prime Minister began to suspect that the Marshal, like the generalissimo, was sinking into defeatism. After a dinner at 10 P.M. Reynaud confirmed this to him.

> M. Reynaud told me that Marshal Pétain had informed him that it would be necessary for France to seek an armistice, and that he had written a paper upon the subject, which he wishes him to read. "He has not," said Reynaud, "handed it to me yet. He is still ashamed to do it."

Late that night of June 11, with the Germans but 60 or 70 miles away, the British party, Churchill remembers, "went unhappily to bed in this disordered château." The French, judging from what had transpired, must have gone to bed even more unhappily.

Early the next morning there was a moment of comic relief. Two French officers finishing their breakfast in the conference room at the château were startled to see appear an apparition in a red silk kimono over a white nightgown. In a loud and clear voice but with an accent difficult to understand the strangely clad figure addressed them: *"Uh ay ma bain?"* It turned out to be the British Prime Minister and the officers finally got it that he wanted a bath.

The Anglo-French meeting on the morning of June 12 was brief. The French renewed their demand for more British planes and troops and Churchill, putting them off, said that the "whole question" would be examined "sympathetically" in London. The Prime Minister did ask for one assurance: that the French government would take no "final decisions" without first conferring with him. On leaving the meeting he asked Admiral Darlan for another. "Darlan," he said, "you must never let them get the French Fleet."

"There's no question of that," the admiral answered. "It would be contrary to our naval traditions and to our honor."[4]

Some historians have contended that despite all that Weygand, Pétain, Georges, and Reynaud said at these two meetings on the Loire June 11–12, Churchill left without fully realizing how critical the French military and political predicament was. Actually, he did realize it. Reporting to the War Cabinet in London on his return the afternoon of June 12, he said:

> General Weygand evidently saw no prospect of the French going on fighting, and Marshal Pétain had quite made up his mind that peace must be made. "There could be no doubt," I said, "that Pétain was a dangerous man at this juncture: he had always been a defeatist, even in the last war."
> . . . It was clear that France was near the end of organized resistance.
> . . . We must now concentrate our main efforts on the defence of our island.[5]

After the British had left Reynaud conferred briefly with Pétain and Weygand. Attempting to counter their insistence that, regardless of Britain, France should now seek an armistice, he reminded them that if the government unilaterally repudiated the agreement of March 28 not to make a separate peace, "England, *ipso facto,* would be liberated from all obligations toward us. In that case we would find ourselves alone at the mercy of Hitler." But the generals were sure by now that Britain too would soon be defeated and that British obligations toward France had no more value. Weygand, supported by Pétain, replied: "The country will never forgive you if, in order to remain faithful to England, you turn down the possibility of peace."[6]

Neither general had dared to put it quite so bluntly in the presence of Churchill. But now to Spears, whom he ran into a few minutes later, the Marshal was quite frank—if shortsighted. They talked for several minutes standing against the wall of the conference room.

"You have left us to fight alone," Pétain said, and the British general detected "an edge of subdued anger" to his words. "Since France cannot continue the struggle," the old soldier went on, "wisdom dictates that England also should seek peace, for certainly she cannot carry on alone. You have no army," he concluded. "What could you achieve where the French Army has failed?"[7]

The answer that history would give to that question could not be foreseen—not even faintly imagined—by the illustrious Marshal who, like so many French generals of limited vision, did not fully comprehend the character of the British race, the infinite possibilities of global war, and the unpredictability of human events. How could the old soldier, for whom the tiny sector of the planet that lay at the western corner of the European continent constituted the only world he knew, the only one in which he had lived and fought, possibly foresee, though the signs were already beginning to appear, that within eighteen months the two most powerful military and industrial powers on the globe would be engaged against the German foe?

All morning long on the 12th the news reaching General Headquarters from the sagging fronts grew worse. General Weygand went over the latest reports with Pétain, Georges, and Doumenc. West of Paris the enemy, after driving south from the lower Seine was across the Eure, pushing on Evreux. East of the capital the main German offensive was in full swing. Eight panzer divisions had cut through the thin French lines on the Aisne and were racing south, below the Marne, below Reims. "It was during this day," says Colonel Lyet, "that the last hope evaporated of pursuing a coordinated defense. . . . From the sea to the Argonne the situation of the armies worsened from hour to hour."[8]

The Supreme Commander drew the consequences. "The limit was reached," Weygand wrote later. "Our last line of defense fell apart everywhere. The Battle of France was lost. At 1:15 P.M. I gave the order to carry out my instructions of June 11 (for a general retreat). . . . My resolve was made. It was unshakable. In a few hours I would ask the government to conclude an armistice."[9]

At 4:30 P.M., with this in mind, he set out on the long drive over roads more encumbered than ever with milling refugees for the Château de Cangé, where the President of the Republic was installed and where a cabinet meeting had been called for 7 P.M. He did not know, he says, how the ministers, other than Reynaud, would react to his demand. But he would insist, he tells us, that it be met "in order to save what could be saved of the territory, the resources, and the military forces of France." The decision, as Weygand well knew, could only be made by the government. Not being a member of it the generalissimo had no constitutional right even to participate in its political discussions, and Reynaud would be much criticized by some of his cabinet colleagues for allowing him to do so—on this evening and during the four crucial days thereafter.

En route to the Château de Cangé, Weygand had been deeply moved, he says, by the plight of the refugees he passed along the roads. "The sad spectacle," he declares, "made me shudder." The twenty-three ministers, gathering in the hall of the château, were affected too. Outside the windows in the early evening they could see an endless stream of refugees shuffling by, pushing their carts and bicycles heaped with miscellaneous belongings, some stopping to eat their dinner in the garden, others preparing to bivouac for the night in the woods beyond, where they thought they might be safe from enemy bombing.

This was the first time the ministers had met together since the evening of June 9 in Paris. Except for Reynaud none of them had any idea of how far the military situation had worsened since their flight from the capital. What the Supreme Commander now proceeded to tell, as Ybarnegaray later related, "overwhelmed them. It was too terrible," he said, "to believe."

According to his own account Weygand got quickly to the main point.

He * concluded that only the cessation of hostilities can permit the maintenance of a little order and cohesion. If the battle continues it means the end of the troops, a military rout and disorder. And not only military disorder but general disorder as the result of the flight and the misery of the refugees mixed with the troops, all without food. In terminating General Weygand demands that the French government ask the German government for an armistice.[10]

According to several present the words of the generalissimo left the ministers in a stupor. That it had come to this so soon—after barely a month of battle—was too overwhelming to believe. Reynaud tried to rally his ministers against the general. Any armistice the Germans might offer, he declared, would be too dishonoring to accept. Looking at Weygand and Pétain, he said: "You take Hitler for Wilhelm I, the old gentleman who only took from us Alsace-Lorraine. But Hitler is a Genghis Khan." In that case, Weygand replied, "the French government would have done its duty and would not be responsible for the continuation of the war." The Premier

---

* Weygand referred to himself in the third person throughout his deposition at Riom, from which this account is taken.

proposed that the government move immediately to the "Breton Redoubt" and that, if it was lost, on to North Africa. Weygand retorted, he says, "that the 'Breton Redoubt' existed only in the mind of the Premier. There are no troops to defend it."

The flood of eloquence [Weygand deposed] continued. The ministers delivered veritable orations, certainly prepared in advance.* No interest in those who were doing the fighting. It was nauseating.

Finally, the generalissimo tracked back to the importance of keeping order in the country—an obsession which had been mushrooming in his mind for several days. "If an armistice is not immediately demanded," he said, "disorder will spread to the armies as it already has to the population."

"Order, disorder," Reynaud comments. "It had become the sole preoccupation of this man who, at that, had assumed the crushing burden of conducting the battle against the enemy."

Despite Weygand's insistence on an immediate armistice, he did not win over the cabinet. "Only Marshal Pétain," he laments, "supported me." He might have added Prouvost. The millionaire textile magnate and press lord would later boast—but only while France was down—that he had staunchly supported the generalissimo both in asking for an armistice and in turning down the idea of moving the government to North Africa. As Spears commented, "Prouvost had too much wealth to like the idea of abandoning it."

One other matter came up before the cabinet meeting adjourned. Reynaud had informed his colleagues of Churchill's request that no vital decision be taken without a further conference with him. The Premier therefore proposed to invite the British Prime Minister back tomorrow. Chautemps suggested that if he came, Churchill be invited to address the Council of Ministers. Reynaud reluctantly agreed. "It was impossible for me to refuse," he says. But this promise to produce Churchill at a full cabinet meeting as well as the implication that he was asking to see him so soon in order to discuss his government's "vital decision" would have consequences that he did not foresee and that would weaken his already shaky position. "You will pose him the question, won't you?" Chautemps had asked Reynaud as the meeting broke up at 11 P.M. The Premier's answer, if any, is not known, but he could have had no doubt what the question was that Chautemps wanted him to ask.

There was no doubt, either, in Baudouin's mind. Driving back at midnight to the Château de Chissay with Reynaud he pled with him to get Churchill's agreement, when they met the next day, to the French government's asking for an immediate armistice. But the tired Premier, says

---

* A typical example of Weygand's prejudice against the Republican politicians. As Marin, who was present, asks: how could the ministers have prepared statements in advance when none of them, except the Premier, even faintly suspected that the generalissimo would ask for an armistice?[11]

Baudouin, put up "an obstinate resistance" to the idea. "His decision is irrevocable." The two men fell into silence. "At 12:30 A.M.," Baudouin records in his journal, "in the vaulted dining room of the château, we dine under the anguished eyes of Madame de Portes, while General de Gaulle paces up and down with giant steps defending obstinately his conception of resistance in Brittany."[12] The Premier's mistress may have been anguished, but she was also determined, as was Baudouin, to wear the head of the government down.

The countess' presence, and determination, grated on the nerves of General Spears when he arrived at the Château de Chissay the next morning. To his "utter astonishment" he found her, as we have seen, garbed in a dressing gown over red pyjamas directing the arriving and departing motorcars from the steps of the main entrance, shouting to the drivers where to park. The astounded British general parked his own car, "so as to avoid the lady," he says, and went inside. Among other things he wanted to see a "Most Secret" telegram from the French Embassy in London which presumably had been repeated to him but which he had not received. He went into the office of Margerie, Reynaud's *chef de cabinet,* to inquire about it. The secretary explained that the telegram had got lost but that they were searching for it. Finally someone brought it in, all crumpled. *"Chut,"* exclaimed Margerie, "it was in Madame de Portes' bed!"

Spears, joined by the British Ambassador, lingered on in Margerie's office to go over telegrams and reports. But they were not alone. "Madame de Portes herself appeared three or four times," says Spears, "this time in normal female garb, whispering mysteriously to one or another." Spears thought he saw "hate in her eyes"—hate for the two Englishmen.

> What a very unattractive woman, [he says he thought]. . . . She was certainly not pretty and quite as certainly untidy. . . .

Later over lunch the Ambassador told Spears that during his private interview with Reynaud, "Madame de Portes had several times popped her head round the door."

> We had all been told [says Spears] that as soon as any of us left the Premier she dashed in, asking what had been said and assailing him with reproaches. "What did he say? What is the sense of going on? . . ."[13]

LAST MEETING OF ALLIED SUPREME COUNCIL, JUNE 13, 1940

Churchill, accompanied by Lords Halifax and Beaverbrook, arrived back at Tours from London shortly before 2 P.M. on June 13. The airport, they noticed as they flew over the field, had been heavily bombed the night before. There was no one to meet them and, viewing the damaged hangars and the nearly deserted airfield and the lack even of transportation to get into town, the Prime Minister sensed, he says, "the increasing degeneration of affairs." Finally he "borrowed" a car from the station commander and drove to the prefecture, where he had heard, he says, the French government had its headquarters. No official was there to greet them either, Mandel, the Minister of Interior, who had set up office there, being momentarily absent. No one knew where Reynaud was. The Prime Minister was hungry, and "insisted" he admits, on luncheon, which was finally found in what he describes as a café (it was actually the Grand Hôtel). Though closed, it opened up after some urging from the hungry visitors.

Paul Baudouin, the first official to arrive on the scene, found them there finishing their modest repast. "He began at once," says the Prime Minister, "in his soft, silky manner about the hopelessness of French resistance." Churchill declined to get into a discussion with him, saying only that he hoped America would come into the war, and that, in any case, Britain "would certainly fight on."

Having appeased their appetites, the British party returned to the prefecture, where they now found Mandel. He was nibbling at what Churchill describes as "an attractive chicken" while constantly talking on the telephone. In the general gloom he struck the British visitor as "a ray of sunshine—he wanted to fight on to the end in France in order to cover the largest possible movement to Africa."

Reynaud arrived at 3:30 P.M. Churchill thought he looked "depressed." The Premier had decided to dispense with the presence of Pétain and Weygand, who had been so defeatist in the meetings with the British the two days before. He feared, he explains, that the two generals would take advantage of Churchill's "nobility of soul and affection for France" in putting their case for an armistice and that the British leader might weaken into assenting. Only Baudouin, and later Margerie, were permitted to accompany him into the conference room, and then only to take notes. In the background, though, according to Elie J. Bois of the *Petit Parisien,* there lurked the ubiquitous Hélène de Portes. She kept flitting about between the hall and the courtyard, sending for Baudouin and insisting that he keep the Premier informed of her views.

Tell Paul that we must give up. We must make an end of it. There must be an armistice!

Finally, says the journalist, some official lost his patience. When Baudouin made one of his forays to the hallway, the official grabbed him and angrily said: "Get that woman out of here! If you don't, I'll do it myself."[14] Perhaps he did not know whose mistress she was.

Inside the prefecture, in Mandel's office, which the Minister of Interior, having devoured his chicken, vacated, the discussions between Reynaud and Churchill began. There is much controversy about them. Reynaud claims that there never was a question of his asking the British to release France from its obligation not to make a separate peace. Churchill and Spears say flatly that Reynaud did indeed pose the question. And Baudouin, certainly without foundation, maintained afterward that Churchill had agreed to France giving up unless the United States entered the war. Actually the French minutes kept by Margerie accord with those of the British cited by Churchill and Spears. It is only the interpretation of them by Reynaud, anxious for his place in history, that seems at fault and that led to so much recrimination among the French.

What he did, he says, was simply to inform Churchill "loyally" that Pétain and Weygand at the cabinet meeting the night before had demanded an armistice and that he had rejected it. "Thus it can be seen," he states, "that the question of France reneging on its engagement was not posed."

Churchill and Spears say it was, and the French minutes bear them out for the most part, though with a subtle difference. This was that while Reynaud did pose the question, he put it hypothetically.

If a French government, which would not include me—a hypothetical French government, let us say—said to the British government that it did not believe it had the right to abandon all of France to Germany . . . that it saw no hope, no light at the end of the tunnel . . . would not the British government agree that France, which had sacrificed the largest and the best part of its youth, while conserving Anglo-French solidarity, be authorized by Great Britain to make a separate peace? That is the question I pose.

"Under no circumstances," the French minutes say Churchill replied, "will we waste time in reproaches and recriminations. But that is a very different thing from becoming a consenting party to a separate peace made in contravention to the agreements we have made."

However hypothetically Reynaud may have put the question it seemed clear to Churchill that Reynaud was asking him to release France from her obligations. The Prime Minister asked for a recess to consult his colleagues. Returning from the garden, after talking things over with Halifax and Beaverbrook,* he left no doubt in Reynaud's mind what the British government's answer was.

On our return [Churchill says] I restated our position. We could not agree on a separate peace, however it might come. . . . We were not in a position to release France from her obligation.

Two of Reynaud's parliamentary colleagues, joined by Mandel, had tried to buck up the Premier during the recess. These were Herriot, Speaker of the Chamber, and Jeanneney, President of the Senate. According to Baudouin, all three violently reproached Reynaud when he told them what he had said to the British.

---

* The impetuous press lord, who was Churchill's Minister of Aircraft Production and a close friend, stoutly supported the Prime Minister. "Don't commit yourself to anything. . . . We are doing no good here. . . . Let's get along home."[15]

They will not accept that the President of the Council should have allowed it to be understood that one day France will decide on a separate armistice. All three are violently opposed to an armistice and they reproach the Premier for his "weakness."[16]

This scolding by three such prominent men is further evidence of what Reynaud actually told the British.

Searching desperately for some means of shoring up the faltering French leader, Churchill dangled the prospect of immediate and massive American aid. "The first thing to do," he proposed, "is to appeal to Roosevelt." Perhaps America would intervene "even in an election year." They should await the American President's response before "confronting the grave and decisive question you have posed." Regardless of Roosevelt's answer, Churchill assured Reynaud, "The cause of France will always be dear to us. We shall restore her *in all her power and dignity* (the words are in English in the French minutes) if we triumph. But that is a very different thing from asking our consent (to an armistice) before consultations with Roosevelt."

Reynaud grasped at the straw, fragile as he knew it to be. He would wire Roosevelt immediately, and he proceeded to outline what he would say. He would warn the President that if France went down Hitler would attack not only Britain but the United States. He asked Churchill to send a similarly strongly worded cable to Washington, and this was agreed. One wonders at the British leader raising such false hopes in the desperate French Premier, whose army was collapsing and whose government was in disarray. For Churchill, better than anyone else in Europe, knew the American political situation and could not have believed that Roosevelt, despite his sympathies for France and Britain, could take the United States into the war in time to save the French.

In his own mind he seems to have acknowledged this, for next he turned to Reynaud with stern words of warning of what might happen to France if she gave up and were occupied by the enemy while Britain continued fighting.

For the war will continue and will be more and more terrible. We are fast approaching a blockade of all of Europe. Famine and desperate suffering will certainly ensue. . . . France will not be able to escape the consequences. It is to be feared that a Franco-British antagonism will develop as a result. We must face up to that problem too.

The prospect of the British ally blockading France and thus compounding the sufferings of the wounded country did not cheer Reynaud up. It would be catastrophic, he said. "It would produce a new and grave situation in Europe."

The Prime Minister was now becoming brutally frank. He seemed to accept, despite or because of what Reynaud said, that France would soon throw in the sponge.

"How much time do we have before you ask for an armistice?" he snapped. "A week? Or more?"

Reynaud evaded a direct answer. It would be a terrible thing, he said, if France and Britain separated. It worried him deeply to think that if the war continued Great Britain "would indirectly inflict more suffering on the French people." Finally the talk returned to how Roosevelt would respond to their appeal. Both men blew hot and cold. "If he consents to come into the war," Churchill said, "then victory is assured." But he did not really believe that America would come in, at least for the time being. "If his response is unfavorable," the Prime Minister said a few minutes later, "and then if you announce your decision to treat separately (with the Germans) we shall have many problems to consider." For his part Reynaud declared that he was "convinced that Roosevelt would take a step forward. . . . I shall try to get him to declare war. . . . We can then discuss with the British government the conditions under which we can continue the war." But Reynaud, who also knew the United States well, did not really believe that Roosevelt would declare war—any more than Churchill did.

Make no mistake, if Roosevelt's response is negative [Reynaud said in conclusion] that will create a new situation with grave consequences. I have to tell you that.

It was agreed in the end that they would await the response of the American President and then meet again in the light of that. Churchill brought up one question before adjournment. He asked Reynaud to turn over to Britain some 400 German fliers shot down over France, many or most of them by the RAF. The Premier readily agreed.* It was now ten minutes to six, and Churchill and his party drove off to the airfield and boarded their plane for London.

That evening in a long cable to Roosevelt the Prime Minister informed him of the meeting at Tours.

I cannot exaggerate its critical character. They were very nearly gone. Weygand had advocated an armistice while he still had enough troops to prevent France from lapsing into anarchy. Reynaud asked us whether, in view of the sacrifices and sufferings of France, we would release her from the obligation about not making a separate peace. . . . I did not hesitate in the name of the British Government to refuse consent to an armistice or separate peace. . . .[18]

Back at Tours de Gaulle, who had arrived at the prefecture during

---

* Because of the confusion of the French government and Army—to put the best possible face on it—the German pilots were not delivered to the British. They all became, Churchill comments wryly, "available for the Battle of Britain, and we had to shoot them down a second time."[17]

the recess, emerged from the meeting depressed—with both Reynaud and Churchill. He thought the Prime Minister had shown too much "comprehension, full of pity" for the idea of France seeking an armistice. He resented Churchill's "bargaining for the French fleet against an armistice while there was still time."* He thought Reynaud was weakening. Accosting him in the corridor he asked, "not without vivacity," he says: "Is it possible that you conceive of France asking for an armistice?"

"Certainly not!" Reynaud answered. "But I had to impress the British in order to obtain more aid."[19]

The gloomy young general became more depressed when he learned, he told Spears, that Baudouin was telling the newspaper correspondents that "Churchill had shown complete comprehension of the French situation and would understand if France concluded an armistice and a separate peace." He asked Spears if the Prime Minister had said that and received a resounding no. But it was not enough. That evening de Gaulle wrote out his resignation from the government. But summoned late in the night by Mandel he tore it up. The stern Minister of Interior insisted that he stay in the government to help counter the defeatists. On such a slender thread his whole subsequent career hung that night.

Reynaud deliberately had not invited Churchill to attend the French cabinet meeting, as he had promised to his colleagues the night before that he would do. As he hurried now to the Château de Cangé, where the Council of Ministers was meeting under Lebrun, he did not realize what a storm this omission would blow up. His lack of candor about it, and about his talk with the Prime Minister, only made his difficulties worse.[20]

A STORMY CABINET MEETING

The Premier found his colleagues and the generalissimo in no mood for harmony and brotherly love. The cabinet meeting had been called for 3 P.M. and notice of its postponement to 5 o'clock—it was now nearly 6 P.M.—had not reached the scattered ministers. Since 3 o'clock most of them had been cooling their heels in the garden of the Château de Cangé, resentful of the delay, their nerves on edge at the prospect of military collapse and perhaps capture by the approaching enemy. Pétain and Weygand, strolling together on the lawn and occasionally dropping a word to a minister, had not cheered them up, and the old Marshal, attired in a gray flannel suit and sporting a straw hat and a cane, had further depressed their spirits by spreading dark rumors of what was happening this very day in Paris, and which, when solemnly palmed off as fact later during the session by Weygand, would panic them until the truth was established.

"Great uproar!" Thus Weygand described the cabinet's reaction at the sight of Reynaud showing up without Churchill. Chautemps protested

---

* It is almost certain that de Gaulle errs here. There is no mention in either the French minutes or in that part of the British record published of Churchill having raised the question of the French fleet. Reynaud specifically denies it.

bitterly and was joined by Bouthillier, the new Minister of Finance, whom Reynaud had recently rescued from obscurity and who, as so often happens in life, apparently had not forgiven him for it. The Premier was less than frank in his explanation of why he had not brought Churchill along. He himself says that he simply mentioned that Churchill had had to return to London "without having said any more about his desire to see my colleagues." Weygand says he understood him to add "in a very embarrassed manner," that he "did not dispose of the person of Winston Churchill, who was very pressed to return to England." In his memoirs Reynaud gives contradictory versions. In Volume I (*Cœur* . . . , p. 765) he says he would have brought Churchill along "if he had persisted in his desire to appear before the cabinet." In Volume II (*Envers* . . . , p. 405) he states: "I did not ask Churchill, who had not expressed the desire, to come to Cangé because I intended to tell the cabinet that the accord between Churchill and me to continue the war was complete and because it would have been repugnant to make him listen to a plea of Weygand for an armistice. I already had told him enough on that."

For his part, Churchill says he and his colleagues "should have been very willing" to go to Cangé "no matter how late we had to fly home. But we were never invited; nor did we know there was to be a French cabinet meeting."*[21]

A number of those present and the President of the Republic himself, who presided at the meeting, later testified that if the indomitable British Prime Minister had come to Cangé ánd with his dynamism fired up his faltering French friends to stay in the fight, history might have taken another course. They believed that Reynaud's failure to produce him was a turning point in the events that would now follow.

Churchill's absence was not the only occasion for a row that evening in the Château de Cangé. Reynaud immediately provoked a second one by telling his colleagues that he had informed the Prime Minister that the government had decided the evening before to continue the war at Britain's side. As we have seen, Reynaud had told him anything but that. The statement, at any rate, raised a new uproar. Bouthillier pulled out of his pocket a written statement, which he proceeded to read, vehemently attacking the Premier and claiming that the cabinet the night before had pronounced for an armistice. This time Lebrun, who rarely intervened in the debates of his quarreling ministers, spoke up. "How can you

---

* Much later when I pointed out to Reynaud the discrepancy between his version and Churchill's, he responded in a letter of August 29, 1965:

Churchill is right. Instead of asking him to be present at the humiliating spectacle of Pétain, Weygand, and certain of my colleagues reproaching him for the insufficiency of British help, such as sending only 10 divisions, I preferred to tell the cabinet that the accord between Churchill and me was perfect on continuing the war. I recognize that perhaps it would have been better for me to ask him to attend the cabinet meeting.

say that the Council of Ministers yesterday came out in favor of an armistice?" He had heard no such thing. On the contrary, he said, the government had taken a stand against an armistice.

Weygand was next called on to report on the military situation. As on the previous evening, the generalissimo, who had no constitutional right to participate in a cabinet debate, launched into a long harangue, arguing not only that an immediate armistice was necessary but that the members of the government were shirking their duty in not asking for it. Caustically and with increasing vehemence, according to many present, he lambasted the ministers for their lack of courage. Carried away by the torrent of his own words he also said some things that he would later rue. He recalled his "remarks" in his deposition at Riom, speaking always of himself in the third person.

General Weygand last night in this assembly said that France no longer had the means of continuing the struggle with any hope of defending the rest of her territory. The ministers who made speeches affirmed the contrary. General Weygand found himself the sole "jerk" in face of so many courageous men. General Weygand could also make capital out of such verbal courage. From the châteaux where he set up he could easily pose as a hero . . .

Soon he was back on his old aberration that the government should never have left Paris in the first place. He repeated his historic analogy of the Roman senators remaining in Rome when the barbarian Gauls arrived. This was preparatory to introducing a new argument which would weigh heavily on the government and the military in the next few days: that, come what might, the government must never leave the soil of France to try to continue the war from French North Africa across the Mediterranean.

Paris has been abandoned. But at least the government must have the courage to remain in France no matter what happens. And for two reasons.

First, it is at this price only that the French will accept the heavy sacrifices demanded of them. You may say that it is a greater sacrifice for the ministers to abandon the soil of the country. No one will accept that. The people will say that the ministers are continuing to insist that the population be killed, bombed, and burned after having taken care to put themselves tranquilly in the shelter of Africa or some other place.

"Secondly"—and now the generalissimo poured out his sarcasm and scorn on the civilian ministers.

Secondly, in admitting that they would be well received in our colonies—which is by no means certain—what authority do they think they would conserve in France? How long would they remain outside it? The time necessary for the American factories to turn out the planes and tanks permitting them to reconquer it? That would take several years. Do they imagine that anyone in France will even remember them? And then how will they reconquer France? By bombing and bombarding our towns, our compatriots? That is an absurd and odious program. The Commander in Chief, at least, will not follow it.

He would not follow it, but that "absurd and odious program" was precisely the one by which France eventually would be liberated.

Weygand fired one last shot of defiance. He himself would never leave the soil of France, he said—"even if they put him in irons."

This was more than a gesture of defiance. It was notice of a refusal to obey the orders of the constitutional government by the Commander in Chief of the armed forces. It challenged the authority of the Republic. It raised the age-old question (which the German generals would bring up—for opposite reasons—at the end of the war) of whether a soldier's obedience was absolute or subject to the dictates of his conscience. Before the Parliamentary Investigating Committee after the war Weygand was pressed on the question and when cornered, became confused and contradictory. Asked whether he thought he had the right to disobey the laws of the nation, which gave the government sole authority to carry on war, he responded: "If the government had given me the order to quit the armies (and go to North Africa) I would have refused." During his questioning he raised the problem of one's conscience justifying disobedience. He claimed the right for himself but denied it to the troops under him.

THE PRESIDENT: Then you do not accept total obedience to the government?

WEYGAND: . . . I am a free man. Consequently, when my conscience forbids me to do something I cannot do it.

LOUIS MARIN: For the soldier on the battlefield do you admit his right to disobey when his conscience so demands?

WEYGAND: Ah, no!

THE PRESIDENT: Your conception of obedience, general, strikes me as a little curious.[22]

It would become even more curious in the days immediately following this cabinet meeting when the generalissimo would refuse to obey an even more important order of the government.

The issue raised by Weygand—and by Pétain a little later in the cabinet meeting—produced a profound conflict between the civilian government and the military which was now grafted on that between the ministers. Later, on reflection, many of the Ministers saw that it should have been resolved then and there, on June 13 at Cangé. But the Premier and his government were too shaky to force the issue and stand up to the generals. "I must say," Georges Monnet, Minister of Blockade, told the Investigating Committee, "I was a little surprised that General Weygand was not put in his place at this meeting." After the session was over Reynaud told the President of the Republic that it would no longer be possible for him to admit Weygand to the cabinet meetings. "We will keep him outside in a nearby room and call him in, if necessary, to report on the military situation. As soon as he has given this he will have to retire." Reynaud says that the attitude of Weygand at the cabinet meetings would have justified the government in relieving him of his command. But in this perilous hour, when the stock of the government of a country going down to defeat was at its lowest ebb in the minds of the people, he hesitated to take such a drastic step.

Weygand was not quite finished talking. He now provoked a new scene that for a moment sent shivers down the spines of the uneasy ministers. In a dramatic tone, as Reynaud remembered it, the generalissimo declared he had just received information that the Communists had taken over in Paris, disarmed the police, and put Thorez, their leader, in the Elysée, the presidential palace. This startling news appeared to bolster Weygand in his demand, ceaselessly repeated for several days, that he needed what was left of the army to maintain order and put down red revolution. No one seems to have thought for a minute that even if the report was true the Communists would not long remain in power in Paris. The Germans had reached the outskirts of the capital and would have no trouble in putting them down when they moved in the next day. Nevertheless, the ministers were thunderstruck.

The source of Weygand's information, as even his faithful aide, Colonel Bourget, writes, remains "dubious." According to the later testimony of Mattéo Connet, *chef de cabinet* of the Minister of Marine, Pétain had told Weygand of a Communist takeover in Paris while they strolled in the garden at Cangé waiting for Reynaud to show up at the cabinet meeting. Not content with telling the generalissimo the news, the Marshal spread it to all who would listen. Alarmed, Connet says he asked Lebrun's Secretary-General to phone Roger Langeron, the Paris Prefect of Police, to see if it was true. The police chief responded that it was nonsense. His force had not been disarmed, there was no Communist uprising, and all was calm in the capital. A note with this information was sent in to President Lebrun during the cabinet meeting but the officer carrying it mistakenly handed it to Weygand.[23]

Now Mandel, as Minister of Interior, intervened. Before leaving Tours shortly before 6 o'clock he had instructed an aide to call Langeron in Paris for the latest information, and the police chief's response had been telephoned to him at the château. He now strode out of the cabinet meeting and put through another call to Paris on the sole telephone in the castle. Langeron again confirmed that all was quiet in Paris. Returning to the meeting room and addressing the President of the Republic, Mandel said:

"I have Langeron on the line. Would you like to speak to him?" Lebrun nodded no and Mandel then reported that there was no truth to the rumor that Weygand had peddled.* Later that evening Mandel told Spears that "Weygand had tried to panic the cabinet" with his tale of a Communist uprising in Paris. "He was," said Mandel, "beside himself with excitement."[25]

The generalissimo had no great love for Mandel and this state of affairs provided one final scene at the cabinet meeting that, in contrast with all that had gone before, was not without its element of comedy— though this may not have been apparent to the distraught ministers. Suddenly General Weygand stalked angrily out of the conference room claiming that Mandel was *smiling* at him. The President of the Republic tried to stop him. As Lebrun recounted the incident to the Parliamentary Investigating Committee:

> He got up brusquely, saying: "I'm leaving. A minister laughed at me." This was supposedly Mandel. Mandel had a rictus in his face sometimes that one mistook for a smile. Mandel had not really laughed, and I said to the general: "Really, no one has laughed. Everyone in fact is saddened by your report. Pray, continue."[26]

But the Supreme Military Commander would not continue. He stomped out.

> We could hear him shouting [Georges Monnet later testified] as he left the Council of Ministers with a rare insolence before the ministerial secretaries in the vestibule of the château. Pardon me for quoting him exactly . . . he said: "They sit with their asses on their chairs, and they don't give a damn that all this time the French army is being massacred. They choose not to get it through their heads that it is time to make an armistice."

The generalissimo was so beside himself, Mandel told Spears that evening in recounting the incident, "that he remarked before my private secretary that the ministers were mad and ought to be arrested."[27]

The usually silent Pétain had also spoken up at the cabinet meeting in support of the Supreme Commander—or rather, he had solemnly read a statement which he had written out the night before. His eyesight none

---

* Weygand in his memoirs and in his postwar testimony states that he also left the room to telephone to General Dentz, who assured him there was no revolutionary happening in Paris. Weygand recounts a somewhat mysterious story that his first report of a Communist takeover came from one of his aides, who got it over the telephone from the Ministry of Marine in Paris. Since this Ministry, like all the others, had moved to the Loire three days before, one wonders if anyone more important than a concierge was left at the Ministry in Paris. Weygand swears a "service officer" gave the report to his aide.[24] If so, it is strange this officer had not informed his naval superiors on the Loire.

too good at his advanced age—he was also becoming a little hard of hearing—he had moved to the window so as to get enough light from the waning summer afternoon to make out his written words. He too was firmly against the government quitting France and, at any rate, would not himself leave it. The only way out, he declared, was to ask for an armistice. For the first time the Marshal developed at some length before the cabinet the ideas which would dominate him and his course of action from now on to the end. They had been slowly turning over in his mind, as we have seen, since the beginning of the war. After dismissing the idea that a prolonged stand could be made in a "redoubt"—in Brittany or elsewhere, he went on:

It is impossible for the government to emigrate, to desert, to abandon the territory of France. The duty of the government, regardless of what happens, is to remain in the country or else it will not be recognized as such. To deprive France of her natural defenders in a period of general disarray is to deliver it to the enemy. It is to kill the soul of France and consequently to render impossible its renaissance.

The renewal of France can only be obtained eventually by remaining where we are rather than by depending on a reconquest of our territory by Allied guns under conditions and with a delay which it is impossible to foresee.

I am therefore against abandoning French soil. We must accept the sufferings which will be imposed on the country and on her sons. The French renaissance will be the fruit of this suffering. . . . As far as I am concerned, and outside the government if necessary, I shall refuse to leave the metropolitan soil. I shall rest among the French people to share its pains and miseries.

The armistice, in my opinion, is the necessary condition for the perpetuity of an eternal France.[28]

The eighty-four-year-old Marshal, it seems obvious from these remarks and from what happened the next day, the last one for the government on the Loire, felt history breathing down his neck. Indeed he had begun to sense it since leaving Madrid the middle of May, as his parting remark to Franco that he soon might be called to power showed.

The cabinet meeting on the late afternoon of June 13, like that of the evening before, had decided nothing. But the intervention of Weygand and Pétain had shown the government where the military stood and what it intended to do. It had impressed at least some of the civilian ministers and succeeded in opening a split between them. Bouthillier, Baudouin, Prouvost, and others had been won over to the side of the generals, and Chautemps, though he later denied it, was leaning that way. Jean Ybarnegaray, a right-wing deputy and Minister of State, later summed up what was happening to the civilians in the cabinet. Until now he had been a fiercely anti-German nationalist, determined to fight on. Testifying after the war before the High Court at his own trial he explained: "When I heard General Weygand, for me the incarnation of the great Foch, say: 'We can no longer fight on, we are defeated'; when I saw Marshal Pétain rally to this view, my resistance completely collapsed. From then on I was for an armistice."[29]

Pétain, with a boldness he had not previously shown in political affairs, now took the initiative. On the morning of June 14 he saw Admiral Darlan, whose magnificent fleet had scarcely fired a shot so far in the war— even against the vulnerable Italians. The canny sailor, like almost everyone else, was wavering and the Marshal apparently knew it. "We are lost," Pétain told the admiral. "We must therefore envisage forming a Consulate. Why shouldn't you, Darlan, become the first Consul?" According to Connet, of the Ministry of Marine, to whom Darlan recounted the conversation immediately afterward, the admiral told him: "I'm becoming the *chouchou* of the Marshal." And Connet adds that perhaps it was from this moment on that Darlan believed he "could get to the top without ever aspiring to descend from it."[30] So on June 14 the Commander in Chief of the Navy was won over.

Pétain left immediately for Bordeaux, where the government would meet the next day. By now he seems to have become fascinated by the new role he was envisaging for himself. Before departing the Loire he had a talk with Baudouin, who he knew had also come over on his side.

The Marshal tells me [Baudouin recounts] that he has decided to finish with it all, that he finds the attitude of the Cabinet "ignoble and cowardly." He has fixed as the last deadline Saturday at noon. (June 15, that is, the next day.) He is going to send a message to General Weygand to tell him that his presence at Bordeaux is necessary.[31]

The message reached the Commander in Chief at 5:30 P.M. on June 14. It read:

The Council of Ministers decided last evening not to take a decision on asking Germany for an armistice until after the response of Roosevelt to a telegram sent him last night asking that he declare war on Germany.

The Marshal considers that the last deadline for reaching a decision is Saturday noon. The Council of Ministers will meet tomorrow at the end of the morning to decide. The presence of General Weygand is necessary. The Commander in Chief should present himself at Bordeaux, 58 rue Saint-Genès, the domicile of Baudouin, telephone 868-20, *before 10:30.*[32]

The conspirators appeared to be moving fast. As Louis Marin points out in his study of them, the Vice-Premier, the Marshal of France, was, behind the back of the Chief of Government, ordering the Commander in Chief to leave his command post (which was being moved that day to Vichy) to participate in resolving a question which was essentially the business of the government and to come to see him personally before appearing at a cabinet meeting.*[33]

On the morning of June 14, before departing Tours for Bordeaux, Reynaud, weary from fighting his own generals and depressed, as were all the Ministers, at the news that the Germans had just entered Paris, got off his last appeal to President Roosevelt. He was desperate.

> I know that a declaration of war does not lie within your hands alone. But I have to tell you that . . . if you cannot give France in the coming days a positive assurance that the United States will come into the struggle within a short space of time . . . you will then see France go under like a drowning man after having thrown a last look toward the land of liberty from which she was expecting salvation.[35]

There could be no question, as Reynaud well knew, of the United States declaring war on Germany in an immediate future. Neither the Congress nor the American people yet had the faintest idea that the fall of France, which might well bring down Great Britain, mortally endangered American survival in a world which then would be at the mercy of the totalitarian powers. Was the harassed Premier making this emotional appeal for the record?† And more—since he knew what the answer would have to be for the time being—to serve as one excuse for his abandoning the struggle himself?

His nervous powers near exhaustion,‡ Paul Reynaud, along with the members of his government, his mistress, and the President of the Republic, set out from Tours on the morning of June 14 for Bordeaux, inching their way in their cars through the endless streams of forlorn refugees encumbering the roads. Anthony J. Drexel Biddle, who was acting as

---

* Weygand relates in his memoirs that before answering Pétain's call he "loyally" telephoned Reynaud, told him of the message and asked his assent to going to Bordeaux. He says the Premier told him he was "always welcome at a cabinet meeting."[34]

† Secretary of State Cordell Hull and Ambassador Bullitt thought so—even before this. Apprised by Bullitt on May 18 that Reynaud intended that evening to send a personal appeal to Roosevelt asking that he induce Congress to declare war on Germany, Hull noted with approval Bullitt's rejoinder to Léger that "it would be purely for the record—Reynaud wishes some day to be able to show he had appealed to the President of the United States and the President had rejected his appeal."[36]

‡ Spears, who saw Reynaud late the night before, says he "looked ghastly . . . still and white." The Premier had stopped at Mandel's office in the prefecture at Tours where the British general was conferring. Reynaud, unusually silent, soon left. "He had not been gone five minutes," Spears recounts, "before Madame de Portes threw the door open. Mandel and I stared in astonishment. . . . She [looked] hostile and aggressive. . . . Her swift glance searched every corner, it darted under the table as if the Premier might have been hiding there. She then stepped back into the shadowy corridor. . . . As the door closed Mandel said: 'Her influence has been sinister this day.' "[37]

U.S. Chargé d'Affaires in the absence of Ambassador Bullitt, who foolishly had decided to remain in Paris, where there was nothing to do and from which he could no longer exercise his considerable influence on the French government, saw the Premier just before he left.

He found him, he reported to Washington, "in a state of profound depression and anxiety." It was clear to Biddle, as he duly reported, that "in the absence of some positive action by us within the next 48 hours the French government will feel that there is no course left but surrender."[38]

34

THE AGONY OF BORDEAUX
THE FALL OF REYNAUD
PETAIN TAKES OVER
June 14–16, 1940

Toward evening of Friday, June 14, the haggard members of the French government straggled into Bordeaux. Though it had served as the provisional capital in 1871 when the Germans had taken Paris and again briefly in the autumn of 1914, when the same enemy had almost taken it, this great port city in the southwest seemed to those who wanted to continue the struggle to be the worst possible place for the shaky, harassed government to set up office. It was in a state of chaos. An air of defeatism, of despair, hung heavy over the city. Those who were there that fateful mid-June weekend remembered afterward that one could feel, could almost smell, the decomposition of the government, the High Command, the Army, the State, the flesh and bones of society, setting in.

Bordeaux was overflowing with refugees clamoring for shelter and food, besieging the hotels and restaurants. The streets were blocked by thousands of cars whose fleeing owners could not find accommodation, who when night came simply slept in their vehicles parked at the curbs. Others slept on park benches or on chairs or on the floors in the halls of beleaguered hotels. Tempers were short. Fear spread: fear of being bombed, fear of being overtaken by the advancing Germans, fear for the fate of one's family left behind in the disordered flight. For most this was the end of the road. For some it was the beginning. The Jews, especially those who had fled from Germany and from the other lands taken by Hitler, scrambled for passports and visas that would permit them to escape the clutches of the approaching German Nazis. Most of them got short shrift. Anti-Semitism, latent since the Dreyfus days but rekindled by Nazi propaganda and by an aberration that the Jews had pushed France into the disastrous war, grew in the swollen, uneasy city. Léon Blum, despite his eminence in French politics, could not at first find lodgings even in a shabby hotel because he was a Jew regarded as a "warmonger." The deputy Audeguil finally took him in.

The regional military governor, the regional prefect, the mayor of Bordeaux, struggled to restore some sort of order in the chaotic city, requisitioning headquarters for the displaced ministries, rooms for the ministers and their families and for the 200-odd members of Parliament who had managed to reach the provisional capital. The mayor was the most successful. This was Adrien Marquet, a dentist by profession, the leader in the Chamber, where he was a deputy, of the Neo-Socialist faction, and who for years, after he left the Socialist Party in 1933, had been increasingly fascinated by Fascism and National Socialism and who now had joined those demanding an armistice. An energetic man, he took over the problem of lodging, assigning the "hawks" to hotels in the vicinity of the railroad station where the danger of bombing was the greatest, and finding accommodation for the "doves"—those who wanted to capitulate—in better hotels in safer parts. Thus for his friend Pierre Laval, who was originally given quarters in a second-class hotel, he found a suite in the finest hostelry in town, the Splendide, removing the former Queen of Portugal from that accommodation and indeed from the hotel. In fairness to the mayor it should be added that he also found a room at the Splendide for the Countess de Portes. Reynaud, after all, was still the head of the government. Marquet did another favor for Laval. He installed him in an office next to his at the Hôtel de Ville, which, beginning the next day, June 15, would become the center for intrigues against Reynaud, against continuing the war, and for the hoisting of Pétain to the top. The last objective, as we have seen, had long been on Laval's mind.

Laval believed his hour had come. Resentful at having been kept out of power since 1936, blaming the "Left" and the British for his eclipse, he now felt that the disaster which had befallen France offered him a golden personal opportunity. On the 14th at his office in his newspaper *Moniteur* at Clermont-Ferrand, he had conferred with numerous politicians, including Colonel de La Rocque, who might be helpful to him. To his friend Senator Jacques Bardoux he said:

> Let Reynaud bear the shame of asking for a capitulation. But he must not be allowed to negotiate it. . . . He has insulted Hitler and Mussolini and will receive the hardest conditions. I'm going to ask Marshal Pétain to let me do it.[1]

Reynaud arrived at Bordeaux at 6:30 P.M. to find the city already seething with intrigues against him among the defeatist ministers and politicians.* He was lodged in the residence of the general commanding

---

* The Countess de Portes followed him in a separate car loaded with her belongings. She was not the only mistress accompanying a cabinet minister. Mandel had brought along Béatrice Bretty, a charming actress. A statesman's mistress does not concern a historian unless her influence on him and on others influences events. Madame de Portes, unlike Madame Bretty, exercised that influence—hence her part in this narrative.

the 18th military region in the rue Vital-Carles. Nearby, President Lebrun was given quarters in the home of the regional prefect. Mandel installed himself in the prefecture. Marshal Pétain preferred to lodge in a private home in the Boulevard Wilson at the other end of town but he held court mostly at the Hôtel de Ville where Laval and Marquet were busy rounding up supporters for him.

Though utterly exhausted by the long automobile trip through the throngs of refugees along the roads and by the mounting pressures on him, the Premier still seemed full of fight. He recognized at once the defeatism rampant among his ministers and the 200 members of Parliament. "The intrigues," he says, "were already developing" and he felt himself being spied upon. His telephones, as he learned two days later, were being tapped by the military. Despite his weariness and discouragement he saw quite clearly, as he took stock of the situation that evening, that the Battle of France was irretrievably lost. The retreating army was fast disintegrating and was no longer capable of making a sustained stand. But he believed that France, behind the protection of its unscathed navy, could continue to wage war from its North African possessions—from Morocco, Tunisia, and Algeria, the last juridically a part of metropolitan France.

He discussed it that evening with General de Gaulle, who in his best obstreperous manner tried to buck him up. The young general and undersecretary already had made up his mind about what had to be done and what he himself would do.

> For the last three days [de Gaulle says he told him] we have been speedily rolling toward capitulation. . . . I myself refuse to submit to an armistice. If you remain here you are going to be submerged by the defeat. You must go to Algeria at once. Are you—yes or no—decided on that?
>
> "*Oui!*", Reynaud responded.
>
> In that case, I said, I should go tomorrow to London to arrange for British shipping to help us. Where will I find you again?
>
> "You will find me in Algeria," the Premier said.[2]

De Gaulle arranged to drive to Brittany and take a destroyer from there to London. Dining in the restaurant of the Hôtel Splendide that evening just before his departure, he saw Pétain at a nearby table. "I went over to him," de Gaulle recounts, "to greet him silently. He shook my hand but without saying a word. I would never see him again, ever."[3]

He thought a good deal about the illustrious old soldier, he says, as he drove throughout the night toward Brittany.

> What current was carrying him along, and toward what fatal destiny? The whole career of this exceptional man had been a long effort to repress his feelings. Too proud to intrigue, too strong for mediocrity, too ambitious to be *arriviste,* he nourished in his solitude a passion to dominate, hardened for a long time by the sense of his own value, the obstacles he had encountered, the scorn

he had of others. Military glory had washed away his bitterness. But it had not satisfied him because he had not loved it alone. Now, suddenly, in the extreme winter of his life, events offered to his gifts and to his pride the occasion—so long awaited!—to bloom again without limits: on one condition, however, that he accept the disaster as the steppingstone to his elevation and decorate it with his glory.[4]

Toward midnight, after de Gaulle had left, Reynaud received the British Ambassador, Sir Ronald Campbell, and General Spears, who brought him a personal message of encouragement from Churchill coupled with a warning that Britain expected France to abide by her pledge not to make a separate peace. Spears found the Premier "worn out . . . forlorn and undecided."[5]

But one thing Reynaud knew. The weekend that was now dawning, Saturday and Sunday, June 15 and 16, would see the supreme test— for him, his government, his country. One way or the other a final, fateful decision would have to be made. Arrayed against him would be Pétain and Weygand, the military power against the civilian. And the latter, as the last cabinet meetings at Cangé had shown, was becoming divided and weakened. He was no longer sure that his own ministers or the President of the Republic would back him. And Parliament, the supreme arbiter in the Republic, which might have sustained him in this hour of uncertainty, could not be called for lack of a quorum. In the disorder of the debacle not enough members had been able to reach Bordeaux. The Chamber and Senate had ceased to function.

BORDEAUX, SATURDAY, JUNE 15: REYNAUD ATTACKED, OUTMANEUVERED, WEAKENED

General Weygand, after a tedious sixteen hour journey by train from Briare, arrived at Bordeaux at 2:30 P.M. on June 15 and, as the Marshal had directed, went first to see him. He found Pétain at the Grand Hôtel in conference with Admiral Darlan, Bouthillier, and Baudouin. The last two, though political protégés of Reynaud, had now turned against their benefactor and were staunchly supporting the two generals. At the beginning of this day no one knew where Darlan stood. The Commander in Chief of the Navy, who regarded the fleet as his private fief and brooked no interference from his superiors, political or military, had met Herriot, the Speaker of the Chamber, that very morning and asked him: "Is it true that those bastards Pétain and Weygand wish to conclude an armistice? If so, I'm leaving with the fleet."[*6] Darlan, as everyone recognized, was a

---

* On May 28, when the evacuation at Dunkirk was getting under way and the possibility of an armistice first loomed, Admiral Darlan had sent a highly secret order to Admiral Le Luc, his Chief of Staff, advising him what to do if an armistice with Germany stipulated handing over the fleet.

"I do not intend," he said, "to carry out that order." He instructed Le Luc to prepare orders directing the fleet, in such a case, to sail to *British* ports, underlining

key figure in the situation. If he made off with the fleet it would be impossible for the generals to get an armistice. Hitler would not be interested in granting one. He had already as good as conquered France. But he needed to get the French fleet, or at least to neutralize it, so that it could not be used by the French to make a stand in North Africa or to help the British in warding off an attack on the British Isles.

Like almost everyone else in Bordeaux this Saturday, however, the salty admiral was beginning to cave in. At 9 A.M., in answer to a summons, he had seen Reynaud, who urged him to get a move on in assembling shipping to carry troops and supplies over the Mediterranean to North Africa. The admiral had responded that little could be done. The "ambitious" government plan, as he had got it from de Gaulle, he said, was "ridiculous." Now, in midafternoon, at the Grand Hôtel, he was consorting with those very two "bastards" he had denounced to Herriot in the morning. As the latter would remark the next day when Darlan's position became clear to all: "This admiral certainly knows how to swim." His meeting with the Marshal and the generalissimo and their two civilian supporters in the cabinet did not last long. It was quickly agreed that an armistice must be demanded at once. The military chiefs seemed heartened by Baudouin's assertion, which was false, that Churchill at Tours two days before had told Reynaud he "fully understood the painful necessity for France to ask for an armistice."[7] This lie seems to have eased the consciences of the two old soldiers and the admiral, who were well aware of France's solemn obligations to Britain not to make a separate peace.

Earlier in the day the Marshal had reiterated his demand for an armistice when he called on Reynaud and read him a declaration. He had also repeated his opposition to the government moving to North Africa. If it did, he said again, he would not accompany it. Reynaud listened without saying a word. There had ceased to be any meeting ground between the Premier and the illustrious soldier. Pétain departed in silence.

But the real showdown in Bordeaux this crucial weekend was between the head of government and the head of the fighting forces. This was inevitable not only because of their respective positions in a conflict that essentially was between the civil and military authorities but because of their clashing temperaments. The first row began just prior to the cabinet meeting called for 4 P.M. when Weygand, after his visit to Pétain, called on Reynaud. There was something of the manner of fighting cocks in these bitter adversaries, both diminutive, trim and cocky, like the bird, and they were soon at each other, with the fiery little general, in a characteristically violent mood, leading the attack. They were no longer, as Weygand

---

the word. It was in this message that Darlan laid it down that no order for the disposal of the fleet must be obeyed unless it carried the signature *"Xavier-François,"* which he would adopt for his own in case of necessity. It was part of his string of middle names.

later said, speaking the same language. And the generalissimo's arrogance, his undisguised contempt from the bottom of his royalist heart for the Republic and its politicians, further widened the gulf between the two antagonists.

The dispute between them was not over whether the army in France was finished. They agreed that it was, and that the consequences must now be faced. What divided them, and indeed what divided the cabinet itself and the government and the High Command, was something else—simple but fundamental. It now came out as the two men flew at each other.

"I have made up my mind," Reynaud said. "You must ask for a cease-fire as did the Commander in Chief of the Dutch Army." He recalled that this had enabled Queen Wilhelmina and her government to move to London, escape the Germans, and continue at the side of the Allies. As for him, Reynaud said, he was moving the government to North Africa and it would be up to Weygand to fix the time for the cease-fire, endeavoring to hold out as long as possible so as to enable the maximum number of troops to elude the Germans and to be transported across the Mediterranean to the new base of operations.

"The government," said Weygand angrily, "cannot leave France."

"But what is Algeria but three French *départements?*"

"It is not the same thing," Weygand rejoined.

The Premier came back to the cease-fire, insisting that it was up to the army chief to demand it.

"Never!" Weygand stormed. "Never will I bring such shame to the colors of the French Army." It would dishonor his soldiers, he said. He would never accept such a responsibility.

"If that is stopping you," Reynaud says he retorted, "I will take the whole responsibility on myself. I will give you a written order."

The generalissimo made it clear he would not obey it. He was also outraged, ardent royalist that he was, at the very idea of Reynaud comparing the Dutch queen and the Dutch monarchy to the French premier and the Republic. By his own account in his deposition at Riom, given, as we have seen, in the third person, usually used only by monarchs

General Weygand replied that there was no similarity between a monarch and a premier. The former could rightly claim to represent a country over which his dynasty had reigned from father to son. What similarity was there between him and a premier when the Third Republic had already counted more than a hundred of them in its seventy years of existence? Once the head of government in France has gone he was soon replaced and forgotten.[8]

Weygand's defiance of the lawful government and his scorn for the French Republic, to which as a soldier he had sworn an oath of loyalty, was thus again made clear. Like a growing number of French leaders in Bordeaux this weekend, the Army chief appears to have begun to think that some good might come out of the military debacle after all. It would bring down the despised Republic.

Reynaud declares that after this stormy encounter he decided to fire the generalissimo at the very cabinet meeting which the two men now entered. But like other resolves of this well-meaning but weakening Premier in these tortured days that were inexorably crushing him, it was, if not forgotten, not carried out.

Instead, once the cabinet meeting began at 4 P.M. at the prefecture under the chair of the President of the Republic, the Premier tried once again to persuade Weygand to agree to a cease-fire. First, though, the cabinet listened to the generalissimo's report on the military situation. It was even more desperate than the last time he had reported to it. The center of the front had become completely ruptured. To the east the Sixth Army was cut in two. Further east the three armies of the Maginot Line, whose retreat had been held up until the 12th by General Weygand, were facing encirclement. At 9:30 A.M. General Georges had got off a wire to Weygand, which the generalissimo now read to the cabinet: "The cutting to pieces of our armies is now a *fait accompli.*"

After sending the wire Georges had met with a number of his Army Group and Army commanders at Briare, which the High Command was preparing to evacuate that evening with the approach of the enemy. According to General Roton, the Chief of Staff, there was "unanimous agreement that hostilities must be stopped at the earliest possible moment." General Besson, commander of Army Group 3, insisted on it. "When are they going to decide," he exclaimed, "to put a stop to the butchery!" And General Georges, testifying about this day at the trial of Pétain, explained: "In all conscience I concluded at this moment that it was impossible to continue the struggle, that our armies, torn to shreds, were no longer capable of putting up a fight against the enemy."[9] The military commanders in the field as well as General Georges, who was still in charge of actual operations, were "unanimous" then, by their own admission, that the French Army must give up. Their conclusions were wired to General Lafont, Commander of the 18th Military Region at Bordeaux, to be transmitted to Weygand. Reynaud later remembered that General Lafont asked to be heard in the cabinet meeting and delivered his news "in a melodramatic tone deliberately assumed." This moved Weygand to again demand an immediate armistice. "I'm being asked if I'm a fool to keep on fighting," he said with what the Premier thought was "his customary exaggeration."

After making his report and reiterating his demand, Weygand retired from the cabinet room at the request of Lebrun, making himself available, if need be, in an adjoining *salle.* After the experiences at Cangé, Lebrun had agreed with Reynaud that the Army chief must no longer be permitted to disrupt a cabinet meeting. The President of the Republic, timorous though he was, had become fed up himself with the recalcitrant generalissimo.

With Weygand out of sight and hearing Reynaud tried to rally the cabinet to his side. France must remain in the war, he said, come what might. It was at this juncture that Chautemps made his first, but not the most important, intervention in the debate. Painting the sad plight of the beaten soldiers and the millions of helpless refugees milling down the clogged roads, he appealed, says Reynaud, to the feelings of humanity of his colleagues. As it turned out, this was just a warm-up for his second intervention, which would prove decisive. Reynaud replied that it was more humane to order a cease-fire, which he had been urging on Weygand, then to negotiate an armistice. A cease-fire, he said, would bring hostilities to a stop immediately and save much bloodshed and suffering. An armistice would take at least four days to conclude, during which the slaughter would go on. The cabinet seemed to agree. For once even Pétain seemed in accord. "The Marshal appeared convinced," Lebrun later recalled. Seizing his opportunity, Reynaud asked the Marshal to step outside, speak to Weygand and convince him not only that a cease-fire would stop the butchery the quickest but would not dishonor the Army. Pétain assented and left the room. When he returned fifteen minutes later he announced that he had been unable to change Weygand's mind. Had he tried? The answer to that question will never be known, for sure.*

But the answer to the more important question was clear. The Commander in Chief refused to ask for a cease-fire or to surrender the armies in the field. Even the venerable Marshal had been unable to move him. His failure convinced Reynaud that Weygand would have to be relieved. "That decision implied," he argues, not very logically, "that the question of an armistice be considered." That and the consequence: that if an armistice were not asked, the government move to North Africa to continue the war. "I now," he says, "put it squarely up to the cabinet." It was at this moment that Camille Chautemps intervened for the second time and by a typically deceitful move, which it is a wonder the cabinet members did not immediately see through, swung the government fatally and swiftly down the road to surrender. Up to this moment, says Louis Marin, who was present, "the partisans of a demand for an armistice were a tiny minority. Then came the Chautemps operation."

---

* During his testimony at the Pétain trial, Weygand first swore that this reported meeting "actually never took place." But then the Marshal, breaking the silence which he maintained throughout most of the proceedings, crossed him up.

PÉTAIN: I want to ask the general a question. When I stepped out to see him did I agree with him about a cease-fire? Perhaps we discussed the question, but I am not sure that I agreed with him about the cease-fire.

WEYGAND: I don't recall having had a conversation with the Marshal on this subject, but I could be wrong. . . . Even if the Marshal had asked me to agree to capitulate, I would not have accepted.[10]

THE CHAUTEMPS PROPOSAL

"A *coup de théâtre*," most members called it afterward. Chautemps, like Pétain a Vice-Premier, and still a force in the Radical Party, was a born compromiser whose reputation for subtlety—if that is the word—was so great that few, even in his own party, knew where he stood on anything. Reynaud and his colleagues knew him well. But what they did not know was that behind the Premier's back he had secretly gone over to Pétain weeks before. Baudouin knew it. He had, as we have seen, noted it in his journal. But he had not told his chief.

What Chautemps, in his most persuasive manner, now proposed was that to justify continuing the war from North Africa to the French people, who would consider that the government was irresponsibly deserting them in the hour of national calamity, France should ask Germany—not for an armistice, but for its *conditions* for an armistice.*

If, contrary to what we expect [he says he explained], the conditions appear moderate, our British friends will no doubt agree that we should study them.

If, on the other hand, as you and I expect, the conditions are catastrophic or dishonorable, I hope the Marshal, cured of his illusions, will agree with us that we must continue the war. . . . And the French people, when they learn that an honorable peace is impossible, will be ready to support the supreme sacrifices which we will have to ask of them.

This was a trick. As Reynaud immediately pointed out, to ask for the *terms* of an armistice was the same thing as asking for an armistice. Once engaged in talks to stop the fighting there could be no pulling back. The very announcement that conditions had been asked, Reynaud argued, would break what was left of the morale of the retreating troops and of the bewildered people. It would destroy the possibility of moving troops and the government to the African colonies. What soldier in the field would risk getting killed in further fighting when he learned that his government had asked for terms for halting the struggle?

It was a trick. But it worked.† Reynaud immediately sensed that a majority of the cabinet members, who, he rightly believed, had been with him in refusing to ask for an armistice, had in the instant swung behind the Chautemps proposal. Frossard, Minister of Public Works, who had started his political career as a Communist, then became a Socialist, and who for some time had been veering further right, warmly supported Chautemps.

---

* Actually in his own version of what he proposed Chautemps says he advocated asking for the "eventual conditions for a *peace*."[11]

† "The truth is," says Reynaud, "that Chautemps was trying to deceive me. I am obliged to admit he succeeded. . . . Whereas we believed that we had only to safeguard ourselves against his weakness, it was really against his duplicity that we should have been on guard. . . . I did not learn until later that the man had already passed over to Pétain's camp."[12]

The Marshal nodded his agreement. Reynaud grabbed a sheet of note-paper and jotted down what appeared to be the lineup: thirteen ministers for the Chautemps proposal, six against. He pushed the note over the table to Lebrun. "Then I turned to him," Reynaud says, "and told him that, in these conditions, I was resigning."

The emotional President of the Republic jumped to his feet. "If you go, I shall go too!" he exclaimed. Reynaud says the usually timid Lebrun was "even violent, rapping his hands on the table"; and the chief magistrate admitted to the Pétain trial court later that he had been "perhaps a little impulsive, because if others could go, I could not." Still the President, says Reynaud, insisted that he "give way" to the majority sentiment in the cab-inet and, as a first step, ask Great Britain to agree to France asking for the conditions for an armistice.

I then had [writes Reynaud] a few seconds of debate within myself which were the gravest of my public life. . . . If I resigned I would be playing Chautemps' game. My successor would open the way for Pétain and his partisans to make an armistice. . . .

I therefore agreed to transmit the demand [to the British], but on condition that I specified it came from the majority of the cabinet.[13]

This proved to be a fatal compromise that next day would precipitate the very events which he hoped to avoid. Reynaud argues that he felt sure the British government would refuse to agree to the French asking the Ger-mans for terms and that he would then be in a strong position to continue the war.

Though outwardly he still seemed full of fight, inwardly he was near-ing the end of his rope. He was losing the battle with the military, now openly supported by Chautemps and a growing number of cabinet min-isters, who wanted out of the war. It was not only they who were working against him. His own immediate circle, Baudouin, Bouthillier, and the Countess de Portes, especially the countess, was working on him. As H. Freeman Matthews, the First Secretary of the U.S. Embassy, the most able and experienced of American diplomats on the scene, would later put it, "Madame de Portes hung on to the Premier's coattails, begging him to accept an armistice." The redoubtable lady even made her way to Matthews' office in Bordeaux, weeping profusely, and hysterically urging him to bring pressure on Reynaud to give up. To those of us who knew "Doc" Matthews, a dry-mannered and prosaic man in public, it would be difficult to imagine a diplomat less likely to be moved by a woman crying on his shoulders. But the countess tried. In a confidential memorandum* recounting this crucial weekend in Bordeaux Matthews wrote of Madame de Portes:

---

* Which he kindly put at the disposal of the author after the State Department had declassified it.

I don't think her role in encouraging the defeatist elements during Reynaud's critical last days as Prime Minister should be underestimated. She spent an hour weeping in my office to get us to urge Reynaud to ask for an Armistice. She knew that our efforts were all in the opposite direction but she was in such a state of panic that she would leave no stone unturned to get Reynaud to surrender. Mr. Biddle and I saw Reynaud at least four times a day during his last few days as Prime Minister; never once did we see him that Hélène de Portes was not just coming out of or going into his office, and I think his gradual . . . loss of nerve was in large part due to her influence on him.

Laval too was at work to undermine Reynaud, to achieve his old goal of making Pétain Premier, to get an armistice and to prevent the government from moving to North Africa. From his office at the City Hall he moved prudently for the first couple of days, lining up right-wing politicians, cultivating Raphaël Alibert, the old Marshal's chief counselor and an even more fanatical royalist than Weygand. Alibert, whose narrow pedantic mind had never emerged from the age of Louis XIV, wanted not only to topple the Reynaud government but the Republican regime itself. Laval had the same ambition, but, shrewd tactician that he was, held his own counsel for the time being. He did not want to tip his hand too soon. For this reason he avoided seeing Pétain directly. He worked through Alibert and others. As Admiral Darlan told Baudouin after the Saturday cabinet meeting, Laval was becoming "very active. He is sending one emissary after another to the Marshal."[14]

Not to be left out was Anatole de Monzie, still nursing a grudge at having been kicked out of the government by Reynaud ten days before. His diary entry of June 15 at Bordeaux tells of his sitting up "past midnight" with the Spanish Ambassador, José Felix de Lequerica, at the latter's office "trying to work out the procedure for an armistice."[15]

Of the extent of the intrigues of the politicians against him Reynaud was still largely unaware. Pétain and Weygand and the military they dominated were still his most formidable opponents on this weekend in Bordeaux. This the Premier fully realized.* It was brought home to him as soon as he left the cabinet meeting when he ran into the generalissimo and an even more violent altercation than the one just prior to the session ensued. It was now 8 P.M. on Saturday, June 15, and Weygand had been cooling his heels for more than two hours outside the cabinet room, from which he had been excluded. The long wait had not sweetened his temper and what Reynaud now said to him caused it to explode anew.

"The ministers," the Premier told him, "favor a capitulation by the army and believe it is up to the generalissimo to ask the Germans for it." Weygand claims Reynaud added a "hint" that the Army chief had already

---

* "I was quite aware," says Reynaud in describing the events of this day, "that the conflict between Weygand and me would be unyielding to the very end."[16]

assented to it.* The fiery old general admits that he exploded. He concedes he also raised his voice so that the several officers and officials in the room could be witnesses to his words. "The silence of those around us," says he, "gave more resonance to my words." Other witnesses say he screamed that he would never agree to surrender his armies.

> Reynaud . . . [Weygand recounts in his memoirs] invited me to calm myself. These words exacerbated my indignation. Certainly not, I declared. I would not calm myself, nor would I hold my tongue. Let me be dismissed, but I would never accept such an infamy. Never would I inflict such shame on our colors. . . . The cessation of hostilities, like the entry into the war, was up to the government. Let it take its responsibilities. Reynaud walked away, saying he would take them.

The general was still fuming. "The thing," he says, "could not be left there." Weygand thereupon strode into the cabinet room to repeat his views to President Lebrun, who already, like Reynaud, knew them and who, on constitutional grounds, refused to listen to him except in the presence of the Premier. Reynaud was fetched and the enraged generalissimo then lit into them both, the President of the Republic and the head of the government. Lebrun, like Reynaud before him, tried to calm down the hysterical Commander in Chief.

> The President of the Republic [Weygand recounts] reproached me for my vivacity and tried to silence me, but I reminded him that when I commanded the army in 1933 I had appealed to him as Supreme Chief of the Armed Forces of the Nation in regard to certain measures taken against my advice and against the interests of national defense. He had refused to listen to me.

"Those were questions of little importance," Lebrun responded coolly.

Of little importance! Weygand was again beside himself. Though one might have thought that the Commander in Chief would have more important matters on his mind at this moment in the debacle of his armies, he now proceeded at length to recall to the startled President how the Republican governments seven years before had refused to grant the army the credits it needed for rearming and once had gone to the length of "irregularly suppressing 5,000 officers." The stormy meeting finally concluded, Weygand himself recounts, "by my renewed affirmation that no one could make me carry out a dishonorable deed. I would refuse to do it." His defiance of the government, his refusal to obey it, was again made clear beyond any doubt to the two highest authorities of the Republican regime.

In his memoirs Weygand concludes that it was a "painful scene" but he does not seem to realize that it was he who provoked it and who made it

---

* Which Reynaud denies. "A few hours before, he had already made himself clear on the cease-fire, turning it down categorically," he writes. But the Premier was not quite straightforward in saying the cabinet favored a cease-fire. The members had not given their opinions on that.

so painful. If the President or the Premier were to relieve the overwrought general, who was flaunting his disobedience, of his command, as Reynaud had said he would do this very day, now, one would think, would have been the appropriate moment. They did not even throw him out of the room. Weygand departed in a huff. After stopping over at Pétain's residence to tattle to the Marshal the tale of his encounters with the head of government and the head of state—"I wanted to make him *au courant* of this incident," he says—he boarded his special train at 9 P.M. for a leisurely overnight journey to his new headquarters at Vichy to resume command of the demoralized and retreating (when they were not encircled) armies.[17]

In vehemently refusing to order his troops in France to stop fighting at the very moment he was demanding an armistice, which would produce the same result, General Weygand, no doubt, sincerely believed that he was upholding the honor of the French Army. It has been difficult for many others to appreciate the difference. General Georges, in his postwar testimony, staunchly supported Weygand's conception. General Gamelin did not. And Reynaud contended that he could never understand why capitulation of an army by order of its commander was any worse than capitulation under the terms of an armistice.

It is true that no expression in the French language denotes such shame, such disgrace, as capitulation *"en rase campagne"*—in the open field. General Georges dwelt on this when questioned by the Parliamentary Investigating Committee.

A capitulation *en rase campagne* is infamous for the chief of an army. Our laws forbid it. . . . Article 234 of the Code of Military Justice punishes it with death and with military degradation.* It is contrary to all the traditions of our Army.

He recalled the example of Marshal Bazaine, who surrendered his army at Metz to the Prussians in 1870 and was condemned to death for it by a court-martial.† "I belong to the generation," he said, "which grew

---

* Article 234 reads: "Any general, any commander of army troops, who capitulates *en rase campagne* is punished with the sentence of death with military degradation if the capitulation results in his troops laying down their arms, or if, before treating verbally or in writing, he has not done everything which duty and honor prescribe." Thus, the second "*if*" does permit a way out "with honor." In a letter to the author of March 28, 1966, Reynaud in discussing the article pointed this out and added: "It is thus clear that Article 234 has nothing to do with a cease-fire for the whole French Army ordered by the government. . . . Our glorious military men thus had no right whatsoever to risk France falling completely under the Nazi yoke on the pretext that in carrying out an order for cease-fire they would be violating their personal honor."

† It will be recalled that Marshal Bazaine, whose sentence was commuted to twenty years, escaped from prison and lived a long and comfortable life in exile in Spain.

up in the shadow of the war of 1870 and I always remembered Bazaine and the capitulation of Metz. That remained engraved in the minds of us all."[18]

And yet, it was General Georges who on June 22, with the approval of General Weygand, authorized General Condé, Acting Commander of Army Group 2, to surrender three French armies (the Second, Third, and Fifth) comprising 400,000 men encircled behind the Maginot Line.[19] Weygand notes that the three armies laid down their arms at 2 P.M. that day but he does not regard this as an "infamy" or contrary to Article 234. He quotes his own telephone instructions to General Georges, who had asked for them, that

When these troops have exhausted all means to live and to fight, they shall ask for an end to the fighting with honors of war which they have largely merited.[20]

Those three battered, encircled French armies were doomed but the fact is they (wisely, in my opinion) did not wait until their means of "living and fighting" had been exhausted, as Weygand laid down. Actually they surrendered eight hours before the generalissimo's formal authorization was made—on the instructions of Georges. They capitulated *en rase campagne* just as Marshal Bazaine's surrounded force at Metz had done in 1870. Some scattered units in the Maginot Line refused to obey their commanders and fought on. A week later they were summarily ordered by General Huntziger to hoist the white flag. "This surrender of fortified places which had not been taken," comments Colonel Lyet, "was *contrary to all military tradition*."*[21] Apparently he takes Weygand literally at his word.

But other French officers disagree. Weygand's predecessor as Commander in Chief, for one. "I must confess," General Gamelin wrote later,

that I do not understand the thesis which differentiated between "the armistice" and "capitulation." For, if the government had withdrawn to Algeria would it have been necessary to have a "capitulation" of the French Army? Would it not have been better to withdraw to England and Africa all the elements possible and on the other hand to ask each of the fighting groups remaining in France to struggle to the last cartridge, each chief trying to obtain the most honorable conditions possible, once duty and honor were satisfied?[22]

To Colonel Goutard, the military historian, who later fought with the Free French,

it would have been in no way dishonorable to stop the fighting by a cease-fire or even capitulate in metropolitan France with the debris of the Army,

---

* The emphasis is Lyet's.

which was in no condition to combat further, in order to continue the struggle elsewhere at the side of our allies.*[23]

It is difficult to escape the conclusion that General Weygand, in refusing to ask for a cease-fire and in insisting instead on an armistice, was concerned mainly with putting the onus of surrender on the government rather than on the Army.

Another consideration weighed heavily on him and on Pétain. They believed with absolute certainty that not only was the Battle of France lost, which it was, but that the war itself was lost. Reynaud opposed an armistice because it would necessarily bring about, if not the surrender of the fleet and of the land and air forces overseas, at least their demobilization under German supervision. That would take France out of the war. But that was precisely what the Marshal and the generalissimo wanted. They were sure that Great Britain either would be quickly conquered or would avert conquest by suing Hitler for peace. With the British Navy, Air Force, and Empire intact, Britain, as we have seen Pétain pointing out to Ambassador Bullitt and General Spears, would get better terms than defeated France. This was uppermost in the Marshal's mind this June weekend in Bordeaux as he and his followers maneuvered for an armistice. And it seems to have weighed heavily on Weygand.

"In three weeks' time," Mandel that Saturday quoted Weygand as saying, "England's neck will be wrung like a chicken's."† Such prophecies, Reynaud remarked later, "were common currency in Bordeaux at that time." Senator Tony Révillon noted some of them in his diary, beginning on June 15 with the above remark attributed to Weygand. On the 18th, Senator Charles Reibel, who had become the parliamentary spokesman for Weygand, told him: "General Weygand is sure that the British are incapable of resisting an invasion of their isle by the Germans." The same day a Colonel "X" accosted Révillon: "Believe me, Senator," he said, "England will be put *hors de combat* in a few weeks. What's the use of continuing the war?"[26]

The expert opinion of the French military, above all that of the Marshal and the Commander in Chief, that Great Britain would go under in a few weeks if it did not seek peace in the meantime, strengthened the defeatists in Bordeaux in their demand for an armistice as the Saturday of the long weekend neared its end.

---

* To Churchill, "Weygand's position . . . finds no foundation in the law and practice of civilized states or in the professional honor of a soldier."[24]

† In a talk with Spears.[25] Churchill made a famous reply in a speech to the Canadian House of Commons on December 30, 1941. "Some chicken!", he said, and when the laughter had died away added: "Some neck!" At the trial of Pétain, Weygand denied having made the statement. By this time his denials of anything that seemed to put him in a bad light in view of subsequent events, did not carry great weight with many Frenchmen.

As the evening passed, Reynaud himself, weary from his two encounters with Weygand and the cabinet meeting, and discouraged by the maneuver of Chautemps, began to cave in. During the day he had clung to some hope from America. "Everything depends on Roosevelt's answer to my last telegram," he told Campbell and Spears. Ambassador Biddle agreed. Endeavoring to impress the American President with the critical nature of the situation in Bordeaux he cabled Roosevelt at 5 P.M.

I feel that I should make it entirely clear that the French Government is now faced with only two alternatives, namely to sue for peace, which of course would have to be unconditional, or to move to North Africa and continue the fight.

The decision . . . will depend on the nature of your reply.[27]

Early in the evening Reynaud called in the British Ambassador and General Spears to discuss with them the message he had promised to send to London in accordance with the Chautemps proposal. The Englishmen noted that the Premier looked "pale, washed-out." Before scarcely a minute had ensued they saw with consternation that he was weakening. Prior to penning his note to Churchill, Reynaud said, he wished to tell them what the government had decided. "As Mr. Churchill stated at Tours," he began, "he would agree that France should sue for an armistice——"

"That's untrue!" Spears, who was taking down the Premier's words, snapped.

"But Baudouin asserted at the Cabinet meeting today that Churchill did say so and that he had made a note of it at the time." This was astonishing to the British diplomats. They knew that Baudouin had been peddling this falsehood ever since but they were surprised that Reynaud, who had heard exactly what Churchill had said at Tours, should swallow it. Baudouin and Madame de Portes, who were working in tandem on the Premier, seemed to have been more successful than Spears and Campbell had expected.

"All three of us were at the meeting and all three of us know that the Prime Minister never said anything of the sort," Spears answered.

Finally, after some argument, the French minutes of the Tours conversation kept by Margerie were fetched by Margerie himself and the facts ascertained.

Paul Reynaud, the British visitors thought, was acting strangely. After Baudouin's lie had been disposed of, the Premier then asserted, according to Spears, that the message he would now draft for London conveyed a formal decision of the cabinet at a meeting "presided over by the President of the Republic." This remark seems inexplicable since Reynaud had insisted in the cabinet session that he would transmit the Chautemps proposition to the British only on condition that he explain it came from a majority of the Council of Ministers, with which he obviously disagreed.*

The Premier now took pen and paper and began to write out the message to Churchill.

At the meeting of the cabinet this afternoon it was held that at a moment when the enemy is on the point of occupying the entire country, which will mean inflicting cruel privations and suffering on the French nation, the departure of the government would be considered by the people as desertion. This might give rise to violent reactions on the part of the public unless it has been established that the peace conditions imposed by Hitler and Mussolini were unacceptable as being contrary to the vital and honorable interests of France.

The cabinet does not doubt that these conditions will in any event be unacceptable, but has decided that it is indispensable that this should be proved beyond doubt. If this course is not adopted the government will break up, as many of its members would, in that case, refuse to leave the soil of France.

With a view to ascertaining German and Italian conditions, the cabinet decided to seek leave of the British government to inquire through the United States government what armistice terms would be offered to France by the German and Italian governments.

The President of the Council is authorized, if the British government will agree to the French government taking this step, to declare to the British government that the surrender of the French fleet to Germany would be held to be an unacceptable condition.

Should the British government withhold its consent to this step, it seems likely, in view of the opinions expressed at the cabinet meeting, that the President of the Council would have no alternative but to resign.

In view of Reynaud's stand up to now this was a strange message for him to pen, and Campbell and Spears, the latter says, took "strong objection to it," firing their arguments "in relays" against asking the British to agree to France seeking armistice terms. The Premier, as a reading of the note shows, was expressing Chautemps' views more forcefully than the slippery Vice-Premier himself had done and he was palming off to Churchill what he himself had labeled a deceitful trick as the considered view of the French government.† During the heated argument with the two British envoys, it is true, he explained that he had resisted the Chautemps proposal but had been overruled. But when he turned over the message to the two Englishmen for transmittal to London he "insisted" again that it repre-

---

* Biddle, who saw the Premier immediately after the cabinet meeting at 7 P.M. and again at midnight, reported that he had told him "the decision of the government to ask for the terms of an armistice was unanimous." He so cabled Washington at 1 A.M.[28]

† To Ambassador Biddle he seems to have made Chautemps' line his own. The Ambassador cabled Roosevelt that night:

> The Cabinet unanimously decided to ask for the terms of an armistice. They have asked the British . . . for their concurrence. . . . Reynaud explained (to me) that only by such a move could he show the French people . . . the severity of German terms and justify a flight of the Government to Africa or England. ("I only hope they won't be too moderate," he said.)[29]

sented the "formal decision of the cabinet"—as indeed the wording made clear. To the American Ambassador, as we have seen, he made it even stronger, telling him that it was "unanimous."

Equally perplexing is his warning in his last paragraph that if the British government withheld its consent to France asking for armistice conditions he would have no alternative but to resign. Perplexing because in his memoirs and his postwar testimony he argues not only that he hoped but that he expected that Churchill would turn down the request so that he could put an end to the intrigues for an armistice, move the government to North Africa, and keep France in the war. "Everyone from Lebrun on down knew," he says, "that I was irrevocably opposed to an armistice." But now he was telling the Prime Minister that unless Britain agreed to his government's asking for one he would have to resign. He told his British visitors frankly that if he went, Pétain would undoubtedly replace him and that this would mean a certain armistice. Either way then, whether he resigned or stayed, the conclusion he left with the British diplomats was that France would ask for conditions for an armistice.*

As Reynaud was drafting the last lines of his note to London, Ambassador Biddle delivered the tensely awaited reply of Roosevelt to the Premier's fervent call for help which he had dispatched from Tours on the morning of June 14. "As he read it," say Spears, "he grew still paler, his face contracted, his eyes became just slits. 'Our appeal has failed,' he said in a small toneless voice, 'the Americans will not declare war.' "† He had known that all along. But still the message, ringing with typical Rooseveltian rhetoric expressing America's "increasing admiration" and "utmost sympathy" for France but concluding coolly that his declarations did "not imply military commitments" since "only Congress" could make them, depressed the worn-out Premier further. His spirits were not raised by the American President saying also that the United States would not "recognize the validity of any attempt to impair the independence of France" and that

in these hours, so heart-rending for the French people and yourself, I can assure you . . . that as long as the French people continue in defense of their liberty they [may] rest assured that matériel and supplies will be sent to them from the United States in ever-increasing quantities and kinds.[32]

---

* In his memoirs Reynaud is remarkably reticent about this evening meeting on June 15 with the British envoys. He disposes of it in three lines, writing merely that "after the cabinet meeting I called in the British Ambassador and Spears. I made them *au courant* of the situation in all its gravity and declared that it was in the name of the majority of the cabinet that I was presenting this demand."[30] And though his lengthy book is crowded with the texts of documents he does not mention the message he drafted for Churchill.

† Reynaud publishes the text in his memoirs without comment.[31]

Reynaud knew it would make no difference to Hitler whether the United States recognized France's loss of independence or not. He knew too, as Franklin Roosevelt must have known, that "ever-increasing" American material aid would now be too late. The French government had to make a decision this weekend, as Biddle had warned the President, and the Saturday was now giving way to Sunday.

The exhausted Premier put Roosevelt's message down and added a paragraph to his note to Churchill.

It was agreed last Thursday at your suggestion that the question of authorizing a request for an armistice would be reconsidered if President Roosevelt's reply was negative. This eventuality having materialized, I think the question must now be put afresh.

Requesting that the British reply by the following morning, Sunday, Reynaud handed over the completed message to Campbell and Spears, who got it off to London in code by telephone at 1:30 A.M.[33]

Sunday, which promised to be so fateful for France, had now come. Much depended on the British response.

BORDEAUX, SUNDAY, JUNE 16: THE FALL OF REYNAUD

Crucial though it promised to be, indeed had to be, with the country's fate hanging in the balance, the day of Sunday, June 16, 1940, began in Bordeaux on a bizarre note. That at least was the way it seemed to the two anxious British diplomats, who, like the American Ambassador, were trying desperately to buck up the sagging Reynaud to keep France in the war.* Campbell and Spears had sat up in the early morning hours before going to bed to try to assess, Spears says, "what resources were left to Reynaud in the conflict of wills with Weygand. . . . We concluded that he had just about reached the end of his tether. . . . The President of the Republic meant well but was weak. . . ." Still, they would continue to work on both of them. "Before going to bed after 4 A.M.," says Spears, "we resolved to strain every nerve to prevent the French Government from asking for an armistice."

Reynaud, impatient to receive an answer from London, called in Campbell and Spears early on the Sabbath morning but they could only tell him that they had not yet received a reply. There had not been time. Reynaud seemed "nervously exhausted" to his British callers.

But what depressed them more, for the moment, was not the President of the Council but his mistress. Hélène de Portes kept opening the door and poking her head in, and once, according to Spears, showed her impatience

---

* At his midnight meeting with Reynaud, Biddle says he pointed out the "danger" of asking for armistice terms, "emphasizing the vital importance of maintaining the freedom of the French fleet . . . and the maintenance of a free and untrammeled Government."[34]

of the English visitors taking so much of the Premier's time—though it was he who had invited them—"by stamping her foot and closing the door none too gently." At the next intrusion, the British general recalled, she made faces at Reynaud "as if she had some vital news to impart." The well-born Englishmen were irritated and shocked—"almost beyond endurance," Spears swears. But they could not have been surprised. They had noticed her in the secretaries' room as they waited to see the Premier, "talking at the top of her voice" to one and the other and pointedly ignoring their very existence.

As they left, Spears stopped off in the office of Roland de Margerie to complain. The Premier's *chef du cabinet* could only commiserate with him, "reiterating," says Spears, "his little saying about her: 'She is ugly, *mal soignée,* dirty, nasty, and half-demented, and a sore trial to me.' " The general was thankful for the sympathy and, he indicates, for the sound of so many telling adjectives. "As we drove away," he says, "I thought once more that Hélène de Portes had done Paul Reynaud more harm than anyone."[35]

True as that may be, there were others in Bordeaux that Sunday who, if they did not have more power over him, had more influence over the weakening President of the Republic and the increasingly defeatist members of the government, and who were determined to force a favorable decision on the armistice before the day was out. In the temporary absence of Weygand, Marshal Pétain took the lead.

The first cabinet meeting of the day, convoked shortly before noon, had hardly begun before the Marshal arose and proceeded to read a letter of resignation.* He could no longer remain in a government, he said, which refused to bring an end to hostilities which were destroying the nation. Nor would he have any part in a government which contemplated leaving the soil of France. The country, he concluded, would have to rise again by itself and not by counting on foreign countries. If, as the Marshal's followers seem to have calculated, the maneuver was intended to bring down the Reynaud government then and there, it failed. The President of the Republic was the first to protest. "Ah! You are not going to do that to us at a moment like this!" he exclaimed.

Reynaud answered "in a deliberately glacial tone," he says, that since the Marshal was submitting his resignation to him in writing, the least he could do was to wait for a written answer before acting on it. The old soldier relented but declared he would not sit down again. Like a spoiled child when crossed, though he was eighty-four, he remained standing, brandishing his letter in one hand.

I told him [says Reynaud] that since we had asked Great Britain to release us from the engagement we had with her, the least we could do was to give her

---

* According to Kammerer, several witnesses later contended that the letter had been written for the Marshal the night before in the office of Laval at the City Hall, which by now had become the headquarters for the capitulationists.[36]

time to answer. I was certain that I would have it during the afternoon. Rather crestfallen, Pétain put his letter in his pocket and sat down. The cabinet thereupon adjourned until 5 P.M.[37]

The cabinet was adjourned but not the bitter struggle between Frenchmen. Hardly had the ministers dispersed before Reynaud and Weygand were at each other again in their third and what would prove to be the last row of the weekend. The generalissimo had not remained long at Supreme Headquarters at Vichy. Arriving there from Bordeaux by train at 7 A.M. on the 16th he had conferred with General Georges, who conveyed to him, he says, the views of the remaining generals in the field. This was that "the continuation of the struggle was impossible." What was left of the French Army, said Georges, "was in danger of dissolving into the flood of refugees."[38] Weygand needed no more prompting. He decided to return immediately to Bordeaux to have it out with the government and force it to ask for an armistice. His special trains having proved too slow, he took off from Vichy at 10 A.M. in a plane and by noon was in the prefect's residence at Bordeaux.

Reynaud found him there as he emerged from the cabinet session. The Supreme Commander was already conversing with Lebrun and two ministers, Mandel and Paul Thellier, Minister of Agriculture—the latter apparently invited to counsel on one point in Pétain's letter of resignation in which the Marshal had asserted that the country would face a famine if it did not give up. A discussion of a cease-fire had already begun, with Weygand again vehemently rejecting it.

"General Weygand tells us," Lebrun said, "that a complete disintegration of the army threatens us if we don't ask for an armistice at once."

"You know my position on that," Reynaud snapped. He explains that he thought further talk with the general on the subject was futile, and that the only way of getting out of the impasse was to relieve him of his command. That, he says, he intended to do at the cabinet meeting that afternoon. As we have seen, he had had the same resolve the day before and had let the occasion slip by.*

Lebrun, in his ineffective way, tried to reconcile the irreconcilable gladiators or at least their views. "But General Weygand," he went on, "says that capitulation would be contrary to the honor of the Army."

Reynaud turned to the general. "If capitulation is laid down in the conditions for an armistice, as it certainly will be, would you reject such an armistice as contrary to the honor of the Army?"

"I will tell you that when the time comes," Weygand said.

"No," said Lebrun with unaccustomed spunk, "you must tell us right

---

* In a letter to the author, March 28, 1966, Reynaud recounts that immediately after this encounter he wrote out in his own hand an order "prescribing the cease-fire which I intended to give to the new Commander in Chief as soon as he was designated." This intention, too, was never carried out.

now." But the general was not to be caught in that trap. He merely reiterated that an armistice was an act of the government, a capitulation that of the military authority.

"If that is what is stopping you," Reynaud said once more, "I am prepared to give you a written order to carry it out."

Weygand again refused.[39] They were back at the impasse which had deadlocked them for a week. But each seems to have understood as the futile meeting broke up that it could not outlast the day. Someone had to break in this clash of wills. Or perhaps events would resolve it. Reynaud confesses he thought the British government might save him.

While the French leaders were quarreling in Lebrun's office, Churchill's reply had come over the wires at the British consulate.

Mr. Churchill to M. Reynaud. London, 16th June, 1940. 12:35 P.M.

Our agreement forbidding separate negotiations, whether for armistice or peace, was made with the French Republic, and not with any particular French Administration or statesman. It thereby involves the honor of France. Nevertheless, provided, *but only provided, that the French Fleet is sailed forthwith for British harbors pending negotiations* His Majesty's Government give their full consent to an inquiry by the French Government to ascertain the terms for an armistice for France. . . .

Spears and Ambassador Campbell read the message as soon as it had been decoded. It perturbed them. Once the door leading to an armistice was opened, they thought, it would never be closed again. Spears was also sure that Darlan, no lover of the British, would feel insulted by the peremptory demand that the French fleet sail forthwith to British ports and would never accept it. The two discouraged envoys discussed first getting the admiral's reaction and then consulting London before delivering the note to Reynaud. "But neither of us," says Spears, "trusted him." They finally agreed to see Jeanneney, the venerable old President of the Senate, on their way to Reynaud's office. That morning, they knew, the presidents of the two chambers had given their assent, as the Constitution required, to the government moving to North Africa. Both men opposed an armistice. But Jeanneney, "frail and thin" and wearied, Spears thought, from "the strain and his age" would not commit himself to approving the French fleet sailing to British waters. That was for the government, not for him, to decide. The British diplomats thereupon drove to Reynaud's office to deliver their message.

The Premier did not like it. "It is really too silly," he remarked, "to ask the French fleet to sail to British harbors when it is needed to protect the Mediterranean and North Africa against the Italians." When the British callers pointed out that there were British naval bases in the Mediterranean from which the two fleets could protect North Africa, Reynaud was unmoved. He was in an unwonted surly mood and even when Madame de Portes poked her head into the room, Spears recounts, he glared at her and she retreated. As Campbell and Spears got up to leave, Reynaud informed them that Churchill had just telephoned him and that they had agreed to meet the next day on a British cruiser off Concarneau in Brittany.*[40]

Shortly before 4 P.M. a second message from London arrived for Campbell. This was from the Foreign Office.

> You should inform M. Reynaud [it said] that we expect to be consulted as soon as any armistice terms are received.
>
> You should impress on French Government that in stipulating for removal of French Fleet to British ports we have in mind French interests as well as our own, and are convinced that it will strengthen the hands of the French Government in any armistice discussions if they can show the French Navy is out of reach of the German forces,†[42]

The British diplomats hurried to deliver it to the Premier. They found him, says Spears, "perhaps more tired . . . certainly more difficult and petulant than at the previous interview." Reynaud cared no more for the second note than for the first, and said so. He would not discuss the fleet going to British ports. The British callers repeated their arguments for it. Spears thought Reynaud appeared to be "at the end of his tether."

In the midst of the rather acrimonious argument a telephone call came from London. General de Gaulle was on the other end of the line and though he was the most taciturn of officers, he was plainly excited. He had a statement, he said, of the greatest importance and urgency from the British government. Reynaud grabbed paper and pencil and began to take it down word for word, repeating each phrase back to de Gaulle so that there would be no error, becoming more and more excited each moment. What he was scrawling on his sheets of paper was a proposal for a Declaration of Union between Great Britain and France.

> At this most fateful moment in the history of the modern world, the Governments of the United Kingdom and the French Republic make this declaration of indissoluble union and unyielding resolution in their common defense of justice and freedom. . . .
>
> The two Governments declare that France and Great Britain shall no longer be two nations but one Franco-British Union.
>
> The constitution of the Union will provide for joint organs of defense, foreign, financial and economic policies.

---

* Weygand claims that on his arrival at Lebrun's office earlier both the President of the Republic and the Premier told him Churchill "had refused to come." This could not be true, as the Prime Minister had not yet telephoned. As we shall see, Churchill actually set off for the meeting.[41]

† Pétain, Weygand, and Darlan believed just the opposite. They intended to use the French fleet as their chief bargaining point for better terms from the Germans. If the fleet were in British waters they would lose this trump.

Every citizen of France will enjoy immediately citizenship of Great Britain; every British subject will become a citizen of France.

Both countries would share the cost of repairing the devastation of war "wherever it occurs." There would be a single War Cabinet to direct the prosecution of the war. It would govern "from wherever it best can." The two Parliaments would be "formally associated." "And thus," it concluded, "we shall conquer."

Reynaud was electrified. "I will die defending these proposals," he said exultantly. In London de Gaulle passed the telephone to Churchill. The Prime Minister and Reynaud both believed they had surmounted the crisis for France with this daring proposal. They confirmed their agreement to meet the next day off Brittany. There they would proclaim the indissoluble Union. *"Alors, à demain! . . . à Concarneau!",* de Gaulle heard the British Prime Minister say in his best French as he hung up. The happy general immediately took off by plane for Bordeaux carrying a copy of the Declaration.[43]

The idea for this bold, last-minute proposal came from a group of Frenchmen in London: Charles Corbin, the French Ambassador, and Jean Monnet and René Pleven, members of the French Economic Mission in London. For some days they had been discussing it with Sir Robert Vansittart, the Chief Diplomatic Adviser to the British Foreign Secretary, and Major Desmond Morton, the Prime Minister's secretary. Their object was to produce a *coup de théâtre,* as de Gaulle puts it, which would keep France in the war.

"I was not the prime mover," says Churchill. He first got wind of it at a luncheon the day before (June 15) at the Carlton Club with Lord Halifax, the Foreign Secretary, Vansittart, Corbin, Monnet, and Pleven. "My first reaction," Churchill admits, "was unfavorable." De Gaulle's too. Arriving in London early on the 16th he was shown the proposed text by Corbin and his colleagues. Though the idea was grandiose, which appealed to him, he thought at first glance that it was in fact too much so to be realized in time—"by a simple exchange of notes." Still, as a manifestation of solidarity it had "real significance," he concluded and would encourage Reynaud to stick to his guns.[44]

The first thing was to get the British to make the proposal—at once. Time was running out. "You alone can get Churchill to do it," de Gaulle says Corbin told him, adding that he had arranged for the general to lunch with the Prime Minister. Churchill concedes that de Gaulle made a strong case and the general in his memoirs agrees. "He impressed on me," the Prime Minister later remembered, "that some dramatic gesture was essential to give Reynaud the support he needed to keep his government in the war." De Gaulle, pursuing tactics which were then new to the British but which later would become only too familiar—and sometimes painful—to them and to others in the long years to come, began by dressing down the Prime Minister for his attitude at Tours.

"I must tell you," he said, "that it surprised me—unpleasantly. You seemed to cheapen our alliance. . . ." Then he got to the main business and strongly urged an immediate Declaration of Union between the two countries.

"It's a big piece to chew on," he quotes Churchill as responding. But de Gaulle persisted and in the end, he says, "Churchill came around to my point of view."*45

Back in Bordeaux Reynaud's office was the scene of great excitement. Spears was in such a state of exultation that, perhaps unconsciously, he took it upon himself to speed the typing of the French translation of the Declaration so that the Premier could distribute it at the cabinet meeting, which was about to convene, it being nearly 5 P.M. on this Sunday afternoon. Gathering Reynaud's script he "dashed off," he says, for the secretaries' room. There

stood the inevitable Madame de Portes. As I handed a secretary the paper she stepped behind him and read over his shoulder, holding his arm to prevent his turning the pages too fast for her to read them. It was difficult to tell from her expression whether rage or amazement prevailed. But both feelings were apparent. As she went on delaying the secretary to read herself, I told him curtly the message must be typed without a moment's delay.†47

The British general then returned to Reynaud's office where there arose a matter which would be the subject of much misunderstanding and controversy for a long time among the French themselves, the British, and between the French and the British—and which would have considerable consequences. The dispute concerns the question of what happened to the two British telegrams earlier on this Sunday stating that Great Britain assented to France asking for conditions of an armistice only if the French fleet were first sailed to British ports, and stressing that London "expected" to be consulted as soon as any armistice terms were received.

Spears contends that immediately after the proposal for a Union had been received Reynaud turned to him and Ambassador Campbell and said he "presumed this offer superseded the two telegrams on the subject of the fleet." Both envoys agreed that it did. If accepted, France would remain

---

* While the War Cabinet assembled to make its decision on the Union proposal, de Gaulle, confident that he had persuaded Churchill, telephoned Reynaud to advise him that he "hoped" before the end of the afternoon to send him "a very important communication."46

† Spears suspects that it was the Countess who leaked out the substance of the proposal to Reynaud's enemies. The Premier, who does not mention Madame de Portes in his lengthy memoirs, believed that his opponents learned of the message through his telephone, which they were tapping. At any rate, they knew of it by the time the cabinet assembled and had made up their minds about it.

in the war, and there would be no question of an armistice and the fleet. But what if it were turned down? This seemed out of the question to both Reynaud and the two British diplomats. "It did not occur to us," says Spears, "that it might not be accepted." But it occurred to the hardheaded British Prime Minister, who, skeptical of the proposal from the first, had only reluctantly gone along with it. To him it seemed self-evident, he says, "that if our offer did not find favor, our rights and claims would revive in their full force." But—strangely—it did not seem self-evident to the French.

The failure of the British Foreign Office in its telegrams to Bordeaux to make its government's position absolutely clear on the point added to the appalling misunderstanding.* When Campbell and Spears, the latter reports, got back to the British consulate they found a telegram from the Foreign Office asking them to "suspend action" on the telegrams. They immediately dispatched a note to Reynaud saying that the two messages should be considered "canceled." ("Suspended," Churchill commented later, "would have been a better word.")

Reynaud's version is quite different from the British. He declares that Campbell and Spears "an hour after delivering the second telegram" came to him and asked him to return the two messages, "explaining to me," he says, "that their government had withdrawn their consent (for an armistice)." Reynaud says he believed it was his initial objections to the two British telegrams which caused the British government to withdraw them. And it was only long after the war, he claims, on reading Churchill's memoirs that he learned that the reason the British government had suspended them was solely because the offer of Union *ipso facto* nullified them.† This explanation is not very convincing. It is difficult to believe that a man of Reynaud's intelligence and clarity of mind did not see the connection.

The cabinet convened at 5 P.M. There was a feeling among all the ministers present that at last there would be a showdown. Either France would ask for the conditions of an armistice, as Chautemps proposed, or the government would move to Africa and continue the war from there. There could be no further postponing a decision. The disintegration of the army, the advance of the Germans toward Bordeaux threatening the government with capture, made that obvious to all. The first thing for the

---

* It would not have been difficult, one would think, for the Foreign Office to have made the government's position quite clear by simply adding that if the offer of Union were rejected, the British conditions for approving of France asking for an armistice would be automatically reinstated. A halfhearted attempt to do this was made at 8 P.M. in a telegram from the Foreign Office to its Ambassador at Bordeaux but even then the point was not made explicitly. And by that time it was too late.[48]

† De Gaulle thought that "perhaps" Churchill withdrew the telegrams earlier as the result of their luncheon talk.[49]

cabinet to know was the British response to the government's request of the night before. But on this crucial point, the weary Premier was less than responsive—or frank. He opened the meeting, he states in his memoirs, by informing the cabinet of the result of his communication to London. "I indicated," he says, "that the British government had given its conditional assent and then withdrawn it." According to President Lebrun and Marin, among others present, he did not mention the two British telegrams.

"I did not know of the two telegrams," says Lebrun who was presiding. "They were not read to the cabinet."

"I did not have to read the telegrams," Reynaud explained to this author.* "They had been withdrawn, and I don't believe I even had the texts with me. I simply alluded to them as quickly as I could, happy that I had obtained their withdrawal."

At the Pétain trial Reynaud was sharply cross-examined about this by Isorni, the Marshal's chief defense lawyer.

"Did you read the telegrams?"

"No. That was completely useless."

"You thought it was useless to deprive the government of such important information?" Isorni persisted.

"Entirely useless," Reynaud responded, "since I had given a résumé of the two telegrams. There was nothing in them that I did not mention."

But wasn't there? Chautemps swears that in telling the Council of the British response Reynaud never mentioned the British reservation about the French fleet sailing to British ports. The Premier merely told them, he says, that the British government had refused its consent to the French asking for armistice conditions, which was not true. Marin, who had no use for Chautemps, agrees with him on that. He stresses that it was all the more important for Reynaud to acquaint the government with the full content of the two British messages because at this point Baudouin intervened to reiterate his by now shopworn—but widely believed—falsehood that at Tours Churchill had consented to France asking for an armistice. Though Reynaud again categorically denied it ("I put Baudouin down brutally," he says) he muffed the opportunity, Marin thinks, of really disposing of it once and for all by telling the Council that the British this very day had stated they would go along with an armistice demand only on condition that the French fleet sailed to British waters beforehand and that they had emphasized that the "honor of France" was involved in the treaty of March 28 not to make a separate peace.

Reynaud was anxious to press on to what he considered the much more important matter: the British offer of Union. He was supremely confident that it would be enthusiastically welcomed by his colleagues, thus putting an end to the endless wrangling about an armistice and restoring a unanimous determination to continue the war from North Africa. In a

---

* In a letter of August 29, 1965.

vibrant voice, his slit eyes lighting up, he announced that General de Gaulle had just telephoned him from London the text of a proposal from the British government which was of the highest importance. He read out the note slowly, emphasizing the salient points. "I underlined," he says, "the tremendous importance of a union with England, not only for the further prosecution of the war, but for the postwar years. I terminated by announcing that I had arranged to see Churchill the next day at a port in Brittany to proclaim the union of France and Great Britain."

To the Premier's utter stupefaction his words were greeted with a stony, hostile silence.

> There was no response [says Reynaud]. Not even from Campinchi, Mandel, or Louis Marin! No one spoke up to support me. . . . I was left absolutely alone. . . .

Finally some did speak up, but only to indignantly reject the very idea of a union with Great Britain. Ybarnegaray seemed to sum up the reaction of most of the cabinet. He accused the British of wanting to reduce France "to the status of a dominion." Others argued that it was like proposing uniting with a cadaver, for they were sure that Britain too would soon be finished.

Outside the cabinet room, from which since the day before he had been barred except when a military report was called for, General Weygand was fuming. He had got wind of the British proposal—through the Premier's tapped telephone, Reynaud charges—and had been busy rounding up his supporters to reject it. "Everyone I talked to," he later testified, "rejected it with indignation."

> The feeling of disapproval was unanimous. It could not be otherwise . . . for acceptance of the proposal would have placed France in a state of vassalage impossible to conceive.

The Commander in Chief, in his excitement, gripped as he was that weekend by an anti-British phobia,* does not seem to have given thought to the vassalage in which France would be placed by the Germans in the

---

* He was still seething at the British for reneging on an agreement he and Georges had signed with General Brooke at Briare two days before (June 14) for a common defense of Brittany. The controversy over this event caused further bad blood between the Allies. Brooke, after signing the accord, reported to London that Weygand had told him on the 14th that organized French resistance had come to an end, that the French army was disintegrating into "disconnected groups." He therefore urged London to disregard the agreement and to withdraw the British troops, numbering some 150,000 men. Weygand vehemently denied that he had told Brooke any such thing. On the night of the 14th the British War Office, without consulting the French, released General Brooke from French command and instructed him to pull out all the troops he could. Weygand angrily protested to London. To him it seemed one more example of British bad faith.[50]

event of an armistice, though he surely knew, for he was not unintelligent or unworldly. But one must not lose sight of the overriding reason for his indignant rejection of the British offer: his certainty that Britain's defeat and downfall would follow that of France within a few weeks. To make a union with her at this juncture was ridiculous. As Charles-Roux, the level-headed permanent secretary of the French Foreign Office, points out, "the plan was imaginative and unprecedented, but it presupposed faith in the final victory of the British, and this faith was lacking."

"Actually, it came late," says Marin, who declares that he and Mandel *did* support it at the cabinet meeting.

If Churchill had proposed it three days before at Tours, or better still, on the Monday at Briare, it would have aroused the almost unanimous enthusiasm of the Cabinet. Neither Pétain nor Weygand would have dared oppose it. But since the Thursday the partisans of an armistice had gained strength and the military situation had worsened. The decision which had to be taken immediately was either to depart for North Africa, in which case the project for Union would have taken on great value, or to ask for an armistice, in which case the project fell through. Actually the proposal of Union was considered only as a corollary of the principal decision.[51]

"My setback was thus total," says Reynaud. "It was the greatest disappointment of my life." From this moment of discouragement he began rapidly to lose his nerve and his resolve. "I now felt isolated," he confessed later. "My position was weakened. . . . I let the talk turn again to the question of an armistice."

This was a tactical blunder. Chautemps was only too anxious to take advantage of it. Backed by Frossard, the shifty Vice-Premier demanded that the cabinet come to a decision on his proposal of the day before: to ask the Germans for their terms. In retreating, Reynaud fired a few more shots —perhaps for the record, for he makes much of them in his memoirs.

"It is a question of France's honor," he kept insisting, "since England has not given her consent," which was not quite accurate. Marin spoke up. "I asked Reynaud," he says, "whether in his conscience he considered the honor of France to be implacably engaged. In an absolute silence he answered: 'Of course. Totally.'"

Though he did not say so, Lebrun, who like Reynaud was beginning to lose heart, did not agree. He now felt that France should not shrink from thinking of her own interests first, despite what Britain might say about France honoring the treaty. He revealed his attitude at the trial of Pétain.

From the moment that one of the two signatories to a convention such as that of March 28 retains a part of its forces for its own defense instead of risking it in the common combat, as the British Empire did, it can always remind us of the obligations we incurred but it has no moral right to say: "We cannot release you from your engagement."

Hélène de Portes went further. If some sources can be believed, she sent in to Reynaud at this moment a hastily scrawled note: *"I hope you are not going to play the role of Isabeau of Bavaria!"* [52] It was this lady, consort of Charles VI of France, who at the Treaty of Troyes in 1420 was instrumental in making Henry V of England regent of France.

Mandel, who though determined to keep France in the war had held back because, he told his friends, he was a Jew and did not think he should take the lead, spoke up. "The question," he said, "is really quite simple. There are those here who want to fight and others who don't want to." Chautemps thought the barb was directed against him. "I do not have to take lessons from M. Mandel," he said heatedly.

It was now 6 P.M. and still no decision had been taken. At this point another message was brought in which helped to make one inevitable and to determine which it would be. It was a telephoned telegram to General Weygand from General Georges. Instead of sending it in to the Premier, as was his duty, the generalissimo marked it for the President of the Republic. Dated 5 P.M., June 16, it gave a succinct outline of what Georges called the "worsening situation." The troops were falling back in disorder everywhere when they were not being encircled. Food was lacking not only for the troops but for the civilian refugees along the roads. "Maneuvers difficult because of clogged roads and bombing of railways and bridges. *Absolutely necessary to take decision.*"[53]

Decision for an armistice, that is. There is no doubt that this message from General Georges contributed a great deal to what now took place in Bordeaux. It settled the question for the wavering President of the Republic, who, ineffectual though he was, might have turned the scales by the power of his office if Reynaud failed to use his greater power as Premier to the full. Later at the Pétain trial Lebrun confessed that the message from General Georges had greatly moved him. "You would have had to be made of stone or steel," he testified, "not to have been affected by it in approaching the decisions that now had to be made. It was a very troubling telegram."

It was Georges' message, more than anything else, Reynaud thought afterward, which enabled Weygand "to win." How could a political leader, from the President of the Republic on down through all the cabinet ministers, disregard the anguished cry of the commander of the troops at the front, who only yesterday, as the Council was told, had been unanimously backed by all the top generals still in the field in insisting that the slaughter be stopped? The answer to that question was soon to come. In the greatest confusion, to be sure, but nevertheless.

The cabinet meeting, called to decide the most momentous issue the Third Republic had ever faced, petered out. There was no serious discussion of the British proposal for Union nor any effort to decide one way or the other on the armistice. Reynaud felt that the majority of the ministers were still for asking Germany's terms. Others believed just the opposite. Reynaud never posed the essential question: how many were for and how many were against asking an armistice? Instead, as he himself recounts, "I put an end to the debate by declaring that I wished to confer with the President of the Republic about the situation. I asked the ministers to come back at 10 P.M."[54]

His intention at this moment is shrouded in confusion. His own explanations of it are far from convincing. He flounders in contradictions. Nor does the testimony of the other figures involved clear up—or even agree on—what now happened. In the agony and disarray and decomposition at Bordeaux that Sunday evening it was difficult for any human being to think clearly or to retain in his mind the memory of exactly what happened. Marin says that most of the ministers left the cabinet meeting, which adjourned at 8 P.M., believing, from what the Premier had told them, that they would reassemble at 10 o'clock to take the final decision for or against an armistice. Reynaud had other thoughts.

He first conferred alone with Lebrun, and we have only the testimony of the two men as to what ensued. "Having been put in a minority," Reynaud explains, "my only chance was to get from Lebrun the go-ahead to form a new government of 'resisters.' "[55] In his memoirs and postwar testimony he tells what was in his mind. But his recollections are contradictory. "Actually," he recalls thinking, "the question for me at the moment is simple:

> Can I obtain from this cabinet, where since yesterday I am in a minority and where I have just been beaten, the head of Weygand and the departure of the government for North Africa? Because the answer is plainly "No," I ask for a suspension of the meeting to talk with the President of the Republic. It is up to him and to him alone to allow me to reshuffle my government so that I can make it one of resistance.[56]

But was Reynaud in a minority late on Sunday afternoon when the cabinet adjourned? The evidence is against him here. On the Saturday a majority, as he believed, may have fallen for the Chautemps proposal to ask the British to agree to France seeking armistice conditions. But now on Sunday, after he had told the Council (not very truthfully) that Britain had refused its assent, there seems little doubt that the majority of ministers were behind him in opposing an armistice. Two ministers who opposed it, Marin and Alphonse Rio, later testified that the majority against was either 15 to 9 (Marin) or 14 to 10 (Rio) with the rest undecided. Even Pomaret, Minister of Labor, who was for an armistice, admitted that his side was outnumbered 12 to 8.[57]

When confronted with such evidence after the war Reynaud wavered. After first maintaining he was in a minority he then argued that whether he was or not was irrelevant, and finally admitted that he was not.

A government profoundly divided on a vital question is condemned to paralysis and ceases to be a government. At that moment it is no longer a question of numbers, and the problem for the President of the Council who takes note of this lack of unity in viewpoints is not to know whether he has or has not a majority. . . .[58]

Cross-examined before the Parliamentary Investigating Committee after the war by Marin, he denied ever having said that he was in a minority at the Sunday cabinet meeting.

"You made a terrible mistake," Marin told him, "in misjudging where the majority stood." As to Reynaud's insistence that he could not govern with a divided cabinet, Marin added: "You say that in these circumstances you could not govern. On the contrary, when you have fifteen ministers with you, you can eliminate two or three others. It is not difficult. . . . I think you could have carried on, for we faced the hypothesis of giving way to Pétain, which meant hurling France toward catastrophe. I believed that you were keeping your position when the cabinet suddenly adjourned and you declared you had to talk with the President of the Republic."

Reynaud's response seems lame, in view of all he had said.

But I never said at all that on June 16 there was a majority against me. It was Lebrun who said that, not I. . . . It was not at all a case of a majority against me determining what I did. . . . But one cannot govern when one has against him the two vice-premiers, especially of the "standing" [he used the English word] of Pétain and Chautemps.[59]

So now, to Reynaud, it is no longer a matter of the majority of the cabinet being against him but only two Vice-Premiers. Unfortunately for him—and for the country—the President of the Republic now convinced himself that the majority *was* against Reynaud and that he must conform to it. The fact seems pretty well established, however, that whereas Reynaud may well have been beaten on the Chautemps proposal the day before, he could have carried his colleagues with him the next afternoon on the more crucial question of refusing to ask for an armistice. Ironically, it appears to have been Reynaud himself, fighting for his own survival and, as he thought, that of the country, who helped to convince Lebrun of the contrary.

The President of the Republic says he had sensed at the cabinet meeting that a majority had formed for an armistice and that Reynaud, when they met alone immediately thereafter, strengthened that feeling.

The views expressed, the reflections made by one and the other [he wrote in his memoirs], showed that a very clear majority had formed in favor of the Chautemps proposal. The Premier recognized it. He told me his decision. Because he was in a minority he declared that his government was resigning.[60]

In his testimony at the Pétain trial, Lebrun was more explicit.

> After the Council meeting, Reynaud said to me: "You see, I'm in a minority. I cannot continue." I told him I agreed he was in a minority. "But my dear President," I added, "we have always been in accord. Yesterday I used all my force to prevent you from resigning. I make the same plea today." He then said: "But what will happen? I'm in a minority. I cannot go out and pose the question on which Chautemps has obtained the majority of the cabinet. It is against my policy. Consequently I can't do it. That's my position."[61]

Asked by Senator Tony Révillon, one of the jurors at the Pétain trial, why at this juncture he did not ask Reynaud to form a new government pledged not to seek an armistice, Lebrun replied:

> Oh, in those troubled times anything was possible. There was no Chamber of Deputies sitting. There was nothing. Finally, I admit I was impressed by this majority which had formed in the cabinet. The President of the Republic is the arbiter. I arbitrated in the sense of the vote which had just been taken.[62]

No vote had been taken. It was contrary to the Cabinet's unwritten rules, a fact which a few minutes before Lebrun himself had explained to the court.

At this point in his discussion with the President of the Republic, Reynaud took a fatal step. He was weary, he admits, and thought that "it would be a waste of time" to prolong the talk with all the arguments he had been making in the cabinet meetings in the hearing of Lebrun since June 12. The battered Premier was perhaps more exhausted and discouraged than he realized—or later admitted. Ambassador Biddle had conferred briefly with him as he emerged from the cabinet meeting. "He was in a state of fatigue and despondency," Biddle cabled Washington.

More important, the American Ambassador got the impression that Reynaud was throwing in the sponge. This came as a shock, for Biddle and Matthews had been doing their best at Tours and Bordeaux to buck him up and encourage him to keep France in the war. To the Ambassador's surprise, Reynaud, on his way to see Lebrun, had again painted the disastrous situation in colors more vivid than even Chautemps had used.

> He said [Biddle cabled] that the position [of] the French people was becoming more horrible by the hour. "Masses of refugee women, children and old men were dying on the roads of starvation and illness. . . . The supplies of food had long since been devoured." This "heartrending situation," he claimed, has so affected many members of the cabinet that the pressure to "ask for armistice terms" was too strong to be held down. . . .

So he was confiding to the American Ambassador that France, because of the pitiful plight of its people, would have to ask for an end of hostilities. He would not do it himself, he assured Biddle, because he had signed the pledge to Britain. At any rate, he concluded, the "final decision" would be made at the meeting of the Council "tonight." That was what the cabinet ministers had understood, and that was what Reynaud was saying. But it was not what was in his mind. Biddle seems to have felt that the Premier was being less than frank.

I said that he must now know what his decision would be. In reply he shrugged his shoulders with a gesture of fatigue and said that he had done what he could and the cabinet would decide.

Biddle once more tried to put iron into the faltering head of the French government.

I said that I assumed of course a French Government would continue the fight from other shores even if metropolitan France was occupied by the German Army. He shrugged again and looked away. I stressed the necessity for the continuance of a free Government and the saving of the French Fleet. . . .

This cabled report from an objective, neutral, but sympathetic observer gives probably the most accurate picture there will ever be of the true state of the troubled French Premier as he left the cabinet meeting to confer alone with the President of the Republic that fatal Sunday evening. Margerie, whom Biddle saw for a moment just before, was more frank with him than Reynaud had been.

He said [Biddle cabled] that in all probability Reynaud would tender his resignation when the Council reconvened tonight. As to who would head the new Cabinet he could not say: there was great pressure by certain Cabinet members to have Pétain head the new Cabinet to ask for armistice terms.[63]

Closeted with the President of the Republic, Paul Reynaud now gave in to that pressure. "It did not take me long to see," he says, "that Lebrun had made up his mind. He declared he was for asking an armistice. Nevertheless, he asked me again, as he had the day before, to bend myself to the majority of the Council, that is, to rally to the Chautemps proposal and to remain in power so as to carry it out." This, Reynaud told the President, he could not do.

"To carry out that policy," he says he told Lebrun, *"go and ask Marshal Pétain!"*

This was a fatal pronouncement and his delivering it at this moment would plague him all the remaining days of his life. It gave his enemies (not to mention objective historians) ground for saying that, after all, it was Reynaud himself who advised Lebrun to pick the Marshal as his successor in the full knowledge that Pétain, as head of government, would immediately ask for an armistice. In his postwar memoirs, in his later testimony at the Pétain trial and before the Parliamentary Investigating Committee, and in letters to and conversations with this author and with others, he tried to explain away the phrase, so fraught with consequences; and on occasions he vehemently denied that he had ever suggested Pétain to succeed him.

At a session of the Parliamentary Investigating Committee on December 12, 1950, more than ten years after the event, Paul Bastid, one of the members, asked Reynaud:

> You never advised [Lebrun] to call on Pétain?
> REYNAUD: Never in my life! It was absolutely contrary to my attitude.[64]

Yet nearly a year after his fall, on May 18, 1941, Reynaud wrote a letter to Pétain from a prison in which the old Marshal had confined him, reminding him: "A year ago I took the responsibility . . . of advising the President of the Republic to designate you as my successor. . . . I do not deny the responsibility which I took but I ask *France to forgive me*."*[65]

Why, asks Reynaud in his memoirs, did he not suggest as his successor Chautemps instead of Pétain? Chautemps was the originator of the proposal to ask for conditions for an armistice, which Lebrun now wanted carried out, and besides, unlike the Marshal, he was a veteran officeholder, having been Premier four times and a cabinet minister thirteen other times since 1925.

"Chautemps," answers Reynaud, "represented in my eyes a greater danger than Pétain." He concluded, he says, that Pétain at least would have the character to stand up to Hitler and refuse to deliver the French fleet as part of an armistice agreement, whereas Chautemps would lack the strength to do so. There was, he admits, another consideration. He thought that since Hitler would insist on having the fleet, Pétain would never get an armistice. In that case he, Reynaud, would most probably be called back to form a new government to continue the war.

Be that as it may, at this hour on Sunday evening at Bordeaux—it was nearly 9 o'clock—Reynaud had one last hope of remaining in power. Pétain had not yet been formally named to succeed him. Before that could be done Lebrun, in conformance to the Constitution, had to call in the Presidents of the two chambers and listen to their advice about whom to choose as Premier. Jeanneney, President of the Senate, and Herriot, Speaker of the Chamber, were summoned. Since they also opposed an armistice they would surely, Reynaud thought, urge Lebrun to retain him.

The indefatigable British diplomats, Campbell and Spears, had been working on Jeanneney for two days, pressing him to use his influence and stout heart in keeping Reynaud in power and France in the war. They too had seen the Premier as he emerged from the cabinet meeting and had

---

* The emphasis is Reynaud's.

been consternated to learn that apparently he was giving up. Margerie had tipped them off, as he had Biddle, that the Premier probably was going to resign.

"I asked him," says Spears, "whether he had resigned or not. He said he had not, but intended doing so, as the majority of the cabinet was against him."

"We worked on him for half an hour," Ambassador Campbell, in unwonted language for him, reported to Churchill by telephone, "encouraging him to try to get rid of the evil influences among his colleagues."[66] But they got the impression he was beyond saving.

On leaving Reynaud the Ambassador had telephoned Downing Street that a "ministerial crisis" had developed and that the meeting arranged for the morrow of Churchill with Reynaud off Concarneau consequently was off. The British Prime Minister, with the leaders of the Labor and Liberal Parties and the three Chiefs of Staff, had already boarded a special train at Waterloo Station in London which was to take them to Southampton, where they would leave on a cruiser for their rendezvous with the French.

"We had taken our seats in the train," Churchill recalled later. ". . . There was an odd delay in starting. Evidently some hitch had occurred." Presently his private secretary arrived with the message from Campbell. "On this," writes the Prime Minister, "I returned to Downing Street with a heavy heart."[67]

In Bordeaux Campbell and Spears set off to see Jeanneney before he was called in by Lebrun. On the way they stopped off for a word with Mandel. "He was in a cold rage," Spears reports, fuming that there was nothing to do with *"ces gens là."* Reynaud, he said, "had lost all authority. . . . He can't make up his mind to leave France. . . . You should have held France to her signature." Mandel described Lebrun as stretched out on a sofa sobbing, "incapable of taking anything in," though Spears says he doubted it. The President of the Republic, he believed, had made up his mind to take France out of the war.

A few moments later the British diplomats were with Jeanneney. They found the venerable President of the Senate "even frailer" than the day before but "clearer-minded and calmer than ever." He knew nothing of what had transpired at the cabinet meeting and Campbell and Spears filled him in from what Reynaud had told them and from their handling of the British offer of Union. "We begged him," Spears relates, to find means of influencing the President of the Republic in favor "of asking Reynaud to form a new government." Jeanneney, rather guardedly, said he would do what he could. "We left this fine old man, a monument of rectitude, with a slight feeling of comfort," says Spears. "We were . . . certain that he and Herriot would do all in their power to keep France in the war."[68]

They tried. But it is doubtful if they did all in their power. Here again the testimony of the men involved is conflicting. In the presence of Reynaud, Lebrun explained to the two parliamentary leaders that the Premier refused to carry out the Chautemps proposal despite its backing by the majority of the cabinet, and was resigning. He had asked him to stay on, but on condition he ask for an armistice.

"It will not be asked by me," Reynaud reiterated.

"Who then, tomorrow?" Lebrun asked, turning to the Senate and Chamber chiefs.

"M. Herriot and I at once, and I think in the same breath," Jeanneney told the Pétain court, "answered: 'Paul Reynaud.' "

"But he refuses to treat with Germany," Lebrun said, according to Herriot. "So, I still ask 'who?' "

"That's your affair," Herriot says he replied, unaware perhaps that he and his Senate colleague were, in effect, washing their hands of the problem—after such a feeble effort.

Herriot swore to the Pétain court that neither he nor Jeanneney "pronounced another name. We never mentioned the name of Pétain."

"But didn't President Lebrun indicate to you that he was thinking of Pétain?" one of the Marshal's lawyers asked.

"No," Herriot replied. "He never mentioned the name."

Lebrun's recollection was quite the contrary.

"I told the Presidents of the two Chambers," he testified at the same trial, "of the offer I was going to make to Pétain. While affirming that they remained strongly attached to the former policy [of Reynaud], I cannot say that they offered any opposition to the proposition that I was going to make [to Pétain] and which I confided to them."

Whichever version one accepts it is obvious that Jeanneney and Herriot, who were in close touch with what was going on, knew by this time that if Reynaud went, Pétain would succeed him and that the Marshal would at once ask for an armistice. Everyone in Bordeaux that Sunday agreed at least on that. Chautemps, Bouthillier, Baudouin, Frossard, and Prouvost in the cabinet, Weygand in the army, Laval among the disgruntled politicians, and others had for days—if not longer—been pressing or conniving for the old war hero to take over and end the war. The fact that the Senate and Chamber presidents refrained from mentioning the Marshal's name suggests that they were deliberately evading the issue—and their responsibility. Otherwise, one would think, they would have made a fight of it not only to persuade the vacillating President of the Republic to keep Reynaud but, even more, if that failed, to reject the idea of naming Pétain. It can scarcely be said that at this decisive moment, when so much hung in the balance, these two elder statesmen, with all their prestige and political power, waged much of a battle for what they believed in.

Why did Lebrun decide on the old Marshal so quickly? After the war he told the Parliamentary Investigating Committee that up to an hour before the idea had never entered his head.

I must confess that on leaving the cabinet meeting, I had never thought that Pétain could be a chief of government. To put a soldier, loaded with honors though he be because of his military past, at the head of a government at the tragic moment we had arrived at—that could not have entered my head. Besides, I had been struck by the fatigue of the Marshal during the last cabinet meetings.

Whereupon he blamed Paul Reynaud for his fateful choice! (After the war most of the leading figures in this drama, anxious to improve their niche in history, would heap blame on others.)

Reynaud said to me [Lebrun continued]: "Call on Pétain. He has, I'm told, his cabinet list in his pocket." I did not doubt it. That was how my mind turned in this direction. I said to myself: Well, if everyone thinks Pétain is the man we need. After all, he has his honor.

And he reminded the Committee of the immense prestige and popularity of the old war hero in Parliament, in the press and in the country. "So finally, this was it." Pétain was his choice.[69]

It is puzzling that such veteran politicians and parliamentarians as Reynaud, Jeanneney, and Herriot left the choice up to Lebrun. Since the time of Marshal MacMahon, as we have seen, the President of the Republic had been a figurehead. He could not pressure, much less force, a Premier to step down. Only an adverse vote in the Chamber or Senate could do that. Lebrun possessed no constitutional authority to put conditions to Reynaud for staying on. Nor was the President bound in any way by the Premier's suggestion for his successor. Reynaud, an experienced and skilled politician, knew this, and the wonder is that he gave in so easily, unless he was, as many later would charge, too weary to continue to shoulder the awesome burdens at so disastrous a moment in the nation's history.[70]

The four most responsible officeholders of the Republic, in truth, faltered at this critical point. Louis Marin endeavored after the war to find some rational explanation for it, cross-examining Lebrun and Reynaud before the Parliamentary Investigating Committee, studying the testimony of Jeanneney and Herriot and pondering his own notes and memories as a member of the ill-fated cabinet whose majority, he shows, tried to stick to Reynaud against an armistice to the end. The quest was not very successful.

One continues to ask oneself [he finally wrote in 1951, eleven years after the event] by what mystery and by what aberration the President of the Republic and the President of the Council, both hostile to the armistice, after having consulted the Presidents of the Senate and Chamber, who were equally hostile to it, called to power the man whose first move, they knew, would be to ask for an armistice?[71]

Despite all the torrents of words which the four men, Reynaud especially, uttered by way of explanation and in self-defense in their postwar testimony and memoirs, the mystery remains, the aberration confounds. One can only set down what on this crucial Sunday in Bordeaux these harassed, confused, crumbling human beings did when cornered by fate and the excuses they later offered for it.

Shortly before 10 P.M. the cabinet members began to gather outside Lebrun's office. Ignorant of what had just taken place within they had arrived in the expectation that the cabinet would meet at 10 o'clock, as Reynaud had promised, and that it would at last take a decision on the armistice. Since they felt that the majority of members were behind the Premier they were fairly certain of what the decision would be. Reynaud emerged. "I crossed the room where the ministers were waiting," he recounts, "and merely said: 'Marshal Pétain is forming a government,' and left. The formality of handing in the resignation of the government seemed to me a useless ritual."[72]

The ministers were speechless. It took some time before Reynaud's own supporters felt their indignation welling up.

One of them, Louis Marin, commented later, "The ministers themselves never gave in their resignations. The Premier alone handed in the resignation of the cabinet, without consulting his colleagues, and after having convoked them for an ultimate meeting, which never took place. . . . I do not believe that ever in our history a situation so dramatic and so profoundly grave in its immediate and ultimate consequences was accompanied by such an imbroglio."[73]

The President of the Republic came out to calm and comfort the flabbergasted ministers. Georges Monnet recalled the scene.

Gentlemen, [Lebrun said] the cabinet will not be meeting now. Excuse me for not having given you notice. I was unable to change Reynaud's mind. He insisted on resigning. Consequently, there will be no session of the cabinet. But I ask you to remain with me. A new government is going to be formed by Marshal Pétain. A certain number of you will be called by the new President of the Council to become his collaborators. But I ask the rest of you to remain also. I want all of us to be united this evening in the same sentiment of sadness.

"I believe," Monnet adds, "that all of us remained there with Lebrun, some because they knew they would be called, the others because they wished to be witnesses of such a dramatic event."[74]

There were no witnesses to what had just happened in the President's office except the participants themselves. Lebrun described it at the Pétain trial. He was closeted alone with the Marshal, whom he had hastily summoned.

It was perhaps 11 o'clock in the evening and I was preoccupied with seeing to it that France had a government by the morrow. I greeted the marshal and

said: "Well, now. Form a government." Instantly the Marshal opened his briefcase and pulled out a list. "There is my government," he said.

The President admitted he was pleasantly surprised. "I remembered
how difficult it had been during my eight years in office to constitute a government. It had usually taken three or four days. But here I had one in a
minute. I found that splendid."

No one has revealed so well the kind of man Lebrun was as he himself
in that recitation.

Since Pétain knew few politicians and had nothing but contempt for
most of them, it seemed surprising to some that he would have a list of
ministers in his pocket. It seemed obvious to others that someone in the
camarilla that had been pushing the Marshal to take over power had drawn
up the list for him. They suspected Raphaël Alibert, his political mentor
for many years, who now became Undersecretary of the Premier's office.
A fanatical royalist whose mind still dwelt in the seventeenth century and
who, as someone said, belonged to that dangerous race of scholars who
transformed their chimeras into action, he was now in a position, at the
Marshal's elbow, to take his revenge on the hated Republic.

"Why did you pick *him*?" the President of the Parliamentary Investigating Committee asked Pétain many years afterward.

"Because I didn't know anyone," he replied.

"My memory has become fugitive. I'm ninety-one," the Marshal told
the Committee when its members called on him one July day in 1947 at
the Fortress of *l'Ile d'Yeu* where he was then confined. Still, he tried to recall how he had made up his cabinet list so quickly on the evening of June
16, 1940, at Bordeaux.

"I did it successively," he said. "The first called upon called in a
second. Soon there were many."

"Who was the first? Pierre Laval?"

"No. It was those who showed up themselves."[75]

Many "showed up themselves." In fact there was a rush of defeatist
politicians and defeated generals toward the Marshal's office and a loud
clamor among some of them for important posts in a government resolved
to surrender. Pierre Laval, despite what Pétain remembered, was among
the first. And Camille Chautemps.

Paul Reynaud seemed immensely relieved to be free of his crushing
burden. Ambassador Biddle, who saw him at 11 o'clock, found him "calm
and entirely himself—a man relieved of an enormous weight."

"I have remained faithful to my word," he said, "and loyal to my policy
of closest collaboration with Great Britain and the United States. . . . The
majority felt the sacrifices France is being called to make are too great to con-

tinue. I have resigned and the President has appointed Marshal Pétain in my place. . . ."

In his cable, dashed off to Washington at midnight, Biddle added: "Pétain will of course immediately seek an armistice."[76]

Campbell and Spears, who sought out Reynaud shortly after 10 o'clock, also were struck by his sense of relief that his ordeal was over. It had taken some doing to find him, as Spears later reported in his usual picturesque manner. He and the Ambassador found the large hall of the Premier's residence dark. "There was absolutely no one about," Spears says. For some minutes the British diplomats poked around in the shadows until they finally spied light behind the crack of a door, shoved it open and discovered Reynaud chatting with Margerie. Though the retiring Premier was at first reserved with his British visitors, he soon, says Spears, began to chat easily with them, filling them in on what had happened. He thought that Pétain's advent was inevitable, that he himself had done all he could to keep France in the war, but that "a majority" of the cabinet had turned against him. The Marshal had been most friendly toward him, he said, and the President of the Republic had asked him to remain at hand. "The President thought he might resort to me once more," he said, explaining that if the German armistice terms were unacceptable, as he thought they were bound to be, he would again be asked to take over.

"Reynaud," say Spears, "seemed to gain solace from just talking," but the impression the British general got was that the man was slipping "into a world of unreality." Spears was certain of it when Reynaud suddenly proposed that he keep his rendezvous with Churchill in Brittany the next day. He would ask the Marshal, he said, for a plane to take him there.

" 'Tomorrow there will be another Government and you will no longer speak for anyone,' " Spears says he replied "perhaps unduly brutally. 'The meeting has been cancelled.' "*

On this note the interview ended. Spears recounts that Margerie told him in London a few days later that on the departure of the British envoys Reynaud had gone into the drawing room where Countess de Portes and "the beautiful Countess de Montgomery" were awaiting him. The ex-Premier was in good spirits and took pleasure in reading out to the two ladies the text of an emotional telegram he was drafting to Roosevelt, expressing his gratitude for the American President's encouragement given to him and the country. After the solace of conversation, the solace of women. It seems doubtful whether Paul Reynaud even then realized how much the woman he loved had contributed to his downfall and to all that would now beset the wounded beaten country.

---

* Reynaud confirms the incident with a naiveté unusual for so sophisticated a man. "I was so convinced at that moment," he writes, "that I would resume power that I put the question as to whether I could keep the rendezvous with Churchill the next day. But Spears objected with reason that this was not possible as I was no longer President of the Council."[77]

Spears next sought out Mandel. He had asked Reynaud in vain to come to England to set up a French resistance movement. He now wanted to put the same request to Mandel. The prefecture too was dark but Spears finally discovered the Minister of Interior sitting at a small table at one end of a long gallery, lit only by a single candle. Mandel also declined to leave the country. "Because I am a Jew it would look as if I were running away," he said. A door opened on the other side of the hall. Out of a room brightly lit with candles stepped a woman. Spears was struck by her "plump, pleasant features and fair hair." This was Madame Béatrice Bretty, the actress.

"The trunks are packed, Georges," she said. Spears thought that "the inflection of slight urgency and pleading" in her voice perhaps meant that she had overheard them and that she was suggesting that with their trunks packed they could well get away to England, as he had pled. This was a false impression. The good lady, it is more probable, was simply saying that in the turgid, growingly anti-Semitic atmosphere in Bordeaux it would be well for Mandel to get out of town as soon as possible. Sooner than she perhaps expected, she proved to be right.[78]

While groping about in the obscurity of the Premier's residence in search of Reynaud earlier in the evening, Spears had bumped into de Gaulle, who was leaning his tall frame against a large pillar in the hall. He had landed at the airport at 9:30 P.M in the British plane which Churchill had lent him in London. As he stepped off the aircraft two aides gave him the news. "That meant certain capitulation," he says he realized, and in the instant he made up his mind. "My decision," he recalled later, "was taken at once. I was going to pull out next morning." He drove into the city and first called on Reynaud.

"I found him," he relates, "without illusions about what the advent of the Marshal meant. He himself seemed relieved at shedding his insupportable burden."[79]

According to Spears, whose dramatic version of his encounters with de Gaulle during the next eleven hours is disputed by French historians and brushed aside by the general himself in his own account, de Gaulle, propped up against the column in the darkened hall, whispered to him that he wanted to get back to England but that he feared General Weygand might arrest him before he could get away. They agreed to meet later in the evening at the Hôtel Montré, where the British diplomats were staying. There in the middle of the night they had a further talk. De Gaulle was determined to go to London and organize what resistance he could to the Pétain regime. His only fear, he repeated, was that Weygand, who he now learned was to be the Marshal's Minister of Defense, would arrest him before he could depart. He would try to lie low the rest of the night, meet Spears at the latter's hotel at 7 A.M., and drive with him in an Embassy car to the airport where they would board the British plane.

Spears telephoned Churchill the news. Both realized that de Gaulle

could do nothing further in France. He was the most junior of all the brigadier generals. Weygand would easily suppress him. Also he was quite unknown to the general public in France and had no political following
whatsoever. But he was all there was. Reynaud and Mandel had refused to
leave the country. Churchill agreed that Spears should bring de Gaulle out.
The general in the meantime called again on Reynaud. His wallet was
almost empty. Reynaud gave him, de Gaulle says, 100,000 francs out of
"secret funds." Margerie arranged to send passports to de Gaulle's wife and
children in Brittany and to try to get them passage on a boat from Brest to
England.* Then de Gaulle went to a small inconspicuous hotel near the
Splendide to spend the rest of the night.

He met Spears at the latter's hotel at 7:30 the next morning and the
Englishman's tale of what followed is so melodramatic that one French historian of the day's events, who quotes it in his own book, suggests that it
has "all the allure of a scenario in a spy film" and "might have been taken
from *The Three Musketeers*."†

De Gaulle had brought quite a lot of luggage, Spears says, and this
was crammed into the Embassy car by Lieutenant Geoffroy de Courcel, a
young career diplomat serving as his aide. The three men then set off for
the airfield at Mérignac—but not directly. "At de Gaulle's request," Spears
swears, "a curious little comedy was played." In order to throw Weygand
off the scent, de Gaulle had the car driven first to the temporary army headquarters in the rue Vital-Carles where he stopped long enough to make
several appointments for himself with various officers and officials for later
in the day. Spears, impatient to get way with his charge, feared that de
Gaulle would be arrested by the military any moment. His appointments
duly made, de Gaulle directed the French chauffeur to drive on to the airport.

The guard at the entrance let them through without trouble and they
drove their small car past the hangars onto the field to find the British plane.
This proved difficult. Spears says the field was packed with more planes
than he had ever seen, lined up wing to wing over the whole airdrome. He
wondered why they had not been thrown into the battle at the moment
when Reynaud and Weygand were crying for more British aircraft. But at
least, he thought, they were being assembled to fly to North Africa, where
they would be safe from the Germans. After a search they located the small
British plane. The pilot was reconnoitering the field to find a few hundred
yards of clearance in which to take off. While he was away Spears and de
Gaulle worked out the final plan. The latter would act as if he had come
to see his English friend off, and at the last moment, as the plane started to
move, Spears would pull him aboard. This would take some doing since de
Gaulle was tall and heavy and Spears rather the opposite.

---

* They got out, he says, on the last boat.
† Henri Amouroux in *Le 18 juin 1940,* pp. 352, 354.

Then a new complication arose. The British pilot declared that de Gaulle's luggage was so heavy and in so many pieces it would have to be lashed down. But there was no rope or twine aboard. Courcel set off to a hanger to try to find some. The new delay gave Spears the jitters. He was almost certain that some official would show up to apprehend the fleeing general. French accounts, in fact, say that just before Courcel set off in a frantic search for some rope two Army officers who had been attached to Reynaud's office did arrive and asked the young lieutenant where de Gaulle was going. Courcel explained that he had "been charged with a mission to London." The two officers seemed satisfied with the explanation and withdrew.

Courcel finally returned with a ball of twine, the luggage was lashed, the propellers started turning, Spears climbed into the machine, the plane began to move. "With hooked hands," Spears tells, "I hoisted de Gaulle on board. Courcel, more nimble, was in in a trice. The door slammed. I just had time to see the gaping face of the chauffeur and one or two more beside him. Gingerly we taxied till the pilot found the space he had located, then with great skill, in a very short distance, he took off."[80]

De Gaulle in his memoirs describes leaving Bordeaux on the journey that would take him so far in history in one laconic sentence: "The departure took place without romanticism and without difficulty."[81]

In the little bobbling plane, as it passed over the shores of Brittany where ships bombed by the Germans could be seen afire and sinking, and then headed inland across the peninsula above the smoke from burning towns and woods, flying at one moment over Paimpont, where de Gaulle's mother lay ill, the fugitive general sat back in his seat and began to meditate on what had happened to France, to Reynaud, to Pétain, and finally on his own destiny. He was carrying with him, Churchill believed, "in this small plane the honor of France."

Though still highly confused and embittered by what had taken place at Bordeaux with such terrifying rapidity that weekend, his thoughts seemed to clear up as the plane plugged on toward England. He put them down later in his memoirs, and no one else on the French side has quite so well, so eloquently and with such perception, described this turning point in the nation's history.

He felt compassion and understanding for Reynaud, with whom for years he had worked, however vainly, to modernize the Army and to prepare the divided country for a conflict that had seemed to both of them inevitable once Hitler began feverishly to rearm and to expand the German frontiers.

All along the days without respite and the nights without sleep the President of the Council felt the entire responsibility for the fate of France weighing heavily on him. . . . He had not taken over the government until the eve of our misfortunes, with no time to face them and after having for so long proposed a military policy which might have prevented them. He met the torment with a solidity of spirit which cannot be denied. Never, during these dramatic days, did Paul Reynaud cease to be master of himself. One never saw him let himself be carried away, become indignant, complain. It was a tragic spectacle which saw this man of such worth unjustly crushed by events beyond his control.

No finer tribute was ever paid Paul Reynaud.

To de Gaulle, the Republic itself had failed to stand the test of adversity.

At a moment when the problem was posed on which depended all the present and all the future of France, the Parliament did not sit, the government showed itself incapable of taking a drastic solution, the President of the Republic abstained from raising his voice, even in a cabinet meeting, to express the superior interests of the country. This collapse of the state was at the bottom of the national drama. At the first flash of lightning, the regime, in its terrible infirmity, had no measure of, and no *rapport* with, the defense, the honor, the independence of France.[82]

As for Pétain, de Gaulle was inclined to blame his resolve to surrender on old age.

Alas! The years had corroded his character. Age delivered him to the maneuvers of men skillful in taking advantage of his majestic lassitude. Old age is a shipwreck. So that nothing should be spared us, the old age of Marshal Pétain was going to identify itself with the shipwreck of France.[83]

Shortly after noon the plane set down at Heston airport outside London. Spears took de Gaulle to Downing Street. "Winston," he reports, "was sitting in the garden enjoying the sunshine. He got up to greet his guest, and his smile of welcome was very warm and friendly."[84] They arranged for the general to broadcast to his people from London the next day.

What would he say? A couple of telephone calls to the French Embassy and the French mission had indicated that his fellow countrymen in London did not share the Prime Minister's warm feelings toward him. While he unpacked his belongings in a small apartment in Seamore Place lent to him by a friend, this man of overpowering self-confidence was overcome by self-doubts.

"I appeared to myself," he says, "alone and deprived of everything, like a man on the shore of an ocean which he pretended he could cross by swimming."[85]

Marshal Pétain at the Helm

The alacrity with which Pétain was named to succeed Reynaud and with which he produced a list of ministers for his new government was now matched that Sunday evening in Bordeaux by the speed with which he arranged his first cabinet meeting and, more important, by the swiftness with which it reached the great decision.

There were a couple of momentary hitches amidst the confusion in the prefecture, where, in Lebrun's office, the Marshal was seeing in rapid turn one politician after another. Weygand was also very much present. When he saw that de Gaulle had been retained as Undersecretary of War he exclaimed to the Marshal: "Ah! No! Not that one! I don't get along with a character like that."[86] The name was scratched off.

More difficult was the case of Pierre Laval. The intriguing senator, like the Marshal, believed his time had come. Throughout the weekend he had been busy in his office next to Mayor Marquet's at the Hôtel de Ville rounding up support for a Pétain government and an armistice. When he called on the Marshal at 10:30 he was shocked to find that he had been named Minister of Justice. He at once demanded to be made Minister of Foreign Affairs. Believing that the old soldier would be only a figurehead in the new government, he wanted to direct the negotiations with Germany and he wanted to break with Britain, against which he had been nursing his grudges since the Italo-Abyssinian affair.

According to his own account at the Pétain trial Laval addressed the old man:

> *Monsieur le Maréchal,* I thank you. I have been Minister of Justice. I'm sorry, but at the present moment I cannot render you any service in that department. . . . I have been Minister of Foreign Affairs. I would prefer that post.
> "I have already given that place to Baudouin," he said.
> I regret it.
> "All right. I will give it to you," he responded.
> So he gave me the Ministry of Foreign Affairs. . . . While we were talking General Weygand entered and asked to speak to the Marshal in private. . . .[87]

Outside the Marshal's office the generalissimo had been chatting with Charles-Roux. Suddenly Baudouin emerged and told them that Pétain had given in to Laval and was giving him the Foreign Ministry. He himself had stepped down. Charles-Roux thought that Laval would be a disaster to the country in such an office.

> I had no personal animosity against Laval [says Charles-Roux]. But I knew that since arriving at Bordeaux he had made himself the interpreter of all the recriminations against England, of all the criticisms of the British alliance, and had been crying to the rooftops that the sole means of saving France was to throw her into the arms of Germany.[88]

He begged General Weygand, he says, to tell Pétain of his "objections." The generalissimo, who had no love for Laval, was pleased to do so.

It was at this moment that Laval, none too happily, saw Weygand approach. According to Charles-Roux, the generalissimo was twice rebuffed by Pétain. At the end of the second encounter the Marshal himself stepped out of his room to tell them: "Laval won't give in. He persists in refusing the Ministry of Justice and demands the Foreign Office." Nevertheless, Charles-Roux got the impression that Pétain was annoyed at Laval's stubbornness. A few moments later Laval himself emerged. "He walked across the room muttering," says the Secretary, "and went out slamming the door."

Laval himself told the Pétain trial court: "After further talk with Weygand, the Marshal came back and said to me: 'You cannot be Minister of Foreign Affairs because your nomination to that post would be considered a provocation by Great Britain.' "

"I replied," says Laval: "Marshal, I do not object. I'm very sorry, but in these conditions I cannot enter your government."[89]

Laval was out. But not for long. His friend Marquet, who had been named Minister of Interior, also withdrew. The old Marshal had survived his first ministerial crisis. And within half an hour. His new government of seventeen ministers included eleven who had been in the Reynaud government. Camille Chautemps, to no one's surprise, was named Vice-Premier and accepted. Frossard, the former Communist and Socialist, who had given him such staunch support in tricking Reynaud, was made Minister of Public Works. Baudouin was promoted to Foreign Minister and Bouthillier remained as Finance Minister—such was the reward to Reynaud's former friends and, in the case of the last two, his protégés. Two Socialists entered the cabinet, Albert Rivière, who had been in the old one and who had favored an armistice, and André Février, a newcomer. They did it with the anguished approval of the Socialist leader, Léon Blum, who since arriving at Bordeaux had been stunned and then overwhelmed by the events of the weekend. Thus the Left added its support to Pétain and his program.*

---

* The Communist Party, which had the bulk of the organized workers, was outlawed at the beginning of the war because of its support of the Soviet-Nazi Pact and its opposition to the war, for which it blamed, not the Germans, but the "British and French imperialists." Its clandestine propaganda during the phony war contributed a good deal, especially among the workers and soldiers, to a growing desire in France to halt the war before the real fighting started. All through the disastrous Battle of France *Humanité,* the party's official newspaper, which was published clandestinely, called for "a government of peace." On June 17, the day the forming of the Pétain government was announced in the press, *Humanité* appealed for the end of the fighting, saying: "Is the City of London (the financial district) going to obtain the continuation of the massacre of our brothers and sons in order to permit England, with its 40 million people, to exploit 400 million?"

When this author entered Paris in June he noticed a surprising fraternal feeling between the French Communists and the Nazi occupiers. On July 4 *Humanité* appeared with an appeal to the French workers to fraternize more with the German soldiers. "It is particularly encouraging," it wrote, "to see the number of Parisian workers meeting in the most friendly way with the German soldiers." During the

It was plain that the new government would be dominated by the military. Besides the Marshal, three generals and one admiral entered the government. Weygand was Minister of National Defense; General Colson, the Chief of the General Staff for the Interior, was Minister of War; General Pujo was Minister of Air. Admiral Darlan, who a day before had told Herriot he would sail away with the fleet if "those bastards" made an armistice, was Minister of Marine.

"It is not the first time in our history," Jean Zay, who had resigned as Minister of Education the previous September to go to the front as a soldier, commented, "that the military men lost a war by their incapacity and their lack of imagination. But it is without doubt the first time that in sanctioning disaster they seize power. The Republic has often feared the dictatorship of conquering generals. It never dreamt of that of the defeated."*[90]

The new cabinet met for the first time shortly before midnight and disposed of its business in thirty minutes. It approved the text of an official communiqué for the morning papers telling of the change of government.

In the present grave circumstances the Council of Ministers, on the recommendation of M. Paul Reynaud, President of the Council, estimated that the government of France should be entrusted to a high personality having the unanimous respect of the nation.†

In consequence M. Paul Reynaud has handed in the resignation of his government to the President of the Republic and M. Lebrun has accepted it, in rendering homage to the patriotism which dictated it, and has immediately called on Marshal Pétain, who has agreed to form a new ministry.

The President of the Republic has thanked Marshal Pétain, who in assum-

---

first days of the occupation of Paris three members of the Central Committee called on the German military command to ask permission for *Humanité* to appear openly. The request was granted but before the journal could reappear the permission was sabotaged by the Paris police, who arrested the three.

The Communist underground press welcomed Pétain's desire for an armistice. After the German attack on Russia in 1941 the French Communists, like those of other lands, reversed their stand on the war and made of it a holy crusade. It was only after this that the French Communists, like other Frenchmen, began to organize resistance to the Germans. Once they had flopped, they fought courageously in the Resistance.

* Zay overlooked the role of the military after the Franco-Prussian War, about which Clemenceau had been so eloquent and bitter. At the time of the Dreyfus Affair, the old Tiger wrote: "The Franco-Prussian war brought the bankruptcy of our military organization. It would appear natural for the French people to condemn unanimously the incompetent generals. . . . Nothing of the sort happened. The ensuing civil war permitted the soldiers to return as victors drunk with vengeance instead of coming home with their faces hidden in shame after the saddest of all capitulations in history. They were praised to the skies. . . . They have been the rulers of France ever since."[91]

† "A lie!" said Reynaud when he learned of the communiqué. "A complete lie!"[92]

ing the heaviest responsibility which has ever weighed on a French statesman, manifested once more his devotion to the country.

In less time than it took to read out this official version of events, the 107th and last government of the Third Republic then took its decision.

"The government," said Pétain "has been formed. Its essential task, without losing time—too much has already been lost—is to ask the German government under what conditions it will stop hostilities."[93]

There was no debate, not even any discussion. Unanimously the ministers agreed.

35

ARMISTICE!
JUNE 17–29, 1940

No time was lost. The cabinet adjourned at midnight and Baudouin, the new Minister of Foreign Affairs, immediately sent for the Spanish Ambassador. While waiting for him he hastily scribbled a note.

José Felix de Lequerica was not surprised by his summons. He had been, as we have seen, working with a number of French defeatists such as Monzie on the proposal for an armistice. So sure was he that he would be called before the night was over that he had arranged to telephone any message the French government might have for the Germans to Hendaye, where messengers were waiting to carry it over the frontier to Irún and telephone it from there to Madrid. When Lequerica arrived Baudouin had finished penning his note.

The French government of Marshal Pétain requests the Spanish government to act as rapidly as possible as intermediary with the German government with a view to the cessation of hostilities and the settlement of conditions for peace. The French government hopes that the German government, as soon as it takes note of this request, will give its Air Force orders to stop the bombing of cities.

The new Pétain government, then, in the belief that the war was as good as over, was asking not only for the terms of an armistice to halt the hostilities but for the conditions of a *peace* settlement.*

According to Lequerica he himself, after reading the note, asked

---

* After the war Baudouin strenuously denied that he had ever asked for peace conditions. In his note to the Papal Nuncio on the morning of the 17th asking the Holy See to act as intermediary with the Italian government Baudouin reiterated his government's desire to "examine the bases for a durable peace between the two countries." He repeated the phrase in a broadcast later in the day.

Baudouin: "Do you mean to speak of conditions for an armistice or for a peace, or for both?" The Ambassador says Baudouin replied: "An armistice is always a temporary expedient. The government would also like to know the conditions for peace." That matter cleared up, Lequerica rushed back to the Spanish consulate and got off the French note to Madrid.[1]

The British Ambassador was the next caller. He listened to Baudouin's feverish explanations in cold silence. Baudouin confesses he spoke with great emotion, expressing the hope that Britain would now show its compassion "for its bleeding and trampled ally." He promised that France would never deliver its fleet to the Germans and that he would keep Campbell fully informed of the armistice negotiations as they proceeded. The Ambassador spoke scarcely a word. "The dryness and cold haughtiness of the man was atrocious," Baudouin recorded in his journal. The reserve of the veteran British diplomat was natural. Spears stresses how cool he was under pressure. But it turned out to be excessive and in one important respect a serious error. He made no mention of the two telegrams of Sunday afternoon giving British assent to France asking for an armistice only on condition that the French fleet was sailed to British waters. The sober-minded Charles-Roux, who was present, confirms this.[2] Nor did the Ambassador deign to say that in asking for an armistice without British agreement, France was breaking its word to Britain. Imperturbable, Campbell took his leave without uttering a word.

The amiable Anthony J. Drexel Biddle, who arrived at 2 A.M., as the British Ambassador departed, was a relief to the anguished Baudouin. The American Ambassador listened with more sympathy to the Foreign Minister's tale of woe about the French army being "completely smashed" and on how "imperative" it was "to stop the slaughter." Baudouin assured him, as he had Campbell, that "the fleet would never be surrendered to Germany." That was why Admiral Darlan, he said, had been named Minister of Marine. Amiable though he was, Biddle was not taken in. "The Admiral's new government associates," he cabled Washington, "hardly inspire complete confidence that the French fleet will remain a bulwark against Nazi aggression."[3] The question of what would happen to the French navy was becoming almost as perturbing to Washington as to London. Before the day was out Roosevelt and Secretary Hull would make that clear to the Bordeaux government.

Churchill too. During the day of the 17th he sent a personal message to Pétain and Weygand, instructing Campbell to give copies to Lebrun and Darlan.

I wish to repeat to you my profound conviction that the illustrious Marshal Pétain and the famous General Weygand . . . will not injure their ally by delivering over to the enemy the fine French Fleet. Such an act would scarify their names for a thousand years of history. Yet this result may easily come by frittering away these few precious hours when the Fleet can be sailed to British or American ports, carrying with it the hope and the honor of France.[4]

As Churchill pointed out to the French Ambassador in London, he did not believe France would dishonor itself by giving up the fleet to the enemy. What he feared was that in the disorder and confusion of defeat the French fleet would be taken by the Germans by surprise before it could be moved out of their reach.[5] Two new 35,000-ton battleships the *Richelieu* and the *Jean-Bart,* which were almost completed, were, he knew, still in the ports of Brittany, which was being rapidly overrun by the German panzers. To stress the necessity of speedy action, Churchill asked A. V. Alexander, the First Lord of the Admiralty, Admiral Sir Dudley Pound, the First Sea Lord, and Lord Lloyd, the Secretary for the Colonies and a personal friend of Weygand, to fly to Bordeaux.

Even before the Germans had time to answer the French request for an armistice, Pétain took a precipitate step. At 12:30 P.M. on June 17, in the midst of a sudden, violent thunderstorm, the first to break the long spell of spring and summer sunshine since the debacle began, the new head of government stepped up to a microphone installed in a classroom of the Lycée Longchamps to broadcast to his fellow countrymen. After telling them that he had taken over power ("I have made a gift of my person to France," he said), he announced that he had asked for armistice terms. "With a heavy heart," he said, *"I tell you today that it is necessary to stop the fighting."*

Stop the fighting—even before the armistice talks had begun and before the French could know whether the German conditions were acceptable? That was the way the troops in the field interpreted the Marshal's statement. "They took it literally," Weygand concedes. By midafternoon General Georges was complaining to the generalissimo that the Marshal's broadcast had "broken the last resistance of the French army." Whole regiments, he said, were ceasing to fight. Other units made haste to surrender. Joyously the soldiers threw away their arms. Colonel Passy noted near Brest on the afternoon of the broadcast "the ditches along the roads strewn with arms lamentably abandoned by men shouting: 'The war is over! Pétain has just said so. Why get killed when the war is over?' " In some cases commanding officers simply ordered their men to lay down their arms. In Brittany, for example, the order went out from the 10th Military District: "Confine your men to barracks, collect all arms in the casernes, and await the arrival of the Germans." A similar order was issued by the general commanding the 18th Military District at Bordeaux, where, one would have thought, every possible preparation would have been taken to defend the seat of government. "Disarm everyone," it said. "Consign

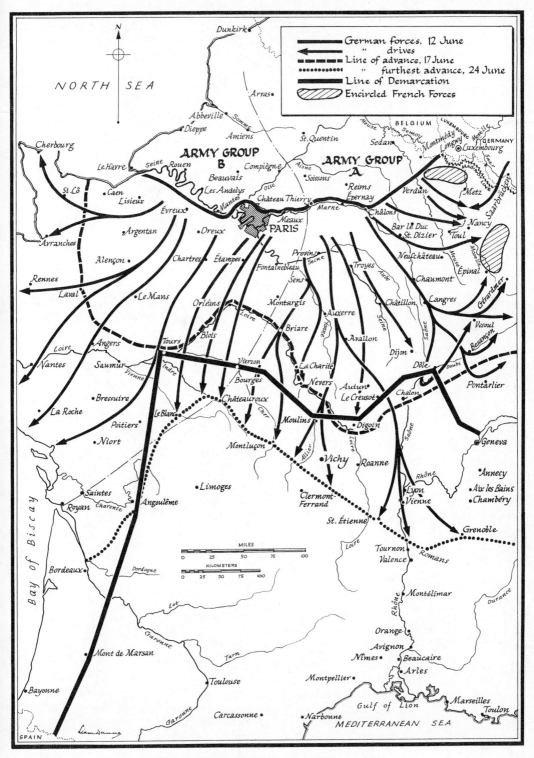

THE END FOR THE FRENCH ARMY
JUNE 14-25, 1940

officers and men to quarters. Remain where you are, without firing. Officers who do not execute these orders will be haled before a court-martial!"

The Germans lost no time in propagating the message of the Marshal. His words were rebroadcast by loudspeakers to French troops.* Leaflets were dropped over them by plane quoting Pétain as saying: "France must abandon the struggle" and calling on them to lay down their arms. Rommel, closing in on Cherbourg with his 7th Panzer Division, spread the news by leaflets happily distributed by French prisoners. He himself drove through villages in a tank waving a white flag and shouting: *"Guerre finie! Krieg fertig! War's over."* At La Ferté-Saint-Aubin, French troops which had been assigned to defend the place let a column of 100 German tanks and vehicles pass by without firing a shot. Near Caen, German and French soldiers began fraternizing in the cafés. At Laval on the afternoon of the 17th three German officers were captured by a French squad which must not have heard the broadcast. The Germans were unarmed and had come into town to shop. "The war is finished for you," they explained to their captors. "The armistice is signed."[6] In vain Weygand issued an order to all forces informing them that there was as yet no armistice and that they must continue to fight.

Darlan similarly instructed the navy in two messages sent out between 1 and 7:30 P.M. He added that however the armistice talks came out "the navy can be certain that in no case will it be delivered intact."

Twice during the day Baudouin tried to diminish the damage caused by the Marshal's careless phrasing—if it was that. An aide of General Weygand telephoned him, he says, that "certain elements" of the army considered that the Marshal had given a veritable order for a cease-fire. The generalissimo demanded a clarification for the army and the populace. Baudouin hastened to issue a "correction" to the press. The Marshal had not said, it explained, that "it is necessary to stop the fighting" but that "it is necessary to *try* to stop the fighting." In an emotional broadcast at 9:30 P.M., the text of which, Baudouin says, was approved by Pétain, he tried to explain to the French people why the new government had asked the enemy for its "conditions for *peace*." In doing so he laid down the line that the Pétain regime would take in its own defense from then on to the bitter end. This was that the "heroic" French army, with little help from the Allies and lacking the necessary tanks, guns, and planes, had done what it could as the *"advance guard."* The government had now "united around our glorious military chiefs, who are the incarnation [of France's] tradition and soul." To Reynaud, as he says in his memoirs, the defeated generals seemed a little less than "glorious," but few in Bor-

---

* The author, who entered Paris that day, heard Pétain's recorded radio address over a loudspeaker from a German army sound truck parked in the Place de la Concorde. It was repeated to the crowds every few minutes throughout the afternoon and evening.

deaux, or in the country, were in a state at this disastrous moment to be so realistic. France, Baudouin concluded in the most flowery and hypocritical language,

has not abandoned the struggle nor laid down its arms. . . . It is not ready and will never be ready to accept dishonorable terms, to abandon the spiritual freedom of its people, to betray the soul of France.

During the day Baudouin had had more prosaic tasks to perform. The British were far from pleased with the French going ahead with an armistice without their accord and especially without honoring the condition which London had put in its two telegrams of the day before. The British Ambassador, who on the Sunday had withdrawn the telegrams and who had not mentioned them to Baudouin at their morning meeting in the first hour of Monday, now reinstated them. Or did he? On this the French and British disagree. Lord Halifax, the British Foreign Secretary, maintains that Campbell not only delivered the two telegrams to the French government but insisted to Pétain that the French fleet be sent to British ports before armistice negotiations began. Moreover Campbell was assured by Baudouin that a decision to do so had already been taken and that it only remained for the cabinet to confirm it.[7]

The French version is quite otherwise. And though Baudouin, who gives it, is not always trustworthy, in this case he is confirmed in part by Charles-Roux, whose word is good. Baudouin being occupied by a conference with the Marshal, the British Ambassador saw Charles-Roux on the afternoon of June 17 and presented him the two telegrams stipulating Britain's assent to France asking for armistice conditions *only* if the French fleet took refuge in British ports. It was the first time the Secretary had seen them, or even heard of them. An hour later he turned them over to Baudouin, who also said he was seeing them for the first time.

Early the next morning, the 18th, they called in Reynaud, who explained that the messages had been withdrawn by Campbell and that, Charles-Roux adds, for that reason he had not brought them to the attention of the cabinet on the Sunday evening. When Baudouin conferred with Campbell later in the morning he asked him, he says, whether he had reinstated the telegrams "for the record" or because they now represented the views of the British government. Campbell, after returning to the consulate to check on his instructions, returned and, according to Baudouin, told him that the two messages should be considered as part of the record of the negotiations on the 16th "which ended in Churchill's offer of Union."[8] This is an unlikely story and Charles-Roux, who was not present, does not vouch for it. Nor did the Parliamentary Investigating Committee give it any credence when they questioned Baudouin after the war. It is important only because Baudouin convinced Pétain and his government that it was true.

The British were becoming tougher on the problem of the disposal of the French fleet than the French realized. They were not content just to appeal to a government in which they were losing trust. On that very day, the 17th, Admiral Cunningham, Commander of the British Mediterranean Fleet, received a message from London.

If France concludes a separate peace, every effort must be employed to see that the French Fleet passes under our authority—or, if not, *to sink it*.[9]

This ominous message presaged a chain of events which would result in one of the most lamentable episodes of the war.

President Roosevelt also got tough during the day with the new French government about the fleet and other matters. Early on the morning of June 17 the American government showed its distrust of the new Pétain regime by ordering all French assets in the United States frozen. But it was the French fleet which most concerned the naval-minded American President. If it were put at the disposal of the British it would increase their chances of successfully defending their island from German assault. More than anyone else in Washington Roosevelt realized that the survival of the United States depended to a large extent on the survival of Britain. If the French fleet were now to be added to the navies of Germany and Italy it would give the Axis a strength on the sea which would not only threaten Britain's security, but directly from across the Atlantic that of the United States, whose Navy was concentrated in the Pacific because of the threat of Japan. Finally Roosevelt was keenly aware of something that in the debacle had escaped the attention of Pétain, Weygand, and Darlan: that if France were eventually to reenter the war, with the help of America and Britain, from bases in North Africa, the French fleet could play a vital role.

At 5 P.M. Roosevelt got off to Bordeaux a stiff note about the fleet. Secretary Hull, who drafted it, recalled later that it "was one of the strongest cables of my career." Biddle was instructed to see Admiral Darlan and Baudouin "immediately" and tell them that in the opinion of the American government

should the French government, before concluding any armistice . . . fail to see that the fleet is kept out of the hands of her opponents, [it] will . . . fatally impair . . . the eventual restoration of French independence. . . .

Furthermore should the French government . . . permit the French Fleet to be surrendered to Germany, the French government will permanently lose the friendship and goodwill of the government of the United States.[10]

The next morning, in Bordeaux, Biddle caught Admiral Darlan as he was going into a cabinet meeting and handed him Roosevelt's sharp note. Missing Baudouin, he called him out of the session and presented him with a copy. Both recipients reacted with ill-concealed irritation. "I told

Biddle," says Baudouin, "that the government refused to accept the second paragraph, which was injurious to Franco-American amity." "He must tell me," Biddle cabled Washington, "that the last sentence of the message had 'deeply pained' the French Government." In parentheses the Ambassador added: "I believe, however, that in spite of this natural feeling the effect thereof was highly salutary." Baudouin assured the Ambassador "in the most solemn manner that the French Fleet would never be surrendered to the enemy. There is no question of that."*

> Baudouin added that he could not, however, say that the French Fleet would join the British Fleet. It might be sent overseas or it might be sunk. . . . I urged . . . that the fleet be moved to safety rather than destroyed.[11]

To the Americans, and more importantly to the British, scuttling the French fleet would be better than handing it over intact to the Germans; and Ambassador Campbell made clear in his dispatches to London that scuttling was all that could be hoped for, given the zeal of the Pétain government to surrender as quickly as possible. But this would deprive the Allies and especially France herself, if she eventually resumed resistance, of a powerful weapon. This eventuality, however, never entered the mind of the Marshal, the generalissimo, or the admiral. They had had enough of fighting the Germans.

Darlan did not like the American note at all. "And now Roosevelt is shitting on me," he told a naval aide. To the cabinet his language was more circumspect but still haughty. "The chief of the French Navy," he said, "needs no advice from the United States about what to do to defend its honor."[12]

Still, the question dogged the government all day of June 18. Shortly after noon the British delegation dispatched by Churchill arrived at Bordeaux to press the matter. Admiral Darlan assured them on his word of honor that his fleet would never fall into German hands and that if the enemy demanded it the armistice negotiations would be broken off. According to the French, Alexander, Admiral Pound, and Lord Lloyd departed "apparently satisfied" with this assurance. Actually they were far from satisfied, especially after seeing Pétain and Weygand the next day. Lord Lloyd was especially disillusioned. An old friend and admirer of Weygand, Lloyd reported finding the generalissimo "a crumpled, broken little man completely finished and filled with vague but bitter recriminations. It was a pathetic sight. I hope never to see him again." Pétain struck Lloyd as "vain, senile, and dangerously ga-ga." As for Lebrun, the Presi-

---

* During the night of June 17–18, the Admiralty sent out orders to the Brittany naval bases that no warship must fall intact into enemy hands. The 35,000-ton battleship *Richelieu* at Brest, which had just completed its first trials, and its sister ship, *Jean-Bart* at St.-Nazaire, which was not quite finished, were ordered to sail to Morocco. They got away on June 18 and 19, respectively.

dent of the Republic "was tearful as usual and quite futile." The British party, it is evident, had little faith in the assurances of such men.[13]

The French, for their part, were greatly annoyed at the British for their concern about the French navy. As Darlan noted sarcastically in his diary after the three men departed: "They gave me the impression of heirs coming to reassure themselves that the dying man has indeed bequeathed in their favor without even inquiring about the state of his health."[14] His experience with his visitors from London seems to have prompted Darlan to take measures to see that no French naval vessel got into, or remained in, the hands of the British. On June 18 and on the following days, several messages were sent out to this effect. On the 21st, the day after Lloyd departed, Darlan ordered all French warships in British ports, particularly in Plymouth and Portsmouth, to leave immediately and head for North Africa.[15] At Portsmouth the British admiral commanding forbade them to leave, as did the naval authorities at other ports in Britain and in the Mediterranean. When a French admiral complained to Admiral Cunningham about the British preventing French ships from leaving British bases, the latter responded: "We have to win the war, not only for us but for you, and all these trivialities and sob stuff about friendship and feelings must be swept aside."[16] The allies of two world wars were nearing a breaking point. On the question of the French fleet they were on a collision course.

One lonely French figure tried to keep the Alliance afloat and his countrymen in the war. Late on the afternoon of June 18 General de Gaulle drove to Broadcasting House in London to address his people over the radio. Since arriving in the British capital from Bordeaux the day before he had crossed his own Rubicon. Now, at 6 P.M., sitting alone in a BBC studio with only a British announcer at his side, the rebellious junior French general began, at a signal, to speak.

The chiefs who have been at the head of the French armies for many years have formed a government. This government, alleging the defeat of our armies, has made contact with the enemy to put an end to the fighting. . . .

But has the last word been said? Is all hope gone? Is the defeat final? No! . . . For France is not alone. . . . She has a vast empire behind her. She can form a bloc with the British Empire, which holds the seas and continues the struggle. She can, like England, utilize without limits the immense industry of the United States.

As the words came out, de Gaulle recalled later, "I felt in myself the termination of a life, one which I had led within the framework of a solid France and an indivisible army. At forty-nine I plunged into an adventure, like a man whom destiny was casting off from all previous connections."[17] He tried to convey to his fellow countrymen a world view of the war, one which was beyond the comprehension of Pétain and Weygand.

This war has not been decided by the Battle of France. This war is a world war. All our mistakes, all our delays, all our suffering, do not alter the fact that there is in the universe all the means needed to crush our enemies one day. . . . The destiny of the world is there.

At the height of the debacle and on the eve of surrender de Gaulle's defiant words seemed to be uttered in a void. The British Broadcasting Corporation, to its later embarrassment, regarded the broadcast as of such little importance that it did not even make a recording. *The Times* of London gave it but a few lines and the *Daily Express* buried it on page 8 with a couple of short sentences. Very few persons in France heard it. With electricity cut off in so many towns, not many radio sets were in operation and those that were were tuned in on Bordeaux, where the decisions for peace or continued war were being made.* Not one single French military or political figure of any consequence, even in London, offered to join the defiant general. He was utterly alone. But undaunted! "Before the terrifying emptiness of general renouncement," de Gaulle says, "my mission suddenly appeared to me, clear and terrible. At this moment, the worst in our history, it was up to me to assume that I was France."[19]

The government in Bordeaux picked up the rebellious broadcast and moved quickly to squelch any effect it might have had on the population and to squelch the defiant general himself. From Pétain's office, Alibert hastened to get out a clumsy communiqué to the press saying that de Gaulle had no "qualification" for making public statements since he was no longer a member of the government. The general, it said, had been summarily ordered home. That very evening, in fact, General Colson, the new Minister of War, got off an urgent wire to the French military attaché in London: "Inform General de Gaulle that he must return without delay." On June 20 de Gaulle replied in a letter to General Weygand transmitted by the French military attaché saying he was ready to return within 24 hours "if an armistice were not signed." He begged the generalissimo to "escape the disaster, go to the Empire overseas and continue the struggle" and pledged his support to him if he did. Idle words! Later the letter was returned to him with a scribbled note: "If the retired *Colonel* de Gaulle wishes to communicate with General Weygand, he must do it through regular channels." Soon afterward Weygand showed his spleen. When a court-martial sentenced de Gaulle to four years in prison, Weygand had

---

* The indefatigable Henri Amouroux discovered that several French newspapers, including two in Marseilles and one in Lyon, the largest cities not yet occupied, published all or part of de Gaulle's broadcast the next day. He is puzzled that it had so small an echo.[18]

another military tribunal at Clermont-Ferrand on August 2 condemn him to death *in absentia* for desertion.

The Pétain-Weygand government lost no time in cracking down on its opponents. Less than 24 hours after Mandel had given up his Ministry of Interior, he was arrested while lunching on June 17 at the elegant restaurant Chapon Fin with Madame Bretty. He and General Bührer, director of colonial troops in his Ministry, were carted off to jail. Alibert, the evil genius of the Marshal, was responsible. Acting on a denunciation from a right-wing journalist, who charged that Mandel was assembling arms to assassinate certain members of the government, Alibert quickly drew up the papers for the arrests and got Pétain to sign them. Later in the day, on the intervention of Lebrun, the two men were released. They went immediately to Pétain and demanded an apology, which, in the case of Mandel, the Marshal wrote out in the most abject terms. But the incident was a warning of the arbitrary nature of the new government. Within ten days Mandel would be arrested again, incarcerated for years, then delivered to the Germans and finally turned over by them to the militia of the Pétain government, which murdered him in cold blood on July 7, 1944. The Marshal's letter of apology to him, dated June 17, 1940, was found on his body. Mandel would be only one of many victims of the Pétain regime. Soon all the leaders of the last Republican governments, Reynaud, Daladier, Blum, and even General Gamelin, would be arbitrarily imprisoned by the Marshal and then turned over to the tender mercies of the Germans. He even turned over poor Lebrun.

At 10:30 on the morning of June 18, Pétain called in the Spanish Ambassador and asked him if there was any word from the Germans. Lequerica had none. Not only the Marshal but Lebrun, Herriot, and Jeanneney were increasingly concerned about the German advance on Bordeaux. Within two or three days the temporary capital might be captured, and with it the government, unless it got away in time. There would be no sense in conducting armistice negotiations if the French government was captive. The rest of the day pressure built up to move the government to Africa after all. At 5 P.M. the Presidents of the two chambers, who had taken the initiative, met with Lebrun and Pétain and insisted that the government depart.

"I shall never leave France," the old soldier said once more.

Jeanneney and Herriot then offered a solution. The Marshal and Weygand, along with two or three ministers, would stay. The President of the Republic, the two heads of the assemblies, and the rest of the cabinet would depart for North Africa. Pétain would delegate his powers to the Vice-Premier, Chautemps, the Marshal remaining in France as a sort of regent. Skeptical at first, Pétain finally assented. "We considered," says Herriot, "Jeanneney and I, that the question was formally settled. The sovereignty of the nation was safeguarded."[20] The next morning the cabinet approved.* Lebrun, Herriot, and Jeanneney and the ministers would leave during the day for Perpignan and thence to Port-Vendres, from which they would embark for North Africa. The members of Parliament would leave directly from Bordeaux on the steamer *Massilia*. But Lebrun and his colleagues had overlooked the scheming of Pierre Laval and Alibert, the capacity of the aged Marshal to vacillate, and the intrigues of all the frightened politicians who opposed setting up the government in Algeria because it might jeopardize the surrender and keep France in the war.

While Pétain, Weygand, and Baudouin waited impatiently but in vain throughout the day of June 18 for some sign of response from the Germans, Hitler was meeting with Mussolini in Munich to discuss the armistice terms for France. The demands of the Duce, whose troops after a week of "fighting" had been unable to advance against the French, though outnumbering them 5 or 6 to 1, were enormous. On the train the night before, going up from Rome to Munich, Mussolini told Ciano, his son-in-law and Italian Foreign Minister, that he would demand "the total occupation of French territory and the surrender of the French fleet."†

Hitler quickly deflated the Italian Caesar as soon as the meeting opened at the Fuehrer House in Munich, where Chamberlain and Daladier had been so accommodating to the two dictators regarding Czechoslovakia less than two years before. He made it clear that he did not intend, for the moment at least, to destroy France as he had Czechoslovakia. He wanted to separate France from Britain and "secure, if possible," he said, "a French government functioning on French territory. This would be far preferable to a situation in which the French might reject the German proposals and flee abroad to London to continue the war from there." He abruptly dismissed Mussolini's demands for the Italian occupation of the Rhône valley, including Toulon, the great French Mediterranean naval

---

* Over the "vehement opposition" of Weygand, according to Chautemps. The Vice-Premier quotes a novel argument of the generalissimo that it was not where a government functioned that made it free but solely its courage. "One is always free when one has courage," Weygand argued. "As for me, they can make me prisoner, torture me even, but I will never sign anything contrary to the honor and the interests of France."[21]

† Another Fascist neighbor that had refrained from fighting was suddenly prey to a strong appetite for spoils at the expense of beaten France. The next day, June 19, the Spanish government of Franco, which on June 14 had taken advantage of the French predicament by occupying the international city of Tangiers, sent Berlin a memorandum of its claims: "Western Algeria, all of Morocco under a Spanish protectorate, a part of the Sahara, and additional territory in West Africa." Franco urged that France be deprived of its entire empire in North Africa. If England continued the war after France ceased fighting, Franco declared that "Spain would be willing to enter the war—after a short period of preparing the public."[22] The vultures were losing no time.

base, and Marseilles, and the disarming of Corsica, Tunisia, and Djibouti. The last town, the gateway to Italian-held Ethiopia, was thrown in by Ciano, say the secret German notes of the meeting, "in an undertone."

Above all, Hitler (like the British) was concerned with the disposal of the French fleet. The captured German memorandum of the parley reveals that most of the Fuehrer's remarks were devoted to that.

The Fuehrer explained in detail what a great increase in strength the French fleet would represent for England, if it were to put itself at Britain's disposal. In certain categories the present strength of the British fleet would be practically doubled or trebled, especially in destroyers. . . .

It would therefore be best to try to reach agreement with a French government to neutralize the fleet. . . . As an inducement Germany might offer a guarantee that the entire fleet would be restored to France when peace was concluded.

With unaccustomed frankness Hitler conceded that "it was doubtful whether France would put any faith in a guarantee by the Fuehrer." In that case, he said, the "remedy" might be internment of the fleet in a neutral country such as Portugal or Spain.

Above all [Hitler concluded] the French fleet must be prevented from reaching England. . . . It would also be a favorable solution if the French fleet scuttled itself.

Hitler's moderation surprised and disappointed his Italian guest. "Mussolini is very much embarrassed," Ciano recorded in his journal at the end of the meeting. "He feels that his role is secondary. . . . In truth, the Duce fears that the hour of peace is growing near and sees fading once again that unattainable dream of his life: glory on the field of battle."

There was one final humiliation for the Italians. When Ciano proposed joint armistice negotiations with the French, the Fuehrer answered that "he did not suppose Italy would wish to negotiate *at the place* where the Franco-German negotiations for the armistice would be held." He did not name it; that was his secret. But as a sop to the Italians he promised that his armistice with France would not become effective until the French had also signed one with Italy. Though the Fuehrer had already drawn up the 23 articles of the proposed Franco-German armistice, which the French would have to take or leave, he did not communicate them to Rome until three days later.[23]

At 6:25 on the morning of June 19 Baudouin was awakened at his domicile by the Spanish Ambassador, who brought with him the German reply. The Reich government, it said, was "prepared to make known the conditions for the cessation of hostilities" and would announce the meeting place as soon as it was informed of the names of the French delegates. The German note added that it would consider an armistice agreement only on condition that one was also reached with Italy. It proposed that the French establish contact with Rome through Spain. Baudouin had already tried to reach Rome through the Vatican but no response had come. Hitler now made it clear that he wanted the Holy See left out.

A hastily convoked meeting was held in Pétain's office at 9 A.M., attended by Weygand, Darlan, Baudouin, Chautemps, Charles-Roux, and Alibert. Who would carry out the thankless task of representing the country at the armistice talks? According to one source, Baudouin suggested Weygand. The generalissimo responded that while "personally willing to make any sacrifice," he recalled that at the armistice negotiations at Rethondes in 1918, which he conducted for the Allies, the Germans had not sent a top general.[24] Chautemps says that "to his great surprise," the Marshal asked him to head the delegation. "I declined this unenviable mission," he says, "for I had no desire to make contact with the Nazi chiefs and I thought my place was in the cabinet."[25] In the absence of volunteers, Pétain named General Huntziger to lead the delegation. Others appointed were Admiral Le Luc, deputy Chief of Staff of the Navy, General Jean Bergeret, Chief of Staff of the Air Force, and General Henri Parisot, former military attaché in Rome. One lone civilian was tacked on: Léon Noël, the former Ambassador to Poland. None of the delegates was asked in advance if he wished to serve. They were given orders to. By 10:15, Baudouin was able to hand the list over to Lequerica. Whatever its shortcomings, the Pétain government could act, when it came to capitulating, with dispatch.

It did make one request. It asked the Germans to halt their advance "in order that a completely independent decision may be reached." Not even Pétain and Weygand wanted to make it if the government at Bordeaux was captured.* Lequerica pointed this out to Madrid in a later message that day, which the German Ambassador there promptly passed on to Berlin, as he was doing with all of Lequerica's dispatches. The Spanish Ambassador painted a bleak picture of the situation in Bordeaux and stressed the danger if the Germans continued their advance and especially if they delayed any longer the start of armistice talks.

The French government hardly has the situation in hand anymore. Although Pétain is acting with great energy, there is the danger that if German troops advance further on Bordeaux and if the start of the armistice is delayed,

---

* The request was of course ignored and the German advance continued almost unimpeded. But Hitler did give one response. That night shortly after midnight the Luftwaffe heavily bombed Bordeaux for the first time, one bomb exploding near Weygand's headquarters. Sixty-three civilians were killed and 180 injured. Charles-Roux called it a "villainy."

the Reynaud faction . . . may gain the upper hand again. The government would not be able to survive a threat to Bordeaux by German troops.[26]

Late that night of the 19th Lequerica telephoned another urgent warning to Madrid, which the German Ambassador also immediately transmitted to Berlin.

The situation is continually deteriorating. . . . If Germany and Italy are interested in concluding a treaty with the French government it appears necessary to do this as quickly as possible, and a zone must be established in which the French government can function freely and with security.

The French Foreign Minister has just told me that in view of the fear and the danger that the government will fall into the hands of the Germans . . . it is intended to take the President of the Republic, the Presidents of the Chamber and Senate, Vice-Premier Chautemps and a few other ministers to Algiers tomorrow, June 20.[27]

That seemed to be the intention in Bordeaux throughout the day and into the next. The cabinet confirmed it at the morning meeting on the 19th and preparations for the exodus of the government were begun. Early in the evening Darlan informed the heads of the two chambers that the liner *Massilia* would be put at the disposal of members of Parliament and would sail from Bordeaux for Morocco at 4 P.M. the next day. Lebrun and most of the ministers would go overland via Perpignan to Port-Vendres, where a destroyer would await them to carry them to Algiers.

So, on the morning of June 20, all seemed ready for the departure of the government, minus Pétain, who had delegated his powers to Chautemps. Then confusion again swamped the anxious leaders and it was compounded by trickery and treachery. At 12:30 P.M. the old Marshal went on the air for the second time to explain to the people again why he was seeking an armistice and to reiterate that he himself, as head of the government, was remaining in France. That did not facilitate the task of those who were trying to get the government to hasten its moves to Africa. But they kept trying. Lebrun packed his bags. Herriot sent his luggage down the river to the *Massilia*. Jeanneney left by car for Perpignan, where a cabinet meeting was scheduled for 9 A.M. the next day. The hotels in that town, but a short distance from Port-Vendres, were requisitioned for the notables. Even the Duke and Duchess of Windsor, halting in their flight toward safety in Spain, were kicked out of the Grand Hôtel to make way for the President of the Republic and his Ministers. The exodus from Bordeaux was to begin at 2:30 P.M.

At 2 o'clock, just as the President of the Republic was about to step into his car for the getaway, a phone call informed him that a special meeting of the ministers had just been called by Pétain. Lebrun called Alibert in the Marshal's office. Alibert confirmed it. "There are new developments," he said. Lebrun, exasperated, decided to wait. It was at this juncture that Alibert, a twisted little man, torpedoed the departure of most of the government by what he later boasted was a lie followed by a forgery.

The lie consisted of telling Lebrun, when the President arrived at the Marshal's office, that he had just received news that French forces were holding the Germans on the Loire. There was therefore no threat to Bordeaux and no need for the President and the ministers to hurry their departure. Pétain nodded his assent. Lebrun, says Alibert, sighed but declared that he still intended to leave with the others.

"That lie," Alibert confided to Deputy Fernand-Laurent two years later, "was the first round. The second was yet to be won. Hence my forgery." Having delayed the departure Alibert was now determined to prevent it altogether.

After I got back to the prefecture [he recounts] I was bombarded with telephone calls from Jeanneney, Herriot, Campinchi, all wanting to know whether the order for departure had finally been given. Something had to be done and I made my decision. Taking the Marshal's personal notepaper I dictated an order for each of the ministers to remain in his lodgings until 8 o'clock the next morning . . . and not to leave town for any reason before receiving instructions. I took the Marshal's seal, stamped the orders, and signed them. That was my forgery.[28]

It worked. General Weygand took the forgery for the real thing. He speaks of the "order" of the Marshal and adds that it was delivered to the ministers by General Henri Bineau, who told the startled members of the government "they were not to budge" until further advised.[*][29]

Thus ended the last hope of Lebrun and the others to move the government to North Africa.[†] The liner *Massilia* did weigh anchor the next day, the 21st, for Casablanca, but only twenty-nine deputies and one senator were aboard. They included most of the "resisters," Daladier, Mandel, Senator Révillon, Campinchi, Delbos, and four deputies still in uniform,

---

* In his testimony at the Pétain trial, Lebrun mentions Alibert's claim of forgery. "But I did not know of it at the time," he told the court. "I didn't know what was going on, in truth. No one told me anything. It was, gentlemen, a rather peculiar situation for the President of the Republic."[30]

† Lequerica, who had reported to Madrid earlier in the day that the government was moving to Perpignan, got off a message during the afternoon saying "the move to Perpignan has been abandoned." This was promptly relayed to Berlin by the German Ambassador in Madrid.[31] Thus by the evening of June 20 the German government, which had begun to worry that the French government might flee to North Africa, knew that it had abandoned the idea.

Berlin apparently did not bother to tell Rome. The next day the Italian government informed the German Foreign Office of reports it had that the French government was about to go to North Africa. Mussolini asked Hitler's approval for "suggesting" to Franco that the Spaniards "immediately occupy French Morocco" so as to cut it off from French Algeria. Without waiting for the Fuehrer's approval, the Italians sounded out Franco, who told them he lacked sufficient forces to take French Morocco.[32]

including Jean Zay and Mendés-France, both lieutenants and both Jews, who later, as the anti-Semitism of the Pétain regime waxed, would be court-martialed for desertion. At first the officers and crew of the ship refused to sail. Some of the sailors booed the parliamentarians and Zay was slapped. Finally Campinchi, who had been Minister of Marine until five days before, harangued the officers and crew and the boat finally got under way. Léon Blum and Herriot decided to follow the government to Perpignan and Port-Vendres. Louis Marin, after putting his luggage aboard, got off before the ship sailed. Learning at the last moment that the government was not leaving Bordeaux he feared a ruse on the part of Pétain and Weygand to remove the parliamentarians from the scene. Pomaret, who as Minister of Interior was in a position to know, later admitted that such was indeed the intention, though he put most of the blame on Darlan. Indeed, three days later the Pétain government was branding the poor parliamentarians as "deserters" and "traitors."

The senators were more shrewd. Suspecting a trap they voted not to embark on the *Massilia* but to follow the government to Perpignan, estimating, in the words of their resolution

that if the government did not leave France they would find themselves in a singular situation, floating on the sea while important decisions were taken.

Laval, who had savagely attacked his fellow members of Parliament for wanting to leave, now turned his guns on the President of the Republic, whom he still suspected of wanting to make away with the government. Early on the afternoon of June 21 a parliamentary delegation headed by Laval "burst" in on Lebrun, as the latter puts it, without notice.* The swarthy senator and former Premier, whose influence had been gaining in Bordeaux, was in a violent mood. "I suddenly had before me," says the President of the Republic, "madmen, who had lost control of themselves, gesticulating, speaking loudly all at once." At one point, he says, Laval shouted so loudly that he had to stop him: "Lower your voice. The more you cry out the less I hear." But Laval could not control himself.

"You cannot, you must not leave," Laval shouted. "We will not accept the fraud of a government continuing from North Africa a war that has become impossible."

Then, according to Deputy Jean Montigny, who was present and applauding, Laval with even more "vehemence" said:

"There's something more. The President of the Republic, in taking the seals of state, will take with him the government. . . . I deny you the right to do it under any pretext." Shaking his finger at the unhappy President and, says Montigny, in a "paroxysm of emotion," Laval went on:

---

* It included Georges Bonnet, the former Foreign Minister, still resentful at having been kicked out of Reynaud's government, and still for "peace."

"Two men only, General Weygand and Marshal Pétain, are qualified to say whether the war should go on. If they think it must cease, we must all bow to them. . . . I've seen the spectacle of our defeat. We are beaten."

Lebrun tried to reason with the aroused defeatist, explaining that if the government departed it was because it had to remain free to deliberate. This only served to incense Laval further.

"If you leave the soil of France," he fumed, "you will never set foot on it again! Yes, when it is learned that you have left, a word will be on everyone's lips: 'defection,' perhaps even 'treason.' "

"I have certain obligations to the Constitution," Lebrun answered.

"I hate it," cried Laval, "for all the harm it has done to France!" This was his first warning that now that surrender was at hand he envisaged getting rid of the Republican Constitution. Out of his well-nourished grudge against the Republic for keeping him out of office so long, his thoughts were already turning, as would be manifest shortly, toward emulating the totalitarian regime of the German conquerors.

"One can understand," Lebrun wrote in his memoirs, "why I still retain in my mind the painful memory of this scene."[33]

That evening after dinner, Baudouin, accompanied by Bouthillier—the two protégés of Reynaud had now become the Whiz Kids of the new government—went to see Pétain at his home.

"What are you going to do with the President of the Republic, who appears bent on leaving?" Baudouin asked the Marshal.

"Very simple," replied Pétain. "I'll have him arrested."[34]

Even before he knew that the departure for Africa was definitely off, Ambassador Biddle cabled Washington during the day that the surge in Bordeaux for capitulation would probably prevent it. He painted a somber picture of the situation on the 21st.

The atmosphere of capitulation grows apace. Such will to resist as still remained is being sapped by the buzzing stories of collapse at the front; the tales of wholesale disintegration; by the anti-British feeling I have just reported.* General Weygand . . . has stopped further shipment of materiel to Africa; the sinking rather than escape of the fleet . . . seems more probable. I am reluctantly reaching the conclusion that the passing of time has ill served the supporters of a free government in Africa. . . . The order to unpack may be expected.[35]

Paul Reynaud, who had seemed so determined to move the government he had headed a few days before to North Africa, took no part in the planning of his old supporters for the departure. His thoughts were on an-

---

* Biddle had reported in an earlier cable that day the growing phobia in Bordeaux against Britain.

other place: Washington. All through the week, while Pétain and Weygand sought to get the armistice talks started and Lebrun, Herriot, and the others pressed the government to leave Bordeaux, Reynaud mulled over an offer by the Marshal to represent the new government as ambassador to the United States.

It had been made to him on June 18, the day Roosevelt's sharp cable on the fleet was read to the cabinet. To allay American fears and suspicions, Pétain suggested to Baudouin after the session that Reynaud might prove useful as ambassador in Washington. He sent for Reynaud after lunch and asked him to accept the post.

"When you called on me," the Marshal told him, "I answered 'Present.' Today I call on you, and you refuse me your help. It is true that France has changed her policies . . . but the country must be served. . . . At such an hour you cannot turn me down."

According to Baudouin, Reynaud accepted "in principle" but asked for a few days to think it over. He would have to see first how the armistice talks came out. If the terms were humiliating but accepted, he would refuse the ambassadorship. Reynaud adds that he did not want to precipitate "a rupture" with the Marshal, who might prove useful in case he, Reynaud, were recalled to power if and when the armistice negotiations failed. Some of his friends, who found it difficult to comprehend how Reynaud could possibly agree to represent a government which he so despised, thought that he was attracted by the offer partly because Countess de Portes liked it. She had already sent her two children to America and felt it would be a good place to sit out the war.* At any rate, at the end of this meeting on the 18th Reynaud agreed that Baudouin should ask for the American government's agreement to his nomination. The former Premier, astute though he was, did not seem to suspect, though others did, that Pétain wanted to send him to Washington to get him out of the way.

---

* So sure was she that Reynaud would accept the Embassy in Washington that she sent her jewelry and gold out with two former aides of the Premier, Leca and Devaux, who departed Bordeaux on June 22 for diplomatic posts in Washington which Reynaud had procured for them. A couple of days later they were arrested in Madrid. In their suitcases police found 18 million francs, the jewelry of the countess, and bundles of highly confidential Foreign Office documents which Reynaud had accumulated as Foreign Minister. Reynaud, highly embarrassed by the news, admitted to Baudouin that since he expected to go to Washington, he had entrusted his former aides, who were traveling on diplomatic passports, with some of his personal papers. Their money had come from "secret funds" of the government and was to be used to finance the Embassy and French missions in America. Baudouin questioned Reynaud again on the 26th about the matter at the latter's suite at the Hôtel Splendide. Countess de Portes was with him.

> She is in tears [Baudouin wrote in his journal] and explains to me that she confided her gold and jewelry to Leca to take to the United States. She did it behind Reynaud's back. . . . M. Reynaud, very pale, very moved, impresses the countess with the gravity of her imprudence. . . .

Returned to France and jailed, their case cited by the Pétain government as evidence of corruption during Reynaud's regime, the two men were later acquitted by a French court.[36]

It seems to have occurred to Lebrun, a far less astute man. When Reynaud's nomination came up to him the next day he refused to sign it.

> I admit [says Lebrun] that this proposition surprised me. I may not have a very critical mind, but I said to myself: "They want to get rid of Reynaud by sending him far away." I opposed that. If the armistice talks failed and France resumed its resistance I intended to ask Reynaud to form a new government.

Lebrun opposed it, but not Reynaud himself. He was saved from later embarrassment by the Marshal, who on June 21 told Baudouin that he had decided to "postpone" Reynaud's nomination. He did not think it was a good time, he said, at the moment when the armistice delegations were meeting, to send to Washington "a man who had made a supreme effort with President Roosevelt to bring the United States into the war against Germany."

"It would have been a terrible mistake," Reynaud admitted at the Pétain trial, "to have represented the Marshal's government in Washington." Roosevelt thought so too. He could not believe, he told Secretary Hull when Reynaud's name was suggested as ambassador, "that Paul Reynaud would agree to representing a government dominated by Germany."[37]

The French delegation to the armistice negotiations left Bordeaux at 2 P.M. on June 20. Apparently alarmed by the messages of Lequerica warning that unless the talks began at once the Pétain government could not survive, the Germans radioed Bordeaux directly during the morning to present its party at a Loire bridge near Tours at 5 P.M. Before leaving, General Huntziger and his colleagues were instructed by Pétain and Weygand to break off the talks if the Germans demanded (1) the fleet, (2) the occupation of all of metropolitan France, and (3) any part of the French overseas empire. They were also told not to sign any agreement unless and until the government approved.

Once they had departed there was a frantic search in Bordeaux for the text of the 1918 armistice, which the French, on behalf of the Allies, had dictated to the Germans. Weygand, who had conducted the armistice talks then, wanted to know exactly what he might expect from the same enemy now that the positions were reversed. The town's libraries were searched for the 1918 text but it could not be found. Finally the municipal archivist located it in *Larousse,* a popular contemporary encyclopedia. Léon Noël, the civilian member of the delegation, says that it had also been instructed to learn, if possible, the German conditions not only for an armistice but for a peace settlement.[38] Naively, Pétain believed that it might be obtained too. As a result, there was also a scramble in Bordeaux that afternoon to find the text of the Versailles Treaty. This too proved difficult in the disordered provisional capital. Ironically, the *original* copy of the Treaty of Versailles (as well as of the Treaty of Westphalia) was at that moment reposing at the American consulate in the hands of H. Freeman Matthews, who had been given it for safekeeping by two officials of the French Foreign Office.*

The government at Bordeaux first believed from the German radio communication received during the morning that the armistice talks would take place in the vicinity of Tours, with which it was still in telephone communication. But that was to underestimate Adolf Hitler's memory, his ingrained vindictiveness and his resolve to humiliate the beaten foe. The French caravan, moving with difficulty over the roads clogged with refugees and retreating troops, did not reach Tours, a part of which was in flames, until 10 P.M. After crossing the Loire the delegation was met at Vendôme by General Kurt von Tippelskirch of the German Army General Staff. He directed the party to continue immediately toward Chartres. Noël surmised that the Germans had selected Versailles, where the 1919 Treaty of Peace had been signed and where, also, the King of Prussia had been crowned German Emperor in 1871. But the exhausted group reached Chartres and then Versailles and drove on to Paris, which was reached at 7:30 A.M. on the 21st. After 17 hours of driving, without sleep or food, the French delegates were put up at the Hôtel Royal-Monceau, given a light breakfast, and told to be ready to proceed further at 1:30 P.M. Their destination still remained unknown.

All day long of June 21 Weygand waited impatiently in Bordeaux for news of the whereabouts of the armistice delegation. At 8:30 in the evening his telephone rang. General Huntziger was on the line.

"I'm in the *wagon!*" he began.†

"*Mon pauvre ami!*" Weygand cried.[39]

On their way north toward Tours the members of the French armistice delegation had seen at first hand the disintegration of the retreating armies. The enemy had not advanced nearly so far toward Bordeaux as they had been told at General Weygand's headquarters. The Germans were

---

* Letter of Matthews to the author. "I sent them by courier pouch to Washington," he writes, "and they were turned over to the French Ambassador after the war."

† The *wagon-lit*. Weygand grasped at once that this was the famous sleeping car at Rethondes in the middle of the Forest of Compiègne, where he himself, at Foch's behest, had dictated the Allied armistice terms to the Germans in November 1918 and in which the document ending hostilities in the first war had been signed at 5 A.M. on November 11. Later the car had been placed in a museum a few yards away from the original railway siding.

On the afternoon of June 19 I had driven out from Paris to Compiègne and found German army engineers, working with pneumatic drills, cutting out one wall of the museum. Soon they were nudging the car through it to the historic siding, marked by a granite stone. The rusty railroad tracks were still there and onto them the engineers finally moved the *wagon-lit*. To one side stood the white marble statue of Marshal Foch, whose private car had been used for the armistice talks.

still on the Loire around Tours, where the remnants of the Seventh Army and the Army of Paris had fought a sharp delaying action. But a hundred miles south of the Loire Ambassador Noël was surprised to see "a flood" of French soldiers, nearly all without arms, "distancing themselves from the front by the thousands." It struck him as a "lamentable spectacle, which awakened the delegates to the state of a large part of our armies."[40]

Pétain's broadcast of June 17 saying that the combat must cease had, as we have seen, sapped what little fight was left in the beaten troops. A government decree the next day, the 18th, proclaiming that all communities of 20,000 or more were "open towns" and, like Paris, would not be defended, had further contributed to halting any resistance. General Georges had protested bitterly to Weygand on the 19th that the proclamation "rendered a coordinated defense impossible." He reported that in many towns the civilian authorities "were insisting that the troops be withdrawn without delay" and that many conflicts between the military and civilian authorities had ensued. Georges also pointed out that in most of these "open towns" there were not only important road and rail junctions but vital bridges and that if the former were not defended and the latter not destroyed the German advance could not even be slowed down. At the moment two thirds of the country was still unoccupied. The question of the bridges within the towns was especially important at Lyon, the second largest city in France, where there were thirty-one bridges across the swift-flowing Rhône. Unless Lyon were defended and the bridges blown the whole Rhône valley to the south would be open to the Germans, and the Army of the Alps, which was still holding up the Italians, threatened from the rear.

Herriot, who had tried to get the government to move to North Africa and continue the war, was aghast at the prospect of the war taking place in his home town of Lyon, of which he had been mayor for thirty-five years. Apprised at 12:30 A.M. on the night of June 17–18 by a telephone call from Lyon that the Germans were approaching the city, that a small force of 3,000 troops—mostly blacks, says Herriot—seemed determined to defend the place and blow the thirty-one bridges and that the entire town was likely to be destroyed in the fighting, Herriot got Pétain out of bed at 1 o'clock in the morning and demanded that his city be spared. The sleepy Marshal, somewhat surprised at the request from one of the most ardent antagonists to an armistice, assented. Lyon was proclaimed an "open city" and orders were dispatched at 3 A.M. to the garrison not to try to defend it or to destroy the bridges. From a military point of view, says Weygand, "it was a detestable measure. It delivered the passage of the Rhône and deprived the Army of the Alps of its principal protection on its northern flank."[41] General Orly, commander of the Army, which had been holding out so valiantly against the Italians, protested that the order "sacrificed" his troops.

The mayors of other towns, learning that Lyon would be spared, besieged Bordeaux with demands that their municipalities also be declared "open cities" and that no warlike acts and particularly no bridge blowing or other destruction of public or private property be permitted within their corporate limits. The government readily assented.

The consequences of the "open city" proclamation on June 18 were predictable. And they were compounded by a strange order issued on the same day by General Colson, the new Minister of War.

The withdrawal of all civil and military authorities is formally prohibited. All must remain at their posts even in case of the arrival of the enemy. Any infraction of this order will bring those concerned before a military tribunal.[42]

This was tantamount to an order to army units to surrender "on the arrival" of the Germans. It was obeyed with alacrity and relief in numerous places. At Rennes in Brittany, where not a shot was fired in defense of the town, the entire General Staff of the French Tenth Army along with several hundred officers surrendered to a German corporal. The deputy Hutin-Desgrees, who was present, thought it a "scandalous scene."[43] There were others. At Clermont-Ferrand General de Laclos and all his officers and men waited until the Germans arrived and then surrendered. The general later affirmed he was merely obeying the order not to withdraw but to await the arrival of the enemy. "This profoundly painful scene," says an official military report, "was filmed by the Germans."[44]

There were other "painful scenes"—or at least they seemed so to later investigators though at the moment, it must be remembered, the commanding officers not only seemed relieved to surrender but believed that in so doing they were conforming to General Colson's orders. The authorization from higher quarters seems to have erased from their minds any sense of shame, which had so horrified Generals Weygand and Georges, of committing the unpardonable crime of surrendering *en rase campagne* and to have freed them from any fear of having to face the death penalty prescribed for such an act. At Nantes, at the mouth of the Loire, where orders and counterorders had confused the command as to what to do, a single German tank arrived before the gateway to the caserne, packed with French soldiers, and settled the matter. A German soldier stuck his head out of the turret, observed that all was peaceful, and proceeded to distribute cigarettes to his willing captives.[45]

At La Rochelle on the coast north of Bordeaux the commanding general on the night of June 19 issued the following order to his troops:

Disarm everyone. Collect all arms and ammunition in one place. Consign officers and troops to quarters. Wait where you are without firing or offering resistance of any kind. Officers who do not carry out these orders will be haled before a court-martial.

The town actually was not immediately threatened. The Germans did not arrive until June 23. For four days the French troops waited patiently in their barracks to surrender.[46] Some generals were more impatient to give up. Colonel Goutard tells of one corps commander, during the retreat south of the Loire, surrendering *over the telephone* to a German unit which was still some distance away.[47]

In one town after another, while General Georges in vain urged his armies to continue to fight until the results of the armistice talks became known, the surrenders proceeded. At Brest various military commanders confined their men to barracks, collected their arms, locked them up and issued orders to await the arrival of the enemy, which came on the evening of June 19.[48] Witnesses testified later that at a number of places the surrender of the troops was hailed by soldiers and civilians alike as a deliverance. At Lorient, south of Brest, one officer who had wanted to fight reported: "The arrival of the Germans on June 21 was welcomed as a deliverance." A young artillery lieutenant at the same place reports his commanding officer telling the men, after he had disarmed them: "Remain where you are and observe perfect discipline. When the Germans arrive they will see we are a disciplined unit." The commander forbade his men to try to escape capture and when some soldiers tried to get away he called out the military police to prevent them. Finally the commanding general addressed the disarmed troops: "Marshal Pétain has asked for an armistice. . . . Now that the war is finished we must face the domestic enemy."[49] The Communists perhaps? Or maybe the horde of disorganized troops who here and there had got out of hand?

French observers have told of bands of French soldiers, often drunk, without a cadre of officers—the officers had often been the first to flee—pillaging the deserted towns whose inhabitants had also fled. "There was pillaging everywhere," says Amouroux, "of food, of gold and silver, of jewelry in the shops, and of many less likely objects." One priest in Normandy reported that his church had been ransacked by the passing troops, who had even made off with the suitcases containing the belongings of refugees who had taken shelter there.[50]

That was why the inhabitants and the officials of many towns sometimes welcomed the arrival of the Germans, who quickly restored order and stopped the pillaging. Senator Bardoux was told by the Ministry of Interior how at Royan, at the mouth of the Gironde estuary, the populace, frightened by the behavior of the refugees and the undisciplined soldiers passing through, "cordially welcomed the German troops. Toasts were exchanged between German officers and local officials. The German army appeared as a guarantee of order and discipline."[51]

The inhabitants of the towns threatened by battle now seemed more determined to oppose their own troops than the enemy. At Vienne, south of Lyon, the mayor stationed several hundred persons around the only bridge across the Rhône to prevent the troops from blowing it. When General Husson, commanding the defense of the town, started to make preparations to dynamite the bridge, the mayor threatened the general with an assault by the women of the community.

"If you persist," he warned, "I have around me 1,000 women of Vienne who are going to prevent you from carrying out this foolishness." The mayor stationed himself on the bridge surrounded by his women warriors. Finally a more senior general arrived on the spot and acceded to this female threat. The bridge remained intact—for the advancing Germans.[52]

Some brave officers did try to continue to resist the Germans. In one case the general who did so was reprimanded by General Weygand (or his ministry), and in two others one officer was killed by the populace and the second by his own men.

The scattered French forces around Tours had held up the Germans there for three days, fighting valiantly. But on June 21, General Vary, who commanded the 9th Military District, was called on the telephone by General Weygand's Ministry of Defense and, according to his own testimony, "asked by whose orders he had defended the bridges of the Loire and for what reasons he had left Tours instead of waiting for the Germans and surrendering to them." Fortunately for General Vary, in the new order of things which Pétain and Weygand were putting so rapidly into shape, he had a good excuse. He told Weygand's ministry that he had left Tours on the orders of General Antoine Besson, Commander of Army Group 3, one of the ranking generals of the French Army.[53]

At least two other officers with a will to resist were less fortunate. General Beaufre (then a captain on General Georges' staff) tells of a tank officer who insisted on defending the outskirts of Vierzon. "He was killed," says Beaufre, "by the populace, which wished to prevent the destruction of the town."[54]

The other case was that of Colonel Charly. It attracted front page attention in the Paris press in 1949 when a military tribunal at Metz brought out the facts and circumstances, reviving memories of the demoralization of the French armies in the terrible June of 1940. Lieutenant Colonel Charly was acting commander of the remnants of the 23rd and 153rd artillery regiments, which had begun to retreat from the Maginot Line and on the evening of June 20, 1940, found themselves encircled in the village of Tantimont. The colonel realized that the war in France was lost. But "as a matter of honor," he wanted his unit to fight its way out through the German lines. Not only his men but his officers rebelled. Angry words were exchanged in a confrontation in an orchard on the outskirts of the hamlet. Officers and men, who had heard on the radio that Marshal Pétain had asked for an armistice, refused to obey the colonel's order to attempt a sortie. Charly became angry, accused them of cowardice, and threatened them with court-martial.

As he walked back to his command post in the village a shot rang out in the dark. Colonel Charly fell dead, a bullet in his back. The Germans arrived a few minutes later, found the dead colonel and buried him with military honors. But they were perplexed by his death, since they had not fired a shot. Nine years later the Military Court at Metz drew out what had happened. A gunner named Fernand Buret had been arrested and accused of the murder. He readily confessed that he had fired the shot that had killed the colonel but he denied any moral guilt. Most of the others, officers and men, would have fired if he hadn't, he said, to prevent the needless slaughter of hundreds of men.

> For several days [he testified] we have been falling back. We kept asking why we weren't fighting. We never once fired our guns. [On June 20] some of the officers said to the colonel: "If we now fire a single cannon we'll all be massacred." He answered: "The first who refuses to obey I'll blow his brains out.". . . Somebody handed me a rifle, saying: "Kill him! He's going to have us all massacred!" I fired in the direction of the colonel. . . . I had never fired a rifle before.

Thirty former members of the regiment testified in Buret's favor. All seemed to believe that Colonel Charly had it coming. His death saved hundreds of lives.

The Military Court showed great understanding. The prosecutor did not demand a severe sentence for this murder which had occurred in the midst of so much killing. It was as if the French Army realized that in the debacle of 1940, in the terrible disorder, many an officer and man had merely given way to human weakness. In defeat and retreat they had lost the old determination to defend their soil to the bitter end. They saw no sense in it now, wanting only—and desperately—to survive, to have a life still on this mad planet. Gunner Buret, who for ten years thereafter had had a life, with a wife and two children, and work as a mason, was sentenced to five years in prison.[55]

In North Africa there were French generals who wanted to continue the war regardless of what happened in the homeland. On June 17, after listening in tears to Pétain's broadcast announcing that the new government was asking for an armistice, General Auguste Noguès, Resident-General of Morocco and Commander in Chief of the North African Theater of Operations, got off a sharply worded protest to General Weygand. "All North Africa is consternated," he wired.

> All land, air, and naval forces ask to continue the struggle to save honor and preserve North Africa for France.
> I am ready, if the government agrees, to take separately from it the responsibility for this attitude. . . With the aid of the naval squadrons and the air forces promised me we can hold out.[56]

In Bordeaux the generalissimo was not pleased by this unusual show of resistance by the military in North Africa. He and the Marshal were resolved, if the Germans agreed, to halt hostilities not only in the homeland but in the Empire. He replied sarcastically to General Noguès the next evening.

Commander in Chief is astonished by the message of General Noguès. French troops continue to resist in all parts of France.[57]

Undaunted by this rebuke, General Noguès on the 18th appealed over the head of Weygand to Pétain.

All the troops as well as the French and Muslim population beg me to respectfully ask the government to continue the struggle and defend the soil of North Africa. . . . To cede the two Protectorates . . . without fighting would be considered treason. . . .
With our fleets intact, with the planes which are now arriving,* and with some additional reinforcements in cadres and materiel, we can hold out a long time—long enough, no doubt, to contribute to the defeat of our enemies.

"Respectfully, but with a burning insistence," Noguès asked the government "to come and pursue, or to let us pursue, the struggle in North Africa."[59]

Such determination of the Commander in Chief in North Africa was not at all to the liking of General Weygand. On June 21 the generalissimo sent Noguès a curt telegram instructing him in the name of the Marshal and himself "to come to Bordeaux, today, by the quickest means."[60]

After first replying that though he could not make it "today" he would fly to Bordeaux the next day "weather permitting," General Noguès had second thoughts.

After having reflected and in view of the situation [he wired Weygand that evening] I consider that it is impossible for me at the present hour to abandon my post without risking very grave events.

He was just barely able, he explained, "to keep the French and native population behind the government." If he left, he said, it would be considered a desertion and the place would explode in revolt. "If the government has an important communication to make to me," he concluded tartly, "it would be better for it to send me a qualified emissary."[61]

The French government had to send "an emissary" to a French general in the field? This sounded in Bordeaux like rebellion. Weygand, however, gave in and replied that he was sending over General Koeltz by air. This was the situation at noon on June 22 when Weygand dispatched

---

* More than 2,000 aircraft. The Italian control commission found a few weeks later that the French had collected 2,648 modern planes in North Africa, of which 710 were the latest-model fighters and 431 were bombers.[58]

this last wire. The armistice had not yet been signed. But the Marshal and the generalissimo knew the German terms. These had been received the night before. A revolt of the armed forces in North Africa under the prestigious leadership of General Noguès, a ranking officer with long experience in the African empire, where he was a popular and respected figure, would sabotage the armistice just at the moment that the government in Bordeaux had decided to accept it. Weygand was greatly concerned.

Early on the evening of June 21 he had learned of the German armistice conditions from General Huntziger. Weygand at once objected to having to take down the terms over the telephone—and on a bad line at that. "There is no one in the office to take them down," he snapped. "All the secretaries have left. The text should be sent by air. You don't bind the fate of a country to a text dictated over the telephone." But when Huntziger explained to him that this was the only means the Germans had left them and that moreover they expected a reply—one way or the other—by 9 A.M. the next day, he reluctantly gave in. He himself repeated the words telephoned by Huntziger so that Captain Gasser, his aide, could take them down in longhand.

First, though, Weygand asked for Huntziger's general impression of the German terms. "Harsh," said the latter, "but there is nothing in them directly against honor."

"What was the tone of the Germans?" Weygand asked.

"Very hard," Huntziger responded. "A great deal of cordiality was hardly to be expected."

The conversation, which the Germans tapped and recorded in a nearby army communications truck,* makes clear that the Pétain government, despite all its later denials, had hoped to get the German conditions not only for an armistice but for a peace settlement.

"I have not been able to learn anything about the peace terms," said Huntziger. "The German delegation flatly refuses to discuss them. We have simply been given an armistice convention of twenty-four articles and told that it cannot be modified. I am permitted only to ask questions to clear up various points. I've done so."[62]

He thereupon proceeded to dictate the German terms to the generalissimo. The process took more than an hour.

Adolf Hitler, at the moment of his greatest triumph, was in a truculent and arrogant mood as he arrived at the little clearing in the woods at

---

* Since my job as a radio correspondent necessitated working close to the German communications truck, which I hoped I could get to relay a broadcast to America, I heard a good deal of the recordings of the French telephone talks with Bordeaux, though my notes of them were lost. The German and French notes on them are given, respectively, in *DGFP,* Vol. IX and Kammerer. See Note 62.

Rethondes at 3:15 P.M. on June 21, followed by the German members of the armistice delegation, his Army, Navy, and Air Force commanders and the insufferable Ribbentrop, the Foreign Minister. To dictate an armistice in this historic place was sweet revenge for the man who had been a lowly corporal in the army which had been forced to give up in 1918, and he did not hide his feelings. Standing a few feet away, I saw his face light up, successively, with hate, scorn, revenge, triumph, as he strode to the little marble block that marked the spot where Foch's *wagon-lit* had stood in 1918 and read the lettering:

> HERE ON THE ELEVENTH OF NOVEMBER 1918 SUC-
> CUMBED THE CRIMINAL PRIDE OF THE GERMAN
> EMPIRE . . . VANQUISHED BY THE FREE PEOPLES
> WHICH IT TRIED TO ENSLAVE.*

The German party, which included Goering, General Brauchitsch, Grand Admiral Raeder and Rudolph Hess, then climbed into the *wagon-lit* followed by the dejected members of the French delegation. On a gesture from Hitler, General Wilhelm Keitel, the chief of the German High Command and the least mentally gifted of the top German generals, opened the proceedings by reading a declaration which could only have been written by Hitler—so full was it of his customary historical distortions, his blinding hatred of the French, his passion for revenge. Going back to the terrible "wrongs" done the Germans by the Allies in 1918 (as Hitler did in dozens of speeches I had had to listen to during my stay in Nazi Germany), blaming France and Britain for having started the present war, it explained that Rethondes had been selected for the second armistice meeting

to efface once and for all by an act of reparative justice a memory which was not for France a glorious page in her history and which was resented by the German people as the greatest shame of all time.

This was unadulterated Hitleriana. And Keitel, a notorious toady to the Fuehrer, read it, Ambassador Noël remembered, "with vehemence, insolence and brutality." Whereupon Hitler departed, leaving the meeting in charge of Keitel. The German general then distributed copies of the German terms along with a French translation, emphasizing as he did so that the provisions of the treaty "were inalterable and must be accepted or rejected as they are." All he could do, he said, was to answer questions and clear up any points which the French might raise.

The terms seemed clear enough, though the French delegates haggled over a few points—without obtaining any important changes. As the French

---

* In *Berlin Diary* I gave in some detail my firsthand observations of Hitler and his entourage in these opening ceremonies at Rethondes. The marble block, whose lettering so offended the Nazi dictator, was blown up, on his orders, three days later.

surely had to expect, the document was, as they said, a *Diktat*. General Huntziger, after hastily reading its twenty-four clauses, told Keitel they were "hard and merciless."

The most crucial clause concerned the disposal of the French fleet. Huntziger told Weygand on the telephone it was "better than expected." It provided that the French fleet, except for those ships needed for the defense of the colonial empire, would be demobilized and disarmed under German or Italian supervision and laid up in their home ports. The fleet would be lost, then, as a weapon for the Allies or for any future French government that might reenter the war, but at least it would not be turned over intact to the Germans, as the British had first feared. On this the Germans gave a solemn promise.

> The German government solemnly declares to the French government that it does not intend to use for its own purposes in the war the French fleet which is in ports under German supervision. . . . Furthermore they solemnly and expressly declare that they have no intention of raising any claim to the French fleet at the time of conclusion of peace.

The Bordeaux government took more seriously a "solemn promise" of Nazi Germany than others which from bitter experience had learned better. Weygand did ask that the French warships, after being disarmed, be permitted to remain in the North African ports, but this, as Huntziger told Keitel, was largely because the French feared the British would bomb vessels returning to their home ports in the Atlantic and the Channel. They would be more safe from British attack, he emphasized, in the African harbors—a proposition that proved illusory in the end.[63] At any rate the French request was refused.

The most odious clause in the proposed agreement, and the most dishonoring to France, was one which obligated the French to turn over all anti-Nazi German refugees. Weygand protested that this was "contrary to honor" because it violated the historic right of asylum, and he demanded its deletion. When the Germans refused the French asked that the clause be amended to say that "the position of foreign nationals who have sought asylum in France will form the subject of a later agreement on the basis of honor and humanity."[64] But Hitler had no intention of treating the anti-Nazi refugees honorably or humanely. Keitel, speaking for him, answered

> that the extradition article applied to the greatest of warmongers, the German emigrés who had betrayed their own people . . . and that the extradition of this category of persons . . . must be insisted upon at all costs.[65]

And it was. Finally accepting a clause that he himself said was "contrary to honor" did not prevent General Weygand from arguing later that there was "nothing dishonorable" in the German armistice conditions. Perhaps he and the other members of the Pétain government felt that de-

livering a few thousand German refugees to face the Nazi executioner's ax
—as some eventually did—was a small price to pay for stopping the killing
of Frenchmen. But as two French ambassadors, Kammerer and Noël,
pointed out, the way this odious article was carried out by the Pétain-Weygand government "was even more odious." The archives of the French
Ministry of Interior and of the secret police are full of orders to track down
the German refugees named by Hitler and to hand them over. And they
were. Among them were two old and honored German Socialist leaders,
Breitscheid and Hilferding, who were objects of a special search by the
French police. Delivered to Hitler, they were axed. At the Pétain trial Noël
told the court that it would have been easy for the French government to
facilitate the escape of the principal German refugees between June 21,
when the German conditions became known, and June 25 when the armistice went into effect. But the opposite was done.[66]

Not very honorable either was a clause in Article 10 under which the
French government undertook to forbid its nationals to fight against Germany in the service of other states. It was agreed that those who did so
would be treated by the Germans as *francs-tireurs*—that is, shot upon capture. This stipulation was aimed at de Gaulle, who was trying to organize a
Free French force in Britain and in the French Empire. Pétain and Weygand knew that to treat their fellow countrymen in such service as *francs-
tireurs* was a crude violation of the rules of war. But they made no protest
over this clause. Perhaps they thought it would frighten de Gaulle, whom
they had summarily called home and whom, on June 23, they stripped of
his rank in the French Army and ordered court-martialed.

Nor did they raise any objections to Article 20, which provided that
French prisoners of war, of whom there were now nearly a million and a
half, would remain in German hands until the conclusion of peace. No
doubt this was because, as Pétain, Weygand, and Darlan believed, the
British would be defeated in a matter of weeks, the war would then be
over, peace made, and the French prisoners released. As it turned out,
they would be held in captivity for five years.

The other clauses of the German terms effectively took France militarily out of the war, providing for a cessation of hostilities not only in
France proper but in its colonial empire, demobilizing and disarming all
its "armed forces on land, at sea, and in the air" except for a few units
necessary to maintain "internal order." Two fifths of metropolitan France
lying to the south and southeast and forming the poorest part of the country
was left unoccupied. The entire Atlantic coast was taken over by the
Germans. Paris remained occupied though the French government was
permitted to have its seat there if it desired. Since nothing was said in the
treaty about North Africa or other possessions except that their armed
forces must be demobilized, they presumably would be free—a presump-
tion that did not last very long. In short, as might have been expected,
France and its Empire were left at the mercy of Nazi Germany.

Weygand would later argue that the armistice was "merely a temporary suspension of arms which permitted France to regain her breath and reenter the war." But in the face of the facts this was ridiculous. He would not have sacrificed the fleet and the relatively strong military position in North Africa, which General Noguès had assured him he could hold, if he had had the slightest thought of France getting back into the war. The shameful decree of the Pétain-Weygand government on August 1 haling before a special court the French leaders such as Reynaud, Daladier, Blum, and General Gamelin, who were accused of having plunged the country into war, was done not only out of revenge but more importantly to prevent the possibility of France ever fighting again in this war. In truth, as the disastrous month of June 1940 neared its end, Weygand and his colleagues, especially Pétain and Darlan, wanted the war to be over once and for all. Then there would be no war for France to "reenter."

From the moment Weygand received the German terms on the evening of June 21 the cabinet ministers sat in long sessions, adjourning at 3 A.M. on the 22nd to meet again at 8 A.M. and continue until the late afternoon when word came through from Huntziger that Keitel had given him an ultimatum granting one more hour in which to sign.

But to what purpose—the round-the-clock discussions? Everyone around the table knew that an armistice between a victor and a vanquished had to be what the Germans called a *Diktat*, to be accepted or rejected as it was. There could be no meaningful negotiation. Chautemps, whose proposal on June 15 to ask for the conditions of an armistice had won the day, seemed at first surprised at this. "It did not take us long to learn," he says, "that you do not negotiate an armistice." He called the German terms "terrible." But he who had argued so suavely in the last hours of the Reynaud government that if they were so, the government could reject them, now had no such thought.* No French minister or general had. Only Charles-Roux of the Foreign Office, who was not a cabinet minister, but who sat in on the first impromptu meeting of Pétain, Weygand, Darlan, Baudouin, Bouthillier, and Alibert that began at 10:30 P.M. as soon as the generalissimo had taken down the German conditions and had got them typed out, was opposed. And he was quickly squelched by the Marshal.

"If these are the German conditions," he exclaimed, "it would be better to leave for Africa!"

"Still that idea!" Pétain responded exasperatedly, raising his hands, Charles-Roux remembered, "to the sky." The Marshal made it clear, says the Foreign Office Secretary, that the question of moving the govern-

---

* Baudouin says that at the first full cabinet meeting called at 1 A.M. to discuss the German terms Chautemps at first opposed acceptance. But Chautemps in his memoirs, written to justify his action at the time, does not even pretend that he did.[67]

ment to North Africa was closed.[68] That could only mean that Pétain was determined to sign the armistice no matter what the terms.

Shortly after midnight the ministers moved over to Lebrun's office so that a full-dress cabinet meeting could be held. It began at 1 A.M. and lasted until 3 o'clock. The President of the Republic, prostrate, his head buried in his hands, declared the German conditions "unacceptable," but he did not push his opposition further.[69]

The British Ambassador had got wind that the German terms had arrived in Bordeaux and he hurried off in the middle of the night to see Pétain and Baudouin, neither of whom could receive him since they were in the midst of the meeting. The day before, on the 20th, he had sent the Foreign Minister a curt note reminding him that his government "expected to be consulted as soon as any armistice terms are received." Baudouin had responded that this was understood. But he was not the man to keep his word, nor when he broke it, to admit it.

Unable to see the Premier or the Foreign Minister the stubborn Ambassador stationed himself outside the cabinet room. Once, at 1:30 A.M., he sent in a note to Baudouin:

I have no doubt that the cabinet will recognize the insidious character of the condition concerning the fleet. No confidence can be given to the word of the Germans. They always break it.

Baudouin says he read out the note to the ministers.[70]

Actually at that moment on the night of June 21–22 Campbell did not know what the Germans had laid down about the French fleet. The terms had not yet been given him. At 3 A.M., when the cabinet adjourned until 8 A.M., the Ambassador collared the slippery Baudouin and tried to obtain them. Baudouin refused. A painful scene ensued. Each man later accused the other of rudeness. However that may have been, Baudouin lied about what happened, even in his own confidential journal. In this he confides that not only had Charles-Roux given Campbell the gist of the German terms when they conversed briefly outside the cabinet room but that he himself at the end of the session gave the Ambassador a copy of them, along with the changes which the government was demanding.

This was false. Charles-Roux finally revealed this in his own memoirs in 1949 (after many a French historian, including even the skeptical Kammerer, had been led astray). The respected Foreign Office Secretary says that early on the morning of the 22nd he learned that his chief "had refused" to give the Ambassador a text. He soon received confirmation. On his way to the Foreign Office that morning Campbell stopped off to see Pétain to protest that Britain was not even being consulted, as promised. The old Marshal tried to brush him off, though he too declined to give his visitor a copy of the armistice document.

"Your government," said Pétain, "need have no fear. We hope the fleet can go to North Africa. The Germans won't touch it there. If they try, it will be scuttled."[71]

This did not greatly reassure the Ambassador, and he hastened off to see Charles-Roux, desperately determined to find out what the German terms actually were. At this early hour, the Foreign Office Secretary believed that his chief had given Campbell a copy of the treaty the night before; Baudouin, he says, had told him so. But as he launched into an explanation of the proposed French amendments he perceived, he recounts, that the Ambassador was not following him, being obviously still ignorant of the German conditions. Charles-Roux, on his own responsibility, then handed him a text to read, and the Ambassador began feverishly to scribble it down. When he came to Clause 8 he stopped and exclaimed:

"But you're delivering your fleet!"

"No, we are not delivering it," Charles-Roux said.

Campbell insisted that the French were putting their warships at the mercy of the Germans, who could grab them any time they wanted. The Secretary answered that Darlan had assured the government that the fleet would be scuttled first. The two diplomats could not agree, and Charles-Roux says he sensed a "fatal break" between the two Allies that would lead to Mers-el-Kébir.

The Ambassador finished copying the text and stood up to go. "Poor France," he said. "She will never rise from this fall."

François-Poncet, the former French Ambassador to Berlin and Rome, who had been standing at a window in the room overhearing the conversation, could take it no longer.

The scene [he later recounted] became so poignant, my conscience was so troubled by what it signified in the break between the two allies, that I quickly left the room in order to hide my tears.

He returned after Campbell had departed.

"*They* will never forgive us for this," he said to the Secretary.[72]

Thanks to Charles-Roux, acting over the head of his Foreign Minister and the government, the British government learned the German terms by noon on the 22nd. Too late. France had not yet put its signature to the treaty, but Campbell apparently advised London that she would before the day was out. The British sense of hopelessness and despair was aired in a telegram to Campbell from London during the afternoon.

French government apparently helpless. Our only hope is Admiral Darlan. Proposed terms put Fleet entirely at German command. No reliance possible on German promises. Campbell must insist to Admiral Darlan that if Fleet cannot be surrendered to Great Britain or United States, it must be scuttled.[73]

British fears about putting the French fleet at the mercy of the Germans and British resentment that the Pétain-Weygand-Darlan government was breaking its word in making a separate armistice, and breaking it further by refusing to consult beforehand, did not greatly concern the

French cabinet in its deliberations throughout the day of June 22. Like any government, it was thinking of its own nation's interests first. The ministers, without exception, believed that France had kept her word to Britain in so far as seeing to it that the fleet would not be used by the Germans to wage war against an ally. As to reneging on the treaty not to make a separate peace, they believed that Britain's failure to throw all its air force into the Battle of France gave them a justified out. And they chose to believe, though some knew it was false, Baudouin's repeated assertion that at Briare on June 11 Churchill himself had agreed to let France out of the war.* Above all, at a moment when the survival of the nation was at stake, the Bordeaux government insisted that it alone would determine the nation's course. As the old Marshal said in a broadcast the next day:

> M. Churchill is the judge of the interests of his own country but not of ours. He is still less the judge of French honor.

The rupture between the Allies of two world wars against Germany was almost complete. Toward midnight of the 22nd the British Ambassador took his leave. Calling on the President of the Republic to bid him farewell he was told that the chief executive could not receive him without a prior request for an audience.[75] The Premier could not see him either. Marshal Pétain had gone to bed. Campbell finally drove to the residence of Baudouin, who had also gone to bed. But Baudouin awaked, put on a dressing gown, and went down to receive him. Campbell, says Baudouin, "was even more nervous and fatigued than before. His features were drawn, the color of his face yellow and his hands trembled." The French Foreign Minister protested his leaving. Campbell replied that he was leaving to make a report to his government. He was also following instructions not to allow himself to be captured by the Germans, who were now approaching the estuary of the Gironde above Bordeaux, where a British destroyer was waiting to take him off. In the early morning hours, the destroyer having moved out of the estuary and down the coast, Campbell boarded it off Saint-Jean-de-Luz and sailed for England.

"It was," says Charles-Roux, "a unilateral rupture of Anglo-French diplomatic relations." The two Western democracies, allies for so long, were drifting toward armed conflict.

The French cabinet was in almost continuous session throughout the day of June 22, but an air of unreality hung over the deliberations. The

---

* Admiral Darlan the next day, the 23rd, radioed a message to all warships warning that the British were trying "to get their hands on the French fleet and the French colonies" and repeating the falsehood that on "June 11 the [British] Prime Minister said he understood the necessity of France ceasing to fight and agreed to it. . . . He is thus not qualified to speak otherwise today."[74]

ministers kept formulating demands for changes in the armistice clauses, though they knew, as even Chautemps finally saw, that these were not negotiable. Still, they went through the motions, no doubt for the record. They wanted the French people—and the outside world—to know that they had struggled for better terms. General Weygand made this clear when toward the end of the afternoon he telephoned Huntziger and insisted that the text of the French demands and the German responses to them be attached to the armistice treaty as a protocol. Huntziger replied that such a demand would be "dangerous" and that it certainly would be turned down by the Germans. He begged his chief not to insist.*

At any rate, the French government submitted their amendments. They were telephoned by Colonel Bourget, Weygand's aide, to Huntziger at 10 A.M. and discussed at the morning meeting in the armistice car. They asked for a bigger unoccupied zone, including Paris, so that the capital could be moved back there. They requested tthat the French fleet be permitted to disarm under German supervision in the North African ports instead of in those of France proper; that all military aircraft instead of being turned over, as the Germans had asked, be destroyed under German supervision;† that the provisions for surrendering German refugees be deleted. The Germans were deaf to all the demands except the one on handing over military aircraft, on which they made a surprisingly generous concession. Huntziger so informed Weygand by telephone at 4 P.M. The chief of the French delegation made something else clear, as a telephone conversation between the two generals, which the Germans recorded, reveals. Huntziger told Weygand he wanted "not merely an authorization to sign, but an order from the French government" to do so. He did not intend to share the government's responsibilities. Furthermore, said Huntziger, the Germans were getting impatient for his signature.

So impatient, in fact, that at 6:30 P.M. General Keitel sent Huntziger a written ultimatum. The French must accept or reject the armistice terms within an hour—by 7:30, to be exact. Otherwise the parleys were off. Huntziger got Weygand on the line and put it up to him. The fiery little generalissimo instantly capitulated. Over the phone he dictated a formal order. "No. 43/DN. Order is given to the French delegation . . . to sign the armistice convention with Germany."

At 6:42 P.M. the two delegations assembled in Marshal Foch's old railroad car for the signing. Through the windows I could see General Huntziger's drawn, ashen face. He fought to keep back the tears. In signing the treaty, he said, he had a statement to make.

---

* Hitler refused to allow the French demands even to be annexed to the treaty, but instructed that the German answers should be considered as binding. The German memorandum on this exchange figures among the captured German documents.[76]

† The Germans more than met the French on this request. Instead of having French planes destroyed, they agreed merely to have them disarmed "and placed in safe custody under German supervision."

Forced by the fortunes of war to give up the struggle in which she was engaged on the side of her Allies, France sees very hard demands imposed on her under conditions which underline their severity. She has a right to expect that in future negotiations Germany will be guided by a spirit which will permit the two great neighboring peoples to live and work in peace.

After a word from General Keitel that "it was honorable for a victor to honor the vanquished," the armistice agreement was signed at 6:50 P.M. on June 22. The French delegation was then driven to Paris and the next day taken in a German plane to Rome. Article 23 had stipulated that the Franco-German armistice would not come into force until six hours after the French had concluded a similar agreement with Italy.*[77]

In a brief private conversation with Keitel after the signing that was highly emotional, Huntziger had said: "We French soldiers hope that we shall never have to repent the step we have just taken." From all that he and Weygand said and did later it is fair to say that neither of them ever repented it. At the time and for long afterward Weygand stoutly defended the armistice, claiming that it saved France from utter disaster. As later head of the French delegation to the Armistice Commission Huntziger proved extremely accommodating to the Germans. As for the beaten, exhausted French soldiers in the field and the weary French people themselves, millions of them still milling about on the roads or trying to survive in their demolished towns and villages, they greeted the news of the armistice with immense relief.

In London, Winston Churchill and Charles de Gaulle were outraged. The defiant general again that night, the 22nd, took to the airwaves over the BBC to address his fellow countrymen. The armistice terms (which he had learned from the British government) were not only a "capitulation but an enslavement," he said. The demobilization of all French military forces would put France "completely under the domination of Germany and Italy." Stressing, as he had in his first appeal on the 18th, the global nature of the war, he said: "The war is not lost. . . . It is not a Franco-German war that can be decided by a single battle. It is a world war." And at the risk of being called a traitor he appealed to all Frenchmen, especially those in the armed service, to join him.

Churchill expressed the "sadness and the stupefaction" of his government at learning that the French government had accepted the German terms for an armistice.

It could not believe that these conditions would be accepted by any French Government in possession of its freedom, its independence and its constitutional

---

* This condition had embittered Huntziger, who told Keitel: "Although Italy has declared war on France, she has not waged war. France in fact does not have to ask Italy for an armistice because the armistice has actually existed since the day of the declaration of war." At one point he said he would refuse to sign an armistice with Germany if this clause was retained, but in the end he gave in on this, as he was forced to do on all the others.[78]

authority. . . . A victory of Great Britain constitutes the only hope for the restoration of the grandeur of France and the freedom of her people.

This last seemed self-evident to the Prime Minister, and history would bear him out, but it did not seem evident at all to the Bordeaux government. Nor did Pétain and Baudouin take kindly to Churchill's closing appeal to "all Frenchmen" to join "the forces of liberation."

Next day, the 23rd, the Marshal broadcast over the radio an angry protest of the Prime Minister's statement and Baudouin got off by wire a stiffly worded official complaint to London. Pétain's words were unusually sharp for him and were believed inspired by Alibert and Laval, the latter having joined the cabinet that morning and immediately demanded a formal diplomatic rupture with Britain and the recall of the French Ambassador in London.*

The government and the people of France [said Pétain] have heard with saddened amazement the words of M. Churchill. . . . The French can but protest the lessons given by a foreign minister. . . . The French will be saved by their own efforts. M. Churchill should know this. . . . He should know that the French are showing more grandeur by admitting defeat than in trying to avoid it by vain and illusory efforts.

Baudouin's note affirmed that Churchill's words had "created the most painful impression in France, showed an absolute lack of *sang-froid,* and contained affirmations directly contrary to reality." And having accused Churchill of prevarication the French Foreign Minister proceeded to repeat—for the *n*th time!—his old lie that the Prime Minister at Briare and Tours

had shown a friendly comprehension of the necessity for France to put an end to hostilities.

The violence of his words and their excess, which go so far as to put in doubt the constitutional authority of the French government, thus cannot be excused by surprise. . . . The Prime Minister speaks as though he considers that the present government of France does not represent French public opinion. The Prime Minister is wrong. . . .[79]

The angry exchange of words between the two Allies went back and forth. On June 24 an official statement of the British government declared that "the government of Marshal Pétain" had broken its "solemn word" by concluding a separate peace. It asserted—with some exaggeration— that the armistice "obliged France to hand over to Germany all her armed forces, all of her arms and war materiel, and the largest part of her territory for the conduct of the war against Great Britain." Next day Havas, the official French news agency and mouthpiece of the government,

---

* Actually, Charles Corbin resigned that day and retired from the diplomatic service.

blamed Britain for the "harshness" of the German terms. "General Keitel explained at Compiègne," Havas said, "that the severity of the terms imposed by Germany on France were rendered necessary by Great Britain's continuation of the war." Ambassador Biddle, who cabled Washington the text of the Havas statement, which was published in the French newspapers, could not refrain from commenting: "The *volte-face* of the French press is revolting."[80]

On the 25th Churchill devoted a long speech to the consequences of the armistice. After expressing his compassion for the French and his scorn for "the Bordeaux government," he exposed Baudouin's falsehood about having released the French from their treaty obligations during his visits on the Loire. But above all, he was concerned about the French fleet. Analyzing Article 8 of the armistice convention, he said:

From this text it is clear that the French war vessels pass into German and Italian control while fully armed. We note, of course, the solemn declaration of the German Government that they have no intention of using them for their own purposes during the war. What is the value of that? Ask half a dozen countries.

In Bordeaux Ambassador Biddle shared the British distrust.

As to the Fleet, I am frankly anxious [he cabled Washington on the 22nd]. Baudouin said the Germans had "agreed" to permit French maintenance of crews and withdrawal of the Fleet to African ports. I pinned him down however to the fact that the Fleet is first to return to ports in metropolitan France for disarmament under German control. While he insisted that in case of last-minute German treachery the ships would be sunk, the value of such a last-minute safeguard seems pitifully small.[81]

Even Darlan at this time seems to have felt little trust in the Germans —or in the British either. On June 24 he sent out his last coded message to all warships and stations:

Secret precautions for scuttling must be taken in case the enemy or the ex-ally* tries to take over a ship and use it. [In this case] without a new order all ships must sail to the United States or scuttle themselves. . . . In no case must they be left intact for the enemy.[84]

Prostrate though the armistice left the country, with the fleet sacrificed

---

* According to Kammerer, the word "ex-ally" was omitted from the text when it was transmitted to the British admiralty the next day.[82] Also not sent the British, naturally, was the text of a secret order to the French fleet which Darlan issued the same day: "Disembark immediately all British liaison officers and personnel. . . . *Watch out for possible British attacks.*"[83]

and North Africa disarmed—the last two sources of military power left to France with which to resist and remain free—no politician or soldier in the homeland protested against its being signed. De Gaulle in London, fulminating against it in his daily broadcasts, was a lonely figure of a Frenchman. Few of his compatriots in the British capital would have anything to do with him. Alexis Léger, André Maurois, Pertinax, Jean Monnet, among others, refused to join him, and thousands of French troops and sailors and their officers, including three generals and two admirals, clamored for repatriation to the subjected motherland.* They had no stomach for continuing the fight under the banner of the general's Free French. In his broadcast on the evening of June 24 de Gaulle could not hide his sense of loneliness—and frustration.

I will say this evening, simply because someone has to say it, what shame, what revolt rises in the hearts of decent Frenchmen. . . . France and the French have been delivered hand and foot to the enemy.

But if decent Frenchmen were filled with shame and revolt no one else publicly expressed it. "The fact was," de Gaulle recalled in his memoirs, "that not a single public figure raised his voice to condemn the armistice."[85]

Not even Paul Reynaud. Baudouin saw his old chief on the afternoon of the 23rd, the day after the armistice was signed, and recorded in his diary:

He disassociates himself from his former collaborator, General de Gaulle, who on the London radio has taken a position against the government of Marshal Pétain. He deplores the speech pronounced by Churchill yesterday. He gives me a personal message for Churchill, which I agree to forward.[86]

That message, which Reynaud later published in his memoirs, read in part:

I appeal to your friendship and to the confidence which you have always accorded me. Nothing would make Hitler happier than a falling out, public and permanent, between our two countries. Your declaration yesterday so moved me that I discussed it with Marshal Pétain.

Reynaud said he understood the Prime Minister's anguish about the French fleet.

The stipulations of the armistice accord on this subject are of a nature, I admit, to disquiet you. But I have just questioned Admiral Darlan, in the presence of the Marshal, about it. Darlan assures me that . . . dispositions will be

---

* They were part of the forces withdrawn from Narvik or taken off at Dunkirk and not yet sent home. Several warships had taken temporary refuge in British ports.

taken so that in no case can the enemy use our fleet against England contrary to the engagements taken by him.

So that must reassure you on this point.

The former Premier closed with a reminder that

at Briare and at Tours, you told me that if another government . . . asked for an armistice, not only would England not waste its time in vain recriminations but that . . . when final victory came France would be restored in her power and dignity. I am sure that these sentiments are always at the bottom of your heart.[87]

So Reynaud joined his political enemies, Pétain, Weygand, Darlan, and Baudouin, in asking Churchill to trust Darlan and the Germans on the navy, and to cease criticizing France for having deserted Britain in the war. On this, at least, there was great unity in France.

Unity too, for the moment, in the feeling that the Marshal's government had done the right thing in abandoning the struggle despite the military strength the country still had in the possession of an intact and powerful fleet and considerable armed forces in North Africa, which the Navy, with the help of the British Mediterranean Fleet, could have protected against German and Italian attack. General Weygand, the principal architect of capitulation through an armistice, staunchly defended it on the grounds that not only was it necessary but that it gave France advantages it would not have had if there had been a simple, unconditional surrender.

The armistice [he declared] preserved for France a part of its territory, a government, men, her possessions overseas, her warships, her armed forces.[88]

If the French army had simply surrendered unconditionally, he argued, all of France would have been overrun and occupied and all the troops made prisoners of war. The country would have lain prostrate. With the armistice, France retained considerable treaty rights which gave it some protection against further German encroachment.

The opposite view, and a minority one, was that France had put herself at the mercy of the Nazi Germans, had sacrificed the considerable military assets she had in the fleet and North Africa, had given up when she still could have fought on the seas and in the Empire, and had broken her solemn word to Britain not to make a separate peace. Moreover the idea that a French government in the unoccupied zone could be free and independent was a fiction. It would be under the heel of Hitler.

Lebrun, who had failed to use his high office to prevent the armistice, saw this only after the lapse of time. Testifying in the Laval trial after the war he said:

It would have been better for France . . . that the country be administered directly by a *Gauleiter* than by a French government, which was not going to have power any longer *except in appearance* and whose essential role would consist, in sum, in guaranteeing all the decisions of the occupation authorities.[89]

"At least our honor is safe," the old Marshal said in a broadcast on June 25. "No one will make use of our planes and our fleet. . . . The government remains free. France will be administered only by the French."

De Gaulle replied in a broadcast directed to Pétain in which he summed up better than anyone else the case against the French capitulation.

You were led to believe, Marshal, that an armistice . . . would be honorable. . . . This armistice is dishonorable. Two thirds of our territory occupied by the enemy—and what an enemy! Our entire army demobilized, our officers and men prisoners. Our fleet, our planes, our tanks, our arms, handed over intact so that the enemy may use them against our own Allies. The country, the government, you yourself, reduced to servitude.

Ah! to obtain and accept such an enslavement, we did not need the Conqueror of Verdun. Anyone else would have sufficed.

Scoring him for not having continued the war from North Africa, for having failed to understand the power and the resolve of Britain to remain in the struggle and for "having rejected beforehand the great amount of help offered by America," the obstreperous general continued:

You played a losing hand, threw in your cards, emptied your pockets as though we didn't have a single trump left. . . . You call upon France, Marshal —a France surrendered, pillaged, and enslaved—to go back to work to build anew and rise from her ruins. But in what atmosphere, by what means, in the name of what, do you expect her to rise again under the German jackboot and the Italian heel?[90]

The venerable Marshal and the rebellious young general, often at odds during the prewar years, had now drifted to opposite poles in their conceptions of how France could best survive. The split would further divide the divided country. For the moment, though, in that disastrous summer of 1940 the overwhelming majority of Frenchmen sided with the hero of Verdun.

So did all but two or three members of the venerable Académie Française, of which the Marshal and the generalissimo were members. So did most of the important writers. The poet-diplomat Claudel wrote an impassioned ode in praise of Pétain.* But there were a few who could

---

* Later, when the course of events took a turn he had not anticipated, Claudel wrote an ode to General de Gaulle in almost identical words. François Mauriac, immensely influential through his novels and journalism, went into ecstasies at the sound of the voice of the hero-marshal calling on the country to accept defeat and to get back to work. In an article in *Le Figaro* on July 3 Mauriac wrote that "the words of Marshal Pétain on the evening of June 25 had a sound that was almost

not go along. They recalled the past. Kammerer remembered the words of the German philosopher Fichte after Jena, where Napoleon had humbled the Prussians:

A cowardly surrender will not save you from destruction! You will get from it only a short respite for a dishonorable existence. . . . What you believe to be a peace with honor is not peace! It leaves the enemy, as soon as this shameful peace is signed, complete power to resume his crushing march against you at the point where he left off.[91]

André Truchet, a combat and badly wounded officer in the first war, recalled a famous exchange between General Ducrot and Thiers in 1870 when the general had advised defending Paris against the Germans even though final victory seemed improbable. At least it would wipe out the shame of the surrenders at Sedan and Metz.

"General," said Thiers, "you speak like a soldier, and that's good. But you do not speak like a political man."

"Monsieur," replied General Ducrot, "I believe I also speak as a political man because a great nation such as ours rises always from her material ruins, but it will never rise from her moral ruins."[92]

I myself in that bleak summer thought of the reply of the Melian delegates to the Athenians of Pericles, who had sent an ultimatum demanding surrender of the island state of Melos. The Athenians had behaved a good deal like Hitler, telling the Melians: "You know as well as we do that right, as the world goes, is only in question between equals in power, while the strong do what they can and the weak suffer what they must."

Thucydides had given the Melian answer.

. . . It were surely great baseness and cowardice in us who are still free not to try everything that can be tried before submitting to your yoke. . . . We know that the fortune of war is sometimes more impartial than the disproportion of numbers might lead one to suppose; to submit is to give ourselves over to despair, while action still preserves for us a hope that we may stand erect.[93]

---

intemporal. It was not a man who spoke to us, but something out of the profound depths of our History. This old man was delegated to us by the dead of Verdun. . . ." Later, when the tide turned, Mauriac, like Claudel, became just as ecstatic over General de Gaulle.

Paul Valéry, the eminent poet and, like Mauriac, a member of the Academy, exulted that the Marshal "has offered himself in order to maintain in the midst of a disorder without example the unity, indeed the existence, of the country." André Gide was not far behind his fellow writers. He thought Pétain's first broadcast, which had called on the French to cease fighting even before the Germans had agreed to discuss an armistice, "simply admirable." On July 10 he confided to his journal: "I would accept a dictatorship, which alone, I fear, can save us from decomposition." He thought on July 9 that "if the German domination assured us abundance, nine out of ten French would accept it." By July 17, he says, he was doing "a lot of reading in German." Goethe attracted him. And by July 19 Gide had "almost come to believe that France did not merit victory" and he was rehashing Laval's line that "it appears she threw herself into the adventure, or rather, let herself be drawn into it, with a perilous imprudence."

In his postwar memoirs and testimony General Weygand went to extreme—and absurd—lengths to try to show that the armistice had saved North Africa and that when the Anglo-American forces came in 1942 they found a French army there "ready for combat." This was too much for one member of the Parliamentary Investigating Committee, who retorted: "Yes, ready for combat—against our friends who were coming to try to liberate us."*

General Weygand not only opposed—successfully—the French government moving to North Africa; he not only convinced the Pétain government that the defense of the Empire across the Mediterranean was impossible and that, as he said, "to move the war to North Africa would be to lose it"; he not only squelched General Noguès, the Commander in Chief on the spot, who at first wanted to continue the war from there; but he misrepresented Noguès' views to the cabinet at a crucial moment when the decision to go or not to go to Africa hung in the balance. One former military officer, an authority on the Empire, even suggests that Weygand, in reporting to the Council of Ministers, distorted the dispatches of Noguès because they opposed his views and because they threatened to wreck the armistice with Germany, which he was determined to get.[94] That was not all. Weygand, along with Baudouin and Bouthillier, who were his principal political henchmen, concocted in their postwar testimony a tale about General Koeltz's role in the matter that was so far from the truth that Koeltz, on his word of honor as an officer and under oath, told the Parliamentary Investigating Committee after the war that it was without foundation whatsoever.

Irritated by General Noguès' telegrams and by his insistence that he could hold North Africa if the fleet were not surrendered, Weygand had sent General Koeltz to Algiers on June 22 to confer with the recalcitrant commander. Koeltz returned to Bordeaux the next day and, according to Weygand, Baudouin, and Bouthillier, made a lengthy report to the cabinet to the effect that Noguès had agreed that his forces were too weak to repel a German attack from Spanish Morocco and an Italian attack from Tripolitania against Tunisia.

"General Koeltz made his report to the cabinet meeting," Weygand swore to the Parliamentary Investigating Committee. "General Noguès had told him what was possible to do. That showed the government all the more that North Africa did not have the means of defending itself."[95]

Baudouin reported on Koeltz's "exposé" in his journal for June 23.

General Koeltz, back from Algeria, made a long report [to the cabinet].

---

* On November 8, 1942, French troops and naval forces, on the orders of the Pétain government and of General Noguès, opposed the landing of an Anglo-American army in North Africa. At Casablanca, where Noguès was installed, there was heavy fighting in which the French lost 1,500 dead and the Americans almost as many. It was a strange welcome to Allied forces which had come to liberate the French.

The information furnished by General Noguès confirms our fears: the military potential is very weak. It would be impossible to resist the German tanks which, in agreement with Spain, could cross . . . the strait [of Gibraltar] and land in Spanish Morocco easily.[96]

Bouthillier reported the declaration of Koeltz at length.

General Koeltz was heard by the cabinet June 23 at 5 P.M. He reported on his talk with General Noguès. Two facts emerged from the declarations of the Commander in Chief in North Africa:
1. The extreme weakness of the army there. . . .
2. The impossibility, in case of attack from the Spanish Rif, of holding on a line along the Wadi Sebou.
To withdraw into the heart of Africa would only serve to attract the Germans and Italians and provoke the entry of Spain into the war . . . and thus prolong it.

Bouthillier summed up the views of Noguès, as given the cabinet by Weygand.

To set up the capital in Algiers appears to be impossible. The President of the Republic would risk being assassinated. . . . In Morocco resistance is inconceivable. . . .
The report of General Koeltz on the 23rd to Marshal Pétain's cabinet, assembled to hear him, destroyed the illusions of those who had nourished them up to now. The idea of a French bastion in North Africa was a chimeric dream. And worse, it was dangerous.[97]

But did General Koeltz report to the cabinet on June 23, and did he tell it that it was Noguès' conclusion that French North Africa could not hold out?

General Koeltz was questioned about that by the Parliamentary Investigating Committee after the war. He had explained that his interview with Noguès at Algiers on the 22nd had not lasted "more than ten or fifteen minutes" because the North African commander had already explained in a telegram to Weygand the same day what his situation was. Later in the evening Noguès gave Koeltz a list of arms he needed. The next day, the 23rd, Koeltz testified, he flew back to Bordeaux, made a brief report to Weygand, and handed him the list of arms which Noguès had given him.

Professor Dhers, a member of the Committee, citing the journal of Baudouin describing Koeltz's appearance before the cabinet that day, asked: "You did not go to that cabinet meeting?"

GENERAL KOELTZ: I give you my word of honor as an officer that I did not go to that cabinet meeting . . . I didn't even know where it met in Bordeaux.

Having cleared up that point, General Koeltz disposed of another: "I declare upon my honor that I never told General Weygand that North Africa could not resist. This is an invention. . . . General Noguès never told me that."[98]

Lebrun confirmed to the Committee that Weygand had never communicated Noguès' defiant telegrams to the cabinet. "Normally," he said, "the President of the Republic should be given these telegrams. I never saw them. I was left ignorant of so many things."[99]

Noguès began to weaken. He had sent three of his staff officers to southern France to scrounge for men and arms and get them on ships at Port-Vendres and off to Algeria. They had found at Toulouse a regiment of artillery, which had been evacuated from Dunkirk, and some guns in the military depot there, but when they tried to get them aboard ships at Port-Vendres, they were arrested on the orders of General Colson, the new Minister of War, and incarcerated in the fortress at Perpignan. Admiral Darlan also intervened not only to stop ships from embarking for North Africa but to recall several vessels en route.*[100] All this was discouraging to General Noguès.

Still, he continued to send telegrams to Bordeaux that sounded almost mutinous to the generalissimo and the Marshal. On the 23rd he got off a wire on his first reactions to the armistice with the Germans.

It is not possible to demobilize the troops in North Africa. They are the last guarantee, with the Air Force and the Navy, of an honorable peace.

He warned that if the armistice did not provide for the integrity of North African soil, not only the native Moslems but the "totality of the armed forces" would continue the struggle.

If the government [he added] does not have the certainty of honorable conditions of peace in order to save the future of the country, it must come and continue the struggle in North Africa.

He supplemented this message with a personal appeal to Weygand to come to North Africa himself and take over the defense of the Empire. Noguès, in his anguish, did not yet realize how committed his Commander

---

* There was much confusion in Bordeaux about sending off to North Africa as many men and as much arms as possible. Thus, after ordering the arrest of General Noguès' staff officers, General Colson sent an order at 11:30 P.M. the same night (the 23rd) to "urgently dispatch" to North Africa all the men and arms "assembled in the Mediterranean ports." But next day Weygand countermanded it and laid it down that only a few ships could depart. Actually, due either to confusion or to disobedience—probably both—a number of ships carrying several thousand troops and supplies got away. Twenty-four ships sailed from Marseilles between June 15 and 24. Fourteen vessels reached Algeria or Morocco between June 24 and 28, with 8,000 men and several thousand tons of arms.[101]

in Chief was to getting out of the war. But he was soon to learn. On the 24th Weygand wired him that "in view of the attitude of the British government and the activity of its diplomatic agents in trying to organize a rebellion against the French government," he was to expel the British liaison mission in North Africa "with the briefest delay." Shortly before midnight came a sharp message from Weygand to Noguès advising him that the cessation of hostilities was imminent.

The elements of appreciation which you possess do not permit you to judge the situation which the government has to face or appreciate the decisions which this situation imposes on it, none of which, however, are contrary to the honor of the country.

Weygand was not quite sure that General Noguès would bow to the dictates of the government, and after admonishing him on his ignorance of the true situation he thought it wise to add:

The government appeals to your sense of duty to maintain the strictest discipline in your troops . . . and to have confidence in the government.

Early on the evening of June 25 Noguès, "with despair in his soul," assured Weygand that his orders would be carried out. But a few hours later he had some doubts, and at 11 P.M. wired the generalissimo:

I make the most express reservations about the measures of demobilization and the conditions under which they will be controlled. . . . I spent most of last night trying to calm the delegations demanding that I take command of the unvanquished forces of the Empire. . . .
The government, acting as it has in the atmosphere of panic, has not been able to recognize the moral element and force which North Africa represents and which, with Navy and Air Force, could hold out until our enemies are exhausted. It will bitterly regret it.
Personally I shall remain at my post so long as there is danger to fulfilling my sacrificial mission, which covers my face with shame, in order not to cut France in two. But as soon as I estimate that calm is assured, I shall ask you to relieve me of my post.

Weygand, always sensitive to criticism, did not care for the African commander's sharp words against his government. On June 28 he replied that

he considers inadmissible the words employed by General Noguès with regard to the government and he considers them as nonexistent.

Weygand in fact was so furious that two days before, on June 26, he had dissolved the North African Command and ordered General Noguès back to Morocco as Resident-General. The possibility of the French fighting in North Africa was smothered by Bordeaux. Noguès finally gave in.[102]

Lebrun recounts that Noguès' tart telegram of the 25th *was* read to the cabinet, "where it provoked much bad feeling. 'It is intolerable,' said some. 'We must dissolve the North African Command and send General Noguès back to Rabat,' which was done."[103]

Thus in the midst of a good deal of skulduggery and deception unusual for the government of a great nation headed by such illustrious military heroes as Pétain and Weygand, the North African trump was thrown away.

Could North Africa, contrary to what Weygand convinced himself of, have held out? General Noguès, the best authority on the subject, thought so. And this is the conclusion of the author of the most objective, thoroughly documented, and exhaustive study of the problem. This is André Truchet, a career army officer and graduate of St.-Cyr, who retired from the army after the first war, in which he was severely wounded, and took up residence in North Africa. In his book, *L'Armistice de 1940 et L'Afrique du Nord,* written after years of research in all the available records, he concludes that North Africa could have held out, that its strength was far greater than Weygand wanted to admit. He cites the facts and the figures.

Weygand contended to his dying breath at the age of ninety-eight in 1965 that the Germans could easily have sent a few panzer divisions through Spain, ferried them across the Strait of Gibraltar under the umbrella of the Luftwaffe, which would have annihilated the French and British fleets there, landed them in Spanish Morocco, and quickly overrun French Morocco and Algeria while the Italians pressed from the other side against Tunisia.

But this thesis is easily refuted. In the first place, the Spaniards had no shipping with which to carry several divisions over the strait. And it is far from certain that Franco, friendly though he was to Hitler and anxious to share in the North African spoils, would have permitted transit to the Germans. At this time Spain, exhausted from the Civil War, was facing starvation and depended upon American shipments of food through the British blockade to survive. These would have been cut off immediately by both Britain and the United States had Franco allowed the Germans to move south through his country. But could the Germans have done it? They were about to assault Great Britain and needed every available plane in that venture. Few fighters and bombers could have been spared for a secondary field of operations. As it was, the French had 700 new fighters to oppose the Luftwaffe—more than Britain had in the first weeks of the Battle of Britain. With such fighter cover the French and British fleets could easily have destroyed any ship trying to cross from Spain to North Africa.

Perhaps one can leave the last word to General Halder, Chief of the German Army General Staff at the time. "It would have been impossible," he concluded, "to conquer England and North Africa at the same time," underlining the words himself.[104]

THE FRANCO-ITALIAN ARMISTICE AND THE END OF HOSTILITIES

The Italians, not having fought, as General Huntziger reminded General Keitel at Rethondes, swallowed their pride, renounced their grandiose ideas of occupying a good deal of France and most of the French African Empire, and signed in Rome on June 24 at 6:35 P.M. an innocuous armistice with France. Hitler had no intention of having his victory, in which Italy had played no part, spoiled by the Duce's illusions of grandeur. The German dictator wanted the armistice because it took France out of the war completely, even in the Empire, and left him free to attack Britain and later Russia.

Mussolini understood his own position. In a humble message to Hitler on June 22, just after the Franco-German armistice was signed, he said:

> Fuehrer: In order to facilitate the acceptance of the armistice by the French I have not included . . . the occupation of the left side of the Rhône, or of Corsica, Tunis, and Djibouti, as we had intended in Munich. I have limited myself to a minimum—a demilitarized zone of 50 kilometers. . . . For the rest, I have used the clauses of the German armistice.[105]

The strutting Italian dictator had been quickly deflated—all the more so because of the miserable showing of the Italian army against a handful of French troops on the Alpine frontier. Ciano, his son-in-law and the Foreign Minister, who led the Italian armistice delegation, recorded in his diary the sinking spirits of the Duce.

> June 21. Mussolini is quite humiliated because our troops have not made a step forward. . . .
> June 23. The French plenipotentiaries have arrived in German planes. . . . I report [the first meeting] to the Duce by telephone. He is bitter because he had wanted to reach the armistice after a victory by our own armed forces.

At 6:35 P.M. on June 24 the Franco-Italian armistice was signed. Six hours later, at 35 minutes past midnight on the 25th, according to the agreement at Rethondes, the armistice went into effect. All over France the guns lapsed into silence, the disorderly retreat of the remnants of the once great French army mercifully ended, and the stricken country breathed a sigh of relief that the killing had stopped.

Some 84,000 soldiers had been killed in the forty-six days of battle,

120,000 wounded and a million and a half made prisoner—most of them in the last few days of the campaign. Bad as the losses were, bad as the death of any young man is before his time, they were but a fraction of those in the first war when a million and a half Frenchmen had been slain on the battlefield.

June 25, when the slaughter came officially to an end, was proclaimed a day of mourning in France and the notables of the government, led by Marshal Pétain, attended a solemn ceremony at the Cathedral of Saint-André. Paul Reynaud joined them and listened to the archbishop admonish that "the French must learn the lessons of their misfortunes and, in accepting the test, try to create a New Order, more just and more sane than that which has crumbled."[106] This was a theme that the Church quickly took up: that an atheistic France under the Third Republic had but received "divine retribution" for its Godless ways. And that it must now atone for its long years of pleasures, frivolities, and lack of Christian faith.[107]

"The New Order." The concept was sprouting not only in the warped mind of Adolf Hitler but in the minds of the new French leaders. In his broadcast on the Day of Mourning, June 25, Marshal Pétain sounded the new line.

Our defeat came because of our slackness. The seeking of pleasures destroyed what the spirit of sacrifice had built up. I call upon you first of all for intellectual and moral redress. . . . *A New Order* begins. . . .

A New Order. Pierre Laval, who had wormed his way into a cabinet post on June 23, began to intrigue for it. To him it must replace the hated Republic. To General Weygand too. On June 28 he, who swore that he never mixed in politics, handed Pétain a grandiose—and foolish—pronunciamento which exposed the kind of future France the new regime would strive for.

The former order of things, a political regime of masonic, capitalist, and international compromises, has led us to where we are.

France wants no more of it. . . . We must return to the cult and the practice of God, Country, Family. We need new programs, new men. . . . Time presses. . . . Tomorrow it will be too late.[108]

It sounded to some as though the generalissimo had recently been reading Hitler's *Mein Kampf.*

This was what was in the air when, at the end of the momentous month of June 1940, German troops moved into Bordeaux and the French government moved out, setting forth for a new provisional capital in the so-called free zone. The last days of the Third Republic had come. Born of disaster at Sedan in 1870 it had begun to expire from disaster at Sedan in 1940, after a tumultuous life of seventy years.

BOOK FIVE

The Collapse
of the Third Republic

36

THE END AT VICHY
June–July 1940

The government of Marshal Pétain abandoned Bordeaux to the Germans on June 29 and set out for Clermont-Ferrand, the fief of Pierre Laval, who owned there a newspaper, a radio station, a printing plant, and other business interests which had made this once penniless politician a millionaire.

Laval had forced his way into the government six days before, on June 23. Swallowing his pride and overcoming his resentment at not having been made Foreign Minister when Pétain came in on the 17th, he had importuned the Marshal to take him back in any capacity. He did not want to be left out of a government which was going his way, which for more than a year he had envisaged and promoted, and of which he planned to become the real chief, pulling the strings behind the figurehead of the eighty-four-year-old, politically inexperienced, and somewhat senile Marshal.

The old soldier consented to make him a Minister of State, explaining to Charles-Roux, who deplored the decision, that "Laval had bitten his fingers for having turned down the Justice Ministry and had pestered him to take him on in no matter what position." Pétain admonished the Foreign Office Secretary "to keep an eye on Laval to see that he doesn't interfere in foreign affairs." Charles-Roux says he replied that, in his opinion, the Marshal "was enrolling a bad recruit."[1]

To Baudouin, who was flabbergasted at the unpleasant news, the Marshal explained that it was better to have Laval in the government, "where his intrigues would be less dangerous than outside." Within a few minutes Baudouin and Laval, who had no intention of refraining from mixing in foreign policy, were clashing.

903

A violent scene between Laval and me [Baudouin noted in his journal of the 23rd]. He insists on a rupture with the British. I tell the Marshal I shall resign if that is done. . . . The Marshal tells Laval to quiet down. . . . Weygand is furious and scornful.[2]

Violent though he was because of his temperament and because of his rage at having been left out of office for so long, Laval nevertheless kept a cool head about his objectives. That, and an iron determination to achieve them quickly now that, as he realized, a golden opportunity had finally come. He confided his thoughts on June 26 to Baudouin and Bouthillier. The Marshal, said Laval, must be given exceptional constitutional powers.

It is impossible to govern with Parliament [Laval said], especially with the Chamber of the Popular Front of 1936.* . . . We must revise the Constitution and put an end to the present political regime.[3]

The two young ministers thought that was going too far and suggested that Parliament be asked to grant the Marshal powers of decreeing laws, such as it had given other premiers in times of emergency. In the meantime the Senate and Chamber would take "a long vacation."

"That is not enough," Laval replied. He took up the thread again four days later, the last day of June, at Clermont-Ferrand, where the government was trying to establish itself in "unimaginable disorder," as Baudouin puts it, his Foreign Office having been installed in a shabby little hotel, he says, "containing a total of seven rooms, without electricity or even a telephone." Pétain met informally with Laval, Alibert, Baudouin, and Bouthillier. The last two suggested that the Marshal simply adjourn Parliament for six months and rule by decree. "By then," said Bouthillier, "the situation will have evolved. We'll know more clearly where we are. And you can tell Parliament what you've done." The Marshal seemed to agree.

Then Laval, backed by Alibert, intervened. This was no time for half measures, he declared. Vanquished France needed a regime that could negotiate with Nazi Germany. The Republic would not be acceptable to Hitler. The National Assembly (comprising the two chambers sitting as one) must be immediately convoked and forced to vote complete power to the Marshal to draw up a new constitution for a new kind of regime. Baudouin objected that it would be difficult to get a majority of the members of Parliament "to commit suicide."

The Marshal [Baudouin reported in his journal] is very indecisive. His personal tendency is to limit himself to sending the Chambers on vacation. . . .

---

* The Chamber, elected in 1936 with a Popular Front majority, now long since dissolved, had had its mandate prolonged because of the war.

He does not wish, at least for now, to reform the Constitution. "To do that," he says, "we would have to be in Paris, in a free Paris. We shall have to see about that later." But the obstinacy of Laval shakes him. Finally he takes refuge behind the President of the Republic.

It was not much of a refuge. Laval volunteered to take care of the President of the Republic. "I will obtain immediately," he cried, "the full agreement of Lebrun to disappear!" And off he rushed to Royat, a nearby resort, where the President was installed, to fulfill his boast. He was back in an hour and, by Baudouin's account, "described how he had routed the President of the Republic and obtained his assent to modifying the Constitution."*

The Marshal [says Baudouin] regarded Laval with astonishment and admiration. Laval is certain of success. He hates the present Chamber. He despises Lebrun. Let the Marshal allow him to settle these matters. He promises success.[5]

And Pétain did. "All right," he told Laval. "Go ahead and try." That was all that Laval needed to proceed with the scrapping of the Republic. The old soldier had given him the green light.

What Laval was up to, what indeed Pétain and Weygand and Darlan and even Lebrun were up to, became quickly evident to Ambassador Bullitt, who, finally seeing the folly of his decision to remain in Paris, where he had nothing to do, had caught up with the French government on July 1 at Clermont-Ferrand and talked at length with most of its leaders. From the nearby resort of La Bourboule, he filed a long dispatch that evening to Washington, "personal for the Secretary and the President," telling at length of his conversations. Bullitt's report gives better than any other contemporary record I have seen the state of mind and heart and soul of the tattered men who controlled the French government at this hour of adversity and trial. Perhaps only a knowledgeable foreigner could have given an objective, true account of the situation in the midst of what the Ambassador called "mental and physical disorder" with "the French completely crushed." Bullitt, who loved France and the French, as these pages have shown, was sympathetic to those he interviewed and to their plight but he himself was crushed by what they said of their country—and of Britain and Germany—and by what they told him they intended to do. One gets the impression that it was the most disillusioning day of his life. But it produced what must be by far the most enlightening diplomatic dispatch he ever wrote. In view of all the denials the chief figures in the French drama would later make of what they thought, said,

---

* Lebrun says that Pétain accompanied Laval to the meeting. "The Marshal," he writes, "says nothing. He acts as if he were absent. He seems to disinterest himself in this grave question." Nevertheless Lebrun confirms that he gave in. He told Laval to bring him the "text" of his proposed law for a new constitution. Like everyone else, the ineffectual President of the Republic was giving way.[4]

and intended at this most crucial moment, it helps to set the historical record—and all of us—straight.[6]

The impression which emerges from these conversations [Bullitt cabled] is the extraordinary one that the French leaders desire to cut loose from all that France has represented during the past two generations, that their physical and moral defeat has been so absolute that they have accepted completely for France the fate of becoming a province of Nazi Germany. Moreover, in order that they may have as many companions in misery as possible they hope that England will be rapidly and completely defeated by Germany. . . . Their hope is that France may become Germany's favorite province—a new *Gau* which will develop into a new Gaul.

The Ambassador had first called on Lebrun, who complained bitterly "that the United States had done nothing to help France." About the British, the President of the Republic, Bullitt reported,

flew into a passion and said that the British had given almost no help whatsoever to the French. They had sent 10 divisions. . . . They had run from the Somme. . . . The British would soon suffer the same fate that the French had suffered.

The usually suave American Ambassador was shocked at the President's language. "I have never seen Lebrun," he commented, "in such a state of nervous excitement."

The theme that "the British had run" and that now Britain would quickly suffer the same fate as France, was repeated to Bullitt almost word for word by Pétain and then by Darlan. The Ambassador talked with the Marshal for three hours and stayed for lunch. He found the old soldier "calm, serious and altogether dignified"—in contrast to the President of the Republic. But just as defeatist and just as bitter against the British and just as certain that Britain was finished. The Marshal had no illusions about what Germany had in store for France. "It would attempt to reduce France to a province of Germany." But he had illusions about Germany's word. "He did not believe," Bullitt reported, "that the Germans would break the terms of the armistice." As to the British, he reiterated what Lebrun had said. "Their troops had run, and although they had 40 squadrons of pursuit planes in England they had sent only 6 to participate in the battle."

He said he expected Germany to crush England rapidly and he believed that Germany would make her chief demands at the expense of England. Germany probably would annex certain portions of France and would probably control the whole of France through economic arrangements, but he felt that England would be destroyed by Germany. . . . He expressed great bitterness against Churchill and General de Gaulle.

The Marshal was frank with the Ambassador about the changes he intended to make in France herself and of his contempt for the parliamentary Republic.

He said he thought it would be a good thing for France if the parliamentarians who had been responsible not only for the policies which had led to the war but also for the relative unpreparedness of France should be eliminated from the French government.

The idea that Hitler, not the French "parliamentarians," might have been responsible for the war did not enter the old soldier's head, and, like Weygand, he blamed the "politicians" for the failures of the French Army, choosing to dodge the terrible responsibilities of himself and the generalissimo and of the High Command.

He intended to dismiss every politician who had been connected with the Blum Government. He felt that the system of government in France must be changed.

And having heaped blame on the "politicians" for the sorry showing of the French Army, he added that the *schoolteachers* also bore a grave responsibility.

In his opinion one of the chief causes of the collapse of the French Army was that the reserve officers, who had been educated by schoolteachers who were Socialists and not patriots, had deserted their men and shown no fighting spirit whatsoever. A sense of courage and duty must be reintroduced into France.

No better account of the muddled thoughts of the old man who now presided over the destiny of France was ever given.

Admiral Darlan too gave vent to his thoughts to the American Ambassador. "He was intensely bitter against Great Britain," Bullitt reported, saying that the British fleet "had proved to be as great a disappointment as the French Army. It was directed not by a man but by a Board of Directors." And the Admiral told of the experience of his son, a marine, with the British troops on the Somme, who "had run . . . and blown up the bridges behind the French marines."

At any rate, said Darlan, scarcely disguising his glee, the British were through.

He felt absolutely certain that Great Britain would be completely conquered by Germany within five weeks, unless Britain should surrender sooner. It would be, in his opinion, entirely impossible for the British to send a single ship into the port of London or into the ports of Plymouth, Southampton and Portsmouth. The Germans could take Ireland easily and close the ports of Glasgow, Liverpool, Cardiff, and Bristol. Great Britain would die of asphyxiation even without a German invasion.

The Admiral had a low opinion of the British character.

He did not believe that the British government or people would have the courage to stand up against serious German air bombing, and he expected a surrender after a few heavy air attacks.

Bullitt was so taken aback that he remarked to Darlan

that he seemed to regard this prospect with considerable pleasure. . . . He did not deny this remark but smiled.

Darlan's hatred of the British was matched by his distrust of them.

Under no condition [he told Bullitt] would he send the Fleet to England since he was certain that the British would never return a single vessel of the Fleet to France, and that if Britain should win the war the treatment which would be accorded to France by Britain would be no more generous than the treatment accorded by Germany.

That "treatment" by Germany, Darlan concluded, would probably result in Hitler making France "his leading vassal state. France could do nothing but accept such a position for the moment." As a parting shot, he subscribed to the desires of Pétain, Weygand, and Laval to rid France of the hated Republic.

The entire system of parliamentary government [Bullitt reported him as saying] in France had been rotten. . . . A complete change in French ways of life was needed.

As the depressed Ambassador got up to leave, Darlan told him that he had just been informed "authoritatively that German troops had already crossed into Spain"—a statement that Lequerica, the Spanish Ambassador, told Bullitt a few minutes later was completely untrue.

After seeing briefly General Weygand and some of the lesser cabinet ministers—he apparently did not call on the new key man, Laval—Bullitt saw Camille Chautemps, who though still Vice-Premier was on his way out, knew it, and had asked Baudouin for the ambassadorship in Washington, which Reynaud had at first been offered. Chautemps told the Ambassador that he was being "shoved aside by Laval." He also told him of what the ruling clique had decided to do.

He said that Pétain, Weygand, and Laval intended to abolish the Constitution and to introduce a semi-dictatorial state. . . . Pétain, Weygand and Laval all believed that if a dictatorship of this kind were introduced in France before the peace, France would obtain much better terms than could be obtained under a parliamentary regime.

The Pétain government, then, was not only resigned to knuckling under to Hitler but thought that by emulating his totalitarian regime it would curry enough favor with him to lead him to be easy on the French. He could then vent his wrath on the British.

Such were the thoughts, exposed in all their nakedness to the American Ambassador, of the men who now were in control of the great country—to the extent that Hitler granted. On this same day, July 1, unable to get the government services functioning for lack of facilities in Clermont-Ferrand, the government moved on to the watering place of Vichy, where the great tourist hotels provided ample accommodation. Baudouin says he urged the Marshal to settle the government in Lyon, the largest city in France next to Paris, "where the government would not be isolated." Pétain bridled. He would not hear of it. He did not wish, he said, to have "any contact" with the Mayor of Lyon, who was Edouard Herriot, the distinguished Speaker of the Chamber of Deputies.

So it was in the isolated unreality of the resort town of Vichy, famed for its curative spring water, which was bottled and drunk all over the country, and a popular spot to which the well-to-do came to take the "cure," a town bristling with deluxe hotels whose regular guests were now hastily removed to make room for the notables, that the burial of the Third Republic was planned to take place. Ambassador Bullitt did not have the heart to go there and witness it. He remained at La Bourboule, a few miles away.

Several staunch defenders of the Republic, who might have been able to counter the intrigues of Laval, could not get to Vichy. They were forcibly detained by the Pétain government in North Africa. These were the ill-fated members of Parliament who, with the blessings of the Marshal and Darlan, had embarked on the *Massilia* at Bordeaux and arrived at Casablanca in Morocco on the morning of June 24. Among them were veteran Republican ministers such as Mandel, Daladier, Campinchi, and Delbos. They received a cool reception from the French authorities, were put under police surveillance, confined for several days to their steamer anchored offshore in the harbor, and Mandel was arrested for having tried to get in contact with the British consul general.

The British consuls in Morocco, Algeria, and Tunisia had indeed been busy, trying to get the French authorities there to break away from Bordeaux, set up an independent government in North Africa, and continue in the war. Arms and planes were promised them if they did. Learning that the *Massilia* was landing in Morocco with a load of members of Parliament apparently resolved to lead the resistance there, Churchill hastily dispatched Lord Gort and Duff Cooper, the latter his Minister of Information, to Rabat, the Moroccan capital, to encourage them and promise them all possible British help. The two envoys were greeted frostily at Rabat, forbidden to get in touch with Mandel or any of the others, and after being forced to spend a night on their hydroplane, packed off to England by the French authorities.*

Attacked by the Bordeaux radio for having "fled" the homeland and branded as traitors, the duped members of Parliament appealed to the government first in Bordeaux and later at Vichy to bring them back to France. When they learned of the convocation of the National Assembly for July 10 at Vichy they demanded transportation to take them back in time to take part in the deliberations. This was refused, and they were held in Algiers until after that meeting. Finally all but Mandel were allowed to return home but confined for several weeks to Marseilles. Mandel, who was acquitted by a military court at Meknès in July,† was rearrested, brought back to France, imprisoned there, then delivered to the Germans, and, as mentioned, handed back to the French after two years in Nazi concentration camps, and murdered by Pétain's French militia in cahoots with the Gestapo.

Mandel was a Jew, and his first arrest in Bordeaux less than twenty-four hours after the advent of Pétain to power had indicated at once the extent of anti-Semitism in the new French regime. Soon it would be trying to emulate that of Hitler. Deputy and former minister Jean Zay and Deputy Mendès-France, among the *Massilia*'s passengers, were also Jews. They were arrested in North Africa, and since they were soldiers haled before a military court on the charge of desertion in the face of the enemy. Zay was sentenced to deportation and national degradation, imprisoned at Riom, where he soon was joined by Léon Blum, also a Jew, and by Reynaud, Daladier, and General Gamelin. Zay was murdered on June 21, 1944, as Mandel was, by the Pétain government's French militia. Mendès-France, being less prominent at the time, got six years in prison.

The saga of the *Massilia* and its members of Parliament, many of whom had played leading roles in the Republican governments between the wars, is only a footnote to history. But it attests to the shabby beginnings of the new French government, now in the hands of four men: Pétain, Weygand, Darlan, and Laval. What now happened at Vichy in the first ten days of July could not have greatly surprised the few who had taken the measure of the new regime. In this last and sorriest chapter in the history of the Third Republic, chicanery, dupery, and every other imaginable kind of deceit, coupled with fear, cowardice, and abjectness, ran rampant and had predictable consequences.

---

* Churchill says that on July 1 he instructed the Admiralty "to try to cut out the *Massilia* and rescue those on board." But since the ship lay under the batteries of Casablanca, the attempt was abandoned.[7]

† Colonel Loireau, the presiding judge, was immediately relieved of his functions and retired from the Army by Vichy.

In the new seat of government at Vichy, Pierre Laval immediately put his fine talents at intrigue to work to inter the Republic and to replace it with a dictatorship of the old Marshal, behind whom he himself intended to rule what was left of France in close and friendly collaboration with the German conquerors and in enmity to the British ally, which he hated. Growing bolder by the hour, cajoling one minute and threatening the next, stooping to the lowest trickery when necessary, he began to win over the deputies and senators to voting themselves and the Parliament— and the Republic—out of existence. He was immensely helped by a sudden, violent act of war by the British against the French on July 3, three days after the arrival of the government in Vichy. This—for the Allies—was the most lamentable event of World War II, closing in inexorably toward its terrible climax with all the stark inevitability of Greek tragedy.

THE BRITISH NAVAL ATTACK AT MERS-EL-KÉBIR, JULY 3, 1940

Toward the end of June the government in London, fearful that, under the terms of the armistice, the French fleet would fall fully armed into German control and be used against now-beleaguered Britain, despite Hitler's promises, in which it did not for a moment believe, took what Churchill would call "a hateful decision, the most unnatural and painful in which I have ever been concerned."

That decision was taken on June 27 by the War Cabinet, which thereafter, Churchill says, never hesitated, though the admirals who had to carry it out did. It called for the seizure, control, or effective disablement or destruction of all the French fleet the British could get their hands on. The code name was *Operation Catapult*. It was to be launched and completed on July 3.

At the beginning of July most of the great warships of the French Navy were still in the reach of the British. At the home ports of Plymouth and Portsmouth were two French battleships, four light cruisers, eight destroyers, several submarines, including the *Surcouf,* the world's largest, and two hundred smaller craft. Most of these had taken refuge in England after the German army swept down the Channel and through Brittany. At the British naval base at Alexandria in Egypt was a French squadron of one battleship, four cruisers (three of them new with 8-inch guns), three destroyers, one submarine, and smaller ships. The cream of the French navy was in Algeria, near Gibraltar. The powerful Atlantic Fleet had moved from its bases in Brittany to Oran and the adjacent naval base of Mers-el-Kébir. This consisted of two battleships; two modern battle cruisers, the *Dunkerque* and the *Strasbourg,* which were superior to the German *Scharnhorst* and *Gneisenau,* having been built especially to outmatch them; four light cruisers; several destroyers; and lesser craft. At nearby Oran were seven cruisers, four of them with 8-inch guns.

If the British could take or put out of action all these warships they could still keep their lifelines in the Mediterranean and Atlantic open and defend their island against the inferior naval forces of Germany and Italy. But if the French fleet were to be added to the Axis fleets, British prospects for survival were bleak. "The life of the State and salvation of our cause," says Churchill, "were at stake." At 2:25 A.M. on July 1, at his prompting, the Admiralty sent out the definite order: *"Be prepared for 'Catapult' July 3."*

At Alexandria, Admiral Sir Andrew Cunningham, who was on excellent terms with the French commander, Admiral René Godfroy, protested against the operation in his port. He radioed London he was convinced that the French would never deliver the ships in Alexandria to the Germans, that to attack them would turn the French against the British in Syria and Africa, and that if force were resorted to the consequences might be disastrous. From Gibraltar Vice-Admiral Sir James Somerville made a similar protest to London. He was in command of "Force H," consisting of the battle cruiser *Hood,* the most powerful warship in the British navy; the battleships *Valiant* and *Resolution;* the aircraft carrier *Ark Royal;* two cruisers; and eleven destroyers. This was the fleet which would have to carry out the most important operation of all—at Mers-el-Kébir. Among Somerville's officers was Captain Holland, former British naval attaché in Paris, more recently chief liaison officer at Admiral Darlan's headquarters, a man who knew the French, liked them, spoke their language, and in turn was liked and respected by them.

Somerville conferred with Holland and other officers. All of them opposed the proposed action. As a result the Admiral radioed London:

After talk with Holland and others Vice-Admiral "Force H" is impressed with their view that the use of force should be avoided at all costs. Holland considers offensive action on our part would alienate all French wherever they are.

But Churchill was adamant. "No act was ever more necessary," he says he was convinced, "for the life of Britain." At his behest, the Admiralty replied curtly to Somerville:

Firm intention of His Majesty's Government that if French will not accept any of your alternatives they are to be destroyed.

What alternatives? The admiral received the message on the evening of July 1. Shortly after midnight the text of the ultimatum which he was to present to the French commander at Mers-el-Kébir, Admiral Marcel-Bruno Gensoul, on July 3 was radioed to him. He then learned the alternatives which were to be offered the French fleet and what he had to do if one of them were not quickly accepted. All the other British admirals, at

Alexandria, at Plymouth, at Portsmouth, knew what they had to do on the morning of July 3, and it stuck in their mouths.

Churchill, who felt a special closeness to the Navy—he had been First Lord of the Admiralty during the first nine months of the war— understood the feelings of his admirals but he was determined that they carry out his orders, however distasteful these were. At 10:55 P.M. on July 2 he requested the Admiralty to send a message to Admiral Somerville, who faced the most difficult task of all.

You are charged with one of the most disagreeable and difficult tasks that a British admiral has ever been faced with, but we have complete confidence in you and rely on you to carry it out relentlessly.

Early on the morning of July 3 and for as many hours as was necessary it was carried out—relentlessly. At the British home bases at Plymouth and Portsmouth the operation went quickly and smoothly though the French complained that their ally was brutal enough. Admiral Cayol, commanding the French squadron at Plymouth, had sniffed what was in the air and on July 1 had ordered his crews to be ready to scuttle their ships should "a foreign force" try to seize them. He explained to his men: "England is no longer our ally, but our ex-ally."

Nevertheless the French crews were taken by surprise when British armed patrols boarded their vessels at 3:45 A.M., shortly before dawn, overpowered those on watch, seized the ships, and ordered the sleepy crews ashore. Only on the giant submarine *Surcouf* was there a scuffle, in which one British and one French sailor were killed and three British wounded. Within an hour all French warships in the British Isles were firmly in the hands of the British Navy and by the day's end their crews were on land, momentarily interned, but given the choice of rallying to General de Gaulle's Free French forces or being sent home. Not many rallied to the general. Despite a plea from Vice-Admiral Muselier, whom de Gaulle had hastily named as commander of his naval forces, only some 900 sailors, few of them officers, responded. All the rest, some 19,000 men, chose repatriation to German-controlled France. French sailors, like French soldiers and civilians, had no more stomach for the war. The pleas of de Gaulle, whom most of the naval personnel frowned on as a rebel, even a traitor, were fruitless.

At Alexandria the respect of Admiral Cunningham and Admiral Godfroy for each other and their coolheadedness averted a massacre which surely would have ensued had the two fleets fired point-blank at each other. Both commanders refused to carry out their orders to the letter. Though commanded by his Admiralty to fight his way out of the harbor, Godfroy declined. He could not bring himself to risk the slaughter of his crews or to inflict heavy casualties on the British. Cunningham felt the same way. He told Godfroy:

We do not want to sink your ships. Why sacrifice uselessly lives in fighting? Our regrets for what has happened are as genuine as yours.

He asked only that the French warships discharge their fuel oil so that they could not get away and remove parts of the gun mechanisms so that they could not fire. He promised repatriation to France of the crews. After parleying all day and night and into the next morning, Godfroy accepted. "Admiral Cunningham," he said later, "behaved throughout like a *gentleman*," employing the English word. "I felt that he had no illusions about the odious role he was forced to take and that he was going through one of the worst moments of his career."

At Mers-el-Kébir events took an opposite turn. Unlike Alexandria, this was a French base and when Admiral Somerville's powerful "Force H" hove over the horizon about 9 A.M. on July 3 Admiral Gensoul, the French commander, decided at once to defend himself if necessary, though at first he could not believe that a British squadron could have hostile intentions. He had received an order from Admiral Darlan "not to have any relations with the British" and when Captain Holland in the destroyer *Foxhound* arrived at a quay and asked to see him, Gensoul refused. He sent a lieutenant to the destroyer to inquire what the British fleet was doing there. He soon learned, and it consternated him. Holland had brought a written ultimatum of unusual length—Churchill says it had been "carefully conceived"—which after explaining that

it is impossible for us, your comrades up to now, to allow your fine ships to fall into the power of the German or Italian enemy. . . . We must make sure that [they] are not used against us by the common foe,

and adding that after victory France and the French Navy would be fully restored, offered the French fleet three alternatives:

(a) Sail with us and continue to fight for victory against the Germans and Italians.
(b) Sail with reduced crews under our control to a British port. . . .
(3) Sail with us . . . to some French port in the West Indies—Martinique for instance . . . or perhaps to the United States. . . .

If you refuse these fair offers, I must, with profound regret, require you to sink your ships within six hours. Failing that, I have the orders . . . to use whatever force may be necessary to prevent your ships from falling into German or Italian hands.

Admiral Gensoul immediately radioed the French Admiralty saying that a British squadron of three battleships, one aircraft carrier and cruisers and destroyers had appeared and given him an ultimatum: *"Sink your ships within six hours or we shall use force to make you. My response: Force will be met by force."*

The Admiral made no mention of the three alternatives to sinking his ships which the British had offered, and he was later reproached—even by the Vichy government—for this omission, especially for not citing the third condition that permitted the fleet to sail to a French port in the West Indies. Both at the trial of Baudouin and at a hearing before the Parliamentary Investigating Committee, Admiral Gensoul was questioned as to why he had failed to inform the Admiralty and government of the three alternatives and, above all, the last. His reply was that he had a lot to do at the moment, that communications with the Admiralty that day were difficult because its offices were being moved. For that reason he had kept his message brief, giving only a bare résumé. Brief, but misleading, though in the end it probably would not have made any difference. Neither the French government nor the Admiralty nor Admiral Gensoul was prepared to accept an ultimatum from the "ex-ally," as they called her.

Admiral Gensoul offered another explanation of why he at first on his own and then with the approval of the Admiralty rejected the British demands. "I realized," he told the Parliamentary Investigating Committee, "that if I accepted them it would rupture the armistice agreement." The French by now were more concerned with keeping their word to the Germans on the armistice than they had been to the British on making the armistice.

"You could have saved your ships!" Michel Clemenceau exclaimed to Admiral Gensoul during the latter's questioning, meaning if he had taken them to French ports in the West Indies. But neither the admirals nor the generals nor the Pétain government had any thought whatsoever that if one day the Germans broke *their* word on the armistice, it would be helpful to France's liberation to have as many warships as possible to turn on them. All they could think of in that case was to scuttle them, thus depriving not only Germany but France of their use.

Having advised his Admiralty of his situation Admiral Gensoul replied to the British. He assured them that no French warships would fall into the hands of the Germans or Italians "intact," that he could not accept the ultimatum, and that he would "reply to force by force." He ordered his own ships to prepare for action. They were in a disadvantageous position to fire back. The big battleships were moored closely together behind a mole, a perfect target. Their forward guns were pointed to the shore. Rising ground between them and the sea made it difficult for even the rear guns to fire at the British ships. Moreover the Admiral had taken the first steps toward disarming his ships. Steam was low in the boilers, some gun mechanisms had been removed, half of the crews were on shore leave prior to being sent home. The men were hastily rounded up, the boilers fired, the missing parts of the gun mechanisms restored.

In the meantime Admiral Gensoul, he admits, played for time. For hours no response came from the French Admiralty. But he felt that the powerful cruiser squadron at nearby Oran and perhaps other ships in the

Mediterranean must have picked up his message and would be coming to his aid. And the French Air Force, with hundreds of new planes at hand ferried over the Mediterranean in recent days, would certainly help. The aircraft carrier *Ark Royal* would be vulnerable to land-based bombers.

None of this help materialized, though late in the afternoon he received a message from the Admiralty instructing him to tell the British

that Darlan has ordered all French forces in the Mediterranean to rally to you immediately. . . . Call on all submarines and planes if necessary.

It added that the Armistice Commission was "being informed." In the face of the British threat the French were appealing to the Germans. At 5 o'clock that day General Huntziger informed the German Armistice Commission in writing of the British ultimatum at Mers-el-Kébir and declared that orders had been given to the French Navy and Air Force in North Africa to respond with force against the British. General Huntziger was most deferential to the Germans.

He told General von Stuelpnagel [say the German minutes] that the French Government now realized that by giving its orders, it was exceeding the scope of the Armistice Agreement. It hoped, however, that the German Government would understand that it was fighting for its life.[8]

Understand! The Germans were delighted at seeing the French, who had ceased fighting against them, taking up battle with their ancient ally. Hitler himself replied to General Huntziger the next day, informing him that the provisions of the armistice calling for the disarmament of the French fleet and the Air Force were temporarily suspended so far as North Africa was concerned so that they might be employed to repel "unjustified and dishonorable aggression by other powers."[9]

It is interesting that the French authorities thought it necessary to get German permission and approval to respond with force to British attacks. At any rate, the permission arrived too late.

All day long Admiral Gensoul, playing for time, parleyed with the British at Mers-el-Kébir. Though the first response of the French Admiralty to his morning's message had been a curt order: "Cease speaking with the enemy," he had continued to exchange messages with Admiral Somerville. Finally at 2:30, an hour and a half before the time limit on the British ultimatum ran out, he radioed Somerville that he was ready, after all, to receive Captain Holland, whom he personally knew well. At 3 o'clock the Captain arrived aboard Gensoul's flagship, the *Dunkerque,* and the Admiral noted that the sole decoration on his white coat was the red ribbon of the Legion of Honor. The two men argued back and forth in the cabin of the Admiral. The heat in the room was sweltering and both men perspired profusely from it—and perhaps from the sad impasse they had reached. Gensoul insisted that measures had been taken to see that no French warship fell intact into German or Italian hands. He showed Holland Admiral Darlan's secret message of June 24 prescribing scuttling if the enemy tried to seize any ship. Moreover he offered to disarm his ships and he gave his personal word of honor that if they were menaced he would sail them to the West Indies. Holland reported this back to the *Hood* by radio, adding: "This is not quite our proposition. Can get no nearer."

As the captain was leaving, a radio message was delivered to the French Admiral from Somerville.

If one of our propositions is not accepted by 5:30 P.M., British Summer Time,* I shall have to sink your ships.

Gensoul handed the message without a word to Holland. The latter glanced at it in silence and then took his leave. He did not hide how wretched he felt.

Back at the Admiralty in London Churchill followed impatiently the messages from the *Hood*. "The distress of the Admiral [Somerville] and his officers," he later recounted, "was evident to us from the signals that had passed." Nothing but the most direct orders, he realized, would compel them to open fire. One was sent at 6:26 P.M.

French ships must comply with our terms or sink themselves or be sunk by you *before dark*.

But Admiral Somerville had already gone into action. At 5:54 P.M. the British fleet, standing off the shore behind a smoke screen spread by destroyers, opened fire with its big guns against the helpless French warships. Planes from the *Ark Royal* flew over and added their bombs to the carnage. In a quarter of an hour the unequal engagement was over. The French battleship *Bretagne* blew up and sank. The battleship *Provence* and the battle cruiser *Dunkerque,* badly damaged, were beached. The battle cruiser *Strasbourg* got away and, though damaged by several salvos and from later attacks by British aircraft and destroyers, made its way, crippled, to Toulon.

Damage to British ships was minor and there was little loss of life. The French lost three capital ships and many smaller ones. Some 1,297 French sailors perished and 341 were wounded. In the course of this single summer day the British had taken over or destroyed the bulk of the French fleet. It could never be used to help defeat them. When, the next day, July 4, Churchill rose in the House of Commons "with profound

---

* An hour ahead of French time.

sadness" to recount the details of the tragedy and to defend what was done on the ground that it was necessary for the survival of Britain, the members listened silently and when he had ended stood up and loudly cheered. Painful though such an action against the old ally was, it somehow gave a shot in the arm to the British people, who now faced the Germans alone. Churchill later commented on how the swift naval action on July 3 had bucked up his fellow countrymen and impressed the world.

Here was this Britain which so many had counted down and out, which strangers had supposed to be quivering on the brink of surrender, . . . striking ruthlessly at her dearest friends of yesterday. . . . It was plain that the British War Cabinet feared nothing and would stop at nothing.

The French would have welcomed such British ruthlessness had it been struck against the Germans before France was struck down. There had been very little British ruthlessness, it seemed to them, about fighting in northern France or earlier in Norway. The French military, government, and people were dumbfounded by the news from Mers-el-Kébir and then wildly angry and finally deeply resentful that an ally, or an ex-ally, could commit such a bloody deed against them. "Monsieur Winston Churchill," wrote François Mauriac in *Le Figaro,* "has arrayed against England—for how many years?—a unanimous France."[10]

In Vichy Laval and Darlan, in a paroxysm of rage, called for a declaration of war against Great Britain. Baudouin found them at a meeting with Pétain at 8:30 A.M. on July 4. The admiral was livid.

"I've been betrayed by my brothers in arms," he cried out. "They did not believe in my word." On the latter point, at least, he was right. He then told of an order he had just given for the cruiser squadron, which had got away from Oran, reinforced by the *Strasbourg,* crippled though it was, to carry out a surprise attack on Admiral Somerville's squadron returning to Gibraltar.

"But that means war with England!" Baudouin says he exclaimed. The Marshal, he adds, turned to Laval, who replied: "We have decided to respond to the attack of yesterday by an attack of our own." A heated debate ensued, with Baudouin insisting to the Marshal that retaliation would be catastrophic for France. For Laval, the enemy was no longer Germany but Britain. As he told an informal meeting of the Chamber deputies the next day: "France has never had, and will never have, a more relentless enemy than Great Britain. All our history attests to it." His venom against the British, like that of Darlan, was spilling out. Two days later the admiral informed the cabinet that he had asked the Italian Admiralty to join him in a joint naval attack on Alexandria to free the French fleet bottled up there. He also proposed a French attack on the British African colony of Sierra Leone and a bombing of Gibraltar.*

The full cabinet met at 10 A.M. and after further heated discussion cooler heads prevailed. Pétain accepted Baudouin's proposal that formal diplomatic relations with Great Britain be broken off but that there be no military reprisal.[11]

Laval grudgingly went along. He realized that the British action on July 3 had come as a godsend to him, uniting the wounded country behind whatever the government proposed to do. As much as Laval loathed the British he was now more concerned with destroying the French Republic than with trying to destroy Britain. The members of the cabinet were in a mood to accept what he now sprang on them. For some days, in collaboration with Alibert, the old royalist hater of the Republic, he had been working on what he called a "project of reform," and on July 2 he had secretly obtained the Marshal's approval of it. Now suddenly, after debate on Mers-el-Kébir had finished, Laval read it to the ministers. It boldly called for a meeting of the National Assembly on July 10 to abolish the 1875 Constitution of the Third Republic. The text had only one brief article:

The National Assembly gives all powers to the Government of the Republic, under the signature and authority of Marshal Pétain, President of the Council, to promulgate by one or several Acts the new Constitution of the French State.

This Constitution will guarantee the rights of work, of family, and of the country. It will be ratified by the Assembly which it will set up.

Laval read it to the cabinet and before a single minister could raise his voice—the President of the Republic, who presided, seemed on the point of raising his—departed.

"You must excuse me for not letting you open a discussion about it," he said. "But sixty senators are waiting for me, and I owe them an explanation." His high-handedness left some of the ministers breathless. A few minutes later it left the august senators in the same state. He did not argue with them; he laid down crisply what had to be done.

Parliament [he said] must be dissolved. The Constitution must be reformed. It must align itself with the totalitarian states. . . . If Parliament does not consent to it Germany will impose it on us, with the immediate consequence of an occupation of all of France.

The senators were stunned. Not a one of them said a word.

---

* After much debate in the cabinet the bombing of Gibraltar was carried out in September by a few French planes, which did little damage, and perhaps by that time were not intended to.

Thus on July 4 at Vichy, Pierre Laval, who had begun his political life as a left-wing Socialist during the first war, had moved, like so many Leftists, steadily toward the Right, had become wealthy, had become three times Prime Minister of a conservative government, had been kept out of office since 1936 by a liberal Parliament and by, he thought, the machinations of Albion, embarked on the greatest—and in the end, the most disastrous—adventure of his strange career. Unlike almost all the other politicians in Vichy at the beginning of the hot summer month, he knew exactly what he wanted—for himself, for the country. And he knew how to achieve it: by audacity. Everyone else was still stunned by the catastrophe. He was at the top of his form, coolly and cynically calculating, supremely confident.

Above all—and this was his greatest trump—Laval had the support of the doddering Marshal, who was lost in the sea of politics, but whom even the staunchest Republicans, even those on the Left, now regarded as the savior of the country to whom they were ready to give their allegiance. Though Laval's supporters in Parliament were at the moment in the minority, they were a determined band and came from all parties—from the Socialists to the extreme Right. Charles Spinasse, a Socialist minister in the two Blum cabinets, Marcel Déat, a former Socialist of "Die for Danzig?" fame, Marquet, an ex-Socialist whom Laval had bludgeoned Pétain into taking into the cabinet a few days before as Minister of the Interior, Jean Montigny, a Radical-Socialist, Gaston Bergery, the former darling of the Left, were among them, making common cause with their reactionary enemies in the Chamber. Not surprisingly, Georges Bonnet, the old Foreign Minister, joined the group, and, according to Montigny, went around "confirming" all that Laval said about it having been criminal for France to have entered the war and explaining how Britain and Poland had sabotaged his own last-minute efforts in September 1939 to save the peace.[12]

The majority of the members of Parliament, who opposed scrapping the Republic, had no leadership. Daladier, Mandel, and Campinchi were confined to North Africa. Reynaud, victim of a motor accident a few days before on leaving Bordeaux, had not yet appeared. Blum, who had to be protected by bodyguards from the street mobs, maintained a dignified silence. Herriot and Jeanneney, the presidents of the two chambers and regarded as pillars of the Republic, were shying away from trying to save it, being content to vie with almost everyone else in their praise of the Marshal and their undying support for him. Lebrun would not even protest Laval's scheme to get rid of him and his high office.

No wonder Laval moved ahead with confidence. He had six days—until July 10—to convince, one way or another, the majority of the 700-odd members of Parliament to destroy themselves and the Republic and to accept for the democratic land a totalitarian dictatorship modeled on that of his masters, Hitler and Mussolini. He set about his task with great skill and energy and aplomb.

Léon Blum, the old Socialist leader, insulted and spat upon in the streets by ruffian gangs from Doriot's Fascist league and by the Cagoulards, ran into Laval in Vichy on July 4. Laval was rather surprised to see him, for Prouvost's *Paris-Soir* had announced that Blum had fled the country and arrived in New York. Laval greeted his old political foe with a gibe against the Parliamentarians who had "fled" on the *Massilia*.

"They are the ones," he said, "who wanted war, this foolish, this criminal war."

"It wasn't France that wanted the war?" Blum responded.

Though he knew the man well from a quarter of a century in the Chamber of Deputies, Blum was shocked by Laval's manner.

An unbelievable arrogance puffed up his small person. In a dry voice and with an irritated glance he flung out verdicts and orders . . . "I do . . . I say . . . I refuse . . . that's the way it is" . . .

Blum asked him when the Socialist newspaper *Le Populaire* would be permitted to reappear.

"When I decide," Laval told him. "No newspaper will appear if it shows the slightest reticence about my policies. The press must follow me absolutely, without reserve—and I will not let myself be duped."

Blum, in a stupor, he says, finally concluded the conversation.

What struck me most [Blum says] was the acrid malice which all his gestures, all his words, exhaled. . . . His fall (in 1936) had nourished in him a deep passion for revenge and for reprisals. His hates, for long dissimulated, now found the occasion to assert themselves. . . . Laval always recalled to me the atrocious words of the great Retz on Mazarin: "He is the first to have introduced cheating into the Ministry."[13]

Vincent Auriol, a former Socialist Minister and destined to become President of the Republic after the war, recalled Laval in those early July days: "Everything about him is black: his clothes, his face, his soul."

On July 5 some opposition began to sprout against Laval among the still-bewildered Parliamentarians. It began with the senators. During the morning a group of twenty-five war veterans in the Senate, led by Senator Jean Taurines, a badly wounded and much decorated soldier from the last war, and by Senator Paul-Boncour, drew up an Order of the Day. After "saluting with emotion and pride their venerated chief, Marshal Pétain," they expressed their confidence in him to rebuild France "within Republican legality." Like everyone else in Vichy, the senatorial ex-soldiers wanted to turn over power to the old Marshal. Unlike Laval, they insisted on preserving the Republic. Could the two desires be reconciled? The senators decided to take their resolution to Pétain in the belief that they could win him over and stop Laval. But the Marshal was a difficult man to get to see. Alibert and Laval had him boxed in. Taurines telephoned his office at 3 P.M. and was told by Alibert he would try to arrange a meeting that evening. Actually Alibert succeeded in putting them off twenty-seven hours, until the evening of July 6.

Nettled at this show of dissent from the senators, Laval went to work on the deputies of the Chamber. Some eighty of them were meeting on July 5 at the Petit Casino. Apprised of Laval's outburst to the Senate the day before, a good many deputies were ready to counter him. Marcel Héraud, an independent from Paris, began the attack with an emotional defense of the Republic.

If the Republic has lost one war, did it not win another? You must attribute our misfortunes to men, not to the Republican regime.

But then the deputy, as so many others would do, played into the hands of the shrewd Laval. He appealed to him to protect the Republic against a possible military coup led by Weygand. The day before at Clermont-Ferrand, the generalissimo was reported to have said, after reviewing the troops of the 14th Division: "Your task is not finished. Perhaps you will have to intervene in the interior." Laval himself had spread the report, which Weygand later denied, using it to warn the deputies that unless they accepted his proposal, Weygand would take over.

After Héraud's speech, the opposition seemed to melt away. To his surprise, Laval began to receive support from the Socialists, the last ones, it would have seemed, to favor a Fascist dictatorship. François Chasseigne, a Socialist deputy, who had gone to the front as a soldier and been wounded in Flanders a few weeks before, jumped up to express the new line of his Socialist comrades—and also the disillusionment of the beaten soldiers.

The old political parties must be liquidated! The times demand a profound change. All the soldiers at the front understand that. And you must. Parliament has but one duty: to put itself in the hands of Marshal Pétain.

Encouraged by these words from a Socialist and wounded war hero, Laval resumed his offensive, first disposing of Héraud.

You made a beautiful speech. But do you think we still have time to listen to speeches? You're wrong. We're finished with speeches. . . . We have to rebuild France.

How? Laval was again brutally frank.

We are going to destroy the totality of what was. We're going to create something entirely different. Either you accept what we demand and align your-

THE END AT VICHY 923

self with a German or Italian constitution, or Hitler will impose it on you. . . . Chasseigne was right. Henceforth there will be only one party, that of all the French.

After a long diatribe against the British, whom he blamed for wrecking his own policies, which, he said, would have spared France a war, he concluded:

We are paying today for the fetish which chained us to democracy and led us to the worst excesses of capitalism, while all around us Europe was forging, without us, a new world.

Georges Monnet, the staunch Socialist, who had opposed an armistice when he was in Reynaud's cabinet, spoke up, but only to say he joined all the others in wishing to "rally around Pétain." However, one thing bothered him: If the Marshal were to be made dictator, who would succeed him "in case of accident?"

Laval fielded that question easily—and with a typical evasion. "The Marshal himself," he replied, "will name his successor."[14]

Actually, Laval was already working on Pétain to name him. The next day he confided this to Baudouin, who noted in his journal:

Lunch with Pierre Laval. He is very much preoccupied with the succession to the Marshal. He wishes to appear in the eyes of the National Assembly as the man designated by the Marshal to carry out the constitutional reform if anything should happen to Pétain. General Weygand would be designated as second in line.

That afternoon, Baudouin says, he informed the Marshal about Laval's ambitions. "He shows very little enthusiasm," he noted in his diary, "about making Laval his successor. I supported him and said there was only one man for that: General Weygand."[15]

Laval was not the man to confuse his priorities. His first job, he realized, was to get rid of the parliamentary Republic and set up Pétain as dictator. Then, because of his ascendancy over the Marshal, he could talk him into doing the right thing about the succession. All through the next day, July 6, Laval labored quietly and shrewdly to convince the members of Parliament to vote themselves and the regime out. What seems to have encouraged him most was that support for him was growing not only on the Right, which was glad to be rid of the Republic, but on the Left, especially among the Socialists, who he had at first feared would stick by the regime to the bitter end.

He met first with the Senate and then with the Chamber in informal sessions. Léon Bérard, one of the most prominent members of the Senate, a distinguished lawyer and author, and a fervent Republican, capitulated to him without an argument. Bérard succeeded in one breath in praising the Republic and sounding its death knell. He supported Laval in rendering to Pétain "the destinies of the country."

In the Chamber, Charles Spinasse, a former Socialist minister and right-hand man of Blum during the Popular Front, made an even more spectacular about-face. While still a minister he had been seduced, as has been mentioned, by the technocrat ideas of Jean Coutrot, the inspirer of the strange cult of *synarchie*—a sort of first step toward the half-baked idea of the Fascist corporate state. Now Spinasse rose in the Chamber, after Georges Bonnet had spoken in support of Laval's assessment of the foreign policy of Daladier and Reynaud as disastrous, to outdo Laval in his denunciation of the democratic regime and in his desire to see it replaced by a fascist New Order.

Parliament is going to indict itself for all its faults. This crucifixion is necessary to prevent the country from foundering in violence and anarchy. Our duty is to allow the government to make a revolution without bloodshed.

After pleading with his colleagues to let the Marshal carry out the revolution—he seems to have forgotten the old Socialist goal of quite a different kind of revolution*—he rolled into his peroration.

We must break with the past. It was full of illusions. . . . We believed in individual freedom, in the independence of man. It was but an anticipation of the future which was beyond our grasp. We must have a new faith based on new values. . . . France abandoned itself. It must now begin anew.

The Chamber was gripped by his unexpected words. Xavier Vallat, an extreme right-wing deputy, who had planned to attack his old Socialist enemy, got up only to applaud him. "I rejoice," he said, "to see all the parties united to wipe out the differences that have separated us." And he joined Spinasse in calling for the downfall of the Republic and its replacement by a dictatorship. Republican France had never seen such a spectacle. Those who had served it and benefited from it were abjectly joining those who, like Vallat, had always detested it, to bury it. Laval's task was turning out to be easier than he had expected.

That evening the senatorial war veterans were finally received by Pétain. After asserting their "full faith" in him and their willingness to hand over power to him, they expressed their fears of Laval's project because of its totalitarian aspects. The Marshal assured them that he had no wish

---

* Charles-Roux, whose job at the Foreign Ministry did not permit him to interfere in domestic matters, nonetheless mused on all the talk in Vichy that week by Socialists and Conservatives in support of the Pétain government carrying out a "national revolution." He summed up his thoughts:

Governments which are not of revolutionary origin—and that of Pétain was not—are inept at making revolutions. When they try, they are not taken seriously, being a little like firemen who set fire to something or to professors who kick up a shindy.[16]

to be a dictator. If he were given power, he would act in the open. He had no wish "to transform the nation without the approval of Parliament." He merely wished to govern until peace was made without the interference of the Presidency and the political parties. Then he would retire—"to Antibes."

The handsome silver-haired and silver-tongued Paul-Boncour, who called himself an "independent Socialist" and prided himself on his Republicanism, answered the old man in a most effusive manner, saying how relieved they were by the Marshal's assurances. Then he went as far as Laval in proposing that Pétain, in effect, become an absolute dictator!

"We shall not hesitate," said the Senator, "to suspend the Constitution in order to give you—you, alone—a dictatorship, as was done under Roman law."

"I am not a Caesar, nor do I wish to be," the old man smiled.

"Marshal," Paul-Boncour went on, "to show you how far we are willing to go, we are willing to give you—I say, you—all the powers—I say, all—you deem necessary to maintain order, reestablish, liberate, and reconstitute this country and conclude the peace."

"Now, that's a proposition," Pétain said. He seemed to be enjoying the interview, and perhaps he mused that in politics he was no more stupid than the politicians. The senators departed completely satisfied. By his demeanor and his words, the Marshal was no less so.

Next day, having revised their Order, the senators brought it back to Pétain. It provided for the suspension of the Constitution until peace was concluded, with the Marshal given "all powers to govern by decree and to prepare a new constitution in consultation with the Legislative Committees." This would be "ratified by the Nation when the circumstances permitted a free consultation."

"It's good. I accept it," the Marshal said. "But you must now clear it with Laval. He's the government's lawyer."

A few minutes later the jubilant senators were with Laval.

"I do not accept your text," Laval told them simply, and when the senators tried to remonstrate he cut them short. "If your counter-project is voted I shall resign and you will then have a dictatorship of General Weygand." It was a line he had been having a good deal of success with in his talks to the Parliamentarians, but Senator Taurines did not like it.

"Mr. President," he retorted, "yesterday you raised the spectre of the Germans. Today it is General Weygand. Whom will you find tomorrow?"[17]

The senators were not so happy after this interview. But Laval was really not worried by them. For the moment he was more concerned with a new and unexpected threat. Pierre-Etienne Flandin, former Premier and Foreign Minister, who like him had been let out to pasture since 1936 and who did not much more like it, had suddenly arrived in Vichy and immediately moved against him. Flandin had certain advantages over Laval. He engendered more trust among the members of Parliament and his devotion to the Republic was not in doubt. If someone was needed at this juncture to appease the Germans and Italians, he filled the bill perhaps better than Laval. He had personally congratulated Hitler (as well as Chamberlain) on Munich. He was on good terms with the Italians. He had long advocated better relations with Nazi Germany.

Hurrying on his arrival at Vichy to a meeting of the deputies at 4 P.M. on July 7 he found them at once receptive to what he had to say. He told them he had been overwhelmed by the plight of his compatriots in the occupied zone. What was the French government doing for them?

Nothing! It convokes us here not to help them—but to modify the Constitution! . . . Change the Constitution? But why? What need is there to change our institutions? The reproach is that we did not respect them.

There was loud applause. It seemed to many that at last a leader had appeared who would get the better of Laval and his intrigues to overthrow the Republic, while at the same time rallying the country around the Marshal.

In sum, [Flandin continued] what does the government wish, what do we all wish? That Marshal Pétain be placed at our head to negotiate with the Germans and to cover with his name and prestige the reorganization of the country. To achieve that, what need is there to change the Constitution? We are all here, the senators and deputies, the President of the Republic. And the National Assembly is convoked.

There is nothing more simple in these conditions than to ask the President of the Republic to resign and then to name the Marshal to replace him. Thus, we shall obtain the result we seek while completely respecting the Constitution.

By their applause the deputies seemed to approve Flandin's words unanimously. This was the way out most of them had been searching. It preserved the Republic, its Parliament, its other institutions. Yet it provided for the Marshal to take over provisionally to guide the conquered country until better days came.

Laval realized that Flandin's proposals would wreck his own plans for destroying the Republic and setting up a dictatorship. But he was too shrewd a tactician to oppose Flandin head on, as he had the senatorial war veterans. He first advised his opponent to see Pétain, who, he warned, would reject his idea. But the Marshal accepted it, as he had the war veterans' proposal. Jubilantly Flandin returned to Laval to say that he now had Pétain's backing. Laval was not impressed.

"The Marshal," he told Flandin, "gave you his accord? But he gives his accord to everyone and then forgets it. Don't count on it. But we need Lebrun's accord. If you can get me his resignation I will support your project."

The wily Laval was setting a trap for his unsuspecting rival. Lebrun might be a weak sister but he had a stubborn pride in his office and in his devotion to the Constitution. Flandin, accompanied by two deputies, saw the President of the Republic at 6:30 P.M. and tried to explain to him that it was his duty to resign. The gentle President was outraged. His first impulse, he later told the Pétain court, was to throw his callers out, but somehow, he added, he managed to keep calm. He told Flandin his request "was strange" and when Flandin persisted, he replied: "My answer very simply is No. . . . I shall not desert my post."*[18]

Flandin was not only rebuffed. He realized that in the face of Lebrun's stubbornness†—after all, most of the members of Parliament seemed ready to vote themselves out of existence—his bold plan to seize the initiative from Laval was falling apart. He was not the man to pursue his course with iron resolve, as the events of the next three days would show. Laval was quick to perceive this—much to his relief. The next day he sent word to Flandin, through Marquet, that he would be happy to reserve a place for him in the new government.

July 8 was a decisive day for Laval. He resumed the offensive, resorting to deceit, threats, persuasion—to anything that would further his purposes. He began at the morning cabinet meeting with a typical piece of trickery. When a Socialist minister, Albert Rivière, asked that the Taurines project of the senatorial war veterans be considered, Laval answered him suavely:

I've just been talking with the group of ex-soldiers from the Senate. I gave them entire satisfaction. They have withdrawn their counter-project. Thus the proposition of Rivière need no longer be considered.

The war veterans had not withdrawn their project, but Rivière did not know this. A few minutes later he joined his colleagues in unanimous approval of Laval's motion to liquidate the Republic and turn over the country to the Marshal's rule. President Lebrun signed it without a word, making it an official government proposal. Vincent Auriol met Rivière later. "Laval lied to you," he said. "You were swindled." But it was too late. Laval had now eliminated the war veterans, Lebrun, and Flandin from his path. Confidently he strode over to the Casino to confront the deputies of the Chamber. One of them, Vincent Badie, had obtained several signatures for a resolution which—such was the confusion in Vichy—went as far as Laval in turning over power to the Marshal but added that the Republican

---

* One is puzzled by the importance Flandin and the deputies gave to replacing Lebrun as President by Pétain. Since the resignation of Marshal MacMahon the President of the Republic had become a figurehead and the real power had been held by the Premier, who on several occasions had been authorized by Parliament to govern by decree laws. This power could easily have been obtained by Pétain, as Premier, from the two Chambers in Vichy, if that was all he—and Laval—wanted, without disturbing the structure or the institutions of the Republic.

† "Either Lebrun understands nothing, or he does not wish to understand," Deputy Jean Mistler, who had accompanied Flandin to the meeting, complained.

regime, "to whose democratic liberties they remain attached," must be preserved.

Laval ignored it, as he rose once more to address the deputies. For the first time he read the text of the government resolution which the National Assembly would be asked to approve, and then gave a long exposition of its "motives." Though this was somewhat vague as to details, and was meant to be, it left no doubt that the Republic was to be abolished and a totalitarian regime set up. "Firmness will be the law," Laval said. "But it will conciliate authority with respect for necessary freedoms." Some of the deputies wanted more specific information before transforming the democratic state into a dictatorship. Laval made short shrift of their questions.

Parliamentary democracy lost the war. It must give way to a new regime: audacious, authoritarian, social and national.

If the members objected that this was a dictatorship, at least, said Laval, it preserved "civilian power." Let the deputies beware, he again warned, of something worse, a military dictatorship. If the members of Parliament did not do their duty, that was what they would get.

Laval, it must be said, was frank enough about what foreign policy the new French regime would follow. France would no longer remain, he said, "in the tow" of England. "Nothing was more humiliating than to see our political figures go to London to ask permission to be a French minister." Those days, he said, were over.

We have only one road to follow, and that is a loyal collaboration with Germany and Italy. We must practice it with honor and dignity. And I am not embarrassed to say so. I urged it during the days of peace.

That was clear enough, and several deputies rose to object. But they were shouted down by the delirious applause and yells of Laval's growing number of supporters. It was a tactic which would become increasingly effective in the next couple of days. One of its instigators was Gaston Bergery, once of the Left, the only man to rise in the Chamber on September 2, 1939, to oppose voting the war credits. He had been howled down then, and he remembered the experience. Now he was employing the same tactics on those who dared to speak up against Laval. During the day he had circulated a resolution, which he had written in the most purple prose, savagely denouncing the Republic and frankly calling for a government based on that of Nazi Germany, whose Hitlerian New Order it demanded that France now try to join. It was signed by 17 deputies and "adhered to" by 51 others, including several Socialists.

After giving the senators the same treatment as he had the deputies, Laval called it a day. Jean Montigny, a Radical-Socialist deputy and sycophant of Laval, thought the decisive battle had been won. "During the course of this day," Montigny wrote, "Laval, in despite of the fears of some and against the hopes of others, has triumphed and triumphed alone."[19] It seemed true.

That evening at 9 P.M. the last cabinet meeting over which Lebrun would preside was held. Laval, says Baudouin, did all the talking. Triumphant, he explained the agenda for the next two days. The Chamber of Deputies and the Senate would meet separately on the morrow, July 9, to vote on the "constitutional reforms." On June 10 the National Assembly (comprising both houses sitting as one) would meet: in the morning in secret session to debate the issue, in the afternoon publicly and without discussion to cast its vote. No minister spoke up to argue or question or comment. As for the unhappy President of the Republic, who now knew he was on the way out, Baudouin recorded in his journal: "The President of the Republic says not a word. His silence, his passivity, stupefies me."[20] The brash young Foreign Minister does not seem to have been stupefied by his own—or the other ministers'—silence and passivity. If not stupefied, Lebrun was at least depressed. But, like everyone else, resigned.

Laval explains the resolution for revision to be submitted tomorrow to the two Chambers [Lebrun records]. Everyone feels that a debate would be useless. All know from the events of the past few days that the game is over. We are submerged in a heavy and mephitic atmosphere which annihilates you.[21]

In this atmosphere of threats and fears and defeatism and baseness and dupery and confusion, all but a handful of the politicians, who only ten months before had enthusiastically and unanimously voted the credits for war, who all their political life had thought, almost all of them, that the Third Republic was the best possible form of government for France and its democracy and freedoms a cherished blessing, were now intent, with whoops of enthusiasm, to destroy it and substitute a copy of the barbarian totalitarianism of the Nazi German conqueror, cutting suddenly loose, as Ambassador Bullitt had reported in his dispatch of July 1, after talking with the leaders, from all that France had been and meant and stood for for so long.

How was it possible? Léon Blum later tried to account for it, but he succeeded only in describing it.

The men whom I had seen the day before and with whom I had talked and shaken hands, were no longer the same men. . . . They seemed plunged in some horrible mixture, in a corrupting bath of such power that those who touched it for a moment emerged poisoned. . . . Within a few hours their thoughts, their words, their faces even, became practically unrecognizable. . . . The poison that one now beheld was fear, quite simply the panic of fear.

Fear, he says, that if they didn't follow Laval, the Germans or General Weygand, as Laval warned, would take over.

The nature of fear permits no reasoning. If the pitiful victims of Laval had been capable of a reflection, of a critical examination, this whole structure of artifices would immediately have crumbled into dust. . . . To escape from the whirlwind there was only needed a moment of *sang-froid,* an effort for reflection. But no one reflected. One let himself be carried away, like a crowd in panic, by the collective currents of dread and cowardice.

The ease with which men can be corrupted counted too.

Laval did not so much convince them as infect them. . . . He offered them jobs, as formerly he promised portfolios. Every revolution produces a scramble for spoils. . . . Laval offered embassies, prefectures. . . .

What hurt Blum most was the baseness with which the French politicians endeavored to ape Hitler and his totalitarian regime, thinking they could thereby curry his favor.

To be vanquished does not mean that you have to become a vassal. To imagine that by being obliging to Hitler one could appease his scorn or moderate his hate was a senseless chimera. . . . Why suppose that if there existed a means of softening or seducing Hitler, it could only be by baseness?

Still, the old Socialist leader kept silent there in Vichy. Not out of fear, he says, but because he was deserted by most of his Socialist "comrades." It "paralyzed" him, he says. Blum silent, and Herriot and Jeanneney silent too, and even Paul Reynaud, who arrived in Vichy on July 8—not to oppose Laval but only to defend his two aides who had been arrested in Spain.

"The spectacle which I now describe," writes Blum, as he reaches the eve of July 9 and 10, "is terrible What a scene!"[22]

We now come to it ourselves, the last and the most lamentable in the seventy years of the Third Republic.

THE END AT VICHY. JULY 9–10, 1940

The rites began at 9:30 on the morning of July 9 when the Chamber of Deputies met to vote on a simple resolution declaring that there was need of revising the constitutional laws. This had to be affirmed separately by each House before the National Assembly could take up the matter of actually changing the Constitution. Since the Grand Casino was the only hall in town large enough to accommodate a meeting of Parliament, it was reserved for the deputies in the morning and for the senators in the afternoon.

Those who were in Vichy that morning remembered the splendor of the weather, the sun out brightly, the sky cloudless, the air balmy, much like the fine days of May and early June when the Battle of France was unfolding. The women, wives and others, were out in all their summer finery, strolling along the broad avenue under the shade of trees toward the

Casino and a seat in the galleries. Baudouin watched them disapprovingly. The ladies looked "too elegant, too happy," he thought, and displayed too much jewelry for such a somber occasion.[23]

All the prominent deputies except the *Massilia* passengers detained in North Africa were present, and among them was Paul Reynaud, his head swathed in bandages. On June 28, while driving from Bordeaux with the Countess de Portes to a country house at Ste.-Maxime, he had been badly injured in an automobile accident. The Countess had been killed, fatally struck in the neck when the brakes were applied too suddenly and the luggage in the back seat was hurled upon her. Against his doctor's orders, Reynaud had made his way to Vichy—not to try to save the Republic against the machinations of Laval, as many hoped and some expected, but merely, as he informed the Marshal in a cordial letter on July 8, to defend two of his former aides, Leca and Devaux, who had been arrested in Madrid with a large amount of money from secret government funds and the gold and jewelry of Madame de Portes in their luggage.

When asked by some of his supporters in the Chamber if he was going to intervene in the debate, Reynaud replied: "No. I've come here solely to defend the honor of my collaborators." Like Herriot, Jeanneney, Lebrun, and others who had opposed the Armistice, he had narrowed his sights. Like them, he seemed resigned to seeing the Republic destroyed without raising his voice in protest. He says he left Vichy without waiting for the decisive meeting of the National Assembly the next day.* He had not uttered one word publicly. His silence was impressive.†

---

* In fact, he remained there during the morning when the secret and most important session of the Assembly was held, but he did not attend. He departed after lunch, just before the final meeting began.

† Reynaud is extremely reticent in his memoirs in discussing his brief appearance in Vichy, and what little he says is not very convincing. "Not having been present at the preliminary meetings," he writes, "I had no more reason to prolong my stay in Vichy, to which my doctor had strongly objected. I therefore left without attending the meeting of the National Assembly, where I had nothing to do." "I cannot go on," he told Vincent Auriol. "Excuse me, but I have to go." He left without any hard feelings for Pétain. Those came later, after the old soldier imprisoned him. At the trial of the Marshal in 1945, Isorni, the chief lawyer for the defense, read into the record a letter Reynaud had written Pétain on July 8, the day he arrived in Vichy. It concluded: "I have retained from our work in common such warm memories that it would be odious to me if they were tarnished by any suspicion."

Robert Murphy, who was in charge of the American Embassy at Vichy, tells in his memoirs of a "very human incident" in connection with Reynaud that might sound like the tale of a sensationalist were it not for the fact that Murphy was one of the most sober-minded of our diplomats—he later became a diplomatic adviser of every President from Roosevelt to Nixon. Lunching with Guy La Chambre and his wife on July 10, Murphy noticed M. and Mme. Paul Reynaud at a nearby table, the former Premier "swathed in bandages." Everyone, says Murphy, was somber and dispirited—

> except Mme. Reynaud, who came over to our table and recounted to Mme. La Chambre the pungent details of the highway accident which took the life of her husband's mistress. As she rose to rejoin M. Reynaud, she exclaimed with some emotion: "And now, *chérie*, for my revenge!"[24]

Even then, the very presence in the Chamber of the former Premier on the morning of the 9th was protested by the reactionaries. One of them, Pierre Tixier-Vignancour, a young Turk of the extreme Right, shouted that Reynaud's appearance was a "provocation" and demanded that he be forbidden to take his seat. Herriot, the Speaker, ignored the rumpus and opened the proceedings with the traditional address from the Chair. Many members, conscious of Herriot's opposition to the Armistice, his efforts to move the government from Bordeaux to North Africa so that the war could be continued from there, and above all his fanatical devotion to the Republic and especially to its parliamentary institutions, in which he had served with distinction for a quarter of a century, thought he would take this opportunity to express a determined opposition to destroying the Third Republic and making the Marshal dictator.

On the contrary. He paid eloquent homage to Pétain and appealed pathetically to the Chamber to approve unanimously the motion before it.

Around the Marshal, in the veneration which his name inspires in us all, our nation has rallied in its distress. Let us be careful not to trouble the accord which has been established under his authority.[25]

So the eminent Speaker of the Chamber and lifelong Republican was publicly capitulating to those who were determined to destroy his beloved Republic. During the afternoon, Jeanneney, the President of the Senate and just as staunch a Republican, would follow his example. The fever to surrender was contagious.

Since no one rose to debate the motion, Herriot announced that, according to the rules, it would be considered by the Committee on Universal Suffrage. Immediately there were cries from the Right: "No! No! Vote right away!" Even Jean Mistler, a Radical-Socialist and the chairman of the committee, joined in. "Enough of your rulings!" he shouted. "The time for that is past! Let us vote!" The galleries, packed with supporters of Laval, applauded loudly. Herriot may have capitulated to Laval, but he insisted on doing so according to parliamentary procedure. The motion went to the committee. It came back an hour later with the unanimous approval of all twenty-three members.

"In the stupor which has followed our disaster," Mistler told the Chamber, "the conscience of the country has felt the necessity of profoundly reforming our political institutions." To add to the confusion—or to the hypocrisy—the committee affirmed that the "reconstruction" of the country must be carried out in "republican legality and order." Every member knew that republican "legality and order" was about to be abolished by their own doing.

Tixier-Vignancour, a brilliant young orator who later would become an eminent lawyer and defender of right-wing leaders and causes, tried to stir up one more rumpus before the Chamber adjourned for the last time in its history. He attempted to introduce a resolution calling for the trial and punishment of those "responsible for the disaster." Herriot ruled him out of order. The young Turk tried to persist. "I contest a ruling," he shouted, "that prevents us from discussing the punishment of the guilty, while you make a ruling that permits Paul Reynaud to come and show himself in this Assembly." Reynaud did not defend himself. Herriot, amidst the tumult, pounded his gavel and called for a vote on the government motion. It carried, 395 to 3. Two Socialists and one Radical voted against.

The vote in the Senate that afternoon was even more overwhelming but, as was usual, its meeting was more decorous than that of the Chamber. The President, Jeanneney, outdid Herriot in his homage to the Marshal.

> I attest to Marshal Pétain our veneration and the gratitude which is due to him for making a gift of his person to the country. . . . We know the nobility of his soul. . . . Let us get to work! . . . To forge a new soul for our country . . . and finally reestablish the authority of moral values, in short, authority.

Those were the words Laval had been employing all week and it was evident to the senators that their President was now backing him. This seems to have smothered any voice of revolt. Jeanneney sent the motion to the committee and back it came in a few minutes also unanimously approved. The committee chairman, Senator Boivin-Champeaux, a member of an old Norman family, gave some dignity to his report, in contrast to the groveling Mistler in the Chamber. He reported the committee's finding that the government motion to reform the constitution was "legal and regular." But personally he was sorry to see the Republic go. He spoke a few words that not many others dared to utter.

> It is not without sadness that we shall bid adieu to the Constitution of 1875. It made France a free country. . . . It died less from its imperfections than from the fault of men who were charged with guarding it and making it work.

It was not a bad epitaph.

When the senator had finished speaking the vote was taken and counted—229 to 1. The lone dissenting vote was cast not by a Socialist or a Radical but by the *Marquis* de Chambrun. Ironically, he was the brother of the father-in-law of Josée Laval, the daughter of the man who was now at the point of his greatest achievement, the wiping out of the hated Republic.

To the Chamber and to the Senate Laval had sketched the final ceremonies for the morrow, July 10. In the morning the National Assembly would meet in secret session to discuss the government motion to give Pétain complete powers to govern and to promulgate the new constitution of "the French State"—even the word "Republic" was to be dropped. Debate,

Laval assured the members of Parliament, would be permitted at the secret session. In the privacy of such a meeting every member would be allowed to say what he wished. In the afternoon the National Assembly would reconvene in public session for a formal vote. Laval hoped that in the glare of the public the members would refrain from debate and simply vote. So the elected representatives of the people were still free, if they wished, to save the Third Republic, to which they had pledged their allegiance, and to vote down Laval's attempt to set up a dictatorship.

THE LAST DAY OF THE THIRD REPUBLIC. JULY 10, 1940

To impress the confused and cowed members of Parliament that the Pétain government meant business, Laval had thrown around the Casino an impressive cordon of gendarmes and *gardes mobiles,* the latter with fixed bayonets, through which the deputies and senators filed for the morning secret session of the National Assembly. Reinforcing them were a number of leaders of the anti-Republican, terrorist Cagoule, many of whom had been released from prison a few months before to serve in the army and who wore their soldiers' uniforms. At their head was Eugène Deloncle, the chief of the band, who had gone from jail to the front and thence to Vichy to lend his hand to the overthrow of the Republic.* None of course were permitted inside to the secret session but in the afternoon the Cagoulards, joined by Doriot's Fascist thugs, would help fill the galleries, from which they planned to shout down any opposition to the proposed dictatorship. "The grenadiers of Murat on 18 Brumaire," Blum mused, "never carried out a more decisive policing."

Jeanneney, who as President of the Senate was supposed to preside over the National Assembly, declined to take the chair on the grounds that a secret session was "irregular." His place was taken by a senator named Valadier. When Laval entered the hall he impressed everyone with his self-confidence. Actually he foresaw only minor trouble: from Flandin, whom he was already trying to soften by offering him a cabinet post; from the senatorial war veterans; and from a group of twenty-seven deputies who had signed a motion drawn up by Vincent Badie, himself just released from the Third Army to attend the session. Laval was prepared to make a small concession to the former and to ignore or trick the latter.† Both groups were agreed with him in turning over power to the Marshal. They differed with him only in that they wished to preserve the Republic. Laval was sure he could handle that. And he promptly did.

After Senator Taurines, on behalf of the war veterans, had introduced his counterresolution, explaining that Pétain had approved it but that Laval

---

* "Finally, the Republic is overthrown," Deloncle wrote his wife that night, "and I played my small part in it."[26]

† That morning Marquet, on behalf of Laval, had offered Badie a high government post if he would withdraw his project. "You're a promising young man," Marquet said. "Think it over." Badie says he replied that he "could not be bought."[27]

had then rejected it, the latter reacted instantly. He seems to have sensed that the Taurines motion impressed the Assembly more than his own, because while acceding to the general desire to hand over power to the Marshal, it maintained the Republic. In his most oily manner he thanked the war veterans for their intervention and agreed to give them "satisfaction"— by a minor concession. He would change the last sentence of the government motion which had provided for the new constitution to "be ratified by the assemblies it created" to read: "ratified by the nation and applied by the assemblies which it will create."

"What is the nation?" several members shouted. "Don't we represent the nation?"

The meeting was getting out of hand. Laval acted swiftly to bring it around. He sprang what many present later branded as a "veritable coup." He was only asking the Assembly, he said, to do what the Marshal demanded. Whereupon he drew out a letter which Pétain had written him July 7, and read it.

> The constitutional project of the government over which I preside will come before the Assemblies July 9 and 10. As it is difficult for me to participate in the meetings I ask you to represent me. The voting of the government project submitted to the National Assembly appears to me to be necessary for the salvation of the country.

That did it. The members were stunned into silence. The Marshal, whom almost all of them supported, indeed worshiped, wanted the government motion adopted to save the country and he had named Laval to put it through for him. Who dared oppose it now? Sensing his easy triumph Laval said softly: "Thus there can be no doubt that it is the thought of the Marshal about the project that I express here." Laval had won. But to administer the *coup de grâce* to the Republic, he now launched into a long discourse which those who heard it, even those who despised him, agreed was the greatest of his career. It took up more than half the time of the morning secret session, leaving few moments for anyone else to speak up. He remained seated, so that the debate, he said, smiling benignly, "could be of a family nature." Soon though, his voice was swelling out over the chamber, as in point after point, in this hour of triumph, he dragged up all his bitter resentments against a regime which for so long had kept him out of power. In the abjectness which defeat and disaster had brought, the overwhelming majority began wildly applauding him. The Third Republic, in all its tumultuous years, had never seen quite such an exhibition.

Why was the Marshal asking for this act? he began.

> The greatest crime . . . was to have declared war [*Prolonged applause*]* without having prepared [*New applause*] either diplomatically [*Interruptions*]—

---

* The official stenographic account, which came to light after the war, is punctuated with notations of applause and other reactions.

Listen to me, I speak without passion—or militarily, but you well know we did not know why we were fighting.

[*From various seats*] For England!

The man could scarcely go on because of the applause and the shouted comments and he appealed for order and calm. Nonetheless he seemed to savor the shouting. He recounted all the faults of "democratic France's" foreign policy: over Austria, Czechoslovakia, Danzig. "Then came Poland and we were in the war."

I do not believe we have ever suffered a greater disaster in our history. . . . Ah! It was a war of democracy against the dictators. We had to defeat Nazism. We had to down Fascism. . . . So we launched this defy with criminal imprudence. We hurled our defy and we were beaten. . . . Now we have to draw the consequences.

He spoke next of England and all his bile against that country oozed out.

Be assured. We do not intend to declare war on England. But we are going to return blow for blow. [*Applause. Interruptions*] I'm going to give you the facts. England dragged us into this war; then, having dragged us in, she did nothing to help us win it. [*Applause. Interruptions from some seats.*] . . . We were considered as her mercenaries.

That led the orator naturally to Mers-el-Kébir.

It was not a battle which His Majesty's Navy gave us. It was a murder. [*Heavy applause.*]

MONTIGNY: It was a disgrace!

LAVAL: I refrain from comment.

Then he turned to domestic affairs.

Some say our project is a condemnation of the parliamentary regime. Never! Why? Because it is a condemnation not only of the parliamentary regime but of all that was and can no longer be.

Laval ranted on and on. Returning to France's foreign policy, he went into great detail to show how he had for years tried to line up the country with the dictators: Hitler, Mussolini, Franco. But the Republican governments would have no dealings with the Fascists.

Look back! With us you could deal with a robber, a crook, a pimp. But it was unpardonable to deal with a Fascist. Anti-Fascism was the base of all our activity—at home and abroad.

And he launched into a paean of praise for the Fascist dictatorships for reestablishing order and "restoring love of country." It was evident what sort of dictatorship he had in mind for France.

France abused its freedom. . . . That is why we have arrived at where we are. A great disaster such as we suffered cannot allow the institutions which were responsible for it to survive.

This did not go down too well and Laval hastened to assure the Assembly. While he refused, he said, to accept any amendments to the government proposal because the Marshal would not stand for it, he promised that the two Chambers would "subsist until the new assemblies are created—so that there will be no hiatus—though their activity will be necessarily reduced." It was a promise quickly broken. When he sat down there was thunderous applause.

A few members placed a little hope in Flandin, who next spoke. But the wind had been taken out of his sails by the refusal of Lebrun to resign and by the realization that Laval was the master of the hour. Flandin was not the man, in any case, to fight heroically against great odds—even at this last opportunity of his life to save the Republic, which had honored him with its highest offices, and of which his forebears had been stout defenders. He spoke long and eloquently of the greatness of Pétain and the need to remake France in the face of German occupation. At one point he seemed to turn against Laval.

One thing disturbed me in your speech, Monsieur Laval, and that was the allusion you made to a sort of necessity of aligning us with other regimes. Nothing would be worse [A voice: Vive la France!] than a servile copy of the institutions of others. . . . You must never try to extinguish freedom of thought, which has been the glory of France.

And then he pulled back and urged everyone to support the government proposal. He too! He, who two days before had tried to torpedo Laval, wreck his plans and who seemed to have won over perhaps a majority of deputies by his plea to place confidence in the Marshal but not to destroy the Republic!* Laval could not disguise his triumphant joy. Flandin had capitulated to him in the end. And Herriot. Paul Reynaud had not even shown up. And Jeanneney, the revered President of the Senate, had done him a favor by persuading Deputy Badie not to bring up *his* counter-project. The President had promised Badie he could bring it up in the afternoon and

---

* Next day Flandin called on Baudouin, who noted their conversation in his journal: "He [Flandin] told me he was entirely at the disposition of the Marshal. He said that did not mean that he expected a post in the cabinet but that he would be happy to serve the government. What he would like was an important post in North Africa, perhaps as delegate-general of the government to the three colonies there."[28] He did not get that post, but he got another. Five months later Pétain named him Foreign Minister in place of Laval.

that he would recognize him for that purpose from the chair—another promise that day that was not kept.

Now before the Assembly recessed Laval turned to thank Flandin for his support and to praise him for his words. "I listened," he said, "with profound emotion to the peroration of my friend Flandin. I accept without a change the conclusion of his speech."

There were cries of "cloture!"—"Close the debate!" but now that he had won the battle Laval wished to say one little thing more. Almost coyly, he proceeded.

Do you know what is at the bottom of all I have told you? Do you know why, especially, we have presented our project? Consider it well before coming to the public session. It is to gain a peace that will hurt France the least.[29]

His meaning could not have been lost on the parliamentary members. Laval would emulate the dictatorships of his German and Italian conquerors in order to get better peace terms from them. If any deputy or senator thought that was a base and servile thing to do, he did not speak up. Flandin alone had objected out loud.*

The National Assembly was adjourned until 2 P.M. for the public session. It would be but a formality so the public could see how the representatives of the people had rallied round their great war hero and at his behest were sacrificing themselves and the Republic. Laval could not be blamed for the look of satisfaction on his face as he left the Assembly at noon for lunch. He had achieved his goal, and though he had had to employ all his guile, victory had come more easily than he anticipated. No one else had ever felled a French republic, or any other French regime, with such finesse and ease, and amid so little tumult. No physical violence had been necessary, and no bloodshed.

Everyone took a leisurely lunch, most of them at the fashionable Restaurant Chantecler, where a French journalist noted that, besides the politicians and ambassadors, "there were a great many ladies, beautifully gotten up and shining." It seemed to be somewhat of a gala occasion for them. (It was here that Murphy had witnessed the "very human incident" with M. and Mme. Reynaud.)

---

* The Nazi German government, in fact, greeted the crawling of Laval and his supporters with contempt. I had returned to Berlin by that time. On July 9, when the dispatches from Vichy made clear what was happening, I noted this contempt in my diary. That day the Wilhelmstrasse had given us some hints as to what the German attitude would be toward the Vichy dictatorship. My diary quotes them.

The change of the former regime in France to an authoritarian form of government will not influence in any way the political liquidation of the war. The fact is that Germany does not consider the Franco-German accounts as settled yet. Later they will be settled with historical realism . . . not only on the basis of the two decades since Versailles, but they will also take into account much earlier times.[30]

When the National Assembly reconvened in public session shortly after 2 P.M., Jeanneney, the venerable President of the Senate, was finally in the chair. He read the government resolution, the last sentence of which Laval had revised in deference to the war veterans' group in the Senate.

> The National Assembly gives all powers to the Government of the Republic under the authority and the signature of Marshal Pétain to promulgate by one or several acts a new constitution of the French State. This constitution will guarantee the rights of Work, Family and Country.
> It will be ratified by the nation and applied by the assemblies which it will create.

Literally, the wording of the resolution gave the Marshal power merely to draw up a new constitution—and nothing more. But Laval shortly would slyly contrive to increase that power. First, though, he launched two parliamentary maneuvers to make his task easier. Before he could put them over, however, there was a slight breath of opposition. Herriot demanded the right to read to the Assembly a telegram of protest from the unhappy members who had set out for North Africa on the *Massilia* and were still detained there by the Pétain government. Herriot warmly defended them against the accusation of certain government members that they had "fled" and put themselves outside the law. His words were greeted with ironic laughter from the floor. And though Laval announced that he accepted the explanation, he could not refrain from remarking that the French people "would understand" why the Marshal, he himself, and others had refused to leave the sacred soil of France. As it turned out, Herriot's intervention, limited as it was to a peripheral affair, was the only one permitted. Laval and his henchmen were now in firm control of the Assembly. They quickly put over two parliamentary maneuvers. The first, carried out by Senator Emile Mireaux, was a motion to provide that a majority of those attending, and not a majority of the membership of the two Assemblies, should decide the vote. The membership was 850; present and voting were 666. Laval was sure he had a majority of the latter—334 votes. He was not so certain about a majority of the former—426 votes. Only 241 votes would defeat him in that case. Jeanneney tried to rule that the senator's motion was unconstitutional but it was quickly put to a vote and approved. Senator Mireaux, a director of *Le Temps,* which had been the semiofficial organ of the Third Republic, no doubt wanted his newspaper to retain that status under the new regime At any rate, Laval rewarded him personally for his intervention by having him appointed to the cabinet three days later. The second maneuver was more important. This was put across by Fernand Bouisson, once a Socialist, once Speaker of the Chamber, who showed during the afternoon that he could stifle the opposition not only by his skill at parliamentary procedure but by the exercise of physical violence. He proposed that the government motion be voted on first. That meant that if it were passed, the two opposition motions—that of the war-veteran group of the Senate and that of Deputy Badie—would not even be considered. The proposal was highly irregular, but the Assembly approved it.

There remained now only the formality of having the government resolution sent to committee for approval, after which, if Laval had his way, it would be voted by the Assembly without debate. It was in committee that Laval pulled another coup. He slipped in, without the members apparently being aware of it, a demand that the Marshal be accorded not only the power to make a new constitution but all executive and *legislative* powers to govern the country as well. He did not want it in the government resolution, he said, but in the report of the committee, which, if accepted by the Assembly, presumably would have the force of law. There was no objection, and it was adopted. This provision gave Pétain the power of an absolute monarch. Not even Hitler's dictatorial authority was more complete.

After the war the Parliamentary Investigating Committee raked Senator Bouvin-Champeaux, the Joint Committee's *rapporteur,* over the coals for letting this be put over on him. Louis Marin read to the senator his committee report giving the Marshal complete executive and legislative powers "without restriction and in the most extended fashion."

MARIN: Now neither the project presented by Pétain nor the project voted by the Assembly gave Pétain such full powers. They gave him power only to make a constitution. That's completely different. . . .

BOUVIN-CHAMPEAUX: Not one voice was raised against it. There was not a single objection. The question was not even discussed.

To the senator's argument that Parliament had often accorded *plein pouvoirs* to a premier and that Pétain was Premier at the moment, Marin exclaimed.

When was a government ever given, except at that moment, full legislative powers? Never! And full executive powers? Never were they given to a man! . . . What you gave was very far from what was once given to a Poincaré or a Daladier. . . . The powers given Pétain gave us a totalitarian regime.[31]

Shortly after 5 P.M. on July 10, after a recess for the Joint Committee to deliberate, the National Assembly reconvened to hear its report and cast the vote on whether to turn the country over to Pétain and Laval. The committee report, going much farther than the government resolution in giving Pétain complete power, was approved without debate. The senators and deputies were now completely cowed. From Laval's supporters came cries of "Vote! Vote!" There was an organized confusion. Jeanneney, trying to observe parliamentary rules of procedure, finally got the hall quieted down enough to announce: "Before the vote I must call on those who asked to be heard to explain their vote." This was the only way the opposition could raise its voice since the two countermotions could not be made until after the vote on the government proposal. But the Casino was filled with cries of *Cloture! Vote!*

The President tried to give the floor to a deputy named Margaine, who supported the Badie resolution. He was howled down in the cries of "*Cloture!* Vote! Vote!"

> THE PRESIDENT: I hear a demand for cloture. That means suppression of the explanations of the vote.
> CRIES: *Oui! Oui!*
> THE PRESIDENT: I will consult the Assembly.

That proved impossible in the well-orchestrated tumult. No vote was taken on closing the debate. It was simply closed by the shouting of Laval's men and by the impotence of the Chair. Paul Boulet, a professor of history and a deputy who supported Badie's motion, later described the scene to the Parliamentary Investigating Committee.

> Every time someone wanted to speak, his voice was drowned out by 400 voices against 20 or 30! You have to imagine what it was like in this Assembly where there were 400 members who did not want anyone to speak.

Did President Jeanneney, who had a great reputation for fairness after years of presiding over the Senate, wish anyone to speak? "We did not have the impression," Boulet testified, "that the President helped very much those who did want to speak."[32]

Amidst the yelling for a vote, Deputy Badie rose to speak on behalf of the twenty-seven deputies who had signed his counterproposal. Jeanneney had promised to give him the floor but so far had not done so. Badie got up anyway and tried to push his way to the rostrum. He was met there by a phalanx of Laval's supporters who barred the way, led by former Speaker Fernand Bouisson, a man of some girth and weight.

> I was seized by two or three of my parliamentary colleagues [Badie later testified]. One of them was especially furious, his face turned to scarlet. This was the former Speaker, Fernand Bouisson.
> He grabbed my coat, pummeled me and tried to force me down the stairs from the rostrum. I said to Bouisson: "You can't do that to me! Leave off, or I'll punch you!" He let go and drew back,
> At this moment President Jeanneney called for the vote on the government project. He would not let me speak.
> He did not keep his promise. If he had wished, despite all the yelling, I would at least have been able to read our motion of protest.[33]

So Jeanneney, who had been a close collaborator of Clemenceau during the first war, being the Undersecretary of State in charge of his office, and who had a sterling reputation over a long parliamentary life for integrity and devotion to the Republic, gave in, as had Herriot, Reynaud, Blum, and all the other pillars of the regime. He refused to recognize Badie. He refused to allow debate. He called for the vote that everyone now knew would sound the death knell of his beloved Republic.

It was overwhelming: 569 for, 80 against and 17 declared abstentions. The majority of Socialists, the majority of Radical-Socialists, the two parties that had been the mainstay of the Republic for two generations, joined the majority of conservatives to swell the affirmative vote.

"I didn't know there were so many cowards and traitors in my party," said Le Troquer, a Socialist deputy detained in Algiers with the *Massilia* passengers. Badie told the Parliamentary Investigating Committee:

> Those who had profited most from the Third Republic, who had been most honored by it, who often had been ministers, who should have, by their training, their education, and their sentiments, defended the Republic, cowardly let it be assassinated.[34]

General Weygand had a different feeling. He was quoted as saying: "I didn't get the Boches, but I got the regime."[35]

The 80 senators and deputies who voted No were later honored. They included Blum, Louis Marin, Paul-Boncour, Auriol, Marx Dormoy (later assassinated by the Vichy militia), and the Marquis de Chambrun. Herriot and Georges Monnet abstained. Georges Bonnet and Anatole de Monzie were among the large majority voting out the Republic, in which they had made a certain mark. "After much reflection," wrote Monzie in his diary two days later, "I do not regret having voted for this 'change.'"

When the vote was announced Laval rose and said: "I have only one word to say in the name of Marshal Pétain. I thank you for France."

As the members filed out Senator Astier, a conservative, who had voted No, cried out: "*Vive la République* just the same!" His cry brought no response.

The Third Republic was dead. It had committed suicide.

Proclaimed on September 4, 1870, after the disastrous defeat by Prussia, it had lasted 70 years, longer than any other regime since the glorious Revolution. And then, as suddenly as it had been born, it fell apart after being crushed by the same enemy from across the Rhine.

In 1961 I sat in the apartment of an eminent French historian overlooking the Seine and as we watched the motorcars below speeding down the new highway along the river he remarked: "If we had not surrendered so quickly in 1940, most of the people in those cars would be dead today. Perhaps it was for the best. If we had stopped the Germans, as we did in 1914, and fought on, we would have had another terrible bloodletting.

I doubt if France could have survived a second one." This was probably true, but I wondered if my distinguished friend had forgotten—so soon— that in the end France survived because she was liberated not by her own efforts but by those of other nations? Had that not happened, the good people scooting about in their cars below might still be alive—but living as slaves of the so-called Master German Race. Over the long run, certainly, over the centuries, a nation's decent survival depended upon itself.

I recalled the words of Freycinet, who was Premier in 1890, when France was attempting to come back after the defeat by Prussia twenty years before.

The security of a great people must not repose on the good will of others; it must reside in themselves, in their own means, in the precautions they take in their armaments and alliances.

I remembered too what Marc Bloch, the French historian, had written before he was tortured and murdered by the German Gestapo:

We find ourselves today (1940) in this appalling situation—that the fate of France no longer depends upon the French. . . . There can be no national freedom in the fullest sense unless we ourselves have worked to bring it about.

To do so he, a professor and no longer young, had served in the Army, as he had in the first war, and then fought in the Resistance, dying a hero's death.

In the end France had been saved by the victory of British, Russian, and American arms, as in a sense she had in the first world conflict, though then she had done more fighting than the others. But how many times in history, I wondered, can a nation be rescued from defeat and collapse by other countries? In July 1940, Pétain, Weygand, and Laval did not believe it could happen again. They were certain that Great Britain would be conquered, as France had been, in a few weeks and they did not foresee the intervention of Russia and the United States. They had resigned them- selves to a France whose survival depended, not on itself, not on an ultimate victory of allies, but on the crumbs from Hitler's table. Laval himself not only believed in German victory but desired it and said so publicly.*

---

* Laval's defenders have claimed that he said this in public in order to hide from the Germans his real intentions, but the fact is that he said it off the record. He told the American Ambassador in Vichy, Admiral William D. Leahy, on April 27, 1942, that "he would prefer Germany to win the war."[36] A fortnight after the overthrow of the Republic, on July 29, 1940, Laval told Robert Murphy, the American chargé, that he "hoped ardently that the English would be defeated."[37] He even told this to Hitler on October 22, declaring: "England will be defeated, and as a Frenchman he could only add that he desired the defeat of Britain with all his heart."[38] He once told Pétain at a cabinet meeting that he would "hail the day when Churchill, Eden, Duff Cooper, and Hore-Belisha were lynched."[39]

Was the action of the National Assembly in voting out the Republic and voting in a dictatorship legal? Constitutional? French lawyers, jurists and historians have been debating the question ever since. That the National Assembly had the right to revise the Constitution is not contested. Article 6 of the Constitutional Laws of February 25, 1875, stipulated it, being in this respect similar to the American Constitution, which authorized the Congress and the state legislatures to make changes in it by amendment. But that the National Assembly had the right to abolish the Constitution (and thereby the Republic) by turning over to a dictator whom it created the right to promulgate a new one is disputed by many. They argue that the Assembly alone had the power to change the Constitution and that it could not delegate it. But even if it is held that the Assembly did have the authority to ask Pétain to draw up a new Constitution, many have argued that it granted him that authority only, and that the report of the Joint Committee which, at Laval's request, accorded to the Marshal sole executive and legislative power without restriction, had no force of law and that its exercise by Pétain was therefore illegal and unconstitutional.

As it turned out, Pétain availed himself of the latter but not the former. He never got around to making a new Constitution. He did arrogate to himself the right to govern absolutely, to decree the laws and to carry them out. He became, like Hitler, the law itself, imprisoning men, especially the leaders of the Third Republic, without trial (or with a disgraceful sham trial such as that at Riom, which was suddenly called off before its end, though the accused, Reynaud, Blum, Daladier, Gamelin, and others were kept thereafter behind bars). The illustrious Marshal even revived a form of the old *lettres de cachet* which the Bourbon kings had used and sold and by which innocent men were imprisoned indefinitely without trial on the grudge or at the whim of the ruler or his henchmen or anyone else who purchased the letters. Vichy, to be sure, did not sell them. It merely issued them.

Robert Murphy questioned Laval about the contemplated arbitrary arrests, on July 29.

He said [Murphy cabled Washington] that Mandel . . . , Daladier, Reynaud, Blum . . . and many others would be tried before the tribunals established for this purpose. He said: "I do not want their lives, but the country demands that the responsibility for the errors committed in persuading France to enter the war . . . be fixed and that those responsible be punished."[40]

Much was made by the defenders of Vichy of the fact that the proceedings of the National Assembly on July 9–10 took place legally and constitutionally, and that its decision was therefore valid. But this overlooks the panicky state of the members of Parliament when they arrived, demoralized by the lightning defeat, the occupation, and the chaos of the stricken country. It ignores the enormous pressures brought upon them, the psychological terror, the threats of Laval that if they didn't adopt his form of dictatorship the Germans or General Weygand would impose one of their own. Those who dared to oppose Laval realized that they probably would be imprisoned for it, and many of them were.

A good many senators and deputies are said to have felt that the stunned French people held the regime responsible for the debacle and for their own sorry plight and that their resentment against Parliament was so deep and bitter that they demanded its abolition. Blum himself would write de Gaulle in 1942 that "at the moment of the armistice the parliamentary system was condemned in France almost unanimously." This probably was true, though there was no way really to know the thoughts of the people, absorbed in scrounging around in their destroyed towns for enough to eat and for shelter under which to sleep. I myself talked to a number of them in the battered towns of northern France, where the main battles had been fought, and they struck me as being so taken up in the struggle for mere physical survival that they gave little thought to what the government or the Parliament was up to. For the old Marshal, there was undoubted veneration. He seemed to most a sort of father-figure, who would help the country through this misery. And though there were the usual gibes against the "politicians," this was not new—it had been going on for ages in France, as elsewhere—and I never heard a word from anyone about wanting a servile French dictatorship, or, for that matter, about wanting Laval in power. He was not a popular figure in the country.

At any rate, to the more articulate it seemed no time to abolish the Republic and its democratic ways, while the hated Germans occupied three fifths of the country and dominated the whole, and the war itself was not over and no permanent peace in sight. The elected representatives of the people bore a heavy responsibility for their abdication in a moment of fear and panic—a judgment made by the French themselves after the war when they barred forever from public life all those who had voted the death of the Republic.

The Third Republic was dead. It remained only to bury it. This was done in great haste, as though the little men of Vichy feared the body might somehow show signs of coming back to life. The day after the Assembly vote, Pétain promulgated his first three Constitutional Acts, drafted by Laval and Alibert, as "Chief of the French State."* Reviving the old form used by the absolute monarchs they began: "We, Philippe Pétain, Marshal of France, assume the functions of Chief of the French State, and decree . . ."

---

* "Alibert and Laval drafted them," says Baudouin. "Neither General Weygand, Marquet, Bouthillier, nor I had the least idea of these texts. They surprised us."[41]

He decreed the end of the Republican Constitution, the assumption of all executive and legislative powers, and the authority "to make the laws and assure their execution." Article 3 sent the Senate and Chamber packing until he himself should convoke it, which he never did.

After much backing and filling, the Marshal issued Act 4 on the following day, July 12, about the succession to the throne. Baudouin described his hesitation, in his diary that evening.

Laval asks me to insist with the Marshal that he put out a Constitutional Act this evening designating him as heir presumptive. I tell him it is not up to me to mix in such business. . . . [Later] The Marshal does not want Laval as his successor. He tells me he has hit upon a formula which reserves to the cabinet the right to choose a new Chief of State. . . . [Later that evening] The Marshal tells me he has changed his mind and that he is designating Pierre Laval as his successor. I lower my voice and ask Laval how he got the Marshal to change his mind. He says he put it to the Marshal firmly, and that that sufficed.[42]

Publication of Act 4 that evening made it official.

There remained only the weak but stubborn President of the Republic to be got rid of, now that the Republic was no more. On the morning of July 13 Pétain called on him.

"Mr. President," said the Marshal, "the painful moment has come. You have served the country well, but in the meantime the vote of the National Assembly creates a new situation. I am not your successor because a new regime begins."

"Do not trouble yourself about me," Lebrun responded. "All my life I have been the faithful servitor of the law, even when it did not have my moral support. I shall have no trouble in obeying it once more. The National Assembly has spoken. All the French must submit."[43]

Albert Lebrun stepped down, and, like the Third Republic, of which he was the last and perhaps the most typical President, passed into history.

EPILOGUE

Of the principal figures in the last act of the drama of the Third Republic before the curtain fell, Pétain and Laval were tried for treason after the war, convicted and sentenced to death. The sentence of the Marshal was commuted by the then Provisional President, General de Gaulle, to life imprisonment on the Island of Yeu, where he died on July 23, 1951, at the age of ninety-six. Laval was executed by a firing squad at the Prison of Fresnes on October 15, 1945. He was sixty-two.

General Weygand was arrested at the end of the war but his trial was quashed and he lived an active life of retirement in Paris, writing his memoirs and books of history, peppering the newspapers with tart comments about Reynaud and de Gaulle and in defense of himself, and attending meetings of the Academy. He died in Paris on January 28, 1965, at the age of ninety-eight. Admiral Darlan, who for a time became the head of government at Vichy under Pétain and pursued a vigorous policy of collaboration with the Germans, was assassinated on Christmas Eve, 1942, in Algiers, where in the last about-face of his life, he had aligned himself with the Allies following the Anglo-American landings in French North Africa. Flandin, after serving briefly as Pétain's Foreign Minister, also went to Algiers to try to get on the Allied bandwagon, but was arrested there and imprisoned. Later he was barred from public life. Alibert was condemned to death *in absentia,* having escaped to Spain, where he lived to a ripe age. Baudouin tried to slip over the French border to Spain at the end of the war but was caught, arrested, tried for treason, and in 1947 sentenced to five years at hard labor. He was released a year later. Camille Chautemps sat out most of the war in Washington, where he first acted for the Vichy government in a semiofficial capacity. He broke with Pétain when the tide of war changed. After the war he was tried for collaboration with the enemy, convicted *in absentia,* and sentenced to five

947

years in prison and national degradation for life. The sentence was later quashed.

Of those who opposed the armistice and were later incarcerated by the Pétain government, and then deported to Germany, Mandel, as has been mentioned, was murdered in 1944 by the Vichy militia in collaboration with the Gestapo. Daladier reentered politics briefly after the war and then retired. Paul Reynaud also returned to politics, which he greatly enlivened, poured out books of memoirs explaining and justifying his career, and feuded with General Weygand in the press, exchanging blow for blow. He died on September 21, 1966, at the age of eighty-seven, robust and active to the very last.

As for Charles de Gaulle, he returned in triumph as head of the Free French forces to Paris after its liberation in August, 1944, became head of the provisional government and then of the government set up by the elected Constituent Assembly in November, 1945, suddenly resigning in January, 1946, and retiring to his country home at Colombey-les-Deux Eglises in northeastern France. Two years later he launched a Right-Wing movement called the Rally of the French People, saw it become a major political party with mass support and then quickly decline, and in July, 1955, he again announced he was retiring from public life. Back in his rural retreat he finished his three-volume memoirs, a work of stunning literary quality and the French equivalent to Churchill's memoirs.

Called back to political power in 1958 as the result of the French military revolt in Algeria, he became first Premier of the last government of the Fourth Republic and then President of the Fifth Republic. For ten years in this last post he reigned supreme in France, a subject of much controversy within his country and without it, settling the problem of Algeria by granting it independence, restoring to France a good deal of its old *grandeur* and giving it a decade of unaccustomed stability. On April 28, 1969, at the age of seventy-eight, he once more suddenly resigned after a defeat in a plebiscite over a relatively minor matter of constitutional reform.

For a quarter of a century he had made his mark as one of the great statesmen of French history. It had, after all, largely vindicated him.

NOTES

1. DEBACLE! SUMMER 1940

1. Marc Bloch: *L'Etrange défaite*, p. 21. There is an English-language translation: *Strange Defeat*.
2. Jacques Maritain: *A travers le désastre*, p. 14.
3. William L. Shirer: *Berlin Diary*, p. 330.
4. Major-General Sir Edward Spears: *Assignment to Catastrophe*. Vol. I, pp. 205–206.
5. Henri Amouroux: *La Vie des français sous l'occupation*, p. 69.
6. Jean Vidalenc: *L'Exode de mai-juin 1940*, p. 262, from E. Dubois: *Paris sans lumières*, p. 60.
7. Paul Reynaud: *Au Cœur de la mêlée, 1930–1945*, p. 452.
8. Vincent Sheean: *Between the Thunder and the Sun*, pp. 145–148.
9. Vidalenc, *op. cit.*, p. 263. From information supplied by the S.N.C.F., the French National Railways.
10. Shirer: *The Rise and Fall of the Third Reich*, p. 957.
11. Vidalenc, *op. cit.*, p. 269. From an eyewitness account.
12. *Ibid.*, pp. 273, 286. See appendix, pp. 421–424, for detailed documented study of Italian air attacks on refugees in France.
13. Albert Lebrun: *Témoignage*, p. 79.
14. Cited by Vidalenc, *op. cit.*, p. 273, from the records of the Seventh Army General Staff, Third Bureau.
15. Cited by Vidalenc, *op. cit.*, p. 316, from G. Charpentier: *Au service de la liberté*, p. 88; and J. Albert-Sorel: *Le Chemin de Croix*, pp. 137–138, respectively.
16. Paul Baudouin: *Neuf mois au gouvernement, avril-décembre 1940*, pp. 145–146. This is a published daily journal of a man who was a close aide to Reynaud during the last crucial weeks and then turned on him and became the first Foreign Minister of the Vichy government. While extremely valuable, it must be taken with a grain of salt and is sometimes inaccurate and misleading.
17. Testimony of Senator Louis Rollin, former Minister of Colonies, before the postwar Parliamentary Investigating Committee. *Les Evénements survenus en France de 1933 à 1945: Témoignages et documents recueillis par la Commission d'Enquête Parlementaire*. Vol. VII, p. 2136.

The Commission was set up by the National Assembly in 1946

to study the causes of the Fall of France in 1940. Half of its members, chosen from the Resistance organizations, were not members of the Assembly. Though the Commission was unable to finish its task before its mandate ran out, its report, published in eleven volumes, is an invaluable source of material for the events recounted in this book. It contains not only the testimony of most of the chief figures concerned as well as that of many key witnesses, but a good many important secret documents, especially the minutes of meetings of the cabinet and the Conseil Supérieur de la Guerre. The testimony, taken under oath, was heard for five years, from 1946 to 1951, by the Commission, and most witnesses were subjected to long cross-examination. Many of them during their testimony pulled out of their pockets or their briefcases important confidential documents which otherwise might not have come to light for decades—if ever. This Parliamentary Report will hereafter be cited as *Evénements*. It is available only in French.

For Rollin's testimony, which will be cited more fully in the concluding chapters of this work, see also his journal, quoted by Reynaud, *op. cit.,* p. 571.

18. Spears, *op. cit.,* Vol. II, pp. 190–191.
19. *Ibid.,* p. 243.
20. Baudouin, *op. cit.,* p. 219.

2. A FREAKISH BIRTH AND EARLY GROWING PAINS 1871–1891

1. René Rémond: *La droite en France.* Second edn., 1963, p. 147.
2. Alexandre Zevaës: *Histoire de la troisième république. 1870–1926.* First edn., p. 126.
3. *Ibid.,* pp. 126–127.
4. *Ibid.,* p. 290.
5. *Ibid.,* p. 303.

6. David Thomson: *Democracy in France,* p. 156.

3. THE DREYFUS AFFAIR
   1894–1906

1. Aside from a large number of papers and documents at the Archives Nationales and the Bibliothèque Nationale in Paris there is a vast literature on the Dreyfus Affair. The most exhaustive study is Joseph Reinach: *Histoire de l'affaire Dreyfus,* 7 vols. (1901–11). Reinach was an active leader of the revisionists. The best anti-Dreyfus work in French is Henri Dutrait-Crozon: *Précis de l'affaire Dreyfus* (1909). Dreyfus himself described his prison life in *Cinq Années de ma vie,* with a preface by François Mauriac in the 1962 edition.

More recent books in French include: Maurice Baumont: *Aux Sources de l'affaire* (1959); Giscard d'Estaing: *D'Esterhazy à Dreyfus* (1960); H. Guillemin: *L'Enigme Esterhazy* (1962); H. Mazel: *Histoire et psychologie de l'affaire Dreyfus* (1934); Pierre Miquel: *L'Affaire Dreyfus* (1959); G. Charensol: *L'Affaire Dreyfus et la troisième république* (1930); and Jacques Kayser: *L'Affaire Dreyfus* (1946).

One of the most moving recent books in English is Nicholas Halasz: *Captain Dreyfus: the Story of a Mass Hysteria* (1955). Guy Chapman: *The Dreyfus Case* (1955) and Douglas Johnson: *France and the Dreyfus Affair* (1967) are based on much solid research in new as well as old material but seem to me to be prejudiced in favor of those who railroaded Dreyfus to Devil's Island and against those who opposed them, especially Colonel Picquart, to whom Johnson especially is less than just. They tend to play down the havoc wrought in French society by the Affair as well as the consequent swelling of anti-Semitism. For a much better account of that swelling see Robert F. Byrnes: *Antisemitism in Modern France,* Vol. II (1950).

Patrice Boussel: *L'Affaire Dreyfus et la presse* (1960) is excellent and contains a useful summary bibliography. Finally, the records of the hearings and trials have all been published.

2. See François Goguel: *La Politique des partis sous la IIIe République,* 3rd edn., 1958, pp. 98–100.
3. Shirer: *The Rise and Fall of the Third Reich,* p. 933.
4. Léautaud's letter of protest and Valéry's remark are quoted in Patrice Boussel: *op. cit.,* pp. 196–197.
5. Saul K. Padover: *France in Defeat,* p. 312.
6. Nicholas Halasz: *Captain Dreyfus: the Story of a Mass Hysteria,* p. 124.
7. Max von Schwartzkoppen: *The Truth about the Dreyfus Affair—from the Schwartzkoppen Papers.* New York, 1931.
8. Henriette Dardenne: *Lumières sur l'affaire Dreyfus* (1964).

4. THE CONSOLIDATION OF THE
   REPUBLIC 1880–1914

1. Herbert Luethy: *France Against Herself,* p. 25.
2. E. Beau de Loménie: *Les Responsabilités des dynasties bourgeoises.* Vol. I, p. 21.
3. See Dudley Kirk's "Population and Population Trends in Modern France," pp. 313–316, in Edward Mead Earle, ed.: *Modern France.* Also: Paul Leroy-Beaulieu: *La Question de la population* (1913) and J. Bertillon: *La Dépopulation de la France* (1911).
4. For the latest studies of the subject, see Alfred Sauvy: *Théorie générale de la population* (2 vols.), 1952–1959; *De Malthus à Mao*

Tse-Toung, 1959; *La Montée des jeunes,* 1959.
5. All three quotations from Maurice Ribet: *Le procès de Riom,* p. 461. A prominent Paris lawyer, Ribet defended Daladier at the Riom Trial.
6. Barbara W. Tuchman: *The Guns of August,* p. 38.

5. CLASSES AND CONFLICT
   1875–1914

1. The quotation is from Gaëtan Pirou: *Georges Sorel* (1927), pp. 52–53. Cited by Scott H. Lytle in Earle, ed., *op. cit.,* p. 288.

6. THE PERMANENT POLITICAL CRISIS
   1875–1914

1. Jacques Ollé-Laprune: *La Stabilité des ministres sous la troisième république, 1879–1940,* p. 11.
2. *Ibid.,* p. 299.
3. Carlton Hayes: *A Political and Social History of Modern Europe, 1815–1915,* Vol. II, p. 362.
4. Goguel, *op. cit.,* p. 26.
5. Ollé-Laprune, *op. cit.* This section on the "stability of ministers" is based on his detailed, statistical study. He lists each cabinet minister from 1879 to 1940 with the number and name of the ministries he held.
6. I am indebted to Herbert Luethy, a Swiss historian, and his lively book, *France Against Herself* (the original was entitled *Frankreichs Uhren Gehen Anders*—a much better title than the English translation), for his penetrating and sometimes humorous account of the French *Administration* and for his reminder of how some of its bureaucrats worked and looked.
7. Quoted by David Thomson, *Democracy in France. The Third Republic,* p. 55, from Daniel Halévy: *Décadence de la liberté.*
8. Albert Guérard: *The France of Tomorrow,* p. 144.
9. "Alain": *Eléments d'une doctrine radicale,* p. 25.

7. THE ACHIEVEMENTS OF THE
   THIRD REPUBLIC   1875–1914

1. Most of the figures on economic
   and colonial development are
   taken from Hayes, *op. cit.*, pp.
   356–357, and from Gordon
   Wright: *France in Modern Times*,
   pp. 343–353, 380–384.
2. Cited by Wright, *op. cit.*, p. 377,
   from Maurice Reclus: *Grandeur
   de la troisième* (1948).
3. *Histoire des littératures, Vol. III,
   Encyclopédie de la Pléiade*, pp.
   1259–1260.

8. THE COMING OF THE FIRST WORLD
   WAR   1905–1914

1. Tuchman, *op. cit.*, p. 44, from
   Péguy's review: *Cahiers de la
   quinzaine*, October 22, 1905.
2. *Ibid.*, pp. 10–11, from Bernhardi's
   book.
3. Winston Churchill: *The World
   Crisis*, Vol. I, p. 207. Churchill
   says Albert Ballin quoted it to him
   in London in July 1914.
4. Jacques Madaule: *Histoire de
   France*, Vol. II, pp. 301–302.

9. THE THIRD REPUBLIC'S FINEST
   HOUR   1914–1918

1. Tuchman, *op. cit.*, p. 348.
2. Interview given by Kluck in 1918
   to a Swedish journalist, quoted in
   Gabriel Hanotaux: *Histoire illustrée de la guerre de 1914*, Vol. IX,
   p. 103; cited by Tuchman, *op. cit.*,
   p. 436.
3. *Encyclopaedia Britannica*, Vol. 14,
   p. 929.
4. Clemenceau: *Grandeurs et misères d'une victoire*, p. 22.
5. *Ibid.*, p. 22.
6. World War I casualty figures, as
   compiled by the U.S. War Department.

10. VICTORIOUS FRANCE—"THE
    GREATEST POWER IN EUROPE"
    1919–1931

1. The casualty figures are from U.S.

War Department tables; Jacques
Chastenet: *Histoire de la troisième république*, Vol. V, pp. 14–15;
This Age of Conflict, p. 315; Alfred Sauvy: *Histoire économique
de la France entre les deux guerres,
1918–39*, Vol. I, pp. 19–24, 438–
441. Sauvy has drawn from the
most exhaustive work on the subject, Michel Huber: *La population
de la France pendant la guerre*.
Huber was director of the Statistique Générale.
2. The demographic statistics are
   from: *Encyclopédie politique de
   la France et du monde*, Vol. II, pp.
   201–215; Chastenet, *op. cit.*, Vol.
   V, pp. 233–234; Earle, ed.: *Modern France*, article by Dudley
   Kirk: "Population and Population
   Trends in Modern France," pp.
   316–318; Alfred Sauvy: *La Montée des jeunes*, especially pp. 59–
   60 on the preponderance of the
   aged.
3. See the author's: *The Rise and
   Fall of the Third Reich*, p. 212.
4. Reparation figures are from J.-B.
   Duroselle: *Histoire diplomatique
   de 1919 à nos jours*, and from
   Sauvy: *Histoire économique*, Vol.
   I. Both authors have taken their
   figures from the authoritative work
   on the subject, Etienne Weill-Raynal: *Les réparations allemandes
   et la France*, 3 vols.
5. Inter-Allied war debt figures are
   from *Encyclopaedia Britannica*,
   Vol. 12, pp. 462–467, article on
   "Inter-Allied Debts"; Walter C.
   Langsam: *The World Since 1914*,
   pp. 165–169; Sauvy, *op. cit.*, pp.
   168–183.

11. DECLINE, I: POLITICAL AND
    FINANCIAL CHAOS, AND THE
    POINCARÉ RECOVERY 1924–1930

1. Quoted from the *Journal des Finances*, July 23, 1936, by Beau de
   Loménie: *Les Responsabilités des
   dynasties bourgeoises*, Vol. IV, p.
   222.
2. If this evaluation of the French

bourgeoisie seems extreme to some readers, they are referred to a number of French and even American historians: Madaule, Loménie, Goguel, and the *Encyclopédie Politique*, Vol. I, in France, to cite but a few; and to Albert Guérard and Charles A. Micaud, both French-born American historians, in the United States.

3. This was Professor Alfred Sauvy, of the Collège de France. See his *Histoire économique . . . op. cit.*, Vol. I, p. 363. His researches led him to conclude that "at the Ministry of Finance they could not even add correctly."

4. Article by Germaine Martin in the *Revue de Paris*, August 15, 1926. Quoted by Sauvy, *op. cit.*, Vol. I, p. 84.

5. From the figures of the *Statistique Générale* and other sources, quoted by Sauvy, *op. cit.*, pp. 349–350, 353–354.

6. Goguel, *op. cit.*, pp. 271–273.

12. DECLINE, II: THE EROSION OF MILITARY POWER   1925–1934

1. Testimony of Marshal Pétain before the Parliamentary Investigating Committee, July 10, 1947, *Evénements, op. cit.*, Vol. I, p. 170.

2. Exposé made by General Weygand to the War Council on January 15, 1935. Text in *Evénements, op. cit., Rapport*, pp. 121–125. The specific statement is on p. 122.

3. General Erich Ludendorff: *Meine Kriegserinnerungen, 1914–1918*, pp. 547–551.

4. J.-R. Tournoux: *Pétain et de Gaulle*, pp. 156–157.

5. General Estienne's statements are taken from Major Eddy Bauer: *La Guerre des blindés*, Vol. I, pp. 27–28, who followed the text of the Brussels version; and from J.-R. Tournoux: *Pétain et de Gaulle*, pp. 154–155, who followed the Paris version of the lecture.

6. Testimony of Germain Martin, former Finance Minister, *Evéne-*

ments, op. cit., Vol. III, p. 702; of Jacomet, Secretary-General of the Ministry of National Defense, *ibid.*, Vol. I, pp. 196–198.

7. General Tony Albord: *Pourquoi cela est arrivé*, p. 30; General André Beaufre: *Le Drame de 1940*, pp. 56–60.

8. Text quoted from Manual, *Evénements, op. cit., Rapport*, p. 76.

9. Report of the Committee, *Ibid.*, p. 67.

10. Article by General Paul-Emile Tournoux: "Les Origines de la Ligne Maginot," *Revue d'Histoire de la Deuxième Guerre Mondiale*, No. 33, January, 1959, p. 14.

11. *Ibid.*, p. 14.

13. DECLINE, III: THE WORLD DEPRESSION SHAKES THE THIRD REPUBLIC   1931–1934

1. Pertinax: *The Gravediggers of France*, p. 89, footnote.

14. A FATEFUL TURNING POINT FEBRUARY 6, 1934

1. Rémond: "Les Anciens combattants et la politique," *Revue Française de Science Politique*, 1955, p. 290, and Rémond: *La Droite en France*, p. 213, footnote.

2. The quotations are from *Evénements, Rapport*, pp. 13–14.

3. Loustaunau-Lacau: *Mémoires d'un français rebelle*, p. 84. A major on Pétain's personal staff, he maintained contact with the leagues and later with the terrorist Cagoule. He also formed his own secret network in the Army, which, though ostensibly only anti-Communist, was believed by the government, which finally dismissed him from the service, to be anti-Republican as well.

4. Eugen Weber: *Action française*, pp. 333–334. Weber says that much of his information about this meeting was given to him by the Comte de Paris.

5. *Rapport général* on the Stavisky

Affair by Deputy Ernest Lafont. Document No. 4886, p. 287.

6. Alexander Werth: *The Twilight of France*, p. 15.

7. François Goguel, *op. cit.*, p. 485.

8. Edouard Bonnefous: *Histoire politique de la troisième république*, Vol. V, p. 210, footnote. This testimony was given the author by the Radical deputy André Cornu.

9. Paul Reynaud: *Mémoires:* Vol. I. *Venu de ma montagne*, pp. 367–368. Reynaud says he told the Speaker "what I thought of this." Georges Suarez in *Les heures héroïques du Cartel*, p. 252, confirms the story.

10. Weber, *op. cit.*, p. 331, footnote.

11. *Evénements, op. cit.*, Vol. I, p. 123.

12. Laurent Bonnevay: *Les journées sanglantes de février: 1934*, pp. 167–170. The *Commission d'Enquête*, which Bonnevay headed, gives slightly different figures. *Supplément*, Doc. 3386, p. 16.

13. J. C. Fernand-Laurent: *Gallic Charter*, pp. 127–128, and Chastenet, *op. cit.*, Vol. VI, p. 84, among others, recount Laval's telephone call from the Elysée Palace. Fernand-Laurent was a deputy at the time.

14. Pertinax, *op. cit.*, pp. 336–338.

15. Jacques Debu-Bridel: *L'Agonie de la troisième république*, p. 261; Pierre Lazareff: *Dernière Edition*, p. 238.

16. Bonnevay, *op. cit.*, pp. 22, 244. President Lebrun's testimony that February 6 was an "assault against republican institutions" and that he advised Daladier to resign to avert "a civil war" is in, respectively, *Evénements*, Vol. IV, pp. 95, 951.

17. *Evénements*, Vol. I, p. 13. *Rapport* of the President of the Committee, M. Charles Serre.

18. General Maxime Weygand: *Mémoires*, Vol. II. *Mirages et Réalité*, p. 409.

19. Gamelin, *Servir*, Vol. II, p. 106.

20. Georges Suarez, *op. cit.*, p. 272.

21. Gamelin, *op. cit.*, Vol. II, p. 109.

22. Testimony of Blum, *Evénements*, Vol. I, p. 123.

23. Robert Aron: *Histoire de Vichy, 1940–1944*, pp. 30–33.

24. John Gunther: *Inside Europe* (1936), p. 141.

25. Weber, *op. cit.*, p. 508.

26. Rémond, *op. cit.*, pp. 228–229.

27. The chief sources for the Stavisky Affair and the February 6 riots are the reports, minutes of evidence, and the documents submitted by the two Investigating Committees of the Chamber, the first under the presidency of Deputy Ernest Lafont (on Stavisky) and the second under the presidency of Deputy Laurent Bonnevay (on the February 6 riots). For background and specific facts I have drawn on them to refresh my memory and supplement my own coverage of the events. As indicated in the footnotes, the testimony contained in the voluminous report of the National Assembly's Committee to investigate the events from 1933 leading up to the collapse of the Republic has proved valuable. An excellent summary of February 6 is contained in a paper by Max Beloff published in *The Decline of the Third Republic*, edited by James Joll.

15. Aftermath: Widening of the Gulf 1934–1936

1. René Rémond, *op. cit.*, p. 222.

2. The complete text of the Pact— *Pacte Synarchiste Révolutionnaire pour L'Empire Français*—is published in Geoffroy de Charnay: *Synarchie;* in Roger Mennevée: *Documents politique et financier*, published by his Agence Independante d'Informations Internationales; and by Henry Coston: *Les Technocrates et la synarchie*. The studies of de Charnay and Mennevée are the best on the subject. Lilian T. Mowrer, in a bro-

chure "Concerning France," published in 1944 by the Union for Democratic Action, was the first to call attention in this country to the Synarchist movement in France.

3. Shirer: *The Rise and Fall of the Third Reich*, p. 212.
4. *Ibid.*, pp. 279–281, for one account.
5. Gamelin, *op. cit.*, Vol. II, pp. 162–167. The Chief of the French Army covers the conversations in Rome in great detail. Flandin: *Politique française, 1919–1940*, gives further details on the military talks and claims credit for pushing them.
6. Gamelin, *op. cit.*, Vol. II, pp. 178–179.
7. Debate in the Senate, acting as a Secret Committee, March 14, 1940. The stenographic account was published after the war, on August 2, 1948, in a special number of the *Journal Officiel*. Laval's statement appears on page 7 of the proceedings of March 14. The debate continued the next day. On April 7, 1948, the *Journal Officiel* had published the stenographic account of the secret debates in the Chamber, acting as a Secret Committee, on March 19 and April 19, 1940. So few copies of these highly important papers were printed that I found (in 1965) that even the Library of Congress did not have them. I unearthed a copy in Paris that year and had it photographed.
8. Pierre Renouvin: *Les Crises du XXᵉ siècle, Vol. II, de 1929 à 1945*, p. 80.
9. *The Memoirs of Anthony Eden, Earl of Avon. Facing the Dictators. 1923–1928*, p. 251.
10. Flandin, *op. cit.*, pp. 104–105, footnote.
11. *Ibid.*, pp. 170, 194.
12. Gamelin, *op. cit.*, Vol. II, p. 180. The meeting took place on November 21, 1935.
13. The text of the secret note is published in *Documents Diplomatiques Français* (hereafter referred to as DDF), 1932–1939, 2ᵉ Série (1936–1939), Tome I (January 1–March 31, 1936), Document No. 227, pp. 322–333.

A footnote says the document was found in the archives of the Ministry of War but that "it was not possible to determine its origin or to whom it was given." But General Gamelin, Vol. II, pp. 198–200, clears the matter up. He states the note was drafted by the General Staff at the request of the War Minister for the French Foreign Ministry.

14. In the words of Jacques Madaule, the French historian. Madaule, *op. cit.*, pp. 380–381.
15. Flandin, *op. cit.*, pp. 183–185.

16. COUP IN THE RHINELAND: THE LAST CHANCE TO STOP HITLER AND AVERT A MAJOR WAR MARCH 1936

1. Shirer, *op. cit.*, p. 290. The German documentary sources are therein given.
2. Testimony of Jean Dobler before the Parliamentary Investigating Committee after the war, *Événements*, Vol. II, pp. 469–515, esp. 504–505.
3. Gamelin, *op. cit.*, Vol. II, pp. 194–195.
4. André François-Poncet: *The Fateful Years. Memoirs of a French Ambassador in Berlin. 1931–1938*, pp. 188–189.
5. Gamelin, *op. cit.*, Vol. II, p. 195.
6. DDF, Vol. I, Doc. No. 36, pp. 52–54.
7. Flandin, *op. cit.*, pp. 194–195. Also, his testimony before the Parliamentary Investigating Committee, July 4, 1947, *Événements*, Vol. I, p. 138.
8. Eden, *op. cit.*, pp. 373–376.
9. Testimony of Flandin, *Événements*, Vol. I, p. 144.
10. Shirer, *op. cit.*, p. 291.
11. General Maurin to M. Flandin,

February 12, 1936. DDF, Vol. I, Doc. No. 170, pp. 245–247.

12. General Maurin to M. Flandin, February 17, 1936. DDF, Vol. I, Doc. No. 196, pp. 290–293.

13. M. Flandin to General Maurin, February 14, 1936. DDF, Vol. I, Doc. No. 186, pp. 277–278. The question is on the latter page.

14. Gamelin, *op. cit.,* Vol. II, p. 197. Also, testimony of General Gamelin before the Parliamentary Investigating Committee on December 16 and 23, 1947, *Evénements,* Vol. II, pp. 451, 517.

15. Gamelin, *op. cit.,* Vol. II, pp. 197–198.

16. *Evénements, Rapport,* p. 50.

17. Text of dispatch, DDF, Vol. I, Doc. No. 63, pp. 91–93.

18. *Ibid.,* Doc. No. 62, pp. 89–90.

19. *Ibid.,* Doc. No. 82, pp. 116–120.

20. Minutes, marked "Secret," of the meeting. *Ibid.,* Doc. No. 83, pp. 121–124.

21. Minutes of the meeting of February 19. *Ibid.,* Doc. No. 203, p. 301.

22. *Ibid.,* Doc. No. 269, pp. 277–278.

23. *Ibid.,* Doc. No. 126, p. 177.

24. *Ibid.,* Doc. No. 175, p. 253.

25. Testimony of Sarraut, February 3, 1948, *Evénements,* Vol. III, pp. 620–621.

26. DDF, Vol. I, Doc. No. 241, p. 339. Sarraut also gives it in slightly different words in his testimony on January 13, 1948, *Evénements,* Vol. III, p. 574.

27. DDF, Vol. I, Doc. No. 283, p. 397. Flandin tells of this meeting at Geneva with Eden in a dispatch to Ambassador Corbin in London on March 5. Apparently this is the first the Ambassador heard of the decision of the government.

28. Eden, *op. cit.,* pp. 378–379.

29. François-Poncet, *op. cit.,* pp. 191–192. The Ambassador's dispatch reporting the interview, DDF, Vol. I, Doc. No. 265, pp. 373–375, and a further report on, Doc. No. 272, pp. 381–385.

30. Shirer, *op. cit.,* p. 291. The documentary evidence is therein cited.

31. DDF, Vol. I, Doc. No. 297, p. 409.

32. *Ibid.,* Doc. No. 242, p. 344.

33. *Ibid.,* Doc. No. 294, p. 405.

34. Shirer, *Berlin Diary,* pp. 39–40.

35. François-Poncet, *op. cit.,* p. 193.

36. Shirer, *Berlin Diary,* pp. 40–45; *The Rise and Fall of the Third Reich,* pp. 291–292.

37. Testimony of Sarraut, February 3, 1948, before the Parliamentary Investigating Committee, *Evénements,* Vol. III, pp. 622ff.

38. General Gamelin reports the questions of Paul-Boncour and Sarraut and his answers in his memoirs. Gamelin, *op. cit.,* Vol. II, p. 201.

39. Testimony of Flandin, July 4, 1947, *Evénements,* Vol. I, p. 201.

40. Eden in his memoirs and Corbin in his two dispatches are in substantial agreement on what was said at their meeting. See Eden, *op. cit.,* p. 383. Corbin's dispatches, DDF, Vol. I, Doc. No. 301, pp. 413–414, Doc. No. 316, pp. 426–427.

41. Flandin to Corbin, March 8, 1936. DDF, Vol. I, Doc. No. 317, pp. 427–428.

42. Eden, *op. cit.,* p. 389.

43. *Ibid.,* p. 386.

44. Flandin to Avenol, Secretary-General of the League of Nations, dated Paris, March 8, 6:15 P.M., DDF, Vol. I, Doc. No. 321, pp. 430–431. Flandin's contention that he acted "without losing an hour" is in his book, *op. cit.,* p. 198.

45. I am indebted for *Le Matin* headlines to Charles A. Micaud: *The French Right and Nazi Germany, 1933–1939. A Study of Public Opinion,* p. 89. Quotations from other newspapers were read during the testimony of Sarraut and Flandin before the Investigating Committee. See *Evénements,* respectively, Vol. III, pp. 566–567, Vol. I, p. 151.

46. Jean Zay: *Souvenirs et Solitude,* p. 66.
47. Paul-Boncour, *op. cit.,* p. 35.
48. Shirer, *Berlin Diary,* p. 45.
49. Jean Zay, *op. cit.,* p. 67.
50. Minutes of the meeting at headquarters of General Gamelin, March 8, DDF, Vol. I, Doc. No. 334, pp. 444–446.
51. Guderian: *Panzer Leader,* p. 27 (paperback edn.).
52. Eden, *op. cit.,* pp. 387–388.
53. Corbin to Flandin, March 8, 5 P.M. DDF, Vol. I, Doc. No. 322, pp. 431–432.
54. Corbin to Flandin, March 8, later. The text of this dispatch is given by Sarraut in testimony before the Investigating Committee on January 27, 1948, *Evénements,* Vol. III, pp. 591–592. It is not given in the DDF volume.
55. Testimony before the Investigating Committee, February 10, 1948, *Evénements,* Vol. III, pp. 656–657. Details of "Plan D" are given in *Evénements, Rapport,* pp. 47–50.
56. Sarraut testimony, *Evénements,* Vol. III, pp. 601–618.
57. General Gamelin's own notes on the meeting are published in his memoirs, *op. cit.,* Vol. II, pp. 204–207. The minutes of the meeting, drawn up by Gamelin and signed by General Maurin, Minister of War, are given in the former's memoirs, *op. cit.,* Vol. II, pp. 208–211; also in *Evénements, Rapport,* pp. 51–52, and in DDF, Vol. I, Doc. No. 392, pp. 504–506. General Gamelin's ideas that evening are further elaborated in a note "On the Subject of an Eventual Penetration of the Rhineland by French Troops," which he drew up for the Supreme War Council on March 28, 1936. Text in *Evénements, Rapport,* pp. 53–56, and in DDF, Vol. I, Doc. No. 525, pp. 696–700.
58. Sarraut testimony, *Evénements,* Vol. III, p. 604.
59. Testimony of Jean Dobler, December 19, 1947, before the Parliamentary Investigating Committee, *Evénements,* Vol. II, pp. 510–511.
60. In his note of March 28, 1936. DDF, Vol. I, Doc. No. 525, p. 698.
61. Testimony of Dobler, *Evénements,* Vol. II, pp. 513–514.
62. Testimony of Sarraut, *Evénements,* Vol. III, p. 646.
63. General Tony Albord: *Pourquoi cela est arrivé, ou les responsabilités d'une génération militaire, 1919–1939,* pp. 49–52. Sarraut quotes it in full in his testimony, *Evénements,* Vol. III, pp. 644–645.
64. A paper by W. F. Knapp: "The Rhineland Crisis of March 1936," in James Joll, ed.: *The Decline of the Third Republic,* p. 83.
65. Eden, *op. cit.,* pp. 390–397; Flandin, *op. cit.,* pp. 202–204.
66. Eden, *op. cit.,* pp. 398–399.
67. Flandin, *op. cit.,* pp. 207–208; Testimony of Flandin, *Evénements,* Vol. I, pp. 135–154.
68. Churchill, *op. cit.,* Vol. I, p. 197.
69. Minutes of a meeting on March 13, 1936, in the office of General Georges, attended by three other generals and an admiral. DDF, Vol. I, Doc. No. 425, pp. 549–552.
70. Eden, *op. cit.,* pp. 400, 402, 403.
71. *Ibid.,* p. 418.
72. Flandin testimony, *Evénements,* Vol. I, pp. 157–158.
73. Testimony of General Maurin, May 20, 1948, *Evénements,* Vol. IV, pp. 912–919.
74. Testimony of General Gamelin, December 16, 1947. *Ibid.,* Vol. II, p. 450.
75. Testimony of Sarraut, *ibid.,* Vol. III, p. 619ff; and p. 668 on British responsibility.
76. Churchill, *op. cit.,* Vol. I, p. 193.
77. *Evénements, Rapport,* p. 81.
78. *Ibid.,* p. 65; pp. 79–80.
79. Paul Schmidt: *Hitler's Interpreter,* p. 41.

80. *Trial of the Major War Criminals* (hereafter referred to as TMWC). Nuremberg Documents and Testimony. Vol. XV, p. 352.
81. Paul Schmidt, *op. cit.*, p. 41; *Hitler's Secret Conversations*, pp. 211–212. I have combined quotations from the two sources.
82. Testimony of Sarraut, *Evénements,* Vol. III, pp. 670–671.
83. Gamelin himself recounts the incident, *op. cit.*, Vol. II, pp. 212–213.
84. *Evénements, Rapport,* pp. 83–85.

17. FRANCE FURTHER DIVIDED—THE FRONT POPULAIRE AND THE SPANISH CIVIL WAR   1936–1937

1. Madaule, Vol. II, *op. cit.*, p. 381.
2. Lebrun, *op. cit.*, pp. 233–234.
3. Blum's version of his talk with President Lebrun is given in *L'Oeuvre de Léon Blum, Vol. V, 1940–1945*, pp. 259–260. This is a work of seven volumes containing Blum's writings and speeches. Volume V was also published separately under the title: *Mémoires, La Prison et le procès, A l'échelle humaine, 1940–1945.*
4. Quoted in L. Bodin and J. Touchard: *Front populaire.* 1936, from Gide: *Œuvres complètes,* Vol. VIII, pp. 574–577.
5. *Ibid.,* p. 89, from Gide's article in *Vendredi,* June 5, 1936, the day after Blum took office.
6. Pertinax (André Géraud): *Les Fossoyeurs,* Vol. II, pp. 74–75.
7. *Evénements,* Vol. I, p. 215. This and other facts of the impact of the Spanish Civil War on his government and country are taken from his testimony before the Parliamentary Investigating Committee in 1947. See *ibid.,* pp. 215–220, 251–254.
8. Lebrun, *op. cit.*, p. 244.
9. Jean Zay, *op. cit.*, p. 114.
10. Blum testimony, *Evénements,* Vol. I, pp. 218–219.
11. Hugh Thomas: *The Spanish Civil War,* pp. 258–259. His main source is the unpublished memoirs of Pablo Azcárate, p. 257. Azcárate was the Republican Spanish Ambassador in London. I am indebted to Thomas and also to Joel Colton's excellent biography, *Léon Blum,* for a good deal of material on the impact of the Spanish Civil War on France, and of the farce of "nonintervention," though I have consulted the documents wherever available, especially the testimony in *Evénements,* and I followed these events closely from Berlin at the time. My conclusions are my own.
12. *Foreign Relations of the United States, 1936,* Vol. II, p. 481.
13. *Documents on German Foreign Policy* (hereafter referred to as DGFP). Series D, Vol. III, p. 60.
14. Thomas, *op. cit.*, p. 263. From General Warlimont's affidavit to U.S. Military Intelligence, 1946. UN Security Council Report on Spain, p. 76.
15. Shirer: *Berlin Diary, op. cit.*, pp. 55–56.
16. Eden, *op. cit.*, p. 453.
17. Text of Gamelin's note, Gamelin, *op. cit.*, Vol. II, pp. 329–331.
18. Colton, *op. cit.*, p. 264. From a letter to Suzanne Blum, then in New York. Madame Blum, a lawyer, was a friend but not a relative of the Premier.
19. *Ibid.,* p. 265. Speech to the International Socialist Conference, 1946.
20. *Evénements,* Vol. II, pp. 177–181.
21. My chief sources for the Salengro tragedy: Gamelin, *op. cit.*, Vol. II, pp. 255–258; Bodin and Touchard, *op. cit.*, pp. 210–220; Jean Zay, *op. cit.*, pp. 116–117.
22. Shirer: *The Rise and Fall of the Third Reich, op. cit.*, p. 298.
23. Blum testimony, *Evénements,* Vol. I, p. 131.
24. Robert Coulondre: *De Staline à Hitler. Souvenirs de deux ambassades, 1936–1939,* p. 17.
25. Blum testimony, *Evénements,* Vol. I, p. 128.

26. Gamelin, *op. cit.,* Vol. II, p. 230.
27. Coulondre, *op. cit.,* p. 13.
28. Testimony of General Ville-lume, who accompanied General Schweisguth to Russia, *Evéne-ments,* Vol. IX, p. 2742. Also, Pierre Renouvin, in lectures given in Paris, March 26 and 27, 1965, published in Edouard Bonnefous, *op. cit.,* Vol. VI, p. 405.
29. Published by Gamelin, *op. cit.,* Vol. II, pp. 286–287.
30. Note of April 10, 1936, General Gamelin to War Minister Dala-dier. Gamelin, *op. cit.,* Vol. II, pp. 286–287.
31. Blum testimony, *Evénements,* Vol. I, p. 129.
32. Churchill, *op. cit.,* Vol. I, pp. 288–289, footnote.
33. *Evénements, Rapport,* pp. 132–133.
34. De Gaulle to Reynaud, letter of August 26, 1936, published by Reynaud, *Mémoires,* Vol. II, p. 84. This volume is entitled: *Envers et contre tous.*
35. Minutes of meeting, Superior War Council, April 29, 1936. *Evénements,* Vol. II, pp. 182–183.
36. Minutes of meeting, Superior War Council, December 15, 1937. *Evénements,* Vol. II (Docs.), pp. 186–187.
37. Extracts from minutes of meeting, Superior War Council, October 14, 1936. Cited by Reynaud, *Evénements,* Vol. I, p. 107, and in his *Au Coeur de la mêlée, 1930–1945.*
38. Minutes of meeting, Superior War Council, December 15, 1937. *Evénements,* Vol. II (Docs.), pp. 184–186.
39. Report of General Renondeau, November 20, 1935, on the Ger-man armored divisions. *Evénements, Rapport,* pp. 164–167.
40. Minutes of meeting. *Evénements,* Vol. II (Docs.), p. 185. Also, Daladier testimony, *Evénements,* Vol. I, p. 25.
41. De Gaulle: *Mémoires,* Vol. I, *op. cit.,* pp. 18–20; Blum: *Mémoires, L'Oeuvre,* Vol. V, *op. cit.,* pp.

113–115; Blum testimony, *Evéne-ments,* Vol. I, p. 223.
42. *Evénements, Rapport,* pp. 89–90.
43. Blum testimony, *ibid.,* Vol. I, pp. 115 and 223, respectively.
44. Auriol: *Hier . . . demain,* Vol. II, pp. 127, note 1.
45. *Morgenthau Diaries,* p. 474, cited by Colton, *op. cit.,* p. 273.
46. *A l'échelle humaine*—a moving book. Published in *L'Oeuvre,* Vol. V, p. 440.
47. Quoted by Weber, *op. cit.,* p. 402, footnote, from *Action fran-çaise,* January 1, 1938.
48. Blum testimony, *L'Oeuvre,* Vol. V, p. 289. Blum's New Year's Eve broadcast remarks are in Bodin and Touchard, *op. cit.,* p. 165, which also reprints Blum's Riom testimony on the subject.
49. As Bodin and Touchard, *op. cit.,* p. 221, point out.

18. DISSENSION AND DISARRAY: FRANCE AND THE ANSCHLUSS MARCH 1938

1. For a detailed account of the secret meeting of November 5, 1937, and the shakeup in the Army and Foreign Office, based on the captured German docu-ments, see Shirer: *The Rise and Fall of the Third Reich,* pp. 303–308 and 309–321, respectively.
2. For further details, *ibid.,* pp. 325–330.
3. Gamelin, *op. cit.,* Vol. II, p. 315.
4. DGFP, Vol. I, p. 263.
5. Daladier testimony, *Evénements,* Vol. I, p. 26.
6. Gamelin, *op. cit.,* Vol. II, p. 316.
7. Dispatches of Count Welczeck to Berlin, March 12, 14, DGFP, Series D, Vol. I, pp. 581–582, 596–597, respectively.
8. *Ibid.,* pp. 590, 592, respectively.
9. *Ibid.,* p. 611.
10. Coulondre, *op. cit.,* pp. 132–136.
11. Churchill, *op. cit.,* Vol. I, p. 282.
12. Blum, *L'Oeuvre,* Vol. V, p. 241.
13. Reynaud, *Mémoires,* Vol. II (*Envers*), *op. cit.,* pp. 197–198.

14. DGFP, Vol. I, p. 683.
15. They are given in full in Gamelin, *op. cit.,* Vol. II, pp. 322–331.
16. DGFP, Vol. III, pp. 623–624.
17. Bonnefous, *op. cit.,* Vol. VI, p. 298.
18. Testimony of Paul-Boncour, *Evénements,* Vol. III, p. 804. Also his *Mémoires,* Vol. III, pp. 96–101.

19. THE ROAD TO MUNICH, I
APRIL 27–SEPTEMBER 13, 1938

1. Gamelin, *op. cit.,* Vol. II, p. 318.
2. Bonnet, *op. cit.,* Vol. I, p. 101.
3. Text of "Note on the Possible Action of France in Favor of Czechoslovakia." Gamelin, *op. cit.,* Vol. II, pp. 318–319.
4. Daladier testimony, *Evénements,* Vol. I, pp. 29–30. He was quoting, he said, from the French *procès-verbal* of the meeting. The British stenographic account is given in *Documents on British Foreign Policy* (hereafter referred to as DBrFP), Third Series, Vol. I, pp. 198–223.
5. Keith Feiling: *Life of Neville Chamberlain,* pp. 347–348.
6. DGFP, Series D, Vol. II, pp. 246–247.
7. *Ibid.,* pp. 263–264.
8. *Ibid.,* pp. 265–266.
9. The Hitler-Keitel discussion is the second paper in the file for *Case Green* and is given in DGFP, Vol. II, pp. 239–240. The entire file was introduced in evidence at Nuremberg as N.D. 388–PS.
10. DGFP, Vol. II, pp. 197–198.
11. Text of four telegrams exchanged. *Nazi Conspiracy and Aggression* (hereafter referred to as NCA), Vol. III, pp. 308–309 (N.D. 388–PS).
12. Text of Directive, DGFP, Vol. II, pp. 299–303.
13. Gamelin, *op. cit.,* Vol. II, pp. 334–335. He reproduces his notes of the meeting jotted down immediately afterwards.
14. Text in DBrFP, Third Series, Vol.

I, Doc. No. 271, pp. 346–347. It is dated "Foreign Office, May 22, 1938, 4:30 P.M." Bonnet gives a French translation, Bonnet, *op. cit.,* Vol. I, pp. 129–130.
15. DBrFP, Vol. I, Doc. No. 286, p. 357.
16. *Ibid.,* Doc. No. 301, pp. 366–367.
17. See *The Rise and Fall of the Third Reich,* pp. 365–366, for the account of Hitler's resolve of May 28. The sources are therein given.
18. Bonnet testimony, *Evénements,* Vol. IX, pp. 2, 618; Bonnet, *op. cit.,* Vol. I, pp. 124–127.
19. Gamelin, *op. cit.,* Vol. II, p. 360.
20. Coulondre, *op. cit.,* p. 135.
21. Bonnet, *op. cit.,* Vol. I, pp. 152–154.
22. Coulondre, *op. cit.,* pp. 142–146. Coulondre says he reproduces here "textually" the notes he made at the time. Bonnet, in his postwar testimony before the Parliamentary Investigating Committee, said, when questioned, that he did not "remember exactly" the May talks with Coulondre. Closely questioned, he finally remembered them, but wiggled out.
23. Coulondre, *op. cit.,* pp. 152–154.
24. DGFP, Vol. II, p. 395.
25. *Ibid.,* pp. 547–549.
26. Bonnet, *op. cit.,* Vol. I, pp. 195–196.
27. Testimony of Bonnet, *Evénements,* Vol. IX, pp. 2600–2601.
28. Conversation of General Paul Stehlin with the author. See also his book: *Témoignage pour l'histoire,* pp. 90–92.
29. Testimony of François-Poncet, *Evénements,* Vol. III, p. 773.
30. Gamelin, *op. cit.,* Vol. II, p. 341.
31. From Jodl's diary, TMWC, Vol. XXVIII, p. 373.
32. The texts of the memoranda are given by Wolfgang Foerster in *Ein General kämpft gegen den Krieg,* pp. 81–119.
33. From Jodl's diary, TMWC, Vol. XXVIII, p. 374.
34. The quotation is from Jodl's diary, TMWC, Vol. XXVIII, p. 375.

General Adam describes the scene at greater length in his unpublished memoirs, cited by Telford Taylor in his *Sword and Swastika.*

35. Gamelin, *op. cit.,* Vol. II, pp. 344–347.
36. Daladier article in *Candide,* number dated September 7–14, 1961. Also, testimony of Bonnet, *Evénements,* Vol. IX, p. 2624; Bonnet, *op. cit.,* Vol. I, p. 212.
37. Daladier article, *ibid.*
38. DBrFP, Vol. II, Doc. No. 807, pp. 269–270.
39. Bonnet, *op. cit.,* Vol. I, pp. 217–219. In an Annex, pp. 360–361, Bonnet publishes a facsimile of the original letter in English.
40. DBrFP, Vol. II, Doc. No. 852, p. 309.
41. *Ibid.,* Doc. No. 855, pp. 310–311.
42. *Ibid.,* p. 444. Footnote describing contents of letter of Phipps to Halifax, September 16.
43. *Ibid.,* Doc. No. 857, pp. 311–312.
44. Daladier article, *op. cit., Candide,* number dated September 7–14, 1961.
45. Phipps to Halifax, September 13, DBrFP, Vol. II, Doc. No. 861, pp. 313–314.
46. DGFP, Vol. II, p. 754.
47. *Ibid.,* p. 754.

20. THE ROAD TO MUNICH, II
SEPTEMBER 15–28, 1938

1. The German minutes of the meeting, as drawn up by the official interpreter, Paul Schmidt, are printed in DGFP, Vol. II, pp. 786–798. Foreign Minister Ribbentrop refused to provide Chamberlain with a copy, and the latter had to depend on his own memory for his account, which is published in DBrFP, Vol. II, pp. 338–341.
2. Feiling, *op. cit.,* p. 367.
3. The text of Runciman's report was made public on September 28, when it had only academic interest. It was published as a White Paper, Cmd. 5847, No. 1. There is reason to believe that it was partly rewritten after it had been submitted informally to the cabinet on the 15th and formally on the 21st.
4. DBrFP, Vol. II, p. 444, footnote. Letter of Phipps to Halifax, September 16.
5. The British minutes of the meeting are published in DBrFP, Vol. II, pp. 379–399. The French minutes have not yet been published, but Bonnet gives a few extracts from them in Vol. I of his memoirs, pp. 234–241, and Daladier recounts the meeting in his article in *Candide, op. cit.,* issue of September 7–14, 1961.
6. The English text of the joint note is printed in the British White Paper, Cmd. 5847, No. 2, and in DGFP, Vol. II, pp. 831–832. The French text is given in Bonnet, *op. cit.,* Vol. I, pp. 244–246, and in Henri Noguères: *Munich, ou la drôle de paix,* pp. 407–408.
7. Testimony of General Foucher, *Evénements,* Vol. IV, pp. 1202–1203. He says General Gamelin had simply acknowledged receipt of the request and passed it on to the government, which did not reply.
8. *Ibid.,* p. 1203, and Gamelin, *op. cit.,* Vol. II, p. 340.
9. Gamelin, *op. cit.,* Vol. II, pp. 340–350.
10. Testimony of Lacroix, *Evénements,* Vol. II (Docs.), p. 268.
11. Bonnet, *op. cit.,* Vol. I, p. 248.
12. This text is given in Bonnet, *op. cit.,* Vol. I, p. 248, and in *Evénements,* Vol. II (Docs.), p. 273, which prints a number of documents which Bonnet returned to the Foreign Office after the war but whose authenticity is suspected by many French historians, especially since Lacroix's testimony.
13. Bonnet, *op. cit.,* Vol. I, p. 252.
14. DBrFP, Vol. II, Doc. No. 1012, p. 454.
15. *Evénements,* Vol. II (Docs.), p. 275.

16. *Evénements,* Vol. IX, p. 2639.
17. DBrFP, Vol. II, Doc. No. 979, p. 425.
18. *Ibid.,* Doc. No. 991, pp. 437–438.
19. Churchill, *op. cit.,* Vol. I, pp. 303–304.
20. Dr. Schmidt's German minutes of the Godesberg meetings are in DGFP, Vol. II, pp. 870–879, 898–908. The British minutes kept by Kirkpatrick are in DBrFP, Vol. II, pp. 463–473, 499–508. Texts of letters exchanged by Chamberlain and Hitler are in DGFP, Vol. II, pp. 887–892, and also in the British White Paper, Cmd. 5847, Doc. No. 3.
21. Jodl's diary, September 26. Nuremberg Doc. 1780–PS.
22. DGFP, Vol. II, p. 931.
23. DBrFP, Vol. II, Doc. No. 1075, pp. 509–510.
24. *Ibid.,* Doc. No. 1094, p. 535.
25. *Ibid.,* Doc. No. 1099, p. 544.
26. *Ibid.,* Doc. No. 1076, p. 510.
27. Gamelin, *op. cit.,* Vol. II, p. 350.
28. The British minutes of the meeting and of the second one the day after are published in DBrFP, Vol. II, Doc. No. 1093, pp. 520–535, and Doc. No. 1096, pp. 536–541, respectively. The French minutes have not yet been published but a footnote in DBrFP, Vol. II, p. 520, reveals that the French record of the talks was given the British government later and agrees with the British version except for one passage. For this the British have inserted in their minutes the French version in French. Daladier in his postwar testimony before the Parliamentary Investigating Committee (*Evénements,* Vol. I, pp. 34–35) and in *Candide,* issue of September 14–21, 1961, and Bonnet in his memoirs, Vol. I, pp. 267–271, give brief accounts.
29. Daladier article, *Candide,* issue of September 14–21, 1961.
30. Notes of General Gamelin on his talks in London, September 26, 1938, *op. cit.,* Vol. II, pp. 350–354.
31. DBrFP, Vol. II, p. 575, footnote.
32. Gamelin, *op. cit.,* Vol. II, pp. 348, 350.
33. Daladier article, *Candide,* September 14–21, 1961; Bonnet, Vol. I, p. 271; DBrFP, Vol. II, Doc. No. 1129, pp. 565–566, the latter in the form Wilson tried to give it amid angry interruptions from Hitler.
34. DBrFP, Vol. II, Doc. No. 1106, pp. 546–547.
35. *Ibid.,* Vol. II, Doc. No. 1122, p. 560.
36. *Ibid.,* Doc. No. 1111, footnote, p. 550.
37. Bonnet, *Le Quai d'Orsay sous trois républiques,* pp. 216–218.
38. *Ibid.*
39. Testimony of Pierre Comert, *Evénements,* Vol. VII, p. 2177. Hamilton Fish Armstrong wrote an interesting article on the subject in the January 1939 issue of *Foreign Affairs.* His account holds up well in the light of the postwar documentation.
40. Paul Schmidt: *Statist auf diplomatischer Bühne, 1923–45,* pp. pp. 407–408.
41. The telegrams of Wilson on his two meetings with Hitler and the notes of them kept by Kilpatrick are published in DBrFP, Docs. Nos. 1115, 1116, 1118, 1127, 1128, 1129, pp. 552–567.
42. Daladier article, *Candide, op. cit.,* issue of September 14–21, 1961.
43. Items 31–33 of "Green File." NCA, Vol. III, pp. 350–352. Nuremberg Doc. 388–PS.
44. Dispatch from Paris. DGFP, Vol. II, p. 977.
45. Dispatch from Stockholm, *ibid.,* p. 974.
46. Dispatch from Washington, *ibid.,* p. 982.
47. Dispatch from Prague, *ibid.,* p. 976.
48. Text of Hitler's letter to Chamberlain, September 27, 1938. DGFP, Vol. II, pp. 966–968.
49. Chamberlain's message to Beneš and a second one sent shortly

thereafter are quoted by Wheeler-Bennett in *Munich,* pp. 151–152, 155, from the Czech archives. Interestingly, they are omitted from the confidential British Foreign Office Papers published after the war.

50. Noguères, *op. cit.,* pp. 214–215.
51. Dispatch from Paris, DGFP, Vol. II, pp. 978–979.
52. Renouvin, Vol. II, *op. cit.,* p. 129.
53. DBrFP, Vol. II, Doc. No. 1139, pp. 571–572.
54. *Ibid.,* Doc. No. 1140, pp. 572–573.
55. *Ibid.,* Doc. No. 1155, pp. 584–586.
56. See Gamelin, *op. cit.,* Vol. II, pp. 353–357, for his account of this affair, and Bonnet's answer in his postwar testimony before the Parliamentary Investigating Committee, *Evénements,* Vol. IX, p. 2642.
57. DBrFP, Vol. II, *op. cit.,* Doc. No. 1143, pp. 575–576.
58. *Ibid.,* Doc. No. 1150, p. 582.
59. *Ibid.,* Doc. No. 1160, p. 588.
60. Testimony of Daladier, *Evénements,* Vol. I, p. 35.
61. Letter of General Vuillemin to Guy La Chambre, September 26, 1938. A photographed copy is in the possession of the author. It bears the number 127 E.M.G.A.A. / S
62. Gamelin, *op. cit.,* Vol. II, p. 358.
63. Text of Chamberlain's letter to Hitler, DBrFP, Vol. II, Doc. No. 1150, p. 587.
64. Daladier in *Candide,* issue of September 14–21, 1961. The British telegrams to Paris: DBrFP, Vol. II, Docs. Nos. 1156, 1158, pp. 586–587.
65. Text of Chamberlain's appeal to Mussolini, telephoned from London to Rome. DBrFP, Vol. II, Doc. No. 1159, pp. 587–588.
66. Henderson: *The Failure of a Mission,* p. 144. DBrFP, Vol. I, p. 614.
67. Jodl's Diary, September 28, 1938. NCA, Vol. IV, p. 368. Nuremberg Doc. 1780–PS.

68. François-Poncet, *op. cit.,* p. 266.
69. Erich Kordt's memorandum, made available to the writer.
70. Schmidt, *op. cit.,* p. 412.
71. From Halder's interrogation at Nuremberg, February 25, 1946. NCA, Suppt. B, pp. 1553–1558.
72. DBrFP, Vol. II, Doc. No. 1194, p. 604.
73. *Ibid.,* Doc. No. 1206, p. 613.
74. Gamelin, *op. cit.,* Vol. II, p. 358.

21. THE CONFERENCE AT MUNICH SEPTEMBER 29–30, 1938

1. *Ciano's Hidden Diary, 1937–1938,* p. 166. In a telegram dated June 20, 1940, Mussolini reminded Hitler that at Munich he had promised to take part in the attack on Britain. The text of the telegram is in DGFP, Vol. X, p. 27. By this time Mussolini had already fulfilled, in a way, the first part of the promise, to join in the attack against France, though he did so only after Germany had decisively defeated the French and British armies.
2. Wilson's comment is in DBrFP, Vol. II, p. 631, from a note he wrote from memory on the conference; Henderson, *op. cit.,* p. 171; François-Poncet, *op. cit.,* p. 271.
3. Text of the Munich Agreement, DGFP, Vol. II, pp. 1014–1016.
4. From the official report of Dr. Masarik to the Czech Foreign Office.
5. Shirer: *Berlin Diary,* p. 145.
6. DGFP, Vol. IV, pp. 287–293.
7. Bonnet, *op. cit.,* Vol. I, pp. 296–297.
8. Schmidt, *op. cit.,* p. 417.
9. DBrFP, Doc. No. 1225, pp. 629–630.
10. Noguères, *op. cit.,* pp. 301–302.
11. Daladier article, *Candide,* issue of September 21–28, 1961.
12. Noguères, *op. cit.,* p. 134. He cites four different sources for the remark.

13. Gamelin, *op. cit.*, Vol. II, p. 359.
14. Quoted from *Le Petit Parisien* by Alexander Werth: *France and Munich*, p. 345.
15. Renouvin, *op. cit.*, p. 129.
16. Keitel's testimony, April 4, 1946, at the Nuremberg Trial, TMWC, Vol. X, p. 509.
17. Manstein's testimony, August 9, 1946, TMWC, Vol. XX, p. 606.
18. Pertinax, *op. cit., The Gravediggers of France*, p. 5.
19. Jodl's testimony, June 4, 1946, TMWC, Vol. XV, p. 361.
20. Gamelin, *op. cit.*, Vol. II, pp. 345–347.
21. DBrFP, Vol. II, Doc. No. 1221, pp. 623–624.
22. Coulondre, *op. cit.*, pp. 165–171.
23. DGFP, Vol. III, pp. 602–604.
24. Gamelin, *op. cit.*, Vol. II, p. 356.
25. Testimony of Pierre Comert, *Evénements*, Vol. VII, p. 2176.
26. Goguel, *op. cit.*, pp. 539–540.
27. Coulondre, *op. cit.*, p. 181.

22. THE TURN OF POLAND 1939

1. Churchill, *op. cit.*, Vol. I, p. 323.
2. Quoted by Telford Taylor in *Sword and Swastika*, p. 41, from the Seeckt papers now at the National Archives in Washington.
3. DBrFP, Vol. IV, Doc. No. 270, p. 263.
4. Bonnet, *op. cit.*, Vol. II, p. 153.
5. Quoted by Gamelin, *op. cit.*, Vol. II, pp. 410–411.
6. Minutes of the meeting of December 5, 1938. Gamelin, *op. cit.*, Vol. II, pp. 371–378.
7. Minutes of the meeting of December 3, 1938. *Evénements*, Vol. II (Docs.), pp. 188–197.
8. Gamelin, *op. cit.*, Vol. I, pp. 133–135.
9. *Ibid.*, Vol. II, p. 413.
10. Halifax statement to Maisky, DBrFP, Vol. IV, Doc. No. 433. Maisky to Boothby in latter's book: *I Fight to Live*, p. 189.
11. Minutes of the meeting, April 9, 1939. Gamelin, *op. cit.*, Vol. II, pp. 403–407.

12. *Ibid.*, p. 406.
13. Bonnet, *op. cit.*, Vol. II, p. 184.
14. Coulondre, *op. cit.*, p. 270.
15. DGFP, Vol. VI, p. 429.
16. *Ibid.*, pp. 266–267.
17. General Paul Stehlin: *Témoignage pour l'histoire*, pp. 376–377.
18. DGFP, Vol. VI, pp. 535–536.
19. *Nazi-Soviet Relations, 1939–1941*, pp. 5–7, 8–9.
20. *Le Livre Jaune Français. Documents Diplomatiques, 1938–1939.* Doc. No. 120, pp. 153–155. Hereafter referred to as LJ. This is the original French edition of *The French Yellow Book*.
21. Stehlin, *op. cit.*, pp. 151–152.
22. LJ, Doc. No. 125, pp. 164–165.
23. *Ibid.*, Doc. No. 127, pp. 172–173.
24. *Ibid.*, Doc. No. 132, pp. 180–181.
25. Shirer: *The Rise and Fall of the Third Reich*, p. 531. The sources for the meeting of Hitler with his generals are given on p. 529, footnote.
26. Minutes of the meeting, DGFP, Vol. VI, pp. 574–580.
27. Gamelin recounts it in full, as well as the story of his negotiations with the Poles, in his memoirs, *op. cit.*, Vol. II, pp. 413–426. Bonnet gives his version in *his* memoirs, *op. cit.*, Vol. II, pp. 217–233, and in Vol. III, pp. 266–267.
28. Bonnet, *op. cit.*, Vol. II, pp. 223–232.
29. Gamelin, *op. cit.*, Vol. II, pp. 424–425.
30. Text of letter from Lukasiewicz to Bonnet, May 26, 1939, in L. B. Namier: *Europe in Decay*, pp. 310–312.
31. Gamelin, *op. cit.*, Vol. II, p. 423.
32. Gamelin, *op. cit.*, Vol. II, p. 426, footnote. Bonnet, *op. cit.*, Vol. II, pp. 227–232, and Vol. III, pp. 266–267. Bonnet's interview is cited by Namier, *op. cit.*, p. 72, from *Le Temps* of November 3, 1940.
33. Gamelin, *op. cit.*, Vol. II, pp. 418–421.
34. Shirer: *Berlin Diary*, pp. 131–132.

35. Gamelin, *op. cit.,* Vol. II, pp. 414–415.

23. A SUMMER'S INTERLUDE IN PARIS MAY–JULY 1939

1. Pierre Lazareff: *De Munich à Vichy,* pp. 121–125.
2. Bonnet, *op. cit.,* Vol. II, p. 257.
3. Weygand: *En lisant les Mémoires de Général de Gaulle,* p. 17.
4. Bonnet, *op. cit.,* Vol. II, pp. 258–259.
5. Lazareff, *op. cit.,* p. 132.
6. Quoted by Bonnefous, *op. cit.,* Vol. VII, p. 90.
7. *Ibid.,* p. 90.
8. Flandin, *op. cit.,* p. 283.
9. Welczeck dispatch, August 11, 1939. DGFP, Vol. VII, Doc. No. 22, p. 22. The telegrams between Ribbentrop and Welczeck on the matter are given in DGFP, Vol. VII, Doc. No. 640, pp. 886–888; No. 658, pp. 907–908; No. 664, pp. 913—914; No. 690, pp. 946–947.
10. Henri de Kerillis: *Français, voici la vérité,* pp. 170–178.
11. Weber, *op. cit.,* pp. 248–251. The author gives as his sources dispatches of the French Foreign Office, copies of which he obtained, and also a note by Bonnet summarizing his part in the negotiations.

24. THE TALKS WITH RUSSIA SUMMER 1939

1. Anatole de Monzie, *Ci-devant,* p. 121.
2. DBrFP, Vol. IV, Doc. No. 183.
3. DGFP, Vol. VI, Doc. No. 458, pp. 616–617.
4. DBrFP, Vol. V, Doc. No. 5.
5. Eden confirms this in his memoirs: *The Reckoning,* pp. 64–65.
6. Churchill, *op. cit.,* Vol. I, p. 389.
7. Bonnet, *op. cit.,* Vol. II, pp. 196–198.
8. *Ibid.,* p. 198.
9. *Ibid.,* pp. 199–200.
10. *Ibid.,* pp. 200–201.
11. DBrFP, Vol. VI, Doc. No. 376.

12. Two dispatches, August 1. DGFP, Vol. VI, Docs. Nos. 752, 753, pp. 1033–1035.
13. DBrFP, Vol. VI, Appendix V, p. 763.
14. General André Beaufre: *Le Drame de 1940,* pp. 123–124.
15. DBrFP, Vol. VII, Appendix II, p. 600.
16. Beaufre, *op. cit.,* p. 122.
17. *Ibid.,* p. 124.
18. *Ibid.,* pp. 127–128. The complete text of the draft is given in DBrFP, Vol. VII, pp. 595–597.
19. *Ibid.,* Vol. VII, p. 598.
20. The dispatches, DGFP, Vol. VI, pp. 1047, 1049–1050, 1048–1049, respectively.
21. LJ, pp. 250–251.
22. DGFP, Vol. VII, p. 49.
23. *Ibid.,* pp. 58–59, and footnote No. 13, p. 48.
24. *Ibid.,* pp. 62–64.
25. There is considerable first-hand material on the military talks in Moscow from the Allied, especially the British, side. The latter is contained in DBrFP, Third Series, Appendix II, pp. 558–614, which reproduces the British minutes of all the meetings as well as reports by the three principal officers, Admiral Drax, Air Marshal Burnett and General Heywood. Included also is a verbatim account, from the Russian minutes, of the dramatic meeting of General Doumenc with Marshal Voroshilov on the evening of August 22. The first half of Vol. VII contains the texts of confidential telegrams on the military negotiations exchanged between the British Embassy in Moscow and the Foreign Office in London.

The best French source is General Beaufre, a member of the French mission, who gives his account in his book, *op. cit.* General Doumenc gave his own account briefly in an article in *Carrefour,* May 21, 1947, and in a statement on February 16, 1948, at Lille, published in *Le Monde* the next day. Both accounts are disappointingly brief and shed little light. Bonnet, *op. cit.*, Vol. II, Chapters 10 and 15, covers the diplomatic side in Paris and prints a number of dispatches to and from Moscow and Warsaw. Daladier's testimony published in *Evénements*, Vol. I, pp. 39 ff., is valuable but uneven. The French government, at this writing, has not yet got around to publishing the French minutes of the meeting nor the military and diplomatic dispatches on it, though Beaufre presents a number of both, as does Bonnet.

Unfortunately, the Russians, so far as I know, have never published their documents on the meeting, though a Soviet account is given in Niknov's *Origins of World War II*, in which much use of the British Foreign Office documents is made. A Soviet version is also given in *Histoire de la diplomatie,* edited by V. Potemkin.

26. Text of Lindsay's air-mailed dispatch of August 17, DBrFP, Vol. VII, Doc. No. 41, pp. 41–42. A footnote, p. 42, discloses the time of receipt by the Foreign Office.
27. DGFP, Vol. VII, Doc. No. 75, pp. 84–85.
28. *Ibid.,* Doc. No. 105, pp. 114–116.
29. *Ibid.,* Doc. No. 113, pp. 121–123.
30. *Ibid.,* Doc. No. 125, p. 134.
31. *Ibid.,* Doc. No. 132, p. 150.
32. Daladier testimony, *Evénements, op. cit.,* Vol. I, pp. 49–50.
33. Churchill, *op. cit.,* p. 391.
34. Text of Hitler's telegram to Stalin, August 20, DGFP, Vol. VII, Doc. No. 142, pp. 156–157.
35. Text of Stalin's reply, August 21, *ibid.,* Doc. No. 159, p. 168.
36. Daladier's testimony, *Evénements, op. cit.,* Vol. I, p. 47.
37. DBrFP, Vol. VII, Doc. No. 130, and footnote, p. 119.
38. DGFP, Vol. VII, pp. 225–229.
39. Naggiar's dispatch is quoted by Bonnet, *op. cit.,* Vol. II, pp. 295–296.

40. Beaufre, *op. cit.,* pp. 173–174. Gamelin makes no mention of this telegram in his memoirs.
41. *Ibid.,* p. 287.

25. ON THE EVE OF WAR
AUGUST 23–31, 1939

1. Bonnefous, *op. cit.,* Vol. VII, p. 327, from Bonnet's note to the author, written in the third person.
2. Bonnet, *op. cit.,* Vol. II, pp. 301–302.
3. Gamelin, *op. cit.,* Vol. I, pp. 23–34.
4. Text of minutes, *Evénements,* Vol. II (Docs.), pp. 276–278. Bonnet also publishes it in his memoirs, *op. cit.,* Vol. II, pp. 305–308.
5. Gamelin testimony, *Evénements,* Vol. II, p. 398.
6. Daladier quoted General Vuillemin's letter in his postwar testimony before the Parliamentary Investigating Committee. *Evénements,* Vol. I, pp. 55–56.
7. Gamelin testimony, *ibid.,* Vol. II, p. 398.
8. Daladier testimony, *ibid.,* Vol. I, p. 50.
9. Halder Diary, entry of August 23, 1939. In the German edition of this diary, published in 1962, it may be found in Vol. I, pp. 27–28. The sources for Hitler's meeting with his generals on August 22 are given fully, and analyzed, in *The Rise and Fall of the Third Reich,* p. 529, footnote. The sources include notes made by Admiral Hermann Boehm, Chief of the High Seas Fleet, published in TMWC, Vol. XLI, pp. 16–25; General Halder's diary for August 22, published in the volume cited above, pp. 22–26, and also (in English) in DGFP, Vol. VII, pp. 557–559. An unsigned memorandum of the meeting, used as evidence at the Nuremberg trial, is published (in English) in DGFP, Vol. VII, pp. 200–206, and in NCA, Vol. III, pp. 581–586. In two parts, it is listed as Nuremberg

Documents (N.Ds.) 798–PS and 1014–PS.

10. DBrFP, Vol. VII, Doc. No. 201, pp. 163–164.

11. LJ, Doc. No. 213, p. 296.

12. DBrFP, Vol. VII, Doc. No. 308, p. 249.

13. Gamelin, *op. cit.*, Vol. II, p. 448.

14. *Ibid.*, p. 445.

15. DBrFP, Vol. VII, Doc. No. 203, p. 166.

16. Henderson's dispatch, August 23. *British Blue Book,* pp. 98–100.

17. Text of declaration of Hitler to Henderson, DGFP, Vol. VII, pp. 279–284. Henderson's dispatch describing the interview, *British Blue Book,* pp. 122–123. Also see his *Failure of a Mission,* p. 270.

18. Coulondre dispatch, August 25, LJ, Doc. No. 242, pp. 312–314. See also Coulondre, *op. cit.*, pp. 287–289.

19. Bonnet, *op. cit.*, Vol. II, p. 319.

20. Schmidt, *op. cit.*, pp. 450–451.

21. Text of Hitler's letter to Mussolini, August 25, DGFP, Vol. VII, Doc. No. 266, pp. 281–283.

22. Text of Mussolini's letter to Hitler, August 25, *ibid.*, Doc. No. 271, pp. 285–286.

23. Keitel's testimony, TMWC, Vol. X, pp. 514–515.

24. NCA, Vol. VI, pp. 977–978. N.D. C–170.

25. DBrFP, Vol. VII, Doc. No. 244, p. 206.

26. Flandin, *op. cit.*, p. 283.

27. *Ibid.*, p. 317, footnote.

28. Gamelin, *op. cit.*, Vol. I, pp. 41–42.

29. DGFP, Vol. VII, Doc. No. 300, p. 308.

30. DBrFP, Vol. VII, Doc. No. 305, pp. 244–245.

31. Beau de Loménie, *op. cit.*, p. 116.

32. Pertinax, *op. cit.*, Vol. I, p. 131; Amer. edn., p. 104.

33. *Ibid.*, pp. 130–131, 104, respectively.

34. André Maurois: *Tragedy in France,* p. 67.

35. Lazareff, *Munich, op. cit.*, p. 103.

36. Spears, *op. cit.*, Vol. I, pp. 90–91.

37. Lazareff, *op. cit.*, p. 104.

38. Clare Boothe: *Europe in the Spring,* p. 147, footnote.

39. Maurois, *op. cit.*, p. 68.

40. Lazareff, *op. cit.*, pp. 104–105.

41. Pertinax: *Les Fossoyeurs, op. cit.*, Vol. II, pp. 37–38.

42. DGFP, Vol. III, Doc. No. 244, pp. 270–271.

43. Alfred Mallet: *Pierre Laval,* Vol. I, p. 135.

44. Testimony of Major Loustauneau-Lacou, Pétain trial, July 30, 1935, pp. 355–357, stenographic account.

45. Text of letter. Louis Noguères: *Le Véritable Procès du Maréchal Pétain,* Annexes, pp. 631–634.

46. Text of Daladier's letter to Hitler, August 26, LJ, Doc. No. 253, pp. 321–322. An English translation is given in DGFP, Vol. VII, Doc. No. 324, pp. 330–331.

47. Coulondre's dispatch, LJ, Doc. No. 261, pp. 328–329. The ambassador's description of the meeting is in his memoirs, *op. cit.*, pp. 290–291.

48. Henderson, *op. cit.*, p. 280.

49. Coulondre's dispatches, August 30, 2 A.M. and 1:30 P.M., LJ, Doc. No. 296, pp. 352–353, and No. 300, p. 367, respectively.

50. Kennard's dispatch reporting talk with Beck, August 29, DBrFP, Vol. VII, Doc. No. 482, pp. 370–371.

51. Two dispatches of Halifax to Henderson, August 30, DBrFP, Vol. VII, Doc. No. 504, p. 391; No. 538, p. 410.

52. Ribbentrop testimony, TMWC, Vol. X, p. 275. Schmidt's testimony, *ibid.*, pp. 196–222. Also Schmidt, *op. cit.*, pp. 456–460.

53. DBrFP, Vol. VII, Doc. No. 604, p. 449.

54. Bonnet, *op. cit.*, Vol. II, p. 335.

55. Monzie, *op. cit.*, p. 149, footnote. He gives as his source Jean Zay.

56. Coulondre, *op. cit.*, p. 299, footnote.

57. Monzie, *op. cit.*, pp. 148–149.

58. The German text of Hitler's di-

rective is in TMWC, Vol. XXXIV, pp. 456–459 (N.D. C–126). English translations are given in NCA, Vol. VI, pp. 935–939, and in DGFP, Vol. VII, pp. 477–479.

26. THE LAUNCHING OF WORLD WAR II
SEPTEMBER 1–3, 1939

1. Reynaud, *Cœur, op. cit.*, p. 334.
2. Dispatch of Noël, September 1, LJ, Doc. No. 343, pp. 388–389.
3. DBrFP, Vol. VII, Doc. No. 749, pp. 530–531.
4. *Ibid.*, Doc. No. 704, p. 503.
5. LJ, Doc. No. 345, p. 390.
6. Bonnet himself supplies this exchange. *Op. cit.*, Vol. II, p. 353.
7. DBrFP, Vol. VII, Doc. No. 718, p. 514.
8. Reynaud, *Cœur, op. cit.*, p. 336.
9. DBrFP, Vol. VII, Doc. No. 699, p. 501. It is misdated as having been sent September 1.
10. Gamelin, *op. cit.*, Vol. II, p. 456.
11. Text in DGFP, Vol. VII, Doc. No. 535, pp. 509–510.
12. LJ, p. 431.
13. Though Bonnet states that it was Halifax who called him, the British minutes of the call say it was Cadogan. DBrFP, Vol. VII, Doc. No. 718, pp. 513–514. Bonnet's note on the call is in LJ, p. 431, and his account in his memoirs, *op. cit.*, Vol. II, p. 358.
14. *The Ciano Diaries, 1939–1943*, pp. 136–137.
15. Reynaud, *Cœur, op. cit.*, p. 336.
16. Lebrun, *op. cit.*, p. 32.
17. Quoted by Bonnefous, *op. cit.*, Vol. VII, pp. 108–109, from Benoist-Méchin: *Histoire de l'armée allemande*, Vol. VI.
18. Beau de Loménie: *La Mort de la Troisième République,* p. 136.
19. DBrFP, Vol. VII, Doc. No. 718, pp. 513–514.
20. Bonnet, *op. cit.*, pp. 358–359.
21. DBrFP, Vol. VII, Doc. No. 727, p. 518.
22. Monzie, *op cit.*, pp. 157, 152.

23. DBrFP, Vol. VII, Doc. No. 740, pp. 524–525.
24. The British minute on the Halifax-Bonnet telephone conversation is given in DBrFP, Vol. VII, Doc. No. 741, pp. 525–526. Bonnet's account is in his memoirs, *op. cit.*, pp. 362–363.
25. Bonnet, *op. cit.*, Vol. II, p. 364.
26. *The Ciano Diaries, op. cit.*, p. 137.
27. DGFP, Vol. VII, Doc. No. 538, pp. 511–512.
28. Bonnet gives the text in his memoirs, *op. cit.*, Vol. II, p. 366. The text in LJ, Doc. No. 365, p. 411, carries the time limit of 5 P.M., September 3, which was inserted at the last minute.
29. Schmidt, *op. cit.*, p. 466; also his testimony at Nuremberg, TMWC, Vol. X, pp. 200–201.
30. Coulondre's dispatch describing his final meeting with Ribbentrop is in LJ, Doc. No. 367, pp. 412–413. He also recounts it in his memoirs, *op. cit.*, p. 314. The German account, a memorandum by Schmidt, is given in DGFP, Vol. VII, Doc. No. 563, pp. 533–534. Weizsaecker's report on his receiving Coulondre is in the same volume, Doc. No. 562, p. 532. The Ambassador recounts it briefly in his memoirs, *op. cit.*, p. 313.
31. Gamelin, *op. cit.*, Vol. II, p. 457.
32. Bonnefous, *op. cit.*, Vol. VII, p. 114.
33. Monzie, *op. cit.*, p. 150.
34. Flandin, *op. cit.*, pp. 336–339.
35. Beau de Loménie, *Mort, op. cit.*, pp. 128–129.
36. Bonnefous, *op. cit.*, Vol. VII, p. 114.

27. LA DRÔLE DE GUERRE.
SEPTEMBER 3, 1939–
APRIL 9, 1940

1. DGFP, Vol. VII, p. 105.
2. *Ibid.*, p. 130.
3. The text of the Polish protests and questions is given from the

French military archives by Colonel Jacques Minart, an aide to Gamelin, in his memoirs: *P. C. Vincennes,* Vol. I, pp. 19–20.

4. Gamelin gives the text of his reply in his memoirs, Vol. III, pp. 60–61.

5. *Ibid.,* p. 55.

6. De Gaulle, *op. cit.,* Vol. I, p. 22; Beaufre, *op. cit.,* p. 189.

7. *The Central Blue: The Autobiography of Sir John Slessor, Marshal of the R.A.F.,* p. 243.

8. Text of Gamelin's Personal Instruction No. 4, September 21, 1939. Gamelin, *op. cit.,* Vol. III, pp. 66–67.

9. *Ibid.,* p. 67.

10. Gamelin's Order, September 21, 1939. Gamelin, *op. cit.,* Vol. III, p. 70; Minart, *op. cit.,* Vol. I, p. 29.

11. Gamelin, *op. cit.,* Vol. III, p. 87.

12. Gamelin's "Note" of September 30, 1939. Gamelin, *op. cit.,* pp. 88–89.

13. Goutard: *1940: La Guerre des Occasions Perdues,* p. 125. All references are to this French edition, which is more complete than the English-language edition published as *The Battle of France, 1940.*

14. Daladier testimony, *Evénements,* Vol. I, pp. 65–67.

15. Churchill, *op. cit.,* Vol. I, p. 384.

16. Testimony of Halder, *Trials of War Criminals* (hereafter referred to as TWC), Vol. XII, p. 1086; of Jodl, TMWC, Vol. XV, p. 350; of Keitel, *ibid.,* Vol. X, p. 519. The quotation from General Westphal is from his book: *The German Army in the West,* pp. 71–72; from General Giraud from a typewritten copy of his *Report to M. Pétain on the Causes of the Defeat of France,* dated July 26, 1940. I found it in the Hoover Library at Stanford.

17. DGFP, Vol. VIII, p. 24.

18. *Ibid.,* pp. 197–198.

19. Brauchitsch's testimony at Nuremberg, TMWC, Vol. XX, p. 573. A note in the OKW War Diary confirms Hitler's words.

20. Hitler's memorandum, NCA, Vol. VII, pp. 800–814 (N. D. L–52); Directive No. 6, *ibid.,* Vol. VI, pp. 880–881 (N. D. NOKW–3433).

21. Bonnet, *op. cit.,* Vol. III, pp. 314–315.

22. Monzie, *op. cit.,* pp. 169–172.

23. Gamelin, *op. cit.,* Vol. III, p. 107.

24. *Foreign Relations of the United States, 1940,* Vol. I, p. 469.

25. Gamelin, *op. cit.,* Vol. III, p. 106.

26. Quoted by the defense in Pétain's subsequent trial.

27. J.-R. Tournoux: *Pétain et de Gaulle,* pp. 189–190.

28. Elie J. Bois: *Truth on the Tragedy of France,* pp. 140–142.

29. DGFP, Vol. VIII, p. 414.

30. Quoted by Goutard, *op. cit.,* p. 131.

31. *Evénements,* Vol. II (Docs.), pp. 281–282.

32. Gamelin testimony, *ibid.,* Vol. II, pp. 413–414, 439–440.

33. Spears, *op. cit.,* Vol. I, pp. 49–50.

34. The quotations from Generals Laffargue, Ruby, Menu, and Grandsard are from Goutard, *op. cit.,* pp. 132–133. For further details see the books of these officers: General Laffargue: *Justice pour ceux de 1940;* General Ruby: *Sedan, terre d'épreuve;* General Menu: *Lumière sur les ruines;* General Grandsard: *Le 10e Corps d'armée dans la bataille.*

35. Shirer: *Berlin Diary, op. cit.,* p. 234.

36. Goutard, *op. cit.,* p. 133.

37. Gamelin, *op. cit.,* Vol. III, pp. 195–199.

38. Daladier to the secret session of the Chamber of Deputies, March 19, 1940, *Journal Officiel* (hereafter listed as *J.O.*), p. 67. It was published after the war, on April 7, 1948, as a "special number," but in so few copies that it is virtually unobtainable, even in some of our best libraries.

39. Note of Gamelin, March 10, 1940. Published in *Documents Secrets de l'Etat Major Général Français* (hereafter listed as the *Wilhelmstrasse Documents*). These French confidential papers, mostly from General Gamelin's headquarters, were captured by the Germans near the end of the Battle of France and were published by the German Foreign Office in Berlin in 1941. See also Gamelin, *op. cit.*, Vol. III, p. 201.

40. See the author's *The Rise and Fall of the Third Reich,* Chapter 20, for the sources for the German plans to invade Norway.

41. Text of Daladier's note of March 14, 1940. *Evénements,* Vol. II (Docs.), pp. 349–350.

42. Text of British reply, March 27, 1940, *ibid.,* pp. 354–357.

43. Note of Daladier, January 19, 1940, *Wilhelmstrasse Documents,* p. 45.

44. Gamelin, *op. cit.,* Vol. III, p. 199.

45. De Gaulle: *Mémoires de Guerre,* Vol. I, p. 26.

46. General Paul Stehlin, *op. cit.,* pp. 215–216.

47. Steinhardt to the Secretary of State, February 2, 1940, *Foreign Relations of the United States,* 1940, Vol. I, pp. 590–591.

48. Bullitt to the Secretary of State, January 15, 1940, *ibid.,* pp. 276–277.

49. Note of General Gamelin, February 22, 1940, *Wilhelmstrasse Documents,* pp. 50–52.

50. Gamelin to Daladier ("Very Secret"), March 12, 1940, *ibid.,* pp. 59–61.

51. Steinhardt to the Secretary of State, March 9, 1940, *Foreign Relations of the United States, 1940,* Vol. I, pp. 276–277.

52. French minutes of the meeting of the Allied Supreme Council, March 28, 1940, at London, *Wilhelmstrasse Documents,* p. 74.

53. Reynaud, *Cœur, op. cit.,* p. 371.

54. Communication of Paul Reynaud to the British Government, March 25, 1940, *Evénements,* Vol. II (Docs.), pp. 351–354.

55. *J.O.,* Secret session of the Senate, March 14, 1940. Speeches of Reibel, pp. 2–5; of Laval, pp. 5–12, 30–31; of Lémery, p. 30.

56. *J.O.,* Secret session of the Chamber of Deputies, March 19, 1940. Speech of Flandin, pp. 88–93.

57. Speeches of Daladier. To the Senate, March 14, 1940, *J.O.,* pp. 21–27; to the Chamber, March 19, *ibid.,* pp. 66–71.

58. Daladier to the Senate, March 14, 1940, *J.O.,* p. 27.

59. Beau de Loménie, *Mort, op. cit.,* pp. 194–195.

60. Churchill, *op. cit.,* Vol. I, pp. 575–576.

61. *Ibid.,* p. 576.

62. Reynaud, *Cœur, op. cit.,* p. 376.

63. Bois, *op. cit.,* p. 205.

64. Pertinax, *op. cit.,* Vol. I, p. 226. (American edn., p. 189.)

65. Reynaud, *Cœur, op. cit.,* p. 379.

66. *Ibid.,* p. 379.

67. Pertinax, *op. cit.,* Vol. I, p. 211. (American edn., p. 171.)

68. DGFP, Vol. IX, p. 73.

69. De Gaulle, *op. cit.,* Vol. I, p. 25.

70. DGFP, Vol. IX, p. 19.

71. Deposition of General Vauthier at the Pétain trial. What the Marshal was up to in Paris during the January visit is related in Louis Noguères: *Le Véritable Procès du Maréchal Pétain, op. cit.,* pp. 20–27; and in Beau de Loménie, *Mort, op. cit.,* pp. 192–193.

72. De Gaulle, *op. cit.,* Vol. I, pp. 25–26.

73. *Ibid.,* pp. 23–24.

74. *J.O.,* Secret session of the Senate, April 16–19, 1940, pp. 92–93.

75. *Ibid.,* Secret session of the Chamber, April 19, p. 114.

76. De Gaulle, *op. cit.,* Vol. I, p. 27.

77. Monzie, *op. cit.,* p. 266.

78. See Baudouin's article in the February 1, 1938, number of the *Revue de Paris* entitled "Les Données du problème français" ("Basic Aspects of the French Problem"). The last comment is

from the Christmas 1939 number of a deluxe review which Baudouin got out entitled *Messages.*

79. Third issue of *Messages,* Spring, 1940. Bois, *op. cit.,* pp. 255–256, quotes it.

80. Bois, *op. cit.,* p. 240.

81. Pertinax, *op. cit.,* Vol. I, p. 285. (American edn., p. 235.)

82. Testimony of Paul-Boncour, *Événements,* Vol. III, pp. 815–816.

83. Memorandum of Welles to President Roosevelt, dated Paris, March 8, 1940. *Foreign Relations of the United States, 1940,* Vol. I, p. 69.

84. Gamelin, *op. cit.,* Vol. III, pp. 304–314.

85. *Ibid.,* p. 313.

86. Reynaud, *Cœur, op. cit.,* pp. 387–388.

28. ON THE EVE: THE WAR IN NORWAY, THE THREAT TO BELGIUM AND THE CRISIS IN PARIS SPRING 1940

1. The account of the meeting is taken from Baudouin: *Neuf mois au gouvernement, avril-décembre 1940,* pp. 22–24; Reynaud, *Cœur,* p. 388; Gamelin, *op. cit.,* Vol. III, pp. 314–315.

2. Gamelin, *op. cit.,* Vol. III, p. 318.

3. Testimony of General de Villelume before the Parliamentary Investigating Committee on April 12, 1951, *Evénements,* Vol. IX, pp. 2, 757.

4. Baudouin, *op. cit.,* p. 25.

5. Gamelin, *op. cit.,* Vol. III, p. 332.

6. *Ibid.,* p. 336.

7. Baudouin, *op. cit.,* pp. 26–33, and Reynaud, *Cœur, op. cit.,* pp. 391–397, give text of minutes of the War Cabinet meeting of April 12, 1940, drawn up by Baudouin. Baudouin, *op. cit.,* pp. 33–34, discusses the meeting and his talks with the three ministers afterward. Gamelin's account of the meeting and of his writing out his resignation is in his memoirs, *op. cit.,* Vol. III, pp. 336–338.

8. Baudouin, *op. cit.,* p. 41.

9. Gamelin, *op. cit.,* Vol. III, p. 366.

10. Baudouin, *op. cit.,* p. 37.

11. *Ibid.,* pp. 37–40.

12. Pierre Lazareff: *De Munich à Vichy,* pp. 228–229.

13. Monzie, *op. cit.,* p. 216.

14. *Ibid.,* pp. 208–209.

15. *Le Procès Laval.* Stenographic Account, pp. 239–241.

16. Louis Noguères: *Le Véritable Procès du Maréchal Pétain,* pp. 27–35.

17. Darlan interview with Henri Béraud, published in *Gringoire,* May 30, 1941.

18. Reynaud, *Cœur, op. cit.,* pp. 917–918.

19. Louis Noguères, *op. cit.,* p. 32.

20. Gamelin, *op. cit.,* Vol. III, p. 381.

21. Shirer: *Rise and Fall . . . ,* pp. 651, 715.

22. Ciano's warnings are given in his diary, *op. cit.,* December 26, 1939, p. 183; December 30, p. 186; January 2, 1940, p. 191. For these and other warnings mentioned, see J. Wullus-Rudiger: *Les Origines internationales du drame belge de 1940,* pp. 183–185; and an article by Jean Vanwelkenhuyzen, "L'alerte du 10 janvier 1940," in the *Revue d'histoire de la Deuxième Guerre Mondiale,* October 1953, No. 12, pp. 33–54.

23. See Halder's diary for January 8 and 9, 1940 (Vol. I, pp. 151–152), and Hans-Adolf Jacobsen: *Fall Gelb. Der Kampf um den Deutschen Operationsplan zur Westoffensive, 1940,* p. 89, from the Bock papers.

24. Vanwelkenhuyzen, *op. cit.,* p. 48.

25. Gamelin, *op. cit.,* Vol. III, pp. 155–156; Minart, *op. cit.,* Vol. I, p. 121.

26. General Oscar Michiels: *18 jours de guerre en Belgique,* p. 54; Jacobsen, *op. cit.,* p. 287, footnote 28; Wullus–Rudiger, *op. cit.,* p. 185.

27. Minart, *op. cit.,* Vol. I, pp. 123–124, gives the text of the Ambassador's dispatch.
28. Gamelin, *op. cit.,* Vol. III, p. 16.
29. *Ibid.,* pp. 157–158.
30. Minart, *op. cit.,* Vol. I, p. 133.
31. Gamelin, *op. cit.,* Vol. III, pp. 159–160.
32. Minart, *op. cit.,* Vol. I, p. 138.
33. Wullus–Rudiger, *op. cit.,* pp. 188, 191.
34. DGFP, Vol. VIII, pp. 674–675.
35. *Ibid.,* p. 660.
36. *Ibid.,* p. 658, footnote 2.
37. Jodl's diary for January 13, 1940; Halder's diary for same day (Vol. I, p. 157); Jacobsen, *op. cit.,* p. 92.
38. Dispatches from Brussels and The Hague, DGFP, Vol. VIII, pp. 666–667; Jodl's diary for January 14; Jacobsen, *op. cit.,* p. 92.
39. Jodl's diary for January 16; Jacobsen, *op. cit.,* p. 93.
40. Gamelin, *op. cit.,* Vol. III, p. 6.
41. Reynaud, *Cœur, op. cit.,* pp. 122–123.
42. Report of General Lelong, French military attaché in London, to General Gamelin, May 5, 1939. *Wilhelmstrasse Documents,* p. 20.
43. Churchill, *op. cit.,* Vol. I, p. 481; Colonel Lugand in *La Campagne de France mai–juin 1940,* p. 19.
44. Telegram of General Gamelin to General Lelong in London, November 13, 1939. *Wilhelmstrasse Documents,* p. 39.
45. Commandant Pierre Lyet: *La Bataille de France, mai–juin 1940,* p. 19. He quotes from a handwritten note of General Georges'.
46. *Ibid.,* p. 25; Lugand, *op. cit.,* pp. 22, 25; testimony of General Villelume, *Evénements,* Vol. IX, pp. 2765–2766.
47. Testimony of General Georges, *Evénements,* Vol. III, p. 684.
48. G.Q.G.N.E. (General Headquarters, Northeast Front), Note No. 941 3/NE of General Georges, November 5, 1939. Quoted by Lyet, *op. cit.,* p. 22; and Lugand, *op. cit.,* p. 26.

49. Major L. F. Ellis: *The War in France and Flanders, 1939–1940,* pp. 317–318. This is the official British account.
50. Goutard, *op. cit.,* p. 147; Lyet, *op. cit.,* p. 25.
51. Major Eddy Bauer: *La Guerre des blindés,* Vol. I, pp. 90–91. Bauer is a Swiss military historian.
52. *Ibid.,* p. 91; Reynaud: *Cœur, op. cit.,* p. 422.
53. Bauer, *op. cit.,* Vol. I, p. 87.
54. Field Marshal Erich von Manstein: *Lost Victories,* p. 99.
55. N.D. (Nuremberg Document) NOKW-511 (6). It is summarized by Manstein, *op. cit.,* pp. 105–107.
56. Manstein, *op. cit.,* p. 106.
57. Jodl's diary, February 13, 1940. TMWC, Vol. XXVIII, p. 402, and N.D. PS–1783.
58. Manstein's own account of the meeting is in his book, *op. cit.,* pp. 120–122, and in his diary entry for this day. Jacobsen, *op. cit.,* pp. 115–116, gives a detailed account from numerous German sources. Also, Jodl's diary for February 17, 1940.
59. General Heinz Guderian: *Panzer Leader* (paperback edn.), p. 73.
60. General Gamelin's testimony, *Evénements,* Vol. II, p. 411; Gamelin, *op. cit.,* Vol. I, p. 88.
61. André Maurois: *Tragedy in France,* p. 85.
62. Reynaud quotes the letter in full in *Cœur, op. cit.,* pp. 410–411. De Gaulle does not mention it in his three volumes of memoirs.
63. General Armengaud: *Batailles politiques et militaires sur l'Europe. Témoignages (1932–1940),* p. 219.
64. The Taittinger report is given verbatim in *Evénements,* Vol. II (Docs.), pp. 359–360.
65. Text of General Huntziger's reply, *Evénements,* Vol. II (Docs.), pp. 361–363.
66. Maurice Ribet: *Le procès de Riom.* p. 460; *Le Procès du Maréchal Pétain,* p. 141.

67. Reynaud: *Cœur, op. cit.*, p. 132, footnote.
68. Pertinax, *op. cit.*, Vol. I, p. 223.
69. Shirer: *Rise and Fall* . . . , *op. cit.*, p. 716. Also Wullus-Rudiger, *op. cit.*, pp. 204–205.
70. S.D. 740,0011: Eur. War. 1939/2637 and 2737. Dispatches of Bullitt, May 3, 8, 1940.
71. Testimony of Daladier at the Pétain trial and his deposition at the Riom trial. See *Le Procès du Maréchal Pétain*, Vol. I, p. 141; and Maurice Ribet: *Le procès de Riom*, p. 496.
72. The text of the "indictment" is given by General Villelume in his testimony before the Parliamentary Investigating Committee, *Evénements*, Vol. IX, pp. 2758–2760. He says he wrote it.
73. Monzie, *op. cit.*, p. 44.
74. The account of the meeting is taken mostly from Baudouin, *op. cit.*, pp. 44–48.
75. Reynaud: *Cœur, op. cit.*, p. 412; Baudouin, *op. cit.*, p. 47.
76. Gamelin tells of his resigning again in his memoirs, *op. cit.*, Vol. III, p. 383. He told of receiving the first report on the German offensive in his testimony before the Parliamentary Investigating Committee, *Evénements*, Vol. II, p. 519.

29. THE BATTLE OF FRANCE, I: THE ARMIES CLOSE IN MAY 10–15, 1940

1. Clare Boothe: *Europe in the Spring*, pp. 126–127, 246.
2. Henri de Kerillis: *Français, voici la vérité*, p. 247.
3. Gamelin, *op. cit.*, Vol. III, p. 389.
4. Baudouin, *op. cit.*, pp. 49–50.
5. Beaufre, *op. cit.*, p. 230.
6. Gamelin, *op. cit.*, Vol. III, p. 384.
7. Bouthillier, *op. cit.*, p. 19.
8. Commandant Lyet's detailed and documented study appeared in the *Revue historique de l'Armée*, No. 1, February 1960.
9. Benoist-Méchin: *Les soixante jours qui ébranlèrent l'Occident. 10 mai–10 juillet 1940*, Vol. I, p. 93. The author says General Colson told him the story.
10. General Gauché: *Le deuxième bureau au travail*, p. 212.
11. Lyet, *Bataille, op. cit.*, p. 30.
12. Testimony of Gamelin, *Evénements*, Vol. II, p. 520.
13. Testimony of Gamelin and de Barrell, *ibid.*, pp. 519–520.
14. General d'Astier de la Vigerie: *Le ciel n'était pas vide. 1940*, pp. 83–84.
15. Major L. F. Ellis: *The War in France and Flanders, 1939–1940*, p. 37. This is the official British war history.
16. D'Astier, *op. cit.*, pp. 87–88.
17. The quotations attributed to Gamelin on air warfare are given, respectively, in d'Astier, *op cit.*, p. 23; Goutard, *op. cit.*, p. 39; Ribet, *op. cit.*, p. 470.
18. The two incidents are described, respectively, by Colonel R. Villate in an article, *L'Entrée des français en Belgique et en Holland en mai 1940* in the book *La Campagne de France mai–juin 1940*, p. 72, and by Major Ellis, *op. cit.*, p. 36.
19. Introduction of General Georges to General Roton's *Années cruciales*, pp. ix, xiii.
20. This brief calculation of the strength of the opposing armies is based on Gamelin, *op. cit.*, Vol. I, pp. 309–314; on Colonel Lugand's study, *Les Forces en présence au 10 mai, 1940*, published in *La Campagne, op. cit.*, pp. 5–48; and on two works of the German military historian, Hans-Adolph Jacobsen: *Der Zweite Weltkrieg in Chronik und Documenten* and *Fall Gelb*, especially the latter, pp. 244–259.
21. Gamelin, *op. cit.*, Vol. I, p. 314.
22. Testimony of General Keller at Riom. Mazé and Genebrier, *Les grandes Journées du procès de Riom*, p. 253.
23. Testimony of Gamelin, *Evénements*, Vol. II, pp. 382–383.

24. Gamelin, *op. cit.,* Vol. I, p. 155.
25. Jacobsen: *Der Zweite Weltkrieg.*
26. General Heinz Guderian, *op. cit.,* p. 72.
27. From a study of the official British military histories made by General de Cossé-Brissac and cited by him in an article in the *Revue d'Histoire de la Deuxième Guerre Mondiale,* No. 53, January 1964, p. 5.
28. Gamelin, *op. cit.,* Vol. I, p. 157.
29. Quoted by Goutard, *op. cit.,* p. 84.
30. Jacobsen's estimate in *Der Zweite Weltkrieg;* Cossé-Brissac in the *Revue de Défense Nationale,* June 1948; Kesselring's in *A Soldier's Record.*
31. Ellis, *op. cit.,* pp. 309–312. His figures do not include Coastal Command, which lost 46 out of 73 planes.
32. Colonel Pierre Paquier: *Les forces aériennes françaises de 1939 à 1945,* pp. 23–24.
33. General d'Astier de la Vigerie, *op. cit.,* p. 74.
34. The testimony of the two Air Force generals at Riom is quoted by Gamelin, *op. cit.,* Vol. I, p. 282.
35. Deposition of General Massenet de Marancour at Riom. Quoted by La Chambre, *Evénements,* Vol. II, pp. 354–355.
36. Testimony of Gamelin, *Evénements,* Vol. II, p. 388. His comment, *Mémoires, op. cit.,* Vol. I, pp. 275, 282.
37. From General Vuillemin's Order of the Day, July 29, 1940, quoted by Guy La Chambre in his testimony before the Parliamentary Investigating Committee, *Evénements,* Vol. II, p. 343.
38. Guy La Chambre gave a detailed account of the purchase of American planes and of the number that were ready for action in his testimony before the same body: *Evénements,* Vol. II, pp. 307–309, 334–337. See also an account of the difficulties encountered in the United States in the *Revue d'Histoire de la Deuxième Guerre Mondiale,* No. 58, April 1965, by John McV. Haight, Jr., of the University of Lehigh.
39. Testimony of General Mittelhauser. Ribet, *op. cit.,* p. 257.
40. Testimony of General Georges, *Evénements,* Vol. III, p. 690.
41. General Maxime Weygand: *Mémoires: Rappelé au Service,* pp. 89–90; Reibel's remark is in *J.O.,* p. 47, stenographic account of the secret session of the Senate, April 16, 1940; Roton, *op. cit.,* p. 121.
42. Gamelin, *op. cit.,* Vol. II, p. 456.
43. Beaufre, *op. cit.,* p. 232.
44. Minart, *op. cit.,* Vol. II, p. 103.
45. Letter of Gamelin to *L'Aurore,* November 8, 1949.
46. The questioning of Dhers and the answering testimony of Gamelin: *Evénements,* Vol. II, p. 463.
47. Gamelin, *op. cit.,* Vol. I, p. 320.
48. Churchill, *op. cit.,* Vol. II: *Their Finest Hour,* p. 40.
49. Gamelin, *op. cit.,* Vol. I, p. 335; Vol. III, p. 290; Vol. I, pp. 318–321, on the first three days, respectively.
50. Denis Richards: *Royal Air Force. 1939–1945,* Vol. I, *The Fight at Odds,* pp. 116–118.
51. General Prioux: *Souvenirs de guerre, 1939–1943,* pp. 63–70.
52. Testimony of Daladier, *Evénements,* Vol. I, pp. 75–76.
53. Quoted by Theodore Draper: *The Six Weeks' War,* p. 113.
54. Colonel Villate, *op. cit.,* pp. 73–74; General Emile Wanty: "La Défense des Ardennes en 1940" in the *Revue d'Histoire de la Deuxième Guerre Mondiale,* No. 42, April 1961, p. 13.
55. General Wanty: "Improvisation de la liaison belgo-britannique du 10 au 18 mai 1940" in the above-mentioned *Revue,* No. 55, January 1964, p. 31. General Wanty was Chief of Staff of the Belgian VIth Corps. General Alan Brooke, Commander of the British IInd

Corps, told of it in his memoirs. See Arthur Bryant: *The Turn of the Tide*, p. 93.

56. *The Memoirs of Field Marshal Montgomery* (paperback edn.), pp. 52–53.

57. General Wanty, "Improvisation," *op. cit.*, pp. 33–35.

58. Gamelin, *op. cit.*, Vol. III, p. 393.

59. General Wanty disclosed this information in two studies in the *Revue d'Histoire de la Deuxième Guerre Mondiale:* "Les relations militaires franco-belges, 1936–octobre 1939," No. 31, July 1958, p. 18; "La Défense des Ardennes en 1940," No. 42, April 1961, p. 8.

60. Goutard, English edn., *The Battle of France, 1940*, pp. 85–86. I do not find it in the French edition.

61. Lieutenant Colonel Le Goyet: "La percée de Sedan (10–15 mai, 1940)" in the *Revue d'Histoire* . . . , No. 59, July 1965, p. 30.

62. Goutard, *op. cit.* (French edn.), p. 140.

63. Le Goyet, *op. cit.*, p. 26, from an article in the German military review *Wehrkunde*, July 1958, by General Hoth, who commanded the German XVth Armored Corps, which attacked over the Meuse at Dinant.

64. General Wanty, article in the *Revue d'Histoire* . . . , *op. cit.*, No. 42, pp. 9–10.

65. General Doumenc: *Histoire de la 9ᵉ armée*, p. 52.

66. Testimony of Gamelin, *Evénements*, Vol. II, p. 429.

67. General Oscar Michiels: *18 jours de guerre en Belgique*, p. 123, footnote.

68. B. H. Liddell Hart: *The German Generals Talk* (paperback edn.), p. 106.

69. *Ibid.*, p. 107.

70. Gamelin, *op. cit.*, Vol. I, pp. 337–338.

71. Reynaud, *Cœur, op. cit.*, pp. 437–438; Le Goyet, *op. cit.*, p. 36 and footnote.

72. Doumenc, *op. cit.*, pp. 81–82.

73. General d'Astier de la Vigerie, *op. cit.*, pp. 89–103.

74. Testimony of General Georges, *Evénements*, Vol. III, p. 688.

75. Gamelin, *op. cit.*, Vol. I, p. 336.

76. Testimony of Daladier at Riom. Mazé and Genebrier, *op. cit.*, p. 235.

77. General Bernhard von Lossberg: *Im Wehrmacht Fuehrungsstab*, p. 78.

78. From the Bormann papers. Quoted by Goutard, *op. cit.*, p. 183.

79. General Adolf Heusinger: *Befehl im Widerstreit—Schicksalstunden der Deutschen Armee 1923–1945.* Quoted by Goutard, *op. cit.*, pp. 182–183.

80. War Diary, Army Group B, May 14, 1940. Jacobsen, *op. cit.*, pp. 30–31.

81. War Diary, Army Group B, May 15, 1940. Jacobsen, *op. cit.*, p. 33.

30. THE BATTLE OF FRANCE, II: DISASTER AT SEDAN. THE BREAKTHROUGH AT THE MEUSE MAY 13–16, 1940

1. Gamelin, *op. cit.*, Vol. I, p. 322 and footnote; Goutard, *op. cit.*, p. 204.

2. Gamelin, *op. cit.*, Vol. I, p. 323.

3. *Ibid.*, pp. 324–326.

4. General C. Grandsard: *Le 10ᵉ Corps d'armée dans la bataille*, p. 89.

5. *Ibid.*, pp. 132–133 and footnote.

6. *Ibid.*, pp. 119–120.

7. *Ibid.*, p. 119 and footnote.

8. Guderian, *op. cit.*, p. 79.

9. General Edmond Ruby: *Sedan, terre d'épreuve.* Cited by Goutard, *op. cit.*, p. 211.

10. Testimony of Gamelin, *Evénements*, Vol. II, p. 435.

11. Grandsard, *op. cit.*, pp. 132–137.

12. *Ibid.*, p. 141.

13. General Grandsard, *op. cit.*, pp. 141–142, 160–161, gives a graphic account of the panic, as does General Ruby, *op. cit.*, cited by Goutard, *op. cit.*, p. 215.

14. Grandsard, *op. cit.,* pp. 146–147, 160–161.
15. Minart, *op. cit.,* Vol. II, p. 138.
16. D'Astier, *op. cit.,* p. 107.
17. Grandsard, *op. cit.,* pp. 161–165.
18. Ruby, *op. cit.,* quoted by Goutard, *op. cit.,* pp. 219–220.
19. Richecourt: *La Guerre de cent heures.* Quoted by Goutard, *op. cit.,* p. 220.
20. Grandsard, *op. cit.,* p. 175.
21. Le Goyet, *op. cit.,* p. 44.
22. Note of General Flavigny to the Committee, July 1948. *Evénements,* Vol. V, pp. 1253–1256. Also Flavigny letter of May 13, 1948, quoted by General Devaux, Chief of Staff of the 3rd Armored Division, to the Committee on December 21, 1948, *Evénements,* Vol. V, p. 1342.
23. Ellis, *op. cit.,* pp. 55–56, gives the figures on British aircraft engaged and lost; *Evénements,* Vol. II, p. 346, gives the official French Air Force Table of Bombing Missions and Losses. Its figures differ slightly from those of General d'Astier, *op. cit.,* pp. 109–111.
24. Guderian, *op. cit.,* p. 85; Le Goyet, *op. cit.,* pp. 43–44, quotes the War Diary of the German XIXth Armored Corps on the dispute between the two generals.
25. Roton, *op. cit.,* p. 177.
26. Minart, *op. cit.,* Vol. II, p. 144.
27. Note of General Flavigny. *Evénements,* Vol. V, p. 1345, footnote.
28. *Ibid.,* p. 1255.
29. Roton, *op. cit.,* p. 182.
30. Testimony of General Georges, *Evénements,* Vol. III, p. 694.
31. Testimony of General Devaux, *Evénements,* Vol. V, p. 1345, footnote 5.
32. Text of General Flavigny's message, *Evénements,* Vol. V, p. 1353.
33. Testimony of General Devaux, *Evénements,* Vol. V, p. 1345, footnote 5.
34. Testimony of General Lacaille, *Evénements,* Vol. IV, pp. 939–940.
35. *Ibid.,* p. 942.
36. *The Rommel Papers,* edited by B. H. Liddell Hart, pp. 8–9.
37. *Ibid.,* pp. 10–11.
38. Testimony of General Véron, *Evénements,* Vol. V, pp. 1269ff.
39. *Ibid.,* pp. 1292–1293.
40. Testimony of General Vallet, *ibid.,* p. 1387.
41. Roton, *op. cit.,* p. 162.
42. Goutard, *op. cit.,* p. 247.
43. Roton, *op. cit.,* p. 163.
44. Testimony of General Véron, *Evénements,* Vol. V, p. 1294.
45. *Ibid.,* p. 1295; Roton, *op. cit.,* p. 166.
46. Testimony of General Bruneau, *Evénements,* Vol. V, p. 1187.
47. *Ibid.,* pp. 1172–1173.
48. Goutard, *op. cit.,* p. 249.
49. Roton, *op. cit.,* p. 165.
50. Testimony of General Georges, *Evénements,* Vol. III, p. 715.
51. Colonel Fox and Squadron Leader d'Ornano in a study *La Percée des Ardennes,* in *La Campagne, op. cit.,* p. 111.
52. *Ibid.,* p. 108.
53. General Menu: *Lumière sur les ruines,* p. 11.
54. Testimony of General Gamelin, *Evénements,* Vol. II, pp. 525–526; also Gamelin, *op. cit.,* Vol. I, pp. 340–341.
55. Testimony of General Georges, *Evénements,* Vol. III, pp. 715–717.
56. Goutard, *op. cit.,* p. 258.
57. Testimony of General Bruneau, *Evénements,* Vol. V, p. 1182.
58. Colonel de Bardies: *La Campagne, 1939–40,* p. 138.
59. Quoted by Goutard, *op. cit.,* p. 259.
60. Minart, *op. cit.,* Vol. II, pp. 146–147.
61. Quoted by Goutard, *op. cit.,* p. 260.
62. Minart, *op. cit.,* Vol. II, p. 144.
63. Gamelin, *op. cit.,* Vol. I, p. 349.
64. Beaufre, *op. cit.,* pp. 232–235.
65. Gamelin, *op. cit.,* Vol. III, pp. 406–407.
66. *Ibid.,* p. 407.

67. Minart, *op. cit.*, Vol. II, pp. 152–153.
68. Gamelin, *op. cit.*, Vol. III, p. 412.
69. Minart, *op. cit.*, Vol. II, p. 156.
70. *Ibid.*, p. 159.
71. *Ibid.*, p. 153.
72. *Ibid.*, p. 161.
73. *Ibid.*, p. 163.
74. Baudouin, *op. cit.*, p. 53.
75. Reynaud, *Cœur, op. cit.*, pp. 449–450.
76. *Ibid.*, pp. 450–451; Churchill's version of the telephone conversation: *Memoirs*, Vol. II: *Their Finest Hour*, p. 42.
77. Churchill, *op. cit.*, p. 43.
78. Reynaud, *Cœur, op. cit.*, p. 452.
79. Bullitt telegram, No. 690, May 15, 1940. Pertinax, *op. cit.*, Vol. I, pp. 91–92. He gives the version as he got it from the Ambassador.
80. Gordon Wright: "Ambassador Bullitt and the Fall of France." Article in *World Politics*, No. 1, October 1957, p. 83.
81. Bullitt telegram, No. 646, May 13, 1940.
82. Bullitt telegram, No. 692, May 16. *Foreign Relations, 1940*, Vol. I, pp. 200–201.
83. Bullitt telegram, No. 728, May 17. *Ibid.*, p. 226.
84. Monzie, *op. cit.*, pp. 226–227.
85. Bullitt telegram, No. 728. *Foreign Relations, 1940*, Vol. I, pp. 226–227.
86. Bullitt telegram, No. 665. This one is in *Foreign Relations of the United States, 1940*, Vol. I, pp. 220–222. His previous telegram describing the Gamelin-Daladier telephone conversation is not published in this volume. A good many of Bullitt's dispatches during these days, including some of the most important and dramatic, are not—for unaccountable reasons—published in the State Department volumes. I learned this while perusing all of them at the National Archives. In this respect the Department does not seem to have given a damn for historians, or for their readers.

87. Baudouin, *op. cit.*, p. 54.
88. Gamelin, *op. cit.*, Vol. III, p. 408.
89. Baudouin, *op. cit.*, p. 55.
90. Monzie, *op. cit.*, pp. 220–223, for his account of the morning of May 16.
91. Pertinax, *op. cit.*, Vol. I, pp. 287–288 and footnote.
92. Letter of Gamelin to *L'Aurore*, a Paris newspaper, November 21, 1949.
93. Churchill's account of the meeting in Paris, May 16, 1940, is given in his *Memoirs*, Vol. II, *op. cit.*, pp. 45–61; the French minutes of the meeting, kept by Margerie, are given textually in Reynaud, *Cœur, op. cit.*, pp. 454–457; Reynaud adds commentary of his own, *ibid.*, pp. 458–461. Baudouin's account is in his memoirs, *op. cit.*, pp. 56–58.
94. Lyet, *op. cit.*, pp. 64–65; Roton, *op. cit.*, p. 186, gives the text of Order No. 14.
95. Roton, *op. cit.*, p. 194.

31. THE BATTLE OF FRANCE, III: DISASTER IN FLANDERS AND THE SURRENDER OF BELGIUM MAY 16–JUNE 4, 1940

1. General Bruché gave a detailed account of the fate of the 2nd Armored Division in his testimony before the Parliamentary Investigating Committee. *Evénements*, Vol. V, pp. 1213–1252.
2. De Gaulle, *op. cit.*, Vol. I, pp. 30–31.
3. De Gaulle gives an account of his two armored attacks on May 17 and 20, and of his thoughts during the battles, in his memoirs, *op. cit.*, Vol. I, pp. 31–34.
4. Hitler to Mussolini, May 18, 1940. DGFP, Vol. IX, p. 375.
5. War Diary, Army Group B, May 16, 1940. Jacobsen, *op. cit.*, p. 38, gives the text.
6. Guderian, *op. cit.*, pp. 87–88.
7. Marcel Thiry: *La Belgique pendant la guerre*, p. 68. Quoted by Reynaud, *Cœur, op. cit.*, p. 447.

8. *Rapport de la Commission d'Information instituée par S.M. Léopold III,* 1947, p. 203. Quoted by Reynaud, *Cœur, op. cit.,* pp. 447–448. The Ambassador's letter was dated September 12, 1940, after Belgium had been occupied by the Germans. The quotations of the King and Premier Pierlot are taken from Articles V and VI in a series the latter wrote after the war for *Le Soir* of Brussels which was published in that newspaper between July 5 and 19, 1947, under the title: *Pages d'histoire.* The Premier gives a good many quotations from the official *Rapport.*

9. Roton, *op. cit.,* pp. 199–200.

10. Pierlot, Article VI, *op. cit.*

11. General Pierre Héring: *La Vie exemplaire de Philippe Pétain,* p. 77.

12. Pertinax, *op. cit.,* Vol. I, p. 244.

13. Langer: *Our Vichy Gamble,* pp. 10–11. Langer says Léger told him this in a conversation on July 3, 1944. Léger confirmed this to me in a talk in Washington on February 27, 1964.

14. Bullitt telegram, May 18, 1940. *Foreign Relations,* Vol. I. pp. 228–229.

15. Bullitt telegram, May 18, 1940. Unpublished. Quoted by Wright in article, *op. cit.,* p. 82.

16. Churchill, *op. cit.,* Vol. II, p. 56.

17. Reynaud publishes the text of Nordling's statement in Vol. II of his memoirs, *Envers et contre tous,* p. 509.

18. Gamelin, *op. cit.,* Vol. III, p. 415.

19. *Ibid.,* pp. 416–419.

20. Reynaud, *Cœur, op. cit.,* p. 462.

21. Gamelin, *op. cit.,* Vol. III, p. 417.

22. *Ibid.,* p. 427.

23. Minart, *op. cit.,* Vol. II, pp. 184–185.

24. General Georges' deposition at Riom. The text is given in Reynaud, *Cœur, op. cit.,* pp. 500–504.

25. Testimony of General Georges, February 12, 1948, *Evénements,* Vol. III, pp. 689–691.

26. Testimony of General Gamelin, *Evénements,* Vol. II, pp. 403–404.

27. General Georges' deposition at Riom. Cited by Reynaud, *Cœur, op. cit.,* p. 502.

28. Gamelin, *op. cit.,* Vol. III, p. 430.

29. General Beaufre, *op. cit.,* pp. 238–239.

30. Gamelin, *op. cit.,* Vol. III, p. 431.

31. Baudouin, *op. cit.,* p. 60.

32. Gamelin, *op. cit.,* Vol. I, pp. 5–8; Vol. III, pp. 432–434.

33. Colonel de Bardies, *op. cit.,* pp. 191–192.

34. Testimony of Guy La Chambre, former Air Minister, *Evénements,* Vol. II, pp. 353–354.

35. Gamelin, *op. cit.,* Vol. III, p. 434.

36. Colonel R. Villate: "Le Changement de commandement de mai 1940," in the *Revue d'Histoire de la Deuxième Guerre Mondiale,* No. 5, January 1952, pp. 28–29.

37. Gamelin's account of his last meeting with Weygand is given in his memoirs, *op. cit.,* Vol. III, pp. 435–437; Weygand's version is in his *Mémoires: Rappelé au Service,* p. 87.

38. Gamelin, *op. cit.,* Vol. III, p. 437.

39. De Gaulle, *op. cit.,* Vol. I, pp. 40–41.

40. Ellis, *op. cit.,* pp. 77–81.

41. Testimony of General Georges, *Evénements,* Vol. III, p. 738.

42. Roton, *op. cit.,* p. 207; Villate, *op. cit.,* p. 32.

43. Lyet, *op. cit.,* pp. 84–85.

44. Report of Major Vautrin. Quoted by Reynaud, *Cœur, op. cit.,* pp. 557–558.

45. Sources for the conference at Ypres, May 21, 1940. *Belgian:* King Leopold's version is given in the Report of the Committee of Inquiry, *op. cit.,* under *Rapport . . . , Annexes,* pp. 56–59, 67–68. Reynaud, *Cœur, op. cit.,* pp. 511–521, quotes its pages on the conference. The texts of letters exchanged between the King and Premier Pierlot are given in the *Rapport* and also published by Reynaud, *Cœur, op. cit.,* pp. 518–

521. Pierlot's own version is given in Article VII of his series in *Le Soir*, this one published on July 12, 1947, entitled *La Conférence d'Ypres*. General Van Overstraeten gives his account in his *Albert I–Léopold III. Vingt ans de politique militaire Belge, 1920–1940*, p. 649 and Annex II, p. 379. General Michiels, *op. cit.*, pp. 136–142, also covers it.

French: Weygand's own account is in his *Rappelé, op. cit.*, pp. 95–105. Reynaud, *Cœur, op. cit.*, pp. 551–563, gives two reports of Major Vautrin, liaison officer of the French First Army with the BEF, depicting the behavior of the leading French and British generals at this time.

British: Ellis, *op. cit.*, pp. 106–111, gives a detailed account of the meeting. Gort gives a briefer one in his Report, Second Dispatch, published as a supplement to the *London Gazette*, October 17, 1941, p. 5918.

46. Bloch, *op. cit.*, pp. 147–148.
47. Bardies, *op. cit.*, p. 219.
48. General Nyssens: "Lord Gort avait raison," an article in the review, *L'Armée, La Nation*, May 1, 1953; and General Michiels, *op. cit.*, p. 142.
49. Gort Report, *op. cit.*, pp. 5920–5921.
50. Gamelin, *op. cit.*, Vol. I, pp. 15–16.
51. The text is in Churchill, *op. cit.*, Vol. II, p. 65; and in the French minutes of the meeting which the Germans published in the *Wilhelmstrasse Documents, op. cit.*, p. 134.
52. Commandant J. Weygand: *The Role of General Weygand*, p. 65. Quoted by Ellis, *op. cit.*, p. 125.
53. Churchill, *op. cit.*, Vol. II, p. 64.
54. Lyet, *op. cit.*, p. 96.
55. Text in Reynaud, *Cœur, op. cit.*, pp. 533–534; Churchill, *op. cit.*, Vol. II, p. 71; Ellis, *op. cit.*, pp. 141–142.
56. Lyet, *op. cit.*, pp. 93–94.
57. *Ibid.*, p. 96.
58. *Ibid.*, p. 98.
59. Gort Report, *op. cit.*, p. 5921.
60. *Ibid.*, p. 5920.
61. Spears, *op. cit.*, Vol. I, pp. 181–185.
62. Lyet, *op. cit.*, p. 99. General Spears' account of the meeting, Spears, *op. cit.*, Vol. I, pp. 182–196; Baudouin's version in Baudouin, *op. cit.*, pp. 78–81.
63. Louis Marin: "Gouvernement et commandement (mai–juin 1940)," an article in the *Revue d'Histoire de la Deuxième Guerre Mondiale*, No. 8, October 1952, p. 5.
64. Baudouin, *op. cit.*, pp. 74–76.
65. *Ibid.*, p. 77.
66. Cross-examination of Baudouin by Dhers, *Evénements*, Vol. VII, pp. 2108–2109.
67. Baudouin, *op. cit.*, p. 72.
68. Testimony of General Weygand, *Evénements*, Vol. VI, p. 1695.
69. Testimony of Baudouin, *Evénements*, Vol. VII, p. 2044.
70. Baudouin's minutes of the meeting of the Comité de Guerre on May 25, as corrected by Reynaud and added to by the version in *L'Aurore*, are published by Professor Dhers in an article "Le Comité de Guerre du 25 mai 1940" in *Campagne, op. cit.*, pp. 165–183. Like all the other articles in this book, it was originally published in the *Revue d'Histoire de la Deuxième Guerre Mondiale*, Nos. 10–11, June 1953. Reynaud, *Cœur, op. cit.*, pp. 584–589, in a section subheaded "Le procès-verbal du Comité de Guerre du 25 mai est un faux," and Baudouin, *op. cit.*, pp. 81–89, give the text as corrected by Reynaud. General Weygand, with evident satisfaction, publishes a photographed copy, plainly showing what the Premier crossed out, in his *Mémoires: Rappelé, op. cit.*, Appendix IX.
71. Baudouin, *op. cit.*, p. 92.
72. Reynaud, *Cœur, op. cit.*, p. 601; Churchill, Vol. II, *op. cit.*, p. 123.

73. *Ibid.*, pp. 89–91, on his talks May 26 with Weygand, Pétain, and Chautemps.
74. *Ibid.*, p. 93.
75. *GAI Ordre No. 30–4517*, 25 mai, 23 h. 50. Cited by Lyet, *op. cit.*, p. 103, and published in full by Ellis, *op. cit.*, p. 172.
76. Roton, *op. cit.*, p. 234. Roton, p. 234, and Lyet, *op. cit.*, p. 106, in footnotes give the numbers of two messages from Weygand and GHQ approving Blanchard's move.
77. Roton, *op. cit.*, pp. 234–235.
78. Text in Gort Report, p. 5924, and in Ellis, *op. cit.*, pp. 173–174.
79. Eden memoirs, *The Reckoning*, p. 128.
80. Gort Report, *op. cit.*, p. 5924.
81. Bourget, *De Beyrouth à Bordeaux*, p. 53.
82. Reynaud, *Cœur, op. cit.*, p. 694.
83. The King's own account of the meeting is given in the Belgian *Rapport, op. cit., Annexes*, pp. 69–70. Pierlot's more detailed account, *ibid.*, pp. 71–75. Pierlot also wrote a long article on it in his series *Pages d'histoire*. It is No. VIII, entitled "La Dernière audience a Wynendaele" and published in *Le Soir*, July 14, 1947. Reynaud, using the Belgian *Rapport* and information provided him in subsequent conversations by Pierlot and Spaak, devotes a long section to the meeting in *Cœur, op. cit.*, pp. 628ff. Spaak's version is published in the Belgian *Rapport, Annexes*, pp. 156–163.
84. General Michiels, *op. cit.*, pp. 208–209.
85. *Ibid.*, pp. 210–211.
86. *Ibid.*, p. 211; and in Gort Report, *op. cit.*, pp. 5924–5925.
87. General Michiels, *op. cit.*, p. 211.
88. *Ibid.*, p. 243; a fuller text is given by Ellis, *op. cit.*, p 198.
89. General Michiels, *op. cit.*, p. 243.
90. Testimony of General Koeltz, *Evénements*, Vol. IX, pp. 2804–2805.
91. *Ibid.*, p. 2806.
92. Gort Report, *op. cit.*, p. 5927.
93. *Ibid.*, p. 5927.
94. Spears, *op. cit.*, Vol. I, p. 248.
95. General Michiels, *op. cit.*, pp. 243–250.
96. Texts of message to diplomatic missions and of Leopold's notes on his meeting with Hitler are in the Belgian *Rapport, op. cit., Annexes*, pp. 202 and 206ff. Both are cited by Pierlot in Article XII of his series in *Le Soir*, July 19, 1947. The Premier's comments are from the same source.
97. Churchill, *op. cit.*, Vol. II, pp. 90, 100.
98. Testimony of General Koeltz, *Evénements*, Vol. IX, p. 2806.
99. Weygand, *Rappelé, op. cit.*, p. 127.
100. Churchill, *op. cit.*, Vol. II, p. 86.
101. Weygand, *Rappelé, op. cit.*, p. 126.
102. General Pownall's account of the meeting is quoted by Churchill, *op. cit.*, Vol. II, pp. 92–95.
103. Gort Report, *op. cit.*, p. 5927, para. 52.
104. The French version of the meeting is given in a report by Colonel Humbert, Chief of Staff of Army Group 1, and quoted in part by Lyet, *op. cit.*, p. 109, footnote No. 66.
105. Blanchard's telegram, No. 1229 D/3 of May 28, and Weygand's reply, telegram No. 1237 FT of May 29, are quoted by Lyet, *op. cit.*, p. 111, footnote.
106. Bardies, *op. cit.*, p. 244.
107. Barlone: *A French Officer's Diary*, pp. 56–57.
108. Sources for the meeting: Reynaud, *Cœur, op. cit.*, pp. 694–697; Weygand, *Rappelé*, pp. 129–130; Baudouin, who reproduces his notes on the session, *op. cit.*, pp. 107–114; Churchill, *op. cit.*, Vol. II, pp. 109–113; Spears, *op. cit.*, Vol. I, pp. 294–317.
109. The text of the notes exchanged is given by Reynaud, *Cœur, op. cit.*, pp. 684–687.

110. General Colson, *Chef d'état-major de l'armée,* disclosed this to General Spears on May 26. Spears, *op. cit.,* Vol. I, p. 220.
111. Baudouin, *op. cit.,* p. 118.
112. Churchill, *op. cit.,* Vol. II, p. 115; Ellis, *op. cit.,* p. 245.
113. Dispatch of Bullitt, June 4, 1940. *Foreign Relations of the United States, 1940,* Vol. I, pp. 238–239.
114. Dispatch of Bullitt, June 5, 1940, *ibid.,* pp. 240–241.
115. Weygand, *Rappelé, op. cit.,* p. 132.

32. THE FALL OF PARIS
    JUNE 5–14, 1940

1. Minutes of the meeting of the War Committee, May 25. Dhers article, *op. cit.,* p. 171.
2. Testimony of General Bertrand, *Evénements,* Vol. VI, p. 1800.
3. The quotations from de Gaulle and General Prételat are in Goutard, *op. cit.,* pp. 338–339. General Bührer's declaration to Mandel is cited by Goutard, p. 339, from Bührer's book: *Aux heures tragiques de l'empire.*
4. De Gaulle, *op. cit.,* Vol. I, p. 39.
5. Ellis, *op. cit.,* pp. 319–320.
6. Testimony of Rollin, *Evénements,* Vol. VII, p. 2136; also Rollin's *Journal,* cited by Reynaud, *Cœur, op. cit.,* p. 571.
7. Baudouin, *op. cit.,* p. 89.
8. *Ibid.,* p. 126.
9. Baudouin, *op. cit.,* p. 130.
10. Spears, *op. cit.,* Vol. II, p. 85. Weygand on De Gaulle: Reynaud, *Cœur, op. cit.,* p. 707; Baudouin, *op. cit.,* p. 143.
11. Report of General Georges to General Weygand. Lyet, *op. cit.,* pp. 130–131, footnote No. 31.
12. Reynaud, *Cœur, op. cit.,* p. 715.
13. Sources for the meetings, June 5, 6: *ibid.,* pp. 715–726; Baudouin, *op. cit.,* pp. 120–125, 127–130, respectively; Spears, *op. cit.,* Vol. II, pp. 51–58, 74–80, respectively.
14. De Gaulle, *op. cit.,* Vol. I, pp. 50–51.
15. *Ibid.,* pp. 44–45.
16. *Ibid.,* p. 49.
17. *Ibid.,* p. 60.
18. Baudouin, *op. cit.,* pp. 133–134.
19. *Ibid.,* pp. 134–135.
20. Albert Lebrun, *op. cit.,* p. 73.
21. Baudouin, *op. cit.,* pp. 138–144, on the meeting of June 10 and Weygand's remarks afterward. Baudouin, *op. cit.,* pp. 140–142, and Reynaud, *Cœur, op. cit.,* pp. 728–729, give the text of Weygand's note to the Premier.
22. De Gaulle, *op. cit.,* Vol. I, p. 55.
23. Spears, *op. cit.,* Vol. II, pp. 162–163, and Churchill, *op. cit.,* pp. 127, 156, recount Anglo-French plans for operations against Italy and General Vuillemin's refusal to let the bombers take off. For the French naval bombardment and Darlan's orders forbidding a further one, Draper, *op. cit.,* p. 267, and Ciano, *op. cit.,* diary entry for June 15, p. 264.
24. De Gaulle, *op. cit.,* Vol. I, pp. 49–50; Alexander Werth: *The Last Days of Paris,* p. 156.
25. Dispatch of Bullitt to Roosevelt, June 10, 1940. *Foreign Relations, op. cit.,* Vol. I, pp. 244–245.
26. The text of Reynaud's message to Roosevelt is given in a second dispatch of Bullitt to the President, June 10, *ibid.,* pp. 245–246.
27. GQG Order No. 1210–3/F.T. Cited by Commandant Pierre Lyet in an article in the *Revue Historique de l'Armée,* June 1948, entitled "Paris 'Ville Ouverte,' " p. 84.
28. Lyet article, *op. cit.,* p. 85, from army records.
29. GQG Instruction No. 1430–3/F.T. Cited in Lyet article, *op. cit.,* p. 85.
30. General Héring's records, cited in Lyet article, *op. cit.,* pp. 86–87.
31. Churchill, *op. cit.,* Vol. II, p. 153.
32. GQG *Lettre* No. 1503–3/F.T. Quoted in Lyet article, *op. cit.,* p. 85.
33. *Ibid.,* p. 88.

34. Testimony of General Georges, *Evénements*, Vol. III, pp. 739–740.
35. Testimony of General Weygand at Pétain's trial on July 31, 1945, p. 388 of the stenographic account.
36. From General Dentz's report, quoted in Lyet article, *op. cit.*, p. 90.
37. The German terms are given in Lyet article, *op. cit.*, p. 88.
38. Lyet, *Bataille, op. cit.*, p. 131.
39. *Ibid.*, p. 89.

33. THE FLIGHT TO BORDEAUX
    JUNE 11–14, 1940

1. Baudouin, *op. cit.*, p. 146.
2. Spears, *op. cit.*, Vol. II, pp. 190–192.
3. Weygand's "Secret and Personal Instruction," No. 1444–3/F.T., June 11, 1940. Cited by Lyet, *op. cit.*, pp. 131–132; Roton; Goutard; and others.
4. The French minutes of the meeting of the Supreme Council at Briare on June 11, kept by Roland de Margerie, Reynaud's *chef de cabinet,* are given textually in Reynaud, *Cœur, op. cit.*, pp. 747–757; Reynaud's own account of both meetings, *ibid.*, pp. 740–747; Weygand's account, *Rappelé, op. cit.*, pp. 200–206. Churchill's report is given in his memoirs, *op. cit.*, Vol. II, pp. 152–160; it is based, he says, on the record kept by General Ismay. Spears' colorful account is in his journal, *op. cit.*, Vol. II, pp. 138–171.
5. Churchill, *op. cit.*, Vol. II, pp. 158–160.
6. Reynaud, *Cœur, op. cit.*, p. 747.
7. Spears, *op. cit.*, Vol. II, pp. 174–177.
8. Lyet, *op. cit.*, p. 132.
9. Weygand, *Rappelé, op. cit.*, pp. 206–208.
10. Deposition of Weygand at Riom, August 26, 1940. Text in *Evénements*, Vol. II (Docs.), p. 410.

11. Louis Marin: "Contribution à l'étude des prodromes de l'armistice," an article in the *Revue d'Histoire de la Deuxième Guerre Mondiale*, No. 3, June 1951, p. 4. (Hereafter referred to as Marin: Armistice article.)
12. Sources for the cabinet meeting, June 12, 1940: besides Weygand's Riom deposition, *op. cit.*, see his *Rappelé, op. cit.*, pp. 209–214; Reynaud, *Cœur, op. cit.*, pp. 759–762; Baudouin, *op. cit.*, pp. 147–152, including his account of the midnight repast; Camille Chautemps: *Cahiers secrets de l'armistice, 1939–1940*, pp. 118–130; Marin: Armistice article, *op. cit.*, pp. 4–5.
13. Spears, *op. cit.*, Vol. II, pp. 190–196.
14. Bois, *op. cit.*, pp. 354–355.
15. Spears, *op. cit.*, Vol. II, p. 215.
16. Baudouin, *op. cit.*, p. 159.
17. Churchill, *op. cit.*, Vol. II, p. 182.
18. Cable, Churchill to Roosevelt, *ibid.*, pp. 184–185. The text is also in *Foreign Relations, op. cit.*, Vol. I, pp. 250–251.
19. De Gaulle, *op. cit.*, Vol. I, pp. 57–58.
20. Sources for the last Allied Supreme Council meeting at Tours, June 13, 1940: the French minutes, drawn up by Margerie, were first published by him in *Le Figaro*, May 30, 1948. Reynaud, *Cœur, op. cit.*, pp. 769–774, publishes the text; his own account, *ibid.*, pp. 764–769; Baudouin's account, with its glaring omission of Churchill's repeated refusal to release France from its obligations, is given in his journal, *op. cit.*, pp. 153–159. Churchill's account is in his memoirs, *op. cit.*, Vol. II, pp. 178–183; Spears' version is in his journal, *op. cit.*, Vol. II, pp. 199–220.
21. Churchill, *op. cit.*, Vol. II, p. 183.
22. Cross-examination of Weygand, June 21, 1949, *Evénements*, Vol. VI, p. 1844ff.

23. Testimony of Mattéo Connet, *Evénements,* Vol. VII, pp. 2187–2188.
24. Testimony of Weygand, *Evénements,* Vol. VI, p. 1565; *Rappelé op. cit.,* p. 216.
25. Spears, *op. cit.,* Vol. II, p. 222.
26. Testimony of Lebrun, *Evénements,* Vol. IV, p. 996.
27. Spears, *op. cit.,* p. 223.
28. The text of the paper read by Pétain is given in Kammerer: *La Vérité sur l'armistice,* Annexe XVI, p. 408.
29. Quoted by Reynaud, *Cœur, op. cit.,* p. 781, footnote. The sources for the cabinet meeting at Cangé, June 13, 1940: Reynaud, *Cœur, op. cit.,* pp. 777–784, and *Envers, op. cit.,* p. 405; Weygand, *Rappelé, op. cit.,* pp. 215–220; Weygand's deposition at Riom, *op. cit.;* Weygand's testimony before the Parliamentary Investigating Committee, *Evénements,* Vol. VI, pp. 1564–1565; testimony of Lebrun, *ibid.,* Vol. IV, p. 996; testimony of Georges Monnet, *ibid.,* Vol. V, p. 1424; testimony of Mattéo Connet, *ibid.,* Vol. VII, pp. 2187–2195; Baudouin, *op. cit.,* pp. 159–164; two articles by Louis Marin: Armistice article, *op. cit.,* pp. 8–11, and "Gouvernement et commandement (mai–juin 1940)" in the *Revue d'Histoire de la Deuxième Guerre Mondiale,* No. 8, October 1952, pp. 7–22 (hereafter noted as Marin: Article I); Kammerer, *op. cit.,* pp. 125–135; Chautemps, *op. cit.,* pp. 130–136; Robert Aron: *Histoire de Vichy, 1940–1944,* pp. 19–23; Spears, *op. cit.,* Vol. II, pp. 222–229, recounting what Mandel told him of the cabinet meeting.
30. Testimony of Connet, *Evénements,* Vol. VII, p. 2188.
31. Baudouin, *op. cit.,* p. 166.
32. Weygand gives the text of Pétain's message in *Rappelé, op. cit.,* p. 224.
33. Marin: Armistice article, *op. cit.,* p. 11.
34. Weygand, *Rappelé, op. cit.,* pp. 224–225.
35. Reynaud gives the text of his appeal to Roosevelt in *Cœur, op. cit.,* pp. 789–790.
36. Cordell Hull, *Memoirs,* Vol. I, pp. 767–768.
37. Spears, *op. cit.,* Vol. II, p. 228.
38. Dispatch of Biddle, June 14, 1940. *Foreign Relations, op. cit.,* Vol. I, pp. 253–254.

34. THE AGONY OF BORDEAUX. THE FALL OF REYNAUD. PÉTAIN TAKES OVER   JUNE 14–16, 1940

1. Jacques Bardoux: *Journal d'un témoin de la Troisième, 1ᵉʳ septembre 1939–15 juillet 1940,* p. 363.
2. De Gaulle, *op. cit.,* Vol. I, p. 59.
3. *Ibid.,* p. 60.
4. *Ibid.,* p. 60.
5. Spears, *op. cit.,* Vol. II, p. 243.
6. Edouard Herriot: *Episodes. 1940–1944,* p. 65.
7. Baudouin himself recounts telling the tale, in his journal, *op. cit.,* p. 168.
8. Weygand's deposition at Riom, August 26, 1940. *Evénements,* Vol. II (Docs.), p. 412.
9. Testimony of General Georges at the Pétain trial. Albin Michel transcript, Vol. I, p. 400. (Though this transcript purports to be the *"compte rendu sténographique,"* it is slightly abridged.) The text of General Georges' telegram to Weygand and his account of his meeting with his generals are given in Roton, *op. cit.,* pp. 285–287.
10. Exchange between Pétain and Weygand at the former's trial, session of July 31, 1945. Transcript, Vol. I, pp. 421–422. Reynaud, *Cœur, op. cit.,* pp. 821–822, gives a somewhat fuller version from the official transcript.
11. Chautemps, *op. cit.,* p. 155.
12. Reynaud, *Cœur, op. cit.,* pp. 809–810.
13. Reynaud, *Cœur, op. cit.,* pp. 807–808. Sources for the cabinet meeting and particularly for the Chau-

temps proposal and the scene it provoked: Chautemps, *op. cit.*, pp. 154–164; Reynaud, *Cœur, op. cit.*, pp. 802–813, and *Envers, op. cit.*, pp. 418–424; also his "Reply to Chautemps," in *Le Monde*, November 23, 1963, p. 10; testimony of Lebrun at the Pétain trial, July 25, 1945, Transcript, Vol. I, p. 155; Marin: Armistice article, *op. cit.*, p. 13. Marin, a minister, was present; Baudouin, *op. cit.*, pp. 169–170. He also was present.

14. Baudouin, *op. cit.*, p. 170.

15. Monzie, *op. cit.*, p. 248.

16. Reynaud, *Cœur, op. cit.*, p. 818.

17. There are several versions of the row. Weygand, *Rappelé, op cit.*, pp. 227–228; his deposition at the Riom trial, *Evénements*, Vol. II (Docs.), pp. 412–413; and Weygand's testimony at the Pétain trial on July 31, 1945, and before the Parliamentary Investigating Committee in 1949; Reynaud, *Cœur, op. cit.*, pp. 813–817, and his testimony at the Pétain trial and before the Parliamentary Investigating Committee; Bouthillier, *op. cit.*, p. 25 (he was a witness to the scene); Bourget, *op. cit.*, pp. 130–132 (he was also a witness).

18. Testimony of General Georges, *Evénements*, Vol. III, p. 742.

19. Telegram of General Georges, No. 2115–3/Op., June 22, 1940. Cited by Lyet, *op. cit.*, p. 146, footnote.

20. Weygand, *Rappelé, op. cit.*, pp. 266–267 and footnote.

21. Lyet, *op. cit.*, p. 149.

22. Gamelin, *op. cit.*, Vol. III, p. 459.

23. Goutard, *op. cit.*, p. 394.

24. Churchill, *op. cit.*, Vol. II, p. 202.

25. Spears, *op. cit.*, Vol. II, p. 272. Tony Révillon: *Mes Carnets (juin-octobre 1940)*, p. 15. Senator Révillon noted the statement of Weygand in his diary for June 15.

26. Révillon, *op. cit.*, diary entries for June 15, 18, pp. 15–16; 44, 48, respectively.

27. Dispatch of Biddle, June 15, 1940, 5 P.M. *Foreign Relations, op. cit.*, Vol. I, pp. 256–257.

28. Dispatch of Biddle, June 16, 1940, 1 A.M. *Ibid.*, p. 258.

29. *Ibid.*

30. Reynaud, *Cœur, op. cit.*, p. 808.

31. *Ibid.*, pp. 823–824.

32. The text of Roosevelt's cable to Reynaud, June 15, 1940, is given in *Foreign Relations, op. cit.*, Vol. I, pp. 255–256; Reynaud gives a French translation in *Cœur, op. cit.*, pp. 823–824.

33. Since Reynaud in his memoirs and postwar testimony refrained from more than barely mentioning his meeting with Campbell and Spears on Saturday evening, June 15, the principal source remains Spears, *op. cit.*, Vol. II, pp. 263–273. He gives the "sense" of Reynaud's note to Churchill, though it appears to be the text. Spears' journal, in the view of some French historians and of Reynaud, as he himself told me, is not always accurate. ("He is a bit romantic," Amouroux complains.) But his notes for this meeting are largely substantiated by Ambassador Biddle's two telegrams of the day— see *Foreign Relations, op. cit.*, Vol. I, pp. 256–257 and 258–259, respectively. Biddle got his account from two meetings with Reynaud, one just after the cabinet meeting at 7 P.M. and the other at midnight after the Premier's long session with the two British envoys, with whom, Biddle says, he also talked.

34. Dispatch of Biddle, 1 A.M., June 16. *Foreign Relations, op. cit.*, Vol. I, pp. 258–259.

35. Spears, *op. cit.*, Vol. II, pp. 278–280.

36. Kammerer, *op. cit.*, pp. 174–175. See also confirmation from Henri Queuille, Minister of Food, in the June 8, 1943, number of *France*, a French language daily published in London during the war. Pertinax, *op. cit.*, Vol. I, p. 356, believed Laval was the author of the letter.

37. Reynaud, *Cœur, op. cit.*, p. 819;

Lebrun, *op. cit.*, p. 82, and testimony at the Pétain trial, July 25, 1945, Transcript, Vol. I, p. 156; Kammerer, *op. cit.*, pp. 174–175. Baudouin and Bouthillier also recount the meeting but their version differs so much from the others that it seems worthless on this occasion at least. Baudouin's time sequence for the two crucial days is completely muddled.

38. Weygand, *Rappelé, op. cit.*, pp. 229–233.

39. Reynaud, *Cœur, op. cit.*, pp. 819–820.

40. Reynaud, *Cœur, op. cit.*, pp. 823, 826; Spears, *op. cit.*, Vol. II, pp. 282–286.

41. Weygand, *Rappelé, op. cit.*, pp. 232–233.

42. The texts of the two British telegrams on Sunday, June 16, 1940, are given in Churchill, *op. cit.*, Vol. II, pp. 206–207, and in Spears, *op. cit.*, Vol. II, pp. 282, 289–290.

43. Sources for the telephone call between London and Bordeaux, Sunday, June 16: Reynaud, *Cœur, op. cit.*, pp. 827–830; De Gaulle, *op. cit.*, Vol. I, pp. 64–65; Spears, *op. cit.*, Vol. II, pp. 291–293. Churchill, *op. cit.*, Vol. II, pp. 208–209, gives the text of the proposed Declaration of Union.

44. On the origins of the Declaration: De Gaulle, *op. cit.*, Vol. I, pp. 61–63; Churchill, *op. cit.*, Vol. II, pp. 204–209. Memorandum of René Pleven, London, June 22, 1940.

45. De Gaulle, *op. cit.*, Vol. I, pp. 63–65; Churchill, *op. cit.*, Vol. II, p. 207.

46. De Gaulle, *op. cit.*, Vol. I, p. 64; Reynaud, *Cœur, op. cit.*, p. 827.

47. Spears, *op. cit.*, Vol. II, pp. 292–293.

48. Text of message telephoned by the Foreign Office to Bordeaux at 8 P.M., June 16. Churchill, *op. cit.*, Vol. II, p. 211.

49. De Gaulle, *op. cit.*, Vol. I, p. 64.

50. Weygand, *Rappelé, op. cit.*, pp. 223, 230–231; Ellis, *op. cit.*, pp.

297–300; Churchill, *op. cit.*, Vol. II, pp. 192–194.

51. Marin: Armistice article, *op. cit.*, p. 17.

52. Pertinax, *op. cit.*, Vol. I, p. 365.

53. The message from Georges was telephoned to General Lafont at 5:35 P.M. for communication to General Weygand, who sent it in to Lebrun by Lafont. The text is given in many works, i.e., Reynaud, *Envers, op. cit.*, p. 433, and *Cœur, op. cit.*, pp. 836–837; Robert Aron, *Vichy, op. cit.*, p. 49; Lyet, *op. cit.*, p. 140.

54. There are many sources for the last Reynaud cabinet session on Sunday, June 16: Reynaud, *Cœur, op. cit.*, pp. 830–838; *Envers, op. cit.*, pp. 429–433; testimony of Reynaud at the Pétain trial, Transcript, Vol. I, p. 94; his testimony before the Parliamentary Investigating Committee, *Evénements,* Vol. VIII, pp. 2421–2430; letters from Reynaud to the author, August 29, 1965, and March 28, 1966; Lebrun, *op. cit.*, p. 97; his testimony at the Pétain trial, Transcript, Vol. I, pp. 156–158, 181, and before the Parliamentary Investigating Committee, *Evénements,* Vol. VI, p. 976. Also: Marin: Armistice article, *op. cit.*, pp. 14–21; testimony of Georges Monnet before the Parliamentary Investigating Committee, *Evénements,* Vol. V, pp. 1427–1430; Chautemps, *op. cit.*, pp. 159–180; all the above were participants. For others: Charles-Roux, *Cinq mois tragiques aux affaires étrangères,* pp. 45–47; Spears, *op. cit.*, Vol. II, pp. 296–299; Amouroux, *Le 18 juin,* pp. 63–72; Robert Aron, *Vichy, op. cit.*, pp. 49–51; Kammerer, *op. cit.*, pp. 188–195.

55. Letter of Reynaud to author, August 29, 1965.

56. Reynaud, *Envers, op. cit.*, p. 432.

57. Marin: Armistice article, *op. cit.*, pp. 22–23; Amouroux, *op. cit.*, p. 69, footnote.

58. Reynaud, *Cœur, op. cit.*, p. 835.

59. Exchange between Marin and Reynaud before the Parliamentary Investigating Committee, *Evénements,* Vol. VIII, pp. 2422–2426.
60. Lebrun, *op. cit.,* p. 84.
61. Quoted by Reynaud, *Cœur, op. cit.,* pp. 839–840, from the unabridged stenographic account. See Transcript, Vol. I, p. 167ff.
62. Quoted by Reynaud from the Pétain trial in his testimony before the Parliamentary Investigating Committee, *Evénements,* Vol. VIII, p. 2424.
63. Dispatch of Biddle, June 16, 1940, 9 P.M. *Foreign Relations, op. cit.,* Vol. I, pp. 260–261.
64. Exchange between Paul Bastid and Paul Reynaud during the latter's testimony before the Parliamentary Investigating Committee, December 12, 1950. *Evénements,* Vol. VIII, p. 2426.
65. The text of Reynaud's letter to Pétain is given in Kammerer, *op. cit.,* pp. 216–217.
66. Spears, *op. cit.,* Vol. II, pp. 297–299; the text of Campbell's telephoned message is given in Churchill, *op. cit.,* Vol. II, p. 214.
67. *Ibid.,* pp. 211–212.
68. Spears, *op. cit.,* Vol. II, pp. 300–301.
69. Testimony of Lebrun, *Evénements,* Vol. IV, p. 1086.
70. Sources for the meeting of Lebrun, Reynaud, Jeanneney, and Herriot: Reynaud, *Cœur, op. cit.,* pp. 838–853; his testimony at the Pétain trial, Transcript, Vol. I, pp. 67–68, and before the Parliamentary Investigating Committee, *Evénements,* Vol. VIII, pp. 2422–2429; Lebrun, *op. cit.,* p. 85; his testimony at the Pétain trial, session of July 26, 1945, and before the Parliamentary Investigating Committee, *Evénements,* Vol. IV, pp. 1086–1087; testimony of Herriot at the Pétain trial, session of July 30, 1945, and of Jeanneney, session of July 26, 1945; Spears, *op. cit.,* Vol. II, pp. 297–303.

71. Marin: Armistice article, *op. cit.,* pp. 23–24.
72. Reynaud, *Cœur, op. cit.,* p. 847.
73. Marin: Armistice article, *op. cit.,* pp. 19, 21.
74. Testimony of Georges Monnet before the Parliamentary Investigating Committee. *Evénements,* Vol. V, pp. 1429–1430.
75. Testimony of Pétain before the Parliamentary Investigating Committee, July 10, 1947. *Evénements,* Vol. I, p. 175.
76. Dispatch of Biddle, June 16, 1940, midnight. *Foreign Relations, op. cit.,* Vol. I, pp. 261–262.
77. Reynaud, *Cœur, op. cit.,* p. 855.
78. The meetings of Campbell and Spears with Reynaud and of Spears with Mandel are described in Spears, *op. cit.,* Vol. II, pp. 303–317.
79. De Gaulle, *op. cit.,* Vol. I, p. 65.
80. Spears, *op. cit.,* Vol. II, pp. 320–322; Amouroux, *op. cit.,* pp. 350–355, gives Spears' account and also the quite different French version, which he says he got from De Gaulle and Courcel.
81. De Gaulle, *op. cit.,* Vol. I, p. 67.
82. *Ibid.,* pp. 65–67.
83. *Ibid.,* p. 61.
84. Spears, *op. cit.,* Vol. II, p. 323.
85. De Gaulle, *op. cit.,* Vol. I, p. 67.
86. Amouroux, *op. cit.,* p. 78. The author says that Baudoin confirmed the story to him and that Weygand, while saying he did not recall it, declared that if Baudouin said it, "it was accurate." The generalissimo had more faith in Baudouin's accuracy than a good many others had.
87. Testimony of Pierre Laval at the Pétain trial, Transcript, Vol. I, p. 511.
88. Charles-Roux: *Cinq mois tragiques aux affaires étrangères,* p. 50.
89. Testimony of Laval at the Pétain trial, Transcript, Vol. I, p. 511.
90. Jean Zay, *op. cit.,* p. 387.
91. Quoted by Halasz, *op. cit.,* p. 249.
92. Testimony of Reynaud before the

Parliamentary Investigating Committee. *Evénements*, Vol. IX, p. 2853.

93. Amouroux, *op. cit.*, p. 12.

35. ARMISTICE! JUNE 17–29, 1940

1. Lequerica's account is given in his dispatch to Madrid and was found in the captured German documents, for his messages were immediately turned over to the German Ambassador by the Spanish government and transmitted to Berlin. Text of Lequerica's dispatch and text of French note are given in DGFP, Series D, Vol. IX, p. 590 and footnote.

2. Baudouin's account of his meeting with Campbell: *Journal, op. cit.*, pp. 177–178; also, an essay by Baudouin entitled "A propos d'un nouveau livre de M. Kammerer," published by Kammerer, *op. cit.*, 2nd edn., pp. 532–540. His statement that Campbell did not mention the two British telegrams is on p. 538. This is confirmed by Charles-Roux, *op. cit.*, p. 53.

3. Dispatch of Biddle, June 17, 1940, 2 A.M. *Foreign Relations, op. cit.*, Vol. II, pp. 455–456.

4. Churchill, *op. cit.*, Vol. II, pp. 216–217.

5. Telegram of Ambassador Corbin from London, filed June 18, 4:09 A.M. Text in *Evénements*, Vol. II (Docs.), p. 432.

6. *Evénements*, Vol. II (Docs.), pp. 384–404. In these pages the Parliamentary Investigating Committee cites a number of cases of surrender or ceasing to fight, some culled from an army investigation late in 1940. Colonel Passy's description is from his *Souvenirs de deuxième Bureau*, cited by Goutard, *op. cit.*, p. 370, footnote.

7. Memorandum of Halifax, July 12, 1940, delivered to the French chargé d'affaires in London. The essential part is given in a memorandum of Charles-Roux, August 14, 1940, *Evénements*, Vol. VII,

pp. 2077–2080. I have translated it from the French.

8. Baudouin, *op. cit.*, pp. 181–182, 184. His testimony before the Parliamentary Investigating Committee, *Evénements*, Vol. VII, pp. 2077–2080. Memorandum of Charles-Roux, *ibid.*; his book, *op. cit.*, pp. 56ff.

9. Cunningham of Hyndhope: *A Sailor's Odyssey*, p. 240.

10. Text of Roosevelt's note. *Foreign Relations, op. cit.*, Vol. II, p. 456; Hull's comment on it is in his *Memoirs, op. cit.*, Vol. I, p. 792.

11. Dispatch of Biddle, June 18, 1940, noon. *Foreign Relations, op. cit.*, Vol. II, p. 457. Baudouin, *op. cit.*, pp. 183–184.

12. Amouroux, *op. cit.* (*18 juin*), p. 246.

13. Captain (later Admiral) Auphan's report was given by Baudouin during cross-examination before the Parliamentary Investigating Committee. *Evénements*, Vol. VII, p. 2080. It is also in Auphan's book, *Histoire de mes 'trahisons.'* A British account is given in an article by P. M. H. Bell in the *Revue d'Histoire de la Deuxième Guerre Mondiale*, No. 33, January 1959, pp. 24–26. He cites from C. F. Adams: *Life of Lord Lloyd*, p. 299. See also Kammerer, *op. cit.*, pp. 264–266, 274.

14. Cited by Kammerer, *op. cit.*, p. 265, footnote, from a note of July 9, 1940, in the French Admiralty records.

15. Dispatches from the French Admiralty, June 18–21. Texts in *Evénements*, Vol. II (Docs.), pp. 447–458.

16. Amouroux, *op. cit.* (*18 juin*), pp. 248–249, footnote.

17. De Gaulle, *op. cit.*, Vol. I, p. 71.

18. Amouroux, *op. cit.* (*18 juin*), pp. 366–370.

19. De Gaulle, *op. cit.*, Vol. I, p. 74.

20. Jeanneney described the scene and furnished the dialogue, as he remembered it, in his testimony at

the Pétain trial, Vol. I, p. 188; Herriot recounted it in his memoirs, *Episodes. 1940–1944*, pp. 84–85.

21. Chautemps, *op. cit.*, pp. 193–194.
22. Memorandum of the Spanish government to Germany, June 19, 1940. Text in DGFP, Vol. IX, pp. 620–621.
23. The confidential German memorandum of the meeting of Hitler and Mussolini on June 18, 1940, at Munich is among the captured documents. Text in DGFP, Series D, Vol. IX, pp. 608–611. Ciano's account is in *The Ciano Diaries*, pp. 265–266.
24. Kammerer, *op. cit.*, p. 286.
25. Chautemps, *op. cit.*, pp. 205–206.
26. Dispatch of Lequerica, June 19. DGFP, Vol. IX, p. 622.
27. Dispatch of Lequerica, June 19. *Ibid.*, p. 629.
28. Alibert gave this account to J. C. Fernand-Laurent, who published it in his book *Gallic Charter*, which he wrote in English and which was first published in the United States in 1944, pp. 178–182. He swore to it in a deposition to the High Court.
29. Weygand, *Rappelé, op. cit.*, p. 248. *Journal* of Weygand, June 20, quoted by Lyet, *op. cit.*, p. 160.
30. Testimony of Lebrun at the Pétain trial, Vol. I, p. 160.
31. Dispatch of Lequerica, June 20. DGFP, Vol. IX, pp. 631–632.
32. Memorandum of State Secretary Weizsaecker, June 21, DGFP, Vol. IX, p. 641.
33. Jean Montigny gives an account of the scene, with direct quotations, in *Toute la vérité sur un mois dramatique de notre histoire*, pp. 25–30. Lebrun describes it in his memoirs, *op. cit.*, pp. 91–94.
34. Baudouin, *op. cit.*, p. 195.
35. Dispatch of Biddle, June 21, 1940. Quoted by Langer, *op. cit.*, pp. 52–53.
36. Baudouin, *op. cit.*, pp. 218–219, 220–221; Pertinax, *op. cit.*, Vol. I, pp. 367–368. Reynaud does not mention the affair in his *Memoirs,* but testified on it under cross-examination before the Parliamentary Investigating Committee. *Evénements*, Vol. IX, pp. 2855–2856. He was not very responsive, pleading "professional secrets."
37. On the case of Reynaud and the Washington embassy: Reynaud, *Cœur, op. cit.*, pp. 883–885; his testimony at the Pétain trial, Vol. I, pp. 71–100. Lebrun, *op. cit.*, p. 90; testimony before the Parliamentary Investigating Committee, *Evénements*, Vol. IV, p. 1017. Baudouin, *op. cit.*, pp. 185–196; Charles-Roux, *op. cit.*, p. 58; Kammerer, *op. cit.*, pp. 241ff. Matthews has confirmed to me that Reynaud discussed the ambassadorship with him and Biddle. Reynaud himself quoted Roosevelt's comment on the matter at the Pétain trial.
38. Léon Noël: *Le Diktat de Rethondes,* p. 26. Though it was published anonymously (in Paris in 1954), Noël later confirmed his authorship.
39. Charles-Roux, *op. cit.*, p. 83, quotes the exchange. It is confirmed in the German record of the telephone talk between Huntziger and Weygand on the evening of June 21. DGFP, Vol. IX, p. 652.
40. Léon Noël, *op. cit.*, p. 30.
41. Weygand, *Rappelé, op. cit.*, p. 241.
42. Orders 4 and 5 SC, June 18, signed by General Colson. *Evénements*, Vol. II (Docs.), p. 391.
43. Goutard, *op. cit.*, p. 376.
44. *Evénements*, Vol. II (Docs.), p. 401.
45. Amouroux, *Vie, op. cit.*, p. 204.
46. *Evénements*, Vol. II (Docs.), p. 403.
47. Goutard, *op. cit.*, p. 376.
48. *Evénements*, Vol. II (Docs.), p. 396.
49. *Ibid.*, pp. 397–398.
50. Amouroux, *Le 18 juin 1940, op. cit.*, pp. 129–130, 147.

51. Bardoux, *op. cit.*, p. 378.
52. *Ibid.*, pp. 128–129.
53. *Evénements,* Vol. II (Docs.), p. 394.
54. Beaufre, *op. cit.*, p. 265.
55. The trial was given full coverage in *Le Monde* of April 27 and 28, 1949, and in *France-Soir* of April 28. Saul K. Padover has given a moving account of the case in an article in *World Politics,* April 1950, "France in Defeat," pp. 324–326. Amouroux, *Vie, op. cit.*, p. 44, also gives a vivid account.
56. Telegram of General Noguès to General Weygand, June 17, 1940, No. 645 Cab/C. *Evénements,* Vol. II (Docs.), p. 416.
57. Telegram of General Weygand to Noguès, June 18, 1940, No. 2,006 3/Ft. *Ibid.*, p. 416.
58. André Truchet: *L'Armistice de 1940 et l'Afrique du Nord,* p. 116. This is the best work on the subject of North Africa.
59. Telegram of General Noguès to Pétain, June 18, 1940, Nos. 54–55–56. *Evénements,* Vol. II (Docs.), pp. 417–418.
60. Telegram of General Weygand to Noguès, June 21, 1940, No. 22/D.N. *Ibid.*, p. 418.
61. Telegram of General Noguès to Weygand, June 21, 1940, No. 674 Cab/C. *Ibid.*, pp. 418–419.
62. The French notes on the telephone talk of Huntziger and Weygand on the evening of June 21 are given in Kammerer, *op. cit.*, pp. 428–430; the German notes are in DGFP, Vol. IX, pp. 652–654. A German army communications truck recorded them.
63. DGFP, Vol. IX, pp. 665, 678.
64. Weygand, *Rappelé, op. cit.*, p. 262. Colonel Bourget to Huntziger on the telephone, June 22, DGFP, Vol. IX, pp. 663–664. Huntziger to Keitel, June 22, *ibid.*, p. 667.
65. *Ibid.*, p. 667.
66. Kammerer, *op. cit.*, p. 300. Noël testimony at Pétain trial, Vol. I, pp. 475–476. Geneviève Noel, *op. cit.*, pp. 231–232, quotes various orders of the Ministry of Interior to track down the German refugees.
67. Baudouin, *op. cit.*, p. 107; Chautemps, *op cit.*, pp. 207–210.
68. Charles-Roux, *op. cit.*, p. 84.
69. Kammerer, *op. cit.*, p. 292.
70. Baudouin, *op. cit.*, p .197.
71. Kammerer, *op. cit.*, p. 305.
72. Baudouin's false assertion that he gave the British Ambassador a copy of the armistice treaty is given in his journal, *op. cit.*, p. 198. It is interesting that this man, who lied on occasion to his ministerial colleagues, would lie to himself in his own diary. Charles-Roux's account, which sets the record straight, is given in his memoirs, *op. cit.*, pp. 87–90. François-Poncet's remarks are given in his journal, *op. cit.*, p. 89, and in Kammerer, *op. cit.*, p. 303.
73. The British message was quoted in a dispatch of Ambassador Kennedy to Hull, June 22, 1940. *Foreign Relations,* Vol. II, p. 458.
74. Darlan to all French warships and naval stations, June 23, 1940, 5:30 P.M. *Evénements,* Vol. II (Docs.), p. 464.
75. Kammerer, *op. cit.*, p. 313.
76. DGFP, Vol. IX, pp. 676–679.
77. The French minutes of the meetings of the armistice delegations, of the telephone conversations between General Huntziger and Bordeaux, of the changes asked by the French and the German responses are given in Kammerer, *op. cit.*, Annexes, pp. 421–446. The German minutes of the above are in DGFP, Vol. IV, pp. 643–679. Weygand, *Rappelé,* op. cit., pp. 258–261, gives his version of the French demands and the German answers. The text of the armistice treaty is in DGFP, Vol. IX, pp. 671–676, in English translation. The French-language text is in Kammerer, pp. 442–446.
78. DGFP, Vol. IX, pp. 646–647, 668–669.

79. The text of the French note is given in *Evénements*, Vol. II (Docs.), pp. 434–435.
80. Dispatches of Biddle, June 23, 26. *Foreign Relations*, Vol. I, p. 268 and footnote.
81. Dispatch of Biddle, June 22. Archives, Washington.
82. Kammerer, *op. cit.*, p. 324.
83. Darlan order No. 7025, June 24. *Evénements*, Vol. II (Docs.), p. 465.
84. *Ibid*. The text of Darlan's secret order to the fleet on June 24 is also given in *Evénements*, Vol. II (Docs.), p. 466, with the word "ex-ally" replaced by "foreign power."
85. De Gaulle, *op. cit.*, Vol. I, p. 73.
86. Baudouin, *op. cit.*, p. 207.
87. Reynaud, *Cœur, op. cit.*, p. 888.
88. Weygand, *Rappelé, op. cit.*, p. 285; his testimony before the Parliamentary Investigating Committee, *Evénements*, Vol. VI, pp. 1760–1761. He testified similarly at the Pétain trial.
89. Testimony of Lebrun at the Laval trial. Stenographic record published by Albin Michel, p. 211.
90. Quoted by Philippe Barrès in his *Charles de Gaulle*, pp. 128–129.
91. Kammerer, *op. cit.*, p. 235.
92. Truchet, *op. cit.*, p. 350.
93. Thucydides: *The Peloponnesian War*, Modern Library edition, pp. 331–333.
94. Truchet, *op. cit.*, p. 368.
95. Testimony of General Weygand, *Evénements*, Vol. VI, pp. 1780, 1782.
96. Baudouin, *op. cit.*, p. 207.
97. Bouthillier, *op. cit.*, pp. 107–108.
98. Testimony of General Koeltz, *Evénements*, Vol. IX, pp. 2810–2816.
99. Testimony of Lebrun, *Evénements*, Vol. IV, pp. 998–999.
100. Report of Colonel Loiret to the Parliamentary Investigating Committee, *Evénements*, Vol. II (Docs.), pp. 429–431.
101. General Colson to General Staff, No. 72 SP, June 23. Cited by Lyet, *op. cit.*, pp. 168–169. On p. 169 Lyet also gives figures on ships that sailed to North Africa.
102. The texts of the telegrams exchanged between Generals Weygand and Noguès are given in *Evénements*, Vol. II (Docs.), pp. 416–429; by Truchet, *op. cit.*, pp. 91–99; by Lyet, *op. cit.*, pp. 161–173.
103. Testimony of Lebrun, *Evénements*, Vol. IV, p. 999.
104. Halder: *Hitler als Feldherr* (Hitler as War Lord), p. 66 of the French-language edition.
105. Mussolini to Hitler, June 22, 1940. DGFP, Vol. IX, pp. 679–680.
106. Bouthillier, *op. cit.*, p. 114.
107. Jean Vidalenc, *L'Exode de mai–juin 1940, op. cit.*, pp. 359ff, gives a number of quotations on the subject from the Catholic clergy.
108. Weygand himself gives the text in his memoirs, *Rappelé, op. cit.*, pp. 298–299, remarking in retrospect that "it was not a model of political skillfulness."

36. THE END AT VICHY
JUNE–JULY 1940

1. Charles-Roux, *op. cit.*, p. 95.
2. Baudouin, *op. cit.*, pp. 204–205.
3. *Ibid.*, p. 219.
4. Lebrun, *op. cit.*, p. 102.
5. Baudouin, *op. cit.*, pp. 227–228.
6. Dispatch of Bullitt from La Bourboule, July 1, 1940, 9 P.M. *Foreign Relations*, Vol. II, pp. 462–469.
7. Churchill, *op. cit.*, Vol. II, p. 221.
8. DGFP, Vol. X, pp. 103–104.
9. *Ibid.*, pp. 124, 127.
10. French sources of Mers-el-Kébir include the testimony of Admiral Gensoul, *Evénements*, Vol. VI, pp. 1897–1916; Kammerer: *Mers-el-Kébir*; Varillon: *Mers-el-Kébir*; Admiral Godfroy: *L'Aventure de la Force X*; Robert Aron, *op. cit.*, p. 104ff; Benoist-Méchin, *op. cit.*, Vol. III, pp. 62–141. Churchill re-

counts the event in his memoirs, *op. cit.,* Vol. II, pp. 231–239. P. M. H. Bell: "Prologue de Mers-el-Kébir," an article in the *Revue d'Histoire de la Deuxième Guerre Mondiale,* No. 33, January 1959.

11. Baudouin, *op. cit.,* pp. 231–235; Bouthillier, *op. cit.,* pp. 152–153.
12. Montigny, *op. cit.,* p. 59.
13. Blum, *Mémoires,* in *L'Oeuvre de Léon Blum,* pp. 68–73.
14. Testimony of Marcel Héraud, *Evénements,* Vol. VI, pp. 1511–1512; testimony of Louis No-guères, *Evénements,* Vol. VII, pp. 2230–2232.
15. Baudouin, *op. cit.,* p. 238.
16. Charles-Roux, *op. cit.,* p. 163.
17. The account of the senatorial war veterans, their Resolution and their visits to Pétain and Laval is told in a pamphlet written by their leader, Senator Taurines, entitled *Tempête sur la République.* Written at the end of 1940 from notes he made from day to day in Vichy, it was read into the record when he testified before the Parliamentary Investigating Committee. *Evénements,* Vol. VIII, pp. 2330–2351. Louis Marin gave him a rough cross-examination.
18. Testimony of Lebrun, Pétain trial, Vol. I, pp. 163–164; his memoirs, *op. cit.,* pp. 104–106.
19. The events of July 8 are recounted by two deputies who took part in them: Montigny, *op. cit.,* pp. 61–65, 139–154; testimony of Louis Noguères, *Evénements,* Vol. VII, pp. 2238–2243.
20. Baudouin, *op. cit.,* p. 240.
21. Lebrun, *op. cit.,* p. 107.
22. Blum, *op. cit.,* pp. 82–87.
23. Baudouin, *op. cit.,* p. 241.
24. Reynaud explained his brief sojourn at Vichy in *Cœur, op. cit.,* p. 977 and footnote, and at the Pétain trial, Vol. I, pp. 100–105. Letter of Reynaud to Pétain, *ibid.,* p. 102. Robert Murphy's story is in his *Diplomat Among Warriors,* pp. 61–62.
25. Herriot proudly publishes the entire text of his address in his memoirs, *Episodes. 1940–1944,* pp. 132ff. He explains that at that moment he did not suspect that Pétain was going "to abuse the confidence accorded him." *Ibid.,* pp. 136–137.
26. Beau de Loménie, *Mort, op. cit.,* p. 398.
27. Testimony of Badie, *Evénements,* Vol. VIII, pp. 2272–2273.
28. Baudouin, *op. cit.,* p. 242.
29. The stenographic account of the morning secret session of the National Assembly was put in the State Archives, survived the Nazi occupation, and was turned over to the Parliamentary Investigating Committee in 1948. It is published in *Evénements,* Vol. II (Docs.), pp. 479–497.
30. The author's *Berlin Diary, op. cit.,* entry for July 9, 1940.
31. The cross-examination of Senator Boivin-Champeaux, *Evénements,* Vol. VII, pp. 2202–2206.
32. Testimony of Deputy Paul Boulet, *Evénements,* Vol. VII, pp. 2213ff.
33. Testimony of Deputy Vincent Badie, *ibid.,* Vol. VIII, p. 2274.
34. *Ibid.,* p. 2275.
35. Roger Stéphane: *Chaque homme est lié au monde,* p. 148.
36. Leahy File, April 27, 1941. Quoted by Langer, *op. cit.,* p. 250.
37. Dispatch of Murphy, July 29, 1940. *Foreign Relations,* Vol. II, p. 379.
38. Minutes of the meeting in the captured German documents, quoted by Langer, *op. cit.,* p. 90.
39. Testimony of Peyrouton, Pétain trial, quoted by Langer, *op. cit.,* p. 105.
40. Dispatch of Murphy, July 29, 1940. *Foreign Relations,* Vol. II, p. 379.
41. Baudouin, *op. cit.,* p. 243.
42. *Ibid.,* pp. 244–245.
43. Lebrun, *op. cit.,* pp. 109–110. His testimony at the Pétain trial, Vol. I, pp. 164–166.

ACKNOWLEDGMENTS

In the research and writing of this book I owe much to many. Since most of the digging for material was done in Paris, the cooperation of the French was all-important. It turned out to be beyond my fondest expectations.

In Paris I worked mostly at the Bibliothèque de Documentation Internationale Contemporaine, or BDIC, as it was known for short. This is a unique library, and, as its name suggests, is devoted to documentation of contemporary history, especially that of World War II and the events which led up to it. Though it was housed in a ramshackle old palace off the Etoile, much too small to provide space for its holdings, it had a warehouse on the outskirts of the capital and a motorcyclist raced to and fro all day long through the mad Parisian traffic fetching what you needed. In some miraculous way the BDIC was also able to obtain for you material from the Bibliothèque Nationale and from the libraries of the University of Paris in much less time than you could get it directly from these great but ancient institutions, where speed is frowned upon and never employed.

M. Henri Roux, the director of BDIC, and M. Hornung, the assistant director, provided me with a desk, and the latter, who had a remarkable memory of bibliography, guided me to much valuable material. The learned lady librarians were superbly helpful in a dozen ways, Mlle. Marcelle Adler-Bresse and Mlle. Sylviane Couve de Murville (as she then was), especially, and also Mme. Wellhof and Mlle. Suzanne Guyotat. I am greatly in debt to them all.

There was, in fact, a multitude of persons in Paris who greatly helped. A number of eminent French historians, none of whom share the disdain their American academic colleagues have for former journalists breaking into their sacred field—that stupidity is unknown in Europe, where *teaching* history is not considered the only qualification for *writing* it—talked with me about my problems and suggested sources to look into. Among these were Professors Pierre Renouvin, Maurice Baumont and J.-B. Duroselle of the Sorbonne; René Rémond, director of Studies and Research at the Fondation Nationale des Sciences Politiques; François Goguel, professor at the Institut d'Etudes Politiques of the University of Paris; and Pierre Dhers, who had also been, as a young deputy in the National Assembly, a member of the Parliamentary In-vestigating Committee which conducted a five-year inquiry into the reasons for the fall of the Third Republic. His work on the committee and his writings have earned him a reputation as an authority on the subject. Over the years I had numerous talks—and arguments—about my work with Dhers, who also led me to much material, some of it in his own library.

Philippe Barrès, son of the great novelist Maurice Barrès, and an old friend from our journalist days in Paris and Berlin and during the war, a former editor of *Le Matin* and, after the war, of *Paris-Presse,* and also a writer, proffered much good advice in long and pleasant conversations at the old family home facing the Bois and in lengthy memoranda, though, like old friends, we did not always agree. Another friend of Paris days, Pierre Lazareff, who had been the boy-wonder editor of *Paris-Soir* before the war, and, after it, of *France-Soir,* dug up material for me and arranged for meetings with numerous persons. It was he who persuaded Daladier to come up to Paris from his home in the south to talk to me.

Usually reticent generals and other military officers, for whom the debacle of 1940 is understandably a painful subject, were generous in the help they gave me. Colonel A. Goutard, whose book on the Battle of France, *1940: La Guerre des Occasions Perdues* ("The War of Lost Opportunities"), was one of the best on the subject—he did not spare the generals for their bumbling—provided me with much information and many ideas in letters and especially in our conversations. Commandant Pierre Lyet, the brilliant *officieux* military historian, whose book on the battle provides much source material to which only he had access, answered my queries during a talk and generously guided me to valuable sources. I also · had long talks with General André Beaufre, a young General Staff officer in 1940, who was in the center of things during the battle, and with General Paul Stehlin of the Air Force, a former air attaché in Berlin, who, like Beaufre, was a captain in 1940, and who flew combat missions. Both are caustic in their books and in their conversation about the Army and Air Force brass during the great test after the Germans invaded.

I spent hours with the genial General de Cossé-Brissac, chief of the Service Historique de l'Armée, at the gloomy dungeon of Vincennes, where General Gamelin had functioned during the war. Though under the wraps of the "law of fifty years" and forbidden by his superiors to make available any secret military papers, he did his best, under these restrictions, to answer my questions, some-times aided by officers of his staff. He also gave me copies of studies he himself had made, especially on the controversial question of French tanks in the battle. The Army Historical Section has been laboring for years on the official publica-tion of the history of the Battle of France. But progress is slow and I got the impression this was due mainly to lack of funds and shortage of personnel. In the meantime studies by the general and other officers of the Historical Section percolate into the military and historical reviews. They are crumbs, but appreci-ated.

There were many others in Paris to whom I am indebted. Professor Alfred Sauvy, who occupies the Chair of Social Demography at the Collège de France —he is often called the father of the postwar French population explosion—and who is also an eminent economist, gave freely of his time and advice over many a good luncheon and rushed to me his monumental two-volume *Histoire économique de la France entre les deux guerres* as soon as each volume was off the press. Henri Michel, director and editor of the *Revue d'Histoire de la Deuxième Guerre Mondiale,* the best single source of published information on France in the second war, was helpful in many ways. As the bibliography at the end of this book indicates, I have gleaned much from his Review, which also publishes in each issue an extensive up-to-date bibliography prepared by the BDIC. Others who volunteered help of all kinds included Henri Noguères, a gifted author of several books, who doubles as chief editor of Flammarion; Jean-Jacques Servan-Schreiber, the publisher and editor of *L'Express,* who collected his colleagues to discuss my project with me; Madame Yvonne Michel of *France-Soir;* and Professor Jean Réal of the Institut d'Etudes Politiques of Grenoble, with whom I have had a fruitful correspondence.

The editors and directors of Stock, my French publisher, nursed me along throughout the work on this book, procuring material and out-of-print books, arranging interviews, proffering advice. Among them were Guy Schoeller, the head of the firm, and François Martineau, a director. Most helpful was André Bay, chief editor, who devoted much of his time to me when I was in Paris, and Mlle. Sabine Delattre, an energetic editor who labored industriously in my behalf.

There were still others, but there are two more persons who must be singled out—not without a tinge of sadness. One was Pierre Comert, the former chief of the Press Department of the French Foreign Office, whom I had known and admired for years. He invited to his apartment overlooking the Tuileries a number of persons to talk to me. He died suddenly in March 1964, a few hours before one of these sessions was to take place. Alexander Werth, author of a number of fine books on France and Russia, who had spent most of his adult life in Paris as a correspondent of the Manchester *Guardian* and the *New Statesman,* and whose friendship goes back to the 1920s, died in Paris as these last lines were being written in 1969. Over the time I was working on this book, we often sat up most of the night discussing and arguing over the subject of this work. I learned much from him. And finally, my thanks to the editors of *Le Soir* of Brussels for digging out of their files the series of articles by Hubert Pierlot, the Belgian Premier in 1940, which shed much light on the controversial action of King Leopold in surrendering the Belgian Army in May 1940.

At home I was also fortunate in receiving the help and advice of many. Donald Wasson, director of the Foreign Relations Library at the Council on Foreign Relations, photographed documents for me, procured material, and showed monumental patience in letting me keep at home, for my writing, volumes of historical papers and other tomes for an unpardonably long time. Roger Vours, director of the French Information Service in New York at the time I began my labors, and later chief of the Press Department at the French Foreign Office, lent me out-of-print books and other material and guided me to a number of historians and officials in Paris. His assistants in New York, Mme. Monique Polgar and Mlle. Yvonne Daumarie, also aided me in procuring material and in discussing certain aspects of my work.

With Professor Stanley Hoffman, of Harvard, I had long talks about the book over the years and he had many penetrating observations to make. In Paris I met up with Professor Eugen Weber of the University of California, Los Angeles, author of *Action française,* a fascinating work on the modern

Royalist movement in France, where the book was a best seller. He gave me learned counsel. Professor John M. Hyde, of Williams College, read part of the manuscript, and Professor Robert G. L. Waite, also of Williams, gave counsel. Professor Erik H. Erikson, of Harvard, and I traded observations about our respective works in progress, he being then in the midst of a book about Gandhi. In Washington I had a long and illuminating conversation with Alexis Léger, secretary-general of the French Foreign Office in the last years before the debacle and a key figure in those days in formulating French foreign policy. In 1960 he won the Nobel Prize in Literature for his poetry, which he writes under the name of Saint-John Perse. In Washington, too, I made some use of the vast resources of the Library of Congress. Even more valuable to me was the National Archives, where, after a hard-to-get approval of the State Department, I was allowed to peruse the dispatches, many of them still classified, from the American embassies in Paris, Brussels, and London. For reasons difficult to fathom many of the most important dispatches were omitted from the volumes published by the State Department under the title *Foreign Relations of the United States, 1940*. At the Hoover Library at Stanford I was able to see a number of French documents. At the New York Public Library I obtained books and back copies of the *Journal Officiel*.

H. Freeman Matthews, who was first secretary of our embassy in Bordeaux during the last crucial days that saw there the fall of Paul Reynaud and the advent of Marshal Pétain, and who wrote most of the hour-to-hour dispatches to Washington on that climactic event, kindly furnished me with memoranda which supplement his dispatches, which themselves are invaluable. Gordon Wright of Stanford, author of several books on France, took time out to discuss my work. Among old friends who did likewise were Telford Taylor, historian and Professor of Law at Columbia, Hamilton Fish Armstrong, editor of *Foreign Affairs*, whose book on the Fall of France written immediately afterward holds up remarkably well in the light of postwar documentation, and Kay Boyle, the novelist, who spent much of her life in France and was there at its fall in 1940. To three members of the Pelton family my thanks are due: to Catherine for typing, to Suzanne for working out the bibliography from my undecipherable handwriting, to Martha for checking the manuscript and typescript and performing many other important chores.

Finally, but far from least, I owe a special debt to Joseph Barnes, my editor at Simon and Schuster, and friend from our days in Europe as correspondents. A man of long experience in Europe and immense learning in contemporary history, he recovered from the long haul of working with me on the *Reich* book, and labored with infinite patience with me on this one, providing new insights, turning up new material and old books, and urging me on. With the two books, this turned out to be for him a fifteen-year hitch. My literary agent Paul R. Reynolds, himself an author, also stuck with me over a number of obstacles and discouragements, as he had with the German book.

To all these, persons and institutions, my gratitude for having made this book possible. The errors therein, of course, are my own.

BIBLIOGRAPHY

The problem of source material for this book was touched on in the Foreword. A lengthier explanation of each specific bit of documentary evidence will be found in the source footnotes as each item appears for the first time. Similarly the evaluation of memoirs, diaries, journals and of their authors is given in the text and in the source footnotes. See also *Acknowledgments*.

PUBLISHED DOCUMENTARY MATERIAL

Belgium—The Official Account of What Happened in 1939–1940. Published for the Belgian Ministry of Foreign Affairs by Didier Publishers, New York, 1942. (The *Belgian Gray Book*.)

Débats Parlementaires, Chambre des Députés, Comités Secrets, Journal Officiel. Numéro spécial, April 7, 1948. (Stenographic accounts, meetings of *Chambre des Députés*, sitting as a secret committee, February 9, March 19, April 19, 1940.)

Débats Parlementaires, Sénat, Comités Secrets, Journal Officiel. Numéro spécial, April 7, 1948. (Stenographic accounts, meetings of Senate, sitting as secret committee, March 14, 15, and April 17, 18, 1940.)

Documents concerning German-Polish Relations and the Outbreak of Hostilities between Great Britain and Germany on September 3. London, 1939. (The *British Blue Book*.)

Documents Diplomatiques Français. 2e Série (1936–1939). Vols. I, II. Paris, 1963. (Referred to in notes as DDF.)

Documents on British Foreign Policy, 1919–39. London, 1947. (Referred to in notes as DBrFP.)

Documents on German Foreign Policy, 1918–1945. Series D, 1937–45. 10 vols. Washington: U.S. Department of State. (Referred to as DGFP.)

Documents Secrets de l'Etat Major Général Français. Berlin, 1941. (Documents captured by the Germans and published by the Auswärtiges Amt [Foreign Office]. Referred to in notes as "the Wilhelmstrasse Documents.")

Foreign Relations of the United States. Diplomatic Papers, 1936 (in 5 vols.). Vols. I and II. Washington, 1957, 1959.

GIRAUD, H. Honoré: "Memorandum from Général Giraud to Maréchal Pétain. July 26, 1940." (Unpublished.)

GORT, John Standish, Lord, Commander of the BEF: Two dispatches of Lord Gort on the operations of the British army in France, 1939–1940. Published as a supplement to the *London Gazette,* October 17, 1941.

La Campagne de mai 1940 (twenty maps and comments), published by La Section historique de l'Armée Belge.

Le Livre Jaune Français. Documents Diplomatiques, 1938–39. Paris, 1939. Ministère des Affaires Etrangères. (*The French Yellow Book.*)

Le Procès du Maréchal Pétain. Compte Rendu Sténographique. 2 vols. Paris, 1945.

Le Procès du Maréchal Pétain devant la Haute Cour de Justice. (Textes officiels du Réquisitoire et des Plaidoiries.) Montreal, 1946.

Le Procès Laval. Compte Rendu Sténographique. Paris, 1946.

Les Evénements survenus en France de 1933 à 1945: Témoignages et documents recueillis par la Commission d'Enquête Parlementaire. 10 vols. Paris, 1947–54. (Referred to as *Evénements.*)

Rapport au nom de la Commission chargée d'enquête sur les événements survenus en France de 1933 à 1945. "Les Evénements du 7 mars 1936." No. 2344 Assemblée Nationale. Première Législature. Session de 1947.

These last two are the work of the Committee set up by the National Assembly in 1946 to inquire into the causes of the fall of France in 1940. The volumes contain the *verbatim* text of the testimony under oath before the Committee over a five-year period of most of the principal figures of the Republic's last years, as well as that of other key witnesses. They also contain a great number of secret documents. Since the policy of French governments since 1945 has been to hold back publication of confidential state papers covering the last decade of the Third Republic, the Committee's volumes, and especially Volume II (Documents), contain the most substantial collection available.

Nazi Conspiracy and Aggression. 10 vols. Washington: U.S. Government Printing Office, 1946. (Referred to as NCA.)

Peace and War. U.S. Foreign Policy, 1931–41. Washington: U.S. Government Printing Office, 1942.

Rapport de la Commission d'Information instituée par S.M. le roi Léopold III. Bruxelles, 1947. (In English: Report by the Commission of Information constituted by Leopold III on July 14, 1946. *The Royal Question,* London, 1949.)

Recueil de documents établi par le secrétariat du roi concernant la période 1936–1949.

Supplement au Recueil de documents établi par le secrétariat du roi concernant la période 1936–1949. Bruxelles, 1950.

BIBLIOGRAPHICAL MATERIAL

Bibliographie Annuelle de l'Histoire de France. Published by Centre Nationale de la Recherche Scientifique. Paris, 1955.

Bulletin Analytique de documentation politique, économique et sociale contemporaine. Paris, 1946.

Bulletin bibliographique. Published by the Bibliothèque de Documentation Internationale Contemporaine et Musée de la Grande Guerre. Publication started in 1946.

DEBYSER, F.: "Bibliographie des ouvrages parus en France sur la Guerre 1939–

1940 et l'Armistice." Published in *Cahiers d'Histoire de la Guerre,* publication du Comité d'Histoire de la Guerre. Paris, January 1949.
Foreign Affairs Bibliography, 1942–1952. New York, 1952.

PAMPHLETS

KENNEDY, Robert M.: *The German Campaign in Poland, 1939.* Department of the Army, 1956.
MOWRER, Lillian T.: *Concerning France.* Washington, 1944.
WARABIOT, Général Louis: *Le 1er Bataillon de Chars dans la Bataille de Noyon.*

PERIODICALS

ALBORD, Général Tony: "Appel à l'Imagination." *Revue de Défense Nationale,* August–September 1949.
ANONYMOUS: "Histoire de la 2ème guerre mondiale. Première période, 1939–1940." *Revue historique de l'armée,* Nos. 1–4, 1948.
ANONYMOUS: "La Guerre jusqu'en 1940." *Revue historique de l'armée,* No. 4, 1955.
ANONYMOUS: "Pétain et le cinquième colonne." *Publications Clandestine.* Editions du Franc-Tireur, February 1944.
BANKWITZ, Philip C. F.: "Maxime Weygand and the Fall of France: a Study in Civil-Military Relations." *The Journal of Modern History,* Vol. XXXI, No. 4, September 1959.
BAUMONT, Maurice: "French Critics and Apologists Debate Munich." *Foreign Affairs,* Vol. XXV, 1947.
CAIRNS, John C.: "Along the Road Back to France, 1940." *The American Historical Review,* Vol. LXIV, April 1959.
———: "Great Britain and the Fall of France—a Study in Allied Disunity." *The Journal of Modern History,* Vol. XXVII, No. 4, December 1955.
DALADIER, Edouard: "Munich." Three articles by the former Premier on the Munich crisis, published in successive issues of *Candide,* September 7, 14, 21, 1961.
DHERS, Pierre: "Les Fables de M. Pierre-Etienne Flandin." *Terre Humaine,* Paris, June 1952.
DUVAL, Général Maurice: "L'Armée française de 1938." *Revue de Paris,* August 15, 1938.
GIDE, André: "Léon Blum." *Vendredi,* June 5, 1936.
GRASSET, Colonel Alphonse Louis: "La Défense nationale et l'effort necessaire." *Revue des Deux Mondes,* June 15, 1938.
GUILLAUMAT, Général: "L'Armée française devant le réarmement allemand." *Revue Politique et Parlementaire,* May 10, 1935.
HAIGHT, John McVickar, Jr.: "France, the United States and the Munich Crisis." *The Journal of Modern History,* Vol. XXVII, No. 4, December 1960.
LYET, Colonel J.: "Le 10 mai 1940. Français et Allemands ont les uns et les autres joué leurs chances sur une seule carte." *Le Monde,* Paris, May 11, 1960.
MADY, J.: "Les Fonds d'archives concernant la deuxième guerre mondiale aux archives nationales." *Cahiers d'Histoire de la Guerre,* No. 1, January 1949.

NIESSEL, Général Henri Albert: "Les Besoins militaires de la France." *Revue Universelle,* December 1, 1937.

PÉGUY, Charles: *Cahiers de la Quinzaine,* October 22, 1905.

PIERLOT, Hubert: "Pages d'histoire." A series of twelve articles in *Le Soir,* Brussels, July 5–19, 1947.

RÉMOND, René: "Les anciens combattants et la politique." *Revue Française de Science Politique,* 1955.

REYNAUD, Paul: "Reply to Weygand." *Le Figaro,* Paris, June 29, 1963.

SONTAG, Raymond J.: "Between the Wars." *Pacific Historical Review,* February 1960.

WEYGAND, Général Maxime: "Open Letter to Paul Reynaud." *Le Figaro,* Paris, June 29, 1963.

————: "L'Etat militaire de la France." *Revue des Deux Mondes,* October 15, 1936.

————: "La Sécurité française." *Revue Hebdomadaire,* February 6, 1937.

————: "L'Unité de l'armée." *Revue Militaire Générale,* January 1937.

WRIGHT, Gordon: "Ambassador Bullitt and the Fall of France." *World Politics,* No. 1, October 1957.

Articles in
Revue D'Histoire de la Deuxième Guerre Mondiale
Presses Universitaires de France, Paris.

ARMENGAUD, Général André: "L'enfer de Dunkerque." No. 2, juin 1948.

BELL, P. M. H.: "Prologue de Mers-el-Kébir." No. 33, janvier 1959.

BONOTAUX, Lt.-Col., and others: "Avec la 3e D. I. M. à Stonne"; "Avec les Chasseurs et les Artilleurs à Blaregnies"; "Avec les Cavaliers et les Chars"; "Avec les défenseurs de Villy et la Ferté." No. 2, juin 1950.

COSSÉ-BRISSAC, Général Philippe de: "L'Allemagne et son armée." No. 1, mars 1949.

————: "L'armée allemande dans la campagne de France de 1940." No. 53, janvier 1964.

————: "Nouvelles précisions allemandes sur la manoeuvre de mai-juin 1940." No. 1, janvier 1948.

DAUTRY, R.: "Note au Président du Conseil (13 juin 1940)." No. 3, juin 1951.

DE JONG, C. T.: "L'attaque allemande sur la Hollande en 1940." No. 20, octobre 1955.

DHERS, P.: "Du 7 mars, 1936, à l'Île d'Yeu." No. 5, janvier 1952.

d'HOOP, J. M.: "La politique française de réarmement (1933–1939)." No. 14, avril 1954.

GOUTARD, Colonel A.: "La menace allemande sur l'A.F.N." No. 44, octobre 1961.

HAIGHT, J. McV., Jr.: "Les achats d'avions américains par la France." No. 58, avril 1965.

LE GOYET, Lieutenant Colonel: "La percée de Sedan (10–15 mai 1940)." No. 59, juillet 1965.

LÉVY, Colonel Paul: "L'organisation de la propagande allemande en France." No. 64, octobre 1966.

LYET, Commandant Pierre: "Des documents secrets voyagent." No. 3, septembre 1948.

————: "Paris 'ville ouverte.'" No. 2, juin 1948.

MARIN, Louis: "Contribution à l'étude des prodromes de l'armistice." No. 3, juin 1951.

————: "Gouvernement et commandement (mai–juin 1940). No. 8, octobre 1952.

————: "Gouvernement et commandement." No. 9, janvier 1953.

MEDLICOTT, W. N.: "De Munich à Prague." No. 13, janvier 1956.

MEGRET, M.: "Les origines de la propagande de guerre française." No. 41, janvier 1961.

MER, Général: "La Bataille des Alpes." No. 2, juin 1948.

————: "La Bataille des Alpes (Fin)." No. 3, septembre 1948.

MICHEL, Henri: "La Commission parlementaire d'enquête." No. 3, juin 1951.

NOËL, Léon: "Le projet d'union franco-britannique de juin 1940." No. 21, janvier 1956.

POSTEL, M. Claude: "Contre les ponts de la Meuse." No. 1, mars 1949.

ROLLOT, Général: "L'offensive de Sedan: les rapports franco-belges." No. 38, avril 1960.

SOUCY, Dr. R.: "Le facisme de Drieu La Rochelle." No. 66, avril 1967.

TOURNOUX, Général: "Les origines de la ligne Maginot." No. 33, janvier 1959.

TRUCHET, A.: "L'Armistice et l'Afrique du Nord." No. 3, juin 1951.

VANWELKENHUYZEN, Jean: "L'alerte du 10 janvier 1940." No. 12, octobre 1953.

VIAL, J.: "La Défense nationale: son organisation entre les deux guerres." No. 18, avril 1955.

VIAULT, B. S.: "Les démarches pour le rétablissement de la paix (septembre 1939–août 1940)." No. 67, juillet 1967.

VILLATE, R.: "Le changement de commandement de mai 1940." No. 5, janvier 1952.

WANTY, Général Emile: "Improvisation de la liaison belgo-britannique du 10 au 18 mai 1940." No. 55, janvier 1964.

————: "La Défense des Ardennes en 1940." No. 42, avril 1961.

————: "Les relations militaires franco-belges, 1936–octobre 1939." No. 31, juillet 1958.

WILLEQUET, J.: "La politique belge d'indépendance, 1936–40." No. 31, juillet 1958.

————: "Les fascismes belges." No. 66, avril 1967.

GENERAL WORKS

ABETZ, Otto: *Pétain et les Allemands. Memorandum sur les rapports franco-allemands.* Paris, 1948.

————: *D'une Prison.* Paris, 1949.

————: *Histoire d'une politique franco-allemande. 1930–1950. Mémoires d'un Ambassadeur.* Paris, 1953.

"ALAIN": *Eléments d'une doctrine radicale.* Paris, 1925.

ALBERT-SOREL, Jean: *Le Chemin de Croix, 1939–1940.* Paris, 1943.

ALBORD, Général Tony: *Pourquoi cela est arrivé, ou les responsabilités d'une génération militaire, 1919–1939.* Nantes, 1946.

ALERME, Colonel M. E. M.: *Les causes militaires de notre défaite.* Paris, 1940.

AMOUROUX, Henri: *La Vie des Français sous l'occupation.* Paris, 1961.

————: *Le 18 juin 1940.* Paris, 1964.

ANONYMOUS: *Feue l'armée française.* Paris, 1929.

ANONYMOUS: *L'armée française.* Paris, 1936.

ANONYMOUS: *Un témoignage: Le Diktat de Rethondes et l'Armistice franco-italien de juin 1940.* Paris, 1954.

ANTHÉRIEU, E.: *Grandeur et sacrifice de la ligne Maginot.* Paris, 1962.

ARANGO, E. Ramon: *Leopold III and the Belgian Royal Question.* Baltimore, 1963.

ARENSTAM, Arned: *Tapestry of a Debacle. From Paris to Vichy.* London, 1942.

ARMENGAUD, Général André: *Batailles politiques et militaires sur l'Europe. Témoignages (1932–1940).* Paris, 1948.

ARMSTRONG, Hamilton Fish: *Chronology of Failure.* New York, 1940.

ARON, Raymond: *Le Grand Schisme.* Paris, 1948.

————: *France, the New Republic.* New York, 1960.

ARON, Robert: *Le Piège où nous a pris l'Histoire.* Paris, 1950.

————: *Histoire de Vichy, 1940–1944.* Paris, 1954. English edition: *The Vichy Regime.*

————: *Les grands Dossiers de l'Histoire contemporaine.* Paris, 1962.

————: *Nouveaux grands Dossiers de l'Histoire contemporaine.* Paris, 1964.

AUDRY, Colette: *Léon Blum, ou la politique du juste: essai.* Collection: *Les Temps Modernes dirigée par Jean-Paul Sartre.* Paris, 1955.

AURIOL, Vincent: *Hier . . . demain.* 2 vols. Paris, 1945.

BAINVILLE, Jacques: *Histoire de France.* Paris, 1924.

BARADUC, Jacques: *Dans la cellule de Pierre Laval.* Paris, 1948.

BARDIES, Colonel de: *La Campagne, 1939–40.* Paris, 1947.

BARDOUX, Jacques: *Journal d'un témoin de la Troisième, 1er septembre 1939– 15 juillet 1940.* Paris, 1957.

BARLONE, D.: *A French Officer's Diary (23 August 1939–1 October 1940).* Cambridge University Press, 1942.

BARRÈS, Philippe: *Charles de Gaulle.* New York, 1941.

BAUDOUIN, Paul: *Neuf mois au gouvernement, avril–décembre 1940.* Paris, 1948.

English translation: *The Private Diaries of Paul Baudouin.* London, 1953.

BAUER, Major Eddy: *La Guerre des blindés.* 2 vols. 2nd edn. Paris, 1962.

BAUMONT, Maurice: *La Faillite de la paix, 1918–39.* 2 vols. Paris, 1945, 1950.

————: *Aux Sources de l'affaire.* 1959.

BEAU DE LOMÉNIE, Emmanuel: *La Mort de la Troisième République.* Paris, 1951.

————: *Les Responsabilités des dynasties bourgeoises.* 4 vols. Paris, 1954.
Vol. I. De Bonaparte à Mac-Mahon.
Vol. II. De Mac-Mahon à Poincaré.
Vol. III. Sous la Troisième République.
Vol. IV. Du Cartel à Hitler.

BEAUFRE, Général André: *Le Drame de 1940.* Paris, 1965.

————: *Introduction à la strategie.* Paris, 1963.

BECHTEL, Guy: *Laval 20 ans après.* Paris, 1963.

BECKER, Carl L.: *Modern History.* New York, 1931.

BECQUART, Henry: *Au Temps du silence. De Bordeaux à Vichy. Souvenirs et réflexions.* Paris.

BENAZET, P.: *Défense nationale, notre sécurité.* Paris, 1938.

BENOIST-MÉCHIN, Jacques: *Les soixante jours qui ébranlèrent l'Occident.* 3 vols. Paris, 1946–1956.

BERL, Emmanuel: *La France irréelle.* Paris, 1957.

BERTILLON, J.: *La Dépopulation de la France.* Paris, 1911.

BIDOU, Henri: *Blitzkrieg.* Vol. I: *Eyewitness History of World War II.* Various contributors. New York, 1962.

BLOCH, Marc: *L'Etrange défaite.* Paris, 1957. English edn., *Strange Defeat. A Statement of Evidence Written in 1940.* London, 1949.

BLUM, Léon: *L'Oeuvre de Léon Blum.* 7 vols. Paris, 1954–1963. Vol. V: *Mémoires, La Prison et le procès, A l'échelle humaine, 1940–1945.* Paris, 1955.

————: *For All Mankind* (English translation of *A l'échelle humaine*). London, 1946.

BODIN, Louis, and TOUCHARD, Jean: *Front populaire. 1936.* Paris, 1961.

BOIS, Elie J.: *Truth on the Tragedy of France.* London, 1941.

BONNEFOUS, Edouard: *Histoire politique de la troisième république.* 7 vols. Paris, 1952–1967.

BONNET, Georges: *Défense de la paix.* 2 vols. Geneva, 1946, 1948.

Vol. I: *De Washington au Quai d'Orsay.*

Vol. II: *Fin d'une Europe (de Munich à la guerre).*

————: *Le Quai d'Orsay sous trois républiques.* Paris, 1961.

BONNEVAY, Laurent: *Les Journées sanglantes de février: pages d'histoire, 1934.* Paris, 1935.

BOOTHE, Clare: *Europe in the Spring.* New York, 1940.

BOURGET, P. A.: *De Beyrouth à Bordeaux.* Paris, 1946.

BOURRET, Général Victor: *La Tragédie de l'armée française.* Paris, 1947.

BOUSSEL, Patrice: *L'Affaire Dreyfus et la presse.* Paris, 1960.

BOUTHILLIER, Yves: *Le Drame de Vichy. Face à l'énnemi, face à l'allié.* Paris, 1950.

BRET, Paul-Louis: *Au feu des événements. Mémoires d'un journaliste.* Londres–Alger (1929–1944). Paris, 1959.

BROGAN, Denis William: *France under the Republic: The Development of Modern France (1870–1939).* New York and London, 1942.

————: *French Personalities and Problems.* New York, 1947.

————: *The French Nation: From Napoleon to Pétain, 1814–1940.* New York and London, 1957.

BROSSE, Général: *Les Eléments de notre défense nationale 1936.* Paris, 1936.

BRYANT, Arthur: *The Turn of the Tide.* New York, 1957. (Based on the diaries of Field Marshal Lord Alanbrooke.)

BYRNES, Robert F.: *Antisemitism in Modern France.* 2 vols. New Jersey, 1950.

Vol. I: *The Prologue to the Dreyfus Affair.*

CARR, Edward Hallet: *The Twenty Years' Crisis, 1919–39.* London, 1942.

CARRIAS, Eugene: *La pensée militaire française.* Paris, 1960.

CHALLENER, Richard D.: *The French Theory of the Nation in Arms. 1866–1939.* New York, 1955.

CHAMBE, Général René: *Histoire de l'aviation.* Paris, 1949.

CHAMBORD, Marcel: *Ombres et clartés de la campagne belge de 1940.* Brussels, 1946.

CHAPMAN, Guy: *The Third Republic of France. The First Phase, 1871–1894.* New York, 1950.

————: *The Dreyfus Case: A Reassessment.* London, 1955.

CHARENSOL, Georges: *L'Affaire Dreyfus et la troisième république.* Paris, 1930.

CHARLES-ROUX, F.: *Cinq mois tragiques aux affaires étrangères (21 mai–1 novembre, 1940).* Paris, 1949.

CHARNAY, Geoffroy de: *Synarchie.* (Fifty-four articles, including documents, published by Roger Mennevée through his Agence Indépendante d'Information Internationale.)

CHARPENTIER, Georges: *Au service de la liberté.*

CHASTENET, Jacques: *Histoire de la troisième république.* 7 vols. Paris, 1952–1963.

CHAUTEMPS, Camille: *Cahiers secrets de l'armistice, 1939–1940.* Paris, 1963.

CHURCHILL, Sir Winston: *The Second World War*. 6 vols. Boston, 1948–1953.
   Vol. I: *The Gathering Storm*.   Vol. II: *Their Finest Hour*.
CIANO, Count Galeazzo: *The Ciano Diaries, 1939–1943*. Edited by Hugh Gibson. New York, 1946.
———: *Ciano's Hidden Diary, 1937–1938*. New York, 1953.
CLEMENCEAU, Georges: *Grandeurs et misères d'une victoire*. Paris, 1930.
COLE, Hubert: *Laval, A Biography*. London, 1963.
COLTON, Joel: *Léon Blum. Humanist in Politics*. New York, 1966.
CONQUET, Général: *L'Enigme de notre manque de divisions blindés. 1932–1940*. Paris, 1956.
COSTON, Henry: *Les Technocrates et la synarchie*. Paris, 1962.
COT, Pierre: *Triumph of Treason*. Chicago, 1944.
COULONDRE, Robert: *De Staline à Hitler. Souvenirs de deux ambassades, 1936–1939*. Paris, 1950.
CRAIG, Gordon A., and GILBERT, Felix (eds.): *The Diplomats. 1919–1939*. Princeton, 1953.
CRANE, Milton (ed.): *The Roosevelt Era*. New York, 1947.
CUGNAC, Général Gaspar Jean Marie de: *Les quarante jours (10 mai–19 juin 1940)*. Paris, 1947.
DARDENNE, Henriette: *Lumières sur l'affaire Dreyfus*. Paris, 1964.
D'ASTIER DE LA VIGERIE, Général: *Le ciel n'était pas vide. 1940*. Paris, 1952.
DAVIS, Forrest, and LINDLEY, Ernest K.: *How War Came*. New York, 1942.
DEBU-BRIDEL, Jacques: *L'Agonie de la troisième république, 1925–1935*. Paris, 1948.
DE JONG, Louis: *The German 5th Column in the Second World War*. London, 1956.
DE JONG, Louis, and STOPPELMAN, Joseph W. F.: *The Lion Rampant*. New York, 1943.
D'ESTAING, Giscard: *D'Esterhazy à Dreyfus*. Paris, 1960.
DHERS, Pierre: *Regards nouveaux sur les années quarante*. Paris, 1958.
———: "L'Armistice. L'Assemblée nationale," in *La France sous l'occupation*. Paris, 1959.
DOLLÉANS, Edouard: *Histoire du mouvement ouvrier, 1830 à nos jours*. 3 vols. Paris, 1947–1953.
DOUMENC, Général André: *Histoire de la 9e armée*. Paris, 1945.
DRAPER, Theodore: *The Six Weeks' War. France, May 10–June 26, 1940*. New York, 1944.
DREYFUS, Alfred: *Cinq Années de ma vie*. Paris, 1962.
DUROSELLE, J.-B.: *Histoire diplomatique de 1919 à nos jours*. Paris, 1957.
DUTOURD, Jean: *The Taxis of the Marne*. New York, 1957.
DUTRAIT-CROUON, Henri: *Précis de l'affaire Dreyfus*. 1909.
EARLE, Edward Mead (ed.): *Makers of Modern Strategy. Military Thought from Machiavelli to Hitler*. Princeton, 1943.
———: *Modern France. Problems of the Third and Fourth Republics*. Princeton, 1951.
EDEN, Anthony: *The Memoirs of Anthony Eden, Earl of Avon*. 3 vols. Boston, 1965.
   Vol. I. *Facing the Dictators. 1923–1938*.
   Vol II. *The Reckoning*.
EHRMANN, Henry W.: *The French Labor Movement from the Popular Front to Liberation*. New York, 1947.
ELLIS, Major L. F.: *The War in France and Flanders, 1939–1940*. London, 1953.

Encyclopédie Politique de la France et du monde. 2 vols. Paris, 1946.
FABRE-LUCE, Alfred: *Au nom des silencieux.* Paris, 1945.
————: *Journal de la France. 1939–1944.* Paris, 1946.
FABRY, J.: *De la place de la Concorde au cours de l'intendance. février 1934–juin 1940.* Paris, 1942.
FARRÈRE, Claude: *Histoire de la Marine.* Paris, 1956.
FAUVET, Jacques: *Histoire du parti communiste français.* 2 vols. Paris, 1964.
FEILING, Keith: *The Life of Neville Chamberlain.* London, 1946.
FERNAND-LAURENT, J. C.: *Gallic Charter.* Boston, 1944.
FEUCHTER, Georg W.: *Geschichte des Luftkriegs.* Bonn, 1954.
FISHER, H. A. L.: *A History of Europe.* London, 1936.
FLANDIN, Pierre-Etienne: *Politique française, 1919–1940.* Paris, 1947.
FOERSTER, Wolfgang: *Ein General kämpft gegen den Krieg.* (The papers of General Beck.) Munich, 1949.
FRANÇOIS-PONCET, André: *De Versailles à Potsdam.* Paris, 1948.
————: *The Fateful Years. Memoirs of a French Ambassador in Berlin. 1931–1938.* New York, 1949.
FULLER, Major General J. F. C.: *The Second World War, 1939–1945.* New York, 1949.
FURNIA, Arthur H.: *The Diplomacy of Appeasement: Anglo-French Relations and the Prelude to World War II, 1931–1938.* Washington, D.C., 1960.
GAMELIN, Général Maurice Gustave: *Servir.* 3 vols. Paris, 1947.
   Vol. I. *Les armées françaises de 1940.*
   Vol. II. *Le prologue du drame (1930–août 1939).*
   Vol. III. *La guerre septembre 1939–19 mai 1940.*
GANNETT, Lewis (ed.): *I Saw It Happen. Eyewitness Accounts of the War.* New York, 1942.
GARNETT, David: *War in the Air. September 1939–May 1941.* New York, 1941.
GAUCHÉ, Général Fernand Georges: *Le deuxième bureau au travail.* Paris, 1953.
GAULLE, Général Charles de: *Le fil de l'épée.* Paris. 1932. (In English, *The Edge of the Sword,* 1960.)
————: *Vers l'armée de métier.* Paris, 1934. (In English, *The Army of the Future,* Philadelphia, 1941.)
————: *La France et son armée.* Paris, 1938. (In English, *France and her Army,* London, 1948.)
————: *Mémoires de Guerre.* 3 vols. Paris, 1954. (In English, *War Memoirs.* 3 vols. London, 1955–1960.)
   Vol. I. *L'Appel 1940–1942.*
   Vol. II. *L'Unité. 1942–1944.*
   Vol. III. *Le Salut 1944–1946.*
GIDE, André: *Journal 1939–1949 Souvenirs.* Paris, 1954.
GOGUEL, François: *La Politique des partis sous la IIIe République.* 3rd edn. Paris, 1958.
GOGUEL, François, and GROSSER, Alfred: *La politique en France.* Paris, 1964.
GORCE, Paul-Marie de la: *The French Army, a Military-Political History.* New York, 1963.
————: *De Gaulle entre deux mondes.* Paris, 1964.
GOUTARD, Colonel Alphonse: *1940: La Guerre des Occasions Perdues.* Paris, 1956. (English title: *The Battle of France, 1940.* London, 1958.)
GRANDSARD, Général C.: *Le 10e Corps d'armée dans la bataille.* Paris, 1949.
GUDERIAN, General Heinz: *Panzer Leader.* New York, 1957.
GUÉRARD, Albert: *The France of Tomorrow.* Cambridge, 1942.

GUILLEMIN, Henri: *L'Enigme Esterhazy*. Paris, 1962.

GUITARD, Louis: *La petite histoire de la IIIe République: Souvenirs de Maurice Colrat*. Paris, 1959.

GUNTHER, John: *Inside Europe*. New York, 1936.

HALASZ, Nicholas: *Captain Dreyfus: the Story of a Mass Hysteria*. New York, 1955.

HALDER, General Franz: *Hitler als Feldherr*. Munich, 1949.

——: *Kriegstagebuch*. 3 vols. Stuttgart, 1962.

HANOTAUX, Gabriel: *Histoire illustrée de la guerre de 1914*.

HATCH, Alden: *The de Gaulle Nobody Knows*. New York, 1960.

HAYES, Carlton J. H.: *A Political and Social History of Mordern Europe, 1815–1915*. 2 vols. New York, 1922, 1929.

HEADINGS, Mildred J.: *French Free-Masonry Under the Third Republic*. Baltimore, 1949.

HENDERSON, Sir Nevile: *The Failure of a Mission*. New York, 1940.

HÉRING, General Pierre: *La Vie exemplaire de Philippe Pétain*. Paris, 1952.

HERRIOT, Edouard: *Episodes. 1940–1944*. Paris, 1950.

——: *Jadis. D'une Guerre à l'autre, 1914–1936*.

Histoire des littératures, Vol. III, Encyclopédie de la Pléiade. Paris, 1958.

HOOVER WAR LIBRARY, Stanford University: *France During the Occupation*. 1957.

HORNE, Alistair: *The Price of Glory: Verdun, 1916*. New York, 1963.

HOWE, Quincy: *A World History of Our Times*, New York, 1949. Vol. I. *The World Between the Wars*. New York, 1953.

HUBER, Michel: *La Population de la France pendant la guerre*. Paris, 1931.

HUDDLESTON, Sisley: *France: The Tragic Years, 1939–1947*. Chicago, 1955.

HULL, Cordell: *The Memoirs of Cordell Hull*. 2 vols. New York, 1948.

ICKES, Harold L.: *The Secret Diary of Harold L. Ickes*. New York, 1953, 1954.
  Vol. I. *The First Thousand Days*.
  Vol. II. *The Lowering Clouds*.

JACOBSEN, Hans-Adolf: *Fall Gelb. Der Kampf um den Deutschen Operationsplan zur Westoffensive, 1940*. Wiesbaden, 1957.

——: *Dokumente zum Westfeldzug 1940*. Berlin, 1960.

JACOMET, Robert: *L'Armement de la France 1936–1940*. Paris, 1945.

JOHNSON, Douglas: *France and the Dreyfus Affair*. New York, 1967.

JOLL, James (ed.): *The Decline of the Third Republic*. St. Anthony's Papers, No. 5, London, 1955. 1. "The Sixth of February" by Max Beloff. 2. "The Making of the Popular Front" by James Joll. 3. "The Rhineland Crisis of March 1936" by W. F. Knapp. 4. "The Tiger's Cub: the last years of Georges Mandel" by John Sherwood.

JOLL, James: *Intellectuals in Politics: Three Biographical Essays*. London, 1960.

JULLIAN, Camille: *Extraits des historiens français du XIXème siècle*. Paris, 1898.

KAMMERER, Albert: *Les Responsables*. Paris, 1938.

——: *La Vérité sur l'armistice*. Paris, 1944.

——: *La Tragédie de Mers-el-Kébir. (L'Angleterre et la flotte française.)* Paris, 1945.

KAYSER, Jacques: *L'Affaire Dreyfus*. Paris, 1946.

KERILLIS, Henri de: *Français, voici la vérité*. New York, 1942.

KIRK, Dudley: "Population and Population Trends in Modern France," in *Modern France*, edited by Edward Mead Earle. Princeton, 1951.

KOELTZ, Général L.: *Comment s'est joué notre destin*. Paris, 1957.

KORDT, Erich: Unpublished memorandum.

LABARTHE, A.: *La France devant la guerre. La Balance des forces*. Paris, 1939.

LABARTHÈTE, H. du Moulin de: *Le Temps des illusions*. Geneva, 1946.

LABUSQUIÈRE, Jean: "Vérité sur les Combattants," in *Grandes Batailles de mai et juin 1940*. (Ed.: H. Lardanchet.) Paris, 1941.

La Campagne de France mai–juin 1940, Lieutenant Colonel Lugand and others. Paris, 1953.

LAFFARGUE, Général André Charles Victor: *Justice pour ceux de 1940*. Paris, 1952.

LANGER, William L.: *Our Vichy Gamble*. New York, 1947.

LANGER, William L., and GLEASON, S. Everett: *The Challenge to Isolation 1937–1940*. New York.

LANGSAM, Walter Consuelo: *The World Since 1914*. New York, 1954.

———: *Historic Documents of World War II*. New York, 1958.

LAUNAY, Jacques de: *Les Grandes Controverses de l'histoire contemporaine*. Lausanne, 1964.

———: *Histoire contemporaine de la diplomatie secrète, 1914–1945*. Lausanne, 1965.

LAVAL, Josée (ed.): *The Diary of Pierre Laval* (English translation of *Laval parle . . . notes et mémoires rédigés à Fresnes d'août à octobre 1945*). New York, 1948.

LAZAREFF, Pierre: *De Munich à Vichy*. New York, 1944.

———: *Dernière Edition: Histoire d'une époque*. Canada.

LEBRUN, Albert: *Témoignage*. Paris, 1945.

LEROY-BEAULIEU, Paul: *La Question de la population*. Paris, 1913.

LIDDELL HART, B. H.: *The German Generals Talk*. New York, 1948.

LIGOU, Daniel: *Histoire du socialisme en France 1871–1961*. Paris, 1961.

LORWIN, Val R.: *The French Labor Movement*. Cambridge, 1954.

LOSSBERG, General Bernhard von: *Im Wehrmacht Fuehrungsstab*. Hamburg, 1950.

LOUCHEUR, Louis: *Carnets secrets de Louis Loucheur*. Lausanne, 1962.

LOUIS, Paul: *Histoire du socialisme en France*. Paris, 1946.

LOUSTAUNAU-LACAU, Georges: *Mémoires d'un français rebelle. 1914–1948*. Paris, 1948.

LUETHY, Herbert: *France Against Herself*. New York, 1955.

LYET, Commandant Pierre: *La Bataille de France, mai–juin 1940*. Paris, 1947.

MADAULE, Jacques: *Histoire de France de 1715 à nos jours. Vol. II*. Paris, 1945.

MALLET, Alfred: *Pierre Laval*. 2 vols. Paris, 1955.

MANEVY, Raymond: *Histoire de la presse. 1914–1939*. Paris, 1945.

———: *La presse de la IIIe République*. Paris, 1955.

MARITAIN, Jacques: *À travers le désastre*. Paris, 1942.

MARTIN DU GARD, Maurice: *Chronique de Vichy*. Paris, 1948.

MAURIN, Général Georges: *L'armée moderne*. Paris, 1938.

MAUROIS, André: *Tragedy in France*. New York, 1940.

MAZÉ, Pierre, and GENEBRIER, Roger: *Les grandes Journées du procès de Riom*. Paris, 1945.

MAZEL, H.: *Histoire et psychologie de l'affaire Dreyfus*. Paris, 1934.

McINNES, Edgar: *The War: First Year*. Canada, 1940.

MENU, Général: *Lumière sur les ruines*. Paris.

MICAUD, Charles A.: *The French Right and Nazi Germany, 1933–1939*. Durham, N.C., 1943.

MICHEL, Henri: *Histoire de la résistance, 1940–1944*. Paris, 1950.

MICHELS, Spencer Allen: *Façade—a study of Public Opinion in France in 1940*. Unpublished senior thesis, Princeton, 1959.

MICHIELS, Général Oscar: *18 jours de guerre en Belgique*. Paris, 1947.

MINART, Colonel Jacques: *P. C. Vincennes, Secteur 4*. 2 vols. Paris, 1945.

MIQUEL, Pierre: *L'Affaire Dreyfus*. Paris, 1959.

MONTGOMERY, Field Marshal Bernard: *The Memoirs of Field Marshal Montgomery*. New York, 1958.

MONTIGNY, Jean: *Toute la vérité sur un mois dramatique de notre histoire. De l'Armistice à l'Assemblée Nationale, 15 juin–15 juillet, 1940.* Paris, 1940.

MONTMORENCY, Alec: *The Enigma of Admiral Darlan.* New York, 1943.

MONZIE, Anatole de: *Ci-devant.* Paris, 1942.

MORDACQ, Général Jean Jules Henri: *La défense nationale en danger.* Paris, 1938.

MORGENTHAU, Henry, Jr.: *The Morgenthau Diaries.* New York, 1947.

MÜLLER, Klaus-Jürgen: *Das Ende der Entente Cordiale.* Frankfurt.

MURPHY, Robert: *Diplomat Among Warriors.* New York, 1964.

NAMIER, L. B.: *Diplomatic Prelude, 1938–39.* New York, 1948.

———: *Europe in Decay. A Study in Disintegration, 1936–1940.* London, 1950.

———: *In the Nazi Era.* London, 1952.

NOEL, Geneviève: *La Mort étrange de la IIIᵉ république.* Paris, 1960.

NOËL, Léon: *Une Ambassade à Varsovie, 1935–1939.* Paris, 1944.

NOGUÈRES, Henri: *La République accuse. Au Procès de Riom.* Paris, 1945.

———: *Munich, ou la drôle de paix.* Paris, 1963.

———: *Histoire de la résistance en France, juin 1940–juin 1941.* Paris, 1967.

NOGUÈRES, Louis: *Un Défi à la Résistance: M. Jules Jeanneney, Ministre d'État.*

———: *Le Véritable Procès du Maréchal Pétain.* Paris, 1955.

———: *La dernière étape Sigmaringen.* Paris, 1956 .

———: *La haute Cour de la libération, 1944–1949.* Paris, 1965.

NOLTE, Ernst: *Der Faschismus in seiner Epoche.* Munich, 1963.

OLLÉ-LAPRUNE, Jacques: *La Stabilité des ministres sous la troisième république, 1879–1940.* Paris, 1962.

OVERSTRAETEN, General Raoul van: *Albert I–Léopold III. Vingt ans de politique militaire Belge, 1920–1940.* Brussels, 1946.

PADOVER, Saul K.: *France in Defeat: Causes and Consequences.* (Reprinted from *World Politics,* Vol. II, No. 3, April 1950.)

———: *France: Setting or Rising Star?* (Headline Series, No. 81. Foreign Policy Association. May 20, 1950.)

PAQUIER, Colonel Pierre: *Les forces aériennes françaises de 1939 à 1945.* Paris, 1949.

PASSY, Colonel: *Souvenirs. (De la résistance.)* 2 vols. Paris, 1946–1947.

PAUL-BONCOUR, Joseph: *Entre Deux Guerres: souvenirs sur la IIIᵉ République.* 3 vols. Paris 1945–1946.

PERTINAX: *Les Fossoyeurs. Défaite militaire de la France, armistice, contre-révolution.* 2 vols. New York, 1943. (English translation: *The Gravediggers of France.* New York, 1944.)

PIROU, Gaëtan: *Georges Sorel.* Paris, 1927.

PLUMYÈNE, J., and LASIERRA, R.: *Les Fascismes français. 1923–1963.* Paris, 1963.

POTEMKIN, V. V., ed: *Histoire de la diplomatie.* Paris, 1946–1947. (A French edition of a Soviet work.)

PRÉTELAT, Général André Gaston: *Le déstin tragique de la ligne Maginot.*

PRIOUX, Général A.: *Souvenirs de guerre 1939–1943.* Paris.

QUÉVAL, Jean: *Première Page, Cinquième Colonne.* Paris, 1945.

RAUCH, Basil: *Roosevelt: From Munich to Pearl Harbor.* New York, 1950.

RECLUS, Maurice: *Grandeur de la troisième.* Paris, 1948.

REINACH, Joseph: *Histoire de l'affaire Dreyfus.* 7 vols. Paris, 1901–1911.

RÉMOND, René: *Les Catholiques, le communisme et les crises, 1929–1939.* Paris, 1960.

———: *La Droite en France—de la première restauration à la Vᵉ république.* Paris, 1963.

RENOUVIN, Pierre: *Les Relations internationales, 1914–1945.* (Eight lectures at the Institut d'études politiques de Paris, 1948–1949.)

————: *Les crises du XXe siècle, Vol. II, de 1929 à 1945*. Paris, 1958.

RÉQUIN, Général Edouard Jean: *D'une Guerre à l'autre. 1919–1939*. Paris 1949.

RÉVILLON, M.-M. Tony: *Mes Carnets (juin–octobre 1940)*. Paris, 1945.

REYNAUD, Paul: *Le Problème militaire français* Paris, 1937.

————: *La France a sauvé l'Europe*. 2 vols. Paris, 1947.

————: *Au Cœur de la mêlée, 1930–1945*. Paris, 1951. Eng. trans.: *In the Thick of the Fight*. New York, 1955. (*Cœur* is a revised and vastly improved version of *La France a sauvé l'Europe*.)

————: *Mémoires*. 2 vols. Paris, 1960, 1963.

Vol. I. *Venu de ma montagne*.

Vol. II. *Envers et contre tous, 7 mars 1936–16 juin 1940*.

RIBET, Maurice: *Le procès de Riom*. Paris, 1945.

RICHARDS, Denis: *Royal Air Force. 1939–1945*. London, 1953.

RONSE, Edward: *Le Procès de Léopold III*. Brussels, 1945.

ROTON, Général Gaston René: *Années cruciales, 1939–1940*. Paris, 1947.

ROUGIER, Louis: *Les Accords Pétain-Churchill*. Montreal, 1945.

ROUSSY DE SALES, Raoul de: *The Making of Yesterday*. New York, 1947.

RUBY, Général Edmond: *Sedan, terre d'épreuve*. Paris.

SAINT-EXUPÉRY, Antoine de: *Flight to Arras*. New York, 1942.

SAINTSBURY, George: *French Literature and its Masters*. New York, 1946.

SALESSE, Lieutenant-Colonel Charles: *L'Aviation de chasse française en 1939–1940*. Paris, 1949.

SAUVY, Alfred: *Histoire économique de la France entre les deux guerres, 1918–1939*. 2 vols. Paris, 1965, 1967.

————: *La Montée des jeunes*. Paris, 1959.

————: *Théorie général de la population*. 2 vols. Paris, 1952–1959.

SCHAPIRO, J. Salwyn: *Modern and Contemporary European History*. New York, 1931.

SCHMIDT, Paul: *Statist auf diplomatischer Bühne, 1923–45*. Bonn, 1949.

Abridged English edn.: *Hitler's Interpreter*. New York, 1951.

SCHMITT, Général: *Toute la Vérité sur le procès Pucheu par un des juges*. Paris, 1963.

SCHWARTZKOPPEN, Max von: *The Truth about the Dreyfus Affair—from the Schwartzkoppen Papers*. New York, 1931.

SEIGNOBOS, Charles: *L'Evolution de la troisième République*. Paris, 1921.

SHEEAN, Vincent: *Between the Thunder and the Sun*. New York, 1943.

SHERWOOD, Robert E.: *Roosevelt and Hopkins*. New York, 1948.

SHIRER, William L.: *Berlin Diary*. New York, 1941.

————: *The Rise and Fall of the Third Reich*. New York, 1960.

SHULMAN, Milton: *Defeat in the West*. New York, 1948.

SLESSOR, Sir John: *The Central Blue: The Autobiography of Sir John Slessor, Marshal of the R.A.F.* New York, 1957.

SOLTAU, Roger: *French Political Thought in the 19th Century*. 1931.

SPEARS, Sir Edward L.: *Assignment to Catastrophe*. 2 vols. New York, 1955.

Vol. I. *Prelude to Dunkirk, July 1939–May 1940*.

Vol. II. *The Fall of France, 1940*.

————: *Two Men Who Saved France: Pétain and De Gaulle*. New York, 1966.

STEHLIN, Général Paul: *Témoignage pour l'histoire*. Paris, 1964.

STÉPHANE, Roger: *Chaque homme est lié au monde*. Paris, 1946.

SUAREZ, Georges: *Briand, sa vie, son œuvre*. 5 vols. Paris, 1938–1941.

TAYLOR, Edmond: *The Strategy of Terror*. Boston, 1940.

TAYLOR, Telford: *Sword and Swastika*. New York, 1952.

————: *The March of Conquest*. New York, 1958.

TELPUCHOWSKI, B. S.: *Die Sowjetische Geschichte des Groszen Vaterlandischen Krieges 1941–1945*. Frankfurt, 1961.

TEMPERLEY, Harold W.: *A History of the Peace Conference of Paris*. 6 vols. London, 1920–1924.

THIERS, Adolphe: *History of the French Revolution*. English translation, 5 vols., 1895.

THOMAS, Hugh: *The Spanish Civil War*. London and New York, 1961.

THOMAS, L.: *Documents sur la guerre 1939–1940*. 2 vols. Paris, 1941.

THOMSON, David: *Democracy in France. The Third Republic*. New York, 1950.

————: *Two Frenchmen: Pierre Laval and Charles de Gaulle*. London, 1951.

TISSIER, Pierre: *Le Procès de Riom*. Paris, 1943.

TOMPKINS, Peter: *The Murder of Admiral Darlan*. New York, 1965.

TORRÈS, Henry: *La France Trahie. Pierre Laval*. New York, 1941.

TOURNOUX, J.-R.: *L'Histoire secrète*. Paris, 1962.

————: *Pétain et de Gaulle*. Paris, 1964.

TOURNOUX, Général Paul-Emile: *Défense des frontières. Haut Commandement. Gouvernement 1919–1939*. Paris, 1960.

TRACOU, Jean: *Le Maréchal aux Liens*. Paris, 1940.

TRUCHET, André: *L'Armistice de 1940 et l'Afrique du Nord*. Paris, 1955.

TUAILLON, Général Jean Louis Georges: *Les Dangers extérieurs et le moral de notre armée nationale*. Paris, 1936.

TUCHMAN, Barbara W.: *The Guns of August*. New York, 1962.

VALÉRY, Paul: *Reflections on the World Today*. New York, 1948.

VIDALENC, Jean: *L'Exode de mai–juin 1940*. Paris, 1957.

WARLIMONT, General Walter: *Inside Hitler's Headquarters, 1939–1945*. New York, 1964.

WEBER, Eugen: *Action française: Royalism and Reaction in Twentieth-Century France*. Stanford, 1963.

WEILL-RAYNAL, Etienne: *Les Réparations allemandes et la France*. 2 vols. Paris, 1947.

WERTH, Alexander: *France and Munich: Before and After the Surrender*. London, 1939.

————: *The Last Days of Paris*. London, 1940.

————: *France 1940–1955*. New York, 1956.

————: *De Gaulle, a Political Biography*. New York, 1965.

WESTPHAL, General Siegfried: *The German Army in the West*. London, 1951.

WEYGAND, Commandant J.: *The Role of General Weygand*. London, 1948.

WEYGAND, Général Maxime: *Le Général Frère—un chef, un héros, un martyr*. Paris, 1949.

————: *Mémoires: Rappelé au Service*. Paris, 1950.

————: *Mémoires: Mirages et Réalité*. Paris, 1957.

————: *Histoire de l'armée*. Paris, 1961.

————: *En lisant les Mémoires de Général de Gaulle*. Paris, 1965.

WHEELER-BENNET, John W.: *Munich, Prologue to Tragedy*. New York, 1948.

WILMOT, Chester: *The Struggle for Europe*. New York, 1952.

WOLFERS, Arnold: *Britain and France between Two Wars: Conflicting Strategies of Peace since Versailles*. New York, 1940.

WRIGHT, Gordon: *The Reshaping of French Democracy*. London, 1950.

————: *France in Modern Times. 1760 to the Present*. Chicago, 1960.

WULLUS-RUDIGER, J.: *Les Origines internationales du drame belge de 1940*. Brussels, 1950.

YOUNG, Desmond: *Rommel, the Desert Fox*. New York, 1950.

ZAY, Jean: *Souvenirs et Solitude*. Paris, 1945.

ZEVAËS, Alexandre: *Histoire de la troisième république. 1870–1926*. 1st edn. Paris, 1926.

INDEX